What are the monetary policy tools used by the Federal Reserve? (pages 100–109)
How do monetary policy changes affect key economic variables? (pages 109–115)
How do U.S. monetary policy initiatives affect foreign exchange rates? (pages 116–118)

Pertinent Websites

Bank of Japan	www.boj.or.jp/
Board of Governors of the Federal Reserve	www.bog.frb.fed.us/
Federal Deposit Insurance Corporation	www.fdic.gov/
Federal Reserve Bank of New York	www.ny.frb.org/
Financial Times	www.ft.com/
Office of the Comptroller of the Currency	www.occ.treas.gov/
The Wall Street Journal	www.wjs.com/

The Financial Markets (Chapters 5–10)

What are money markets, bond markets, mortgage markets, stock markets, foreign exchange markets, and derivative security markets? (pages 122–125, 154, 190, 201–202, 219, 257–258, 280–281)

What are the major types of securities traded in each of these markets? (pages 125–142, 154–178, 191–211, 219–240, 258–273, 282–312)

What is the process used to issue and trade securities in various markets? (pages 126–130, 132–134, 138–142, 162–165, 168–171, 176, 191–196, 203, 207–208, 226–237, 267–273, 284, 287–289, 298–300, 309–310)

Who are the main participants in the various financial markets? (pages 143–145, 176, 212–213, 244–245, 267–273, 280–281)

To what extent do foreign investors participate in U.S. financial markets? (pages 145–151, 181–187, 213–216, 250–253, 258–278)

Pertinent Websites

American Banker	www.americanbanker.com/
Bank for International Settlements	www.bis.org/
Bureau of Economic Analysis	www.bea.doc.gov/
Board of Governors of the Federal Reserve	www.bog.frb.fed.us/
Chicago Board of Options Exchange	www.cboe.com/
Chicago Board of Trade	www.cbot.com/
Chicago Mercantile Exchange	www.cme.com/
Commodity Futures Trading Commission	www.cftc.gov/
Deutsche Bank	www.bundesbank.de/
Dow Jones & Company	www.dowjones.com/
Federal Home Loan Mortgage Corporation	www.freddiemac.com/
Federal Housing Finance Board	www.fhfb.gov/
Federal National Mortgage Association	www.fanniemae.com/
Federal Reserve Bank of New York	www.ny.frb.org/
Financial Times	www.ft.com/
Government National Mortgage Association	www.ginniemae.gov/
International Swaps and Derivatives Association	www.isda.org/
London International Financial Futures Exchange	www.liffe.com/
Merrill Lynch	www.ml.com/
Moody's	www.moodys.com/
Mortgage Bankers Association	www.mbaa.org/
Nasdaq-Amex Market Group	www.nasdaq.com/
New York Stock Exchange	www.nyse.com/
Securities and Exchange Commission	www.sec.gov/
Standard & Poor's	www.standardandpoors.com/
The Wall Street Journal	www.wjs.com/
Thompson Financial Securities Data	www.tfsd.com/
U.S. Treasury	www.ustreas.gov/
Veterans Administration	www.va.com/

Financial Markets and Institutions

A Modern Perspective

The McGraw-Hill/Irwin Series in Finance, Insurance and Real Estate

Stephen A. Ross
Franco Modigliani Professor of Finance
and Economics
Sloan School of Management
Massachusetts Institute of Technology
Consulting Editor

FINANCIAL MANAGEMENT

Benninga and Sarig
Corporate Finance:
A Valuation Approach

Block and Hirt
Foundations of Financial Management
Ninth Edition

Brealey and Myers
Principles of Corporate Finance
Sixth Edition

Brealey, Myers and Marcus
Fundamentals of Corporate Finance
Third Edition

Brooks
FinGame Online 3.0

Bruner
Case Studies in Finance: Managing for
Corporate Value Creation
Third Edition

Chew
The New Corporate Finance:
Where Theory Meets Practice
Third Edition

Graduate Management Admissions
Council, Robert F. Bruner, Kenneth Eades
and Robert Harris
Essentials of Finance: With an
Accounting Review
Fully interactive CD-ROM derived from
Finance Interactive 1997
Pre-MBA Edition
Finance Interactive: Pre-MBA
Series 2000
Second Edition

Grinblatt and Titman
Financial Markets and
Corporate Strategy

Helfert
Techniques of Financial Analysis:
A Guide to Value Creation
Tenth Edition

Higgins
Analysis for Financial Management
Sixth Edition

Hite
A Programmed Learning
Guide to Finance

Kester, Fruhan, Piper and Ruback
Case Problems in Finance
Eleventh Edition

Nunnally and Plath
Cases in Finance
Second Edition

Ross, Westerfield and Jaffe
Corporate Finance
Fifth Edition

Ross, Westerfield and Jordan
Essentials of Corporate Finance
Third Edition

Ross, Westerfield and Jordan
Fundamentals of Corporate Finance
Fifth Edition

Smith
The Modern Theory of
Corporate Finance
Second Edition

White
Financial Analysis with an
Electronic Calculator
Fourth Edition

INVESTMENTS

Bodie, Kane and Marcus
Essentials of Investments
Fourth Edition

Bodie, Kane and Marcus
Investments
Fourth Edition

Cohen, Zinbarg and Zeikel
Investment Analysis and
Portfolio Management
Fifth Edition

Corrado and Jordan
Fundamentals of Investments:
Valuation and Management

Farrell
Portfolio Management:
Theory and Applications
Second Edition

Hirt and Block
Fundamentals of
Investment Management
Sixth Edition

Jarrow
Modelling Fixed Income Securities and
Interest Rate Options

Shimko
The Innovative Investor
Excel Version

FINANCIAL INSTITUTIONS
AND MARKETS

Cornett and Saunders
Fundamentals of Financial
Institutions Management

Rose
Commercial Bank Management
Fourth Edition

Rose
Money and Capital Markets:
Financial Institutions and Instruments
in a Global Marketplace
Seventh Edition

Rose and Kolari
Financial Institutions: Understanding
and Managing Financial Services
Fifth Edition

Santomero and Babbel
Financial Markets, Instruments,
and Institutions
Second Edition

Saunders
Financial Institutions Management:
A Modern Perspective
Third Edition

INTERNATIONAL FINANCE

Eun and Resnick
International Financial Management
Second Edition

Kester and Luehrman
Case Problems in International Finance
Second Edition

Levi
International Finance
Third Edition

Financial Markets and Institutions

A Modern Perspective

Anthony Saunders

Stern School of Business
New York University

Marcia Millon Cornett

Southern Illinois University

Boston Burr Ridge, IL Dubuque, IA Madison, WI
New York San Francisco St. Louis
Bangkok Bogotá Caracas Lisbon London Madrid Mexico City
Milan New Delhi Seoul Singapore Sydney Taipei Toronto

McGraw-Hill Higher Education

*A Division of The **McGraw-Hill** Companies*

FINANCIAL MARKETS AND INSTITUTIONS
Published by McGraw-Hill/Irwin, an imprint of The McGraw-Hill Companies, Inc. 1221
Avenue of the Americas, New York, NY, 10020. Copyright © 2001 by The McGraw-
Hill Companies, Inc. All rights reserved. No part of this publication may be reproduced
or distributed in any form or by any means, or stored in a database or retrieval system,
without the prior written consent of The McGraw-Hill Companies, Inc., including, but
not limited to, in any network or other electronic storage or transmission, or broadcast for
distance learning.
Some ancillaries, including electronic and print components, may not be available to
customers outside the United States.

This book is printed on acid-free paper.

1 2 3 4 5 6 7 8 9 0 VNH/VNH 0 9 8 7 6 5 4 3 2 1 0

ISBN 0-07-234892-5

Vice president/Editor-in-chief: *Michael W. Junior*
Publisher: *John E. Biernat*
Executive editor: *Stephen M. Patterson*
Developmental editor: *Sarah Pearson*
Executive marketing manager: *Rhonda Seelinger*
Senior project manager: *Susan Trentacosti*
Production supervisor: *Melonie Salvati*
Senior designer: *Jennifer McQueen Hollingsworth*
Lead supplement coordinator: *Cathy L. Tepper*
Media technology producer: *Barb Block*
Interior design: *Lloyd Lemna Design*
Cover image: *©Rob Colvin/SIS*
Compositor: *GAC Indianapolis*
Typeface: *10.5/12 Times Roman*
Printer: *Von Hoffmann Press, Inc.*

Library of Congress Cataloging-in-Publication Data

Saunders, Anthony, (date)
    Financial markets and institutions : a modern perspective / Anthony Saunders, Marcia
Millon Cornett.
        p. cm.
    Includes bibliographical references and index.
    ISBN 0-07-234892-5
    1. Securities—United States. 2. Stock exchanges—United States. 3. Financial
institutions—United States. 4. Rate of return—United States. 5. Interest rates—United
States. I. Cornett, Marcia Millon. II. Title.

HG4910 .S28 2001
332—dc21

00-064750

www.mhhe.com

To my father, Myer Saunders (1919–1998).

To Galen

About the Authors

ANTHONY SAUNDERS

Anthony Saunders is the John M. Schiff Professor of Finance and Chair of the Department of Finance at the Stern School of Business at New York University. Professor Saunders received his Ph.D. from the London School of Economics and has taught both undergraduate and graduate level courses at NYU since 1978. Throughout his academic career, his teaching and research have specialized in financial institutions and international banking. He has served as a visiting professor all over the world, including INSEAD, the Stockholm School of Economics, and the University of Melbourne. He is currently on the Executive Committee of the Salomon Center for the Study of Financial Institutions, NYU.

Professor Saunders holds positions on the Board of Academic Consultants of the Federal Reserve Board of Governors as well as the Council of Research Advisors for the Federal National Mortgage Association. In addition, Dr. Saunders has acted as a visiting scholar at the comptroller of the Currency and at the Federal Monetary Fund. He is the editor of the *Journal of Banking and Finance* and the *Journal of Financial Markets, Instruments and Institutions,* as well as the associate editor of eight other journals, including *Financial Management* and the *Journal of Money, Credit and Banking.* His research has been published in all of the major money and banking journals and in several books. He has just published a book on *Financial Institutions Management: A Modern Perspective* with McGraw-Hill/Irwin.

MARCIA MILLON CORNETT

Marcia Millon Cornett is a Professor of Finance at Southern Illinois University at Carbondale. She received her B.S. degree in Economics from Knox College in Galesburg, Illinois, and her M.B.A. and Ph.D. degrees in Finance from Indiana University in Bloomington, Indiana. Dr. Cornett has written and published several articles in the areas of bank performance, bank regulation, corporate finance, and investments. Articles authored by Dr. Cornett have appeared in such academic journals as the *Journal of Finance,* the *Journal of Money, Credit, and Banking,* the *Journal of Financial Economics, Financial Management,* and the *Journal of Banking and Finance.* She served as an Associate Editor of *Financial Management* and is currently an Associate Editor for the *Multinational Finance Journal.* Dr. Cornett is currently a member of the Board of Directors and the Finance Committee of the Southern Illinois University Credit Union. Dr. Cornett has also taught at the University of Colorado, Boston College, and Southern Methodist University. She is a member of the Financial Management Association, the American Finance Association, and the Western Finance Association.

Preface

The 1990s was characterized as a period in which financial markets in the United States boomed. The Dow Jones Industrial Average rose from a level of 2,800 in January 1990 to more than 11,000 by the end of the decade; this compared to a move from 100 at its inception in 1906 to 2,800 thirty-four years later. While security values in U.S. financial markets rose dramatically, financial markets in Southeast Asia, South America, and Russia plummeted. For example, on July 2, 1997, the Thai baht fell nearly 50 percent in value relative to the U.S. dollar. Countries such as Russia, Thailand, and South Korea required an international bailout by the International Monetary Fund to prevent a complete collapse of their financial markets and their economies. Nevertheless, Indonesia had to declare a moratorium on some of its debt repayments, while Russia defaulted on payments on its short-term government bonds.

Meanwhile, the financial services industry is approaching a full historical cycle. Originally, the banking industry operated as a full-service industry, performing directly or indirectly all financial services (commercial banking, investment banking, stock investing, insurance provision, etc.). In the early 1930s, the economic and industrial collapse resulted in the separation of some of these activities. In the 1970s and 1980s, new, relatively unregulated financial services industries sprang up (e.g., mutual funds, brokerage funds) that separated the financial service functions even further. Now, at the turn of the century, regulatory barriers via the Financial Services Modernization Act of 1999, technological innovation, and financial innovation have resulted in changes such that a full set of financial services may again be offered by a single financial institution (FI) such as Citigroup. Not only are the boundaries between traditional industry sectors weakening but competition is becoming global in nature, as the Germans, French, and other Europeans enter into U.S. financial service markets, and vice versa.

As the economic and competitive environments change, attention to profit and, more than ever, risk becomes increasingly important. This book offers a unique analysis of the risks faced by investors and savers interacting through both financial institutions and financial markets, as well as strategies that can be adopted for controlling and managing these risks. Special emphasis is also put on new areas of operations in financial markets and institutions, such as asset securitization, off-balance-sheet activities, and globalization of financial services.

While maintaining a risk measurement and management framework, *Financial Markets and Institutions: A Modern Perspective* provides a broader application of this important perspective. This book recognizes that domestic and foreign financial markets are increasingly connected and that financial intermediaries are evolving towards a single financial services industry. The analytical rigor is mathematically accessible to all levels of students, undergraduate and graduate, and is balanced by a comprehensive discussion of the unique environment within which financial markets and institutions operate. Important practical tools such as how to issue and trade financial securities or how to analyze financial statements and loan applications will arm students with skills necessary to understand and manage financial market and institution risks in this dynamic environment. While descriptive concepts, so important to financial management (financial market securities, regulation, industry trends, industry characteristics, etc.) are included in the book, ample analytical techniques are also included as practical tools to help students understand the operation of modern financial markets and institutions.

Intended Audience

Financial Markets and Institutions: A Modern Perspective is aimed at the first course in financial markets and institutions at both the undergraduate and MBA levels. While topics covered in this book are found in more advanced textbooks on financial markets and institutions, the explanations and illustrations are aimed at those with little or no practical or academic experience beyond the introductory level in financial courses. In most chapters, the main relationships are presented using figures, graphs, and simple examples. The more complicated details and technical problems related to in-chapter discussion are provided in appendixes to the chapters.

Organization

Since our focus is on return and risk and the sources of that return and risk in domestic and foreign financial markets and institutions, this book relates ways in which a modern financial manager, saver, and investor can expand return with a managed level of risk to achieve the best, or most favorable, return-risk outcome.

The book is divided into five major sections. Part One provides an introduction to the text and an overview of financial markets and institutions. Chapter 1 defines and introduces the various domestic and foreign financial markets and describes the special functions of FIs. This chapter also takes an analytical look at how financial markets and institutions benefit today's economy. In Chapter 2, we provide an in-depth look at interest rates. We first review the concept of time value of money. We then look at factors that determine interest rate levels, as well as their past, present, and expected future movements. Chapter 3 then applies these interest rates to security valuation. In Chapter 4, we describe the Federal Reserve System and how monetary policy implemented by the Federal Reserve affects interest rates and, ultimately, the overall economy.

Part Two of the text presents an overview of the various securities markets. We describe each securities market, its participants, the securities traded in each, the trading process, and how changes in interest rates, inflation, and foreign exchange rates impact the FI managers' decisions to hedge risk. These chapters cover the money markets (Chapter 5), bond markets (Chapter 6), mortgage markets (Chapter 7), stock markets (Chapter 8), foreign exchange markets (Chapter 9), and derivative securities markets (Chapter 10).

Part Three of the text summarizes the operations of depository institutions. Chapter 11 describes the key characteristics and recent trends in the commercial banking sector. Chapter 12 does the same for the thrift institution sector. Chapter 13 describes the financial statements of a typical depository institution and the ratios used to analyze those statements. This chapter also analyzes actual financial statements for representative financial institutions. Chapter 14 provides a comprehensive look at the regulations under which these financial institutions operate and, particularly, at the effect of recent changes in regulation.

Part Four of the text provides an overview describing the key characteristics and regulatory features of the other major sectors of the U.S. financial services industry. We discuss insurance institutions in Chapter 15, securities firms and investment banks in Chapter 16, finance companies in Chapter 17, mutual fund firms in Chapter 18, and pension funds in Chapter 19.

Part Five concludes the text by examining the risks facing a modern FI and FI managers, and the various strategies for managing these risks. In Chapter 20, we preview the risk measurement and management chapters that follow with an overview of the risks facing a modern FI. We divide the chapters on risk measurement and management along two lines: measuring and managing risks on the balance sheet, and managing risks off the balance sheet. In Chapter 21, we begin the on-balance-sheet risk measurement and management section by looking at credit risk on individual loans and bonds and how these risks adversely impact an FI's profits and value. The chapter also discusses the lending process, including loans made to small households and small, medium-sized, and large corporations. Chapter 22 covers liquidity risk in financial institutions. This chapter includes a detailed analysis of ways in which FIs can insulate themselves from liquidity risk, and the key role deposit insurance and other guarantee schemes play in reducing liquidity risk.

In Chapter 23, we investigate the net interest margin as a source of profitability and risk, with a focus on the effects of interest rate risk and the mismatching of asset and liability maturities on FI risk exposure. At the core of FI risk insulation is the size and adequacy of the owner's capital stake, which is also a focus of this chapter.

The management of risk off the balance sheet is examined in Chapter 24. The chapter highlights various new markets and instruments that have emerged to allow FIs to better manage three important types of risk: interest rate risk, foreign exchange risk, and credit risk. These markets and instruments and their strategic use by FIs include forwards and futures, options, and swaps.

Finally, Chapter 25 explores ways of removing credit risk from the loan portfolio through asset sales and securitization.

Anthony Saunders
Marcia Millon Cornett

Walkthrough Main Features

The following special features have been integrated throughout the text to encourage student interaction and to aid them in absorbing the material.

Reserve System, Monetary Policy, *and* Interest Rates

Chapter Navigator

1. What are the major functions of the Federal Reserve System?
2. What is the structure of the Federal Reserve System?
3. What are the monetary policy tools used by the Federal Reserve?
4. How do monetary policy changes affect key economic variables?
5. How do U.S. monetary policy initiatives affect foreign exchange rates?

Responsibilities of the Federal Reserve System: Chapter Overview

Structure of the Federal Reserve System
- Federal Reserve Banks
- Board of Governors of the Federal Reserve System
- Federal Open Market Committee
- Balance Sheet of the Federal Reserve

Monetary Policy Tools
- Open Market Operations
- The Discount Rate
- Reserve Requirements (Reserve Ratios)

The Federal Reserve, the Money Supply, and Interest Rates

Chapter-Opening Outlines

These outlines offer students a snapshot view of what they can expect to learn from each chapter's discussion.

Chapter Navigators

The chapter navigators list the chapter topics in order, providing numbers that correspond with the section in which they can be found in the chapter.

3   Monetary Policy Tools

In the previous section of this chapter, we referred briefly to tools or instruments that the Federal Reserve uses to implement its monetary policy. These included open market operations, the discount rate, and reserve requirements. Regardless of the tool the Federal Reserve uses to implement monetary policy, the major link by which monetary policy impacts the macroeconomy occurs through the Federal Reserve influencing the market for bank reserves (required and excess reserves held as depository institution reserves balances in accounts at Federal Reserve Banks plus vault cash on hand of commercial banks). Specifically, the Federal Reserve's

7. The minimum daily average reserves that a bank must maintain are computed as a percentage of the daily average net transaction accounts held by the bank over the two-week computation period, called the reserve computation period. Transaction accounts include all deposits on which an accountholder may

Bold Key Terms and a Marginal Glossary

The main terms and concepts are emphasized throughout the chapter by the bold key terms and a marginal glossary.

Pertinent Website Addresses

Website addresses are also referenced in the margins throughout each chapter providing additional resources to aid in the learning process.

www.ny.frb.org/

Federal Reserve Board Trading Desk
Unit of the Federal Reserve Bank of New York through which open market operations are conducted.

policy directive
Statement sent to the Federal Reserve Board Trading Desk from the FOMC that specifies the money supply target.

Open Market Operations

When a targeted monetary aggregate (M1, M2, etc.—see definition below) or interest rate level is determined by the FOMC, it is forwarded to the **Federal Reserve Board Trading Desk** at the Federal Reserve Bank of New York (FRBNY) through a statement called the **policy directive**. The manager of the Trading Desk uses the policy directive to instruct traders on the amount of open market purchases or sales to transact. Open market operations are the Federal Reserves' purchases or sales of securities in the U.S. Treasury securities market. This is an over-the-counter market in which traders are linked to each other electronically (see Chapter 5).

Open market operations are particularly important because they are the primary determinant of changes in bank excess reserves in the banking system and thus directly impact the size of the money supply and/or the level of interest rates (e.g., the fed funds rate). When the Federal Reserve purchases securities, it pays for the securities by either writing a check on itself or directly transferring funds (by wire transfer) into the seller's account. Either way, the Fed credits the reserve deposit account of the bank that sells it (the Fed) the securities. This transaction increases the bank's excess reserve levels. When the Fed sells securities, it either collects checks received as payment or

Gold and Foreign Exchange and Treasury Currency. The Federal Reserve holds Treasury gold certificates that are redeemable at the U.S. Treasury for gold. The Fed also holds small amounts of Treasury-issued coinage and foreign-denominated assets to assist in foreign currency transactions or currency swap agreements with the central banks of other nations.

Do You Understand?

1. What the main functions of Federal Reserve Banks are?
2. What the main responsibilities of the Federal Reserve Board are?
3. How the FOMC implements monetary policy?
4. What the main assets and liabilities in the Federal Reserve System are?

Loans to Domestic Banks. As mentioned earlier, in a liquidity emergency, depository institutions in need of additional funds can borrow at the Federal Reserve's discount window (discussed in detail below). The interest rate or discount rate charged on these loans is often lower than other interest rates in the short-term money markets (see Chapter 5). To prevent excessive borrowing from the discount window, the Fed discourages borrowing unless a bank is in serious liquidity need (see Chapters 14 and 22). As a result, (discount) loans to domestic banks are normally a relatively small portion of the Fed's total assets.[8]

"Do You Understand?" Boxes

These boxes allow students to test themselves on the main concepts within each major chapter section.

Example 4–1 Purchases of Securities by the Federal Reserve

Suppose the FOMC instructs the FRBNY Trading Desk to purchase $500 million of Treasury securities. Traders at the FRBNY call primary government securities dealers of major commercial and investment banks (such as Goldman Sachs and Chase)[9] who provide a list of securities they have available for sale, including the denomination, maturity, and the price on each security. FRBNY traders then seek to purchase the target number of securities (at the desired maturities and lowest possible price) until they have purchased the $500 million. The FRBNY then notifies its government bond department to receive and pay the sellers for the securities it has purchased. The securities dealer sellers (such as banks) in turn deposit these payments in their accounts held at their local Federal Reserve Bank. As a result of these purchases, the Treasury securities account balance of the Federal Reserve System is increased by $500 million and the total reserve accounts maintained by these banks and dealers at the Fed is increased by $500 million. We illustrate these changes to the Federal Reserve's balance sheet in Table 4–6. In addition, there is also an impact on commercial bank balance sheets. Total reserves (assets) of commercial banks will increase by $500 million due to the purchase of securities by the Fed, and demand deposits (liabilities) of the securities dealers (those who sold the securities) at their banks will increase by $500 million.[10] We also show the changes to commercial banks' balance sheets in Table 4–6.

Note the Federal R... ...f Treasury sec... ...reased the total

In-Chapter Examples

These examples provide numerical demonstrations of the analytical material described in many chapters.

In the News
4-1

Alan Greenspan, U.S. Federal Reserve Chairman, said yesterday he expected "a lot of problems" to emerge in the global financial payments system because of the Year 2000 computer problem. The Fed had already or... ...the printing of extra

U.S. Prints Cash to Cope with Demands of Millennium Bomb

is we are going to run into a lot of problems. And as a ... ...we are doi...

for banknotes between July and the end of 1999. In July, the Fed estimated it had $460 billion in banknotes in circulation with an additional $153 billion in its vaults, a total of $613 billion. As part of the Fed's contingency planning, it had ordered increased printing ...t currency for th...

"In the News . . ." Boxes

These boxes demonstrate the application of chapter material to real, current events.

Main Features

End-of-Chapter Problems

At least 20 problems per chapter are written for varied levels of difficulty.

Summary

This chapter described the Federal Reserve System in the United States. The Federal Reserve is the central bank charged with conducting monetary policy, supervising and regulating depository institutions, maintaining the stability of the financial system, and providing specific financial services to the U.S. government, the public, and financial institutions. We reviewed the structure under which the Fed provides these functions, the monetary policy tools it uses, and the impact of monetary policy changes on credit availability, interest rates, money supply, security prices, and foreign exchange rates.

Questions

1. Describe the functions performed by Federal Reserve Banks.
2. Define the discount window and the discount rate.
3. Describe the structure of the Board of Governors of the Federal Reserve System.
4. What are the primary responsibilities of the Federal Reserve Board?
5. What are the primary responsibilities of the Federal Open Market Committee?
6. What are the major liabilities of the Federal Reserve System? Describe each.
7. What are the major assets of the Federal Reserve System? Describe each.
8. What are the tools used by the Federal Reserve to implement monetary policy?
9. Suppose the Federal Reserve instructs the Trading Desk to purchase $1 billion of securities. Show the result of this transaction on the balance sheets of the Federal Reserve System and commercial banks.
10. Suppose the Federal Reserve instructs the Trading Desk to sell $850 million of securities. Show the result of this transaction on the balance sheets of the Federal Reserve System and commercial banks.
11. Explain how a decrease in the discount rate affects credit availability and the money supply.
12. Why does the Federal Reserve rarely use the discount rate to implement its monetary policy?
13. What is the difference between an adjustment credit, a seasonal credit, and an extended credit discount window loan?
14. Bank Three currently has $600 million in transaction deposits on its balance sheet. The Federal Reserve has currently set the reserve requirement at 10 percent of transaction deposits.
    a. If the Federal Reserve decreases the reserve requirement to 8 percent, show the balance sheet of Bank Three and the Federal Reserve System just before and after the full effect of the reserve requirement change. Assume Bank Three withdraws all excess reserves and gives out loans, and that borrowers eventually return all of these funds to Bank Three in the form of transaction deposits.
    b. Redo part (a) using a 12 percent reserve requirement.
15. National Bank currently has $500 million in transaction deposits on its balance sheet. The current reserve requirement is 10 percent, but the Federal Reserve is decreasing this requirement to 8 percent.
    a. Show the balance sheet of the Federal Reserve and National Bank if National Bank converts all excess reserves to loans, but borrowers return only 50 percent of these funds to National Bank as transaction deposits.
    b. Show the balance sheet of the Federal Reserve and National Bank if National Bank converts 75 percent of its excess reserves to loans and borrowers return 60 percent of these funds to National Bank as transaction deposits.
16. Which of the monetary tools available to the Federal Reserve is most often used? Why?
17. Describe how expansionary activities conducted by the Federal Reserve impact credit availability, the money supply, interest rates, and security prices. Do the same for contractionary activities.

Supplements

The Wall Street Journal Edition

Through a unique arrangement with Dow Jones, McGraw-Hill/Irwin is able to offer your students a 10-week subscription to *The Wall Street Journal* as part of the purchase price of the WSJ Edition text. The WSJ will keep students up to date on the world of finance. (ISBN 007239708X)

Instructor's Manual

The Instructor's Manual, prepared by Tim Manuel of the University of Montana, includes detailed chapter contents, additional examples for use in the classroom, and complete solutions to end-of-chapter question and problem materials. (ISBN 0072397047)

Test Bank

Also prepared by Tim Manuel, the Test Bank includes nearly 1,000 additional problems to be used for test material. (ISBN 0072397055)

Brownstone Diploma Testing System

Our Brownstone Diploma Testing System offers the test items for *Financial Markets and Institutions* on computer disk. This program makes it possible to create tests based on chapter, type of questions, and difficulty level. It allows instructors to combine their own questions with test items created by the Test Bank author. This system can be used to edit existing questions and create several different versions of each test. The program accepts graphics, allows password protection of saved tests, and may be used on a computer network. (ISBN 0072397063)

Study Guide

William Lepley, University of Wisconsin–Green Bay, has written a Study Guide that speaks directly to the student. It provides a conceptual outline and applications that include definitional and quantitative problems for each chapter. Detailed solutions explain how answers were derived. (ISBN 0072397039)

PowerPoint

The PowerPoint Presentation, prepared by Joseph Ogden of the State University of New York–Buffalo, includes full-color slides featuring lecture notes, figures, and tables. Found only on the book's website, the slides can be easily downloaded and edited for a specific course.

Instructor's CD-ROM

The Instructor's CD-ROM provides the instructor with one resource for all supplementary material, including the Instructor's Manual, Test Bank, and PowerPoint. (ISBN 0072397071)

Website

The Saunders/Cornett Custom Crafted Website is found at www.mhhe.com/sc1e. In addition to information on the book and its features, the site also includes downloadable PowerPoint slides and sample chapters from both the text and the Study Guide.

PageOut

PageOut: The Course Website Development Center and PageOut Lite

www.pageout.net

This Web page generation software, free to adopters, is designed to help professors just beginning to explore website options. In just a few minutes, even a novice computer user can have a course website.

Simply type your material into the template provided and PageOut Lite instantly converts it to HTML—a universal Web language. Next, choose your favorite of three easy-to-navigate designs and your Web homepage is created, complete with online syllabus, lecture notes, and bookmarks. You can even include a separate instructor page and an assignment page.

Contents in Brief

Contents

Introduction *and* Overview *of* Financial Markets

P art One of the book provides an introduction to the text and an overview of financial markets. Chapter 1 defines and introduces the various financial markets and describes the special functions of financial institutions. In Chapter 2, we provide an in-depth look at interest rates; Chapter 3 then applies these interest rates to security valuation. In Chapter 4, we describe the Federal Reserve System and how monetary policy implemented by the Federal Reserve affects interest rates, and, ultimately, the overall economy.

chapter one

Introduction

Chapter Navigator

1. What is the difference between primary and secondary markets?

2. What is the difference between money and capital markets?

3. What are foreign exchange markets?

4. What are the different types of financial institutions?

5. What services do financial institutions perform?

6. Why are financial institutions regulated?

7. Why are financial markets increasingly becoming global?

Why Study Financial Markets and Institutions?: Chapter Overview

This book provides a detailed overview and analysis of the financial system in which financial managers operate. Making investment and financing decisions requires managers to understand the flow of funds throughout the economy as well as the operation and structure of domestic and international financial markets. In the 1990s, financial markets in the United States boomed. The Dow Jones Industrial Index—a widely quoted index of the values of 30 large corporations (see Chapter 8)—rose from a level of 2,800 in January 1990 to more than 11,000 by the end of the decade; this compares to a move from 100 at its inception in 1906 to 2,800 thirty-four years later. While security values in U.S. financial markets rose dramatically in the 1990s, markets in Southeast Asia, South America, and Russia were much more volatile. The Thai baht,

In the News

1-1

I t was just hours after a second, tumultuous day in the U.S. stock market had come to an end. To the relief of investors around the world, the market last Tuesday had risen sharply, the first blessed evidence in three trading days that stocks weren't headed for the abyss. The day before, the Dow Jones industrial average had plunged 554 points before the New York Stock Exchange, like a referee finally stepping in a bloody and brutally one-sided fight, had for the second time that day called a halt to trading. Since the close of business on Wednesday, October 22, the Dow had plummeted 863

Source: Bill Powell, *Newsweek*, November 10, 1997, p. 32. From Newsweek, 1998. © 1997, Newsweek, Inc. All rights reserved. Reprinted by permission.

The Globe Shudders

The Asian Contagion Spreads, Sending the World's Markets on a Wild Ride

points—a response, in part, to increasing fears that the unfolding economic debacle in East Asia would inevitably damage many American companies. . .

It was not the week's only important lesson. The other was an indelible reminder—delivered with the subtlety of a wrecking ball—of just how interlinked global markets have become. Market signals whip around the world instantaneously, and for an economy as large as the United States', with its

globally integrated corporations earning more and more overseas, that means there is hardly a place on the planet completely irrelevant to its economic health. At the end of the 20th century, the business of America is business everywhere. Monday's Dow sell-off was triggered by yet another stunning rout in the troubled Hong Kong stock market; by Thursday, what just two weeks ago most analysts thought was a localized event (the Asia melt-down) had suddenly become the "Asian contagion"—a virus that had spread violently to South America's largest economy. Brazil, with large current account deficits and a flagging currency (just like some of East Asia's emerging economies), watched its stock market decline nearly 10 percent on Thursday.

www.dowjones.com/

www.newsweek.com/

for example, fell nearly 50 percent in value relative to the U.S. dollar on July 2, 1997. In the News box 1–1 highlights how a financial system crisis in Asian countries impacted the U.S. stock market.

Do You Understand?

1. What the Asian contagion is?
2. Why the Asian crisis affected the values of U.S. company stocks?

Meanwhile, the financial institutions industry is approaching a full historical cycle. Originally the banking industry operated as a full-service industry, performing directly or indirectly all financial services (commercial banking, investment banking, stock investing, insurance provision, etc.). In the early 1930s, the economic and industrial collapse resulted in the separation of some of these activities. In the 1970s and 1980s new, relatively unregulated financial services industries sprang up (e.g., mutual funds, brokerage funds) that separated the financial service functions even further. Now, at the beginning of the new millennium, regulatory changes, technology, and financial innovation are interacting such that a full set of financial services may again be offered by a single financial institution (FI) such as Citigroup. Not only are the boundaries between traditional industry sectors weakening, but competition is becoming global in nature, as German, French, and other international FIs enter into U.S. financial service markets and vice versa.

As economic and competitive environments change, attention to profit and, more than ever, risk becomes increasingly important. This book offers a unique analysis of the risks faced by investors and savers, as well as strategies that can be adopted for controlling and managing these risks. Newer areas of operations such as asset securitization, derivative securities, and internationalization of financial services also receive special emphasis.

This introductory chapter provides an overview of the structure and operations of various financial markets and financial institutions. Financial markets are differentiated by the characteristics (such as maturity) of the financial instruments, or securities that are exchanged. Moreover, each financial market, in turn, depends in part or in whole on financial institutions. Indeed, FIs play a special role in the functioning of financial markets. In particular, FIs often provide the least costly and most efficient way to channel funds to and from financial markets.

Overview of Financial Markets

financial markets

The arenas through which funds flow.

Financial markets are structures through which funds flow. Financial markets can be distinguished along two major dimensions: (1) primary versus secondary markets and (2) money versus capital markets. The next sections discuss each of these dimensions.

Primary Markets versus Secondary Markets

primary markets

Markets in which corporations raise funds through new issues of securities.

Primary Markets.   **Primary markets** are markets in which users of funds (e.g., corporations) raise funds through new issues of financial instruments, such as stocks and bonds. New issues of financial instruments are sold to the initial suppliers of funds (e.g., households) in exchange for funds (money) that the issuer or user of funds needs.[1] Most primary market transactions in the United States are arranged through financial institutions called investment banks—for example, Morgan Stanley or Lehman Brothers—who serve as intermediaries between the issuing corporations (fund users) and investors (fund suppliers). Figure 1–1 illustrates a time line for the primary market exchange of funds for a new issue of corporate bonds or equity. Normally, an investment bank facilitates this transfer of funds by *underwriting* the financial instruments issued by a corporation. The investment bank seeks to guarantee a fixed price for the corporation for its newly issued financial instruments. It does this by buying the whole issue at a single price from the corporate issuer. It then seeks to resell these securities to suppliers of funds (investors) at a slightly higher price. This process is called **firm commitment underwriting** and is discussed in more detail in Chapter 8. When acting as an underwriter, the investment bank takes a risk that it may be unable to resell the instruments to investors at a price equal to or above that paid to the corporation. If this occurs, the investment bank takes a loss on its underwriting. The corporation, however, is assured of a fixed cash inflow from the sale of the financial instrument.

firm commitment underwriting

The issue of financial instruments by an investment bank in which the investment bank guarantees the corporation a price for newly issued instruments by buying the whole issue at a fixed price from the corporate issuer. It then seeks to resell these instruments to suppliers of funds (investors) at a higher price.

initial public offerings (IPOs)

The first public issue of financial instruments by a firm.

Primary market financial instruments include issues of equity by firms initially going public (e.g., allowing their equity—shares—to be publicly traded on stock markets for the first time). These first-time issues are usually referred to as **initial public offerings (IPOs).** For example, on July 24, 1998, theglobe.com, Inc., announced a $27.9 million IPO of its common stock at $9 per share. The company's stock was underwritten by several investment banks, including Bear, Stearns & Co. Inc.

1. We discuss the users and suppliers of funds in more detail in Chapter 2.

Figure 1–1 Primary and Secondary Market Transfer of Funds Time Line

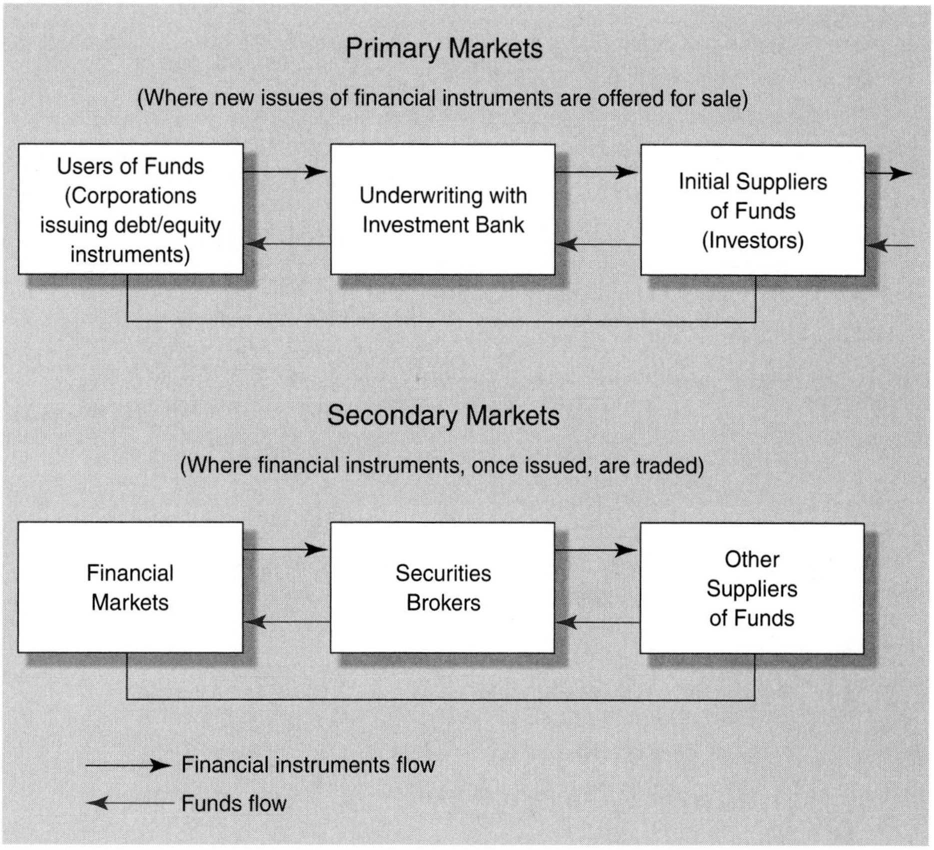

Primary market securities also include the issue of additional equity or debt instruments of an already publicly traded firm. For example, on November 20, 1998, Fox Entertainment Group, Inc., announced the sale of an additional 124,800,000 shares of common stock (at $22.50 per share) underwritten by investment banks such as Merrill Lynch & Co., Allen & Co., Goldman Sachs & Co., and Morgan Stanley Dean Witter. The **tombstone** (the public announcement of the issue in the financial press) for this sale is presented in Figure 1–2. Other investment banks (such as Bear, Stearns; Donaldson, Lufkin & Jenrette; J.P. Morgan; NationsBanc Montgomery Securities; and Salomon Smith Barney) also participated in the sale and distribution of the new issue but were not the main or lead underwriters.

tombstone

A public announcement of a new issue of financial instruments in the financial press.

Secondary Markets. Once financial instruments such as stocks are issued in primary markets, they are then traded—that is, rebought and resold—in secondary markets. For example, on the first day of trading the price of theglobe.com rose over 600 percent, as new investors bought the shares from the original investors in the IPO. The New York Stock Exchange (NYSE), the American Stock Exchange (AMEX), and the National Association of Securities Dealers Automated Quotation (NASDAQ)[2] system are three well-known examples of secondary markets for trading stocks.[3] We discuss

2. On October 30, 1998, the National Association of Securities Dealers, Inc. (NASD), the world's first electronic stock market, and the American Stock Exchange (AMEX), the nation's second largest floor-based exchange, merged to form the Nasdaq-Amex Market Group. Each market continues to function as an independent subsidiary.

3. Most bonds are not traded on floor-based exchanges. Rather, FIs trade them over the counter (OTC) using telephone and computer networks (see Chapter 6). For example, less than 1 percent of corporate bonds outstanding are traded on organized exchanges such as the NYSE.

Figure 1-2 Tombstone Announcing the Primary Issue of Common Stock

This announcement is under no circumstances to be construed as an offer to sell or as a solicitation of an offer to buy any of these securities. The offering is made only by the Prospectus.

New Issue   November 20, 1998

$2,808,000,000

Fox Entertainment Group, Inc.
124,800,000 Shares
Class A Common Stock

———————

Price $22.50 Per Share

———————

The New York Stock Exchange symbol is FOX

Copies of the Prospectus may be obtained in any State or jurisdiction in which this announcement is circulated from only such of the undersigned or other dealers or brokers as may lawfully offer these securities in such State or jurisdiction.

106,080,000 Shares
The above shares were underwritten by the following group of U.S. Underwriters.

Merrill Lynch & Co.
     Allen & Company Incorporated
          Goldman Sachs & Co.
              Morgan Stanley Dean Witter
Bear, Stearns & Co. Inc.
     Donaldson, Lufkin & Jenrette
          J.P. Morgan & Co.
             NationsBanc Montgomery Securities LLC
                Salomon Smith Barney

ABN AMRO Incorporated	BT Alex. Brown Incorporated	Credit Lyonnais Securities (USA) Inc.	Credit Suisse First Boston
A.G. Edwards & Sons, Inc.	ING Barings Furman Selz LLC	Lazard Freres & Co. LLC	Lehman Brothers
PaineWebber Incorporated		Prudential Securities Incorporated	Schroder & Co. Inc.
TD Securities		Warburg Dillon Read LLC	Wasserstein Perella Securities, Inc.
Sanford C. Bernstein & Co., Inc.		Blaylock & Partners, L.P.	Chatsworth Securities LLC
Crowell, Weedon & Co.	Dain Rauscher Wessels A division of Dain Rauscher Incorporated	Doley Securities, Inc.	Gerard Klauer Mattison & Co., Inc.
Guzman & Company	Interstate/Johnson Lane Corporation	Janney Montgomery Scott Inc.	Legg Mason Wood Walker Incorporated
May Davis Group		Neuberger Berman, LLC	Pryor, McClendon, Counts & Co., Inc.
Raymond James & Associates, Inc.		The Robinson-Humphrey Company	Sands Brothers & Co., Ltd.
Tucker Anthony Incorporated		Utendahl Capital Partners, L.P.	Wheat First Union A Division of Wheat First Securities, Inc.

Source: Fox Entertainment Group, Prospectus.

the details of each of these markets in Chapter 8. Buyers of secondary market securities are economic agents (consumers, businesses, and governments) with excess funds. Sellers of secondary market financial instruments are economic agents in need of funds. Figure 1–1 illustrates a secondary market transfer of funds. When an economic agent buys a financial instrument in a secondary market, funds are exchanged, usually with the help of a securities broker such as Schwab acting as an intermediary between the buyer and the seller of the instrument (see Chapter 8). The original issuer of the

Table 1-1 Top NYSE Volume Days

Date	Volume (in thousands)
December 17, 1999	1,349,711
October 1, 1998	1,216,325
April 19, 1999	1,213,763
October 28, 1997	1,201,347
June 30, 1999	1,150,172
October 29, 1999	1,143,115
October 28,1999	1,134,675
December 9, 1999	1,122,007
October 8, 1998	1,114,368
April 15, 1999	1,088,806
October 16, 1998	1,022,181
April 29, 1999	1,001,926
April 16, 1999	1,001,752
January 6, 1999	986,640
October 7, 1998	976,816
October 20, 1998	958,065
October 15, 1997	937,417
August 31, 1998	917,250
October 2, 1998	902,729
September 23, 1998	900,003

Source: The New York Stock Exchange website, Data Library, January 2000. *www.nyse.com/*

instrument (user of funds) is not involved in this transfer. In addition to stocks and bonds, secondary markets also exist for financial instruments backed by mortgages and other assets (see Chapter 7), foreign exchange (see Chapter 9), and futures and options (i.e., derivative securities—see Chapter 10). As we will see in Chapter 10, derivative securities have existed for centuries, but the growth in derivative securities markets occurred mainly in the 1970s, 1980s, and 1990s. As major markets, therefore, the derivative securities markets are among the newest of the financial security markets.

secondary market

A market that trades financial instruments once they are issued.

Secondary markets offer benefits to both investors (suppliers of funds) and issuing corporations (users of funds). For investors, secondary markets provide liquidity and diversification benefits (see Chapter 2). Corporate security issuers are not directly involved in the transfer of funds or instruments in the secondary market. However, the issuer does obtain information about the current market value of its financial instruments, and thus the value of the corporation as perceived by investors such as its stockholders, through tracking the prices at which its financial instruments are being traded on secondary markets. This price information allows issuers to evaluate how well they are using the funds generated from the financial instruments they have already issued and provides information on how well any subsequent offerings of debt or equity might do in terms of raising additional money (and at what cost).

Trading volume in secondary markets can be large. Some of the top volume trading days on the NYSE are listed in Table 1–1; on October 28, 1997, NYSE trading volume exceeded 1 billion shares for the first time ever. In the mid-1980s, a NYSE trading day involving 250 million shares was considered to be heavy.

Secondary markets offer buyers and sellers liquidity—the ability to turn an asset into cash quickly—as well as information about the prices or the value of their investments. Increased liquidity makes it more desirable and easier for the issuing firm to sell a security initially in the primary market. Further, the existence of centralized markets for buying and selling financial instruments allows investors to trade these instruments at low transaction costs.

Figure 1–3 Money versus Capital Market Maturities

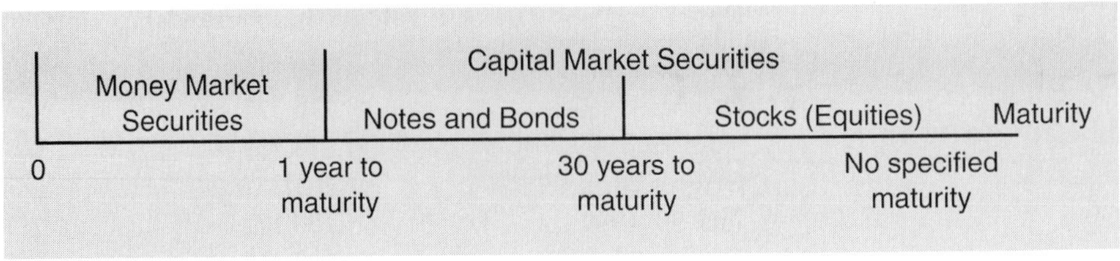

	Capital Market Securities		
Money Market Securities	Notes and Bonds	Stocks (Equities)	Maturity
0	1 year to maturity	30 years to maturity	No specified maturity

Money Markets versus Capital Markets

money markets

Markets that trade debt securities or instruments with maturities of less than one year.

Money Markets. **Money markets** are markets that trade debt securities or instruments with maturities of one year or less (see Figure 1–3). In the money markets, economic agents with short-term excess supplies of funds can lend funds (i.e., buy money market instruments) to economic agents who have short-term needs or shortages of funds (i.e., they sell money market instruments). The short-term nature of these instruments means that fluctuations in their prices in the secondary markets in which they trade are usually quite small (see Chapters 3 and 20 on interest rate risk). In the United States, money markets do not operate in a specific location—rather, transactions occur via telephones, wire transfers, and computer trading. Thus, most U.S. money markets are said to be **over-the-counter** (OTC) **markets.**

over-the-counter market

Markets that do not operate in a specific fixed location—rather, transactions occur via telephones, wire transfers, and computer trading.

FIs frequently transact in money markets. Depository institutions such as commercial banks are required by regulators (such as the Federal Reserve) to hold a minimum proportion of their deposits as cash reserves. Since these cash reserves bear no interest, depository institutions invest any excess short-term fund holdings in short-term money market instruments. Other financial institutions, especially money market mutual funds (see Chapter 18), also invest heavily in money market instruments.

Money Market Instruments. Table 1–2 lists outstanding amounts of money market instruments in the United States in 1990, 1995, and 1999. Notice that in 1999 commercial paper, followed by federal funds and repurchase agreements, negotiable CDs, and Treasury bills, had the largest amounts outstanding. Money market instruments and the operation of the money markets are described and discussed in detail in Chapter 5.

capital markets

Markets that trade debt (bonds) and equity (stock) instruments with maturities of more than one year.

Capital Markets. **Capital markets** are markets that trade equity (stocks) and debt (bonds) instruments with maturities of more than one year (see Figure 1–3). Given their longer maturity, these instruments experience wider price fluctuations in the secondary markets in which they trade than do money market instruments.[4]

Capital Market Instruments. Table 1–3 lists the major capital market instruments and their outstanding amounts by value. Notice that corporate stocks or equities represent the largest capital market instrument, followed by securitized residential mortgages and corporate bonds. Securitized mortgages are those mortgages that FIs have packaged together and sold as bonds backed by mortgage cash flows (such as interest and principal repayments—see Chapters 7 and 25). The relative size of capital market instruments outstanding depends on two factors: number of securities issued and their market prices. One reason for the sharp increase in the amount of equities outstanding is the bull market in stock prices in the 1990s. Capital market instruments and their operations are discussed in detail in Chapters 6 through 8.

---

4. For example, their longer maturities subject these instruments to both higher credit (or bankruptcy) risk and interest rate risk than money market instruments.

Table 1–2 Money Market Instruments Outstanding, 1990–1999
(in billions of dollars)

	1990	1995	1999 (third quarter)
Commercial paper	$557.8	$677.7	$1,284.5
Federal funds and repurchase agreements	372.3	660.1	1,006.1
U.S. Treasury bills	527.4	760.7	647.8
Negotiable CDs	546.9	476.9	836.8
Banker's acceptances	52.1	22.6	8.3

Source: Federal Reserve Board, "Flow of Fund Accounts," *Statistical Releases,* Washington, D.C., various issues. *www.bog.frb.fed.us/*

Table 1–3 Capital Market Instruments Outstanding, 1990–1999
(in billions of dollars)

	1990	1995	1999 (third quarter)
Corporate stocks	$3,524.8	$8,389.9	$16,008.3
Residential mortgages	2,966.5	3,921.6	5,020.9
Commercial and farm mortgages	837.7	787.8	1,160.3
Corporate bonds	1,703.1	2,776.0	4,534.6
Treasury securities	1,653.4	2,531.5	2,956.7
State and local government bonds	1,184.4	1,304.0	1,518.1
U.S. government owned agencies	1,043.5	1,570.3	2,246.2
U.S. government sponsored agencies	393.7	806.7	1,499.8
Bank and consumer loans	1,626.1	2,075.8	2,571.8

Source: Federal Reserve Board, "Flow of Fund Accounts," *Statistical Releases,* Washington, D.C., various issues. *www.bog.frb.fed.us/*

Financial Market Regulation

www.sec.gov/

Financial instruments are subject to regulations imposed by regulatory agencies such as the Securities and Exchange Commission (SEC), as well as the exchanges (if any) on which the instruments are traded. For example, the main emphasis of SEC regulations is on full and fair disclosure of information on securities issues to actual and potential investors. Those firms planning to issue new stocks or bonds to be sold to the public at large (public issues) are required by the SEC to register their securities with the SEC and to fully describe the issue, and any risks associated with the issue, in a legal document called a prospectus.[5] The SEC also monitors trading on the major exchanges (along with the exchanges themselves) to ensure that stockholders and managers do not trade on the basis of inside information about their own firms (i.e., information prior to its public release). SEC regulations are not intended to protect investors against poor investment choices but rather to ensure that investors have full and accurate information available about corporate issuers when making their investment decisions. The SEC has also recently imposed regulations on financial markets in an effort to reduce excessive price fluctuations. For example, the NYSE now operates under a series of "circuit breakers" that require the market to shut down for a period of time when prices drop by large amounts during any trading day. The details of these circuit breaker regulations are listed in Chapter 8.

www.nyse.com/

---

5. Those issues not offered to the public at large but rather sold to a few large investors are called private placements and are not subject to SEC regulations (see Chapter 6).

Foreign Exchange Markets

In addition to understanding the operations of domestic financial markets, a financial manager must also understand the operation of foreign exchange markets and foreign capital markets. Today's U.S.-based companies operate globally. It is therefore essential that financial managers understand how events and movements in financial markets in other countries affect the profitability and performance of their own companies. For example, a currency and economic crisis in Russia in the late 1990s adversely impacted U.S. markets in the summer and fall of 1998.

Cash flows from the sale of securities (or other assets) denominated in a foreign currency expose U.S. corporations and investors to risk regarding the value at which foreign currency cash flows can be converted into U.S. dollars. For example, the actual amount of U.S. dollars received on a foreign investment depends on the exchange rate between the U.S. dollar and the foreign currency when the nondollar cash flow is converted into U.S. dollars. If a foreign currency depreciates (declines in value) relative to the U.S. dollar (say from $.1679 per unit of foreign currency to $.1550 per unit of foreign currency) over the investment period (i.e., the period between the time a foreign investment is made and the time it is terminated), the dollar value of cash flows received will fall. If the foreign currency appreciates, or rises in value, relative to the U.S. dollar, the dollar value of cash flows received on the foreign investment will increase.

While foreign currency exchange rates are often flexible—they vary day to day with demand and supply of foreign currency for dollars—central governments sometimes intervene in foreign exchange markets directly or affect foreign exchange rates indirectly by altering interest rates. We discuss the motivation and effects of these interventions in Chapters 4 and 9. The sensitivity of the value of cash flows on foreign investments to changes in the foreign currency's price in terms of dollars is referred to as *foreign exchange risk* and is discussed in more detail in Chapter 9. Techniques for managing, or "hedging," foreign exchange risk, such as using foreign exchange (FX), futures, options, and swaps, are discussed in Chapter 24.

Two major types of foreign exchange market transactions are spot transactions and forward transactions. These transactions are illustrated in Figure 1–4. **Spot foreign exchange transactions** involve the immediate exchange of currencies at the current (or spot) exchange rate. For example, a U.S. investor wishing to buy Italian lira through a local bank essentially has the dollars transferred from his or her bank account to the dollar account of a lira seller. Simultaneously, lira are transferred from the seller's account into a lira account designated by the U.S. investor. Moreover, many large FIs continuously trade foreign currencies among themselves, seeking to profit on movements in spot exchange rates. Thus, foreign exchange markets, like corporate bond and money markets, operate mainly over the counter (OTC), rather than through organized exchanges.

A second type of transaction, a **forward foreign exchange transaction,** is the exchange of currencies at a given exchange rate (forward exchange rate) at some prespecified date in the *future*. Forward contracts are typically written for one-, three-, or six-month periods into the future, but in practice they can be written for any future time period. For example, a U.S. investor can enter into a 27-day forward contract to sell the French franc at the same time it purchases spot francs (see Figure 1–4). As a result, the U.S. investor is guaranteed an exchange rate of French francs for U.S. dollars in 27 days time at a fixed (forward) rate regardless of what happens to the spot exchange rate over the intervening 27 days.

spot foreign exchange transaction

A transaction that involves the immediate exchange of currencies at the current (or spot) exchange rate.

forward foreign exchange transaction

A transaction that involves the exchange of currencies at a specified date in the future and at a specified rate (or forward exchange rate).

Do You Understand?

1. The difference between primary and secondary markets?
2. The major distinction between money markets and capital markets?
3. What the major instruments traded in the capital markets are?
4. The difference between a spot transaction and a forward transaction in foreign currency markets?
5. What happens to the dollar value of a U.S. investor's holding of British pounds if the pound appreciates (rises) in value against the dollar?

Figure 1–4   Time Line Illustrating a Spot versus Forward Foreign Exchange
Transaction

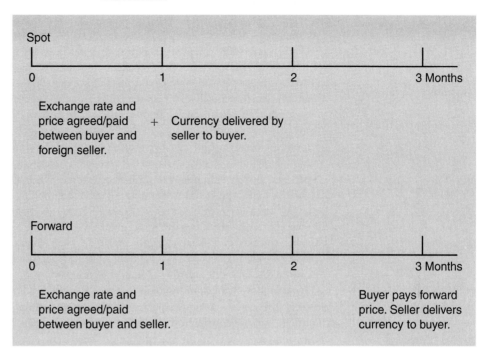

Overview of Financial Institutions

financial institutions

Institutions that perform
the essential function of channeling funds from those with
surplus funds to those with
shortages of funds.

Financial institutions (e.g., banks, credit unions, insurance companies, mutual funds) perform the essential function of channeling funds from those with surplus funds (suppliers of funds) to those with shortages of funds (users of funds). Chapters 11 through 19 discuss the various types of FIs in today's economy, including (1) the size, structure, and composition of each type of FI, (2) their balance sheets and recent trends, (3) FI performance, and (4) the regulators who oversee each type of FI. Table 1–4 lists and summarizes the FIs discussed in detail in later chapters.

In Table 1–5, we show the changing shares of total assets of FIs in the United States from 1860 to 1999. A number of important trends are clearly evident; most apparent is the decline in the total share of depository institutions—commercial banks and thrifts—since World War II. Specifically, the share of commercial banks declined from 55.9 to 35.0 percent between 1948 and 1999, while the share of thrifts (savings banks, savings associations, and credit unions) fell from 12.3 to 10.3 percent over the same period.[6] Similarly, insurance companies also witnessed a decline in their share, from 24.3 to 18.2 percent. The most dramatic trend involves the increasing share of pension funds and investment companies. Pension funds (private plus state and local)

---

6. Although bank assets as a percentage of total assets in the financial sector may have declined in recent years, this does not necessarily mean that banking activity has decreased. Boyd and Gertler show that banking activity has risen, albeit moderately, when measured against the growth of gross domestic product (GDP) (see J. H. Boyd and M. Gertler, "Are Banks Dead? Or, Are the Reports Greatly Exaggerated?" Federal Reserve Bank of Minneapolis, Research Department, working paper, May 1994). In addition, off-balance-sheet activity has replaced some of the traditional activities of commercial banks (see Chapter 13).

Table 1–4 Types of Financial Institutions

Commercial banks—depository institutions whose major assets are loans and whose major liabilities are deposits. Commercial banks' loans are broader in range, including consumer, commercial, and real estate loans, than are those of other depository institutions. Commercial banks' liabilities include more nondeposit sources of funds, such as subordinate notes and debentures, than do those of other depository institutions.

Thrifts—depository institutions in the form of savings and loans, savings banks, and credit unions. Thrifts generally perform services similar to commercial banks, but they tend to concentrate their loans in one segment, such as real estate loans or consumer loans.

Insurance companies—financial institutions that protect individuals and corporations (policyholders) from adverse events. Life insurance companies provide protection in the event of untimely death, illness, and retirement. Property casualty insurance protects against personal injury and liability due to accidents, theft, fire, and so on.

Securities firms and investment banks—financial institutions that underwrite securities and engage in related activities such as securities brokerage, securities trading, and making a market in which securities can trade.

Finance companies—financial intermediaries that make loans to both individuals and businesses. Unlike depository institutions, finance companies do not accept deposits but instead rely on short- and long-term debt for funding.

Mutual funds—financial institutions that pool financial resources of individuals and companies and invest those resources in diversified portfolios of asset.

Pension funds—financial institutions that offer savings plans through which fund participants accumulate savings during their working years before withdrawing them during their retirement years. Funds originally invested in and accumulated in a pension fund are exempt from current taxation.

increased their asset share from 3.1 to 13.1 percent, while investment companies (mutual funds and money market mutual funds) increased their share from 1.3 to 16.6 percent over the 1948 to 1999 period.

To understand the important economic function FIs play in the operation of financial markets, imagine a simple world in which FIs did not exist. In such a world, suppliers of funds (e.g., households), generating excess savings by consuming less than they earn, would have a basic choice: They could either hold cash as an asset or directly invest that cash in the securities issued by users of funds (e.g., corporations or households). In general, users of funds issue financial claims (e.g., equity and debt securities) to finance the gap between their investment expenditures and their internally generated savings such as retained earnings. As shown in Figure 1–5, in such a world we have a **direct transfer** of funds (money) from suppliers of funds to users of funds. In return, financial claims would flow directly from users of funds to suppliers of funds.

In an economy without FIs, the level of funds flowing between suppliers of funds and users of funds through financial markets is likely to be quite low. There are several reasons for this. Once they have lent money in exchange for financial claims, suppliers of funds need to monitor continuously the use of their funds. They must be sure that the user of funds neither steals the funds outright nor wastes the funds on projects that have low or negative returns, since this would lower the chances of being repaid and/or earning a positive return on their investment (such as through the receipt of dividends or interest). Such monitoring is often extremely costly for any given fund supplier because it requires considerable time, expense, and effort to collect this information relative to the size of the average fund supplier's investment.

As mentioned earlier, the SEC requires and monitors the full and fair disclosure of information on securities to actual or potential investors (suppliers of funds)—such as in quarterly and annual reports. Many investors, however, do not have the financial training to analyze this information in order to determine whether a securities issuer is

direct transfer

A corporation sells its stock or debt directly to investors without going through a financial institution.

Table 1–5 Percentage Shares of Assets of Financial Institutions in the United States, 1860–1999

	1860	1880	1900	1912	1922	1929	1939	1948	1960	1970	1980	1990	1999[†]
Commercial banks	71.4%	60.6%	62.9%	64.5%	63.3%	53.7%	51.2%	55.9%	38.2%	37.9%	34.8%	36.8%	35.0%
Thrift institutions	17.8	22.8	18.2	14.8	13.9	14.0	13.6	12.3	19.7	20.4	21.4	16.5	10.3
Insurance companies	10.7	13.9	13.8	16.6	16.7	18.6	27.2	24.3	23.8	18.9	16.1	18.2	18.2
Investment companies	—	—	—	—	0.0	2.4	1.9	1.3	2.9	3.5	3.6	9.5	16.6
Pension funds	—	—	0.0	0.0	0.0	0.7	2.1	3.1	9.7	13.0	17.4	11.2	13.1
Finance companies	—	0.0	0.0	0.0	0.0	2.0	2.2	2.0	4.6	4.8	5.1	5.8	5.0
Securities brokers and dealers	0.0	0.0	3.8	3.0	5.3	8.1	1.5	1.0	1.1	1.2	1.1	1.3	1.2
Mortgage companies	0.0	2.7	1.3	1.2	0.8	0.6	0.3	0.1	*	*	0.4	0.6	0.3
Real estate investment trusts	—	—	—	—	—	—	—	—	0.0	0.3	0.1	0.1	0.3
Total (percent)	100.0%	100.0%	100.0%	100.0%	100.0%	100.0%	100.0%	100.0%	100.0%	100.0%	100.0%	100.0%	100.0%
Total (trillion dollars)	.001	.005	.016	.034	.075	.123	.129	.281	.596	1.328	4.025	8.122	13.207

Columns may not add to 100% due to rounding.

*Data not available.

[†]As of March 31, 1999.

Source: Randall Kroszner, "The Evolution of Universal Banking and Its Regulation in Twentieth Century America," in *Universal Banking Financial System Design Reconsidered*, ed. Anthony Saunders and Ingo Walter, (Burr Ridge, IL: Irwin, 1996), and *Federal Reserve Bulletin*, Table 1.60, November, 1999. *www.bog.frb.us/*

Figure 1–5   Flow of Funds in a World without FIs

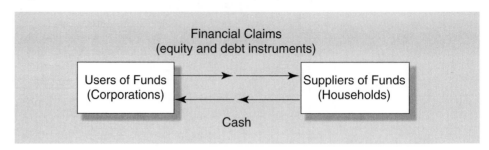

making the best use of its funds. Further, there is such a large number of investment opportunities available to fund suppliers that even those trained in financial analysis rarely have the time to monitor the use of funds for all of their investments. Given this, fund suppliers would likely prefer to leave, or delegate, the monitoring of fund borrowers to others. The resulting lack of monitoring increases the risk of directly investing in financial claims.

The relatively long-term nature of many financial claims (e.g., mortgages, corporate stock, and bonds) creates a second disincentive for suppliers of funds to hold the direct financial claims issued by users of funds. Specifically, given the choice between holding cash and long-term securities, fund suppliers may well choose to hold cash for **liquidity** reasons, especially if they plan to use their savings to finance consumption expenditures in the near future and financial markets are not very developed, or deep, in terms of the number of active buyers and sellers in the market. Moreover, even though real-world financial markets provide some liquidity services, by allowing fund suppliers to trade financial securities among themselves, fund suppliers face a **price risk** upon the sale of securities. In addition, the secondary market trading of securities involves various transaction costs. The price at which investors can sell a security on secondary markets such as the New York Stock Exchange (NYSE) may well differ from the price they initially paid for the security either because investors change their valuation of the security between the time it was bought and when it was sold and/or because dealers, acting as intermediaries between buyers and sellers, charge transaction costs for completing a trade.[7]

Unique Economic Functions Performed by Financial Institutions

Because of (1) monitoring costs, (2) liquidity costs, and (3) price risk, the average investor may view direct investment in financial claims and markets as an unattractive proposition and prefer to hold cash. As a result financial market activity (and therefore savings and investment) would likely remain quite low.

However, the financial system has developed an alternative and indirect way for investors (or fund suppliers) to channel funds to users of funds. This is the **indirect transfer** of funds to the ultimate user of funds via FIs. Due to the costs of monitoring, liquidity risk, and price risk, as well as for other reasons explained later, fund suppliers often prefer to hold the financial claims issued by FIs rather than those directly issued by the ultimate users of funds. Consider Figure 1–6, which is a closer representation than Figure 1–5 of the world in which we live and the way funds flow in the U.S. financial system. Notice how financial intermediaries or institutions are standing, or intermediating between, the suppliers and users of funds—that is, channeling funds from ultimate suppliers to ultimate users of funds.

liquidity

The ease with which an asset can be converted into cash.

price risk

The risk that an asset's sale price will be lower than its purchase price.

indirect transfer

A transfer of funds between suppliers and users of funds through a financial intermediary.

---

7. On organized exchanges such as the NYSE, the price difference between a buy and sell price is called the bid-ask spread.

Figure 1–6 Flow of Funds in a World with FIs

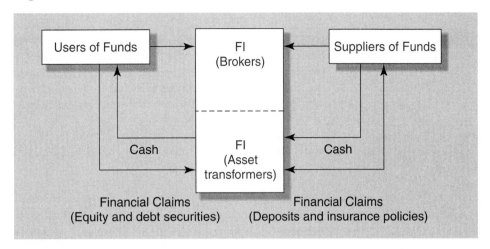

Table 1–6 Services Performed by Financial Intermediaries

Services Benefiting Suppliers of Funds

Monitoring Costs—Aggregation of funds in an FI provides greater incentive to collect a firm's information and monitor actions. The relatively large size of the FI allows this collection of information to be accomplished at a lower average cost (economies of scale).

Liquidity and Price Risk—FIs provide financial claims to household savers with superior liquidity attributes and with lower price risk.

Transaction Cost Services—Similar to economies of scale in information production costs, an FI's size can result in economies of scale in transaction costs.

Maturity Intermediation—FIs can better bear the risk of mismatching the maturities of their assets and liabilities.

Denomination Intermediation—FIs such as mutual funds allow small investors to overcome constraints to buying assets imposed by large minimum denomination size.

Services Benefiting the Overall Economy

Money Supply Transmission—Depository institutions are the conduit through which monetary policy actions impact the rest of the financial system and the economy in general.

Credit Allocation—FIs are often viewed as the major, and sometimes only, source of financing for a particular sector of the economy, such as farming and residential real estate.

Intergenerational Wealth Transfers—FIs, especially life insurance companies and pension funds, provide savers with the ability to transfer wealth from one generation to the next.

Payment Services—Efficiency with which depository institutions provide payment services directly benefits the economy.

How can an FI reduce the monitoring costs, liquidity risks, and price risks facing the suppliers of funds compared to when they directly invest in financial claims? We look at each of these services next and summarize them in Table 1–6.

Monitoring Costs. As mentioned above, a supplier of funds who directly invests in a fund user's financial claims faces a high cost of monitoring the fund user's actions in a timely and complete fashion. One solution to this problem is for a large number of small investors to group their funds together by holding the claims issued by an FI. In turn the FI invests in the direct financial claims issued by fund users. This aggregation of funds by fund suppliers in an FI resolves a number of problems. First, the "large" FI now has a much greater incentive to collect information and monitor the ultimate fund user's actions because the FI has far more at stake than any small individual fund supplier. Second, the monitoring function performed by the FI alleviates the "free-rider" problem that exists when small fund suppliers leave it to each other to collect information and monitor a fund user. In an economic sense, fund suppliers have appointed the FI as a **delegated monitor** to act on their behalf. For example, full-service securities firms such as Merrill Lynch carry out investment research on new issues and make investment recommendations for their retail clients (or investors), while commercial banks collect deposits from fund suppliers and lend these funds to ultimate users such as corporations. An important part of these FIs' functions is their ability and incentive to monitor ultimate fund users.

Liquidity and Price Risk. In addition to improving the quality and quantity of information, FIs provide additional claims to fund suppliers, thus acting as **asset transformers.** FIs purchase the financial claims issued by users of funds—primary securities such as mortgages, bonds, and stocks—and finance these purchases by selling financial claims to household investors and other fund suppliers in the form of deposits, insurance policies, or other *secondary securities.*

Often claims issued by FIs have liquidity attributes that are superior to those of primary securities. For example, banks and thrift institutions (e.g., savings associations) issue transaction account deposit contracts with a fixed principal value and often a guaranteed interest rate that can be withdrawn immediately, on demand, by investors. Money market mutual funds issue shares to household savers that allow them to enjoy almost fixed principal (depositlike) contracts while earning higher interest rates than on bank deposits, and that can be withdrawn immediately by writing a check. Even life insurance companies allow policyholders to borrow against their policies held with the company at very short notice. How can FIs such as depository institutions offer highly liquid, low price-risk securities to fund suppliers on the liability side of their balance sheets while investing in relatively less liquid and higher price-risk securities—such as the debt and equity—issued by fund users on the asset side? Furthermore, how can FIs be confident enough to guarantee that they can provide liquidity services to fund suppliers when they themselves invest in risky assets? Indeed, why should fund suppliers believe FIs' promises regarding the liquidity and safety of their investments?

The answers to these three questions lie in FIs' ability to **diversify** away some, but not all, of their investment risk. The concept of diversification is familiar to all students of finance. Basically, as long as the returns on different investments are not perfectly *positively* correlated, by spreading their investments across a number of assets, FIs can diversify away significant amounts of their portfolio risk. (We discuss the mechanics of diversification in the loan portfolio in Chapter 21.) Indeed, experiments in the United States and the United Kingdom have shown that diversifying across just 15 securities can bring significant diversification benefits to FIs and portfolio managers.[8] Further, for equal investments in different securities, as the number of securities in an FI's asset portfolio increases, portfolio risk falls, albeit at a diminishing rate. What is really going on here is that FIs can exploit the law of large numbers in making their investment decisions, whereas due to their smaller wealth size, individual fund suppliers are constrained to holding relatively undiversified portfolios. As a result, diversification allows an FI to predict more accurately its expected return and risk on its investment portfolio so that it can credibly fulfill its promises to the suppliers of funds to provide highly liquid claims with little price risk. A good example of this is a bank's ability to offer highly liquid, instantly withdrawable demand deposits as liabilities

delegated monitor

An economic agent appointed to act on behalf of smaller investors in collecting information and/or investing funds on their behalf.

asset transformers

Financial claims issued by an FI that are more attractive to investors than are the claims directly issued by corporations.

diversify

The ability of an economic agent to reduce risk by holding a number of securities in a portfolio.

---

8. For a review of such studies, see E. J. Elton and M. J. Gruber, *Modern Portfolio Theory and Investment Analysis,* 6th ed. (New York: John Wiley & Sons, 1998), Chapter 2.

while investing in risky, nontradable, and often illiquid loans as assets. As long as an FI is large enough to gain from diversification and monitoring on the asset side of its balance sheet, its financial claims (its liabilities) are likely to be viewed as liquid and attractive to small savers—especially when compared to direct investments in the capital market.

Additional Benefits FIs Provide to Suppliers of Funds

The indirect investing of funds through FIs is attractive to fund suppliers for other reasons as well. We discuss these below and summarize them in Table 1–6.

Reduced Transaction Cost.   Not only do FIs have a greater incentive to collect information, but also their average cost of collecting relevant information is lower than for the individual investor (i.e., information collection enjoys **economies of scale**). For example, the cost to a small investor of buying a $100 broker's report may seem inordinately high for a $10,000 investment. For an FI with $10 billion of assets under management, however, the cost seems trivial. Such economies of scale of information production and collection tend to enhance the advantages to investors of investing via FIs rather than directly investing themselves.

Nevertheless, due to technological advances, the costs of direct access to financial markets by savers is ever falling and the relative benefits to the individual savers of investing through FIs is narrowing. In the News box 1–2 gives an example of this ability to reduce transactions costs with an **etrade** on the Internet rather than using a traditional stockbroker and paying brokerage fees (see Chapter 8). Another example is the private placement market, in which corporations such as General Electric sell securities directly to investors often without using underwriters. In addition, a number of companies allow investors to buy their stock directly without using a broker. Among well-known companies that have instituted such stock purchase plans are Bell Atlantic, BellSouth, IBM, Walt Disney Co., Royal Dutch Petroleum, Warner-Lambert, and Tribune Co., a Chicago-based entertainment and media company.

Maturity Intermediation.   An additional dimension of FIs' ability to reduce risk by diversification is their greater ability to bear the risk of mismatching the maturities of their assets and liabilities than can small savers. Thus, FIs offer maturity intermediation services to the rest of the economy. Specifically, by maturity mismatching, FIs can produce new types of contracts such as long-term mortgage loans to households, while still raising funds with short-term liability contracts such as deposits. In addition, although such mismatches can subject an FI to interest rate risk (see Chapters 3 and 20), a large FI is better able than a small investor to manage this risk through its superior access to markets and instruments for hedging the risks of such loans (see Chapters 7, 10, 23, and 25).

Denomination Intermediation.   Some FIs, especially mutual funds, perform a unique service because they provide services relating to denomination intermediation. Because many assets are sold in very large denominations, they are either out of reach of individual savers or would result in savers holding very undiversified asset portfolios. For example, the minimum size of a negotiable CD is $100,000, while commercial paper (short-term corporate debt) is often sold in minimum packages of $250,000 or more. Individual small savers may be unable to purchase such instruments directly. However, by buying shares in a mutual fund with other small investors, small savers overcome constraints to buying assets imposed by large minimum denomination size. Such indirect access to these markets may allow small savers to generate higher returns (and lower risks) on their portfolios as well.

---

economies of scale

The concept that cost reduction in trading and other transaction services results from increased efficiency when FIs perform these services.

etrade

Buying and selling shares on the Internet.

Do You Understand?

1. What actions brokers and investment companies are taking to attract online trading customers to their firms?

In the News

Online Investment Services Boom

Internet securities brokering and investment information services look likely to be the biggest growth area by far for online financial services over the next five years . . . Online brokerage services are already growing rapidly in the U.S. and latest research demonstrates that many of the Internet brokerage pioneers like Merrill Lynch, Fidelity, and Donaldson, Lufkin, Jenrette are already reaping the rewards.

Global sales of business and professional information disseminated by computer systems, like the Internet, will grow to $37.5 billion in 2001 from $24 billion last year. . . This near 60 percent increase will be led by growth in sales of brokerage service information, which will expand to $14.8 billion from $8.4 billion over the next four years, according to Cowles-Simba Information (a U.S.

research consultancy company). Forrester Research, another U.S. consultancy, forecast that online investing accounts in the U.S. are set to increase from 3 million by the end of this year to 14.4 million in 2002. During this period, assets managed online are predicted to grow by 473 percent to $688 billion . . .

Online discount brokerages are . . . trying to brand name themselves to preserve their market share. ETrade and Fidelity Investments both gave the go-ahead to large, broad-range advertising campaigns recently. This is a significant departure from smaller and more limited brand awareness campaigns like the sponsorship of web banners on the Internet. ETrade's $25 million campaign will include commercials on prime-time TV, pages in business publica-

tions, and billboards at national sporting events. Fidelity Investments will launch its TV advertisements during commercial breaks in the Major League Basketball play-offs. This is the first time that Fidelity has launched any kind of corporate advertising campaign . . .

Aside from offering competitive commissions, the simplest way to attract investors is the age-old way—add value to the service, experts said. This has been the preferred manner of traditional proprietary brokerage houses for a number of years and they have significantly profited from the strategy. It is likely that the majority of future online brokerages will offer free, centralized, web-site research facilities to customers in the future. This trend has already started to occur, despite protests to the contrary by Internet discount brokerages that the Web provides investors with enough information for their investment decisions.

Source: Christopher Jeffery, *Funds International,* November 1997, p. 14.

Economic Functions FIs Provide to the Financial System as a Whole

In addition to the services FIs provide to suppliers and users of funds in the financial markets, FIs perform services that improve the operation of the financial system as a whole. We discuss these next and summarize them in Table 1–6.

Table 1–7 Money Stock, Liquid Assets, and Debt Measures

(billions of dollars, averages of daily figures, seasonally adjusted)

Measures	December 1991	1992	1993	1994	1995	1996	1997	1998	November 1999
M1	897.7	1,024.8	1,128.4	1,148.7	1,124.8	1,081.1	1,076.0	1,093.4	1,108.6
M2	3,455.2	3,509.0	3,567.9	3,509.0	3,657.4	3,834.5	4,040.2	4,401.0	4,627.6
M3	4,180.4	4,183.0	4,232.0	4,319.4	4,572.4	4,933.2	5,423.7	5,995.8	6,385.5
Debt	11,171.1	11,706.1	12,335.4	13,153.2	13,866.9	14,485.7	15,228.1	16,244.9	17,164.4

Composition of the money stock measures and debt is as follows:

M1: 1. Currency outside the U.S. Treasury, Federal Reserve Banks, and the vaults of depository institutions.
2. Traveler's checks of nonbank issuers.
3. Demand deposits at all commercial banks other than those owed to depository institutions, the U.S. government, and foreign banks and official institutions, less cash items in the process of collection and Federal Reserve float.
4. Other checkable deposits (OCDs).

M2: M1 plus
1. Savings and small time deposits (time deposits in amounts of less than $100,000).
2. Other nondeposit obligations of depository institutions.

M3: M2 plus
1. Large time deposits (in amounts of $100,000 or more) issued by all depository institutions.
2. Other nondeposit obligations of depository institutions.

Debt: The debt aggregate is the outstanding credit market debt of the domestic nonfinancial sectors.

Source: *Federal Reserve Bulletin*, January 2000, Table A12, Publication Services, Washington D.C. *www.bog.frb.fed.us/; www.ustreas.gov/; www.treas.gov/*

The Transmission of Monetary Policy. The highly liquid nature of bank and thrift deposits has resulted in their acceptance by the public as the most widely used medium of exchange in the economy. As the notes to Table 1–7 indicate, at the core of the three most commonly used definitions of the money supply—M1, M2, and M3—are bank and/or thrift deposit contracts. Because deposits are a significant component of the money supply, which in turn directly impacts the rate of inflation, depository institutions—particularly commercial banks—play a key role in the *transmission of monetary policy* from the central bank (the Federal Reserve) to the rest of the economy (see Chapter 4 for a detailed discussion of how the Federal Reserve implements monetary policy through depository institutions). Because depository institutions are instrumental in determining the size and growth of the money supply, depository institutions have been designated as the primary conduit through which monetary policy actions by the Federal Reserve impact the rest of the financial sector and the economy in general.

Credit Allocation. Additionally, FIs provide a unique service to the economy in that they are the major source of financing for particular sectors of the economy preidentified by society as being in special need of financing. For example, policymakers in the United States and a number of other countries such as the United Kingdom have identified *residential real estate* as needing special attention. This has enhanced the specialness of those FIs that most commonly service the needs of that sector. In the United States, savings associations and savings banks must emphasize mortgage lending. Sixty-five percent of their assets must be mortgage related for thrifts to maintain their charter status (see Chapter 12). In a similar fashion, farming is an especially important area of the economy in terms of the overall social welfare of the population. Thus, the U.S. government has directly encouraged financial institutions to specialize in financing this area of activity through the creation of Federal Farm Credit Banks.

Intergenerational Wealth Transfers or Time Intermediation. The ability of savers to transfer wealth from their youth to old age as well as across generations is also of

Table 1–8   Risks Faced by Financial Institutions

1. **Interest Rate Risk**—risk incurred by an FI when the maturities of its assets and liabilities are mismatched.
2. **Foreign Exchange Risk**—risk that exchange rate changes can affect the value of an FI's assets and liabilities located abroad.
3. **Market Risk**—risk incurred in trading assets and liabilities due to changes in interest rates, exchange rates, and other asset prices.
4. **Credit Risk**—risk that promised cash flows from loans and securities held by FIs may not be paid in full.
5. **Liquidity Risk**—risk that a sudden surge in liability withdrawals may require an FI to liquidate assets in a very short period of time and at low prices.
6. **Off-Balance-Sheet Risk**—risk incurred by an FI as the result of activities related to contingent assets and liabilities.
7. **Technology Risk**—risk incurred by an FI when its technological investments do not produce anticipated cost savings.
8. **Operational Risk**—risk that existing technology or support systems may malfunction or break down.
9. **Country or Sovereign Risk**—risk that repayments to foreign borrowers may be interrupted because of interference from foreign governments.
10. **Insolvency Risk**—risk that an FI may not have enough capital to offset a sudden decline in the value of its assets.

great importance to a country's social well-being. Because of this, special taxation relief and other subsidy mechanisms encourage investments by savers in life insurance and pension funds. For example, pension funds offer savings plans through which fund participants accumulate tax exempt savings during their working years before withdrawing them during their retirement years.

Payment Services.   Depository institutions such as banks and thrifts are also special in that the efficiency with which they provide payment services directly benefits the economy. Two important payment services are check-clearing and wire transfer services. For example, on any given day, over $2 trillion of payments are directed through Fedwire and CHIPS, the two largest wholesale payment wire network systems in the United States. Any breakdowns in these systems would likely produce gridlock to the payment system, with resulting harmful effects to the economy.

FIs face various risks that affect their ability to perform the services described above. These include interest rate risk, foreign exchange risk, market risk, credit risk, liquidity risk, off-balance-sheet risk, technology risk, operational risk, sovereign risk, and insolvency risk. Chapters 20 through 25 provide an analysis of how FIs measure and manage these risks. We summarize these in Table 1–8.

Regulation of Financial Institutions

6   The preceding section showed that FIs provide various services to sectors of the economy. Failure to provide these services, or a breakdown in their efficient provision, can be costly both to the ultimate suppliers of funds and users of funds as well as to the economy overall. For example, bank failures may destroy household savings and at the same time restrict a firm's access to credit. Insurance company failures may leave household members totally exposed in old age to the cost of catastrophic illnesses and to sudden drops in income on retirement. In addition, individual FI failures may create doubts in savers' minds regarding the stability and solvency of FIs and

Do You Understand?

1. The three major reasons that suppliers of funds would not want to directly purchase securities?
2. What the asset transformation function of FIs is?
3. What delegated monitoring function FIs perform?
4. What the link is between asset diversification and the liquidity of deposit contracts?
5. What maturity intermediation is?
6. Why the need for denomination intermediation arises?
7. The two major sectors that society has identified as deserving special attention in credit allocation?
8. Why monetary policy is transmitted through the banking system?
9. The payment services that FIs perform?

Table 1–9   World Financial Markets

(in billions of dollars)

| Country | Long-Term Debt | | | | Money Market Securities |
	1996	1997	1998	September 1999	September 1999
Argentina	$ 10.8	$ 15.4	$ 17.5	$ 18.8	—
Australia	51.5	53.3	61.7	73.9	5.5
Austria	33.6	36.0	40.0	44.5	N/A
Belgium	29.0	30.9	33.4	39.9	N/A
Brazil	25.9	31.3	32.2	30.1	—
Canada	48.1	55.6	68.3	80.7	0.9
France	198.4	199.0	234.1	274.2	N/A
Germany	325.4	325.4	491.0	637.2	N/A
Hong Kong	16.7	24.5	24.2	28.8	13.7
Ireland	11.4	13.3	17.1	20.5	N/A
Italy	39.3	41.9	51.5	84.6	N/A
Japan	317.1	293.3	293.3	307.2	4.0
Luxembourg	11.3	13.6	17.2	17.1	N/A
Mexico	18.5	22.6	25.7	30.3	—
Netherlands	116.4	135.2	182.9	222.9	N/A
Norway	12.3	18.7	28.4	32.2	—
South Korea	28.9	31.9	30.6	26.9	—
Spain	25.4	30.3	46.3	68.8	N/A
Sweden	24.8	26.1	29.0	37.6	0.5
Switzerland	39.4	61.8	78.9	81.7	7.3
United Kingdom	254.9	294.4	350.5	443.8	20.5
United States	353.4	502.8	714.3	929.3	115.0
Total private sector debt	$2,092.9	$2,446.1	$3,025.4	$4,095.4	$243.7

Source: Bank for International Settlements, "International Banking and Financial Market Developments,"
Quarterly Review, November 1999. *www.bis.org/*

the financial system in general and cause panics and even withdrawal runs on sound institutions. FIs are regulated in an attempt to prevent these types of market failures. Chapter 14 describes the regulations (past and present) that have been imposed on FIs.

Globalization of Financial Markets and Institutions

Financial markets and institutions in the United States have their counterparts in many foreign countries. Table 1–9 lists U.S. dollar equivalent values of money market and debt securities outstanding in countries throughout the world from 1996 through 1999. Prior to the 1980s, U.S. financial markets were much larger in value size and trading volume than any foreign market. Financial markets became truly global in the 1980s when the values of stocks traded in foreign markets soared. For example, the value of stocks traded in the Japanese stock market has, at times, exceeded that of stocks traded in the United States. Likewise, foreign bond markets have served as a major source of international capital. For example, **Eurodollar bonds** are dollar-denominated bonds issued mainly in London and other European centers such as Luxembourg. Since they are issued outside U.S. territory, Eurodollar bonds are not required to be registered with the U.S. SEC (the regulator of domestic securities' issues). Eurodollar bonds account for over 80 percent of new issues in the international bond market. Globalization of financial markets is also evident

Eurodollar bond

Dollar-denominated bonds issued mainly in London and other European centers such as Luxembourg.

Table 1–10 Financial Market Securities Holdings
(in billions of dollars)

	1992	1993	1994	1995	1996	1997	1998	1999*
U.S. Financial Market Instruments Held by Foreign Investors								
Open market paper	12.9	18.8	24.9	43.4	57.9	77.8	114.8	105.3
U.S. government securities	595.0	702.4	757.7	995.3	1,293.9	1,498.1	1,617.7	1,690.1
U.S. corporate bonds	251.5	273.3	311.4	369.5	453.2	540.0	628.7	775.9
Loans to U.S. corporate businesses	129.9	114.2	122.1	122.1	126.2	142.6	142.5	131.1
Total	989.3	1,108.7	1,216.0	1,530.3	1,931.2	2,258.4	2,503.5	2,702.4
U.S. corporate equities held	329.0	373.5	397.7	527.6	656.8	915.9	1,115.4	1,168.1
Total financial assets held	2,247.0	2,605.3	2,852.5	3,423.1	4,133.2	4,845.7	5,616.6	6,164.8
Foreign Financial Market Instruments Held by U.S. Investors								
Commercial paper	78.4	68.8	42.7	56.2	67.5	65.1	72.9	81.8
Bonds	147.2	230.1	242.3	291.9	347.7	394.4	420.2	424.4
Bank loans	23.9	24.6	26.1	34.6	43.7	52.1	58.9	58.8
U.S. government loans	55.1	54.1	51.9	51.1	50.1	48.3	47.2	46.7
Acceptance liabilities to banks	11.3	8.2	7.9	8.2	9.9	9.7	4.7	3.1
Total	315.8	385.8	370.8	441.9	518.8	569.6	603.9	614.8
Foreign corporate equities held	314.3	543.9	586.6	699.1	876.8	1,001.3	1,407.1	1,667.2
Total financial assets held	1,712.3	2,118.1	2,291.7	2,663.5	3,117.0	3,504.3	4,074.9	4,365.5

*As of the third quarter of 1999.
Source: Federal Reserve Board, "Flow of Fund Accounts," *Statistical Releases,* December 1999. *www.bog.frb.fed.us/*

in the derivative securities markets (discussed in Chapter 10). Eurodollar futures and options contracts (futures and options in which the underlying index is the three-month Eurodollar deposit rate or the LIBOR rate) are major contributors to these markets, often dominating in terms of the number of contracts and notional value outstanding.[9]

The significant growth in foreign financial markets is the result of several factors. First is the increase in the pool of savings in foreign countries (e.g., Japan). Second, international investors have turned to U.S. and other markets to expand their investment opportunities and improve their investment portfolio risk and return characteristics. This is especially so as the value of public pension plans has declined in many European countries and investors have turned to private pension plans instead. Third, information on foreign investments and markets is now more accessible and thorough—for example, via the Internet. Fourth, some U.S. FIs—such as specialized mutual funds—offer their customers opportunities to invest in foreign securities and emerging markets at relatively low transaction costs. Finally, deregulation in many foreign countries has allowed international investors greater access and allowed the deregulating countries to expand their investor bases (e.g., until 1997, foreign investors faced severe restrictions on their ability to buy Korean stocks). As a result of these factors, the overall volume of investment and trading activity in foreign securities is increasing, as is the integration of U.S. and foreign financial markets.

9. For example, on September 24, 1999, 503,842 Eurodollar futures contracts were traded on the Chicago Mercantile Exchange, each with a face value of $1 million. U.S. Treasury bond futures, each with a face value of $100,000, were the second most active financial future traded, with a volume of 400,000 contracts.

Table 1–11 The 20 Largest Banks in the World
(in millions of dollars)

	Total Assets	Capital and Reserves
1. Deutsche Bank (Germany)	$735,171	$20,697
2. UBS Group (Switzerland)	687,380	22,704
3. Citigroup (United States)	668,641	48,630
4. Bank of America (United States)	617,679	51,220
5. Bank of Tokyo-Mitsubishi (Japan)	579,791	22,015
6. HypoVereinsbank (Germany)	540,851	15,192
7. ABN-Amro Bank (Netherlands)	507,217	17,701
8. HSBC Holdings (United Kingdom)	482,921	28,455
9. Credit Suisse Group (Switzerland)	475,018	16,178
10. ING Group (Netherlands)	463,598	34,863
11. Crédit Agricole Mutual (France)	457,037	26,437
12. Dai-Ichi Kangyo Bank (Japan)	455,900	17,393
13. Société Générale (France)	450,225	11,640
14. Dresdner Bank (Germany)	429,027	12,666
15. Sumitomo Bank (Japan)	428,001	13,891
16. Sanwa Bank (Japan)	418,373	17,705
17. Westdeutsche Landesbank Girozentrale (Germany)	415,954	9,242
18. Norinchukin Bank (Japan)	407,624	N/A
19. Sakura Bank (Japan)	392,099	17,959
20. Fuji Bank (Japan)	385,253	18,088

Source: *American Banker,* August 5, 1999. *www.americanbanker.com/.* Reprinted with permission—American Banker.

Table 1–12 Foreign Bank Offices Assets and Liabilities Held in the United States
(in billions of dollars)

	1992	1994	1996	1998	1999*
Financial Assets					
Total financial assets	$509.3	$589.7	$714.8	$806.3	$757.0
Financial Liabilities					
Total financial liabilities	519.3	602.8	731.9	828.6	781.6

*As of the third quarter of 1999.
Source: Federal Reserve Board, "Flow of Fund Accounts," *Statistical Releases,* December 1999. *www.bog.frb.fed.us/*

Table 1–10 shows the extent of the growth in foreign investment in U.S. financial markets. From 1992 to the third quarter of 1999, foreign investors' holdings of U.S. financial market debt securities outstanding increased 173.2 percent, from $989.3 billion to $2,702.4 billion, while foreign financial market debt securities held by U.S. investors increased 94.7 percent, from $315.8 billion to $614.8 billion.

For the same reasons discussed earlier (i.e., monitoring costs, liquidity risk, and price risk), financial institutions are of central importance to the development and integration of markets globally. However, U.S. FIs must now compete not only with other domestic FIs for a share of these markets but increasingly with foreign FIs. Table 1–11 lists the 20 largest banks in the world, measured by total assets, as of 1999. Only 2 of the top 20 banks are U.S. banks. Table 1–12 lists foreign bank offices' assets and

Table 1–13   Top Global Banks

Banks	Home Country	Percentage of Overseas Business*
1. Standard Chartered	United Kingdom	74.3%
2. Credit Suisse	Switzerland	74.2
3. Union Bank of Switzerland	Switzerland	71.0
4. Credit Agricole Indosuez	France	71.0
5. Swiss Bank Corporation	Switzerland	64.4
6. HSBC Holdings	United Kingdom	62.8
7. Citigroup	United States	59.6
8. Comp Financiere de Paribas	France	55.6
9. Credit Lyonnais	France	52.5
10. Creditanstalt-Bankverein	Austria	52.3
11. Erste Bank	Austria	51.0
12. J. P. Morgan & Co.	United States	50.9
13. Bankers Trust	United States	49.5
14. ABN-Amro Bank	Netherlands	49.4
15. Allied Irish Bank	Ireland	48.8

* Overseas business refers to the percentage of assets banks hold outside their home country.
Source: "Top 50 Global Banks," *The Banker,* February 1998, p. 41–42.

liabilities held in the United States from 1992 through the third quarter of 1999. Total foreign bank assets over this period increased from $509.3 billion to $757.0 billion.

The world's most active 15 banks, based on the percent of their assets held outside their home countries, are listed in Table 1–13. These include the big Swiss banks[10] as well as U.S. banks such as J. P. Morgan and Citigroup. Interestingly, although prior to 1998 Japanese banks occupied 7 of the top 20 banks in the world in terms of asset size (see Table 1–11), they are absent from the list of banks with the most active international operations. Indeed, domestic problems, including record bad loans (especially in real estate) and a recession, induced Japanese banks to contract their foreign assets and international activities, as well as to merge. For example, the three-way merger between Industrial Bank of Japan, Fuji Bank, and Dai-Ichi Kangyo Bank in 2000 created the world's largest banking group, with assets of over $1,372 billion. Chapter 14 discusses regulatory differences among countries' FIs and recent changes towards implementing a regulatory "level playing field."

As a result of the increased globalization of financial markets and institutions, U.S. financial market movements now have a much greater impact on foreign markets than historically. Moreover, referring back to In the News box 1–1, foreign financial market movements also have a much greater impact on U.S. markets. Thus, the ability of managers to maximize value for an FI's shareholders not only depends on their knowledge of the operations of domestic financial markets and institutions but increasingly on their knowledge of the operations of overseas financial markets and institutions.

Do You Understand?

1. What the trends are in the growth of global financial markets since the 1980s?
2. What a Eurodollar bond is?

10. Union Bank of Switzerland and Swiss Bank Corporation merged in 1998.

Summary

This introductory chapter reviewed the basic operations of domestic and foreign financial markets and institutions. It described the ways in which funds flow through an economic system from lenders to borrowers and outlined the markets and instruments that lenders and borrowers employ to complete this process. In addition, the chapter discussed the need for FI managers to understand the functioning of both the domestic as well as the international markets in which they participate.

The chapter also identified the various factors impacting the specialness of the services FIs provide and the manner in which they improve the efficiency with which funds flow from suppliers of funds to the ultimate users of funds. Currently, however, there are a number of forces—such as technology and especially the Internet—that are so powerful that in the future FIs that have historically relied on making profits by performing traditional special functions such as brokerage will need to expand the array of financial services they sell as well as the way that such services are distributed or sold to their customers.

End-of-Chapter Questions

1. Classify the following transactions as taking place in the primary or secondary markets:
   a. IBM issues $200 million of new common stock.
   b. The New Company issues $50 million of common stock in an IPO.
   c. IBM sells $5 million of GM preferred stock out of its marketable securities portfolio.
   d. The Magellan Fund buys $100 million of previously issued IBM bonds.
   e. Prudential Insurance Co. sells $10 million of GM common stock.

2. Classify the following financial instruments as money market securities or capital market securities:
   a. Bankers Acceptances
   b. Commercial Paper
   c. Common Stock
   d. Corporate Bonds
   e. Mortgages
   f. Negotiable Certificates of Deposit
   g. Repurchase Agreements
   h. U.S. Treasury Bills
   i. U.S. Treasury Notes
   j. Federal Funds

3. How does the location of the money market differ from that of the capital market?

4. Which of the money market instruments has grown fastest since 1990?

5. What are the major instruments traded in capital markets?

6. Classify the following transactions as occurring in the spot or forward markets.
   a. A U.S. bank sells $2 million of DM (deutsche marks).
   b. A U.S. bank agrees to sell $4 million of Japanese yen in 2 months at a price agreed upon today.
   c. A German bank buys $50 million.
   d. An Italian bank agrees to buy $100 million in 6 months at a price agreed upon today.

7. If a U.S. bank is holding Japanese yen in its portfolio, what type of exchange rate movement would the bank be most concerned about?

8. What are the different types of financial institutions? Include a description of the main services offered by each.

9. How would economic transactions between suppliers of funds (e.g., households) and users of funds (e.g., corporations) occur in a world without FIs?

10. Why would a world limited to the direct transfer of funds from suppliers of funds to users of funds likely result in quite low levels of fund flows?

11. How do FIs reduce monitoring costs associated with the flow of funds from fund suppliers to fund investors?

12. How do FIs alleviate the problem of liquidity risk faced by investors wishing to invest in securities of corporations?

13. How do financial institutions help individuals to diversify their portfolio risks? Which financial institution is best able to achieve this goal?

14. What is meant by maturity intermediation?

15. What is meant by denomination intermediation?

16. What services do FIs provide to the financial system?

17. Why are FIs regulated?

18. What countries have the most international debt securities outstanding?

19. What countries have the largest commercial banks?

20. Go to the Federal Reserve Board's website and find the latest figures for Foreign Bank Office Assets and Liabilities Held in the United States.

chapter two

Determinants *of* Interest Rates

Chapter Navigator

1. How are interest rates used to determine present and future values?

2. Who are the main suppliers of loanable funds?

3. Who are the main demanders of loanable funds?

4. How are equilibrium interest rates determined?

5. What factors cause the supply and demand curves for loanable funds to shift?

6. How do interest rates change over time?

7. What specific factors determine interest rates?

8. What are the different theories explaining the term structure of interest rates?

9. How can forward rates of interest be derived from the term structure of interest rates?

Interest Rate Fundamentals: Chapter Overview

Nominal interest rates are the interest rates actually observed in financial markets. These nominal interest rates (or just interest rates) directly affect the value (price) of most securities traded in the money and capital markets, both at home and abroad. As will be discussed later, they affect the relationship between spot and forward foreign

nominal interest rates

The interest rates actually observed in financial markets.

exchange rates as well. This chapter examines the link between the time value of money and interest rates, as well as the factors that drive the level of current and future interest rates.

Time Value of Money and Interest Rates

Chapter 1 introduced the different types of financial markets that exist and the securities that trade in these markets. Interest rates have a direct and immediate effect on the value of virtually all of these securities—that is, interest rates affect the price or value the seller of a security receives and the buyer of a security pays in organized financial markets. In this section, we review the time value of money concepts that link interest rates to the valuation of securities.[1]

Time Value of Money

Time value of money is the basic notion that a dollar received today is worth more than a dollar received at some future date. This is because a dollar received today can be invested and its value enhanced by an interest rate of return such that the investor receives more than a dollar in the future. The interest rate of return reflects the fact that people generally prefer to consume now rather than wait until later. To compensate them for delaying consumption (i.e., saving), they are paid a rate of interest by those who wish to consume more today than their current resources permit (dissavers). Dissavers are willing to pay this rate of interest because they plan to productively use the borrowed funds such that they will earn even more than the rate of interest promised to the savers (lenders of the funds).

compound interest

Interest earned on an investment is reinvested.

simple interest

Interest earned on an investment is not reinvested.

The time value of money concept specifically assumes that any interest or other return earned on a dollar invested over any given period of time (e.g., two, three, four, . . . years) is immediately reinvested—that is, the **interest** return is **compounded.** This is in contrast to the concept of **simple interest,** which assumes that interest returns earned are not reinvested over any given time period.

Example 2–1 Calculation of Simple and Compounded Interest Returns

Suppose you have $1,000 to invest for a period of two years. Currently, default risk-free one-year securities (such as those issued by the U.S. Treasury) are paying a 12 percent interest rate per year, on the last day of each of the two years over your investment horizon. If you earn simple annual interest on this investment, or you do not reinvest the annual (12 percent) interest earned, the value of your investment at the end of the two-year investment horizon would be determined as follows:

$$\text{Value in 2 years (simple interest)} = \text{Principal} + \text{Interest}$$
$$= \$1,000 + \$1,000(.12)(2)$$
$$= \$1,240$$

If, instead, the annual interest earned is reinvested immediately after it is received at 12 percent (i.e., interest is compounded), the value of the investment at the end of the two-year investment horizon would be:

---

1. The time value of money concept is a topic that finance students probably studied in introductory financial management courses. However, its use in the valuation of financial instruments created, traded, and held by financial institutions is critical to financial managers. Therefore, in this chapter, we review and provide a reference guide to the general relationships between interest rates and security valuation. In Chapter 3, we use these general relationships to determine values of specific securities (e.g., equities and bonds).

Value in 2 years $\quad$ = Principal + Interest + Compounded interest
(compounded interest) $\qquad$ (or interest on interest)
$$= \$1,000 + \$1,000(.12)(2) + 1,000(.12)(.12)$$
$$= \$1,000[1+2(.12) + (.12)^2] = \$1,000(1.12)^2$$
$$= \$1,254.40$$

By compounding interest using time value of money principles, an investor increases his or her return compared to the simple interest return. In the example above using a two-year investment horizon, a 12 percent annual interest rate, and an initial investment of $1,000, the investment is worth $1,254.40 at the end of two years under compounded returns rather than $1,240 using simple interest to calculate returns.

The time value of money concept can be used to convert cash flows earned over an investment horizon into a value at the end of the investment horizon. This is called the investment's future value (FV) and is the same as that in the compounded return example above. Alternatively, the time value of money concept can be used to convert the value of future cash flows into their current or present values (PV) (i.e., future dollars converted into their equivalent present value or current dollars). We illustrate the FV and PV scenarios in Figure 2–1.

Present Values

lump sum payment

A single cash flow occurs at the beginning and end of the investment horizon with no other cash flows exchanged.

annuity

A series of equal cash flows received at fixed intervals over the investment horizon.

The present value function converts cash flows received over a future investment horizon into an equivalent (present) value as if they were received at the beginning of the current investment horizon. This is done by discounting future cash flows back to the present using the current market interest rate. Two forms of present value calculations are commonly used in finance for security valuation purposes: the present value of a lump sum and the present value of annuity payments. A **lump sum payment** is a single cash payment received at the end of some investment horizon (e.g., $100 at the end of five years). **Annuity** payments are a series of equal cash flows received at fixed intervals over the entire investment horizon (e.g., $100 a year received each year for five years). In actual practice, "annuity" payments can be paid more frequently than once a year—so that the term *annuity* really means a constant payment received at equal intervals throughout an investment horizon (e.g., twice, three times, . . . a year). The

Figure 2–1   Time Value of Money Concepts

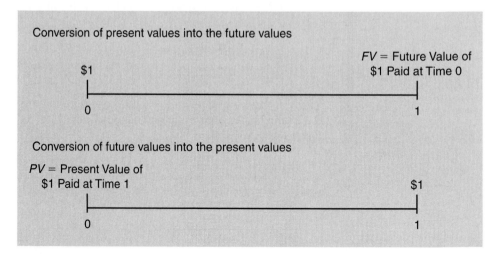

Figure 2–2   Present Value of a Lump Sum versus an Annuity
(invested at the rate of i *per year)*

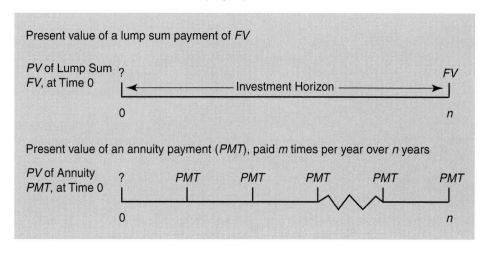

time value of money equations used to calculate these values are illustrated in Figure 2–2 and can be represented as follows.

Present value (*PV*) of a *lump sum* (*FV*) received at the end of the investment horizon:

$$PV = FV_n\,(1/(1\,+\,i/m))^{nm} = FV_n(PVIF_{i/m,nm})$$

Present value (*PV*) of an annuity stream (*PMT*) received in the future:

$$PV = PMT \sum_{t\,=\,1}^{nm} (1/(1\,+\,i/m))^t = PMT\,(PVIFA_{i/m,nm})$$

where

$\qquad PV = $ Present value of cash flows
$\qquad FV = $ Future value of cash flows (lump sum) received in *n* years
$\qquad PMT = $ Periodic annuity payment received during an investment horizon
$\qquad i = $ Simple annual interest rate earned on investments
$\qquad n = $ Number of years in investment horizon
$\qquad m = $ Number of compounding periods in a year (i.e., frequency with which cash flows are received—e.g., daily, weekly, monthly, quarterly, semi-annually)
$\qquad PVIF = $ Present value interest factor of a lump sum
$\qquad PVIFA = $ Present value interest factor of an annuity[2]

Example 2–2   Calculation of Present Value of an Annuity

You have been offered a security investment such as a bond that will pay you $10,000 (on the last day of[3]) every quarter for the next six years in exchange for a fixed payment today. We illustrate this investment in Figure 2–3. If the appropriate annual

---

2. Interest factor formulas are programmed in a business calculator—a tool with which every finance student should be familiar. The interest factor tables for *PVIF* and *PVIFA* are presented in the appendix to the textbook.

3. Had the annuity been paid on the first day of each quarter, an extra interest payment would be received for each $10,000 payment. Thus, the time value of money equation for the present value of an annuity becomes:

$$PV = PMT\,(PVIFA_{i/m,nm})(1\,+\,i/m)$$

Figure 2–3 Present Value of $10,000 Received on the Last Day of Each Quarter for Six Years

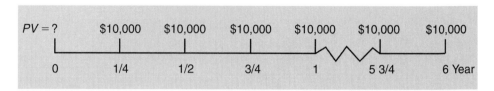

interest rate on the investment is 8 percent, the present value of this investment is computed as follows:

$$PV = PMT\,(PVIFA_{i/m,nm})$$
$$= \$10,000\,(PVIFA_{8\%/4,6(4)})$$
$$= \$10,000\,(18.913926) = \$189,139.26$$

If the annual interest rate on the investment rises to 12 percent, the present value of this investment becomes:

$$PV = \$10,000\,(PVIFA_{12\%/4,6(4)})$$
$$= \$10,000\,(16.935542) = \$169,355.42$$

If the annual interest rate rises to 16 percent, the present value of this investment becomes:

$$PV = \$10,000\,(PVIFA_{16\%/4,6(4)})$$
$$= \$10,000\,(15.246963) = \$152,469.63$$

Notice from the examples above that the *present values* of the security investment *decrease as interest rates increase.* For example, as the interest rate rose from 8 percent to 12 percent, the (present) value of the security investment fell $19,783.84 (from $189,139.26 to $169,355.42). As interest rates rose from 12 percent to 16 percent, the value of the investment fell $16,885.79 (from $169,355.42 to $152,469.63). This is because as interest rates increase, fewer funds need to be invested at the beginning of an investment horizon to receive a stated amount at the end of the investment horizon. This inverse relationship between the value of a financial instrument—for example, a bond—and interest rates is one of the most fundamental relationships in finance and is evident in the swings that occur in financial asset prices whenever major changes in interest rates arise. Indeed, even the hint of an announcement of a change in interest rate targets by the chairman of the Federal Reserve Board (the Fed)—(see Chapter 4 for an explanation of when and why the Fed changes interest rate targets) can send financial markets around the world reeling (see In the News box 2–1).

Note also that *as interest rates increase,* the *present values* of the investment *decrease at a decreasing rate.* The fall in present value is greater when interest rates rise from 8 percent to 12 percent compared to when they rise from 12 percent to 16 percent—the inverse relationship between interest rates and the present value of security investments is neither linear nor proportional.

Future Values

Future value equations translate cash flows received during an investment period to a terminal (future) value at the end of an investment horizon (e.g., 5 years, 10 years).

In the News

Greenspan Launches Shares on Roller-Coaster

World markets underwent a roller-coaster day yesterday as hints by Alan Greenspan, Chairman of the U.S. Federal Reserve, of a possible cut in interest rates led first to an upward surge in equity prices, followed by profit-taking and concern over bank exposure to global economic turmoil. Mr. Greenspan's remarks on Wednesday before a congressional committee prompted a big rally late that day on Wall Street, with Dow Jones Industrial Average up 257.21 points at 8,154.41.

His comments, and Wall Street's rally, buoyed Asian stocks at the start of yesterday's trading. In Japan, the

Nikkei closed up 3 percent at 14,205.78, even though the head of the country's main opposition Democratic party said it could not accept the prime minister Keizo Obochi's latest proposal on banking reform. In Hong Kong, the Han Seng index jumped 4.4 percent while Thailand's SET index leaped 18.90 points, or 8.2 percent, to close at 250.18.

European markets also opened bullishly, with many indices putting on more than 2 percent in early trading, but then reversed to close sharply lower. Measured by their main stock market indices, Frankfurt fell

by 2.36 percent, Switzerland was down by 2.46 percent, Paris dropped 1.25 percent and Milan was 1.07 percent lower. Europe had already been troubled by the overnight rescue of Long-Term Capital Management, the U.S. hedge fund, thanks to a $3.5 billion bailout led by a group of American and international banks and coordinated by the U.S. Federal Reserve . . .

By the end of the European trading day, Wall Street was busily taking profits from Wednesday's rally, while the mood was more downbeat, focusing more on the potential for further international economic gloom. However, some analysts saw scope for gains in the run-up to the U.S. Fed meeting next week which will consider interest rate policy.

Source: *Financial Times*, September 25, 1998, p. 44.

Similar to present value, two forms of future value equations are commonly used to value security investments: the future value of a lump sum payment received today and the future value (terminal value) of annuity payments received over an investment period. The future value (*FV*) equations are illustrated in Figure 2–4 and can be represented as follows.

Future value of a lump sum received at the beginning of the investment horizon:

$$FV_n = PV(1 + i/m)^{nm} = PV\,(FVIF_{i/m,nm})$$

Future value of an annuity payment stream received over an investment horizon:[4]

$$FV_n = PMT \sum_{t=0}^{nm-1} (1 + i/m)^t = PMT\,(FVIFA_{i/m,nm})$$

4. The interest factor tables for *FVIF* and *FVIFA* are listed in the appendix to the textbook.

Figure 2–4   Future Value of a Lump Sum versus an Annuity
(invested at the rate of i per year)

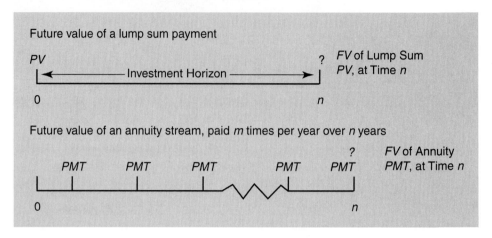

where

$$FVIF_{i/m,nm} = \text{Future value interest factor for a lump sum}$$
$$FVIFA_{i/m,nm} = \text{Future value interest factor of an annuity payment stream}$$

Example 2–3   Calculation of the Future Value
of an Annuity Payment

You plan to invest $10,000 (on the last day of[5]) every quarter for the next six years. If the interest rate on the investment is 8 percent, the future value of your investment in six years is computed as follows:

$$FV = \$10,000\,(FVIFA_{8\%/4,6(4)})$$
$$= \$10,000\,(30.421862) = \$304,218.62$$

If the interest rate on the investment rises to 12 percent, the future value of this investment becomes:

$$FV = \$10,000\,(FVIFA_{12\%/4,6(4)})$$
$$= \$10,000\,(34.426470) = \$344,264.70$$

If the interest rate rises to 16 percent, the future value of this investment becomes:

$$FV = \$10,000\,(FVIFA_{16\%/4,6(4)})$$
$$= \$10,000\,(39.082604) = \$390,826.04$$

Notice that the *future value* of an investment *increases as interest rates increase.* As interest rates rose from 8 percent to 12 percent, the (future) value of the investment of $10,000 per quarter for six years rose by $40,046.08 (from $304,218.62 to $344,264.70). As rates rose from 12 percent to 16 percent, the (future) value of the investment rose $46,561.34 (from $344,264.70 to $390,826.04). Note also that *as interest*

---

5. Had the annuity been paid on the first day of each quarter, an extra interest payment would be earned on each $10,000 investment. Thus, the time value of money equation for the future value of an annuity becomes:

$$FV = PMT(FVIFA_{i/m,nm})(1 + i/m)$$

Figure 2–5   Relation between Interest Rates and Present and Future Values

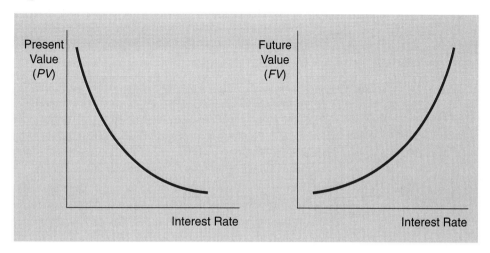

rates increase, future values increase at an increasing rate.[6] This is because as interest rates increase, a stated amount of funds invested at the beginning of an investment horizon accumulates to a larger amount at the end of the investment horizon. By contrast, as stated earlier, as interest rates increase, the present value of an investment decreases at a decreasing rate. These nonlinear relationships are illustrated in Figure 2–5.

The annual interest rate, *i,* used in the time value of money equations in Example 2–3, is the simple (nominal or 12-month) interest rate on default risk free securities (e.g., Treasury securities). However, if interest is paid or compounded more than once per year, the true annual rate earned or paid will differ from the simple annual rate. The **equivalent annual return** (EAR) is the return earned over a 12-month period taking any within-year compounding of interest into account. Specifically, the EAR can be written as follows:

$$EAR = (1 + i/m)^m - 1$$

In Example 2–3, the EAR on the 8 percent simple return is computed as:

$$EAR = (1 + .08/4)^4 - 1 = 8.24\%$$

and on the 12 percent simple return it is computed as:

$$EAR = (1 + .12/4)^4 - 1 = 12.55\%$$

Thus, for each dollar invested at the beginning of the year, at 8 percent and 12 percent respectively, you would have earned $8.24 and $12.55 at the end of the year. Accordingly, the EAR provides a more accurate measure of annual returns in time value of money calculations.

Interest Rates on Securities with a Maturity of Less than One Year

Many of the financial securities mentioned in Chapter 1 and discussed in detail in later chapters have maturities of less than one year. In particular, money markets are financial markets that trade debt securities with maturities of less than one year. For these securities, we need to calculate an equivalent annual interest rate that depends on the

---

6. That is, as rates go from 8 percent to 12 percent (an increase in interest rates of 4 percent), the future value increases by $40,046.08; as interest rates go from 12 percent to 16 percent (an increase in interest rates of 4 percent), the future value increases by $46,561.34.

equivalent annual return

Rate earned over a 12-month period taking the compounding of interest into account.

maturity and compounding period of the security. As mentioned above, the equivalent annual return is the return earned over a 12-month period taking any within-year compounding of interest into account. Such a calculation allows a comparison of their returns with those on investments with horizons longer than one year (such as most bonds).

Further, many of these short-maturity securities' returns are measured and quoted in a manner that does not allow them to be evaluated using the time value of money equations above. For example, some securities' interest rates or returns are based on a 360-day year, while others are based on a 365-day year. It is therefore inappropriate to compare annual interest rates on short-term and long-term securities without adjusting their interest rates for differences in the securities' characteristics with regard to the number of days in an interest rate year that are assumed.

Securities with Less than One Year to Maturity. The quoted annual nominal interest rate on securities with a maturity of less than one year can be converted to an equivalent annual interest return (*EAR*) using the following equation

$$EAR = (1 + i/(365/h))^{365/h} - 1$$

where

h = number of days to maturity

Example 2–4   Calculation of EAR on a Security with Less than One Year to Maturity

Suppose you can invest in an investment security that matures in 75 days and offers a 7 percent annual interest rate. The effective annual interest return on this security is

$$EAR = (1 + (.07)/(365/75))^{365/75} - 1 = 7.20\%$$

Discount Yields. Some money market instruments (e.g., Treasury bills and commercial paper—see Chapter 5) are bought and sold on a discount basis. Rather than directly receiving interest payments over the investment horizon, the return on these securities results from the purchase of the security at a discount from its face value (P_0) and the receipt of face value (P_f) at maturity, as we show in the following time line.

$$P_0 \rule{3cm}{0.4pt} P_f$$
$$0 \qquad\qquad\qquad\qquad \text{Maturity}$$
$$\text{(days)}$$

Further, yields on these securities normally use a 360-day year rather than a 365-day year to calculate interest return. Interest rates on discount securities, or discount yields (i_{dy}), are quoted on a discount basis using the following equation:

$$i_{dy} = [(P_f - P_0)/P_f](360/h)$$

where

P_f = Face value
P_0 = Discount price of the security

There are several features of a discount yield that make it difficult to compare with yields on other (nondiscount) securities—for example, U.S. Treasury bonds—that pay a (coupon) interest payment semiannually. The annual interest rate on nondiscount securities (such as U.S. Treasury bonds) is often referred to as the bond equivalent yield

(i_{bey}).[7] The bond equivalent yield used for comparison with a discount money market instrument of short (less than one year) maturity can be calculated as follows:

$$i_{bey} = [(P_f - P_0)/P_0](365/h)$$

Notice the discount yield uses the terminal price, or the security's face value (P_f), as the base price in calculating an annualized interest rate. By contrast, bond equivalent yields are based on the purchase price (P_0) of a security. Further, and as already mentioned, discount yields often use a 360-day rather than a 365-day year to compute interest returns. An appropriate comparison of interest rates on discount securities versus nondiscount securities, adjusting for both the base price and days in the year differences, requires converting a discount yield into a bond equivalent yield in the following manner:

$$i_{bey} = i_{dy}(P_f/P_0)(365/360)$$

Finally, neither of these interest rates considers the effects of compounding of interest during the less than one year investment horizon. The EAR on a discount security would be calculated by applying the calculated bond equivalent yield (i_{bey}) for the discount security to the EAR equation, as illustrated in Example 2–4 (i.e., setting i equal to i_{bey} in Example 2–4).

Example 2–5 Comparison of Discount Yield,
Bond Equivalent Yield, and EAR

Suppose you can purchase a $1 million Treasury bill that is currently selling on a discount basis (i.e., with no explicit interest payments) at 97½ percent of its face value. The T-bill is 140 days from maturity (when the $1 million will be paid). Depending on the setting in which you are interested, any one of the following three yields or interest rates could be appropriate

Discount yield: $i_{dy} = (($1m. - $975,000)/$1m.)(360/140) = 6.43\%$
Bond equivalent yield: $i_{bey} = (($1m. - $975,000)/$975,000)(365/140) = 6.68\%$
EAR: $EAR = (1 + .0668/(365/140))^{365/140} - 1 = 6.82\%$

Single-Payment Yields. Some money market securities (e.g., jumbo CDs, fed funds) pay interest only once during their lives: at maturity. Thus, the single-payment security holder receives a terminal payment consisting of interest plus the face value of the security, as we show in the following time line. Such securities are special cases of the pure discount securities that only pay the face value on maturity.

Invest $1   Receive $1 + Interest

0   Maturity
(days)

Further, quoted nominal interest rates on single-payment securities (or single-payment yield, i_{spy}) normally assume a 360-day year. In order to compare interest rates on these securities with others, such as U.S. Treasury bonds, that pay interest based on a 365-day year, the nominal interest rate must be converted to a bond equivalent yield in the following manner:

$$i_{bey} = i_{spy}(365/360)$$

7. We describe bond equivalent yields and bond valuation in detail in Chapter 3.

Further, allowing for interest rate compounding, the EAR for single-payment securities must utilize the bond equivalent yield as follows:

$$EAR = (1 + (i_{spy} (365/360))/(365/h))^{365/h} - 1$$
$$EAR = (1 + (i_{bey}/(365/h))^{365/h} - 1$$

Example 2–6   Comparison of Single-Payment Yield, Bond Equivalent Yield, and EAR

Suppose you can purchase a $1 million jumbo CD that is currently 105 days from maturity. The CD has a quoted annual interest rate of 5.16 percent for a 360-day year. The bond equivalent yield is calculated as:

$$i_{bey} = 5.16\%(365/360) = 5.232\%$$

The EAR on the CD is calculated as:

$$EAR = (1 + (.05232)/(365/105))^{365/105} - 1 = 5.33\%$$

Do You Understand?

1. The difference between simple interest and compounded interest?
2. What should happen to the future value of an annuity stream of cash flows as interest rates increase?
3. How an EAR differs from a simple rate of return?
4. What characteristics of a bond equivalent yield prevent it from being directly compared to an EAR?

loanable funds theory

A theory of interest rate determination that views equilibrium interest rates in financial markets as a result of the supply and demand for loanable funds.

Depending on the setting in which an investor is analyzing interest rates, any one of the above rates could be appropriate.

Loanable Funds Theory

So far we have shown the technical details of how interest rates play a part in the determination of the value of financial instruments. Given the impact a change in interest rates has on security values, financial institution and other managers spend much time and effort trying to identify the factors that determine the level of interest rates at any moment in time, as well as what causes interest rate movements over time. One model that is commonly used to explain interest rates and interest rate movements is **loanable funds theory**. The loanable funds theory of interest rate determination views the level of interest rates in financial markets as resulting from factors that affect the supply and demand for loanable funds. This is similar to the way that the prices for goods and services in general are viewed as being the result of the forces of supply and demand for those goods and services. The *supply of loanable funds* is a term commonly used to describe funds provided to the financial markets by net suppliers of funds. The *demand for loanable funds* is a term used to describe the total net demand for funds by fund users. The loanable funds framework categorizes financial market participants—suppliers and demanders of funds—as consumers, businesses, governments, and foreign participants. Table 2–1 summarizes the factors that affect the supply and demand for loanable funds discussed in this section, their impact on the supply and demand for loanable funds for a specific security, and the impact on the market clearing (or equilibrium) interest rates holding all other factors constant.

Supply of Loanable Funds

In general, the quantity of loanable funds supplied increases as interest rates rise. Figure 2–6 illustrates the supply curve for loanable funds. Other factors held constant, more funds are supplied as interest rates increase (the reward for supplying funds is higher). Table 2–2 presents data on the supply of loanable funds from the various groups of market participants from U.S. flow of funds data as of December 1999.

The household sector (consumer sector) is the largest supplier of loanable funds in the United States—$31,866.4 billion in 1999. Households supply funds when they

Table 2–1 Factors that Affect the Supply of and Demand for Loanable Funds for a Financial Security

Panel A: The Supply of Funds

Factor	Change in Factor	Impact on Supply of Funds	Impact on Equilibrium Interest Rate
Interest rate	Increase	Movement up along the supply curve	Increase
	Decrease	Movement down along the supply curve	Decrease
Total wealth	Increase	Shift supply curve down and to the right	Decrease
	Decrease	Shift supply curve up and to the left	Increase
Risk of financial security	Increase	Shift supply curve up and to the left	Increase
	Decrease	Shift supply curve down and to the right	Decrease
Near-term spending needs	Increase	Shift supply curve up and to the left	Increase
	Decrease	Shift supply curve down and to the right	Decrease
Monetary expansion	Increase	Shift supply curve down and to the right	Decrease
	Decrease	Shift supply curve up and to the left	Increase
Economic conditions	Increase	Shift supply curve up and to the left	Increase
	Decrease	Shift supply curve down and to the right	Decrease

Panel B: The Demand for Funds

Factor	Change in Factor	Impact on Demand for Funds	Impact on Equilibrium Interest Rate
Interest rate	Increase	Movement up along the demand curve	Increase
	Decrease	Movement down along the demand curve	Decrease
Utility derived from asset purchased with borrowed funds	Increase	Shift demand curve up and to the right	Increase
	Decrease	Shift demand curve down and to the left	Decrease
Restrictiveness of nonprice conditions	Increase	Shift demand curve down and to the left	Decrease
	Decrease	Shift demand curve up and to the right	Increase
Economic conditions	Increase	Shift demand curve up and to the right	Increase
	Decrease	Shift demand curve down and to the left	Decrease

Figure 2–6 Supply of and Demand for Loanable Funds

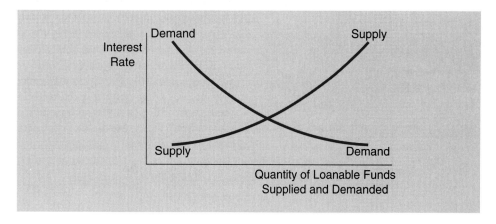

have excess income or want to reallocate their asset portfolio holdings. For example, during times of high economic growth, households may replace part of their cash holdings with earning assets (i.e., by supplying loanable funds in exchange for holding securities). As the total wealth of a consumer increases, the total supply of loanable

Table 2–2   Funds Supplied and Demanded by Various Groups
(in billions of dollars)

	Funds Supplied	**Funds Demanded**
Households	$31,866.4	$ 6,624.4
Business—nonfinancial	7,400.0	30,356.2
Business—financial	27,701.9	29,431.1
Government units	6,174.8	10,197.9
Foreign participants	6,164.8	2,698.3

Source: Federal Reserve Board, website, "Flow of Fund Accounts," December 15, 1999. *www.bog.frb.fed.us/*

funds from that consumer will also generally increase. Households determine their supply of loanable funds not only on the basis of the general level of interest rates and their total wealth, but also on the risk of securities investments. The greater the perceived risk of securities investments, the less households are willing to invest at each interest rate. Further, the supply of loanable funds from households also depends on their immediate spending needs. For example, near-term educational or medical expenditures will reduce the supply of funds from a given household.

Higher interest rates will also result in higher supplies of funds from the U.S. business sector ($7,400.0 billion from nonfinancial business and $27,701.9 billion from financial business in 1999) who often have excess cash, or working capital, that they can invest for short periods of time in financial assets. In addition to the interest rates on these investments, the expected risk on financial securities and their businesses' future investment needs will affect their overall supply of funds.

Loanable funds are also supplied by some governments ($6,174.8 billion in 1999). For example, some governments (e.g., municipalities) temporarily generate more cash inflows (e.g., through local taxes) than they have budgeted to spend. These funds can be loaned out to financial market fund users until needed.

Finally, foreign investors increasingly view U.S. financial markets as alternatives to their domestic financial markets ($6,164.8 billion of funds supplied to the U.S. financial markets in 1999). When interest rates are higher on U.S. financial securities than they are on comparable securities in their home countries, foreign investors increase their supply of funds to U.S. markets. Indeed the high savings rates of foreign households (such as Japanese households) combined with relatively high U.S. interest rates (compared to foreign rates) has resulted in foreign market participants being major suppliers of funds to U.S. financial markets in recent years. Similar to domestic suppliers of loanable funds, foreigners assess not only the interest rate offered on financial securities, but also their total wealth, the risk on the security, and their future expenditure needs. Additionally, foreign investors alter their investment decisions as financial conditions in their home countries change relative to the U.S. economy and the exchange rate of their country's currency vis-à-vis the U.S. dollar (see Chapter 9). For example, in the late 1990s, the severe financial downturn in Southeast Asia, South America, and Russia resulted in a flow of funds out of financial markets in these countries and into those in the United States and Europe (see In the News box 2–2).

Do You Understand?

1. What is meant by the phrase "investors take flight to safe haven"?
2. Why such a flight occurred from Brazilian markets in late 1998?

Demand for Loanable Funds

In general, the quantity of loanable funds demanded is higher as interest rates fall. Figure 2–6 also illustrates the demand curve for loanable funds. Other factors held constant, more funds are demanded as interest rates decrease (the cost of borrowing funds is lower).

Households (although they are net suppliers of funds) also borrow funds in financial markets ($6,624.4 billion in 1999). The demand for loanable funds by households

In the News

Investors Take Flight to Safe Haven

Government bond markets soared yesterday as investors sought safe havens after Brazil's surprise de facto devaluation and the resignation of Gustavo Franco, head of the country's central bank. The 30-year U.S. Treasury bond, the benchmark for U.S. interest rates, jumped by more than 200 basis points in early trading as investors sold shares and fled to bonds in a kneejerk reaction. The Brazilian stock market initially fell 10 percent while the country's benchmark "C" Brady bond dropped by 450 basis points. The decision to widen the trading band for the real against the U.S. dollar from 1.12–1.20 to 1.20–1.32—effectively devaluing the currency by 8.3 percent—did not con-

Source: *Financial Times,* January 14, 1999, p. 42, by Arkady Ostrovsky and John Labate.

vince everyone. Analysts said it was enough to scare off foreign investors but not enough to cut Brazilian interest rates, which would boost domestic demand . . .

In the U.S., by early afternoon the 30-year bond was off its morning highs, with a gain of at 101 $^{17}/_{32}$, sending the yield down to 5.149 percent. Among shorter term issues the 10-year note had gained to 100 ¼, yielding 4.717 percent, and the two-year note climbed $^{7}/_{32}$ to 100 $^{5}/_{32}$, yielding 4.540 percent. Hedge funds and banks fled to Treasuries, sparking a slide in equities in early trading, although the Dow Jones Industrial Average was recovering in afternoon trading. "The outlook is good for

Treasuries," said Richard Gilhooly at Paribas Capital Markets. "There is concern that Argentina, Mexico and Peru will be forced to devalue their currencies, and that Brazil could be forced to devalue again or to float its currency."

The flight to safety and the strong performance in the U.S. also pushed up the European markets, which saw a sharp rise in trading activity. The German bond future closed 0.27 higher at 117.03. The U.K. gilt future rose by 0.78 to 119.51.

The Brazilian crisis had knock-on effects on other emerging markets, Argentina being one of the worst hit. But analysts said the Brazilian devaluation is unlikely to be as contagious as the Russian crisis has been. Argentine and Mexican Brady bonds were down sharply at one stage but recovered as investors took stock of the developments.

reflects the demand for financing purchases of homes (with mortgage loans), durable goods (e.g., car loans, appliance loans), and nondurable goods (e.g., education loans, medical loans). Additional nonprice conditions and requirements (discussed below) also affect a household's demand for loanable funds at every level of interest rates.

Businesses demand funds to finance investments in long-term (fixed) assets (e.g., plant and equipment) and for short-term working capital needs (e.g., inventory and accounts receivable) usually by issuing debt and other financial instruments ($30,356.2 billion for nonfinancial businesses and $29,431.1 for financial businesses in 1999). When interest rates are high (i.e., the cost of loanable funds is high), businesses prefer to finance investments with internally generated funds (e.g., retained earnings) rather than through borrowed funds. In addition to interest rates, nonprice conditions directly affect businesses' demand for funds. For example, the more restrictive the contractual conditions (borrower covenants discussed below) relating to borrowed funds, the less businesses prefer to borrow at any given interest rate. Further, the greater the number of profitable projects available to businesses, or the better the overall economic conditions, the greater the demand for loanable funds.

Governments also borrow heavily in the markets for loanable funds ($10,197.9 billion in 1999). For example, state and local governments often issue debt instruments to finance temporary imbalances between operating revenues (e.g., taxes) and budgeted expenditures (e.g., road improvements, school construction). Higher interest rates can cause state and local governments to postpone borrowings and thus capital expenditures. Similar to households and businesses, governments' demand for funds varies with general economic conditions. The federal government is also a large borrower partly to finance current budget deficits (expenditures greater than taxes) and partly to finance past deficits. The cumulative sum of past deficits is called the national debt, which in the United States at the end of 1999 stood at $5.738 trillion. Thus, the national debt and especially the interest payments on the national debt have to be financed in large part by government borrowing.

www.ustreas.gov/

Finally, foreign participants (households, businesses, and governments) might also borrow in U.S. financial markets ($2,698.3 billion in 1999). Foreign borrowers look for the cheapest source of dollar funds globally. Most foreign borrowing in U.S. financial markets comes from the business sector. In addition to interest costs, foreign borrowers consider nonprice terms on loanable funds as well as economic conditions in the home country and the general attractiveness of the U.S. dollar relative to their domestic currency (e.g., the euro or the yen).

Equilibrium Interest Rate

4

The aggregate supply of loanable funds is the sum of the quantity supplied by the separate fund supplying sectors (e.g., households, business, governments, foreign agents) discussed above. Similarly, the aggregate demand for loanable funds is the sum of the quantity demanded by the separate fund demanding sectors. As illustrated in Figure 2–7, the aggregate quantity of funds supplied is positively related to interest rates, while the aggregate quantity of funds demanded is inversely related to interest rates. As long as competitive forces are allowed to operate freely in a financial system, the interest rate that equates the aggregate quantity of loanable funds supplied with aggregate quantity of loanable funds demanded for a financial security, Q^*, is the equilibrium interest rate for that security, i^*, point E in Figure 2–7. For example, whenever the rate of interest is set higher than the equilibrium rate, such as i^H, there is a surplus of loanable funds in the financial system. As a result, some suppliers of funds will lower the interest rate at which they are willing to lend and the demanders of funds will absorb the loanable funds surplus. In contrast, when the rate of interest is lower than the equilibrium interest rate, such as i^L, there is a shortage of loanable funds in the financial system. Some borrowers will be unable to obtain the funds they need at current rates. As a result, interest rates will increase, causing more suppliers of loanable funds to enter the market and some demanders of funds to leave the market. These competitive forces will cause the quantity of funds supplied to increase and the quantity of funds demanded to decrease until a shortage of funds no longer exists.

Factors that Cause the Supply and Demand Curves for Loanable Funds to Shift

5

While we have alluded to the fundamental factors that cause the supply and demand curves for loanable funds to shift, in this section we formally summarize these factors. We then examine how shifts in the supply and demand curves for loanable funds determine the market changing or equilibrium interest rate on a specific

Figure 2–7   Determination of Equilibrium Interest Rates

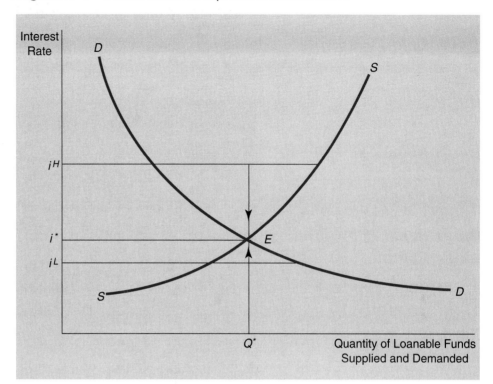

financial instrument. A shift in the supply or demand curve occurs when the quantity of a financial security supplied or demanded changes at every given interest rate in response to a change in another factor besides the interest rate. In either case, a change in supply or demand causes interest rates to move.

Supply of Funds.   We have already described the positive relation between interest rates and the supply of loanable funds. Factors that cause the supply curve of loanable funds to shift include the wealth of fund suppliers, the risk of the financial security, future spending needs, monetary policy objectives, and economic conditions.

Wealth.   As the total wealth of financial market participants (households, business, etc.) increases, the absolute dollar value available for investment purposes increases. Accordingly, at every interest rate, the supply of loanable funds increases, or the supply curve shifts down and to the right. For example, as the U.S. economy grew in the 1990s, total wealth of U.S. investors increased as well. Consequently, the supply of funds available for investing (e.g., in stock and bond markets) increased at every available interest rate. We show this shift (increase) in the supply curve in Figure 2–8 (a) as a move from SS to SS''. The shift in the supply curve creates a disequilibrium between demand and supply. To eliminate the imbalance or disequilibrium in this financial market, the equilibrium interest rate falls, from i^* to $i^{*''}$, which is associated with an increase in the quantity of funds traded, from Q^* to $Q^{*''}$.

Conversely, as the total wealth of financial market participants decreases, the absolute dollar value available for investment purposes decreases. Accordingly, at every interest rate, the supply of loanable funds decreases, or the supply curve shifts up and to the left. The decrease in the supply of funds due to a decrease in the total wealth of market participants results in an increase in the equilibrium interest rate and a decrease in the equilibrium quantity of funds traded.

Figure 2–8   The Effect on Interest Rates from a Shift in the Demand Curve for or Supply Curve of Loanable Funds

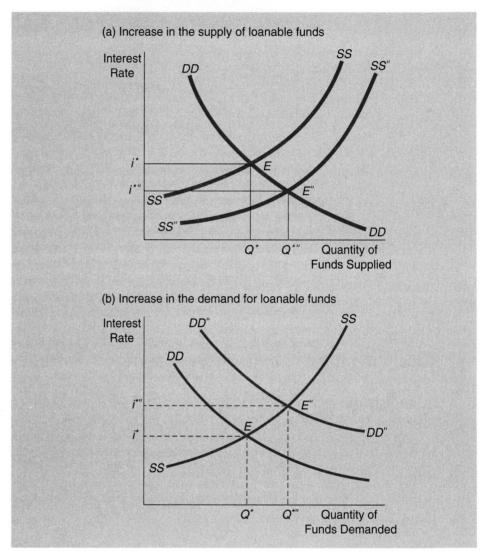

(a) Increase in the supply of loanable funds

(b) Increase in the demand for loanable funds

Risk.   As the risk of a financial security decreases (e.g., the probability that the issuer of the security will default on promised repayments of the funds borrowed), it becomes more attractive to suppliers of funds. At every interest rate, the supply of loanable funds increases, or the supply curve shifts down and to the right, from *SS* to *SS″* in Figure 2–8(a). Holding all other factors constant, the increase in the supply of funds, due to a decrease in the risk of the financial security, results in a decrease in the equilibrium interest rate, from *i** to *i*″*, and an increase in the equilibrium quantity of funds traded, from *Q** to *Q*″*.

Conversely, as the risk of a financial security increases, it becomes less attractive to suppliers of funds. Accordingly, at every interest rate, the supply of loanable funds decreases, or the supply curve shifts up and to the left. For example, in the last half of 1999, Raytheon Co.'s stock price dropped from $76.50 per share (in July) to $6.38 per share (in January 2000) as investors sold shares (decreased the supply of funds) on news of continued decreases in earnings, heavy debt burdens, and a credit rating downgrade that left investors concerned about the default or credit risk of the defense contractor. Holding all other factors constant, the decrease in the supply of funds due to an increase in the financial security's risk results in an increase in the equilibrium interest rate and a decrease in the equilibrium quantity of funds traded.

Near-Term Spending Needs. When financial market participants have few near-term spending needs, the absolute dollar value of funds available to invest increases. For example, when a family's son or daughter moves out of the family home to live on his or her own, current spending needs of the family decrease and the supply of available funds (for investing) increases. At every interest rate, the supply of loanable funds increases, or the supply curve shifts down and to the right. The financial market, holding all other factors constant, reacts to this increased supply of funds by decreasing the equilibrium interest rate and increasing the equilibrium quantity of funds traded.

Conversely, when financial market participants have increased near-term spending needs, the absolute dollar value of funds available to invest decreases. At every interest rate, the supply of loanable funds decreases, or the supply curve shifts up and to the left. The shift in the supply curve creates a disequilibrium in this financial market that results in an increase in the equilibrium interest rate and a decrease in the equilibrium quantity of funds traded.

www.bog.frb.fed.us/

Monetary Expansion. One method used by the Federal Reserve to implement monetary policy is to alter the availability of funds, the growth in the money supply, and thus inflation and economic expansion (we explain this process in detail in Chapter 4). When monetary policy objectives are to allow the economy to expand, the Federal Reserve increases the supply of funds available in the financial markets. At every interest rate, the supply of loanable funds increases, the supply curve shifts down and to the right, and the equilibrium interest rate falls, while the equilibrium quantity of funds traded increases.

Conversely, when monetary policy objectives are to restrict the rate of economic expansion (and thus inflation), the Federal Reserve decreases the supply of funds available in the financial markets. At every interest rate, the supply of loanable funds decreases, the supply curve shifts up and to the left, and the equilibrium interest rate rises, while the equilibrium quantity of funds traded decreases.

Economic Conditions. Finally, as the underlying economic conditions (e.g., inflation rate, unemployment rate, economic growth) improve in a country relative to other countries, the flow of funds to that country increases. This reflects the lower risk (country or sovereign risk) that the country, in the guise of its government, will default on its obligation to repay funds borrowed. For example, the severe economic crisis in Southeast Asia, South America, and Russia in the 1990s resulted in a decrease in the supply of funds to these countries and an increase in the supply of funds to financial markets in the United States (review again In the News box 2–2). The inflow of foreign funds to U.S. financial markets increases the supply of loanable funds at every interest rate and the supply curve shifts down and to the right. Accordingly, the equilibrium interest rate falls and the equilibrium quantity of funds traded increases.

Conversely, when economic conditions in foreign countries improve, domestic and foreign investors take their funds out of domestic financial markets (e.g., the United States) and invest abroad. Thus, the supply of funds available in the financial markets decreases and the equilibrium interest rate rises, while the equilibrium quantity of funds traded decreases.

Demand for Funds. We explained above that the quantity of loanable funds demanded is negatively related to interest rates. Factors that cause the demand curve for loanable funds to shift include the utility derived from assets purchased with borrowed funds, the restrictiveness of nonprice conditions on borrowing and economic conditions.

Utility Derived from Asset Purchased with Borrowed Funds. As the utility (i.e., satisfaction or pleasure) derived from an asset purchased with borrowed funds increases, the willingness of market participants (households, business, etc.) to borrow increases and the absolute dollar value borrowed increases. Accordingly, at every interest rate, the demand for loanable funds increases, or the demand curve shifts up and to the right. For example, suppose a change in jobs takes an individual from Arizona to Minnesota. The individual currently has a convertible automobile. Given the move to Minnesota, the individual's utility from the convertible decreases, while it would increase for a car with heated seats. Thus, with the increased utility from the purchase of a new car, the individual's demand for funds in the form of an auto loan increases. We showed this shift (increase) in the demand curve in Figure 2–8(b) as a move from DD to DD''. The shift in the demand curve creates a disequilibrium in this financial market. Holding all other factors constant, the increase in the demand for funds due to an increase in the utility from the purchased asset results in an increase in the equilibrium interest rate, from i^* to $i^{*''}$, and an increase in the equilibrium quantity of funds traded, from Q^* to $Q^{*''}$.

Conversely, as the utility derived from an asset purchased with borrowed funds decreases, the willingness of market participants (households, business, etc.) to borrow decreases and the absolute dollar value borrowed decreases. Accordingly, at every interest rate, the demand for loanable funds decreases, or the demand curve shifts down and to the left. The shift in the demand curve again creates a disequilibrium in this financial market. As competitive forces adjust, and holding all other factors constant, the decrease in the demand for funds due to a decrease in the utility from the purchased asset results in a decrease in the equilibrium interest rate and a decrease in the equilibrium quantity of funds traded.

Restrictiveness on Nonprice Conditions on Borrowed Funds. As the nonprice restrictions put on borrowers as a condition of borrowing decrease, the willingness of market participants to borrow increases and the absolute dollar value borrowed increases. Such nonprice conditions may include fees, collateral, requirements or restrictions on the use of funds (covenants, see Chapter 6). The lack of such restrictions makes the loan more desirable to the user of funds. Accordingly, at every interest rate, the demand for loanable funds increases, or the demand curve shifts up and to the right, from DD to DD''. As competitive forces adjust, and holding all other factors constant, the increase in the demand for funds due to a decrease in the restrictive conditions on the borrowed funds results in an increase in the equilibrium interest rate, from i^* to $i^{*''}$, and an increase in the equilibrium quantity of funds traded, from DD to DD''.

Conversely, as the nonprice restrictions put on borrowers as a condition of borrowing increase, market participants' willingness to borrow decreases and the absolute dollar value borrowed decreases. Accordingly, the demand curve shifts down and to the left. The shift in the demand curve results in a decrease in the equilibrium interest rate and a decrease in the equilibrium quantity of funds traded.

Economic Conditions. When the domestic economy is experiencing a period of growth, such as that in the United States in the 1990s, market participants are willing to borrow more heavily. For example, state and local governments would be more likely to repair and improve decaying infrastructure when the local economy is strong. Accordingly, the demand curve for funds shifts up and to the right. Holding all other factors constant, the increase in the demand for funds due to economic growth results in an increase in the equilibrium interest rate and an increase in the equilibrium quantity of funds traded.

Conversely, when domestic economic growth is stagnant, market participants reduce their demand for funds. Accordingly, the demand curve shifts down and to the left, resulting in a decrease in the equilibrium interest rate and a decrease in the equilibrium quantity of funds traded.

Do You Understand?

1. Who the main suppliers of loanable funds are?
2. Who the major demanders of loanable funds are?

Movement of Interest Rates over Time

6

As demonstrated in the previous section of this chapter, the loanable funds theory of interest rates is based on the supply and demand for loanable funds as functions of interest rates. The equilibrium interest rate (point E in Figure 2–7) is only a temporary equilibrium. Changes in underlying factors that determine the demand and supply of loanable funds can cause continuous shifts in the supply and/or demand curves for loanable funds. Market forces will react to the resulting disequilibrium with a change in the equilibrium interest rate and quantity of funds traded in that market. Refer again to Figure 2–8(a), which shows the effects of an *increase in the supply curve* for loanable funds, from SS to SS'' (and the resulting *decrease in the equilibrium interest rate*, from E to E''), while Figure 2–8(b) shows the effects of an *increase in the demand curve* for loanable funds, from DD to DD'' (and the resulting *increase in the equilibrium interest rate,* from E to E'').

Changes in interest rates influence the performance and decision making for individual investors, businesses, and governmental units alike. Figure 2–9 illustrates the movement in several key U.S. interest rates over the past 30 years: the prime commercial loan rate, the three-month T-bill rate, the high-grade corporate bond rate, and the home mortgage rate. Notice in Figure 2–9 the variability over time in interest rate levels. For example, the prime rate hit highs of over 20 percent in the early 1980s, yet was as low as 4.75 percent in the early 1970s, and was well below 10 percent throughout much of the 1990s.

Do You Understand?

1. What will happen to the equilibrium interest rate when the demand for loanable funds increases?
2. What will happen to the equilibrium interest rate when the supply of loanable funds increases?
3. How supply and demand, together, determine interest rates?

Determinants of Interest Rates for Individual Securities

7

In previous sections, we looked at the general determination of equilibrium (nominal) interest rates for financial securities in the context of the loanable demand and supply theory of the flow of funds. In this section, we provide details of the specific factors that affect interest rates in different financial markets (i.e., differences among interest rates on individual securities, given the underlying level of interest rates determined by the demand and supply of loanable funds). These factors include inflation, the "real" interest rate, default risk, liquidity risk, special provisions regarding the use of funds raised by a security issuance, and the term to maturity of the security. We discuss each of these in this section and summarize them in Table 2–3.

Inflation

The first factor to affect interest rates is the *actual or expected inflation rate* in the economy. Specifically, the higher the level of actual or expected inflation, the higher will be the level of interest rates. The intuition behind the positive relationship between interest rates and inflation rates is that an investor who buys a financial asset must earn a higher interest rate when inflation increases to compensate for the increased cost of forgoing consumption of real goods and services today. In other words, the higher the rate of inflation, the more expensive the same basket of goods and services will be in the future. **Inflation** of the general price index of goods and services (IP) is defined as the (percentage) increase in the price of a standardized basket of goods and services over a given period of time. In the United States, inflation is measured using indexes such as the consumer price index (CPI) and the producer price index (PPI). For example, the annual inflation rate using the CPI index between years t and $t + 1$ would be equal to:

inflation

The continual increase in the price level of a basket of goods and services.

$$\text{Inflation } (IP) = \frac{CPI_{t+1} - CPI_t}{CPI_t} \times \frac{100}{1}$$

Figure 2–9 Key U.S. Interest Rates, 1970–1999

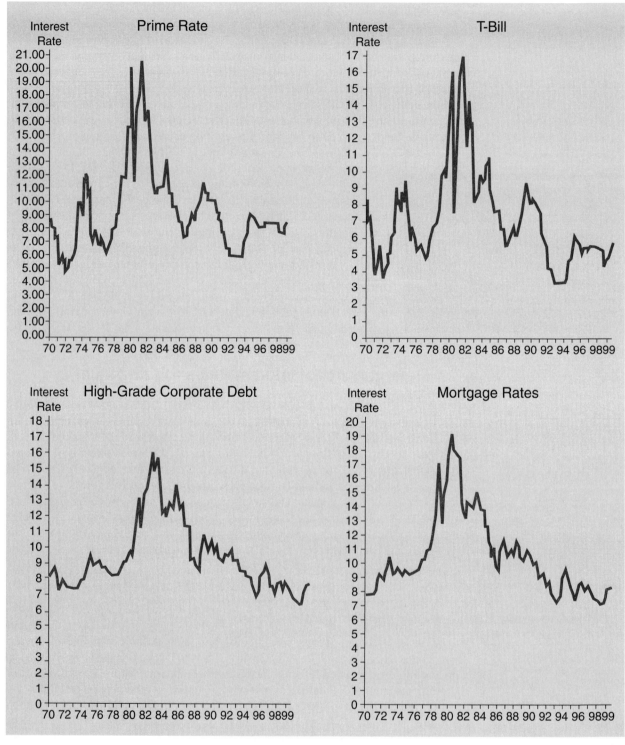

Source: Federal Reserve Board website, December 15, 1999. *www.bog.frb.fed.us/*

Table 2–3 Factors Affecting Nominal Interest Rates

Inflation—continual increase in the price level of a basket of goods and services.
Real Interest Rate—nominal interest rate that would exist on a security if no inflation were expected.
Default Risk—risk that a security's issuer will default on the security by missing an interest or principal payment.
Liquidity Risk—risk that a security cannot be sold at a predictable price with low transaction costs at short notice.
Special Provisions—provisions (e.g., taxability, convertibility, and callability) that impact the security holder beneficially or adversely and as such are reflected in the interest rates on securities that contain such provisions.
Time to Maturity—length of time a security has until maturity.

Real Interest Rates

real interest rate

The interest rate that would exist on a default free security if no inflation were expected.

A **real interest rate** is the interest rate that would exist on a security if no inflation were expected over the holding period (e.g., a year) of a security. As such, it measures society's relative time preference for consuming today rather than tomorrow. The higher society's preference to consume today (i.e., the higher its time value of money or rate of time preference), the higher the real interest rate (RIR) will be.

Example 2–7 Calculation of Real Interest Rates

Suppose one-year Treasury bills issued by the U.S. government had a bond equivalent yield (or nominal interest rate of return) of 3 percent. If the expected inflation rate over the next year was zero percent, the real interest rate would be 3 percent. If expected inflation over the next year was 2 percent, the real interest rate would be 1 percent. That is:

$$RIR = i_{bey} - \text{Expected } (IP)$$

Fisher Effect

The relationship among nominal interest rates, real interest rates, and expected inflation described above is often referred to as the Fisher effect, named for the economist Irving Fisher, who identified these relationships early last century. The Fisher effect theorizes that nominal interest rates observed in financial markets must compensate investors for (1) any reduced purchasing power due to inflationary price changes and (2) an additional premium above the expected rate of inflation for forgoing present consumption (which reflects the real interest rate discussed above).

$$i = \text{Expected}(IP) + RIR$$

Thus, the nominal interest rate will be equal to the real interest rate only when market participants expect inflation to be zero—Expected $(IP) = 0$. Similarly, nominal interest rates will be equal to the expected inflation rate only when real interest rates are zero. Note that we can rearrange the nominal interest rate equation to show the determinants of the real interest rate:

$$RIR = i - \text{Expected}(IP)$$

For example, one-year Treasury bill rates in 1999 averaged 5.08 percent and inflation (measured by the consumer price index) for the year was 2.70 percent. If investors had expected the same inflation rate as that actually realized (i.e., 2.70 percent), then according to the Fisher effect the real interest rate for 1999 was:

$$5.08\% - 2.70\% = 2.38\%$$

Because the expected inflation rate is difficult to estimate accurately, the real interest rate can be difficult to measure accurately as well, since investors' expectations are not always realized.

http://stats.bls.gov/cpih
ome.htm

Default or Credit Risk

default risk

The risk that a security's issuer will default on that security by being late on or missing an interest or principal payment.

Default risk is the risk that a security's issuer will default on making its promised interest and principal payments to the buyer of a security. The higher the default risk, the higher the interest rate that will be demanded by the buyer of the security to compensate him or her for this default (or credit) risk exposure. Not all securities exhibit default risk. For example, U.S. Treasury securities are regarded as having no default risk since they are issued by the U.S. government, and the probability of the U.S. government defaulting on its debt payments is practically zero given its taxation powers and its ability to print currency. Some borrowers, however, such as corporations or individuals, have less predictable cash flows (and no taxation powers), and therefore investors charge them an interest rate premium reflecting their perceived probability of default and the potential recovery of the amount loaned. The difference between a quoted interest rate on a security (security j) and a Treasury security with similar maturity, liquidity, and other features is called a *default* or *credit risk premium* (DRP_j). That is:

$$DRP_j = i_{jt} - i_{Tt}$$

where

www.moodys.com/

www.standardandpoors.
com/

$i_{jt} = $ interest rate on a security issued by a non-Treasury issuer (issuer j) of maturity m at time t

$i_{Tt} = $ interest rate on a security issued by the U.S. Treasury of maturity m at time t

The default risk on many corporate bonds is evaluated and categorized by various bond rating agencies such as Moody's and Standard & Poor's. (We discuss these ratings in more detail in Chapter 6). For example, in December 1999, the 30-year Treasury rate was 6.35 percent. Moody's ratings on Aaa-rated and Baa-rated corporate debt were 7.55 percent and 8.15 percent, respectively. Thus, the average default risk premiums on the Aaa-rated and Baa-rated corporate debt were:

$$DRP_{Aaa} = 7.55\% - 6.35\% = 1.20\%$$
$$DRP_{Baa} = 8.15\% - 6.35\% = 1.80\%$$

Liquidity Risk

liquidity risk

The risk that a security can be sold at a predictable price with low transaction costs on short notice.

A highly liquid asset is one that can be sold at a predictable price with low transaction costs and thus can be converted into its full market value at short notice. The interest rate on a security reflects its relative liquidity, with highly liquid assets carrying the lowest interest rates (all other characteristics remaining the same). Likewise, if a security is illiquid, investors add a **liquidity risk** premium (LRP) to the interest rate on the security. In the United States, liquid markets exist for most government securities and the stocks and bonds issued by large corporations. Securities issued by small companies are relatively less liquid.

A different type of liquidity risk premium may also exist (see below) if investors dislike long-term securities because their prices (present values) are more sensitive to interest rate changes than short-term securities (see Chapter 3). In this case, a higher liquidity risk premium may be added to a security with a longer maturity because of its greater exposure to price risk (loss of capital value) on a security as interest rates change.

Special Provisions or Covenants

Numerous special provisions or covenants that may be written into the contracts underlying the issuance of a security also affect the interest rates on different securities. Some of these special provisions include the security's taxability, convertibility, and callability.

For example, for investors, interest payments on municipal securities are free of federal, state, and local taxes. Thus, the interest rate demanded by a municipal bond holder is smaller than that on a comparable taxable bond—for example, a Treasury bond, which is taxable at the federal level but not at the state or local (city) levels, or a corporate bond, whose interest payments are taxable at the state and local levels as well as federal levels. Specifically:

$$i_c = i_m/(1 - t_s - t_F)$$

or

$$i_m = i_c(1 - t_s - t_F)$$

where

i_c = Interest rate on a corporate bond
i_m = Interest rate on a municipal bond
t_s = State plus local tax rate
t_F = Federal tax rate

Example 2–8   Calculation of the Equilibrium Interest Rate on a Municipal Bond

You are considering investing in either a corporate bond that currently pays an interest rate of 8 percent, or a municipal bond. The two bonds have the same maturity, credit risk, and liquidity risk characteristics. Thus, in equilibrium they should pay the same tax-adjusted returns. The state and local tax rate is 4 percent and the federal tax rate is 31 percent. We can compare interest rates on the two bonds as follows:

$$i_m = 8\%(1 - .04 - .31) = 5.2\%$$

or the municipal bond should pay an interest rate of 5.2 percent to provide the same after-tax return as that on the corporate bond.

A convertible (special) feature of a security offers the holder the opportunity to exchange one security for another type of the issuer's security at a preset price. Because of the value of this conversion option, the convertible security holder requires a lower interest rate than a comparable nonconvertible security holder (all else equal). In general, special provisions that provide benefits to the security holder (e.g., tax-free status and convertibility) are associated with lower interest rates, and special provisions that provide benefits to the security issuer (e.g., callability, by which an issuer has the option to retire—call—a security prior to maturity at a preset price) are associated with higher interest rates. Specifically:

$$i_{cvb} = i_T - OP_{cvb}$$

and

$$i_{cb} = i_T + OP_{cb}$$

where

i_{cvb} = Interest rate on convertible bond
i_{cb} = Interest rate on callable bond
i_T = Interest rate on a nonconvertible/noncallable bond
OP_j = Option premium on a convertible (*cvb*) or callable (*cb*) bond

---

Example 2–9 Calculation of Convertible and Callable Bond Rates

A particular company has three types of bonds outstanding: nonconvertible-noncallable (or straight) bonds, convertible bonds (*cvb*), and callable bonds (*cb*). All three bond issues have comparable maturities, default risks, and liquidity risks. The straight debt pays an interest rate of 8 percent. The required premium for the option of the buyer to convert his or her debt into another security (such as another bond of the same issuer with a higher coupon) is (minus) 3 percent and for the security issuer to "call" in debt early (for example, at a price equal to its face value) is (plus) 0.15 percent.[8] The current equilibrium interest rates on the convertible and callable bonds are calculated as follows:

$$i_{cvb} = 8\% - 3\% = 5\%$$

and

$$i_{cb} = 8\% + 0.15\% = 8.15\%$$

Table 2–4 presents yield to maturities on straight debt, callable debt, and convertible debt issues outstanding for several companies as of June 1999. Notice the callable debt issues have higher yields to maturity than the same firm's straight debt issue (e.g., Adelphia Communications' three straight debt issues have yields ranging from 8.53 percent to 8.63 percent; Adelphia's callable debt issue has a yield to maturity of 10.53 percent.) Notice also that convertible debt issues have lower yield to maturities than the firm's straight debt (e.g., AES Corp.'s straight debt yields range from 8.93 percent to 9.49 percent, while its convertible debt has a yield to maturity of 6.50 percent).

Term to Maturity

term structure of interest rates

A comparison of market yields on securities, assuming all characteristics except maturity are the same.

There is also a relationship between interest rates and the term to maturity of a security.[9] This relationship is often called the **term structure of interest rates** or the yield curve. The term structure of interest rates compares the interest rates on securities, assuming that all characteristics (i.e., default risk, liquidity risk) *except maturity* are the same. The change in required interest rates as the maturity of a security changes is called the maturity premium (MP). The MP, or the difference between the required yield on long and short securities of the same characteristics except maturity, can be positive, negative, or zero. The interest or yield to maturity curve for U.S. Treasury securities is the most commonly reported and analyzed yield to maturity curve. The shape of the yield curve on Treasury securities has taken many forms over the years, but the four most common shapes are shown in Figure 2–10. In graph (a), yields rise steadily with maturity when the yield curve is upward sloping. This is the most common yield curve, so that on average the MP is positive. Graph (b) shows an inverted or downward-sloping yield curve for which yields decline as maturity increases. Inverted yield curves most recently

---

8. In practice, analysts and traders use formal models to calculate the values of these options—see Cox and Rubenstein, *Options Markets* (Englewood Cliffs, NJ: Prentice-Hall, 1985).

9. As we discuss in Chapter 3, only debt securities have an identifiable maturity date; equity securities do not. Thus, the maturity risk premium would only be relevant when evaluating interest rates on debt.

Table 2–4 Yield to Maturity on Straight versus Callable and Convertible
Corporate Bonds

Firm Name	Type of Debt	Yield to Maturity
Adelphia Communications Corporation	Straight	8.53%
	Straight	8.63
	Straight	8.56
	Callable	10.53
AES Corporation	Straight	9.49
	Straight	9.19
	Straight	8.93
	Convertible	6.50
Caterpillar	Straight	5.83
	Straight	5.83
	Straight	6.01
	Callable	8.80
CKE Restaurants	Straight	9.59
	Convertible	9.30
Comcast Corporation	Straight	7.14
	Straight	7.52
	Callable	8.09
	Callable	8.04
	Callable	8.75

Source: Author's research.

Figure 2–10 Common Shapes for Yield Curves on Treasury Securities

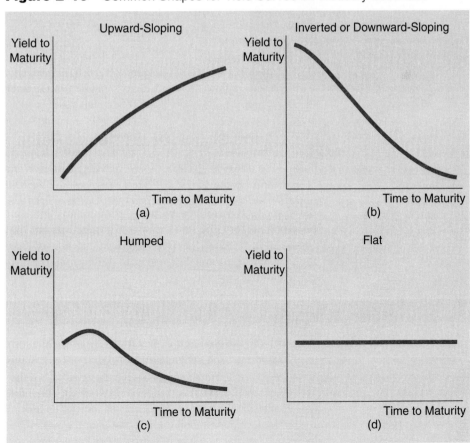

appeared in February 2000. Graph (c) shows a humped yield curve, one most recently seen in mid- to late 1991. Finally, graph (d) shows a flat yield curve in which the yield to maturity is virtually unaffected by the term to maturity. This shape of the yield curve was last seen in fall 1989.

Note that these yield curves may reflect factors other than investor's preferences for the maturity of a security, since in reality there may be liquidity differences among the securities traded at different points along the yield curve. For example, newly issued 30-year Treasury bonds offer a rate of return less than (seasoned issues) 20-year Treasury bonds if investors prefer new ("on the run") securities to previously issued ("off the run") securities. Specifically, since the Treasury only issues new 10-year notes and 30-year bonds at the long end of the maturity spectrum, an existing 20-year Treasury bond would have to have been issued 10 years previously (i.e., it was originally a 30-year bond when it was issued 10 years previously). The increased demand for the newly issued "liquid" 30-year Treasury bonds relative to the less liquid 20-year Treasury bonds can be large enough to push the equilibrium interest rate on the 30-year Treasury bonds below that on the 20-year Treasury bonds and even below short-term rates, as happened in early 2000. In the next section, we review three major theories that are often used to explain the shape of the yield to maturity curve.

Putting the factors that impact interest rates in different markets together, we can use the following general equation to determine the factors that functionally impact the fair interest rate (i_j^*) on an individual (jth) financial security.

$$i_j^* = f(IP, RIR, DRP_j, LRP_j, SCP_j, MP_j)$$

where

$$
\begin{aligned}
IP &= \text{Inflation premium} \\
RIR &= \text{Real interest rate} \\
DRP_j &= \text{Default risk premium on the } j\text{th security} \\
LRP_j &= \text{Liquidity risk premium on the } j\text{th security} \\
SCP_j &= \text{Special covenant premium on the } j\text{th security} \\
MP_j &= \text{Maturity premium on the } j\text{th security}
\end{aligned}
$$

The first two factors, *IP* and *RIR,* are common to all financial securities, while the other factors can be unique to each security.

Do You Understand?

1. What the difference is between inflation and real interest rates?
2. What should happen to a security's equilibrium interest rate as the security's liquidity risk increases?
3. What term structure of interest rates means?

8 Term Structure of Interest Rates

As discussed above in the context of the maturity premium, the relationship between a security's interest rate and its remaining term to maturity (the term structure of interest rates) can take a number of different shapes. Explanations for the shape of the yield curve fall predominantly into three theories: the unbiased expectations theory, the liquidity premium theory, and the market segmentation theory. Figure 2–11 presents the Treasury yield curve as of January 6, 2000. As can be seen, the yield curve on this date reflected the normal upward-sloping relationship between yield and maturity.[10]

Unbiased Expectations Theory

According to the unbiased expectations theory of the term structure of interest rates, at a given point in time the yield curve reflects the market's current expectations of future

---

10. Approximately one month later (in February 2000), however, the yield curve showed an inverted shape.

Figure 2–11 Treasury Yield Curve, January 6, 2000

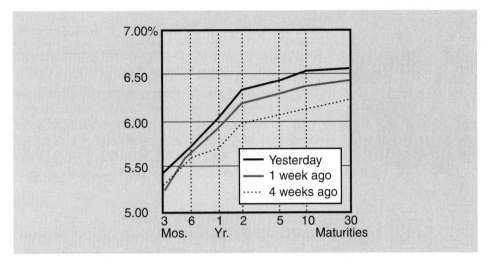

short-term rates. The intuition behind the unbiased expectations theory is that if investors have a 30-year investment horizon, they could either buy a current 30-year bond and earn the current yield on a 30-year bond (R_{30}, if held to maturity) each year, or could invest in 30 successive one-year bonds (of which they only know the current one-year rate (R_1), but form expectations of the unknown future one-year rates). In equilibrium, the return to holding a 30-year bond to maturity should equal the expected return to investing in 30 successive one-year bonds. Similarly, the return on a 29-year bond should equal the expected return on investing in 29 successive one-year bonds. If future one-year rates are expected to rise each successive year into the future, then the yield curve will slope upwards. Specifically, the current 30-year T-bond rate or return will exceed the 29-year bond rate, which will exceed the 28-year bond rate, and so on. Similarly, if future one-year rates are expected to remain constant each successive year into the future, then the 30-year bond rate will be equal to the 29-year bond rate—that is, the term structure of interest rates will remain constant over the relevant time period. Specifically, the unbiased expectation theory posits that current long-term interest rates are geometric averages of current and expected *future* short-term interest rates. The mathematical equation representing this relationship is:

$$(1 + R_N)^N = (1 + R_1)(1 + E(r_2)) \ldots (1 + E(r_N))$$

therefore:

$$\bar{R}_N = [(1 + \bar{R}_1)(1 + E(\tilde{r}_2)) \ldots (1 + E(\tilde{r}_N))]^{1/N} - 1$$

where

$\bar{R}_N$ = Actual N-period rate today
N = Term to maturity
$\bar{R}_1$ = Actual 1-year rate today
$E(\tilde{r}_i)$ = Expected one-year rates for years 2, 3, 4, ..., N in the future

Notice that uppercase interest rate terms, $\bar{R}_t$, are the actual current interest rates on securities purchased today with a maturity of t years. Lowercase interest rate terms, $\tilde{r}_t$, are estimates of future one-year interest rates starting t years into the future.

Example 2–10   Construction of a Yield Curve Using the Unbiased Expectations Theory of the Term Structure of Interest Rates

Suppose that the current one-year rate (one-year spot rate) and expected one-year T-bond rates over the following three years (i.e., years 2, 3, and 4, respectively) are as follows:

$$\bar{R}_1 = 6\%, E(\tilde{r}_2) = 7\%, E(\tilde{r}_3) = 7.5\%, E(\tilde{r}_4) = 7.85\%$$

Using the unbiased expectations theory, current (long-term) rates for one-, two-, three-, and four-year maturity Treasury securities should be:

$$\bar{R}_1 = 6\%$$
$$\bar{R}_2 = [(1 + .06)(1 + .07)]^{1/2} - 1 = 6.499\%$$
$$\bar{R}_3 = [(1 + .06)(1 + .07)(1 + .075)]^{1/3} - 1 = 6.832\%$$
$$\bar{R}_4 = [(1 + .06)(1 + .07)(1 + .075)(1 + .0785)]^{1/4} - 1 = 7.085\%$$

and the current yield to maturity curve will be upward sloping as shown:

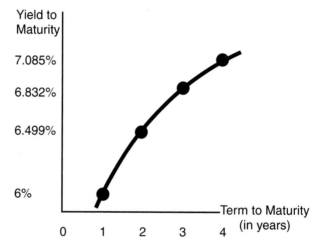

This upward-sloping yield curve reflects the market's expectation of persistently rising one-year (short-term) interest rates over the future horizon.[11]

Liquidity Premium Theory

The second theory, the liquidity premium theory of the term structure of interest rates, is an extension of the unbiased expectations theory. It is based on the idea that investors will hold long-term maturities only if they are offered at a premium to compensate for future uncertainty in a security's value, which increases with an asset's maturity. The liquidity premium theory states that long-term rates are equal to geometric averages of current and expected short-term rates (as under the unbiased expectations theory), plus liquidity risk premiums that increase with the maturity of the security. For example, according to the liquidity premium theory, an upward-sloping yield curve may reflect investors' expectations that future short-term rates will be flat, but because liquidity premiums increase with maturity, the yield curve will nevertheless be upward sloping. The liquidity premium theory may be mathematically represented as:

$$\bar{R}_N = [(1 + \bar{R}_1)(1 + E(\tilde{r}_2) + L_2) \ldots (1 + E(\tilde{r}_N) + L_N)]^{1/N} - 1$$

---

11. That is, $E(\tilde{r}_4) > E(\tilde{r}_3) > E(\tilde{r}_2) > R_1$.

Figure 2–12　Market Segmentation and Determination of the Slope of Yield Curve

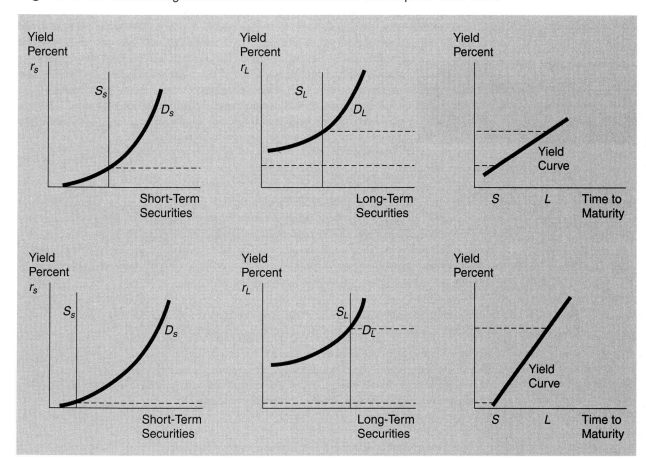

where

L_t = Liquidity premium for a period t
$L_2 < L_3 < \ldots L_N$

Market Segmentation Theory[12]

The market segmentation theory argues that individual investors and FIs have specific maturity preferences, and to get them to hold securities with maturities other than their most preferred requires a higher interest rate (maturity premium). Accordingly, the market segmentation theory does not consider securities with different maturities as perfect substitutes. Rather, individual investors and FIs have preferred investment horizons (habitats) dictated by the nature of the liabilities they hold. For example, banks might prefer to hold relatively short-term U.S. Treasury bonds because of the short-term nature of their deposit liabilities, while insurance companies may prefer to hold long-term U.S. Treasury bonds because of the long-term nature of their life insurance contractual liabilities. Accordingly, interest rates are determined by distinct supply and demand conditions within a particular maturity segment (e.g., the short end and long end of the bond market). The market segmentation theory assumes that investors and borrowers are generally unwilling to shift from one maturity sector to another without adequate compensation in the form of an interest rate premium. Figure 2–12 demonstrates how changes in the supply curve for short- versus long-term bond segments of the market results in

12. Also called preferred habitat theory.

56

www.ustreas.gov/

changes in the shape of the yield to maturity curve. Specifically in Figure 2–12, the higher the yield on securities (the lower the price), the higher the demand for them.[13] Thus, as the *supply* of securities *decreases in the short-term* market and *increases in the long-term* market, the *slope* of the yield curve *becomes steeper.* If the *supply* of *short-term* securities had *increased* while the *supply* of *long-term* securities had *decreased,* the *yield curve would have a flatter slope* and might even have sloped downward. Indeed, the large-scale repurchases of long-term Treasury bonds (i.e., reductions in supply) by the U.S. Treasury in early 2000 has been viewed as the major cause of the inverted yield curve that appeared in February 2000.

forward rate

An expected rate (quoted today) on a security that originates at some point in the future.

Forecasting Interest Rates

The unbiased expectations hypothesis can be used to forecast interest rates in the future (i.e., forward interest rates). A **forward rate** is an expected or "implied" rate on a security that is to be originated at some point in the future. Using the equations representing unbiased expectations theory, the market's expectation of forward rates can be derived directly from existing or actual rates on securities currently traded in the spot market.

Example 2–11 Calculation of Implied Forward Rates Using the Unbiased Expectations Hypothesis

To find an implied forward rate on a one-year security to be issued one year from today, the unbiased expectations hypothesis equation can be rewritten as follows:

$$\bar{R}_2 = [(1 + \bar{R}_1)(1 + (f_2))]^{1/2} - 1$$

where

f_2 = Expected one-year rate for year 2, or the implied forward one-year rate for next year

Therefore, f_2 is the market's estimate of $E(\tilde{r}_2)$ for a particular security being analyzed. Solving for f_2, we get:

$$f_2 = [(1 + \bar{R}_2)^2/(1 + \bar{R}_1)] - 1$$

In general, we can find the forward rate for any year N years into the future using the following equation:

$$f_N = [(1 + \bar{R}_N)^N/(1 + \bar{R}_{N-1})^{N-1}] - 1$$

For example, on August 13, 1999, the existing or current (spot) one-year, two-year, three-year, and four-year zero-coupon Treasury security rates were as follows:

$$\bar{R}_1 = 5.46\% \quad \bar{R}_2 = 5.76\%, \quad \bar{R}_3 = 5.87\%, \quad \bar{R}_4 = 5.97\%$$

Using the unbiased expectations theory, one-year forward rates on zero-coupon Treasury bonds for years two, three, and four as of August 13, 1999, were:

$$f_2 = [(1.0576)^2/(1.0546)] - 1 = 6.061\%$$
$$f_3 = [(1.0587)^3/(1.0576)^2] - 1 = 6.090\%$$
$$f_4 = [(1.0597)^4/(1.0587)^3] - 1 = 6.271\%$$

13. In general, the price and yield on a bond are inversely related. Thus, as the price of a bond falls (becomes cheaper), the demand for the bond will rise. This is the same as saying that as the yield on a bond rises, it becomes cheaper and the demand for it increases.

Summary

This chapter reviewed the determinants of nominal interest rates and their effects on security prices and values in domestic and foreign financial markets. It described the way funds flow through the financial system from lenders to borrowers and how the level of interest rates and its movements over time are determined. The chapter also introduced theories regarding the determination of the shape of the term structure of interest rates.

End-of-Chapter Questions

1. What is the difference between simple interest and compound interest?

2. You are considering an investment that offers the following cash flows paid on the last day of the year:

Year	Cash Flow
1–5	$10,000
6	5,000
7–10	6,000

If the required interest rate on this investment is 15 percent, what would you be willing to pay?

3. Calculate the future value at the end of year 10 on the cash flows received in Question 2, assuming you can reinvest the cash flows at 12 percent.

4. Calculate the effective annual return on an investment offering a 12 percent interest rate, compounded monthly.

5. Why can discount yields not generally be compared to yields on other (nondiscount) securities?

6. What is the discount yield, bond equivalent yield, and effective annual return on a $1 million Treasury bill that currently sells at 97⅞ percent of its face value and is 65 days from maturity?

7. Calculate the bond equivalent yield and effective annual yield on a jumbo CD that is 115 days from maturity and has a quoted nominal yield of 6.56 percent.

8. You would like to purchase a Treasury bill that has a $10,000 face value and is 68 days from maturity. The current price of the Treasury bill is $9,875. Calculate the discount yield on this Treasury bill.

9. Who are the suppliers of loanable funds?

10. Who are the demanders of loanable funds?

11. What factors cause the supply of funds curve to shift?

12. What factors cause the demand for funds curve to shift?

13. A particular security's equilibrium rate of return is 8 percent. For all securities, the inflation risk premium is 1.75 percent and the real interest rate is 3.5 percent. The security's liquidity risk premium is 0.25 percent and maturity risk premium is 0.85 percent. The security has no special covenants. Calculate the security's default risk premium.

14. If we observe a one-year Treasury security rate higher than the two-year Treasury security rate, what can we infer about the one-year rate expected one year from now?

15. Suppose we observe the following rates: $\bar{R}_1 = 8\%, \bar{R}_2 = 10\%$. If the unbiased expectations theory of the term structure of interest rates holds, what is the one-year interest rate expected one year from now, $E(\tilde{r}_2)$?

16. Suppose we observe the three-year Treasury security rate ($\bar{R}_3$) to be 12 percent, the expected one-year rate next year—$E(\tilde{r}_2)$—to be 8 percent, and the expected one-year rate the following year—$E(\tilde{r}_3)$—to be 10 percent. If the unbiased expectations theory of the term structure of interest rates holds, what is the one-year Treasury security rate?

17. Based on economists' forecasts and analysis, one-year Treasury bill rates and liquidity premiums for the next four years are expected to be as follows:

$$\bar{R}_1 = 5.65\%$$
$$E(\tilde{r}_2) = 6.75\% \qquad L_2 = 0.05\%$$
$$E(\tilde{r}_3) = 6.85\% \qquad L_3 = 0.10\%$$
$$E(\tilde{r}_4) = 7.15\% \qquad L_4 = 0.12\%$$

Using the liquidity premium hypothesis, plot the current yield curve. Make sure you label the axes on the graph and identify the four annual rates on the curve both on the axes and on the yield curve itself.

18. Suppose we observe the following rates: $\bar{R}_1 = .10, \bar{R}_2 = .14$, and $E(\tilde{r}_2) = .10$. If the liquidity premium theory of the term structure of interest rates holds, what is the liquidity premium for year 2?

19. If you note the following yield curve in *The Wall Street Journal*, what is the one-year forward rate for the period beginning two years from today, according to the unbiased expectations hypothesis?

Maturity	Yield
One day	2.00%
One year	5.50
Two years	6.50
Three years	9.00

20. Assume the current interest rate on a one-year Treasury bond ($\bar{R}_1$) is 4.50 percent, the current rate on a two-year Treasury bond ($\bar{R}_2$) is 5.25 percent, and the current rate on a three-year Treasury bond ($\bar{R}_3$) is 6.50 percent. If the unbiased expectations theory of the term structure of interest rates is correct, what is the one-year interest rate expected on Treasury bills during year 3 ($E(\tilde{r}_3)$)?

chapter three

Interest Rates *and* Security Valuation

Chapter Navigator

1. What are the differences in the required rate of return, the expected rate of return, and the realized rate of return?

2. How are bonds valued?

3. How are security prices affected by interest rate changes?

4. How do the maturity and coupon rate on a security affect its price sensitivity to interest rate changes?

5. What is duration?

6. How do maturity, yield to maturity, and coupon interest affect the duration of a security?

7. What is the economic meaning of duration?

Interest Rates as a Determinant of Financial Security Values: Chapter Overview

In Chapter 2, we introduced the basic concepts of time value of money and how time value of money equations can be used to convert cash flows received or paid over an investment horizon into either a present value or future value. Of particular importance was the fact that interest rate levels, and changes in interest rate levels, affect security values. We also reviewed the factors that determine the level of interest rates, changes in interest rates, and interest rate differences among securities (e.g., default risk, callability).

With this understanding of how and why interest rates change, in this chapter we apply time value of money principals to the valuation of specific financial securities,

In the News

3-1

World government bond prices fell yesterday amid uncertainty about the direction of U.S. interest rates before today's Federal Open Market Committee meeting. Analysts appeared to be evenly split as to whether or not the committee would raise interest rates. Although the U.S. economy has shown impressive growth in recent months, signs of inflation have been scarce.

Many believe a 25 basis point increase by the Fed could generate a mild relief

Source: *Financial Times*, November 16, 1999, p. 40, by Sathnam Sanghera.

International Capital Markets: Fed Watching Lowers Prices

rally for Treasuries, as was the case when the European Central Bank raised rates earlier in the month. If the Fed leaves rates unchanged, however, the uncertainty may linger as investors turn their attention to forthcoming consumer price index data and Thursday's release of minutes from today's meeting. In midday trading on Wall Street, the benchmark 30-year Treasury fell $\frac{1}{32}$ to 101$\frac{5}{32}$, pushing its yield up to 6.040 percent.

Similarly, the ten-year and five-year notes each lost $\frac{1}{32}$ to yield 5.934 percent and 5.868 percent, respectively.

Euro-zone government bond prices also ended lower, weighed down about the U.S. rate uncertainty and weakness in the euro. The ten-year bond future eventually settled 0.35 lower at 107.58. The yield on the ten-year bond rose by 2 basis points to 4.90.

"It has been very, very quiet in Europe," said Graham McDevitt, head of fixed income at ABN Amro. "But after the rally over the last few weeks, the market has generally drifted lower and is experiencing a bit of consolidation."

www.ft.com/

paying particular attention to the change in a security's value when interest rates change. For example, In the News box 3–1 provides an example of how prices on government bonds reacted to the speculation of interest rate changes in late 1999. We examine how characteristics specific to a financial security (e.g., its coupon rate and remaining time to maturity) also influence a financial security's price. We conclude the chapter with an analysis of the duration of a security. Duration, which measures the weighted-average time to maturity of an asset or liability, also has economic meaning as the sensitivity of an asset or liability's value or price to a small interest rate change.

Do You Understand?

1. How world bond markets responded to speculation that interest rates would increase in late 1999?

Various Interest Rate Measures

In Chapter 2, we presented a general discussion of interest rates and how they are determined. The term *interest rates* can actually have many different meanings depending on the time frame used for analysis and the type of security being analyzed. In this chapter, we start off by defining the different interest rate measures employed in the valuation of financial securities by market participants. These definitions are summarized in Table 3–1.

Table 3–1   Various Interest Rate Measures

Required Rate of Return—interest rate an investor *should* receive on a security given its risk. Required rate of return is used to calculate the fair present value on a security.

Expected Rate of Return—interest rate an investor *would* receive on a security if he or she buys the security at its current market price, receives all expected payments, and sells the security at the end of his or her investment horizon.

Realized Rate of Return—actual interest rate earned on an investment on a financial security. Realized rate of return is a historical (ex post) measure of the interest rate.

Coupon Rate—interest rate on a bond instrument used to calculate the annual cash flows the bond issuer promises to pay the bond holder.

Required Rate of Return

Market participants use time value of money equations to calculate the fair present value of a financial security over an investment horizon. As we discussed in Chapter 2 and will see later on in this chapter, this process involves the discounting of all projected cash flows (CFs)[1] on the security at an appropriate interest rate. The interest rate used to find the fair present value of a financial security is called the **required rate of return** (rrr). This interest rate is a function of the various risks associated with a security (discussed in Chapter 2) and is thus the interest rate the investor *should* receive on the security given its risk (default risk, liquidity risk, etc.). The required rate of return is thus an ex ante (before the fact) measure of the interest rate on a security. The *fair present value (FPV)* is determined by the following formula:

$$FPV = \frac{\widetilde{CF}_1}{(1 + rrr)^1} + \frac{\widetilde{CF}_2}{(1 + rrr)^2} + \frac{\widetilde{CF}_3}{(1 + rrr)^3} + \ldots + \frac{\widetilde{CF}_n}{(1 + rrr)^n}$$

where

rrr = Required rate of return

$\widetilde{CF}_t$ = Cash flow projected in period t ($t = 1, \ldots, n$)

$\sim$ = Indicates that projected cash flow is uncertain (due to default and other risks)

n = Number of periods in the investment horizon

Once an *FPV* is calculated, market participants then compare this fair present value with the *current market price* (*P*) at which the security is trading in a financial market (the current market price). If the current market price of the security (*P*) is less than its fair value (*FPV*), the security is currently undervalued. The market participant would want to buy more of this security at its current price. If the current market price of the security is greater than its fair present value, the security is overvalued. The market participant would not want to buy this security at its current price. If the fair present value of the security equals its current market price, the security is said to be fairly priced given its risk characteristics. In this case, *FPV* equals *P*.

Expected Rate of Return

The **expected rate of return** (Err) on a financial security is the interest rate a market participant *would* earn if he or she buys the security at its *current market price* (P), receives all the projected cash flow payments ($\widetilde{CF}$s) on the security, and sells the security or the security matures at the end of his or her investment horizon. Thus, the expected

required rate of return

The interest rate an investor should receive on a security given its risk.

expected rate of return

The interest rate an investor would earn on a security if he or she buys the security at its current market price, receives all promised or expected payments on the security, and sells the security at the end of his or her investment horizon.

---

1. The projected cash flows used in these equations may be those promised by the security issuer or expected cash flows estimated by the security purchaser (or some other analyst) from a probability distribution of the possible cash flows received on the security. In either case, the cash flows received are not ex ante known with perfect certainty due to default and other risks.

Table 3–2   The Relation between Required Rate of Return and Expected Rate of Return

$Err \geq rrr$, or $P \leq FPV$	The present value of the cash flows received on the security is greater than or equal to that required to compensate for the risk incurred from investing in the security. Thus, buy this security.
$Err < rrr$, or $P > FPV$	The present value of the cash flows received on the security is less than that required to compensate for the risk incurred from investing in the security. Thus, do not buy this security.

rate of return is also an ex ante measure of the interest rate on a security. However, the expected rate of return on an investment is based on the current market price rather than fair present value. As discussed above, these may or may not be equal.

Again, time value of money equations are used to calculate the expected rate of return on a security. In this case, the current market price of the security is set equal to the present value of all projected cash flows received on the security over the investment horizon. The expected rate of return is the discount rate in the present value equations that just makes the present value of projected cash flows equal to its current market price (P). That is:

$$P = \frac{\tilde{CF}_1}{(1 + Err)^1} + \frac{\tilde{CF}_2}{(1 + Err)^2} + \frac{\tilde{CF}_3}{(1 + Err)^3} + \ldots + \frac{\tilde{CF}_n}{(1 + Err)^n}$$

where

Err = Expected rate of return
$\tilde{CF}_t$ = Cash flow projected in period t ($t = 1, \ldots, n$)
n = Number of periods in the investment horizon

Once an expected rate of return (Err) on a financial security is calculated, the market participant compares this expected rate of return to its required rate of return (rrr). If the expected rate of return is greater than the required rate of return, the projected cash flows on the security are greater than is required to compensate for the risk incurred from investing in the security. Thus, the market participant would want to buy more of this security. If the expected rate of return is less than the required rate of return, the projected cash flows from the security are less than those required to compensate for the risk involved. Thus, the market participant would not want to invest more in the security.[2] We summarize these relationships in Table 3–2.

Required versus Expected Rates of Return: The Role of Efficient Markets

We have defined two ex ante (before the fact) measures of interest rates. The *required* rate of return is used to calculate a *fair* present value of a financial security, while the *expected* rate of return is a discount rate used in conjunction with the *current* market price of a security to calculate an ex ante (or before the fact) return. As long as financial markets are efficient (see below), the current market price of a security tends to equal its fair price present value. This is the case most of the time. However, when an event occurs that unexpectedly changes interest rates or a characteristic of a financial security (e.g., an unexpected dividend increase, an unexpected decrease in default risk), the current market price of a security can temporarily diverge from its fair present value. When investors determine a security is undervalued (i.e., its current market

---

2. Note also that by implication, if $Err > rrr$, then the market price of a security *(P)* is less than its fair present value *(FPV)* and vice versa if $Err < rrr$.

price is less than its fair present value), demand for the security increases, as does its price. Conversely, when investors determine a security is overvalued (i.e., its current market price is greater than its fair present value), they will sell the security, resulting in a price drop. The speed with which financial security prices adjust to unexpected news, so as to maintain equality with the fair present value of the security, is referred to as **market efficiency**. We examine the three forms of market efficiency (weak form, semistrong form, and strong form) in Chapter 8.

market efficiency

The process by which financial security prices move to a new equilibrium when interest rates or a security-specific characteristic changes.

Realized Rate of Return

Required and expected rates of return are interest return concepts pertaining to the returns expected or required just prior to the investment being made. Once made, however, the market participant is concerned with how well the financial security actually performs. The **realized rate of return** (rr) on a financial security is the interest rate *actually* earned on an investment in a financial security. The realized rate of return is thus a historical interest rate of return—it is an ex post (after the fact) measure of the interest rate on the security.

realized rate of return

The actual interest rate earned on an investment in a financial security.

To calculate a realized rate of return (rr), all cash flows actually paid or received are incorporated in time value of money equations to solve for the realized rate of return. By setting the price actually paid for the security (P) equal to the present value of the realized cash flows ($RCF_1, RCF_2, \ldots, RCF_n$), the realized rate of return is the discount rate that just equates the purchase price to the present value of the realized cash flows. That is:

$$P = \frac{RCF_1}{(1+rr)^1} + \frac{RCF_2}{(1+rr)^2} + \cdots + \frac{RCF_n}{(1+rr)^n}$$

where

RCF_t = Realized cash flow in period t ($t = 1, \ldots, n$)
rr = Realized rate of return on a security

If the realized rate of return (rr) is greater than the required rate of return (rrr), the market participant actually earned more than was needed to be compensated for the ex ante or expected risk of investing in the security. If the realized rate of return is less than the required rate of return, the market participant actually earned less than the interest rate required to compensate for the risk involved.

Coupon Rate

coupon interest rate

Interest rate used to calculate the annual cash flow the bond issuer promises to pay the bond holder.

A final variation on the meaning of the term *interest rate* specific to debt instruments is the **coupon interest rate** paid on a bond. As discussed in detail in the next section, the coupon rate on a bond instrument is the annual (or periodic) cash flow that the bond issuer contractually promises to pay the bond holder. This coupon rate is only one component of the overall return (required, expected, or realized rate of return) the bond holder earns on a bond, however. As discussed above, required, expected, or realized rates of return incorporate not only the coupon payments but all cash flows on a bond investment, including full and partial repayments of principal by the issuer.

Example 3–1   Application of Required, Expected, and Realized Rates of Return

A bond you purchased two years ago for $890 is now selling for $925. The bond paid $100 per year in coupon interest on the last day of each year (the last payment made today). You intend to hold the bond for four more years and project that you will be able to sell it at the end of year 4 for $960. You also project that the bond will continue paying $100 in interest per year. Given the risk associated with the bond, its required rate of return (*rrr*) over the next four years is 11.25 percent. Accordingly, the bond's fair present value is:

$$FPV = \frac{100}{(1 + .1125)^1} + \frac{100}{(1 + .1125)^2} + \frac{100}{(1 + .1125)^3} + \frac{100 + 960}{(1 + .1125)^4}$$

$$= \$935.31$$

Further, the expected rate of return on the bond, using its current market price, is calculated as follows:

$$925 = \frac{100}{(1 + Err)^1} + \frac{100}{(1 + Err)^2} + \frac{100}{(1 + Err)^3} + \frac{100 + 960}{(1 + Err)^4}$$

$$\Rightarrow Err = 11.607\%$$

Given the current selling price of the bond, $925, relative to the fair present value, $935.31, this bond is currently undervalued. Finally, the realized rate of return you have earned on this bond over the last two years is calculated as follows:

$$890 = \frac{100}{(1 + rr)^1} + \frac{100 + 925}{(1 + rr)^2}$$

$$\Rightarrow rr = 13.08\%$$

Do You Understand?

1. The difference between a required rate of return and an expected rate of return?
2. The difference between the coupon rate on a bond and the realized rate of return on a bond?

Bond Valuation

The valuation of a bond instrument employs time value of money concepts. The fair value of a bond reflects the present value of all cash flows promised or projected to be received on that bond discounted at the required rate of return (rrr). Similarly, the expected rate of return (Err) is the interest rate that equates the current market price of the bond with the present value of all promised cash flows received over the life of the bond. Finally, a realized rate of return (rr) on a bond is the actual return earned on a bond investment that has already taken place. We will limit our present discussion of bond valuation to required and expected rates of return. The appendix to this chapter reviews the valuation of equity instruments (such as common stock). Promised cash flows on bonds come from two sources: (1) interest or coupon payments paid over the life of the bond and (2) a lump sum payment (face or par value) when a bond matures.

coupon bonds

Bonds that pay interest based on a stated coupon rate. The interest paid or coupon payments per year is generally constant over the life of the bond.

zero-coupon bonds

Bonds that do not pay interest.

Bond Valuation Formula Used to Calculate Fair Present Values

Most bonds pay a stated coupon rate of interest to the holders of the bonds. These bonds are called **coupon bonds**. The interest, or coupon, payments per year are generally constant (are fixed) over the life of the bond.[3] Thus, the fixed interest payment, INT, is essentially an annuity paid to the bond holder periodically (normally semiannually) over the life of the bond. Bonds that do not pay coupon interest are called **zero-coupon bonds**. For these bonds, INT is zero. The face or par value of the bond, on the other hand, is a lump sum payment received by the bond holder when the bond matures. Face value is generally set at $1,000 in the U.S. bond market.

---

3. Variable rate bonds pay interest that is indexed to some broad interest rate measure (such as Treasury bills) and thus experience variable coupon payments. Income bonds pay interest only if the issuer has sufficient earnings to make the promised payments. Index (or purchasing power) bonds pay interest based on an inflation index. Both these types of bonds, therefore, can have variable interest payments.

Using time value of money formulas, and assuming that the bond issuer makes its promised coupon and principal payments, the present value of the bond can be written as:

$$V_b = \frac{INT/m}{(1 + i_d/m)^1} + \frac{INT/m}{(1 + i_d/m)^2} + \ldots + \frac{INT/m}{(1 + i_d/m)^{Nm}} + \frac{M}{(1 + i_d/m)^{Nm}}$$

$$= \frac{INT}{m} \sum_{t=1}^{Nm} \left(\frac{1}{1 + i_d/m}\right)^t + \frac{M}{(1 + i_d/m)^{Nm}}$$

$$= \frac{INT}{m} (PVIFA_{i_d/m,\ Nm}) + M(PFIV_{i_d/m,\ Nm})$$

where

V_b = Present value of the bond

M = Par or face value of the bond

INT = Annual interest (or coupon) payment per year on the bond; equals the par value of the bond times the (percentage) coupon rate

N = Number of years until the bond matures

m = Number of times per year interest is paid

i_d = Interest rate used to discount cash flows on the bond

Example 3–2   Calculation of the Fair Value of a Coupon Bond

You are considering the purchase of a bond that pays 10 percent coupon interest per year, with the coupon paid semiannually (i.e., 5 percent over the first half of the year and 5 percent over the second half of the year). The bond matures in 12 years and has a face value of $1,000. If the required rate of return (rrr) on this bond is 8 percent, the fair market value of the bond is calculated as follows:

$$V_b = \frac{1,000(.1)}{2} (PVIFA_{8\%/2,12(2)}) + 1,000(PVIF_{8\%/2,12(2)})$$

$$= 50 (15.24696) + 1,000 (0.39012) = \$1,152.47$$

or an investor would be willing to pay no more than $1,152.47 for this bond.

If the required rate of return on this bond is 10 percent, the fair market value of the bond is calculated as follows:

$$V_b = \frac{1,000(.1)}{2} (PVIFA_{10\%/2,12(2)}) + 1,000(PVIF_{10\%/2,12(2)})$$

$$= 50 (13.79864) + 1,000 (0.31007) = \$1,000.00$$

or an investor would be willing to pay no more than $1,000.00 for this bond.

If the required rate of return on this bond is 12 percent, the fair market value of the bond is calculated as follows:

$$V_b = \frac{1,000(.1)}{2} (PVIFA_{12\%/2,12(2)}) + 1,000(PVIF_{12\%/2,12(2)}) = \$874.50$$

$$= 50 (12.55036) + 1,000 (0.24698) = \$874.50$$

or an investor would be willing to pay no more than $874.50 for this bond.

In the preceding example, notice that when the required rate of return (*rrr*) on the bond is 8 percent, the fair value of the bond, $1,152.47, is greater than its face value of $1,000. When this relationship between the fair value and the face value of a bond

Table 3–3   Description of a Premium, Discount, and Par Bond

Premium Bond—when the *coupon rate* on a bond is greater than the *required rate of return* on the bond, the *fair present value* is greater than the *face value* of the bond.

   When the *coupon rate* on a bond is greater than the *yield to maturity* on the bond, the *current market price* is greater than the *face value* of the bond.

Discount Bond—when the *coupon rate* on a bond is less than the *required rate of return* on the bond, the *fair present value* is less than the *face value* of the bond.

   When the *coupon rate* on a bond is less than the *yield to maturity* on the bond, the *current market price* is less than the *face value* of the bond.

Par Value—when the *coupon rate* on a bond is equal to the *required rate of return* on the bond, the *fair present value* is equal to the *face value* of the bond.

   When the *coupon rate* on a bond is equal to the *yield to maturity* on the bond, the *current market price* is equal to the *face value* of the bond.

premium bond

A bond in which the present value of the bond is greater than its face value.

discount bond

A bond in which the present value of the bond is less than its face value.

par bond

A bond in which the present value of the bond is equal to its face value.

exists, the bond is referred to as a **bond** that should sell at a **premium**. This premium occurs because the coupon rate on the bond is greater than the required rate of return on the bond (a 10 percent coupon rate versus an 8 percent required rate of return in our example). When the required rate of return on the bond is 12 percent, the present value of the bond is less than its face value, and the bond is referred to as a **bond** that should sell at a **discount**. This discount occurs because the coupon rate on the bond is less than the required rate of return on the bond.

Finally, when the required rate of return on the bond is 10 percent, the present value of the bond is equal to its face value, and the bond is referred to as a **bond** that should sell at **par**. This par occurs because the coupon rate on the bond is equal the required rate of return on the bond. To achieve the required rate of return on the bond, the bond holder experiences neither a gain nor a loss on the difference between the purchase price of the bond and the face value received at maturity. We summarize the scenarios for premium, discount,[4] and par bonds in Table 3–3.

It should be noted that the designation as a premium, discount, or par bond does not necessarily assist a bond holder in the decision to buy or sell a bond. This decision is made on the basis of the relationship between the fair present value and the actual current market price of the bond. Rather, premium, discount, and par bonds are descriptive designations regarding the relationship between the fair present value of the bond and its face value. As stated above, the fair present value of the bond will only equal the bond's price in an efficient market where prices instantaneously adjust to new information about the security's value.

Bond Valuation Formula Used to Calculate Yield to Maturity

The present value formulas can also be used to find the expected rate of return (Err) or, assuming all promised coupon and principal payments are made with a probability of 100 percent, what is often called the **yield to maturity** (ytm) on a bond (i.e., the return the bond holder would earn on the bond if he or she buys the bond at its current market price, receives all coupon and principal payments as promised, and holds the bond until maturity). The yield to maturity calculation implicitly assumes that all coupon payments periodically received by the bond holder can be reinvested at the same rate—that is, reinvested at the calculated yield to maturity.

Rewriting the bond valuation formula, where V_b is the current market price that has to be paid to buy the bond, we can solve for the yield to maturity (*ytm*) on a bond as follows (where we write *ytm* instead of *Err*):

$$V_b = \frac{INT}{m}(PVIFA_{ytm/m,Nm}) + M(PVIF_{ytm/m,Nm})$$

yield to maturity

The return or yield the bond holder will earn on the bond if he or she buys it at its current market price, receives all coupon and principal payments as promised, and holds the bond until maturity.

---

4. The term *discount bond* is also used to denote a zero-coupon bond.

Table 3–4   Summary of Factors that Affect Security Prices and Price Volatility When Interest Rates Change

Interest Rate—there is a negative relation between interest rate changes and present value (or price) changes on financial securities.

   As interest rates increase, security prices decrease at a decreasing rate.

Time Remaining to Maturity—the shorter the time to maturity for a security, the closer the price is to the face value of the security.

   The longer the time to maturity for a security, the larger the price change of the security for a given interest rate change.

   The maturity effect described above increases at a decreasing rate.

Coupon Rate—the higher a security's coupon rate, the smaller the price change on the security for a given change in interest rates.

Example 3–3   Calculation of the Yield to Maturity on a Coupon Bond

You are considering the purchase of a bond that pays 11 percent coupon interest per year, paid semiannually (i.e., 5½ percent per semiannual period). The bond matures in 15 years and has a face value of $1,000. If the current market price of the bond is $931.176, the yield to maturity (or *Err*) is calculated as follows:

$$931.176 = \frac{1,000(.11)}{2}(PVIFA_{ytm/2,15(2)}) + 1,000(PVIF_{ytm/2,15(2)})$$

Solving for *ytm*,[5] the yield to maturity (or expected rate of return) on the bond is 12 percent. Equivalently, you would be willing to buy the bond only if the required rate of return (*rrr*) was no more than 12 percent.

As already discussed in this chapter and in Chapter 2, the variability of financial security prices depends on interest rates and the characteristics of the security. Specifically, the factors that affect financial security prices include interest rate changes, the time remaining to maturity, and the coupon rate. We evaluate next the impact of each of these factors as they affect bond prices. Table 3–4 summarizes the major relationships we will be discussing.

Impact of Interest Rate Changes on Security Values

Refer back to Example 3–2. Notice in this example that present values of the cash flows on bonds decreased as interest rates increased. Specifically, when the required rate of return increased from 8 percent to 10 percent, the fair present value of the bond fell from $1,152.47 to $1,000, or by 13.23 percent ((1,000 − 1,152.47)/1,152.47). Similarly, when the required rate of return increased from 10 percent to 12 percent, the fair present value of the bond fell from $1,000 to $874.50, or by 12.55 percent ((874.50 − 1,000)/1,000). This is the inverse relationship between present values and interest rates we discussed in Chapter 2. While the examples refer to the relation between fair values and required

5. Business calculators are programmed to easily solve for the yield to maturity on a security.

Figure 3–1 Relation between Interest Rates and Bond Values

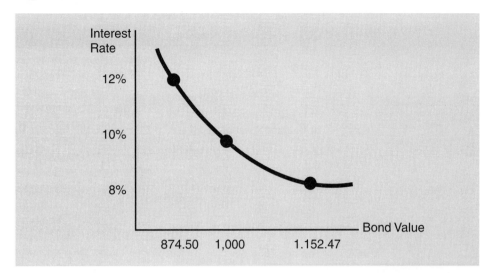

rates of returns, the inverse relation also exists between current market prices and expected rates of return—as yields on bonds increase, the current market prices of bonds decrease. We illustrate this inverse relation between interest rates on bonds and the present value of bonds in Figure 3–1.

Notice too from the earlier example that the inverse relationship between bond prices and interest rates is not linear. Rather, the percentage change in the present value of a bond to a given change in interest rates is smaller when interest rates are higher. When the required rate of return on the bond increased from 8 percent to 10 percent (a 2 percent increase), the fair present value on the bond decreased by 13.23 percent. However, another 2 percent increase in the required rate of return (from 10 percent to 12 percent) resulted in a fair present value decrease of only 12.55 percent. The same nonlinear relation exists for current market prices and yield to maturities. Thus, as interest rates increase, present values of bonds (and bond prices) decrease at a decreasing rate. This is illustrated in Figure 3–1.

The relationship between interest rates and security values is important for all types of investors. Financial institutions (FIs)such as commercial banks, thrifts, and insurance companies are affected because the vast majority of the assets and liabilities held by these firms are financial securities (e.g., loans, deposits, investment securities). When required rates of return rise (fall) on these securities, the fair present values of the FI's asset and liability portfolios decrease (increase) by possibly different amounts, which in turn affects the fair present value of the FI's equity (the difference between the fair present value of an FI's assets and liabilities).

For example, suppose an FI held the 8 percent required return bond evaluated in Example 3–2 (10 percent coupon interest per year paid semiannually, 12 years remaining to maturity, and face value of $1,000) in its asset portfolio and had partly financed the asset purchase by issuing the 10 percent required return bond evaluated in Example 3–2 (the same bond characteristics as above except that the required rate of return is 10 percent) as part of its liability portfolio. In the example, we calculated the fair present values of these bonds as $1,152.47 and $1,000, respectively. The market value balance sheet of the FI is shown in Table 3–5. The market value of the FI's equity is $152.47 ($1,152.47 − $1,000)—the difference between the market values of the FI's assets and liabilities. This can also be thought of as the value of the FI's equity owners' contribution to the financing of the purchase of the asset. If the required rate of return increases by 2 percent on both of these bonds (to 10 percent on the bond in the asset portfolio and to 12 percent on the bond in the liability portfolio), the fair present values of the asset

Table 3–5 Balance Sheet of an FI before and after an Interest Rate Increase

(a) Balance Sheet before the Interest Rate Increase

Assets		Liabilities and Equity	
Bond (8% required rate of return)	$1,152.47	Bond (10% required rate of return)	$1,000
		Equity	$152.47

(b) Balance Sheet after 2 Percent Increase in the Interest Rates

Assets		Liabilities and Equity	
Bond (10% required rate of return)	$1,000	Bond (12% required rate of return)	$874.50
		Equity	$125.50

Do You Understand?

1. What happens to the fair present value of a bond when the required rate of return on the bond increases?
2. What happens to the fair present value of a bond when the required rate of return on the bond decreases?

and liability portfolios fall to $1,000 and $874.50, respectively. As a result, the value of the FI's equity falls to $125.50 ($1,000 − $874.50)—see Table 3–5. Implicitly, the equity owners of the FI have lost $26.97 ($152.47 − $125.50) of the value of their ownership stake in the FI. We examine the measurement and management of an FI's interest rate risk in more detail in Chapter 23.

4 Impact of Maturity on Security Values

An important factor that affects the degree to which the price of a bond changes (or the price sensitivity of a bond changes) as interest rates change is the time remaining to maturity on the bond. A bond's **price sensitivity** is measured by the percentage change in its present value for a given change in interest rates. The larger the percentage change in the bond's value for a given interest rate change, the larger the bond's price sensitivity. Specifically, as is explained below, the shorter the time remaining to maturity, the closer a bond's price is to its face value. Also, the further a bond is from maturity, the more sensitive the price (fair or current) of the bond as interest rates change. Finally, the relationship between bond price sensitivity and maturity is not linear. As the time remaining to maturity on a bond increases, price sensitivity increases but at a decreasing rate. Table 3–6 presents the bond information we will be using to illustrate these relationships.

price sensitivity

The percentage change in a bond's present value for a given change in interest rates.

Maturity and Security Prices

Table 3–6 lists the present values of 10 percent (compounded semiannually) coupon bonds with a $1,000 face value and 12 years, 14 years, and 16 years, respectively, remaining to maturity. We calculate the fair present value of these bonds using an 8 percent, 10 percent, and 12 percent required rate of return. Notice that for each of these bonds, the closer the bond is to maturity, the closer the fair present value of the bond is to the $1,000 face value. This is true regardless of whether the bond is a premium, discount, or par bond. For example, at an 8 percent interest rate, the 12-year, 14-year, and 16-year bonds have present values of $1,152.47, $1,166.63, and $1,178.74, respectively. The intuition behind this is that nobody would pay much more than the face value of the bond and any remaining (in this case semiannual) coupon payments just prior to maturity since these are the only cash flows left to be paid on the bond. Thus, the time value effect is reduced as the maturity of the bond approaches. Many people

Table 3–6 The Impact of Time to Maturity on the Relation between a Bond's Fair Present Value and Its Required Rate of Return

Required Rate of Return	12 Years to Maturity			14 Years to Maturity			16 Years to Maturity		
	Fair Price*	Price Change	Percentage Price Change	Fair Price*	Price Change	Percentage Price Change	Fair Price*	Price Change	Percentage Price Change
8%	$1,152.47			$1,166.63			$1,178.74		
		−$152.47	−13.23%		−$166.63	−14.28%		−$178.74	−15.16%
10%	1,000.00			1,000.00			1,000.00		
		−125.50	−12.55		−134.06	−13.41		−140.84	−14.08
12%	874.50			865.94			859.16		

*The bond pays 10% coupon interest compounded semiannually and has a face value of $1,000.

call this effect the pull to par—bond prices and fair values approach their par values (e.g., $1,000) as time to maturity declines towards zero.

Maturity and Security Price Sensitivity to Changes in Interest Rates

The Percentage Price Change columns in Table 3–6 provide data to examine the effect time to maturity has on bond price sensitivity to interest rates change. From these data we see that the longer the time remaining to maturity on a bond, the more sensitive are bond prices to a given change in interest rates. (Note again that all bonds in Table 3–6 have a 10 percent coupon rate and a $1,000 face value.) For example, the fair present value of the 12-year bond falls 13.23 percent as the required rate of return increases from 8 percent to 10 percent. The same 2 percent increase (from 8 percent to 10 percent) in the required rate of return produces a larger 14.28 percent drop in the fair present value of the 14-year bond, and the 16-year bond's fair present value drops 15.16 percent. This same trend is demonstrated when the required rate of return increases from 10 percent to 12 percent—the longer the bond's maturity, the greater the percentage decrease in the bond's fair present value.

The same relationship occurs when analyzing expected rates of return (or yields to maturity) and the current market price of the bond—the longer the time to maturity on a bond, the larger the change in the current market price of a bond for a given change in yield to maturity.

Incremental Changes in Maturity and Security Price Sensitivity to Changes in Interest Rates.   A final relationship we can examine from Table 3–6 is that between incremental changes in time remaining to maturity and incremental changes in security price sensitivity to a given change in interest rates. Specifically, notice that the maturity effect described above is not linear. For example, a 2 percent increase in the required rate of return (from 8 percent to 10 percent) on the 12-year bond produces a 13.23 percent decrease in the bond's fair present value. The same 2 percent increase (from 8 percent to 10 percent) in the 14-year bond produces a 14.28 percent decrease in the fair present value. The difference, as we move from a 12-year to a 14-year maturity, is 1.05 percent (14.28% − 13.23%). Increasing the time to maturity two more years (from 14 years to 16 years) produces an increase in price sensitivity of 0.88 percent (−14.28% − (−15.16%)). While price sensitivity for a given increase in interest rates increases with maturity, the increase is nonlinear (decreasing) in maturity. We illustrate this relationship in Figure 3–2.

Do You Understand?

1. What happens to a bond's price as it approaches maturity?
2. What happens to a bond's price sensitivity for a given change in interest rates as its time to maturity increases? decreases?

Figure 3–2   The Impact of a Bond's Maturity on Its Interest Rate Sensitivity

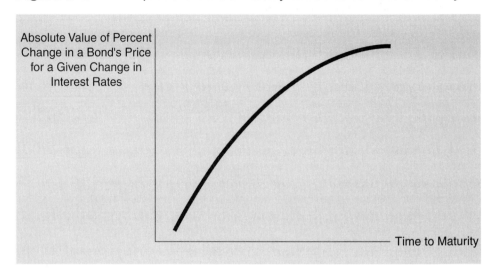

Table 3–7   The Impact of Coupon Rate on the Relation between a Bond's Fair Present Value and Its Required Rate of Return

Required Rate of Return	10 Percent Coupon Bond			12 Percent Coupon Bond		
	Fair Price*	Price Change	Percentage Price Change	Fair Price*	Price Change	Percentage Price Change
8%	$1,152.47			$1,304.94		
		−$152.47	−13.23%		−$166.95	−12.79%
10%	1,000.00			1,137.99		
		−125.50	−12.55		−137.99	−12.13
12%	874.50			1,000.00		

*The bond pays interest semiannually, has 12 years remaining to maturity, and has a face value of $1,000.

Impact of Coupon Rates on Security Values

Another factor that affects the degree to which the price sensitivity of a bond changes as interest rates change is the bond's coupon rate. Specifically, the higher the bond's coupon rate, the higher its present value at any given interest rate. Also, the higher the bond's coupon rate, the smaller the price changes on the bond for a given change in interest rates. These relationships hold when evaluating either required rates of return and the resulting fair present value of the bond or expected rates of return and the current market price of the bond. To understand these relationships better, consider again the bonds in Example 3–2. Table 3–7 summarizes the bond values and value changes as interest rates change.

Coupon Rate and Security Price

In Table 3–7, we first list the fair present values of the bonds analyzed in Example 3–2. We then repeat the present value calculations using two bonds with identical characteristics except for the coupon rate: 10 percent versus 12 percent. Notice that the fair present value of the 10 percent coupon bond is lower than that of the 12 percent coupon bond at every required rate of return. For example, when the required rate of return is 8 percent, the fair value of the 10 percent coupon bond is $1,152.47 and that of the 12 percent coupon bond is $1,304.94.

Figure 3–3 The Impact of a Bond's Coupon Rate on Its Interest
Rate Sensitivity

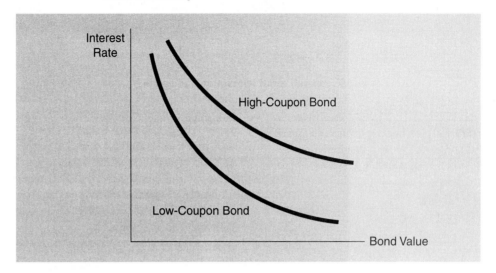

Coupon Rate and Security Price Sensitivity to Changes in Interest Rates

Table 3–7 also demonstrates the effect a bond's coupon rate has on its price sensitivity to a given change in interest rates. The intuition behind this relation is as follows. The higher (lower) the coupon rate on the bond, the larger (smaller) is the portion of the required rate of return paid to the bond holder in the form of coupon payments. Any security that returns a greater (smaller) proportion of an investment sooner is more (less) valuable and less (more) price volatile.

To see this, notice in Table 3–7 that the higher the bond's coupon rate, the smaller the bond's price sensitivity for any given change in interest rates. For example, for a 10 percent coupon bond, a 2 percent increase in the required rate of return (from 8 percent to 10 percent) results in a 13.23 percent decrease in the bond's fair price. A further 2 percent increase in the required rate of return (from 10 percent to 12 percent) results in a smaller 12.55 percent decrease in the fair price.

For a 12 percent coupon bond, notice that the 2 percent increase in the required rate of return (from 8 percent to 10 percent) results in a 12.79 percent decrease in the bond's fair price, while an increase in the required rate of return from 10 percent to 12 percent results in a lower 12.13 percent decrease in the bond's fair price. Thus, price sensitivity on a bond is negatively related to the level of the coupon rate on a bond. The higher the coupon rate on the bond, the smaller the decrease in the bond's fair price for a given increase in the required rate of return on the bond.

We illustrate this relationship in Figure 3–3. The high coupon-paying bond is less susceptible to interest rate changes than the low coupon-paying bond. This is represented in Figure 3–3 by the slope of the line representing the relation between interest rates and bond prices. The sensitivity of bond prices is smaller (the slope of the line is flatter) for high-coupon bonds than for low-coupon bonds.

Do You Understand?

1. Whether a high or low coupon-rate bond experiences a larger price change if interest rates increase?
2. Whether a high or low coupon-rate bond experiences a larger price change if interest rates decrease?

Duration

In this section, we show that the price sensitivity of a bond, or the percent change in the bond's fair present value, for a given change in interest rates (as discussed above) can be more directly measured by a concept called duration (or

In the News

Robert MacIntosh of Eaton Vance

Credit and structure "can go hand in hand," says Robert MacIntosh, portfolio manager with Boston-based Eaton Vance Management. However, he added, it's more often that a portfolio manager is concerned with either duration management or yield gathering—not both. "You may need duration so you may need a lower coupon and/or a longer bond," he said. MacIntosh looks for noncallable bonds but also em-

phasizes a 10-year premium call on a new bond. "It's always helpful to be thinking of doing swaps out of some of the bonds that are a little older and getting a little shorter from a call perspective," he said.

MacIntosh, who manages several state-specific funds from the $340 million New Jersey Tax Free Fund to the $22 million Hawaii Tax Free Fund, said while the smaller states provide fewer opportunities to shape

structure, each fund manager is in the same boat. "You have less paper to choose from, so you're trading less, and swapping less, ending up with structures that might not be ideal," he observed. But, he added, "the same thing is happening to your competitors."

Above all, MacIntosh keeps an eye on his competitors' funds when strategizing his duration. He does not want to be far ahead or far behind the peer group average. "If your duration is where you want it to be, but you want yield, then maybe you look more towards yieldly paper," he said.

Source: *Bond Buyer*, April 19, 1999, p. 7, by Jennifer Karchmer. Reprinted by permission—American Banker.

www.americanbanker. com/

duration

The weighted-average time to maturity on an investment.

elasticity

The percentage change in the price of a bond for any given change in interest rates.

Do You Understand?

1. Why is either duration or yield— but not both—management used as a portfolio management strategy?

Macauley's duration). We also show that duration produces an accurate measure of the price sensitivity of a bond to interest rate changes for relatively small changes in interest rates. The duration measure is a less accurate measure of price sensitivity the larger the change in interest rates. **Duration** is the *weighted-average* time to maturity on a financial security using the relative present values of the cash flows as weights. On a time value of money basis, duration measures the period of time required to recover the initial investment in a bond. Any cash flows received prior to the period of a bond's duration reflect the recovery of the initial investment, while cash flows received after the period of a bond's measured duration and before its maturity are the profits or returns earned by the investor. In addition to being a measure of the average life of an asset or liability, duration also has *economic* meaning as the sensitivity, or **elasticity**, of that asset's or liability's value to small interest rate changes (either required rate of return or yield to maturity). Duration describes the percentage price, or present value, change of a financial security for a given (small) change in interest rates. Thus, rather than calculating present value changes resulting from interest rate changes, as we did in the previous sections, the duration of a financial security can be used to directly calculate the price change.

In this section, we present the basic arithmetic needed to calculate the duration of an asset or liability. Then we analyze the economic meaning of the number we calculate for duration and explain why duration, as a measure of interest rate sensitivity, is most accurate only for small changes in interest rates. In the News box 3–2 illustrates that duration is an important tool used by bond and FI portfolio managers.

Figure 3–4   Promised Cash Flows on the One-Year Bond

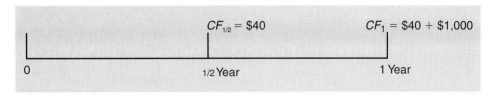

Figure 3–5   Present Value of the Cash Flows from the Bond

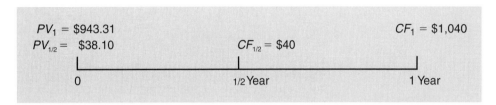

A Simple Illustration of Duration

Duration is a measure that incorporates the time of arrival of all cash flows on an asset or liability along with the asset or liability's maturity date. To see this, consider a bond with one year remaining to maturity, a $1,000 face value, an 8 percent coupon rate (paid semiannually), and an interest rate (either required rate of return or yield to maturity) of 10 percent. The promised cash flows from this bond are illustrated in Figure 3–4. The bond holder receives the promised cash flows (CF) from the bond issuer at the end of one-half year and at the end of one year.

$CF_{1/2}$ is the $40 promised payment of (semiannual) coupon interest ($1,000 $\times$ 8% $\times$ ½) received after six months. CF_1 is the promised cash flow at the end of year; it is equal to the second $40 promised (semiannual) coupon payment plus the $1,000 promised payment of face value. To compare the relative sizes of these two cash flow payments—since duration measures the weighted-average time to maturity of a bond—we should put them in the same dimensions, because $1 of principal or interest received at the end of one year is worth less to an investor in terms of time value of money than is $1 of principal or interest received at the end of six months. Assuming that the current interest rate is 10 percent per year, we calculate the present values (PV) of the two cash flows (CF) as:

$$CF_{1/2} = \$40 \qquad\qquad PV_{1/2} = \$40/(1.05) = \$38.10$$
$$CF_1 = \$1,040 \qquad\qquad PV_1 = \$1,040/(1.05)^2 = \$943.31$$
$$CF_{1/2} + CF_1 = \$1,080 \qquad PV_{1/2} + PV_1 = \$981.41$$

Note that since $CF_{1/2}$, the cash flows received at the end of one-half year, are received earlier, they are discounted at $(1 + R/2)$ (where R is the current annual interest rate on the bond); this discount factor is smaller than the discount rate applied to the cash flow received at the end of the year $(1 + R/2)^2$. Figure 3–5 summarizes the PVs of the cash flows from the bond.[6]

The bond holder receives some cash flows at one-half year and some at one year (see Figure 3–5). Intuitively, duration is the weighted-average maturity on the portfolio

---

6. Here we use the Treasury formula for calculating the present values of cash flows on a security that pays cash flows semiannually. We use $1/(1 + ½R)^2$ to discount the one-year cash flow rather than $1/(1 + R)$. This approach is more accurate, since it reflects the semiannual payment and compounding of interest on the bond.

of zero-coupon bonds, one that has payments at one-half year and at the end of the year (year 1) in this example. Specifically, duration analysis weights the time at which cash flows are received by the relative importance in *present value terms* of the cash flows arriving at each point in time. In present value terms, the relative importance of the cash flows arriving at time $t = \frac{1}{2}$ year and time $t = 1$ year are as follows:

Time (t)	Weight (X)			
$\frac{1}{2}$ year	$X_{1/2} = \dfrac{PV_{1/2}}{PV_{1/2} + PV_1}$	$= \dfrac{38.10}{981.41}$	$= .0388 =$	3.88%
1 year	$X_1 = \dfrac{PV_1}{PV_{1/2} + PV_1}$	$= \dfrac{943.31}{981.41}$	$= .9612 =$	96.12%
			1.0	100%

In present value terms, the bond holder receives 3.88 percent of the cash flows on the bond with the first coupon payment at the end of six months ($t_{1/2}$) and 96.12 percent with the second payment of coupon plus face value at the end of the year (t_1). By definition, the sum of the (present value) cash flow weights must equal 1:

$$X_{1/2} + X_1 = 1$$
$$.0388 + .9612 = 1$$

We can now calculate the duration (D), or the weighted-average time to maturity of the bond, using the present value of its cash flows as weights:

$$D_L = X_{1/2} \times (t_{1/2}) + X_1 \times (t_1)$$
$$= .0388 \times (\tfrac{1}{2}) + .9612 \times (1) = .9806 \text{ years}$$

Thus, although the maturity of the bond is one year, its duration or average life in a cash flow sense is only .9806 years. On a time value of money basis, the initial investment in the bond is recovered (albeit not yet realized) after .9806 years. After that time, the investor earns a profit on the bond. Duration is less than maturity because in present value terms, 3.88 percent of the cash flows are received during the year.

A General Formula for Duration

You can calculate the duration for any fixed income security that pays interest annually using the following formula:

$$D = \frac{\displaystyle\sum_{t=1}^{N} \dfrac{CF_t \times t}{(1 + R)^t}}{\displaystyle\sum_{t=1}^{N} \dfrac{CF_t}{(1 + R)^t}} = \frac{\displaystyle\sum_{t=1}^{N} PV_t \times t}{\displaystyle\sum_{t=1}^{N} PV_t}$$

where

D = Duration measured in years
t = 1 to N, the period in which a cash flow is received
N = Number of years to maturity
CF_t = Cash flow received on the security at end of period t
R = Annual yield to maturity or current required market rate of return on the investment
PV_t = Present value of the cash flow received at the end of the period t

For bonds that pay interest semiannually, the duration equation becomes:[7]

$$D = \frac{\displaystyle\sum_{t=\frac{1}{2}}^{N} \frac{CF_t \times t}{(1 + R/2)^{2t}}}{\displaystyle\sum_{t=\frac{1}{2}}^{N} \frac{CF_t}{(1 + R/2)^{2t}}}$$

where

$$t = \tfrac{1}{2}, 1, 1\tfrac{1}{2}, \ldots, N$$

Notice that the denominator of the duration equation is the present value of the cash flows on the security (which in an efficient market will be equal to the current market price). The numerator is the present value of each cash flow received on the security multiplied or weighted by the length of time required to receive the cash flow. To help you fully understand this formula, we look at some examples next.

The Duration of Bonds Paying Periodic Interest

Example 3–4   The Duration of a Four-Year Bond

Suppose that you have a bond that offers a coupon rate of 10 percent paid semiannually. The face value of the bond is $1,000, it matures in four years, its current yield to maturity (R) is 8 percent, and its current price is $1,067.34.[8] See Table 3–8 for the calculation of its duration, including, in the last column, the percent of the initial investment recovered each year. As the calculation indicates, the duration, or weighted-average time to maturity, on this bond is 3.42 years. In other words, on a time value of money basis, the initial investment of $1,067.34 is recovered after 3.42 years. Between 3.42 years and maturity (4 years), the bond produces a profit or return to the investor. Table 3–9 shows that if the annual coupon rate is lowered to 6 percent, the duration of the bond rises to 3.60 years. Since 6 percent annual coupon payments are smaller than 10 percent coupon payments, it takes longer to recover the initial investment with the 6 percent coupon bond. In Table 3–10, duration is calculated for the original 10 percent coupon bond, assuming that its yield to maturity (discount rate) increases from 8 percent to 10 percent. Now duration falls from 3.42 years (in Table 3–8) to 3.39 years. The higher the yield to maturity on the bond, the more the investor earns on reinvested coupons and the shorter the time needed to recover his or her initial investment. Finally, as the maturity on a bond decreases, in this case to 3 years in Table 3–11, duration falls to 2.67 years (i.e., the shorter the maturity on the bond, the more quickly the initial investment is recovered).

---

7. In general, the duration equation is written as:

$$D = \frac{\displaystyle\sum_{t=1/m}^{N} \frac{CF_t \times t}{(1 + R/m)^{mt}}}{\displaystyle\sum_{t=1/m}^{N} \frac{CF_t}{(1 + R/m)^{mt}}}$$

where m = Number of times per year interest is paid

8. We use the yield to maturity and current market price in our examples. The duration formula can also employ the required rate of return and fair present value.

Table 3–8 Duration of a Four-Year Bond with 10 Percent Coupon Paid Semiannually and 8 Percent Yield

t	CF_t	$\dfrac{1}{(1 + 4\%)^{2t}}$	$\dfrac{CF_t}{(1 + 4\%)^{2t}}$	$\dfrac{CF_t \times t}{(1 + 4\%)^{2t}}$	Percent of Initial Investment Recovered
½	50	0.9615	48.08	24.04	24.04/1,067.34 = 0.02
1	50	0.9246	46.23	46.23	46.23/1,067.34 = 0.04
1½	50	0.8890	44.45	66.67	66.67/1,067.34 = 0.06
2	50	0.8548	42.74	85.48	85.48/1,067.34 = 0.08
2½	50	0.8219	41.10	102.75	102.75/1,067.34 = 0.10
3	50	0.7903	39.52	118.56	118.56/1,067.34 = 0.11
3½	50	0.7599	38.00	133.00	133.00/1,067.34 = 0.13
4	1,050	0.7307	767.22	3,068.88	3,068.88/1,067.34 = 2.88
			1,067.34	3,645.61	3.42

$$D = \frac{3,645.61}{1,067.34} = 3.42 \text{ years}$$

Table 3–9 Duration of a Four-Year Bond with 6 Percent Coupon Paid Semiannually and 8 Percent Yield

t	CF_t	$\dfrac{1}{(1 + 4\%)^{2t}}$	$\dfrac{CF_t}{(1 + 4\%)^{2t}}$	$\dfrac{CF_t \times t}{(1 + 4\%)^{2t}}$	Percent of Initial Investment Recovered
½	30	0.9615	28.84	14.42	14.42/932.68 = 0.01
1	30	0.9246	27.74	27.74	27.74/932.68 = 0.03
1½	30	0.8890	26.67	40.00	40.00/932.68 = 0.04
2	30	0.8548	25.64	51.28	51.28/932.68 = 0.05
2½	30	0.8219	24.66	61.65	61.65/932.68 = 0.07
3	30	0.7903	23.71	71.13	71.13/932.68 = 0.08
3½	30	0.7599	22.80	79.80	79.80/932.68 = 0.09
4	1,030	0.7307	752.62	3,010.48	3,010.48/932.68 = 3.23
			932.68	3,356.50	3.60

$$D = \frac{3,356.50}{932.68} = 3.60 \text{ years}$$

Table 3–10 Duration of a Four-Year Bond with 10 Percent Coupon Paid Semiannually and 10 Percent Yield

t	CF_t	$\dfrac{1}{(1 + 5\%)^{2t}}$	$\dfrac{CF_t}{(1 + 5\%)^{2t}}$	$\dfrac{CF_t \times t}{(1 + 5\%)^{2t}}$	Percent of Initial Investment Recovered
½	50	0.9524	47.62	23.81	23.81/1,000.00 = 0.02
1	50	0.9070	45.35	45.35	45.35/1,000.00 = 0.05
1½	50	0.8638	43.19	64.78	64.78/1,000.00 = 0.07
2	50	0.8227	41.14	82.28	82.28/1,000.00 = 0.08
2½	50	0.7835	39.18	97.95	97.95/1,000.00 = 0.10
3	50	0.7462	37.31	111.93	111.93/1,000.00 = 0.11
3½	50	0.7107	35.53	124.36	124.36/1,000.00 = 0.12
4	1,050	0.6768	710.68	2,842.72	2,842.72/1,000.00 = 2.84
			1,000.00	3,393.18	3.39

$$D = \frac{3,393.18}{1,000.00} = 3.39 \text{ years}$$

Table 3–11   Duration of a Three-Year Bond with 10 Percent Coupon Paid
                     Semiannually and an 8 Percent Yield

t	CF_t	$\dfrac{1}{(1+4\%)^{2t}}$	$\dfrac{CF_t}{(1+4\%)^{2t}}$	$\dfrac{CF_t \times t}{(1+4\%)^{2t}}$	**Percent of Initial Investment Recovered**
½	50	0.9615	48.08	24.04	24.04/1,052.42 = 0.02
1	50	0.9246	46.23	46.23	46.23/1,052.42 = 0.04
1½	50	0.8890	44.45	66.67	66.67/1,052.42 = 0.06
2	50	0.8548	42.74	85.48	85.48/1,052.42 = 0.08
2½	50	0.8219	41.10	102.75	102.75/1,052.42 = 0.10
3	1,050	0.7903	829.82	2,489.46	2,489.46/1,052.42 = 2.37
			1,052.42	2,814.63	2.67

$$D = \frac{2,814.63}{1,052.42} = 2.67 \text{ years}$$

The Duration of a Zero-Coupon Bond.   Zero-coupon bonds sell at a discount from face value on issue and pay their face value (e.g., $1,000) on maturity. These bonds have no intervening cash flows, such as coupon payments, between issue and maturity. The current price that an investor is willing to pay for such a bond, assuming annual compounding of interest, is equal to the present value of the single, fixed (face value) payment on the bond that is received on maturity (here, $1,000):

$$P = \frac{1,000}{(1+R)^N}$$

where

R = Required annually compounded yield to maturity
N = Number of years to maturity
P = Price

Because the only cash flow received on these securities is the final payment at maturity (time N), the following must be true:

$$D_{zc} = N_{zc}$$

That is, the duration of a zero-coupon instrument equals its maturity. Note that it is only for zero-coupon bonds that duration and maturity are equal. Indeed, for any bond that pays some cash flows prior to maturity, its duration will always be less than its maturity.

Example 3–5   The Duration of a Zero-Coupon Bond

Suppose that you have a zero-coupon bond with a face value of $1,000, a maturity of four years, and a current yield to maturity of 8 percent. Since the bond pays no interest, the duration equation consists of only one term—cash flows at the end of year 4:

t	CF_4	$\dfrac{1}{(1+8\%)^4}$	$\dfrac{CF_4}{(1+8\%)^4}$	$\dfrac{CF_4 \times 4}{(1+8\%)^4}$
4	$1,000	0.7350	735	2,940

$$D = \frac{2,940}{735} = 4 \text{ years}$$

or duration equals the maturity of the zero-coupon bond.

Table 3–12   Features of Duration

1. The higher the coupon or promised interest payment on a security, the lower is its duration.
2. The higher the yield on a security, the lower is its duration.
3. Duration increases with maturity at a decreasing rate.

Table 3–13   Duration of a Two-Year Bond with 10 Percent Coupon Paid Semiannually and 8 Percent Yield

t	CF_t	$\dfrac{1}{(1+4\%)^{2t}}$	$\dfrac{CF_t}{(1+4\%)^{2t}}$	$\dfrac{CF_t \times t}{(1+4\%)^{2t}}$	Percent of Initial Investment Recovered
½	50	0.9615	48.08	24.04	24.04/1,036.30 = 0.02
1	50	0.9246	46.23	46.23	46.23/1,036.30 = 0.05
1½	50	0.8890	44.45	66.67	66.67/1,036.30 = 0.06
2	1,050	0.8548	897.54	1,795.08	1,795.08/1,036.30 = 1.73
			1,036.30	1,932.02	1.86

$$D = \frac{1,932.02}{1,036.30} = 1.86 \text{ years}$$

Features of Duration

The preceding examples suggest several important features of duration relating to the time remaining to maturity, yield to maturity, and coupon interest of the underlying bond being analyzed. These features are summarized in Table 3–12.

Duration and Coupon Interest.   A comparison of Tables 3–8 and 3–9 indicates that the higher the coupon or promised interest payment on the bond, the lower its duration. This is due to the fact that the larger the coupon or promised interest payment, the more quickly investors receive cash flows on a bond and the higher are the present value weights of those cash flows in the duration calculation. On a time value of money basis, the investor recoups his or her initial investment faster when coupon payments are higher.

Duration and Yield to Maturity.   A comparison of Tables 3–8 and 3–10 also indicates that duration decreases as yield to maturity increases. This makes intuitive sense since the higher the yield to maturity on the bond, the lower the present value cost of waiting to receive the later cash flows on the bond. Higher yields to maturity discount later cash flows more heavily, and the relative importance, or weights, of those later cash flows decline when compared to cash flows received earlier.

Duration and Maturity.   A comparison of Tables 3–8, 3–11, and 3–13 indicates that duration *increases* with the maturity of a bond, but at a *decreasing* rate. As maturity of a 10 percent coupon bond decreases from four years to three years (Tables 3–8 and 3–11), duration decreases by 0.75 years, from 3.42 years to 2.67 years. Decreasing maturity for an additional year, from three years to two years (Tables 3–11 and 3–13), decreases duration by 0.81 years from 2.67 years to 1.86 years.

Economic Meaning of Duration

So far we have calculated duration for a number of different bonds. In addition to being a measure of the average life of a bond, duration is also a direct measure of its interest rate sensitivity or elasticity.[9] In other words, the larger the numerical value of duration (D), the more sensitive the price of that bond to (small) changes or shocks in interest rates. The specific relationship between these factors for securities with annual compounding of interest is represented as:

$$\frac{\dfrac{dP}{P}}{\dfrac{dR}{(1+R)}} = -D$$

For securities with semiannual receipt (compounding) of interest, it is represented as:

$$\frac{\dfrac{dP}{P}}{\dfrac{dR/2}{(1+R/2)}} = -D$$

The economic interpretation of this equation is that the number D is the interest elasticity, or sensitivity, of the bond's price to small interest rate (either required rate of return or yield to maturity) changes. That is, D describes the percentage fair or current value decrease—capital loss—on the security (dP/P) for any given (discounted) small increase in interest rates ($dR/1 + R$), where dR is the change in interest rates and $1 + R$ is one plus the current level of interest rates.

The definition of duration can be rearranged in another useful way for interpretation regarding interest sensitivity:

$$\frac{dP}{P} = -D \left[\frac{dR}{1+R} \right]$$

or

$$\frac{dP}{P} = -D \left[\frac{dR/2}{(1+R/2)} \right]$$

for annual and semiannual compounding of interest, respectively. This equation shows that for *small changes* in interest rates, bond prices move *in an inversely proportional* manner according to the size of D. Clearly, for any given change in interest rates, long-duration securities suffer a larger capital loss (or receive a higher capital gain) should interest rates fall (rise) than do short-duration securities.[10] The duration equation can be rearranged, combining D and $(1 + R)$ into a single variable $D/(1 + R)$, to produce what practitioners call **modified duration** (MD). For annual compounding of interest:

modified duration

Duration divided by 1 plus the interest rate.

$$\frac{dP}{P} = -MD \times dR$$

where

$$MD = \frac{D}{1+R}$$

9. In Chapter 23, we also make the direct link between duration and the interest rate sensitivity of an asset or liability or of an FI's entire portfolio (i.e., its duration gap). We show how duration can be used to immunize a security or portfolio of securities against interest rate risk.

10. By implication, gains and losses under the duration model are *symmetric*. That is, if we repeated the above examples but allowed interest rates to *decrease* by one basis point annually (or ½ basis point semi-annually), the percentage increase in the price of the bond (dP/P) would be proportionate with D. Further, the capital gains would be a mirror image of the capital losses for an equal (small) increase in interest rates.

For semiannual compounding of interest:

$$\frac{dP}{P} = -MD \times dR/2$$

where

$$MD = \frac{D}{1 + R/2}$$

This form is more intuitive because we multiply *MD* by the simple change in interest rates rather than the discounted change in interest rates as in the general duration equation. Next, we use duration to measure the price sensitivity of different bonds to small changes in interest rates (either required rate of return or yield to maturity).

The Interest-Paying Bond

Example 3–6   Four-Year Bond

Consider a four-year bond with a 10 percent coupon paid semiannually and an 8 percent annual yield to maturity (the discount rate). According to calculations in Table 3–8, the bond's duration is $D = 3.42$ years. Suppose that the yield to maturity increases by 10 basis points (1/10th of 1 percent) from 8 to 8.10 percent (or 5 basis points, .0005, for each semiannual period); then, using the semiannual compounding version of the duration model shown above, the percentage change in the bond's price is:

$$\frac{dP}{P} = -(3.42)\left[\frac{.0005}{1.04}\right]$$

$$= -.00164$$

or

$$= -0.164\%$$

The bond price had been $1,067.34, which was the present value of a four-year bond with a 10 percent annual coupon and an 8 percent annual yield to maturity. However, the duration model predicts that the price of this bond would fall by 0.164 percent, or by $1.75, to $1,065.59 after the increase in the annual yield to maturity on the bond of 10 basis points.[11]

With a lower annual coupon rate of 6 percent, as shown in Table 3–9, the bond's duration, *D,* is 3.6 and the bond price changes by:

$$\frac{dP}{P} = -(3.60)\left[\frac{.0005}{1.04}\right] = -.00173$$

or

$$= -0.173\%$$

for a 5-basis-point increase in the yield to maturity for each semiannual period. The bond's price drops by 0.173 percent, or by $1.61, from $932.68 (reported in Table 3–9) to $931.07. Notice again that, all else held constant, the higher the coupon rate on the bond, the shorter the duration of the bond and the smaller the percentage decrease in a bond's price for a given increase in interest rates.

---

11. That is, a price fall of 0.164 percent in this case translates into a dollar fall of $1.75. To calculate the dollar change in value, we can rewrite the equation as $dP = (P)(-D)((dR/2)/(1+R/2)) + R) = (\$1,067.34)(-3.42)(.0005/1.04) = \$1.75$.

Figure 3–6 Duration Estimated versus True Bond Price

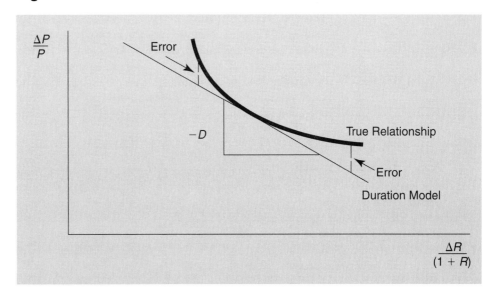

Large Interest Rate Changes and Duration

It needs to be stressed here that duration accurately measures the price sensitivity of financial securities only for small changes in interest rates of the order of one or a few basis points (a basis point is equal to one-hundredth of 1 percent). Suppose, however, that interest rate shocks are much larger, of the order of 2 percent or 200 basis points or more. While such large changes in interest rates are not common, this might happen in a financial crisis or if the central bank (see Chapter 4) suddenly changes its monetary policy strategy. In this case, duration becomes a less accurate predictor of how much the prices of bonds will change, and therefore, a less accurate measure of the price sensitivity of a bond to changes in interest rates. Figure 3–6 is a graphic representation of the reason for this. Note the difference in the change in a bond's price due to interest rate changes according to the proportional duration measure (D), and the "true relationship," using time value of money equations of Chapter 2 (and discussed earlier in this chapter) to calculate the exact present value change of a bond's price to interest rate changes.

Specifically, duration predicts that the relationship between an interest rate change and a security's price change will be proportional to the security's D (duration). By precisely calculating the true change in the security's price, however, we would find that for large interest rate increases, duration overpredicts the *fall* in the security's price, and for large interest rate decreases, it underpredicts the *increase* in the security's price. Thus, duration understates the final value of a security following a large change (either positive or negative) in interest rates. Further, the duration model predicts symmetric effects for rate increases and decreases on a bond's price. As Figure 3–6 shows, in actuality, the *capital loss effect* of large rate increases tends to be smaller than the *capital gain effect* of large rate decreases. This is the result of a bond's price–interest rate relationship exhibiting a property called **convexity** rather than *linearity,* as assumed by the simple duration model. Intuitively, this is because the sensitivity of the bond's price to a change in interest rates depends on the *level* from which interest rates change (i.e., 6 percent, 8 percent, 10 percent, 12 percent). In particular, the higher the level of interest rates, the smaller a bond's price sensitivity to interest rate changes.

convexity

The degree of curvature of the price–interest rate curve around some interest rate level.

Do You Understand?

1. When the duration of an asset is equal to its maturity?
2. What the denominator of the duration equation measures?
3. What the numerator of the duration equation measures?
4. What the duration of a zero-coupon bond is?
5. Which has the longest duration, a 30-year, 8 percent yield to maturity, zero-coupon bond, or a 30-year, 8 percent yield to maturity, 5 percent coupon bond?
6. What the relationship is between the duration of a bond and its interest elasticity?

Summary

This chapter applied the time value of money formulas presented in Chapter 2 to the valuation of financial securities such as equities and bonds. With respect to bonds, we included a detailed examination of how changes in interest rates, coupon rates, and time to maturity affect their price and price sensitivity. We also presented a measure of bond price sensitivity to interest rate changes, called duration. We showed how the value of duration is affected by various bond characteristics, such as coupon rates, interest rates, and time to maturity.

End-of-Chapter Questions

1. You bought a bond five years ago for $935 per bond. The bond is now selling for $980. It also paid $75 in interest per year, which you reinvested in the bond. Calculate the realized rate of return earned on this bond.

2. Refer again to the bond information in Question 1. You expect to hold the bond for three more years, then sell it for $990. If the bond is expected to continue paying $75 per year over the next three years, what is the expected rate of return on the bond during this period?

3. A bond you are evaluating has a 10 percent coupon rate (compounded semiannually), a $1,000 face value, and is 10 years from maturity.
    a. If the required rate of return on the bond is 6 percent, what is its fair present value?
    b. If the required rate of return on the bond is 8 percent, what is its fair present value?
    c. What do your answers to parts (a) and (b) say about the relation between required rates of return and fair values of bonds?

4. For each of the following situations, identify whether a bond would be considered a premium bond, a discount bond, or a par bond.
    a. A bond's current market price is greater than its face value.
    b. A bond's coupon rate is equal to its yield to maturity.
    c. A bond's coupon rate is less than its required rate of return.
    d. A bond's coupon rate is less than its yield to maturity.
    e. A bond's coupon rate is greater than its yield to maturity.
    f. A bond's fair present value is less than its face value.

5. Calculate the yield to maturity on the following bonds.
    a. A 9 percent coupon (paid semiannually) bond, with a $1,000 face value and 15 years remaining to maturity. The bond is selling at $985.
    b. An 8 percent coupon (paid quarterly) bond, with a $1,000 face value and 10 years remaining to maturity. The bond is selling at $915.
    c. An 11 percent coupon (paid annually) bond, with a $1,000 face value and 6 years remaining to maturity. The bond is selling at $1,065.

6. Calculate the fair present values of the following bonds, all of which pay interest semiannually, have a face value of $1,000, have 12 years remaining to maturity, and have a required rate of return of 10 percent.
    a. The bond has a 6 percent coupon rate.
    b. The bond has an 8 percent coupon rate.
    c. The bond has a 10 percent coupon rate.
    d. What do your answers to parts (a) through (c) say about the relation between coupon rates and present values?

7. Repeat parts (a) through (c) of Question 6 using a required rate of return on the bond of 8 percent. What do your calculations imply about the relation between the coupon rates and bond price volatility?

8. Calculate the fair present value of the following bonds, all of which have a 10 percent coupon rate (paid semiannually), face value of $1,000, and a required rate of return of 8 percent.
    a. The bond has 10 years remaining to maturity.
    b. The bond has 15 years remaining to maturity.
    c. The bond has 20 years remaining to maturity.
    d. What do your answers to parts (a) through (c) say about the relation between time to maturity and present values?

9. Repeat parts (a) through (c) of Question 8 using a required rate of return on the bond of 11 percent. What do your calculations imply about the relation between time to maturity and bond price volatility?

10. What is the economic meaning of duration?

11. a. What is the duration of a two-year bond that pays an annual coupon of 10 percent and has a current yield to maturity of 12 percent? Use $1,000 as the face value.
    b. What is the duration of a two-year zero-coupon bond that is yielding 11.5 percent? Use $1,000 as the face value.
    c. Given these answers, how does duration differ from maturity?

12. Consider the following two banks:
    Bank 1 has assets composed solely of a 10-year, 12 percent coupon, $1 million loan with a 12 percent yield to maturity. It is financed with a 10-year, 10 percent coupon, $1 million CD with a 10 percent yield to maturity.

Bank 2 has assets composed solely of a 7-year, 12 percent, zero-coupon bond with a current value of $894,006.20 and a maturity value of $1,976,362.88. It is financed by a 10-year, 8.275 percent coupon, $1,000,000 face value CD with a yield to maturity of 10 percent.

All securities except the zero-coupon bond pay interest annually.

a. If interest rates rise by 1 percent (100 basis points), how do the values of the assets and liabilities of each bank change?

b. What accounts for the differences between the two banks' accounts?

13. Consider the following.

a. What is the duration of a five-year Treasury bond with a 10 percent semiannual coupon selling at par?

b. What is the duration of the above bond if the yield to maturity (ytm) increases to 14 percent? What if the ytm increases to 16 percent?

c. What can you conclude about the relationship between duration and yield to maturity?

14. Consider the following.

a. What is the duration of a four-year Treasury bond with a 10 percent semiannual coupon selling at par?

b. What is the duration of a three-year Treasury bond with a 10 percent semiannual coupon selling at par?

c. What is the duration of a two-year Treasury bond with a 10 percent semiannual coupon selling at par?

d. What conclusions can you draw from these results between duration and maturity?

15. What is the duration of a zero coupon bond that has 8 years to maturity? What is the duration if the maturity increases to 10 years? If it increases to 12 years?

16. Suppose that you purchase a bond that matures in five years and pays a 13.76 percent coupon rate. The bond is priced to yield 10 percent.

a. Show that the duration is equal to four years.

b. Show that if interest rates rise to 11 percent next year and your investment horizon is four years from today, you will still earn a 10 percent yield on your investment.

17. An insurance company is analyzing the following three bonds, each with 5 years to maturity, and is using duration as its measure of interest rate risk:

a. $10,000 par value, coupon rate = 8%, ytm = .10

b. $10,000 par value, coupon rate = 10%, ytm = .10

c. $10,000 par value, coupon rate = 12%, ytm = .10

What are the durations of each of the three bonds?

18. How is duration related to the interest elasticity of a fixed-income security? What is the relationship between duration and the price of a fixed-income security?

19. You have discovered that when the required return of a bond you own fell by 0.50 percent from 9.75 percent to 9.25 percent, the price rose from $975 to $995. What is the duration of this bond?

The following questions are related to appendix material.

20. Calculate the present value on a stock that pays $5 in dividends per year (with no growth) and has a required rate of return of 10 percent.

21. A stock you are evaluating paid a dividend last year of $2.50. Dividends have grown at a constant rate of 1.5 percent over the last 15 years and you expect this to continue.

a. If the required rate of return on the stock is 12 percent, what is its fair present value?

b. If the required rate of return on the stock is 15 percent, what is its expected price four years from today?

22. You are considering the purchase of a stock that is currently selling at $64 per share. You expect the stock to pay $4.50 in dividends next year.

a. If dividends are expected to grow at a constant rate of 3 percent per year, what is your expected rate of return on this stock?

b. If dividends are expected to grow at a constant rate of 5 percent per year, what is your expected rate of return on this stock?

c. What do your answers to parts (a) and (b) say about the impact of dividend growth rates on expected rate of returns on stocks?

23. A stock you are evaluating is expected to experience supernormal growth in dividends of 8 percent over the next six years. Following this period, dividends are expected to grow at a constant rate of 3 percent. The stock paid a dividend of $5.50 last year and the required rate of return on the stock is 10 percent. Calculate the stock's fair present value.

Appendix   Equity Valuation

The valuation process for an equity instrument (such as common stock or a share) involves finding the present value of an infinite series of cash flows on the equity discounted at an appropriate interest rate. Cash flows from holding equity come from dividends paid out by the firm over the life of the stock, which in expectation can be viewed as infinite since a firm (and thus the dividends it pays) has no defined maturity or life. Even if an equity holder decides not to hold the stock forever, he or she can sell it to someone else who in a fair and efficient market is willing to pay the present value of the remaining (expected) dividends to the seller at the time of sale. Dividends on equity are that portion of a firm's earnings paid out to the stockholders. Those earnings retained are normally reinvested to produce future income and future dividends for the firm and its stockholders. Thus, conceptually, the fair price paid for investing in stocks is the present value of its current and future dividends. Growth in dividends occurs primarily because of growth in the firm's earnings, which is, in turn, a function of the profitability of the firm's investments and the percent of these profits paid out as dividends rather than being reinvested in the firm. Thus, earnings growth, dividend growth, and stock value (price) will generally be highly correlated.

We begin by defining the variables we will use to value an equity:

D_t = Dividend paid out to stockholders at the end of the year t
P_t = Price of a firm's common stock at the end of year t
P_0 = Current price of a firm's common stock
i_s = Interest rate used to discount cash flows on an investment in a stock

As described above, time value of money equations can be used to evaluate a stock from several different perspectives. For example, the realized rate of return (rr) is the appropriate interest rate (discount rate) to apply to cash flows when evaluating the historical performance of an equity.

Example 3–7 Calculation of Realized Rate of Return on a Stock Investment

Suppose you owned a stock for the last two years. You originally bought the stock two years ago for $25 ($P_0$) and just sold it for $35 ($P_2$). The stock paid an annual dividend of $1 on the last day of each of the past two years. Your realized rate of return on the stock investment can be calculated using the following time value of money equation:

$$P_0 = D\,(PVIFA_{i_s,2}) + P_2\,(PVIF_{i_s,2})$$

or

$$25 = 1\,(PVIFA_{i_s,2}) + 35\,(PVIF_{i_s,2})$$

Solving for i_s, your annual realized rate of return (rr) on this investment was $i_s = rr = 22.02$ percent.

$$25 = 1\,(1.4912) + 35\,(0.6716)$$

The expected rate of return (Err) is the appropriate interest rate when analyzing the expected future return on stocks, assuming the investor buys the stock at its current market price, receives all promised payments, and sells the stock at the end of his or her investment horizon.

Example 3–8 Calculation of Expected Rate of Return on a Stock Investment

You are considering the purchase of a stock that you expect to own for the next three years. The current market price of the stock is $32 ($P_0$) and you expect to sell it for $45 in three years time ($\tilde{P}_3$). You also expect the stock to pay an annual dividend ($\tilde{D}$) of $1.50 on the last day of each of the next three years. Your expected return on the stock investment can be calculated using the following time value of money equation:

$$P_0 = \tilde{D}\,(PVIFA_{i_s,3}) + \tilde{P}_3\,(PVIF_{i_s,3})$$

or

$$32 = 1.50\,(PVIFA_{i_s,3}) + 45\,(PVIF_{i_s,3})$$

Solving for i_s, your annual expected rate of return (*Err*) on this investment is $i_s = Err = 16.25$ percent.

Finally, the required rate of return (*rrr*) is the appropriate interest rate when analyzing the fair value of a stock investment over its whole lifetime. The fair value of a stock reflects the present value of all relevant (but uncertain) cash flows to be received by an investor discounted at the required rate of return (*rrr*)—the interest rate or return that should be earned on the investment given its risk. Present value methodology applies time value of money to evaluate a stock's cash flows over its life as follows:

$$P_0 = \frac{\tilde{D}_1}{(1 + i_s)^1} + \frac{\tilde{D}_2}{(1 + i_s)^2} + \ldots + \frac{\tilde{D}_\infty}{(1 + i_s)^\infty}$$

The price or value of a stock is equal to the present value of its future dividends ($\tilde{D}_t$), whose values are uncertain. This requires an infinite number of future dividend values to be estimated, which makes the equation above difficult to use for stock valuation and *rrr* calculation in practice. Accordingly, assumptions are normally made regarding the expected pattern of the uncertain flow of dividends over the life of the stock. Two assumptions that are commonly used include (1) zero growth in dividends over the (infinite) life of the stock; and (2) a constant growth rate in dividends over the (infinite) life of the stock.

Zero Growth in Dividends

Zero growth in dividends means that dividends on a stock are expected to remain at a constant level forever. Thus, $D_0 = D_1 = D_2 = \ldots = D_\infty = D$. Accordingly, the equity valuation formula can be written as follows:

$$P_0 = \frac{\tilde{D}_1}{(1 + i_s)^1} + \frac{\tilde{D}_2}{(1 + i_s)^2} + \ldots + \frac{\tilde{D}_\infty}{(1 + i_s)^\infty} = D \sum_{t=1}^{\infty} \frac{1}{1 + i_s}$$

where

$D_1 = $ Current (time 0) value of dividends
$D_t = $ Value of dividends at time $t = 1, 2, \ldots, \infty$

or[12]

$$P_0 = D/i_s$$

This formula can be generalized as follows:

$$P_t = D/i_s$$

The value of a stock with zero growth in dividends is equal to the (current) dividend divided by the return on the stock. If the required rate of return (*rrr*) is applied to the formula ($i_s = rrr$), the price we solve for is the fair market price. If the expected return (*Err*) is applied to the formula ($i_s = Err$), the price we solve for is the current market

---

12. Remember that, in the limit:

$$\sum_{t=1}^{\infty} \left(\frac{1}{1 + x}\right)^t = \left(\frac{1}{1 + x}\right)^1 + \left(\frac{1}{1 + x}\right)^2 + \ldots + \left(\frac{1}{1 + x}\right)^\infty = \frac{1}{x}$$

Thus:

$$\sum_{t=1}^{\infty} \left(\frac{1}{1 + i_s}\right)^t = \frac{1}{i_s}$$

price. Furthermore, the formula can be rearranged to determine a return on the stock if it were purchased at a price, P_0.[13]

$$i_s = D/P_0$$

If the fair market price is applied to this formula, the return we solve for is the required rate of return (*rrr*). If the current market price is applied to the formula, the price we solve for is the expected return (*Err*). Recall from above, in efficient markets the required rate of return equals the expected rate of return and thus the current market price on a security equals its fair market value.

Example 3–9 Calculation of Stock Price with Zero Growth in Dividends

A stock you are evaluating is expected to pay a constant dividend of $5 per year each year into the future. The expected rate of return (*Err*) on the stock is 12 percent. The current market value (or price) of this stock is calculated as follows:

$$P_0 = 5/0.12 = \$41.67$$

Constant Growth in Dividends

Constant growth in dividends means that dividends on a stock are expected to grow at a constant rate, g, each year into the future. Thus, $D_1 = D_0(1 + g)^1$, $D_2 = D_0(1 + g)^2$, ..., $D_\infty = D_0(1 + g)^\infty$. Accordingly, the equity valuation formula can now be written as follows:

$$P_0 = \frac{D_0(1 + g)^1}{(1 + i_s)^1} + \frac{D_0(1 + g)^2}{(1 + i_s)^2} + \ldots + \frac{D_0(1 + g)^\infty}{(1 + i_s)^\infty} = D_0 \sum_{t=1}^{\infty} \left(\frac{(1 + g)}{(1 + i_s)}\right)^t$$

or[14]

$$P_0 = \frac{D_0(1 + g)^1}{i_s - g} = \frac{D_1}{i_s - g}$$

This formula can be generalized as follows:

$$P_t = \frac{D_0(1 + g)^t}{i_s - g} = \frac{D_{t+1}}{i_s - g}$$

If the required rate of return (*rrr*) is applied to the formula ($i_s = rrr$), the price we solve for is the fair market price. If the expected return (*Err*) is applied to the formula ($i_s = Err$), the price we solve for is the current market price. The equity valuation formula can also be rearranged to determine a rate of return on the stock if it were purchased at a price, P_0.

$$i_s = \frac{D_0(1 + g)}{P_0} + g = \frac{D_1}{P_0} + g$$

If the fair market price is applied to the formula, the return we solve for is the required rate of return (*rrr*). If the current market price is applied to the formula, the price we solve for is the expected return (*Err*).

---

13. This is also referred to as the current dividend yield on a stock.

14. Remember that in the limit:

$$\sum_{t=1}^{\infty} \left(\frac{1 + g}{1 + i_s}\right)^t = \sum_{t=1}^{\infty} \left(\frac{1}{1 + \frac{i_s - g}{1 + g}}\right)^t = \frac{1 + g}{i_s - g}$$

Example 3–10   Calculation of Stock Price with Constant Growth in Dividends

A stock you are evaluating paid a dividend at the end of last year of $3.50. Dividends have grown at a constant rate of 2 percent per year over the last 20 years, and this constant growth rate is expected to continue into the future. The required rate of return (*rrr*) on the stock is 10 percent. The fair present value (or price) of this stock is calculated as follows:

$$P_0 = \frac{3.50(1 + .02)}{.10 - .02} = \$44.625$$

The investor would be willing to pay no more than $44.625 for this stock.

Example 3–11   Calculation of the Expected Rate of Return (Err) on a Stock with Constant Growth in Dividends

A stock you are evaluating paid a dividend at the end of last year of $4.80. Dividends have grown at a constant rate of 1.75 percent per year over the last 15 years, and this constant growth rate is expected to continue in the future. The stock is currently selling at a price of $52 per share. The expected rate of return on this stock is calculated as follows:

$$i_s = \frac{4.80(1 + 0.0175)}{52} + .0175 = 11.14\%$$

Supernormal (or Nonconstant) Growth in Dividends

Firms often experience periods of supernormal or nonconstant dividend growth, after which dividend growth settles at some constant rate. The stock value for a firm experiencing supernormal growth in dividends is, like firms with zero or constant dividend growth, equal to the present value of the firm's expected future dividends. However, in this case, dividends during the period of supernormal (nonconstant) growth must be evaluated individually. The constant growth in dividends model can then be adapted to find the present value of dividends following the supernormal growth period.

To find the present value of a stock experiencing supernormal or nonconstant dividend growth, we calculate the present value of dividends during the two different growth periods. A three-step process is used as follows:

Step 1: Find the present value of the dividends during the period of supernormal growth;

Step 2: Find the price of the stock at the end of the supernormal growth period (when constant growth in dividends begins) using the constant growth in dividends model. Then discount this price to a present value.

Step 3: Add the two components of the stock price together.

Example 3–12   Calculation of Stock Price with Supernormal or Nonconstant Growth in Dividends

A stock you are evaluating is expected to experience supernormal growth in dividends of 10 percent, g_s, over the next five years. Following this period, dividends are expected to grow at a constant rate of 4 percent, g. The stock paid a dividend of $4 last year, and the required rate of return on the stock is 15 percent. The fair present value of the stock is calculated as follows:

Step 1: Find the present value of dividends during the period of supernormal growth.

Year	Dividends ($D_0(1 + g_s)^t$)	$PVIF_{15\%,t}$	Present Value
1	$4(1 + .1)^1 = 4.400$	.8696	3.826
2	$4(1 + .1)^2 = 4.840$	.7561	3.659
3	$4(1 + .1)^3 = 5.324$	.6575	3.500
4	$4(1 + .1)^4 = 5.856$	.5718	3.349
5	$4(1 + .1)^5 = 6.442$	.4972	3.203

Present value of dividends during supernormal growth period $17.537

Step 2: Find present value of dividends after period of supernormal growth.
a. Find stock value at beginning of constant growth period.

$$P_5 = \frac{D_6}{k_s - g} = \frac{D_0(1 + g_s)^5 (1 + g)^1}{k_s - g} = \frac{4 (1 + .1)^5 (1 + .04)^1}{.15 - .04} = \$60.906$$

b. Find present value of constant growth dividends.

$$P_0 = P_5(PVIF_{15\%,5}) = 60.906(.4972) = \$30.283$$

Step 3: Find Present value of stock = Value during supernormal growth period + Value during normal growth period.

$$\$17.537 + \$30.283 = \$47.820$$

The Federal Reserve System, Monetary Policy, *and* Interest Rates

Chapter Navigator

1. What are the major functions of the Federal Reserve System?

2. What is the structure of the Federal Reserve System?

3. What are the monetary policy tools used by the Federal Reserve?

4. How do monetary policy changes affect key economic variables?

5. How do U.S. monetary policy initiatives affect foreign exchange rates?

Major Duties and Responsibilities of the Federal Reserve System: Chapter Overview

The Federal Reserve (the Fed) is the central bank of the United States. Founded by Congress under the Federal Reserve Act in 1913, the Fed's original duties were to provide the nation with a safer, more flexible, and more stable monetary and financial system. This was needed following a number of banking crises and panics that had occurred in the first decade of the 20th century (particularly 1907) and the last decades of the 19th century. As time passed, additional legislation, including the Banking Act of 1935, the Full Employment Act of 1946, and the Full Employment and Balanced Growth Act of 1978 (also called the Humphrey-Hawkins Act), revised and supplemented the original purposes and objectives of the Federal Reserve System. These objectives included economic growth in line with the economy's potential to expand, a high level of employment, stable prices, and moderate long-term interest rates.

The Federal Reserve system is an independent central bank in that its decisions do not have to be ratified by the president or another member of the executive branch of the U.S. government. The system is, however, subject to oversight by the U.S. Congress under its authority to coin money. Further, the Federal Reserve is required to work within the framework of the overall objectives of economic and financial policies established by the U.S. government.

1 The Federal Reserve System has evolved such that its duties incorporate four major functions: (1) conducting monetary policy, (2) supervising and regulating depository institutions, (3) maintaining the stability of the financial system, and (4) providing payment and other financial services to the U.S. government, the public, financial institutions, and foreign official institutions.

In this chapter, we present an overview of the Federal Reserve System. We start with a basic description, highlighting its organization and structure. We then examine the monetary policy tools available to the Fed and how the Fed uses these tools to influence the U.S. money supply and interest rates both domestically and internationally. Finally, we look at the impact of U.S. monetary policy on foreign exchange rates.

2 Structure of the Federal Reserve System

www.bog.frb.fed.us/

The Federal Reserve System consists of 12 Federal Reserve Banks located in major cities throughout the United States and a seven-member Board of Governors located in Washington, D.C. This structure was implemented in 1913 to spread power along regional lines, between the private sector and the government, and among bankers, businesspeople, and the public. Federal Reserve Banks and the Federal Reserve Board of Governors together comprise and operate the Federal Open Market Committee (FOMC), which is responsible for the formulation and implementation of monetary policy.

Federal Reserve Banks

Functions Performed by Federal Reserve Banks. As part of the Federal Reserve System, Federal Reserve Banks perform multiple functions. These include assistance in the conduct of monetary policy, supervision and regulation of member banks, and the provision of services such as new currency issue, check clearing, wire transfer, and research services to either the federal government, member banks, or the general public. We summarize these functions in Table 4–1.

Assistance in the Conduct of Monetary Policy. As mentioned above, a primary responsibility of the Federal Reserve System is to influence the monetary (and financial)

Table 4–1 Functions Performed by the Federal Reserve Banks

Assistance in the Conduct of Monetary Policy—Federal Reserve Bank (FRB) presidents serve on the Federal Open Market Committee (FOMC). FRBs set and change discount rates.

Supervision and Regulation—FRBs have supervisory and regulatory authority over the activities of banks located in their district.

Government Services—FRBs serve as the commercial bank for the U.S. Treasury.

New Currency Issue—FRBs are responsible for the collection and replacement of damaged currency from circulation.

Check Clearing—FRBs process, route, and transfer funds from one bank to another as checks clear through the Federal Reserve System.

Wire Transfer Services—FRBs and their member banks are linked electronically through the Federal Reserve Communications System.

Research Services—each FRB has a staff of professional economists who gather, analyze, and interpret economic data and developments in the banking sector in their district and economywide.

discount rate

The interest rate on loans made by Federal Reserve Banks to depository institutions.

discount window

The facility through which Federal Reserve Banks issue loans to depository institutions.

conditions in U.S. financial markets and thus, the economy. Federal Reserve Banks assist in this process in several ways. First, as discussed in more detail later, 5 of the 12 Federal Reserve Bank presidents serve on the Federal Open Market Committee (FOMC), which determines monetary policy with respect to the open market sale and purchase of government securities and therefore, interest rates.[1] Second, the Boards of Directors of each Federal Reserve Bank set and change the **discount rate** (the interest rate on "lender of last resort" loans made by Federal Reserve Banks to depository institutions). As discussed later, any discount rate change must be reviewed by the Board of Governors of the Federal Reserve. These loans are transacted through each Federal Reserve Bank's **discount window** and involve the discounting of eligible short-term securities in return for cash loans. Federal Reserve Bank Boards also have discretion in deciding which banks qualify for discount window loans—since such loans are viewed as available only under emergency or special liquidity situations.

Supervision and Regulation.   Each Federal Reserve Bank has supervisory and regulatory authority over the activities of state-chartered member banks and bank holding companies located in their districts. These activities include (1) the conduct of examinations and inspections of member banks, bank holding companies, and foreign bank offices by teams of bank examiners; (2) the authority to issue warnings (e.g., cease and desist orders should some banking activity be viewed as unsafe or unsound); and (3) the authority to approve various bank and bank holding company applications for expanded activities (e.g., mergers and acquisitions).

Government Services.   As discussed above, the Federal Reserve serves as the commercial bank for the U.S. Treasury (U.S. government). Each year government agencies and departments deposit and withdraw billions of dollars from U.S. Treasury operating accounts held by Federal Reserve Banks. For example, it is the Federal Reserve Banks that receive deposits relating to federal unemployment taxes, individual income taxes withheld by payroll deduction, and so on. Further, some of these deposits are not protected by deposit insurance and must be fully collateralized at all times. It is the Federal Reserve Banks that hold collateral put up by government agencies. Finally, Federal Reserve Banks are responsible for the operation of the U.S. savings bond scheme, the issuance of Treasury securities, and other government-sponsored securities (e.g., Fannie Mae, Freddie Mac—see Chapter 7). Federal Reserve Banks issue and redeem savings bonds and Treasury securities, deliver government securities to investors, provide for a wire transfer system for these securities (the Fedwire), and make periodic payments of interest and principal on these securities.

Do You Understand?

1. Why the Federal Reserve printed additional banknotes at the end of 1999?

New Currency Issue.   Federal Reserve Banks are responsible for the collection and replacement of currency (paper and coin) from circulation. They also distribute new currency to meet the public's need for cash (see In the News box 4–1).

Check Clearing.   Over 60 billion checks are written in the United States each year. About 15 billion of these checks are deposited in the same institution on which the check was written (called "on-us" checks). The Federal Reserve System operates a central check-clearing system for U.S. banks, routing interbank checks to depository institutions on which they are written and transferring the appropriate funds from one bank to another. About 40 percent of these interbank checks, approximately 18 billion per year, are processed by this system.[2] Table 4–2 shows the number and value of checks collected by the Federal Reserve Banks from 1920 through 1998. All

---

1. The president of the New York Federal Reserve Bank always sits on the FOMC. The other four positions are allocated to the other Federal Reserve districts on a rotating annual basis.

2. The remainder are processed through private check-clearing systems.

In the News

4-1

Alan Greenspan, U.S. Federal Reserve Chairman, said yesterday he expected "a lot of problems" to emerge in the global financial payments system because of the Year 2000 computer problem. The Fed had already ordered the printing of extra banknotes for the next year to deal with expected extra demand for the currency that would result, he said.

The Fed was "probably on track" to ensure "that the banking system in the United States—looked at strictly as a domestic operation—is probably going to be OK. But our systems are integrated with the rest of the world and . . . we don't know and may not know until the actual time arises, whether everybody is, as we call it, Y2K compliant. But he said, "My suspicion

Source: *The Financial Times,* September 24, 1998, p. 1, by Stephen Fidler.

U.S. Prints Cash to Cope with Demands of Millennium Bomb

is we are going to run into a lot of problems. And as a consequence we are doing a great deal of planning on what happens if it goes wrong."

The Fed was "reasonably certain" that concerns about whether the banking system was going to work would generate a significant increase in demand for currency towards the end of the next year and a "very major increase" in currency had been ordered. Economists have said extra demand for cash could arise if people expect problems with credit cards and automated bank teller machines and other payment mechanisms.

According to Fed staff, the Fed expects a 14 percent increase in the need

for banknotes between July and the end of 1999. In July, the Fed estimated it had $460 billion in banknotes in circulation with an additional $153 billion in its vaults, a total of $613 billion. As part of the Fed's contingency planning, it had ordered increased printing of currency for the fiscal year starting in October based on the estimated increase to $697 billion by the end of next year. This was a "precautionary exercise" and most of the increase would stay in the vaults unless and until the demand emerges.

Beyond that, Mr. Greenspan told the Senate budget committee that the concerns about just-in-time inventory systems not working would "induce accumulation of inventories in the fourth quarter of next year which would not otherwise have occurred. So even if everything comes out exactly right, there will be a Y2K effect."

www.ft.com/

Do You Understand?

1. What actions banks are taking to reduce check-clearing "float"?
2. How the Federal Reserve is reacting to these actions taken by banks?

depository institutions have accounts with the Federal Reserve Bank in their district for this purpose. As shown in In the News box 4–2, technological advancements in the check-clearing process have allowed banks to profit from the check-clearing function.

Table 4–2   Number and Value of Checks Cleared by the Federal Reserve

Year	Number of Checks Cleared (in millions)	Value of Checks Cleared (in billions of dollars)
1920	424	$ 149.78
1930	905	324.88
1940	1,184	280.44
1950	1,955	856.95
1960	3,419	1,154.12
1970	7,158	3,331.73
1980	15,716	8,038.03
1990	18,598	12,519.17
1993	19,009	14,066.52
1998	16,573	N/A

Source: Federal Reserve Board, website, "Purposes & Functions," July 1999. *www.bog.frb.fed.us/*

Table 4–3   Number and Value of Fedwire Transactions Processed by the Federal Reserve

Year	Number of Transactions (in millions)	Value of Transactions (in billions of dollars)
1920	0.5	$ 30.86
1930	2.0	198.88
1940	0.8	92.11
1950	1.0	509.17
1960	3.0	2,428.08
1970	7.0	12,332.00
1980	43.0	78,594.86
1990	63.0	199,067.20
1993	69.7	207,629.20
1998	98.1	328,748.90

Source: Federal Reserve Board, website, "Purposes & Functions," July 1999. *www.bog.frb.fed.us/*

Wire Transfer Services.   The Federal Reserve Banks and their member banks are linked electronically through the Federal Reserve Communications Systems. This network allows these institutions to transfer funds and securities nationwide in a matter of minutes. Two electronic (wire) transfer systems are operated by the Federal Reserve: Fedwire and the Automated Clearinghouse (ACH). Fedwire allows depository institutions to transfer funds on their own behalf or for their customers. Fedwire transfers are typically large dollar payments (averaging over $3 million per transaction). Table 4–3 shows the number and dollar value of Fedwire transactions processed by Federal Reserve banks from 1920 through 1998. The Automated Clearinghouse (ACH) was developed jointly by the private sector and the Federal Reserve System in the early 1970s and has evolved as a nationwide method to electronically process credit and debit transfers of funds. Table 4–4 shows the number and dollar value of ACH transactions processed by Federal Reserve Banks from 1975 through 1998.

Research Services.   Each Federal Reserve Bank has a staff of professional economists who gather, analyze, and interpret economic data and developments in the banking sector as well as the overall economy. These research projects are often used in the conduct of monetary policy by the Federal Reserve.

In the News

High-Tech Tactics Let Banks Keep the Float

If anybody knows time is money, it's banks. And in the electronic age, banks are becoming more expert at the movement of money: racing it to themselves faster—but sometimes slamming on the brakes when you deposit a check. So don't expect your funds to be available to you any quicker.

To zip checks along and reduce the "float"—or the downtime between when a check is written and when the funds are actually drawn from an account—banks are turning to everything from speedier check-reading machines to zooming jet planes loaded with bundles of checks.

First Union Corp., for one, has begun installing scanning devices at Hair-Cuttery salons so when a patron hands over an ordinary check for a shampoo and a cut, a machine reads it and swiftly deducts the amount from the checking account—just as debit cards currently do.

Source: *The Wall Street Journal,* June 3, 1999, p. B1, by Rick Brooks. Reprinted by permission of *The Wall Street Journal.* © 1999 Dow Jones & Company, Inc. All Rights Reserved Worldwide.

But when it comes to moving funds into a customer's account, sometimes the pace is suddenly a lot slower. Bob Gordon, a chemical-company executive in New Jersey, was hit with six bounced-checks by Chase Manhattan Corp. last year while the bank put a hold on a $9,000 check he deposited from his local employer. Referring to how the bank times its transactions, he says, "It always works for them and never for me." While refusing to discuss that case specifically, a Chase spokeswoman says customers can avoid such mishaps by obtaining "overdraft protection" coverage. And, she adds, "we follow the rules to a T."

There is big business in playing traffic cop to the flow of checks. At any given moment, an estimated $140 billion in checks are en route to a bank—a mountain of paper that could earn roughly $20 million in interest everyday, estimates David Medeiros, an analyst

at Tower Group, a bank consultancy in Needham, Mass.

Banks make no apologies for the practice of holding deposits if a check is unusually large or drawn on a newly opened account. The law specifies that banks can take a "reasonable period" in those cases, though in practice it tends be about 10 days. They note that the delay is allowed under federal rules to protect banks from check fraud, which generates an estimated $615 million in annual losses. "The bank needs to balance that concern against the desire of the customers to have availability of funds," says a spokeswoman for First Union, the nation's sixth-largest bank, which is based in Charlotte, N.C.

Responding to the accelerated movement of money, the government may clamp down on banks. A pending Federal Reserve Board proposal, which banks oppose, would cut the maximum number of days a bank can put a hold on most checks to four business days from the current five day limit. The Fed started putting limits on how long banks can hold customer funds about a decade ago, in response to

In the News continued

numerous customer complaints that deposits are being tied up for no reason.

Clearly, paper checks are moving faster now. About 83 percent of checks currently arrive back at their bank of origin within five business days, up from 73 percent in 1990, according to the Fed. Major banks now use a fleet of 30 Lear jets owned by AirNet Systems Inc. of Columbus, Ohio, to whiz checks across the country.

"Float will disappear," predicts Royce Brown, managing director of Carreker-Antinori Inc., a Dallas company that helps banks manage their flow of checks. And with split-second transactions by banks, managing the timing of deposits is going to get harder and harder for consumers . . .

Other bank-policy changes are reducing the breathing room people have long enjoyed with checks. One new tactic is requiring the loan payments to be received by their due date; in the past, banks usually considered a payment made if it was postmarked by the due date . . .

For the time being, the vast majority of checks are covered by the Fed's five-day rule, but a check may be held longer by the bank under certain circumstances. A check, for instance, might be unusually large or it might be deposited by a customer who has repeatedly overdrawn his account. But even in those cases, the bank must notify the customer when a deposit will be held for a week or longer, and explain

exactly when the funds will be available for withdrawal.

Whether the Fed will take action to ease such consumer problems isn't clear. Banks are attacking the agency's proposed change, saying they are concerned that reducing the holding period could make it easier for bad checks to slip through. "There are probably some in the banking industry that take advantage of float days to their own benefit and profit," acknowledges John E. Lufburrow, chairman of Heritage Saving Bank in Lutherville, Md., in a letter to the Fed. "Please, for the sake of us who are honest, do not shorten float times and play into the hands of the dishonest.

Organization of Federal Reserve Banks.   The Federal Reserve System is divided into 12 Federal Reserve districts that are the "operating arms" of the central banking system (see Figure 4–1). Each district has one main Federal Reserve Bank, some of which also have branches in other cities within the district (identified in Figure 4–1). In addition to carrying out the functions for the central banking system as a whole, each reserve bank acts as a depository institution for the banks in its district. In terms of total assets, the three largest Federal Reserve Banks are the New York, Chicago, and San Francisco banks. Together these three banks hold over 50 percent of the total assets (discussed later) of the Federal Reserve System. The New York Federal Reserve Bank is generally considered the most important of the Federal Reserve Banks because so many of the largest U.S. and international banks are located in the New York district (the so-called money center banks).

www.ny.frb.org/

Table 4–4   Number and Value of ACH Transactions Processed by the Federal
Reserve

Year	Number of Transactions (in millions)	Value of Transactions (in billions of dollars)
1975	6	$ 92.87
1980	227	286.60
1990	1,435	4,660.48
1993	2,100	8,747.32
1998	2,966	N/A

Source: Federal Reserve Board, website, "Purposes & Functions," July 1999. *www.bog.frb.fed.us/*

Figure 4–1   Federal Reserve Districts

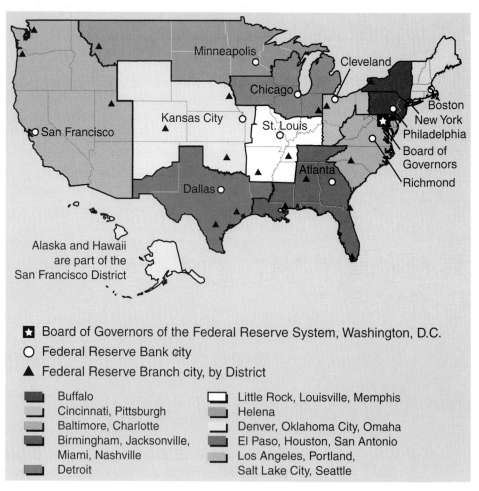

Alaska and Hawaii
are part of the
San Francisco District

★ Board of Governors of the Federal Reserve System, Washington, D.C.
○ Federal Reserve Bank city
▲ Federal Reserve Branch city, by District

Buffalo	Little Rock, Louisville, Memphis
Cincinnati, Pittsburgh	Helena
Baltimore, Charlotte	Denver, Oklahoma City, Omaha
Birmingham, Jacksonville, Miami, Nashville	El Paso, Houston, San Antonio
Detroit	Los Angeles, Portland, Salt Lake City, Seattle

Source: Federal Reserve Board, website, "The Structure of the Federal Reserve System," May 29, 1999.
www.bog.frb.fed.us/

Federal Reserve Banks operate under the general supervision of the Board of Governors of the Federal Reserve based in Washington, D.C. Each Federal Reserve Bank has its own nine-member Board of Directors that oversees its operations: six are elected by member banks in the district (three are professional bankers and three are businesspeople) and three are appointed by the Federal Reserve Board of Governors

www.occ.treas.gov/

(directors in this group are prohibited from being employees, officers, or stockholders of a member bank). These nine directors are responsible for appointing the president of their Federal Reserve Bank.

Nationally chartered banks, those chartered by the federal government through the Office of the Comptroller of the Currency (OCC),[3] are required to become members of the Federal Reserve System (FRS). State chartered banks (those not chartered by the OCC) can also elect to become FRS members if they meet the standards set by the FRS.[4] Commercial banks that become members of the FRS are required to buy stock in their Federal Reserve district bank. Thus, Federal Reserve Banks are quasipublic (part private, part government) entities owned by member commercial banks in their district. Their stock, however, is not publicly traded and pays a predetermined dividend (at a maximum rate of 6 percent annually). Approximately 40 percent of all U.S. banks (holding over 80 percent of the total assets in the U.S. banking system) are currently members of the Federal Reserve System.

Federal Reserve Banks operate as nonprofit organizations. They generate income primarily from three sources: (1) interest earned on government securities acquired in the course of Federal Reserve open market transactions (see below), (2) interest earned on reserves that banks are required to deposit at the Fed (see reserve requirements below), and (3) fees from the provision of payment and other services to member depository institutions.

Board of Governors of the Federal Reserve System

The Board of Governors of the Federal Reserve (also called the Federal Reserve Board) is a seven-member board headquartered in Washington D.C. Each member is appointed by the president of the United States and must be confirmed by the Senate. Board members serve a nonrenewable 14-year term.[5] Board members' terms are staggered so that one term expires every other January. The president designates two members of the Board to be the chairman and vice chairman for four-year terms.

The primary responsibilities of the Federal Reserve Board are the formulation and conduct of monetary policy and the supervision and regulation of banks. All seven Board members sit on the Federal Open Market Committee, which makes key decisions affecting the availability of money and credit in the economy (see below). For example, the Federal Reserve Board, through the FOMC, sets money supply and interest rate targets. The Federal Reserve Board also sets bank reserve requirements (discussed in Chapter 14) and reviews and approves the discount rates (see above) set by the 12 Federal Reserve Banks.

The Federal Reserve Board also has primary responsibility for the supervision and regulation of (1) all bank holding companies (their nonbank subsidiaries and their foreign subsidiaries), (2) state chartered banks that are members of the Federal Reserve System (state chartered member banks), and (3) Edge Act and agreement corporations (through which U.S. banks conduct foreign operations).[6] The Fed also shares supervisory and regulatory responsibilities with state supervisors and other federal supervisors

---

3. The Office of the Comptroller of the Currency (OCC) charters, regulates, and supervises national banks in the United States to ensure a safe, sound, and competitive banking system (see Chapters 11 and 14).

4. These state chartered banks are called state chartered member banks. State chartered banks that are not members of the FRS are called state chartered nonmember banks.

5. The length of the term is intended to limit the president's control over the Fed and thus to reduce political pressure on Board members; the nonrenewable nature of an appointment prevents any incentives for governors to take actions that may not be in the best interests of the economy yet may improve their chances of being reappointed.

6. An Edge Act corporation is a subsidiary of a federally chartered domestic bank holding company that generally specializes in financing international transactions. An agreement corporation operates like an Edge Act but is a subsidiary of a state chartered domestic bank.

www.occ.treas.gov/

www.fdic.gov/

(e.g., the OCC, the FDIC), including overseeing both the operations of foreign banking organizations in the United States and the establishment, examination, and termination of branches, commercial lending subsidiaries, and representative offices of foreign banks in the United States. The Board approves member bank mergers and acquisitions and specifies permissible nonbank activities of bank holding companies. The Board is also responsible for the development and administration of regulations governing the fair provision of consumer credit (e.g., the Truth in Lending Act, the Equal Credit Opportunity Act).

The chairman of the Federal Reserve Board often advises the president of the United States on economic policy and serves as the spokesperson for the Federal Reserve System in Congress and to the public. All Board members share the duties of conferring with officials of other government agencies, representatives of banking industry groups, officials of the central banks of other countries, and members of Congress.

Federal Open Market Committee

Federal Open Market Committee (FOMC)

The major monetary policy-making body of the Federal Reserve System.

The **Federal Open Market Committee (FOMC)** is the major monetary policy-making body of the Federal Reserve System. As alluded to above, the FOMC consists of the seven members of the Federal Reserve Board of Governors, the president of the Federal Reserve Bank of New York, and the presidents of four other Federal Reserve Banks (on a rotating basis). The chairman of the Board of Governors is also the chair of the FOMC. The FOMC is required to meet at least four times each year in Washington, D.C. However, eight regularly scheduled meetings have been held each year since 1980.

The main responsibilities of the FOMC are to formulate policies to promote full employment, economic growth, price stability, and a sustainable pattern of international trade. The FOMC seeks to accomplish this by setting guidelines regarding open market operations. **Open market operations**—the purchase and sale of U.S. government and federal agency securities—is the main policy tool that the Fed uses to achieve its monetary targets (although the operations themselves are normally carried out by traders at the Federal Reserve Bank of New York—see below). The FOMC also sets ranges for the growth of the monetary aggregates and directs operations of the Federal Reserve in foreign exchange markets (see Chapter 9). In addition, although reserve requirements and the discount rate are not specifically set by the FOMC, their levels are monitored and guided by the FOMC.

open market operations

Purchases and sales of U.S. government and federal agency securities by the Federal Reserve.

Balance Sheet of the Federal Reserve

Table 4–5 shows the balance sheet for the Federal Reserve System as of the end of 1999. The conduct of monetary policy by the Federal Reserve involves changes in the assets and liabilities of the Federal Reserve System, which are reflected in the Federal Reserve System's balance sheet.

reserves

Depository institution's vault cash plus reserves deposited at Federal Reserve Banks.

Liabilities. The major liabilities on the Fed's balance sheet are currency in circulation and **reserves** (depository institution reserve balances in accounts at Federal Reserve Banks plus vault cash on hand at commercial banks). Their sum is often referred to as the Fed's **monetary base** or **money base**. We can represent these as follows:

monetary base

Currency in circulation and reserves (depository institution reserves and vault cash of commercial banks) held by the Federal Reserve.

> **Reserves**—depository institution reserve balances at the Fed plus vault cash.
> **Money base**—currency in circulation plus reserves.

As we show below, changes in these accounts are the major determinants of the size of the nation's money supply—increases (decreases) in either or both of these balances (e.g., currency in circulation or reserves) will lead to an increase (decrease) in the money supply (see Chapter 1 and below for a definition of the U.S. money supply).

Table 4–5 Balance Sheet of the Federal Reserve
(in billions of dollars)

Assets

Gold and foreign exchange	$ 27.1
SDR certificates	7.2
Treasury currency	27.4
Federal Reserve float	0.1
Federal Reserve loans to domestic banks	0.5
Security repurchase agreements	22.1
U.S. Treasury securities	489.0
U.S. government agency securities	0.2
Miscellaneous assets	16.3
Total assets	$589.9

Liabilities and Equity

Depository institution reserves	$ 21.7
Vault cash of commercial banks	41.0
Deposits due to federal government	6.7
Deposits due to rest of the world	1.3
Currency outside banks	503.0
Miscellaneous liabilities	8.6
Federal Reserve Bank stock	7.6
Total liabilities and equity	$589.9

Source: Federal Reserve Board, "Flow of Fund Accounts," Monetary Authority, December 15, 1999, p. L.108. *www.bog.frb.fed.us/*

Currency Outside Banks. The largest liability, in terms of percent of total liabilities and equity, of the Federal Reserve System is currency in circulation (85.3 percent of total liabilities and equity). At the top of each Federal Reserve note ($1 bill, $5 bill, $10 bill, etc.) is the seal of the Federal Reserve Bank that issued it. Federal Reserve notes are basically IOUs from the issuing Federal Reserve Bank to the bearer. In the U.S., Federal Reserve notes are recognized as the principal medium of exchange, and therefore function as money (see Chapter 1).

Reserve Deposits. The second largest liability on the Federal Reserve's balance sheet (10.6 percent of total liabilities and equity) is commercial bank reserves. All banks hold reserve accounts at their local Federal Reserve Bank. These reserve holdings are used to settle accounts between depository institutions when checks and wire transfers are cleared (see above). Reserve accounts also influence the size of the money supply (as described below).

required reserves

Reserves the Federal Reserve requires banks to hold.

excess reserves

Additional reserves banks choose to hold.

Total reserves can be classified into two categories: (1) **required reserves** (reserves that the Fed requires banks to hold by law) and (2) **excess reserves** (additional reserves over and above required reserves) that banks choose to hold themselves. Required reserves are reserves banks must hold by law to back a portion of their customer transaction accounts (deposits). For example, the Federal Reserve currently requires 10 cents of every dollar of transaction deposit accounts at U.S. commercial banks to be backed with reserves (see Chapter 14). Thus, required reserves expand or contract with the level of transaction deposits and with the required reserve ratio set by the Federal Reserve Board. Because these deposits do not earn interest, banks try to keep excess reserves to a minimum.[7] Excess reserves, on the other hand, may be lent by banks to other banks that do not have sufficient reserves on hand to meet their required levels. As the Federal Reserve implements monetary policy, it uses the market for excess reserves.

Assets.   The major assets on the Federal Reserve's balance sheet are Treasury securities, Treasury currency, and gold and foreign exchange. While loans to domestic banks are quite a small portion of the Federal Reserve's assets, they play an important role in implementing monetary policy (see below).

Treasury Securities.   Treasury securities (82.9 percent of total assets) are the Fed's holdings of securities issued by the U.S. Treasury (U.S. government). The Fed's open market operations involve the buying and selling of these securities. An increase (decrease) in Treasury securities held by the Fed leads to an increase (decrease) in the money supply.

Gold and Foreign Exchange and Treasury Currency.   The Federal Reserve holds Treasury gold certificates that are redeemable at the U.S. Treasury for gold. The Fed also holds small amounts of Treasury-issued coinage and foreign-denominated assets to assist in foreign currency transactions or currency swap agreements with the central banks of other nations.

Loans to Domestic Banks.   As mentioned earlier, in a liquidity emergency, depository institutions in need of additional funds can borrow at the Federal Reserve's discount window (discussed in detail below). The interest rate or discount rate charged on these loans is often lower than other interest rates in the short-term money markets (see Chapter 5). To prevent excessive borrowing from the discount window, the Fed discourages borrowing unless a bank is in serious liquidity need (see Chapters 14 and 22). As a result, (discount) loans to domestic banks are normally a relatively small portion of the Fed's total assets.[8]

Do You Understand?

1. What the main functions of Federal Reserve Banks are?
2. What the main responsibilities of the Federal Reserve Board are?
3. How the FOMC implements monetary policy?
4. What the main assets and liabilities in the Federal Reserve System are?

Monetary Policy Tools

3

In the previous section of this chapter, we referred briefly to tools or instruments that the Federal Reserve uses to implement its monetary policy. These included open market operations, the discount rate, and reserve requirements. Regardless of the tool the Federal Reserve uses to implement monetary policy, the major link by which monetary policy impacts the macroeconomy occurs through the Federal Reserve influencing the market for bank reserves (required and excess reserves held as depository institution reserves balances in accounts at Federal Reserve Banks plus vault cash on hand of commercial banks). Specifically, the Federal Reserve's

---

7. The minimum daily average reserves that a bank must maintain are computed as a percentage of the daily average net transaction accounts held by the bank over the two-week computation period, called the reserve computation period. Transaction accounts include all deposits on which an account holder may make withdrawals (for example, demand deposits, NOW accounts, and share draft accounts—offered by credit unions). Transaction account balances are reduced by demand balances due from U.S. depository institutions and cash items in process of collection to obtain net transaction accounts. Under the current set of regulations, a lag of 30 days exists between the beginning of the reserve computation period and the beginning of the reserve maintenance period (over which vault cash and deposits at the Federal Reserve Bank must meet or exceed the required reserve target). Thus, the bank's reserve manager knows the value of its target reserves with perfect certainty throughout the reserve maintenance period. See Chapter 14 for more specific details.

8. Such loans could increase rapidly in a major financial crisis or panic (such as the stock market crash of October 1987).

monetary policy seeks to influence either the demand for, or supply of, excess reserves at depository institutions and in turn the money supply and the level of interest rates. Specifically, a change in excess reserves resulting from the implementation of monetary policy triggers a sequence of events that affect such economic factors as short-term interest rates, long-term interest rates, foreign exchange rates, the amount of money and credit in the economy, and ultimately the levels of employment, output, and prices.

fed funds rate

The interest rate on short-term funds transferred between financial institutions, usually for a period of one day.

Depository institutions trade excess reserves held at their local Federal Reserve Banks among themselves. Banks with excess reserves—whose reserves exceed their required reserves—have an incentive to lend these funds (generally overnight) to banks in need of reserves since excess reserves held in the vault or on deposit at the Federal Reserve earn no interest. The rate of interest (or price) on these interbank transactions is a benchmark interest rate, called the federal funds rate or **fed funds rate**, which is used in the U.S. to guide monetary policy. The fed funds rate is a function of the supply and demand for federal funds among banks and the effects of the Fed's trading through the FOMC.

In implementing monetary policy, the Federal Reserve can take one of two basic approaches to affect the market for bank excess reserves: (1) it can target the quantity of reserves in the market based on the FOMC's objectives for the growth in the monetary base (the sum of currency in circulation and reserves) and, in turn, the money supply (see below), or (2) it can target the interest rate on those reserves (the fed funds rate). The actual approach used by the Federal Reserve has varied according to considerations such as the need to combat inflation, or the desire to encourage sustainable economic growth (we discuss the various approaches below). Since 1993, the FOMC has implemented monetary policy mainly by targeting interest rates (mainly using the fed funds rate as a target).

In this section, we explore the tools or instruments used by the Fed to implement its monetary policy strategy. Figure 4–2 illustrates the monetary policy implementation process that we will be discussing in more detail below.

Figure 4–2   Federal Reserve Monetary Policy Activities

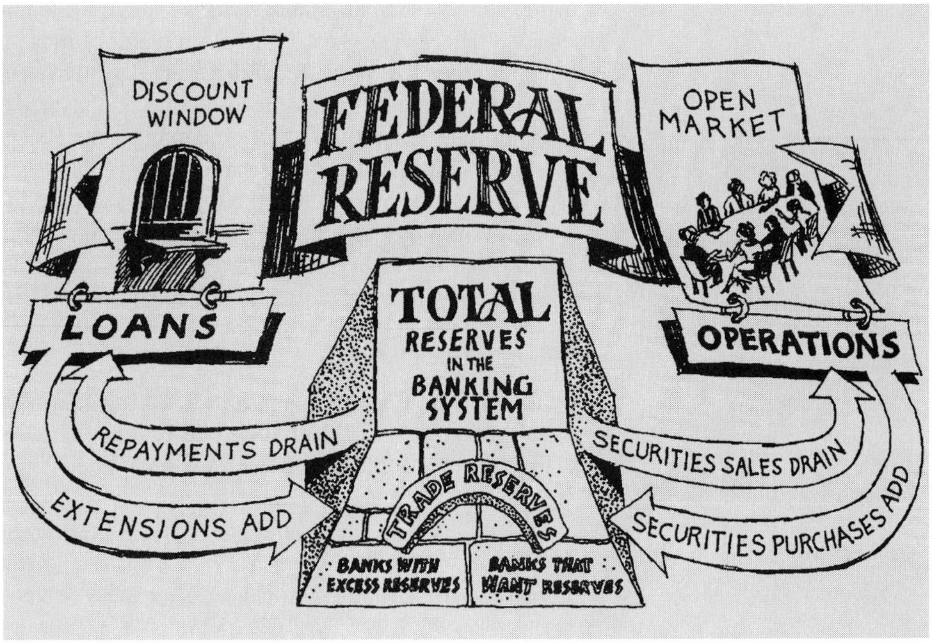

Source: Federal Reserve Board, website, "Purposes & Functions," July 1999. *www.bog.frb.fed.us/*

www.ny.frb.org/

Federal Reserve Board Trading Desk

Unit of the Federal Reserve Bank of New York through which open market operations are conducted.

policy directive

Statement sent to the Federal Reserve Board Trading Desk from the FOMC that specifies the money supply target.

Open Market Operations

When a targeted monetary aggregate (M1, M2, etc.—see definition below) or interest rate level is determined by the FOMC, it is forwarded to the **Federal Reserve Board Trading Desk** at the Federal Reserve Bank of New York (FRBNY) through a statement called the **policy directive**. The manager of the Trading Desk uses the policy directive to instruct traders on the amount of open market purchases or sales to transact. Open market operations are the Federal Reserves' purchases or sales of securities in the U.S. Treasury securities market. This is an over-the-counter market in which traders are linked to each other electronically (see Chapter 5).

Open market operations are particularly important because they are the primary determinant of changes in bank excess reserves in the banking system and thus directly impact the size of the money supply and/or the level of interest rates (e.g., the fed funds rate). When the Federal Reserve purchases securities, it pays for the securities by either writing a check on itself or directly transferring funds (by wire transfer) into the seller's account. Either way, the Fed credits the reserve deposit account of the bank that sells it (the Fed) the securities. This transaction increases the bank's excess reserve levels. When the Fed sells securities, it either collects checks received as payment or receives wire transfers of funds from these agents (such as banks) using funds from their accounts at the Federal Reserve Banks to purchase securities. This reduces the balance of the reserve account of a bank that purchases securities. Thus, when the Federal Reserve sells (purchases) securities in the open market, it decreases (increases) banks' (reserve account) deposits at the Fed.

Example 4–1   Purchases of Securities by the Federal Reserve

Suppose the FOMC instructs the FRBNY Trading Desk to purchase $500 million of Treasury securities. Traders at the FRBNY call primary government securities dealers of major commercial and investment banks (such as Goldman Sachs and Chase)[9] who provide a list of securities they have available for sale, including the denomination, maturity, and the price on each security. FRBNY traders then seek to purchase the target number of securities (at the desired maturities and lowest possible price) until they have purchased the $500 million. The FRBNY then notifies its government bond department to receive and pay the sellers for the securities it has purchased. The securities dealer sellers (such as banks) in turn deposit these payments in their accounts held at their local Federal Reserve Bank. As a result of these purchases, the Treasury securities account balance of the Federal Reserve System is increased by $500 million and the total reserve accounts maintained by these banks and dealers at the Fed is increased by $500 million. We illustrate these changes to the Federal Reserve's balance sheet in Table 4–6. In addition, there is also an impact on commercial bank balance sheets. Total reserves (assets) of commercial banks will increase by $500 million due to the purchase of securities by the Fed, and demand deposits (liabilities) of the securities dealers (those who sold the securities) at their banks will increase by $500 million.[10] We also show the changes to commercial banks' balance sheets in Table 4–6.

Note the Federal Reserve's purchase of Treasury securities has increased the total supply of bank reserves in the financial system. This in turn increases the ability of banks to make new loans and create new deposits.

---

9. As of May 1999, there were 30 primary securities dealers trading, on average, $185 billion securities per day.

10. In reality, not all of the $500 million will generally be deposited in demand deposit accounts of commercial banks, and commercial banks will not generally hold all of the $500 million in reserve accounts of Federal Reserves Banks. We relax these simplifying assumptions and look at the effect on total reserves and the monetary base later in the chapter.

Table 4–6 Purchase of Securities in the Open Market

Change in Federal Reserve's Balance Sheet

Assets		Liabilities	
Treasury securities	+ $500m.	Reserve account of securities dealers' banks	+ $500m.

Change in Commercial Bank Balance Sheets

Assets		Liabilities	
Reserve accounts at Federal Reserve	+ $500m.	Securities dealers' demand deposit accounts	+ $500m.

Example 4–2   Sale of Securities by the Federal Reserve

Suppose the FOMC instructs the FRBNY Trading Desk to sell $500 million of securities. Traders at the FRBNY call government securities dealers who provide a list of securities they are willing to buy, including the price on each security. FRBNY traders sell securities to these dealers at the highest prices possible until they have sold $500 million. The FRBNY then notifies its government bond department to deliver the securities to, and receive payment from, the buying security dealers. The securities dealers pay for these securities by drawing on their deposit accounts at their commercial banks. As a result of this sale, the Treasury securities account balance for the Federal Reserve System is decreased by $500 million (reflecting the sale of $500 million in Treasury securities) and the reserve accounts maintained at the Fed by commercial banks that handle these securities transactions for the dealers are decreased by $500 million. The changes to the Federal Reserve's balance sheet would in this case have the opposite sign (negative) as those illustrated in Table 4–6. In addition, total reserves of commercial banks will decrease by $500 million due to the purchase of securities from the Fed, and demand deposits of the securities dealers at their banks will decrease by $500 million (reflecting the payments for the securities by the securities dealers). Commercial banks' balance sheet changes would have the opposite sign as those illustrated in Table 4–6 for a purchase of securities.

Note that the Federal Reserve's sale of Treasury or other government securities has decreased the total supply of bank reserves in the financial system. This in turn decreases the ability of banks to make loans and create new deposits.

While the Federal Reserve conducts most of its open market operations using Treasury securities, other government securities can be used as well. Treasury securities are used most because the secondary market for such securities is highly liquid and there is an established group of primary dealers who also trade extensively in the secondary market. Thus, the Treasury securities market can absorb a large number of buy and sell transactions without experiencing significant price fluctuations.

At times, the Federal Reserve may want to *temporarily* increase (or decrease) the aggregate level of bank reserves for reasons other than directly impacting monetary targets or interest rates. For example, holiday deposit withdrawals can create temporary imbalances in the level of bank reserves. In this case, the Trading Desk often uses **repurchase agreements** or repos to offset such temporary shortfalls in bank reserves and liquidity. With a repo, the Fed purchases government securities from a dealer or a bank with an agreement that the seller will repurchase them within a stated period of time (generally 1 to 15 days) as specified in the repurchase agreement. When a repurchase

repurchase agreements

Open market transactions in which the Trading Desk purchases government securities with an agreement that the seller will repurchase them within a stated period of time.

agreement is used, the level of bank reserves rises as the securities are sold. They are then reduced when the dealers repurchase their securities a few days later. The objective of such repurchase agreements is to smooth out fluctuations in bank reserves and thus in the nation's money supply and to avoid adverse impacts on interest rates.

The Discount Rate

The discount rate is the second monetary policy tool or instrument used by the Federal Reserve to control the level of bank reserves (and thus the money supply or interest rates). As defined above, the discount rate is the rate of interest Federal Reserve Banks charge on emergency or "lender of last resort" loans to depository institutions in their district. The Federal Reserve can influence the level and price of reserves by changing the discount rate it charges on these loans.

Specifically, changing the discount rate signals to the market and the economy that the Federal Reserve would like to see higher or lower rates in the economy. Thus, the discount rate is like a signal of the FOMC's intentions regarding the tenor of monetary policy. For example, raising the discount rate signals that the Fed would like to see a tightening of monetary conditions and higher interest rates in general (and a relatively lower amount of borrowing). Lowering the discount rate signals a desire to see more expansionary monetary conditions and lower interest rates in general.

While the lowering of the discount rate relative to short-term money market rates in the open market (such as the fed funds rate) may lead to enhanced commercial bank borrowing through the discount window, this is *not* the primary intention of the rate change. Indeed, excessive borrowing by banks for reasons other than *special needs* (described below) is actively discouraged by the Federal Reserve. For example, banks may be tempted to profit from the cheap nature of discount window funds relative to open market (fed) funds. If a bank is caught doing this by the Fed, it can be disciplined, fined, and ultimately have its banking charter revoked.

For two reasons, the Federal Reserve rarely uses the discount rate as a monetary policy tool. First, it is difficult for the Fed to predict changes in bank discount window borrowing when the discount rate changes. There is no guarantee that banks will borrow more (less) at the discount window in response to a decrease (increase) in the discount rate. Thus, the exact direct effect of a discount rate change on the money supply is often uncertain. Second, because of its "signaling" importance, a discount rate change often has great effects on the financial markets. For example, the 0.25 percent decrease in the Fed's discount rate in October 1998 resulted in a 330.58 point increase in the Dow Jones Industrial Average, the third largest point gain in the history of the Dow. Moreover, virtually all interest rates respond in the same direction (if not the same amount) to the discount rate change. For example, Figure 4–3 shows the correlation in four major U.S. interest rates (discount rate, prime rate, three-month CD rate, and three-month T-bill rate) from 1990 through 1999.

In general, discount rate changes are used only when the Fed wants to send a strong message to financial markets to show that it is serious about wanting to implement new monetary policy targets. For example, Federal Reserve Board members commented that the October 1998 discount rate change was intended to stress the Fed's concern that tight credit availability by banks could slow the economy down. Thus, the drop in the discount rate was intended to signal the Fed's strong intention to allow the money supply to increase and to ease credit availability.

The emergency, or lender of last resort, nature of discount window loans can be seen by analyzing the three different types of discount window loans the Federal Reserve offers to depository institutions. **Adjustment credit** is offered for short-term liquidity problems that may have been caused by a *temporary* deposit outflow from a bank. Adjustment credit loans are the major type of discount window loan. The rate of interest on adjustment credit loans is the basic discount rate set by the local Federal

adjustment credit

Discount window loan offered for short-term liquidity problems that may result from a temporary deposit outflow.

Figure 4–3   Various U.S. Interest Rates

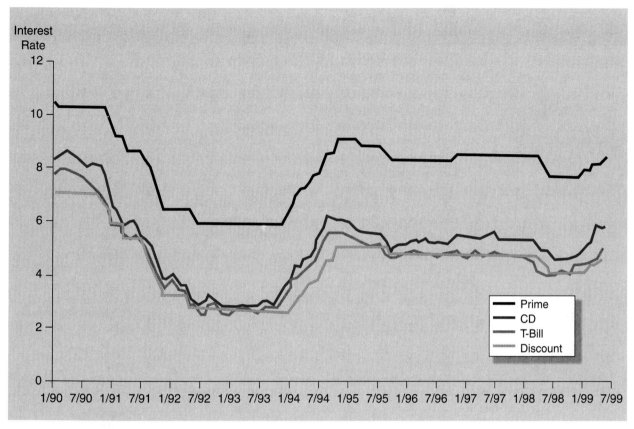

Source: Federal Reserve Board, website, "Research and Data," January 2000. *www.bog.frb.fed.us/*

Reserve Bank. These loans are expected to be repaid quickly, generally by the end of the next business day for the largest banks.

seasonal credit

Discount window loan offered to banks for seasonal liquidity squeezes.

Seasonal credit is offered to banks to offset seasonal liquidity squeezes—for example, for banks in rural areas that experience seasonal deposit flow patterns reflecting the agricultural crop cycle. To qualify for seasonal credit, a bank must be small and able to demonstrate a historical pattern of seasonality in its business. The rate of interest charged on seasonal credit loans is based on the federal funds and certificate of deposit rates and is therefore a bit more expensive than adjustment credit loans.[11]

extended credit

Discount window loan offered to banks with severe liquidity problems due to deposit outflows that will not be resolved in the foreseeable future.

Extended credit is offered by the Federal Reserve to more severely liquidity-constrained banks due to deposit outflows that will not be resolved in the foreseeable future (although the bank must still be seen as solvent). The interest rate charged on extended credit loans is one-half a percentage point above the interest rate charged on seasonal credit loans. Banks applying for extended credit loans must submit a proposal to the Federal Reserve Bank explaining why the extended credit loan is needed, as well as an acceptable plan for restoring the liquidity of the bank.

To protect against losses in the event that a borrower defaults, all discount window loans must be collateralized (generally with U.S. Treasury or federal agency securities) to the satisfaction of the Federal Reserve Bank that provides the discount window loan.

---

11. In the case of seasonal credit, it would be very difficult for a bank to profit by borrowing from the discount window rather than in the open market.

Collateral is generally held in safekeeping at the Federal Reserve Bank or by an acceptable third party. The value of collateral pledged to secure a discount window loan must exceed the amount of the loan.

Reserve Requirements (Reserve Ratios)

The third monetary policy tool available to the Federal Reserve to achieve its monetary targets is commercial bank reserve requirements. As defined above, reserve requirements determine the minimum amount of reserve assets (vault cash plus bank deposits at Federal Reserve Banks) that depository institutions must maintain by law to back transaction deposits held as liabilities on their balance sheets. This requirement is usually set as a ratio of transaction accounts—for example, 10 percent (see Chapter 14). A decrease in the reserve requirement ratio means that depository institutions may hold fewer reserves (vault cash plus reserve deposits at the Fed) against their transaction accounts (deposits). Consequently, they are able to lend out a greater percentage of their deposits, thus increasing credit availability in the economy. As new loans are issued and used to finance consumption and investment expenditures, some of these funds spent will return to depository institutions as new deposits by those receiving them in return for supplying consumer and investment goods to bank borrowers. In turn, these new deposits, after deducting the appropriate reserve requirement, can be used by banks to create additional loans, and so on. This process continues until the banks' deposits have grown sufficiently large such that the bank willingly holds its *current* reserve balance at the new lower reserve ratio. Thus, a decrease in the reserve requirement results in a multiplier increase in the supply of bank deposits and thus the money supply.

Conversely, an increase in the reserve requirement ratio means that depository institutions must hold more reserves against the transaction accounts (deposits) on their balance sheet. Consequently, they are able to lend out a smaller percentage of their deposits than before, thus decreasing credit availability and lending, and eventually, leading to a multiple contraction in deposits and a decrease in the money supply.

Example 4–3   Increasing the Money Supply by Lowering Banks' Reserve Requirements on Transaction Accounts

City Bank currently has $400 million in transaction deposits on its balance sheet. The current reserve requirement, set by the Federal Reserve, is 10 percent. Thus, City Bank must have reserve assets of at least $40 million ($400 million $\times$ .10) to back its deposits. In this simple framework, the remaining $360 million of deposits can be used to extend loans to borrowers. Table 4–7, Panel A, illustrates the Federal Reserve's and City Bank's balance sheets, assuming City Bank holds all of its reserves at the Fed, (i.e., City Bank has no vault cash).

If the Federal Reserve decreases the reserve requirement from 10 percent to 5 percent, City Bank's minimum reserve requirement decreases by $20 million, from $40 million to $20 million ($400 million $\times$ .05). City Bank can now use $20 million of its reserves at its local Federal Reserve Bank (since these are now excess reserves that earn no interest) so as to make new loans. Suppose, for simplicity, that City Bank is the only commercial bank (in practice, the multiplier effect described below will work the same except that deposit growth will be spread over a number of banks). Those who borrow the $20 million from the bank will spend the funds on consumption and investment goods and services and those who produce and sell these goods and services will redeposit the $20 million in funds received from their sale at their bank (assumed here to be City Bank). We illustrate this redeposit of funds in Figure 4–4. As a result, City Bank's balance sheet changes to that shown in Panel B of Table 4–7. Because of the $20 million increase in transaction account deposits, City Bank now must increase its reserves held at the Federal Reserve Bank by $1 million ($20 million $\times$ .05) but still has $19 million in excess reserves with which to make more new loans from the additional deposits of $20 million (see row 2 in Figure 4–4).

Assuming City Bank continues to issue new loans and that borrowers continue to spend the funds from their loans, and those receiving the loanable funds (in exchange for the sale of goods and services) redeposit those funds in transaction deposits at City Bank, City Bank's balance sheet will continue to grow until there are no excess reserves held by City Bank (Panel C in Table 4–7). For this to happen, City Bank must willingly hold the $40 million it has in reserves. This requires City Bank's balance sheet (and its deposits) to double in size as a result of the reserve requirement decrease from 10 percent to 5 percent (i.e., $800 million deposits $\times$ .05 = $40 million). Note that the effect on the size of bank deposits and on City Bank's balance sheet is the inverse of the percentage drop in the reserve requirement (i.e., 1/((Old reserve requirement − New reserve requirement)/old reserve requirement), or 1/((.10 − .05)/.10) = 1/.5 = 2 times).

Table 4–7 Lowering the Reserve Requirement

Panel A: Initial Balance Sheets

Federal Reserve Bank

Assets		Liabilities	
Securities	$40m.	Reserve accounts	$40m.

City Bank

Assets		Liabilities	
Loans	$360m.	Transaction deposits	$400m.
Reserve deposits at Fed	40m.		

Panel B: Balance Sheet Immediately after Decrease in Reserve Requirement

Federal Reserve Bank

Assets		Liabilities	
Securities	$21m.	Reserve accounts	$21m.

City Bank

Assets		Liabilities	
Loans	$380m.	Transaction deposits	$420m.
Reserve deposits at Fed	21m.		
Cash	19m.		

Panel C: Balance Sheet after All Changes Resulting from Decrease in Reserve Requirement

Federal Reserve Bank

Assets		Liabilities	
Securities	$40m.	Reserve accounts	$40m.

City Bank

Assets		Liabilities	
Loans	$760m.	Transaction deposits	$800m.
Reserve deposits at Fed	40m.		

Figure 4–4 Deposit Growth Multiplier

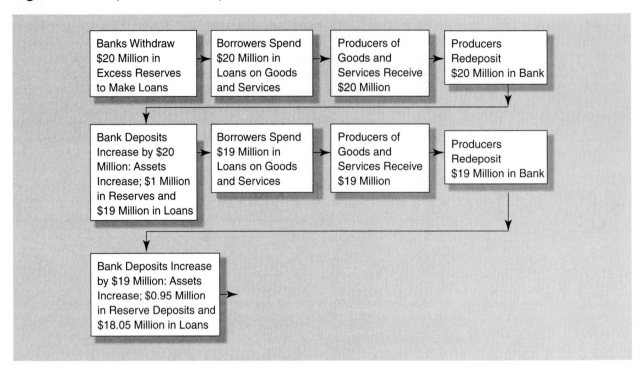

Alternatively, the deposit growth multiplier can be viewed using the excess reserves originally created as a result of the decrease in the reserve requirement from 10 percent to 5 percent (i.e., the $20 million in excess reserves). That is, the bank's deposits grow by 1 divided by the new reserve requirement times the amount of excess reserves created by the reserve requirement change, or in the example above:

$$\text{Change in bank deposits} = 1/.05 \times \$20 \text{ million} = \$400 \text{ million}$$

While the deposit multiplier effect has been illustrated here using the example of a change in reserve requirements, it also holds when other monetary policy tools or instruments are changed as well (e.g., open market operations). For example, suppose the FOMC instructs the FRBNY Trading Desk to purchase $200 million in U.S. Treasury securities. If the reserve requirement is set at 10 percent, the $200 million open market purchase will result in an increase in bank excess reserves of $200 million, and ultimately, via the multiplier (1/.1), an increase in bank deposits and the money supply of $2 billion:

$$1/.1 \times \$200 \text{ million} = \$2,000 \text{ million} = \$2 \text{ billion}$$

We have made some critical assumptions about the behavior of banks and borrowers to simplify our illustration of the impact of a change in open market operations and reserve requirements on bank deposits and the money supply. In Example 4–3 we assumed that City Bank was the only bank, that it converts all (100 percent) of its excess reserve deposits into loans, that all (100 percent) of these funds are spent by borrowers, and that all are returned to City Bank as "new" transaction deposits. If these assumptions are relaxed, the overall impact of a decrease in the reserve requirement ratio, or increase in excess reserves from an open market operation, on the amount of bank deposits and the money supply will be smaller than illustrated above and the precise effect of a change in the reserve base on the money supply is not fully predictable. Nevertheless, as long as some portion of the excess reserves created by the decrease in the reserve requirement are converted into loans and some portion of these loans after being spent are returned to the banking system in the form of transaction deposits, a decease in reserve requirements will result in a multiple (that is, greater than one) increase in bank deposits, the money supply, and credit availability.

Conversely, if the Federal Reserve increases reserve requirement ratios, depository institutions must convert some loans on their balance sheet back into reserves held at their local Federal Reserve Bank. The overall result is that an increase in the reserve requirements will result in a multiple decline in credit availability, bank deposits, and the money supply (i.e., the multiplier effect described above will be reversed). Again, the overall effect on the money supply is not fully predictable.

Because changes in reserve requirements can result in unpredictable changes in the money supply (depending on the amount of excess reserves held by banks, the willingness of banks to make loans rather than hold other assets such as securities, and the predictability of the public willingness to redeposit funds lent at banks instead of holding cash—that is, whether they have a stable cash-deposit ratio or not), the reserve requirement is very rarely used by the Federal Reserve as a monetary policy tool.

Do You Understand?

1. What the major policy tools used by the Federal Reserve to influence the economy are?
2. What the impact is on credit availability and the money supply if the Federal Reserve purchases securities?
3. Why the Federal Reserve is unique in its ability to change the money supply through monetary policy tools?

4   The Federal Reserve, the Money Supply, and Interest Rates

As we introduced this chapter, we stated that the Federal Reserve takes steps to influence monetary conditions—credit availability, interest rates, the money supply, and ultimately security prices—so it can promote price stability (low inflation) and other macroeconomic objectives. We illustrate this process in Figure 4–5. Historically, the Fed has sought to influence the economy by directly targeting the money supply or interest rates. In this section, we take a look at the ultimate impact of monetary policy changes on key economic variables. We also look at the Fed's choice of whether to target the money supply or interest rates in order to best achieve its overall macroeconomic objectives.

Effects of Monetary Tools on Various Economic Variables

The examples in the previous section illustrated how the Federal Reserve and bank balance sheets change as a result of monetary policy changes. Table 4–8 goes one step further and looks at how credit availability, interest rates, the money supply, and security prices are affected by these monetary policy actions. To do this, we categorize monetary policy tool changes into expansionary activities versus contractionary activities.

Expansionary Activities. We described above the three monetary policy tools that the Fed can use to increase the money supply. These include open market purchases of securities, discount rate decreases, and reserve requirement ratio decreases. All else held constant, when the Federal Reserve purchases securities in the open market, the reserve accounts of banks increase. When the Fed lowers the discount rate, this generally results in a lowering of interest rates in the economy. Finally, a decrease in the reserve requirements, all else constant, results in an increase in bank reserves.

In two of the three cases (open market operations and reserve requirement changes), an increase in reserves results in an increase in bank deposits and the money supply. One immediate effect of this is that interest rates fall and security prices start to rise (see Chapters 2 and 3). In the third case (a discount rate change), the impact of a lowering of interest rates is more direct. Lower interest rates encourages borrowing from banks. Economic agents spend more when they can get cheaper funds. Households, business, and governments are more likely to invest in fixed assets (e.g., housing,

Figure 4–5   The Process of Monetary Policy Implementation

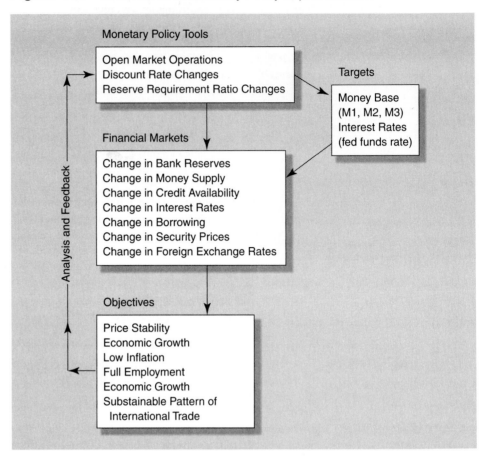

Table 4–8   The Impact of Monetary Policy on Various Economic Variables

	Expansionary Activities	Contractionary Activities
Impact on		
Reserves	↑	↓
Credit availability	↑	↓
Money supply	↑	↓
Interest rates	↓	↑
Security prices	↑	↓

plant, and equipment). Households increase their purchases of durable goods (e.g., automobiles, appliances). State and local government spending increases (e.g., new road construction, school improvements). Finally, lower domestic interest rates relative to foreign rates can result in a drop in the (foreign) exchange value of the dollar relative to other currencies.[12] As the dollar's (foreign) exchange value drops, U.S. goods become relatively cheaper compared to foreign goods. Eventually, U.S. exports increase. The increase in spending from all of these market participants results in economic expan-

---

12. See the discussion of the interest rate parity theorem in Chapter 9.

Table 4–9   Federal Reserve Monetary Policy Targets

Target	Years
Fed funds rate targeted using bank reserves to achieve target	1970–October 1979
Nonborrowed reserves targeted	October 1979–October 1982
Borrowed reserves targeted	October 1983–July 1993
Fed funds rate targeted (rate announced)	July 1993–present

sion, stimulates additional real production, and may cause the inflation rate (defined in Chapter 2) to rise. Ideally, the expansionary policies of the Fed are meant to be conducive to real economic expansion (economic growth, full employment, sustainable international trade) without price inflation. Indeed, price stabilization (low inflation) can be viewed as the primary policy objective of the Fed.

Contractionary Activities.   We also described three monetary policy tools that the Fed can use in a contractionary fashion. These include open market sales of securities, discount rate increases, and reserve requirement ratio increases. All else constant, when the Federal Reserve sells securities in the open market, reserve accounts of banks decrease. When the Fed raises the discount rate, interest rates generally increase in the open market, making borrowing more expensive. Finally, an increase in the reserve requirement ratio, all else constant, results in a decrease in excess reserves for all banks and limits the availability of funds for additional loans.

In all three cases, interest rates will tend to rise. Higher interest rates discourage credit availability and borrowing. Economic participants spend less when funds are expensive. Households, business, and governments are less likely to invest in fixed assets. Households decrease their purchases of durable goods. State and local government spending decreases. Finally, an increase in domestic interest rates relative to foreign rates may result in an increase in the (foreign) exchange value (rate) of the dollar. As the dollar's exchange rate increases, U.S. goods become relatively expensive compared to foreign goods. Eventually, U.S. exports decrease.

Money Supply versus Interest Rate Targeting

As shown in Table 4–9, the Federal Reserve has varied between its use of the money supply and interest rates as the target variable used to control economic activity in the United States. Figure 4–6 illustrates the targeting of money supply (such as M1), while Figure 4–7 shows the targeting of interest rates. For example, letting the demand curve for money be represented as M_D in Figure 4–6, suppose the FOMC sets the target M1 money supply (currency and checkable deposits,[13] see Table 4–10 for the full definition of M1, M2, and other money supply categories) at a level that is consistent with 5 percent growth, line M_S in Figure 4–6. At this M_S level, the FOMC expects the equilibrium interest rate to be i^*. However, unexpected increases or decreases in production, or changes in inflation, may cause the demand curve for money to shift up and to the right, M_D', or down and to the left, M_D''. Accordingly, interest rates will fluctuate between i' and i''. Thus, targeting the money supply can lead to periods of relatively high volatility in interest rates.

---

13. Remember that the money base is currency in circulation plus reserves (depository institution reserves balances in accounts at Federal Reserve Banks plus vault cash on hand of commercial banks). Thus, the money base is a part (subset) of the M1 money supply.

Figure 4–6   Targeting Money Supply

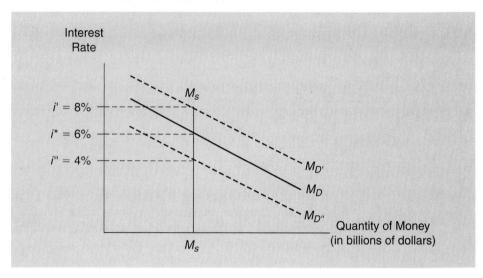

Table 4–10   Money Supply Definitions

Money Base—currency in circulation and reserves (depository institution reserve balances in accounts at Federal Reserve Banks plus vault cash on hand of commercial banks).

M1—(1) currency outside the U.S. Treasury, Federal Reserve Banks, and the vaults of depository institutions, (2) traveler's checks of nonbank issuers, (3) demand deposits at all commercial banks other than those owed to depository institutions, the U.S. government, and foreign banks and official institutions, less cash items in the process of collection and Federal Reserve float, and (4) other checkable deposits (OCDs), consisting of negotiable order of withdrawal (NOW) and automatic transfer service (ATS) accounts at depository institutions, credit union share draft accounts, and demand deposits at thrift institutions.

M2—M1 plus (1) overnight (and continuing contract) repurchase agreements (RPs) issued by all depository institutions and overnight Eurodollars issued to U.S. residents by foreign branches of U.S. banks worldwide, (2) savings (including MMDAs) and small time deposits (time deposits—including retail RPs—in amounts of less than $100,000), and (3) balances in both taxable and tax-exempt general-purpose and broker–dealer money market funds. Excludes individual retirement accounts (IRAs) and Keogh balances at depository institutions and money market funds.

M3—M2 plus (1) large time deposits and term RP liabilities (in amounts of $100,000 or more) issued by all depository institutions, (2) term Eurodollars held by U.S. residents at foreign branches of U.S. banks worldwide and at all banking offices in the United Kingdom and Canada, and (3) balances in both taxable and tax-exempt, institution-only money market funds.

L—M3 plus the nonbank public holdings of U.S. savings bonds, short-term Treasury securities, commercial paper, and bankers acceptances, net of money market fund holdings of these assets.

Debt—debt aggregate is the outstanding credit market debt of the domestic nonfinancial sectors—the federal sector (U.S. government, not including government-sponsored enterprises or federally related mortgage pools) and the nonfederal sectors (state and local governments, households and nonprofit organizations, nonfinancial corporate and nonfarm noncorporate businesses, and farms).

Source: *Federal Reserve Bulletin,* Publication Services, Washington, D.C., June 1999, Table A12.
www.bog.frb.fed.us/

Figure 4–7 Targeting Interest Rates

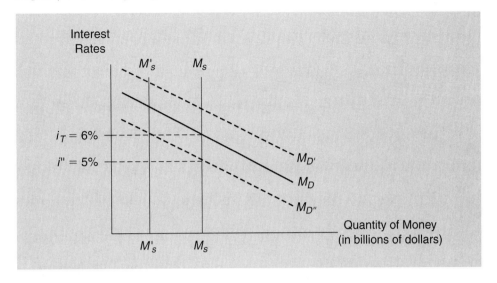

In Figure 4-7, suppose instead the FOMC targets the interest rate, $i_T = 6$ percent. If the demand for money falls, to M_D'', interest rates will fall to $i'' = 5$ percent with no intervention by the Fed. In order to maintain the target interest rate, the FOMC has to conduct monetary policy actions (such as open market sales of U.S. securities) to lower bank reserves and the money supply (to M_S'). This reduction in the money supply will maintain the target interest rate at $i_T = 6$ percent. As should be obvious from these graphs and the discussion, the Federal Reserve can successfully target *only one of these two variables* (money supply or interest rates) at any one moment. If the money supply is the target variable used to implement monetary policy, interest rates must be allowed to fluctuate relatively freely. By contrast, if an interest rate (such as the fed funds rate) is the target, then bank reserves and the money supply must be allowed to fluctuate relatively freely.

In the 1970s, the Fed implemented its monetary policy strategy by targeting the federal funds rate. The Fed allowed the money supply to accommodate flexibly the desired targeted fed funds rate. The Trading Desk at the Federal Reserve Bank of New York was instructed to implement these objectives. Specifically, if the fed funds rate increased above the target level, the Fed would instruct the FRBNY to conduct open market purchases, injecting bank reserves into the system. From Figure 4–7, the increase in bank reserves would result in an increase in the money supply and, in turn, a decrease in the fed funds rate. If the fed funds rate was too low, the Fed would instruct the FRBNY to conduct open market sales, drawing bank reserves out of the system and resulting in an increase in the fed funds rate.

During the 1970s, interest rates rose dramatically (due initially to the oil price shock of 1973–1974). The fed responded to these interest rate increases by increasing bank reserves. However, the relatively large expansion of reserves, and in turn the money supply, led to historically high levels of inflation (e.g., over 10 percent in the summer of 1979). With rapidly rising inflation, Paul Volcker (chairman of the Federal Reserve Board at the time) felt that interest rate targets were not doing an appropriate job in constraining the demand for money (and the inflationary side of the economy). Thus, on October 6, 1979, the Fed chose to completely refocus its monetary policy, moving away from interest rate targets toward targeting the money supply itself, and in particular bank reserves—nonborrowed reserves, which are the difference between total reserves and reserves borrowed through the discount window (see the earlier discussion in this chapter). Essentially, nonborrowed reserves reflect those reserves available for purchase and sale in the federal funds market. Operationally, the Fed

www.ny.frb.org/

Figure 4–8 Federal Fund Rates and Annualized Money Supply Growth Rates, 1975–1999

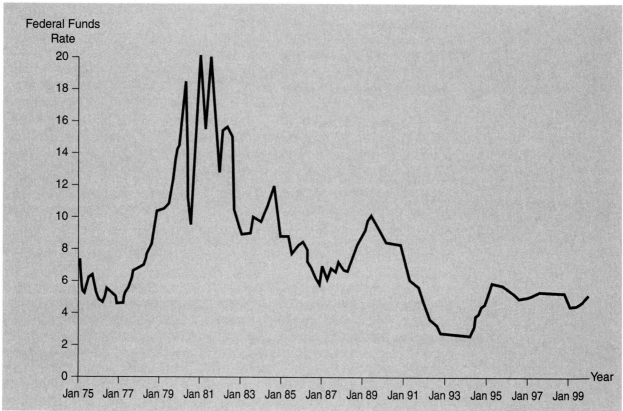

considerably widened the permitted federal funds rate range (with rates being allowed to vary around their current levels anywhere from 10 to 15 percentage points) and initially (for 1980) set the M1 growth rate target range between 4.5 percent and 7.0 percent. As might be expected, volatility in the federal funds rate increased dramatically after October 1979 (see Figure 4–8).

Growth in the money supply, however, did not turn out to be any easier to control when the quantity of (nonborrowed) bank reserves were used as the target variable. For example, the Fed missed its M1 growth rate targets in each of the first three years in which reserve targeting was used (the actual growth in the M1 money supply was 7.5 percent in 1980). Further, in contrast to expectations, volatility in the money supply growth rate grew as well. However, the 1979–1982 experiment of targeting nonborrowed reserves, rather than interest rates, worked to the extent that it rapidly reduced the U.S. inflation rate.

In October 1982, the Federal Reserve abandoned its policy of targeting nonborrowed reserves for a policy of targeting borrowed reserves (those reserves banks borrow from the Fed's discount window). The major reason for this, as reflected in the volatility of the M1 growth rates, was that over the 1979–1982 period many banks had sought to offset the declines in nonborrowed reserves implemented by the Fed (such as shortages of funds in the fed funds market) by borrowing more from the Federal Reserve's discount window. This effectively made the total supply of bank reserves (borrowed plus nonborrowed reserves) endogenous—that is, controllable by the banking system.

The borrowed reserve targeting system lasted from October 1982 until 1993, when the Federal Reserve announced that it would no longer target bank reserves and money

Figure 4–8   Concluded

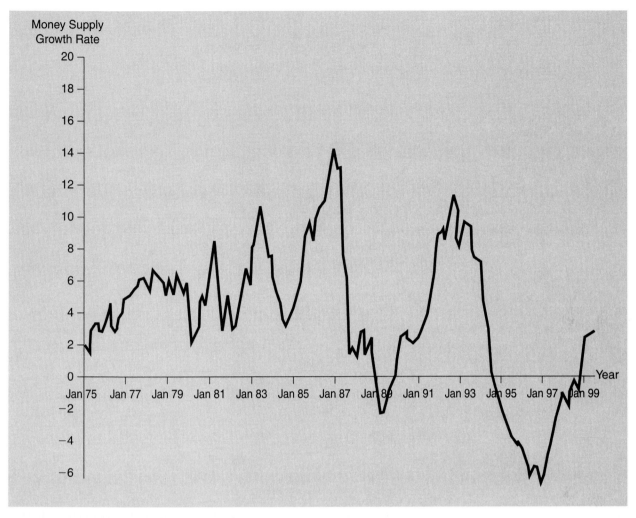

Source: Federal Reserve Board, website, "Research and Data," January 2000. *www.bog.frb.fed.us/*

supply growth at all. At this time, the Fed announced that it would use interest rates—the federal funds rate—as the main target variable to guide monetary policy (initially setting the target rate at a constant 3 percent). Under the current regime, and contrary to previous tradition such as in the 1970s, the Fed simply announces whether the federal funds rate target has been increased, decreased, or left unchanged after every monthly FOMC meeting—previously, the federal funds rate change had been kept secret. This announcement is watched very closely by financial market participants who, as demonstrated in In the News boxes in previous chapters, react quickly to any change in the fed funds rate target.

International Monetary Policies and Strategies

As discussed in Chapter 2, foreign investors are major participants in the financial markets. As such, the Federal Reserve considers economic conditions of other major countries—for example, Japan—when assessing and conducting its monetary policy for the U.S. economy. The

Figure 4–9 Exchange Rate of Japanese Yen for U.S. Dollars in Response to Bank of Japan Intervention

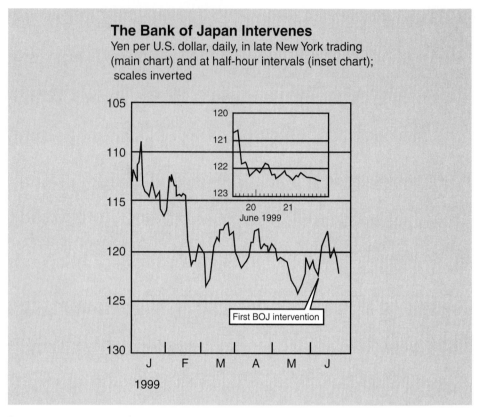

Source: *The Wall Street Journal,* June 22, 1999, p. A16. Reprinted by permission of *The Wall Street Journal,* © 1999 Dow Jones & Company, Inc. All Rights Reserved Worldwide. *www.wsj.com/*

Fed's actions regarding international monetary policy initiatives are most effective if it coordinates its activities and policies with the central banks of other countries. In this section, we look at how U.S. monetary policy initiatives affect foreign exchange rates.

Impact of U.S. Monetary Policy on Foreign Exchange Rates

Central banks in major countries often make commitments to each other about institutional aspects of their intervention (or nonintervention) in the foreign exchange markets. This is done through various forums, including meetings such as the Group of 7 (the meeting of senior government representatives from the seven major industrialized countries of the world). The current U.S. approach is to generally allow exchange rates to fluctuate freely. However, central banks can influence their country's exchange rates by buying and selling currencies, especially if they perceive the market has become unstable (a process called **foreign exchange intervention**). For example, in June 1999, the Bank of Japan (Japan's central bank) bought $5 billion U.S. dollars for yen in the currency markets, thus increasing the supply of yen. The reason for this was that there was wide concern among central bankers that the yen's exchange rate was appreciating (rising) too fast against the dollar and this might be a deterrent to Japanese exports and the movement of the Japanese economy out of recession. The purchase, conducted when Japanese markets were closed for a public holiday, caused the yen to fall in value from 120 yen per dollar (i.e., .00833 dollars for yen) to as high as 122.52 yen per dollar (i.e., .00816 dollars per yen—see Figure 4–9).

www.boj.or.jp/en/

foreign exchange intervention

Commitments between countries about the institutional aspects of their intervention in the foreign exchange markets.

Figure 4–10   Changes in the Equilibrium Foreign Exchange Rate in Response to Purchase of Japanese Yen with U.S. Dollars

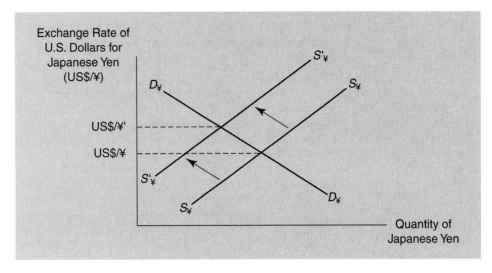

The process of foreign exchange intervention is similar to that of open market purchases and sales of Treasury securities, described earlier. Instead of purchasing or selling securities, the Federal Reserve purchases or sells some of its holdings of foreign currency reserves (listed as part of gold and foreign exchange in Table 4–5) in the foreign exchange markets (see Chapter 9). Specifically, when the Federal Reserve sells domestic currency to purchase foreign currency (e.g., the Japanese yen) in the foreign exchange market,[14] it results in an increase in the Fed's "gold and foreign exchange" and "deposits due to rest of the world" accounts (see Table 4–5). Further, since the Fed's purchasing of yen supplies more dollars to outside holders, this transaction increases the money supply in the United States.

For example, as shown in Figure 4–10, if the Federal Reserve decides to purchase ¥5 billion Japanese yen for dollars, the transaction results in an increase in the U.S. money supply and a decrease in the supply of Japanese yen. Thus, the supply curve for the foreign currency (the Japanese yen) shifts up and to the left, from $S_¥$ to $S'_¥$, and the equilibrium foreign exchange rate of U.S. dollars for Japanese yen (i.e., \$US/¥) rises from \$US/¥ to \$US/¥' in Figure 4–10—that is, the foreign currency (Japanese yen) appreciates in value relative to the U.S. dollar (or the U.S. dollar depreciates in value relative to the Japanese yen). Conversely, when the Federal Reserve purchases domestic currency using foreign exchange as payment, the transaction results in a decrease in the U.S. money supply and an increase in the supply of the foreign currency. As a result, the foreign currency depreciates in value relative to the U.S. dollar or the U.S. dollar appreciates in value relative to the foreign currency.

Do You Understand?

1. How central banks intervene in foreign exchange markets?

Example 4–4   Purchase of Foreign Assets by Selling Domestic Currency

Suppose the Federal Reserve decides to purchase \$5 billion worth of foreign currency in exchange for \$5 billion of its deposit accounts at the Federal Reserve. The Fed's purchase of foreign currency results in two balance sheet changes. First, the Fed's holdings

14. This transaction is completed by the Foreign Exchange Desk at the Federal Reserve Bank of New York.

of foreign exchange increase by $5 billion. Second, the Fed increases its dollar deposit accounts of the foreign currency sellers by $5 billion. Thus, the Fed's purchase of foreign currency and the payment with dollar deposits at the Fed result in a $5 billion increase in U.S. bank reserves.

Summary

This chapter described the Federal Reserve System in the United States. The Federal Reserve is the central bank charged with conducting monetary policy, supervising and regulating depository institutions, maintaining the stability of the financial system, and providing specific financial services to the U.S. government, the public, and financial institutions. We reviewed the structure under which the Fed provides these functions, the monetary policy tools it uses, and the impact of monetary policy changes on credit availability, interest rates, money supply, security prices, and foreign exchange rates.

Questions

1. Describe the functions performed by Federal Reserve Banks.
2. Define the discount window and the discount rate.
3. Describe the structure of the Board of Governors of the Federal Reserve System.
4. What are the primary responsibilities of the Federal Reserve Board?
5. What are the primary responsibilities of the Federal Open Market Committee?
6. What are the major liabilities of the Federal Reserve System? Describe each.
7. What are the major assets of the Federal Reserve System? Describe each.
8. What are the tools used by the Federal Reserve to implement monetary policy?
9. Suppose the Federal Reserve instructs the Trading Desk to purchase $1 billion of securities. Show the result of this transaction on the balance sheets of the Federal Reserve System and commercial banks.
10. Suppose the Federal Reserve instructs the Trading Desk to sell $850 million of securities. Show the result of this transaction on the balance sheets of the Federal Reserve System and commercial banks.
11. Explain how a decrease in the discount rate affects credit availability and the money supply.
12. Why does the Federal Reserve rarely use the discount rate to implement its monetary policy?
13. What is the difference between an adjustment credit, a seasonal credit, and an extended credit discount window loan?
14. Bank Three currently has $600 million in transaction deposits on its balance sheet. The Federal Reserve has

currently set the reserve requirement at 10 percent of transaction deposits.

a. If the Federal Reserve decreases the reserve requirement to 8 percent, show the balance sheet of Bank Three and the Federal Reserve System just before and after the full effect of the reserve requirement change. Assume Bank Three withdraws all excess reserves and gives out loans, and that borrowers eventually return all of these funds to Bank Three in the form of transaction deposits.

b. Redo part (a) using a 12 percent reserve requirement.

15. National Bank currently has $500 million in transaction deposits on its balance sheet. The current reserve requirement is 10 percent, but the Federal Reserve is decreasing this requirement to 8 percent.

a. Show the balance sheet of the Federal Reserve and National Bank if National Bank converts all excess reserves to loans, but borrowers return only 50 percent of these funds to National Bank as transaction deposits.

b. Show the balance sheet of the Federal Reserve and National Bank if National Bank converts 75 percent of its excess reserves to loans and borrowers return 60 percent of these funds to National Bank as transaction deposits.

16. Which of the monetary tools available to the Federal Reserve is most often used? Why?

17. Describe how expansionary activities conducted by the Federal Reserve impact credit availability, the money supply, interest rates, and security prices. Do the same for contractionary activities.

18. How does the purchase and sale of domestic currency to sell and buy foreign currency in the foreign exchange market affect the Federal Reserve's balance sheet, the money supply, and foreign exchange rates?

19. Suppose the Federal Reserve purchases $10 billion worth of foreign currency in exchange for deposit accounts at the Federal Reserve. Show the changes that result from this transaction on the Fed's balance sheet.

20. Go to the Federal Reserve System website and find the most recent level of M1 money growth rates and the fed funds rate.

Securities Markets

Part Two of the book presents an overview of the various securities markets. We describe each securities market, its participants, the securities traded in each, and the trading process in each. These chapters cover the money markets (Chaper 5), bond markets (Chapter 6), mortgage markets (Chapter 7), stock markets (Chapter 8), foreign exchange markets (Chapter 9), and derivative securities markets (Chapter 10).

c h a p t e r   f i v e

Money Markets

Chapter Navigator

1. What are money markets?

2. What are the major types of money market securities?

3. What is the process used to issue Treasury securities?

4. Who are the main participants in money markets?

5. To what extent do foreign investors participate in U.S. money markets?

6. What are the major developments in Euro money markets?

1 Definition of Money Markets: Chapter Overview

Money markets exist to transfer funds from individuals, corporations, and government units with short-term excess funds (suppliers of funds) to economic agents who have *short-term* needs for funds (users of funds). Specifically, in **money markets,** short-term debt instruments (those with an original maturity of one year or less) are issued by economic units that require short-term funds and are purchased by economic units that have excess short-term funds. Once issued, money market instruments trade in active secondary markets. Capital markets serve a similar function for market participants with excess funds to invest for periods of time longer than one year and/or who wish to borrow for periods longer than one year. Market participants who concentrate their investments in capital market instruments also tend to invest in some money market securities so as to meet their short-term liquidity needs (see, for example, In the News box 5–1). The secondary markets for money market instruments are

In the News

Tax-free money market funds grew during the first two weeks of the month as investors moved cash from other accounts to write checks to the Internal Revenue Service (IRS). Others had parked tax refunds in short-term accounts before deciding on their final destination. Peter Crane, editor of IBC's Money Fund Report, said managers are in a holding pattern until summer note season, which typically starts up in June. "You have managers concerned about cash flows and April 15 for a while and I think everyone expects a big lull until summer," he said.

Tax-exempt money market funds posted a record

Money Market Funds Staying Liquid in the Lull between Tax and Note Season

high volume of $199.5 billion in net assets last week, according to IBC Financial Data . . . Fund manager Kevin Shaughnessy of Wells Capital Management Inc. said the period immediately following tax time brings heavy outflows from his $2.4 billion Stage Coach California Tax-Exempt Money Market Fund. This week alone, he lost about $200 million due to IRS filings, which usually occur the first 10 days after April 15. "I think once you start seeing (IRS) checks get cashed . . . you see a steady outflow," he said . . .

Source: *Bond Buyer*, April 23, 1999, by Jennifer Karchmer.

"Unfortunately, you never know how much you will lose in outflows," John Maloney of Back Bay Advisors Inc. says. Early-bird filers parking their tax refunds and investors beefing up their short-term position before paying Uncle Sam contributed to the fund's $14 million increase since January, he said. In addition, equity investors who feared stock market volatility "wanted to take some (cash) off the table" and put it into short-term accounts.

. . . Like most money fund managers, Paul Marandett (of Freedom Capital Management Corp.) will continue to see IRS checks clear. "We're looking for outflows at this point," Marandett said. "How big or how much, I don't know. But that's what we can expect to see."

www.americanbanker.com/

money markets

Markets that trade debt securities or instruments with maturities of less than one year.

Do You Understand?

1. Why money market funds saw a significant inflow of funds in March and April 1999?

extremely important, as they serve to reallocate the (relatively) fixed amounts of liquid funds available in the market at any particular time.

In this chapter, we present an overview of money markets. We define and review the various money market instruments that exist, the new issue and secondary market trading process for each, and the market participants trading these securities. We also look at international money markets and instruments, taking a particularly close look at the Euro markets.

Money Markets

The need for money markets arises because the immediate cash needs of individuals, corporations, and governments do not necessarily coincide with their receipts of cash.

For example, the federal government collects taxes quarterly; however, its operating and other expenses occur daily. Similarly, corporations' daily patterns of receipts from sales do not necessarily occur with the same pattern as their daily expenses (e.g., wages and other disbursements). Because excessive holdings of cash balances involve a cost in the form of forgone interest, called **opportunity cost**, those economic units with excess cash usually keep such balances to the minimum needed to meet their day-to-day transaction requirements. Consequently, holders of cash invest "excess" cash funds in financial securities that can be quickly and relatively costlessly converted back to cash when needed with little risk of loss of value over the short investment horizon. Money markets are efficient in performing this service in that they enable large amounts of money to be transferred from suppliers of funds to users of funds for short periods of time both quickly and at low cost to the transacting parties. In general, a money market instrument provides an investment opportunity that generates a higher rate of interest (return) than holding cash, but it is also very liquid and (because of its short maturity) has relatively low default risk. Table 5–1 describes various money market instruments and their interest rates, as listed in *The Wall Street Journal,* for January 18, 2000.

opportunity cost

The forgone interest cost from the holding of cash balances when they are received.

Notice, from the description above, that money markets and money market securities or instruments have three basic characteristics. First, money market instruments are generally sold in large denominations (often in units of $1 million to $10 million). Most money market participants want or need to borrow large amounts of cash, so that transactions costs are low relative to the interest paid. The size of these initial transactions prohibits most individual investors from investing directly in money market securities. Rather, individuals generally invest in money

Table 5–1   Various U.S. Money Market Security Rates

MONEY RATES

Tuesday, January 18, 2000
The key U. S. and foreign annual interest rates below are a guide to general levels but don't always represent actual transactions.

PRIME RATE: 8.50% (effective 11/17/99). The base rate on corporate loans posted by at least 75% of the nation's 30 largest banks.

DISCOUNT RATE: 5.00% (effective 11/16/99). The charge on loans to depository institutions by the Federal Reserve Banks.

FEDERAL FUNDS: 6 1/4 % high, 5 1/2 % low, 5 3/4 % near closing bid, 6 % offered. Reserves traded among commercial banks for overnight use in amounts of $1 million or more. Source: Prebon Yamane(U.S.A)Inc. FOMC fed funds target rate 5.50% effective 11/16/99.

CALL MONEY: 7.25% (effective 11/17/99). The charge on loans to brokers on stock exchange collateral. Source: Reuters.

COMMERCIAL PAPER: placed directly by General Electric Capital Corp.: 5.62% 30 to 42 days; 5.70% 43 to 73 days; 5.80% 74 to 105 days; 5.83% 106 to 164 days; 5.85% 165 to 186 days; 5.92% 187 to 270 days.

EURO COMMERCIAL PAPER: placed directly by General Electric Capital Corp.: 3.05% 30 days; 3.14% two months; 3.25% three months; 3.32% four months; 3.40% five months; 3.47% six months.

DEALER COMMERCIAL PAPER: High-grade unsecured notes sold through dealers by major corporations: 5.65% 30 days; 5.70% 60 days; 5.82% 90 days.

CERTIFICATES OF DEPOSIT: 5.26% one month; 5.38% two months; 5.45% three months; 5.66% six months; 6.00% one year. Average of top rates paid by major New York banks on primary new issues of negotiable C.D.s, usually in amounts of $1 million and more. The minimum unit is $100,000. Typical rates in the secondary market. 5.76% one month; 5.96% three months; 6.15% six months.

BANKERS ACCEPTANCES: 5.70% 30 days; 5.80% 60 days; 5.90% 90 days; 5.92% 120 days; 5.95% 150 days; 5.97% 180 days. Offered rates of negotiable, bank-backed business credit instruments typically financing an import order.

LONDON LATE EURODOLLARS: 5.81% - 5.69% one month; 5.94% - 5.81% two months; 6.06% - 5.94% three months; 6.13% - 6.00% four months; 6.06% - 6.19% five months; 6.25% - 6.13% six months.

LONDON INTERBANK OFFERED RATES (LIBOR): 5.8075% one month; 6.0350% three months; 6.2150% six months; 6.64125% one year. British Banker's Association average of interbank offered rates for dollar deposits in the London market based on quotations at 16 major banks. Effective rate for contracts entered into two days from date appearing at top of this column.

EURO LIBOR: 3.12000% one month; 3.31000% three months; 3.52688% six months; 3.92375% one year. British Banker's Association average of interbank offered rates for euro deposits in the London market based on quotations at 16 major banks. Effective rate for contracts entered into two days from date appearing at top of this column.

EURO INTERBANK OFFERED RATES (EURIBOR): 3.120% one month; 3.313% three months; 3.529% six months; 3.925% one year. European Banking Federation-sponsored rate among 57 Euro zone banks.

FOREIGN PRIME RATES: Canada 6.50%; Germany 3.00%; Japan 1.375%; Switzerland 3.25%; Britain 5.75%. These rate indications aren't directly comparable; lending practices vary widely by location.

TREASURY BILLS: Results of the Tuesday, January 18, 2000, auction of short-term U.S. government bills, sold at a discount from face value in units of $1,000 to $1 million: 5.350% 13 weeks; 5.535% 26 weeks.

OVERNIGHT REPURCHASE RATE: 5.65%. Dealer financing rate for overnight sale and repurchase of Treasury securities. Source: Reuters.

Source: *The Wall Street Journal,* January 19, 2000, p. C26. Reprinted by permission of *The Wall Street Journal.*
© 2000 Dow Jones & Company, Inc. All Rights Reserved Worldwide. *www.wsj.com/*

market securities indirectly, with the help of financial institutions such as money market mutual funds.

default risk

The risk of late or nonpayment of principal or interest.

Second, money market instruments have low **default risk**; the risk of late or nonpayment of principal and/or interest is generally small. Since cash lent in the money markets must be available for a quick return to the lender, money market instruments can generally be issued only by high-quality borrowers with little risk of default.

Finally, money market securities must have an original maturity of one year or less. Recall from Chapter 3 that the longer the maturity of a debt security, the greater is its interest rate risk and the higher is its required rate of return. Given that adverse price movements resulting from interest rate changes are smaller for short-term securities, the short-term maturity of money market instruments helps lower the risk that interest rate changes will significantly affect the security's market value and price.

Do You Understand?

1. What the three characteristics common to money market securities are?
2. Why it is difficult for individual investors to be involved in the initial sale of a money market security?

Money Market Securities

A variety of money market securities are issued by corporations and government units to obtain short-term funds. These securities include Treasury bills, federal funds, repurchase agreements, commercial paper, negotiable certificates of deposit, and banker's acceptances. In this section, we look at the characteristics of each of these. Table 5–2 defines each of the money market securities and Table 5–3 lists the amounts of each outstanding and the interest rate on each of these instruments at the end of 1990 and 1999.

Table 5–2   Money Market Instruments

Treasury Bills—short-term obligations issued by the U.S. government.
Federal Funds—short-term funds transferred between financial institutions usually for no more than one day.
Repurchase Agreements—agreement involving the sale of securities by one party to another with a promise to repurchase the securities at a specified date and price.
Commercial Paper—short-term unsecured promissory notes issued by a company to raise short-term cash.
Negotiable Certificates of Deposit—bank-issued time deposit that specifies an interest rate and maturity date and is negotiable.
Banker Acceptances—time draft payable to a seller of goods, with payment guaranteed by a bank.

Table 5–3   Money Market Instruments Outstanding, December 1990 and 1999
         (in billions of dollars)

	Amount Outstanding		Rate of Return	
	1990	**1999**	**1990**	**1999**
Treasury bills	$527.0	$ 674.8	7.85%	5.23%
Federal funds and				
repurchase agreements	372.3	1,006.1	8.10	5.30
Commercial paper	537.8	1,284.5	8.06	5.87
Negotiable certificates of deposit	546.9	836.8	8.15	6.05
Banker's acceptance	52.1	8.3	7.93	5.24

Source: Federal Reserve Bulletin, May 1991 and December 1999, various tables. *www.bog.frb.fed.us/*

Treasury Bills

Treasury bills (T-bills) are short-term obligations of the U.S. government issued to cover current government budget shortfalls (deficits)[1] and to refinance maturing government debt. At the end of 1999 there were $674.8 billion of Treasury bills outstanding. As discussed in Chapter 4, T-bills (and other Treasury securities) are also used by the Federal Reserve as a tool in conducting monetary policy through open market operations. T-bills are sold through an auction process (described below). Original maturities are 91 days, 182 days, or 12 months, and they are issued in denominations of multiples of $1,000. The minimum allowable denomination for a T-bill bid is $1,000. A typical purchase in the newly issued T-bill market is a round lot of $5 million. However, existing T-bills can be bought and sold in an active secondary market through government securities dealers who purchase Treasury bills from the U.S. government and resell them to investors. Thus, investors wanting to purchase smaller amounts of T-bills can do so through a dealer for a fee.

Because they are backed by the U.S. government, T-bills are virtually default risk free. In fact, T-bills are often referred to as *the* risk-free asset in the United States. Further, because of their short-term nature and active secondary market, T-bills have little liquidity risk.

The New Issue and Secondary Market Trading Process for Treasury Bills. The U.S. Treasury has a formal process by which it sells new issues of Treasury bills through its regular **Treasury bill auctions**. Every week (usually on a Thursday), the amount of new 13-week and 26-week T-bills the Treasury will offer for sale is announced. Bids may be submitted by government securities dealers, financial and nonfinancial corporations, and individuals and must be received by a Federal Reserve Bank (over the Internet (through Treasury Direct), by phone, or by paper form) by the deadline of 1 P.M. on the Monday following the auction announcement. An auction tender form is presented in Figure 5–1. Allocations and prices are announced the following morning (Tuesday) and the T-bills are delivered on the Thursday following the auction. In addition, auctions of 52-week (1-year) T-bills are conducted by the U.S. Treasury on a monthly basis.

Submitted bids can be either competitive bids or noncompetitive bids. Competitive bids specify the desired quantity of T-bills and the bid price. Any bidder can submit more than one bid and can bid on up to 35 percent of the total issue size. The highest bidder receives the first allocation (allotment) of T-bills, and subsequent bids are filled in decreasing order of the bid until all T-bills auctioned that week are distributed. Thus, the auction takes the form of a "discriminating" price auction in that different bidders pay different prices. No bidder can legally receive more than 35 percent of the T-bills involved in any auction. This rule prevents one bidder from "squeezing" the market. Competitive bids are generally used by large investors and government securities dealers, and make up the majority of the auction market. Table 5-4 shows the results of the Treasury auction on January 20, 2000. At this auction, 46.61 and 39.10 percent of the submitted bids were accepted for the 13- and 26-week T-bills, respectively.

Figure 5–2 illustrates the T-bill auction for the 13-week T-bills. The highest accepted bid on the 13-week T-bills was 98.678 percent of the face value of the T-bills. Bids were filled at prices below the high. The lowest accepted bid price was 98.648 percent. The median accepted price was 98.653 percent. All bidders who submitted prices *above* 98.648 percent (categories 1 through 5 in Figure 5–2) were awarded in full (winning bids). Bidders who submitted a price below 98.648 percent (categories 7 and beyond in Figure 5–2) received no allocation of the auctioned T-bills. A portion, but not all, of the bids submitted at 98.648 were filled (category 6 in Figure 5–2). Bids submitted at 98.648 were filled on a pro rata (proportional) basis until the supply available was exhausted.

---

1. The excess of U.S. government expenditures minus revenues.

Figure 5–1   Treasury Security Auction Tender Form

PD F 5381 (I)
Department of the Treasury
Bureau of the Public Debt
(Revised October 1998)
www.treasurydirect.gov

OMB No. 1535-0069

TREASURY BILL, NOTE & BOND TENDER

TREASURY DIRECT®

For Tender Instructions, See PD F 5382

TYPE OR PRINT IN INK ONLY – TENDERS WILL NOT BE ACCEPTED WITH ALTERATIONS OR CORRECTIONS

1. BID INFORMATION *(Must Be Completed)*

Par Amount: Bid Type: *(Fill in One)*   ○ Noncompetitive
$_____   ○ Competitive at |__|__|__|.|__|__|__| %
(Sold in units of $1,000)   *(Bill bids must end in 0 or 5.)*

DEPARTMENT USE
TENDER NO.
RECEIVED BY/DATE

2. TreasuryDirect ACCOUNT NUMBER
(If NOT furnished, a new account will be opened.)

3. TAXPAYER ID NUMBER *(Must Be Completed)*
|__|__|__|-|__|__|-|__|__|__|__| OR |__|__|-|__|__|__|__|__|__|__|
Social Security Number (First-Named Owner)   Employer ID Number

ENTERED BY
APPROVED BY

4. TERM SELECTION *(Fill in One)*
(Must Be Completed)

Treasury Bill
$1,000 Minimum   Circle the Number of Reinvestments
○ 13-Week.........0 1 2 3 4
                        5 6 7 8
○ 26-Week.........0 1 2 3 4
○ 52-Week.........0 1 2

Treasury Note/Bond
$1,000 Minimum
○ 2-Year Note
○ 5-Year Note
○ 10-Year Note
○ 30-Year Bond
○ Inflation-Indexed _____
                        Term

5. ACCOUNT NAME Please Type or Print! *(Must Be Completed)*

6. ADDRESS *(For new account or if changed.)* ○ New Address?

City   State   ZIP Code

ISSUE DATE
CUSIP 912795-
CUSIP 912827-
CUSIP 912810-
FOREIGN ☐
BACKUP ☐

7. TELEPHONE NUMBERS *(For new account or if changed.)* ○ New Phone Number?

Work ( )   -   Home ( )   -

8. PAYMENT INFORMATION *(For new account only.)* Changes? Submit PD F 5178.

Routing Number |__|__|__|__|__|__|__|__|__|
Financial Institution Name _____
Account Number |__|__|__|__|__|__|__|__|__|__|__|__|
Name on Account _____
Account Type: *(Fill in One)*   ○ Checking   ○ Savings

9. PURCHASE METHOD
(Must Be Completed)

○ **Pay Direct**
   (Existing TreasuryDirect Account Only)
○ Checks: $_____
                          $_____
○ Securities: $_____
○ Other $_____
Total Payment
Attached: $_____
CHECKS ARE DEPOSITED IMMEDIATELY

REVIEW ☐
CHECK #

10. AUTHORIZATION *(Must Be Completed – Original Signature Required)*
Tender Submission: I submit this tender pursuant to the provisions of Department of the Treasury Circulars, Public Debt Series Nos. 2-86 (31 CFR Part 357) and 1-93 (31 CFR Part 356), and the applicable offering announcement. As the first-named owner and under penalties of perjury, I certify that: 1) The number shown on this form is my correct taxpayer identification number (or I am waiting for a number to be issued to me), and 2) I am not subject to backup withholding because: (a) I am exempt from backup withholding, or (b) I have not been notified by the Internal Revenue Service (IRS) that I am subject to backup withholding as a result of a failure to report all interest or dividends, or (c) the IRS has notified me that I am no longer subject to backup withholding. I further certify that all other information provided on this form is true, correct and complete.

Pay Direct: (If using this purchase method.) I authorize a debit to my account at the financial institution I designated in *TreasuryDirect* to pay for this security. I understand that the purchase price will be charged to my account on or after the settlement date. I also understand that if this transaction cannot be successfully completed, my tender can be rejected and the transaction canceled. If there is a dispute, a copy of this authorization may be provided to my financial institution.

Signature(s)   Date

SEE BACK FOR PRIVACY ACT AND PAPERWORK REDUCTION ACT NOTICE

Source: Department of Treasury, website, Bureau of Public Debt, June 1999. *www.ustreas.gov/*

With noncompetitive bids, the bidder indicates the quantity of T-bills he or she wants to buy and agrees to pay the weighted-average price of the winning competitive bids. Noncompetitive bidders get a preferential allocation—that is, all these bids are met before the remaining T-bills are allocated to the competitive bidders. Notice, from Table 5–4, that 10.16 percent ($1,196.2m./$11,778.1m.) and 11.19 percent ($1,095.1m./$9,786.3m.), respectively, of the accepted bids at the January 20, 2000, Treasury auction were noncompetitive for 13- and 26-week T-bills. This resulted in a supply of T-bills available to competitive bidders (S_C) that is lower than the total supply (S_T), because of

Table 5–4   Treasury Auction Results, January 20, 2000

	13-Week Treasury Bill Auction	26-Week Treasury Bill Auction
Bids tendered (in millions)	$25,268.1	$25,031.6
Bids accepted (in millions)	$11,778.1	$ 9,786.3
Noncompetitive bids (in millions)	$ 1,196.2	$ 1,095.1
Price	98.648%	97.202%
High price	98.678%	97.250%
Low price	98.648%	97.202%
Median price	98.653%	97.209%

Source: Department of Treasury, website, Bureau of Public Debt, January 20, 2000. *www.ustreas.gov/*

Figure 5–2   Treasury Auction Results

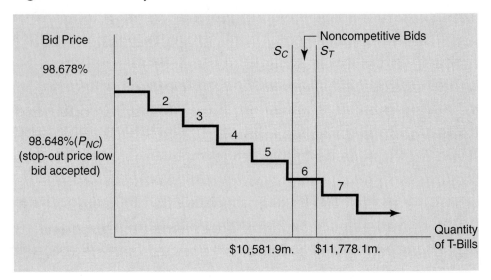

the preferential bidding status of noncompetitive bidders (i.e., noncompetitive bidders always receive a 100 percent allocation of their bids). Noncompetitive bids are limited to $1 million or less and allow small investors to participate in the T-bill auction market without incurring large risks. Small investors who are unfamiliar with money market interest rate movements can use a noncompetitive bid to avoid bidding a price too low to receive any of the T-bills or bidding too high and paying more than the fair market price.

The secondary market for T-bills is the largest of any U.S. money market security. At the heart of this market are those securities dealers designated as primary government securities dealers by the Federal Reserve Bank of New York (consisting of about 30 financial institutions) who purchase the majority of the T-bills sold competitively at auction and who create an active secondary market. In addition, there are many (approximately 500) smaller dealers who directly trade in the secondary market. Primary dealers make a market for T-bills by buying and selling securities for their own account and by trading for their customers, including depository institutions, insurance companies, pension funds, and so on. T-bill transactions by primary dealers averaged $31.03 billion per day in the first half of 1999.

The T-bill market is decentralized, with most trading transacted over the telephone. Brokers keep track of the market via closed circuit television screens located in trading rooms of the primary dealers that display bid and asked prices available at any point in time. Treasury markets are generally open from 9:00 A.M. to 3:30 P.M. EST.

www.ny.frb.org/

Figure 5–3 Secondary Market Treasury Bill Transaction

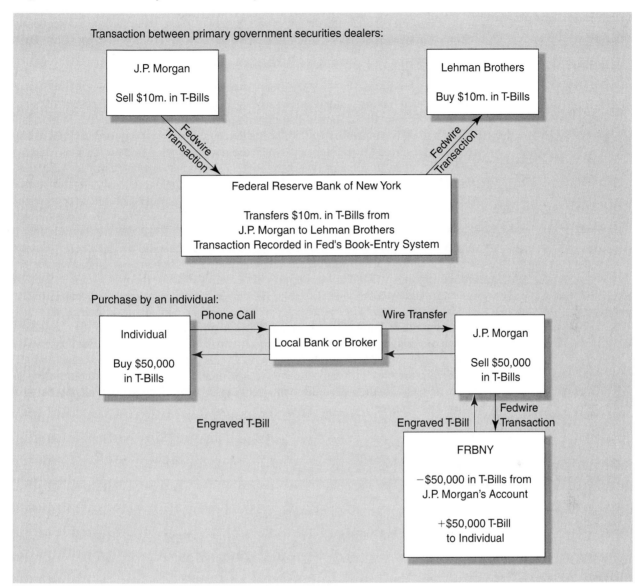

Transaction between primary government securities dealers:

J.P. Morgan		Lehman Brothers
Sell $10m. in T-Bills		Buy $10m. in T-Bills

Fedwire Transaction   *Fedwire Transaction*

Federal Reserve Bank of New York

Transfers $10m. in T-Bills from
J.P. Morgan to Lehman Brothers
Transaction Recorded in Fed's Book-Entry System

Purchase by an individual:

Phone Call   *Wire Transfer*

Individual	Local Bank or Broker	J.P. Morgan
Buy $50,000 in T-Bills		Sell $50,000 in T-Bills

Engraved T-Bill   Engraved T-Bill   Fedwire Transaction

FRBNY

−$50,000 in T-Bills from
J.P. Morgan's Account

+$50,000 T-Bill
to Individual

Secondary market T-bill transactions between primary government securities dealers are conducted over the Federal Reserve's wire transfer service—Fedwire (see Chapter 4)—and are recorded via the Federal Reserve's book-entry system.[2] We illustrate a transaction in Figure 5–3.

For example, if J.P. Morgan wants to sell $10 million of T-bills to Lehman Brothers, J.P. Morgan would instruct its district Federal Reserve Bank—the Federal Reserve Bank of New York (FRBNY)—to electronically transfer the (book-entry) T-bills, via the Fedwire, from its account to Lehman Brothers (also in the district of the FRBNY). The transaction would be recorded in the Fed's book-entry system with no physical transfer of paper necessary. An individual wanting to purchase $50,000 T-bills in the secondary market must contact his or her bank or broker. A bank or broker that is not a primary government securities dealer or a secondary market dealer must contact (via phone, fax,

www.ny.frb.org/

---

2. With a book-entry system, no physical documentation of ownership exists. Rather, ownership of Treasury securities is accounted for electronically by computer record.

or wire) one of these dealers (e.g., J.P. Morgan) to complete the transaction. The T-bill dealer will instruct its local Federal Reserve Bank to increase (credit) its T-bill account at the Fed. In exchange for the investor's $50,000, these securities are subsequently recorded in the dealer's book-entry system as an issue held for the investor. T-bill dealers maintain records identifying owners of all Treasury securities held in its account in the book-entry system.

Treasury Bill Yields.   As we discussed in Chapter 2 and above, Treasury bills are sold on a discount basis. Rather than directly paying interest on T-bills (the coupon rate is zero), the government issues T-bills at a discount from their par (or face) value. The return comes from the difference between the purchase price paid for the T-bill and the face value received at maturity. Table 5–5 lists T-bill rates as quoted in *The Wall Street Journal* for trading on January 18, 2000. Column 1 in the quote lists the maturity date of the T-bill (note the maximum maturity is less than one year). Column 2 specifies the remaining number of days until each T-bill matures. For example, at the close of trading on January 18, 2000, the T-bill maturing on January 27, 2000, would trade for an additional 8 days. Column 3, labeled Bid, is the discount yield (defined below) on the T-bill given the current selling price available to T-bill holders (i.e., the price dealers are willing to pay T-bill holders to purchase their T-bills for them). Column 4, labeled Asked, is the discount yield based on the current purchase price set by dealers that is available to investors (i.e., potential T-bill buyers). The percentage difference in the ask and bid yields is known as the spread. The spread is essentially the profit the dealers charge to conduct the trade for investors. It is part of the transaction cost incurred by investors for the trade. Column 5, labeled Chg., is the change in the Asked (discount) yield from the previous day's closing yield. Finally, the last column (column 6), labeled Ask Yld., is the Asked discount yield converted to a bond equivalent yield (see below and Chapter 2).

Table 5–5   Treasury Bill Rates

	(1)	(2)	(3)	(4)	(5)	(6)

TREASURY BILLS

Maturity	Days to Mat.	Bid	Asked	Chg.	Ask Yld.
Jan 20 '00	1	5.28	5.20	+0.06	5.27
Jan 27 '00	8	4.92	4.84	−0.07	4.91
Feb 03 '00	15	5.12	5.04	−0.05	5.12
Feb 10 '00	22	5.11	5.03	−0.06	5.12
Feb 17 '00	29	5.13	5.05	−0.09	5.14
Feb 24 '00	36	5.12	5.08	−0.07	5.18
Mar 02 '00	43	5.17	5.13	−0.05	5.23
Mar 09 '00	50	5.18	5.14	−0.02	5.25
Mar 16 '00	57	5.18	5.14	−0.03	5.25
Mar 23 '00	64	5.19	5.17	−0.03	5.29
Mar 30 '00	71	5.19	5.17	−0.03	5.30
Apr 06 '00	78	5.23	5.21	−0.02	5.34
Apr 13 '00	**85**	**5.23**	**5.22**	**−0.02**	**5.36**
Apr 20 '00	92	5.31	5.29	....	5.44
Apr 20 '00	92	5.37	5.36	+0.03	5.51
Apr 27 '00	99	5.29	5.27	−0.02	5.42
May 04 '00	106	5.35	5.33	−0.02	5.49
May 11 '00	113	5.38	5.36	−0.01	5.53
May 18 '00	120	5.39	5.37	−0.02	5.54
May 25 '00	127	5.41	5.39	−0.03	5.57
Jun 01 '00	134	5.46	5.44	−0.02	5.63
Jun 08 '00	141	5.47	5.45	−0.01	5.65
Jun 15 '00	148	5.46	5.44	−0.02	5.64
Jun 22 '00	155	5.51	5.49	....	5.70
Jun 29 '00	162	5.48	5.46	−0.02	5.68
Jul 06 '00	169	5.48	5.46	−0.01	5.68
Jul 13 '00	**176**	**5.43**	**5.42**	**....**	**5.64**
Jul 20 '00	183	5.53	5.51	−0.01	5.75
Jul 20 '00	183	5.53	5.52	−0.02	5.76
Aug 17 '00	211	5.59	5.57	+0.01	5.82
Sep 14 '00	239	5.66	5.64	....	5.90
Oct 12 '00	267	5.73	5.71	+0.01	5.99
Nov 09 '00	295	5.77	5.75	+0.01	6.05
Dec 07 '00	323	5.77	5.75	....	6.07

The discount yield (*dy*) on a T-bill is calculated as follows:

$$i_{\text{T-bill}} (dy) = \frac{P_F - P_0}{P_F} \times \frac{360}{h}$$

where

$i_{\text{T-bill}}$ = Annualized yield on the T-bill

P_F = Price (face value) paid to the T-bill holder
P_0 = Purchase price of the T-bill
h = Number of days until the T-bill matures

Example 5–1   Calculating a Treasury Bill Yield

Suppose that you purchase a 182-day T-bill for $9,650. The T-bill has a face value of $10,000. The T-bill's discount yield is calculated as:

$$i_{\text{T-bill}} (dy) = \frac{\$10,000 - \$9,650}{\$10,000} \times \frac{360}{182} = 6.92\%$$

Thus, 6.92 percent is the Asked discount yield on this T-bill.[3]

Remember, from Chapter 2, that the discount yield differs from a true rate of return (or bond equivalent yield) for two reasons: (1) the base price used is the face value of the T-bill and not the purchase price of the T-bill, and (2) a 360-day year rather than a 365-day year is used. The bond equivalent yield uses a 365-day year and the purchase price, rather than the face value of the T-bill, as the base price. Thus, the formula for a bond equivalent yield on a T-bill, $i_{\text{T-bill}}$ (*bey*), is:

$$i_{\text{T-bill}} (bey) = \frac{P_F - P_0}{P_0} \times \frac{365}{h}$$

For example, the bond equivalent yield (or Ask Yld.) in Example 5–1 is calculated as:

$$i_{\text{T-bill}} = \frac{\$10,000 - \$9,650}{\$9,650} \times \frac{365}{182} = 7.27\%$$

A Treasury bill's price can be calculated from the quote reported in the financial press (e.g., *The Wall Street Journal*) by rearranging the yield equations listed above. Specifically, for the Asked discount yield, the required market ask price would be:

$$P_0 = P_F - \left[i_{\text{T-bill}} (dy) \times \frac{h}{360} \times P_F\right]$$

and for the bond equivalent yield:

$$P_0 = P_F \bigg/ \left[1 + \left(i_{\text{T-bill}} (bey) \times \frac{h}{365}\right)\right]$$

Example 5–2   Calculation of Treasury Bill Price from a *Wall Street Journal* Quote

From Table 5–5, the Asked (or discount) yield on the T-bill maturing on January 27, 2000, is 4.84 percent. The T-bill price for these T-bills is calculated as:

---

3. Remember, from Chapter 2, that the effective annual return (over a 12-month investment period) on this T-bill is:

$(1 + .0692/(360/182))^{360/182} - 1 = 7.04\%$

$$P_0 = \$10{,}000 - \left[.0484 \times \frac{8}{360} \times \$10{,}000\right] = \$9{,}989.24$$

or using the Ask Yld. (or the bond equivalent yield) on the T-bill, 4.91 percent:

$$P_0 = \$10{,}000 / \left[1 + \left(.0491 \times \frac{8}{365}\right)\right] = \$9{,}989.25$$

Federal Funds

federal funds

Short-term funds transferred between financial institutions, usually for a period of one day.

federal funds rate

The interest rate for borrowing fed funds.

Federal funds (fed funds) are short-term funds transferred between financial institutions, usually for a period of one day. The institution that borrows fed funds incurs a liability on its balance sheet, "federal funds purchased," while the institution that lends the fed funds records an asset, "federal funds sold." The overnight (or one day) interest rate for borrowing fed funds is the **federal funds rate**.

Federal Funds Yields. Federal funds (fed funds) are single-payment loans—they pay interest only once, at maturity (see Chapter 2). Further, fed fund transactions take the form of short-term (mostly overnight) *unsecured* loans. Quoted interest rates on fed funds, i_{ff}, assume a 360-day year. Therefore, to compare interest rates on fed funds with other securities such as Treasury bills, the quoted fed funds interest rate must be converted into a bond equivalent rate or yield, i_{bey}.

Example 5–3 Conversion of Federal Funds Rate of Interest to a Bond Equivalent Rate

From Table 5–1, the overnight fed funds rate on January 18, 2000, was 6 percent. The conversion of the fed funds rate to a bond equivalent rate is calculated as follows:

$$i_{bey} = i_{ff}\,(365/360)$$
$$= 6.0\%\,(365/360) = 6.083\%$$

In addition to being the cost of unsecured, overnight, interbank borrowing, the federal funds rate is of particular importance because, as was discussed in Chapter 4, the fed funds rate is a focus or target rate in the conduct of monetary policy.

Trading in the Federal Funds Market. Commercial banks conduct the vast majority of transactions in the fed funds market. This is because fed fund transactions are created by banks borrowing and lending excess reserves held at their Federal Reserve Bank (see Chapter 4), using Fedwire, the Federal Reserve's wire transfer network, to complete the transaction. Banks with excess reserves lend fed funds, while banks with deficient reserves borrow fed funds.

Federal funds transactions can be initiated by either the lending or the borrowing bank, with negotiations between any pair of commercial banks taking place directly over the telephone. Alternatively, trades can be arranged through fed funds brokers (such as Garban Ltd. and RMJ Securities Corp), who charge a small fee for bringing the two parties to fed funds together.[4]

Figure 5–4 illustrates a fed funds transaction. For example, a bank that finds itself with \$75 million in excess reserves (e.g., Chase) can call its **correspondent banks** (banks with which it has reciprocal accounts and agreements) to see if they need overnight reserves. The bank will then sell its excess reserves to those correspondent

correspondent banks

Banks with reciprocal accounts and agreements.

---

4. Brokerage fees are often as low as 50 cents per \$1 million.

Figure 5–4 Federal Funds Transaction

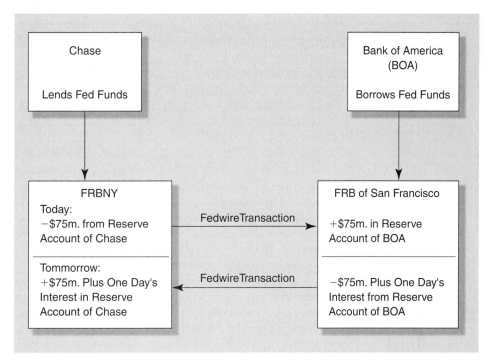

banks that offer the highest rates for these fed funds (e.g., Bank of America). When a transaction is agreed upon, the lending bank (Chase) instructs its district Federal Reserve Bank (e.g., the FRBNY) to transfer the $75 million in excess reserves to the borrowing bank's (Bank of America) reserve account at its Federal Reserve Bank (e.g., the Federal Reserve Bank of San Francisco). The Federal Reserve System's wire transfer network, Fedwire, is used to complete the transfer of funds. The next day, the funds are transferred back, via Fedwire, from the borrowing bank to the lending bank's reserve account at the Federal Reserve Bank plus one day's interest.[5] Overnight fed fund loans will likely be based on an oral agreement between the two parties and are generally unsecured loans.

Repurchase Agreements

repurchase agreement

An agreement involving the sale of securities by one party to another with a promise to repurchase the securities at a specified price and on a specified date.

reverse repurchase agreement

An agreement involving the purchase of securities by one party from another with the promise to sell them back.

A **repurchase agreement** (repo or RP) is an agreement involving the sale of securities by one party to another with a promise to repurchase the securities at a specified price and on a specified date in the future. Thus, a repurchase agreement is essentially a collateralized fed funds loan, with the collateral backing taking the form of securities. The securities used most often in repos are U.S. Treasury securities (e.g., T-bills) and government agency securities (e.g., Fannie Mae). A **reverse repurchase agreement** (reverse repo) is an agreement involving the purchase of securities by one party from another with the promise to sell them back at a given date in the future.

---

5. Increasingly, participants in the fed funds markets do not hold balances at the Federal Reserve (e.g., commercial banks that do not belong to the Federal Reserve System). In this case, the fed funds transaction is settled in immediately available funds—fed funds on deposit at the lending bank that may be transferred or withdrawn with no delay. A federal funds broker, typically a commercial bank, matches up institutions using a telecommunications network that links federal funds brokers with participating institutions. Upon maturity of the fed funds loan, the borrowing bank's fed fund demand deposit account at the lending bank is debited for the total value of the loan and the borrowing bank pays the lending bank an interest payment for the use of the fed funds. Most of these fed fund transactions are for more than $5 million (they averaged around $45 million in the late 1990s) and usually have a one- to seven-day maturity.

Because the parties in every repurchase agreement transaction have opposite perspectives, the titles repo and reverse repo can be applied to the same transaction. That is, a given transaction is a repo from the point of view of the securities' seller and a reverse repo from the point of view of the securities' buyer. Whether a transaction is termed a *repo* or a *reverse repo* generally depends on which party initiated the transaction. Most repos have very short terms to maturity (generally from 1 to 14 days), but there is a growing market for longer-term 1- to 3-month repos). Repos with a maturity of less than one week generally involve denominations of $25 million or more. Longer-term repos are more often in denominations of $10 million.

The Trading Process for Repurchase Agreements. Repurchase agreements are arranged either directly between two parties or with the help of brokers and dealers. Figure 5–5 illustrates a $75 million repurchase agreement of Treasury bonds arranged directly between two parties (e.g., Chase and Bank of America). The repo buyer, Chase, arranges to purchase T-bonds from the repo seller, Bank of America, with an agreement that the seller will repurchase the T-bonds within a stated period of time—one day. In most repurchase agreements, the repo buyer acquires title to the securities for the term of the agreement.

Once the transaction is agreed upon, the repo buyer, Chase, instructs its district Federal Reserve Bank (the FRBNY) to transfer $75 million in excess reserves, via Fedwire, to the repo seller's reserve account. The repo seller, Bank of America, instructs its district Federal Reserve Bank (the FRB of San Francisco) to transfer $75 million from its T-bond account via securities Fedwire to the repo buyer's T-bond account. Upon maturity of the repo (one day in this example), these transactions are

Figure 5–5 A Repurchase Agreement Transaction

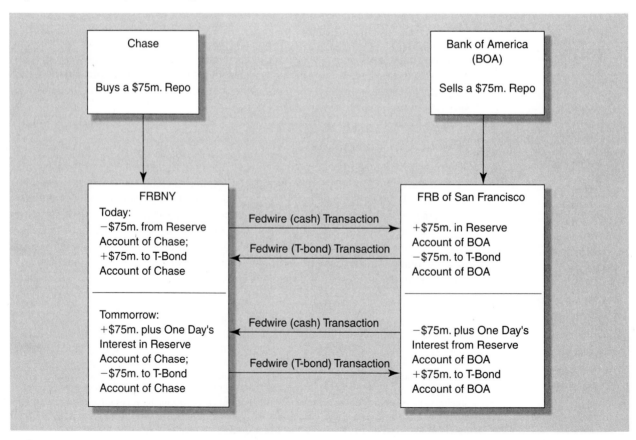

reversed. In addition, the repo seller transfers additional funds (representing the one day's interest) from its reserve account to the reserve account of the repo buyer.

As noted in Chapter 4, repurchase agreements are used by the Federal Reserve to help it conduct open market operations as part of its overall monetary policy strategy. When monetary adjustments are intended to be temporary (often smoothing out fluctuations in interest rates or the money supply), the Fed uses repurchase agreements with dealers or banks. The maturities of the repos used by the Federal Reserve are rarely longer than 15 days. Government securities dealers—such as the largest investment and commercial banks—engage in repos to manage their liquidity and to take advantage of anticipated changes in interest rates.

Repurchase Agreement Yields. Because Treasury securities back repurchase agreements, they are low credit risk investments and have lower interest rates than uncollateralized fed funds.[6] The spread between the rate on collateralized repos versus uncollateralized fed funds has usually been in the order of 0.25 percent, or 25 basis points. The yield on repurchase agreements is calculated as the annualized percentage difference between the initial selling price of the securities and the contracted (re)purchase price (the selling price plus interest paid on the repurchase agreement), using a 360-day year. Specifically:

$$i_{RA} = \frac{P_F - P_0}{P_0} \times \frac{360}{h}$$

where

P_F = Repurchase price of the securities (equals the selling price plus interest paid on the repurchase agreement)
P_0 = Selling price of the securities
h = Number of days until the repo matures

Example 5–4 Calculation of a Yield on a Repurchase Agreement

Suppose a bank enters a reverse repurchase agreement in which it agrees to buy Treasury securities from one of its correspondent banks at a price of $10,000,000, with the promise to sell these securities back at a price of $10,008,548 ($10,000,000 plus interest of $8,548) after five days. The yield on this repo to the bank is calculated as follows:

$$i_{RA} = \frac{\$10,008,548 - \$10,000,000}{\$10,000,000} \times \frac{360}{5} = 6.15\%$$

Because of their common use as a source of overnight funding and the fact that repos are essentially collateralized fed funds, the Federal Reserve generally classifies federal funds and repurchase agreements together in their statistical data. Together, these amounted to $1,006.1 billion outstanding in 1999 (see Table 5–3).

Some notable differences exist, however, between repurchase agreements and fed funds. For example, repurchase agreements are less liquid than fed funds since they can only be arranged after an agreed upon type of collateral is posted (i.e., repos are hard to arrange at the close of the banking day, whereas fed funds can be arranged at

6. There is a one-day interest rate risk that may impact credit risk if interest rates suddenly rise so that the market value of the collateral backing the repo falls. To avoid the risk many repo transactions require a securities "haircut" to be imposed at the time of the transaction—more securities are used to back the cash part of the transaction. For example, Bank A may send $100 million in cash to Bank B. In turn, Bank B sends $105 million in securities as collateral to back the cash loan from A.

Figure 5–6 Commercial Paper and Prime Rate, 1971–1999

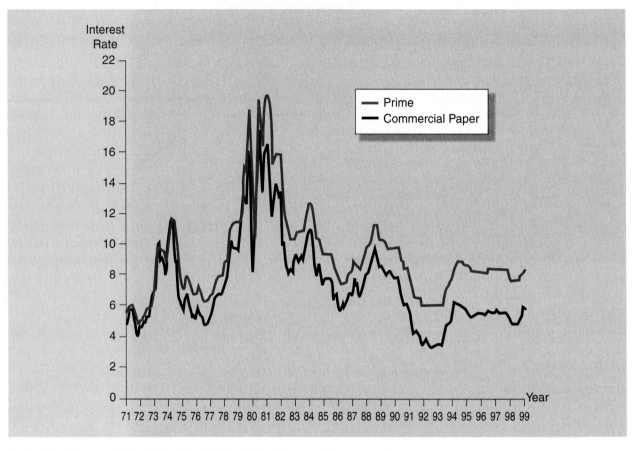

Source: Federal Reserve Board, website, "Selected Interest Rates," January 2000. *www.bog.frb.fed.us/*

very short notice, even a few minutes). Further, nonbanks are more frequent users of repurchase agreements.

Commercial Paper

commercial paper

An unsecured short-term promissory note issued by a company to raise short-term cash, often to finance working capital requirements.

www.sec.com/

Commercial paper is an unsecured short-term promissory note issued by a corporation to raise short-term cash, often to finance working capital requirements. Commercial paper is the largest (in terms of dollar value outstanding) of the money market instruments, with $1,284.5 billion outstanding as of 1999. One reason for such large amounts of commercial paper outstanding is that companies with strong credit ratings can generally borrow money at a lower interest rate by issuing commercial paper than by directly borrowing (via loans) from banks. Figure 5–6 illustrates the difference between commercial paper rates and the prime rate for borrowing from banks from 1971 through 1999.[7]

Commercial paper is generally sold in denominations of $100,000, $250,000, $500,000, and $1 million. Maturities generally range from 1 to 270 days—the most common maturities are between 20 and 45 days. This 270-day maximum is due to a Securities and Exchange Commission (SEC) rule that securities with a maturity of more than 270 days must go through the time-consuming and costly registration

7. It should be noted, however, that the best borrowers from banks can borrow below prime. Prime rate in today's banking world is viewed as a rate to be charged to an average borrower—best borrowers pay prime rate minus some spread.

Figure 5–7   Direct versus Dealer Placements of Commercial Paper

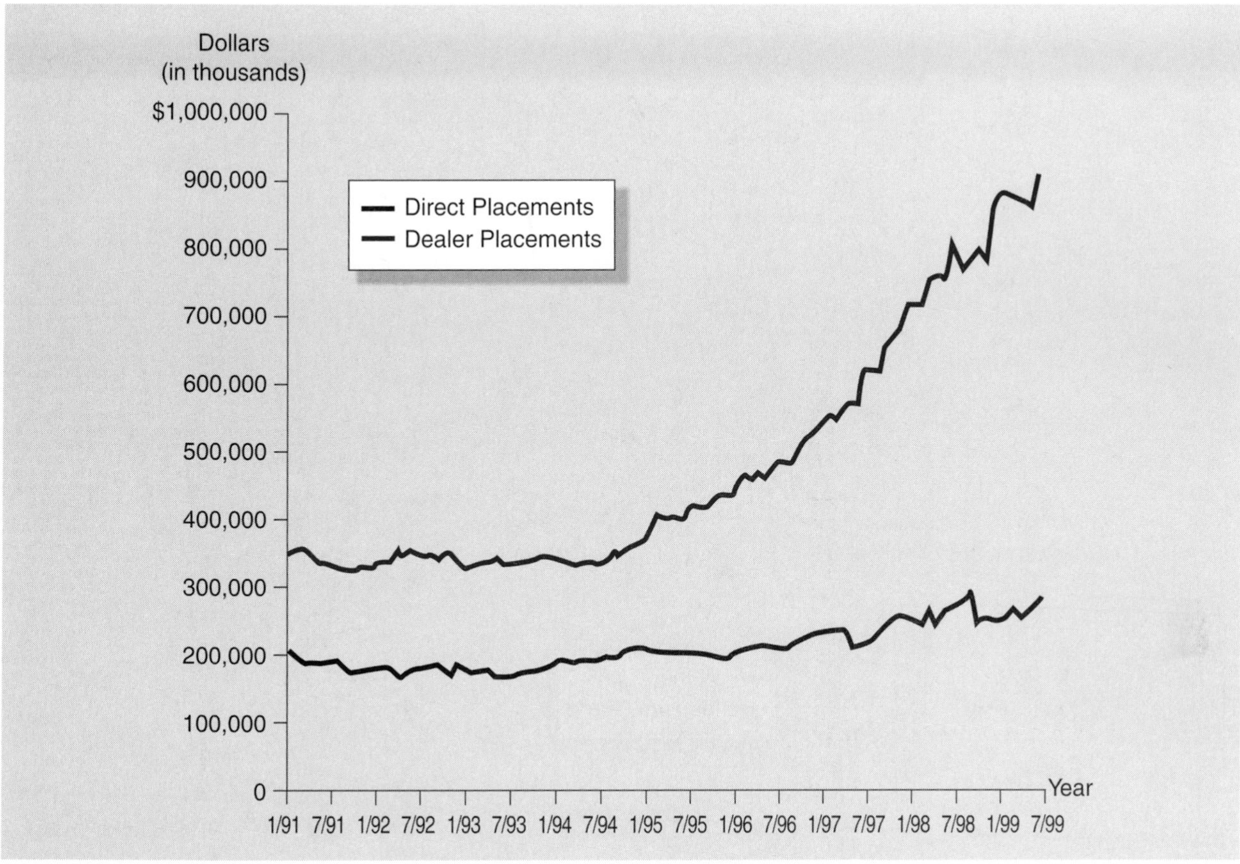

Source: Federal Reserve Board, website, "Research and Data," January 2000. *www.bog.frb.fed.us/*

process to become a public debt offering (i.e., a corporate bond). Commercial paper can be sold directly by the issuers to a buyer such as a mutual fund (a direct placement) or can be sold indirectly by dealers in the commercial paper market. The dollar value (in thousands of dollars) of each method of issue from 1991 through 1999 is reported in Figure 5–7.

Commercial paper is generally held from the time of issue until maturity by investors. Thus, there is not an active secondary market for commercial paper.[8] Because commercial paper is not actively traded and because it is also unsecured debt, the credit rating of the issuing company is of particular importance in determining the marketability of a commercial paper issue. Credit ratings provide potential investors with information regarding the ability of the issuing firm to repay the borrowed funds, as promised, and to compare the commercial paper issues of different companies. Several credit rating firms rate commercial paper issues (e.g., Standard & Poor's, Moody's, and Fitch IBCA, Inc.). Standard & Poor's rates commercial paper from A-1 for highest quality issues to D for lowest quality issues, while Moody's rates commercial paper from P-1 for highest quality issues to "not rated" for lowest quality issues. Virtually all companies that issue commercial paper obtain ratings from at least one rating services company, and most obtain two rating evaluations.

www.standardandpoors. com/

www.moodys.com/

8. This is partly because any dealer that issues (underwrites) commercial paper of a given company will generally buy back that commercial paper should a buyer wish to sell it. Thus, in general, underwriters act as counterparties in any secondary market trade.

Figure 5–8 Rates on Prime versus Medium Grade Commercial Paper, 1997–1999

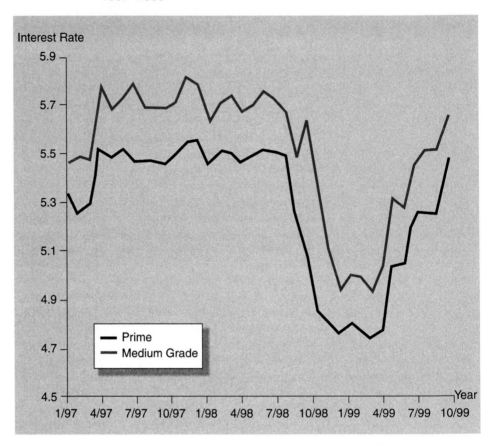

Source: Federal Reserve Board, website, "Research and Data," January 2000. *www.bog.frb.fed.us/*

The better the credit rating on a commercial paper issue, the lower the interest rate on the issue. The spread between the interest rate on medium grade commercial paper and prime grade commercial paper is shown in Figure 5–8 and has generally been on the order of 0.22 percent (22 basis points) per year.

Commercial paper issuers with lower than prime credit ratings often back their commercial paper issues with a line of credit obtained from a commercial bank. In these cases, the bank agrees to make the promised payment on the commercial paper if the issuer cannot pay off the debt on maturity. Thus, a letter of credit backing commercial paper effectively substitutes the credit rating of the issuer with the credit rating of the bank. This reduces the risk to the purchasers of the paper and results in a lower interest rate (and high credit rating) on the commercial paper. In other cases, an issuer arranges a line of credit with a bank (a loan commitment) and draws on this line if it has insufficient funds to meet the repayment of the commercial paper issue at maturity.

The Trading Process for Commercial Paper. Commercial paper is sold to investors either directly (about 25 percent of all issues in 1999—see Figure 5–7), using the issuer's own sales force (e.g., GMAC), or indirectly through brokers and dealers (about 75 percent of all issues in 1999), such as major bank subsidiaries that specialize in investment banking activities (so-called Section 20 subsidiaries) and investment banks underwriting the issues.[9] Commercial paper underwritten and issued through brokers and dealers is more expensive to the issuer, usually increasing the cost of the

---

9. Commercial bank subsidiaries have only been allowed to underwrite commercial paper since 1987.

issue by one-tenth to one-eighth of a percent, reflecting an underwriting cost. In return, the dealer guarantees, through a firm commitment underwriting, the sale of the whole issue. To help achieve this goal, the dealer contacts prospective buyers of the commercial paper, determines the appropriate discount rate on the commercial paper, and relays any special requests for the commercial paper in terms of specific quantities and maturities to the issuer. When a company issues commercial paper through a dealer, a request made at the beginning of the day by a potential investor (such as a money market mutual fund) for a particular maturity is often completed by the end of the day.

When commercial paper is issued directly from an issuer to a buyer, the company saves the cost of the dealer (and the underwriting services) but must find appropriate investors and determine the discount rate on the paper that will place the complete issue. When the firm decides how much commercial paper it wants to issue, it posts offering rates to potential buyers based on its own estimates of investor demand. The firm then monitors the flow of money during the day and adjusts its commercial paper rates depending on investor demand.

Commercial Paper Yields.   Like Treasury bills, yields on commercial paper are quoted on a discount basis—the discount return to commercial paper holders is the annualized percentage difference between the price paid for the paper and the par value using a 360-day year. Specifically:

$$i_{cp}(dy) = \frac{P_F - P_0}{P_F} \times \frac{360}{h}$$

and when converted to a bond equivalent yield:

$$i_{cp}(bey) = \frac{P_F - P_0}{P_0} \times \frac{365}{h}$$

Example 5–5   Calculation of the Yield on Commercial Paper

Suppose an investor purchases 95-day commercial paper with a par value of $1,000,000 for a price of $985,000. The discount yield (dy) on the commercial paper is calculated as:

$$i_{cp}(dy) = \frac{\$1,000,000 - \$985,000}{\$1,000,000} \times \frac{360}{95} = 5.68\%$$

and the bond equivalent yield (bey) is:

$$i_{cp}(bey) = \frac{\$10,000,000 - \$985,000}{\$985,000} \times \frac{365}{95} = 5.85\%$$

Negotiable Certificates of Deposits

negotiable certificate of deposit

A bank-issued, fixed maturity, interest-bearing time deposit that specifies an interest rate and maturity date and is negotiable.

bearer instrument

An instrument in which the holder at maturity receives the principal and interest.

A **negotiable certificate of deposit** (CD) is a bank-issued time deposit that specifies an interest rate and maturity date and is negotiable (i.e., salable) in the secondary market. As of December 1999, there were $836.8 billion of negotiable CDs outstanding. A negotiable CD is a **bearer instrument**—whoever holds the CD when it matures receives the principal and interest. A negotiable CD can be traded any number of times in secondary markets; therefore, the original buyer is not necessarily the owner at maturity.[10] Negotiable CDs have denominations that range from $100,000 to $10 million; $1 million is the most common denomination. The large denominations make negotiable CDs

---

10. By contrast, retail CDs with face values under $100,000 are not traded. Thus, a negotiable CD is more "liquid" to an investor than a retail CD or time deposit.

too large for most individuals to buy. However, negotiable CDs are often purchased by money market mutual funds (see Chapter 18), which pool funds of individual investors and allow this group to indirectly purchase negotiable CDs. Negotiable CD maturities range from two weeks to one year, with most having a maturity of one to four months.

While CDs have been used by banks since the early 1900s, they were not issued in a negotiable form until the early 1960s. Because of rising interest rates in the 1950s and significant interest rate penalties charged on the early withdrawal of funds invested in CDs, large CDs became unattractive to deposit holders. The result was a significant drop in deposits at banks (disintermediation). In 1961, First National City Bank of New York (now known as Citigroup) issued the first negotiable CD, and money market dealers agreed to make a secondary market in them. These negotiable CDs were well received and helped banks regain many of their lost deposits. Indeed, the success of negotiable CDs helped bank managers focus more actively on managing the liquidity side of their portfolios (see Chapter 22).

The Trading Process for Negotiable Certificates of Deposit. Banks issuing negotiable CDs post a daily set of rates for the most popular maturities of their negotiable CDs, normally 1-, 2-, 3-, 6-, and 12-months. Then, subject to its funding needs, the bank tries to sell as many CDs to investors who are likely to hold them as investments rather than sell them to the secondary market.

In some cases, the bank and the CD investor directly negotiate a rate, the maturity, and the size of the CD. Once this is done, the issuing bank delivers the CD to a custodian bank specified by the investor. The custodian bank verifies the CD, debits the amount to the investor's account, and credits the amount to the issuing bank. This is done though the Fedwire system by transferring fed funds from the custodian bank's reserve account at the Fed to the issuing bank's reserve account.

The secondary market for negotiable CDs allows investors to buy existing negotiable CDs rather than new issues. While it is not a very active market, the secondary market for negotiable CDs is made up of a linked network of approximately 15 brokers and dealers using telephones to transact. The secondary market is predominantly located in New York City, along with most of the brokers and dealers.

The mechanics of the secondary market are similar to those of the primary market for negotiable CDs. Certificates are physically transported between traders or their custodian banks. The custodian bank verifies the certificate and records the deposit in the investor's account. Most transactions executed in the morning are usually settled the same day; most transactions executed later in the day are settled the next business day.

Negotiable CD Yields. Negotiable CD rates are negotiated between the bank and the CD buyer. Large, well-known banks can offer CDs at slightly lower rates than smaller, less well-known banks. This is due partly to the lower perceived default risk and greater marketability of well-known banks and partly to the belief that larger banks are often "too big to fail"—regulators will bail out troubled large banks and protect large depositors beyond the explicit ($100,000) deposit cap under the current FDIC insurance program (see Chapter 14). Interest rates on negotiable CDs are generally quoted on an interest-bearing basis using a 360-day year. CDs with a maturity of more than one year generally pay interest semiannually.

Example 5–6 Calculation of the Secondary Market Value of a Negotiable CD

A bank has issued a 6-month, $1 million negotiable CD with a 7 percent annual interest rate. Thus, the CD holder will receive:

$$FV = \$1m. (1 + .07/2) = \$1,035,000$$

in six months in exchange for $1 million deposited in the bank today.

Immediately after the CD is issued, the market rate on the $1 million CD falls to 6 percent. As a result, the secondary market price of the $1 million face value CD increases as follows:

$$PV = 1,035,000/(1 + .06/2) = \$1,004,854$$

Banker's Acceptances

banker's acceptance

A time draft payable to a seller of goods, with payment guaranteed by a bank.

A **banker's acceptance** is a time draft payable to a seller of goods, with payment guaranteed by a bank. There were $8.3 billion banker's acceptances outstanding in 1999. Time drafts issued by a bank are orders for the bank to pay a specified amount of money to the bearer of the time draft on a given date.

The Trading Process for Banker's Acceptances.   Many banker's acceptances arise from international trade transactions and the underlying letters of credit (or time drafts) that are used to finance trade in goods that have yet to be shipped from a foreign exporter (seller) to a domestic importer (buyer). Foreign exporters often prefer that banks act as guarantors for payment before sending goods to domestic importers, particularly when the foreign supplier has not previously done business with the domestic importer on a regular basis. In the United States, the majority of all acceptances are originated in New York, Chicago, and San Francisco. The U.S. bank insures the international transaction by stamping "Accepted" on a time draft written against the letter of credit between the exporter and the importer, signifying its obligation to pay the foreign exporter (or its bank) on a specified date should the importer fail to pay for the goods. Foreign exporters can then hold the banker's acceptance (the accepted time draft written against the letter of credit) until the date specified on the letter of credit. If they have an immediate need for cash, they can sell the acceptance before that date at a discount from the face value to a buyer in the money market (e.g., a bank).

We illustrate the process by which an international trade-related banker's acceptance is created in Figure 5–9. The creation of a banker's acceptance generally begins when a domestic importer, after placing a purchase order from a foreign exporter (1), arranges a letter of credit through its U.S. bank (2). The bank subsequently notifies the foreign exporter (3) that, upon meeting the delivery requirements, the exporter is entitled to draw a time draft against the letter of credit at the importer's bank (i.e., withdraw money) for the amount of the transaction. After the export order is shipped (4), the foreign exporter presents the time draft and the shipping papers to its own (foreign) bank (5), who forwards these to the domestic importer's U.S. bank. The U.S. bank stamps the time draft as accepted and the draft becomes a banker's acceptance (6).

At this point, the U.S. bank either returns the stamped time draft (now a banker's acceptance) to the foreign exporter's bank and payment is made on the maturity date (e.g., in three months' time), or the U.S. bank immediately pays the foreign bank (and implicitly the exporter) the discounted value of the banker's acceptance (7). In either case, the foreign bank pays the foreign importer for the goods (8) (either on the maturity date of the banker's acceptance or immediately based on a discounted value). When the banker's acceptance matures, the domestic importer must pay its U.S. bank for the purchases (9), and the U.S. bank sends the domestic importer the shipping papers (10).

If the U.S. bank pays the foreign exporter's bank for the acceptance before the maturity date (on a discounted basis), the bank can either hold the acceptance as an investment until it matures or sell the banker's acceptance in the secondary market. In this case, the ultimate bearer will receive the face value of the banker's acceptance on maturity.

Further, because banker's acceptances are payable to the bearer at maturity, they can and are traded in secondary markets. Maturities on banker's acceptances traded in

Figure 5–9 Creation of Banker's Acceptance

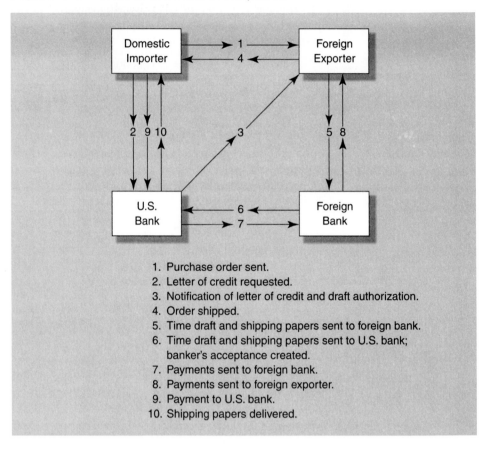

1. Purchase order sent.
2. Letter of credit requested.
3. Notification of letter of credit and draft authorization.
4. Order shipped.
5. Time draft and shipping papers sent to foreign bank.
6. Time draft and shipping papers sent to U.S. bank; banker's acceptance created.
7. Payments sent to foreign bank.
8. Payments sent to foreign exporter.
9. Payment to U.S. bank.
10. Shipping papers delivered.

secondary markets range from 30 to 270 days. Denominations of banker's acceptances are determined by the size of the original transaction (between the domestic importer and the foreign exporter). Once in the secondary markets, however, banker's acceptances are often bundled and traded in round lots, mainly of $100,000 and $500,000.

Only the largest U.S. banks are active in the banker's acceptance market. Because the risk of default is very low (essentially an investor is buying a security that is fully backed by commercial bank guarantees), interest rates on banker's acceptance are low. Specifically, there is a form of double protection underlying banker's acceptances that reduces their default risk. Since it requires both the importer and the importer's bank to default on the transaction before the investor is subject to risk, the investor is also protected by the value of the goods imported to which he or she now has a debtor's claim—the goods underlying the transaction can be viewed as collateral. Like T-bills and commercial paper, banker's acceptances are sold on a discounted basis.

Comparison of Money Market Securities

Having reviewed the different money market securities, it should be obvious that the different securities have a number of characteristics in common: large denominations, low default risk, and short maturities. It should also be noted that these securities are quite different in terms of their liquidity. For example, Treasury bills have an extensive secondary market. Thus, these money market securities can be converted into cash quickly and with little loss in value. Commercial paper, on the other hand, has no organized secondary market. These cannot be converted into cash quickly unless resold to the original dealer/underwriter, and conversion may involve a relatively higher cost. Federal funds also have no secondary market trading, since they are typically overnight loan transactions and are not intended as investments to be held beyond very short horizons (thus, the lack of a secondary market is inconsequential). Indeed, longer-horizon holders simply roll over their holdings or, in the case of those in need of liquidity, simply do not renew their fed fund loans. Bank negotiable CDs can also be traded on secondary markets, but in recent years trading has been inactive, as most negotiable CDs are being bought by "buy and hold" oriented money market mutual funds, as are banker's acceptances.

Money Market Participants

The major money market participants are the U.S. Treasury, the Federal Reserve, commercial banks, money market brokers and dealers, corporations, and other financial institutions such as mutual funds. Table 5–6 summarizes the role (issuer or investor) each of these participants plays in the markets for the various money market securities.

The U.S. Treasury

www.ustreas.gov/

The U.S. Treasury raises significant amounts of funds in the money market when it issues T-bills. T-bills are the most actively traded of the money market securities. T-bills allow the U.S. government to raise money to meet unavoidable short-term expenditure needs prior to the receipt of tax revenues. Tax receipts are generally concentrated around quarterly dates, but government expenditures are more evenly distributed over the year.

Table 5–6   Money Market Participants

Instrument	Principal Issuer	Principal Investor
Treasury bills	U.S. Treasury	Federal Reserve System Commercial banks Brokers and dealers Other financial institutions Corporations
Federal funds	Commercial banks	Commercial banks
Repurchase agreement	Federal Reserve System Commercial banks Brokers and dealers Other financial institutions	Federal Reserve System Commercial banks Brokers and dealers Other financial institutions Corporations
Commercial paper	Commercial banks Other financial institutions Corporations	Brokers and dealers Corporations
Negotiable CDs	Commercial banks	Brokers and dealers Corporations Other financial institutions
Banker's acceptances	Commercial banks	Commercial banks Brokers and dealers Corporations

www.bog.frb.fed.us/

The Federal Reserve

The Federal Reserve is a key (arguably the most important) participant in the money markets. The Federal Reserve holds T-bills (as well as T-notes and T-bonds) to conduct open market transactions—purchasing T-bills when it wants to increase the money supply, and selling T-bills when it wants to decrease the money supply. The Federal Reserve often uses repurchase agreements and reverse repos to temporarily smooth interest rates and the money supply. Moreover, the Fed targets the federal funds rate on interbank loans as part of its overall monetary policy strategy, which can in turn affect other money market rates. Finally, the Fed operates the discount window, which it can use to influence the supply of bank reserves to commercial banks and ultimately the demand for and supply of fed funds and repos.

Commercial Banks

Commercial banks are the most diverse group of participants in the money markets. As Table 5–6 shows, banks participate as issuers and/or investors of almost all money market instruments discussed above. For example, banks are the major issuers of negotiable CDs, banker's acceptances, federal funds, and repurchase agreements.

The importance of banks in the money markets is driven in part by their need to meet reserve requirements imposed by regulation. For example, during periods of economic expansion, heavy loan demand can produce reserve deficiencies for banks (i.e., their actual reserve holdings are pushed below the minimums required by regulation). Additional reserves can be obtained by borrowing fed funds from other banks, engaging in a repurchase agreement, selling negotiable CDs, or selling commercial paper.[11] Conversely, during contractionary periods, many banks have excess reserves that they can use to purchase Treasury securities, trade fed funds, engage in a reverse repo, and so on.

Brokers and Dealers

Brokers' and dealers' services are important to the smooth functioning of money markets. We have alluded to various categories of brokers and dealers in this chapter. First are the 30 primary government security dealers. This group of participants plays a key role in marketing new issues of Treasury bills (and other Treasury securities). Primary government securities dealers also make the market in Treasury bills, buying securities from the Federal Reserve when they are issued and selling them in the secondary market. Secondary market transactions in the T-bill markets are transacted in the trading rooms of these primary dealers. These dealers also assist the Federal Reserve when it uses the repo market to temporarily increase or decrease the supply of bank reserves available.

The second group of brokers and dealers are money and security brokers. The five major brokers in this group are Cantor, Fitzgerald Securities Corp., Garban Ltd., Liberty, RMJ Securities Corp., and Hill Farber. When government securities dealers trade with each other, they often use this group of brokers as intermediaries. These brokers also play a major role in linking buyers and sellers in the fed funds market and assist secondary trading in other money market securities as well. These brokers never trade for their own account, and they keep the names of dealers involved in trades they handle confidential.

The third group of brokers and dealers are the thousands of brokers and dealers who act as intermediaries in the money markets by linking buyers and sellers of money market securities (see Chapter 16). This group of brokers and dealers often act as the intermediaries for smaller investors who do not have sufficient funds to invest in primary issues of money market securities or who simply want to invest in the money markets.

---

11. Only bank holding companies such as Citigroup can issue commercial paper. However, funds so borrowed can be lent (downstreamed) to bank subsidiaries such as Citibank. Currently, the Federal Reserve imposes reserve requirements on such transactions.

Corporations

Nonfinancial and financial corporations raise large amounts of funds in the money markets, primarily in the form of commercial paper. The volume of commercial paper issued by corporations has been so large that there is now more commercial paper outstanding than any other type of money market security. Because corporate cash inflows rarely equal their cash outflows, they often invest their excess cash funds in money market securities, especially T-bills, repos, commercial paper, negotiable CDs, and bankers acceptances.

Other Financial Institutions

Because their liability payments are relatively unpredictable, property-casualty (PC) insurance companies, and to a lesser extent life insurance companies, must maintain large balances of liquid assets (see Chapter 15). To accomplish this, insurance companies invest heavily in highly liquid money market securities, especially T-bills, repos, commercial paper, and negotiable CDs.

Since finance companies are not banks and cannot issue deposits, they raise large amounts of funds in the money markets (see Chapter 17), especially through the issuance of commercial paper.

Finally, money market mutual funds purchase large amounts of money market securities and sell shares in these pools based on the value of their underlying (money market) securities (see Chapter 17). In doing so, money market mutual funds allow small investors to invest in money market instruments and to achieve higher returns compared to investing in retail deposits.

Do You Understand?

1. Who the major money market participants are?
2. Which money market securities commercial banks issue?
3. What services brokers and dealers provide for money market participants?

International Aspects of Money Markets

While U.S. money markets are the largest and most active in the world, money markets across the world have been growing in size and importance. Two forms of growth include (1) U.S. money market securities bought and sold by foreign investors and (2) foreign money market securities. In conjunction with this increased worldwide interest in U.S. money market securities, some of the largest U.S. financial institutions that trade in money markets for themselves and their customers have opened offices in London, Tokyo, and beyond, most recently through mergers and acquisitions (see In the News box 5–2).

Do You Understand?

1. What some of the methods are that U.S. banks have used to access foreign securities markets?

As a result of the growth in money markets worldwide, the flow of funds across borders in various countries has grown as international investors move their funds to money markets offering the most attractive yields. Table 5–7 lists the total amounts of various U.S. money market securities held by foreign investors from 1994 through 1999. Table 5–8 lists the U.S. dollar equivalent amounts of money market instruments traded in international money markets, listed by type of instrument issued and the currency of issue. Table 5–9 shows the variation in central bank interest rates (discount rates for lender of last resort loans) in several countries as of December 1999.

Do You Understand?

1. What the major U.S. money market securities held by foreign investors are?
2. Which currencies most international money market instruments are issued in?

Euro Money Markets

Because of the importance of the U.S. dollar relative to other currencies, many international financial contracts call for payment in U.S. dollars—the U.S. dollar is still the major international medium of exchange. As a result, foreign governments

In the News

American Companies in Japan: Financial Services

A new benchmark has been established for the changes sweeping Japan's limping financial services sector and how American competitors are capitalizing on openings. Financial services powerhouse Travelers Group Inc. will acquire a 25 percent stake in Nikko Securities Co., Ltd., Japan's third biggest brokerage house, for roughly $1.6 billion. That will be the largest investment to date by an American company in a Japanese financial institution. It will make Travelers the top shareholder in Nikko Securities, displacing Bank of Tokyo-Mitsubishi. Ltd. Equally important, Travelers and the securities firm will establish a joint brokerage business in Tokyo capitalized at $1 billion. Nikko Securities will own 51 percent

Source: *Japan-U.S. Business Report*, July 30, 1998.

of Nikko Salomon Smith Barney Ltd., with Travelers' Salomon Smith Barney, Inc. investment banking/securities company putting up 49 percent of the capital but running the show . . .

Merrill Lynch & Co., Inc.—which rocked competitors both in Japan and at home earlier this year by announcing plans to build a nationwide retail brokerage business using offices and employees of failed Yamaichi Securities Co. Ltd.—merged its three Japanese asset management companies effective July 1 . . . The merger follows Merrill Lynch's acquisition last December of London-based Mercury Asset Management Group PLC.

One of America's major mutual fund managers,

Scudder Kemper Investments, Inc., has changed the name of its Japanese operation to reflect its new business direction. Effective July 1, Scudder Stevens & Clark Japan, Inc., an investment advisory firm, became Scudder Investment Japan, Inc. . . . The company will use a variety of wholesale channels to sell its products, including banks and securities firms.

In a first for any state, the New York State Banking Department has opened an office in Tokyo. Its mission is to keep tabs on American financial institutions moving into Japan and other Asian countries to exploit the openings created by the region's financial turmoil and regulatory reform.

Citibank N.A., which sees tie-ups with regional banks as one important way to expand its business in Japan, has signed up Michinoku Bank, Ltd. to market its financial services.

Table 5–7   Foreign Investments in U.S. Money Market Instruments
(in billions of dollars)

	1994	**1995**	**1996**	**1997**	**1998**	**1999***
Treasury securities[†]	$632.6	$840.5	$1,097.7	$1,251.8	$1,316.3	$1,318.9
Repurchase agreements	46.6	67.6	70.9	90.8	72.0	81.9
Negotiable CDs	56.3	49.6	60.6	73.6	86.1	89.7
Open market paper[‡]	24.9	43.4	57.9	77.8	114.8	105.3

*As of September.

†Includes Treasury bills, notes, and bonds.

‡Commercial paper and banker's acceptances.

Source: Federal Reserve Board, website, "Flow of Fund Accounts," December 1999. *www.bog.frb.fed.us/*

Table 5–8 Money Market Instruments Outstanding, September 1999
(in billions of U.S. dollars)

Instrument	Amount Outstanding	
Total Issues	$243.7	
Commercial Paper	$170.9	
Currency type		
U.S. dollar		$ 84.4
Euro area currencies		52.3
Japanese yen		2.5
Other currencies		31.7
Issuer type		
Financial institutions		$107.4
Governments and state agencies		15.1
International institutions		5.1
Corporate issuers		43.2
Other Short-Term Paper	$ 72.8	
Currency type		
U.S. dollar		$ 30.6
Euro area currencies		22.8
Japanese yen		1.5
Other currencies		17.9
Issuer type		
Financial institutions		$ 61.2
Governments and state agencies		10.5
International institutions		—
Corporate issuers		1.1
Currency of Issue		
Australian dollar	$ 5.5	
Canadian dollar	0.9	
ECU	75.1	
Greek drachma	0.2	
Hong Kong dollar	13.7	
Japanese yen	4.0	
New Zealand dollar	0.6	
Pound sterling	20.5	
Swedish krona	0.5	
Swiss franc	7.3	
U.S. dollar	115.0	
Other	0.1	

Source: Bank for International Settlements, "International Banking and Financial Market Developments," *Quarterly Review,* November 1999. *www.bis.org/*

Eurodollar deposits

Dollar-denominated deposits in non-U.S. banks.

Eurodollar market

The market in which Eurodollars trade.

and businesses have historically held a store of funds (deposits) denominated in dollars outside of the United States. Further, U.S. corporations conducting international trade often hold U.S. dollar deposits in foreign banks overseas to facilitate expenditures and purchases. These dollar-denominated deposits held offshore in U.S. bank branches overseas and in other (foreign) banks are called **Eurodollar deposits** and the market in which they trade is called the **Eurodollar market**. Eurodollars may be held by governments, corporations, and individuals from anywhere in the world and are not directly subject to U.S. bank regulations, such as reserve requirements and deposit insurance premiums (or protection).

Table 5–9   Selected Central Bank Interest Rates

	New Rate		Previous Rate	
Country/Interest Rate	**Percent Per Year**	**Applicable From**	**Percent Per Year**	**Applicable From**
1. EU-countries*				
Denmark				
Discount rate	3	Nov. 4, '99	2¾	Apr. 9, '99
Repurchase/CD selling rate	3.30	Nov. 4, '99	2.85	June 17, '99
Greece				
Deposit rate†	11	Oct. 21, '99	11.50	Jan. 14, '99
Repurchase rate	11½	Oct. 21, '99	12	Jan. 13, '99
Lombard rate	13	Oct. 20, '99	13½	Jan. 14, '99
Sweden				
Deposit rate	2¾	Feb. 17, '99	3¼	Nov. 12, '98
Repurchase rate	3.25	Nov. 17, '99	2.90	Mar. 25, '99
Lombard rate	4¼	Feb. 17, '99	4¾	Nov. 12, '98
United Kingdom				
Repurchase rate‡	5½	Nov. 4, '99	5¼	Sep. 8, '99
2. Switzerland				
Discount rate	½	Apr. 9, '99	1	Sep. 27, '96
3. Non-European countries				
Canada§				
Discount rate	5	Nov. 17, '99	4¾	May 4, '99
Japan				
Discount rate	½	Sep. 8, '95	1	Apr. 14, '95
United States				
Discount rate	5	Nov. 16, '99	4¾	Aug. 24, '99
Federal funds rate#	5½	Nov. 16, '99	5¼	Aug. 24, '99

*Only those member countries that are not participating in the euro area for the time being.
†Basic tranche.
‡Bank of England key rate.
§Bank of Canada's ceiling rate for call money.
#Rate targeted for interbank trade in central bank money.
Source: Deutsche Bank, website, Monthly Report, December 1999. *www.bundesbank.de/*

London Interbank Offered Rate (LIBOR)

The rate paid on Eurodollars.

Large banks in London have organized an interbank Eurodollar market. This market is now used by banks around the world as a source of overnight funding. The rate paid on these funds is known as the **London Interbank Offered Rate** (**LIBOR**). As alternative sources of overnight funding, the LIBOR and U.S. federal funds rate tend to be very closely related. Should rates in one of these markets (e.g., the LIBOR market) decrease relative to the other (e.g., the fed funds market), overnight borrowers will borrow in the LIBOR market rather than the fed funds market. As a result, the LIBOR will increase with this increased demand and the fed funds rate will decrease with demand. The ease of transacting in both markets makes it virtually costless to use one market versus the other.

While they are close substitutes for overnight funding, the fed funds rate is generally lower than the LIBOR. This difference is due to the low-risk nature of U.S. bank deposits versus foreign bank deposits. U.S. bank deposits are covered by deposit insurance up to certain levels. Moreover, there is a perception that large U.S. bank depositors and large U.S. banks are implicitly insured via a "too big to fail" guarantee. Such guarantees lower U.S. bank risk and thus, the cost of borrowing in the fed funds

Figure 5–10 Overnight Interest Rates, 1997–1999

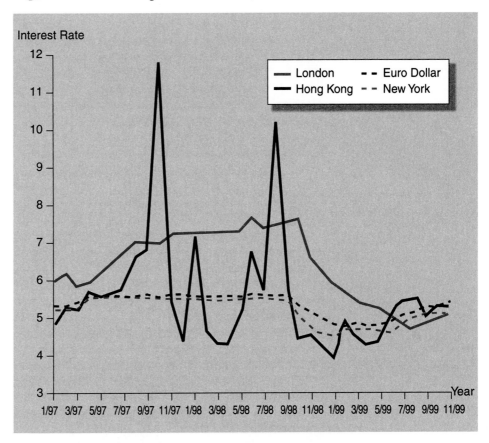

Source: Deutsche Bank, website, Monthly Report, April 1999. *www.bundesbank.de/*

market. Foreign banks have no such explicit or implicit guarantees. As a result, LIBOR is generally higher than the fed funds rate, reflecting higher default risk. Overnight rates, including the fed funds rate (New York) and Eurodollar rate, between 1997 and November 1999 are plotted in Figure 5–10. The spread of the LIBOR over the fed funds rate averaged 0.12 percent over this period, and the correlation between the movements in the two rates was 92 percent.

Euro Money Market Securities

In this section, we look at the characteristics of a number of Euro money market securities. These include Eurodollar certificates of deposit, Euronotes, and Eurocommercial paper.

Eurodollar Certificates of Deposit. Eurodollar certificates of deposits (CDs) are U.S. dollar–denominated CDs in foreign banks. Maturities on Eurodollar CDs are less than one year, and most have a maturity of one week to six months. Because these securities are deposited in non-U.S. banks, Eurodollar CDs are not subject to reserve requirements in the same manner as U.S. deposits (although the reserve requirement on U.S. CDs was set to zero at the beginning of 1991).

Figure 5–11 shows the difference between three-month Eurodollar and U.S. bank issued CDs from 1971 through 1999. As can be seen in this figure, prior to the 1990s, the Eurodollar CD paid consistently higher interest rates than U.S. CDs. In the 1990s, after the reserve requirement on CDs was set to zero, it is difficult to distinguish the

Figure 5–11 Three-Month U.S. Bank Issued versus Eurodollar CD Rates, 1971–1999

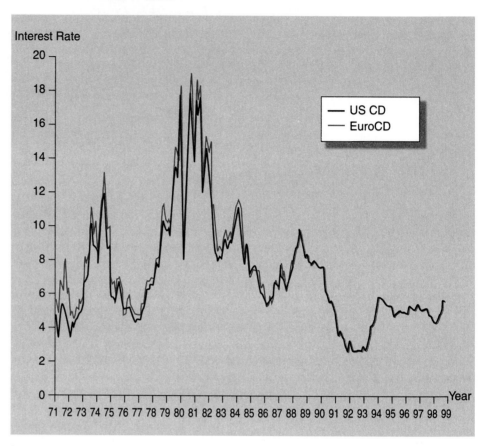

Source: Federal Reserve Board, website, "Research and Data," January 2000. *www.bog.frb.fed.us/*

Euronotes

Short-term notes similar to commercial paper. These instruments are most frequently used by European banks that deal in commercial paper.

Eurocommercial paper

Eurosecurities issued by dealers of commercial paper without involving a bank.

Do You Understand?

1. What the difference is between a Eurodollar CD, Euronote, and Eurocommercial paper?
2. What the relation is between the federal funds rate and the LIBOR?

Eurodollar CD rate from the U.S. CD rate. Indeed, during the 1990s, the average rate paid on three-month Eurodollar CDs was 5.30 percent and on three-month U.S. CDs was 5.31 percent. The correlation on the movements in the two rates was 0.99986—that is, returns on three-month Eurodollar CDs and U.S. CDs were virtually identical in the 1990s.

Euronotes and Eurocommercial Paper. **Euronotes** are short-term notes (maturities of 1, 3, and 6 months) similar to commercial paper. These instruments are most frequently used by European banks that deal in commercial paper. Along the same lines, **Eurocommercial paper** (Euro-CP) is issued by dealers of commercial paper without involving a bank. The Eurocommercial paper rate is generally about one-half to 1 percent above the LIBOR rate. As mentioned above, foreign commercial paper markets are new and small relative to U.S. commercial paper markets. Table 5–10 lists the amount of Euronotes and Eurocommercial paper outstanding in the international money markets from 1995 through September 1999 by currency and type of issuer.

Table 5–10 Euronotes and Eurocommercial Paper Outstanding, 1995–September 1999

(in billions of U.S. dollars)

Type of instrument	Amount Outstanding				
	1995	**1996**	**1997**	**1998**	**1999**
Euronotes	$45.5	$ 68.7	$ 73.5	$ 61.6	$ 72.8
Currency type					
U.S. dollar	27.9	33.1	38.9	33.6	30.6
Euro area currencies*	0.5	0.1	17.9	11.8	22.8
Japanese yen	0.4	1.8	1.6	1.2	1.5
Other currencies	16.7	33.8	15.1	15.0	17.9
Issuer type					
Financial institutions	41.4	49.2	53.2	48.6	61.2
Governments and state agencies	0.4	17.0	16.7	10.2	10.5
International institutions	1.2	0.7	0.9	—	—
Corporate issuers	2.5	1.8	2.7	2.8	1.1
Eurocommercial paper	$87.0	$102.9	$110.4	$132.9	$170.9
Currency type					
U.S. dollar	55.7	64.6	66.6	77.9	84.4
Euro area currencies*	9.1	9.5	14.8	24.1	52.3
Japanese yen	2.1	4.5	5.0	3.5	2.5
Other currencies	20.0	24.3	24.0	27.3	31.7
Issuer type					
Financial institutions	40.5	54.7	60.5	76.2	107.4
Governments and state agencies	14.2	19.3	20.2	19.4	15.1
International institutions	2.1	2.1	2.7	3.2	5.1
Corporate issuers	30.2	26.8	26.9	34.1	43.2

*The BIS used the deutsche mark in 1995 and 1996.

Source: Bank for International Settlements, "International Banking and Financial Market Developments," *Quarterly Review,* November 1999. *www.bis.org/*

Summary

In this chapter, we reviewed money markets, which are markets that trade debt securities with original maturities of one year or less. The need for money markets arises because cash receipts do not always coincide with cash expenditures for individuals, corporations, and government units. Because holding cash involves an opportunity cost, holders of excess cash invest these funds in money market securities. We looked at the various money market securities available to short-term investors and the major borrowers and issuers of each. We also outlined the processes by which each of these securities are issued and traded in secondary markets. We concluded the chapter by examining international issues involving money markets, taking a particular look at Euro money markets.

Questions

1. What are the three characteristics common to money market securities?
2. Describe the T-bill auction process.
3. What is the difference between a competitive bid and a noncompetitive bid in a T-bill auction?
4. What is the difference between a discount yield and a bond equivalent yield? Which yield is used for Treasury bill quotes?
5. Suppose you purchase a T-bill that is 125 days from maturity for $9,765. The T-bill has a face value of $10,000.

a. Calculate the T-bill's quoted yield.

b. Calculate the T-bill's bond equivalent yield.

6. Refer to Table 5–5.

a. Calculate the ask price of the T-bill maturing on March 16, 2000, as of January 18, 2000.

b. Calculate the bid price of the T-bill maturing on May 25, 2000, as of January 18, 2000.

7. What are federal funds? How are they recorded on the balance sheets of commercial banks?

8. Describe the two types of fed fund transactions.

9. What is the difference between a repurchase agreement and a reverse repurchase agreement?

10. Suppose a bank enters a repurchase agreement in which it agrees to buy Treasury securities from a correspondent bank at a price of $24,950,000, with the promise to buy them back at a price of $25,000,000.

a. Calculate the yield on the repo if it has a 7-day maturity.

b. Calculate the yield on the repo if it has a 21-day maturity.

11. Why do commercial paper issues have an original maturity of 270 days or less?

12. Why do commercial paper issuers almost always obtain a rating of their issues?

13. You can buy commercial paper of a major U.S. corporation for $495,000. The paper has a face value of $500,000 and is 45 days from maturity. Calculate the discount yield and bond equivalent yield on the commercial paper.

14. What is the process through which negotiable CDs are issued?

15. You have just purchased a four-month, $500,000 negotiable CD, which will pay a 5.5 percent annual interest rate.

a. If the market rate on the CD rises to 6 percent, what is its current market value?

b. If the market rate on the CD falls to 5.25 percent, what is its current market value?

16. Describe the process by which a banker's acceptance is created.

17. Who are the major issuers of and investors in money market securities?

18. What are Eurodollar CDs, Euronotes, and Eurocommercial paper?

19. Go to the U.S. Treasury website and get the most recent Treasury auction results.

20. Go the Deutsche Bank website and find the most recent rates charged by the major central banks.

Bond Markets

Chapter Navigator

1. What are the major bond markets?

2. What are the characteristics of the various bond market securities?

3. Who are the major bond market participants?

4. What types of securities trade in international bond markets?

Definition of Bond Markets: Chapter Overview

Equity (stocks) and debt (notes, bonds, and mortgages) instruments with maturities of more than one year trade in **capital markets**. In the next three chapters, we look at characteristics of the different capital markets, starting in this chapter with bond markets.[1] In Chapter 7, we look at the mortgage markets (e.g., mortgage-backed securities, asset-backed securities), and in Chapter 8, we describe the equity markets.

Bonds are long-term debt obligations issued by corporations and government units. Proceeds from a bond issue are used to raise funds to support long-term operations of the issuer (e.g., for capital expenditure projects). In return for the investor's funds, bond issuers promise to pay a specified amount in the future on the maturity of the bond (the face value) plus coupon interest on the borrowed funds (the coupon rate times the face value of the bond). If the terms of the repayment are not met by the bond issuer, the bond holder (investor) has a claim on the assets of the bond issuer.

---

1. Although both notes and bonds are issued by agents such as the U.S. government, their characteristics (coupon rate) other than maturity are generally the same. In this chapter, the term *bond* will mean bonds and notes in general, except where we distinguish notes by their special maturity features. For example, U.S. Treasury notes have maturities of over one year up to 10 years. U.S. Treasury bonds have maturities from over 10 years to 30 years at the time of issue.

capital markets

Markets that trade debt (bonds and mortgages) and equity (stocks) instruments with maturities of more than one year.

bonds

Long-term debt obligations issued by corporations and government units.

Table 6–1 Bond Market Instruments Outstanding, 1994–1999
(in billions of dollars)

	1994	1995	1996	1997	1998	1999*
Treasury bonds	$2,377.3	$2,531.5	$2,667.3	$2,693.4	$2,581.9	$2,956.7
Municipal securities	1,341.7	1,293.5	1,269.0	1,367.5	1,464.3	1,518.1
Corporate bonds	2,504.0	2,822.9	3,128.0	3,441.5	3,879.0	4,534.6
Total	$6,223.0	$6,647.9	$7,064.3	$7,502.4	$7,925.2	$9,009.4

*As of the end of the third quarter.

Source: Federal Reserve Board, website, "Flow of Funds Accounts," December 15, 1999. *www.bog.frb.fed.us/*

bond markets

Markets in which bonds are issued and traded.

Bond markets are markets in which bonds are issued and traded. They are used to assist in the transfer of funds from individuals, corporations, and government units with excess funds to corporations and government units in need of long-term debt funding. Bond markets are traditionally classified into three types: (1) Treasury notes and bonds, (2) municipal bonds, and (3) corporate bonds. Table 6–1 lists the amount of each type outstanding from 1994 through September 1999. In this chapter, we look at the characteristics of the various bond securities (including the trading process in bond markets), the participants in the bond markets, and international bond markets and securities.

Bond Market Securities

Government units and corporations are the major bond security issuers. Table 6–1 shows that the dollar amount of bond securities issued by these groups has increased 44.8 percent, from $6,223.0 billion in 1994 to $9,009.4 billion in 1999. In this section, we look at the bond market securities issued by each of these bond issuers: Treasury notes and bonds, municipal bonds, and corporate bonds.

Treasury Notes and Bonds

Treasury notes and bonds

Long-term bonds issued by the U.S. Treasury to finance the national debt and other federal government expenditures.

www.ustreas.gov/

Treasury notes and bonds (T-notes and T-bonds) are issued by the U.S. Treasury to finance the national debt and other federal government expenditures ($2,956.7 billion outstanding in September 1999). The national debt (*ND*) reflects the historical accumulation of annual federal government deficits or expenditures (*G*) minus taxes (*T*) over the last 200-plus years, as follows:

$$ND_t = \sum_{t=1}^{N} (G_t - T_t)$$

Table 6–2 lists the composition of the U.S. national debt from 1994 through September 1999. Notice that over this period, approximately 50 percent of the U.S. national debt consisted of Treasury notes and bonds.

Like T-bills, T-notes and bonds are backed by the full faith and credit of the U.S. government and are, therefore, default risk free. As a result, T-notes and bonds pay relatively low rates of interest (yields to maturity) to investors. T-notes and bonds, however, are not completely risk free. Given their longer maturity (i.e., duration), these instruments experience wider price fluctuations than do money market instruments as interest rates change (and thus are subject to interest rate risk—see Chapter 23). Further, many of the older issued bonds and notes— "off the run issues"—may be less liquid than newly issued bonds and notes— "on the run" issues—in which case they may bear an additional premium for illiquidity risk. Figure 6–1 shows the pattern of 10-year T-note yields versus 3-month T-bill yields from 1980 through 1999.

Table 6–2   Composition of the U.S. National Debt
(in billions of dollars)

	1994	**1995**	**1996**	**1997**	**1998**	**1999***
T-bills	$ 697.3	$ 742.5	$ 761.2	$ 701.9	$ 637.7	$ 653.2
T-notes	1,882.9	1,995.7	2,114.1	2,161.6	2,082.9	1,936.1
T-bonds	511.8	522.6	543.5	576.1	610.5	643.7
U.S. savings securities	176.4	181.2	184.1	182.7	180.8	180.0
Foreign series	42.0	40.9	37.5	34.9	35.1	31.0
Government account securities	1,211.7	1,324.3	1,454.7	1,608.5	1,777.3	2,005.1
State and local government securities	137.4	113.4	95.7	111.8	164.4	168.1
Domestic securities	30.0	30.0	30.0	30.0	30.0	30.0
Total	$4,689.5	$4,950.6	$5,220.8	$5,407.5	$5,518.7	$5,647.2

*As of September.

Source: U.S. Treasury Department, *Treasury Bulletin*, December 1999. *www.ustreas.gov/*

Figure 6–1   T-Bill versus T-Note Yields, 1980–1999

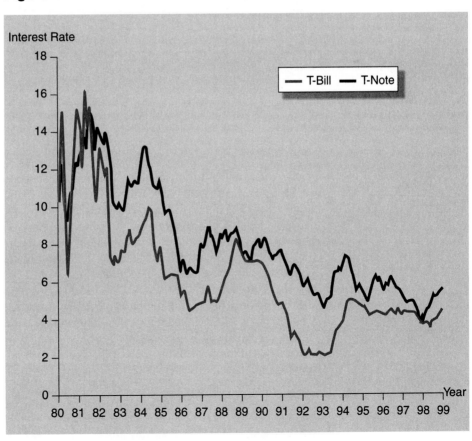

Source: Federal Reserve Board, website, "Research and Data," January 2000. *www.bog.frb.fed.us/*

Table 6–3 Treasury Note and Bond Quote

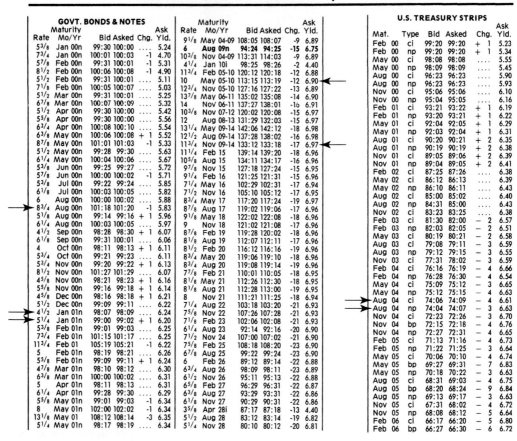

TREASURY BONDS, NOTES

GOVT. BONDS & NOTES

Rate	Maturity Mo/Yr	Bid	Asked	Chg.	Ask Yld.
5 3/8	Jan 00n	99:30	100:00	....	5.24
7 3/4	Jan 00n	100:01	100:03	-1	4.70
5 7/8	Feb 00n	99:31	100:01	-1	5.31
8 1/2	Feb 00n	100:06	100:08	-1	4.90
5 1/2	Feb 00n	99:31	100:01	....	5.11
7 1/8	Feb 00n	100:05	100:07	....	5.03
5 1/2	Mar 00n	99:31	100:01	....	5.25
6 7/8	Mar 00n	100:07	100:09	....	5.32
5 1/2	Apr 00n	99:30	100:00	....	5.42
5 5/8	Apr 00n	99:30	100:00	....	5.56
6 3/4	Apr 00n	100:08	100:10	....	5.54
6 3/8	May 00n	100:06	100:08	+ 1	5.52
8 7/8	May 00n	101:01	101:03	-1	5.33
5 1/2	May 00n	99:28	99:30	....	5.63
6 1/4	May 00n	100:04	100:06	....	5.67
5 3/8	Jun 00n	99:25	99:27	....	5.72
5 7/8	Jun 00n	100:00	100:02	-1	5.71
5 3/8	Jul 00n	99:22	99:24	....	5.85
6 1/8	Jul 00n	100:03	100:05	....	5.82
6	Aug 00n	100:00	100:02	....	5.88
8 3/4	Aug 00n	101:18	101:20	-1	5.83
5 1/8	Aug 00n	99:14	99:16	+ 1	5.96
6 1/4	Aug 00n	100:03	100:05	....	5.97
4 1/2	Sep 00n	98:28	98:30	+ 1	6.07
6 1/8	Sep 00n	99:31	100:01	....	6.06
4	Oct 00n	98:11	98:13	+ 1	6.11
5 3/4	Oct 00n	99:21	99:23	....	6.11
5 3/4	Nov 00n	99:20	99:22	+ 1	6.13
8 1/2	Nov 00n	101:27	101:29	....	6.07
4 5/8	Nov 00n	98:21	98:23	+ 1	6.16
5 5/8	Nov 00n	99:16	99:18	+ 1	6.14
4 5/8	Dec 00n	98:16	98:18	+ 1	6.21
5 1/2	Dec 00n	99:09	99:11	....	6.22
4 1/2	Jan 01n	98:07	98:09	....	6.24
5 1/4	Jan 01n	99:00	99:02	+ 1	6.20
5 3/8	Feb 01n	99:01	99:03	....	6.25
7 3/4	Feb 01n	101:15	101:17	....	6.25
11 3/4	Feb 01	105:19	105:21	-1	6.22
5	Feb 01n	98:19	98:21	....	6.26
5 5/8	Feb 01n	99:09	99:11	+ 1	6.24
4 7/8	Mar 01n	98:10	98:12	....	6.30
6 3/8	Mar 01n	100:00	100:02	....	6.31
5	Apr 01n	98:11	98:13	....	6.31
6 1/4	Apr 01n	99:28	99:30	....	6.29
5 5/8	May 01n	99:01	99:03	-1	6.34
8	May 01n	102:00	102:02	-1	6.34
13 1/8	May 01	108:12	108:14	-3	6.35
5 1/4	May 01n	98:17	98:19	....	6.34

Rate	Maturity Mo/Yr	Bid	Asked	Chg.	Ask Yld.
9 1/8	May 04-09	108:05	108:07	-9	6.89
6	Aug 09n	94:24	94:25	-15	6.75
10 3/8	Nov 04-09	113:31	114:03	-9	6.89
4 1/4	Jan 10i	98:25	98:26	-2	4.40
11 3/4	Feb 05-10	120:12	120:18	-12	6.88
10	May 05-10	113:15	113:19	-12	6.90
12 3/4	Nov 05-10	127:16	127:22	-13	6.89
13 7/8	May 06-11	135:02	135:08	-14	6.90
14	Nov 06-11	137:27	138:01	-16	6.91
10 3/8	Nov 07-12	120:02	120:08	-15	6.97
12	Aug 08-13	131:29	132:03	-15	6.97
13 1/4	May 09-14	142:06	142:12	-18	6.98
12 1/2	Aug 09-14	137:28	138:02	-16	6.98
11 3/4	Nov 09-14	133:12	133:18	-17	6.97
11 1/4	Feb 15	139:14	139:20	-18	6.96
10 5/8	Aug 15	134:11	134:17	-16	6.96
9 7/8	Nov 15	127:18	127:24	-15	6.95
9 1/4	Feb 16	121:25	121:31	-15	6.96
7 1/4	May 16	102:29	102:31	-17	6.94
7 1/2	Nov 16	105:10	105:12	-17	6.95
8 3/4	May 17	117:20	117:24	-19	6.97
8 7/8	Aug 17	119:02	119:06	-17	6.96
9 1/8	May 18	122:02	122:08	-18	6.96
9	Nov 18	121:02	121:08	-17	6.96
8 7/8	Feb 19	119:28	120:02	-18	6.96
8 1/8	Aug 19	112:07	112:11	-17	6.96
8 1/2	Feb 20	116:12	116:16	-19	6.96
8 3/4	May 20	119:06	119:10	-18	6.96
8 3/4	Aug 20	119:08	119:14	-19	6.96
7 7/8	Feb 21	110:01	110:05	-18	6.95
8 1/8	May 21	112:26	112:30	-18	6.95
8 1/8	Aug 21	112:28	113:00	-19	6.95
8	Nov 21	111:21	111:25	-18	6.94
7 1/4	Aug 22	103:18	103:20	-21	6.93
7 5/8	Nov 22	107:26	107:28	-21	6.93
7 1/8	Feb 23	102:06	102:08	-21	6.93
6 1/4	Aug 23	92:14	92:16	-20	6.90
7 1/2	Nov 24	107:00	107:02	-21	6.90
7 5/8	Feb 25	108:18	108:20	-23	6.90
6 7/8	Aug 25	99:22	99:24	-23	6.90
6	Feb 26	89:12	89:14	-22	6.88
6 3/4	Aug 26	98:09	98:11	-23	6.89
6 1/2	Nov 26	95:11	95:13	-22	6.88
6 5/8	Feb 27	96:29	96:31	-22	6.87
6 3/8	Aug 27	93:29	93:31	-22	6.86
6 1/8	Nov 27	90:29	90:31	-22	6.86
3 5/8	Apr 28i	87:17	87:18	-13	4.40
5 1/2	Aug 28	83:12	83:14	-19	6.82
5 1/4	Nov 28	80:10	80:12	-20	6.81

U.S. TREASURY STRIPS

Mat.	Type	Bid	Asked	Chg.	Ask Yld.
Feb 00	ci	99:20	99:20	+ 1	5.23
Feb 00	np	99:20	99:20	+ 1	5.34
May 00	ci	98:08	98:08	....	5.55
May 00	np	98:09	98:09	....	5.45
Aug 00	ci	96:23	96:23	....	5.90
Aug 00	np	96:23	96:23	....	5.93
Nov 00	ci	95:06	95:06	....	6.10
Nov 00	np	95:04	95:05	....	6.16
Feb 01	ci	93:21	93:22	+ 1	6.19
Feb 01	np	93:20	93:21	+ 1	6.22
May 01	ci	92:04	92:05	+ 1	6.29
May 01	np	92:03	92:04	+ 1	6.31
Aug 01	ci	90:20	90:21	+ 2	6.35
Aug 01	np	90:19	90:19	+ 2	6.38
Nov 01	ci	89:05	89:06	+ 2	6.39
Nov 01	np	89:04	89:05	+ 2	6.41
Feb 02	ci	87:25	87:26	....	6.38
May 02	ci	86:12	86:13	....	6.39
May 02	np	86:10	86:11	....	6.43
Aug 02	ci	85:00	85:02	....	6.40
Aug 02	np	84:31	85:00	....	6.43
Nov 02	ci	83:23	83:25	....	6.38
Feb 03	ci	81:30	82:00	− 2	6.57
Feb 03	np	82:03	82:05	− 2	6.51
May 03	ci	80:19	80:21	− 2	6.58
Aug 03	ci	79:08	79:11	− 3	6.59
Aug 03	np	79:12	79:15	− 3	6.55
Nov 03	ci	77:31	78:02	− 3	6.59
Feb 04	ci	76:16	76:19	− 4	6.66
Feb 04	np	76:28	76:30	− 4	6.54
May 04	ci	75:09	75:12	− 3	6.65
May 04	np	75:12	75:15	− 4	6.63
Aug 04	ci	74:06	74:09	− 4	6.61
Aug 04	np	74:04	74:07	− 3	6.63
Nov 04	ci	72:23	72:26	− 3	6.70
Nov 04	bp	72:15	72:18	− 4	6.76
Nov 04	np	72:27	72:31	− 4	6.65
Feb 05	ci	71:13	71:16	− 4	6.73
Feb 05	np	71:22	71:25	− 3	6.64
May 05	ci	70:06	70:10	− 4	6.74
May 05	bp	69:27	69:31	− 7	6.83
May 05	np	70:18	70:22	− 3	6.63
Aug 05	ci	68:31	69:03	− 4	6.75
Aug 05	bp	68:20	68:24	− 9	6.84
Aug 05	np	69:13	69:17	− 3	6.63
Nov 05	ci	67:31	68:02	− 4	6.72
Nov 05	np	68:08	68:12	− 5	6.64
Feb 06	ci	66:17	66:20	− 5	6.80
Feb 06	bp	66:27	66:30	− 6	6.72

In contrast to T-bills, which are sold on a discount basis from face value (see Chapter 5), T-notes and T-bonds pay coupon interest (semiannually). Further, T-bills have an original maturity of less than one year. Treasury notes have original maturities from 1 to 10 years, while T-bonds have original maturities from over 10 to 30 years. T-notes and bonds are issued in minimum denominations of $1,000, or in multiples of $1,000.

Table 6–3 presents part of a T-note and T-bond (including Treasury STRIPS—see below) closing price/interest yield quote sheet from *The Wall Street Journal* for January 18, 2000. Column 1 in the table lists the coupon rate on the Treasury security. Note that coupon rates are set at intervals of 1/8th of 1 percent. Column 2 is the month and year the note or bond matures (an "n" after the year means that the security is a T-note—i.e., having an original maturity of less than 10 years). Column 3, labeled Bid, is the close of the day selling price (in percentage terms) available to T-note and bond holders (i.e., the price dealers are willing to pay T-note and bond holders for their Treasury securities). Prices are quoted as percentages of the face value on the Treasury security, in 32nds. For example, using a face value of $1,000, the bid price on the 8¾ percent coupon, Aug00 T-note was $1,015.625 (101 18/32% × $1,000). Column 4, labeled Asked, is the close of the day purchase price available to investors. Column 5, labeled Chg., is the change in the Asked price from the previous day's close in

Figure 6–2 Creation of a Treasury STRIP

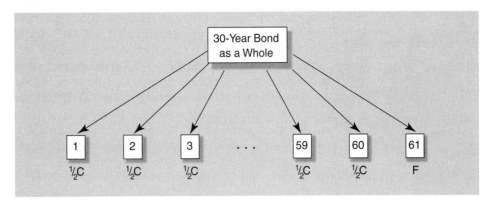

32nds—that is, the November 2009 T-note's price decreased by $^{17}/_{32}$ from the previous day. Finally, the last column, labeled Ask Yld., is the Asked price converted into a rate of return (yield to maturity) on the T-note or T-bond. This yield is calculated using the yield to maturity formulas found in Chapter 3—it is the interest rate or yield (using semiannual compounding) that makes the price of the security just equal to the present value of the expected coupon and face value cash flows on the bond (where this yield is the single discount rate that makes this equality hold).

STRIPS. In 1985, the Treasury began issuing 10-year notes and 30-year bonds to financial institutions using a book-entry system under a program titled Separate Trading of Registered Interest and Principal Securities (STRIPS). A **STRIP** is a Treasury security in which periodic coupon interest payments can be separated from the each other and from the final principal payment. As illustrated in Figure 6–2, a STRIP effectively creates two sets of securities—one set for each semiannual interest payment and one set for the final principal payment. Each of the components of the STRIP are often referred to as "Treasury zero bonds" or "Treasury zero-coupon bonds" because investors in the individual components only receive the single stripped payments (e.g., the third semiannual coupon) in which they invest.

STRIPs were created by the U.S. Treasury in response to the separate trading of Treasury security principal and interest that had been developed by securities firms. Specifically, in the early 1980s, Merrill Lynch introduced Treasury Investment Growth Receipts (TIGRs). Merrill Lynch purchased Treasury securities, stripped them into one security representing the principal component only and a separate security for each coupon payment, and put these individual securities up for resale. The Treasury's creation of the STRIP was meant to offer a competitive product to the market.

The U.S. Treasury does not issue STRIPs directly to investors. Rather, stripped Treasury notes and bonds may be purchased only through financial institutions and government securities brokers and dealers, who create the strip components after purchasing the original T-notes or T-bonds (whole) in Treasury auctions (see below). After the STRIP components have been created, by requesting that the Treasury separate each coupon and face value payment on each bond and recording them as separate securities in its book-entry computer system, they can be sold individually in the secondary markets.[2]

STRIP

A Treasury security in which the periodic interest payment is separated from the final principal payment.

www.ml.com/

---

2. Once a bond is stripped, if an investor purchases each coupon and face value component at a later time, he or she can ask the Treasury to reconstitute the original bond on it's computer system. Thus, the Treasury STRIP program is highly flexible.

Example 6–1   Creation of a STRIP

Suppose the Treasury issues a five-year T-note with a par value of $10,000 and an 8 percent coupon rate (paid semiannually, or $400 is paid to the holder every six months for the next five years) to Citigroup. Citigroup decides to convert the bond into a set of stripped securities by requesting the Treasury to separate the coupons and face value of the note into separate securities on its computer system (basically giving each coupon and face value a separate I.D. or CUSIP number). This means that Citigroup can then sell 11 different securities: 10 securities associated with each of the semiannual coupon payments of $400 and one that pays $10,000 (the face or principal value) in five years to outside investors. We show the value of each of these securities in Table 6–4, assuming the yield to maturity on each of the stripped securities is 7.90 percent.

Notice that the total present value of the 11 different securities involved with the STRIP is the same as that of the original T-note before it is stripped, $10,040.65. However, in general, the bank (Citigroup) will try to sell the 11 stripped securities for a greater total present value than the bond as a whole. The reason for this is that many investors desire particular maturity zero-coupon bonds to meet investment goals and needs. Such goals and needs (such as duration targets—see below) are often harder to achieve through buying whole T-notes or T-bonds.

As mentioned above, STRIPs are attractive investments to investors desiring particular maturity-zero coupon bonds to meet investment goals and needs. For example, STRIPs are used as investment securities for individual retirement accounts, Keogh Plans, and pension funds. Frequently, managers of these types of financial institutions face the problem of structuring their asset investments so they can pay a given cash amount to policyholders in some future period. The classic example of this is an insurance policy that pays the holder some lump sum when the holder reaches retirement age. The risk to the life insurance company manager is that interest rates on the funds generated from investing the holder's premiums could fall. Thus, the accumulated returns on the premiums invested might not meet the target or promised amount. In effect, the insurance company would be forced to draw down its reserves and net worth to meet its payout commitments. (See Chapter 15 for a discussion of this risk.) To

Table 6–4   Present Value of STRIP Components of a 10-Year T-Note with an 8 Percent Coupon Rate and 7.90 Percent Yield to Maturity

Maturity on Security (in years)	Cash flow Received at maturity	Present Value of Cash Flow at 7.90 Percent
0.5	$ 400	$ 384.80
1.0	400	370.18
1.5	400	356.11
2.0	400	342.58
2.5	400	329.56
3.0	400	317.04
3.5	400	304.99
4.0	400	293.40
4.5	400	282.25
5.0	400	271.53
5.0	10,000	6,788.21
Total		$10,040.65

immunize or protect itself against interest rate risk, the insurer can invest in Treasury zero-coupon bonds (or STRIPS).

Example 6–2 Using a STRIP to Immunize against Interest Rate Risk

Suppose that it is 1999 and an insurer must make a guaranteed payment to an investor in five years, 2004. For simplicity, we assume that this target guaranteed payment is $14,690, a lump sum policy payout on retirement, equivalent to investing $10,000 at an annually compounded rate of 8 percent over five years. Of course, realistically, this payment would be much larger, but the underlying principles of the example do not change by scaling up or down the payout amount.

To immunize or protect itself against interest rate risk, the insurer needs to determine which investments would produce a cash flow of exactly $14,690 in five years, regardless of what happens to interest rates in the immediate future. By investing in a five-year maturity (and duration) Treasury zero-coupon bond (or STRIP), the insurance company would produce a $14,690 cash flow in five years, no matter what happens to interest rates in the immediate future.

Given a $1,000 face value and an 8 percent yield and assuming annual compounding, the current price per five-year STRIP is $680.58 per bond:

$$P = 680.58 = \frac{1,000}{(1.08)^5}$$

If the insurer buys 14.69 of these bonds at a total cost of $10,000 in 1999, these investments would produce $14,690 on maturity in five years. The reason is that the duration of this bond portfolio exactly matches the target horizon for the insurer's future liability to its policyholders. Intuitively, since the STRIP pays no intervening cash flows or coupons, future changes in interest rates have no reinvestment income effect. Thus, the return would be unaffected by intervening interest rate changes.

Most T-note and T-bond issues are eligible for the STRIP program. The components of a STRIP are sold with minimum face values of $1,000 and in increasing multiples of $1,000 (e.g., $2,000, $3,000). Thus, the par amount of the securities must be an amount that will produce semiannual coupon payments of $1,000 or a multiple of $1,000. The original Treasury note and bond issues that are eligible for the STRIP program are usually limited to those with large par values.

The T-note and bond quote list in Table 6–3 includes a portion of the Treasury STRIPS that traded on January 18, 2000. Look at the two lines for STRIPS maturing in August 2004. The first column of the quote lists the month and year the STRIP matures (e.g., Aug 04). The second column, labeled Type, indicates whether the instrument represent the coupon payments (ci) or the note's principal value (np) from the original Treasury note. Columns 3 and 4 list the bid and ask prices for the STRIPS. Like the quote for other Treasury securities (discussed above), the Bid is the close of the day selling price (in percentage terms) available to STRIP holders (i.e., the price dealers are willing to pay T-note and bond holders for their Treasury securities). Prices are quoted as percentages of the face value on the Treasury security, in 32nds. The Asked price is the close of the day purchase price available to investors. Column 5, labeled Chg., is the change in the Asked price from the previous day's close in 32nds. Finally, the last column, labeled Ask Yld., is the Asked price converted into a rate of return (yield to maturity) on the STRIP. This yield is calculated using the yield to maturity formulas found in Chapter 3, that is, it is the interest rate or yield (using semiannual compounding) that makes the price of the security just equal to the present value of the expected coupon or face value cash flows on the STRIP.

Part 2 Securities Markets

Example 6–3   Calculation of Yield on a STRIP

For the principal (np) STRIP maturing in August 2004 (reported in Table 6–3), the Asked price at the close on January 18, 2000 (or present value) is 74:07 (= 74⁷⁄₃₂, or 74.21875 percent). When the STRIP matures, on August 15, 2004 (in 4.5726 years), the STRIP holder will receive 100 percent of the face value (or future value). Using semiannual compounding, the yield to maturity (*ytm*), or Ask Yld. is calculated as:

$$74.21875\% = 100\% \, / \, (1 + ytm/2)^{2 \times 4.5726}$$

Solving for *ytm*, we get:

$$ytm = 6.63\%$$

Treasury Note and Bond Yields.   Treasury note and bond yield to maturities and prices are calculated using bond valuation formulas presented in Chapter 3. The general bond valuation formula is:

$$V_b = \frac{INT}{m}(PVIFA_{i_d/m,Nm}) + M(PVIF_{i_d/m,Nm})$$

where

V_b = Present value of the bond
M = Par or face value of the bond
INT = Annual interest (or coupon) payment per year on the bond, equals the par value times the coupon rate
N = Number of years until the bond matures
m = Number of times per year interest is paid
i_d = Interest rate used to discount cash flows on the bond

Example 6–4   Calculation of a T-Note Price from a *Wall Street Journal* Quote

From Table 6–3, there were two T-notes outstanding on January 18, 2000, with a maturity on January 31, 2001 (i.e., they were 1.0356 years from maturity). The first T-note had a coupon rate of 4.50 percent and an Ask Yield of 6.24 percent (*The Wall Street Journal* lists yields and prices to ¹⁄₁₀₀ of 1 percent). Using the bond valuation formula, the Asked price on the bond should have been:

$$V_b = \frac{4.50\%}{2}(PVIFA_{6.24\%/2,\ 1.0356(2)}) + 100(PVIF_{6.24\%/2,\ 1.0356(2)})$$

$$= 98.288$$

or to the nearest ¹⁄₃₂, 98²⁸⁄₃₂. The Asked quote reported in *The Wall Street Journal* was indeed 98²⁸⁄₃₂.

For the second January 2001 maturity T-note, the coupon rate was 5.25 percent and the yield was 6.20 percent. The Asked price on the bond should have been (and was):

$$V_b = \frac{5.25\%}{2}(PVIFA_{6.20\%/2,\ 1.0356(2)}) + 100(PVIF_{6.20\%/2,\ 1.0356(2)})$$

$$= 99.0613$$

or to the nearest ¹⁄₃₂, 99²⁄₃₂.

A limited number of T-note and bond issues are callable prior to maturity. Refer again to the T-note and T-bond quote in Table 6–3. Any quote with two years listed in column 2, labeled Maturity Mo/Yr, is callable. For example, look at the May 05-10 T-bond quote. This bond can be called for 100 percent of its face at any time between 2005 and 2010. T-bonds generally have a five-year call window. In August 1999, the U.S. government announced plans to buy back (or call-back) up to $11 billion in Treasury bonds. The extensive period of economic growth (in the 1990s) and the resulting budget surplus presented an opportunity, for the first time since 1972, to reduce the public debt via a call-back program of some of the outstanding T-bonds. We look at the impact of callability of a bond when we discuss corporate bonds.

Accrued Interest.   When an investor buys a T-note or T-bond between coupon payments, the buyer must compensate the seller for that portion of the coupon payment accrued between the last coupon payment and the settlement day (normally, settlement takes place 1 to 2 days after a trade). This amount is called **accrued interest**. Thus, at settlement, the buyer must pay the seller the purchase price of the T-note or T-bond plus accrued interest. The sum of these two is often called the *full price* or *dirty price* of the security. The price without the accrued interest added on is called the *clean price*.

Accrued interest on a T-note or T-bond is based on the actual number of days the bond was held by the seller since the last coupon payment:

$$\text{Accrued interest} = \frac{INT}{2} \times \frac{\text{Actual number of days since last coupon payment}}{\text{Actual number of days in coupon period}}$$

accrued interest

That portion of the coupon payment accrued between the last coupon payment and the settlement day.

Example 6–5   Calculation of Accrued Interest and Yield to Maturity on a Bond

On August 2, 1999, you purchase a $10,000 T-note that matures on May 15, 2006 (settlement occurs two days after purchase, so you receive actual ownership of the bond on August 4, 1999). The coupon rate on the T-note is 5.875 percent and the current price quoted on the bond is 101-11 (or 101.34375% of the face value of the T-note). The last coupon payment occurred on May 15, 1999 (81 days before settlement), and the next coupon payment will be paid on November 15, 1999 (103 days from settlement). We illustrate this time line in Figure 6–3.

The accrued interest due to the seller from the buyer at settlement is calculated as:

$$(5.875\%/2) \times 81/184 = 1.29314\%$$

of the face value of the bond, or $129.3134. The dirty price of this transaction is:

$$\begin{array}{ccccc}
\text{Clean price} & + & \text{Accrued interest} & = & \text{Dirty price} \\
101.34375\% & + & 1.29314\% & = & 102.63689\%
\end{array}$$

Figure 6–3   Timeline Used to Determine Accrued Interest on a Bond

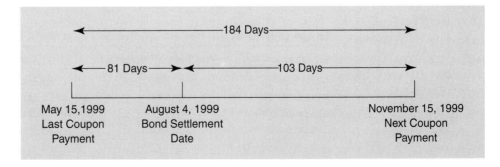

of the face value of the bond, or $10,263.689 per $10,000 face value bond.

The yield to maturity (which is based on the clean price) on the bond received on August 4, 1999, and maturing on May 15, 2006 (a total of 5 years and 285 days, or 5.7808 years) is:

$$101.34375\% = \frac{5.875\%}{2}(\text{PVIFA}_{ytm/2,\ 5.7808(2)}) + 100(\text{PVIF}_{ytm/2,\ 5.7808(2)})$$

Solving for the yield to maturity, we get 5.632 percent.

Do You Understand?

1. What the difference is between a competitive and noncompetitive Treasury auction bid?
2. What percentage of a Treasury auction offering may be awarded to any single bidder?

www.bog.frb.fed.us/

Primary and Secondary Market Trading in Treasury Notes and Bonds. Similar to primary market T-bill sales, the U.S. Treasury sells T-notes and T-bonds through competitive and noncompetitive Treasury auctions (see Chapter 5). Table 6–5 shows a recent auction pattern for T-note and T-bond new issues. The Treasury issues a press release about a week before each auction announcing the details of the auction, including the auction date, the amount to be sold, and other details about the securities to be issued (see In the News box 6–1).

Bids may be submitted by government securities dealers, businesses, and individuals through a Federal Reserve Bank until noon Eastern time for noncompetitive bids and 1 P.M. Eastern time for competitive bids on the day of the auction. Awards are announced the following day. Table 6–6 shows the results of the two-year T-note auction of December 22, 1999. At this auction, 51.07 percent (or $17,176.0 million) of the submitted bids ($33,634.0 million) were accepted. Further, 7.55 percent ($1,296.5 million) of the accepted bids at the December 22, 1999, Treasury auction were noncompetitive. The auction is a discriminating auction—different bidders pay different prices, with priority going to the highest bid prices.

Figure 6–4 illustrates the auction results for the two-year T-notes. The highest price offered on the two-year T-notes was 99.968 percent (or a yield of 6.142 percent) of the face value of the T-notes. Bids were filled at prices below the high. The lowest accepted bid price was 99.800 percent (or a yield of 6.233 percent). At this price, all $17.176 million in two-year T-notes offered were sold. All bidders who submitted prices above 99.800 percent (categories 1 through 5 in Figure 6–4) were awarded in full (winning bids). Bidders who submitted a price below 99.800 percent (categories 7 and beyond in Figure 6–4) received no allocation of the auctioned T-notes. A portion, but not all, of the bids submitted at 99.800 were filled (category 6 in Figure 6–4). These bids are filled pro rata at this price. For example, if total bids in category 6 were $100 million, but only $25 million in notes remained to be allocated to competitive bidders (given the S_C supply curve in Figure 6–4), each bidder would receive 25 percent (¼) of his or her bid quantity at this price. All of the $1,296.5 million noncompetitive bids were accepted at a price of 99.800 percent (which is equal to the weighted-average price paid by the winning competitive bidders). Finally, the median price on the accepted bids was 99.848 percent (for a yield of 6.207 percent).

Table 6–5 Auction Pattern for Treasury Notes and Bonds

Security	Purchase Minimum	General Auction Schedule
2-year note	$1,000	Monthly
5-year note	$1,000	February, May, August, November
10-year note	$1,000	February, May, August, November
30-year bond	$1,000	February, August, November

Source: U.S. Treasury, website, Bureau of Public Debt, May 21, 1999. *www.ustreas.gov/*

In the News

Treasury to Auction $15,000 Million of 2-Year Notes

The Treasury will auction $15,000 million of 2-year notes to refund $27,858 million of publicly held securities maturing May 31, 1999, and to pay down about $12,858 million. In addition to the public holdings, Federal Reserve Banks hold $3,056 million of the maturing securities for their own accounts, which may be refunded by issuing an additional amount of the new security.

The maturing securities held by the public include $3,053 million held by Fed-

Source: U.S. Treasury, website, Bureau of Public Debt, May 19, 1999.

eral Reserve Banks as agents for foreign and international monetary authorities. Amounts bid for these accounts by Federal Reserve Banks will be added to the offering.

TreasuryDirect customers requested that we reinvest their maturing holdings of approximately $670 million into the 2-year note.

The auction will be conducted in the single-price auction format. All competitive and noncompetitive

awards will be at the highest yield of accepted competitive tenders.

The notes being offered today are eligible for the STRIPS program.

Tenders will be received at Federal Reserve Banks and Branches and at the Bureau of the Public Debt, Washington, D.C. This offering of Treasury securities is governed by the terms and conditions set forth in the Uniform Offering Circular for the Sale and Issue of Marketable Book-Entry Treasury Bills, Notes, and Bonds (31 CFR Part 356, as amended).

Details about the new security are given in the attached offering highlights.

www.ustreas.gov/

Attachment

HIGHLIGHTS OF TREASURY OFFERINGS TO THE PUBLIC OF 2-YEAR NOTES TO BE ISSUED JUNE 1, 1999

May 19, 1999

Offering Amount . . . . $15,000 million

Description of Offering:

Term and type of security	2-year notes
Series	Y-2001
CUSIP number	912827 5H 1
Auction date	May 26, 1999
Issue date	June 1, 1999
Dated date	May 31, 1999
Maturity date	May 31, 2001
Interest date	Determined based on the highest accepted competitive bid
Yield	Determined at auction
Interest payment dates	November 30 and May 31
Minimum bid amount and multiples	$1,000
Accrued interest payable by investor	Determined at auction
Premium or discount	Determined at auction

(continues)

In the News continued

STRIPS Information:

Minimum amount required	Determined at auction
Corpus CUSIP number	912820 DW 4
Due date(s) and CUSIP number(s) for additional TINT(s)	Not Applicable

Submission of bids:

Noncompetitive bids: Accepted in full up to $5,000,000 at the highest accepted yield.

Competitive bids:

(1) Must be expressed as a yield with three decimals, e.g., 7.123%.

(2) Net long position for each bidder must be reported when the sum of the total bid amount, at all yields, and the net long position is $2 billion or greater.

(3) Net long position must be determined as of one-half hour prior to the closing time for receipt of competitive tenders.

Maximum Recognized Bid at a Single Yield.	35% of public offering
Maximum Award	35% of public offering

Receipt of Tenders:

Noncompetitive tenders: Prior to 12:00 noon Eastern Daylight Saving time on auction day.

Competitive tenders: Prior to 1:00 p.m. Eastern Daylight Saving time on auction day.

Payment Terms: By charge to a funds account at Federal Reserve Bank on issue date, or payment of full par amount with tender. *TreasuryDirect* customers can use the Pay Direct feature which authorizes a charge to their account of record at their financial institution on issue date.

Most secondary market trading of Treasury notes and bonds occurs directly through broker and dealer trades (see Chapters 5 and 16). For example, according to the Federal Reserve Bank of New York, the average daily trading volume in T-note and T-bond issues for the first half of 1999 was $165.5 billion. The Treasury quotes in Table 6–3 show just a small number of the Treasury securities that traded on January 18, 2000. The full quote listed in *The Wall Street Journal* shows the hundreds of different Treasury securities that trade daily.

municipal bonds

Securities issued by state and local (e.g., county, city, school) governments.

Municipal Bonds

Municipal bonds are securities issued by state and local (e.g., counties, cities, schools) governments ($1,518.1 billion outstanding in September 1999) to fund either temporary imbalances between operating expenditures and receipts or to finance long-term capital outlays for activities such as school construction, public utility construction, or transportation systems. Tax receipts or revenues generated from a project are the source of repayment on municipal bonds.

Municipal bonds are attractive to household investors since interest payments on municipal bonds (but not capital gains) are exempt from federal income taxes and most state and local income taxes (in contrast, interest payments on Treasury securities are exempt only from state and local income taxes). As a result, the interest borrowing cost to state or local government is lower, because investors are willing to accept lower interest rates on municipal bonds relative to comparable taxable bonds such as corporate bonds.

Municipal Bond Yields. To compare returns from tax-exempt municipal bonds with those on fully taxable corporate bonds, the after-tax (or equivalent tax-exempt) rate of return on a taxable bond can be calculated as follows:

$$i_a = i_b \, (1 - t)$$

Table 6–6   Announcement of Treasury Auction Results, December 22, 1999

PUBLIC DEBT NEWS

Department of the Treasury • Bureau of the Public Debt • Washington, DC 20239

```
                 TREASURY SECURITY AUCTION RESULTS
              BUREAU OF THE PUBLIC DEBT - WASHINGTON DC

FOR IMMEDIATE RELEASE                    CONTACT:    Office of Financing
December 22, 1999                                    202-691-3550

           RESULTS OF TREASURY'S AUCTION OF 2-YEAR NOTES

Interest Rate:  6 1/8%              Issue Date:      December 31, 1999
Series:         R-2001              Dated Date:      December 31, 1999
CUSIP No:       9128272E1           Maturity Date:   December 31, 2001


          High Yield:   6.233%    Price:  99.800
```

   All noncompetitive and successful competitive bidders were awarded
securities at the high yield. Tenders at the high yield were
allotted 19%. All tenders at lower yields were accepted in full.

   This offering was announced on December 15, 1999, as a new 2-YEAR NOTES
of Series AG-2001(CUSIP No. 9128275V0). The interest rate determined in
this auction matches that of an outstanding issue with the same maturity and
interest payment dates. ACCORDINGLY, THE SECURITY AUCTIONED TODAY WILL BE
CONSIDERED AN ADDITIONAL ISSUE OF THE 5-YEAR NOTE OF SERIES R-2001
FULLY DESCRIBED ABOVE.

```
              AMOUNTS TENDERED AND ACCEPTED (in thousands)

    Tender Type                 Tendered              Accepted
    -----------              ---------------        ---------------
    Competitive           $    30,162,034       $    13,704,034
    Noncompetitive             1,296,527              1,296,527
                           ---------------        ---------------
       PUBLIC SUBTOTAL         31,458,561             15,000,561 1/

    Federal Reserve             2,175,445              2,175,445
                           ---------------        ---------------
    TOTAL                 $    33,634,006       $    17,176,006
```

   Median yield   6.207%: 50% of the amount of accepted competitive tenders
was tendered at or below that rate. Low yield   6.142%:   5% of the amount
of accepted competitive tenders was tendered at or below that rate.

BID-TO-COVER RATIO = 31,458,561 / 15,000,561 = 2.10, STRIPS MIN: $1,600,000
CORPUS CUSIP: 912820EJ2. ALL AMOUNTS OUTSTANDING FOR CUSIP 9128272E1,
INCLUDING THE 5-YEAR NOTES ISSUED 12-31-96, ARE AVAILABLE FOR STRIPS.

1/ Awards to TREASURY DIRECT = $872,518,000

                http://www.publicdebt.treas.gov

Source: U.S. Treasury, website, Bureau of Public Debt, December 22, 1999. *www.ustreas.gov/*

Figure 6–4   Treasury Auction Results

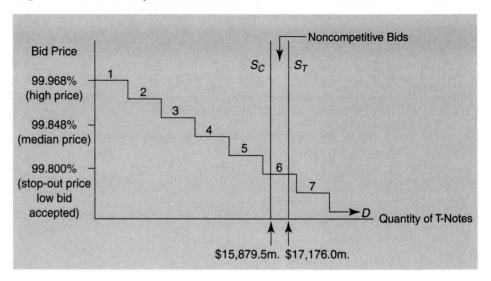

where

     i_a = After-tax (equivalent tax exempt) rate of return on a taxable corporate bond
     i_b = Before-tax rate of return on a taxable bond
     t = Marginal income tax rate of the bond holder (i.e., the sum of his or her marginal federal, state, and local taxes)

Example 6–6   Comparison of Municipal Bonds and Fully Taxable Corporate Bond Rates

Suppose you can invest in taxable corporate bonds that are paying a 10 percent annual interest rate or municipal bonds. If your marginal tax rate is 28 percent, the after-tax or equivalent tax exempt rate of return on the taxable bond is:

$$10\% \ (1 - .28) = 7.2\%$$

Thus, the comparable interest rate on municipal bonds of similar risk would be 7.2 percent.

Alternatively, the interest rate on a tax-exempt municipal bond can be used to determine the tax equivalent rate of return for a taxable security that would cause an investor to be just indifferent between the taxable and tax-exempt bonds of the same default and liquidity risks. Rearranging the equation above,

$$i_b = i_a \, /(1 - t)$$

Example 6–7   Conversion of a Municipal Bond Rate to a Tax Equivalent Rate

You are considering an investment in a municipal bond that is paying i_a = 6.5 percent annually. If your marginal tax rate (t) is 21 percent, the tax equivalent rate of interest on this bond (i_b) is:

$$8.125\% = 6.5\%/(1 - .21)$$

Table 6-7 General Obligation and Revenue Bonds Issued, 1990 and 1999
(in millions of dollars)

	1990	**1999**
General obligation bonds	$39,610	$ 69,924
Revenue bonds	81,295	155,947

Source: Federal Reserve Bulletin, Table 1.45, May 1992; and *Bond Buyer,* January 3, 2000. *www.bog.frb.fed.us/*

general obligation bonds

Bonds backed by the full faith and credit of the issuer.

Two types of municipal bonds exist: general obligation bonds and revenue bonds. Table 6-7 shows the amount of both issued in 1990 and 1999. **General obligation (GO) bonds** are backed by the full faith and credit of the issuer—that is, the state or local government promises to use all of its financial resources (e.g., its taxation powers) to repay the bond. GO bonds have neither specific assets pledged as collateral backing the bond nor a specific revenue stream identified as a source of repayment of the bond's principal and interest. Because the taxing authority of the government issuer is promised to ensure repayment, the issuance of new GO bonds generally requires local taxpayer approval. Possibly because of this requirement, and taxpayers' reluctance to have their taxes increased, general obligation bonds represent a smaller portion of municipal bonds issued (31 percent in 1999).

revenue bonds

Bonds sold to finance a specific revenue-generating project and are backed by cash flows from that project.

Revenue bonds are sold to finance a specific revenue-generating project and are backed by cash flows from that project. For example, a revenue bond may be issued to finance an extension of a state highway. To help pay off the interest and principal on that bond, tolls collected from the use of the highway may be pledged as collateral. If the revenue from the project is insufficient to pay interest and retire the bonds on maturity as promised—perhaps because motorists are reluctant to use the highway and pay the tolls—general tax revenues may not be used to meet these payments. Instead, the revenue bond goes into default and bond holders are not paid. Thus, revenue bonds are generally riskier than GO bonds.

Industrial development bonds (IDBs) are a type of revenue bond issued by municipalities on behalf of a corporation to help build the economic base of the municipality. For example, in December 1998, Sedgwick County's (Kansas) Commission issued $1 billion of taxable industrial development bonds for Raytheon Aircraft Co. over a 10-year period. The issuance of the IDB made Raytheon eligible for $200 million of property tax reductions under Kansas law.

Unlike a revenue bond, however, the municipality gives its approval for the sale of the bonds but assumes no legal liability for repayment. Rather, the company for which the IDBs are issued is liable for repayment. Abuses of the tax exempt or tax reduced status of IDB bonds led to the passage of federal legislation in 1984 that limited the amount of IDBs that could be sold in each state.

Municipal bonds are typically issued in minimum denominations of $5,000. Although trading in these bonds is less active than that of Treasury bonds, a secondary market exists for municipal bonds. Table 6-8 lists a municipal bond quote sheet from *The Wall Street Journal* on January 18, 2000. Column 1 lists the (local) government issuer. Column 2 lists the coupon rate (generally paid semiannually) on the bond issue. Column 3, labeled MAT, is the maturity date of the bond issue. Column 4, labeled PRICE, is the bond price in percentage terms (i.e., 96 = 96 percent of the face value). Column 5, labeled CHG, is the change in the price from the previous day's close. Column 6, labeled BID YLD, is the yield to maturity on the municipal bond based on the current selling price available to the municipal bond holder.

As can be seen in In the News box 6–2, municipal bonds are not default risk free. Defaults on municipal bonds peaked in 1990 at $1.4

Do You Understand?

1. Why the Hesperia Assessment District defaulted on its municipal bonds?

Table 6–8   Municipal Bond Quote

TAX-EXEMPT BONDS

Representative prices for several active tax-exempt revenue and refunding bonds, based on institutional trades.
Changes rounded to the nearest one-eighth. Yield is to maturity. n-New. Source: The Bond Buyer.

ISSUE	COUPON	MAT	PRICE	CHG	BID YLD	ISSUE	COUPON	MAT	PRICE	CHG	BID YLD
Atl Ga Wtr&Wstwtr 99A	5.000	11-01-38	79⅞	....	6.41	Miami-Dade Co Educ	5.750	04-01-29	95½	....	6.08
CA State genl oblig	5.750	12-01-29	95½	....	6.08	Miss Dev Bk Ser99A	5.000	07-01-24	83½	....	6.32
CA State genl oblig	5.750	12-01-24	96	....	6.06	Mmphs-Shlby Airpt	6.000	03-01-24	97	....	6.24
CAHlthFinAuth	6.125	12-01-30	94¼	....	6.56	Monty BMC Spc Care	5.000	11-15-29	80⅞	....	6.45
ClarkCoNV arpt	6.000	07-01-29	97⅛	....	6.21	NJ Hlth Fac Fin Auth	4.750	07-01-28	78½	....	6.39
Del River Prt Auth	5.750	01-01-26	95½	....	6.09	NYC Genl Obl Bds	5.000	03-15-29	80½	....	6.49
Del River Prt Auth	5.750	01-01-22	96	....	6.08	NYC TSASC tobacco	6.250	07-15-34	94½	....	6.66
Det MI sewage disp	6.000	07-01-29	97¼	....	6.21	NYC TSASC tobacco	6.375	07-15-39	95½	....	6.70
EmpireStDevCpNY	6.000	01-01-29	97¼	....	6.20	NYS Dorm Auth	6.000	05-15-39	94¾	....	6.37
Farmington NM	5.125	04-01-29	83⅞	....	6.33	NYS Dorm Auth	5.950	05-15-29	97	....	6.18
FL Pts Fin Comm99	5.500	10-01-29	89⅞	....	6.25	Ohio Air Qty Dev	5.150	05-01-26	85¼	....	6.30
FLStBdEd	5.750	06-01-29	95⅝	....	6.07	OK Indus Auth hlth	5.750	08-15-29	92	....	6.35
Harris Co Hlth Fac Tex	5.375	07-01-29	86	....	6.43	Phila Sch Dist PA	5.750	03-01-29	94¼	....	6.17
IL Hth FacAuth99	6.250	11-15-29	93	....	6.79	San Diego Pub Fac Ca	5.000	05-15-29	83¼	....	6.24
Louisvll&Jeffers Metro	5.750	05-15-33	94	....	6.17	Tampa FL Water	5.750	10-01-29	95⅝	....	6.07
MA Wtr PollTr	5.750	08-01-29	93⅞	....	6.20	Univ IL Bd Trustees	6.000	04-01-30	96⅞	....	6.23
Mass Tpk Auth	5.000	01-01-39	79⅞	....	6.41	VirginIsl PubFinAuth	6.125	10-01-29	96	....	6.43
MDHlth HigherEd	6.000	07-01-39	96⅝	....	6.23	Wash Co Auth PA	6.150	12-01-29	98½	....	6.26
Mesa IndDev AZ	5.625	01-01-29	91⅞	....	6.23	Washoe NV ltd cnv	6.400	07-01-29	98⅞	....	6.48
MI StHosp	6.125	11-15-26	94⅝	....	6.55	Wichita KS hosp	6.250	11-15-24	94⅞	....	6.67

Source: *The Wall Street Journal,* January 19, 2000, p. C20. Reprinted by permission of *The Wall Street Journal.*
© 2000 Dow Jones & Company, Inc. All Rights Reserved Worldwide. *www.wsj.com/*

billion, due mainly to a major economic recession in the United States. Unlike Treasury securities, for which the federal government (in the worst case) can raise taxes or print money to make promised payments, state and local governments are limited to their local tax and revenue base as sources of funds for municipal bond repayment.

The Trading Process for Municipal Bonds.   The initial (primary market) sale for municipal bonds (and corporate bonds, discussed below) occurs either through a public offering, using an investment bank serving as a security underwriter, or through a private placement to a small group of investors (often financial institutions). Generally, when a large state or local governmental unit issues municipals to the public, many investment banks are interested in underwriting the bonds and the municipals can generally be sold in a national market. Total dollar volume of these new issues was $219 billion in 1999, down from $279 billion in 1998. Table 6–9 lists the activity of the top 10 municipal bond underwriters in 1999.

Most smaller municipal bond issues, however, are underwritten by small regional investment banks located in the immediate area of the municipal issuer. Table 6–10 lists the top 10 underwriters of municipals with a face value of less than $10 million in 1999. The high cost of gathering information about smaller municipal issuers limits the interest of smaller investors in the sales of these issues.

firm commitment underwriting

The issue of securities by an investment bank in which the investment bank guarantees the issuer a price for newly issued securities by buying the whole issue at a fixed price from the issuer. It then seeks to resell these securities to suppliers of funds (investors) at a higher price.

Public offerings of municipal (and corporate, see below) bonds are most often made through an investment banking firm (see Chapter 16) serving as the underwriter. Normally, the investment bank facilitates this transfer using a **firm commitment underwriting,** illustrated in Figure 6–5. The investment bank guarantees the municipality (or corporation for a corporate bond) a price for newly issued bonds by buying the whole issue at a fixed price from the municipal issuer (the bid price). The investment bank then seeks to resell these securities to suppliers of funds (investors) at a higher price (the offer price). As a result, the investment bank takes a risk that it may not be able to resell the securities to investors at a higher price. This may occur if prices of municipal bonds suddenly fall due to an unexpected change in interest rates or negative information being released about the issuing municipality. If this occurs, the investment bank takes a loss on its underwriting of the security. However, the municipal issuer is protected by being able to sell the whole issue.

In the News

6-2

Hesperia, California, Suffers State's Largest Municipal Bond Default in 1998

An assessment district set up by the High Desert city of Hesperia suffered the biggest municipal bond default out of 11 reneging institutions in 1998, and seven other local bond issues could be in danger of following suit this year. All told, institutions around the state breached on $89.2 million worth of bonds in 1998, according to the California Municipal Bond Advisor, a Palm Springs-based newsletter that tracks the state's municipal bond market. Moreover, the newsletter named seven other Inland Empire bond issues to a "watch list" of financial instruments that are on shaky ground.

The Hesperia Assessment District, established in 1992, had by far the largest default in the state last year, at $20.6 million, according to the newsletter. The next-highest failures included an $11.6 million default by the

Selma Public Financing Authority and a $10.5 million lapse on a series of Marks-Roos Bonds by the California Public Financing Authority. Besides the Hesperia Assessment District, no other Inland Empire-based institution made the 1998 list of defaults . . .

Mann's newsletter also keeps a "watch list" of institutions throughout California that he believes are in danger of reneging on municipal bonds. Bonds qualify for the list if there are delinquent taxes or if reserve funds have been used to pay bond holders. The current list includes 17 institutions and $433 million in potential defaults statewide, he said. Among those on the "watch list" is a Fontana community facilities district,

which last month threatened to bail on $46.2 million in Mello-Roos bonds as early as April 2000.

In addition to Fontana, six Inland Empire-based institutions could be in danger of defaulting . . .The Fontana district, which has the largest potential default on the local list, was formed to develop Empire Center, a 240-acre parcel off Sierra Avenue that will be a mixed-use commercial and residential development. They blame the default on the developer, Fontana Empire Center LLC, which refused to pay back taxes on the property. That forced the city to foreclose in December 1996.

In Hesperia, the city set up the assessment district to build infrastructure for a 940-acre residential and commercial development in the southwest part of the city, according to Mel Drown, the city's finance director. When developer Hill Williams declared bankruptcy, the city was left holding the bag, he said.

Source: *The Business Press,* Ontario, CA, February 1, 1999, by Joseph Ascenzi.

www.inlandempireonline. com/

The investment bank can purchase the bonds through competitive bidding against other investment bankers or through direct negotiation with the issuer. In a competitive sale, the issuer invites bids from a number of underwriters. The investment bank that submits the highest bid to the issuer wins the bid. The underwriter may use a syndicate of other underwriters and investment banks to distribute (sell) the issue to the public.

Table 6–9   Top Municipal Bond Underwriters

Underwriter	Principal Amount (in millions of dollars)	Market Share	Number of Issues
Salomon Smith Barney	$31,375.4	12.7%	475
Merrill Lynch	22,845.3	9.2	312
Paine Webber	22,089.3	8.9	420
Goldman Sachs	17,314.8	7.0	233
Lehman Brothers	11,039.4	4.5	169
Morgan Stanley Dean Witter	9,518.3	3.8	226
Bear, Stearns	7,642.9	3.1	108
First Union	6,373.8	2.6	393
J.P. Morgan	5,660.7	2.3	106
U.S. Bancorp Piper Jaffray	5,206.8	2.1	538
Industry totals	$219 billion		

Source: Thomson Financial Securities Data, January 2000. *www.tfsd.com/*

Table 6–10   Top Small Issue Municipal Bond Underwriters

Underwriter	Principal Amount (in millions of dollars)	Market Share	Number of Issues
U.S. Bancorp Piper Jaffray	$1,562.6	5.6%	403
First Union Capital Markets	1,188.5	4.3	248
Banc One Capital Markets	1,007.0	3.6	283
Dain Rauscher	910.8	3.3	268
Roosevelt & Cross	875.2	3.2	243
Banc of America Securities	819.7	3.0	176
A.G. Edwards & Sons	772.0	2.8	146
Morgan Keegan	766.1	2.8	199
Salomon Smith Barney	649.1	2.3	119
Robert W. Baird	645.9	2.3	183

Source: Thomson Financial Securities Data, January 2000. *www.tfsd.com/*

Figure 6–5   Firm Commitment Underwriting of a Municipal or Corporate Bond Issue

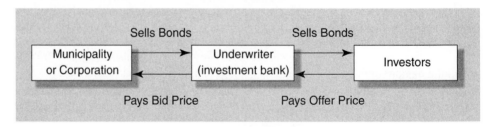

Most state and local governments require a competitive municipal bond issue to be announced in a trade publication, e.g., the *Bond Buyer*. With a negotiated sale, the investment bank obtains the exclusive right to originate, underwrite, and distribute the new bonds through a one-on-one negotiation process. With a negotiated sale, the investment bank provides the origination and advising services to the issuers. Most states require that GO bonds be issued through competitive bids.

best efforts underwriting

The issue of securities in which the underwriter does not guarantee a price to the issuer and acts more as a placing or distribution agent on a fee basis related to its success in placing the issue.

Some municipal (and corporate) securities are offered on a **best efforts (underwriting)** basis in which the underwriter does not guarantee a firm price to the issuer (as with a firm commitment offering) and acts more as a placing or distribution agent for a fee.

In a private placement, a municipality (or corporation), sometimes with the help of an investment bank, seeks to find a large institutional buyer or group of buyers (usually less than 10) to purchase the whole issue. To protect smaller individual investors against a lack of disclosure, the Security and Exchange Act of 1934 requires publicly traded securities to be registered with the Securities and Exchange Commission (SEC). Private placements, on the other hand, can be unregistered and can only be resold to large, financially sophisticated investors (see below). These large investors supposedly possess the resources and expertise to analyze a security's risk.

Privately placed bonds (and stocks) have traditionally been among the most illiquid securities in the bond market, with only the very largest financial institutions or institutional investors being able or willing to buy and hold them in the absence of an active secondary market. In April 1990, however, the Securities and Exchange Commission (SEC) amended its Regulation 144A. This allowed large investors to begin trading these privately placed securities among themselves even though, in general, privately placed securities do not satisfy the stringent disclosure and informational requirements that the SEC imposes on approved publicly registered issues. Rule 144A private placements may now be underwritten by investment banks on a firm commitment basis. Of the total $363.65 billion in private debt (municipal and corporate) placements in 1998, $297.59 billion (82.1 percent) were Rule 144A placements. Goldman Sachs was the lead underwriter of Rule 144A debt placements in 1998 (underwriting $30.25 billion, 10.2 percent of the total placements).

Issuers of privately placed bonds tend to be less well known (e.g., medium-sized municipalities and corporations). As a result of a lack of information on these issues, and the resulting possibility of greater risk, interest rates paid to holders of privately placed bonds tend to be higher than on publicly placed bond issues. Although Rule 144A has improved the liquidity of privately placed bonds, this market is still less liquid than the public placement market. Another result of the increased attention to this market by investment banks is that the interest premiums paid by borrowers of privately placed issues over public issues has decreased.

Although the SEC defined large investors as those with assets of $100 million or more—which excludes all but the very wealthiest household savers—it is reasonable to ask how long this size restriction will remain. As they become more sophisticated and the costs of information acquisition fall, savers will increasingly demand access to the private placement market. In such a world, savers would have a choice not only between the secondary securities from financial institutions and the primary securities publicly offered by municipalities and corporations but also between publicly offered (registered) securities and privately offered (unregistered) securities.

The secondary market for municipal bonds is thin (i.e., trades are relatively infrequent). Thin trading is mainly a result of a lack of information on bond issuers, as well as special features (such as covenants) that are built into those bond's contracts. Information on municipal bond issuers (particularly of smaller government units) is generally more costly to obtain and evaluate, although this is in part offset by bond rating agencies (see below). In a similar fashion, bond rating agencies generate information about corporate and sovereign (country) borrowers as well.

Corporate Bonds

corporate bonds

Long-term bonds issued by corporations.

Corporate bonds are all long-term bonds issued by corporations ($4,534.6 billion outstanding in September 1999, 50.3 percent of all outstanding long-term bonds). The minimum denomination on publicly traded corporate bonds (that, in contrast to privately placed corporate bonds, require SEC registration) is $1,000, and coupon-paying corporate bonds generally pay interest semiannually.

bond indenture

The legal contract that specifies the rights and obligations of the bond issuer and the bond holders.

www.nyse.com/

The **bond indenture** is the legal contract that specifies the rights and obligations of the bond issuer and the bond holders. The bond indenture contains a number of positive and negative covenants associated with a bond issue (rules and restrictions placed on the bond issuer and bond holders, such as the ability to call the bond issue, dividend restrictions on the issuer, etc.). By legally documenting the rights and obligations of all parties involved in a bond issue, the bond indenture helps lower the risk (and therefore the interest cost) of the bond issue. All matters pertaining to the bond issuer's performance regarding any debt covenants as well as bond repayments are overseen by a trustee (frequently a bank trust department) who is appointed as the bond holders' representative or "monitor." The trustee initiates any legal action on behalf of the bond holders against the issuing firm if the terms of a bond's indenture are violated.

Table 6–11 presents a bond market quote sheet from *The Wall Street Journal* for January 18, 2000, for corporate bonds traded on the New York Stock Exchange (NYSE). Look at the first quote posted in Table 6–11. Column 1 of the quote lists the issuer (AES Cp), the coupon rate (8 percent), and the year of maturity (8 = Year 2008). Column 2, labeled Cur Yld., is the current yield on the bond (or the coupon rate divided by the current price, 8 percent ÷ 92 percent = 8.7 percent). Column 3, labeled Vol., is the trading volume for the bond in thousands of dollars (10 = $10,000). Column 4, labeled Close, is the closing price of the bond on January 18 in percentage terms (92 = 92 percent of $1,000 = $920). Column 5, labeled Net Chg., is the change in the closing price from the previous day, in percentage terms (−½ = −0.50%).

Bond Characteristics.   Corporate (and Treasury) bonds have many different characteristics that differentiate one issue from another. We list and briefly define these characteristics in Table 6–12, and we describe them in detail below.

Bearer versus Registered Bonds.   Corporate bonds can be bearer bonds or registered bonds. With **bearer bonds**, coupons are attached to the bond and the holder (bearer) at the time of the coupon payment gets the relevant coupon paid on presentation to the issuer (i.e., gets the bond coupon "clipped"). With a **registered bond**, the bond holder's (or owner's) identification information is kept in an electronic record by the issuer and the coupon payments are mailed or wire-transferred to the bank account of the registered owner. Because of the lack of security with bearer bonds, they have largely been replaced by registered bonds.

bearer bonds

Bonds with coupons attached to the bond. The holder presents the coupons to the issuer for payments of interest when they come due.

registered bond

A bond in which the owner is recorded by the issuer and the coupon payments are mailed to the registered owner.

term bonds

Bonds in which the entire issue matures on a single date.

serial bonds

Bonds that mature on a series of dates, with a portion of the issue paid off on each.

mortgage bonds

Bonds issued to finance specific projects, which are pledged as collateral for the bond issue.

Term versus Serial Bonds.   Most corporate bonds are **term bonds,** meaning that the entire issue matures on a single date. Some corporate bonds (and most municipal bonds), on the other hand, are **serial bonds,** meaning that the issue contains many maturity dates, with a portion of the issue being paid off on each date. For economic reasons, many issuers like to avoid a "crisis at maturity." Rather than having to pay off one very large principal sum at a given time in the future (as with a term issue), many issuers like to stretch out the period over which principal payments are made—especially if the corporation's earnings are quite volatile.

Mortgage Bonds.   Corporations issue **mortgage bonds** to finance specific projects that are pledged as collateral for the bond issue. Thus, mortgage bond issues are secured debt issues.[3] Bond holders may legally take title to the collateral to obtain payment on the bonds if the issuer of a mortgage bond defaults. Because mortgage bonds are backed with a claim to specific assets of the corporate issuer, they are less risky investments than unsecured bonds. As a result, mortgage bonds have lower yields to

---

3. Open-end mortgage bonds allow the firm to issue additional bonds in the future, using the same assets as collateral and giving the same priority of claim against those assets. Closed-end mortgage bonds prohibit the firm from issuing additional bonds using the same assets as collateral and giving the same priority of claim against those assets.

Table 6–11 Corporate Bond Market Quote

NEW YORK EXCHANGE BONDS

Quotations as of 4 p.m. Eastern Time
Tuesday, January 18, 2000

Volume $11,143,000

	Domestic Tue.	Domestic Fri.	All Issues Tue.	All Issues Fri.
Issues Traded	200	169	207	178
Advances	61	69	63	73
Declines	98	67	103	72
Unchanged	41	33	41	33
New highs	1	2	1	3
New lows	33	18	33	20

SALES SINCE JANUARY 1
(000 omitted)

2000	1999	1998
$116,577	$158,476	$230,614

Dow Jones Bond Averages

–1999– High	–1999– Low	–2000– High	–2000– Low		–2000– Close	–2000– Chg.	–2000– %Yld	–1999– Close	–1999– Chg.
106.88	96.80	97.17	94.92	20 Bonds	94.92	−0.88	8.06	106.52	−0.18
104.72	94.96	95.09	93.20	10 Utilities	93.20	−1.08	7.89	104.71	+0.17
109.44	98.31	99.36	96.65	10 Industrials	96.65	−0.67	8.23	108.34	−0.52

CORPORATION BONDS
Volume, $10,645,000

Bonds	Cur Yld.	Vol.	Close	Net Chg.
AES Cp 8s8	8.7	10	92	− ½
ATT 5⅛01	5.2	2	98	...
ATT 7⅛02	7.1	27	100⅛	+ ⅛
ATT 6¾04	6.9	5	97¾	− ¾
ATT 5⅝04	6.0	50	94	− ⅜
ATT 7s05	7.1	20	99	− ⅛
ATT 8.2s05	8.2	72	100½	...
ATT 7½06	7.4	35	101	...
ATT 7¾07	7.6	50	101½	− ½
ATT 6s09	6.8	259	88⅞	− ¼
ATT 8⅛22	8.1	163	100⅜	+ ⅜
ATT 8⅛24	8.1	44	100	...
ATT 8⅝31	8.5	131	102⅛	− ⅛
Aames 10½02	13.8	49	76	+ 1
Aetna 6⅜03	6.6	60	96½	+ 2
Alza 5s06	cv	28	110¾	+ 1¼
AForP 5s30	8.9	2	56¼	− ½
Amresco 10s03	16.6	71	60⅛	+ ⅛
Amresco 10s04	17.0	190	59	...
ARch 10⅞05	9.4	10	115⅞	− ⅛
AutDt zr12	...	65	128½	− 1⅝
BkrHgh zr08	...	6	69½	+ 1½
BankAm 8½07	8.0	10	106⅝	+ 1⅞
BayView 9s07	11.1	6	81	− 1
BellPa 7⅛12	7.6	5	94	− ⅜
BellsoT 6½00	6.5	50	99 15/16	...
BellsoT 6¼03	6.4	10	97⅛	− ⅜
BellsoT 6⅜04	6.6	20	96⅝	− ¼
BellsoT 6½05	6.7	50	96¾	+ 1⅜
BellsoT 5⅞09	6.6	37	88¾	+ ⅜
BellsoT 7s25	7.8	60	90¼	− ¾
BellsoT 8¼32	8.3	407	100	− ⅜
BellsoT 7⅞32	8.2	65	96½	− 1⅝
BellsoT 7½33	8.1	335	92¾	− 1⅜
BellsoT 6¾33	8.1	93	83½	− ¼
BellsoT 7⅝35	8.1	42	93⅝	− 1⅜
BethSt 8⅜01	8.5	15	98⅞	− ⅛
BethSt 8.45s05	8.9	30	94½	− ⅝
Bluegrn 8¼12	cv	42	77	+ 2
Bordn 8⅜16	10.3	130	81⅛	− ⅜
BosCelts 6s38	11.2	2	53⅜	− ⅛
BoydGm 9¼03	9.1	15	102	+ 1
BrnSh 9½06	9.7	20	98⅛	+ ⅞
CaterpInc 6s07	6.7	19	90	− ⅛
CentrTrst 7½01	cv	133	94	...
ChaseM 7½03	7.4	10	101½	...
ChaseM 6¼06	6.8	55	92¼	− 1¾
ChaseM 6⅛08	6.9	8	89⅛	− 1⅞
ChespkE 9⅛06	10.2	98	89½	+ 1
ChiqBr 10s09	13.3	72	75	− 1⅛
ClrkOil 9½04	14.1	225	67½	+ ⅝
Coastl 8⅛02	8.1	8	100½	...
CoeurDA 7¼05	cv	46	53	+ 1¼
Coeur 6⅜04	cv	114	52⅝	+ 1⅛
Consec 8⅛03	8.2	40	99⅛	− ⅞
ConPort 11s06	18.0	20	61⅛	− 8⅞
Convrse 7s04	cv	34	21½	− 1⅛
DelcoR 8⅝07	9.2	16	93⅜	− 1
DevonE 4.9s08	cv	12	94⅝	− ⅜
Dole 7s03	7.4	10	94¼	− ⅛
Dole 7⅞13	8.5	107	92⅞	+ 1⅛
DukeEn 6⅞23	8.1	50	84⅝	− 2
DukeEn 7⅞24	8.0	60	98	...
DukeEn 6¾25	8.0	50	84⅛	− 1⅝
DukeEn 7½25	8.0	93	93½	+ ⅜
DukeEn 7s33	7.8	35	90⅜	+ ⅜
EMC 6s04	cv	10	141	+ 3½
FedDS 8⅛02	8.1	13	100⅜	− ½
FedDS 8½03	8.3	20	102¼	− ¼
Florsh 12¾02	14.8	60	86	+ ½
FordCr 6⅜08	7.0	25	91⅝	− 1
FremntGn zr13	...	70	38	+ 4¼
GBCB 8⅜07	9.0	29	93	− 1½
GECap 7½35	7.6	2	99	+ 2
GMA 9⅝00	9.6	8	100¾	...
GMA 5½01	5.7	45	95⅞	− ⅝
GMA 6⅞01	7.0	17	98⅞	− ¼
GMA 7⅛01	7.1	15	100	+ ⅝
GMA 7s02	7.0	32	99½	− ⅛
GMA 6⅝02	6.8	37	98⅛	+ ⅛
GMA dc6s11	7.1	33	84⅜	+ ⅝
GMA zr12	...	12	355	...
GMA zr15	...	23	291	...
GenesisH 9¾05	25.7	380	38	− 2
HlthcrR 6.55s02	cv	20	85	...
HewlPkd zr17	...	30	66	+ 3
Hilton 5s06	cv	251	75½	...
Hollgnr 9¼07	9.5	55	97⅛	− 1⅞
Honywll zr2000	...	5	95 17/32	− 3/32
Honywll zr01	...	10	88⅜	− ⅜
Honywll zr03	...	10	74⅜	...
Honywll zr05	...	5	66⅜	+ ⅛
Honywll zr07	...	55	54⅝	− ⅛
Honywll zr09	...	100	46⅞	+ ¼
IRT Pr 7.3s03	cv	25	92	...
IllPwr 5⅝00	5.7	25	99 15/32	+ 3/16
InldStl 7.9s07	9.3	10	85	+ 1
IBM 6⅜00	6.4	35	99 27/32	...
IBM 7¼02	7.2	33	100¼	− ⅛
IBM 5⅜09	6.3	5	85	− ½
IBM 7½13	7.6	155	98¾	− 1⅛
IBM 8⅜19	7.9	65	106¾	− ¾
IBM 6½28	7.6	15	86	− ⅛
IPap dc5⅛12	6.9	10	74⅜	− 1⅝
IntShip 9s03	9.3	39	97	− ½
JCPL 7⅛04	7.3	11	98⅜	− 1⅛
KCS En 8⅞08f	...	12	32⅛	− 1⅞
KaufB 9⅜03	9.4	181	99⅜	+ ⅜
KaufB 7¾04	8.2	35	94⅜	+ ⅜
KaufB 9⅝06	9.5	25	101	...
KentE 4½04	cv	30	79½	...
KerrM 7½14	cv	196	95½	...
Lamar 06	...	10	100½	− ⅛
Leucadia 7¾13	8.4	22	92⅜	− ¼
LibPrp 8s01	cv	20	116	− 4
Lilly 8⅛01	7.9	11	102½	+ 1¼
Loews 3⅛07	cv	5	80⅛	− 1⅝
LglsLt 8.2s23	8.3	47	98⅝	+ ¼
Lucent 7¼06	7.4	3	98⅜	− 1⅜
MBNA 8.28s26	9.4	10	88	− 1
MSC Sf 7⅞04	cv	35	89	+ ½
Malan 9½04	cv	49	90	− 1
MarO 7s02	7.1	40	98⅛	− ⅛
Mascotch 03	cv	100	75	− ¾
Medtrst 7½01	cv	10	86⅞	− 3⅝
MPac 4¾30f	...	10	58	− ⅜
Moran 8¾08f	cv	45	94	+ 2
Motrla zr09	...	33	263	+ 13¾
NatData 5s03	cv	18	90	...
NETelTel 6⅞23	8.0	47	86½	...
NJBTl 7¼11	7.4	49	97⅞	− ¼
NYTel 7¼24	8.1	28	89⅜	− ⅞
NYTel 6s07	6.5	2	92⅜	+ 1⅞
NYTel 7⅝23	8.1	52	94¼	− 1¼
NYTel 7s25	8.1	10	86⅞	+ ⅞
NYTel 9⅜31	8.7	10	108	...
NYTel 7s33	8.0	6	87	− ½
Noram 6s12	cv	20	84⅛	− 2⅞
OcciP 10⅛01	9.7	5	104½	...
OcciP 10⅛09	9.0	10	113	− ½
OcciP 11⅛19	10.5	9	105½	− ½
OffDep zr07	...	10	60	− 2⅜
OffDep zr08	...	84	67¼	+ 2
OreStl 11s03	10.8	10	102¼	− ¼
ParkElc 5½06	cv	10	86	...
ParkerD 5½04	cv	23	71	+ ½
PhnxInv 6s15	cv	25	98	...
Polaroid 11½06	11.8	186	97½	− ⅞
PSvEG 7s24	7.9	1	88⅛	− 1
Quest 10¾06	10.4	15	103	− 11½
Rallys 9⅞00	10.3	58	96 5/32	− 5/32
RalsP 9¼09	8.4	20	110½	...
RelGrp 9s00	9.7	153	92 15/32	− ½
RelGrp 9¾03	12.3	72	79	− 1
ReynTob 8s01	8.3	5	96⅞	...
ReynTob 7⅝03	8.2	288	93	− ½
ReynTob 8¾04	9.2	25	95½	...
ReynTob 9¼13	10.1	10	91⅝	− 1
RobMyr 63	cv	100	95½	+ ⅜
Safwy 10s01	9.7	60	103	− ⅝
SearsAc 6¾05	7.2	50	93¼	− 2¾
Shoney zr04	...	100	14	− 1
Simula 8s04	cv	15	68	...
SouBell 6s04	6.4	17	94½	...
SouNG 7.85s02	7.7	20	101½	+ 1⅝
Sprint 6⅞28	8.0	2	86	− 5¼
StdCmcl 07	cv	45	47½	− 1½
StdPac 8½07	9.1	5	93	+ ½
StoneC 9⅞01	9.9	333	100	...
StoneC 10¾02A	10.8	170	100	+ ¼
StoneC 10¾02O	10.5	30	102¾	+ ¼
StoneC 11½04	11.1	5	103¼	+ ⅛
StoneCn 6¾07	cv	18	87	− 1⅞
StoneC 12¼02	11.9	28	103⅛	+ 1⅞
SwiftE 6¼06	cv	70	75¾	+ ¾
TVA 6⅛03	6.4	82	96½	...
TVA 8¼34	8.3	50	99⅝	+ ⅛
TVA 7¼43	7.7	10	93⅞	...
TVA 6⅞43	7.7	5	89¾	− 1
TVA 7.85s44	7.9	50	99⅛	+ ⅛
Tenet 8s03	8.2	20	98	− ⅛
Tenet 8s05	8.4	155	95½	− ⅝
Tenet 8⅝07	9.0	40	95½	+ ⅛
Texco 8½03	8.0	28	105⅞	+ 1⅞
TmeWar 7¾05	7.8	100	100	− 1½
TmeWar 8.11s06	8.0	5	102	+ ½
TmeWar 8.18s07	8.1	7	101½	− ½
TmeWar 7.48s08	7.6	10	99	...
TmeWE 7¼08	7.5	60	97	+ ¾
TmeWar 9⅛13	8.4	9	108½	...
TollCp 8¾06	9.0	50	97½	+ ½
TravPrp 6¾01	6.8	10	98¾	...
Valhi zr07	...	13	60	+ 2¾
WsteM 4s02	cv	20	88	...
Webb 9¾03	9.9	43	98⅝	+ ½
Webb 9s06	10.1	55	88⅞	...
Webb 9¾08	10.7	56	91½	− ⅛
Webb 10¼10	10.6	40	96¼	+ 1
WebbDel 9⅜09	10.5	81	89	...
WhlPit 9⅜03	9.0	100	104	− ¼

EXPLANATORY NOTES
(For New York and American Bonds)

Yield is Current yield.

cv-Convertible bond. cf-Certificates. cld-Called. dc-Deep discount. ec-European currency units. f-Dealt in flat. il-Italian lire. kd-Danish kroner. m-Matured bonds, negotiability impaired by maturity. na-No accrual. r-Registered. rp-Reduced principal. st, sd-Stamped. t-Floating rate. wd-When distributed. ww-With warrants. x-Ex interest. xw-Without warrants. zr-Zero coupon.

vj-In bankruptcy or receivership or being reorganized under the Bankruptcy Act, or securities assumed by such companies.

FOREIGN BONDS
Volume, $498,000

Bonds	Cur Yld.	Vol.	Close	Net Chg.
Inco cv04	cv	10	94⅜	− 1⅝
Inco 7¾16	cv	68	86½	− ⅝
Ivaco 11½05	10.8	5	107	+ 1⅜
RoyBkSc 6⅜11	8.5	4	75	...
SeaCnt 9½03	9.9	147	96⅛	− ⅞
TelArg 11⅞04	11.1	277	106⅞	− ⅞
TrnMarMx 03	...	10	84	+ 1¾
TrnMarMx 06	cv	25	78⅜	− 1⅝

AMEX BONDS

Volume $258,000

SALES SINCE JANUARY 1

2000	1999	1998
$7,474,000	$6,543,000	$18,204,000

	Tue.	Fri	Thu.	Wed.
Issues Traded	7	12	12	8
Advances	3	2	5	2
Declines	4	9	3	6
Unchanged	0	1	5	0
New highs	0	0	2	0
New lows	0	1	0	1

Bonds	Cur Yld.	Vol.	Close	Net Chg.
AltLiv 5¼02	cv	33	62	+ 2½
ArchCm 10⅞08f	...	140	49⅛	− 1⅝
FriedeGld 4½04	cv	3	50	− 3
vjFruitL 7s11f	...	11	30½	− 1¼
TrnsLux 7½06	cv	10	87½	+ ½
TWA 11⅜06	27.4	30	41½	+ ¼
Trump 11¾03f	...	31	80⅛	− ⅝

NASDAQ

Convertible Debentures

Tuesday, January 18, 2000

Issue	Vol.	Close	Net Chg.
Agnico 3½04	113	67¾	− ¼
Avatar05	40	87¾	+ ¼
BankAtl07	115	63	− ¼
DixGrp 7s12	6	69	− 3
DrgEmp 7¾14	43	54	− 2⅞
DuraPh 3½02	10	84½	...
Jacobsn 6¾11	10	65	...
Metamor 2.94s04	2	83¾	...
OHM 8s06	3	86	− ½
PhyCor 4½03	184	53¼	+ ¾
Schuler 6½03	28	78¼	− 3¼
Telxon 7½12	19	89	+ 4½

Source: *The Wall Street Journal,* January 19, 2000, p. C19. Reprinted by permission of *The Wall Street Journal.*

Table 6–12   Bond Characteristics

Bearer Bonds—bonds on which coupons are attached. The bond holder presents the coupons to the issuer for payments of interest when they come due.

Registered Bonds—with a registered bond, the owner's identification information is recorded by the issuer and the coupon payments are mailed to the registered owner.

Term Bonds—bonds in which the entire issue matures on a single date.

Serial Bonds—bonds that mature on a series of dates, with a portion of the issue paid off on each.

Mortgage Bonds—bonds that are issued to finance specific projects that are pledged as collateral for the bond issue.

Equipment Trust Certificates—bonds collateralized with tangible non–real estate property (e.g., railcars and airplanes).

Debentures—bonds backed solely by the general credit of the issuing firm and unsecured by specific assets or collateral.

Subordinated Debentures—unsecured debentures that are junior in their rights to mortgage bonds and regular debentures.

Convertible Bonds—bonds that may be exchanged for another security of the issuing firm at the discretion of the bond holder.

Stock Warrants—bonds that give the bond holder an opportunity to purchase common stock at a specified price up to a specified date.

Callable Bonds—bonds that allow the issuer to force the bond holder to sell the bond back to the issuer at a price above the par value (at the call price).

Sinking Fund Provisions—bonds that include a requirement that the issuer retire a certain amount of the bond issue each year.

---

bond holders than unsecured bonds. Equipment trust certificates are bonds collateralized with tangible (movable) non–real estate property such as railcars and airplanes.

Debentures and Subordinated Debentures.   Bonds backed solely by the general creditworthiness of the issuing firm, unsecured by specific assets or collateral, are called **debentures**. Debenture holders generally receive their promised payments only after the secured debt holders, such as mortgage bond holders, have been paid. **Subordinated debentures** are also unsecured, and they are junior in their rights to mortgage bonds and regular debentures. In the event of a default, subordinated debenture holders receive a cash distribution only after all nonsubordinated debt has been repaid in full. As a result, subordinated bonds are the riskiest type of bond and generally have higher yields than nonsubordinated bonds. In many cases, these bonds are termed *high-yield* or *junk bonds* because of their below investment grade credit ratings (see below).

Convertible Bonds.   **Convertible bonds** are bonds that may be exchanged for another security of the issuing firm (e.g., common stock) at the discretion of the bond holder. If the market value of the securities the bond holder receives with conversion exceeds the market value of the bond, the bond holder can return the bonds to the issuer in exchange for the new securities and make a profit. As a result, conversion is an attractive option or feature to bond holders. It gives the bond holder an investment opportunity (an option) that is not available with nonconvertible bonds. As a result, the yield on a convertible bond is usually lower (generally, 2 to 5 percentage points) than that on a nonconvertible bond:

$$i_{cvb} = i_{ncvb} - op_{cvb}$$

where

debentures

Bonds backed solely by the general credit of the issuing firm, unsecured by specific assets or collateral.

subordinated debentures

Bonds that are unsecured and are junior in their rights to mortgage bonds and regular debentures.

convertible bonds

Bonds that may be exchanged for another security of the issuing firm at the discretion of the bond holder.

op_{cvb} = Value of the conversion option to the bond holder

Example 6–8 Analysis of a Convertible Bond

In 1999, Titan Corporation had a convertible bond issue outstanding. Each bond, with a face value of $1,000, could be converted into common shares at a rate of 285.71 shares of stock per $1,000 face value bond (the conversion rate), or $3.50 per share. In June 1999, Titan's common stock was trading (on the NYSE) at $9.375 per share. While this might look like conversion would be very profitable, Titan's convertible bonds were trading at 267.875 percent of the face value of the bond, or $2,678.75.

To determine whether or not it is profitable to convert the bonds into common stock in Titan Corp., the conversion value of each bond can be calculated as:

$$\text{Conversion value} = \frac{\text{Current market price of common}}{\text{stock received on conversion}} \times \text{Conversion rate}$$

If a bond holder were to convert Titan Corp. bonds into stock, each bond (worth $2,678.75) could be exchanged for 285.71 shares of stock worth $9.375. The conversion value of the bonds is:

$$\$9.375 \times 285.71 = \$2,678.53$$

Thus, there is virtually no difference in dollar value of the investment to the investor if he or she holds Titan's debt or its common stock equivalent.

Most convertible bond issues are set up so that it is not initially profitable to convert to stock. Usually the stock price must increase 15 to 20 percent before it becomes profitable to convert the bond to the new security.

stock warrants

Bonds issued with stock warrants attached giving the bond holder an opportunity to purchase common stock at a specified price up to a specified date.

Stock Warrants. Bonds can also be issued with **stock warrants** attached. Similar to convertible bonds, bonds issued with stock warrants attached give the bond holder an opportunity to detach the warrants to purchase common stock at a prespecified price up to a prespecified date. In this case, however, if the bond holder decides to purchase the stock (by returning or exercising the warrant), the bond holder does not have to return the underlying bond to the issuer (as under a convertible bond). Instead, he or she keeps the bond and pays for additional stock at a price specified in the warrant. Bond holders will exercise their warrants if the market value of the stock is greater than the price at which the stock can be purchased through the warrant. Further, the bond holder may sell the warrant rather then exercise it, while maintaining ownership of the underlying bond.

call provision

A provision on a bond issue that allows the issuer to force the bond holder to sell the bond back to the issuer at a price above the par value (or at the call price).

call premium

The difference between the call price and the face value on the bond.

Callable Bonds. Many corporate bond issues include a **call provision**, which allows the issuer to require the bond holder to sell the bond back to the issuer at a given (call) price—usually set above the par value of the bond. The difference between the call price and the face value on the bond is the **call premium**. Bonds are usually called in when interest rates drop (and bond prices rise) so that the issuer can gain by calling in the old bonds (with higher coupon rates) and issuing new bonds (with lower coupon rates).

For example, in 1999, Union Camp Corporation had a $100 million callable sinking fund (see below) debenture issue outstanding. The face value of each bond was $1,000. The issue, with a maturity date of April 15, 2016, was callable as a whole or in part not less than 30 days nor more than 60 days following April 14 of each year between the years 2000 and 2006, as listed in Table 6–13. Thus, if the bonds are called in 2003, the bond holder will receive $1,017.25 per bond called in.

Table 6–13   Call Schedule for Union Camp Corporation Sinking Fund
Debenture Due 2016

Year	Call Price
2000	103.019%
2001	102.588
2002	102.156
2003	101.725
2004	101.294
2005	100.863
2006	100.431

Source: Union Camp Corporation, Annual Report, 1998.

A call provision is an unattractive feature to bond holders, since the bond holder may be forced to return the bond to the issuer before he or she is ready to end the investment and the investor can only reinvest the funds at a lower interest rate. As a result, callable bonds generally have higher yields (generally between 0.05 and 0.25 percent) than comparable noncallable bonds:

$$i_{ncb} = i_{cb} - op_{cb}$$

where

op_{cb} = Value of the issuer's option to call the debt early

sinking fund provision

A requirement that the issuer retire a certain amount of the bond issue each year.

Sinking Fund Provisions.   Many bonds have a **sinking fund provision,** which is a requirement that the issuer retire a certain amount of the bond issue early over a number of years, especially as the bond approaches maturity. The bond issuer provides the funds to the trustee by making frequent payments to a sinking fund. This sinking fund accumulates in value and is eventually used to retire the specified dollar amount of bonds either by purchasing them in the open market or by calling them. For example, the Union Camp Corporation callable sinking fund debenture issue discussed above required that the firm put $4.5 million per year from 1997 through 2015 (19 years) into a sinking fund, or a total of $85.5 million of the $100 million total would be accumulated before maturity.

Since it reduces the probability of default at the maturity date, (the "crisis at maturity"), a sinking fund provision is an attractive feature to bond holders. Thus, bonds with a sinking fund provision are less risky to the bond holder and generally have lower yields than comparable bonds without a sinking fund provision.

The Trading Process for Corporate Bonds.   Primary sales of corporate bond issues occur through either a public sale (issue) or a private placement in a manner identical to that discussed for municipal bonds (see above). In 1998, a total of $1,065.04 billion of corporate debt was issued, of which $362.65 billion was privately placed.

There are two secondary markets in corporate bonds: the exchange market (e.g., the NYSE) and the over-the-counter (OTC) market. Notice the small trading volume reported for NYSE trading in Table 6–11. The dollar value of trading totaled $11.143 million on January 18, 2000, in a market with $4.53 trillion of bonds outstanding. This is because less than 1 percent of all corporate bonds trade on exchanges such as the NYSE. Rather, most bonds are traded OTC among major bond dealers such as Salomon Smith Barney and Paine Webber. The OTC direct, interdealer market totally dominates trading in corporate bonds.

Table 6–14 Bond Credit Ratings

Explanation	Moody's	S&P
Best quality; smallest degree of risk	Aaa	AAA
High quality; slightly more long-term risk	Aa1	AA+
than top rating	Aa2	AA
	Aa3	AA−
Upper medium grade; possible impairment in the future	A1	A+
	A2	A
	A3	A−
Medium grade; lack outstanding investment characteristics	Baa1	BBB+
	Baa2	BBB
	Baa3	BBB−
Speculative issues; protection may be very moderate	Ba1	BB+
	Ba2	BB
	Ba3	BB−
Very speculative; may have small assurance	B1	B+
of interest and principal payments	B2	B
	B3	B−
Issues in poor standing; may be in default	Caa	CCC
Speculative in a high degree; with marked shortcomings	Ca	CC
Lowest quality; poor prospects of attaining	C	C
real investment standing		D

Source: Moody's and Standard & Poor's websites. *www.moodys.com/; www.standardandpoors.com/*

Bond Ratings

As mentioned above, the inability of investors to get information pertaining to the risk, especially default risk, on bonds, at a reasonable cost, can result in thinly traded markets. In Chapter 3, we examined the impact of interest rate risk (i.e., interest rate changes) on bond prices. Specifically, we demonstrated that bonds with longer maturities (durations) and low coupon rates experience larger price changes for a given change in interest rates than bonds with short maturities and high coupon rates, (i.e., bonds with longer maturities and lower coupon rates are subject to greater interest rate risk). More importantly, bond investors need to measure the degree of default risk on a bond.

Large bond investors, traders, and managers often evaluate default risk by conducting their own analysis of the issuer, including an assessment of the bond issuer's financial ratios (see Chapter 21) and security prices. Small investors are not generally capable of generating the same extensive information and thus frequently rely on bond ratings provided by the bond rating agencies. The two major bond rating agencies are Moody's and Standard & Poor's (S&P).[4] Both companies rank bonds based on the perceived probability of issuer default and assign a rating based on a letter grade. Table 6–14 summarizes these rating systems and provides a brief definition of each. The highest credit quality (lowest default risk) that rating agencies assign is a triple-A (Aaa for Moody's and AAA for S&P). Bonds with a triple-A rating have the lowest interest spread over similar maturity Treasury securities. As the assessed default risk increases, Moody's and S&P lower the credit rating assigned on a bond issue, and the interest spread over similar maturity Treasuries paid to bond holders generally increases.[5]

www.moodys.com/

www.standardand poors.com/

4. Other credit rating agencies include Fitch IBCA, Inc. (www.fitchibca.com/) and Duff and Phelps Credit Rating Services (www.dcrco.com/).

5. Note that S&P and Moody's sometimes disagree on ratings (recently differences occur about 15 percent of the time). When this occurs, a bond is said to have a "split" rating.

Rating agencies consider several factors in determining and assigning credit ratings on bond issues. These factors include the likelihood of payment (i.e., the capacity and willingness of the debt issuer to meet its financial commitment on the debt in accordance with the terms of the obligation), the nature and provisions of the debt issue (e.g., the covenants and callability of the bond), and the protection afforded by, and relative position of, the debt issue in the event of bankruptcy, reorganization, or other arrangements under the laws of bankruptcy and other laws affecting creditors' rights.

Bonds rated Baa or better by Moody's and BBB or better by S&P are considered to be investment grade bonds. Financial institutions (e.g., banks, insurance companies) are generally prohibited by state and federal law from purchasing anything but investment grade bond securities.[6] Bonds rated below Baa by Moody's and BBB by S&P are considered to be speculative grade bonds and are often termed **junk bonds**, or high-yield bonds. The issuance of speculative bonds was rare prior to the economic downturn of the late 1970s. Given the risk involved with speculative bonds and the ready availability of investment grade bonds, investment banks had a difficult time marketing the more speculative bonds to primary bond market investors.

In 1977, however, Michael Milken, an investment banker working for Drexel Burnham Lambert, Inc., developed a way to successfully market primary issues of junk bonds to investors. Throughout the 1980s, Drexel Burnham Lambert captured the bulk of the junk bond market by promising investors to act as a "dealer" for the junk bonds in the secondary market. Investors were, therefore, more willing to purchase these junk securities because Drexel provided an implicit guarantee that it would buy them back or find another buyer at market prices should an investor need to sell. This considerably enhanced the liquidity of such bonds.

The junk bond market experienced difficulties over the 1989–1991 period, however, as bond prices fell, reflecting the economy's move into recession. Serious concerns about the creditworthiness of Drexel's junk bond–laden asset portfolio led creditors to deny Drexel extensions of its vital short-term commercial paper financings. As a result, Drexel declared bankruptcy in February 1991.[7]

Despite a temporary decline in the junk bond market that followed Drexel's demise, the market continued to grow in the late 1990s, with smaller and medium-sized firms, unqualified to issue investment-grade debt securities, issuing long-term debt in this market. For example, in 1990, $503.3 million in corporate "high-yield" straight debt was issued. In 1999, $95.3 billion was issued, an increase of 188 percent.

Bond Market Indexes

Table 6–15 lists major bond market indexes as of January 18, 2000. Data in this table gives investors general information on returns of bonds from various types of issuers (e.g., Treasuries, municipals, and corporate bonds) and various maturities. The indexes are those managed by major investment banks (e.g., Lehman Brothers, Merrill Lynch) and reflect both the monthly capital gain and loss on bonds in the index plus any interest (coupon) income earned. Changes in the values of these broad market indexes can be used by bond traders to evaluate changes in the investment attractiveness of bonds of different types and maturities.

---

junk bond

Bond rated as speculative or less than investment grade (below Baa by Moody's and BBB by S&P) by bond-rating agencies.

Do You Understand?

1. What the different classifications of bonds are? Describe each.
2. What a STRIP security is?
3. What the process is through which Treasury notes and bonds are issued in the primary markets?
4. What the difference is between a general obligation bond and a revenue bond?
5. What the difference is between a firm commitment and a best efforts bond issue offering?
6. What the characteristics are that differentiate corporate bonds?
7. What factors are used to determine a firm's bond issue rating?

---

6. For example, the Financial Institutions Reform, Recovery, and Enforcement Act of 1989 rescinded the ability of Savings and Loans to purchase and hold below-investment-grade bonds (see Chapter 14).

7. For additional discussion of the failure of Drexel Burnham Lambert, see W. S. Haraf, "The Collapse of Drexel Burnham Lambert: Lessons for Bank Regulators," *Regulation*, winter 1991, pp. 22–25.

Table 6–15 Major Bond Market Indexes

MAJOR INDEXES

HIGH	LOW (12 MOS)		CLOSE	NET CHG	% CHG	12-MO CHG	% CHG	FROM 12/31	% CHG
U.S. TREASURY SECURITIES	(Lehman Brothers indexes)								
5680.14	5529.99	Intermediate	5617.79 −	6.30 −	0.11	+ 1.93 +	0.03	− 21.35 −	0.38
8755.95	7817.09	Long-term	7822.71 −	23.58 −	0.30	− 814.91 −	9.43	− 98.52 −	1.24
1728.90	1446.80	Long-term(price)	1446.80 −	5.52 −	0.38	− 262.08 −	15.34	− 23.44 −	1.59
6312.50	6042.87	Composite	6079.95 −	10.42 −	0.17	− 190.92 −	3.04	− 39.87 −	0.65
U.S. CORPORATE DEBT ISSUES	(Merrill Lynch)								
1027.18	976.88	Corporate Master	988.10 −	1.78 −	0.18	− 30.72 −	3.02	− 9.87 −	0.99
733.62	710.98	1-10 Yr Maturities	721.99 −	0.90 −	0.12	− 4.19 −	0.58	− 4.97 −	0.68
827.57	754.03	10+ Yr Maturities	756.06 −	2.27 −	0.30	− 62.05 −	7.58	− 12.69 −	1.65
514.50	498.85	High Yield	505.08 −	0.27 −	0.05	+ 2.70 +	0.54	− 3.03 −	0.60
737.70	707.08	Yankee Bonds	719.08 −	1.12 −	0.16	− 11.63 −	1.59	− 6.73 −	0.93
TAX-EXEMPT SECURITIES	(Bond Buyer Muni Index, from Dec. 22, 1999)								
107-12	91-07	Bond Buyer 6% Muni	91-07	n.a.	n.a.	− 14-29 −	14.05	− 1-01 −	1.12
147.74	141.73	7-12 yr G.O.	143.45 −	0.09 −	0.06	− 2.51 −	1.72	− 0.49 −	0.34
153.73	143.11	12-22 yr G.O.	144.59 −	0.09 −	0.06	− 7.26 −	4.78	− 0.91 −	0.63
147.89	132.83	22+ yr Revenue	133.02 −	0.18 −	0.14	− 13.05 −	8.93	− 1.34 −	1.00
MORTGAGE-BACKED SECURITIES	(current coupon; Merrill Lynch: Dec. 31, 1986 = 100)								
318.57	302.87	Ginnie Mae(GNMA)	312.27 −	0.76 −	0.24	− 3.21 −	1.02	− 3.70 −	1.17
314.29	299.59	Fannie Mae(FNMA)	307.53 −	0.79 −	0.26	− 2.05 −	0.66	− 4.25 −	1.36
190.87	181.90	Freddie Mac(FHLMC)	188.84 −	0.27 −	0.14	+ 0.29 +	0.15	− 0.69 −	0.36
BROAD MARKET	(Merrill Lynch)								
835.13	804.30	Domestic Master	814.66 −	1.49 −	0.18	− 15.53 −	1.87	− 6.70 −	0.82
936.31	896.97	Corporate/Government	904.05 −	1.63 −	0.18	− 26.17 −	2.81	− 6.77 −	0.74

Source: *The Wall Street Journal,* January 19, 2000, p. C20. Reprinted by permission of *The Wall Street Journal.* © 2000 Dow Jones & Company, Inc. All Rights Reserved Worldwide. *www.wsj.com/*

Bond Market Participants

Bond markets bring together suppliers and demanders of long-term funds. We have just seen that the major issuers of debt market securities are federal, state, and local governments and corporations. The major purchasers of capital market securities are households, businesses, government units, and foreign investors. Figure 6–6 shows the percentage of each type of bond security held by each of these groups. Notice that business financial firms (e.g., banks, insurance companies, mutual funds) are the major suppliers of funds for two of the three types of bonds. Financial business firms hold 27.68 percent of all Treasury notes and bonds, 62.62 percent of municipal bonds, and 59.39 percent of the corporate bonds outstanding. In addition to their direct investment reported in Figure 6–6, households often deposit excess funds in financial institutions (such as mutual bond funds and pension funds) that use these funds to purchase bond market securities. Thus, much of the business and financial holdings of bond securities shown in Figure 6-6 reflect indirect investments of households in the bond market.

Do You Understand?

1. Who the major purchasers of bond market securities are?

Comparison of Bond Market Securities

Figure 6–7 shows the yield to maturity on various types of bonds (e.g., 30-year Treasury bonds, municipal bonds, and high-grade corporate bonds) from 1980 through 1999. While the general trends in yields were quite similar over this period (i.e., yield

Figure 6–6 Bond Market Securities Held by Various Groups of Market Participants, September 1999

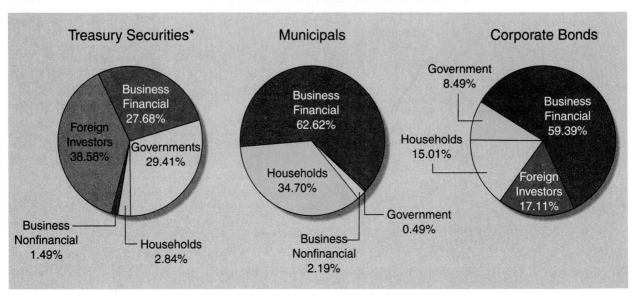

*Includes Treasury bills, notes, and bonds.

Source: Federal Reserve Board, website, "Flow of Funds Accounts," December 1999. *www.bog.frb.fed.us/*

Figure 6–7 Yields on Bond Market Securities, 1980–1999

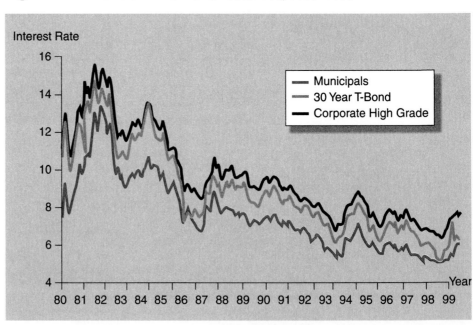

Source: Federal Reserve Board, website, "Research and Data," January 2000. *www.bog.frb.fed.us/*

changes are highly correlated), yield spreads among bonds can vary as default risk, tax status, and marketability change. For example, yield spread differences can change when characteristics of a particular type of bond are perceived to be more or less favorable to the bond holder (e.g., relative changes in yield spreads can result when the default risk increases for a firm that has one bond issue with a sinking fund provision

www.stls.frb.org/

Do You Understand?

1. What events can cause yield spreads on bond securities to change?

and another issue without a sinking fund issue). Economic conditions can also cause bond yield spreads to vary over time. This is particularly true during periods of slow economic growth (e.g., 1982 and 1989–1991), as investors require higher default risk premiums. The St. Louis Federal Reserve Bank offers free online access to its database (called FRED) of U.S. economic and financial data, including daily U.S. interest rates, monetary business indicators, exchange rates, balance of payments, and regional economic data.

International Aspects of Bond Markets

International bond markets are those markets that trade bonds that are underwritten by an international syndicate, offer bonds simultaneously to investors in several countries, issue bonds outside the jurisdiction of any single country, and offer bonds in unregistered form. The rapid growth in international bond markets in recent years can be seen in Table 6–16, which lists the dollar volume of new issues of international bond securities from 1993 through 1998. Much of this growth has been driven by investors' demand for international securities and international portfolio diversification (e.g., the growth of specialized U.S. mutual funds that invest in offshore bond issues). In just six years, new issues have grown from $188.7 billion (in 1993) to $677.7 billion (in 1998). The majority of this growth has been debt issued by developed countries (e.g., the U.S., Europe, and Canada). Notice the drop in debt securities issued by Japan and by "Other countries" (i.e., emerging market countries such as Thailand and Singapore) after the economic crisis in Southeast Asia in 1997. For example, (net) new debt issues for Japan fell from $16.3 billion in 1996 to −$19.8 billion in 1998 (meaning that more Japanese notes and bonds were redeemed than issued). New debt issues in "Other countries" fell from $89.2 billion in 1997 to $40.9 billion in 1998. Notice also the sharp increase in new Euro-denominated debt issues in

Table 6–16 International Debt Securities Issued, 1993–1998
(in billions of U.S. dollars)

	1993	1994	1995	1996	1997	1998
Total net issues	$188.7	$253.6	$263.1	$537.3	$573.3	$677.7
Money market instruments	−6.2	3.3	17.4	41.1	19.8	7.4
Bonds and notes	194.9	250.3	245.8	496.2	553.5	670.3
Developed countries	114.8	205.5	228.4	411.0	449.0	570.2
Europe	147.7	167.1	159.8	243.2	257.9	279.6
Japan	−52.1	−5.9	−2.9	16.3	−0.4	−19.8
United States	−4.0	22.9	56.3	131.8	176.9	282.6
Canada	19.2	16.6	8.7	8.8	10.1	21.5
Offshore centers	10.2	7.2	1.7	16.3	14.5	11.6
Other countries	27.6	32.5	22.1	88.2	89.2	40.9
International institutions	36.2	8.5	11.0	21.8	20.6	55.1
U.S. dollar	28.6	66.5	69.0	261.7	332.0	411.1
Yen	29.3	86.0	81.3	85.3	34.6	−29.3
Euro area currencies	82.6	80.2	84.3	135.8	139.0	220.3
Other currencies	48.3	20.9	28.5	54.4	67.8	75.5
Financial institutions	51.4	136.1	167.9	346.9	360.0	368.3
Public sector	130.7	103.1	73.3	118.5	89.0	182.1
Corporate issuers	6.6	14.4	22.0	71.9	124.3	127.2

Source: Bank for International Settlements, Annual Report, June 1999. *www.bis.org/*

Table 6–17 International Bonds and Notes Outstanding, 1995–1999

Type; Sector and Currency	1995	1996	1997	1998	1999*
Total Issues	$2,209.3	$3,054.1	$3,322.8	$4,121.6	$4,880.3
Floating Rate	326.2	591.9	735.7	925.8	1,153.5
U.S. dollar	181.5	338.9	442.1	550.8	621.8
Euro area currencies	44.2	58.2	130.9	185.3	317.8
Japanese yen	27.0	65.4	69.6	85.2	96.1
Other currencies	73.6	129.4	93.0	104.5	117.8
Financial institutions	203.2	405.1	535.0	709.0	887.2
Government and state agencies	61.9	81.5	83.1	85.9	88.8
International institutions	18.4	24.9	26.9	26.7	25.2
Corporate issuers	42.8	80.3	90.7	104.1	152.3
Straight Fixed Rate	1,712.4	2,284.8	2,389.8	2,974.8	3,499.8
U.S. dollar	490.8	714.7	890.2	1,181.0	1,504.7
Euro area currencies	214.4	270.9	693.1	909.4	1,038.8
Japanese yen	315.4	432.7	368.7	381.1	397.0
Other currencies	691.9	866.5	437.7	503.2	559.3
Financial institutions	501.4	799.2	894.8	1,119.9	1,325.9
Government and state agencies	492.8	633.8	621.3	779.2	906.5
International institutions	268.3	291.2	272.6	341.1	352.3
Corporate issuers	449.3	560.6	601.1	734.5	915.1
Equity Related	170.7	177.4	197.4	221.1	226.9
U.S. dollar	83.1	94.6	123.0	128.7	125.0
Euro area currencies	10.7	8.4	25.0	43.2	55.9
Japanese yen	7.4	13.1	14.8	16.4	18.2
Other currencies	69.5	61.3	34.7	32.8	27.8
Financial institutions	32.5	37.9	45.3	68.9	71.1
Government and state agencies	0.4	3.9	5.9	7.1	7.6
International institutions	—	0.1	0.1	0.2	0.2
Corporate issuers	137.7	135.5	146.1	144.8	148.0

* As of September.

Source: Bank for International Settlements, *Quarterly Review,* November 1999. *www.bis.org/*

1998, $220.3 billion, as investors attempted to position themselves before the introduction of the Euro in 1999.

Table 6–17 lists the values of international debt outstanding by type (e.g., floating-rate, straight fixed-rate, and equity-related debt) from 1995 through September 1999. In September 1999, international bonds and notes outstanding totaled over $4.9 trillion, compared to $2.2 trillion in 1995. Straight fixed-rate securities dominate the market, mainly due to the strong demand for dollar and Euro currency assets. Floating-rate notes were second in size, partly as a result of interest rate uncertainty in the late 1990s.

Notice that the majority of international debt instruments are denominated in U.S. dollars. For example, in September 1999, 53.9 percent of the floating-rate debt, 43.0 percent of the straight fixed-rate debt, and 55.1 percent of the equity-related debt was issued in U.S. dollars. A possible reason for this is that, as seen in Figure 6–8, for 1998 and 1999, U.S. bond yields were consistently the highest among the major countries, and the U.S. dollar continues to be the currency of choice as an international medium of

Figure 6–8 Government Bond Yields in Major Countries

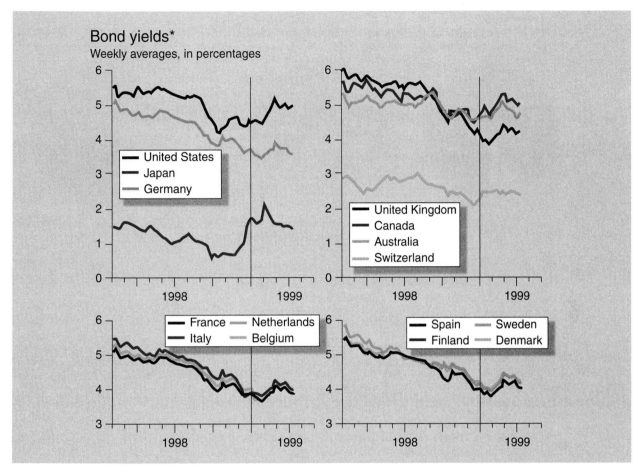

Bond yields*
Weekly averages, in percentages

exchange and store of value. The introduction of the Euro has created significant measurement problems in the international markets, which may account for at least part of the drop in the Euro area currencies reported for 1999. Specifically, the creation of the single currency has compounded the difficulty of distinguishing between domestic and offshore security issues. The markets for emerging market bonds were also affected in the first quarter of 1999 by the possibility of debt restructuring programs in some countries. For example, the IMF suggested that Pakistan and Russia include outstanding international bonds in the restructuring of its external debt. Fear of losses on holdings of these emerging market bonds sparked a wider selloff in the emerging markets.

Figure 6–9 illustrates the distribution of international bonds by type of issuer (e.g., financial institutions, governments). Financial institutions issue the vast majority of floating-rate bonds (76.9 percent) and most of the straight fixed-rate bonds (37.9 percent). Financial institutions had been hampered in 1998 by concerns over their exposures to lower-rated countries. The stabilization of market conditions in 1999 made it easier for U.S. and European financial institutions to issue new debt securities. Public sector issues were largely accounted for by U.S. financing agencies and a few emerging market issues. Corporations, as might be expected, issue the vast majority of the equity-related bonds (65.2 percent).

Do You Understand?

1. The major currency in which international bonds are denominated?
2. What group of market participants is the major issuer of international debt?

Figure 6–9 Distribution of International Bonds Outstanding by Type of Issuer, September 1999

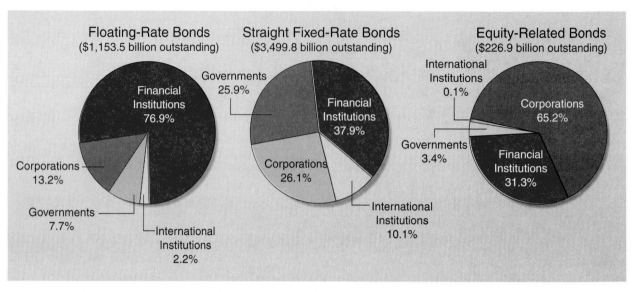

Source: Bank for International Settlements, *Quarterly Review,* November 1999. *www.bis.org/*

4 Eurobonds, Foreign Bonds, and Brady and Sovereign Bonds

International bonds can be classified into three groups: Eurobonds, foreign bonds, and Brady and sovereign bonds.

Eurobonds

Eurobonds are long-term bonds issued and sold outside the country of the currency in which they are denominated (e.g., dollar-denominated bonds issued in Europe or Asia[8]). Eurobonds were first sold in 1963 as a way to avoid taxes and regulation. U.S. corporations were limited by regulations on the amount of funds they could borrow domestically (in the United States) to finance overseas operations, while foreign issues in the United States were subject to a special 30 percent tax on their coupon interest. In 1963, these corporations created the Eurobond, by which bonds were denominated in various currencies and were not directly subject to U.S. regulation. Even when these regulations were abandoned, access to a new and less-regulated market by investors and corporations created sufficient demand and supply for the market to continue to grow.

Eurobonds are generally issued in denominations of $5,000 and $10,000. They pay interest annually using a 360-day year (floating-rate Eurobonds generally pay interest every six months based on a spread over some stated rate, usually the LIBOR rate). Eurobonds are generally *bearer* bonds and are traded in the over-the-counter markets, mainly in London and Luxembourg. Historically, they have been of interest to smaller investors who want to shield the ownership of securities from the tax authorities. The classic investor is the "Belgian dentist" who would cross the border to Luxembourg on the annual coupon date to collect his coupons without the knowledge of the Belgian tax authority. However, today small investors—of the Belgian dentist

---

8. A Eurobond does not have to be issued in Europe.

www.moodys.com/

www.standardand
poors.com/

type—are overshadowed in importance by large investors such as mutual and pension funds. Ratings services such as Moody's and Standard & Poor's generally rate Eurobonds. Equity-related Eurobonds are convertible bonds (bonds convertible into equity) or bonds with equity warrants attached.

Eurobonds are placed in primary markets by investment banks. Often, a syndicate of investment banks works together to place the Eurobonds. Most Eurobonds are issued via firm commitment offerings, although the spreads in this market are much larger than for domestic bonds because of the need to distribute the bonds across a wide investor base often covering many countries. Thus, the underwriters bear the risk associated with the initial sale of the bonds. The Eurobond issuer chooses the currency in which the bond issue will be denominated. The promised payments of interest and principal must then be paid in this currency. Thus, the choice of currency, and particularly the level and volatility in the interest rates of the country of the currency, affect the overall cost of the Eurobond to the bond issuer and the rate of return to the bond holder. However, referring again to Figure 6–8, long-term interest rates across countries tend to move in the same manner.

The introduction of the Euro in 1999 has certainly changed the structure of the Eurobond market and is likely to continue to change it as participating European countries move into full currency union in 2002. Most obvious is that Eurobonds denominated in the individual European currencies will no longer exist but rather will be denominated in a single currency, the ECU. Further, liquidity created by the consolidation of European currencies should allow for the demand and size of Eurobond issues to increase. Such growth was exhibited early in the life of the Euro as the volume of new Euro debt issues in the first and second quarter of 1999 rose 32 percent and 43 percent, respectively, from the same periods in 1998. In January 1999, a record $415 billion in long-term Eurobonds were issued. Finally, Eurobond yields across the European countries should vary only slightly, which should improve Euro-denominated securities' marketability even further. If successful, Euro-denominated notes and bonds could threaten the dollar as the world's most dominant currency. Together, the 11 "Euroland" countries have 20 percent more tradeable debt than the U.S. Treasury markets.

Foreign Bonds

Foreign bonds are long-term bonds issued by firms and governments outside of the issuer's home country and are usually denominated in the currency of the country in which they are issued—for example, a Japanese company issuing a dollar-denominated public bond in the United States. Foreign bonds were issued long before Eurobonds and, as a result, are frequently called traditional international bonds. Countries sometimes name their foreign bonds to denote the country of origin. For example, foreign bonds issued in the United States are called Yankee bonds, foreign bonds issued in Japan are called Samurai bonds, and foreign bonds issued in the United Kingdom are called Bulldog bonds.

Brady Bonds and Sovereign Bonds

Brady bonds

Bonds that are swapped for an outstanding loan to a less developed country.

Brady bonds were created in the mid-1980s through IMF and central bank–sponsored programs under which U.S. and other banks[9] exchanged their dollar loans to emerging market countries for dollar bonds issued by the relevant countries (e.g., the Philippines, Mexico, Brazil). These bonds have a much longer maturity than that promised on the original loans and a lower promised original coupon (yield) than the interest rate on the

9. Major market makers include the Dutch ING bank, Lehman, Salomon Bros., Citibank, J. P. Morgan, Bankers Trust, and Merrill Lynch.

Table 6–18 Debt Reduction Achieved through the Brady Plan
(in billions of dollars)

Country	Debt Reduction
Argentina	$ 29.9
Brazil	45.6
Bulgaria	8.1
Ecuador	8.0
Mexico	33.0
Nigeria	5.8
Panama	3.5
Peru	10.6
Philippines	4.5
Poland	14.0
Venezuela	19.3
Eastern Europe	22.1
Latin America	139.3
Total	206.4

Source: Salomon Brothers.

original loan. In many cases, the bond's principal and interest payments have been partially backed by U.S. T-bonds as collateral to improve their attractiveness to investors.[10] Once banks and other financial institutions have swapped loans for bonds, they can sell them on the secondary market.

Approximately $206.4 billion of less developed countries (LDC) loans has been converted into bonds under the Brady Plan, with the top issuers being Brazil (22.1 percent), Mexico (16.0 percent), Argentina (14.5 percent), Russia (11.7 percent), and Venezuela (12.1 percent). Table 6–18 lists the LDC debt reduction achieved through the Brady Plan through 1998. These bond-for-loan swap programs seek to restore LDCs' creditworthiness and thus the value of bank holdings of such debt by creating longer-term, lower fixed-interest but more liquid securities in place of shorter-term, floating-rate loans.[11]

The creation of these bonds was the result of three factors. First was the fact that LDC central banks assumed the various loans made to individual borrowers in that country. Thus, for example, U.S. financial institutions' loans to Mexico, Brazil, and Argentina were increasingly consolidated at the local central bank. As a result, a foreign financial institution such as Citigroup became the owner or creditor of a consolidated account denominated in dollars at the LDC's central bank.[12]

Second, the frequent restructurings of the stock of LDC loans, along with their consolidation at the local central bank, made loan terms increasingly homogeneous. For example, the August 1987 re-

Do You Understand?

1. What Eurobonds are?
2. How Brady bonds are created?
3. What sovereign bonds are?

10. For example, the face value payment of a 30-year Brady bond may be backed by the issuing government placing a 30-year U.S. zero-coupon T-bond as collateral in an escrow account. Should the issuing government default on its Brady bond, investors would have a claim to the 30-year zero-coupon Treasury bond as collateral.

11. However, even after restructuring their debt into Brady Bonds, Russia and Ecuador defaulted on their outstanding Brady bonds in 1999.

12. Usually, a local company or state organization swaps its dollar loans owed to a U.S. bank for a local currency loan at the central bank. That is, the debt to the U.S. bank is transferred to the central bank of that country.

structuring of Argentinean debt to a maturity of 19 years and an interest rate of LIBOR + $^{13}/_{16}$ percent involved the whole stock of Argentinean loans outstanding as of January 1986, or $30.5 billion.

Third, banks received increasing demands from regulators to make their LDC loan portfolios more liquid. In particular, by converting loans into tradeable Brady bonds, LDCs' assets become more liquid.[13] More recently, as the credit quality of some LDCs has improved, some Brady bonds have been converted back into **sovereign bonds**, whereby U.S. Treasury bond collateral backing is removed and the creditworthiness of the country is substituted instead. Spreads over Treasuries on these bonds are much higher than on Brady bonds (often in the 4 percent plus range). However, countries save by not having to pledge U.S. dollar Treasury bonds as collateral against principal and interest payments.

sovereign bonds

A bond that is swapped for an outstanding loan to a less developed country (LDC), in which the U.S. Treasury secondary collateral backing is removed and the creditworthiness of the country is substituted instead.

13. The Brady bond is usually created on an interest rate rollover date. On that date, the floating-rate loans are usually converted into fixed-rate coupon bonds on the books of an agent bank. The agent bank is the bank that kept the records of loan ownership and distributed interest payments made by the LDC to individual bank creditors. Once converted, the bonds can start trading.

Summary

This chapter looked at the domestic and international bond markets. We defined and discussed the three types of bonds available to long-term debt investors: Treasury notes and bonds, municipal bonds, and corporate bonds. We also reviewed the process through which bonds trade in both primary and secondary bond markets. International bond markets have grown dramatically in recent years. We documented and offered some reasons for this growth. We concluded the chapter with a description of the different types of international bonds: the traditional foreign bonds, the relatively new Eurobonds, Brady bonds, and sovereign bonds.

End-of-Chapter Questions

1. What are capital markets and how do bond markets fit into the definition of capital markets?
2. What is the difference between T-bills, T-notes, and T-bonds?
3. Refer to the T-note and T-bond quote in Table 6–3.
   a. What is the asking price on the 9.25 percent February 2016 T-bond if the face value of the bond is $10,000?
   b. What is the bid price on the 5.5 percent March 2000 T-note if the face value of the bond is $10,000?
4. What is a STRIP? Who would invest in a STRIP?
5. You can invest in taxable bonds that are paying a 9.5 percent annual rate of return or a municipal bond paying a 7.75 percent annual rate of return. If your marginal tax rate is 21 percent, which security bond should you buy?
6. A municipal bond you are considering as an investment currently pays a 6.75 percent annual rate of return.
   a. Calculate the tax equivalent rate of return if your marginal tax rate is 28 percent.
   b. Calculate the tax equivalent rate of return if your marginal tax rate is 21 percent.
7. What is the difference between general obligation bonds and revenue bonds?
8. Refer to Table 6–11.
   a. What was the price on the Ford Credit Corporation bonds on January 18, 2000?
   b. What was the dollar volume of trading in Loews bonds on January 18, 2000?
   c. What was the price on MBNA bonds on January 18, 2000?
9. What is the difference between bearer bonds and registered bonds?
10. What is the difference between term bonds and serial bonds?
11. Which type of bond—a mortgage bond, a debenture, or a subordinated debenture—generally has the
    a. Highest cost to the bond issuer?
    b. Least risk to the bond holder?
    c. Highest yield to the bond holder?
12. What is a convertible bond? Is a convertible bond more or less attractive to a bond holder than a nonconvertible bond?

13. What is a callable bond? Is a call provision more or less attractive to a bond holder than a noncallable bond?

14. Explain the meaning of a sinking fund provision on a bond issue.

15. What is the difference between an investment grade bond and a junk bond?

16. What is the difference between a Eurobond and a foreign bond?

17. How are Brady bonds created?

18. Go to the Bank for International Settlements' website and identify the most recent volume for the issue of new international debt.

19. Go to the Bank for International Settlements' website and find the current distribution of international bonds by type of issuer.

20. Go to the U.S. Treasury's website and obtain the latest T-note and T-bond auction results.

Mortgage Markets

Chapter Navigator

1. What is the difference between a mortgage and a mortgage-backed security?

2. What are the main types of mortgages issued by financial institutions?

3. What are the major characteristics of a mortgage?

4. How is a mortgage amortization schedule determined?

5. What are some of the new innovations in mortgage financing?

6. What is a mortgage sale?

7. What is a pass-through security?

8. What is a collateralized mortgage obligation?

9. Who are the major mortgage holders in the United States?

10. What are the trends in the international securitization of mortgages?

1   Mortgages and Mortgage-Backed Securities: Chapter Overview

Mortgages are loans to individuals or businesses to purchase a home, land, or other real property. As of September 1999, there were over $6.18 trillion of primary mortgages outstanding, held by various financial institutions such as banks and mortgage companies. Table 7–1 lists the major categories of mortgages and the amount of

Table 7–1 Mortgage Loans Outstanding
(in billions of dollars)

Mortgage type	1992	1993	1994	1995	1996	1997	1998	1999*
Home	$2,986.5	$3,148.8	$3,332.1	$3,511.8	$3,721.2	$3,957.0	$4,324.8	$4,648.2
Multifamily residential	269.0	266.6	267.7	277.0	294.8	310.5	341.3	372.7
Commercial	733.1	712.2	712.3	732.1	797.0	855.4	960.9	1,058.5
Farm	79.7	80.7	83.0	84.6	87.1	90.3	95.5	101.8
Total	$4,068.3	$4,208.4	$4,395.1	$4,605.5	$4,900.1	$5,213.2	$5,722.5	$6,181.2

*As of September.

Source: Federal Reserve Board, website, "Flow of Fund Accounts," December 1999. *www.bog.frb.fed.us/*

mortgages

Loans to individuals or businesses to purchase a home, land, or other real property.

securitized

Securities are packaged and sold as assets backing a publicly traded or privately held debt instrument.

each outstanding from 1992 through September 1999. Home mortgages (one to four families) are the largest loan category (75.2 percent of all mortgages in 1999), followed by commercial mortgage bonds (used to finance specific projects that are pledged as collateral for the bond issue—17.1 percent), multifamily dwellings (6.0 percent), and farms (1.7 percent).

Many mortgages, particularly residential mortgages, are subsequently **securitized** by the mortgage holder—they are packaged and sold as assets backing a publicly traded or privately held debt instrument. Securitization allows financial institutions' (FIs') asset portfolios to become more liquid, reduces interest rate risk and credit risk, provides FIs with a source of fee income, and helps reduce the effects of regulatory constraints such as capital requirements, reserve requirements, and deposit insurance premiums on FI profits (see Chapter 14).

We examine mortgage markets separately from bond and stock markets for several reasons. First, mortgages are backed by a specific piece of real property. If the borrower defaults on a mortgage, the financial institution can take ownership of the property. Only mortgage bonds are backed by a specific piece of property that allows the lender to take ownership in the event of a default. All other corporate bonds and stock give the holder a general claim to a borrower's assets. Second, there is no set denomination for primary mortgages. Rather, the size of each mortgage depends on the borrower's needs and ability to repay. Bonds generally have a denomination of $1,000 or a multiple of $1,000 per bond and shares of stock are generally issued in (par value) denominations of $1 per share. Third, primary mortgages generally involve a single investor (e.g., a bank or mortgage company). Bond and stock issues, on the other hand, are generally held by many (sometimes thousands of) investors. Finally, because primary mortgage borrowers are often individuals, information on these borrowers is less extensive and unaudited. Bonds and stocks are issued by publicly traded corporations that are subject to extensive rules and regulations regarding information availability and reliability.

In this chapter, we look at the characteristics and operations of the mortgage and mortgage-backed securities markets. We look at different types of mortgages and the determination of mortgage payments. (We look at the processes used by financial institutions to evaluate mortgage loan applicants in Chapter 21.) We also discuss the agencies owned or sponsored by the U.S. government that help securitize mortgage pools. We briefly describe the major forms of securitization and discuss the process of securitization. More complete details of the securitization process are provided in Chapter 25. We conclude the chapter with a look at international investors in mortgages and mortgaged-backed securities markets, as well as trends in international securitization of mortgage assets.

Primary Mortgage Market

2

Four basic categories of mortgages are issued by financial institutions: home, multifamily dwelling, commercial, and farm. Home mortgages ($4,648.2 billion outstanding in 1999) are used to purchase one- to four-family dwellings. Multi-family dwelling mortgages ($372.7 billion outstanding) are used to finance the purchase of apartment complexes, townhouses, and condominiums. Commercial mortgages ($1,058.5 billion outstanding) are used to finance the purchase of real estate for business purposes (e.g., office buildings, shopping malls). Farm mortgages ($101.8 billion outstanding) are used to finance the purchase of farms. As seen in Table 7–1, while all four areas have experienced tremendous growth, the historically low mortgage rates in the 1990s have particularly spurred growth in the single-family home area (55.6 percent growth from 1992 through 1999), followed by commercial business mortgages (44.4 percent growth), and multifamily residential mortgages (38.6 percent growth).

Mortgage Characteristics

3

As mentioned above, mortgages are unique as capital market instruments because the characteristics (such as size, fees, interest rate) of each mortgage held by a financial institution can differ. A mortgage contract between a financial institution and a borrower must specify all of the characteristics of the mortgage agreement.

When a financial institution receives a mortgage application, it must determine whether the applicant qualifies for a loan. (We describe this process in Chapter 21.) Because most financial institutions sell or securitize their mortgage loans in the secondary mortgage market (discussed below), the guidelines set by the secondary market buyer for acceptability, as well as the guidelines set by the financial institution, are used to determine whether or not a mortgage borrower is qualified. Further, the characteristics of loans to be securitized will generally be more standardized than those that are not to be securitized. When mortgages are not securitized, the financial institution can be more flexible with the acceptance/rejection guidelines it uses and mortgage characteristics will be more varied.

Collateral.   As mentioned in the introduction, all mortgage loans are backed by a specific piece of property that serves as collateral to the mortgage loan. As part of the mortgage agreement, the financial institution will place a **lien** against a property that remains in place until the loan is fully paid off. A lien is a public record attached to the title of the property that gives the financial institution the right to sell the property if the mortgage borrower defaults or falls into arrears on his or her payments. The mortgage is secured by the lien—that is, until the loan is paid off, no one can buy the property and obtain clear title to it. If someone tries to purchase the property, the financial institution can file notice of the lien at the public recorder's office to stop the transaction.

Down Payment.   As part of any mortgage agreement, a financial institution requires the mortgage borrower to pay a portion of the purchase price of the property (a **down payment**) at the closing (the day the mortgage is issued). The balance of the purchase price is the face value of the mortgage (or the loan proceeds).

Down payments decrease the probability that the borrower will default on the mortgage. A mortgage borrower who makes a large down payment is less likely to walk away from the house should property values fall, leaving the mortgage unpaid. As seen in In the News box 7–1, the drop in real estate values in Texas in the 1980s caused many mortgage borrowers to walk away from their homes and mortgages, as well as many mortgage lenders to fail.

The size of the down payment depends on the financial situation of the borrower. Generally, a 20 percent down payment is required (i.e.,

lien

A public record attached to the title of the property that gives the financial institution the right to sell the property if the mortgage borrower defaults.

down payment

A portion of the purchase price of the property a financial institution requires the mortgage borrower to pay up front.

Do You Understand?

1. The condition of savings and loans associations in Texas in the mid and late 1980s?
2. What factors caused the massive lender failures?

In the News

Texas S&L Toll: 80% Likely to Need Aid

The Texas thrift crisis, which has already claimed 87 of the state's savings institutions, has not hit rock bottom yet. Amid rising interest rates and a continuing drop in real estate values comes this sobering prediction: Only one out of five savings and loan associations is expected to survive without federal assistance. "The crisis is worsening at an accelerated pace," said Stuart Chesley, chairman of the Texas Savings and Loan League. "We are unable to contain the losses."

The ailing Federal Savings and Loan Insurance Corp. spent $24.5 billion last year to rescue 87 Texas S&Ls, or about one-third of the state total. But at least 70 more are insolvent and still in need of assistance. And an additional 68 Texas thrifts are in danger of failing, according to a study prepared by Ferguson & Co. for the Texas Savings and

Source: *The American Banker,* February 15, 1989, p. 1, by Steve Klinkerman.

Loan League. That would leave 54 survivors, or 19% of the 279 savings associations that were operating in Texas last March . . .

For many Texas thrift executives, the crisis will bring an end to their institutions and their careers. Dozens upon dozens of managers are throwing their hands up in the face of plummeting real estate values and loan demand. For the national thrift industry, the Texas crisis paints a picture of what could happen in other over-built markets. "To a lesser extent, what we are seeing in Texas probably will be repeated elsewhere," said consultant William Ferguson, principal of Ferguson & Co., Irving, Tex.

Collapsing real estate loans and property values are at the heart of the Texas crisis. The twin evils are symptoms of a vastly over-built market. The poor

performance of the expected survivors—arguably the most conservative lenders—illustrates the troubles of the overall industry. The state's 54 strongest thrifts experienced a 45% increase in repossessed assets during the nine months ended Sept. 30, according to Ferguson & Co.

Losses at these thrifts—largely spurred by loan-loss provisions and write-downs—equaled 53% of the group's total profits from the previous two years. Retained earnings for the group fell by 24%. "We still are seeing significant devaluations in Texas real estate," said James Pledger, Texas savings and loan commissioner. "The depth of the economic hole in this state is hard to comprehend." Damage from the real estate implosion promises to keep regulators on the defensive. Up to 138 more Texas thrifts with combined assets of about $40 billion may need federal assistance before the Texas crisis has run its course.

www.americanbanker.com

private mortgage insurance

Insurance contract purchased by a mortgage borrower guaranteeing to pay the financial institution the difference between the value of the property and the balance remaining on the mortgage.

the loan-to-value ratio may be no more than 80 percent). Borrowers that put up less than 20 percent are required to purchase **private mortgage insurance** (PMI). In the event of default, the PMI issuer (such as Norwest Mortgage Company) guarantees to pay the financial institution the difference between the value of the property and the balance remaining on the mortgage. As payments are made on the mortgage, or if the value of the property increases, a mortgage borrower can eventually request that the PMI requirement be removed.

federally insured mortgages

Mortgages originated by financial institutions, with repayment guaranteed by either the Federal Housing Administration (FHA) or the Veterans Administration (VA).

conventional mortgages

Mortgages issued by financial institutions that are not federally insured.

Insured versus Conventional Mortgages.   Mortgages are classified as either federally insured or conventional. **Federally insured mortgages** are originated by financial institutions, but repayment is guaranteed (for a fee of 0.5 percent of the loan amount) by either the Federal Housing Administration (FHA) or the Veterans Administration (VA). In order to qualify, FHA and VA mortgage loan applicants must meet specific requirements set by these government agencies (e.g., have income below a specified level). Further, the maximum size of the mortgage is limited (the limit varies by state and is based on the cost of housing). FHA or VA mortgages require either a very low or zero down payment.

Conventional mortgages are mortgages held by financial institutions and are not federally insured (but as already discussed, they generally are required to be privately insured if the borrower's down payment is less than 20 percent of the property's value). Secondary market mortgage buyers will not generally purchase conventional mortgages that are not privately insured and that have a loan-to-value ratio of greater than 80 percent.

Mortgage Maturities.   A mortgage generally has an original maturity of either 15 or 30 years. Until recently, the 30-year mortgage was the one most frequently used. However, the 15-year mortgage has grown in popularity. Mortgage borrowers are attracted to the 15-year mortgage because of the potential saving in total interest paid (see below). However, because the mortgage is paid off in half the time, monthly mortgage payments are higher on a 15-year than on a 30-year mortgage.

Financial institutions find the 15-year mortgage attractive because of the lower degree of interest rate risk on a 15-year relative to a 30-year mortgage. To attract mortgage borrowers to the 15-year maturity mortgage, financial institutions generally charge a lower interest rate on a 15-year mortgage than a 30-year mortgage.

amortized

A mortgage is amortized when the fixed principal and interest payments fully pay off the mortgage by its maturity date.

balloon payment mortgages

Mortgage that requires a fixed monthly interest payment for a three- to five-year period. Full payment of the mortgage principal (the balloon payment) is then required at the end of the period.

Most mortgages allow the borrower to prepay all or part of the mortgage principal early without penalty. In general, the monthly payment is set at a fixed level to repay interest and principal on the mortgage by the maturity date (i.e., the mortgage is fully **amortized**). We illustrate this payment pattern for a 15-year fixed-rate mortgage in Figure 7–1. However, other mortgages have interest rates and thus payments that vary (see below).

In addition to 15- and 30-year fixed-rate and variable-rate mortgages, financial institutions sometimes offer **balloon payment mortgages**. A balloon payment mortgage requires a fixed monthly interest payment (and, sometimes, principal payments) for a three- to-five year period. Full payment of the mortgage principal (the balloon payment) is then required at the end of the period, as illustrated for a five-year balloon payment mortgage in Figure 7–1. Because they consist of interest only, the monthly payments prior to maturity are lower than those on an amortized loan. Generally, because few borrowers save enough funds to pay off the mortgage in three to five years, the mortgage principal is refinanced at the current mortgage interest rate at the end of the balloon loan period (refinancing at maturity is not, however, guaranteed). Thus, with a balloon mortgage the financial institution essentially provides a long-term mortgage in which it can periodically revise the mortgage's characteristics.

Interest Rates.   Possibly the most important characteristic identified in a mortgage contract is the interest rate on the mortgage. Mortgage borrowers often decide how much to borrow and from whom solely by looking at the quoted mortgage rates of several financial institutions. In turn, financial institutions base their quoted mortgage rates on several factors. First, they use the market rate at which they obtain funds (e.g., the fed funds rate or the rate on certificates of deposit). The market rate on available

Figure 7–1 Fixed-Rate versus Balloon Payment Mortgage

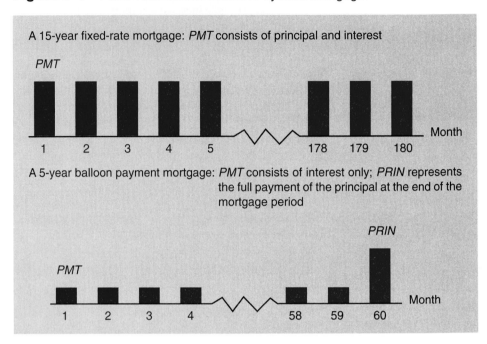

Figure 7–2 30-Year Mortgage versus 30-Year Treasury Rates

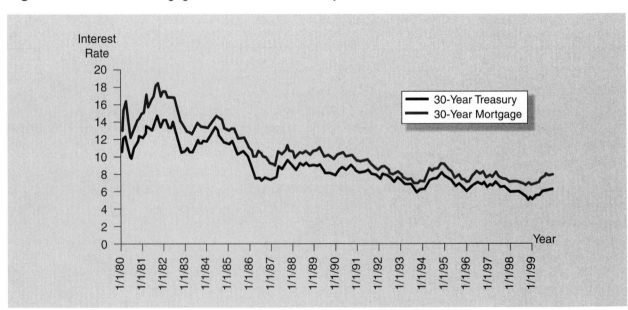

Source: Federal Reserve Board, website, "Research and Data," December 1999. *www.bog.frb.fed.us/*

funds is the base rate used to determine mortgage rates. Figure 7–2 illustrates the trend in mortgage interest rates and 30-year Treasury bond rates from 1980 through 1999. The rate on a specific mortgage is also adjusted for other factors (e.g., whether the mortgage specifies a fixed or variable (adjustable) rate of interest and whether the loan specifies discount points and other fees).

Figure 7–3 ARMs' Share of Total Loans Closed, 1992–1999

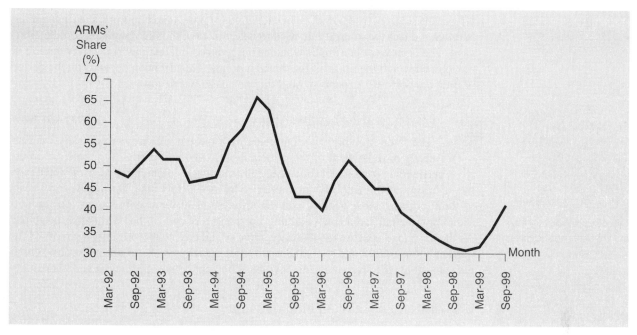

Source: Federal Housing Finance Board, website, December 1999. *www.fhfb.gov/*

fixed-rate mortgage

A mortgage that locks in the borrower's interest rate and thus the required monthly payment over the life of the mortgage, regardless of how market rates change.

adjustable-rate mortgage

A mortgage in which the interest rate is tied to some market interest rate. Thus, the required monthly payments can change over the life of the mortgage.

discount points

Interest payments made when the loan is issued (at closing). One discount point paid up front is equal to 1 percent of the principal value of the mortgage.

Fixed versus Adjustable Rate Mortgages.   Mortgage contracts specify whether a fixed or variable rate of interest will be paid by the borrower. A **fixed-rate mortgage** locks in the borrower's interest rate and thus required monthly payments over the life of the mortgage, regardless of how market rates change. In contrast, the interest rate on an **adjustable-rate mortgage** (ARM) is tied to some market interest rate or interest rate index. Thus, the required monthly payments can change over the life of the mortgage. ARMs generally limit the change in the interest rate allowed each year and during the life of the mortgage (called *caps*). For example, an ARM might adjust the interest rate based on the average Treasury bill rate plus 1.5 percent, with caps of 1.5 percent per year and 4 percent over the life of the mortgage.

Figure 7–3 shows the percentage of ARMs relative to all mortgages closed from 1992 through 1999. Mortgage borrowers generally prefer fixed-rate loans to ARMs, particularly when interest rates in the economy are low. If interest rates rise, ARMs may cause borrowers to be unable to meet the promised payments on the mortgage. In contrast, most mortgage lenders prefer ARMs. When interest rates rise, ARM payments on their mortgage assets will rise. Since deposit rates and other liability rates too will be rising, it will be easier for financial institutions to pay the higher interest rates to their depositors when they issue ARMs. However, higher interest payments mean mortgage borrowers may have trouble making their payments. Thus, default risk increases. As a result, while ARMs reduce a financial institution's interest rate risk, they also increase their default risk.

Note from Figure 7–3 the behavior of the share of ARMs to fixed-rate mortgages over one recent period—1997 to 1999—when interest rates fell dramatically. Notice that borrowers' preferences for fixed-rate mortgages prevailed over this period as a consistently low percentage of total mortgages closed were ARMs (over this period the percentage of ARMs to total mortgages issued averaged only 38 percent).

Discount Points.   **Discount points** (or more often just called points) are fees or payments made when a mortgage loan is issued (at closing). One discount point paid up front is equal to 1 percent of the principal value of the mortgage. For example, if the borrower pays 2 points up front on a $100,000 mortgage, he or she must pay $2,000 at the closing of the mortgage. While the mortgage principal is $100,000, the borrower effectively has received $98,000. In exchange for points paid up front, the financial institution reduces the interest rate used to determine the monthly payments on the mortgage. The borrower determines whether the reduced interest payments over the life of the loan outweigh the up-front fee through points. This decision depends on the period of time the borrower expects to hold the mortgage (see below).

4

Mortgage Amortization

The fixed monthly payment made by a mortgage borrower generally consists partly of repayment of the principal borrowed and partly of the interest on the outstanding (remaining) balance of the mortgage. In other words, these fixed payments fully amortize (pay off) the mortgage by its maturity date. During the early years of the mortgage, most of the fixed monthly payment represents interest on the outstanding principal and a small amount represents a payoff of the outstanding principal. As the mortgage approaches maturity, most of the payment represents a payoff of the outstanding principal and a small amount represents interest. An **amortization schedule** shows how the fixed monthly payments are split between principal and interest.

amortization schedule

Schedule showing how the monthly mortgage payments are split between principal and interest.

Example 7–1   Calculation of Monthly Mortgage Payments

You plan to purchase a house for $150,000 using a 30-year mortgage obtained from your local bank. The mortgage rate offered to you is 8 percent with zero points. In order to forgo the purchase of private mortgage insurance, you will make a down payment of 20 percent of the purchase price ($30,000 = .20 × $150,000) at closing and borrow $120,000 through the mortgage.

The monthly payments on this mortgage are calculated using the time value of money formulas presented in Chapter 2. Specifically, the amount borrowed through the mortgage represents a present value of the principal, and the monthly payments represent a monthly annuity payment. The equation used to calculate your fixed monthly mortgage payments to pay off the $120,000 mortgage at an 8 percent annual interest rate over 30 years is as follows:

$$PV = PMT\,(PVIFA_{i/12,\ n(12)})$$

where

$$PV = \text{Principal amount borrowed through the mortgage}$$

$$PMT = \text{Monthly mortgage payment}$$
$$PVIFA = \text{Present value interest factor of an annuity}$$
$$i = \text{Annual interest rate on the mortgage}$$
$$n = \text{Length of the mortgage in years}$$

For the mortgage in this example:

$$\$120,000 = PMT(PVIFA_{\ 8\%/12,\ 30(12)})$$

or:

$$PMT = \$120,000/(PVIFA_{8\%/12,\ 30(12)})$$

Therefore:

$$PMT = \$120,000/136.2835 = \$880.52$$

Thus, your monthly payment is $880.52.

We now construct the amortization schedule for this mortgage.

Example 7–2 Construction of an Amortization Schedule

Using the monthly payment calculated on the mortgage in Example 7–1, we construct an amortization schedule in Table 7–2. Column 1 is the month in the 360-month loan period. Column 2 is the balance of the mortgage outstanding at the beginning of each month. Column 3 is the monthly payment on the mortgage, calculated in Example 7–1. Column 4, Interest, is the portion of the monthly payment that represents the pure interest payment based on the loan balance outstanding at the beginning of the month (Beginning loan balance $\times$ 8%/12). Column 5, Principal, is the portion of the monthly payment that represents the repayments of the mortgage's principal (monthly Payment − monthly Interest, or in this example for month 1, $880.52 − $800 = $80.52). Column 6 is the balance of the mortgage principal outstanding at the end of the month. This value becomes the beginning balance in the next month.

Notice that the total payments made by the mortgage borrower over the 30-year life of the mortgage are $316,987.20. Of this amount $120,000 is repayment of the original principal. Thus, the borrower paid a total of $196,978.20 in interest over the life of the mortgage.

Table 7–2 Amortization Schedule for a 30-Year Mortgage

Month	Beginning Loan Balance	Payment	Interest	Principal	Ending Loan Balance
1	$120,000.00	$ 880.52	$ 800.00	$ 80.52	$119,919.48
2	119,919.48	880.52	799.46	81.06	119,838.42
•	•	•	•	•	•
•	•	•	•	•	•
•	•	•	•	•	•
59	114,321.37	880.52	762.14	118.38	114,202.99
60 (5 years)	114,202.99	880.52	761.36	119.16	114,083.83
•	•	•	•	•	•
•	•	•	•	•	•
•	•	•	•	•	•
119	105,623.54	880.52	704.16	176.36	105,447.18
120 (10 years)	105,447.18	880.52	702.98	177.54	105,269.64
•	•	•	•	•	•
•	•	•	•	•	•
•	•	•	•	•	•
179	92,665.12	880.52	617.77	262.75	92,402.37
180 (15 years)	92,402.37	880.52	616.02	264.50	92,137.87
•	•	•	•	•	•
•	•	•	•	•	•
•	•	•	•	•	•
239	73,359.08	880.52	489.06	391.46	72,967.62
240 (20 years)	72,967.62	880.52	486.45	394.07	72,573.55
•	•	•	•	•	•
•	•	•	•	•	•
•	•	•	•	•	•
359	1,743.58	880.52	11.63	868.89	874.69
360 (30 years)	874.69	880.52	5.83	874.69	0
Total		$316,987.20	$196,987.20	$120,000.00	

As discussed above, an advantage of a 15-year mortgage to a mortgage borrower is that the total interest paid on a 15-year mortgage is smaller than that paid on a 30-year mortgage.

Example 7–3 Comparison of Interest Paid on a 15-Year Versus a 30-Year Mortgage

Using the information in Example 7–1 but changing the loan maturity to 15 years, the monthly payment on the $120,000 mortgage loan is:

$$\$120,000 = PMT \, (PVIFA_{8\%/12, \, 15(12)})$$

or:

$$PMT = \$120,000/(PVIFA_{8\%/12, \, 15(12)})$$

Therefore:

$$PMT = \$120,000/104.6406 = \$1,146.78$$

Solving for *PMT,* your monthly mortgage payment is $1,146.78. Table 7–3 shows the corresponding loan amortization schedule.

Total payments on the 15-year mortgage are $206,420.85, of which $86,420.85 is interest. This compares to interest of $196,978.20 on the 30-year mortgage (a difference of $110,557.35). The mortgage borrower's interest payments are reduced significantly with the 15-year mortgage relative to the 30-year mortgage. However, the borrower must pay $1,146.78 per month with the 15-year mortgage compared to $880.52 with the 30-year mortgage, a difference of $266.26 per month. This may be difficult if his or her income level is not very high.

Table 7–3 Amortization Schedule for a 15-Year Mortgage

Month	Beginning Loan Balance	Payment	Interest	Principal	Ending Loan Balance
1	$120,000.00	$ 1,146.78	$ 800.00	$ 346.78	$119,653.22
2	119,653.22	1,146.78	797.69	349.09	119,304.13
•	•	•	•	•	•
•	•	•	•	•	•
•	•	•	•	•	•
59	95,542.57	1,146.78	636.95	509.83	95,032.74
60 (5 years)	95,032.74	1,146.78	633.55	513.23	94,519.51
•	•	•	•	•	•
•	•	•	•	•	•
•	•	•	•	•	•
199	58,081.72	1,146.78	387.21	759.57	57,322.15
120 (10 years)	57,322.15	1,146.78	382.15	764.63	56,557.52
•	•	•	•	•	•
•	•	•	•	•	•
•	•	•	•	•	•
179	2,270.83	1,146.78	15.14	1,131.64	1,139.19
180 (15 years)	1,139.19	1,146.78	7.59	1,139.19	0
Total		$206,420.85	$86,420.85	$120,000.00	

Another factor that affects the amortization of a loan is whether the borrower pays discount points up front in exchange for a reduced interest rate and, consequently, reduced monthly payments.

Example 7–4   Analyzing the Choice Between Points and Monthly Payments of Interest

You plan to purchase a house for $150,000 using a 30-year mortgage obtained from your local bank. You will make a down payment of 20 percent of the purchase price, $30,000. Thus, the mortgage loan amount will be $120,000. Your bank offers you the following two options for payment:

Option 1:   Mortgage rate of 8 percent and zero points.

Option 2:   Mortgage rate of 7.75 percent and 2 points ($2,400 = $120,000 × .02).

If option 2 is chosen, you receive $117,600 at closing ($120,000 − $2,400), although the mortgage principal is $120,000.

To determine the best option, we first calculate the monthly payments for both options as follows:

Option 1: $120,000 = PMT \ (PVIFA_{8\%/12,\ 30(12)}) \Rightarrow PMT = \$880.52$

Option 2: $120,000 = PMT \ (PVIFA_{7.75\%/12,\ 30(12)}) \Rightarrow PMT = \$859.69$

In exchange for $2,400 up front, option 2 reduces your monthly mortgage payments by $20.83. The present value of these savings (evaluated at 7.75 percent) over the 30 years is:

$$PV = \$20.83 \ (PVIFA_{7.75\%/12,\ 30(12)}) = \$2,907.54$$

Option 2 is the better choice. The present value of the monthly savings, $2,907.54, is greater than the points paid up front, $2,400.

Suppose, however, you plan on paying off the loan in 15 years (180 months) even though the mortgage has a 30-year maturity. Now the monthly savings from option 2 have a present value of:

$$PV = \$20.83 \ (PVIFA_{7.75\%/12,\ 15(12)}) = \$2,212.95$$

Option 1 becomes the better deal. The present value of the monthly savings, $2,212.95, is less than the points paid up front, $2,400.

Notice that the choice of points (and lower monthly payment) versus no points (and higher monthly payments) depends on how long the mortgage borrower takes to pay off the mortgage. Specifically, the longer the borrower takes to pay off the mortgage, the more likely he or she is to choose points and a lower mortgage rate. Thus, by offering points, the mortgage lender decreases the probability that the mortgage borrower will prepay the mortgage—paying the mortgage off early reduces the present value of the monthly savings to the mortgage borrower.

Other Types of Mortgages

New methods of creative financing have been developed by financial institutions to attract mortgage borrowers. These include automatic rate-reduction mortgages, graduated-payment mortgages, growing-equity mortgages, second mortgages, shared-appreciation mortgages, equity-participation mortgages, and reverse-annuity mortgages.

automatic rate-reduction mortgages

Mortgages in which the lender automatically lowers the rate on an existing mortgage when prevailing rates fall.

Automatic Rate-Reduction Mortgages.   As the name suggests, with automatic rate-reduction mortgages, the lender automatically lowers the rate on an existing mortgage when prevailing rates fall. Unlike variable-rate mortgages, while the interest rate on an automatic rate-reduction mortgage can be adjusted downward, it will not be increased if prevailing rates increase. Thus, interest rates on automatic rate-reduction mortgages can only fall. Mortgage lenders offer automatic rate-reduction mortgages as a way of keeping their mortgage customers from refinancing their mortgages with another mortgage lender when mortgage rates fall.

graduated-payment mortgages

Mortgages in which borrowers make small payments early in the life of the mortgage. Payments then increase over the first 5 to 10 years, and finally payments level off at the end of the mortgage period.

Graduated-Payment Mortgages.   **Graduated-payment mortgages** (GPMs) allow mortgage borrowers to make small payments early in the life of the mortgage. The payments then increase over the first 5 to 10 years, and finally payments level off at the end of the mortgage period. GPMs are used by households that expect their incomes to rise along with the GPM payment. GPMs allow borrowers to qualify for a larger loan than they could get with a conventional mortgage. The risk to the borrower and the financial institution is that, if the expected income increase does not occur, the borrower may default on the mortgage.

growing-equity mortgages

Mortgages in which the initial payments are the same as on a conventional mortgage, but they increase over a portion or the entire life of the mortgage. In contrast to GPMs, which do not affect the time until the mortgage is paid off, the incremental increase in monthly payments on GEMs reduces the principal on the mortgage more quickly. This reduces the actual life of the mortgage.

Growing-Equity Mortgages.   **Growing-equity mortgages** (GEMs) are mortgages in which the initial payments are the same as on a conventional mortgage, but they increase over a portion or the entire life of the mortgage. In contrast to GPMs, which do not affect the time until the mortgage is paid off, the incremental increase in monthly payments on GEMs reduces the principal on the mortgage more quickly. This reduces the actual life of the mortgage. Thus, GEMs are used by borrowers who want to pay off a mortgage in a shorter period of time than stated in the mortgage contract and, like GPMs, borrowers who expect their incomes to rise over the life of the mortgage.

second mortgages

Loans secured by a piece of real estate already used to secure a first mortgage.

Second Mortgages.   **Second mortgages** are loans secured by a piece of real estate already used to secure a first mortgage. Should a default occur, the second mortgage holder is paid only after the first mortgage is paid off. As a result, interest rates on second mortgages are higher than on first mortgages.

About 15 percent of all primary mortgage holders also have second mortgages. Second mortgages provide mortgage borrowers with a way to use the equity they have built up in their homes as collateral on another mortgage, thus allowing mortgage borrowers to raise funds without having to sell their homes. Financial institutions often offer **home equity loans** that let customers borrow on a line of credit secured with a second mortgage on their homes. The dollar value of home equity loans issued by commercial banks and outstanding in 1999 was $98.6 billion, compared to a total of $4,648.2 billion in total home mortgage loans. Further, the rate of interest financial institutions charged on home equity loans was 8.64 percent compared to 6.84 percent on 15-year fixed-rate first mortgage loans.

Interest on all mortgages (first, second, and home equity) secured by residential real estate is tax deductible. Interest on other types of individual loans—such as consumer loans—is not eligible for a tax deduction.

home equity loan

Loans that let customers borrow on a line of credit secured with a second mortgage on their homes.

shared-appreciation mortgage

Allows a home buyer to obtain a mortgage at an interest rate below current market rates in exchange for a share in any appreciation in the property value. If the property is eventually sold for more than the original purchase price, the financial institution is entitled to a portion of the gain.

Shared-Appreciation Mortgages.   A **shared-appreciation mortgage** (SAM) allows a home buyer to obtain a mortgage at an interest rate below current market rates in exchange for a share (given to the lender) in any appreciation in the property value. Thus, the borrower's monthly mortgage payments are smaller. However, if the property is eventually sold for more than the original purchase price, the financial institution is entitled to a portion of the gain. The financial institution has bought, in effect, a call option on the value of the house compared to its purchase price (with the house buyer being viewed as the seller of that option). SAMs are used mainly when interest rates are high because they allow borrowers who would not qualify for high interest rate (high monthly payment) mortgages to do so.

equity-participation mortgage

A mortgage that is similar to a SAM except that an outside investor shares in the appreciation of the property rather than the financial institution.

reverse-annuity mortgage

A mortgage for which a mortgage borrower receives regular monthly payments from a financial institution rather than making them. When the RAM matures (or the borrower dies) the borrower (or the estate of the borrower) sells the property to retire the debt.

Equity-Participation Mortgages. An **equity-participation mortgage** (EPM) is similar to a SAM except that an outside investor shares in the appreciation of the property rather than the financial institution that issues the mortgage. The investor either provides a portion of the down payment on the property or provides monthly payments.

Reverse-Annuity Mortgages. With a **reverse-annuity mortgage** (RAM), a mortgage borrower receives regular monthly payments from a financial institution rather than making them. When the RAM matures (or the borrower dies), the borrower (or the borrower's estate) sells the property to retire the debt. RAMs were designed as a way for retired people to live on the equity they have built up in their homes without the necessity of selling the homes. Maturities on RAMs are generally set such that the borrower will likely die prior to maturity.

Secondary Mortgage Markets

After financial institutions originate mortgages, they often sell or securitize them in the secondary mortgage market. In 1999, approximately 50 percent of all residential mortgages were securitized in this fashion. The sale/securitization of mortgages in the secondary mortgage markets reduces the liquidity risk, interest rate risk, and credit risk experienced by the originating financial institution compared to keeping the mortgage in its asset portfolio. For example, depository institutions obtain the majority of their funds from short-term deposits. Holding long-term fixed-rate mortgages in their asset portfolios subjects them to interest rate risk, particularly if interest rates are expected to increase (see Chapter 23). Moreover, selling/securitizing mortgages can generate fee income for the mortgage-originating financial institution and helps reduce the effects of regulatory constraints (see Chapter 14).

Many financial institutions such as mortgage companies (e.g., Countrywide Credit Industries, North American Mortgage, HomeSide Lending) therefore prefer to concentrate on the servicing of mortgages rather than the long-term financing of them, which occurs if they are kept on the balance sheet. For example, in 1998, mortgage companies originated $880 billion in home mortgages and serviced over $2 trillion in home mortgages. The loan originator prefers to act as a servicer, collecting payments from mortgage borrowers and passing the required interest and principal payments through to the secondary market investor. The servicer also keeps the formal records of all transactions pertaining to the mortgage. In return for these services, the financial institution collects a monthly fee. Mortgage servicers generally charge fees ranging from ¼ to ½ percent of the mortgage balance. Financial institutions can remove mortgages from their balance sheets through one of the two mechanisms. First, they can pool their recently originated mortgages together and sell them in the secondary mortgage market. Second, financial institutions can issue mortgage-backed securities, creating securities that are backed by their newly originated mortgages (i.e., securitization of mortgages).

History and Background of Secondary Mortgage Markets

The secondary mortgage markets were created by the federal government to help boost U.S. economic activity during the Great Depression. In the 1930s, the government established the Federal National Mortgage Association (FNMA or Fannie Mae) to buy mortgages from thrifts so that these depository institutions could make more mortgage loans. The government also established the Federal Housing Administration (FHA) and the Veterans Administration (VA) to insure certain mortgage contracts against default risk (described earlier). This made it easier to sell/securitize mortgages. Financial

Do You Understand?

1. What the function of a lien placed on a mortgage contract is?
2. When private mortgage insurance is required for a mortgage?
3. What the difference is between an insured mortgage and a conventional mortgage?
4. What the typical mortgage maturity is?
5. What graduated-payment mortgages are?

www.fanniemae.com/

www.va.com/

institutions originated the mortgages, and secondary market buyers did not have to be as concerned with a borrower's credit history or the value of collateral backing the mortgage since they had a federal government guarantee protecting them against default risk.

By the late 1960s, fewer veterans were obtaining guaranteed VA loans. As a result, the secondary market for mortgages declined. To encourage continued expansion in the housing market, the U.S. government created the Government National Mortgage Association (GNMA or Ginnie Mae) and the Federal Home Loan Mortgage Corporation (FHLMC or Freddie Mac), which provided direct or indirect guarantees that allowed for the creation of mortgage-backed securities (see below).

As the secondary mortgage markets have evolved, a wide variety of mortgage-backed securities have been developed to allow primary mortgage lenders to securitize their mortgages and to allow a thriving secondary market for mortgages to develop. The organizations involved in the secondary mortgage markets (e.g., GNMA, FNMA) differ in the types of mortgages included in the mortgage pools, security guarantees (or insurance), and payment patterns on the securities.

6   Mortgage Sales

Financial institutions have sold mortgages and commercial real estate loans among themselves for more than 100 years. In fact, a large part of **correspondent banking** involves small banks making loans that are too big for them to hold on their balance sheets—either for lending concentration risk or capital adequacy reasons—and selling parts of these loans to large banks with whom they have had a long-term deposit and lending correspondent relationship. In turn, large banks often sell parts of their loans, called *participations* to smaller banks.

A **mortgage sale** occurs when a financial institution originates a mortgage and sells it with or without recourse to an outside buyer. If the mortgage is sold without recourse, the financial institution not only removes it from its balance sheet but also has no explicit liability if the mortgage eventually goes bad. Thus, the buyer of the mortgage (not the financial institution that originated the loan) bears all the credit risk.[1] If, however, the mortgage is sold with **recourse,** under certain conditions the buyer can return the mortgage to the selling financial institution; therefore, the financial institution retains a contingent credit risk liability. In practice, most mortgage sales are without recourse. For example, in the first quarter of 1999, commercial banks sold $39.5 billion of the primary mortgages from their asset portfolios: $30.8 billion (77.9 percent) of these were sold without recourse. Mortgage sales usually involve no creation of new types of securities, such as those described below. We discuss loan sales in more detail in Chapter 25.

A major reason that financial institutions sell loans is to manage their credit risk better (see Chapter 21). Mortgage sales remove assets (and credit risk) from the balance sheet and allow a financial institution to achieve better asset diversification. Additionally, mortgage sales allow financial institutions to improve their liquidity risk and interest rate risk situations. Other than risk management, however, financial institutions are encouraged to sell loans for a number of other economic (generation of fee income) and regulatory reasons (including reducing the cost of reserve requirements and reducing the cost of holding capital requirement against mortgages[2]). The benefits of loan sales are discussed in detail in Chapter 25.

A wide array of potential buyers and sellers of mortgage loans exist. The five major buyers of primary mortgage loans are domestic banks, foreign banks, insurance companies and pension funds, closed-end bank loan mutual funds, and nonfinancial corporations. The major sellers of mortgage loans are money center banks, small

www.ginniemae.gov/

www.freddiemac.com/

correspondent banking

A relationship between a small bank and a large bank in which the large bank provides a number of deposit, lending, and other services.

mortgage sale

Sale of a mortgage originated by a bank with or without recourse to an outside buyer.

recourse

The ability of a loan buyer to sell the loan back to the originator should it go bad.

---

1. Although the buyer's credit risk is reduced if the mortgage is federally insured against default risk.

2. Under the current BIS scheme (see Chapter 14), this is 4 percent for most residential mortgages.

regional or community banks, foreign banks, and investment banks. We discuss the motivations of each in Chapter 25.

Securitization of Mortgages

In this section, we summarize the three major forms of mortgage securitization—the pass-through security, the collateralized mortgage obligation (CMO), and the mortgage-backed bond. In Chapter 25, we provide a detailed analysis of these securities and the processes by which these mortgage-backed securities are created.

Securitization of mortgages involves the pooling of a group of mortgages with similar characteristics, the removal of these mortgages from the balance sheet, and the subsequent sale of interests in the pool to secondary market investors. Securitization of mortgages results in the creation of mortgage-backed securities (e.g., government agency securities, collateralized mortgage obligations), which can be traded in secondary mortgage markets. For example, there were $2.632 trillion in outstanding mortgage securitization pools at the end of 1998.

pass-through mortgage securities

Mortgage-backed securities that "pass-through" promised payments of principal and interest on pools of mortgages created by financial institutions to secondary market participants holding interests in the pools.

Pass-Through Securities. Financial institutions frequently pool the mortgages and other assets they originate and offer investors an interest in the pool in the form of *pass-through certificates* or *securities*. **Pass-through mortgage securities** "pass through" promised payments of principal and interest on pools of mortgages created by financial institutions to secondary market investors (mortgage-backed security bond holders) holding an interest in these pools. We illustrate this process in Figure 7–4. After a financial institution accepts mortgages (step 1 in Figure 7–4), they pool them and sell interests in these pools to pass-through security holders (step 2 in Figure 7–4). Each pass-through mortgage security represents a fractional ownership share in a mortgage pool.[3] Thus, a 1 percent owner of a pass-through mortgage security issue is entitled to a 1 percent share of the principal and interest payments made over the life of the mortgages underlying the pool of securities. The originating financial institutions (e.g., bank or mortgage company) or a third-party servicer receives principal and interest payments from the mortgage holder (step 3 in Figure 7–4) and passes these payments (minus a servicing fee) through to the pass-through security holders (step 4).

Unlike the primary market issue of a mortgage, pass-through securities are issued in standard denominations. The minimum investment size is $25,000, and investments are in increments of $5,000 beyond the minimum. This, and the backing of pass-through securities by the U.S. government, make pass-through securities highly marketable.

Three agencies, either government-owned or government-sponsored, are directly involved in the creation of mortgage-backed pass-through securities. Informally, they are known as Ginnie Mae (GNMA), Fannie Mae (FNMA), and Freddie Mac (FHLMC). There are also private mortgage issuers, such as banks and thrifts, that purchase mortgage pools that do not conform to government-related issuer standards. Table 7–4 reports the amount of mortgaged-backed pass-through securities outstanding for each from 1995 through 1999.

www.ginniemae.gov/

GNMA. The Government National Mortgage Association (GNMA), or Ginnie Mae, began in 1968 when it split off from the Federal National Mortgage Association (FNMA). GNMA is a government-owned agency with two major functions: sponsoring mortgage-backed securities programs by financial institutions such as banks, thrifts, and mortgage bankers and acting as a guarantor to investors in mortgage-backed securities regarding the timely pass-through of principal and interest payments from the financial institution or mortgage servicer to the bond holder (step 4 in Figure 7–4). In other

---

3. This is a simplification. In actual practice, the mortgages are first sold (placed) in a "special purpose vehicle" (SPV) off the balance sheet, and it is this SPV that issues the bonds backed by the mortgages.

Figure 7–4 Pass-Through Mortgage Security

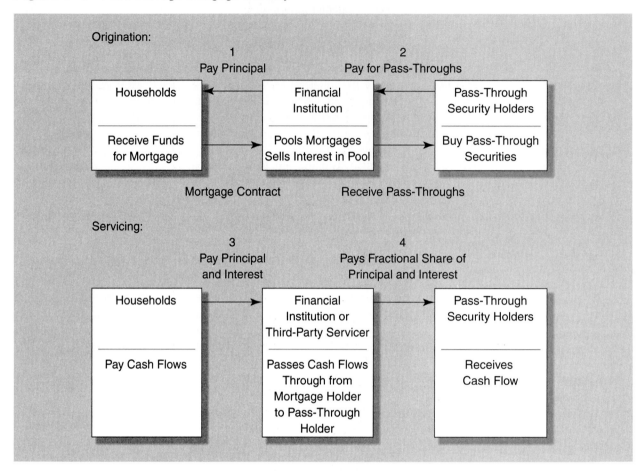

Table 7–4 Government-Related Mortgage-Backed Pass-Through Securities Outstanding
(in billions of dollars)

	1995	1996	1997	1998	1999*
GNMA	$ 472.3	$ 506.3	$ 536.8	$ 537.4	$ 553.3
FNMA	515.1	554.3	579.4	646.5	718.1
FHLMC	583.0	650.8	709.6	834.2	911.4
Private mortgage issuers	292.8	353.5	447.2	613.7	678.6
Total	$1,863.2	$2,064.9	$2,273.0	$2,631.8	$2,861.4

*As of June.

Source: Federal Reserve Bulletin, November 1999, Table 1.54, p. A35. *www.bog.frb.fed.us/*

timing insurance

A service provided by a sponsor of pass-through securities (such as GNMA) guaranteeing the bond holder interest and principal payments at the calendar date promised.

words, GNMA provides **timing insurance**. In acting as a sponsor and payment-timing guarantor, GNMA supports only those pools of mortgage loans whose default or credit risk is insured by one of three government agencies: the Federal Housing Administration (FHA), the Veterans Administration (VA), and the Farmers Home Administration (FMHA). Mortgage loans insured by these agencies target groups that might otherwise be disadvantaged in the housing market, such as low-income families, young families, and veterans. As such, the maximum mortgage under the FHA/VA/FMHA–GNMA securitization program is capped. The cap was $240,000 for a single family home in 1999.

GNMA securities are issued in minimum denominations of $25,000. The minimum pool size for GNMA single-family mortgages is $1 million. Once a pool of mortgages is packaged by a financial institution in accordance with GNMA specifications, pass-through securities can be issued. Cash flows of interest and principal received from the original mortgages are used to pay the promised payments on the GNMA securities (see Figure 7–4). The mortgages from the pool are used as collateral, guaranteeing the promised payments to the GNMA holders.

GNMA requires that all of the mortgages in a pool used to back a particular GNMA pass-through security issue have the same interest rate. Secondary market purchasers of GNMA pass-through securities generally receive 0.50 percent less than the rate on the underlying mortgages. The 0.50 percent is divided between the financial institution that services the mortgages and GNMA, which charges a fee for the provision of its timing insurance.

www.fanniemae.com/

FNMA.   Originally created in 1938, the Federal National Mortgage Association (FNMA or Fannie Mae) is the oldest of the three mortgage-backed security-sponsoring agencies. It is now a private corporation owned by shareholders, with its stock traded on the New York Stock Exchange. However, in the minds of many investors, it still has implicit government backing, which makes it equivalent to a government-owned agency. Indeed, the fact that FNMA has a secured line of credit available from the U.S. Treasury should it need funds in an emergency supports this view. FNMA is a more active agency than GNMA in creating pass-through securities. GNMA merely sponsors such programs and guarantees the timing of payments from financial institution servicers to GNMA investors; FNMA actually helps create pass-throughs by buying and holding mortgages on its balance sheet; it also issues bonds directly to finance those purchases.

Specifically, FNMA creates mortgage-backed securities (MBSs) by purchasing packages of mortgage loans from banks and thrifts; it finances such purchases by selling MBSs to outside investors such as life insurers or pension funds. In addition, FNMA engages in swap transactions by which it swaps MBSs with a bank or thrift for original mortgages. Since FNMA guarantees securities in regard to the full and timely payment of interest and principal, the financial institution receiving the MBSs can then resell them in the capital market or can hold them in its own portfolio. Unlike GNMA, FNMA securitizes conventional mortgage loans as well as FHA/VA insured loans, as long as the conventional loans have acceptable loan-to-value or collateral ratios not normally exceeding 80 percent. Conventional loans with high loan-to-value ratios usually require that the mortgages be insured with private mortgage insurance (see earlier discussion) before they are accepted into FNMA securitization pools.

www.freddiemac.com/

FHLMC.   The Federal Home Loan Mortgage Corporation (FHLMC), or Freddie Mac (FMAC), performs a similar function to that of FNMA except that its major securitization role has historically involved thrifts. Like FNMA, FHLMC is a stockholder-owned corporation with a line of credit from the U.S. Treasury. Further, like FNMA, it buys mortgage pools from financial institutions and swaps MBSs for loans. FHLMC also sponsors conventional mortgage pools and mortgages that are not federally insured as well as FHA/VA mortgage pools and guarantees timely payment of interest and ultimate payment of principal on the securities it issues.

Private Mortgage Pass-Through Issuers.   Private mortgage pass-through issuers (such as commercial banks, thrifts, and private conduits) purchase nonconforming mortgages (e.g., mortgages that exceed the size limit set by government agencies, such as the $240,000 cap set by the FHA), pool them, and sell pass-through securities on

Table 7–5 Pass-Through Securities Quote Sheet

	(1)	(2)	(3)	(4)	(5)	(6)	(7)	(8)

MORTGAGE-BACKED SECURITIES

Indicative, not guaranteed; from Bear Stearns Cos./Street Pricing Service

		PRICE (Feb) (Pts-32ds)	PRICE CHANGE (32ds)	AVG LIFE (years)	SPRD TO AVG LIFE (Bps)	SPREAD CHANGE	PSA (Prepay Speed)	YIELD TO MAT.*
30-YEAR								
FMAC GOLD	6.5%	92-25	– 11	9.4	108	unch	135	7.82%
FMAC GOLD	7.0%	95-14	– 10	9	115	– 1	150	7.88
FMAC GOLD	7.5%	97-28	– 09	8.9	123	– 1	160	7.96
FNMA	6.5%	92-24	– 11	9.4	105	– 1	135	7.79
FNMA	7.0%	95-11	– 11	9	113	– 1	150	7.86
FNMA	7.5%	97-25	– 09	8.8	121	– 1	160	7.94
GNMA	6.5%	92-07	– 12	11	103	unch	100	7.78
GNMA	7.0%	95-04	– 11	10.2	112	– 1	120	7.88
GNMA	7.5%	97-20	– 11	9.6	124	– 1	140	7.98
15-YEAR								
FMAC GOLD	7.0%	97-31	– 05	5.9	86	– 2	150	7.51%
FNMA	7.0%	97-31	– 05	5.9	81	– 2	150	7.46
GNMA	7.0%	97-31	– 05	5.9	86	– 2	145	7.51

*Extrapolated from benchmarks based on projections from Bear Stearns
prepayment model, assuming interest rates remain unchanged.

which the mortgage collateral does not meet the standards of a government-related mortgage issuer. There are a limited number of private conduits—Prudential Home, Residential Funding Corporation, GE Capital Mortgages, Ryland/Saxon Mortgage Countrywide, Chase Mortgage Finance, and Citigroup/Citibank Housing. Private mortgage pass-through securities must be registered with the SEC and are generally rated by a rating agency (such as Moody's) in a manner similar to corporate bonds.

Mortgaged-Backed Pass-Through Quotes. Table 7–5 presents a quote sheet for mortgage-backed pass-through securities traded on January 18, 2000. The quote lists the trades by issuer (e.g., GNMA, FNMA). Column 1 of the quote lists the sponsor of the issue (e.g., FMAC, FNMA, GNMA), the stated maturity of the issue (30 years or 15 years), the mortgage coupons on the mortgages in each pool (e.g., 6.5 percent), and information about the maximum delay between the receipt of interest by the servicer/sponsor and the actual payment of interest to bond holders. The "GOLD" next to FMAC indicates a maximum stated delay of 55 days. The current market price of a bond is shown in column 2, with the daily price change in column 3. Both prices are in percentages, and the number after the dash is in 32nds (e.g., 92–25 = 92 $\frac{25}{32}$ percent). Column 4 shows the average life of the bond reflecting the prepayment patterns of homeowners in the pool as estimated by one investment bank (Bear Stearns). Notice these pools of 15- and 30-year mortgages have an expected weighted-average life[4] of

4. The weighted-average life of these securities is not the same as duration, which measures the weighted-average time to maturity based on the relative present values of cash flows as weights. Rather, the weighted-average life is a significant simplification of the duration measure that seeks to concentrate on the expected timing of payments of principal.

no more than 11.0 years. The fifth column in the quote is a measure of the yield spread of the mortgage-backed security over a Treasury bond with the same average life, and column 6 reports the spread change for the day. Column 7 is a measure of the estimated prepayment speed. The prepayment speeds are shown relative to those normally occurring on pass-through securities as estimated by the Public Securities Association (PSA). Thus, 150 PSA (prepayment speed) means that these MBS mortgage holders are prepaying 1½ times quicker (or 150 percent) than the speed that normally would be expected. One possible reason for this is that current interest rates are low and many mortgage holders are prepaying early to refinance new mortgages at lower rates. Finally, the last column (8) is the yield to maturity on the mortgage-backed pass-through security. This yield is calculated using the yield to maturity formulas found in Chapter 3, given the contractual income, principal cash flows, and the expected prepayment pattern (based on projections made by Bear Stearns).

collateralized mortgage obligation (CMO)

A mortgage-backed bond issued in multiple classes or tranches.

tranches

A bond holder class associated with a CMO.

Collateralized Mortgage Obligations. Although pass-throughs are still the primary mechanism for securitization, the **collateralized mortgage obligation (CMO)** is a second vehicle for securitizing financial institution assets that is increasingly used. Innovated in 1983 by FHLMC and First Boston, the CMO is a device for making mortgage-backed securities more attractive to certain types or classes of investors. The CMO does this by repackaging the cash flows from mortgages and pass-through securities in a different fashion.

A pass-through security gives each investor a pro rata share of any promised and prepaid interest and principal cash flows on a mortgage pool. By contrast, a CMO can be viewed as a multiclass pass-through with a number of different bond holder classes or **tranches**. Unlike a pass-through, which has no guaranteed annual coupon, each bond holder class in a CMO has a different guaranteed coupon (paid semiannually) just as a regular T-bond. More importantly, the allocation of any excess cash flows over and above the guaranteed coupon payments due to increased mortgage prepayments go toward retiring the principal outstanding of only one class of bond holders, leaving all other classes prepayment protected for a period of time. CMOs give investors greater control over the maturity of the mortgage-backed securities they buy. By comparison, for pass-throughs, the mortgage-backed security holder has a highly uncertain maturity date due to the risk of very rapid prepayments (called *prepayment risk by the mortgagees*).

Creation of CMOs. CMOs can be created either by packaging and securitizing whole mortgage loans or, more usually, resecuritizing pass-through securities. In the latter case, a trust or third-party bank holds the GNMA pass-through as collateral against issues of new CMO securities. The trust normally issues a CMO with three or more different classes (or tranches). For example, the first CMO that Freddie Mac issued in 1983, secured by 20,000 conventional home mortgages worth $1 billion, had three classes: A-1, $215 million; A-2, $350 million, and A-3, $435 million. We show a three-class or tranche CMO in Figure 7–5. Class A-1 CMO holders will be the least prepayment protected since after paying any guaranteed coupons to the three classes of bondholders, A-1, A-2, and A-3, all remaining cash flows from the mortgage pool have to be used to repurchase the principal outstanding of Class A-1 bond holders. After Class A-1 bonds have been retired then remaining cash flows (after coupon payments) are used to retire the bonds of Class A-2, and so on. As a result, Class A-2 holders will have higher prepayment protection than Class A-1, and Class A-3 holders will have the greatest prepayment protection. We examine the ability of CMOs to protect against prepayment risk in more detail in Chapter 25.

CMOs can always have more than three classes described above. Indeed, issues of up to 17 different classes have been made. Clearly, the 17th-class bond holders would have an enormous degree of prepayment protection, since the first 16 classes would have had their bonds retired before the principal outstanding on this bond class would

Figure 7–5   The Creation of a CMO

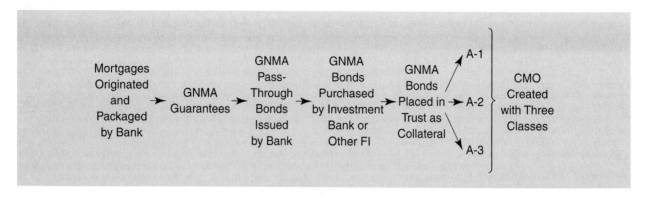

be affected by early prepayments. In addition, trustees have created other special types of classes as products to attract investor interest.

Frequently, CMO issues contain a Z class as the last regular class. The Z implicitly stands for zero, but these are not really zero-coupon bonds. This class has a stated coupon such as 10 percent and accrues interest for the bond holder on a monthly basis at this rate. The trustee does not pay this interest, however, until all other classes of bonds are fully retired. When the other classes have been retired, the Z class bond holder receives the promised coupon and principal payments plus accrued interest payments. Thus, the Z class has characteristics of both a zero-coupon bond (no coupon payments for a long period) and a regular bond.

Issuing CMOs is often equivalent to engaging in "double" securitization. An FI packages mortgages and issues a GNMA pass-through. An investment bank such as Goldman Sachs or another CMO issuer such as FHLMC, a commercial bank, or a savings bank may buy this entire issue or a large part of it. Goldman Sachs, for example, then places these GNMA securities as collateral with a trust and issues three new classes of bonds backed by the GNMA securities as collateral.[5] As a result, the investors in each CMO class have a claim to the GNMA collateral should the issuer fail. The investment bank or other issuer creates the CMO to make a profit by repackaging the cash flows from the single-class GNMA pass-through into cash flows (bonds) more attractive to different groups of investors.

As noted above, CMOs are attractive to secondary mortgage market investors because they can choose a particular CMO class that fits their maturity needs. While there is no guarantee that the CMO securities will actually mature in exact accordance with the horizon desired by the investor, the CMO significantly increases the probability of receiving cash flows over a specified horizon. For example, a third-class CMO holder knows that he or she will not be paid off until all first- and second-class holders are paid in full.

One drawback of CMOs is that originators may not be able to pass through all interest payments on a tax-free basis when they issue multiple debt securities. This creates a tax problem for various originators. A provision of the 1986 Tax Reform Act authorized the creation of a new type of mortgage-backed security called a REMIC (real estate mortgage investment conduit). A REMIC allows for the pass-through of all interest and principal payments before taxes are levied. Today, most CMOs are created as REMICs because of this tax advantage.

Mortgage Pass-Through Strips.   The mortgage pass-through strip is a special type of CMO with only two classes of securities. The fully amortized nature of mortgages means that any given monthly payment contains an interest component and a principal

---

5. These trusts are sometimes called real estate mortgage investment conduits (REMICs).

Figure 7–6 IO/PO Strips

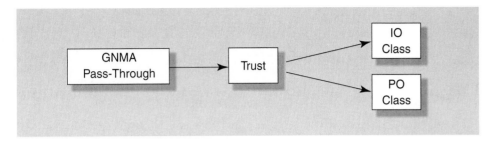

component. Beginning in 1987, investment banks and other financial institution issuers stripped out the interest component from the principal component and sold each payment stream separately to different bond class investors. They sold an interest only (IO) class and a principal only (PO) class. We show this stripping of the cash flows in Figure 7–6.

IO strips

The owner of an IO strip has a claim to the present value of interest payments by the mortgagees in the GNMA pool.

The owner of an **IO strip** has a claim to the interest payments made by the mortgage holder in the GNMA pool—that is, to the IO segments of each month's cash flows received from the underlying mortgage pool. An IO strip has no par value. If interest rates decrease slightly, the value of an IO strip increases (e.g., its present value increases as interest rates decrease). However, an IO investor receives interest only on the amount of the principal outstanding. Thus, he or she hopes prepayments on the mortgage will not occur. If interest rates fall significantly, mortgage borrowers will prepay their mortgages (and refinance them at the lower rate). When prepayments occur, the amount of interest payments the IO investor receives falls as the outstanding principal falls. The decrease in *total* payments reduces the value of the IO, counteracting the positive effect a decrease in interest rates has on the present value of the remaining payments on the IO. If prepayments are large, the IO investor may not recover his or her initial investment in the IO strip. We illustrate this relation in Figure 7–7.

PO strips

Represent the mortgage principal components in each monthly payment by the mortgagee.

The **PO strip** represents the mortgage principal components in each monthly payment by the mortgage holder. This includes both the scheduled monthly amortized principal component and any prepayments of principal by the mortgage holder. As with any security, as interest rates fall, the (present) value of the PO strip increases. In addition, if interest rates fall significantly, mortgage borrowers will prepay their mortgages. As illustrated in Figure 7–7, the faster prepayments occur (i.e., the lower interest rates fall), the faster the PO investor receives a return on his or her investment and the greater the value of the PO. Thus, in contrast to the IO investor, the PO investor hopes for large and speedy prepayments.

The IO-PO strip is a classic example of financial engineering. From a given GNMA pass-through bond, two new bonds have been created. Each class is attractive to different investors and investor segments. The IO is attractive to banks and thrifts as an on-balance-sheet hedging vehicle—as interest rates increase, the gain in value on an IO can offset the loss in value from mortgages and other bonds in the bank or thrift's asset portfolio (see Figure 7–7). The PO is attractive to those financial institutions that wish to increase the interest rate sensitivity in their portfolios in expectation of falling interest rates and to investors or traders who wish to take a speculative position regarding the future course of interest rates. Their high and complex interest sensitivity has resulted in major traders such as J.P. Morgan and Merrill Lynch, as well as many investors such as hedge funds, suffering considerable losses on their investments in these instruments when interest rates move unexpectedly against them.

mortgage- (asset-) backed bonds

Bonds collateralized by a pool of assets.

Mortgage-Backed Bond.   **Mortgage- (asset-)backed bonds** (MBBs) are the third asset-securitization vehicle. These bonds differ from pass-throughs and CMOs in two

Figure 7–7   Price-Yield Curves of IO/PO Strips

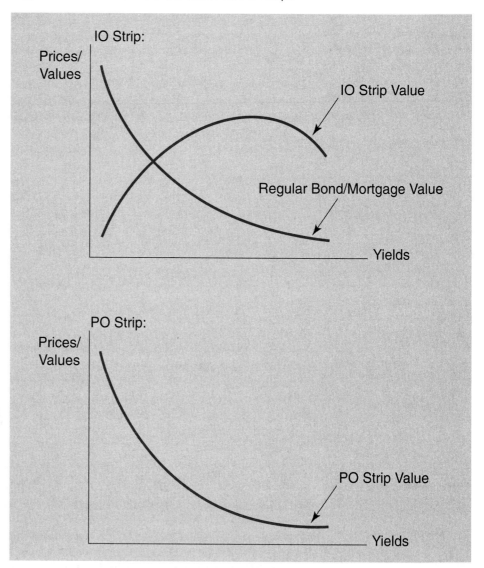

key dimensions. First, while pass-throughs and CMOs help financial institutions remove mortgages from their balance sheets, MBBs normally remain on the balance sheet. Second, pass-throughs and CMOs have a direct link between the cash flows on the underlying mortgages and the cash flows on the bond instrument issued. By contrast, the relationship for MBBs is one of collateralization; the cash flows on the mortgages backing the bond are not necessarily directly connected to interest and principal payments on the MBB.

Essentially, a financial institution issues an MBB to raise long-term low-cost funds. MBB holders have a first claim to a segment of the financial institution's mortgage assets, as illustrated in Table 7–6. Practically speaking, the financial institution segregates a group of mortgage assets on its balance sheet and pledges this group of assets as collateral against the MBB issue. For example, consider a bank with $200 million in long-term mortgages as assets. It is financing these mortgages with $100 million in

Table 7–6 Balance Sheet of Potential MBB Issuer
(in millions of dollars)

Before MBB issue:

Assets		Liabilities	
Long-term mortgages	$200	Insured deposits	$100
		Uninsured deposits	100
	$200		$200

After MBB issue:

Assets		Liabilities	
Collateral = Market value of segregated mortgages	$110	MBB issue	$100
Other mortgages	90	Insured deposits	100
	$200		$200

short-term uninsured deposits (e.g., wholesale deposits over $100,000) and $100 million in insured deposits (e.g., retail deposits under $100,000).

This balance sheet poses problems for the FI manager. First, the bank has a significant interest rate risk exposure due to the mismatch of the maturities of its long-term assets and short-term liabilities (see Chapter 23). Second, because of this interest rate risk, and the potential default risk on the bank's mortgage assets, uninsured depositors are likely to require a positive and potentially significant risk premium to be paid on their deposits. By contrast, the insured depositors may require approximately the risk-free rate on their deposits because they are fully insured by the FDIC (see Chapter 14).

To reduce its interest rate risk exposure and lower its funding costs, the bank can segregate $110 million of the mortgages on the asset side of its balance sheet and pledge them as collateral backing a $100 million long-term MBB issue. Because the $100 million in MBBs is backed by mortgages worth $110 million, the mortgage-backed bond issued by the bank may cost less to issue, in terms of required yield, than *uninsured* deposits—that is, it may well be rated AA while uninsured deposits might be rated BB. As shown in Table 7–6, the FI can then use the proceeds of the $100 million bond issue to replace the $100 million of uninsured deposits.

A trustee normally monitors the segregation of assets and ensures that the market value of the collateral exceeds the principal owed to MBB holders. Financial institutions back most MBB issues by excess collateral. This excess collateral backing of the bond (in the above example, $10 million), in addition to the priority rights of the bond holders, generally ensures the sale of these bonds with a high investment grade credit rating (BBB or better). In contrast, the financial institution, when evaluated as a whole, could be rated as BB or even lower. A high credit rating results in lower coupon payments than would be required if significant default risk had lowered the credit rating.

Weighed against the benefits of MBB issuance are a number of costs. The first cost is that MBBs tie up mortgages on the financial institution's balance sheet for a long time. This decreases the asset portfolio's liquidity. Second, balance sheet illiquidity is enhanced by the need to overcollateralize MBBs to ensure a high-quality credit risk rating for the issue. Third, by keeping the mortgages on the balance sheet, the financial institution continues to be liable for capital adequacy and reserve requirement taxes. Because of these costs, MBBs are the least used of the three basic vehicles of securitization. We discuss MBBs in more detail in Chapter 25.

Do You Understand?

1. Which loans should have the highest yields—loans sold with recourse or loans sold without recourse?
2. The three forms of mortgage loan securitization? What are the major differences in the three forms?
3. Why an investor in a securitized asset who is concerned about prepayment risk would prefer a CMO over a pass-through security?

Figure 7–8   Mortgages Outstanding by Type of Holder, 1992 and
September 1999

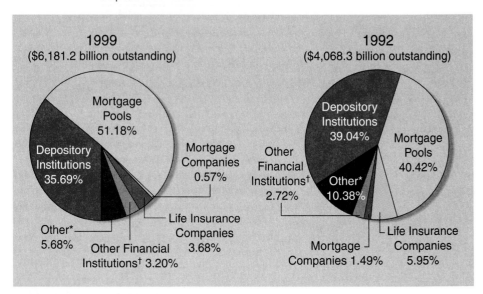

†Includes other insurance companies, pension funds, finance companies, and mortgage companies.
*Includes households, businesses, state and local government, and the federal government.
Source: Federal Reserve Board, website, "Flow of Fund Accounts," December 1999. *www.bog.frb.fed.us/*

9 Institutional Use of Mortgage Markets

In this chapter, we have demonstrated that financial institutions are critical in the operations of both the primary and secondary mortgage markets. Some financial institutions (e.g., banks, savings institutions) contribute mainly to the primary mortgage markets. Others (e.g., mortgage companies) contribute to both the primary and secondary markets. Figure 7–8 shows the distribution of mortgages outstanding in 1992 and September 1999 by type of mortgage holder—the ultimate investor.

Notice in Figure 7–8 the growth in the importance of mortgage securitization pools over the period (40.42 percent of all mortgages outstanding in 1992 versus 51.18 percent in 1999). Remember that government-sponsored mortgage pools were virtually nonexistent before the establishment of GNMA in 1968. By contrast, mortgages held by life insurance companies, households, businesses, and the federal government have fallen as a percentage of the total pool of mortgages outstanding (5.95 percent for life insurance companies in 1992 versus 3.68 percent in 1999; 10.38 percent for households, businesses, and government in 1992 versus 5.68 percent in 1999).

Notice that the actual holdings of mortgages by specialized mortgage companies (such as Atlas Mortgage, Inc., of Texas and Greenwich Home Mortgage Corp. of New Jersey) are small (1.49 percent in 1992 and 0.57 percent in 1999). Mortgage companies, or mortgage bankers, are financial institutions[6] that originate mortgages and collect payments on them. Unlike a bank or thrift, mortgage companies typically do not invest in the mortgages they originate. Instead, they sell the mortgages they originate but continue to service the mortgages by collecting payments and keeping records on each loan, as seen in Figure 7–4. Mortgage companies earn income to cover the costs of originating and servicing the mortgages from the servicing fees they charge the ultimate buyers of mortgages. Figure 7–9 shows the distribution of one- to four-family mortgage originations; mortgage companies originated 56.3 percent of all home mortgages in 1998.

---

6. Most of these mortgage companies are finance companies, which are discussed in Chapter 17.

Figure 7–9   One- to Four-Family Mortgage Originations

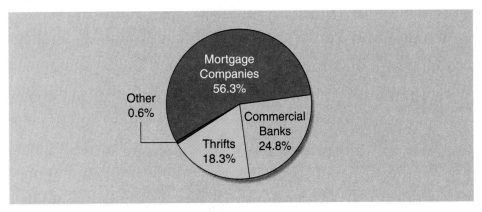

Source: Mortgage Bankers Association of America, website, January 2000. *www.mbaa.org/*

Figure 7–10   Issuers of Ginnie Mae Securities

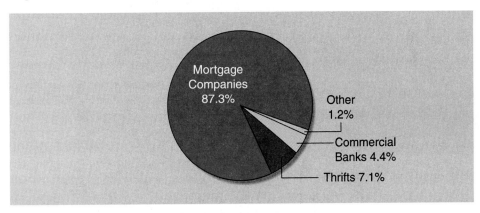

Source: Ginnie Mae, website, January 2000. *www.ginniemae.gov/*

Do You Understand?

1. Who the major holders of mortgages in the United States are?

2. Why mortgage companies hold such a small portion of the mortgage market on their balance sheets?

Mortgage companies are major originators of FHA- and VA-insured mortgage pass-throughs sponsored by GNMA. Figure 7–10 shows the distribution of issuers of GNMA securities; mortgage companies issued 87.3 percent of all GNMA securities in 1998. What should be evident from these figures is that despite originating such a large volume in the mortgage market, the reason for the small investments in mortgages by mortgage companies (as seen in Figure 7–8) is that, while mortgage companies are major *originators* of home mortgages, they generally do not *hold* the mortgage loans in their asset portfolios for a long period of time. Rather, mortgage companies *sell* or *securitize* most of the mortgages they originate in the secondary market.

International Trends in Securitization

Demand by International Investors for U.S. Mortgage-Backed Securities

International investors participate in U.S. mortgage and mortgage-backed securities markets. Table 7–7 lists the dollar value of primary mortgages issued and held by

Table 7–7 Foreign Investments in U.S. Mortgage Markets
(in billions of dollars)

	1992	1993	1994	1995	1996	1997	1998	1999*
Mortgages held by foreign banking offices in the United States	$51.6	$45.1	$40.3	$35.1	$32.2	$26.1	$20.6	$16.9

*As of September.

Source: Federal Reserve Board, website, "Flow of Fund Accounts," December 1999. *www.bog,frb.fed.us/*

foreign banking offices in the United States between 1992 and September 1999. Notice that the value of mortgages held by foreign banks has decreased over this period by 67 percent (from $51.6 billion in 1992 to $16.9 billion in 1999). This compares to primary mortgages issued and held by domestic banks of $2,206.1 billion in 1999 (see Figure 7–8)—foreign bank offices issue and hold less than 1 percent of the total primary mortgage market in the United States.

International Mortgage Securitization

While they have not evolved to the level of U.S. mortgage markets, securitization vehicles have also been developed for mortgages in countries other than the United States. After the United States, Europe is the world's second-largest and most developed securitization market. Although a form of securitization has been in existence in Europe in the German and Danish mortgage markets since the 1700s, securitization as we currently know it has only emerged outside the United States in the mid-1980s. The original growth of "modern" securitization in Europe was based largely upon the activities of a small number of centralized lenders in the booming U.K. residential mortgage market of the late 1980s. In the News box 7–2 explains the hesitance of some European investors to participate extensively in these mortgage-backed securities markets.

Do You Understand?

1. Why German investors were slow to invest in securitized mortgages?

Since mid-1993, the number of European originators of securitized assets has continued to grow, as have the types of assets that can be securitized and the investor base. Further, securitization costs have fallen, and legislative and regulatory changes in European countries have supported this market's growth. The volume of European securitizations skyrocketed in 1996 and 1997, when European countries securitized a total of $41.5 billion assets. Despite the world economic crisis in 1998, the European securitization market fell only slightly to $38.4 billion. More than $22 billion of securitized vehicles were issued in just the first half of 1999 alone, including $3.5 billion in international deals from Japan. Japan and Europe accounted for $16 billion of the first quarter total. Latin America and the emerging markets (still struggling with economic crises) lagged behind, with issues totaling $2.0 billion.

In Europe, the factors driving the securitization market include the conversion to a single currency (a factor driving many European markets at the beginning of the 21st century), the effects of globalization of all markets, and the spread of U.S.-style financial securities. Europe as a whole, and not just the U.K., is increasing its participation in securitization markets—the percentage of the total European securitization deals conducted by European countries other than the U.K. is increasing. For example, in 1997, the U.K. securitized 48 percent of the European new issues. In 1998, the U.K. securitized only 33 percent of the new issues. Germany's share of the European securitization market has grown from nothing in the early 1990s to 15 percent in 1998. In addition, the Italian government has approved new securitization laws, and Greece, Portugal, and Sweden are considering similar changes, which should increase their market shares. The single currency, the Euro, is expected to accentuate the increased trend in securitization in Europe; issuers will be able to securitize combined assets in the Euro with minimal currency risk while benefiting from a bigger and more diversified pool of buyers.

For several reasons, growth of securitization in Japan has also taken hold. Japan recently enacted new laws to facilitate pooling for securitization of assets. Improvements in Japanese economic conditions in 1999 over previous years also has played a role in the increased interest in the securitization market.

In the News

German Investors Seek Safe Home for Cash

Securitized Mortgages May Have Been a German Invention, but the Risk-Averse Nation Is Still Shy of Them

With the onset of the asset pooling and repackaging phenomenon, securitized mortgages throughout Europe were predicted to become a major idea in the banking markets in the 1990s. They signified cheap lending, and, above all, innovation within the rather conservative commercial banking industry. In fact, they may have mushroomed throughout the continent with the exception of Germany. Why is it that securitized mortgages carry a lower weighting there than in investors' portfolios elsewhere in Europe? This is a country where every young person considers himself a potential Hauslebauer—a little homebuilder.

It is ironic considering mortgage-backed papers originated in Germany. The

Source: *Financial Times*, June 21, 1999, p. 39.

first securitized mortgages were issued in 1769, when Frederick the Great, the Prussian King, needed funds to rebuild the devastated areas of his homeland after the Seven Years' War. Frederick ordered local landowners to pool their assets into specialized-purpose vehicles, which were granted loans against their collateral. Two hundred and thirty years later, the product is still around. Banks pool mortgage assets and lend against them. This

enables commercial banks to exclude these refinancing measures from their balance sheets, avoiding the risks of underwriting and protecting their credit ratios against dilution. The resulting price advantage is handed over, raising the investment attractiveness to the retail client. The customer buys it, with an albeit small risk of default.

But the case is different in conservative Germany. Between the end of the first world war and the arrival of the Nazi regime, people saw their modest economic success ravaged by inflation and economic downturn. Risk-aversion prevailed and led, once the second world war was over, to an essentially new and safer instrument in mortgage refinancing, Pfandbriefe. Instead of trading on mortgages only, these bonds appear on the balance sheet of the issuing banks,

(continues)

In the News continued

substantially adding credit quality. Their security was further enhanced by regulation, which stipulated size, duration and currency match between lending issue and collateral backing. That way Germans have jumped into an attractive market, giving them just what they were asking for: predictable returns on a safer investment.

Meanwhile, the market has been innovative enough to introduce Jumbos, pooled issuances under specified conditions, bringing down processing costs. That has further increased retail demand, and in turn has raised liquidity and attracted international interest. But that wide-ranging

attention has also led to the French authorities studying opportunities to replicate Pfandbriefe in their home market.

This is not to say Germans will refuse to invest in mortgage-backed securities (MBS) forever. Demand will rise as soon as pricing is attractive enough, says Erwin Mirkes, a Pfandbriefe trader at Deutsche Bank in Frankfurt. The Jumbos, in many cases additionally backed by German Lander or states, are priced at a spread of only 15–20 basis points to bonds. That creates a gap for riskier investments and such a market should evolve in the future, analysts predict. However, only one such issue has

been made—a 1995 paper issued by Rheinhyp, Commerzbank's mortgage banking subsidiary.

Commercial banks are seeking to broaden their trade base and are sitting on huge potential in their residential mortgages. Securitization helps them to pump up their returns on equity, reducing asset base and underwriting responsibilities. It was only in May 1997 when BAKred, the German banking regulator, authorized banks to securitize their own assets . . . Similarly, regulation has cleared the way for securitization on commercial mortgages, further developing that still tiny market segment.

Summary

In this chapter, we examined the primary and secondary mortgage markets. For several reasons, mortgages are analyzed separately from other capital market securities (e.g., bonds and stocks). We identified several characteristics associated with mortgages and various categories of primary mortgage markets. We also provided an overview of the secondary mortgage markets.

Securitization of mortgages allows financial institutions to reduce interest rate risk exposure experienced when mortgages are left in the asset portfolios for the entire life of the mortgage. We look at the details of the securitization process in a risk-return framework in Chapter 25.

End-of-Chapter Questions

1. Why are mortgage markets studied as a separate capital market?

2. What are the four major categories of mortgages and what percentage of the overall market does each entail?

3. What is the purpose of putting a lien against a piece of property?

4. Explain the difference between a federally insured mortgage and a conventional mortgage.

5. Explain the difference between a fixed-rate mortgage and an adjustable-rate mortgage. Include a discussion of mortgage borrowers' versus mortgage lenders' preferences for each.

6. You plan to purchase a $100,000 house using a 30-year mortgage obtained from your local credit union. The mortgage rate offered to you is 8.25 percent. You will make a down payment of 20 percent of the purchase price.
   a. Calculate your monthly payments on this mortgage.
   b. Calculate the amount of interest and, separately, principal paid in the 25th payment.
   c. Calculate the amount of interest and, separately, principal paid in the 225th payment.
   d. Calculate the amount of interest paid over the life of this mortgage.

7. You plan to purchase a $175,000 house using a 15-year mortgage obtained from your local bank. The mortgage rate offered to you is 7.75 percent. You will make a down payment of 20 percent of the purchase price.
   a. Calculate your monthly payments on this mortgage.
   b. Calculate the amount of interest and, separately, principal paid in the 60th payment.
   c. Calculate the amount of interest and, separately, principal paid in the 180th payment.
   d. Calculate the amount of interest paid over the life of this mortgage.

8. You plan to purchase an $80,000 house using a 15-year mortgage obtained from your local bank. The mortgage rate offered to you is 8.00 percent. You will make a down payment of 20 percent of the purchase price.
   a. Calculate your monthly payments on this mortgage.
   b. Calculate the amount of interest and, separately, principal paid in the 127th payment.
   c. Calculate the amount of interest and, separately, principal paid in the 159th payment.

   d. Calculate the amount of interest paid over the life of this mortgage.

9. You plan to purchase a house for $115,000 using a 30-year mortgage obtained from your local bank. You will make a down payment of 20 percent of the purchase price.
   a. Your bank offers you the following two options for payment:
      Option 1: Mortgage rate of 9 percent and zero points.
      Option 2: Mortgage rate of 8.85 percent and 2 points.
      Which option should you choose?
   b. Your bank offers you the following two options for payments:
      Option 1: Mortgage rate of 10.25 percent and 1 point.
      Option 2: Mortgage rate of 10 percent and 2.5 points.
      Which option should you choose?

10. What is the difference between a graduated-payment mortgage and a growing-equity mortgage?

11. What is the difference between a shared-appreciation mortgage and an equity-participation mortgage?

12. How did the U.S. secondary mortgage markets evolve?

13. What is a mortgage sale? How does a mortgage sale differ from the securitization of mortgage?

14. What is a pass-through security?

15. What is the Government National Mortgage Association? How does this organization play a role in secondary mortgage markets?

16. What is the Federal National Mortgage Association? How does this organization play a role in secondary mortgage markets?

17. Describe a collateralized mortgage obligation. How is a CMO created?

18. What is a mortgage-backed bond? Why do financial institutions issue MBOs?

19. Go to the Federal Housing Finance Board website and find the most recent data on the percentage of mortgages that are adjustable rate.

20. Go to the Federal Reserve System website and find the most recent data on international holdings of the U.S.-based mortgages reported in Table 7–7.

Stock Markets

Chapter Navigator

1. What are the major characteristics of common stock?

2. What are the major characteristics of preferred stock?

3. What is the process by which common stock is issued in primary markets?

4. What are the major secondary stock markets?

5. What is the process by which a trade takes place in the stock markets?

6. What are the major stock market indexes?

7. Who are the major stock market participants?

8. What are the three forms of market efficiency?

9. What are the major characteristics of international stock markets?

The Stock Markets: Chapter Overview

In the 1990s, the market value of corporate stock outstanding increased faster than any other type of financial security. Corporate stock serves as a source of financing for firms, in addition to debt financing or retained earnings financing. Table 8–1 shows the market value of corporate stock issued in the United States from 1994 through September 1999 by type of issuer. Stock values increased over 150 percent over this period compared to 44.8 percent growth in bond values (see Table 6–1) and 40.6 percent growth in primary mortgage market values (see Table 7–1).

Table 8-1 Market Value of Common Stock Outstanding, by Type of Issuer
(in billions of dollars)

	1994	1995	1996	1997	1998	1999
Nonfinancial corporate business	$4,811.9	$6,435.0	$ 7,618.6	$ 9,661.1	$11,561.0	$12,095.0
Financial corporations	893.9	1,284.0	1,634.3	2,319.3	2,445.2	2,246.1
Rest of world	627.5	776.8	1,002.9	1,201.0	1,407.1	1,667.2
Total	$6,333.3	$8,495.7	$10,255.8	$13,181.4	$15,413.4	$16,008.3

*As of September.

Source: Federal Reserve Board, website, "Flow of Fund Accounts," December 1999. *www.bog.frb.fed.us/*

Legally, holders of a corporation's common stock or equity have an ownership stake in the issuing firm that reflects the percentage of the corporation's stock they hold. Specifically, corporate stockholders have the right to a share in the issuing firm's profits after the payment of interest to bond holders and taxes. They also have a residual claim on the firm's assets if the company fails or is dissolved after all debt and tax liabilities are paid. Bond holders, on the other hand, are creditors of the issuing firm. They have no direct ownership interest in the firm, but they have a superior claim to the firm's earnings and assets relative to that of stockholders.

Further, common stockholders have voting privileges on major issues in the firm such as the election of the board of directors. It is the board of directors that oversees the day-to-day operations of the firm. The board is charged with ensuring that the firm is being run so as to maximize the value of the firm (i.e., the value of its equity and debt claims). Thus, while stockholders have no direct control over a firm's day-to-day operations, they do decide on who will oversee these operations and they can replace the board when they feel the firm is not being run efficiently from a value-maximizing perspective.

The secondary market for corporate stock is the most closely watched and reported of all financial security markets. Daily television and newspaper reports include recaps of the movements in stock markets (both in the United States and abroad). This is because stock market movements are sometimes seen as predictors of economic activity and performance. This is also because corporate stocks may be the most widely held of all financial securities. Most individuals own stocks either directly or indirectly through pension fund and mutual fund investments, and thus their economic wealth fluctuates closely with that of the market.

In this chapter, we present a description of equity or stock securities and the markets in which they trade. We begin with a description of the different types of corporate stock. We next look at how they are sold to the public and then traded; first in primary markets (the original sale) and then in secondary markets. We also review the major stock market indexes. We look at the participants in stock markets and other issues relating to those markets, such as the link between stock market indexes and the overall economic activity, the efficiency of the stock market, as well as regulations covering stock market operations. We conclude the chapter with an examination of international participation in U.S. stock markets and some characteristics of foreign stock markets.

Stock Market Securities

Two types of corporate stock exist: common stock and preferred stock. While all public corporations issue common stock, many do not offer preferred stock. Both types of stock offer investors a two-part rate of return. The first part is capital gains if the stock appreciates in price over time.[1] The second part is the periodic (generally quarterly) dividend payments to the stockholder. Preferred stock dividends are generally preset at a fixed rate, while common stock dividends vary over time and are thus uncertain (see below). Thus, the return to a stockholder over a period t-1 to t can be written as:

$$R_t = \frac{P_t - P_{t-1}}{P_{t-1}} + \frac{D_t}{P_{t-1}}$$

where

P_t = Stock price at time t

D_t = Dividends paid over time $t-1$ to t

$\dfrac{P_t - P_{t-1}}{P_{t-1}}$ = Capital gain over time $t-1$ to t

$\dfrac{D_t}{P_{t-1}}$ = Return from dividends paid over time $t-1$ to t

---

Example 8–1   Calculation of Return on a Stock

Suppose you owned a stock over the last year. You originally bought the stock for $40 ($P_{t-1}$) and just sold it for $45 ($P_t$). The stock also paid an annual dividend of $4 on the last day of the year. Your return on the stock investment can be calculated as follows:

$$R_t = \frac{\$45 - \$40}{\$40} + \frac{\$4}{\$40}$$

$$= 12.5\% + 10.0\% = 22.5\%$$

or your return on the stock over the last year was 22.5 percent, 12.5 percent from capital gains and 10.0 percent from dividends.

We also looked at the calculation of the rate of return on corporate stocks in the appendix to Chapter 3.

Table 8–2 shows the annual issuance of new common and preferred stock sold to new and existing stockholders from 1992 through 1998. Notice that preferred stock represents a very small portion of the new issue market. Indeed, the majority of public corporations do not have preferred stock outstanding.

Common Stock

common stock

The fundamental ownership claim in a public corporation.

Common stock is the fundamental ownership claim in a public corporation. There are many characteristics of common stock that differentiate it from other types of financial securities (e.g., bonds, mortgages, preferred stock). These

Table 8–2   New Securities Issued
(in billions of dollars)

	1992	1993	1994	1995	1996	1997	1998
Preferred	$21.33	$18.90	$12.57	$10.96	$33.21	$29.80	$ 21.20
Common	57.10	82.66	47.83	57.81	83.05	82.40	107.60

Source: Federal Reserve Bulletin, Table 1.46, various issues. *www.bog.frb.fed.us/*

---

1. If the stock price falls, then the stock is subject to capital losses.

include (1) discretionary dividend payments, (2) residual claim status, (3) limited liability, and (4) voting rights. These characteristics are described next.

Dividends. While common stockholders can potentially receive unlimited dividend payments if the firm is highly profitable, they have no special or guaranteed dividend rights. Rather, the payment and size of dividends is determined by the board of directors of the issuing firm (who are elected by the common stockholders). Further, unlike interest payments on debt, a corporation does not default if it misses a dividend payment to common stockholders. Thus, common stockholders have no legal recourse if dividends are not received, even if a company is highly profitable and chooses to use these profits to reinvest in new projects and firm growth.[2]

Another drawback with common stock dividends, from an investor's viewpoint, is that they are taxed twice—once at the firm level (at the corporate tax rate, by virtue of the fact that dividend payments are not tax deductible from the firm's profits or net earnings) and once at the personal level (at the personal income tax rate). Investors can partially avoid this double taxation effect by holding stocks in growth firms that reinvest most of their earnings to finance growth rather than paying larger dividends. Generally, the faster a firm's earnings grow, the faster its stock price increases. Thus, stockholders can sell their stock for a profit and pay capital gains tax rather than ordinary income taxes on dividends. Under current tax laws, capital gains tax rates are lower than ordinary income tax rates. For example, in the late 1990s, ordinary income tax rates ranged from 15 percent to 39.6 percent of an individual's taxable income. Long-term (a 12-month or longer investment horizon) capital gains tax rates were capped at 20 percent.

In the context of the return equation above, the reinvestment of earnings (rather than payment of dividends) affects both return components: capital gains and dividends. By reinvesting earnings (rather than paying dividends), the dividend component of returns, D_t/P_{t-1}, decreases. However, the reinvestment of earnings generally results in a relatively larger increase in the capital gains component, $(P_t - P_{t-1})/P_{t-1}$.

Example 8–2 Payment of Dividends versus Reinvestment of Earnings

A corporation has after-(corporate)tax earnings that would allow a $2 dividend per share to be paid to its stockholders. If these dividends are paid, the firm will be unable to invest in new projects, and its stock price, currently $50 per share, probably would not change. The return to the firm's stockholders in this case is:

$$R_t = \frac{50 - 50}{50} + \frac{2}{50} = 4\%$$

Suppose a stockholder bought the stock at the beginning of the year (at $50) and sold it at the end of the year (at $50). The stockholder's ordinary income tax rate is 31 percent and capital gains tax rate is 20 percent. The return to the stockholder in this case is all in the form of ordinary income (dividends). Thus, the after-tax rate of return to the stockholder is 4%(1 − .31) = 2.76%.

Alternatively, rather than pay dividends, the firm can use the earnings to invest in new projects that will increase the overall value of the firm such that the stock price will rise to $52 per share. The return to the firm's stockholders in this case is:

$$R_t = \frac{52 - 50}{50} + \frac{0}{50} = 4\%$$

---

2. Eventually, of course, such profits will be paid out—in the extreme case on dissolution of the corporation.

In this case, the return to the stockholder is all in the form of capital gains, and is thus taxed at a rate of 20 percent. Thus, the after-tax rate of return to the stockholder is $4\%(1 - .20) = 3.2\%$.

residual claim

In the event of liquidation, common stockholders have the lowest priority in terms of any cash distribution.

Residual Claim.   Common stockholders have the lowest priority claim on a corporation's assets in the event of bankruptcy—they have a **residual claim**. Only after all senior claims are paid (i.e., payments owed to creditors such as the firm's employees, bond holders, the government (taxes), and preferred stockholders) are common stockholders entitled to what assets of the firm are left. The residual claim feature associated with common stock makes it riskier than bonds as an investable asset.

limited liability

No matter what financial difficulties the issuing corporation encounters, neither it nor its creditors can seek repayment from the firm's common stockholders. This implies that common stockholder losses are limited to the original amount of their investment.

Limited Liability.   One of the most important characteristics of common stock is its limited liability feature. Legally, **limited liability** implies that common stockholder losses are limited to the amount of their original investment in the firm, I in Figure 8–1, if the company's asset value falls to less than the value of the debt it owes, point B. That is, the common stockholders' personal wealth held outside their ownership claims in the firm are unaffected by bankruptcy of the corporation—even if the losses of the firm exceed its total common stock ownership claims. In contrast, sole proprietorship or partnership stock interests mean the stockholders may be liable for the firm's debts out of their total private wealth holdings, W in Figure 8–1, if the company gets into financial difficulties and its losses exceed the stockholders ownership claims in the firm. This is the case of "unlimited" liability.

Voting Rights.   A fundamental privilege assigned to common stock is voting rights. While common stockholders do not exercise control over the firm's daily activities (these activities are overseen by managers hired to act in the best interests of the firm's common stockholders and bond holders), they do exercise control over the firm's activities indirectly through the election of the board of directors.

dual-class firms

Two classes of common stock are outstanding, with differential voting rights assigned to each class.

The typical arrangement is to assign one vote per share of common stock. However, some corporations are organized as **dual-class firms,** in which two classes of common stock are outstanding, with different voting rights assigned to each class. For example, inferior voting rights have been assigned by (1) limiting the number of votes per share on one class relative to another (e.g., Alberto-Culver Class A shares are entitled to one-tenth vote per share, while Class B shares are entitled to one vote per share), (2) limiting the fraction of the board of directors that one class could elect relative to another (e.g., ICH Corp. allowed one vote per share on both its common and Class B stock, but common shares elect 20 percent of the board, while Class B stockholders elect 80 percent of the board), or (3) a combination of these two (e.g., American Fructose Class A shares elect 25 percent of the board and have one vote per share on all other matters, while Class B shares elect 75 percent of the board and have 10 votes per share on all other matters).

To offset the reduced voting rights, inferior class shares are often assigned higher dividend rights. For example, no dividend is paid on the Class B common shares of Alberto Culver unless an equal or greater dividend is paid on the Class A stock. Bowl America paid its inferior voting rights stock a 20 percent dividend preference for four years after the issuance of the limited voting class of stock.

In 1999, approximately 300 dual-class firms existed. Dual-class firms have often been used in corporations owned and controlled by a single family or group turning to the public market to raise capital through the issue of new shares. To retain voting control over the firm, the family or group issues the dual classes of stock, keeping the high voting stock for themselves and selling the limited voting shares to the public. For example, shares in Class A might carry 5 or 10 votes per share, while shares in Class B carry only 1 vote per share—in all other respects, the shares of the two classes are

Figure 8–1 The Limited Liability Effect

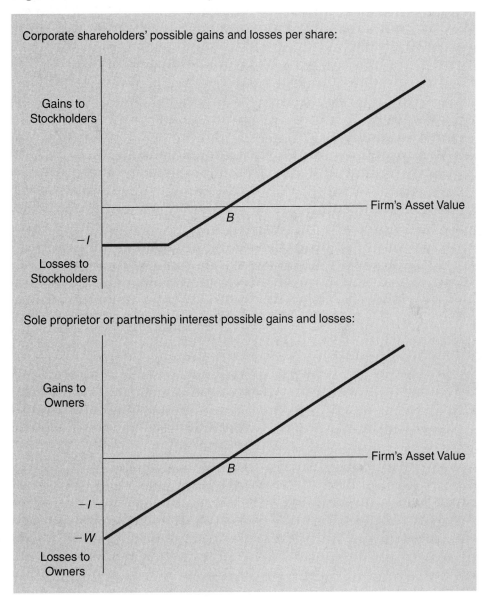

Corporate shareholders' possible gains and losses per share:

Gains to Stockholders

Firm's Asset Value

B

−I

Losses to Stockholders

Sole proprietor or partnership interest possible gains and losses:

Gains to Owners

Firm's Asset Value

B

−I

−W

Losses to Owners

identical. Because dual classes of stock have often been used by a small group (i.e., family members) to entrench themselves in the firm, dual-class firms are controversial. In 1999, Marriott International announced a plan to create two classes of common stock: one class with 1 vote per share and one class with 10 votes per share. Marriott officials argued that the dual-class structure would enable the company to grow through mergers more easily. However, several pension fund groups that owned stock in Marriott argued that the plan would allow the Marriott family (who owned about 20 percent of Marriott's stock) to accumulate higher voting control and still sell common shares in the firm. The dual-class proposal was rejected in a vote of the firm's shareholders.

Shareholders exercise their voting rights, electing the board of directors by casting votes at the issuing firm's annual meeting or by mailing in a proxy vote (see below). Two methods of electing a board of directors are generally used: cumulative voting and straight voting. Cumulative voting is required by law in some states (e.g., California

cumulative voting

All directors up for election are voted on at the same time. The number of votes assigned to each stockholder equals the number of shares held multiplied by the number of directors to be elected.

and Illinois) and is authorized in others. With **cumulative voting**, all directors up for election, as nominated by the shareholders and selected by a committee of the board, are voted on at the same time. The number of votes assigned to each stockholder equals the number of shares held multiplied by the number of directors to be elected. A shareholder may assign all of his or her votes to a single candidate for the board or may spread them over more than one candidate. The candidates with the highest number of total votes are then elected to the board.

Example 8–3 Cumulative Voting of a Board of Directors

Suppose a firm has 1 million shares of common stock outstanding and three directors up for election. With cumulative voting, the total number of votes available is 3,000,000 (= 1 million shares outstanding $\times$ 3 directors).

If there are four candidates for the three board positions, the three candidates with the highest number of votes will be elected to the board and the candidate with the least total votes will not be elected. In this example, the minimum number of votes needed to ensure election is one-fourth of the 3 million votes available, or 750,000 votes. If one candidate receives 750,000, the remaining votes together total 2,250,000. No matter how these votes are spread over the remaining three director candidates, it is mathematically impossible for *each* of the three to receive *more than* 750,000. This would require more than 3 $\times$ 750,000 votes, or more than the 2,250,000 votes that remain.

For example, if candidate 1 receives 750,000 votes and votes for the other three candidates are spread as follows:

$$Candidate\ 2 = 2\ million\ votes$$
$$Candidate\ 3 = 150,000\ votes$$
$$Candidate\ 4 = 100,000\ votes$$

for a total of 3 million votes cast, candidates 1, 2, and 3 are elected to the board. Alternatively, votes for the other three candidates can be spread as:

$$Candidate\ 3 = 751,000\ votes$$
$$Candidate\ 2 = 750,000\ votes$$
$$Candidate\ 4 = 749,000\ votes$$

Again, candidates 1, 2, and 3 are elected. Indeed, any distribution of the remaining 2,250,000 votes will ensure that candidate 1 is one of the top three vote getters and will be elected to the board.

Cumulative voting permits minority stockholders to have some real say in the election of the board of directors, since less than a majority of the votes can affect the outcome.

With straight voting, the vote on the board of directors occurs one director at a time. Thus, the number of votes eligible for each director is the number of shares outstanding. Straight voting results in a situation in which an owner of over half the voting shares can elect the entire board of directors.

proxy

A voting ballot sent by a corporation to its stockholders. When returned to the issuing firm, a proxy allows stockholders to vote by absentee ballot or authorizes representatives of the stockholders to vote on their behalf.

Proxy Votes. Most shareholders do not attend the annual meetings. Most corporations anticipate this and routinely mail proxies to their stockholders prior to the annual meeting. A completed **proxy** returned to the issuing firm allows stockholders to vote by absentee ballot or authorize representatives of the stockholders to vote on their behalf. It is estimated that, on average, less than 40 percent of the total possible votes are cast at corporate meetings. However, use of the Internet may increase this number in the future. In 1999, over 1,000 U.S. firms (such as Alcoa, Federated Investors, Morgan Stanley Dean Witter, and Tyco International) were putting proxy statements on-line and allowing votes to be cast via the Internet. For example, in its first trial at offering on-line proxy voting (in July 1999), 6 percent of Federated Investors' proxy votes were received via the Internet.

Preferred Stock

preferred stock

A hybrid security that has characteristics of both bonds and common stock.

Preferred stock is a hybrid security that has characteristics of both a bond and a common stock. Preferred stock is similar to common stock in that it represents an ownership interest in the issuing firm, but like a bond it pays a fixed periodic (dividend) payment. Preferred stock is senior to common stock but junior to bonds. Therefore, preferred stockholders are paid only when profits have been generated and all debt holders have been paid (but before common stockholders are paid). Like common stock, if the issuing firm does not have sufficient profits to pay the preferred stock dividends, preferred stockholders cannot force the firm into bankruptcy. Further, if the issuing firm goes bankrupt, preferred stockholders are paid their claim only after all creditors have been paid, but before common stockholders are paid.

Dividends on preferred stock are generally fixed (paid quarterly) and are expressed either as a dollar amount or a percent of the face or par value of the preferred stock.

Example 8–4 Calculation of Preferred Stock Dividends

Suppose you own a preferred stock that promises to pay an annual dividend of 5 percent of the par (face) value of the stock (received in quarterly installments). If the par value of the stock is $100, the preferred stockholder will receive:

$$\text{Annual dividends} = \$100 \times .05 = \$5$$

or:

$$\text{Quarterly dividend} = \$5 \div 4 = \$1.25$$

at the end of each quarter.

Alternatively, the preferred stock could promise to pay an annual dividend of $5 per year in quarterly installments.

---

nonparticipating preferred stock

Preferred stock in which the dividend is fixed regardless of any increase or decrease in the issuing firm's profits.

cumulative preferred stock

Preferred stock in which missed dividend payments go into arrears and must be made up before any common stock dividends can be paid.

participating preferred stock

Preferred stock in which actual dividends paid in any year may be greater than the promised dividends.

noncumulative preferred stock

Preferred stock in which dividend payments do not go into arrears and are never paid.

Preferred stockholders generally do not have voting rights in the firm. An exception to this rule may exist if the issuing firm has missed a promised dividend payment. For example, preferred stock in Pitney Bowes, Inc., has no voting rights except when dividends are in arrears for six quarterly payments. In this case, preferred stockholders can elect one-third of the board of directors.

Typically, preferred stock is nonparticipating and cumulative. **Nonparticipating preferred stock** means that the preferred stock dividend is fixed regardless of any increase or decrease in the issuing firm's profits. **Cumulative preferred stock** means that any missed dividend payments go into arrears and *must* be made up before *any* common stock dividends can be paid.

In contrast, **participating preferred stock** means that actual dividends paid in any year may be greater than the promised dividends. In some cases, if the issuing firm has an exceptionally profitable year, preferred stockholders may receive some of the high profits in the form of an extra dividend payment. In others, the participating preferred stock pays and changes dividends along the same lines as common stock dividends. For example, RISCORP, Inc., has participating preferred stock outstanding that pays dividends equal to those on its common stock. If **preferred stock** is **noncumulative**, missed dividend payments do not go into arrears and are never paid. For example, G & L Realty, Inc.'s preferred stock entitles stockholders to monthly dividends based on an annual rate of $2.45 per share. If a dividend payment is missed, the dividends do not go into arrears. Noncumulative preferred stock is generally unattractive to perspective preferred stockholders. Thus, noncumulative preferred stock generally has some other special features (e.g., voting rights) to make up for this drawback.

Corporations find preferred stock beneficial as a source of funds because, unlike coupon interest on a bond issue, dividends on preferred stock can be missed without fear of bankruptcy proceedings. Additionally, preferred stock is beneficial to an issuing firm's debt holders. Funds raised through a preferred stock issue can be used by the firm to fund the purchase of assets that will produce income needed to pay debt holders before preferred stockholders can be paid.

However, preferred stock also has its drawbacks for corporations. The first drawback is that, if a preferred dividend payment is missed, new investors may be reluctant to make investments in the firm. Thus, firms are generally unable to raise any new capital until all missed dividend payments are paid on preferred stock. In addition, preferred stockholders must be paid a rate of return consistent with the risk associated with preferred stock (i.e., dividend payments may be delayed). Therefore, preferred stock is generally a costlier source of funding for the issuing firm than bonds.

A second drawback of preferred stock from the issuing firm's viewpoint is that, unlike coupon interest paid on corporate bonds, dividends paid on preferred stock are not a tax-deductible expense—preferred dividends are paid out of after-tax earnings. This raises the cost of preferred stock relative to bonds for a firm's shareholders. Specifically, this difference in the tax treatment between coupon interest on debt and preferred stock dividends affects the net profit available to common stockholders of the firm. While preferred stock has its strengths and drawbacks as a method of financing a firm's assets, In the News box 8–1 explains that preferred stock has seen a resurgence of interest as an investment opportunity.

Do You Understand?

1. What common stock is?
2. What some of the drawbacks are of dividends paid on common stock from the stockholders' point of view?
3. What the difference is between cumulative voting and straight voting of the board of directors?
4. What preferred stock is? How is preferred stock similar to common stock and bonds?

Primary and Secondary Stock Markets

Before common stock can be issued by a corporation, shares must be authorized by a majority vote of both the board of directors and the firm's existing common stockholders. Once authorized, new shares of stock are distributed to existing and new investors through a primary market sale with the help of investment banks. Once issued, the stocks are traded in secondary stock markets (such as the NYSE or NASDAQ—see below).

In this section, we examine the process involved with the primary sale of corporate stock. We also describe the secondary markets, the process by which stocks trade in these markets, and the indexes that are used to summarize secondary stock market value changes.

Primary Markets

primary markets

Markets in which corporations raise funds through new issues of securities.

Primary markets are markets in which corporations raise funds through *new* issues of stocks. The new stock securities are sold to initial investors (suppliers of funds) in exchange for funds (money) that the issuer (user of funds) needs. As illustrated in Figure 8–2, most primary market transactions go through investment banks (e.g., Morgan Stanley or Lehman Brothers—see Chapter 16), who serve as the intermediary between the issuing corporations (fund users) and ultimate investors (fund suppliers) in securities.

Like the primary sale of bonds (discussed in Chapter 6), the investment bank can conduct a primary market sale of stock using a firm commitment underwriting (where the investment bank guarantees the corporation a price for newly issued securities by buying the whole issue at a fixed price from the corporate issuer) or a best efforts underwriting basis (where the underwriter does not guarantee a price to the issuer and acts more as a placing or distribution agent). In a firm commitment underwriting, the

In the News

Preferred stock. The term evokes a Wall Street era of ticker tape, spittoons and coupon-clipping. These securities, commanding almost no public attention these days, are still around, however, and some professionals think they now offer almost irresistible value. "Yields on preferreds right now on a historical basis make them very advantageous," said Joseph Grunfeld, an adviser to well-to-do investors at Merrill Lynch. Yields are now 8 to 10 percent. According to a Merrill Lynch study, they average about nine-tenths of a percentage point higher than bonds of similar credit quality, a difference that is about three times as much as usual. The spread has been wider: late last year, because of intense tax-loss selling, it hit 1.20 points. But it is still attractive. And the yield to maturity on the Merrill Lynch fixed-rate preferred stock index, meanwhile, at 9.03 percent, is nearly a full percentage point higher than it was a year ago.

Source: *The Wall Street Journal,* January 30, 2000, p. D1, by Robert D. Hershey, Jr. Reprinted by permission of *The Wall Street Journal.* © 2000 Dow Jones & Company, Inc. All Rights Reserved Worldwide.

Slow but Steady Is Looking Flashier

Preferred Stock Makes a Comeback

Preferred shares occupy a clear niche. They are equity shares that rank ahead of common stock in their right to receive dividends and, if the issuer fails, to share in proceeds from its liquidation. With a preferred share of the "cumulative" type, dividend arrears must be paid before holders of common stock get a dime . . . Preferred issues trade like bonds, meaning that their prices move more in response to fluctuations in interest rates than in response to what happens to the companies that issue them . . . Indeed, preferred shares are best considered as substitutes for bonds, a conservative way to raise portfolio income without going into bonds, which are subject to sharp price swings, the volatility becoming progressively greater as maturity lengthens. Preferred shares are somewhat less sensitive to rates than bonds of the same duration because of their subordination to bonds. "They allow us to pump up the yields in

a way that we have a measure of safety," said William C. Newell, president of Atlantic Capital Management in Sherborn, Mass.

Investing in preferred shares is generally safe and easy, with 468 of them listed on the New York Stock Exchange. But they are not for everyone because, except for those convertible into common stock, they are almost guaranteed not to rise much in value. "There's no growth in them," Mr. Newell said, "Absolutely not" . . .

What preferreds do offer, in return for investors' sacrificing the chance for capital gains, are fat yields—9.19 percent, for example, for preferreds of Grand Metropolitan, which merged with Guinness, the Irish brewer, in 1997 to form Diageo. To get as much yield in bonds, Mr. Gurnfeld said, "I've got to buy junk"—that is, drop below investment grade minimums.

Traditionally, most preferred shares were bought by corporations, which until 1994 did not pay taxes on 70 percent of dividends from these shares. The reduced corporate presence since the law was changed has tended to raise yields and produced anomalies that smart investors can exploit.

Figure 8–2   Primary Market Stock Transaction

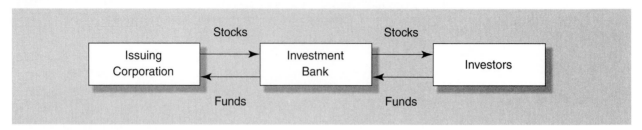

net proceeds

The guaranteed price at which the investment bank purchases the stock from the issuer.

gross proceeds

The price at which the investment bank resells the stock to investors.

underwriter's spread

The difference between the gross proceeds and the net proceeds.

syndicate

The process of distributing securities through a group of investment banks.

originating house

The lead bank in the syndicate negotiates with the issuing company on behalf of the syndicate.

investment bank purchases the stock from the issuer for a guaranteed price (called the **net proceeds**) and resells them to investors at a higher price (called the **gross proceeds**). The difference between the gross proceeds and the net proceeds (called the **underwriter's spread**) is compensation for the expenses and risks incurred by the investment bank with the issue. In the 1990s, the underwriter's gross spread on first-time equity issues (i.e., private firms going public—the initial public offering or IPO) averaged 7.65 percent and on seasoned equity issues (i.e., publicly traded firms issuing additional shares) averaged 5.67 percent.[3] We discuss these costs in more detail in Chapter 16.

Often an investment bank will bring in a number of other investment banks to help sell and distribute a new issue—called a **syndicate.** For example, the tombstone in Figure 8–3 announcing the issue of 5 million shares of common stock in Alteon Web Systems lists the syndicate of 12 investment banks involved in the initial issue. The investment banks are listed according to their degree of participation in the sale of new shares. The lead bank(s) in the syndicate (Lehman Brothers and Robertson Stephens), who directly negotiated with the issuing company on behalf of the syndicate, are called the **originating house(s)** (see Chapter 1). Once an issue is arranged and its terms set, each member of the syndicate is assigned a given number of shares in the issue for which it is responsible for selling. Shares of stock issued through a syndicate of investment banks spreads the risk associated with the sale of the stock among several investment banks. A syndicate also results in a larger pool of potential outside investors, increasing the probability of a successful sale and widening the scope of the investor base.

A primary market sale may be a first-time issue by a private firm going public (e.g., allowing its equity, some of which was held privately by managers and venture capital investors, to be *publicly* traded in stock markets for the first time). These first-time issues are also referred to as initial public offerings (IPOs—see Chapter 16). Alternatively, a primary market sale may be a seasoned offering, in which the firm already has shares of the stock trading in the secondary markets. In both cases, the issuer receives the proceeds of the sale and the primary market investors receive the securities.

Also like the primary sales of corporate bond issues, corporate stocks may initially be issued through either a public sale (where the stock issue is offered to the general investing public) or a private placement (where stock is sold privately to a limited number of large investors). For example, private placements of equity totaled $84.68 billion in 1998, of which $25.49 billion were 144A placements (i.e., private placements that could be subsequently traded—see Chapter 6). Merrill Lynch was the main underwriter of private equity placements—underwriting $23.35 billion (27.6 percent) of the total private placements. Morgan Stanley led the 144A placements, with $3.7 billion (15.8 percent) underwritten.

3. See A. Gande, M. Puri, and A. Saunders, "Bank Entry, Competition and the Market for Corporate Securities Underwriting," forthcoming in *Journal of Financial Economics;* and I. Lee, S. Lockhead, J. Ritter, and Q. Zhao, "The Cost of Raising Capital," *Journal of Financial Research*, Spring 1996, pp. 59–74.

Figure 8–3 Tombstone Announcing the Issuance of Common Stock

This announcement is not an offer to sell or a solicitation of an offer to buy any of these securities. The offering is made only by the Prospectus, copies of which may be obtained in any State in which this announcement is circulated only from such of the several underwriters as may lawfully offer these securities in such State.

February 11, 2000

5,000,000 Shares

Common Stock

Price $103.50 Per Share

Lehman Brothers	Robertson Stephens
Thomas Weisel Partners LLC	Dain Rauscher Wessels

Fidelity Capital Markets
a division of National Financial Services Corporation
    Salomon Smith Barney   SG Cowen   Warburg Dillon Read LLC

Nutmeg Securities, Ltd.   Brad Peery Inc.

Tucker Anthony Cleary Gull   U.S. Bancorp Piper Jaffray

Source: Alteon WebSystems, prospectus.

preemptive rights

A right of existing stockholders in which new shares must be offered to existing shareholders first in such a way that they can maintain their proportional ownership in the corporation.

Corporate law in some states, and some corporate charters, give shareholders **preemptive rights** to the new shares of stock when they are issued. This means that before a seasoned offering of stock can be sold to outsiders, the new shares must first be offered to existing shareholders in such a way that they can maintain their proportional ownership in the corporation. A "rights offering" generally allows existing stockholders to purchase shares at a price slightly below the market price. Stockholders can then exercise their rights (buying the allotted shares in the new stock) or sell them. The result can be a low-cost distribution of new shares for a firm (i.e., the issuing firm avoids the expense of an underwritten offering).

Example 8–5 Calculation of Shares Purchased Through a Rights Offering

Suppose you own 1,000 shares of common stock in a firm with 1 million total shares outstanding. The firm announces its plan to sell an additional 500,000 shares through a rights offering. Thus, each shareholder will be sent 0.5 rights for each share of stock owned. One right can then be exchanged for one share of common stock in the new issue.

Your current ownership interest is 0.1 percent (1,000/1 million) prior to the rights offering and you receive 500 rights (1,000 × 0.5) allowing you to purchase 500 of the new shares. If you exercise your rights (buying the 500 shares), your ownership interest in the firm after the rights offering is still 0.1 percent ((1,000 + 500)/(1 million + 500,000)). Thus, the rights offering ensures that every investor can maintain his or her fractional ownership interest in the firm.

Suppose the market value of the common stock is $40 before the rights offering, or the total market value of the firm is $40 million ($40 × 1 million), and the 500,000 new shares are offered to current stockholders at a 10 percent discount, or for $36 per share. The firm receives $18 million. The market value of the firm after the rights offering is $58 million (the original $40 million plus the $18 million from the new shares), or $38.67 per share ($58 million ÷ 1.5 million).

Your 1,000 shares are worth $40,000 ($40 × 1,000) before the rights offering, and you can purchase 500 additional shares for $18,000 ($36 × 500). Thus, your total investment in the firm after the rights offering is $58,000, or $38.67 per share ($58,000 ÷ 1,500).

Suppose you decide not to exercise your preemptive right. Since each right allows a stockholder to buy a new share for $36 per share when the shares are worth $38.67, the value of one right should be $2.67. Should you sell your rights rather than exercise them, you maintain your original 1,000 shares of stock. These have a value after the rights offering of $38,667 (1,000 × 38.67). You could also sell your rights to other investors for $1,333 (500 × $2.67). As a result, you have a total wealth level of $40,000—you have lost no wealth.

In 1999, AMF Bowling, Inc., announced a rights offering to its common stockholders intended to raise $140 million in new stock at a subscription price of $5 per share—that is, to issue 28 million new shares of common stock. Prior to the rights offering, AMF had 84.6 million shares of common stock outstanding, and each shareholder received 0.331 rights for each share of stock owned. AMF common stock traded between $5.50 and $8.75 per share during the period of the rights offering, from May 5 to July 29, 1999. Thus, right holders could purchase new shares in AMF at a discount of between $0.50 and $3.75 from the market price of the stock. These rights were listed on the NYSE and could be sold by AMF Bowling common stockholders to other investors. Rights are similar to options in that they give the holder the option, but not the obligation, to buy the stock at a fixed price (see Chapter 10). The rights holder has the

Figure 8–4   Getting Shares of Stock to the Investing Public

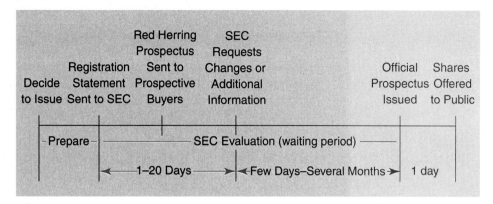

option of buying the new shares at the stated price, selling the rights to other investors, or letting the rights expire at the end of the offering period unused.

In a public sale of stock, once the issuing firm and the investment bank have agreed on the details of the stock issue, the investment bank must get SEC approval in accordance with the Securities and Exchange Act of 1934. Registration of a stock can be a lengthy process. We illustrate the process in Figure 8–4. The process starts with the preparation of the registration statement to be filed with the SEC. The registration statement includes information on the nature of the issuer's business, the key provisions and features of the security to be issued, the risks involved with the security, and background on the management. The focus of the registration statement is on full information disclosure about the firm and the securities issued to the public at large. At the same time that the issuer and its investment bank prepare the registration statement to be filed with the SEC, they prepare a preliminary version of the public offering's prospectus called the **red herring prospectus**. The red herring prospectus is similar to the registration statement but is distributed to potential equity buyers. It is a preliminary version of the official or final prospectus that will be printed upon SEC registration of the issue.

After submission of the registration statement, the SEC has 20 days to request additional information or changes to the registration statement. This period of review is called the waiting period. It generally takes about 20 days for the SEC to approve a new security issue. First-time or infrequent issuers can sometimes wait up to several months for SEC registration, especially if the SEC keeps requesting additional information and revised red herring prospectuses. However, companies that know the registration process well can generally obtain registration in a few days.

Once the SEC is satisfied with the registration statement, it registers the issue. At this point, the issuer (along with its investment bankers) sets the final selling price on the shares, prints the official prospectus describing the issue, and sends it to all potential buyers of the issue. Upon issuance of the prospectus (generally the day following SEC registration), the shares can be sold.

In order to reduce the time and cost of registration, yet still protect the public by requiring issuers to disclose information about the firm and the security to be issued, the SEC passed a rule in 1982 allowing for "shelf registration." As illustrated in Figure 8–5, **shelf registration** allows firms that plan to offer multiple issues of stock over a two-year period to submit one registration statement as described above (called a master registration statement). The registration statement summarizes the firm's financing plans for the two-year period. Thus, the securities are shelved for up to two years until the firm is ready to issue them. Once the issuer and its investment bank decide to issue shares during the two-year shelf registration period, they prepare and file a short form statement with the SEC. Upon SEC approval, the shares can be priced and offered to the public usually within one or two days of deciding to take the shares "off the shelf."

---

red herring prospectus

A preliminary version of the prospectus describing a new security issue distributed to potential buyers prior to the security's registration.

www.sec.com/

shelf registration

Allows firms that plan to offer multiple issues of stock over a two-year period to submit one registration statement summarizing the firm's financing plans for the period.

Figure 8–5   Getting Shelf Registrations to the Investing Public

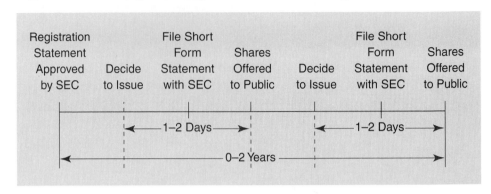

Thus, shelf registration allows a firm to get stocks onto the market quickly (e.g., in one or two days) if they feel conditions (especially the price they can get for the new stock) are right, without the time lag generally associated with full SEC registration. For example, in July 1999, Forest Oil Corp. announced a public offering of 8 million shares of its common stock under its shelf registration filed with the SEC. Salomon Smith Barney and Credit Suisse First Boston jointly led the underwriting of shares that were sold just days after this announcement.

Secondary Markets

secondary stock markets

The markets in which stocks, once issued, are traded—rebought and resold.

www.nyse.com/
www.nasdaq.com/

Secondary stock markets are the markets in which stocks, once issued, are traded—that is, bought and sold by investors. The New York Stock Exchange (NYSE) and the National Association of Securities Dealers Automated Quotation (NASDAQ) system are well-known examples of secondary markets in stocks. On October 30, 1998, the National Association of Securities Dealers, Inc. (NASD), the world's first electronic stock market, and the American Stock Exchange (AMEX), the nation's second largest floor-based exchange, merged to form the Nasdaq-Amex Market Group. Each market continues to function as an independent subsidiary. When a transaction occurs in a secondary stock market, funds are exchanged, usually with the help of a securities broker or firm acting as an intermediary between the buyer and the seller of the stock. The original issuer of the stock is not involved in this transfer of the stocks or the funds. In this section, we look at the major secondary stock markets, the process by which a trade occurs, and the major stock market indexes.

Stock Exchanges.   The three major U.S. stock markets are the New York Stock Exchange (NYSE), the American Stock Exchange (AMEX), and the National Association of Securities Dealers Automated Quotation (NASDAQ) system. Figures 8–6, 8–7 , and 8–8 present data comparing the three stock markets. Figure 8–6 shows dollar volume of trading in each market from 1979 through 1999; Figure 8–7 shows share volume in each market from 1979 through 1999; and Figure 8–8 shows the number of companies listed in each market from 1975 through 1998. Obvious from these trading volume and listing figures is that while the NYSE is the premier stock market and the NASDAQ is growing the quickest, activity on the AMEX is dropping on all accounts. Other smaller stock exchanges include the Pacific Stock Exchange, the Chicago Stock Exchange, the Philadelphia Stock Exchange, the Boston Stock Exchange, and the Cincinnati Stock Exchange. These account for no more than 5 percent of daily U.S. stock market volume.

www.nyse.com/

The New York Stock Exchange.   Worldwide, the New York Stock Exchange (NYSE) is the most well known of all the organized exchanges in the United States. Over 3,700 different stocks are listed and traded on the NYSE. Table 8–3 summarizes

Figure 8–6 Dollar Volume of Trading on the NYSE, AMEX, and NASDAQ

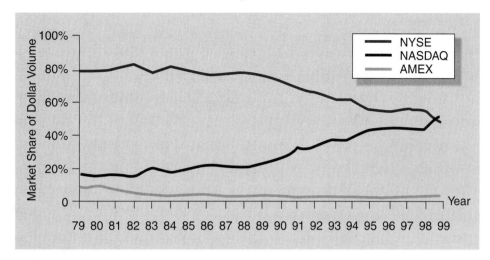

Source: Nasdaq, website, January 2000. © Copyright 2000, The Nasdaq Stock Market Inc. Reprinted with permission. *www.nasdaq.com/*

Figure 8–7 Share Volume of Trading on the NYSE, AMEX, and NASDAQ

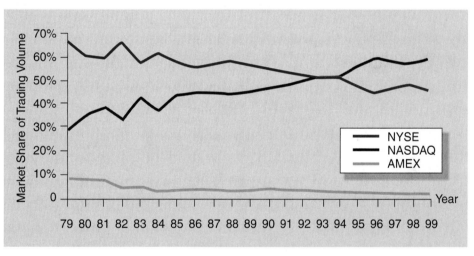

Source: Nasdaq, website, January 2000. © Copyright 2000, The Nasdaq Stock Market Inc. Reprinted with permission. *www.nasdaq.com/*

trading post

A specific place on the floor of the exchange where transactions on the NYSE occur.

specialists

Exchange members who have an obligation to keep the market going, maintaining liquidity in their assigned stock at all times.

the market activity in the NYSE (as well as the AMEX and NASDAQ) as of November 1999. The dollar volume of trading in November 1999 totaled $772.4 billion on 18.3 billion shares traded. In 1999, the NYSE converted from a private company to a publicly traded corporation. The move was prompted by an increasing need for funds to support the rapidly increasing costs of new computers and other technology, as well as increased investor demands. The NYSE hopes to raise the needed funds by selling ownership stakes to public investors.

The Trading Process. All transactions occurring on the NYSE occur at a specific place on the floor of the exchange (called a **trading post**), see Figure 8–9. Each stock is assigned a special market maker (a **specialist**). The market maker is like a monopolist with the power to arrange the market for the stock. In return,

Figure 8–8 Number of Companies Listed on NYSE, AMEX, and NASDAQ

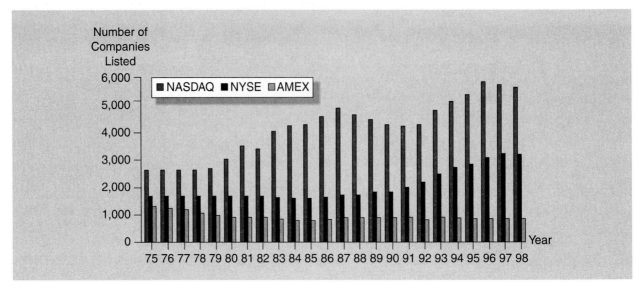

Source: Nasdaq, website, January 2000. © Copyright 2000, The Nasdaq Stock Market Inc. Reprinted with permission. *www.nasdaq.com/*

Table 8–3 Market Activity on the NYSE, AMEX, and NASDAQ

	NYSE	**AMEX**	**NASDAQ**
Share volume (in millions)	18,343	714	29,778
Year-to-date share volume (in millions)	184,180	7,325	240,068
Dollar volume (in millions)	$772,403	$52,758	$1,261,597
Market value (month end) (in billions)	$11,564	$125	$4,226
Number of companies (month end)	3,042	N/A	4,844
Number of issues (month end)	3,765	874	5,234
Average price per shares traded	$42.11	$73.84	$42.37

Source: Nasdaq, website, January 2000. © Copyright 2000, The Nasdaq Stock Market Inc. Reprinted with permission. *www.nasdaq.com/*

Figure 8–9 New York Stock Exchange Trading Post

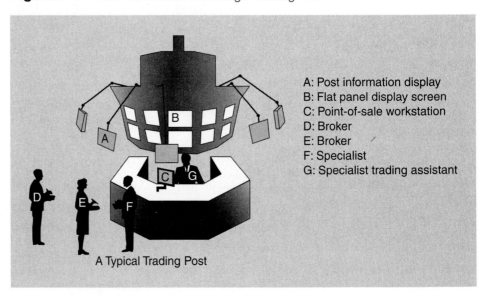

A: Post information display
B: Flat panel display screen
C: Point-of-sale workstation
D: Broker
E: Broker
F: Specialist
G: Specialist trading assistant

A Typical Trading Post

Source: The New York Stock Exchange, website, August 1999. *www.nyse.com/*

the specialist has an affirmative obligation to stabilize the order flow and prices for the stock in times when the market becomes turbulent (e.g., when there is a large imbalance of sell orders, the specialist has an obligation to buy the stock to stabilize the price).

Because of the large amount of capital needed to serve the market-making function, specialists often organize themselves as firms (e.g., Equitrade Partners, JJC Specialists, Inc.). Specialist firms on the NYSE range in size from 2 to over 20 members. Specialist firms may be designated to serve as the market maker for more than one stock. However, only one specialist is assigned to each stock listed on the exchange. In general, because specialists are obligated to establish the fair market price of a stock and must even occasionally step in and stabilize a stock's price, underwriters/investment banks (responsible for getting the best available price for their customers' new issues) cannot be specialists.

Three types of transactions can occur at a given post: (1) brokers trade on behalf of customers at the "market" price (market order); (2) limit orders are left with a specialist to be executed; and (3) specialists transact for their own account. These traders are discussed in more detail below. As of May 1999, 419 firms had representatives "seated" on the floor of the NYSE (273 of the total 1,336 seats dealt with trades sent from the public) at a price as high as $2.6 million per seat.

Generally, as illustrated in Figure 8–10, when individuals want to transact on the NYSE, they contact their broker (such as Merrill Lynch). The broker then sends the order to its representative at the exchange (called a commission broker) or to a floor broker (working for themselves) to conduct the trade with the appropriate specialist or market maker in the stock. Large brokerage firms generally own several "seats" on the floor filled by their commission brokers trading orders for the firm's clients or its own accounts. One of the specialist's jobs is to execute orders for floor and commission brokers. However, these brokers can transact at a post with others without specialist participation. Specialists participate in only about 10 percent of all shares traded. Also, orders are increasingly coming from the public using on-line (Internet) trading, bypassing the broker and going directly to the floor broker (see Chapter 16).

Once the transaction is completed (generally in less than 15 minutes), the investor's broker is contacted and the trade is confirmed. Generally, the transaction is settled in three days—that is, the investor has three days to pay for the stock and the floor or commission broker has three days to deliver the stock to the investor's broker.

The vast majority of orders sent to floor or commission brokers are of two types: market orders or limit orders. A **market order** is an order for the broker and the market specialist to transact at the best price available when the order reaches the post. The

market order

An order to transact at the best price available when the order reaches the post.

Figure 8–10 Purchase of a Stock on the NYSE

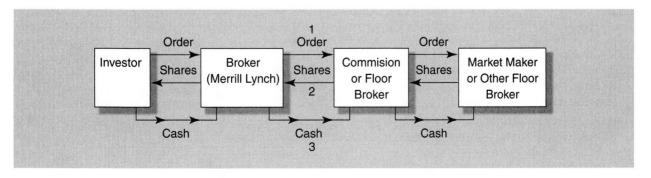

limit order

An order to transact at a specified price.

floor or commission broker will go to the post and conduct the trade. A **limit order** is an order to transact only at a specified price (the limit price). When a floor or commission broker receives a limit order, he or she will stand by the post with the order if the current price is near the limit price. When the current price is not near the limit price, a floor or commission broker does not want to stand at the post for hours (and even days) waiting for the current price to equal the limit price on this single limit order. In this case, the floor broker enters the limit order on the order book of the specialist at the post. The specialist, who is at the post at all times when the market is open, will monitor the current price of the stock and conduct the trade when, and if, it equals the limit price. Some limit orders are submitted with time limits. If the order is not filled by the time date for expiration, it is deleted from the market maker's book. The third type of trade is that of a specialist trading for his or her own account.

Figure 8–11 illustrates the link between a market order and a limit order. When a market order is placed, the transaction occurs at the current market price, $97⅞ per share, determined by the current level of traders' aggregate supply (S) of and demand (D) for the stock. If the limit order price (e.g., 97⅝ per share) differs from the current market price, the order is placed on the specialist's book. If supply and/or demand conditions change (e.g., the demand curve in Figure 8–11 falls to D′) such that the market price falls to $97⅝ per share, the specialist completes the limit order and notifies the floor broker who submitted the order.

Program Trading.   The NYSE has defined program trading as the simultaneous buying and selling of a portfolio of at least 15 different stocks valued at more than $1 million, using computer programs to initiate the trades. For example, program trading can be used to create portfolio insurance. A program trader can take a long position in a portfolio of stocks and a short position in a stock index futures contract (see Chapter 10). Should the market value of the stock portfolio fall, these losses are partly offset by the position in the futures contract. The timing of these trades is determined by the computer program.

In the late 1980s, about 15 million shares were traded per day on the NYSE as program trades. In May 1999, average daily volume of program trading was 151.7 million shares. The most active program traders are investment banks (e.g., Salomon Smith Barney, Morgan Stanley) conducting trades for their own accounts or those of their customers (e.g., insurance companies, hedge funds, pension funds). Much of this program trading involves index funds (e.g., Vanguard's 500 Index Fund that seeks to replicate the

Figure 8–11   Price on a Market Order versus a Limit Order

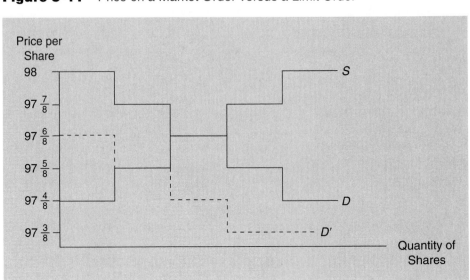

S&P 500 Index—see below) and futures contracts on various indexes (e.g., S&P 500 Index futures). Investment in these index funds grew in the 1980s and 1990s as a result of the relatively poor performance (in terms of returns) of specialized mutual funds (see Chapter 18) and the strong performance in the major indexes.

Stock Market Quote. Table 8–4 presents a small part of a NYSE stock quote list from *The Wall Street Journal* summarizing trading on Tuesday, January 18, 2000. Columns 1 and 2 of the stock quote list show the high and low closing price on the listed stocks over the previous (from January 18) 52 weeks. Share prices and price changes are recorded at intervals of 1/16th of $1 to ease trading. As of September 2000, the NYSE started phasing in decimalization of stock quotes in which equity securities prices were quoted in a decimal format—$97.250, with increments of one-tenth of one cent per share. The change to decimalization of equity prices is expected to cost the securities industry as much as $1 billion to implement and result in more frequent price changes and increased messaging traffic, which the information infrastructure of the exchanges may be unable to handle. Column 3 is the name of the corporation. Column 4, labeled Sym, is the ticker symbol of the stock. When trades are recorded on a stock, the ticker symbol is used rather than the company name. Column 5, labeled Div, is the annual dividend per share based on the most recent dividend payment (e.g., AVX Corp. paid dividends of $0.26 per share on its common stock in 1999). Column 6, labeled Yld %, is the dividend yield on the stock (equal to the annual dividends per year divided by the closing stock price (e.g., for AVX Corp., .26 ÷ 58 11/16 = 0.4 percent)). Column 7 is the firm's P/E ratio—the ratio of the company's closing price to earnings per share over the previous year (e.g., AVX Corp.'s P/E ratio is reported to be 55; AVX's price—the

Table 8–4 Stock Market Quote, January 18, 2000

	52 Weeks Hi	Lo	Stock	Sym	Div	Yld %	PE	Vol 100s	Hi	Lo	Close	Net Chg
	60 3/4	12 9/16	▲AVX Cp	AVX	.26	.4	55	1688	60	58 1/8	58 11/16	– 7/8
	76 3/4	53 3/4	AXA ADS	AXA	.90e	1.3	...	760	68	67	67 7/16	– 1/16
s	38 3/4	25 1/2	▲AXA Fnl	AXF	.10	.3	15	12110	36	34 1/4	34 3/8	– 1/8
	3 1/16	11/16	AamesFnl	AAM		...	dd	635	13/16	3/4	3/4	...
	22 1/4	12 7/8	AaronRent	RNT	.04	.3	12	29	15 1/2	14 15/16	15 1/8	– 3/8
	20	11 5/8	AaronRent A	RNTA	.04	.2	16	21	17 1/2	17 1/2	17 1/2	...
n	24 11/16	19	AbbeyNtl	SUA	1.75	8.8	...	141	20	19 3/4	19 15/16	– 1/8
n	23 15/16	19 13/16	AbbeyNtl 7 1/4%	SUD	.91e	4.4	...	97	20 3/4	20 1/2	20 1/2	– 1/8
	26 3/4	23 1/8	AbbeyNtl pfA		2.19	9.3	...	6	23 1/2	23 1/2	23 1/2	+ 1/8
	53 5/16	33	AbbotLab	ABT	.68	2.0	22	50195	34 1/2	33 1/8	33 3/4	– 3/4
s	50 3/4	21	Abercrombie A	ANF		...	19	9394	23 15/16	22 9/16	23 1/2	– 1/4
	13 13/16	7 5/8	Abitibi g	ABY	.40g	...	...	1246	13 1/16	12 7/8	12 7/8	...
	5 3/4	4 3/8	▲AcadiaRlty	AKR	.48	9.1	33	232	5 5/16	5 1/16	5 1/4	+ 1/16
	18 7/16	4 9/16	▲AcceptIns	AIF		...	dd	1176	4 3/4	4 9/16	4 9/16	...
	20	11 1/8	AckrlyGp	AK	.02	.1	29	63	17 7/8	17 1/2	17 11/16	– 1/4
	32 3/4	19 7/8	ACNielsen	ART		...	20	796	25 1/8	23 15/16	23 15/16	– 1 3/16
	18 1/16	9 13/16	Acuson	ACN		...	17	552	12 15/16	12 1/2	12 11/16	– 3/16
	33 15/16	25 15/16	▲AdamsExp	ADX	2.38e	7.1	...	684	33 11/16	33 3/16	33 11/16	+ 5/16
	34 1/2	**11 1/8**	**Administaff**	**ASF**		**...**	**42**	**1038**	**25 1/2**	**23**	**23 3/8**	**– 2 3/8**
	24 7/16	**12 3/8**	**AFP Prov ADR**	**PVD**	**1.45e**	**6.9**	**...**	**348**	**21**	**20**	**21**	**+ 1**
	13 15/16	3 15/16	AdvCommGp	ADG		...	dd	3540	12 1/4	11 3/8	11 3/4	+ 1/4

EXPLANATORY NOTES

The following explanations apply to New York and American exchange listed issues and the Nasdaq Stock Market. NYSE and Amex prices are composite quotations that include trades on the Chicago, Pacific, Philadelphia, Boston and Cincinnati exchanges and reported by the National Association of Securities Dealers.

Boldfaced quotations highlight those issues whose price changed by 5% or more if their previous closing price was $2 or higher.

Underlined quotations are those stocks with large changes in volume, per exchange, compared with the issue's average trading volume. The calculation includes common stocks of $5 a share or more with an average volume over 65 trading days of at least 5,000 shares. The underlined quotations are for the 40 largest volume percentage leaders on the NYSE and the Nasdaq National Market. It includes the 20 largest volume percentage gainers on the Amex.

The 52-week high and low columns show the highest and lowest price of the issue during the preceding 52 weeks plus the current week, but not the latest trading day. These ranges are adjusted to reflect stock payouts of 1% or more, and cash dividends or other distributions of 10% or more.

Dividend/Distribution rates, unless noted, are annual disbursements based on the last monthly, quarterly, semiannual, or annual declaration. Special or extra dividends or distributions, including return of capital, special situations or payments not designated as regular are identified by footnotes.

Yield is defined as the dividends or other distributions paid by a company on its securities, expressed as a percentage of price.

The P/E ratio is determined by dividing the closing market price by the company's diluted per-share earnings, as available, for the most recent four quarters. Charges and other adjustments usually are excluded when they qualify as extraordinary items under generally accepted accounting rules.

Sales figures are the unofficial daily total of shares traded, quoted in hundreds (two zeros omitted; f-four zeros omitted.)

Exchange ticker symbols are shown for all New York and American exchange common stocks, and Dow Jones News/Retrieval symbols are listed for Class A and Class B shares listed on both markets. Nasdaq symbols are listed for all Nasdaq NMS issues. A more detailed explanation of Nasdaq ticker symbols appears with the NMS listings.

FOOTNOTES: ▲-New 52-week high. ▼-New 52-week low. **a**-Extra dividend or extras in addition to the regular dividend. **b**-Indicates annual rate of the cash dividend and that a stock dividend was paid. **c**-Liquidating dividend. **cc**-P/E ratio is 100 or more. **dd**-Loss in the most recent four quarters. **e**-Indicates a dividend was declared in the preceding 12 months, but that there isn't a regular dividend rate. Amount shown may have been adjusted to reflect stock split, spinoff or other distribution. **ec**-Emerging Company Marketplace issue. **FD**-First day of trading. **f**-Annual rate, increased on latest declaration. **g**-Indicates the dividend and earnings are expressed in Canadian money. The stock trades in U.S. dollars. No yield or P/E ratio is shown. **gg**-Special sales condition; no regular way trading. **h**-Temporary exemption from Nasdaq requirements. **i**-Indicates amount declared or paid after a stock dividend or split. **j**-Indicates dividend was paid this year, and that at the last dividend meeting a dividend was omitted or deferred. **k**-Indicates dividend declared this year on cumulative issues with dividends in arrears. **m**-Annual rate, reduced on latest declaration. **n**-Newly issued in the past 52 weeks. The high-low range begins with the start of trading and doesn't cover the entire period. **p**-Initial dividend; no yield calculated. **pf**-Preferred. **pp**-Holder owes installment(s) of purchase price. **pr**-Preference. **r**-Indicates a cash dividend declared in the preceding 12 months, plus a stock dividend. **rt**-Rights. **s**-Stock split or stock dividend, or cash or cash equivalent distribution, amounting to 10% or more in the past 52 weeks. The high-low price is adjusted from the old stock. Dividend calculations begin with the date the split was paid or the stock dividend occurred. **stk**-Paid in stock in the last 12 months. Company doesn't pay cash dividend. **un**-Units. **v**-Trading halted on primary market. **vj**-In bankruptcy or receivership or being reorganized under the Bankruptcy Code, or securities assumed by such companies. **wd**-When distributed. **wi**-When issued. **wt**-Warrants. **ww**-With warrants. **x**-Ex-dividend, ex-distribution, ex-rights or without warrants. **z**-Sales in full, not in 100s.

Source: *The Wall Street Journal*, January 19, 2000, p. C3. Reprinted by permission of *The Wall Street Journal*. © 2000 Dow Jones & Company, Inc. All Rights Reserved Worldwide. *www.wsj.com/*

numerator of the P/E ratio—is reported as $58\frac{11}{16}$; thus, AVX Corp.'s earnings per share—the denominator of the P/E ratio—over the period January 1999 through January 2000 must have been $1.07 per share: $E = P \div P/E = \$58\frac{11}{16} \div 55$). The P/E ratio is used by traders as an indicator of the relative value of the stock. Looking at the inverse of the P/E ratio (E/P), traders can estimate the number of years (based on the firm's current earnings) that it will take to recoup their investment in the stock (the payback period). High P/E ratio stocks reflect the market's expectation of growth in earnings. Should earnings expectations fail to materialize, these stocks will see a price drop. Low P/E ratio stocks generally have low earnings growth expectations. Column 8, Vol 100s, lists the day's trading volume in 100s of shares (e.g., 168,800 shares of AVX Corp. traded on January 18, 2000). Columns 9 and 10, Hi and Lo, are the high and low prices at which a trade occurred on January 18, 2000. Column 11, Close, is the price on the last transaction to occur (the Close) on January 18, 2000. Normally, shares are traded in "round" lots of 100. Finally, Column 12, Net Chg, is the change in the closing price from the previous day's closing price (in 1/16th of $1).

The American Stock Exchange.   The American Stock Exchange (AMEX), located in New York, generally lists stocks of smaller firms that are of national interest. It is organized as a floor broker-specialist market-maker system like the NYSE. As of November 1999, stocks of 874 issues were trading on the AMEX. Figures 8–6 through 8–8 show the diminishing size and importance of the AMEX. Share volume on the AMEX in November 1999 (714 million shares), as seen in Table 8–3, was less than 4 percent of the total shares traded on the NYSE. Dollar volume on the AMEX through November 1999 ($52,758 billion) was less than 7 percent of that on the NYSE. Possibly as a result of its diminishing prominence as a secondary stock market, the AMEX merged with the NASDAQ market in 1998.

www.nasdaq.com/

The NASDAQ Market.   Securities not sold on one of the organized exchanges such as the NYSE and AMEX, are traded over the counter. Unlike the centralized NYSE and AMEX exchanges, the over-the-counter markets do not have a physical trading floor. Rather, transactions are completed via an electronic market. The NASDAQ (National Association of Securities Dealers Automated Quotation) market is the world's first electronic stock market. The NASDAQ system provides continuous trading for the most active stocks traded over the counter. Indeed, as seen in Figures 8–6 through 8–8, the NASDAQ currently has more firms listed and a higher dollar volume of trading than the NYSE. Like the NYSE, in order to raise funds needed to keep up with the costs of increasing technology and investor demand, the NASDAQ-AMEX Market Group is converting from a private company to a publicly traded corporation.

5   The NASDAQ market is primarily a dealer market, in which dealers are the market makers who stand ready to buy or sell particular securities. Unlike the NYSE (or AMEX), many dealers, in some cases more than 20, will make a market for a single stock—that is, quote a bid (buy) and ask (sell) price. There are no limits on the number of stocks a NASDAQ market maker can trade nor on the number of market makers in a particular stock. A NASDAQ broker or dealer may also be a member of an organized exchange (e.g., the NYSE). Moreover, the original underwriter of a new issue can also become the dealer in the secondary market—unlike the NYSE, which seeks a separation between underwriters and dealers.[4] Anyone who meets the fairly low capital requirements for market makers on the NASDAQ can register to be a broker-dealer.

4. A study by K. Ellis, R. Michaely, and M. O'Hara, "When the Underwriter Is the Market Maker: An Examination of Trading in the IPO Aftermarket," Cornell University working paper, 1999, finds that the lead underwriter always becomes a market maker in a new issue and, in fact, becomes the most active dealer in issues it brings to the NASDAQ market.

An individual wanting to make a trade contacts his or her broker. The broker then contacts a dealer in the particular security to conduct the transaction. In contrast to the NYSE and AMEX, the NASDAQ structure of dealers and brokers results in the NASDAQ being a negotiated market (e.g., quotes from several dealers are usually obtained before a transaction is made). When a request for a trade is received, a dealer will use the computer to find the dealers providing the inside quotes—the lowest ask and the highest bid. The dealer may also request the quotes of every market maker in the stock. The dealer initiating the trade will then contact the dealer offering the best price and execute the order. The dealer will confirm the transaction with the investor's broker and the customer will be charged that quote plus a commission for the broker's services. Like exchange trading, on-line (Internet) trading services now allow investors to trade directly with a securities dealer without going through a personal broker.

Choice of Market Listing. Firms listed with the NYSE and AMEX markets must meet the listing requirements of the exchange. The requirements are extensive and can be found at the websites of the exchanges. The basic qualifications are based on such characteristics as firm market value, earnings, total assets, number of shares outstanding, number of shareholders, and trading volume. An NYSE-listed firm may also have its securities listed on regional exchanges. There are several reasons that NYSE listing is attractive to a firm: improved marketability of the firm's stock (making it more valuable); publicity for the firm, which could result in increased sales; and improved access to the financial markets, as firms find it easier to bring new issues of listed stock to the market.

The requirements for AMEX listing are generally less stringent than those for the NYSE. Thus, AMEX-listed firms tend to be smaller, less well known (therefore less traded), and often younger than NYSE firms.

Firms that do not meet the requirements for exchange listing trade on the NASDAQ. Thus, most NASDAQ firms are smaller, of regional interest, or unable to meet the listing requirements of the organized exchanges. Many NASDAQ companies are newly registered public issues with only a brief history of trading. Over time, many of these apply for NYSE listing. Not all companies eligible to be listed on the NYSE actually do so. Some companies—for example, Microsoft—do not believe that the benefits of exchange listing (improved marketability, publicity) are significant. Others prefer not to release the financial information required by the exchanges for listing.

Twenty-Four Hour Trading and Day Trading. The major stock markets currently open at 9:30 A.M. eastern standard time and close at 4:00 P.M. eastern standard time. Alternative electronic communications networks (ECNs), such as Reuters Group's ECN, offer after-hours trading of some stocks traded on the major stock markets. In response to the increased after-hours trading of their securities, in the early 2000s, the major markets are planning to extend trading hours; with the NYSE planning on moving towards 24-hour trading. While several issues and problems have delayed the start of 24-hour trading on the stock exchanges, it is only a matter of time before 24-hour trading becomes a reality in U.S. stock markets; especially with the increasing volume of block (large) trades that are taking place after market hours and the growing demands of "day" traders.

Day trading is a trading strategy by which traders zip electronically in and out of stock positions (most often high-tech stocks) in split-second trades. Day-trading activity increased significantly in the 1990s as the result of the introduction of powerful computers that can process trades quickly. Thus, small investors were given greater access to the market. Day traders try to make money by quickly buying and selling shares of stock, often holding a stock for just minutes at a time when they see a price move. Day traders sell much of their holdings by the end of the trading day.

In 1999, there were more than 100 day-trading firms in existence. These firms, which generally require at least $5,000 to open an account, offer day traders a desk and a computer with high-speed access to the stock markets. There is often no check of the day trader's trading history or the qualifications of day traders, and some day-trading firms allow traders to borrow money for their trades. An estimated 5,000 people used the facilities offered by day-trading firms in 1999. Thousands more were day trading using their home computers and on-line accounts offered by brokerage houses (e.g., E-Trade Group, Inc.).

Because of the lack of screening of the qualifications of day traders, and the lack of disclosure of the risks of day trading by day-trading firms, day trading and day-trading firms came under fire in the summer of 1999 (see In the News box 8–2). George Ferris, Jr., chair of Ferris Baker Watts (a brokerage house that does not offer on-line trading) commented, "My impression is most of these day traders couldn't analyze a financial statement of a company if they had one." The SEC is currently reviewing the rules and practices for on-line investing to see if new regulations are needed to protect investors. Some members of Congress are moving to increase the SEC's power to restrict on-line activities. State securities dealers also are moving to pass laws preventing various kinds of fraud in on-line trading. Finally, research has shown that those investors who trade most frequently often have the poorest performance in terms of returns.[5]

Do You Understand?

1. Why day-trading firms came under regulatory scrutiny in 1999?

www.dowjones.com/

www.nyse.com/

www.standardandpoors. com/

www.nasdaq.com/

Stock Market Indexes

A stock market index is the composite value of a group of secondary market-traded stocks. Movements in a stock market index provide investors with information on movements of a broader range of secondary market securities. Table 8–5 shows a listing of some major stock market indexes as of January 18, 2000. Figure 8–12 shows the trends in some of these indexes (the Dow Jones Industrial Average, the NYSE Composite Index, the S&P Composite Index, and the NASDAQ Composite Index) from 1989 through 1999. Notice that movements in these indexes are highly correlated over the 10-year period. Notice also that the correlation of the NASDAQ index has deviated from the others in the late 1990s and early 2000s as technology stocks (listed mainly on the NASDAQ) soared in value (rising from 2300 in January 1999 to over 5000 by March 2000) then fell back to 3500 in April 2000.

The Dow Jones Industrial Average.   The Dow Jones Industrial Average (the DJIA or the Dow) is the most widely reported stock market index. The DJIA was first published in 1896 as an index of 12 industrial stocks. In 1928, the Dow was expanded to include the values of 30 large (in terms of sales and total assets) corporations selected by the editors of *The Wall Street Journal* (owned by Dow Jones & Company). In choosing companies to be included in the DJIA, the editors look for the largest companies with a history of successful growth and with interest among stock investors. The composition of the DJIA was most recently revised in 1999, when Chevron, Goodyear Tire & Rubber, Sears, and Union Carbide were replaced by Microsoft, Intel, Home Depot, and SBC Communications. The changes, which for the first time included NASDAQ firms in the DJIA, were made to reflect the growing importance of technology in the U.S. economy. Table 8–6 lists the 30 NYSE and NASDAQ corporations included in the DJIA. Dow Jones and Company has also established and publishes indexes of 20 transportation companies, 15 utility companies, and a composite index consisting of all 65 companies in the industrial, transportation, and utility indexes.

---

5. See B. M. Barber and T. Odean, "Trading Is Hazardous to Your Wealth: The Common Stock Investment Performance of Individual Investors," *Journal of Finance,* April 2000; and T. Odean, "Do Investors Trade Too Much?" *American Economic Review,* forthcoming.

Robert Mahavia

In the News

I n the first significant report on day trading, state regulators blasted broker-dealers for widespread deceptive marketing and possible securities law violations. The study by the North American Securities Administrators Association identified such persistent industry problems as poor screening of customers, questionable loan schemes among customers to finance their trades and firms improperly trading in customer accounts. The study also raised questions about broker-dealers inadequately monitoring employees and failing to keep proper trading records.

"If they don't get their act together, they will be under increasing regulatory pressure" said Peter Hildreth, president of the association and head of New Hampshire's securities division. The NASAA represents

www.wsj.com/

Day Trading Firms Rebuked by Group of State Regulators Over Marketing

regulators from 50 states and parts of Canada and Mexico. Mr. Hildreth said more enforcement actions are likely . . .

The study, which examined a dozen firms, said some firms have resorted to aggressive marketing because of rapid customer turnover and high operating costs. "Some firms have been operating in a very predatory and manipulative way," said William Galven, Massachusetts secretary of the commonwealth who is responsible for securities oversight in his state.

The study rebuts advertising claims that a majority of customers make money from day trading. An analysis of 26 randomly selected day trading accounts at All-Tech Investments Group Inc.'s branch in Watertown, Mass., found that 70 percent were unprofitable, and nearly all lost everything.

Only three accounts consistently made money. The report also found that many investors don't understand how much their trading profits can be depleted by commission costs, because day trading firms charge customers by the transaction. Day traders must make a 56 percent profit to cover commissions and fees, the regulators said . . .

To curb abuses, the NASAA called for more focus on day trading by federal and state enforcement regulators. It also urged the National Association of Securities Dealers to ban loans between day trading customers to cover losses and to enact a rule requiring firms to make sure day trading is appropriate for both new and existing customers. Currently, the NASD, which regulates most of the day trading firms, has proposed only that new customers be screened. The SEC said it expects to receive a proposal from the NASD soon and will seek public comment before deciding whether the rule should be enacted.

Table 8–5   Major Stock Market Indexes

STOCK MARKET DATA BANK   1/18/00

MAJOR INDEXES

†12-MO HIGH	†12-MO LOW		DAILY HIGH	DAILY LOW	CLOSE	NET CHG	% CHG	†12-MO CHG	% CHG	FROM 12/31	% CHG
DOW JONES AVERAGES											
11722.98	9120.67	30 Industrials	11720.12	11546.45	11560.72 −	162.26 −	1.38	+2205.50 +	23.58	+ 63.60 +	0.55
3783.50	2808.44	20 Transportation	2893.31	2838.18	2853.61 −	38.02 −	1.31	− 324.24 −	10.20	− 123.59 −	4.15
333.45	269.20	15 Utilities	302.11	297.46	299.29 −	2.95 −	0.98	− 5.70 −	1.87	+ 15.93 +	5.62
3366.13	2832.10	65 Composite	3271.38	3226.07	3229.20 −	42.70 −	1.31	+ 331.69 +	11.45	+ 14.82 +	0.46
1390.32	1154.51	DJ Global-US	1388.62	1376.28	1380.38 −	7.92 −	0.57	+ 189.85 +	15.95	− 9.94 −	0.71
NEW YORK STOCK EXCHANGE											
663.12	576.17	Composite	649.77	642.90	643.92 −	5.85 −	0.90	+ 49.09 +	8.25	− 6.38 −	0.98
836.88	722.97	Industrials	835.11	826.91	830.40 −	4.71 −	0.56	+ 91.20 +	12.34	+ 2.19 +	0.26
518.74	426.40	Utilities	484.45	479.92	480.14 −	1.53 −	0.32	+ 21.82 +	4.76	− 31.01 −	6.07
560.33	428.31	Transportation	477.09	468.68	469.33 −	7.71 −	1.62	− 8.11 −	1.70	+ 2.63 +	0.56
584.22	457.63	Finance	517.94	504.24	504.65 −	13.29 −	2.57	− 15.67 −	3.01	− 11.96 −	2.32
STANDARD & POOR'S INDEXES											
1469.25	1216.14	500 Index	1465.15	1451.25	1455.14 −	10.01 −	0.68	+ 203.14 +	16.23	− 14.11 −	0.96
1841.92	1466.86	Industrials	1837.90	1816.25	1827.22 −	4.36 −	0.24	+ 313.91 +	20.74	− 14.70 −	0.80
269.98	215.62	Utilities	241.67	237.35	238.02 −	3.65 −	1.51	− 12.91 −	5.14	+ 10.80 +	4.75
449.94	353.14	400 MidCap	450.46	446.16	449.94 +	1.47 +	0.33	+ 64.29 +	16.67	+ 5.27 +	1.19
201.66	154.83	600 SmallCap	201.78	199.61	201.66 +	1.16 +	0.58	+ 25.09 +	14.21	+ 3.87 +	1.96
308.89	255.39	1500 Index	308.40	305.64	306.62 −	1.78 −	0.58	+ 42.68 +	16.17	− 2.27 −	0.73
NASDAQ STOCK MARKET											
4131.15	2248.91	Composite	4148.00	4053.21	4130.81 +	66.54 +	1.64	+1722.64 +	71.53	+ 61.50 +	1.51
3790.55	1888.66	Nasdaq 100	3779.56	3665.87	3757.78 +	53.04 +	1.43	+1724.07 +	84.77	+ 49.95 +	1.35
2286.52	1294.40	Industrials	2268.72	2223.91	2263.92 +	29.33 +	1.31	+ 876.65 +	63.19	+ 24.95 +	1.11
2372.33	1702.46	Insurance	1851.67	1826.72	1830.50 −	10.49 −	0.57	+ 56.53 +	3.19	− 65.78 −	3.47
1898.49	1551.96	Banks	1598.26	1576.83	1587.47 −	11.90 −	0.74	− 222.18 −	12.28	− 103.82 −	6.14
2370.99	1164.77	Computer	2385.88	2317.84	2370.99 +	46.44 +	2.00	+1077.37 +	83.28	+ 45.59 +	1.96
1023.45	542.90	Telecommunications	1011.08	983.29	1007.03 +	14.64 +	1.48	+ 450.29 +	80.88	− 8.37 −	0.82

Source: *The Wall Street Journal,* Tuesday, January 19, 2000, p. C2. Reprinted by permission of The Wall Street Journal © 2000 Dow Jones & Company, Inc. All Rights Reserved Worldwide. *http://www.wsj.com/*

Figure 8–12   DJIA, NYSE Composite Index, S&P Composite Index, and NASDAQ Composite Index Values

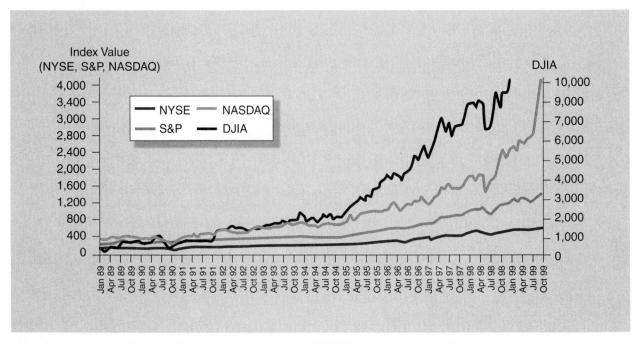

Source: Dow Jones, the New York Stock Exchange, Standard & Poor's, and NASDAQ, websites, January 2000.

Table 8–6   Dow Jones Industrial Average Companies

AT&T	IBM
Allied Signal	Intel
Aluminum Company of America	International Paper
American Express	J. P. Morgan
Boeing	Johnson & Johnson
Caterpillar	McDonald's
Citigroup	Merck
Coca-Cola	Microsoft
DuPont	Minnesota Mining & Manufacturing
Eastman Kodak	Philip Morris
Exxon Mobil	Proctor & Gamble
General Electric	SBC Communications
General Motors	United Technologies
Hewlett-Packard	Wal-Mart
Home Depot	Walt Disney

Source: Dow Jones & Company, website, January 2000. *www.dowjones.com/*

Dow indexes are *price-weighted averages,* meaning that the stock *prices* of the companies in the indexes are added together and divided by an adjusted value, as follows:

$$\sum_{i=1}^{30} P_{it} \text{ / Adjusted value}$$

where

P_{it} = Price of each stock in the Dow index on day t.

The divisor was set at 30 in 1928, but due to stock splits and stock dividends, this value has dropped to 0.17677618 in 2000.

The NYSE Composite Index.   In 1966, the NYSE established the NYSE Composite Index to provide a comprehensive measure of the performance of the overall NYSE market. The index consists of all common stocks listed on the NYSE. In addition to the composite index, NYSE stocks are divided into four subgroups: industrial, transportation, utility, and financial companies. The indexed value of each group is also reported daily.

The NYSE is a *value-weighted index,* meaning that the *current market values* (stock price × number of shares outstanding) of all stocks in the index are added together and divided by their value on a base date (December 31, 1965, for the NYSE). Any changes in the stocks included in the index are incorporated by adjusting the base value of the index.

The Standard & Poor's 500 Index.   Standard & Poor's established the S&P 500 index (a value-weighted index) consisting of the stocks of 500 of the largest U.S. corporations listed on the NYSE and the NASDAQ. The NYSE stocks included in the S&P 500 index account for over 80 percent of the total market value of all stocks listed on the NYSE. Thus, movements in the S&P 500 Index are highly correlated with those of the NYSE Composite Index (see Figure 8–12). Standard & Poor's also reports subindexes consisting of industrials and utilities in the S&P 500 Index.

The NASDAQ Composite Index.   First established in 1971, the NASDAQ Composite Index (a value-weighted index) consists of three categories of NASDAQ companies: industrials, banks, and insurance

Do You Understand?

1. What the purpose of a rights offering is?
2. What the major secondary stock markets in the United States are?
3. What the major U.S. stock indexes are?

Table 8–7 Holders of Corporate Stock
(in billions of dollars)

	1994	1995	1996	1997	1998	1999	Percent of 1999 Total
Household sector	$3,070.9	$4,121.6	$4,642.1	$5,689.6	$6,337.8	$6,599.2	41.2%
State and local governments	10.6	26.2	46.8	79.0	102.0	111.0	0.7
Rest of world	397.7	527.6	656.8	919.5	1,115.4	1,168.1	7.3
Depository institutions	180.6	244.2	273.5	331.4	339.0	327.1	2.0
Life insurance companies	246.1	315.4	414.1	558.6	723.1	795.5	5.0
Other insurance companies	112.1	134.2	148.6	186.0	201.4	198.1	1.2
Private pension funds	996.3	1,238.4	1,490.9	1,863.9	2,232.3	2,211.9	13.8
Public pension funds	557.4	791.1	1,031.6	1,431.7	1,761.5	1,801.4	11.3
Mutual funds	709.6	1,024.9	1,470.0	2,018.7	2,508.5	2,701.5	16.9
Closed-end funds	31.9	38.0	51.1	50.2	40.2	39.4	0.3
Brokers and dealers	20.1	34.2	51.9	51.9	52.1	55.0	0.3

*As of September.

Source: Federal Reserve Board, website, December 1999. *www.bog.frb.fed.us/*

companies. All stocks traded through the NASDAQ in these three industries are included. NASDAQ also reports separate indexes based on industrials, banks, insurance companies, computers, and telecommunications companies.

Stock Market Participants

Table 8–7 shows the holdings of corporate stock from 1994 through September 1999 by type of holder. Households are the single largest holders of corporate stock (holding 41.2 percent of all corporate stock outstanding in September 1999). Mutual funds and private and public pension funds are also prominent in the stock markets (holding 16.9 percent, 13.8 percent, and 11.3 percent of the $16.00 trillion in corporate stock outstanding, respectively).

As a result of the tremendous increase in stock values in the 1990s, most individuals in the United States either directly own corporate stock or indirectly own stock via investments in mutual funds and pension funds. Figure 8–13 shows the age distribution of adult stockholders by percent of all shareholders and percent of shares owned. While over 50 percent of all stockholders are under 45 years of age, this group owns just 20.6 percent of all stock outstanding. The major investors (holding 49.4 percent of all stock outstanding) are those 33.1 percent of the market participants between 45 and 64 years old.

Table 8–8 reports characteristics of adult investors in the stock markets, classified as All Adults, Baby Boomers (between 33 and 48 years old), and Senior Citizens (those 65 years and older). A greater percent of baby boomers hold stock than the average for all age groups. Approximately 40 percent of stock investors are employed as professionals or executives and the same percent have a college degree. The mean family income of stock investors is $72,900, and the mean value of investors' overall investment portfolios is $95,000. Baby boomers have smaller investment portfolios, $62,900, than the average, and senior citizens are the largest group of investors, with a mean investment portfolio valued at $183,300.

Do You Understand?

1. Who the major holders of stock are?
2. What age group of individual investors hold the largest percent of stock outstanding?

Figure 8–13 Distribution of Common Stock Ownership by Age

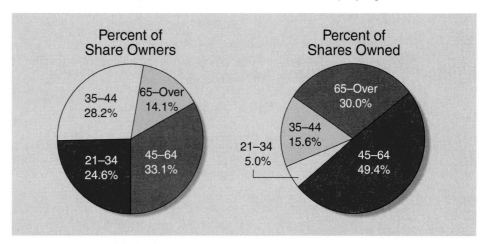

Source: NYSE, *Shareownership,* 1998.

Table 8–8 Profiles of Adult Stockholders

	All Adults	Baby Boomers	Senior Citizens
Employed:	76.4%	89.0%	19.3%
Occupation (conditional on working):			
Professional/Executive	39.9	38.6	52.1
Clerical, technical, or sales	32.4	33.8	29.6
Education:			
Completed college?	39.9	42.8	32.8
Any postgraduate work?	16.1	17.8	14.4
Family status:			
Married	82.0	84.1	71.0
Widowed	4.4	0.9	21.6
Portfolio attributes:			
Has brokerage account	26.5	24.3	37.5
Willing to take risk	76.1	78.7	61.5
Owns IRA or Keogh	49.1	47.6	58.3
Owns mutual fund	27.9	24.1	35.9
Only one stock owned	15.2	15.0	17.9
Median age	43	41	72
Median family income (000s)	$50.0	$57.0	$ 34.0
Mean family income (000s)	$72.9	$74.9	$ 63.1
Median portfolio value (000s)	$15.5	$16.0	$ 29.0
Mean portfolio value (000s)	$95.0	$62.9	$183.3
Mean number of stocks held	1.5	1.0	3.4
Mean number of stocks held if hold stocks directly	3.2	2.0	4.3

Notes: Tabulations from the 1995 Survey of Consumer Finances. Baby Boomer shareholders are those born between 1947 and 1962. Senior citizen shareholders are those aged 65 and above in 1995.

Source: *Stockownership,* 1998, The New York Stock Exchange, 1998. *www.nyse.com/*

Other Issues Pertaining to Stock Markets

Economic Indicators

In the appendix to Chapter 3, we used time value of money equations to determine the fair value of a stock. Specifically, it was shown that the fair value of a stock today (P_0) could be represented as:

$$P_0 = \frac{D_1}{(1 + i_s)^1} + \frac{D_2}{(1 + i_s)^2} + \ldots + \frac{D_\infty}{(1 + i_s)^\infty}$$

The present value of a stock today is the discounted sum of the expected future dividends (D_i) to be paid on the stock. As expected future dividends increase (decrease), stock prices should increase (decrease).

To the extent that today's stock values reflect expected future dividends, stock market indexes might be used to forecast future economic activity. An increase (decrease) in stock market indexes today potentially signals the market's expectation of higher (lower) corporate dividends and profits and in turn, higher (lower) economic growth. To the extent that the market's assessment of expected dividends is correct, stock market indexes can be predictors of economic activity. Indeed, stock prices are one of the 11 variables included in the index of leading economic indicators used by the Federal Reserve as it formulates economic policy (see Chapter 4).[6]

www.bog.frb.fed.us/

Figure 8–14 shows the relation between stock market movements (using the DJIA) and economic cycles in the United States. Notice some recessionary periods (represented in Figure 8–14 by the shaded bars) were indeed preceded by a decline in stock market index values; other recessionary periods were not preceded by a decline in stock market index values; and still other declines in stock market indexes were not followed by recessionary periods. Figure 8–14 suggests that stock market movements are not consistently accurate predictors of economic activity. In fact, a study by researchers at the Federal Reserve Bank of Kansas City found that only 11 of 27 recessions in the United States between 1900 and 1987 were preceded by declines in stock market values.[7]

Market Efficiency

As discussed above (and in Chapter 3), theoretically, the *current* market price of a stock equals the present value of its expected future dividends (or the *fair* market value of the security). However, when an event occurs that unexpectedly changes interest rates or a characteristic of the company (e.g., an unexpected dividend increase or decrease in default risk), the current market price of a stock can temporarily diverge from its fair present value. When market traders determine that a stock is undervalued (i.e., the current price of the stock is less than its fair present value), they will purchase the stock, thus driving its price up. Conversely, when market traders determine that a stock is overvalued (i.e., its current price is greater than its fair present value), they will sell the stock, resulting in a price decline.

The degree to which financial security prices adjust to "news" and the degree (and speed) with which stock prices reflect information about the firm and factors that affect

---

6. The other indicators include average weekly hours of manufacturing production workers, average weekly initial claims for unemployment insurance, manufactures' new orders, time for deliveries, contracts and orders for plant and equipment, building permits for new private housing units, change in manufacturers' unfilled orders for durable goods, change in sensitive materials prices, money supply, and index of consumer expectations. These data, tabulated by the National Bureau of Economic Research (NBER), are available in the *Survey of Current Business*.

7. See Byron Higgins, "Is a Recession Inevitable This Year?" *Economic Review*, Federal Reserve Bank of Kansas City, January 1988, pp. 3–16.

Figure 8–14   The Relation between Stock Market Movements and Economic Activity

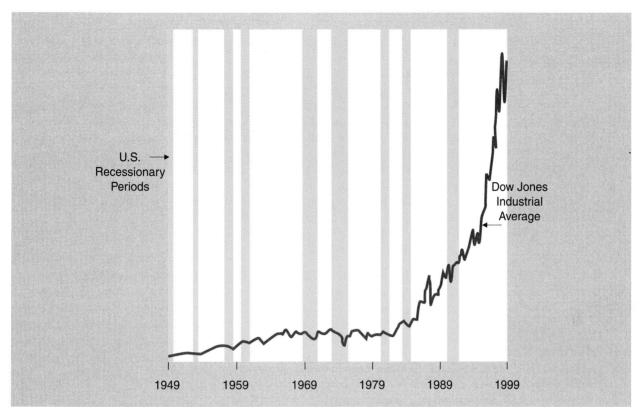

U.S. →
Recessionary
Periods

Dow Jones
Industrial
Average ←

1949   1959   1969   1979   1989   1999

Source: Dow Jones & Company, website, and National Bureau of Economic Research, website, July 6, 1999.

market efficiency

The speed with which financial security prices adjust to unexpected news pertaining to interest rates or a stock-specific characteristic.

firm value is referred to as **market efficiency**.[8] Three measures (weak form, semi-strong form, and strong form market efficiency) are commonly used to measure the degree of stock market efficiency. The measures differ in the type of information or news (e.g., public versus private, historic versus nonhistoric) that is impounded into stock prices.

Weak Form Market Efficiency.   According to the weak form of market efficiency, current stock prices reflect all historic public information about a company. Old news and trends are already impounded in historic prices and are of no use in predicting today's or future stock prices. Thus, weak form market efficiency concludes that investors cannot make more than the fair (required) return using information based on historic price movements.

If markets are weak form efficient, technical analysis used by some investors to identify mispriced stocks is valueless. Technical analysis uses charts of previous stock prices and trading volume (most commonly bar charts indicating a security's high price, low price, and closing price for the day) to pick stock investments. Technical analysts believe that previous prices reflect useful current information about a security. Thus, stock prices tend to form patterns as information flows into the market, allowing future prices to be predicted because these patterns repeat themselves. Trading via technical analysis is in direct contrast to weak form market efficiency.

8. While we discuss market efficiency in the context of stock markets, it also applies to the speed with which any security's price changes in response to new information.

random walk hypothesis

The theory that historical prices on a financial claim cannot help in predicting future prices.

The theory that historic prices of a stock cannot help an investor to predict future stock prices is also consistent with the **random walk hypothesis**. Stock prices follow a "random walk" if changes in the future price of a stock are independent of historical price changes, or the correlation between the return on a stock today and its return yesterday is zero.

Empirical research on weak form market efficiency generally confirms that markets are weak form efficient. Evidence suggests that successive price changes are generally random and that the correlation between stock prices from one day to the next is virtually zero. Thus, historical price trends are of no help in predicting future price movements (and technical analysis has no value as a trading strategy). However, some notable exceptions (anomalies) to weak form market efficiency have been noted. For example, a number of studies have found that abnormal returns (i.e., returns greater than that required for the risk involved on an investment) can consistently be earned over the Friday-Monday period (the "weekend effect") and around the turn of the month, including the end of the year (the "turn of the year effect").[9] Further, studies have revealed that small-capitalization firms and firms with low P/E ratios earn positive abnormal returns compared to large firms.[10]

Semistrong Form Market Efficiency. The semistrong form market efficiency hypothesis focuses on the speed with which public information is impounded into stock prices. According to the concept of semistrong form market efficiency, as public information arrives about a company, it is immediately impounded into its stock price. For example, semistrong form market efficiency states that a common stock's value should respond immediately to unexpected news announcements by the firm regarding its future earnings. Thus, if an investor calls his or her broker just as the earnings news is released, they cannot earn an abnormal return. Prices have already (immediately) adjusted. According to semistrong form market efficiency, investors cannot make more than the fair (required) return by trading on public news releases.

Since historical information is a subset of all public information, if semistrong form market efficiency holds, weak form market efficiency must hold as well. However, it is possible for weak form market efficiency to hold when semistrong form market efficiency does not. This implies that investors can earn abnormal returns by trading on current public news releases. The quicker the stock market impounds this information, the smaller any abnormal returns will be.

Semistrong form market efficiency has been examined by testing how security prices react to unexpected news releases or announcement "events" (event studies—see the appendix to this chapter). If the market is semistrong form efficient, earnings news announcements will be quickly incorporated into the security's price and abnormal returns around the announcement date should fluctuate randomly around zero. Markets are inefficient if abnormal returns are evident after the news announcement.

Some specific announcements that have been tested include macroeconomic events such as interest rate changes, and firm specific announcements such as earnings and dividend changes, stock splits, brokerage house buy and sell recommendations, and mergers and acquisitions. Financial markets have generally been found to immediately reflect information from news announcements. That is, abnormal returns cannot consistently be achieved when news is released. Thus, financial markets are generally semistrong form market efficient.[11]

9. See, for example, J. Lakonishok and S. Smidt, "Are Seasonal Anomalies Real? A Ninety-Year Perspective," *Review of Financial Studies*, Winter 1988, pp. 403–25.

10. See, for example, R. Banz, "The Relationship between Return and Market Value of Common Stocks," *Journal of Financial Economics*, March 1981, pp. 3-18 and S. Basu, "Investment Performance of Common Stocks in Relation to Their Price-Earnings Ratios: A Test of the Efficient Market Hypothesis," *Journal of Finance*, June 1977, pp. 663–82.

11. In some cases where earnings or dividend announcements were significantly different than expected, it takes longer for prices to adjust to the news (in contrast to semistrong form efficiency). See

Strong Form Market Efficiency.   The strong form of market efficiency states that stock prices fully reflect all information about the firm, both public and private. Thus, according to strong form market efficiency, even learning inside information about the firm is of no help in earning more than the required rate of return. As insiders get private information about a firm, the market has already reacted to it and has fully adjusted the firm's common stock price to its new equilibrium level. Thus, strong form market efficiency implies that there is no set of information that allows investors to make more than the fair (required) rate of return on a stock.

If strong form market efficiency holds, semistrong form market efficiency must hold as well. However, semistrong form market efficiency can hold when strong form market efficiency does not. This implies that private information can be used to produce abnormal returns, but as soon as the private or inside information is publicly released, abnormal returns are unobtainable.

Because inside information is not observable to outsiders, it is difficult to test for strong form market efficiency. As a result, there are few studies testing its validity. The limited empirical tests of strong form market efficiency examine information available to insiders. These include tests of the trading behavior of corporate insiders, who include anyone possessing nonpublic information about their firm, the recommendations of security analysts who specialize in particular securities, and economists and other market observers whose job includes forecasting changes in the economy. Empirical evidence suggests that not all insiders (e.g., professional managers, economists, and market observers) have been able to earn abnormal returns using inside information. However, studies have found that corporate insiders (e.g., directors, officers, and chairs) do earn abnormal returns from trading and that the more informed the insider, the more often abnormal returns are earned.[12] Therefore, information possessed by corporate insiders can be used in trading to earn abnormal returns.

Because private information can be used to earn abnormal returns, laws prohibit insiders from trading on the basis of their private information (insider trading) although they can trade, like any investor, based on publicly available information about the firm. To try to ensure that insider trading does not occur, publicly traded companies are required to file monthly reports with the Security and Exchange Commission reporting every purchase and sale of the company's securities by officers and directors of the company. Even with this information, it is often hard to identify trades driven by private (inside) as opposed to public information. It should be noted that some economists argue that trading on private information should not be restricted, since this trading gets information into the market quicker and improves the overall efficiency of the market.

Stock Market Regulations

Stock markets and stock market participants are subject to regulations imposed by the Securities and Exchange Commission (SEC) as well as the exchanges on which stocks are traded. The main emphasis of SEC regulations is on full and fair disclosure of information on securities issues to actual and potential investors. The two major regulations that were created to prevent unfair and unethical trading practices on security

---

D. Peterson, "Security Price Reactions to Initial Review of Common Stock by the Value Line Investment Survey," *Journal of Financial and Quantitative Analysis,* December 1987, pp. 483–94; A. Kalay and U. Lowenstein, "Predictable Events and Excess Returns: The Case of Dividend Announcements," *Journal of Financial Economics,* September 1985, pp. 423–50; and J. Groth, W. Lewellen, G. Schlarbaum, and R. Lease, "An Analysis of Brokerage House Securities Recommendations," *Financial Analysts Journal* (January/February 1979), pp. 32–40.

12. See "Specialists: Special at Exactly What?" *Forbes,* February 1988, pp. 22–23, J. Jaffe "Special Information and Insider Trading," *Journal of Business,* July 1974, pp. 410–428, and K. Nunn, G. Madden, and M. Gombola, "Are Some Insiders More 'Inside' than Others?" *Journal of Portfolio Management,* Spring 1982, pp. 18–22.

exchanges are the Securities Act of 1933 and the Securities Exchange Act of 1934. The 1933 Act required listed companies to file a registration statement and to issue a prospectus that details the recent financial history of the company when issuing new stock. The 1934 Act established the SEC as the main administrative agency responsible for the oversight of secondary stock markets by giving the SEC the authority to monitor the stock market exchanges and administer the provisions of the 1933 Act. SEC regulations are not intended to protect investors against poor investment choices but rather to ensure that investors have full and accurate information available when making their investment decisions.

www.sec.gov/

The SEC has delegated certain regulatory responsibilities to the markets (e.g., NYSE or NASDAQ). In these matters, the NYSE and NASDAQ are self-regulatory organizations (SROs). Specifically, the NYSE has primary responsibility for the day-to-day surveillance of trading activity. It monitors specialists to ensure adequate compliance with their obligation to make a fair and orderly market; monitors all trading to guard against unfair trading practices; monitors broker-dealer activity with respect to minimum net capital requirements, standards, and licensing; and enforces various listing and disclosure requirements.

www.nyse.com/

Do You Understand?

1. Whether movements in stock market indexes are always accurate predictors of changes in economic activity?
2. What the difference is between weak form, semistrong form, and strong form market efficiency?
3. What the purpose of regulations imposed on the stock market participants by the SEC is?

The National Association of Securities Dealers (NASD) has the primary responsibility for regulating brokers and dealers on the NASDAQ market. It requires its members to meet certain standards of conduct in issuing and selling securities and monitors members to prevent them from profiting unreasonably at the expense of their customers. The NASD also conducts field examinations of its member firms at least once a year and can censure, fine, suspend, or expel a broker-dealer from the NASD if violations are found.

The SEC has recently imposed regulations on financial markets intended to reduce excessive price fluctuations. For example, the NYSE now operates under a series of circuit breakers that require the market to shut down for a period of time when prices drop by large amounts during any trading day. The current set of circuit breakers can be found at the NYSE website.

International Aspects of Stock Markets

The U.S. stock markets are the world's largest. However, European markets are becoming an increasing force, and with the introduction of a common currency, the Euro, in 1999, they should continue to grow in importance. Figure 8–15 shows the proportion of stock market capitalization among major countries in 1988, 1996, and 1997. The U.S. dominance in the stock markets is best seen in 1996 and 1997. Note also the stock market developments in Europe and the Pacific Basin countries from 1988 to 1997. While the European markets have increased their market share (from 20.93 to 25.11 percent of the total), the Asian economic problems that started in 1997 reduced the value of these markets significantly (for example, Japanese stock markets decreased from 40.16 percent in 1988 to 9.42 percent in 1997 of the worldwide stock markets).

From an investor's viewpoint, international stock markets are attractive because some risk can be eliminated (diversified away—see Chapter 21) by holding the stocks issued by corporations in foreign countries. For example, while a stock issued by a corporation in one country might be reduced in value by a recessionary slowdown, increases in the value of stocks issued by a corporation in another country (that is experiencing economic growth or an appreciation in the foreign exchange rate of its currency) can offset those losses. A recent (1997–1998) look at correlations in stock returns in the United States, Europe, and the Pacific Basin shows that diversification

Figure 8–15 Worldwide Stock Market Capitalization

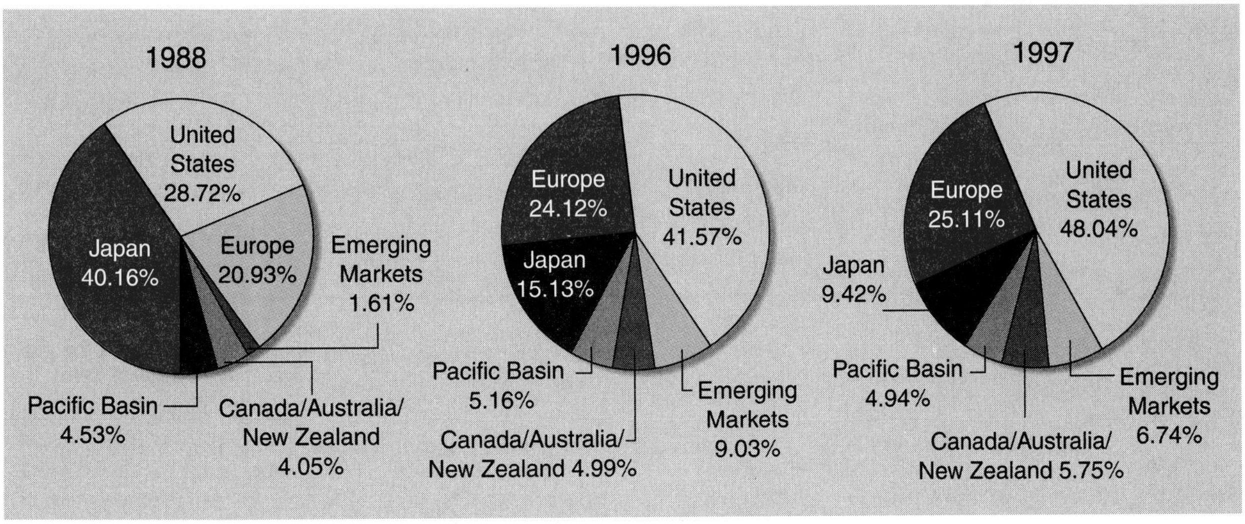

1988

United States 28.72%
Japan 40.16%
Europe 20.93%
Emerging Markets 1.61%
Pacific Basin 4.53%
Canada/Australia/ New Zealand 4.05%

1996

Europe 24.12%
United States 41.57%
Japan 15.13%
Pacific Basin 5.16%
Emerging Markets 9.03%
Canada/Australia/ New Zealand 4.99%

1997

Europe 25.11%
United States 48.04%
Japan 9.42%
Pacific Basin 4.94%
Emerging Markets 6.74%
Canada/Australia/ New Zealand 5.75%

Source: *Emerging Stock Markets Fact Book, 1998.* International Finance Corporation, May 1998.

opportunities do indeed exist.[13] For example, the correlation coefficient on (local currency) stock returns in the United States versus Europe was 0.48, and in the United States versus Pacific Basin countries was 0.30.[14]

Example 8–6 Returns from International Portfolio Diversification

Suppose over the last year you owned stock in a U.S. company and a U.K. company. U.S. dollars were converted to British pounds last year to make the investment, and pounds were converted back to dollars as you liquidated the investment. The exchange rate of British pounds into U.S. dollars was 1.5898 last year and is now 1.6226. Thus, the pound appreciated relative to the dollar over the investment period. The details of the two stock investments are as follows:

	U.S. Stock	U.K. Stock		U.S. Dollar Equivalent for U.K. Stocks
Purchase price, P^C_{t-1}	$50	£60	=	$95.388
Sale price, P^C_t	$48	£64	=	$103.846
Dividends, D^C_t	$1.50	£2.50	=	$4.0565

The return on the U.S. company's stock was:

$$R^{US}_t = \frac{\$48 - \$50}{\$50} + \frac{\$1.5}{\$50} = -1\%$$

and the return on the U.K. company's stock, ignoring the change in the exchange rate, was:

---

13. See T. Lombard, J. Roulet, and B. Solnik, "Pricing of Domestic versus Multinational Companies," *Financial Analysts Journal*, March–April 1999, pp. 35–49.

14. A correlation coefficient of 1 means the returns move exactly together; a correlation coefficient of 0 means there is no relation in the return movements, and a correlation of negative 1 means the returns move in exactly the opposite direction.

$$R^{UK}_t = \frac{£64 - £60}{£60} + \frac{£2.5}{£60} = 10.83\%$$

On a U.S. dollar equivalent basis the return was:

$$R^{UK}_t = \frac{\$103.846 - \$95.388}{\$95.388} + \frac{\$4.0565}{\$95.388} = 13.12\%$$

The loss on the U.S. stock, 1 percent, was offset by an increase in the value of the U.K. stock, reflecting both an increase in its local market value and an appreciation in the pound relative to the dollar.

While international diversification eliminates some risks, it introduces others. For example, for smaller investors, information about foreign stocks is less complete and timely than that for U.S. stocks. Further, international investments introduce foreign exchange risk (see Chapter 9) and political (or sovereign) risk (see Chapter 20).

As seen in Table 8–7 (Rest of world), foreign investors held $1,168.1 billion (or 7.3 percent) of the outstanding stock issued in the U.S. Moreover, foreign companies issued $1,667.2 billion of the stocks in the United States (see Table 8–1). Facilitating U.S. investment in stocks of foreign corporations is the creation of the American Depository Receipt (ADR). An ADR is a certificate that represents ownership of a foreign stock. An ADR is typically created by a U.S. bank, who buys stock in foreign corporations in their domestic currencies and places them with a custodian. The bank then issues dollar ADRs backed by the shares of the foreign stock. These ADRs are then traded in the United States, in dollars, on and off the organized exchanges. The major attraction to U.S. investors is that ADRs are claims to foreign companies that trade on domestic (U.S.) exchanges *and* in dollars.

There are currently about 2,000 ADRs of foreign corporations available to U.S. investors (mainly listed on the NYSE, the AMEX, or the NASDAQ). ADR trading volume in the first half of 1999 exceeded 8.8 billion shares valued at $317 billion. The Bank of New York is the main issuer of ADRs, issuing over 1,300 ADRs representing 69 countries in 1999.

A further advantage of ADRs to U.S. investors is that the SEC requires companies with ADRs trading in the United States to file financial statements that are consistent with U.S. generally accepted accounting principles (GAAP). Thus, unlike direct investments in foreign corporations on their local exchanges, investors in ADRs can obtain and review significant amounts of (audited) information on the foreign firm that appears in a currency, language, and format familiar to U.S. investors.

Similar to domestically traded stock, U.S. investment banks underwrite and sell stock issues globally. For example, Fox Enterprises Group, Inc., issued 124.8 million of its Class A common shares in November 1998: 106.08 million were issued in the United States and 18.72 in international markets. An internationally placed stock issue is attractive to an issuing firm because the shares of stock can reach a much larger market than if they were placed strictly in the United States. Foreign investors (with investment needs that differ from U.S. investors) may buy these stocks even when U.S. investors may not. Foreign issues of stock can also help enhance the international reputation of the firm. This is especially important to firms that concentrate at least a part of their business in international trade.

As noted earlier, U.S. stock exchanges are regulated by the SEC on some matters and are self-regulated organizations for others. Stock market structures in Japan, Canada, Hong Kong, and Australia are similar to the U.S. structure. These exchanges are self-regulating, with the government mainly playing the role of monitor. In Canada, Hong Kong, and Australia, the exchanges determine which securities are listed and the criteria that firms must meet for membership. In Japan, the Ministry of Finance must approve all listed securities.

In France, Belgium, Spain, and Italy, governments exercise the major control over the operations and activities of the exchanges. Membership on these exchanges may require government approval or licensing, and to insure against insolvency government agencies set minimum capital requirements. In Germany, Switzerland, Austria, and Sweden, the majority of the exchange trading is conducted through banks, reflecting regulatory and government policy.

As mentioned earlier, prices on U.S. stock markets are determined continuously throughout the trading day as brokers submit orders. Stock markets in Canada, Japan, Hong Kong, and most of Europe also use continuous trading. Stock markets in Germany and Austria use call-based trading, in which orders are batched for simultaneous execution at the same price and at a particular time during the day.

Only the Montreal Stock Exchange uses a specialist system of trading directly similar to that of the NYSE. The Amsterdam Stock Exchange gives certain firms the specialists duties for small and medium-sized trades. Large trades, however, are transacted directly by the parties involved. On the Toronto Stock Exchange, market makers are similar to specialists. These traders are selected by the exchange to trade for their own accounts and to create an orderly price flow in stocks that the exchange assigns them. These traders are obligated to post bid and ask prices throughout the day and to keep their bid-ask spreads small.

All other continuous trading markets in the world use a competitive dealer system of trading similar to that used by NASDAQ. For example, the London International Stock Exchange allows any well-capitalized firm that follows the regulations to act as a dealer for any security. Market makers publish firm bid-ask quotes for their stocks. One difference in this market is that for a limit order, only the broker-dealer that accepts the order from a customer knows about it. The computerized trading system does not record the existence of an order. The dealer then executes the order when his or her own price reaches the requested level. The Tokyo Stock Exchange uses a variation of the competitive dealer system, in which a broker functions as an intermediary between the dealers and the brokers who are members of the exchange. The brokers cannot buy or sell for their own accounts but can only arrange transactions among dealers, conduct trading auctions, and match buy and sell orders submitted by brokers for their clients.

Do You Understand?

1. What percentage of the world's capital markets are represented by U.S. stocks?
2. What an ADR is?

Summary

In this chapter, we examined corporate stocks and stock markets. Holders of corporate (preferred and common) stock have an ownership interest in the issuing firm based on the percentage of stock held. Stock markets are the most watched and reported of the financial markets. We described the major characteristics of corporate stocks—for example, dividend rights, residual claim status, limited liability, and voting rights of stockholders. We also looked at the primary and secondary markets for stocks, including a description of the trading process. While the NYSE has historically been the major stock market exchange in the United States, we showed that the NASDAQ system is increasing in importance.

We also looked at stock market indexes as predictors of future economic activity, reviewed the speed with which stock market prices adjust to new information, and described the major regulations governing stock market trading. We concluded the chapter with a brief look at international stock market activity—foreign investments in U.S. corporate stocks and U.S. investments in foreign corporate stocks.

End-of-Chapter Questions

1. Why are the stock markets the most watched and reported of the financial security markets?

2. What are some characteristics associated with dividends paid on common stock?

3. What is meant by the statement "common stockholders have a residual claim on the issuing firm's assets?"

4. What is a dual-class firm? Why do firms typically issue dual classes of common stock?

5. Suppose a firm has 15 million shares of common stock outstanding and six candidates are up for election to five seats on the board of directors.
    a. If the firm uses cumulative voting to elect its board, what is the minimum number of votes needed to ensure election to the board?
    b. If the firm uses straight voting to elect its board, what is the minimum number of votes needed to ensure election to the board?

6. What is the difference between nonparticipating and participating preferred stock?

7. What is the difference between cumulative and noncumulative preferred stock?

8. Suppose you own 50,000 shares of common stock in a firm with 2.5 million total shares outstanding. The firm announces a plan to sell an additional 1 million shares through a rights offering. The market value of the stock is $35 before the rights offering and the new shares are being offered to existing shareholders at a $5 discount.
    a. If you exercise your preemptive rights, how many of the new shares can you purchase?
    b. What is the market value of the stock after the rights offering?
    c. What is your total investment in the firm after the rights offering? How is your investment split between original shares and new shares?

    d. If you decide not to exercise your preemptive rights, what is your investment in the firm after the rights offering? How is this split between old shares and rights?

9. What have been the trends in the growth of the NYSE, AMEX, and NASDAQ stock market exchanges?

10. What is a market order? What is a limit order? How are each executed?

11. Refer to the stock market quote in Table 8–4.
    a. What was the closing stock price for AVX Corp. on January 18, 2000?
    b. What were the high and low prices at which Abbot Labs traded between January 19, 1999, and January 18, 2000?
    c. What was the dividend yield on Acadia Realty's stock as of January 18, 2000?

12. What are the major U.S. stock market indexes?

13. Who are the major holders of corporate stock?

14. Are stock market indexes consistently accurate predictors of economic activity?

15. Describe the three forms of stock market efficiency.

16. What are circuit breakers used by the NYSE?

17. What is an ADR? How is an ADR created?

18. Go to the NASDAQ website and find the current levels of dollar value of trading and share volume of trading on the NYSE, AMEX, and NASDAQ stock markets.

19. Go to the NYSE website and find the most recent information on the NYSE market indexes.

20. Go to the Federal Reserve System website and find the most recent data on foreign investor's holdings of U.S. issued corporate stocks and foreign corporate stocks issued in the U.S.

Appendix   Event Study Tests

Event studies use a model, called a market model, to identify the *normal* relationship between a stock's return and the market's return using a period of time prior to a news release (e.g., the year prior). The market model equation is represented as:

$$R_{it} = a_i + \beta_i R_{Mt} + e_{it}$$

where

R_{it} = Return on firm i on day t

R_{Mt} = Return on a market portfolio (e.g., S&P 500 index) in day t

a_i = Regression coefficient representing the intercept term for stock i, the stock's return component that is not related to the market return

β_i = Coefficient representing the slope of the regression, the expected change in stock i for a 1 percent change in the market return (often called the stock's beta or β) [15]

---

15. A stock's beta is a measure of the sensitivity of its return to changes in the return on a market index.

e_{it} = Error term on the regression

On the day of the news release, the actual market return is applied to the market model to calculate the stock's expected return, or $E(R_{it})$, as follows:

$$E(R_{it}) = a_i + \beta_i R_{Mt}$$

An abnormal return on the announcement day, AR_{it}, is then calculated by subtracting the expected return on the stock, $E(R_{it})$, from the actual return, R_{it}, on the stock as follows:

$$AR_{it} = R_{it} - E(R_{it})$$

or:

$$AR_{it} = R_{it} - [a_i + \beta_i R_{Mt}]$$

Market inefficiencies are indicated if the abnormal return is statistically different from zero.

Example 8–7   Calculation of Abnormal Returns at a News
                          Announcement

Suppose that early this morning, a firm in which you own stock released news that earnings for the past quarter increased by 10 percent more than expected. In response to this announcement, the stock price increased 5 percent during today's trading. The return on the S&P 500 index increased by 2 percent during today's trading. You want to use the market model to determine the abnormal return on the stock resulting from this announcement. You have collected the following information on the stock using a simple regression of returns on the stock and the S&P 500 index over the last year:

$1\% = a_s$ = Regression coefficient representing the intercept term for the stock
$1.5 = \beta_s$ = Coefficient representing the slope of the regression (i.e., the β of the
                    stock)

or for this stock:

$$E(R_{it}) = 1\% + 1.5\ (R_{Mt})$$

To calculate the abnormal return on the stock resulting from the earnings announcement, we use this equation, as follows:

$$
\begin{aligned}
AR_{it} &= R_{it} - [1\% + 1.5\ (R_{Mt})] \\
&= 5\% - [\ 1\% + 1.5\ (2\%)] \\
&= 5\% - 4\% = 1\%
\end{aligned}
$$

or you can earn an abnormal return of 1 percent as a result of the news of increased earnings.

chapter nine

Foreign Exchange Markets

Chapter Navigator

1. What are foreign exchange markets and foreign exchange rates?

2. What are the world's largest foreign exchange markets?

3. What is the difference between a spot foreign exchange transaction and a forward foreign exchange transaction?

4. How can return and risk be measured on foreign exchange transactions?

5. What is the role of financial institutions in foreign exchange transactions?

6. What is the relation between interest rates, inflation, and exchange rates?

7. What are the balance of payment accounts of a country?

Foreign Exchange Markets and Risk: Chapter Overview

U.S.-based FIs and companies are more and more frequently operating globally. They may sell their products or services to foreign customers or buy their inputs (labor, capital, raw materials, etc.) from foreign suppliers. It is therefore essential that financial managers understand how events in other countries in which they operate, as well as events in the United States (e.g., a change in interest rates—see In the News box 9–1) affect cash flows received from or paid to other countries and thus their company's or FI's profitability.

In the News

9-1

Fed Funds Rate Cut Leaves Dollar Cold

The U.S. dollar initially weakened on the foreign currency markets after the Federal Reserve nudged interest rates 25 basis points higher yesterday, but tempered the increase by returning to a neutral bias. The Fed said that while U.S. labor markets were tight, productivity gains had contained inflation. Despite the return to a neutral bias, the committee said it would remain alert to inflationary pressures. Immediately after the decision a rally in

Source: *Financial Times*, July 1, 1999, p. 39, by Christopher Swann.

U.S. bonds and stocks failed to translate into dollar strength and the U.S. currency was weaker against the euro and the yen during trading in New York.

The Fed's decision divided analysts over its longer-term impact. "By encouraging a rally in bond markets and avoiding alarm in the equity markets, this move should be good for the dollar," said Paul Chertkow, head of global currency research at Tokyo-

Mitsubishi. But Robert Lynch, currency analyst at Paribas in New York, said most of the good news was now priced into the dollar.

The Fed's decision yesterday overshadowed signs of recovery in one of Europe's most sickly economies, with Italian gross domestic product data coming in above expectations. But the euro failed to take heart, closing the London session at $1.031 against the dollar. However, analysts said the accumulation of positive economic statistics could prevent the euro declining to parity with the dollar.

www.ft.com/

foreign exchange markets

Markets in which cash flows from the sale of products or assets denominated in a foreign currency are transacted.

foreign exchange rate

The price at which one currency can be exchanged for another currency.

Do You Understand?

1. What the effect of the Federal Reserve's interest rate increase on the U.S. currency exchange rate was?

Cash flows from the sale of products, services, or assets denominated in a foreign currency are transacted in **foreign exchange (FX) markets**. A **foreign exchange rate** is the price at which one currency (e.g., the U.S. dollar) can be exchanged for another currency (e.g., the French franc) in the foreign exchange markets. These transactions expose U.S. corporations and investors to **foreign exchange risk** as the cash flows are converted into and out of U.S. dollars. The actual amount of U.S. dollars received on a foreign transaction depends on the (foreign) exchange rate between the U.S. dollar and the foreign currency when the nondollar cash flow is received (and exchanged for U.S. dollars) at some future date. If the foreign **currency** declines (or **depreciates**) in value relative to the U.S. dollar over the period between the time a foreign investment is made and the time it is liquidated, the dollar value of the cash flows received will fall. If the foreign **currency** rises (or **appreciates**) in value relative to the U.S. dollar, the dollar value of the cash flows received on the foreign investment increases.

In this chapter, we examine the operations of foreign exchange markets. We start with a brief look at the history of foreign exchange markets. We define and describe the spot and forward foreign exchange transaction process. We also look at balance of payment accounts that summarize a country's foreign transactions.

foreign exchange risk

Risk that cash flows will vary as the actual amount of U.S. dollars received on a foreign investment changes due to a change in foreign exchange rates.

currency depreciation

When a country's currency falls in value relative to other currencies, meaning the country's goods become cheaper for foreign buyers and foreign goods become more expensive for foreign sellers.

currency appreciation

When a country's currency rises in value relative to other currencies, meaning that the country's goods are more expensive for foreign buyers and foreign goods are cheaper for foreign sellers (all else constant).

Background and History of Foreign Exchange Markets

Foreign exchange markets have existed for some time as international trade and investing have resulted in the need to exchange currencies. The type of exchange rate system used to accomplish this exchange, however, has changed over time. For example, from 1944 to 1971, the Bretton Woods Agreement called for the exchange rate of one currency for another to be fixed within narrow bands around a specified rate with the help of government intervention. The Bretton Woods Agreement, however, led to a situation in which some currencies (such as the U.S. dollar) became very overvalued and others (such as the German mark) became very undervalued. The Smithsonian Agreement of 1971 sought to address this situation. Under this agreement, major countries allowed the dollar to be devalued and the boundaries between which exchange rates could fluctuate were increased from 1 to 2¼ percent.

In 1973, under the Smithsonian Agreement II, the exchange rate boundaries were eliminated altogether. This effectively allowed exchange rates of major currencies to float freely. This free-floating foreign exchange rate system is still partially in place. However, as discussed in Chapter 4, central governments may still intervene in the foreign exchange markets by altering interest rates to affect the value of their currency relative to others, and the major European countries have chosen to peg (fix) their exchange rates with each other as they move towards a single currency and full monetary union in the year 2002. Indeed, on January 1, 1999, 11 major European countries pegged their exchange rates together to create a single currency, called the European Currency Unit or euro.[1] Similar to the government intervention under the Bretton Woods agreement, European governments intervene to ensure that exchange rates between the European Union countries are maintained.

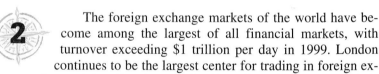

The foreign exchange markets of the world have become among the largest of all financial markets, with turnover exceeding $1 trillion per day in 1999. London continues to be the largest center for trading in foreign exchange; it handles almost twice the daily volume as New York, the second-largest market. Third-ranked Tokyo handles approximately one-third the volume of London. Moreover, the FX market is essentially a 24-hour market, moving from Tokyo, London, and New York throughout the day. Therefore, fluctuations in exchange rates and thus, FX trading risk exposure continues into the night even when some FI operations are closed.

Do You Understand?

1. What the Bretton Woods Agreement did to the ability of foreign exchange rates to fluctuate freely?
2. What the European Currency Unit is?

Foreign Exchange Rates and Transactions

Foreign Exchange Rates

As mentioned above, a foreign exchange rate is the price at which one currency (e.g., the U.S. dollar) can be exchanged for another currency (e.g., the French franc). Table 9–1 lists the exchange rates between the U.S. dollar and other currencies as of 4:00 p.m. eastern standard time on January 18, 2000. Foreign exchange rates are listed in two ways: U.S. dollars received for one unit of the foreign currency exchanged (U.S. $ equiv.) and foreign currency received for each U.S. dollar exchanged (Currency per U.S. $). For example, the exchange rate of U.S. dollars for Canadian dollars on Janu-

---

1. The 11 countries are Austria, Belgium, Finland, France, Germany, Ireland, Italy, Luxembourg, Netherlands, Portugal, and Spain.

Table 9–1 Foreign Currency Exchange Rates

THE WALL STREET JOURNAL WEDNESDAY, JANUARY 19, 2000 **C19**

CURRENCY TRADING

Tuesday, January 18, 2000

EXCHANGE RATES

The New York foreign exchange mid-range rates below apply to trading among banks in amounts of $1 million and more, as quoted at 4 p.m. Eastern time by Reuters and other sources. Retail transactions provide fewer units of foreign currency per dollar. Rates for the 11 Euro currency countries are derived from the latest dollar-euro rate using the exchange ratios set 1/1/99.

Country	U.S. $ equiv. Tue	U.S. $ equiv. Mon	Currency per U.S. $ Tue	Currency per U.S. $ Mon
Argentina (Peso)	1.0002	1.0001	.9998	.9999
Australia (Dollar)	.6660	.6651	1.5016	1.5036
Austria (Schilling)	.07366	.07351	13.576	13.605
Bahrain (Dinar)	2.6525	2.6525	.3770	.3770
Belgium (Franc)	.0251	.0251	39.8006	39.8832
Brazil (Real)	.5579	.5577	1.7925	1.7930
Britain (Pound)	1.6377	1.6320	.6106	.6127
1-month forward	1.6378	1.6321	.6106	.6127
3-months forward	1.6378	1.6321	.6106	.6127
6-months forward	1.6372	1.6317	.6108	.6129
Canada (Dollar)	.6898	.6900	1.4498	1.4492
1-month forward	.6901	.6906	1.4491	1.4480
3-months forward	.6911	.6915	1.4469	1.4461
6-months forward	.6923	.6928	1.4444	1.4434
Chile (Peso) (d)	.001939	.001952	515.75	512.25
China (Renminbi)	.1208	.1208	8.2793	8.2793
Colombia (Peso)	.0005167	.0005196	1935.50	1924.50
Czech. Rep. (Koruna)				
Commercial rate	.02812	.02806	35.562	35.635
Denmark (Krone)	.1362	.1359	7.3437	7.3601
Ecuador (Sucre)				
Floating rate	.00004004	.00004000	24975.00	25002.50
Finland (Markka)	.1705	.1701	5.8662	5.8784
France (Franc)	.1545	.1542	6.4719	6.4853
1-month forward	.1549	.1546	6.4559	6.4696
3-months forward	.1556	.1552	6.4282	6.4416
6-months forward	.1566	.1563	6.3862	6.3996
Germany (Mark)	.5182	.5171	1.9297	1.9337
1-month forward	.5195	.5184	1.9249	1.9290
3-months forward	.5217	.5207	1.9167	1.9206
6-months forward	.5252	.5241	1.9041	1.9081
Greece (Drachma)	.003064	.003057	326.38	327.11
Hong Kong (Dollar)	.1286	.1286	7.7790	7.7789
Hungary (Forint)	.003970	.003966	251.89	252.15
India (Rupee)	.02296	.02297	43.545	43.540
Indonesia (Rupiah)	.0001375	.0001378	7275.00	7255.00
Ireland (Punt)	1.2870	1.2844	.7770	.7786
Israel (Shekel)	.2457	.2449	4.0695	4.0834
Italy (Lira)	.0005235	.0005224	1910.38	1914.35
Japan (Yen)	.009462	.009537	105.69	104.85
1-month forward	.009511	.009588	105.14	104.30

Country	U.S. $ equiv. Tue	U.S. $ equiv. Mon	Currency per U.S. $ Tue	Currency per U.S. $ Mon
3-months forward	.009602	.009679	104.15	103.31
6-months forward	.009754	.009832	102.53	101.71
Jordan (Dinar)	1.4085	1.4085	.7100	7100
Kuwait (Dinar)	3.2819	3.2873	.3047	3042
Lebanon (Pound)	.0006634	.0006634	1507.50	1507.50
Malaysia (Ringgit)	.2632	.2632	3.7999	3.8000
Malta (Lira)	2.4474	2.4426	.4086	.4094
Mexico (Peso)				
Floating rate	.1063	.1061	9.4050	9.4240
Netherland (Guilder)	.4599	.4590	2.1742	2.1788
New Zealand (Dollar)	.5206	.5206	1.9209	1.9209
Norway (Krone)	.1252	.1249	7.9883	8.0066
Pakistan (Rupee)	.01926	.01927	51.925	51.898
Peru (new Sol)	.2865	.2866	3.4905	3.4890
Philippines (Peso)	.02463	.02466	40.595	40.550
Poland (Zloty)	.2446	.2452	4.0875	4.0775
Portugal (Escudo)	.005056	.005045	197.80	198.21
Russia (Ruble) (a)	.03492	.03487	28.635	28.675
Saudi Arabia (Riyal)	.2666	.2666	3.7505	3.7503
Singapore (Dollar)	.5974	.5970	1.6740	1.6750
Slovak Rep. (Koruna)	.02394	.02389	41.764	41.851
South Africa (Rand)	.1641	.1645	6.0925	6.0790
South Korea (Won)	.0008877	.0008925	1126.50	1120.50
Spain (Peseta)	.006092	.006079	164.16	164.50
Sweden (Krona)	.1182	.1182	8.4598	8.4630
Switzerland (Franc)	.6283	.6264	1.5917	1.5963
1-month forward	.6307	.6289	1.5856	1.5900
3-months forward	.6350	.6331	1.5749	1.5796
6-months forward	.6415	.6398	1.5588	1.5631
Taiwan (Dollar)	.03155	.03241	31.700	30.850
Thailand (Baht)	.02678	.02671	37.335	37.445
Turkey (Lira)	.00000183	.00000183	546595.00	546700.00
United Arab (Dirham)	.2723	.2723	3.6726	3.6730
Uruguay (New Peso)				
Financial	.08558	.08571	11.685	11.668
Venezuela (Bolivar)	.001531	.001535	653.10	651.50
SDR	1.3667	n.a.	.7317	n.a.
Euro	1.0136	1.0115	.9866	.9886

Special Drawing Rights (SDR) are based on exchange rates for the U.S., German, British, French , and Japanese currencies. Source: International Monetary Fund.

a-Russian Central Bank rate. Trading band lowered on 8/17/98. b-Government rate. d-Floating rate; trading band suspended on 9/2/99.

The 3-month and 6-month forward rates for France, Germany, Japan and Switzerland appearing in the Foreign Exchange column were incorrectly calculated for the period beginning with August 13 and ending with October 7. Corrected data is available from Readers' Reference Service (413) 592 3600.

OPTIONS
PHILADELPHIA EXCHANGE

		Calls Vol.	Calls Last	Puts Vol.	Puts Last
Euro					101.43
62,500 Euro-cents per unit.					
102	Feb	4	0.95	...	...
102	Mar	24	1.62	...	...
104	Mar	17	0.94	1	3.34
104	Jun	30	2.34	...	0.01
106	Mar	2	0.46	...	0.01
106	Jun	406	1.66	...	0.01
108	Jun	17	1.15	...	0.01
British Pound					163.83
31,250 Brit. Pounds-European Style.					
163	Feb	...	0.01	32	0.78
31,250 Brit. Pounds-cents per unit.					
166	Mar	32	1.09	...	0.01

		Calls Vol.	Calls Last	Puts Vol.	Puts Last
166	Jun	32	2.33	...	0.01
168	Mar	32	0.60	...	0.01
168	Jun	32	1.72	...	0.01
Canadian Dollar					68.91
50,000 Canadian Dollars-cents per unit.					
69½	Mar	20	0.40	...	0.01
50,000 Canadian Dollars-cents per unit.					
69	Feb	...	0.01	10	0.39
Euro					101.43
62,500 Euro-European style.					
102	Feb	16	0.80	...	...

		Calls Vol.	Calls Last	Puts Vol.	Puts Last
Swiss Franc					62.83
62,500 Swiss Francs-European Style.					
62	Feb	...	...	30	0.39
62,500 Swiss Francs-cents per unit.					
62½	Feb	...	0.01	240	0.57
63	Feb	240	0.71	...	...
63½	Mar	...	0.01	59	1.34
64	Jun	1	1.62	...	...
65	Mar	...	...	29	2.48
67½	Mar	1	1.45	...	0.01
Call Vol	1,276			**Open Int**	16,522
Put Vol	2,291			**Open Int**	17,382

ary 18, 2000, was .6898 (US$/C$), or $0.6898 could be received for each Canadian dollar exchanged. Conversely, the exchange rate of Canadian dollars for U.S. dollars was 1.4498 (C$/US$), or 1.4498 Canadian dollars could be received for each U.S. dollar exchanged.

Figure 9–1   Spot versus Forward Foreign Exchange Transaction

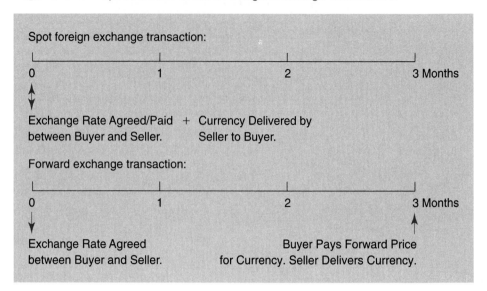

Foreign Exchange Transactions

spot foreign exchange transactions

Foreign exchange transactions involving the immediate exchange of currencies at the current (or spot) exchange rate.

Recall from Chapter 1 that there are two types of foreign exchange rates and foreign exchange transactions: spot and forward. **Spot foreign exchange transactions** involve the immediate exchange of currencies at the current (or spot) exchange rate—see Figure 9–1. Spot transactions can be conducted through the foreign exchange division of commercial banks or a nonbank foreign currency dealer. For example, a U.S. investor wanting to buy Italian lira through a local bank on January 18, 2000, essentially has the dollars transferred from his or her bank account to the dollar account of a lira seller at a rate of $1 per 1910.38 lira (or $0.0005235 per lira).[2] Simultaneously, lira are transferred from the seller's account into an account designated by the U.S. investor. If the dollar depreciates in value relative to the lira (e.g., $1 per 1898.9745 lira or $0.0005266 per lira), the value of the lira investment, if converted back into U.S. dollars, increases. If the dollar appreciates in value relative to the lira (e.g., $1 per 1915.7088 lira or $0.0005220 per lira), the value of the lira investment, if converted back into U.S. dollars, decreases.

The appreciation of a country's currency (or a rise in its value relative to other currencies) means that the country's goods are more expensive for foreign buyers and foreign goods are cheaper for foreign sellers (all else constant). Thus, when a country's currency appreciates, domestic manufacturers find it harder to sell their goods abroad and foreign manufactures find it easier to sell their goods to domestic purchasers. Conversely, depreciation of a country's currency (or a fall in its value relative to other currencies) means the country's goods become cheaper for foreign buyers and foreign goods become more expensive for foreign sellers. Figure 9–2 shows the pattern of exchange rates between the U.S. dollar and several foreign currencies in the mid- and late-1990s.[3] Notice the significant depreciation, in 1997 and 1998, in the value of currencies of countries affected by the Asian crisis relative to the U.S. dollar.

forward foreign exchange transaction

The exchange of currencies at a specified exchange rate (or forward exchange rate) at some specified date in the future.

A **forward foreign exchange transaction** is the exchange of currencies at a specified exchange rate (or forward exchange rate) at some specified date in the future, as

---

2. In actual practice, settlement—exchange of currencies—occurs normally two days after a transaction.

3. Notice that the exchange rate between the U.S. dollar and the Japanese yen is shown as yen for U.S. dollars (¥/US$). For the other graphs, the exchange rates are listed as the U.S. dollar for the foreign currency (US$/fx).

Figure 9–2 Exchange Rate of the U.S. Dollar with Various Foreign Currencies

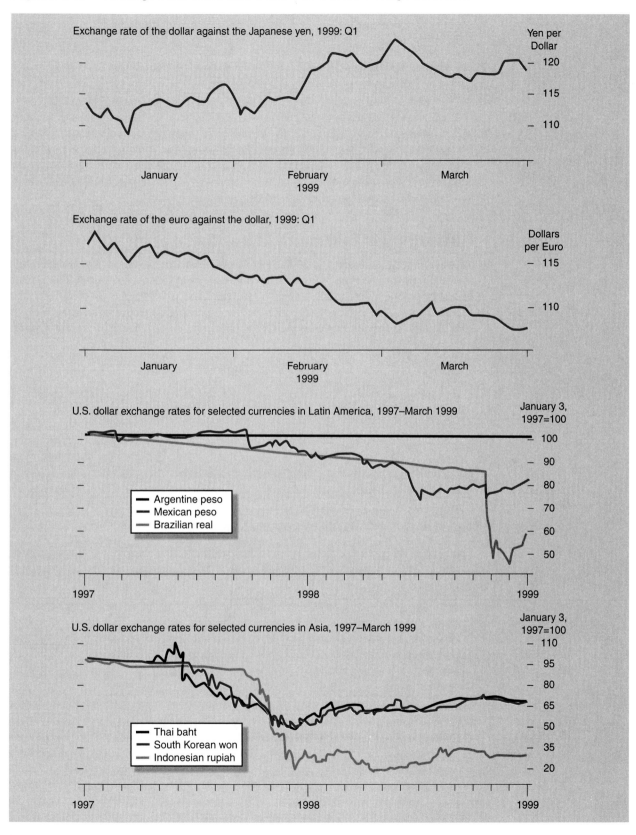

Source: Kathryn A. Morisse, "U.S. International Transactions in 1998," *Federal Reserve Bulletin,* May 1999, pp. 287–99; and Laura F. Ambrosene, "Treasury and Federal Reserve Foreign Exchange Operations," *Federal Reserve Bulletin,* June 1999, pp. 396–400. *www.bog.frb.fed.us/*

illustrated in Figure 9–1. An example is an agreement today (at time 0) to exchange dollars for lira at a given (forward) exchange rate three months into the future. Forward contracts are typically written for one-, three-, or six-month periods, but in practice they can be written over any given length of time.

4   Return and Risk of Foreign Exchange Transactions

This section discusses the extra dimensions of return and risk from foreign exchange transactions. The risk involved with a spot foreign exchange transaction is that the value of the foreign currency may change relative to the U.S. dollar. Further, foreign exchange risk is introduced by adding foreign currency assets and liabilities to an FI's portfolio. Like domestic assets and liabilities, returns result from the contractual income from or costs paid on a security. With foreign assets and liabilities, however, returns are also affected by changes in foreign exchange rates.

Example 9–1   Foreign Exchange Risk

Suppose that on January 18, 2000, a U.S. firm plans to purchase 3 million French francs' (Ff) worth of French bonds from a French FI in one month's time. The French FI wants payment in French francs. Thus, the U.S. firm must convert dollars into French francs. The spot exchange rate for January 18, 2000 (reported in Table 9–1) of U.S. dollars to French francs is .1545, or one franc costs $.1545 in dollars. Consequently, the U.S. firm must convert:

$$\text{U.S.\$/Ff exchange rate} \times \text{Ff 3 million} =$$
$$.1545 \quad\quad \times \quad \text{Ff 3m} \quad = \$463{,}500$$

into French francs today.

One month after the conversion of dollars to French francs, the French bond purchase deal falls through and the U.S. firm no longer needs the French francs it purchased at $.1545 per franc. The spot exchange rate of the French franc to the dollar has fallen or depreciated over the month so that the value of a franc is worth only $.142, or the exchange rate is $.142 per franc. The U.S. dollar value of 3 million French francs is now only:

$$.142 \times \text{Ff 3 million} = \$426{,}000$$

The depreciation of the French franc relative to the dollar over the month has caused the U.S. firm to suffer a $37,500 ($463,500 − $426,000) loss due to exchange rate fluctuations.

To avoid such a loss in the spot markets, the U.S. FI could have entered into a forward transaction, which is the exchange of currencies at a specified future date and a specified exchange rate (or forward exchange rate). Forward exchange rates for January 18, 2000, are also listed in Table 9–1. As mentioned above, forward contracts are typically written for a one-, three-, or six-month period from the date the contract is written, although they can be written for any time period. For example, if the U.S. investor had entered into a one-month forward contract on the French franc on January 18, 2000, at the same time it purchased the spot francs, the U.S. investor would have been guaranteed an exchange rate of .1549 U.S. dollars per French franc, or 6.4559 French francs per U.S. dollar, from selling francs in one month's time. If the U.S. FI had sold francs one month forward at .1549 on January 18, 2000, it would have largely avoided the loss of $37,500 described in Example 9–1. Specifically, by selling francs forward, it would have received:

$$.1549 \times \text{Ff 3 million} = \$464{,}700$$

suggesting a small net profit of $\$464{,}700 - \$463{,}500 = \$1{,}200$ on the combined spot and forward transactions. Essentially, by using the one-month forward contract, the FI hedges its foreign currency risk in the spot market.

Example 9–2 Calculating the Return of Foreign Exchange Transactions of a U.S. FI

Suppose that a U.S. FI has the following assets and liabilities:

Assets	Liabilities

$100 million
  U.S. loans (one year) in dollars
	$200 million
	  U.S. CDs (one year) in dollars

$100 million equivalent
  U.K. loans (one year)
  (loans made in sterling)	

The U.S. FI is raising all of its $200 million liabilities in dollars (one-year CDs), but it is investing 50 percent in U.S. dollar assets (one-year maturity loans) and 50 percent in U.K. pound sterling assets (one-year maturity loans).[4] In this example, the FI has matched the maturity (M) or duration (D) of its assets (A) and liabilities (L):

$$(M_A = M_L = D_A = D_L = 1 \text{ year})$$

but has mismatched the currency composition of its asset and liability portfolios. Suppose that the promised one-year U.S. CD rate is 8 percent, to be paid in dollars at the end of the year, and that one-year, credit risk–free loans in the United States are yielding only 9 percent. The FI would have a positive spread of 1 percent from investing domestically. Suppose, however, that credit risk–free one-year loans are yielding 15 percent in the United Kingdom.

To invest $100 million (of the $200 million in CDs issued) in one-year loans in the United Kingdom, the U.S. FI engages in the following transactions:

1. At the beginning of the year, it sells $100 million for pounds on the spot currency markets. If the exchange rate is $1.60 to £1, this translates into $100 million/1.6 = £62.5 million.
2. It takes the £62.5 million and makes one-year U.K. loans at a 15 percent interest rate.
3. At the end of the year, sterling revenue from these loans will be £62.5(1.15) = £71.875 million.[5]
4. It repatriates these funds back to the United States at the end of the year—that is, the U.S. FI sells the £71.875 million in the foreign exchange market at the spot exchange rate that exists at that time, the end of the year spot rate.

Suppose that the spot foreign exchange rate has not changed over the year—it remains fixed at $1.60/£1. Then the dollar proceeds from the U.K. investment are:

$$£71.875 \text{ million} \times \$1.60/£1 = \$115 \text{ million or as a return}$$

$$\frac{\$115 \text{ million} - \$100 \text{ million}}{\$100 \text{ million}} = 15\%$$

---

4. For simplicity, we ignore the leverage or net worth aspects of the FI's portfolio.
5. No default risk is assumed.

Given this, the weighted return on the FI's portfolio of investments would be:

$$(.5)(.09) + (.5)(.15) = .12, \text{ or } 12\%$$

This exceeds the cost of the FI's CDs by 4 percent (12% − 8%).

Suppose, however, that the exchange rate had fallen from $1.60/£1 at the beginning of the year to $1.45/£1 at the end of the year, when the FI needed to repatriate the principal and interest on the loan. At an exchange rate of $1.45/£1, the pound loan revenues at the end of the year translate into:

$$\text{£}71.875 \text{ million} \times \$1.45/\text{£}1 = \$104.22 \text{ million}$$

or as a return on the original dollar investment of:

$$\frac{\$104.22 - \$100}{\$100} = .0422 = 4.22\%$$

The weighted return on the FI's asset portfolio would be:

$$(.5)(.09) + (.5)(.0422) = .0661 = 6.61\%$$

In this case, the FI actually has a loss or a negative interest margin (6.61% − 8% = −1.39%) on its balance sheet investments.

The reason for the loss is that the depreciation of the pound from $1.60 to $1.45 has offset the attractively high yield on British pound sterling loans relative to domestic U.S. loans. If the pound had instead appreciated (risen in value) against the dollar over the year—say, to $1.70/£1—the U.S. FI would have generated a dollar return from its U.K. loans of:

$$\text{£}71.875 \times \$1.70 = \$122.188 \text{ million}$$

or a percentage return of 22.188 percent.

The U.S. FI would receive a double benefit from investing in the United Kingdom, a high yield on the domestic British loans and an appreciation in sterling over the one-year investment period.

Risk and Hedging.   Since a manager cannot know in advance what the pound/dollar spot exchange rate will be at the end of the year, a portfolio imbalance or investment strategy in which the bank is *net long* $100 million in pounds (or £62.5 million) is risky. As we discussed, the British loans would generate a return of 22.188 percent if the pound appreciated from $1.60 to $1.70 but would produce a return of only 4.22 percent if the pound were to depreciate in value against the dollar to $1.45.

In principle, an FI manager can better control the scale of its FX exposure in two major ways: on-balance-sheet hedging and off-balance-sheet hedging. On-balance-sheet hedging involves making changes in the on-balance-sheet assets and liabilities to protect FI profits from FX risk. Off-balance-sheet hedging involves no on-balance-sheet changes but rather involves taking a position in forward or other derivative securities to hedge FX risk.

On-Balance-Sheet Hedging.   The following example illustrates how an FI manager can control FX exposure by making changes on the balance sheet.

Example 9–3   Hedging on the Balance Sheet

Suppose that instead of funding the $100 million investment in 15 percent British loans with U.S. CDs, the FI manager funds the British loans with $100 million equivalent one-year pound sterling CDs at a rate of 11 percent. Now the balance sheet of the FI would be as follows:

Assets	Liabilities
$100 million	$100 million
U.S. loans (9%)	U.S. CDs (8%)
$100 million	$100 million
U.K. loans (15%)	U.K. CDs (11%)
(loans made in sterling)	(deposits raised in sterling)

In this situation, the FI has both a matched maturity and foreign currency asset–liability book. We might now consider the FI's profitability or spreads between the return on assets and cost of funds under two scenarios: first, when the pound depreciates in value against the dollar over the year from $1.60/£1 to $1.45/£1, and second, when the pound appreciates in value during the year from $1.60/£1 to $1.70/£1.

1. The Depreciating Pound. When the pound falls in value to $1.45/£1, the return on the British loan portfolio is 4.22 percent. Consider what happens to the cost of $100 million in pound liabilities in dollar terms:

1. At the beginning of the year, the FI borrows $100 million equivalent in sterling CDs for one year at a promised interest rate of 11 percent. At an exchange rate of $1.60/£1, this is a sterling equivalent amount of borrowing of $100 million/1.6 = £62.5 million.
2. At the end of the year, the FI must pay the sterling CD holders their principal and interest, £62.5 million (1.11) = £69.375 million.
3. If the pound had depreciated to $1.45/£1 over the year, the repayment in dollar terms would be $100.59 million (= £69.375 million times $1.45/£1), or a dollar cost of funds of 0.59 percent.

Thus, at the end of the year, the following occurs:
Average return on assets:

$$(0.5)(0.9) + (0.5)(.0422) = .0661 = 6.61\%$$
U.S. asset return + U.K. asset return = Overall return

Average cost of funds:

$$(0.5)(.08) + (0.5)(.0059) = .04295 = 4.295\%$$
U.S. cost of funds + U.K. cost of funds = Overall cost

Net return:

$$\text{Average return on assets} - \text{Average cost of funds}$$
$$6.61\% - 4.295\% = 2.315\%$$

2. The Appreciating Pound. When the pound appreciates over the year from $1.60/£1 to $1.70/£1, the return on British loans equals 22.188 percent. Now consider the dollar cost of British one-year CDs at the end of the year when the U.S. FI must pay the principal and interest to the CD holder:

$$£69.375 \text{ million} \times \$1.70/£1 = \$117.9375 \text{ million}$$

or a dollar cost of funds of 17.9375 percent. Thus, at the end of the year:
Average return on assets:

$$(0.5)(.09) + (0.5)(.22188) = .15594 \text{ or } 15.594\%$$

Average cost of funds:

$$(0.5)(.08) + (0.5)(.179375) = .12969 \text{ or } 12.969\%$$

Net return:

$$15.594\% - 12.969\% = 2.625\%$$

Thus, by directly matching its foreign asset and liability book, an FI can lock in a positive return or profit spread whichever direction exchange rates change over the investment period. For example, even if domestic U.S. banking is a relatively low-profit activity (i.e., there is a low spread between the return on assets and the cost of funds), the FI could be very profitable overall. Specifically, it could lock in a large positive spread—if it exists—between deposit rates and loan rates in foreign markets. In our example, a 4 percent positive spread occurred between British one-year loan rates and deposit rates compared to only a 1 percent spread domestically.

Note that for such imbalances in domestic spreads and foreign spreads to continue over long periods of time, financial service firms would have to face significant barriers to entry in foreign markets. Specifically, if real and financial capital is free to move, FIs would increasingly withdraw from the U.S. market and reorient their operations toward the United Kingdom. Reduced competition would widen loan deposit interest spreads in the United States, and increased competition would contract U.K. spreads until the profit opportunities from overseas activities disappeared.

Hedging with Forwards.   Instead of matching its $100 million foreign asset position with $100 million of foreign liabilities, the FI might have chosen to remain unhedged on the balance sheet. Instead, as a lower cost alternative, it could hedge by taking a position in the forward or other derivative markets for foreign currencies—for example, the one-year forward market for selling sterling for dollars. Any forward position taken would not appear on the balance sheet; it would appear as a contingent off-balance-sheet claim, which we describe as an item below the bottom line in Chapter 13. The role of the forward FX contract is to offset the uncertainty regarding the future spot rate on sterling at the end of the one-year investment horizon. Instead of waiting until the end of the year to transfer sterling back into dollars at an unknown spot rate, the FI can enter into a contract to sell forward its *expected* principal and interest earnings on the loan at today's known forward exchange rate for dollars/pounds, with delivery of sterling funds to the buyer of the forward contract taking place at the end of the year. Essentially, by selling the expected proceeds on the sterling loan forward at a known (forward FX) exchange rate today, the FI removes the future spot exchange rate uncertainty and thus the uncertainty relating to investment returns on the British loan.

Example 9–4   Hedging with Forwards

Consider the following transactional steps when the FI hedges its FX risk by immediately selling its expected one-year sterling loan proceeds in the forward FX market:

1. The U.S. FI sells $100 million for pounds at the spot exchange rate today and receives $100 million/1.6 = £62.5 million.
2. The FI then immediately lends the £62.5 million to a British customer at 15 percent for one year.
3. The FI also sells the expected principal and interest proceeds from the sterling loan forward for dollars at today's forward rate for one-year delivery. Let the current forward one-year exchange rate between dollars and pounds stand at $1.55/£ or at a 5 cent discount to the spot rate; as a percentage discount:

$$(\$1.55 - \$1.60)/\$1.6 = -3.125\%$$

This means that the forward buyer of sterling promises to pay:

£62.5 million (1.15) $\times$ \$1.55/£ = £71.875 $\times$ \$1.55/£ = \$111.406 million

to the FI (the forward seller) in one year when the FI delivers the £71.875 million proceeds of the loan to the forward buyer.

4. In one year, the British borrower repays the loan to the FI plus interest in sterling (£71.875 million).
5. The FI delivers the £71.875 million to the buyer of the one-year forward contract and receives the promised $111.406 million.

Barring the sterling borrower's default on the loan or the pound forward buyer's reneging on the forward contract, the FI knows from the very beginning of the investment period that it has locked in a guaranteed return on the British loan of:

$$\frac{\$111.406m. - \$100m.}{\$100m.} = .11406 = 11.406\%$$

Specifically, this return is fully hedged against any dollar/pound exchange rate changes over the one-year holding period of the loan investment. Given this return on British loans, the overall expected return on the FI's asset portfolio is:

$$(.5)(.09) + (.5)(.11406) = .10203, \text{ or } 10.203\%$$

Since the cost of funds for the FI's $200 million U.S. CDs is an assumed 8 percent, it has been able to lock in a return spread over the year of 2.203 percent regardless of spot exchange rate fluctuations between the initial overseas (loan) investment and repatriation of the foreign loan proceeds one year later.

In the preceding example, it is profitable for the FI to drop domestic U.S. loans and to hedge foreign U.K. loans, since the hedged dollar return on foreign loans of 11.406 percent is so much higher than the 9 percent for domestic loans. As the FI seeks to invest more in British loans, it needs to buy more spot sterling. This drives up the spot price of sterling in dollar terms to more than $1.60/£1. In addition, the FI could sell more sterling forward (the proceeds of these sterling loans) for dollars, driving the forward rate to below $1.55/£1. The outcome would widen the dollar forward–spot exchange rate difference on sterling, making forward hedged sterling investments less attractive than before. This process would continue until the U.S. cost of FI funds just equals the forward hedged return on British loans—that is, the FI could make no further profits by borrowing in U.S. dollars and making forward contract–hedged investments in U.K. loans (see also the discussion below on the interest rate parity theorem).

Role of Financial Institutions in Foreign Exchange Transactions

Foreign exchange market transactions, like corporate bond and money market transactions, are conducted among dealers mainly over the counter (OTC) using telecommunication and computer networks. In the News box 9–2 highlights the impact computer technology has made on the trading process. Foreign exchange traders are generally located in one large trading room at a bank or other FI where they have access to foreign exchange data and telecommunications equipment. Traders generally specialize in just a few currencies.

Since 1982, when Singapore opened its FX market, foreign exchange markets have operated 24 hours a day. When the New York market closes, trading operations in San Francisco are still open; when trading in San Francisco closes, the Hong Kong and Singapore markets open; when Tokyo and Singapore close, the Frankfurt market opens; an hour later, the London market opens; and before these markets close, the New York market reopens.

The nation's largest commercial banks are major players in foreign currency trading and dealing, with large money center banks such as Citigroup and J. P. Morgan also taking significant positions in foreign currency assets and liabilities. Smaller banks maintain lines of credit with these large banks for foreign exchange transactions.

Do You Understand?

1. How technology has changed the way companies manage foreign exchange transactions?

In the News

9-2

The Impact of Bank Technology on Foreign Exchange

How Technological Solutions Help Corporations Handle Global Payment Transactions

The foreign exchange market is the largest market in the world. Money changes hands quickly—through explosive moves or steady flow—for an astounding daily average of over $1 trillion per day. Globalization in the business world has created a marketplace where even small transactions, across borders, trigger the exchange of currency. Foreign exchange has become an integral part of a broad range of business transactions for a steadily increasing number of corporations in most industry sectors. These companies need to exchange currency when they make payments for raw materials, labor, legal services, distribution or when they need to repatriate profits. Such companies, challenged with the task of managing foreign currency transactions efficiently, securely and cost effectively, turn to their bank's foreign exchange trading desk for help. And

Source: *Business Credit,* June 1, 1999, p. 26, by Maria Adler. Printed by permission of the National Association of Credit Management.

to handle the increasing volume, volatility and hectic pace of foreign exchange, banks are developing and deploying sophisticated technology.

Here's an example of how technology has revolutionized the way companies transact their foreign exchange business. Not too many years ago, the accounts payable payments process was labor-intensive and time consuming. Executing deals and providing settlement instructions was both slow and error prone. A company's corporate trader would determine its foreign currency needs based on the numerous payments that the company must make to its various suppliers, and then call one or more banks' foreign exchange trading desks

to obtain rates for the aggregate amounts required in each currency. After the trades were completed over the phone, the corporation would confirm each trade with the bank's foreign exchange back office, and then provide settlement instructions, via fax or phone, which specified where the bank must deliver the currency.

No longer. The process of executing foreign exchange for account payable payments has been redefined by technology, making the process faster and more efficient, reducing errors. Businesses now utilize automated dealing and settlements systems to complete the process entirely over a PC, with no need to phone or fax any of the information to the bank. Businesses implement these systems for use by the accounts payable staff, installing a bank-provided software product on the local area network (LAN) so that it is accessed directly from the staff's desktop. The staff accesses the software to input payment instructions for the foreign currency accounts payable payments.

In the News continued

In this environment, the corporation inputs the detailed delivery instructions, with the ability to view the details on screen. Accounts payable payments repeatedly involve payments that are made to the same vendor on a regular basis. For these respective payments, the delivery instructions are saved as a template, eliminating re-keying each time the vendor needs to be paid.

Further enhancing the process is the software's ability to aggregate payment instructions before a trade is executed to purchase the required currency. For example, if the corporation has the need to execute 10 payments in Japanese yen, it will input the delivery instructions, and the software product will then total the 10 amounts. The corporation can contract one trade for the purchase of total Japanese yen needed to make the payments. It is advantageous for corporations to aggregate currency amounts before trading, because the general consensus regarding the prices quoted by banks to corporate customers is that the larger the amounts, the lower the spread on the rate quote.

The trading process is also accomplished utilizing the software package. Corporations utilize the software product to dial-in to the bank to execute trades. The automated dealing process links the two market players, bank and corporate customer, on a one-to-one basis. This is a fast and safe method because the customer is able to see the deals that they are executing, decreasing the risk of errors in amounts traded. Once the trading step is complete, the payment instructions or settlement instructions that were previously input are transmitted to the bank.

In addition to the automation of a previously cumbersome and manually intensive process, the PC products can offer additional efficiencies through integration with a corporation's general ledger and/or accounts payable system. Once all trading is complete and settlement instructions are sent to the bank, the corporation has an electronic record of each payment with the U.S. dollar equivalent amounts. This data can be easily fed into the corporation's general ledger system, to automatically post each vendor payment to the appropriate general ledger account.

The same data can be used to automatically update the corporation's accounts payable system. The electronic movement of data can also create efficiencies on the input side. For example, a file of payment instructions is exported from the accounts payable system and imported into the PC product for the aggregation of the payment instructions, execution of trades, and the transmission of settlement instructions to the bank . . .

With the advent of the euro and the growing number of foreign exchange transactions, technology will play an increasingly significant role in the process of foreign exchange and foreign currency accounts payable execution—providing corporations a fast, reliable and secure process for executing trades and sending payments overseas.

Table 9–2   Liabilities to and Claims on Foreigners Reported by Banks in the United States, Payable in Foreign Currencies

(millions of dollars, end of period)

Item	1993	1994	1995	1996	1997	1998	1999
Banks' liabilities	$78,259	$89,284	$109,713	$103,383	$117,524	$101,125	$97,751
Banks' claims	62,017	60,689	74,016	66,018	83,038	74,013	67,864
Deposits	20,993	19,661	22,696	22,467	28,661	41,846	41,895
Other claims	41,024	41,028	51,320	43,551	54,377	32,167	25,969
Claims of banks' domestic customers*	12,854	10,878	6,145	10,978	8,191	29,975	23,474

Note: Data on claims exclude foreign currencies held by U.S. monetary authorities.

*Assets owned by customers of the reporting bank located in the United States that represents claims on foreigners held by reporting banks for the accounts of the domestic customers.

Source: *Federal Reserve Bulletin*, Table 3.16, various issues. *www.bog.frb.fed.us/*

Table 9–3   Monthly U.S. Bank Positions in Foreign Currencies and Foreign Assets and Liabilities, September 1999

(in currency of denomination)

	(1) Assets	(2) Liabilities	(3) FX Bought*	(4) FX Sold*	(5) Net Position†
Canadian dollars (millions)	61,649	57,989	331,433	329,368	5,725
German marks (millions)	13,875	15,053	47,516	52,399	−6,061
Japanese yen (billions)	28,834	26,540	178,117	181,879	−1,468
Swiss francs (millions)	27,387	29,867	471,174	451,434	17,260
British pounds (millions)	93,162	93,517	546,347	527,938	18,054

*Includes spot, future, and forward contracts.

†Net position = Assets − Liabilities + FX bought − FX sold

Source: *Treasury Bulletin*, December 1999, pp. 99–107. *www.ustreas.gov/*

Table 9–2 lists the outstanding dollar value of U.S. banks' foreign assets and liabilities for the period 1993 to June 1999. The June 1999 figure for foreign assets was $67.9 billion, with foreign liabilities of $97.8 billion.

Table 9–3 gives the categories of foreign currency positions (or investments) of all U.S. banks in five major currencies. Columns 1 and 2 of Table 9–3 refer to the assets and liabilities denominated in foreign currencies that are held in the portfolios of U.S. banks. Columns 3 and 4 refer to foreign currency trading activities (the spot and forward foreign exchange contracts bought—a long position—and sold—a short position—in each major currency). Foreign currency trading dominates direct portfolio investments. Even though the aggregate trading positions appear very large—for example, U.S. banks bought 178,117 billion yen—their overall or net exposure positions can be relatively small (e.g., the net position in yen was −1,468 billion yen).

A financial institution's overall net foreign exchange (FX) exposure in any given currency can be measured by its net book or position exposure, which is measured in column 5 of Table 9–3 as

$$\text{Net exposure}_i = (\text{FX assets}_i - \text{FX liabilities}_i) + (\text{FX bought}_i - \text{FX sold}_i)$$
$$= \text{Net foreign assets}_i + \text{Net FX bought}_i$$

where

$$i = i\text{th country's currency}$$

net exposure

A financial institution's overall foreign exchange exposure in any given currency.

net long (short) in a currency

A position of holding more (fewer) assets than liabilities in a given currency.

Clearly, a financial institution could match its foreign currency assets to its liabilities in a given currency and match buys and sells in its trading book in that foreign currency to reduce its foreign exchange net exposure to zero and thus avoid foreign exchange risk. It could also offset an imbalance in its foreign asset–liability portfolio by an opposing imbalance in its trading book so that its **net exposure** position in that currency would also be zero.

Notice in Table 9–3 that U.S. banks' net foreign exchange exposures in September 1999 varied across currencies: They carried a positive net exposure position in Canadian dollars, Swiss francs, and British pounds, while they had a negative net exposure position in Japanese yen and German marks. A *positive* net exposure position implies that a U.S. financial institution is overall **net long in a currency** (i.e., the financial institution has purchased more foreign currency than it has sold) and faces the risk that the foreign currency will fall in value against the U.S. dollar, the domestic currency. A *negative* net exposure position implies that a U.S. financial institution is **net short** (i.e., the financial institution has sold more foreign currency than it has purchased) in a foreign currency and faces the risk that the foreign currency could rise in value against the dollar. Thus, failure to maintain a fully balanced position in any given currency exposes a U.S. financial institution to fluctuations in the foreign exchange rate of that currency against the dollar. Indeed, the greater the volatility of foreign exchange rates given any net exposure position, the greater the fluctuations in value of a financial institution's foreign exchange portfolio (see Chapter 20, where we discuss market risk).

We have given the foreign exchange exposures for U.S. banks only, but most large nonbank financial institutions also have some foreign exchange exposure either through asset-liability holdings or currency trading. The absolute sizes of these exposures are smaller than for major U.S. money center banks. The reasons for this are threefold: smaller asset sizes, prudent person concerns,[6] and regulations.[7] See Figure 9–3 for foreign investments by U.S. pension fund companies from 1997 to 1999. During the actual period reported, U.S. pension funds invested from 12 to 28 percent of their asset portfolios in foreign securities. Notice the large drop in U.S. pension fund holdings of Japanese securities as a result of the 1997 Asian crisis. These foreign securities were replaced with those of various European countries that were relatively unaffected by the Asian crisis.

The levels of claims in foreign currencies and positions in foreign currencies held by financial institutions have increased in recent years, but the level of foreign currency trading has decreased. For example, in the United Kingdom, the number of foreign exchange traders decreased by 12.5 percent (from 32,000 to 28,000 traders) during the 1990s. Investment bank mergers have reduced the number of computer terminals and thus the number of traders. Further, the increased use of technology links worldwide has increased the efficiency of each foreign exchange trader, reducing the need for as many traders. Finally, reduced volatility in European country foreign exchange rates in the 1990s and the movement toward a single currency in Europe (by 2002) as part of the 1999 European Monetary Union (EMU) have reduced the need for foreign exchange trading with these countries and thus, traders. For example, with the Euro in place, cash flows from subsidiaries based in one European country can be put directly into the accounts of the parent company without complicated foreign exchange adjustments. As a result, as the EMU is fully implemented, in 2002, large multinational companies will likely reduce the number of their banking relationships and foreign exchange transactions.

---

6. *Prudent person concerns*, which require financial institutions to adhere to investment and lending policies, standards, and procedures that a reasonable and prudent person would apply with respect to a portfolio of investments and loans to avoid undue risk of loss and obtain a reasonable return, are especially important for pension funds.

7. For example, New York State restricts foreign asset holdings of New York–based life insurance companies to less than 10 percent of their assets.

Figure 9–3 U.S. Pension Fund International Investments
(in billions of dollars)

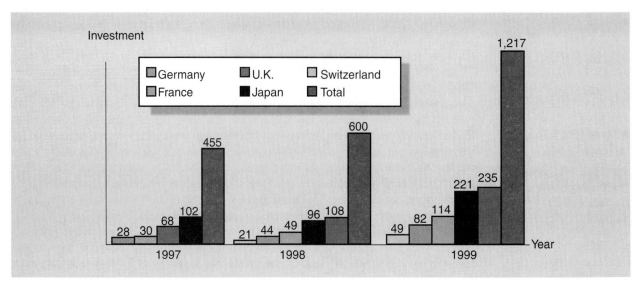

Source: *Pension and Investments*, various issues.

A financial institution's position in the foreign exchange markets generally reflects four trading activities:

1. The purchase and sale of foreign currencies to allow customers to partake in and complete international commercial trade transactions.
2. The purchase and sale of foreign currencies to allow customers (or the financial institution itself) to take positions in foreign real and financial investments.
3. The purchase and sale of foreign currencies for hedging purposes to offset customer (or financial institution) exposure in any given currency.
4. The purchase and sale of foreign currencies for speculative purposes through forecasting or anticipating future movements in foreign exchange rates.

open position

An unhedged position in a particular currency.

In the first two activities, the financial institution normally acts as an *agent* on behalf of its customers for a fee but does not assume the foreign exchange risk itself. Citigroup is the dominant supplier of foreign exchange trading to retail customers in the United States. As of December 31, 1998, the aggregate value of Citigroup's principal amounts of foreign exchange contracts totaled $2,434 billion. In the third activity, the financial institution acts defensively as a hedger to reduce foreign exchange exposure. For example, it may take a short (sell) position in the foreign exchange of a country to offset a long (buy) position in the foreign exchange of that same country. Thus, foreign exchange risk exposure essentially relates to **open** (or speculative) **positions** taken by the FI, the fourth activity. A financial institution usually creates open positions by taking an unhedged position in a foreign currency in its foreign exchange trading with other financial institutions. The Federal Reserve estimates that 200 financial institutions are active market makers in foreign currencies in the U.S. foreign exchange market, with about 30 commercial and investment banks making a market in the five most important currencies. Financial institutions can make speculative trades directly with other financial institutions or arrange them through specialist foreign exchange brokers. The Federal Reserve Bank of New York estimates that approximately 44 percent of speculative or open position trades are accomplished through specialized brokers who receive a fee for arranging trades between financial institutions. Speculative trades can be instituted through a variety of foreign exchange instruments. Spot currency trades are the most common, with financial institutions seeking to make a profit on the difference between buy and sell prices (i.e., movements in the purchase and sale prices over time). However, financial institutions can also take speculative positions in foreign exchange forward contracts, futures, and options (see Chapter 10).

6   Interaction of Interest Rates, Inflation, and Exchange Rates

As global financial markets have become increasingly interlinked, so have interest rates, inflation, and foreign exchange rates. For example, higher domestic interest rates may attract foreign financial investment and impact the value of the domestic currency. In this section, we look at the effect that inflation (or the change in the price level of a given set of goods and services, defined earlier, in Chapter 2, as the variable *IP*) in one country has on its foreign currency exchange rates—purchasing power parity (PPP). We also examine the links between domestic and foreign interest rates and spot and forward foreign exchange rates—interest rate parity (IRP).

Purchasing Power Parity

One factor affecting a country's foreign currency exchange rate with another country is the relative inflation rate in each country (which, as shown below, is directly related to the relative interest rates in these countries). Specifically, from Chapter 2, we showed that:

$$i_{US} = IP_{US} + RIR_{US}$$

and

$$i_F = IP_F + RIR_F$$

where

$$
\begin{aligned}
i_{US} &= \text{Interest rate in the United States} \\
i_F &= \text{Interest rate in France} \\
IP_{US} &= \text{Inflation rate in the United States} \\
IP_F &= \text{Inflation rate in France} \\
RIR_{US} &= \text{Real rate of interest in the United States} \\
RIR_F &= \text{Real rate of interest in France}
\end{aligned}
$$

Assuming real rates of interest (or rates of time preference) are equal across countries:

$$RIR_{US} = RIR_F$$

then:

$$i_{US} - i_F = IP_{US} - IP_F$$

The (nominal) interest rate spread between the United States and France reflects the difference in inflation rates between the two countries.

As relative inflation rates (and interest rates) change, foreign currency exchange rates should adjust to account for relative differences in the price levels (inflation rates) between the two countries. One theory that explains how this adjustment takes place is the theory of **purchasing power parity (PPP)**. According to PPP, foreign currency exchange rates between two countries adjust to reflect changes in each country's price levels (or inflation rates and implicitly interest rates) as consumers and importers switch their demands for goods from relatively high inflation (interest) rate countries to low inflation (interest) rate countries.

purchasing power parity (PPP)

The theory explaining the change in foreign currency exchange rates as inflation rates in the countries change.

Example 9–5   Application of Purchasing Power Parity

Suppose that the current spot exchange rate of U.S. dollars for Russian rubles, $S_{US/R}$, is .17 (i.e., 0.17 dollars, or 17 cents, buys 1 ruble). The price of the Russian-produced goods increases by 10 percent (i.e., inflation in Russia, IP_R, is 10 percent) and the U.S. price index increases by 4 percent (i.e., inflation in the United States, IP_{US}, is 4 percent). According to PPP, the 10 percent rise in the price of Russian goods combined with the 4 percent rise in the price of U.S. goods results in a depreciation of the Russian ruble (by 6 percent). Specifically, the exchange rate of Russian rubles to U.S. dollars should fall, so that:[8]

$$\begin{array}{c} \text{U.S.} \\ \text{inflation rate} \end{array} - \begin{array}{c} \text{Russian} \\ \text{inflation rate} \end{array} = \dfrac{\begin{array}{c}\text{Change in spot exchange rate} \\ \text{of Russian rubles for U.S. dollars}\end{array}}{\begin{array}{c}\text{Initial spot exchange rate} \\ \text{of Russian rubles for U.S. dollars}\end{array}}$$

or:

$$IP_{US} - IP_R = \Delta S_{US/R}/S_{US/R}$$

Also, assuming:

$$RIR_{US} = RIR_R$$
$$i_{US} - i_R = IP_{US} - IP_R = \Delta S_{US/R}/S_{US/R}$$

Plugging in the inflation and exchange rates, we get:

$$.04 - .10 = \Delta S_{US/R}/S_{US/R} = \Delta S_{US/R}/.17$$

or:

$$-.06 = \Delta S_{US/R}/.17$$

and:

$$\Delta S_{US/R} = -(.06) \times .17 = -.0102$$

Thus, it costs 1.02 cents less to buy a ruble (or it costs 15.98 cents [17 cents − 1.02 cents], or .1598 of $1, to buy a ruble). The Russian ruble depreciates in value by 6 percent against the U.S. dollar.[9]

Interest Rate Parity

We discussed above that foreign exchange spot market risk can be reduced by entering into forward foreign exchange contracts. Table 9–1 lists foreign exchange rates on January 18, 2000. Notice that spot rates and forward rates differ. For example, the spot exchange rate between the Canadian dollar and U.S. dollar was .6898 on January 18, 2000, meaning that one Canadian dollar could be exchanged today for .6898 U.S. dollars. The six-month forward rate between the two currencies on January 18, 2000, however, was .6923. This forward exchange rate is determined by the spot exchange rate and the interest rate differential between the two countries.

interest rate parity theorem (IRPT)

The theory that the domestic interest rate should equal the foreign interest rate minus the expected appreciation of the domestic currency.

The relationship that links spot exchange rates, interest rates, and forward exchange rates is described as the **interest rate parity theorem (IRPT)**. Intuitively, the IRPT implies that, by hedging in the forward exchange rate market, an investor realizes the same returns, whether investing domestically or in a foreign country—that is, the hedged dollar return on foreign investments just equals the return on domestic investments. Mathematically, the IRPT can be expressed as:

$$1 + i_{USt} = (1/S_t) \times (1 + i_{UKt}) \times F_t$$
Return on U.S. investment = Hedged return on foreign (U.K.) investment

where

$1 + i_{USt} = 1$ plus the interest rate on a U.S. investment maturing at time t

---

8. This is the relative version of the PPP theorem. There are other versions of the theory (such as absolute PPP and the law of one price); however, the version shown here is the one most commonly used.

9. A 6 percent fall in the ruble's value translates into a new exchange rate of .1598 dollars per ruble if the original exchange rate between dollars and rubles was .17.

$1 + i_{UKt}$ = 1 plus the interest rate on a U.K. investment maturing at time t
S_t = \$/£ spot exchange rate at time t
F_t = \$/£ forward exchange rate at time t

Rearranging, the IRPT can be expressed as:

$$\frac{i_{USt} - i_{UKt}}{1 + i_{UKt}} = \frac{F_t - S_t}{S_t}$$

Example 9–6 An Example of the Interest Rate Parity Theorem at Work

Suppose that on January 18, 2000, a U.S. citizen has excess funds available to invest in either U.S. or British bank time deposits. It is assumed that both types of deposits are credit or default risk free and that the investment horizon is one month. The interest rate available on British pound time deposits, i_{UK}, is 4.5 percent annually. The spot exchange rate of U.S. dollars for British pounds on January 18, 2000 (from Table 9–1) is \$1.6377/£, and the one-month forward rate is \$1.6378/£. According to the IRPT, the interest rate on comparable U.S. time deposits should be:

$$1 + i_{US} = (1/1.6377) \times (1 + .045) \times 1.6378 = 1.045064$$

or 4.5064 percent. We can rearrange this relationship as shown above as:

$$\frac{.045064 - .045}{1 + .045} = \frac{1.6378 - 1.6377}{1.6377}$$

$$.000061 = .000061$$

Thus, the discounted spread between domestic and foreign interest rates is, in equilibrium, equal to the percentage spread between forward and spot exchange rates.

Suppose that, in the preceding example, the annual rate on U.S. time deposits was 4.60 percent (rather than 4.5064 percent). In this case, it would be profitable for the investor to put any excess funds into U.S. rather than U.K. time deposits. In fact, a risk-free (or arbitrage) investment opportunity now exists and will result in a flow of funds out of U.K. time deposits into U.S. time deposits. According to the IRPT, this flow of funds would quickly drive up the U.S. dollar for British pound spot exchange rate until the potential risk-free profit opportunities from investment in U.S. deposits is eliminated. Thus, any arbitrage opportunity should be small and fleeting.[10] Any long-term violations of this relationship are likely to occur only if major imperfections exist in international deposit markets, including barriers to cross-border financial flows.

Balance of Payment Accounts

Transactions between citizens of one country (e.g., the U.S.) with other countries are summarized in the **balance of payment accounts** of that country. Bal-

balance of payment accounts

Summary of all transactions between citizens of two countries.

10. In addition, as funds flowed out of U.K. time deposits, banks in the United Kingdom would have an incentive to raise interest rates. By comparison, as funds flowed into U.S. banks, the banks would have the incentive to lower interest rates. Further, as funds flowed to the United States, British investors would sell dollars forward for pounds (in addition to buying more spot dollars). While the purchase of spot dollars leads to an appreciation in the spot dollar rate, the sale of dollars forward for pounds will lead to a depreciation in the forward rate (F_t). These two effects, combined with the effect on the spot rate of \$/£, would once again equate the returns on domestic and foreign investments.

Table 9–4   U.S. Balance of Payment Accounts, 1999

(in millions of dollars)

Current Accounts

1.	Exports of goods, services, and income		$312,189
2.	Goods, adjusted, excluding military	$173,578	
3.	Services	69,048	
4.	Income receipts on U.S. assets abroad	69,563	
5.	Imports of goods, services, and income		−390,934
6.	Goods, adjusted, excluding military	−265,723	
7.	Services	−50,728	
8.	Income payments on foreign assets in the United States.	−74,483	
9.	Unilateral transfers, net		−11,204
10.	Total current accounts		−$ 89,949
11.	Balance on goods (lines 2 and 6).		−92,145
12.	Balance on services (lines 3 and 7)		18,320
13.	Balance on investment income (lines 4 and 8)		−4,920

Capital Accounts

14.	U.S. assets abroad, net (increase/capital outflow (−))		−$101,483
15.	U.S. official reserve assets, net	$ 1,950	
16.	U.S. government assets, other than official reserve assets, net	−673	
17.	U.S. private assets, net.	−102,760	
18.	Foreign assets in the United States, net (increase/capital inflow (+))		207,319
19.	Foreign official assets in the United States, net.	12,272	
20.	Other foreign assets in the United States, net	195,047	
21.	Statistical discrepancy (sum of above items with sign reversed)		−15,887
22.	Total capital accounts		$ 89,949
23.	Sum of current and capital accounts		$ 0

Source: U.S. Department of Commerce, Bureau of Economic Analysis, December 1999. *www.bea.doc.gov/*

ance of payment accounts use double-entry accounting methods such that debit entries must be matched with offsetting credit entries—the balance of payments must always balance. Table 9–4 shows the U.S. balance of payment accounts in the third quarter of 1999. Debits are designated as negative account balances, credits are designated as positive account balances. The balance of payments is divided into two accounts: (1) a current account and (2) a capital account. As will be explained below, the sum of these two accounts must always be zero—a current account surplus (deficit) must be exactly offset by a capital account deficit (surplus). We first describe these two accounts, and then we explain why the two account balances must offset each other.

Current Account

current account

The section of the balance of payment table that summarizes foreign trade in goods and services, net investment income, and gifts, grants, or aid given to other countries.

The **current account** in the balance of payments table summarizes foreign trade in goods and services, net investment income, and gifts, grants, or aid given to other countries. Lines 1–13 in Table 9–4 show the current accounts for the United States. Notice from lines 2 plus 6 that the United States has a substantial trade deficit in goods, resulting from the import of more foreign goods relative to the export of domestic goods, equal to $92.145 billion in 1999. This deficit has increased in the 1990s. For example, the deficit in the trade of foreign goods was just $19.350 billion in 1991. This is mainly due to the relatively high economic growth rate in the United States compared to the Japanese and European growth rates. As an economy grows relative to other countries, the demand for imports increases relative to the amount exported. In particular, goods that might have been exported get "consumed" at home.

In contrast, from lines 3 plus 7 in Table 9–4, the United States ran a surplus in the services component of the balance of payments current account, $18.320 billion in 1999 versus $13.830 billion in 1991. The U.S. service sector (e.g., financial services, transportation fares, defense expenditures) generally generates a substantial positive balance. Thus, these services have a positive impact on the overall U.S. balance of payment account.

Net investment income, lines 4 plus 8 in Table 9–4, of U.S. citizens contributed negatively, $4.920 billion in 1999, to the balance of payments. Prior to the 1990s, net investment income was generally positive. However, in the late 1980s, the U.S. sold significant amounts of assets (e.g., U.S. government bonds) to finance a large government deficit and deficit in the trade of goods. The interest payments the U.S. must make on these assets has caused the net investment income to contribute negatively to the current account of the balance of payments.[11]

Unilateral transfers are gifts and foreign aid that require no repayment, $11.240 billion in 1999. Because of its relatively large participation in overseas aid programs, the U.S. generally runs a negative balance for unilateral transfers. Thus, overall the U.S. current account had a deficit balance of −$89.949 billion.

Capital Accounts

capital accounts

The section of the balance of payment table that summarizes capital flows into and out of a country.

Capital accounts measure investment capital (principal) flows into and out of a country. A positive balance in these accounts indicates that foreign investors purchased more U.S. assets than U.S. investors purchased foreign assets, creating a capital inflow into the United States. A negative balance in these accounts indicates that U.S. investors purchased more foreign assets than foreign investors purchased U.S. assets, creating a capital outflow on capital accounts. U.S. asset purchases abroad (e.g., a U.S. investor's purchase of foreign stock) include: (1) private asset purchases ($102.760 billion in 1999, line 17 in Table 9–4), and (2) government asset purchases, e.g., SDRs (Special Drawing Rights[12]) or foreign currencies (reserve currencies discussed in Chapter 4) ($1.277 billion in 1999, lines 15 plus 16 in Table 9–4). Foreign purchases of assets in the United States (e.g., Japanese investors buying U.S. Treasury securities) include foreign government assets in the United States, $12.272 billion in 1999 (line 19 in Table 9–4), and other foreign assets in the United States, $195.047 billion in 1999 (line 20 in Table 9–4). The high level of economic growth in the United States in the 1990s has resulted in the United States being an attractive place for foreigners to invest. Other foreign assets in the United States were just $41.910 billion in 1991.

As can be seen in Table 9–4, the capital account surplus is $89.949 billion, which exactly offsets the current account deficit (−$89.949 billion). Thus, overall the balance of payments balances (i.e., line 23 in Table 9–4) must equal $0. An intuitive reason or way to understand why this occurs is to think of the analogy between a country and a single consumer. When an individual spends more on goods and services than he or she earns (runs a current account deficit), he or she must either borrow to finance that deficit or sell some of his or her financial assets. What is true for an individual is also true for a country. In particular, excessive net consumption by a country on foreign goods and services (such that its imports exceed exports) has to be financed by borrowing from abroad or selling off that country's assets (e.g., sale of domestic equities

---

11. However, the recent dramatic improvement in the U.S. budget deficit position suggests that net investment income may well become positive again in the near future.

12. SDRs are used to transfer currencies to central banks through the International Monetary Fund in exchange for domestic currency.

Do You Understand?

1. What balance of payment accounts are?
2. Why the U.S. runs a trade deficit in foreign goods imports relative to domestic goods exports?
3. What balance of payment current accounts and capital accounts are?

and real estate to foreigners such as the Japanese). In other words, sufficient net capital inflows into a country are needed to finance the gap that a country is running in its excessive consumption of foreign goods and services. Thus, in the United States, we have run persistent current account deficits in the 1990s (imported more than we have exported) financed by both borrowing from abroad and selling domestic assets to foreigners (i.e., running a capital account surplus reflected by net capital inflows).

Summary

In this chapter, we reviewed foreign exchange markets. Foreign exchange markets have grown to be among the largest of the world's financial markets. We reviewed the trading process in this market, paying particular attention to the role played by financial institutions in the operations of the foreign exchange market. We concluded the chapter with a look at balance of payment accounts, which summarize the trading activity of one country with all others.

Questions

1. How did the Bretton Woods and the Smithsonian Agreements affect the ability of foreign exchange rates to float freely? How did the elimination of exchange boundaries in 1973 affect the ability of foreign exchange rates to float freely?

2. Refer to Table 9–1.
   a. What was the spot exchange rate of Canadian dollars for U.S. dollars on January 18, 2000?
   b. What was the six-month forward exchange rate of Canadian dollars for U.S. dollars on January 18, 2000?
   c. What was the three-month forward exchange rate of U.S. dollars for Swiss francs on January 17, 2000?

3. Refer to Table 9–1.
   a. On December 18, 1999, you purchased a deutsche mark–denominated CD by converting $1 million to deutsche marks at a rate of 1.9382 deutsche marks for U.S. dollars. It is now January 18, 2000. Has the U.S. dollar appreciated or depreciated in value relative to the deutsche mark?
   b. Using the information in part (a), what is your gain or loss on the investment in the CD? Assume no interest has been paid on the CD.

4. On January 18, 2000, you convert $500,000 U.S. dollars to Japanese yen in the spot foreign exchange market and purchase a 1-month forward contract to convert yen into dollars. How much will you receive in U.S. dollars at the end of the month? Use the data in Table 9–1 for this problem.

5. Sun Bank USA has purchased a 16 million one-year deutsche mark loan that pays 12% interest annually. The spot rate of U.S. dollars for deutsche marks is 0.625. It has funded this loan by accepting a British pound (BP)–denominated deposit for the equivalent amount and maturity at an annual rate of 10%. The current spot rate of U.S. dollars for British pounds is 1.60.
   a. What is the net interest income earned in dollars on this one-year transaction if the spot rate of U.S. dollars for deutsche marks and U.S. dollars for BPs at the end of the year are 0.588 and 1.848, respectively?
   b. What should the spot rate of U.S. dollars for BPs be at the end of the year in order for the bank to earn a net interest income of $200,000 (disregarding any change in principal values)?

6. North Bank has been borrowing in the U.S. markets and lending abroad, thereby incurring foreign exchange risk. In a recent transaction, it issued a one-year $2 million CD at 6% and is planning to fund a loan in deutsche marks at 8% for a 2 percent expected spread. The spot rate of deutsche marks for U.S. dollars is 1.45.
   a. However, new information now indicates that the deutsche mark will depreciate such that the spot rate of deutsche marks for U.S. dollars is 1.47 by year end. What should the bank charge on the loan in order to maintain the 2% spread?
   b. The bank has an opportunity to hedge using one-year forward contracts at 1.46 deutsche marks for U.S. dollars. What is the spread if the bank hedges its forward foreign exchange exposure?

    c. How should the loan rates be increased to maintain the 2% spread if the bank intends to hedge its exposure using the forward rates?

7. How are foreign exchange markets open 24 hours per day?

8. Citibank holds $23 million in foreign exchange assets and $18 million in foreign exchange liabilities. Citibank also conducted foreign currency trading activity in which it bought $5 million in foreign exchange contracts and sold $12 million in foreign exchange contracts.

    a. What is Citibank's net foreign assets?

    b. What is Citibank's net foreign exchange bought?

    c. What is Citibank's net foreign exposure?

9. What are the major foreign exchange trading activities performed by financial institutions?

10. If the interest rate in the United Kingdom is 8 percent, the interest rate in the United States is 10 percent, the spot exchange rate is $1.75/£, and interest rate parity holds, what must be the one-year forward exchange rate?

11. Suppose all of the conditions in Question 10 hold except that the forward rate of exchange is also $1.75/£. How could an investor take advantage of this situation?

12. If a bundle of goods in Japan costs 4,000,000 yen while the same goods and services cost $40,000 in the United States, what is the current exchange rate of U.S. dollars for yen? If, over the next year, inflation is 6 percent in Japan and 10 percent in the United States, what will the goods cost next year? Will the dollar depreciate or appreciate relative to the yen over this time period?

13. What is the implication for cross-border trades if it can be shown that interest rate parity is maintained consistently across different markets and different currencies?

14. What are some reasons why interest rate parity may not hold in spite of the economic forces that should ensure the equilibrium relationship?

15. One form of the interest rate parity equation appears as $1 + r_{ust} = (1/S_t) \times (1 + r_{ukt}) \times F_t$ where both the spot and forward rates are in terms of dollars for pounds or direct exchange rates. How would the equation be written if the exchange rates were indirect—that is, pounds for dollars?

16. Assume that annual interest rates are 8 percent in the United States and 4 percent in Germany. An FI can borrow (by issuing CDs) or lend (by purchasing CDs) at these rates. The spot rate is $0.60/DM.

    a. If the forward rate is $0.64/DM, how could the bank arbitrage using a sum of $1 million? What is the spread earned?

    b. At what forward rate is this arbitrage eliminated?

17. Why has the United States held a trade deficit for most of the 1990s? Make sure you distinguish between the import versus export of goods and services.

18. The following table lists balance of payment current accounts for country A.

Current Accounts

1. Exports of goods, services, and income		$168,953
2. Goods, adjusted, excluding military	$92,543	
3. Services	45,689	
4. Income receipts on U.S. assets abroad	30,721	
5. Imports of goods, services, and income		−150,936
6. Goods, adjusted, excluding military	−84,107	
7. Services	−31,689	
8. Income payments on foreign assets in the United States	−35,140	
9. Unilateral transfers, net		−9,421

    a. What is country A's total current accounts?

    b. What is country A's balance on goods?

    c. What is country A's balance on services?

    d. What is country A's balance on investment income?

19. Why must the current account balance equal the value of the capital account balance (in opposite sign)?

20. Go to the U.S. Treasury website and update the data in Table 9–3.

21. Go to the U.S. Department of Commerce website and find the most recent balance of payment data for the United States.

chapter ten

Derivative Securities Markets

Chapter Navigator

1. What are forward and future contracts?

2. How is a futures transaction conducted?

3. What information can be found in a futures quote?

4. What are option contracts?

5. What information can be found in an options quote?

6. Who are the main regulators of futures and options markets?

7. What is an interest rate swap?

8. What are caps, floors, and collars?

Derivative Securities: Chapter Overview

A **derivative security** is a financial security whose payoff is linked to another, previously issued security. Derivative securities generally involve an agreement between two parties to exchange a standard quantity of an asset or cash flow at a predetermined price and at a specified date in the future. As the value of the underlying security to be exchanged changes, the value of the derivative security changes. A securitized asset such as a mortgage-backed security (see Chapter 7) is a derivative security in that its value is based on the value of an underlying security (e.g., a mortgage). Option contracts are also derivatives since their value depends on the price of some underlying security (e.g., a stock) relative to a reference (or strike) price. **Derivative securities markets** are the markets in which derivative securities trade. While derivative securi-

derivative security

An agreement between two parties to exchange a standard quantity of an asset at a predetermined price at a specified date in the future.

derivative securities markets

The markets in which derivative securities trade.

www.cme.com/

www.bog.fed.frb.us/

www.cbot.com/

ties have been in existence for centuries, the growth in derivative securities markets occurred mainly in the 1970s, 1980s, and 1990s. As major markets, therefore, the derivative securities markets are the newest of the financial security markets.

The first of the modern wave of derivatives to trade were foreign currency futures contracts. These contracts were introduced by the International Monetary Market (IMM), a subsidiary of the Chicago Mercantile Exchange (CME), in response to the introduction of floating exchange rates between currencies of different countries following the Smithsonian Agreements of 1971 and 1973 (see Chapter 9).

The second wave of derivative security growth was with interest rate derivative securities. Their growth was mainly in response to increases in the volatility of interest rates in the late 1970s and after, as the Federal Reserve started to target nonborrowed reserves (see Chapter 4) rather than interest rates. Financial institutions such as banks and savings institutions had many rate-sensitive assets and liabilities on their balance sheets. As interest rate volatility increased, the sensitivity of the net worth (equity) of these institutions to interest rate shocks increased as well. In response, the Chicago Board of Trade (CBT) introduced, in the 1970s, numerous short-term and long-term interest rate futures contracts, and in the 1980s, stock index futures and options. Accordingly, financial institutions are the major participants in the derivative securities markets (see In the News box 10–1). Financial institutions can be either users of derivative contracts for hedging (see Chapter 24) or dealers that act as counterparties in trades with customers for a fee. It has been estimated that only 600 U.S. banks use derivatives and that only seven large dealer banks—Bank of America Corp., Bank One Corp., Deutsche Bank (incorporating Bankers Trust), Chase Manhattan Corp., Citigroup Inc., First Union Corp., and J. P. Morgan—account for some 90 percent of the derivatives that user banks hold.[1]

Do You Understand?

1. What the level of derivatives trading by banks in the first quarter of 1999 was?
2. What the concentration of derivatives trading across the banking industry is?

A third wave of derivative security innovations occurred in the 1990s with credit derivatives (e.g., credit forwards, credit risk options, and quality swaps). For example, a credit forward is a forward agreement that hedges against an increase in default risk on a loan (a decline in the credit quality of a borrower) after the loan rate is determined and the loan is issued. In September 1999, the notional value of credit derivatives held by U.S. banks was approximately $234 billion. These derivative securities have become particularly useful for managing credit risk of emerging market countries and credit portfolio risk in general.

In this chapter, we present an overview of the derivative securities markets. We look at the markets for forwards, futures, options, swaps, and some special derivative contracts (caps, floors, and collars). We define the various derivative securities and focus on the markets themselves—their operations and trading processes. In Chapter 24, we describe how these securities can be used to manage and hedge the foreign exchange, interest rate, and credit risks of financial institutions.

Forwards and Futures

To present the essential nature and characteristics of forward and futures contracts and markets, we compare them with spot contracts. We show appropriate time lines for each of the three contracts using a bond as the underlying financial security to the derivative contract in Figure 10–1 and define each in Table 10–1.

Spot Markets

spot contract

An agreement to transact involving the immediate exchange of assets and funds.

A **spot contract** is an agreement between a buyer and a seller at time 0, when the seller of the asset agrees to deliver it immediately and the buyer agrees to pay for that asset

---

1. See Office of the Comptroller of the Currency, "Bank Derivatives Report," First Quarter, July 1999.

In the News

Bank trading revenues spiked 77 percent in the first quarter to a record $3.6 billion, the Office of the Comptroller of the Currency announced Thursday. "That's a big number," said Mike Brosnan, deputy comptroller for risk evaluation. "It would be unrealistic to assume there is going to be a quarter like this repeated on a regular basis" . . .

The notional, or aggregate, amount of derivatives . . . increased 27 percent in the first quarter compared

Source: *American Banker*, June 25, 1999, p. 2, by Barbara A. Rehm.

Industry Trading Revenue Rose 77 Percent in First Quarter, to a Record $3.6 Billion

to the year earlier period. The notional amount of credit derivatives, while still just a sliver of the overall total, jumped 33 percent to a record $191 billion in the first quarter. Banks bought $110.6 billion of credit derivatives, which provide insurance against a decline in a loan's value, and collected fees to provide $80.4 billion of this credit protection. Credit derivatives totaled

$91 billion on March 31, 1998 . . .

Seven banks continued to dominate the derivatives market, with 93 percent of the industry's share of this business. On average, trading revenues contributed to 9.6 percent of gross revenues at these seven banks, up from 5.1 percent in the fourth quarter. But among the seven banks it ranged from J.P. Morgan gaining more than 30.9 percent of its gross revenues from trading to 4 percent at Banc One Corp. Among all banks, derivatives accounted for 3.7 percent of gross revenues, up from 2.1 percent in the fourth quarter.

www.americanbanker. com/

immediately.[2] Thus, the unique feature of a spot market is the immediate and simultaneous exchange of cash for securities, or what is often called *delivery versus payment.* A spot bond quote of $97 for a 20-year maturity bond is the price the buyer must pay the seller, per $100 of face value, for immediate (time 0) delivery of the 20-year bond.

Forward Markets

forward contract

An agreement to transact involving the future exchange of a set amount of assets at a set price.

Forward Contracts.   A **forward contract** is a contractual agreement between a buyer and a seller at time 0 to exchange a prespecified asset for cash at some later date. Market participants take a position in forward contracts because the future (spot) price or interest rate on an asset is uncertain. Rather than risk that the future spot price will move against them—that the asset will become more expensive to buy in the future—forward traders pay a financial institution a fee to arrange a forward contract. Such a contract lets the market participant hedge the risk that future spot prices on an asset will move against him or her by guaranteeing a future price for the asset *today*.

For example, in a three-month forward contract to deliver $100 face value of 10-year bonds, the buyer and seller agree on a price and amount today (time 0), but the

---

2. Technically, physical settlement and delivery may take place one or two days after the contractual spot agreement in bond markets. In equity markets, delivery and cash settlement normally occurs three business days after the spot contract agreement (T+3 settlement).

Figure 10–1 Contract Time Lines

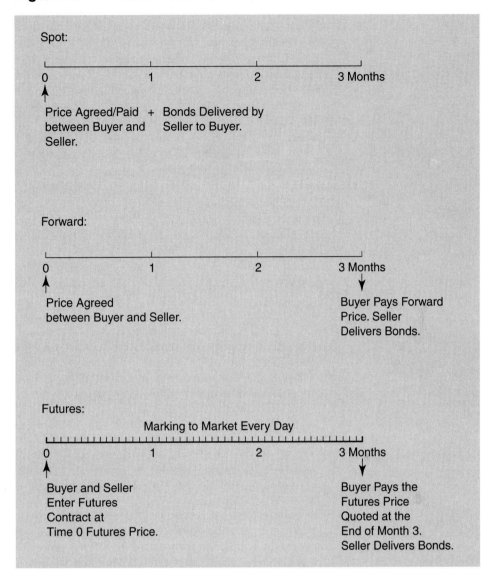

Table 10–1 Spot, Forward, and Futures Contracts

Spot Contract—agreement made between a buyer and a seller at time 0 for the seller to deliver the asset immediately and the buyer to pay for the asset immediately.

Forward Contract—agreement between a buyer and a seller at time 0 to exchange a nonstandardized asset for cash at some future date. The details of the asset and the price to be paid at the forward contract expiration date are set at time 0. The price of the forward contract is fixed over the life of the contract.

Futures Contract—agreement between a buyer and a seller at time 0 to exchange a standardized asset for cash at some future date. Each contract has a standardized expiration, and transactions occur in a centralized market. The price of the futures contract changes daily as the market value of the asset underlying the futures fluctuates.

delivery (or exchange) of the 10-year bond for cash does not occur until three months into the future. If the forward price agreed to at time 0 was $98 per $100 of face value, in three months' time the seller delivers $100 of 10-year bonds and receives $98 from the buyer. This is the price the buyer must pay and the seller must accept no matter what happens to the spot price of 10-year bonds during the three months between the time the contract was entered into and the time the bonds are delivered for payment (i.e., whether the spot price falls to $97 or below or rises to $99 or above).

In Chapter 9, we discussed the market for forward foreign currency exchange contracts, which allows market participants to buy or sell a specified currency for a specified price at a specified date (e.g., one-month, three-month, or six-month contracts are standard). Forward contracts can also be based on a specified interest rate (e.g., LIBOR) rather than a specified asset (called forward rate agreements, or FRAs). The buyer of an FRA agrees to pay the contract rate based on some notional principal amount (e.g., $1 million)—he or she buys the notional amount at the stated interest rate. The seller of an FRA agrees to sell the funds to the buyer at the stated rate. For example, for a three-month FRA written today with a notional value of $1 million and a contract rate of 5.70 percent, the buyer of the FRA agrees to pay 5.70 percent (the current three-month LIBOR rate) to borrow $1 million starting three months from now. The seller of the FRA agrees to lend $1 million to the buyer at 5.70 percent starting three months from now. If interest rates rise in the next three months, the FRA buyer benefits from the FRA. He or she can borrow $1 million at the rate stated on the FRA (5.70 percent) rather than the higher market rate (say, 7 percent).

Forward contracts often involve underlying assets that are nonstandardized, because the terms of each contract are negotiated individually between the buyer and the seller (e.g., a contract between Bank A to buy from Bank B, six months from now, $1 million in 30-year Treasury bonds with a coupon rate of 6.25 percent). As a result, the buyer and seller involved in a forward contract must locate and deal directly with each other in the over-the-counter market to set the terms of the contract rather than transacting the sale in a centralized market (such as a futures market exchange).

Forward Market Operations.   Commercial banks (see Chapter 11) and investment banks and broker–dealers (see Chapter 16) are the major forward market participants, acting as both principals and agents. These financial institutions make a profit on the spread between the price at which they buy and sell the asset underlying the forward contracts.

Each forward contract is originally negotiated between the financial institution and the customer, and therefore the details of each (e.g., price, expiration, size, delivery date) can be unique. As the forward market has grown over the last decade, however, traders have begun making secondary markets in some forward contracts, communicating the buy and sell price on the contracts over computer networks. As of September 1999, U.S. commercial banks held over $8.4 trillion of forward contracts that were listed for trading in the over-the-counter markets. The advent of this secondary market trading has resulted in an increase in the standardization of forward contracts. It has also become increasingly easy to get out of a forward position by taking an offsetting forward position in the secondary market. Secondary market activity in forward contracts has made them more attractive to firms and investors that had previously been reluctant to get locked into a forward contract until expiration. Secondary market activity has also resulted in a situation in which the differences between forward and future contracts have significantly narrowed.

Futures Markets

futures contract

An agreement to transact involving the future exchange of a set amount of assets for a price that is settled daily.

Futures Contracts.   A **futures contract** is normally traded on an organized exchange such as the New York Futures Exchange (NYFE). A futures contract, like a forward contract, is an agreement between a buyer and a seller at time 0 to exchange a standardized, prespecified asset for cash at some later date. Thus, a futures contract is

marked to market

Describes the prices on outstanding futures contracts that are adjusted each day to reflect current futures market conditions.

initial margin

A deposit required on futures trades to ensure that the terms of any futures contract will be met.

maintenance margin

The margin a futures trader must maintain once a futures position is taken. If losses on the customer's futures position occur and the level of the funds in the margin account drop below the maintenance margin, the customer is required to deposit additional funds into his or her margin account, bringing the balance back up to the initial margin.

very similar to a forward contract. The difference relates to the contract's price, which in a forward contract is fixed over the life of the contract (e.g., $98 per $100 of face value for three months to be paid on expiration of the forward contract), whereas a futures contract is **marked to market** daily. This means that the contract's price is adjusted each day as the futures price for the contract changes and the contract approaches expiration. Therefore, actual daily cash settlements occur between the buyer and seller in response to these price changes (this is called marking-to-market). As illustrated in Figure 10-1, this can be compared to a forward contract, for which cash payment from buyer to seller occurs only at the end of the contract period.[3]

Brokerage firms require their customers to post only a portion of the value of the futures contracts, called an **initial margin,** any time they request a trade. The amount of the margin varies according to the type of contract traded and the quantity of futures contracts traded (e.g., 5 percent of the value of the underlying asset). Minimum margin levels are set by each exchange. If losses on the customer's futures position occur (when their account is marked to market at the end of the trading day) and the level of the funds in the margin account drops below a stated level (called the **maintenance margin**), the customer receives a margin call. A margin call requires the customer to deposit additional funds into his or her margin account, bringing the balance back up to the initial level. The maintenance margin is generally about 75 percent of the initial margin. If the margin is not maintained, the broker closes out (sells) the customer's futures position. Any amount of cash received above the initial margin may be withdrawn by the customer from his or her account. Brokerage firms are responsible for ensuring that their customers maintain the required margin requirements.

In a futures contract, like a forward contract, a person or firm makes a commitment to deliver an asset (such as foreign exchange) at some future date. If a counterparty were to default on a futures contract, however, the exchange would assume the defaulting party's position and payment obligations. Consider the case of Barings, the 200-year-old British merchant bank that failed as a result of trading losses in February 1995 (see In the News box 10–2). In this case, Barings (specifically, one trader, Nick Leeson) bought $8 billion worth of futures on the Japanese Nikkei Stock Market Index, betting that the Nikkei index would rise. For a number of reasons, the index actually fell and the bank lost more than $1.2 billion on its trading position over a period of one month. When Barings was unable to meet its margin calls on Nikkei Index futures traded on the Singapore futures exchange (SIMEX) in 1995, the exchange stood ready to assume Barings' futures contracts and ensure that no counterparty lost money. Thus, unless a systematic financial market collapse threatens an exchange itself, futures are essentially default risk free.[4] In addition, the daily marking to market of future contracts prevents the accumulation of losses and gains that occur with forward contracts, which reduces default risk.

Do You Understand?

1. How Barings, and Nick Leeson, incurred derivatives trading losses of £1 billion?

www.cbot.com/

www.cme.com/

Futures Markets. Futures trading occurs on organized exchanges—for example, the Chicago Board of Trade (CBT) and the Chicago Mercantile Exchange (CME). Financial futures market trading was introduced in 1972 with the establishment of foreign exchange future contracts on the International Money Market (IMM). By 1998, five

---

3. Another difference between forwards and futures is that forward contracts are bilateral contracts subject to counterparty default risk, but the default risk on futures is significantly reduced by the futures exchange guaranteeing to indemnify counterparties against credit or default risk.

4. More specifically, the default risk of a futures contract is less than that of a forward contract for at least four reasons: (1) daily marking to market of futures (so that there is no buildup of losses or gains), (2) margin requirements on futures that act as a security bond should a counterparty default, (3) price movement limits that spread extreme price fluctuations over time, and (4) default guarantees by the futures exchange itself.

In the News

Barings Pays the Price of Ignoring Warning Signs

As a Bank of England inquiry got under way into the collapse of Barings, the City dismissed the official line that Nick Leeson's trading losses of up to 1 billion pounds were simply the work of a "rogue trader" which could not have been foreseen. "They're bound to say this," said one banking analyst. "It gets Barings off the hook."

But the City remains unconvinced. Derivatives market insiders claim that responsibility for the bank's collapse lies squarely with Barings' management, which ignored a series of warning signs. This has been compounded by unsubstantiated reports that Mr. Leeson's 24-year-old wife, Lisa, worked in the back office of the bank's Singapore operation which monitored the trading activities of her husband.

While the financial markets had been agog with rumors of Mr. Leeson's colossal 27 billion dollars (17 billion pounds) market position days before the crisis came to a head, Barings either knew nothing of it or failed to react to the danger signs. "Any professional

Source: *Investors Chronicle* (London: The Financial Times Limited, March 3, 1995).

follower of the derivatives market and many of the integrated securities houses were more than aware some time ago of the large positions Barings was building up," said Martin Burton, managing director of derivatives trader Monument Derivatives.

To discover this position, management need have looked no further than the data published by the Osaka Securities Exchange, one of the two exchanges where Mr. Leeson traded heavily. Between early January and mid-February, Barings' "buy" futures commitments on the Nikkei 225 spiraled from a sizeable 3,000 contracts to an amazing 20,000. The Singapore International Monetary Exchange (Simex) must also have known.

But Barings failed to act. Fellow traders speculate that this was because the bank believed the position to be hedged—largely balanced by offsetting positions—or that it was being built for a client. But as one dealer points out: "This is still a huge position to build for a client." And Barings should have checked it out.

That it didn't illustrates the breakdown of control systems throughout the bank, and particularly in the Singapore office. Mr. Leeson was invested with trust way beyond his youth. As one Barings trader put it: "He'd taken big positions before, some long, some short. And management just assumed they were covered."

But there was also a more fundamental problem. In the Singapore office, according to persistent market rumors, Mr. Leeson was also allowed to settle his own transactions—banks normally keep trading and settlement rigidly apart. "This is so basic, it's unbelievable," commented the head of market risk at one London bank.

Blaming Barings' collapse on the failure of its internal control systems in Singapore, Derek Ross, a leading consultant on capital markets operations at Touche Ross, says: "As in the past, where there have been huge losses in the derivatives market, they have not been due to the complexity of the derivatives contracts or the failure of computer systems. They have been due to a lack of control at a very fundamental level."

major exchanges existed in the United States[5] and several exchanges exist abroad.[6] Table 10–2 lists the characteristics of the most widely traded financial futures contracts. Table 10–3 lists the average month-end contracts outstanding, number of contracts traded, and number of contracts settled from 1992 through 1999. The terms of futures contracts (e.g., contract size, delivery month, trading hours, minimum price fluctuation, daily price limits, and process used for delivery) traded in the United States are set by the exchange and are subject to the approval of the Commodity Futures Trading Commission (CFTC), the principal regulator of futures markets.

In recent years, "off-market" trading systems have sprung up in which institutional investors and money managers can continue to trade during, as well as after, futures exchanges operating hours. Indeed, it is estimated that trading volume in off-market currencies, interest rate swaps, and Eurodollars has grown 3 to 10 times faster than trading volume on futures exchanges.

2

Trading on the largest exchanges such as the CBT takes place in trading "pits." A trading pit consists of circular steps leading down to the center of the pit. Traders for each delivery date on a futures contract informally group together in the trading pit. Futures trading occurs using an **open-outcry auction** method where traders face each other and "cry out" their offers to buy or sell a stated number of futures contracts at a stated price.

Only futures exchange members are allowed to transact on the floor of futures exchanges. Trades from the public are placed with a **floor broker.** When an order is placed, a floor broker may trade with another floor broker or with a professional trader. **Professional traders** are similar to specialists on the stock exchanges in that they trade for their own account. Professional traders are also referred to as position traders, day traders, or scalpers. **Position traders** take a position in the futures market based on their expectations about the future direction of prices of the underlying assets. **Day traders** generally take a position within a day and liquidate it before day's end. **Scalpers** take positions for very short periods of time, sometimes only minutes, in an attempt to profit from this active trading. Scalpers do not have an affirmative obligation to provide liquidity to futures market but do so in expectation of earning a profit. Scalper's profits are related to the bid-ask spread and the length of time a position is held. Specifically, it has been found that scalper trades held longer than three minutes, on average, produce losses to scalpers. Thus, this need for a quick turnover of a scalper's position enhances futures market liquidity and is therefore valuable.[7]

Similar to trading in the stock market, futures trades may be placed as market orders (instructing the floor broker to transact at the best price available) or limit orders (instructing the floor broker to transact at a specified price). The order may be for a purchase of the futures contract in which the futures holder takes a **long position** in the futures contract, or the order may be for a sale of the futures contract in which the futures holder takes a **short position** in the futures contract.

Once a futures price is agreed upon in a trading pit, the two parties do not complete the deal with each other but rather (as illustrated in Figure 10–2) with the clearinghouse overseeing the exchange. The exchange's **clearinghouse** guarantees all trades made by exchange traders. The clearinghouse breaks up every trade into a buy and sell transaction and takes the opposite side of the transaction, becoming the buyer for every futures contract seller (transaction 1 in Figure 10–2) and the seller for every

---

www.cftc.gov/

open-outcry auction

Method of futures trading where traders face each other and "cry out" their offer to buy or sell a stated number of futures contracts at a stated price.

floor broker

Exchange members who place trades from the public.

professional traders

Exchange members who trade for their own account.

position traders

Exchange members who take a position in the futures market based on their expectations about the future direction of the prices of the underlying assets.

day traders

Exchange members who take a position within a day and liquidate it before day's end.

scalpers

Exchange members who take positions for very short periods of time, sometimes only minutes, in an attempt to profit from this active trading.

long position

A purchase of a futures contract.

short position

A sale of a futures contract.

clearinghouse

The unit that oversees trading on the exchange and guarantees all trades made by the exchange traders.

---

5. These include the Chicago Board of Trade, the Chicago Mercantile Exchange, the New York Futures Exchange, the MidAmerica Commodity Exchange, and the Kansas City Board of Trade.

6. These include the London International Financial Futures Exchange (LIFFE), the Singapore International Monetary Exchange (SIMEX), the Marche a Terme International de France (MATIF), and the Montreal Exchange.

7. See W.L. Silber, "Marketmaker Behavior in an Auction Market: An Analysis of Scalpers in Futures Markets," *Journal of Finance*, September 1984, pp. 937–53.

Table 10–2 Characteristics of Actively Traded Futures Contracts

Type of Futures	Contract Size	Exchange*	Open Interest
Interest Rates			
Treasury bonds	$100,000	CBT	681,466
Treasury bonds	$50,000	CME	11,401
Treasury notes	$100,000	CBT	577,559
Treasury notes—5 year	$100,000	CBT	330,503
Treasury notes—2 year	$200,000	CBT	35,262
Federal funds—30 days	$5,000,000	CBT	33,862
Municipal bond index	$1,000	CBT	18,235
Treasury bills	$1,000,000	CME	44,623
Eurodollars	$1,000,000	CME	3,097,987
Euroyen	¥100,000,000	CME	85,211
Short sterling	£500,000	LIFFE	988,255
Long gilt	£50,000	LIFFE	102,141
Eurolibor-3 month	Euro1,000,000	LIFFE	1,108,953
Euroswiss-3 month	Sfr1,000,000	LIFFE	208,024
Euro BTP Italian government	Euro100,000	LIFFE	30,513
Canadian banker's acceptances	C$1,000,000	ME	185,100
Canadian government bonds—10 year	C$100,000	ME	41,300
Eurobonds—5 year	Euro100,000	MATIF	2,362
Euro national bond	Euro100,000	MATIF	59,767
Eurobond	Euro1,000,000	MATIF	83,488
Commonwealth T-bonds—3 year	A$100,000	SFE	128,015
Euroyen	¥100,000,000	SIMEX	491,089
German Euro-government bonds—5 year	Euro 100,000	EUREX	370,169
German Euro-government bonds—10 year	Euro 100,000	EUREX	820,558
German Euro-government bonds—2 year	Euro 100,000	EUREX	170,684
Currency			
Japanese yen	¥12,500,000	CME	112,138
Deutsche mark	125,000 marks	CME	24,400
Canadian dollar	C$100,000	CME	62,430
British pound	£62,500	CME	70,859
Swiss franc	Sfr 125,000	CME	68,736
Australian dollar	A$ 100,000	CME	34,351
Mexican peso	500,000 peso	CME	27,974
Euro FX	Euro 125,000	CME	43,555
Index			
DJIA	$10 times average	CBT	21,397
S&P 500 index	$250 times index	CME	372,185
Mini S&P index	$50 times index	CME	15,309
S&P midcap 400	$500 times index	CME	14,511
Nikkei 225 stock average	$5 times index	CME	22,241
Nasdaq 100	$100 times index	CME	22,159
GSCI	$1,000 times index	CME	33,304
Russell 200	$500 times index	CME	14,762
U.S. dollar index	$1,000 times index	NYBOT	11,013

*CBT = Chicago Board of Trade, CME = Chicago Mercantile Exchange, LIFFE = London International Financial Futures Exchange, ME = Montreal Exchange, MATIF = Marche a Terme International de France, SFE = Sydney Futures Exchange, SIMEX = Sinagpore International Monetary Exchange, EUREX = The European Derivatives Market, and NYBOT = New York Board of Trade.

Table 10–3 Futures Market Activity, 1992–1999

	1992	1993	1994	1995	1996	1997	1998	1999
Average month end contracts outstanding (in thousands):								
Financial instruments	2,037.8	2,758.5	3,799.0	3,749.8	3,776.6	4,052.6	5,337.4	5,372.6
Currencies	385.5	318.0	338.8	299.2	335.6	413.1	515.2	477.5
Number of contracts traded (in millions):								
Financial instruments	148.17	185.40	252.58	259.03	234.26	250.14	319.92	303.66
Currencies	38.66	28.81	30.37	24.29	21.21	25.21	27.59	23.56
Number of contracts maturing (in thousands):								
Financial instruments	965.4	1,035.4	1,809.4	1,939.9	1,904.0	2,385.9	2,705.7	2,230.0
Currencies	503.1	503.8	578.2	521.5	502.5	670.7	865.9	837.9

Source: Commodity Futures Trading Commission, January 2000. *www.cftc.gov/*

Figure 10–2 Clearinghouse Function in Futures Markets

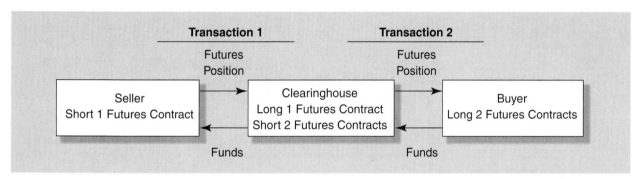

futures contract buyer (transaction 2 in Figure 10–2). Thus, the clearinghouse ensures that all trading obligations are met. Clearinghouses are able to perform their function as guarantor of an exchange's futures contracts by requiring all member firms to deposit sufficient funds (from customers' margins) to ensure that the firm's customers will meet the terms of any futures contract entered into on the exchange.

3   Table 10–4 shows a futures quote from *The Wall Street Journal* for January 18, 2000. The three types of futures contracts are interest rate futures, currency futures, and equity stock index futures. The underlying asset on an interest rate futures contract is a bond or a short-term fixed-interest security's price or interest rate (e.g., Treasury securities, Eurodollar CDs); on a currency contract it is an exchange rate (e.g., yen to U.S. dollar); and on an index futures contract it is a major U.S. or foreign stock market index (e.g., the Dow Jones Industrial Average—see Chapter 8). Look at the quote for Treasury bond interest rate futures contracts. The bold heading of each quote contains information about the underlying deliverable asset (e.g., Treasury bonds) on the futures contract, the exchange on which the futures is traded (e.g., CBT), the face value of a contract (e.g., $100,000), and the basis for the quoted prices (e.g., pts, 32nds of 100%, or 89-07 = 89$\frac{7}{32}$%). Each row of the quote provides information for a specific delivery month (e.g., Mar = March 2000). The first column of the quote lists the delivery month. The second through fourth columns, labeled Open, High, and Low, are the opening price, high price, and low price at which trades occurred during

Table 10–4   Futures Quote

INTEREST RATE

TREASURY BONDS (CBT)-$100,000; pts. 32nds of 100%

	Open	High	Low	Settle	Change	Lifetime High	Lifetime Low	Open Interest
Mar	89-22	89-27	89-00	89-07	— 17	101-07	89-00	597,119
June	89-16	89-16	88-22	88-28	— 18	99-15	88-22	45,348
Sept	88-16	88-19	88-16	88-19	— 18	93-28	88-16	626

Est vol 260,000; vol Fri 475,394; open int 643,134, +16,738.

TREASURY BONDS (MCE)-$50,000; pts. 32nds of 100%

Mar	89-16	89-19	89-00	89-08	— 17	96-01	89-00	8,706

Est vol 2,600; vol Fri 5,445; open int 8,714, +100.

TREASURY NOTES (CBT)-$100,000; pts. 32nds of 100%

Mar	94-19	94-23	93-32	94-04	— 16	100-11	93-32	567,863
June	94-06	94-07	93-32	93-26	— 17	96-10	93-22	22,052

Est vol 170,000; vol Fri 177,212; open int 589,915, +13,495.

5 YR TREAS NOTES (CBT)-$100,000; pts. 32nds of 100%

Mar	97-105	97-125	97-00	97-035	— 7.5	00-055	97-00	379,607

Est vol 65,000; vol Fri 77,308; open int 388,545, +1,878.

2 YR TREAS NOTES (CBT)-$200,000; pts. 32nds of 100%

Mar	98-31	98-312	98-267	98-287	— 2.2	00-035	98-267	32,502

Est vol 3,000; vol Mon 1,943; open int 32,502, −32.

30-DAY FEDERAL FUNDS (CBT)-$5 million; pts. of 100%

Jan	94.550	94.550	94.530	94.545	−.015	95.260	94.400	8,871
Feb	94.22	94.22	94.21	94.21	−.01	94.75	94.17	8,095
Mar	94.13	94.14	94.13	94.13	....	94.50	94.10	3,640
Apr	94.00	94.01	94.00	94.00	....	94.45	93.98	1,884
May	93.91	93.91	93.91	93.91	....	94.20	93.91	468

Est vol 2,100; vol Fri 5,826; open int 22,969, +913.

MUNI BOND INDEX (CBT)-$1,000; times Bond Buyer MBI

Mar	90-25	90-30	90-17	90-18	— 14	97-00	90-17	21,237

Est vol 1,400; vol Fri 1,817; open int 21,318, −255.
Index: Close 91-07; Yield 6.69.

TREASURY BILLS (CME)-$1 mil.; pts. of 100%

	Open	High	Low	Settle		Discount Settle	Chg	Open Interest
Mar	....	....	....	94.43	....	5.57	....	2,411

Est vol 0; vol Fri 3; open int 2,411, +3.

LIBOR-1 MO. (CME)-$3,000,000; points of 100%

						Yield		
Feb	94.04	94.04	94.03	94.04	....	5.96	....	12,439
Mar	93.91	93.92	93.91	93.91	....	6.09	....	4,599
Apr	93.84	93.85	93.84	93.84	....	6.16	....	1,278
May	93.73	93.73	93.73	93.73	+ .01	6.27	− .01	134
June	....	....	....	93.56	....	6.44	....	138
July	....	....	....	93.47	....	6.53	....	447
Aug	....	....	....	93.40	....	6.60	....	334
Sept	....	....	....	93.32	− .01	6.68	+ .01	450
Oct	93.24	93.24	93.22	93.23	....	6.77	....	275
Nov	....	....	....	93.18	− .01	6.82	+ .01	400

Est vol 3,019; vol Fri 4,819; open int 34,586, +1,416.

EURODOLLAR (CME)-$1 million; pts of 100%

	Open	High	Low	Settle		Yield Settle	Chg	Open Interest
Feb	93.85	93.86	93.85	93.85	....	6.15	....	17,431
Mar	93.76	93.77	93.76	93.77	....	6.23	....	496,047
Apr	93.65	93.65	93.65	93.65	....	6.35	....	454
May	93.52	93.53	93.52	93.52	....	6.48	....	185
June	93.41	93.43	93.39	93.41	....	6.59	....	462,186
Sept	93.16	93.17	93.12	93.16	− .01	6.84	+ .01	387,544
Dec	92.94	92.95	92.90	92.94	−.02	7.06	+ .02	287,625
Mr01	92.88	92.89	92.85	92.88	−.03	7.12	+ .03	236,869
June	92.80	92.81	92.76	92.78	−.04	7.22	+ .04	170,063
Sept	92.75	92.75	92.70	92.73	−.04	7.27	+ .04	121,621
Dec	92.66	92.67	92.61	92.64	−.05	7.36	+ .05	99,806
Mr02	92.69	92.70	92.65	92.67	−.05	7.33	+ .05	94,781
June	92.68	92.69	92.63	92.65	−.05	7.35	+ .05	67,739
Sept	92.67	92.67	92.61	92.63	−.05	7.37	+ .05	63,676
Dec	92.58	92.58	92.55	92.57	−.06	7.43	+ .06	62,115
Mr03	92.64	92.64	92.58	92.60	−.06	7.40	+ .06	57,411
June	92.61	92.62	92.55	92.57	−.06	7.43	+ .06	51,091
Sept	92.59	92.59	92.53	92.54	−.07	7.46	+ .07	35,645
Dec	92.50	92.51	92.44	92.45	−.07	7.55	+ .07	30,504
Mr04	92.49	92.49	92.42	92.46	−.07	7.54	+ .07	26,709
June	92.44	92.44	92.39	92.41	−.07	7.59	+ .07	22,829
Sept	92.40	92.40	92.35	92.36	−.07	7.64	+ .07	17,419
Dec	92.32	92.33	92.26	92.27	−.07	7.73	+ .07	17,664
Mr05	....	....	....	92.27	−.07	7.73	+ .07	12,384
June	92.23	92.24	92.22	92.23	−.07	7.77	+ .07	11,281
Sept	92.26	92.26	92.18	92.19	−.07	7.81	+ .07	10,702
Dec	....	....	....	92.10	−.07	7.90	+ .07	6,262
Mr06	92.17	92.17	92.09	92.11	−.07	7.89	+ .07	5,955
June	92.12	92.12	92.05	92.06	−.07	7.94	+ .07	5,047
Sept	92.09	92.09	92.01	92.03	−.07	7.97	+ .07	4,816
Dec	....	....	....	91.93	−.07	8.07	+ .07	3,938
Mr07	91.96	91.96	91.93	91.94	−.08	8.06	+ .08	3,929
June	....	....	....	91.89	−.08	8.11	+ .08	3,279
Sept	....	....	....	91.86	−.08	8.14	+ .08	3,455
Dec	....	....	....	91.76	−.08	8.24	+ .08	5,028
Mr08	....	....	....	91.77	−.08	8.23	+ .08	3,362
June	....	....	....	91.72	−.08	8.28	+ .08	4,084
Sept	....	....	....	91.69	−.08	8.31	+ .08	3,603
Dec	....	....	....	91.59	−.08	8.41	+ .08	2,934
Mr09	....	....	....	91.60	−.08	8.40	+ .08	2,187
June	....	....	....	91.55	−.08	8.45	+ .08	1,864
Sept	....	....	....	91.52	−.08	8.48	+ .08	1,582
Dec	....	....	....	91.42	−.08	8.58	+ .08	793

Est vol 262,109; vol Fri 524,222; open int 2,986,753, +4,953.

EUROYEN (CME) -Yen 100,000,000; pts. of 100%

	Open	High	Low	Settle	Change	Lifetime High	Lifetime Low	Open Interest
Mar	99.84	99.84	99.83	99.83	+ .01	99.88	96.92	21,182
June	99.77	99.78	99.77	99.77	+ .04	99.80	98.09	15,197
Sept	99.61	99.62	99.61	99.61	+ .04	99.71	98.00	12,155
Dec	99.45	99.45	99.44	99.45	+ .05	99.57	97.92	7,055
Mr01	99.33	99.33	99.33	99.33	+ .05	99.54	98.07	7,934
June	99.21	99.21	99.21	99.21	+ .05	99.41	98.20	3,717
Sept	....	....	....	99.06	+ .05	99.30	98.05	4,710
Dec	....	....	....	98.89	+ .05	99.15	97.89	8
Mr02	....	....	....	98.76	+ .06	98.86	97.97	179

Est vol 2,724; vol Fri 2,713; open int 72,186, +1,150.

SHORT STERLING (LIFFE)-£500,000; pts of 100%

	Open	High	Low	Settle	Change	Lifetime High	Lifetime Low	Open Interest
Jan	93.89	93.90	93.89	93.90	....	94.28	93.80	14,514
Feb	93.71	93.71	93.71	93.71	− .01	93.92	93.67	490
Mar	93.54	93.55	93.53	93.54	− .01	95.17	91.96	184,584
June	93.12	93.13	93.09	93.11	− .02	95.17	92.47	166,124
Sept	92.85	92.86	92.81	92.83	− .03	95.13	92.81	115,229
Dec	92.67	92.67	92.63	92.64	− .04	98.40	92.63	69,716
Mr01	92.63	92.63	92.57	92.58	− .06	95.08	92.57	60,725
June	92.58	92.58	92.51	92.53	− .06	95.08	92.50	49,535
Sept	92.54	92.55	92.50	92.51	− .06	95.09	92.41	37,366
Dec	92.51	92.51	92.45	92.46	− .07	95.07	92.31	21,272
Mr02	92.55	92.55	92.51	92.51	− .06	95.13	92.34	17,555
June	92.59	92.59	92.54	92.55	− .07	95.10	92.39	9,736
Sept	92.66	92.66	92.63	92.60	− .08	95.11	92.38	5,936
Dec	92.68	92.68	92.66	92.65	− .08	95.11	92.45	4,397
Mr03	....	....	....	92.78	− .04	94.69	92.49	1,677
June	92.91	92.91	92.90	92.90	− .08	93.88	92.83	137
Sept	....	....	....	92.98	− .08	93.56	93.54	470
Dec	....	....	....	93.03	− .06	93.23	93.20	425

Est vol 79,689; vol Mon 38,810; open int 759,888, +6,233.

LONG GILT (LIFFE) (Decimal)-£50,000; pts of 100%

Mar	108.98	109.06	108.15	108.36	− .76	115.66	108.15	69,479

Est vol 22,338; vol Mon 6,116; open int 69,479, +87.

3 MONTH EURIBOR (LIFFE) Euro 1,000,000; pts of 100%

Feb	96.57	96.58	96.56	96.57	− .01	96.60	96.52	10,172
Mar	96.41	96.41	96.39	96.40	− .02	97.38	96.22	346,400
June	96.04	96.04	96.00	96.01	− .03	97.27	95.90	234,169
Sept	95.75	95.75	95.70	95.72	− .03	97.16	95.64	184,177
Dec	95.40	95.41	95.35	95.38	− .04	97.00	95.36	126,104
Mr01	95.26	95.26	95.19	95.23	− .05	96.96	95.18	88,884
June	95.08	95.08	95.00	95.03	− .05	96.98	94.98	69,767
Sept	94.89	94.89	94.82	94.85	− .06	96.75	94.82	54,091
Dec	94.67	94.67	94.58	94.61	− .06	96.58	92.57	23,560
Mr02	94.59	94.61	94.53	94.54	− .07	96.48	94.50	16,192
June	94.50	94.53	94.44	94.44	− .07	96.37	94.40	15,929
Sept	94.14	94.42	94.33	94.35	− .06	96.25	94.28	9,399
Dec	94.24	94.24	94.16	94.18	− .06	96.06	94.15	6,490
Mr03	....	....	....	94.13	− .06	96.01	94.13	2,362
June	....	....	....	94.06	− .06	95.45	94.02	3,238
Sept	....	....	....	94.01	− .06	95.15	93.97	2,908
Dec	....	....	....	93.88	− .06	95.07	94.15	116
Mr04	....	....	....	93.91	− .06	94.50	94.00	510
June	....	....	....	93.88	− .06	94.43	94.04	505
Sept	....	....	....	93.82	− .06	94.40	93.91	660

Est vol 189,294; vol Mon 96,338; open int 1,195,633, +3,722.

3-MONTH EUROSWISS (LIFFE) SFr 1,000,000; pts of 100%

Mar	97.93	97.93	97.88	97.90	− .04	98.67	97.10	79,878
June	97.47	97.47	97.42	97.45	− .05	98.51	96.90	33,069
Sept	97.13	97.13	97.10	97.12	− .06	98.36	96.63	22,475
Dec	96.78	96.80	96.75	96.77	− .06	98.12	96.30	13,364
Mr01	96.70	96.70	96.69	96.66	− .06	98.04	96.20	12,027
June	96.51	96.51	96.51	96.49	− .06	97.47	96.20	2,372
Sept	96.37	96.39	96.37	96.36	− .05	96.76	95.88	4,885
Dec	96.21	96.21	96.20	96.17	− .05	96.46	96.20	4,714

Est vol 26,834; vol Mon 13,287; open int 172,784, −1,225.

EURO BTP ITALIAN GOVT. BOND (LIFFE) Euro 100,000; pts of 100%

Mar	101.31	101.31	100.98	101.05	− .72	106.70	100.98	4,213

Est vol 124; vol Mon 59; open int 4,213, −3.

CANADIAN BANKERS ACCEPTANCE (ME)-C$1,000,000

Feb	....	....	....	94.59	− .04	94.70	94.60	425
Mar	94.51	94.51	94.45	94.46	− .04	95.55	93.85	113,011
June	94.01	94.01	93.94	93.97	− .05	95.34	93.73	54,826
Sept	93.67	93.69	93.62	93.62	− .08	95.24	93.50	24,327
Dec	93.45	93.46	93.38	93.39	− .07	95.13	93.38	13,965
Mr01	93.28	93.28	93.25	93.25	− .08	95.10	93.25	7,066
June	93.19	93.19	93.19	93.16	− .08	95.07	93.19	5,169
Sept	93.15	93.15	93.13	93.10	− .08	93.73	93.13	2,239
Dec	....	....	....	93.05	− .08	94.74	93.11	730
Mr02	....	....	....	93.00	− .08	94.73	93.30	175
June	....	....	....	92.95	− .08	93.42	93.37	1,675
Sept	....	....	....	92.90	− .08	93.39	93.30	365

Est vol 30,179; vol Mon 1,154; open int 224,023, −14,318.

10 YR. CANADIAN GOVT. BONDS (ME)-C$100,000

Mar	116.65	116.75	116.07	116.26	− 0.48	120.80	116.07	33,820

Est vol 4,907; vol Mon 238; open int 33,800, −3,000.

10 YR. EURO NOTIONAL BOND(MATIF)-Euros 100,000

Mar	84.05	84.15	83.46	83.56	− 0.57	87.92	83.46	59,936

Est vol 171,942; vol Mon 116,954; open int 59,936, +1,838.

3 MONTH EURIBOR (MATIF)-Euros 1,000,000

Feb	....	....	....	96.56	− 0.01	....	....	0
Mar	96.39	96.40	96.39	96.39	− 0.01	97.26	94.36	14,972
June	96.01	96.01	96.00	96.01	− 0.02	97.14	95.00	6,246
Sept	95.72	95.73	95.71	95.71	− 0.03	97.00	95.23	4,179
Dec	95.39	95.39	95.36	95.37	− 0.03	96.95	95.24	7,712
Mr01	95.22	95.22	95.20	95.22	− 0.04	96.85	95.15	2,704
June	95.03	95.03	95.02	95.03	− 0.05	96.75	94.47	1,866
Sept	94.87	94.87	94.83	94.84	− 0.05	96.58	94.83	1,394
Dec	94.60	94.60	94.60	94.61	− 0.05	96.48	94.60	391
Mr02	94.58	94.58	94.55	94.54	− 0.05	95.55	94.55	549
June	94.45	94.45	94.45	94.43	− 0.07	95.10	94.45	201
Sept	94.38	94.38	94.38	94.35	− 0.05	95.40	94.34	170
Dec	....	....	....	94.17	− 0.05	94.73	94.27	105

Est vol 1,717; vol Mon 2,177; open int 40,511, −5,389.

3 YR. COMMONWEALTH T-BONDS (SFE)-A$100,000

Mar	93.05	93.10	93.04	93.09	+ 0.04	93.78	92.98	277,909

Est vol 20,730; vol Mon 15,767; open int 277,909, +236.

CURRENCY

	Open	High	Low	Settle	Change	Lifetime High	Lifetime Low	Open Interest

JAPAN YEN (CME)-12.5 million yen; $ per yen (.00)

Mar	.9617	.9625	.9540	.9548	+ .0001	1.0018	.8369	95,344
June	.9724	.9725	.9712	.9705	+ .0001	1.0175	.8619	3,247
Sept	....	....	....	.9860	+ .0001	1.0272	.9825	244

Est vol 11,175; vol Fri 16,771; open int 98,924, −198.

DEUTSCHEMARK (CME)-125,000 marks; $ per mark

Mar	.5228	.5228	.5162	.5196	− .0012	.5611	.5144	5,434

Est vol 4,548; vol Fri 8,936; open int 63,087, −1,299.

CANADIAN DOLLAR (CME)-100,000 dlrs.; $ per Can $

Mar	.6902	.6919	.6896	.6903	+ − .0004	.6952	.6425	55,744
June	.6926	.6932	.6915	.6918	+ .0004	.6964	.6547	5,500
Sept	.6948	.6948	.6927	.6930	+ .0004	.6970	.6630	1,299
Dec	.6957	.6957	.6938	.6941	+ .0004	.6980	.6640	510

Est vol 4,548; vol Fri 8,936; open int 63,087, −1,299.

BRITISH POUND (CME)-62,500 pds.; $ per pound

Mar	1.6342	1.6392	1.6306	1.6362	+ .0016	1.6810	1.5570	36,581

Est vol 3,785; vol Fri 10,821; open int 36,596, −1,368.

SWISS FRANC (CME)-125,000 francs; $ per franc

Mar	.6299	.6325	.6285	.6313	− .0009	.7086	.6278	56,970
June	.6369	.6394	.6357	.6383	− .0011	.7040	.6357	222

Est vol 8,405; vol Fri 27,956; open int 57,224, +2,065.

AUSTRALIAN DOLLAR (CME)-100,000 dlrs.; $ per A.$

Mar	.6638	.6662	.6630	.6656	− .0017	.6704	.6268	39,831

Est vol 906; vol Fri 2,012; open int 39,853, −63.

MEXICAN PESO (CME)-500,000 new Mex. peso; $ per MP

Mar	.10390	.10450	.10370	.10433	+ .00450	.10450	.08135	13,847
June	.10155	.10645	.10090	.10095	+ .00425	.10105	.08350	2,758
Sept	.09780	.09780	.09780	.09790	+ .00450	.10295	.08500	169
Dec	.09475	.09475	.09475	.09520	+ .00450	.09475	.09200	81

Est vol 2,419; vol Fri 4,004; open int 16,855, +697.

EURO FX (CME)-Euro 125,000; $ per Euro

Mar	1.0166	1.0185	1.0113	1.0163	− .0022	1.1242	1.0089	61,233
June	1.0225	1.0250	1.0199	1.0235	− .0022	1.1077	1.0166	212
Sept	....	....	....	1.0302	− .0022	1.1136	1.0226	99

Est vol 13,767; vol Fri 37,627; open int 61,558, −4,822.

INDEX

DJ INDUSTRIAL AVERAGE (CBOT)-$10 times average

	Open	High	Low	Settle	Change	Lifetime High	Lifetime Low	Open Interest
Mar	11832	11625	11655	....	− 180	11853	10091	13,333
June	11895	11895	11770	11796	− 181	11980	10275	762
Sept	....	....	....	11945	− 181	12126	11282	257
Dec	....	....	....	12105	− 182	12180	8100	226

Est vol 10,000; vol Fri 14,449; open int 14,578, +299.
Idx prl: HI 11720.12; Lo 11546.45; Close 11560.72, −162.26.

S&P 500 INDEX (CME)-$250 times index

Mar	147810	147940	146200	146950	− 850	149650	97000	354,678
June	148250	149450	148150	148840	− 870	151450	98000	8,458
Sept	....	....	....	150870	− 880	153200	99000	2,602
Dec	152750	153580	152580	152990	− 890	155290	126650	2,554
Mr01	....	....	....	155290	− 890	157590	132430	154
June	....	....	....	157590	− 890	159890	134280	119

Est vol 97,178; vol Fri 88,488; open int 368,570, −2,574.
Idx prl: HI 1465.15; Lo 1447.50; Close 1455.14, −10.01.

MINI S&P 500 (CME)-$50 times index

Mar	147875	148025	146200	146950	− 850	149950	125850	16,088

Vol Mon 57,421; open int 16,106, +100.

S&P MIDCAP 400 (CME)-$500 times index

Mar	449.50	455.00	449.00	453.50	+ 1.00	456.00	367.70	12,834

Est vol 623; vol Fri 538; open int 12,834, +3.
Idx prl: HI 450.46; Lo 446.16; Close 449.94, +1.50.

NIKKEI 225 STOCK AVERAGE (CME)-$5 times index

Mar	19060.	19085.	18980.	19030.	− 30	19200.	15290.	18,169
June	19000.	19100.	19000.	18990.	− 30	19100.	16790.	96

Est vol 1,175; vol Fri 1,243; open int 18,265, +153.
Idx prl: HI 19412.47; Lo 19145.17; Close 19196.57, −240.66.

NASDAQ 100 (CME)-$100 times index

Mar	375775	381800	369000	380700	− 5250	388500	219700	25,273

Est vol 20,031; vol Fri 15,589; open int 25,327, +156.
Idx prl: HI 4148.00; Lo 4053.21; Close 4130.76, +66.49.

GSCI (CME)-$250 times nearby index

Jan	204.30	209.00	204.30	....	na	na	209.00	167.50	1,183
Feb	204.50	205.20	202.20	205.70	+ 2.70	205.80	174.00	41,367

Est vol 2,087; vol Fri 4,246; open int 42,611, +257.
Idx prl: HI 4148.00; Lo 4053.21; Close 4130.76, +66.49.

RUSSELL 2000 (CME)-$500 times index

Mar	506.00	518.40	506.00	518.40	+ 7.85	518.40	393.50	13,402

Est vol 798; vol Fri 800; open int 13,402, −118.
Idx prl: HI 513.44; Lo 506.20; Close 513.43, +5.87.

U.S. DOLLAR INDEX (NYBOT)-$1,000 times USDX

Mar	101.43	101.86	101.38	101.65	− .14	102.90	96.40	6,156

Est vol na; vol Fri na; open int na, na.
Idx prl: HI 102.11; Lo 101.64; Close 101.86, −.19.

the day (e.g., 89-22 = $89^{22}/_{32}\%$ of $100,000 = $89,687.50 at the open of trading on January 18, 2000). The fifth column, labeled Settle, is a representative price at which a trade occurs at the end of the day. If trading in a futures contract is active, the Settle price is the price on the last trade of the day. If, however, the contract does not trade actively, the settlement price is determined by a committee of the exchange immediately after the market's close. The settlement price is the price used to determine the value of a trader's position at the end of each trading day. The sixth column, labeled Change, is the change in the futures price quote from the previous day's settlement price. Columns 7 and 8, labeled Lifetime High and Low, are the highest and lowest price at which a trade has occurred over the life of the futures contract. Finally, the last column, labeled **Open Interest,** is the total number of long positions in the futures contract outstanding at the beginning of the day. The bottom line of the futures quote lists the estimated trading volume for the day (e.g., 260,000 contracts), the volume of trading in the contract the previous day (e.g., 475,394), and the number of contracts outstanding for that type (T-bonds), regardless of expiration month (e.g., 643,134).

open interest

The total number of the futures, put option, or call option contracts outstanding at the beginning of the day.

A holder of a futures contract has two choices for liquidating his or her position: liquidate the position before the futures contract expires, or hold the futures contract to expiration. To liquidate before the expiration date, the futures holder simply calls his or her broker and requests on offsetting trade to his or her original position, an opposite position. For example, if the original transaction was a buy or long position, the trader can sell or short the same futures contract. Thus, any losses on the buy position will be exactly offset by gains on the sell position over the remaining life (time) to expiration of the contract.

If the futures holder keeps the futures contract to expiration, the parties will either (as specified in the futures contract) conduct a cash settlement where the traders exchange cash based on the final price of the underlying asset relative to the futures price, or the futures holder will take delivery of the underlying asset (e.g., a T-bond) from the futures seller.

Do You Understand?

1. What the difference is between a spot contract, a forward contract, and a futures contract?
2. What the major futures exchanges in the United States are?
3. What position traders, day traders, and scalpers are?
4. When a futures trader would buy (long) a futures contract? Sell (short) a futures contract?

Profit and Loss on a Futures Transaction.   In Table 10–4, a March 2000 Treasury bill futures contract traded on the CME could be bought (long) or sold (short) on January 18, 2000, for 94.43 percent of the face value of the T-bill—or the yield on the T-bill deliverable in March 2000 was 5.57 percent (100% − 94.43%). The minimum contract size on one of these futures is $1,000,000, so a position in one contract can be taken at a price of $944,300.

The subsequent profit or loss from a position in March 2000 T-bills taken on January 18, 2000, is graphically described in Figure 10–3. A long position in the futures market produces a profit when the value of the underlying T-bill increases (i.e., interest rates fall).[8] A short position in the futures will produce a profit when the value of the underlying T-bill decreases (i.e., interest rates rise).

option

A contract that gives the holder the right, but not the obligation, to buy or sell the underlying asset at a specified price within a specified period of time.

Options

An **option** is a contract that gives the holder the right, but not the obligation, to buy or sell an underlying asset at a prespecified price for a specified time

---

8. Notice that if rates move in an opposite direction from that expected, losses are incurred on the futures position. That is, if rates rise and futures prices drop, the long investor loses on his or her futures position. Similarly, if rates fall and futures prices rise, the short investor loses on his or her futures position.

Figure 10–3 Profit or Loss on a Futures Position in Treasury Bills Taken on January 18, 2000

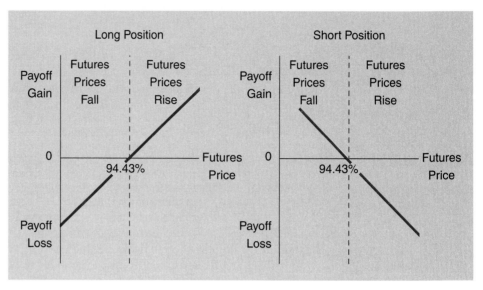

Figure 10–4 Exercise of an American Option versus a European Option

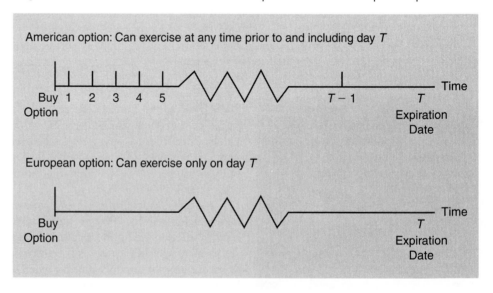

American option

An option that can be exercised at any time before and on the expiration date.

European option

An option that can be exercised only on the expiration date.

period. An **American option** gives the option holder the right to buy or sell the underlying asset at *any time* before and on the expiration date of the option. A **European option** (e.g., options on the S&P 500 Index) gives the option holder the right to buy or sell the underlying option *only* on the expiration date. Figure 10–4 illustrates the difference in the exercise opportunities with an American versus a European option. Most options traded on exchanges in the United States and abroad are American options. Options are classified as either call options or put options. We discuss both of these below, highlighting their payoffs in terms of price movements on the underlying asset. These relationships are summarized in Table 10–5.

Table 10–5   Summary of Gains and Losses on Option Contracts

Position	Change in Price of Underlying Assets	Gain/Loss
Buy call option	Decrease	Loss limited to option premium
	Increase	Gain unlimited
Write call option	Decrease	Gain limited to option premium
	Increase	Loss unlimited
Buy put option	Decrease	Gain unlimited
	Increase	Loss limited to option premium
Write put option	Decrease	Loss unlimited
	Increase	Gain limited to option premium

Figure 10–5   Payoff Function for the Buyer of a Call Option on a Stock

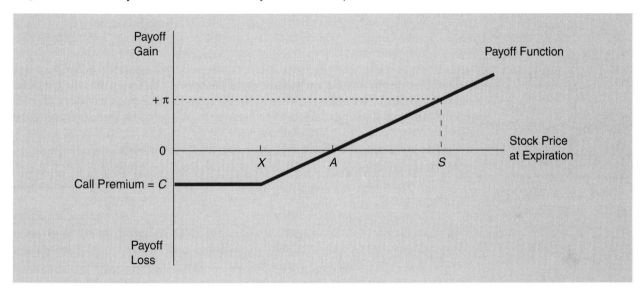

Call Options

call option

An option that gives a purchaser the right, but not the obligation, to buy the underlying security from the writer of the option at a prespecified exercise price on a prespecified date.

A **call option** gives the purchaser (or buyer) the right to buy an underlying security (e.g., a stock) at a prespecified price called the *exercise* or *strike* price (X). In return, the buyer of the call option must pay the writer (or seller) an up-front fee known as a *call premium (C)*. This premium is an immediate negative cash flow for the buyer of the call option. However, he or she potentially stands to make a profit should the underlying stock's price be greater than the exercise price (by an amount exceeding the premium) when the option expires. If the price of the underlying stock is greater than X (the option is referred to as "in the money"), the buyer can exercise the option, buying the stock at X and selling it immediately in the stock market at the current market price, greater than X. If the price of the underlying stock is less than X when the option expires (the option is referred to as "out of the money"), the buyer of the call would not exercise the option (i.e., buy the stock at X when its market value is less than X). In this case, the option expires unexercised. The call buyer incurs a cost C for the option, and no other cash flows result.

Buying a Call Option.   The profit or loss from buying a call option is illustrated in Figure 10–5. As Figure 10–5 shows, if, as the option expires, the price of the stock underlying the option is S, the buyer makes a profit of π, which is the difference between

Figure 10–6 Payoff Function for the Writer of a Call Option on a Stock

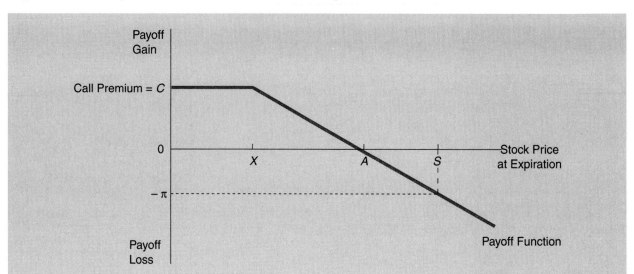

the stock's price (S) and the exercise price of the option (X) minus the call premium paid to the writer of the option ($C = A - X$). If the underlying stock's price rises to A, the buyer of the call has just broken even because the net proceeds from exercising the call ($A - X$) just equals the premium payment for the call (C).

Notice two important things about call options in Figure 10–5:

1. As the underlying stock's price rises, the call option buyer has a large profit potential: The higher the underlying stock's price at expiration, the larger the profit on the exercise of the option.
2. As the underlying stock's price falls, the call option buyer has a higher potential for losses, but they are limited to the call option premium. If the underlying stock's price at expiration is below the exercise price, X, the call buyer is not obligated to exercise the option. Thus, the buyer's losses are truncated by the amount of the up-front premium payment (C) made to purchase the call option.

Thus, buying a call option is an appropriate position when the underlying asset's price is expected to rise.

Writing a Call Option. The writer of a call option sells the option to the buyer (or is said to take a short position in the option). In writing a call option on a stock, the writer or seller receives an up-front fee or premium (C) and must stand ready to sell the underlying stock to the purchaser of the option at the exercise price, X. Note the payoff from writing a call option on a stock in Figure 10–6.

Notice two important things about this payoff function:

1. As the underlying stock's price falls, the potential for a call option writer to receive a positive payoff (or profit) increases. If the underlying stock's price is less than the exercise price (X) at expiration, the call option buyer will not exercise the option. The call option writer's profit has a maximum profit equal to the call premium (C) charged up front to the buyer of the option.
2. As the underlying stock's price rises, the call option writer has unlimited loss potential. If the underlying stock's price is greater than the exercise price (X) at expiration, the call option buyer will exercise the option, forcing the option writer to buy the underlying stock at its high market price and then sell it to the call option buyer at the lower exercise price. Since stock prices are theoretically unbounded in the upward direction, these losses could be very large.

Figure 10–7   Payoff Function for the Buyer of a Put Option on a Stock

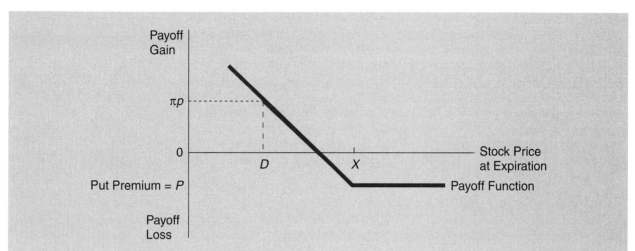

Thus, writing a call option is an appropriate position when the underlying asset's price is expected to fall. Caution is warranted, however, because profits are limited but losses are potentially unlimited. A rise in the underlying stock's price to S results in the writer of the option losing π (in Figure 10–6).

Put Options

put option

An option that gives a purchaser the right, but not the obligation, to sell the underlying security to the writer of the option at a prespecified price on a prespecified date.

A **put option** gives the option buyer the right to sell an underlying security (e.g., a stock) at a prespecified price to the writer of the put option. In return, the buyer of the put option must pay the writer (or seller) the put premium (P). If the underlying stock's price is less than the exercise price (X) when the option expires (the put option is "in the money"), the buyer will buy the underlying stock in the stock market at less than X and immediately sell it at X by exercising the put option. If the price of the underlying stock is greater than X when the option expires (the put option is "out of the money"), the buyer of the put option never exercises the option (i.e., selling the stock at X when its market value is more than X). In this case, the option expires unexercised. The put option buyer incurs a cost P for the option, and no other cash flows result.

Buying a Put Option.   The buyer of a put option on a stock has the right (but not the obligation) to sell the underlying stock to the writer of the option at an agreed exercise price (X). In return for this option, the buyer of the put option pays a premium (P) to the option writer. We show the potential payoffs to the buyer of the put option in Figure 10–7. Note the following:

1. The lower the price of the underlying stock at the expiration of the option, the higher the profit to the put option buyer upon exercise. For example, if stock prices fall to D in Figure 10–7, the buyer of the put option can purchase the underlying stock in the stock market at that price and put it (sell it) back to the writer of the put option at the higher exercise price X. As a result, after deducting the cost of the put premium, P, the buyer makes a profit of πp in Figure 10–7.
2. As the underlying stock's price rises, the probability that the buyer of a put option has a negative payoff increases. If the underlying stock's price is greater than the exercise price (X) at expiration, the put option buyer will not exercise the option. As a result, his or her maximum loss is limited to the size of the up-front put premium (P) paid to the put option writer.

Figure 10–8 Payoff Function for the Writer of a Put Option on a Stock

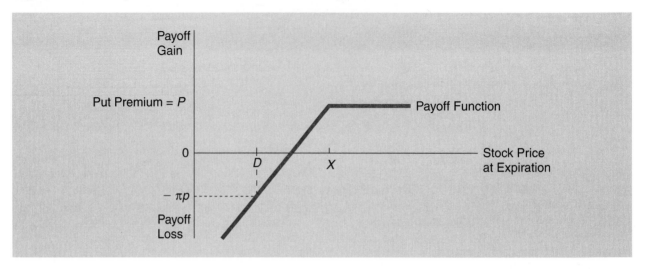

Thus, buying a put option is an appropriate position when the price on the underlying asset is expected to fall.

Writing a Put Option. The writer or seller of a put option receives a fee or premium (P) in return for standing ready to buy the underlying stock at the exercise price (X) should the buyer of the put choose to exercise the option at expiration. See the payoff function for writing a put option on a stock in Figure 10–8. Note the following:

1. When the underlying stock's price rises, the put option writer has an enhanced probability of making a profit. If the underlying stock's price is greater than the exercise price (X) at expiration, the put option buyer will not exercise the option. The put option writer's maximum profit, however, is constrained to equal the put premium (P).
2. When the underlying stock's price falls, the writer of the put option is exposed to potentially large losses. If the price of the underlying stock is below the exercise price (e.g., D in Figure 10–8), the put option buyer will exercise the option, forcing the option writer to buy the underlying stock from the option buyer at the exercise price (X) when it is worth only D in the stock market. The lower the stock's price at expiration relative to the exercise price, the greater the losses to the option writer.

Thus, writing a put option is an appropriate position if the price on the underlying asset is expected to rise. However, profits are limited and losses are potentially large.

Notice from the above discussion that an option holder has three ways to liquidate his or her position. First, if conditions are never profitable for an exercise (the option remains "out of the money"), the option holder can let the option expire unexercised. Second, if conditions are right for exercise (the option is "in the money"), the holder can take the opposite side of the transaction: thus, an option buyer can sell options on the underlying asset with the same exercise price and the same expiration date. Third, if conditions are right for exercise, the option holder can exercise the option, enforcing the terms of the option. For an American option, this exercise can theoretically occur any time before the option expires, while for a European option this exercise can occur only as the option expires.

Option Values

Notice in the discussion above that we examined the profit and loss from exercising an option *at expiration*. The profit and loss on an option was a function of the price of the

Figure 10–9   The Intrinsic Value versus the Before Exercise Value of a Call Option

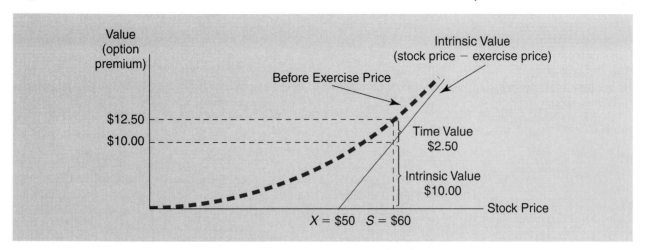

intrinsic value of an option

The difference between an option's exercise price and the underlying asset's price.

option's underlying asset and the exercise price on the option. The difference between the underlying asset's price and an option's exercise price is called the option's **intrinsic value**. For a call option, the intrinsic value is:

Stock price − Exercise price	if Stock price ≥ Exercise price (option is in the money)
Zero	if Stock price < Exercise price (option is out of the money)

For a put option, the intrinsic value is:

Exercise price − Stock price	if Stock price ≤ Exercise price (option is in the money)
Zero	if Stock price > Exercise price (option is out of the money)

At expiration, an option's value is equal to its intrinsic value.

We limited the analysis of the profit and loss on an option to exercise at expiration because research has found that it is generally not optimal to exercise an option before its expiration date.[9] Specifically, exercising a call option early (prior to expiration) is only appropriate if the value of the option before expiration is less than its intrinsic value, which is rarely the case.

Figure 10–9 illustrates this relation for a call option. For example, suppose you have a call option on a stock with an exercise price of $50 and an expiration in three months. The underlying stock's price is currently $60. The intrinsic value of the option is $10 ($60 − $50). The option is currently selling on the Chicago Board of Trade for $12.50. Thus, the value of the call option is greater than its intrinsic value by $2.50. The difference between an option's price (or premium) and its intrinsic value is called its **time value**. If you exercise the option today (prior to expiration), you receive the intrinsic value but give up the time value.

time value of an option

The difference between an option's price (or premium) and its intrinsic value.

The time value of an option is the value associated with the probability that the intrinsic value (i.e., the stock price) *could* increase (if the underlying asset's price moves favorably) between the option's purchase and the option's expiration date itself. It is this "time value" that allows an out of the money option to have value and trade on the option markets. As noted above, a call option is out of the money if the exercise price

9. See J. Cox and M. Rubinstein, *Options Markets* (Englewood Cliffs, NJ: Prentice-Hall, 1985).

Table 10-6 Options Market Activity, 1992–1999

	1992	1993	1994	1995	1996	1997	1998	1999
Average month end contracts outstanding (in thousands)	1,585.8	2,155.4	2,961.6	3,285.4	3,514.8	3,920.5	4,983.3	5,176.0
Number of contracts traded (in thousands)	39,928.1	46,814.0	66,937.1	65,502.6	62,667.3	69,337.9	86,884.6	86,708.8

Source: Commodity Futures Trading Commission, website, January 2000. *www.cftc.gov/*

is greater than the underlying stock's price, or the intrinsic value of the option is zero. This option still has "time" value and will trade at a positive price or premium, however, if investors believe that prior to the option's expiration, the stock price will increase (to a value greater than the exercise price).

As an option moves towards expiration, its time value goes to zero. At any point in time, the time value of an option can be calculated by subtracting its intrinsic value (e.g., $10) from its current market price or premium (e.g., $12.50). The model most commonly used by practitioners and traders to price and value options is the Black-Scholes option pricing model. We show how to calculate an option's time value and, in turn, its overall value for any price of the underlying asset (at any point in time prior to maturity for a European option) using the Black-Scholes option pricing model in the appendix to this chapter.

Option Markets

www.cboe.com/

The Chicago Board of Options Exchange (CBOE) opened in 1973. It was the first exchange devoted solely to the trading of stock options. In 1982, financial futures options contracts (options on financial futures contracts, e.g., Treasury bond futures contracts) started trading. Options markets have grown rapidly since the mid-1980s.

Table 10–6 shows the level of trading activity in the options markets from 1992 through 1999. Table 10–7 lists the characteristics of the most active option contracts. The largest option exchange is the Chicago Board Options Exchange (CBOE).[10] The first option exchanges abroad were the European Options Exchange and the London Interna-

www.liffe.com/

tional Financial Futures Exchange (LIFFE). Options exchanges have more recently been opened in Paris, Sweden, Switzerland, Germany, and Japan. As with futures trading, many options also trade over the counter. Thus, the volume of trade in options is more than what is reported in the option quotes (see below) for the organized exchanges.

The trading process for options is the same as that for futures contracts. An investor desiring to take an option position calls his or her broker and places an order to buy or sell a stated number of call or put option contracts with a stated expiration date and exercise price. The broker directs this order to its representative on the appropriate exchange for execution. Trading on the largest exchanges such as the CBOE takes place in trading pits, where traders for each delivery date on an option contract informally group together. Like futures contracts, options trading generally occurs using an open-outcry auction method.

Only option exchange members are allowed to transact on the floor of option exchanges. Trades from the public are placed with a floor broker, professional trader, or a market maker for the particular option being traded. Option trades may be placed as market orders (instructing the floor broker to transact at the best price available) or limit orders (instructing the floor broker to transact at a specified price).

---

10. Other major exchanges are the American Stock Exchange, CBT, CME, IMM, Pacific Stock Exchange, Philadelphia Exchange, New York Stock Exchange, and the Financial Instrument Exchange of the New York Cotton Exchange.

Table 10–7 Characteristics of Actively Traded Options on Futures

Type of Option	Exchange*	Contract Traded
Stock options	CBOE	Stock options
	AM	Stock options
	PB	Stock options
	PC	Stock options
	NY	Stock options
Stock index options	CBOE	Dow Jones Industrial Average
	CBOE	Dow Jones Transportation Average
	CBOE	Dow Jones Utility Average
	CBOE	Nasdaq 100
	CBOE	Russell 2000
	CBOE	S&P 100 Index
	CBOE	S&P 500 Index
	AM	Mexico Index
	AM	Computer Technology Index
	AM	Institutional
	AM	Japan Index
	AM	Major Market Index
	AM	MS Cyclical
	AM	MS Hitech
	AM	Pharmaceutical
	AM	S&P Midcap
	PB	Gold/Silver
	PB	Oil Service
	PB	PHLX KBW Bank
	PB	Semiconductor
	PB	Street.com
	PB	Utility Index
	PB	Value Line
Financial futures options:		
Interest rate	CBT	T-bonds
	CBT	T-notes
	CBT	T-notes—5 year
	CBT	Muni bond index
	CME	Eurodollar
	CME	Mid-Curve Eurodollar—1 year
	CME	Mid Curve Eurodollar—2 year
	LIFFE	Eurolibor
	LIFFE	Long Gilt
	EUREX	German Eurogovernment bond—10 year
Currency	CME	Japanese yen
	CME	Deutsche mark
	CME	Canadian dollar
	CME	British pound
	CME	Swiss franc
Stock index	CBT	DJIA
	CME	S&P 500 Index
Currency options	PB	Canadian dollar EOM
	PB	Euro
	PB	Australian dollar
	PB	British pound
	PB	Canadian dollar-European style

continued

Table 10–7   *concluded*

Type of Option	Exchange*	Contract Traded
	PB	Canadian dollar
	PB	Euro-European Style
	PB	Japanese yen
	PB	Swiss franc-European Style
	PB	Swiss franc

*CBOE= Chicago Board of Option Exchange, AM= American Exchange, PB= Philadelphia Stock Exchange, PC= Pacific Stock Exchange, NY= New York Stock Exchange, CBT= Chicago Board of Trade, CME= Chicago Mercantile Exchange, LIFFE= London International Financial Futures Exchange, and EUREX= The European Derivatives Market.

Source: *The Wall Street Journal*, January 19, 2000, p. C17. Reprinted by permission of *The Wall Street Journal*. © 2000 Dow Jones & Company, Inc. All Rights Reserved Worldwide. *www.wsj.com/*

Once an option price is agreed upon in a trading pit, the two parties send the details of the trade to the option clearinghouse (the Options Clearing Corporation), which breaks up trades into buy and sell transactions and takes the opposite side of each transaction—becoming the seller for every option contract buyer and the buyer for every option contract seller. The broker on the floor of the options exchange confirms the transaction with the investor's broker.

Table 10–8 shows portions of an option quote table from *The Wall Street Journal* for January 18, 2000. Four types of options trade: stock options, stock index options, options on futures contracts, and currency options. More "exotic" or special types of options (e.g., credit options—see Chapter 24) tend to trade over the counter rather than on organized exchanges. We discuss the four major types of exchange traded options next.

Stock Options.   The underlying asset on a stock option contract is the stock of a publicly traded company. One option generally involves 100 shares of the underlying company's stock. As mentioned earlier, options on U.S. option exchanges are American options. Look at the options quotes for AT&T in Table 10–8. The first column lists the name of the company and its closing stock price for the day (e.g., $53.375). The second column lists the strike price on the different options on AT&T stock (e.g., $45). Note that the same stock can have many different call and put options differentiated by expiration and strike price. The third column is the expiration month on the option (e.g., January). Columns 4 and 5 give data on the call options: volume (e.g., 877 call options traded) and call price (or premium) of the option (e.g., 8⅝ = $8.625 × 100 per option).[11] Columns 6 and 7 list the same type of data for put options traded.

Stock Index Options.   The underlying asset on a stock index option is the value of a major stock market index (e.g., the DJIA or the S&P 500 index). An investor would buy a call (put) option on a stock index when he or she thinks the value of the underlying stock market index will rise (fall) by the expiration date of the option. If the index does indeed rise above (fall below) the exercise price on the option, the call (put) option holder can profit by an amount equal to the intrinsic value when the option expires. A difference between a stock option and a stock index option is that at expiration, the stock index option holder cannot settle the option contract with the actual purchase or sale of the underlying stock index. Rather, at expiration, stock index options are settled in cash (i.e., the option holder receives the intrinsic value if the option is in the money and nothing if the option is out of the money). Except for the S&P 500 (which is a European option), stock index options are American options.

11. Times 100 since each option contract is for 100 shares.

Table 10–8 Option Quote, January 18, 2000

STOCK OPTIONS

Option/Strike		Exp.	Call Vol.	Call Last	Put Vol.	Put Last
ACTV	35	Jan	817	3½	38	1
AT&T Cda	40	Apr	450	8	...	...
AT&T	45	Jan	877	8⅝	20	1/16
53⅜	50	Jan	579	3⅝	212	3/16
53⅜	55	Jan	1165	5/16	51	1¾
53⅜	55	Feb	574	2 1/16	60	3⅛
53⅜	60	Jan	599	1/16	309	6⅝
AT&T o	63⅜	Jan	550	1/16	...	...
Abbt L	35	Jan	106	¼	632	1 9/16
33¾	35	Feb	82	1 5/16	525	2¼
ActPerf	10	Feb	...	...	500	7/16
13⅝	12½	Feb	500	2	...	...
AdvCmG	10	Apr	500	3⅞	...	...
A M D	7½	Jan	1771	3¼	295	1¾
39	20	Jan	405	19⅝	...	...
39	27½	Apr	1812	13⅞	...	...
39	30	Jan	704	9¼	172	¼
39	32½	Jan	411	7	81	7/16
39	35	Jan	1309	4⅞	770	15/16
39	40	Jan	2017	2¼	683	2⅞
39	40	Feb	852	4	80	5
39	42½	Feb	548	3⅛	...	...
39	45	Jan	2771	1	10	6
39	50	Jan	1887	½	...	...
39	55	Jan	641	3/16	...	...

Option/Strike		Exp.	Call Vol.	Call Last	Put Vol.	Put Last
Airtouch	35	Jan	2093	117⅛	...	...
AirbFr	25	Jan	892	1¼	10	1
25⅜	25	Feb	549	2¾	71	1⅜
Alcoa	75	Feb	...	...	1054	1⅞
AllianSemi	17½	Jan	423	1¼	245	¼
Altera	60	Jan	1237	2	134	1½
60⅜	65	Jan	452	7/16	...	...
Alza	42½	Feb	1046	1	...	...
Amazon	42½	Apr	...	...	700	2¾
64⅛	62½	Jan	582	2¾	75	1⅝
64⅛	65	Jan	303	1¾	416	2¼
64⅛	70	Jan	232	⅜	611	6¼
64⅛	70	Apr	80	10¼	464	15
64⅛	80	Jan	81	⅛	699	16⅛
Amdocs	25	Apr	1952	20	10	5/16
44	30	Apr	1879	16	10	15/16
44	40	Jan	693	3⅝	...	...

FUTURES OPTIONS

INTEREST RATE

T-BONDS (CBT)
$100,000; points and 64ths of 100%

Strike Price	Calls-Settle Feb	Calls-Settle Mar	Calls-Settle Jun	Puts-Settle Feb	Puts-Settle Mar	Puts-Settle Jun
87	2-16	2-34	....	0-02	0-21	....
88	1-20	1-50	2-38	0-06	0-37	1-47
89	0-34	1-10	....	0-20	0-61	....
90	0-08	0-45	1-37	0-57	1-30	2-45
91	0-01	0-24	....	1-51	2-10	....
92	0-01	0-12	0-58	2-50	2-62	4-00

Est vol 100,000;
Fr vol 68,655 calls 74,913 puts
Op int Fri 473,764 calls 369,200 puts

T-NOTES (CBT)
$100,000; points and 64ths of 100%

Strike Price	Calls-Settle Feb	Calls-Settle Mar	Calls-Settle Jun	Puts-Settle Feb	Puts-Settle Mar	Puts-Settle Jun
92	....	....	....	....	0-11	0-53
93	....	....	....	0-03	0-23	1-11
94	0-23	0-54	1-27	0-16	0-46	1-40
95	0-03	0-26	1-00	0-59	1-18	2-12
96	0-01	0-11	0-44	1-56	2-02	2-55
97	0-01	0-04	0-29	2-56	2-59	....

Est vol 40,000 Fr 24,851 calls 31,369 puts
Op int Fri 266,081 calls 191,986 puts

5 YR TREAS NOTES (CBT)
$100,000; points and 64ths of 100%

Strike Price	Calls-Settle Feb	Calls-Settle Mar	Calls-Settle Jun	Puts-Settle Feb	Puts-Settle Mar	Puts-Settle Jun
9600	....	....	....	....	0-09	0-40
9650	....	0-55	....	0-02	0-16	....
9700	0-16	0-34	....	0-09	0-27	....
9750	0-03	0-18	....	0-28	0-43	....
9800	0-01	0-09	0-28	0-58	1-01	1-43
9850	0-01	0-04	....	1-25	1-28	....

Est vol 18,000 Fr 3,703 calls 2,478 puts
Op int Fri 91,380 calls 114,849 puts

CURRENCY

JAPANESE YEN (CME)
12,500,000 yen; cents per 100 yen

Strike Price	Calls-Settle Feb	Calls-Settle Mar	Calls-Settle Apr	Puts-Settle Feb	Puts-Settle Mar	Puts-Settle Apr
9450	1.55	....	....	0.57	1.14	....
9500	1.25	1.84	....	0.77	1.36	....
9550	0.98	....	....	1.00	1.61	....
9600	0.77	1.38	....	1.29	1.90	1.75
9650	0.60	1.19	....	1.62	2.20	....
9700	0.47	1.03	....	1.99	2.54	....

Est vol 1,042 Fr 228 calls 189 puts
Op int Fri 21,322 calls 28,664 puts

DEUTSCHEMARK (CME)
125,000 marks; cents per mark

Strike Price	Calls-Settle Feb	Calls-Settle Mar	Calls-Settle Apr	Puts-Settle Feb	Puts-Settle Mar	Puts-Settle Apr
5100	....	....	....	....	0.42	....
5150	....	....	....	....	....	....
5200	....	0.78	....	0.53	0.82	....
5250	....	....	....	....	....	....
5300	0.18	0.41	....	1.22	1.44	....
5350	....	....	....	....	....	....

Est vol 50 Fr 1 calls 90 puts
Op int Fri 2,241 calls 249 puts

INDEX

DJ INDUSTRIAL AVG (CBOT)
$100 times premium

Strike Price	Calls-Settle Jan	Calls-Settle Feb	Calls-Settle Mar	Puts-Settle Jan	Puts-Settle Feb	Puts-Settle Mar
115	19.05	35.25	45.80	3.55	19.50	30.40
116	12.10	29.00	39.75	6.60	23.00	34.40
117	6.75	23.25	34.10	11.25	27.25	38.50
118	3.20	18.25	28.90	17.70	32.25	43.30
119	1.25	14.00	24.10	25.75	37.75	....
120	0.40	10.25	19.80	34.85	....	54.10

Est vol 500 Fr 516 calls 676 puts
Op int Fri 7,329 calls 13,801 puts

S&P 500 STOCK INDEX (CME)
$250 times premium

Strike Price	Calls-Settle Jan	Calls-Settle Feb	Calls-Settle Mar	Puts-Settle Jan	Puts-Settle Feb	Puts-Settle Mar
1460	18.00	38.00	51.40	8.50	28.60	42.00
1465	14.90	35.10	48.50	10.40	30.60	44.00
1470	12.00	32.20	45.50	12.50	32.70	46.00
1475	9.40	29.50	42.70	14.90	35.00	48.10
1480	7.20	26.90	40.00	17.70	37.30	50.40
1485	5.40	24.40	37.40	20.90	....	....

Est vol 11,202 Fr 6,797 calls 15,643 puts
Op int Fri 77,633 calls 188,406 puts

CURRENCY

OPTIONS
PHILADELPHIA EXCHANGE

		Calls Vol.	Calls Last	Puts Vol.	Puts Last
Euro					101.43
62,500 Euro-cents per unit.					
102	Feb	4	0.95	...	...
102	Mar	24	1.62	...	...
104	Mar	17	0.94	1	3.34
104	Jun	30	2.34	...	0.01
106	Mar	2	0.46	...	0.01
106	Jun	406	1.66	...	0.01
108	Jun	17	1.15	...	0.01
British Pound					163.83
31,250 Brit. Pounds-European Style.					
163	Feb	...	0.01	32	0.78
31,250 Brit. Pounds-cents per unit.					
166	Mar	32	1.09	...	0.01
166	Jun	32	2.33	...	0.01
168	Mar	32	0.60	...	0.01
168	Jun	32	1.72	...	0.01
Canadian Dollar					68.91
50,000 Canadian Dollars-cents per unit.					
69½	Mar	20	0.40	...	0.01
50,000 Canadian Dollars-cents per unit.					
69	Feb	...	0.01	10	0.39
Euro					101.43
62,500 Euro-European style.					
102	Feb	16	0.80	...	...
Swiss Franc					62.83
62,500 Swiss Francs-European Style.					
62	Feb	...	...	30	0.39
62,500 Swiss Francs-cents per unit					
62½	Feb	...	0.01	240	0.57
63	Feb	240	0.71	...	...
63½	Mar	...	0.01	59	1.34
64	Jun	1	1.62	...	...
65	Mar	...	...	29	2.48
67½	Mar	1	1.45	...	0.01

Call Vol ...... 1,276 Open Int ... 16,522
Put Vol .... 2,291 Open Int ... 17,382

STOCK INDEX OPTIONS

DJ INDUS AVG(DJX)

	Strike	Vol.	Last	Net Chg.	Open Int.
Mar	76p	40	1/16	− 1/16	514
Jun	90p	20	⅞	+ ⅛	245
Mar	92p	850	¼	− ¼	1,719
Jun	92p	10	⅞	− 1/16	9,197
Mar	96p	70	¼	− ⅛	10,642
Jun	96p	10	1 3/16	+ 3/16	6,822
Mar	100p	105	½	− ⅛	10,398
Jun	100p	70	1¾	+ 5/16	5,149
Feb	102p	100	3/16	− ⅛	1,879
Jan	104c	11	12⅜	+ ⅞	2,610
Mar	104c	2	13½	− ⅞	823
Mar	106c	57	12	− 1	388
Mar	106p	600	1	+ ⅛	2,614
Jan	108c	3	8	− ½	738
Feb	108c	2	9½	+ ¼	2,207
Mar	108p	301	1⅜	+ ¼	5,645
Jun	108c	1	13	− 1	600
Jun	108p	3	3	+ ⅛	2,920
Jan	110c	31	6⅛	− 1⅜	1,626
Feb	110p	305	⅞	+ ⅛	2,134
Mar	110c	12	8¼	− ¾	7,009
Mar	110p	5	1 7/16	− 1/16	7,851
Jun	110c	74	11⅝	− ⅞	1,921
Jun	110p	10	3⅝	+ ⅝	1,036
Jan	112c	10	4¾	− ¾	1,998
Jan	112p	18	1/16	...	2,782
Feb	112c	120	5⅝	− ⅝	596
Feb	112p	38	1¼	+ ¼	911
Mar	112c	2	7¼	− ¾	1,057
Mar	112p	1	2	+ ¼	1,043
Jun	112c	328	10⅜	− ⅝	1,421
Jun	112p	10	4	...	134
Jan	113p	70	¼	+ ⅛	3,778
Jan	114c	37	2	− 1¼	1,573
Jan	114p	428	⅜	+ ⅛	6,421
Feb	114c	10	4⅛	− 1	2,009
Feb	114p	22	1¾	+ ½	950
Mar	114c	49	5¾	− ⅜	315
Mar	114p	7	2¾	+ ⅜	637
Jan	115c	106	1¾	− ¾	486
Jan	115p	92	⅝	+ 5/16	2,335
Jan	116c	107	13/16	− 1 1/16	2,093
Jan	116p	508	1	+ ½	1,298
Feb	116c	20	2 11/16	− 15/16	1,555
Feb	116p	101	2⅝	+ ¾	432
Mar	116c	61	4	− 1	490
Mar	116p	93	3¼	+ 7/16	793
Jan	117c	58	11/16	− 7/16	178
Jan	117p	52	1⅝	+ 13/16	1,313
Jan	118c	73	3/16	− ⅜	758
Jan	118p	19	2	+ 11/16	116
Feb	118c	6	1 9/16	− 9/16	246
Feb	118p	10	3	+ ¼	223
Mar	118c	2	3⅜	− ½	526
Mar	118p	61	4⅜	+ ⅝	26
Jan	119c	5	⅛	− ¼	671
Jan	119p	2	2⅞	+ 9/16	155
Feb	119p	2	4¼	+ 1	3
Mar	119p	50	4⅝	...	...
Jan	120c	347	1/16	− 1/16	11,100
Jan	120p	8	4	+ 1⅛	1,183
Feb	120c	14	1	− ⅜	338
Feb	120p	16	4½	+ ⅝	29
Mar	120c	10	2 5/16	− 5/16	2,777
Mar	120p	15	5½	+ 1	251
Mar	121c	320	1 13/16	...	...
Mar	123p	1	7⅝	...	...
Feb	124c	30	¼	− ⅛	288
Feb	128c	250	1/16	− 1/16	340
Feb	128p	1	11¼	− 1	20

Call Vol. ....2,195 Open Int. 151,595
Put Vol. ....4,149 Open Int. 324,361

S & P 500 INDEX-AM(SPX)

	Strike	Vol.	Last	Net Chg.	Open Int.
Mar	750c	500	717⅛	− ⅞	2,386
Mar	750p	1,560	⅛	− ⅛	5,383
Mar	800p	100	⅛	− ⅛	2,530
Mar	975p	40	½	...	1,997
Mar	1025p	100	¾	− 1⅞	16,766
Jan	1050c	2	407	+ 40	5
Mar	1050c	2	414	+ 36	805
Mar	1075p	20	1¼	− ¼	1,422
Mar	1100p	51	1½	+ ¼	6,847
Jan	1125p	50	1/16	...	1,548
Mar	1150p	6	2 7/16	− 1 9/16	12,689
Mar	1175p	23	3	+ ⅝	5,924
Jan	1200c	1	254½	− 11½	610
Feb	1200p	4	⅞	...	3,988
Mar	1225p	404	4¾	+ ¾	9,848
Jan	1250p	42	⅛	− ⅛	21,740
Feb	1250p	67	1¾	− ⅛	2,263
Mar	1250p	26	5⅛	...	24,676
Jan	1275p	11	1/16	− 1/16	22,237
Feb	1275p	22	2½	+ ¼	8,025
Mar	1275p	140	7½	− 2	11,402
Jan	1300c	6	157	+ 12	15,326
Jan	1300p	10	¼	...	23,727
Feb	1300p	1,019	3⅜	+ ⅜	12,864
Mar	1300c	17	170½	+ 9½	22,205
Mar	1300p	2,731	8½	− ¼	13,476
Jan	1325c	106	130	− 13	29,224
Jan	1325p	76	3/16	− 5/16	32,721
Feb	1325p	2	5¼	+ 1⅛	5,893
Mar	1325p	32	12¼	+ ⅞	14,577
Jan	1350c	161	112	− 5½	15,233
Jan	1350p	120	⅜	...	22,401
Feb	1350c	6	122	+ 1	4,877
Feb	1350p	49	7	+ ¾	12,132
Mar	1350c	14	130½	− 9½	16,904
Jan	1360p	126	⅜	− 1⅞	201
Jan	1375c	48	83	− 12	7,624
Jan	1375p	5,131	½	...	18,799
Feb	1375c	221	100½	+ 5½	1,199
Feb	1375p	1,594	10	+ 2	15,167
Mar	1375p	25	18¾	+ 1¾	7,673
Jan	1380p	211	1	− 1⅛	1,911
Jan	1390c	220	1¼	− 1⅞	753
Jan	1390p	2	32¾	− 5¼	401
Mar	1390c	5	34	+ 4⅞	11
Jan	1400c	167	60	− 6½	21,302
Jan	1400p	1,499	1⅛	+ ⅛	28,349
Feb	1400c	20	76	− 5	6,365
Feb	1400p	905	14¼	+ 2	13,888
Mar	1400c	57	93	− 3	29,515
Mar	1400p	39	24	+ 1⅜	33,924
Jan	1405p	152	1 3/16	− 1/16	362
Jan	1410c	50	46	+ 13	1,155
Jan	1410p	104	1⅝	+ ½	1,803
Mar	1410p	1	27½	− 10½	2,584
Jan	1415p	53	1¼	− ⅝	858
Jan	1420c	17	42	− 9¼	1,100
Mar	1420p	1	30⅞	+ 5⅜	2,297
Jan	1425c	662	35⅝	− 8⅞	38,234
Jan	1425p	1,110	2	− ⅛	37,420
Feb	1425c	226	61⅝	− 1¾	8,210
Feb	1425p	577	19⅛	+ 2⅛	10,851
Mar	1425c	2	74	− 10	36,784
Mar	1430p	20	30½	− 13½	5,818
Jan	1440c	6	21	− 9	3,814
Jan	1440p	2,981	4	+ ¼	3,883
Mar	1440p	800	36¼	− 9¾	3,821
Jan	1450c	1,692	15	− 8	17,087
Jan	1450p	3,160	6¾	+ ¾	18,638
Feb	1450c	4,737	44	− 2	9,603
Feb	1450p	6,565	27	+ 2⅛	14,751
Mar	1450c	6,846	55½	− 5½	20,666
Mar	1450p	7,290	39⅞	+ 5⅜	23,500
Jan	1460c	896	10	− 6	2,564
Jan	1460p	554	11½	+ 2½	871
Mar	1460c	811	50	+ 2	1,301
Mar	1460p	811	43⅛	+ 3¼	2,192
Jan	1465c	85	7	− 5¼	374
Jan	1465p	850	13¾	+ ¼	416
Feb	1465c	254	30¾	− 8¼	882
Feb	1465p	320	30½	− ⅝	659
Jan	1470c	370	5	− 3⅜	2,446
Jan	1470p	124	14½	+ 1	2,103
Feb	1470c	105	30	− 2¼	707
Feb	1470p	12	35½	+ 5¼	1,343
Mar	1470c	866	46	− 1	2,270
Mar	1470p	674	47	+ 3½	2,263
Jan	1475c	5,415	4	− 3⅞	16,136
Jan	1475p	1,434	22	+ 7	11,806
Feb	1475c	2,002	27	− 3	6,052
Feb	1475p	1,351	39¼	+ 6⅜	2,767
Mar	1475c	314	42¼	− 5¾	11,659
Mar	1475p	212	46	+ 1	11,313
Jan	1480c	111	3⅛	− 1	1,552
Jan	1485c	211	1⅜	− 2⅝	1,496
Jan	1500c	1,559	7/16	− 15/16	9,713
Jan	1500p	72	37½	+ 2⅝	684
Feb	1500c	704	17	− 1⅜	8,808
Feb	1500p	95	53½	+ 7¾	1,323
Mar	1500c	1,075	29	− 7	18,510
Mar	1500p	3	62	+ 4	753
Jan	1525c	296	⅛	− ¼	6,350
Jan	1525p	1	72	+ 14½	682
Feb	1525c	1,161	8	− 1⅜	11,113
Feb	1525p	45	67	+ 8½	176
Mar	1525c	200	19¼	− 1¼	9,898
Jan	1550c	145	1/16	− 1/16	13,649
Feb	1550c	867	4	− ¾	10,324
Feb	1550p	15	86	+ 4	248
Mar	1550c	1,835	13	− 2	6,120
Mar	1550p	234	97	+ 11	820
Feb	1575c	10	1 7/16	− 9/16	3,456
Mar	1575c	262	6⅝	− 1⅞	3,208
Feb	1675c	20	⅛	+ 1/16	489
Mar	1750c	250	⅛	− ¼	2,740
Mar	1750p	500	273	+ ¾	2,394

Call Vol.......48,111 Open Int..1,022,753
Put Vol. ......62,451 Open Int..1,231,338

Source: *The Wall Street Journal,* January 19, 2000, p. C23. Reprinted by permission of *The Wall Street Journal.* *www.wsj.com/*

Options on stock indexes allow investors to invest indirectly in a diversified portfolio that replicates a major market index (e.g., the S&P 500 index). If an investor thinks the S&P 500 index will rise in the future, he or she can buy a call option on the S&P 500 Index. If the S&P 500 index does rise, the value of the call option also rises. Thus, the investor can earn returns based directly on the S&P 500 index without investing the large amounts of money needed to directly buy every stock in the index.

The dollar value associated with each stock index option is established by a particular multiplier—the value of a stock index option is equal to the index times its multiplier. For example, the multiplier on the S&P 500 index option is 500, on the S&P 100 index option is 100, on the DJIA option is 100, and on the NYSE Composite index option is 500. Thus, if an S&P 500 index option has an exercise price of 1,400, the dollar amount involved with the exercise of this option is $1,400 \times \$500 = \$700,000$.

Options on stock indexes also give investors a way to hedge their existing stock portfolios.

Example 10–1   Using a Stock Index Option to Hedge a Stock Portfolio

Suppose that over the last seven years an investor's stock portfolio increased in value from $250,000 to $2.79 million. The stock portfolio was originally set up so as to (virtually) replicate the S&P 500 index. The investor believes that due to expected rising interest rates in the next three months, stock market indexes (including the S&P 500 index, currently at 1,395.0) will soon experience sharp declines in value and his stock portfolio will experience the same percentage drop in value. The investor has thought of liquidating his stock portfolio but is in the 20 percent capital gains tax bracket and does not want to incur such high tax payments.

Instead, the investor takes a long position in (or buys) put options on the S&P 500 index with a three-month expiration and an exercise price of 1,395. Incorporating the S&P 500 multiplier of $500, this is equivalent to $697,500 (1,395 × $500). To hedge his $2.79 million stock portfolio, the investor would buy 4 ($2.79 million ÷ (1,395 × $500)) put options on the S&P 500 index.

Suppose the investor was correct in his expectations. In three months' time (as the put option on the S&P 500 index expires), the S&P 500 index has dropped 25 percent to 1,046.25, as has the value of his stock portfolio (now valued at $2,092,500 million). The investor has lost $697,500 in value on his stock portfolio. However, the investor can settle the put options he purchased for cash—the intrinsic value at the option's expiration is $697,500 ((1,395 − 1,046.25 per option) × $500 × 4 options).

The investor was able to take a position in the stock index option market such that any losses on his stock portfolio were offset with gains on the put option position in stock index options. We ignored transaction costs in this example (i.e., the premiums required to purchase the four put options), but they would be small relative to the losses the investor would have incurred had he not hedged his stock portfolio with stock index options.

5   Stock index option quotes (in Table 10–8) list the underlying index (e.g., DJ INDUS AVG = DJIA). The first column lists the expiration month of the option contract and the second column lists the exercise price, often listed in some submultiple of the actual value of the index (e.g., 76 = 7,600 for the DJIA), including a designation for put, p, or call, c, options traded. Column 3 is the trading volume (e.g., 40 = 40 options traded). Column 4 lists the settlement price (or premium) on the option (e.g., 1/16 = 100 x .0625 = $6.25), and Column 5 is the change in this settlement price (or premium) from the previous day. Finally, the last column of the quote table reports the number of contracts outstanding at the beginning of the day.

Options on Futures Contracts. The underlying asset on a futures option is a futures contract (e.g., $100,000 Treasury bond futures—discussed above). The buyer of a call (put) option on a futures contract has the right to buy (sell) the underlying futures contract before expiration (i.e., an American option). The seller of a call (put) option on a futures contract creates the obligation to sell (buy) the underlying futures contract on exercise by the option buyer. If exercised, a call (put) option holder can buy (sell) the underlying futures contracts at the exercise price. Options are currently written on interest rate, currency, and stock index futures contracts.

Look at the first futures option quote listed in Table 10–8 (for T-bonds). The bold heading for each quote lists the type of option (e.g., on T-bond futures contracts), face value of each option contract (e.g., $100,000), and the basis for the quote (e.g., points and 64ths of 100% means 2-16 = $2^{16}\!/_{64}$%). Each row in the quote then lists trading results for a specific exercise price (e.g., 87, 88). Column 1 lists the strike price (e.g., 87 = 87%); Columns 2 through 4 list settlement prices on call options traded, by expiration month of the option contract (e.g., February, March, and June). The last three columns list settlement prices for the various expiration put options.[12]

Currency Options. The underlying asset on a currency option contract is a foreign currency exchange rate. Most foreign currency option contracts trade on the Philadelphia Options Exchange. Foreign currency options include both American and European options. A call (put) option on a foreign currency exchange rate gives the option holder the right to buy (sell) a designated quantity of a foreign currency (e.g., £31,250 British pounds) for a given price in dollars—that is, the strike price of the option contract.

Look at the quote for British pound currency options in Table 10–8. The bold heading for each quote states the currency (i.e., British pound), the current spot exchange rate of U.S. dollars for the foreign currency times 100 (e.g., 163.83 = 1.6383 U.S. dollars for British pounds), the face value on the option contract or the amount of the foreign currency to be delivered (e.g., £31,250 British pounds), and the basis for the quoted prices (e.g., cents per British pound). If the option is a European option, this will also be stated in the header information (look at the first entry for the British pound option). Each row in the quote sheet then lists trading results for a separate option exercise price and expiration month on the currency option contracts (e.g., 166 Mar). The first column lists the exercise price (e.g., 166 = 1.6600 U.S. dollars for British pounds); the second column is the option expiration month (e.g., March). The third and fourth columns summarize the call options: the trading volume (e.g., 32 March expiration British pound call contracts traded on January 18, 2000) and the settlement price (e.g., 1.09 U.S. dollars for British pounds). Columns 5 and 6 list the same information for put option contracts.

The value of a foreign currency call (put) option increases (decreases) if the foreign currency appreciates (depreciates) in value relative to the dollar (e.g., the exchange rate of U.S. dollars for British pounds goes up to 1.76 or down to 1.51).

Example 10–2 Change in the Value of a Currency Option as Foreign Exchange Rates Change

Suppose a U.S. investor buys the February British pound currency call option with an exercise price of 163 (i.e., $1.63 U.S. dollars for £1 British pound) and a face value of £31,250. As listed in the option quote, the current exchange rate of U.S. dollars for

---

12. Contracts with other maturities also trade but are not reported in *The Wall Street Journal*.

British pounds is 1.6383 (or £1 can be exchanged for $1.6383). Suppose that on or before the option expires, the British pound appreciates in value relative to the U.S. dollar such that the exchange rate of dollars for pounds rises to 1.76. The call option holder can exercise the option, receive the £31,250 (in return for $1.63 × 31,250 = $50,937.50), and convert them into dollars, receiving $55,000 (1.76 × £31,250). The call option holder makes $4,062.50 (= (1.76 − 1.63) × £31,250) as a result of the appreciation of the British pound relative to the U.S. dollar.

Do You Understand?

1. What the difference is between a call option and a put option?
2. When an option trader would want to buy a call option on a stock?
3. When an option trader would want to buy a put option on a stock?
4. What the four types of options traded in the United States are?

www.cftc.gov/

www.sec.gov/

www.cftc.gov/

6 Regulation of Futures and Options Markets

The Commodity Futures Trading Commission (CFTC), formed in 1974, is the primary regulator of futures markets. The CFTC's major mission is to protect the trading public by seeking to prevent misrepresentations and/or market manipulation by exchange participants. The CFTC approves new or proposed contracts to ensure they have an economic purpose, conducts economic studies of the markets, enforces the rules set by the individual exchanges, and provides regulatory surveillance of futures market participants. The CFTC also monitors futures trading in an attempt to identify market manipulation. One way the CFTC monitors trading is by obtaining information on positions of all large market participants in an attempt to identify unusual activity. The CFTC also puts limits on the number of futures contracts any trader can hold and monitors the time stamping of trades, where traders must record the time at which a trade occurs to identify irregularities.

The Securities and Exchange Commission (SEC) is the main regulator of stock options in which delivery is based on a stock or stock index (e.g., stock options and stock index options). The CFTC is the main regulator of options on futures contracts in which delivery involves a futures contract. For example, the SEC regulates trading of S&P 500 futures options traded on the CBT, the value of which is determined by the value of the S&P 500 Index, but the CFTC regulates trading of S&P 500 futures options traded on the CME, the value of which is determined by the futures contract on the S&P 500 Index. This distinction has often caused confusion for both regulators and traders alike.

The individual futures and option exchanges also set and enforce many rules on their members designed to ensure the smooth operations and financial solvency of the exchange. As mentioned above, exchanges also are responsible for setting trading procedures, hours of trading, contract characteristics, margin requirements, and so on for contracts traded on the individual exchanges.

Do You Understand?

1. Who the main regulators of futures and option exchanges are?

---

7 Swaps

swap

An agreement between two parties to exchange assets or a series of cash flows for a specific period of time at a specified interval.

A **swap** is an agreement between two parties (called counterparties) to exchange specified periodic cash flows in the future based on some underlying instrument or price (e.g., a fixed or floating rate on a bond or note). Like forward, futures, and option contracts, swaps allow firms to better manage their interest rate, foreign exchange, and credit risks. Swaps were first introduced in the early 1980s, and the market for swaps has grown enormously in recent years—the notional value of swap contracts outstanding by U.S. commercial banks (by far the major participant in the swap markets) was $17.36 trillion in September 1999, making them the largest of all the derivative markets. The five generic types of swaps, in order of quantitative importance, are interest rate swaps, currency swaps, credit risk swaps, commodity swaps, and equity swaps.[13] The asset or instrument underlying the swap may change, but the basic principle of a swap agreement is the same in that it involves the transacting parties restructuring their asset or liability cash flows in a preferred direction. In this section, we consider the role of the two major generic types of swaps—interest rate and currency. We also look at other types of swaps and describe the ability of swaps to hedge various kinds of risk in more detail in Chapter 24.

Interest Rate Swaps

By far the largest segment of the swap market comprises **interest rate swaps**. Conceptually, an interest rate swap is a succession of forward contracts on interest rates arranged by two parties.[14] As such, it allows the swap parties to put in place long-term protection (sometimes for as long as 15 years) against interest rate risk (see Chapter 23). The swap reduces the need to "roll over" contracts from old ones into new ones if futures or forward contracts had been relied on to achieve such long-term hedging protection.[15]

In a swap contract, the **swap buyer** agrees to make a number of fixed interest rate payments based on a principal contractual amount (called the **notional principal**) on periodic settlement dates to the **swap seller**. The swap seller, in turn, agrees to make floating-rate payments, tied to some interest rate, to the swap buyer on the same periodic settlement dates. In undertaking this transaction, the party that is the fixed-rate payer is seeking to transform the variable-rate nature of its liabilities into fixed-rate liabilities to better match the fixed returns earned on its assets. Meanwhile, the party that is the variable-rate payer seeks to turn its fixed-rate liabilities into variable-rate liabilities to better match the variable returns on its assets.

interest rate swap

An exchange of fixed-interest payments for floating-interest payments by two counterparties.

swap buyer

By convention, a party that makes the fixed-rate payments in an interest rate swap transaction.

notional principal

The principal amount involved in a swap.

swap seller

By convention, a party that makes the floating-rate payments in an interest rate swap transaction.

Example 10–3 Hedging Interest Rate Risk with an Interest Rate Swap

To explain the role of a swap transaction in protecting a firm against interest rate risk, we use a simple example of an interest rate swap. Consider two financial institutions. The first is a money center bank that has raised $50 million of its funds by issuing five-year, medium-term notes with 10 percent annual fixed coupons (see Table 10–9). On the asset side of its portfolio, the bank makes commercial and industrial (C&I) loans whose rates are indexed to annual changes in the London interbank offered rate (LIBOR). Banks index most large commercial and industrial loans to either LIBOR or the federal funds rate in the money market.

As a result of having floating-rate loans and fixed-rate liabilities in its asset–liability structure, the money center bank is exposed to interest rate risk. Specifically, if interest rates decrease, the bank's interest income decreases, since the variable interest return on loans (assets) will fall relative to the fixed cost of its funds (liabilities).

One way for the bank to hedge the risk of this exposure is to alter the interest rate sensitivity of its liabilities by transforming them into floating-rate liabilities that better match the (floating) rate sensitivity of its asset portfolio. The bank can make changes either on or off the balance sheet. On the balance sheet, the bank could attract an additional $50 million in short-term deposits that are indexed to the LIBOR rate in a manner

---

13. There are also *swaptions,* which are options to enter into a swap agreement at some preagreed contract terms (e.g., a fixed rate of 10 percent) at some time in the future in return for the payment of an up-front premium.

14. For example, a four-year swap with annual swap dates involves four net cash flows between the parties to a swap. This is essentially similar to arranging four forward rate agreement (FRA) contracts: a one-year, a two-year, a three-year, and a four-year contract.

15. For example, futures contracts are offered usually with a maximum maturity of 2 years or less.

Table 10–9   Money Center Bank Balance Sheet

Assets		Liabilities	
C & I Loans (rate indexed to LIBOR)	$50 million	Medium-term notes (coupons) fixed at 10% annually	$50 million

Table 10–10   Savings Bank Balance Sheet

Assets		Liabilities	
Fixed-rate mortgage	$50 million	Short-term CDs (one year)	$50 million

similar to its loans. The proceeds of these deposits can be used to pay off its medium-term notes. This reduces the difference in the interest rate sensitivity between the bank's assets and liabilities. Alternatively, the bank could go off the balance sheet and sell an interest rate swap—that is, enter into a swap agreement to make the floating-rate payment side of a swap agreement.

The second party to the swap in this example is a thrift institution (a savings bank) that has invested $50 million in fixed interest rate residential mortgage assets of long maturity. To finance this residential mortgage portfolio, the savings bank has had to rely on short-term certificates of deposit with an average duration of one year (see Table 10–10). On maturity, these CDs must be "rolled over" at the current market rate.

Consequently, the savings bank's asset–liability balance sheet structure is the reverse of the money center bank's—if interest rates increase, the bank's interest expense increases. Since its assets (mortgages) are fixed rate, while its liabilities (deposits) are floating, the bank's net income falls.

The savings bank could hedge this interest rate risk exposure by transforming the short-term floating-rate nature of its liabilities into fixed-rate liabilities that better match the long-term maturity structure of its assets by either on- or off-balance-sheet hedging. On the balance sheet, the thrift could issue long-term notes (or bonds) with a maturity equal (or close to equal) that on the mortgages. The proceeds of the sale of the notes can be used to pay off the CDs. As a result, it would be funding long-term mortgages with long-term notes. Alternatively, the thrift could go off the balance sheet and buy a swap—that is, the thrift could enter into a swap agreement to make the fixed-rate payment side of a swap agreement.

The opposing balance sheet and interest rate risk exposures of the money center bank and the savings bank provide the necessary conditions for an interest rate swap agreement between the two parties. This swap agreement can be arranged directly by the two parties themselves—for example, by direct telephone contact. However, it is likely that a third financial institution—another commercial bank or an investment bank—would act either as a broker or an agent, receiving a fee[16] for bringing the two parties together or intermediating fully by accepting the credit risk exposure and guaranteeing the cash flows underlying the swap contract. We illustrate these swap transactions in Figure 10–10. By acting as a principal as well as an agent in arranging the swap, the third party financial institution can add a credit risk premium to the fee.

---

16. One way the fees are reflected is in swap bid-ask spreads. For example, a bank can either make fixed-rate payments (buy a swap) or receive fixed-rate payments (sell a swap). Generally, the fixed rate for selling a swap is set at a margin above the fixed rate for borrowing.

Figure 10–10   A Swap Transaction

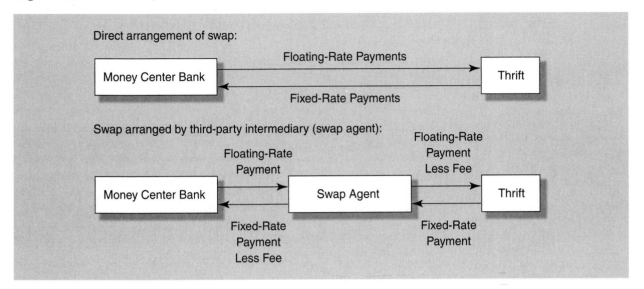

Direct arrangement of swap:

Money Center Bank → Floating-Rate Payments → Thrift

Thrift → Fixed-Rate Payments → Money Center Bank

Swap arranged by third-party intermediary (swap agent):

Money Center Bank → Floating-Rate Payment → Swap Agent → Floating-Rate Payment Less Fee → Thrift

Thrift → Fixed-Rate Payment → Swap Agent → Fixed-Rate Payment Less Fee → Money Center Bank

Figure 10–11   Fixed-Floating Rate Swap

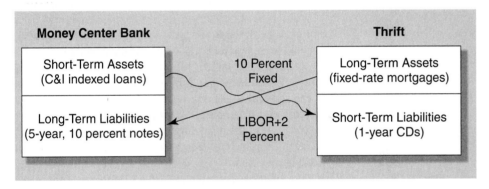

Money Center Bank

| Short-Term Assets (C&I indexed loans) |
| Long-Term Liabilities (5-year, 10 percent notes) |

10 Percent Fixed

LIBOR+2 Percent

Thrift

| Long-Term Assets (fixed-rate mortgages) |
| Short-Term Liabilities (1-year CDs) |

However, the credit risk exposure of a swap to a financial institution is somewhat less than that on a loan (see Chapter 24). Conceptually, when a third-party financial institution fully intermediates the swap, that institution is really entering into two separate swap agreements—in this example, one with the money center bank and one with the savings bank.

The swap agreement that is arranged might dictate that the thrift send fixed payments of 10 percent per annum of the notional $50 million value of the swap to the money center bank to allow the money center bank to cover fully the coupon interest payments on its note issue. In return, the money center bank sends annual payments indexed to the one-year LIBOR to help the thrift better cover the cost of refinancing its one-year renewable CDs. Suppose that the money center bank agrees to send the thrift annual payments at the end of each year equal to the one-year LIBOR plus 2 percent.[17] We depict this fixed-floating rate swap transaction in Figure 10–11.

As a result of the swap, the money center bank has transformed its four-year, fixed-rate liability notes into a variable-rate liability matching the variability of returns

17. These rates implicitly assume that this is the cheapest way each party can hedge its interest rate exposure. For example, LIBOR plus 2 percent is the lowest cost way that the money center bank can transform its fixed-rate liabilities into floating-rate liabilities.

on its C&I loans. Further, through the interest rate swap, the money center bank effectively pays LIBOR plus 2 percent for its financing. The thrift has also transformed its variable-rate CDs into fixed-rate payments similar to those received on its fixed-rate mortgages.

Currency Swaps

currency swap

A swap used to hedge against exchange rate risk from mismatched currencies on assets and liabilities.

Interest rate swaps are long-term contracts that can be used to hedge interest rate risk exposure. This section considers a simple example of how **currency swaps** can be used to immunize or hedge against exchange rate risk when firms mismatch the currencies of their assets and liabilities.

Fixed-Fixed Currency Swaps.   Consider a U.S. financial institution with all of its fixed-rate assets denominated in dollars. It is financing part of its asset portfolio with a £100 million issue of five-year, medium-term British pound sterling notes that have a fixed annual coupon of 10 percent. By comparison, a financial institution in the United Kingdom has all its assets denominated in sterling; it is partly funding those assets with a $200 million issue of five-year, medium-term dollar notes with a fixed annual coupon of 10 percent.

These two financial institutions are exposed to opposing currency risks. The U.S. institution is exposed to the risk that the dollar will depreciate (decline in value) against the pound over the next five years, which would make it more costly to cover the annual coupon interest payments and the principal repayment on its pound-denominated note liabilities. On the other hand, the U.K. institution is exposed to the risk that the dollar will appreciate against the pound, making it more difficult to cover the dollar coupon and principal payments on its five-year, $200 million note liabilities.

These financial institutions can hedge their exposures either on or off the balance sheet. Assume that the dollar/pound exchange rate is fixed at $2/£1. On the balance sheet, the U.S. financial institution can issue $200 million in five-year, medium-term dollar notes. The proceeds of the sale can be used to pay off the £100 million of five-year, medium-term sterling notes. Similarly, the U.K. financial institution can issue £100 million in five-year, medium-term sterling notes, using the proceeds to pay off the $200 million of five-year, medium-term dollar notes. Both institutions have taken actions on the balance sheet so that they are no longer exposed to movements in the exchange rate between the two currencies (i.e., their assets and liabilities are currency matched).

Example 10–4   Expected Cash Flows on Fixed-Fixed Currency Swap

Alternatively, the U.K. and U.S. financial institutions can enter into a currency swap by which the U.K. institution sends annual payments in pounds to cover the coupon and principal repayments of the U.S. financial institution's pound sterling note issue, and the U.S. financial institution sends annual dollar payments to the U.K. financial institution to cover the interest and principal payments on its dollar note issue.[18] We summarize this currency swap in Figure 10–12. As a result of the swap, the U.K. financial institution transforms its fixed-rate dollar liabilities into fixed-rate sterling liabilities that better match the fixed-rate sterling cash flows from its asset portfolio. Similarly, the U.S. financial institution transforms fixed-rate sterling liabilities into fixed-rate dollar liabilities that better match the fixed-rate dollar cash flows on its asset portfolio. In undertaking this exchange of cash flows, the two parties normally agree on a fixed

---

18. In a currency swap, it is usual to include both principal and interest payments as part of the swap agreement. For interest rate swaps, it is usual to include only interest rate payments. The reason for this is that both principal and interest are exposed to foreign exchange risk.

Figure 10–12 Fixed-Fixed Pound/Dollar Currency Swap

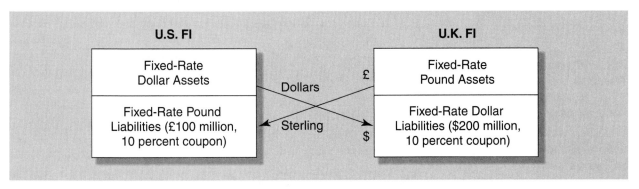

exchange rate for the cash flows at the beginning of the period.[19] In this example, the fixed exchange rate is $2/£1.

Note in the example above that should the exchange rate change from the rate agreed in the swap ($2/£1), either one or the other side would be losing in the sense that a new swap might be entered into at a more favorable exchange rate to one party. Specifically, if the dollar were to appreciate against the pound over the life of the swap, the agreement would become more costly for the U.S. financial institution. If, however, the dollar depreciated, the U.K. financial institution would find the agreement increasingly costly over the swap's life.

Swap Markets

Swap transactions are generally heterogeneous in terms of maturities, indexes used to determine payments, and timing of payments—there is no standardized contract. Swap dealers exist to serve the function of taking the opposite side of each transaction in order to keep the swap market liquid by locating or matching counterparties, or in many cases, taking one side of the swap themselves. In a direct swap between two counterparties, each party must find another party having a mirror image financing requirement—for example, a financial institution in need of swapping fixed-rate payments, made quarterly for the next 10 years, on $25 million in liabilities must find a counterparty in need of swapping $25 million in floating-rate payments made quarterly for the next 10 years. Without swap dealers, the search costs of finding such counterparties to a swap can be significant.

A further advantage of swap dealers is that they generally guarantee swap payments over the life of the contract. If one of the counterparties defaults on a direct swap, the other counterparty is no longer adequately hedged against risk and may have to replace the defaulted swap with a new swap at less favorable terms (replacement risk). By booking a swap with a swap dealer, a default by a counterparty will not affect the other counterparty. The swap dealer incurs any costs associated with the default (the fee or spread charged by the swap dealer to each party in a swap incorporates this default risk).[20] Commercial and investment banks have evolved as the major swap dealers, mainly because of their close ties to the financial markets and their specialized

19. As with interest rate swaps, this exchange rate reflects the contracting parties' expectations as to future exchange rate movements.

20. For interest rate swaps where the dealer intermediates, a different (higher) fixed rate will be set for receiving fixed rate payments compared to paying fixed rate.

skills in assessing credit risk. Each swap market dealer manages a "book" of swaps listing its swap positions.

In contrast to futures and options markets, swap markets are governed by very little regulation—there is no central governing body overseeing swap market operations. However, the International Swaps and Derivatives Association (ISDA) is a global trade association with over 425 members (including most of the world's major financial institutions) that sets codes and standards for swap markets. Established in 1985, the ISDA establishes, reviews, and updates the code of standards (the language and provisions) for swap documentation. The ISDA also acts as the spokesgroup for the industry on regulatory changes and issues, promotes the development of risk management practices for swap dealers (for example, the ISDA was instrumental in helping to develop the guidelines set by the Basle committee on capital adequacy in financial institutions—see Chapter 14), provides a forum for informing and educating swap market participants about relevant issues, and sets standards of commercial conduct for its members.

Further, because commercial banks are the major swap dealers, the swap markets are subject, indirectly, to regulations imposed by the Board of Governors of the Federal Reserve, the FDIC, and other bank regulatory agencies charged with monitoring bank risk. For example, commercial banks must include swap risk exposure when calculating risk-based capital requirements (see Chapter 14). To the extent that swap activity is part of a bank's overall business, swap markets are monitored for abuses. Investment banks and insurance companies have recently become bigger players in the swap markets, however, and these dealers are subject to few regulations on their swap dealings.

www.isda.org/

www.bog.frb.fed.us/

www.fdic.gov/

Do You Understand?

1. Which party in a swap is the swap buyer and which party is the swap seller?
2. What the difference is between an interest rate swap and a currency swap?

Caps, Floors, and Collars

8

Caps, floors, and collars are derivative securities that have many uses, especially in helping an FI to hedge interest rate risk. In general, FIs purchase interest rate caps if they are exposed to losses when interest rates rise. Usually, this happens if FIs are funding assets with floating-rate liabilities such as notes indexed to the London Interbank Offered Rate (or some other cost of funds) and they have fixed-rate assets or they are net long in bonds. By contrast, FIs purchase floors when they have fixed costs of debt and have variable rates (returns) on assets or they are net short in bonds. Finally, FIs purchase collars to finance cap or floor positions or are concerned about excessive interest rate volatility.

www.isda.org/

As of the end of June 1998, the ISDA reported a total of $4.92 trillion notional value outstanding worldwide in caps, floors, and collars (51.6 percent issued in the United States and 48.4 percent issued outside the United States). The maturity on these contracts was distributed as 35.5 percent with less than one year to maturity; 45.6 percent with between one and five years to maturity; and 18.9 percent with greater than five years to maturity. The market for caps, floors, and collars is operated over the counter by financial institutions.

cap

A call option on interest rates, often with multiple exercise dates.

Buying a **cap** means buying a call option or a succession of call options on interest rates.[21] Specifically, if interest rates rise above a cap rate, which acts in a similar fashion to a strike price in an option contract, the seller of the cap—usually a bank—compensates the buyer—for example, another financial institution—in return for an up-front premium. Suppose that two firms enter a two-year cap agreement with a no-

---

21. Note that a cap can be viewed as a call option on interest rates (as discussed here) or as a put option on bond prices, since rising interest rates mean falling bond prices. Similarly, a floor (discussed in the next paragraph) can be viewed as a put option on interest rates or a call option on bond prices. We follow market convention and discuss caps and floors as options on interest rates rather than on bond prices.

Figure 10–13   Hypothetical Path of Interest Rates during a Cap Agreement

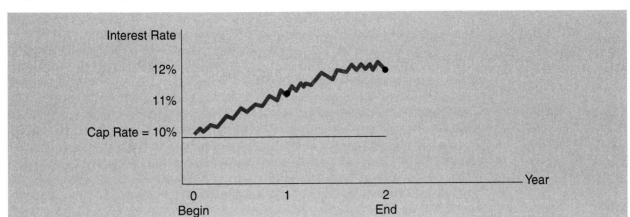

Figure 10–14   Hypothetical Path of Interest Rates during a Floor Agreement

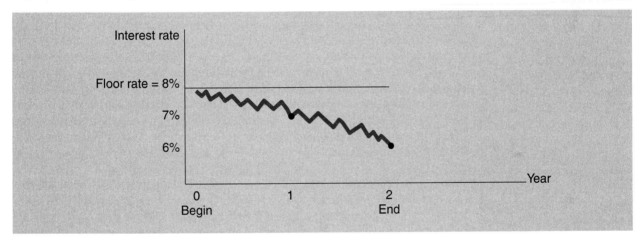

tional value of $1 million. The cap rate is 10 percent and payments are settled once a year based on year-end interest rates. For the interest rate movements shown in Figure 10–13, the cap writer owes the cap buyer (11% − 10%) × $1 million, or $100,000, at the end of year 1, and (12% − 10%) × $1 million, or $200,000, at the end of year 2. As a result, buying an interest rate cap is like buying insurance against an (excessive) increase in interest rates. A cap agreement can have one or many exercise dates.

floor

A put option on interest rates, often with multiple exercise dates.

Buying a **floor** is similar to buying a put option on interest rates. If interest rates fall below the floor rate, the seller of the floor compensates the buyer in return for an up-front premium. For example, suppose that two financial institutions enter a two-year floor agreement with a notional value of $1 million. The floor rate is 8 percent, and payments are settled once a year based on year-end rates. For the interest rate movements shown in Figure 10–14, the floor writer owes the floor buyer (8% − 7%) × $1 million, or $100,000, at the end of year 1, and (8% − 6%) × $1 million, or $200,000, at the end of year 2. As with caps, floor agreements can have one or many exercise dates.

collar

A position taken simultaneously in a cap and a floor.

A **collar** occurs when a firm takes a simultaneous position in a cap and a floor, usually *buying* a cap and *selling* a floor. The idea here is that the firm wants to hedge

Figure 10–15 Hypothetical Path of Interest Rates during a Collar Agreement

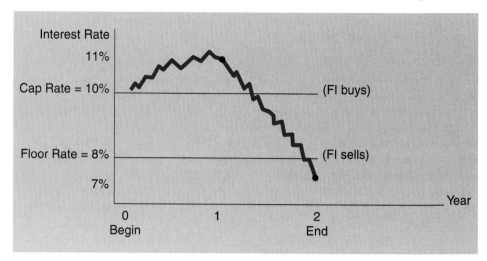

itself against rising rates but wants to finance the cost of the cap. One way to do this is to sell a floor and use the premiums earned on the floor to pay the premium on the purchased cap. For example, suppose that a financial institution enters into a two-year collar agreement with a notional value of $1 million. The floor rate is 8 percent and the cap rate is 10 percent. Payments are settled once a year based on year-end rates. For the interest rate movements shown in Figure 10–15, the collar buyer, the financial institution, gains (11% − 10%) × $1 million, or $100,000, at the end of year 1. However, since the financial institution has written or sold a floor to another financial institution to finance the cap purchase, it pays (8% − 7%) × $1 million, or $100,000, at the end of year 2.

Many firms invested in caps and collars at the end of the 1990s in expectation that interest rates would increase. For example, Credit Suisse Asset Management arranged a $1.5 billion collar for an (unnamed) Fortune 500 company that wanted to hedge a large portfolio of equities against interest rate increases with minimal costs. Also, as euro interest rates hit historical lows (e.g., the six-month euro-CD rate was as low as 2.6 percent in May 1999), many European corporations (e.g., Endesa, a Spanish electric company, and Kemira, a Finnish chemical and fertilizer company) turned to European banks to purchase caps and collars to hedge against interest rate increases.

Do You Understand?

1. What the difference is between a cap and a collar?
2. The conditions under which a firm would buy a floor?

Summary

In this chapter, we introduced the major derivative securities and the markets in which they trade. Derivative securities (forwards, futures, options, and swaps) are securities whose value depends on the value of an underlying asset but whose payoff is not guaranteed with cash flows from these assets. Derivative securities can be used as investments on which a trader hopes to directly profit or as hedge instruments used to protect the trader against risk from another asset or liability held. We examined the characteristics of the various securities and the markets in which each trade. We look at how these securities are used by financial institutions to hedge various risks in Chapter 24.

End-of-Chapter Questions

1. What is a derivative security?
2. What is the difference between a spot contract, a forward contract, and a futures contract?
3. What are the functions of floor brokers and professional traders on the futures exchanges?
4. What is the purpose of requiring a margin on a futures or option transaction? What is the difference between an initial margin and a maintenance margin?
5. When is a futures or option trader in a long versus a short position in the derivative contract?
6. Refer to Table 10–4.
    a. What was the settlement price on the December 2000 Eurodollar futures contract on Tuesday, January 18, 2000?
    b. How many 30-day federal fund futures contracts traded on Friday, January 14, 2000?
    c. What is the face value on a Swiss franc currency futures contract on January 18, 2000?
    d. What was the settlement price on the June 2000 DJIA futures contract on January 14, 2000?
7. Refer to Table 10–4.
    a. If you think two-year Treasury note prices will fall between January 18, 2000 and March 2000, what type of futures position would you take?
    b. If you think inflation in Japan will increase by more than that in the U.S. between January and March 2000, what type of futures position would you take?
    c. If you think stock prices will fall between January and March 2000, what type of position would you take in the March S&P 500 Index futures contract? What happens if stock prices actually rise?
8. What is an option? How does an option differ from a forward or futures contract?
9. What is the difference between a call option and a put option?
10. You have taken a long position in a call option on IBM common stock. The option has an exercise price of $136 and IBM's stock currently trades at $140. The option premium is $5 per contract.
    a. What is your net profit on the option if IBM's stock price increases to $150 at expiration of the option and you exercise the option?
    b. What is your net profit if IBM's stock price decreases to $130?

11. You have purchased a put option on Pfizer common stock. The option has an exercise price of $38 and Pfizer's stock currently trades at $40. The option premium is $0.50 per contract.
    a. What is your net profit on the option if Pfizer's stock price does not change over the life of the option?
    b. What is your net profit on the option if Pfizer's stock price falls to $34 and you exercise the option?
12. What are the three ways an option holder can liquidate his or her position?
13. Refer to Table 10–8.
    a. How many Amazon.com April 70 put options traded on Tuesday, January 18, 2000?
    b. What was the closing price of a T-note February 94 futures call option on January 18, 2000?
    c. How many call options on the DJIA futures contract traded on Friday, January 14, 2000?
    d. What was the exchange rate between the Canadian dollar and the U.S. dollar on January 18, 2000?
14. Who are the major regulators of futures and options markets?
15. What is a swap?
16. What is the difference between an interest rate swap and a currency swap?
17. Which party is the swap buyer and which is the swap seller in a swap transaction?
18. A commercial bank has fixed-rate long-term loans in its asset portfolio and variable-rate CDs in its liability portfolio. Bank managers believe interest rates will increase in the future. What side of a fixed-floating rate swap would the commercial bank need to take to protect against this interest rate risk?
19. An American firm has British pound–denominated accounts payable on its balance sheet. Managers believe the exchange rate of British pounds to U.S. dollars will depreciate before the accounts will be paid. What type of currency swap should the firm enter?
20. What is the difference between a cap, a floor, and a collar? When would a firm enter any of these derivative security positions?
21. Go to the Commodity Futures Trading Commission website and get the most recent information on futures and options trading volume.

Appendix   Black-Scholes Option Pricing Model

In 1973, Fisher Black and Myron Scholes published their option pricing model.[22] Since its publication, improvements and extensions have been made to the model and it is

22. See F. Black and M. Scholes, "The Pricing of Options and Corporate Liabilities," *Journal of Political Economy* 81, (May–June, 1973), pp. 637–54.

now used by most professional option traders. The Black-Scholes option pricing model used to value European options is presented in the following equation:

$$C = N(d_1)S - E(e^{-rT})N(d_2)$$

$$d_1 = \frac{\ln(S/E) + (r + \sigma^2/2)T}{\sigma\sqrt{T}}$$

$$d_2 = d_1 - \sigma\sqrt{T}$$

where

C = Call option price
S = Price on the asset underlying the option
E = Exercise price of the option
r = Riskless rate of interest over one year
σ = Standard deviation of the underlying asset's return
T = Time to expiration of the option as a fraction of one year
e = Base of the natural logarithm, or the exponential function
$\ln(S/E)$ = Natural log of S/E
$N(d)$ = Value of the cumulative normal distribution evaluated at d_1 and d_2

The Black-Scholes option pricing formula assumes the following:

- Capital markets are frictionless (i.e., there are no transaction costs or taxes and all information is simultaneously and freely available to all investors).
- The variability in the underlying asset's return is constant.
- The probability distribution of the underlying asset's price is log normal.
- The risk-free rate is constant and known over time.
- No dividends are paid on the underlying asset.
- No early exercise is allowed on the option.

Example 10–5   Using the Black-Scholes Formula to Value a Call Option

Suppose you own a call option on a stock for which the following applies:

Underlying stock's price = $60
Exercise price on the option = $58
Annual risk-free rate = 5 percent
Time to expiration on the option = 3 months
Standard deviation of the underlying stock's return = .12

To calculate the value of the option, we first calculate d_1 and d_2 as follows:

$$d_1 = \frac{\ln(S/E) + (r + \sigma^2/2)T}{\sigma\sqrt{T}}$$

$$= \frac{\ln(60/58) + (.05 + (.12)^2/2)(3/12)}{.12\,(3/12)^{1/2}} = .8034$$

$$d_2 = d_1 - \sigma\sqrt{T}$$

$$= .8034 - .12\,(3/12)^{1/2} = .7434$$

Next, the values of $N(d_1)$ and $N(d_2)$ are found from Table 10–A1, which shows the cumulative normal distribution. Interpolation from the values in Table 10–A1 give $N(d_1)$:

Table 10–A1   Values of the Cumulative Normal Distribution

d	N(d)	d	N(d)	d	N(d)	d	N(d)	d	N(d)	d	N(d)
		−2.00	.0228	−1.00	.1587	.00	.5000	1.00	.8413	2.00	.9773
−2.95	.0016	−1.95	.0256	−.95	.1711	.05	.5199	1.05	.8531	2.05	.9798
−2.90	.0019	−1.90	.0287	−.90	.1841	.10	.5398	1.10	.8643	2.10	.9821
−2.85	.0022	−1.85	.0322	−.85	.1977	.15	.5596	1.15	.8749	2.15	.9842
−2.80	.0026	−1.80	.0359	−.80	.2119	.20	.5793	1.20	.8849	2.20	.9861
−2.75	.0030	−1.75	.0401	−.75	.2266	.25	.5987	1.25	.8944	2.25	.9878
−2.70	.0035	−1.70	.0446	−.70	.2420	.30	.6179	1.30	.9032	2.30	.9893
−2.65	.0040	−1.65	.0495	−.65	.2578	.35	.6368	1.35	.9115	2.35	.9906
−2.60	.0047	−1.60	.0548	−.60	.2743	.40	.6554	1.40	.9192	2.40	.9918
−2.55	.0054	−1.55	.0606	−.55	.2912	.45	.6735	1.45	.9265	2.45	.9929
−2.50	.0062	−1.50	.0668	−.50	.3085	.50	.6915	1.50	.9332	2.50	.9938
−2.45	.0071	−1.45	.0735	−.45	.3264	.55	.7088	1.55	.9394	2.55	.9946
−2.40	.0082	−1.40	.0808	−.40	.3446	.60	.7257	1.60	.9459	2.60	.9953
−2.35	.0094	−1.35	.0855	−.35	.3632	.65	.7422	1.65	.9505	2.65	.9960
−2.30	.0107	−1.30	.0968	−.30	.3821	.70	.7580	1.70	.9554	2.70	.9965
−2.25	.0122	−1.25	.1057	−.25	.4013	.75	.7734	1.75	.9599	2.75	.9970
−2.20	.0139	−1.20	.1151	−.20	.4207	.80	.7831	1.80	.9641	2.80	.9974
−2.15	.0158	−1.15	.1251	−.15	.4404	.85	.8023	1.85	.9678	2.85	.9973
−2.10	.0179	−1.10	.1337	−.10	.4502	.90	.8159	1.90	.9713	2.90	.9931
−2.05	.0202	−1.05	.1469	−.05	.4301	.95	.8289	1.95	.9744	2.95	.9984

d_1	$N(d_1)$
.80	.7831
.8034	?
.85	.8023

or:

$$N(d_1) = .7844$$

and

$$N(d_2):$$

d_1	$N(d_1)$
.70	.7580
.7434	?
.75	.7734

or:

$$N(d_2) = .7713$$

Next, these values are plugged into the Black-Scholes formula to get the call option's price as follows:

$$C = N(d_1)S - E(e^{-rT})N(d_2)$$

$$= .7844(60) - 58(e^{-.05(3/12)}).7713$$

$$= 47.0640 - 44.1797 = 2.884$$

The Black-Scholes model can also be used to price European put options. The put pricing model is presented in the following equation:

$$P = -N(-d_1)S + E(e^{-rT})N(-d_2)$$

where

P = put option price

All other variables are the same as above

Example 10–6 Using the Black-Scholes Formula to Value a Put Option

Suppose you own a put option on the stock described in Example 10–5. The put option has an exercise price of $65. The values of $d_1 = -.8034$ and of $d_2 = -.7434$. The values of $N(d_1)$ and $N(d_2)$ are found from Table 10–A1, which shows the cumulative normal distribution. Interpolation from Table 10–A1 gives $N(d_1)$:

d_1	$N(d_1)$
−.85	.1977
−.8034	?
−.80	.2119

or,

$N(d_1) = .2109$

and

$N(d_2)$:

d_1	$N(d_1)$
−.75	.2266
−.7434	?
−.70	.2420

or

$N(d_2) = .2286$

Next, these values are plugged into the Black-Scholes formula to get the call option's price as follows:

$$P = -N(-d_1)S + E(e^{-rT})N(-d_2)$$

$$= -.2109(60) + 65\,(e^{-.05(3/12)}).2286$$

$$= -12.654 + 14.674 = 2.020$$

Depository Institutions

Part Three of the text summarizes the operations of depository institutions. Chapter 11 describes the key characteristics and recent trends in the commercial banking sector. Chapter 12 does the same for the thrift institution sector. Chapter 13 describes the financial statements of a typical depository institution and the ratios used to analyze those statements. Chapter 14 provides a comprehensive look at the regulations under which these financial institutions operate and, particularly, at the effect of recent changes in regulations.

chapter eleven

Commercial Banks

Chapter Navigator

1. What is a commercial bank?

2. What are the main assets held by commercial banks?

3. What are the main liabilities held by commercial banks?

4. What types of off-balance-sheet activities do commercial banks undertake?

5. What factors have motivated the significant decrease in the number of commercial banks?

6. How has the commercial banking industry performed in recent years?

7. Who are the main regulators of commercial banks?

Commercial Banks as a Sector of the Financial Institutions Industry: Chapter Overview

The products that modern financial institutions sell and the risks they face are becoming increasingly similar, as are the techniques they use to measure and manage these risks. The two panels in Table 11–1 indicate the products sold by the financial services industry in 1950 and in 2000. Three major FI groups—commercial banks, savings institutions, and credit unions—are also called *depository institutions* because a significant proportion of their funds come from customer deposits. Chapters 11 through 14 describe depository institutions, their financial statements, and the regulations that govern their operations.

Table 11-1 Products Sold by the U.S. Financial Services Industry

	Function															
Institution	Payment Services		Savings Products		Fiduciary Services		Lending				Underwriting Issuance of				Insuarance and Risk Management Products	
							Business		Consumer		Equity		Debt			
	1950	2000	1950	2000	1950	2000	1950	2000	1950	2000	1950	2000	1950	2000	1950	2000
Depository institutions	X	X	X	X	X	X	X	X	X	X		X		X		X
Insurance companies		X	X	X		X	*	X		X		†		†	X	X
Finance companies		X		X		X	*	X	X	X		†		†		X
Securities firms		X	X	X	X	X		X		X	X	X	X	X		X
Pension funds			X	X		X		X								X
Mutual funds		X	X	X		X										

*Minor involvement.
†Selective involvement via affiliates.

Figure 11-1 Differences in Balance Sheets of Depository Institutions and Nonfinancial Firms

Depository Institutions

Assets	Liabilities and Equity
Loans	Deposits
Other financial assets	
Other nonfinancial assets	Other liabilities and equity

Nonfinancial Firms

Assets	Liabilities and Equity
Deposits	Loans
Other financial assets	
Other nonfinancial assets	Other liabilities and equity

As we examine the structure of depository institutions and their financial statements, notice a distinguishing feature between them and nonfinancial firms illustrated in Figure 11–1. Specifically, depository institutions' major assets are loans (financial assets) and their major liabilities are deposits. Just the opposite is true for nonfinancial firms, whose deposits are listed as assets on their balance sheets and whose loans are listed as liabilities. In contrast to depository institutions, nonfinancial firms' major assets are nonfinancial (tangible) assets such as buildings and machinery. Indeed, as illustrated in Figure 11–2, depository institutions provide loans to, and accept deposits from, nonfinancial firms (and individuals), while nonfinancial firms provide deposits to, and obtain loans from, depository institutions.

Figure 11–2   Interaction Between Depository Institutions and Nonfinancial Firms

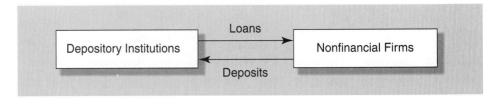

Our attention in this chapter focuses on the largest sector of the depository institutions group, commercial banks, and in particular: (1) the size, structure, and composition of this industry group, (2) its balance sheets and recent trends, (3) the industry's recent performance, and (4) its regulators.

Definition of a Commercial Bank

Commercial banks represent the largest group of depository institutions measured by asset size. They perform functions similar to those of savings institutions and credit unions—they accept deposits (liabilities) and make loans (assets). Commercial banks are distinguishable from savings institutions and credit unions, however, in the size and composition of their loans and deposits. Specifically, while deposits are the major source of funding, commercial bank liabilities usually include several types of *non*deposit sources of funds (such as subordinated notes and debentures). Moreover, their loans are broader in range, including consumer, commercial, international, and real estate loans. Commercial banks are regulated separately from savings institutions and credit unions. Within the banking industry, the structure and composition of assets and liabilities also varies significantly for banks of different asset sizes.

Do You Understand?

1. What the three categories of depository institutions are?
2. What distinguishes a commercial bank from other types of depository institutions?

Balance Sheets and Recent Trends

Chapter 13 provides a detailed discussion of the financial statements (balance sheets and income statements) of commercial banks and how financial statements are used by regulators, stockholders, depositors, and creditors to evaluate bank performance. In this chapter, we present a brief introduction to commercial bank balance sheets and their recent performance, highlighting trends in each.

Assets

Consider the aggregate balance sheet (in Table 11–2) and the percentage distributions (in Figure 11–3) for all U.S. commercial banks as of May 26, 1999. The majority of the assets held by commercial banks are loans. Total loans amounted to $3,478.6 billion, or 66.0 percent of total assets, and fell into four broad classes: business or commercial and industrial loans; commercial and residential real estate loans; individual loans, such as consumer loans for auto purchases and credit card loans; and all other loans, such as loans to emerging market countries.[1]

---

1. The reserve for loan and lease losses is a contra-asset account representing an estimate by the bank's management of the percentage of gross loans (and leases) that will have to be "charged-off" due to future defaults (see Chapter 13).

Table 11–2 Balance Sheet

(all U.S. commercial banks, in billions of dollars)

Assets

Total cash assets			$ 253.8
U.S. government securities		$ 801.4	
Other		391.6	
Investment securities			1,193.0
Interbank loans		223.0	
Loans excluding interbank		3,314.3	
Commercial and industrial	$ 948.5		
Real estate	1,343.0		
Individual	496.4		
All other	526.4		
Less: Reserve for loan losses		58.7	
Total loans			3,478.6
Other assets			347.6
Total assets			$5,273.0

Liabilities and Equity

Transaction accounts	$ 667.4	
Nontransaction accounts	$2,688.5	
Total deposits		$3,355.9
Borrowings		1,006.0
Other liabilities		462.3
Total liabilities		$4,824.2
Equity		448.8

Source: Federal Reserve Bulletin, May 26, 1999, seasonally adjusted. *www.bog.frb.fed.us/*

Figure 11–3 Distribution of Commercial Bank Assets, Liabilities, and Equity, May 1999

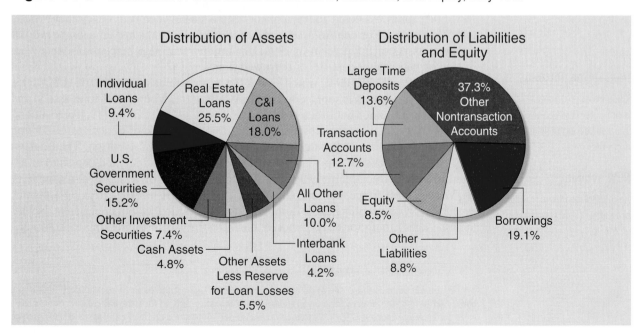

Source: Federal Deposit Insurance Corporation, *Quarterly Banking Profile*, Second Quarter 1999. *www.fdic.gov/*

Investment securities consist of items such as interest-bearing deposits purchased from other FIs, federal funds sold to other banks, repurchase agreements (RPs or repos),[2] U.S. Treasury and agency securities, municipal securities issued by states and political subdivisions, mortgage-backed securities, and other debt and equity securities. In 1999, the investment portfolio totaled $1,193.0 billion, or 22.6 percent of total assets. U.S. government securities such as U.S. Treasury bonds totaled $801.4 billion, with other securities making up the remainder. Investment securities generate interest income for the bank and are also used for trading and liquidity management purposes. Many investment securities held by banks are highly liquid, have low default risk, and can usually be traded in secondary markets (see Chapter 13).

A major inference we can draw from this asset structure (and the importance of loans in this asset structure) is that the major risk faced by modern commercial bank managers is credit or default risk and, ultimately, insolvency risk (see Chapters 20 and 21). Because commercial banks are highly leveraged and therefore hold little equity (see below) compared to total assets, even a relatively small amount of loan defaults can wipe out the equity of a bank, leaving it insolvent.[3] We look at recent loan performance below.

Figure 11–4 shows broad trends over the 1951–1999 period in the four principal earning asset areas of commercial banks: business loans (or commercial and industrial loans), securities, mortgages, and consumer loans. Although business loans were the major asset on bank balance sheets between 1965 and 1990, they have dropped in importance (as a proportion of the balance sheet) since 1990. At the same time, mortgages have increased in importance. These trends reflect a number of long-term and temporary influences. Important long-term influences have been the growth of the commercial paper market (see Chapter 5) and the public bond markets (see Chapter 6), which have become competitive and alternative funding sources to commercial bank loans for major corporations. Another factor has been the securitization of mortgage loans (see Chapter 7), which entails the pooling and packaging of mortgage loans for sale in the form of bonds.

Liabilities

Commercial banks have two major sources of funds (other than the equity provided by owners and stockholders): (1) deposits and (2) borrowed or other liability funds. As noted above, a major difference between banks and other firms is their high leverage or debt-to-assets ratio. For example, banks had an average ratio of equity to assets of 8.5 percent in 1999; this implies that 91.5 percent of assets were funded by debt, either deposits or borrowed funds.

Note that in Table 11–2, which shows the aggregate balance sheet of U.S. banks, in May 1999, deposits amounted to $3,355.9 billion (63.6 percent of total assets) and borrowings and other liabilities were $1,006.0 and $462.3 billion (19.1 percent and 8.8 percent of total assets), respectively. Of the total stock of deposits, transaction accounts represented 19.9 percent of total deposits, or $667.4 billion. **Transaction accounts** are checkable deposits that either bear no interest (demand deposits) or are interest bearing (most commonly called negotiable order of withdrawal accounts or **NOW accounts**). Since their introduction in 1980, interest-bearing checking accounts, especially NOW accounts, have dominated the transaction accounts of banks. Nevertheless, since limitations are imposed on the ability of corporations to hold such

transaction accounts

The sum of noninterest-bearing demand deposits and interest-bearing checking accounts.

NOW account

An interest-bearing checking account.

---

2. Federal funds and repos are described in detail in Chapter 5.

3. Losses such as those due to defaults are charged off against the equity (stockholders' stake) in a bank. Additions to the reserve for loan and lease losses accounts (and, in turn, the expense account "provisions for losses on loans and leases") to meet *expected* defaults reduce retained earnings and, thus, reduce equity of the bank. *Unexpected* defaults (e.g., due to a sudden major recession) are meant to be written off against the remainder of the bank's equity (e.g., its retained earnings and funds raised from share offerings).

Figure 11–4 Portfolio Shift: U.S. Commercial Banks' Financial Assets

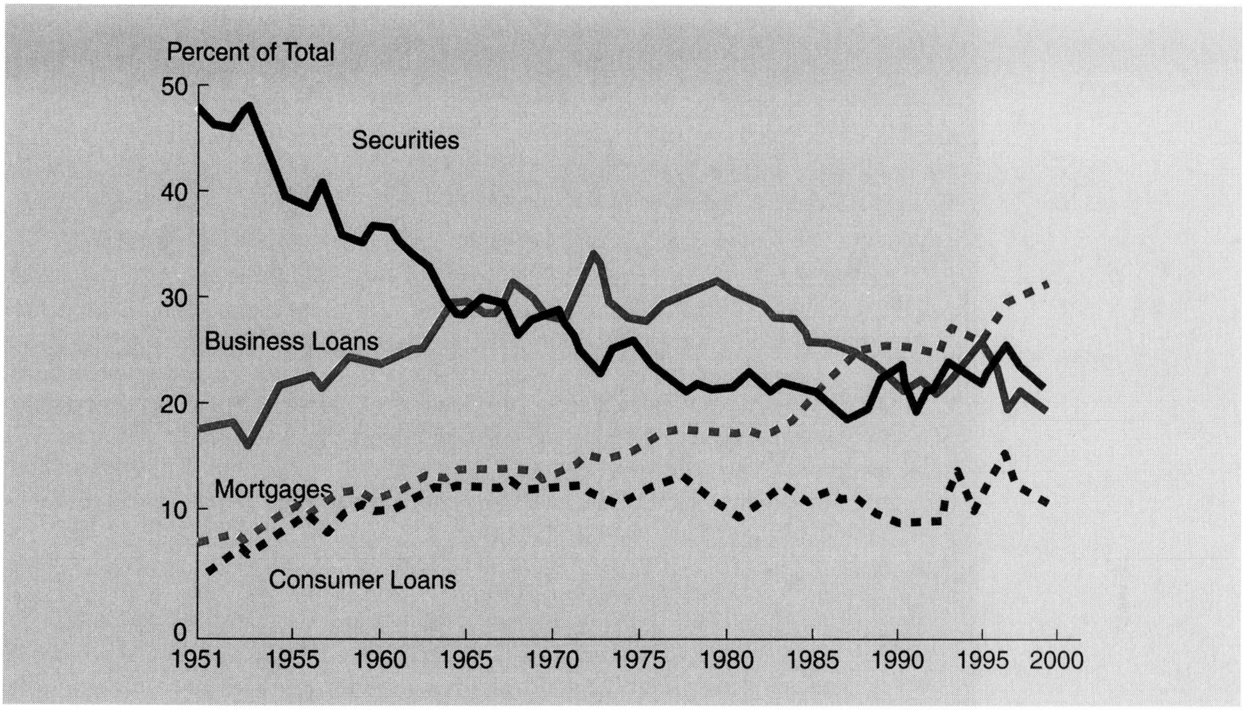

Source: Federal Deposit Insurance Corporation, *Statistics on Banking*, various issues. *www.fdic.gov/*

accounts, and NOW accounts have minimum balance requirements, noninterest-bearing demand deposits are still held. The second major segment of deposits is retail or household savings and time deposits, normally individual account holdings of less than $100,000. Important components of bank retail savings accounts are small non-transaction accounts, which include passbook savings accounts and retail time deposits. Small nontransaction accounts compose 58.7 percent of total deposits. However, this disguises an important trend in the supply of these deposits to banks. Specifically, the amount held of retail savings and time deposits has been falling in recent years, largely as a result of competition from money market mutual funds.[4] These funds pay a competitive rate of interest based on wholesale money market rates by pooling and investing funds (see Chapter 18) while requiring relatively small-denomination investments.

The third major segment of deposit funds is large time deposits ($100,000 or more);[5] these deposits amounted to $719.1 billion, or approximately 21.4 percent of total deposits, in May 1999. These are primarily **negotiable certificates of deposit** (deposit claims with promised interest rates and fixed maturities of at least 14 days) that can be resold to outside investors in an organized secondary market. As such, they are usually distinguished from retail time deposits by their negotiability and secondary market liquidity.

Nondeposit liabilities comprise borrowings and other liabilities that total 30.4 percent of all bank liabilities, or $1,486.3 billion. These categories include a broad array of instruments, such as purchases of federal funds (bank reserves) on the interbank market and repurchase agreements (temporary swaps of securities for federal funds) at the short end of the maturity spectrum, to the issuance of notes and bonds at the longer

negotiable CDs

Fixed-maturity interest-bearing deposits with face values of $100,000 or more that can be resold in the secondary market.

---

4. See U.S. General Accounting Office, "Mutual Funds: Impact on Bank Deposits and Credit Availability," GAO/GGD-95-230 (Washington, D.C.: Government Printing Offices, 1995).

5. $100,000 is the cap for explicit coverage under bank deposit insurance. We discuss this in more detail in Chapter 14.

end (see Chapters 5 and 6). We discuss commercial banks' use of each of these in Chapter 13.

Overall, the liability structure of banks' balance sheets tends to reflect a shorter maturity structure than that of their asset portfolio. Further, relatively more liquid instruments such as deposits and interbank borrowings are used to fund relatively less liquid assets such as loans. Thus, interest rate risk—or maturity mismatch risk—and liquidity risk are key exposure concerns for bank managers (see Chapters 20 through 25).

Equity

Commercial bank equity capital (8.51 percent of total liabilities and equity in May 1999) consists mainly of common and preferred stock (listed at par value), surplus[6] or additional paid-in capital, and retained earnings. Regulators require banks to hold a minimum level of equity capital to act as a buffer against losses from their on- and off-balance-sheet activities (see Chapter 14). Because of the relatively low cost of deposit funding, banks tend to hold equity close to the minimum levels set by regulators. As we discuss in Chapters 14 and 23, this impacts banks' exposure to risk and their ability to grow—both on and off the balance sheet—over time.

Off-Balance-Sheet Activities

The balance sheet itself does not reflect the total scope of bank activities. Banks conduct many fee-related activities off the balance sheet. Off-balance-sheet (OBS) activities are becoming increasingly important, in terms of their dollar value and the income they generate for banks—especially as the ability of banks to attract high-quality loan applicants and deposits becomes ever more difficult. OBS activities include issuing various types of guarantees (such as letters of credit), which often have a strong insurance underwriting element, and making future commitments to lend. Both services generate additional fee income for banks. Off-balance-sheet activities also involve engaging in derivative transactions—futures, forwards, options, and swaps.

off-balance-sheet (OBS) asset

When an event occurs, this item moves onto the asset side of the balance sheet or income is realized on the income statement.

off-balance-sheet liability

When an event occurs, this item moves onto the liability side of the balance sheet or an expense is realized on the income statement.

Under current accounting standards, such activities are not shown on the current balance sheet. Rather, an item or activity is an **off-balance-sheet asset** if, when a contingent event occurs, the item or activity moves onto the asset side of the balance sheet or an income item is realized on the income statement. Conversely, an item or activity is an **off-balance-sheet liability** if, when a contingent event occurs, the item or activity moves onto the liability side of the balance sheet or an expense item is realized on the income statement.

By moving activities off the balance sheet, banks hope to earn additional fee income to complement declining margins or spreads on their traditional lending business. At the same time, they can avoid regulatory costs or "taxes" since reserve requirements and deposit insurance premiums are not levied on off-balance-sheet activities (see Chapter 14). Thus, banks have both earnings and regulatory "tax-avoidance" incentives to undertake activities off their balance sheets.

Off-balance-sheet activities, however, can involve risks that add to the overall insolvency exposure of a financial intermediary (FI). Indeed, the failure of the U.K. investment bank Barings and the bankruptcy of Orange County in California in the 1990s have been linked to FIs' off-balance-sheet activities in derivatives. More recently, the 1997–1998 Asian crisis left banks that had large positions in the Asian-related derivative securities markets with large losses. For example, Chase Manhattan Corp. announced a 1998 third quarter earnings decrease of 15 percent, due to losses in global markets, including derivative securities. However, off-balance-sheet activities and instruments have both risk-reducing as well as risk-increasing attributes, and,

---

6. Surplus or additional paid-in capital shows the difference between the stock's par value and what the original stockholders paid when they bought the newly issued shares.

when used appropriately, they can reduce or hedge an FIs' interest rate, credit, and foreign exchange risks.

We show the notional, or face, value of bank OBS activities, and their distribution and growth, for 1992 to 1999 in Table 11–3. Notice the relative growth in the notional dollar value of OBS activities in Table 11–3. By the first quarter of 1999, the notional value of OBS bank activities was $36,978.0 billion compared to the $5,409.7 billion value of on-balance-sheet activities. It should be noted that the notional or face value of OBS activities does not accurately reflect the risk to the bank undertaking such activities. The potential for the bank to gain or lose on the contract is based on the possible change in the market value of the contract over the life of the contract rather than the notional or face value of the contract, normally less than 3 percent of the notional value of an OBS contract.[7]

The use of derivative contracts accelerated during the 1992–1999 period and accounted for much of the growth in OBS activity (see Figure 11–5). Figure 11–5 shows that this growth has occurred for all types of derivative contracts: futures and forwards, swaps, and options. As we discuss in detail in Chapter 24, the significant growth in derivative securities activities by commercial banks has been a direct response to the increased interest rate risk, credit risk, and foreign exchange risk exposures they have faced, both domestically and internationally. In particular, these contracts offer banks a way to hedge these risks without having to make extensive changes on the balance sheet.

www.occ.treas.gov/

Although the simple notional dollar value of OBS items overestimates their risk exposure amounts, the increase in these activities is still nothing short of phenomenal.[8] Indeed, this phenomenal increase has pushed regulators into imposing capital requirements on such activities and into explicitly recognizing an FI's solvency risk exposure from pursuing such activities. We describe these capital requirements in Chapter 14.

4   As noted in Table 11–3 and Figure 11–5, major types of OBS activities for U.S. banks include the following:

- Loan commitments.
- Standby letters of credit and letters of credit.
- Derivative contracts: futures, forwards, swaps, and options.
- When-issued securities.
- Loans sold.

We discuss each of these in Chapter 13.

Other Fee-Generating Activities

Commercial banks engage in other fee-generating activities that cannot easily be identified from analyzing their on- and off-balance-sheet accounts. Two of these include trust services and correspondent banking.

Trust Services.   The trust department of a commercial bank holds and manages assets for individuals or corporations. Only the largest banks have sufficient staff to offer trust services. Individual trusts represent about one-half of all trust assets managed by commercial banks. These trusts include estate assets and assets delegated to bank trust departments by less financially sophisticated investors. Pension fund assets are the second largest group of assets managed by the trust departments of commercial banks. The banks manage the pension funds, act as trustees for any bonds held by the

---

7. The market value of a swap (today) is the difference between the present value of the cash flows (expected) to be received minus the present value of cash flows expected to be paid.

8. This overestimation of risk exposure occurs because the risk exposure from a contingent claim (such as an option) is usually less than its face value (see Chapter 13).

Table 11–3 Aggregate Volume of Off-Balance-Sheet Commitments and Contingencies by U.S. Commercial Banks, Annual Data as of December*
(in billions of dollars)

	1992	1993	1994	1995	1996	1997	1998	1999	Distribution 1999
Commitments to lend	$ 1,272.0	$ 1,455.3	$ 1,768.3	$ 2,157.4	$ 2,528.7	$ 3,084.9	$ 3,478.7	$ 3,749.2	10.1%
Future and forward contracts (exclude FX)									
On commodities and equities	26.3	43.9	54.3	115.0	101.6	108.9	122.3	115.0	0.3
On interest rates	1,738.1	2,496.7	3,434.3	3,063.1	3,201.2	4,082.8	4,817.7	5,595.1	15.1
Notional amount of credit derivatives									
Bank is guarantor	4.1	10.4	7.6	4.1	14.1	14.3	59.0	80.5	0.2
Bank is beneficiary	4.5	8.0	8.4	7.9	14.5	40.4	70.2	110.6	0.3
Standby contracts and other option contracts									
Written option contracts on interest rates	504.7	950.2	1,024.4	1,261.7	1,588.6	2,087.9	2,567.9	2,791.3	7.6
Purchased option contracts on interest rates	508.0	818.8	1,015.0	1,223.8	1,567.6	1,896.6	2,503.1	2,850.8	7.7
Written option contracts on foreign exchange	245.7	263.3	341.4	406.6	529.9	756.4	879.5	664.0	1.8
Purchased option contracts on foreign exchange	249.1	254.5	312.0	409.9	502.6	700.9	840.0	645.4	1.7
Written option contracts on commodities	30.9	50.3	77.5	111.6	106.8	165.4	200.4	274.0	0.8
Purchased option contracts on commodities	29.4	46.3	71.1	102.6	97.1	146.4	206.2	277.2	0.8
Commitments to buy FX (includes $U.S.), spot, and forward	3,015.5	3,689.4	4,620.4	4,525.4	5,000.8	5,675.6	5,724.9	5,184.0	14.0

Standby LCs and foreign office guarantees									
To U.S. addressees	128.0	130.8	140.3	150.2	166.5	182.7	193.0	244.9	0.7
To non-U.S. addressees	34.5	32.2	35.7	39.6	44.5	47.7	47.5	51.8	0.1
(Amount of these items sold to others via participations)	(14.9)	(15.0)	(19.7)	(20.8)	(21.8)	(26.9)	(25.4)	(26.7)	
Commercial LCs	28.1	28.0	32.5	31.9	30.9	29.3	32.7	25.7	0.1
Participations in acceptances sold to others	0.8	0.9	0.8	1.1	1.2	1.5	0.7	0.5	0.0
Participations in acceptances bought from others	0.2	0.2	0.2	0.3	0.2	0.2	0.2	0.2	0.0
Securities borrowed	10.8	21.4	14.6	17.9	25.5	21.6	23.5	24.5	0.1
Securities lent	96.4	127.0	140.4	149.8	208.0	297.3	348.4	373.9	1.0
Other significant commitments and contingencies	8.7	7.8	3.5	3.6	14.0	6.2	N/A	31.4	
Memoranda									
Notional value of all outstanding interest rate swaps	2,122.0	2,946.3	4,451.1	5,546.8	7,069.4	9,018.0	10,164.0	13,839.8	37.4
Mortgages sold, with recourse Outstanding principal balance of mortgages sold or swapped	10.7	8.8	7.5	9.4	11.4	18.6	32.3	39.5	0.1
Amount of recourse exposure on these mortgages	6.3	4.9	4.2	5.6	8.2	8.8	8.5	8.7	0.0
Total, including memoranda items	$10,200.3	$13,496.3	$17,549.4	$19,345.3	$22,833.3	$28,392.4	$32,320.7	$36,978.0	100.0%
Total assets (on-balance-sheet items)	$ 3,476.4	$ 3,673.7	$ 3,972.9	$ 4,312.7	$ 4,578.3	$ 5,014.9	$ 5,182.8	$ 5,409.7	

FX = Foreign exchange, LC = Letter of credit.

*1999 figures are as of March.

Sources: FDIC, *Statistics on Banking*, various issues. *www.fdic.gov/*

Figure 11–5 Derivative Contracts by Product*

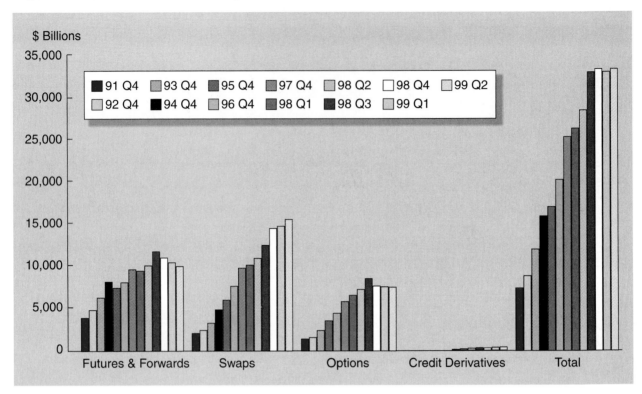

*In billions of dollars; notional amount of futures, total exchange-traded options, total swaps. Note that data after 1994 do not include spot FX in the total notional amount of derivatives.

Credit derivatives were reported for the first time in the first quarter of 1997. Currently, the Call Report does not differentiate credit derivatives by product, which have therefore been added as a separate category. As of 1997, credit derivatives have been included in the sum of total derivatives in this chart.

Note: numbers may not add due to rounding.

Source: Call Reports.

---

pension funds, and act as transfer and disbursement agent for the pension funds. We discuss pension funds in more detail in Chapter 19.

Correspondent Banking. Correspondent banking is the provision of banking services to other banks that do not have the staff resources to perform the service themselves. These services include check clearing and collection, foreign exchange trading, hedging services, and participation in large loan and security issuances. Correspondent banking services are generally sold as a package of services. Payment for the services is generally in the form of noninterest bearing deposits held at the bank offering the correspondent services (see Chapter 13).

5 Size, Structure, and Composition of the Industry

As of June 1999, the United States had 8,675 commercial banks. Even though this may seem to be a large number, in fact the number of banks has been decreasing. For example, in 1984, the number of banks was 14,483; in 1989, it was 12,744.

Figure 11–6 Structural Changes in the Number of Commercial Banks, 1980–1999

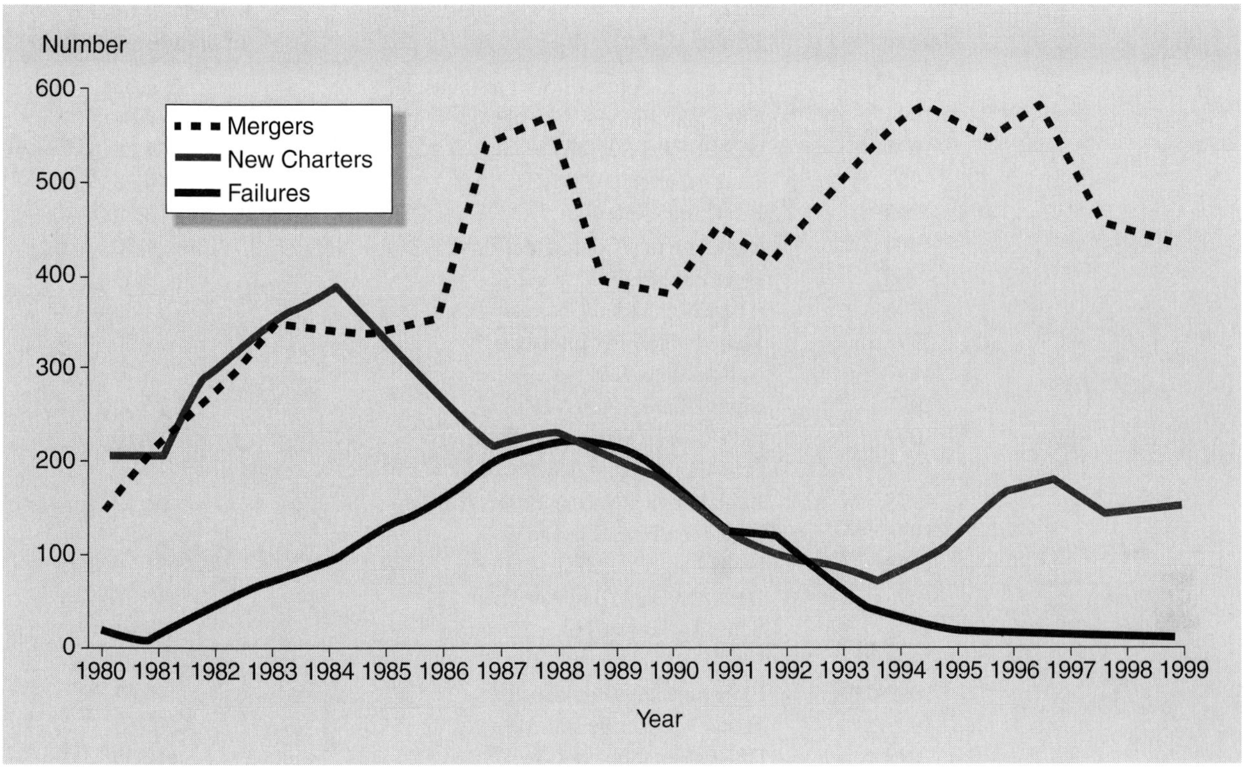

Source: Federal Deposit Insurance Corporation, *Quarterly Banking Profile*, Fourth Quarter 1994 and Fourth Quarter 1999. *www.fdic.gov/*

megamerger

The merger of banks with assets of $1 billion or more.

economies of scale

The degree to which a firm's average unit costs of producing financial services fall as its output of services increase—for example, cost reduction in trading and other transaction services resulting from increased efficiency when these services are performed by FIs.

economies of scope

The degree to which a firm can generate cost synergies by producing multiple financial service products.

Figure 11–6 illustrates the number of bank mergers, bank failures, and new charters for the period 1980 through June 1999. Notice that much of the change in the size, structure, and composition of this industry is the result of mergers and acquisitions. It was not until the 1980s and 1990s that regulators (such as the Federal Reserve or state banking authorities) allowed banks to merge with other banks across state lines (interstate mergers), and it has only been since 1994 that Congress has passed legislation (the Reigle-Neal Act) easing branching by banks across state lines. Finally, it has only been since 1987 that banks have possessed (limited) powers to underwrite corporate securities. Full authority to enter the investment banking (and insurance) business was only received with the passage of the Financial Services Modernization Act in 1999. We discuss the impact that changing regulations have had on the ability of commercial banks to merge and branch in Chapter 14. Table 11–4 lists some of the largest bank mergers in recent years.

Economies of Scale and Scope

An important reason for the consolidation of the banking industry is the search by banks to exploit potential cost and revenue economies of scale and scope. Indeed, **megamergers** (mergers involving banks with assets of $1 billion or more) are often driven by the desire of managers to achieve greater cost and revenue economies. Cost economies may result from **economies of scale** (where the unit or average cost of producing the bank's services falls as the size of the bank expands), **economies of scope**

Table 11–4   Large U.S. Bank Mergers, 1990–1999

Year	Banks	Price Paid for Target (in billions of dollars)
1990	Citizens & Southern/Sovran Financial	$ 2.05
1991	Chemical/Manufacturers Hanover	2.04
1991	NCNB/C&S Sovran	4.26
1991	BankAmerica/Security Pacific	4.21
1993	KeyCorp/Society	3.88
1994	BankAmerica/Continental Bank	1.90
1995	Fleet Financial/Shawmut	4.50
1996	Chase Manhattan/Chemical Bank	11.36
1996	Wells Fargo/First Interstate	11.20
1997	NationsBank/Boatmens Bancshares	8.70
1997	NationsBank/Barnett Banks	15.50
1997	First Union/CoreStates Financial	17.10
1997	First Bank System/US Bancorp	19.20
1998	BankAmerica/NationsBank	66.62
1998	Banc One/First Chicago	29.52
1998	Wells Fargo/Norwest	31.71
1998	Deutsche Bank/Bankers Trust[*]	10.28
1998	Suntrust Banks/Crestar Financial	9.61
1998	Star Banc/Firstar	7.23
1999	Fleet Financial/BankBoston	16.02
1999	Firstar/Mercantile Bancorp	10.69
1999	HSBC/Republic New York[*]	10.30
1999	Amsouth/First American	6.38
1999	Zions Bancorp/First Security	5.76

[*]International acquisitions.

Source: Securities Data Corp. and *The Wall Street Journal*, various issues.

X efficiencies

Cost savings due to the greater managerial efficiency of the acquiring firm.

(where banks generate synergistic cost savings through joint use of inputs such as computer systems in producing multiple products), or managerial efficiency sources (often called **X efficiencies**[9] because they are difficult to specify in a quantitative fashion).

Economies of Scale.   As financial firms become larger, the potential scale and array of the technology in which they can invest generally expands (see In the News box 11–1). The largest FIs generally have the largest expenditures on technology-related innovations. For example, the Tower Group (a consulting firm specializing in information technology) estimated that technology expense as a percent of noninterest expense would be as high as 22 percent at the largest U.S. banks in the three-year period 1999–2001. Internet banking is sure to be one of the major factors shaping the banking industry in the 21st century. The Internet offers financial institutions a channel to customers that enables them to react quickly to customer needs, bring products to the market quickly, and respond more effectively to changing business conditions. However, this capability will come at a cost to financial institutions as they invest in the necessary technology.

9. X efficiencies are those cost savings not directly due to economies of scope or economies of scale. As such, they are usually attributed to superior management skills and other difficult-to-measure managerial factors. To date, the explicit identification of what composes these efficiencies remains to be established in the empirical banking literature.

In the News

11-1

Technology the Pivot of Is Bigger Better?

Retired banker Thomas Storrs reignited a controversy last week that never seems to die and may continue to rage well into the next century. Mr. Storrs, a giant of regional banking in the 1980s when he headed NCNB Corp., told the Bank Administration Institute's (BAI) Retail Delivery '99 Conference that the biggest banks have gained a technological, and therefore competitive, advantage over others. "New technology has loaded the game in favor of large organizations," said Mr. Storrs, whose North Carolina-based company evolved into a nationwide organization—Bank of America Corp.—that he said proves his point perfectly . . .

Last year Bank One Corp. chief executive officer John B. McCoy said that smaller banking organizations had no chance to keep up with the technology and branding investments necessary to establish a lasting presence and impression on the Internet . . .The big bank cause was taken up . . . by chairman P. Jan Kalff of

Source: *American Banker*, December 13, 1999, p. 1, by Jeffrey Kutler.

ABN Amro. Explaining how the Dutch institution intends to be one of the few truly global banks, he said the Internet and other new market realities call for "marketing and technology (that) require large commitments. Big will be beautiful in banking."

Chase Manhattan Corp. president and chief executive officer William B. Harrison then told of his personal conversion over the last year into an Internet believer and of the "full-court press and sense of urgency" that he has instilled in the organization. The most obvious manifestation is the Chase.com business unit under vice chairman Joseph Sponholz, designed to have a Silicon Valley mentality liberated from banking bureaucracy . . .

Debates about size are not new. Academic studies have consistently undermined the assumption that bigness in banking correlates with either operating efficiency or superior shareholder returns. But it is also widely accepted that economies of scale accrue

to the biggest participants in such profitable businesses as credit cards and securities processing. Geographical and business-line diversification are considered desirable, and pro-bigness assertions have grown more insistent since the most recent wave of megamergers.

"There will always be a place for community banks" is a common refrain. Even Mr. Storrs said "there is room for banks of every size." But the smaller ones in these scenarios are relegated to specialties or niches far from a national or superregional stage . . . "Small banks can do very well as fast followers" of those that are first to take advantage of innovations, (banking consultant) Mr. (David) Kerstein said. "What they don't have is the kind of distribution that a Chase has." They don't have money in money center quantities.

Tower Group of Needham, Mass., projected that Citigroup next year will spend $5.9 billion on information technology. Five other holding companies would spend $900 million to $4 billion apiece—Bank of America, Chase, Bank

(continues)

In the News continued

One, Wells Fargo & Co., and First Union—and then the amount would drop more precipitously—to PNC Bank Corp. at $500 million and KeyCorp at $420 million. The data show a "technology gap" is opening up, and "the big banks that do the tech spending have the best chance," said Tower Group founder and president Diogo Teixeira. "They may not do a lot of the innovative things that new entrants in the market do, but they will do a lot better than small banks" . . . "It will be interesting to watch what size means on the Internet," said Earl Fischl Jr., a former PNC executive who is BAI's executive director of strategic research. "I think banks will find there are lots of ways to stay in the game."

Do You Understand?

1. How bank size is related to technological innovation?
2. Why such a relation exists?

If enhanced or improved technology lowers an FI's average costs of financial service production, larger FIs may have an economy of scale advantage over smaller financial firms. Economies of scale imply that the unit or average cost of producing FI services in aggregate (or some specific activity such as deposits or loans) falls as the size of the FI expands.

Figure 11–7 depicts economies of scale for three FIs of different sizes. The average cost of producing an FI's output of financial services is measured as:

$$AC_i = \frac{TC_i}{S_i}$$

where

AC_i = Average costs of the ith bank
TC_i = Total costs of the ith bank
S_i = Size of the bank measured by assets, deposits, or loans

The effect of improving operations or technology over time is to shift the AC curve downward; see Figure 11–8. AC_1 is the hypothetical AC curve prior to cost-reducing innovations. AC_2 reflects the cost-lowering effects of technology and consolidation on FIs.

The average cost to the largest FI in Figure 11–7 (size C) to produce financial services is lower than the cost to smaller firms B and A. This means that at any given price for financial service firm products, firm C can make a higher profit than either B or A. Alternatively, firm C can undercut B and A in price and potentially gain a larger market share.

Cost Economies of Scope. FIs are multiproduct firms producing services involving different technological and personnel needs. Investments in one financial service area (such as lending) may have incidental and synergistic benefits in lowering the costs to produce financial services in other areas (such as securities underwriting or brokerage). In 1999, regulators passed the Financial Services Modernization Act, which repealed laws that prohibited mergers between commercial banks and investment banks (as well as insurance companies). The bill, touted as the biggest change in the regulation of financial institutions in over 60 years, created a "financial services holding company" that can engage in banking activities *and* securities *and* insurance underwriting. Mergers of FIs that produce different services, such as the 1998 merger of Travelers Corp.

Figure 11–7   Economies of Scale in FIs

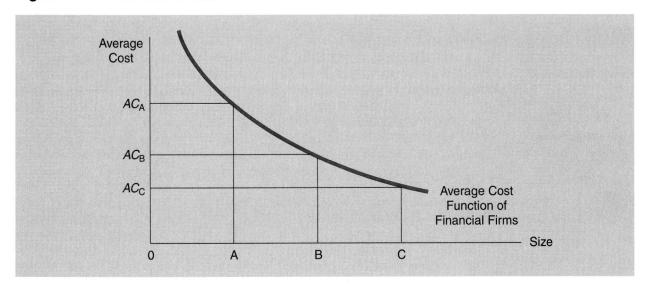

Figure 11–8   The Effects of Technological Improvement

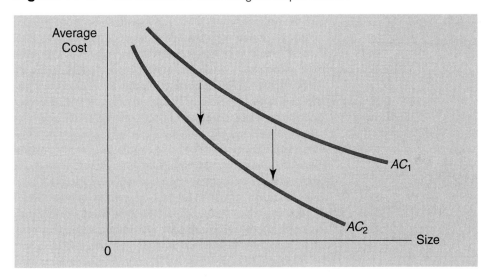

and Citicorp to form Citigroup, may allow two FIs to jointly use their input resources to produce a set of financial services at a lower cost than if the financial service products were produced independently of one another. Similarly, computerization allows the storage of important information on customers and their needs that can be used by more than one service area. FIs' abilities to generate synergistic cost savings through joint use of inputs in producing multiple products is called economies of scope, as opposed to economies of scale.

For example, in 1996, Chase Manhattan and Chemical Bank announced a megamerger, creating the (then) largest banking organization in the United States, with assets of $300 billion. Annual cost savings from the merger were estimated at $1.5 billion, to be achieved by consolidating certain operations and eliminating redundant costs, including the elimination of some 12,000 positions from a combined staff of 75,000 located in 39 states and 51 countries. Similarly, the merger of Banc One and First Chicago in 1998 (valued at $30 billion) was estimated to produce $930 million in cost savings and $275 million in additional revenue resulting from synergies among their credit card, retail banking, and commercial banking businesses. The combined Banc One-First Chicago had 2,000 offices in 14 states and became the nation's second largest credit card issuer.

Although the Chase-Chemical Bank and Banc One-First Chicago mergers are interesting examples of megamergers, they are still essentially mergers in the same or closely related geographic banking markets. Whether similar cost savings are available for more geographically dispersed mergers and acquisitions is important. For example, the retail-oriented, California-based Bank of America acquired the wholesale-oriented, Chicago-based Continental Bank for $1.9 billion in 1994. Bank of America's objective was to sell fee-based services—especially those with a strong technology base—to Continental's corporate customers. Research has shown that corporate customers stay very loyal to a bank even postacquisition. Another example is North Carolina–based NationsBank's acquisition of Boatmen's Bancshares of St. Louis, Missouri. The acquisition gave NationsBank entry into markets in Missouri, Arkansas, Kansas, Oklahoma, and New Mexico. The shift to statewide banking groups and the use of technology as a result of the acquisition were expected to produce cost savings of $335 million. These two banks (Bank of America and NationsBank) became the first truly nationwide bank when they merged in 1998, a transaction valued at over $66 billion, giving them a share of approximately 9 percent of the national commercial bank deposit base. The banks estimated the merger would cut their combined annual expenses by $1.3 billion and would eliminate between 5,000 to 8,000 jobs (3 to 4 percent of their work force).

Geographic diversification was also a major factor in late 1998 when Deutsche Bank (of Germany) announced the acquisition of Bankers Trust to create the world's largest financial services company as measured by assets (the combined bank would have over $843 billion in total assets). Together, the two banks became one of the global leaders in investment banking. They also have one of the largest global trading businesses. At the time of the acquisition, it was expected to produce a gain of $1 billion through new revenue and cost savings.

Revenue Economies of Scope.   In addition to economies of scope on the cost side, there are also economies of scope (or synergies) on the revenue side that can emanate from mergers and acquisitions. Revenue synergies have three potential dimensions. First, acquiring an FI in a growing market may produce new revenues. For example, acquisitions of banks in Florida and the Southwest in the 1980s and 1990s by NationsBank of North Carolina was apparently a key component of its strategy to expand its retail banking network nationwide and thus, increase revenues.

Second, the acquiring bank's revenue stream may become more stable if the asset and liability portfolio of the acquired (target) institution exhibits different credit, interest rate, and liquidity risk characteristics than the acquirer. For example, real estate loan portfolios have shown very strong regional cycles. Specifically, in the 1980s, U.S. real estate declined in value in the Southeast, then in the Northeast, and then in California with a long and variable lag. Thus, a geographically diversified real estate portfolio may be far less risky than one in which both acquirer and target specialize in a single region.[10] Recent studies confirm risk diversification gains from geographic expansions.[11]

Third, expanding into markets that are less than fully competitive offers an opportunity for revenue enhancement. That is, banks may be able to identify and expand ge-

10. As a result, the potential revenue diversification gains for more geographically concentrated mergers such as the 1991 merger of Bank of America and Security Pacific are likely to be relatively low because both are heavily exposed to California real estate loans.

11. See Y. Brook, R. Hendershott, and D. Lee, "The Gains from Takeover Deregulation: Evidence from the End of Interstate Banking Restrictions," *Journal of Finance* 53, no. 6 (1998), pp. 2185–204.

www.mybank.com/

www.aba.com/aba/

Table 11-5 U.S. Bank Asset Concentration, 1984 versus 1999

	1999				1984			
	Number	**Percent of Total**	**Assets***	**Percent of Total**	**Number**	**Percent of Total**	**Assets***	**Percent of Total**
All FDIC-insured Commercial Banks	8,675		$5,467,745		14,483		$2,508,871	
1. Under $100 million	5,303	61.1%	247,002	4.5%	12,044	83.2%	404,223	16.1%
2. $100 million–$1 billion	2,978	34.3	736,506	13.5	2,161	14.9	513,912	20.5
3. $1–$10 billion	317	3.4	872,507	15.9	254	1.7	725,947	28.9
4. $10 billion or more	77	0.9	3,611,730	66.1	24	0.2	864,789	34.5

*In millions of dollars.

Source: General Accounting Office, *Interstate Banking*, GAO/GGD, 95-35, December 1994, p. 101; and *FDIC Quarterly Banking Profile*, Second Quarter 1999. *www.fdic.gov/*

ographically into those markets in which *economic rents* potentially exist but in which regulators will not view such entry as potentially anticompetitive. Indeed, to the extent that geographic expansions are viewed as enhancing an FI's monopoly power by generating excessive rents, regulators may act to prevent a merger unless it produces potential efficiency gains that cannot be reasonably achieved by other means.[12] In recent years, the ultimate enforcement of antimonopoly laws and guidelines has fallen to the U.S. Department of Justice. In particular, the Department of Justice has established guidelines regarding the acceptability or unacceptability of acquisitions based on the potential increase in concentration in the market in which an acquisition takes place.

Bank Size and Concentration

Interestingly, a comparison of asset concentration by bank size (see Table 11–5) indicates that the recent consolidation in banking appears to have reduced the asset share of the smallest banks (under $1 billion) from 36.6 percent in 1984 to 18.0 percent in 1999. These small or **community banks**—with less than $1 billion in asset size—tend to specialize in retail or consumer banking, such as providing residential mortgages and consumer loans, and accessing the local deposit base. Clearly, this group of banks is decreasing both in number and importance.

The relative asset share of the largest banks (over $1 billion in size), on the other hand, increased from 63.4 percent in 1984 to 82.0 percent in 1999. The largest 10 U.S. banks as of the second quarter 1999 are listed in Table 11–6. Large banks engage in a more complete array of wholesale commercial banking activities, encompassing consumer and residential lending as well as commercial and industrial lending (C&I loans) both **regionally, superregionally,** and nationally. In addition, big banks have access to the markets for purchased funds, such as the interbank or **federal funds market,** to finance their lending and investment activities. Some of the very biggest banks are often classified as being **money center banks.** For example, in 1999, the *American Banker* identified six banking organizations in its money center bank group: Bank of America, Bankers Trust,[13] Chase Manhattan, Citigroup, J. P. Morgan, and Republic NY Corporation.

It is important to note that asset or lending size does not necessarily make a bank a money center bank. Thus, Bank One Corporation, with $256.0 billion in assets in 1999 (the fifth largest U.S. bank organization), is not a money center bank, but

community bank

A bank that specializes in retail or consumer banking.

regional or superregional bank

A bank that engages in a complete array of wholesale commercial banking activities.

federal funds market

An interbank market for short-term borrowing and lending of bank reserves.

money center bank

A bank that relies heavily on nondeposit or borrowed sources of funds.

12. U.S. Department of Justice, "Horizontal Merger Guidelines," April 2, 1992.

13. Bankers Trust was purchased by Deutsche Bank (a German bank) in 1998. The Bankers Trust name, however, has been retained for U.S. operations.

Table 11–6   Top Ten U.S. Banks Listed by Total Asset Size, Second - Quarter 1999

Bank	Total Assets (in billions of dollars)
Citigroup	$689.6
Bank of America	614.1
Chase Manhattan	356.9
J.P. Morgan	269.4
Bank One	256.0
First Union	224.5
Wells Fargo	205.4
Fleet	106.9
Suntrust	93.2
National City	84.0

Source: Bank Call Reports, Second Quarter 1999.

Republic NY Corporation (with only $51.2 billion in assets) is a money center bank. The classification as a money center bank is partly based on the physical location of the bank and partly based on the geographic area in which the bank offers services. Specifically, a money center bank is a bank located in a major financial center (e.g., New York) and participates in both national and international money markets. In fact, because of its extensive retail branch network, Bank One tends to be a net supplier of funds on the interbank market (federal funds market). By contrast, money center banks such as J. P. Morgan have no retail branches and rely almost entirely on wholesale and borrowed funds as sources of funds or liabilities.

Do You Understand?

1. Which banks performed the best/worst in the third quarter of 1998?

interest rate spread

The difference between lending and deposit rates.

Do You Understand?

1. What economies of scale and scope are?
2. What the three dimensions to revenue synergy gains are?
3. What the features are that distinguish a money center bank from other banks?
4. Which size banks generally have the highest ROA? ROE?

Bank Size and Activities

Bank size has traditionally affected the types of activities and financial performance of commercial banks (see In the News box 11–2). Large banks' relatively easy access to purchased funds and capital markets compared to small banks' access is a reason for many of these differences. For example, large banks with easier access to capital markets operate with lower amounts of equity capital than do small banks. Also, large banks tend to use more purchased funds (such as fed funds) and have fewer core deposits (deposits such as demand deposits that are stable over short periods of time, see Chapter 13) than do small banks. At the same time, large banks lend to larger corporations. This means that their **interest rate spreads** (i.e., the difference between their lending rates and deposit rates) have usually been narrower than those of smaller regional banks, which are more sheltered from competition in highly localized markets and lend to smaller, less sophisticated customers.

In addition, large banks tend to pay higher salaries and invest more in buildings and premises than small banks do. They also tend to diversify their operations and services more than small banks do. Large banks generate more noninterest income (i.e., fees, trading account, derivative security, and foreign trading income) than small banks. Although large banks tend to hold less equity, they do not necessarily return more on their assets. However, as the barriers to regional competition and expansion in banking have fallen in recent years, the largest banks have generally improved their return on equity (ROE) and return on asset (ROA) performance relative to small banks (see Figure 11–9). We discuss the impact of size on bank financial statements and performance in more detail in Chapter 13.

In the News

11-2

Old-fashioned banking—hoarding deposits, issuing mortgages and small-business loans and staying close to home—is looking good. As the nation's banks report earnings for the third quarter over the next few weeks, those with the best results are expected to be the ones that rely on plain-vanilla businesses that aren't connected to the uncertainty battering global markets. So-called money-center banks, which operate in both domestic and overseas financial markets, have been hammered by loan losses in Russia and trading losses in other teetering securities markets around the world. They are expected to report sharp declines in third-quarter earnings, or even losses for the quarter.

Analysts say the split between the earnings performance of the two groups is likely to be one of the widest in memory. At re-

Source: *The Wall Street Journal,* October 7, 1998, p. A3, by Rick Brooks. Reprinted by permission of *The Wall Street Journal.* © 2000 Dow Jones & Company, Inc. All Rights Reserved Worldwide.

Regional Banks Had Strong Quarter, Avoiding Overseas Woes of Bigger Firms

gional banks, which generally do a primarily domestic business in no more than a handful of states, per-share earnings are expected to grow about 11 percent in the third quarter, says Michael L. Mayo, a banking analyst at Credit Suisse First Boston Corp. In contrast, he predicts about a 38 percent decline in third-quarter earnings for money-center banks . . .

And though most of the regional and even smaller banks haven't yet been directly affected by the global turmoil—meaning strong double-digit third-quarter earnings growth for banks ranging from superregional U.S. Bancorp to Midwestern stalwart Fifth Third Bancorp—some regionals are seeing a slowdown in the demand for loans to local companies doing business overseas . . .

One of the biggest banks to be hit by trading losses

in Russia, Chase Manhattan Corp., is expected to see third-quarter net income tumble 31 percent to about $682 million, or 78 cents a share, primarily because of sharply lower trading revenue and higher commercial charge-offs . . .

The profit picture for Bankers Trust Corp., also with substantial exposure to the deteriorating Russian economy, is even bleaker. Bradley G. Ball, a Credit Suisse First Boston analyst, expects Bankers Trust, which has disclosed a $350 million trading loss in July and August alone, to post a loss of about $400 million, or $3.75 a share, compared with year-earlier net income of $235 million, or $2.16 a share . . .

David Berry of Keefe, Bruyette & Woods Inc. calculates that in all, third-quarter earnings for six big banks with exposure to the continuing turmoil—BankAmerica, Bankers Trust, Chase, Citicorp, J.P. Morgan & Co., and Republic New York Corp.—will total about $2 billion, compared with the $5 billion in quarterly profit "we might have expected five or six weeks ago," Mr. Berry says.

Figure 11–9   ROA and ROE on Different Size Banks, 1990–1999

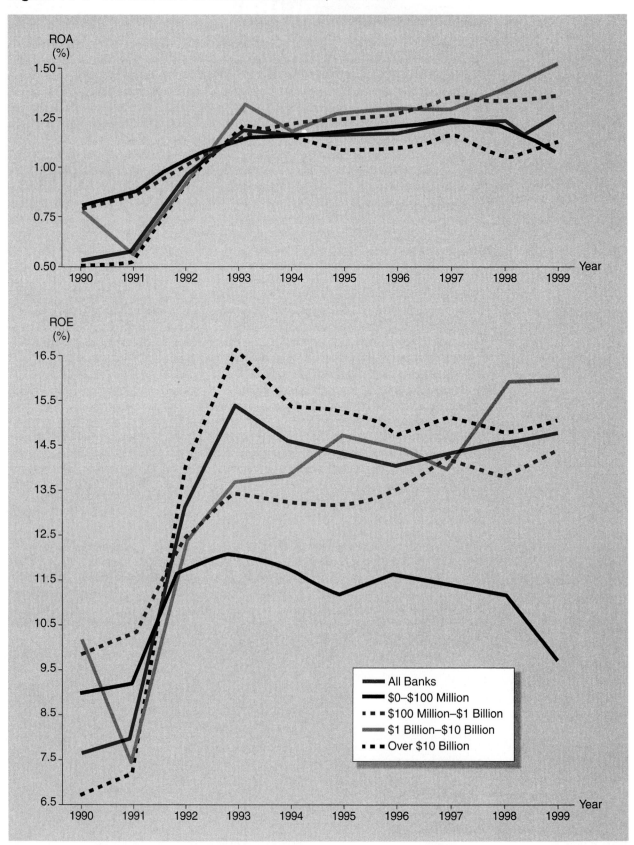

Source: Federal Deposit Insurance Corporation, *Quarterly Banking Profile*, Second Quarter 1999. *www.fdic.gov/*

Table 11–7 Selected Indicators for U.S. Commercial Banks, 1989, 1993 through June 1999

	1999*	1998	1997	1996	1995	1994	1993	1989
Number of institutions	8,675	8,984	9,143	9,528	9,940	10,451	10,958	12,709
Return on assets (%)	1.28	1.19	1.24	1.19	1.17	1.17	1.22	0.49
Return on equity (%)	14.97	13.93	14.71	14.40	14.68	14.90	15.67	7.71
Provision for loan losses to total assets (%)	0.19	0.41	0.39	0.36	0.29	0.27	0.45	0.94
Net charge-offs to loans (%)	0.59	0.67	0.64	0.58	0.49	0.50	0.85	1.16
Asset growth rate (%)	5.52	8.50	9.54	6.16	7.53	8.21	5.72	5.38
Net operating income growth (%)	12.89	2.29	12.48	6.44	7.48	16.18	35.36	−38.70
Number of failed/assisted institutions	2	3	1	5	6	11	42	206

*Through June 30, ratios annualized where appropriate. Asset growth is for 12 months ending June 30.

Source: FDIC, *Quarterly Banking Profile,* Second Quarter 1999; and *Historical Statistics,* 1989. *www.fdic.gov/*

Industry Performance

provision for loan losses

Bank management's recognition of expected bad loans for the period.

net charge-offs

Actual losses on loans and leases.

net operating income

Income before taxes and extraordinary items.

Do You Understand?

1. What the trends in ROA and ROE have been in the commercial banking industry over the last decade or so?
2. What the trend in loan performance has been in the commercial banking industry over the last decade or so?

Table 11–7 presents selected performance ratios for the commercial banking industry for 1989 and 1993 through June 1999. With the economic expansion in the U.S. economy and falling interest rates throughout most of the 1990s, U.S. commercial banks have flourished for most of the 1990s. In the first half of 1999 commercial bank earnings were a record $35 billion. More than two-thirds of all U.S. banks reported an ROA of 1 percent or higher, and the average ROA for all banks was 1.28 percent, up from 1.19 percent for the year 1998.[14] This, despite continued financial problems in Southeast Asia, Russia, and South America.

This performance is quite an improvement from the recessionary and high interest rate conditions in which the industry operated in the late 1980s. As reported in Table 11–7, the average ROA and ROE for commercial banks in June 1999 was 1.28 percent and 14.97 percent, respectively, compared to 1989 when ROA and ROE averaged 0.49 percent and 7.71 percent, respectively. **Provision for loan losses** (bank management's expectations of losses on the current loan portfolio, see Chapter 13) to assets ratio and **net charge-offs** (actual losses on loans and leases) to loans ratio averaged 0.19 percent and 0.59 percent, respectively, in 1999, versus 0.94 percent and 1.16 percent, respectively, in 1989. **Net operating income** (income before taxes and extraordinary items) grew at an annualized rate of 12.89 percent in the first half of 1999 versus a *drop* of 38.70 percent in 1989. Finally, note that in 1999 (through June 1999), only two U.S. commercial banks failed versus 206 in 1989. As a result of such massive losses and failures in the industry, several regulations were proposed and enacted to prevent such occurrences from happening again. (We discuss the major changes in regulation and their impact in Chapter 14.) As a result of these changes and the strong U.S. economy, in the last decade or so the commercial banking industry essentially has gone from the brink of disaster to a period of almost unprecedented profit and stability.

14. ROA is calculated as net income divided by the book value of total assets. It reflects the earnings per dollar of assets for the bank. ROE is calculated as net income divided by common equity of the bank and measures the return to the bank's common stockholders. We discuss ROA and ROE in more detail in Chapter 13.

Regulators

While Chapter 14 provides a detailed description of the regulations governing commercial banks and their impact on the banking industry, this section provides a brief overview of the regulators of this group of FIs. Unlike other countries that have one or sometimes two regulators, U.S. banks may be subject to the supervision and regulations of as many as four separate regulators. The key commercial bank regulators are the Federal Deposit Insurance Corporation (FDIC), the Office of the Comptroller of the Currency (OCC), the Federal Reserve System (FRS), and state bank regulators. The next sections discuss the principal role that each plays.

Federal Deposit Insurance Corporation

www.fdic.gov/

Established in 1933, the Federal Deposit Insurance Corporation (FDIC) insures the deposits of commercial banks.[15] In so doing, it levies insurance premiums on banks, manages the deposit insurance fund (that is, generated from those premiums and their reinvestment), and conducts bank examinations. In addition, when an insured bank is closed, the FDIC acts as the receiver and liquidator, although the closure decision itself is technically made by the bank's chartering or licensing agency (see below). Because of problems in the thrift industry and the insolvency of the savings and loan (S&L) insurance fund (FSLIC) in 1989 (see Chapter 14), the FDIC now manages both the commercial bank insurance fund and the S&L insurance fund. The Bank Insurance Fund is called *BIF* and the S&L fund is called the Savings Association Insurance Fund, or *SAIF* (see Chapter 12). The number of FDIC-BIF insured banks and the division between nationally and state-chartered banks is shown in Figure 11–10.

Office of the Comptroller of the Currency

www.occ.treas.gov/

The Office of the Comptroller of the Currency (OCC) is the oldest U.S. bank regulatory agency. Established in 1863, it is organized as a subagency of the U.S. Treasury. Its primary function is to charter national banks as well as to close them. In addition, the OCC examines national banks and has the power to approve or disapprove their merger applications. Instead of seeking a national charter, however, banks can seek to be chartered by 1 of 50 individual state bank regulatory agencies.

Historically, state chartered banks have been subject to fewer regulations and restrictions on their activities than national banks. This lack of regulatory oversight was a major reason many banks chose not to be nationally chartered. Many more recent regulations (such as the Depository Institutions Deregulation and Monetary Control Act of 1980) attempted to level the restrictions imposed on federal and state chartered banks (see Chapter 14). Not all discrepancies, however, were changed and state chartered banks are still generally less heavily regulated than nationally chartered banks. The choice of being a nationally chartered or state-chartered bank lies at the foundation of the **dual banking system** in the United States. Most large banks, such as Citibank, choose national charters, but others have state charters. For example, Morgan Guaranty, the money center bank subsidiary of J. P. Morgan, is chartered as a state bank under State of New York law. In the second quarter of 1999, 2,409 banks were *nationally* chartered and 6,266 were *state* chartered, representing 27.8 percent and 72.2 percent, respectively, of all commercial bank assets.

dual banking system

The coexistence of both nationally and state-chartered banks, as in the United States.

Federal Reserve System

www.bog.frb.fed.us/

In addition to being concerned with the conduct of monetary policy, the Federal Reserve, as this country's central bank, also has regulatory power over some banks and, where relevant, their holding company parents. All 2,409 nationally chartered banks

---

15. Virtually all U.S. banks are members of the FDIC's insurance fund.

Figure 11–10   Bank Regulators

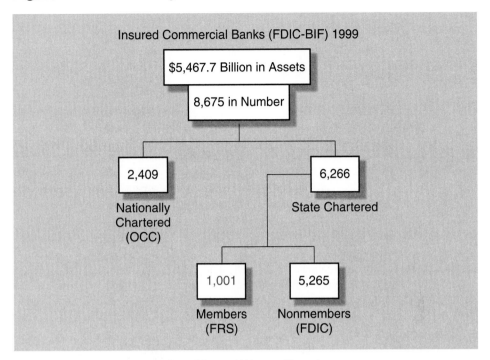

Insured Commercial Banks (FDIC-BIF) 1999

$5,467.7 Billion in Assets

8,675 in Number

2,409

Nationally
Chartered
(OCC)

6,266

State Chartered

1,001

Members
(FRS)

5,265

Nonmembers
(FDIC)

Source: FDIC, *Statistics on Banking*, Second Quarter 1999. *www.fdic.gov/*

holding company

A parent company that owns a controlling interest in a subsidiary bank or other FI.

shown in Figure 11–10 are automatically members of the Federal Reserve System (FRS). In addition, 1,001 of the state-chartered banks have also chosen to become members. Since 1980, all banks have had to meet the same noninterest-bearing reserve requirements whether they are members of the FRS or not. The primary advantage of FRS membership is direct access to the federal funds wire transfer network for nationwide interbank borrowing and lending of reserves. Finally, many banks are often owned and controlled by parent **holding companies**—for example, Citigroup is the parent holding company of Citibank (a national bank). Because the holding company's management can influence decisions taken by a bank subsidiary and thus influence its risk exposure, the FRS regulates and examines bank holding companies as well as the banks themselves.

Do You Understand?

1. Who the major regulators of commercial banks are?
2. Which of all commercial banks the OCC regulates?

State Authorities

As mentioned above, banks may chose to be state-chartered rather than nationally chartered. State-chartered commercial banks are regulated by state agencies. State authorities perform similar functions as the OCC performs for national banks.

Summary

This chapter provided an overview of the major activities of commercial banks and recent trends in the banking industry. Commercial banks rely heavily on deposits to fund their activities, although borrowed funds are becoming increasingly important for the largest institutions. Historically, commercial banks have concentrated on commercial or business lending and on investing in securities. Differences between the asset and liability portfolios of commercial banks and other financial institutions, however, are being eroded due to competitive forces, consolidation, regulation, and changing financial and business technology. Indeed, in the late 1990s, the largest group of assets in commercial bank portfolios were mortgage related. The chapter examined the relatively large decline in the number of commercial banks in the last decade and reviewed reasons for the recent wave of bank mergers. Finally, the chapter provided an overview of this industry's performance over the last decade.

End-of-Chapter Questions

1. What is meant by the term *depository institution?* How does a depository institution differ from an industrial corporation?

2. What are the major sources of funds for commercial banks in the United States? What are the major uses of funds for commercial banks in the United States? For each of your answers, specify where the item appears on the balance sheet of a typical commercial bank.

3. What are the principal types of financial assets for commercial banks? How has the relative importance of these assets changed over the past five decades? What are some of the forces that have caused these changes? What are the primary types of risk associated with these types of assets?

4. Why do commercial banks hold investment securities?

5. What are the principal liabilities for commercial banks? What does this liability structure tell us about the maturity of the liabilities of banks? What types of risks does this liability structure entail for commercial banks?

6. What type of transaction accounts do commercial banks issue? Which type of accounts have dominated transaction accounts of banks?

7. Compare and contrast the profitability ratios (ROE and ROA) of banks with assets below and above $100 million in Figure 11–9 from 1990 through 1999. What conclusions can you derive from those numbers?

8. What is meant by an off-balance-sheet activity? What are some examples of them? What are some of the forces responsible for them?

9. How does one distinguish between an off-balance-sheet asset and an off-balance-sheet liability?

10. What has been the recent trend in the number of commercial banks in the United States? What factors account for this trend?

11. What is the difference between economies of scale and economies of scope?

12. What are the three revenue synergies that an FI can obtain from expanding geographically?

13. What is a money center bank and a regional bank?

14. How has the performance of the commercial banking industry changed in the last decade?

15. Which commercial banks are experiencing the highest profitability and why? Which commercial banks are experiencing the lowest profitability?

16. Who are the major regulators of commercial banks? Which banks does each agency regulate?

17. What are the major functions performed by the FDIC?

18. What are the main advantages of being a member of the Federal Reserve System?

19. Go to the Federal Reserve Board's website and find the latest figure for the total assets of all U.S. commercial banks. How does this compare with the figure from Table 11–2?

20. Go to the Office of the Comptroller of the Currency's website and find the latest distribution of derivative contracts by product and by type. What are the major components of each breakdown?

Thrift Institutions

Chapter Navigator

1. What is the difference between a savings association and a savings bank?

2. Why did savings institutions experience such high failure rates in the 1980s?

3. What are the main assets held by savings institutions?

4. What are the main liabilities held by savings institutions?

5. Who regulates thrift institutions?

6. How did savings institutions perform in the late 1990s?

7. How are credit unions different from commercial banks and savings institutions?

8. What are the main assets and liabilities held by credit unions?

1   Three Categories of Thrift Institutions: Chapter Overview

Thrift institutions are comprised of three different groups of FIs: savings associations, savings banks, and credit unions. Thrift institutions were first created in the early 1800s in response to commercial banks' failure to adequately serve the needs of individuals requiring borrowed funds to purchase homes. Thus, while today's thrifts

Figure 12–1   Major Services Offered by the Different Types of Thrifts

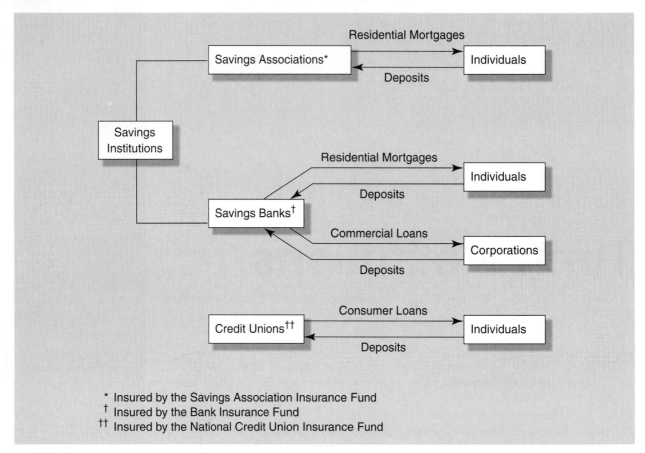

* Insured by the Savings Association Insurance Fund
† Insured by the Bank Insurance Fund
†† Insured by the National Credit Union Insurance Fund

generally perform services similar to commercial banks, they are still grouped separately because they provide important residential mortgage and other lending services to households. Figure 12–1 illustrates key asset side differences among the three types of thrift institutions. Historically, savings associations have concentrated primarily on residential mortgages, while savings banks have been operated as more diversified institutions, with a large concentration of residential mortgage assets but holding commercial loans, corporate bonds, and corporate stock as well. Credit unions have historically focused on consumer loans funded with member deposits. Each category of thrift includes federally chartered and state chartered institutions. Table 12–1 shows the number of each type of thrift as of the second quarter of 1999. This chapter reviews these three types of depository institutions. For each group, we examine (1) their size, structure, and composition, (2) their balance sheets and recent trends, (3) their regulators, and (4) recent industry performance.

Savings Associations

Size, Structure, and Composition of the Industry

The savings associations industry prospered throughout most of the 20th century. Savings associations were historically referred to as savings and loan (S&L) associations. However, in the 1980s, federally chartered savings banks appeared in the United

Table 12–1 Number of Thrift Institutions, Second Quarter 1999

Type	Federally Chartered	State Chartered	Total
Savings associations	1,073	217	1,290
Savings banks	41	321	362
Credit unions	6,707	4,134	10,841

Source: FDIC, *Quarterly Banking Profile*, Second Quarter, 1999; and National Credit Union Association, *Quick Facts*, June 1999. *www.fdic.gov/; www.ncua.gov/*

States.[1] These institutions have the same regulators and regulations as the traditional savings and loans. Together they are referred to as savings associations. These specialized institutions in this industry made long-term residential mortgages usually backed by the short-term deposits of small savers. This strategy was successful largely because of the Federal Reserve's policy of smoothing or targeting interest rates, especially in the post-World War II period up until the late 1970s, and the generally stable and upward-sloping shape of the yield curve or the term structure of interest rates (see Chapter 2). During some periods, such as the early 1960s, the yield curve did slope downwards, but for most of the post–World War II period, the upward-sloping yield curve meant that the interest rates on savings associations' 30-year residential mortgage assets exceeded the rates they paid on their short-term deposit liabilities. Moreover, significant shocks to interest rates were generally absent due to the Fed's policy of interest rate smoothing and the fact that the world's economies were far less integrated when compared with today's economies.

2 At the end of the 1970s, slightly fewer than 4,000 S&Ls existed, with assets of approximately $0.6 trillion. During the October 1979 to October 1982 period, however, the Federal Reserve radically changed its monetary policy strategy by targeting bank reserves rather than interest rates, in an attempt to lower the underlying rate of inflation (see Chapter 4 for more details). The Fed's restrictive monetary policy actions led to a sudden and dramatic surge in interest rates, with rates on T-bills and bank certificates of deposits rising as high as 16 percent. This increase in short-term rates and the cost of funds had two effects. First, many savings associations faced negative interest spreads or **net interest margins** (interest income minus interest expense divided by earning assets) in funding much of their long-maturity, fixed-rate residential mortgages in their portfolios. For example, a 12 percent 30-year mortgage was having to be funded by a 15 percent 3-month CD. Second, they had to pay more competitive interest rates on deposits to prevent **disintermediation** and the reinvestment of these funds in money market mutual fund accounts. Their ability to do this was constrained by the Federal Reserve's **Regulation Q ceilings**, which limited (albeit to a lesser extent for savings institutions than commercial banks) the interest rates that savings associations could pay on the traditional passbook savings account and retail time deposits that small savers held.[2] Thus, many small depositors, especially the more sophisticated, withdrew their funds from savings association deposit accounts (that were paying less than market interest rates due to Regulation Q)

net interest margin

Interest income minus interest expense divided by earning assets.

disintermediation

Withdrawal of deposits from depository institutions to be reinvested elsewhere, e.g., money market mutual funds.

regulation Q ceiling

An interest ceiling imposed on small savings and time deposits at banks and thrifts until 1986.

---

1. The term *savings association* has replaced S&L association to capture the change in the structure of the industry. In 1978, the Federal Home Loan Bank Board (FHLBB), at the time the main regulator of savings associations, began chartering federal savings banks insured by the Federal Savings and Loan Insurance Corporation (FSLIC). In 1982, the FHLBB allowed S&Ls to convert to federal savings banks with bank (rather than S&L) names. As more and more S&Ls converted to savings banks, the title associated with this sector of the thrift industry was revised to reflect this change.

2. In the 1970s, these Regulation Q ceilings were usually set at rates of 5¼ or 5½ percent.

Table 12–2 Balance Sheets of Savings Associations (percentage of total assets and liabilities)

Item	1977	1982
Liabilities		
Fixed ceiling liabilities	87.3%	22.0%
Passbook and NOW accounts	33.9	15.6
Fixed ceiling time deposits	53.4	6.4
Market ceiling small time deposits	0.0	52.8
Money market certificates	0.0	28.6
Small saver certificates	0.0	19.3
Other small time deposits	0.0	4.9
Discretionary liabilities	8.6	23.2
Large time deposits	2.1	8.1
FHLB advances	4.7	10.3
Other borrowings	1.8	4.6
Other liabilities	4.0	2.0
Assets		
Mortgage assets	86.0	81.1
Fixed rate	86.0	74.9
Adjustable rate	0.0	6.2
Nonmortgage loans	2.3	2.6
Cash and investments	9.2	11.2
Other assets	2.5	5.1

Source: *Federal Reserve Bulletin*, December 1982. *www.bog.frb.fed.us/*

and invested directly in unregulated money market mutual fund accounts (where they could earn market interest rates).

Partly to overcome the adverse effects of rising rates and disintermediation on the savings association industry, Congress passed two major acts in the early 1980s revising the permitted scope of savings associations' activities: the Depository Institutions Deregulation and Monetary Control Act (DIDMCA) of 1980 and the Garn-St. Germain Depository Institutions Act (DIA) of 1982 (see Chapter 14); these expanded savings associations' deposit-taking and asset investment powers. On the liability side, savings associations were allowed to offer interest-bearing transaction accounts, called NOW accounts, and to issue more market rate–sensitive liabilities such as money market deposit accounts (MMDAs) to limit disintermediation and to compete with mutual funds. On the asset side of the balance sheet, they were allowed to offer floating- or adjustable-rate mortgages and, to a limited extent, expand into consumer real estate development and commercial lending. Note the structural shifts in savings association balance sheets between 1977 and 1982 in Table 12–2. For many savings associations, the new powers created safer and more diversified institutions.

For a small but significant group, however, whose earnings and shareholders' capital was being eroded in traditional areas of asset and liability business, the new regulations meant the opportunity to take more asset side risks which, if they paid off, could return the institution to profitability. However, in the mid-1980s, real estate and land prices in Texas and the Southwest collapsed. This was followed by economic downturns in the Northeast and Western states of the U.S. Many borrowers with mortgage loans issued by savings associations in these areas defaulted. In other words, the risks incurred by many of these institutions did not pay off. This risk-taking behavior was accentuated by the policies of the federal insurer of savings associations' deposits, FSLIC. It chose not to close capital-depleted, economically insolvent savings associa-

Figure 12–2 Structural Changes in the Number of Savings Institutions, 1984–1999

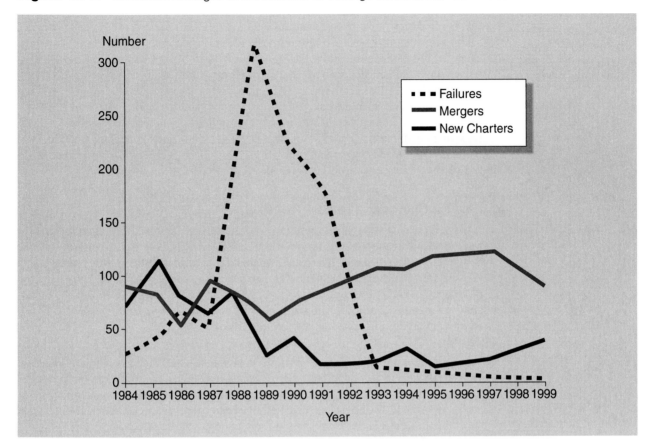

Source: Federal Deposit Insurance Corporation, *Quarterly Banking Profile,* Fourth Quarter 1994 and Second Quarter 1999, and *Historical Statistics,* various years. *www.fdic.gov/*

regulator forbearance

A policy not to close economically insolvent FIs, allowing them to continue in operation.

savings institutions

Savings associations and savings banks combined.

tions (a policy of **regulator forbearance**) and to maintain deposit insurance premium assessments independent of the risk taken by the institution (see Chapter 14). As a result, an alarming number (1,248) of savings association failures occurred in the 1982–1992 period (peaking at 316 in 1989), alongside a rapid decline in asset growth of the industry. Figure 12–2 shows the number of failures, mergers, and new charters of **savings institutions** (savings associations and savings banks combined) from 1984 through June 1999. Notice the large number of failures from 1987 through 1992 and the decline in the number of new charters.

In the 1980s, the large number of savings association failures depleted the resources of the FSLIC to such an extent that by 1989 it was massively insolvent. As a result, Congress passed an additional piece of legislation: the Financial Institutions Reform, Recovery, and Enforcement Act (FIRREA) of 1989. This legislation abolished the FSLIC and created a new savings association insurance fund (SAIF) under the management of the FDIC. FIRREA also replaced the Federal Home Loan Bank Board with the Office of Thrift Supervision (OTS) as the main regulator of federally chartered savings associations. In addition, the act created the Resolution Trust Corporation (RTC) to close and liquidate the most insolvent S&Ls.[3] The FIRREA also strengthened the capital requirements of savings associations and constrained their nonmortgage-related asset investment powers under a revised qualified thrift lender test, or **QTL test**

3. At the time of its dissolution in 1995, the RTC had resolved or closed more than 700 savings associations and savings banks at an estimated cost of $200 billion to U.S. taxpayers.

QTL test

Qualified thrift lender test that sets a floor on the mortgage-related assets that thrifts can hold (currently, 65 percent).

(discussed below). Following FIRREA, Congress further enacted the Federal Deposit Insurance Corporation Improvement Act (FDICIA). The FDICIA of 1991 introduced risk based deposit insurance premiums (starting in 1993) to limit excess risk taking by savings association owners. It also introduced a prompt corrective action (PCA) policy, such that regulators could close thrifts and banks faster (see Chapter 14). In particular, if a savings association's ratio of its owners' equity capital to its assets fell below 2 percent, it had to be closed down or recapitalized within three months.

As a result of closing weak savings associations and strengthening their capital requirements, the industry is now significantly smaller both in terms of numbers and asset size. Specifically, the number of savings associations decreased from 2,600 in 1989 to 1,290 in 1999 (by 50 percent) and assets have decreased from $1.2 trillion to $779 billion (by 35 percent) over the same period.

Balance Sheets and Recent Trends

Even in its new smaller state, the future viability of the savings association industry in traditional mortgage lending areas is a matter of concern. This is due partly to intense competition for mortgages from other financial institutions such as commercial banks and specialized mortgage bankers. It is also due to the securitization of mortgages into mortgage-backed security pools by government-sponsored enterprises, which we discuss in Chapters 7 and 25.[4] In addition, long-term mortgage lending exposes FIs to significant credit, interest rate, and liquidity risks.

Column (1) of Table 12–3 shows the balance sheet for the savings association industry in 1999. On this balance sheet, mortgages and mortgage-backed securities (securitized pools of mortgages) represent 79.05 percent of total assets. Figure 12–3 shows the distribution of mortgage-related assets for all savings institutions (savings associations and savings banks) as of June 1999. As noted earlier, the FIRREA uses the QTL test to establish a minimum holding of 65 percent in mortgage-related assets for savings associations.[5] Reflecting the enhanced lending powers established under the 1980 DIDMCA and 1982 DIA, commercial loans and consumer loans amounted to 1.90 and 5.59 percent of savings association assets, respectively. Finally, savings associations are required to hold cash and investment securities for liquidity purposes and to meet regulator-imposed reserve requirements (see Chapter 14). In June 1999, cash and U.S. Treasury securities holdings amounted to 4.26 percent of total assets.

On the liability side of the balance sheet, small time and savings deposits are still the predominant source of funds, with total deposits accounting for 62.16 percent of total liabilities and net worth. The second most important source of funds is borrowing from the 12 Federal Home Loan Banks (FHLBs),[6] which the institutions themselves own. Because of their size and government-sponsored status, FHLBs have access to wholesale money markets for notes and bonds and can relend the funds borrowed in these markets to savings associations at a small markup over wholesale cost. Other borrowed funds include repurchase agreements and direct federal fund borrowings.

---

4. The major enterprises are GNMA, FNMA, and FHLMC.

5. Failure to meet the 65 percent QTL test results in the loss of certain tax advantages and the ability to obtain Federal Home Loan Bank advances (loans).

6. The Federal Home Loan Bank System, established in 1932, consists of 12 regional Federal Home Loan Banks (set up similar to the Federal Reserve Bank system) that borrow funds in the national capital markets and use these funds to make loans to savings associations that are members of the Federal Home Loan Bank. The Federal Home Loan Banks are supervised by the Federal Home Loan Bank Board.

Table 12–3 Assets and Liabilities of Savings Associations and Savings Banks

	(1) SAIF-Insured Savings Associations		(2) BIF-Insured Savings Banks	
	($ Millions)	(Percent)	($ Millions)	(Percent)
Cash and due from	$ 18,600	2.39%	$ 6,321	1.82%
U.S. treasury and federal agency obligations	14,562	1.87	3,284	0.95
Federal funds and repos	4,797	0.61	7,710	2.22
Bonds, notes, debentures, and other securities	20,585	2.64	22,084	6.37
Corporate stock	4,122	0.53	6,478	1.87
Mortgage loans	456,823	58.64	199,631	57.58
MBS (includes CMOs, POs, IOs)	158,986	20.41	61,361	17.70
Commercial loans	14,834	1.90	9,303	2.68
Consumer loans	43,536	5.59	14,085	4.06
Other loans and financing leases	1,876	0.24	1,453	0.42
Less: Allowance for loan losses and unearned income	4,687	0.60	2,299	0.66
Other assets	45,010	5.78	17,306	4.99
Total assets	$779,044	100.00	$346,717	100.00
Total deposits	$484,259	62.16	$214,995	62.01
Federal funds and repos	54,655	7.02	21,411	6.17
Other borrowed money	164,591	21.13	73,805	21.29
Other liabilities	10,934	1.40	4,888	1.41
Total liabilities	714,439	91.71	315,099	90.88
Net worth*	64,605	8.29	31,618	9.12
Total liabilities and net worth	$779,044	100.00	$346,717	100.00
Number of banks	1,290		362	

*Includes limited life preferred stock for BIF-insured state chartered savings banks and redeemable preferred stock and minority interest for SAIF-insured institutions and BIF-insured FSBs.
Source: FDIC, *Statistics on Banking*, Second Quarter 1999. *www.fdic.gov/*

Figure 12–3 Real Estate Assets as a Percent of Total Assets at Savings Institutions

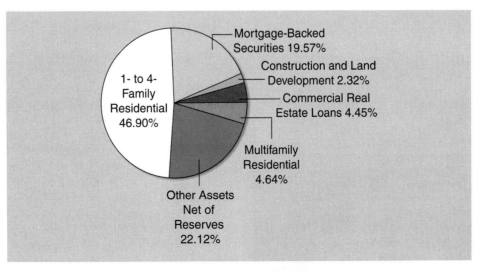

Source: Federal Deposit Insurance Corporation, *Quarterly Banking Profile*, Second Quarter 1999. *www.fdic.gov/*

mutual organization

An institution in which the liability holders are also the owners—for example, in a mutual savings bank, depositors also own the bank.

Finally, net worth is the book value of the equity holders' capital contribution; it amounted to 8.29 percent in 1999. Historically, most savings associations (and savings banks) were established as **mutual organizations** (in which the depositors are the legal owners of the institution and no stock is issued). As a mutual organization, member deposits represent the equity of the savings association. Since there are no stockholders, and thus no demand for equity investment returns, mutual organizations are generally less risky than stock-chartered organizations—mutual savings association managers can concentrate on low-risk investments and the prevention of failure rather than higher risk investments needed to produce higher required returns on stockholders' investments. However, through time many savings associations (and savings banks) have switched from mutual to stock charters (in which the holders of the stock or equity are the legal owners of the institution rather than depositors as under the mutual charter). This is mainly because stock ownership allows savings institutions to attract capital investment from outside stockholders beyond levels achievable at a mutual institution. Figure 12–4 shows this trend in mutual versus stock charters and asset size for savings institutions from 1988 through 1999.

Do You Understand?

1. Why the savings association industry prospered throughout most of the 20th century (until the late 1970s)?
2. Why the performance of savings associations deteriorated in the 1970s and 1980s?
3. What was done to rescue the savings associations industry in the 1980s?
4. What the major assets and liabilities of savings associations are?

Savings Banks

Size, Structure, and Composition of the Industry

Traditionally, savings banks were established as mutual organizations in states that permit such organizations. These states were largely confined to the East Coast—for example, New York, New Jersey, and the New England states. As a result, savings banks (unlike savings associations) were not affected by the oil-based economic ups and downs of Texas and the Southwest in the 1980s. The crash in New England real estate values in 1990–1991 presented equally troubling problems for this group, however. Indeed, many of the failures of savings institutions (see Figure 12–2) were of savings banks rather than savings associations. As a result, like savings associations, savings banks have decreased in both size and number. In June 1999, 362 savings banks had $346 billion in assets: their deposits of $215 billion are insured by the FDIC under the BIF (Bank Insurance Fund). FDIC insurance under the BIF is just one characteristic that distinguishes savings banks from savings associations, whose deposits are insured under by the FDIC under the SAIF (Savings Association Insurance Fund).

Balance Sheets and Recent Trends

3   **4**

Notice the major similarities and differences between savings associations and savings banks in Table 12–3, which shows their respective assets and liabilities as of June 1999. Savings banks (in the second column of Table 12–3) have a heavy concentration (75.28 percent) of mortgage loans and mortgage-backed securities (MBSs). This is slightly less than the savings associations' 79.05 percent in these assets. Over the years, savings banks have been allowed greater freedom to diversify into corporate bonds and stocks; their holdings are 8.24 percent compared to 3.17 percent for savings associations. On the liability side, the major difference is that savings banks generally (although this was not the case in 1999, as shown in Table 12–3) rely more on deposits than savings associations and therefore savings banks have fewer borrowed funds. Finally, the ratio of the book value of net worth to total assets for savings banks stood at 9.12 percent (compared to 8.29 percent for savings associations) in 1999.

Do You Understand?

1. Where savings banks were originally established?
2. The asset and liability characteristics that differentiate savings banks from savings associations?

Figure 12–4 Assets and Number of Mutual and Stock Savings Institutions

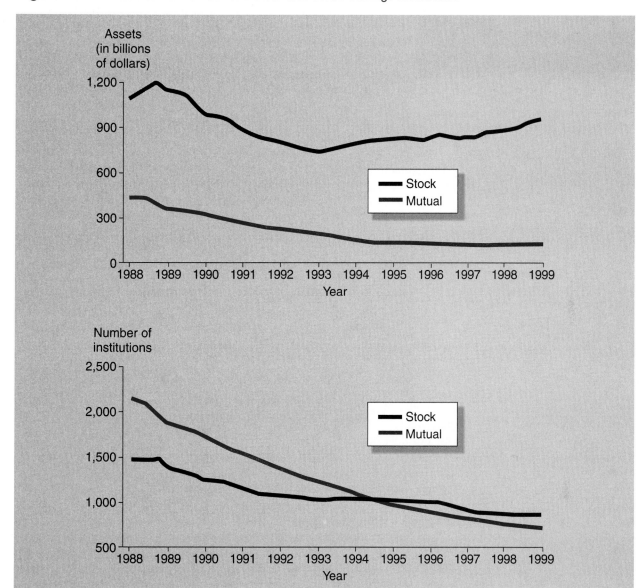

Source: Federal Deposit Insurance Corporation, *Quarterly Banking Profile,* Fourth Quarter 1994 and Second Quarter 1999. *www.fdic.gov/*

Regulators of Savings Institutions

The three main regulators of savings institutions are the Office of Thrift Supervision (OTS), the FDIC, and state regulators.

www.ots.treas.gov/

The Office of Thrift Supervision. Established in 1989 under the FIRREA, this office charters and examines all *federal* savings institutions. It also supervises the holding companies of savings institutions.

www.fdic.gov/

The FDIC. The FDIC oversees and manages the Savings Association Insurance Fund (SAIF), which was established in 1989 under the FIRREA in the wake of FSLIC insolvency. The SAIF provides insurance coverage for savings associations. Savings banks are insured under the FDIC's Bank Insurance Fund (BIF) and are thus also subject to supervision and examination by the FDIC.

Other Regulators. State chartered savings institutions are regulated by state agencies—for example, the Office of Banks and Real Estate in Illinois—rather than the OTS.

Do You Understand?

1. Who the regulators of savings institutions are?

---

6 Savings Association and Savings Bank Recent Performance

Like commercial banks, savings institutions (savings associations and savings banks) experienced record profits in the mid- to late 1990s as interest rates (and thus the cost of funds to savings institutions) remained low and the U.S. economy (and thus the demand for loans) prospered. The result was an increase in the spread between interest income and interest expense for savings institutions and consequently an increase in net income. Figure 12–5 reports ROAs and ROEs for the industry from 1988 through June 1999.[7] In the second quarter of 1999, savings institutions reported $2.9 billion in net income and an annualized ROA of 1.03 percent (this compares to an ROA of 1.28 percent over the same period for commercial banks—see Chapter 11). Only the $3.0 billion of net income reported in the third quarter of 1998 exceeded these results. In 1999, over 93 percent of savings institutions were profitable and 29 percent had an ROA of 1 percent or better. Asset quality improvements were widespread during the second quarter of 1999, providing the most favorable net operating income that the industry had ever reported. The loan loss reserves to total assets ratio was also at its lowest level since 1990 at 0.94 percent. Noncurrent loans (those with an interest payment over 90 days past due) as a percent of total loans remained below 1 percent (0.76 percent). Equity capital as a percent of total assets was 8.55 percent, down from its all time high of 8.94 percent in 1998, largely due to rapid asset growth by these banks. Table 12–4 presents several performance ratios for the industry for 1989 and 1993 through 1999.

Like the commercial banking industry, savings institutions have experienced substantial consolidation in the 1990s. For example, the 1998 acquisition of H.F. Ahmanson & Co. by Washington Mutual Inc. for almost $10 billion was the fourth largest bank/thrift merger completed in 1998.[8] Washington Mutual was the third largest savings institution in the United States early in 1997, while Ahmanson was the largest savings institution. In 1997, Washington Mutual bought Great Western to become the largest thrift in the country. Then, in March 1998, Washington Mutual bought Ahmanson to combine the two largest U.S. thrifts. Table 12–5 shows the industry consolidation in number and asset size over the period 1992–1999. Notice that over this period, the biggest savings institutions (over $10 billion) grew in number from 8 to 35 and their control of industry assets grew from 17.8 percent to 55.9 percent.

Larger savings institutions have also enjoyed superior profitability compared to smaller savings institutions. The 681 small thrifts (with assets less than $100 million) had an average annualized ROA of 0.67 percent for the second quarter of 1999, while the larger (stock-owned) institutions reported a record ROA of 1.05 percent. One major reason for this size-based difference in ROA is that larger savings institutions (unlike money center banks relative to smaller commercial banks) have virtually no asset investments or offices in foreign markets and countries and have consequently

---

7. The sharp drop in ROA and ROE in 1996 was the result of a $3.5 billion special assessment on SAIF deposits. Without these one-time charges, ROA would have been 0.89 percent rather than the −0.02 percent in Figure 12–5, while ROE would have been 10.36 percent rather than −0.26 percent.

8. Behind Travelers Group/Citicorp ($74 billion), NationsBank/BankAmerica ($62 billion), and BancOne/First Chicago NBD ($30 billion).

Figure 12–5 ROA and ROE for Savings Institutions, 1988 through 1999

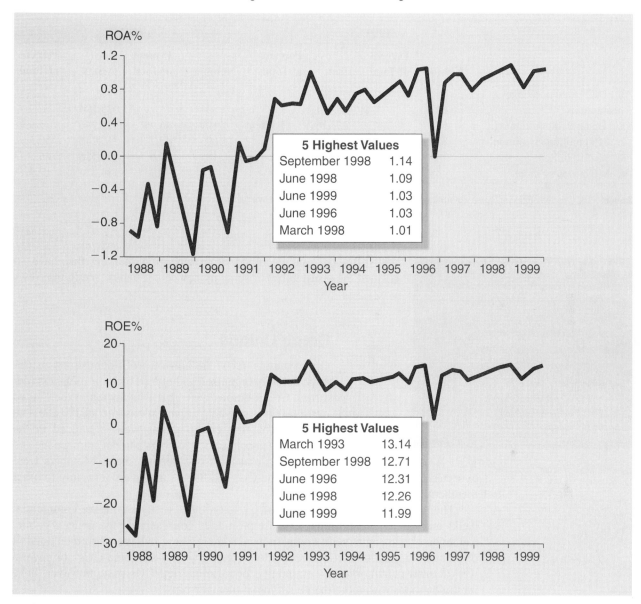

Source: Federal Deposit Insurance Corporation, *Quarterly Banking Profile,* Second Quarter 1999. *www.fdic.gov/*

Table 12–4 Selected Indicators for U.S. Savings Institutions, 1989 and 1993 through June 1999

	1999*	1998	1997	1996	1995	1994	1993	1989
Number of institutions	1,652	1,687	1, 779	1,924	2,030	2,152	2,262	3,086
Return on assets (%)	1.01	1.01	0.93	0.70	0.77	0.66	0.71	−0.39
Return on equity (%)	11.70	11.35	10.84	8.40	9.40	8.28	9.32	−8.06
Noncurrent assets plus other real estate owned to assets (%)	0.62	0.72	0.95	1.09	1.20	1.38	2.10	2.78
Asset growth rate (%)	7.74	6.05	−0.21	0.25	1.70	0.77	−2.85	−11.14
Net operating income growth (%)	8.69	7.69	20.07	−13.99	13.81	22.24	21.16	−58.95
Number of failed institutions	0	0	0	1	2	4	8	331

*Through June 30, ratios annualized where appropriate. Asset growth is for 12 months ending June 30.

Source: FDIC, *Quarterly Banking Profile,* Second Quarter 1999; and *Historical Statistics,* 1989. *www.fdic.gov/*

Table 12–5 U.S. Savings Institution Asset Concentration, 1992 versus 1999
(in millions of dollars)

	1999				1992			
	Number	**Percent of Total**	**Assets**	**Percent of Total**	**Number**	**Percent of Total**	**Assets**	**Percent of Total**
All FDIC-insured savings institutions	1,652		$1,125,761		2,391		$1,035,194	
1. Under $100 million	681	41.2%	35,116	3.1%	1,109	46.4%	55,946	5.4%
2. $100 million–$1 billion	828	50.1	241,379	21.4	1,093	45.7	315,246	30.5
3. $1–$10 billion	108	6.5	220,556	19.6	181	7.6	479,526	46.3
4. $10 billion or more	35	2.1	628,710	55.9	8	0.3	184,476	17.8

Source: *FDIC Quarterly Banking Profile*, Fourth Quarter 1992 and Second Quarter 1999. *www.fdic.gov/*

Do You Understand?

1. The recent performance of savings institutions?
2. The ways that profit trends for savings institutions have been similar to those of commercial banks in the 1990s?
3. Why profits for large savings institutions have outperformed those of large commercial banks in the late 1990s?

---

not suffered from recent crises in emerging markets that have so harmed the profitability of some money center banks (see In the News box 12–1).

Credit Unions

Credit unions (CUs) are not-for-profit depository institutions mutually organized and owned by their members (depositors). Credit unions were first established in the United States in the early 1900s as self-help organizations intended to alleviate widespread poverty. The first credit unions were organized in the Northeast, initially in Massachusetts. Members paid an entrance fee and put up funds to purchase at least one deposit share. Members were expected to deposit their savings in the CU, and these funds were lent only to other members.

This limit in the customer base of CUs continues today as, unlike commercial banks and savings institutions, CUs are prohibited from serving the general public. Rather, in organizing a credit union, members are required to have a common bond of occupation (e.g., police CUs), association (e.g., university-affiliated CUs), or cover a well-defined neighborhood, community, or rural district. CUs may, however, have multiple groups with more than one type of membership.

The primary objective of credit unions is to satisfy the depository and borrowing needs of their members. CU member deposits (called shares, representing ownership in the CU) are used to provide loans to other members in need of funds. Earnings from these loans are used to pay interest on member deposits. Because credit unions are not-for-profit organizations, their earnings are not taxed. This tax-exempt status allows CUs to offer higher rates on deposits and charge lower rates on some types of loans compared to banks and savings institutions, whose earnings are taxable.

Size, Structure, and Composition of the Industry

Do You Understand?

1. Why thrifts remained relatively unaffected by volatile global markets in 1998?

Credit unions are the most numerous of the institutions (10,841 in 1999) that comprise the depository institutions segment of the FI industry. (Figure 12–6 shows the number of credit unions, their total assets, and number of members from 1993 through 1999.) Moreover, CUs were less affected by the crisis that affected commercial banks and savings institutions in the 1980s. This is because traditionally more than 40 percent

In the News

T hough big banks are reeling from volatile global markets, the nation's thrifts are posting stellar profits. The Office of Thrift Supervision said Wednesday that the industry earned $2.23 billion in the third quarter, up 66 percent from a year earlier. It was the eighth consecutive quarter of record results, and it put the industry on track for a record year.

Thrift executives said the results show that old-fashioned banking can produce more profits than foreign lending and securities dealings. "Well-managed institutions are doing well in basic banking—taking deposits and lending money," said David E.A. Carson, chairman and chief executive of People's Bank, a state-chartered thrift in Bridgeport, Conn. "They haven't been caught in the trading problems of many of the commercial banks."

Commercial banks, stung by trading losses in Russia and other developing markets, are expected to see their own string of

Source: *The American Banker*, December 3, 1998, by Dean Anason.

Market Woes Leave Thrifts Unfazed;

Net Surged in Third Quarter

record earnings broken when the Federal Deposit Insurance Corp. releases its third-quarter report on December 16. Already, Bankers Trust Corp. and Republic New York Corp. have collectively reported more than $581 million of losses for the third quarter.

The strong results for thrifts stand in sharp contrast to the late 1980s and early 1990s, when the industry collapsed. "The resurgence of the thrift industry continues," said Paul A. Schosberg, president of America's Community Bankers. "The performance for virtually half a decade now underscores how significant the charter is and how good a job of managing business opportunities . . . the executives, trustees, and directors are doing."

Industry officials said the results show that thrifts have retooled themselves, diversified their mortgage products, and successfully expanded into other retail

services. "The late 1980s and early 1990s were an extremely difficult time for the industry," said William A. Fitzgerald, chairman and chief executive of Commercial Federal Bank, Omaha. "Those that survived had to restructure their financial institutions to compete in an environment with greater volatility in interest rate movements."

Ellen S. Seidman, director of the OTS, lauded thrift executives for managing the liability side of their balance sheets well and reacting to declines in deposits with less costly, longer-term borrowings. Yet, she said, regulators are worried about declining deposits bases, weaker operating efficiencies, expansions into riskier product lines, and the flattening yield curve between long-term and short-term rates.

All the same, thrift executives took clear pride in comparing the recent results with those of commercial banks. "I am just going to smile," said Lee Beard, president and chief executive of First Federal Bank in Hazleton, PA. "I am not going to have to say anything. The numbers speak for themselves."

Figure 12–6 Characteristics of Credit Unions, 1993 through 1999

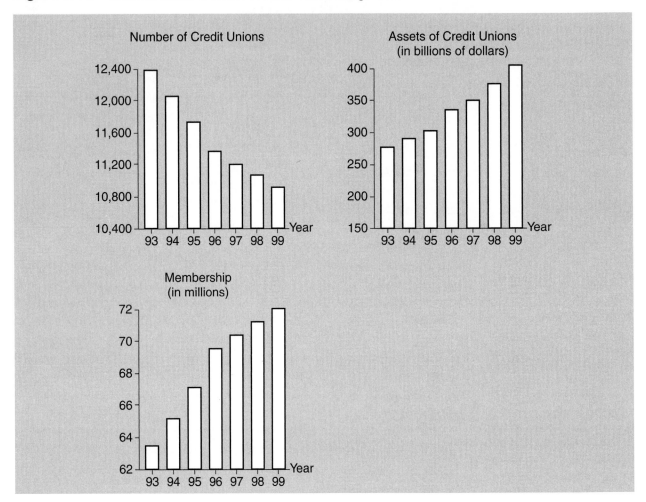

Source: National Credit Union Association, *Midyear Statistics,* 1999. *www.ncua.gov/*

of their assets have been in small consumer loans, often for amounts less than $10,000, which are funded mainly by member deposits. This combination of relatively matched credit risk and maturity in the asset and liability portfolios left credit unions less exposed to credit and interest rate risk than commercial banks and savings institutions. In addition, CUs tend to hold large amounts of government securities (almost 20 percent of their assets in 1999) and relatively small amounts of residential mortgages. CUs' lending activities are funded mainly by deposits contributed by their 70 million members.

The nation's credit union system consists of three distinct tiers: the top tier at the national level (U.S. Central Credit Union); the middle tier at the state or regional level (corporate credit unions); and the bottom tier at the local level (credit unions). Figure 12–7 illustrates this structure, with the services conducted between various entities identified via arrows. Corporate credit unions are financial institutions that are cooperatively owned by their member credit unions.[9] Corporate credit unions serve their members primarily by investing and lending excess funds (unloaned deposits) that

9. Ownership in corporate credit unions is represented by the deposit accounts of their member credit unions, with each member having equal voting rights.

Figure 12–7 The Structure of the Credit Union System

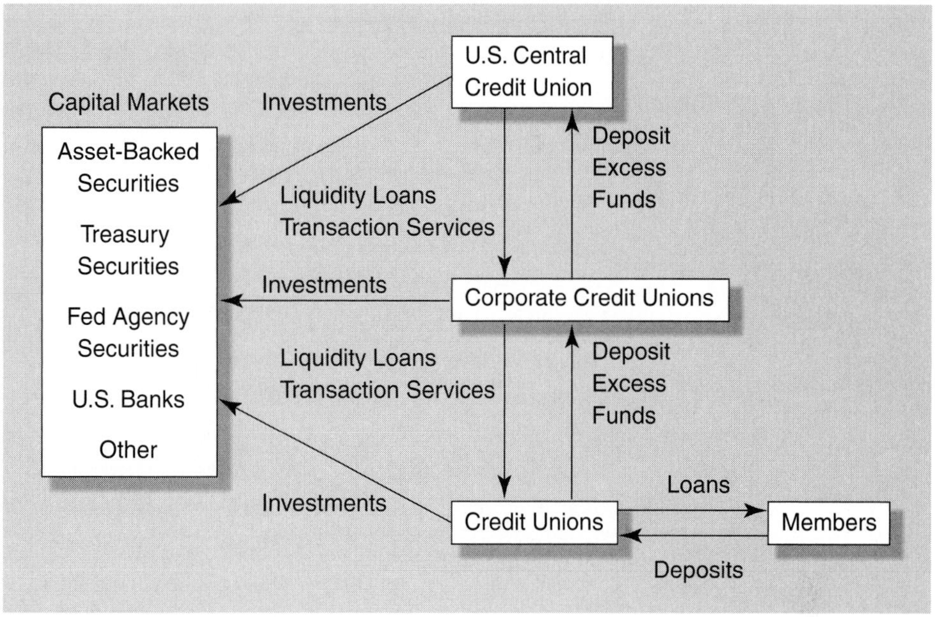

Source: *Credit Unions*, U.S. Department of Treasury, December 1997, p. 86. *www.ustreas.gov/*

member credit unions place with them. Additional services provided by corporate credit unions include automated settlement, securities safekeeping, data processing, accounting, and payment services. As of 1999, credit unions had over $35 billion (9.3 percent of total assets) invested in corporate credit unions. The U.S. Central Credit Union serves as a "corporate's corporate"—providing investment and liquidity services to corporate credit unions.

In recent years, to attract and keep customers, CUs have expanded their services to compete with commercial banks and savings institutions. For example, many CUs now offer mortgages, credit lines, and automated teller machines. Some credit unions also offer business and commercial loans to their employer groups. For example, in the late 1990s, AWANE (Automotive Wholesalers Association of New England) Credit Union's[10] business loans represented 13.6 percent of its lending and the CU participated actively in the Small Business Administration loan programs, which enabled it to sell a portion of those loans. In addition, commercial real estate lending accounted for 29.5 percent of AWANE's total lending. An example of the success of one military base–related credit union is discussed in In the News box 12–2.

As CUs have expanded in membership, size, and services, bankers claim that CUs unfairly compete with small banks that have historically been the major lender in small towns and local communities. For example, the American Bankers Association claimed that the tax exemption for CUs gives them the equivalent of a $1 billion a year

Do You Understand?

1. How PMFCU created such rapid growth in assets and membership in 1997 through 1999?

---

10. AWANE is a trade association of companies that serve the automotive after-market through sales of auto parts and other items. It is the association member companies and firms related to the automotive business, as well as their owners and employees, who AWANE Credit Union serves through its common bond.

In the News

Lessons Offered by a New Community Charter

When Point Mugu (Federal Credit Union) PMFCU applied for community charter, it prepared to serve what was at that time among the largest and most diverse fields of membership among credit unions. To attract some of the county's 750,000 residents, the (credit union) CU launched a home-spun marketing campaign combining traditional advertising and community involvement to carve a wildly—maybe even overly—successful member-service niche.

The 1996 application for community charter arose from the threatened closure of Point Mugu Naval Air Warfare Center Weapons Division, one of the largest employers in Ventura County and PMFCU's core membership. Though the military base did not close, a 50% workforce reduction hurt the credit union and caused a ripple effect

among members. "Some of the other groups that we had brought in to our field of membership through the (secondary employment group) SEG program we found out were more defense-related than we thought," said Ron McDaniel, president of PMFCU. "So as the base downsized a lot of their work went to other parts of the county. We determined that it was going to have a major impact on the credit union so we looked at options and the option we chose was community charter." . . .

The conversion resulted in a stabilized growth rate of 12% to 15% from 1997 through 1999 versus the flat 2% the three years prior. Assets climbed from $125 million to $180 million and membership grew from 31,000 to 37,000 . . . Rapid growth resulted from awareness marketing, product-specific loan marketing

and, finally, an indirect lending program with local automobile dealers that has really blossomed. "The reason it's been so successful is we've been able to go out and build relationships with those dealers so that we did become a business partner from both sides of the relationship," McDaniel said. "We've found ways to go out and leverage each other's business position in the marketplace."

Experiments in billboard, radio and TV advertising co-marketed with the automobile dealers resulted in several successful models. The strategy succeeded in recapturing the bread-and-butter auto loans that have slowly been eroded by the aggressive financing practices by auto manufacturers' lending arms. McDaniel said the change was significant for PMFCU. "We've gone from being a credit union with a stagnant future to a credit union that is going to have to manage its growth," he said. "It's a total flip-flop from where we were in 1996 before we got the community charter."

Source: *Credit Union Journal*, March 27, 2000, p. 1, by Tina Carlson.

www.americanbanker.com/

subsidy. The response of the Credit Union National Association (CUNA) is that any cost to taxpayers from CUs' tax-exempt status is more than passed on to their members and society at large through favorable interest rates on deposits and loans. For example, CUNA estimates that the benefits of CU membership can range from $200 to $500 a year per member or, with almost 70 million members, a benefit of $14 billion to $35 billion per year.

In 1997, the banking industry filed two lawsuits in its push to restrict the growing competitive threat from credit unions. The first lawsuit (filed by four North Carolina banks and the American Bankers Association) challenged an occupation-based credit union's (the AT&T Family Credit Union based in North Carolina) ability to accept members from companies unrelated to the firm that originally sponsored the credit union. In the second lawsuit, the American Bankers Association asked the courts to bar the federal government from allowing occupation-based credit unions to convert to community-based charters. Bankers argued in both lawsuits that such actions, broadening the membership base of credit unions, would further exploit an unfair advantage allowed through the credit union tax-exempt status. In February 1998, the Supreme Court sided with the banks in its decision that credit unions could no longer accept members that were not a part of the "common bond" of membership. In April 1998, however, the U.S. House of Representatives overwhelmingly passed a bill that allowed all existing members to keep their credit union accounts. The bill was passed by the Senate in July 1998 and signed into law by the president in August 1998. This legislation not only allowed CUs to keep their existing members but allowed CUs to accept new groups of members—including small businesses and low-income communities—that were not considered part of the "common bond" of membership by the Supreme Court ruling.

Balance Sheets and Recent Trends

As of 1999, 10,841 credit unions had assets of $412.3 billion. This compares to $192.8 billion in assets in 1988, or a growth rate of 114 percent over the period 1988–1999. Individually, credit unions tend to be very small, with an average asset size of $38.0 million in 1999 compared to $630.3 million for banks. The total assets of all credit unions are smaller than the largest U.S. banking organization(s). For example, Citigroup had $689.6 billion in total assets, BankAmerica had $614.1 billion in total assets, and Chase had $356.9 billion in assets compared to *total* credit union assets of $412.3 billion in 1999.

Table 12–6 shows the breakdown of financial assets and liabilities for credit unions as of June 30, 1999. Given their emphasis on retail or consumer lending, discussed above, 38.1 percent of CU assets are in the form of small consumer loans and another 25.2 percent are in the form of home mortgages. Together these member loans comprise 63.3 percent of total assets. Figure 12–8 provides more detail on the composition of the loan portfolio for all CUs. Because of the common bond requirement on credit union customers, few business or commercial loans are issued by CUs.

Credit unions also invest heavily in investment securities (28.1 percent of total assets in 1999). Figure 12–9 shows that 50.5 percent of the investment portfolio of CUs is in U.S. government Treasury securities or federal agency securities, while investments in other FIs (such as deposits of banks) totaled 41.2 percent of their investment portfolios. Their investment portfolio composition along with cash holdings (2.1 percent of total assets) allow credit unions ample liquidity to meet their daily cash needs—such as share (deposit) withdrawals. Some CUs have also increased their off-balance-sheet activities. Specifically, unused loan commitments, including credit card limits and home equity lines of credit, totaled over $80 billion in 1999.

Table 12–6   Assets and Liabilities of Credit Unions, June 30, 1999

	Billions of dollars	Percentage
Assets		
Checkable deposits and currency	$ 8.8	2.1%
Time and savings deposits	27.2	6.6
Federal funds and security RPs	7.1	1.7
Open market paper	0.8	0.2
U.S. government securities	80.9	19.6
Treasury	14.9	3.6
Agency	66.0	16.0
Home mortgages	104.0	25.2
Consumer credit	156.8	38.1
Credit market instruments	$342.5	83.1%
Mutual fund shares	3.9	1.0
Miscellaneous assets	22.8	5.5
Total assets	$412.3	100.0%
Liabilities and Equity		
Checkable	$ 43.1	10.4%
Small time and savings	305.0	74.0
Large time	20.6	5.0
Shares/deposits	$368.6	89.4%
Other loans and advances	1.8	0.4
Miscellaneous liabilities	4.8	1.2
Total liabilities	$375.2	91.0%
Total ownership shares	$ 37.1	9.0%

Source: *Federal Reserve Bulletin*, September 1999, p. 74. *www.bog.frb.fed.us/*

Figure 12–8   Composition of Credit Union Loan Portfolio, 1999

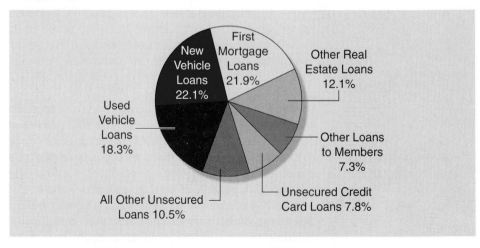

Source: National Credit Union Association, *Midyear Statistics,* 1999. *www.ncua.gov/*

Figure 12–9   Composition of Credit Union Investment Portfolio, 1999

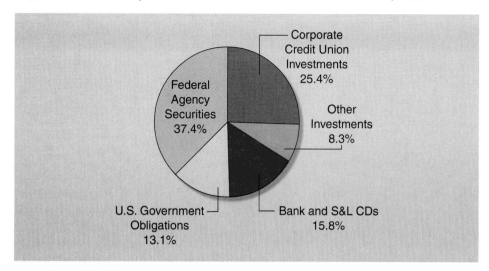

Source: National Credit Union Association, *Midyear Statistics,* 1999. *www.ncua.gov/*

Figure 12–10   Composition of Credit Union Deposits, 1999

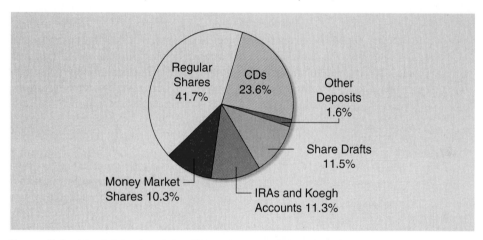

Source: National Credit Union Association, *Midyear Statistics,* 1999. *www.ncua.gov/*

Credit union funding comes mainly from member deposits (almost 90 percent of total funding in 1999). Figure 12–10 presents the distribution of these deposits in 1999. Regular share draft transaction accounts (similar to NOW accounts at other depository institutions—see Chapters 11 and 13) accounted for 41.7 percent of all CU deposits, followed by certificates of deposits (23.6 percent of deposits) and share accounts (similar to passbook savings accounts at other depository institutions but so named to designate the deposit holders' ownership status) (11.5 percent of deposits). Credit unions tend to hold higher levels of equity than other depository institutions. Since CUs are not stockholder owned, this equity is basically the accumulation of past earnings from CU activities that is "owned" collectively by member depositors. As will be discussed in Chapters 20 and 23, this equity protects a CU against losses on its loan portfolio as well as other financial and operating risks. In June 1999, CUs capital-to-assets ratio was 10.73 percent compared to 8.29 percent for S&Ls, 9.12 percent for savings banks, and 8.51 percent for commercial banks.

Figure 12–11   Return on Assets for Credit Unions, 1993 through 1999

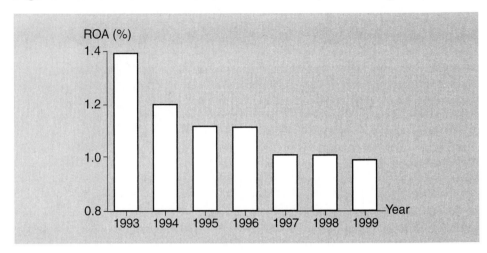

Source: National Credit Union Association, *Midyear Statistics,* 1999. *www.ncua.gov/*

5 Regulators

www.ncua.gov/

Like savings banks and savings associations, credit unions can be federally or state chartered. As of 1999, 61.9 percent of the 10,841 CUs were federally chartered and subject to National Credit Union Administration (NCUA) regulation (see Table 12–1), accounting for 59.1 percent of the total membership and 60.0 percent of total assets. In addition, through its insurance fund (the National Credit Union Share Insurance Fund, or NCUSIF), the NCUA provides deposit insurance guarantees of up to $100,000 for insured credit unions. Currently, the NCUSIF covers 98 percent of all credit union deposits.

Industry Performance

Like other depository institutions, the credit union industry has grown in asset size in the 1990s. Asset growth in 1998 and 1999 topped 6 percent and 9 percent, respectively. In addition, CU membership increased from 72.6 million to over 74.6 million over the 1998–1999 period. Asset growth was especially pronounced among the largest CUs (the 1,516 CUs with assets of over $50 million) as their assets increased by 10 and 12 percent in 1998 and 1999, respectively. Figure 12–11 shows the trend in ROA for CUs from 1993 through 1999. The decrease in ROA over the period is mostly attributed to earnings decreases at the smaller CUs. For example, the 75 largest credit unions (that serve 17 percent of the industry's customers) experienced an ROA of 3.41 percent in the first half of 1999, while ROA for the whole industry was 1.03 percent. Smaller CUs generally have a smaller customer base with which to issue quality loans and have higher overhead expenses per dollar of assets. Thus, their ROAs have been hurt.

Given the mutual-ownership status of this industry, however, growth in ROA (or profits) is not necessarily the primary goal of CUs. Rather, as long as capital or equity levels are sufficient to protect a CU against unexpected losses on its credit portfolio as well as other financial and operational risks, this not-for-profit industry has a primary goal of serving the deposit and lending needs of its members. This contrasts with the emphasis placed on profitability by stockholder-owned commercial banks and savings institutions.

Do You Understand?

1. How credit unions differ from commercial banks and savings institutions?
2. Why credit unions have prospered in recent years in comparison to savings associations and savings banks?
3. How the credit union industry is organized?
4. Why commercial banks and savings institutions claim that credit unions have an unfair advantage in providing bank services?
5. The main assets and liabilities credit unions hold?

Summary

This chapter provided an overview of the major activities of savings associations, savings banks, and credit unions. Each of these institutions relies heavily on deposits to fund loans, although borrowed funds are becoming increasingly important for the largest of these institutions. Historically, while commercial banks have concentrated on commercial or business lending and on investing in securities, savings institutions have concentrated on mortgage lending and credit unions on consumer lending. These differences are being eroded due to competitive forces, regulation, and the changing nature of financial and business technology, so that the types of interest rate, credit, liquidity, and operational risks faced by commercial banks, savings institutions, and credit unions are becoming increasingly similar.

Questions

1. How do the balance sheets of savings associations and savings banks differ from those of commercial banks? How do their sizes compare?

2. What were the reasons for the crisis of the thrift industry in the late 1970s and early 1980s?

3. What two major pieces of legislation were adopted in the early 1980s to ameliorate the thrift crisis? Explain.

4. What shortcoming in the Depository Institutions Deregulation and Monetary Control Act of 1980 (DIDMCA) and the Garn-St. Germain Depository Institutions Act of 1982 (DIA) contributed to the failure of the thrift industry?

5. How did the Financial Institutions Reform, Recovery, and Enforcement Act (FIRREA) of 1989 reverse some of the key features of earlier legislation?

6. What are the main assets held by savings associations?

7. What are the main liabilities issued by savings associations?

8. What are the similarities and differences among savings institutions (savings associations and savings banks)?

9. What regulatory agencies oversee deposit insurance services to savings associations and saving banks?

10. What happened to the value of the savings institutions' charters in the period of time since October 1979? How did this shift contribute to the crisis in the savings institutions industry?

11. What does it mean when a savings bank is a mutual organization?

12. What is the trend in mutual versus stock charters (in number and asset size) for savings institutions?

13. Why have size-based differences in ROA existed in the savings institutions industry relative to the commercial banking industry in the late 1990s?

14. What explanations can be provided for the recent decline in the size of the savings institutions industry?

15. How do credit unions differ from other thrift institutions?

16. Why were credit unions less affected by the sharp increase in interest rates in the late 1970s and early 1980s than the savings institutions industry?

17. What are the main assets and liabilities held by credit unions?

18. Why did commercial banks pursue legal action against the credit union industry in the late 1990s? What was the result of this legal action?

19. Who are the regulators of credit unions?

20. Go to the Federal Deposit Insurance Corporation's website and find the latest figure for the total assets of all U.S. savings institutions. How does this compare with the figure from Table 12–3?

Depository Institutions' Financial Statements *and* Analysis

Chapter Navigator

1. What are the four major categories of assets on a depository institution's balance sheet?

2. What are core deposits and purchased funds?

3. What off-balance-sheet activities do depository institutions undertake?

4. What are the major categories on a depository institution's income statement?

5. What ratios can be used to analyze a depository institution?

Why Evaluate the Performance of Depository Institutions: Chapter Overview

Unlike other private corporations, depository institutions (DIs) are unique in the special services they perform (e.g., assistance in the implementation of monetary policy) and the level of regulatory attention they receive (see Chapters 1 and 14). DIs are, as a result, unique in the types of assets and liabilities they hold. Like any for profit corporation, however, the ultimate measure of a DI's performance is the value of its common equity to its shareholders.[1] This chapter discusses the financial statements of these institutions. Managers, stockholders, depositors, regulators, and other parties use performance, earnings, and other measures obtained from financial statements to evaluate

---

1. Nevertheless, some DIs that adopt the mutual form of ownership (such as credit unions) have objectives other than value maximization—for example, the provision of relatively low-cost loans to their members (see Chapter 12).

In the News

13-1

Top Regional Banks Draw Attention from Investors

Investors are expected to become much more selective about bank stocks this year because of the dark clouds from abroad that are hanging over the industry, analysts say. "Top-quality names will move further ahead of the pack," said Sean J. Ryan of Bear, Stearns & Co. "We are going into 1999 with slower economic growth and continued disinflation that should feed into the continuing bifurcation of bank stocks." Indeed, some regional banks' stocks outpaced the industry group last week as value investors began funneling their money into what many analysts call "quality names"— banks with strong business operations and little exposure to foreign markets and hedge funds . . .

"The market has been awarding higher valuations to only those banks that have demonstrated the greatest ability to sustain high profitability and growth rates, while the rest of the group has languished at lower valuations," Mr. Ryan wrote in a recent report. The analyst said he expects investors' enthusiasm for bank stocks to continue, regardless of the year 2000 issue or a slowing economy.

In 1996 and 1997, Mr. Ryan said, banks as a group behaved homogeneously. In those years, he said, "we had a strong economy and inflation, which masks many of the blemishes of the banking industry. A strong economy will bail you out of the bad loans

and inflation will allow you to profit just from playing the yield curve." That, however, was not the case in 1998, Mr. Ryan said. "There has been more disparity in the performance of the bank stocks, and that trend is here to stay." Banks that continue to deliver so-so performances or continue to take a "business as usual" approach are going to see their earnings growth dissipate very rapidly, he said. "Good banks, as opposed to great banks, also have potential in the new year, either because they are not too far behind the great performers or because they are acquisition targets," he said . . .

Bank analyst Frank J. Barkocy of Josephthal & Co. said he expects bank stocks with medium-sized market capitalization to move ahead of the pack because consolidation and business operations are still going strong.

Source: *American Banker*, January 4, 1999, p. 12, by Tania Padgett.

www.americanbanker. com/

Do You Understand?

1. Why investors were expected to be cautious about investments in bank stocks in the late 1990s?
2. Which banks were expected to perform the best over the period of the late 1990s?

which DI stocks they will purchase (see In the News box 13-1). Given the extensive level of regulation and the accompanying requirements for public availability of financial information, the financial statements of commercial banks are ideal candidates to use in examining the performance of depository institutions.

This chapter uses commercial banks to illustrate a return on equity (ROE) framework as a method of evaluating depository institutions' profitability. The ROE framework decomposes this frequently used measure of profitability into its various component parts to identify existing or potential financial management and risk exposure problems.[2] The fact that bank size and/or niche (i.e., the financial market segment the bank specializes in servicing) may affect the evaluation of financial statements is also highlighted.

Financial Statements of Commercial Banks

report of condition

Balance sheet of a commercial bank reporting information at a single point in time.

report of income

Income statement of a commercial bank reporting revenues, expenses, net profit or loss, and cash dividends over a period of time.

www.ffiec.gov/

Financial information on commercial banks is reported in two basic documents. The **report of condition** (or balance sheet) presents financial information on a bank's assets, liabilities, and equity capital. The balance sheet reports a bank's condition at a single point in time. The **report of income** (or the income statement) presents the major categories of revenues and expenses (or costs) and the net profit or loss for a bank over a period of time. Financial statements of commercial banks must be submitted to regulators and stockholders at the end of each calendar quarter—March, June, September, and December. The Federal Financial Institutions Examination Council (FFIEC), based in Washington, D.C., prescribes uniform principles, standards, and report forms for depository institutions.

Financial institutions are also engaging in an increased level of off-balance-sheet (OBS) activities. These activities produce income (and sometimes losses) for the FI that are reported on the income statement. This chapter summarizes off-balance-sheet activities (and the risks involved with such activities), which are discussed in more detail in Chapters 7, 10, 24, and 25.

To evaluate the performance of commercial banks, we use two bank holding companies of varying sizes and market niches: North Fork Bancorporation and Bank One Corporation.

North Fork Bancorp (NFB) is a publicly traded commercial bank holding company headquartered in Melville, New York; in 1997, it had $6.7 billion in assets. It is Long Island's largest independent commercial bank, operating 85 branch locations throughout New York and Connecticut. NFB, by emphasizing retail banking, has been one of the most efficient and profitable banks in the country. **Retail banks** focus on individual consumer banking relationships, such as residential mortgages and consumer loans on the asset side of the portfolio, and individual demand, NOW, savings, and time deposits on the liability side. In contrast, **wholesale banks** focus their business activities on business banking relationships; they hold more business loans and fewer mortgages and consumer loans and use fewer consumer deposits and more purchased funds than retail banks do. In addition to providing a range of personal and commercial banking products, NFB also offers an array of financial services, including trust, asset management, and brokerage services. NFB invests heavily in real estate loans and attempts to fund assets as much as possible with core deposits. At the end of 1997, multifamily mortgage loans constituted more than 80 percent of the bank's loan portfolio. In 1998, NFB acquired New York Bancorp, which increased its size to $10.1 billion in assets and 108 branch locations.

Bank One Corporation (BOC), headquartered in Chicago, Illinois, is the nation's fifth largest bank, with assets of $118 billion as of December 1997. The merger of Bank One and First Chicago NBD in 1998 brought this asset value up to $235 billion, with more than 2,000 offices in the United States and 11 foreign countries. Bank One is the nation's second largest credit card company, the leading retail bank in the midwest and Arizona, and manages the third largest bank-sponsored mutual fund family. Bank One operates nationally in many business lines, including retail and wholesale banking, investment and trust management, and credit card company business.

retail bank

A bank that focuses its business activities on consumer banking relationships.

wholesale bank

A bank that focuses its business activities on commercial banking relationships.

www.bankone.com/

Balance Sheet Structure

Table 13–1 presents December 31, 1997, balance sheet information for the two commercial bank holding companies (hereafter called *banks*). As stated in Chapter 11,

2. This decomposition is often termed *DuPont* analysis.

Table 13–1 Balance Sheet for Two Commercial Banks on
December 31, 1997

(in millions of dollars)

	North Fork Bancorp[*]	Bank One Corporation[*]
Assets		
1. Vault cash	$ 43.94	$ 1,883.01
2. Deposits at Federal Reserve	7.05	1,406.10
3. Deposits at other financial institutions	2.88	1,063.63
4. Cash items in process of collection	99.09	4,097.65
5. Cash and balances due from depository institutions	$ 152.96	$ 8,450.39
6. Interest-bearing deposits at other FIs	8.74	4,180.29
7. Federal funds sold and RPs	58.97	3,706.84
8. U.S. Treasury and U.S. agency securities	173.22	3,910.60
9. Securities issued by states and political subdivisions	114.51	2,248.60
10. Mortgage-backed securities	2,297.10	9,213.89
11. Other debt and equity securities	52.35	3,095.70
12. Investment securities	$2,704.89	$ 26,355.92
13. Commercial and industrial loans	393.97	18,063.56
14. Loans secured by real estate	2,986.75	26,463.85
15. Consumer loans	265.04	25,363.93
16. Other loans	36.46	2,870.58
17. Leases	47.06	8,748.94
18. Gross loans and leases	$3,729.28	$ 81,510.86
19. Less: Unearned income	14.63	3.79
20. Reserve for loan and lease losses	84.96	1,325.90
21. Net loans and leases	3,629.69	80,181.17
22. Premises and fixed assets	63.50	282.19
23. Other real estate owned	4.71	9.24
24. Investments in unconsolidated subsidiaries	0.00	6.76
25. Intangible assets	68.30	321.35
26. Other	80.32	2,284.46
27. Other assets	$ 216.83	$ 2,904.00
28. Total assets	$6,704.37	$117,891.48
Liabilities and Equity Capital		
29. Demand deposits	$ 321.63	$ 19,883.93
30. NOW accounts	35.23	1,878.61
31. MMDAs	1,135.55	24,493.64
32. Other savings deposits	1,427.68	8,282.35
33. Retail CDs	1,378.33	16,930.87
34. Core deposits	$4,298.42	$ 71,469.40
35. Wholesale CDs	344.51	5,640.50
36. Total deposits	$4,642.93	$ 77,109.90

continued

Table 13–1 *concluded*

	North Fork Bancorp*	Bank One Corporation*
37. Federal funds purchased and RPs	1,413.68	12,755.50
38. Other borrowed funds	68.28	4,722.49
39. Subordinated notes and debentures	0.00	11,066.40
40. Other liabilities	29.02	1,861.19
41. Total liabilities	$6,153.91	$107,515.48
42. Preferred stock	0.00	135.40
43. Common stock	7.06	3,229.80
44. Surplus and paid-in capital	265.02	6,650.00
45. Retained earnings	278.38	360.80
46. Total equity capital	$ 550.46	$ 10,376.00
47. Total liabilities and equity capital	$6,704.37	$117,891.48

*Values are taken from the 1997 FDIC report of condition data tapes and annual reports.

www.fdic.gov/

many banks are owned by parent bank holding companies. One-bank holding companies control only one subsidiary commercial bank; multiple bank holding companies control two or more subsidiary commercial banks (see Chapter 14). The financial statements reported in this chapter are for the consolidated multiple bank holding company, which includes the parent holding company plus bank subsidiaries. These data are taken from the Federal Deposit Insurance Corporation call reports and from annual reports. Pay particular attention to the fact that, unlike manufacturing corporations, the majority of a commercial bank's assets are financial assets rather than physical or fixed assets (such as buildings or machines). Additionally, a relatively large portion of a commercial bank's liabilities are short-term deposits and borrowings. In general, banks have higher leverage than manufacturing corporations do.

Assets.   A bank's assets are grouped into four major subcategories: (1) cash and balances due from other depository institutions, (2) investment securities, (3) loans and leases, and (4) other assets. Investment securities and loans and leases are the bank's earning assets. Cash and balances due from depository institutions (item 5 in Table 13–1) consist of vault cash, deposits at the Federal Reserve (the central bank), deposits at other financial institutions, and cash items in the process of collection. None of these items generates much income for the bank, but each is held because they perform specific functions. Vault cash (item 1) is composed of the currency and coin needed to meet customer withdrawals. Deposits at the Federal Reserve (item 2) are used primarily to meet legal reserve requirements (see Chapter 14), to assist in check clearing, wire transfers, and the purchase or sale of Treasury securities. Deposits at other financial institutions (item 3) are primarily used to purchase services from those institutions. These banks generally purchase services such as check collection, check processing, fed funds trading, and investment advice from **correspondent banks**. Cash items in the process of collection (item 4) are checks written against accounts at other institutions that have been deposited at the bank. Credit is given to the depositor of these checks only after they clear.

Investment securities (item 12 in Table 13–1) consist of items such as interest-bearing deposits at other FIs, federal funds sold, repurchase agreements (RPs or repos), U.S. Treasury and agency securities, securities issued by states and political subdivisions (municipals), mortgage-backed securities, and other debt and equity securities.

correspondent bank

A bank that provides services to another commercial bank.

These securities generate some income for the bank and are used for liquidity risk management purposes. Investment securities are highly liquid,[3] have low default risk, and can usually be traded in secondary markets. Banks generally maintain significant amounts of these securities to ensure that they can easily meet liquidity needs that arise unexpectedly.[4] However, because the revenue generated from investment securities is low compared to that from loans and leases, many (particularly larger) banks attempt to minimize the amount of investment securities they hold.

Short-maturity (less than one year to maturity) investments include interest-bearing deposits at other FIs (item 6), federal funds sold and repurchase agreements (item 7), and U.S. Treasury bills and agency securities (item 8). Returns on these investments vary directly with changes in market interest rates. Although banks with excess cash reserves invest some of this in interest-earning liquid assets such as T-bills and short-term securities, they have the option to lend excess reserves for short intervals to other banks seeking increased short-term funding. The interbank market for excess reserves is called the federal funds (fed funds) market. In the United States, federal funds are short-term uncollateralized loans made by one bank to another; more than 90 percent of such transactions have maturities of one day. Repurchase agreements (RPs or repos) can be viewed as collateralized federal funds transactions. In a federal funds transaction, the bank with excess reserves sells fed funds for one day to the purchasing bank. The next day, the purchasing bank returns the fed funds plus one day's interest reflecting the fed funds rate. Since credit risk exposure exists for the selling bank, because the purchasing bank may be unable to repay the fed funds the next day, the seller may seek collateral backing for the one-day fed funds loan. In an RP transaction, the funds-selling bank receives government securities as collateral from the funds-purchasing bank—that is, the funds-purchasing bank temporarily exchanges securities for cash. The next day, this transaction is reversed—the funds-purchasing bank sends back the fed funds it borrowed plus interest (the RP rate); it receives in return (or repurchases) its securities used as collateral in the transaction.

Long-maturity investments such as U.S. Treasury bonds and U.S. agency securities (item 8), municipals (item 9), mortgage-backed securities (item 10), and most other securities (item 11) usually offer somewhat higher expected returns than short-maturity investments since they are subject to greater interest rate risk exposure—see Chapter 23. U.S. Treasury securities and Government National Mortgage Association (agency) bonds are fully backed by the U.S. government and thus carry no default risk. Other U.S. government agency securities, such as those of the Federal National Mortgage Association and the Federal Home Loan Mortgage Corporation, are not directly backed by the full faith and credit of the U.S. government and therefore carry some default risk (see Chapter 7). Municipal securities held by commercial banks are generally high-rated, investment-grade (i.e., low-risk) securities, issued by municipalities as either general obligation or revenue bonds.[5] Interest paid on municipals is exempt from federal income tax obligations. Mortgage-backed securities include items such as collateralized mortgage obligations and mortgage-backed bonds (see Chapter 7). Other investment securities include investment-grade corporate bonds, foreign debt securities, and securities such as U.S. Treasury securities and municipals held for short-term

www.ginniemae.gov/

www.fanniemae.com/

www.freddiemac.com/

---

3. Not all of a bank's investment securities can be sold immediately. Some securities, such as U.S. Treasury securities and municipals, can be pledged against certain types of borrowing by the bank and, therefore, must remain on the bank's books until the debt obligation is removed or another security is pledged as collateral.

4. Most investment securities are debt rather than equity instruments, because current regulations generally prohibit banks from owning equity securities as investments. Banks can hold equity securities only if they are acquired as collateral on a loan or if they are stocks issued by the Federal Reserve Bank.

5. Payments of principal and interest on general obligation bonds are backed by the full faith, credit, and taxing authority of the issuer. Payments of principal and interest on revenue bonds are backed only by the revenues generated from the facility or project that the proceeds of the bonds are financing.

trading purposes. These trading account securities earn interest for the bank and generate capital gains or losses from changes in the market values of these securities.[6]

Loans (items 13–16 in Table 13–1) are the major items on a bank's balance sheet and generate the largest flow of revenue income. However, loans are also the least liquid asset item and the major source of credit and liquidity risk for most banks. Leases (item 17) are used as alternatives to loans when the bank, as owner of a physical asset, allows a customer to use an asset in return for periodic lease payments. Loans are categorized as commercial and industrial (C&I) loans (item 13), loans secured by real estate (item 14), individual or consumers loans (item 15), and other loans (item 16). Foreign loans often carry an additional risk for the bank—called *country* or *sovereign risk* (see Chapters 9 and 20).

C&I loans are used to finance a firm's capital needs, equipment purchases, and plant expansion. They can be made in quite small amounts such as $100,000 to small businesses or in packages as large as $10 million or more to major corporations. Commercial loans can be made at either fixed rates or floating rates of interest. The interest rate on a fixed-rate loan is set at the beginning of the contract period. This rate remains in force over the loan contract period no matter what happens to market rates. The interest rate on a floating-rate loan can be adjusted periodically according to a formula so that the interest rate risk is transferred in large part from the bank to the borrower. As might be expected, longer-term loans are more likely to be made under floating-rate contracts than are relatively short-term loans. In addition, commercial loans can be made for periods as short as a few weeks to as long as eight years or more. Traditionally, short-term commercial loans (those with an original maturity of one year or less) are used to finance firms' working capital needs and other short-term funding needs, while long-term commercial loans are used to finance credit needs that extend beyond one year, such as the purchase of real assets (machinery), new venture start-up costs, and permanent increases in working capital. Commercial loans can be secured or unsecured. A *secured loan* (or asset-backed loan) is backed by specific assets of the borrower, while an *unsecured loan* (or junior debt) gives the lender only a general claim on the assets of the borrower should default occur.

Real estate loans are primarily mortgage loans and some revolving home equity loans (see Chapter 7). For banks (as well as savings institutions), residential mortgages are the largest component of the real estate loan portfolio; until recently, however, commercial real estate mortgages had been the fastest-growing component of real estate loans. Residential mortgages are very long-term loans with an average maturity of approximately 25 years. As with C&I loans, the characteristics of residential mortgage loans differ widely. As discussed in Chapter 7, these include the size of loan, the loan-to-value ratio, and the maturity of the mortgage. Other important characteristics are the mortgage interest (or commitment) rate and fees and charges on the loan, such as commissions, discounts, and points paid by the borrower or the seller to obtain the loan. In addition, the mortgage rate differs according to whether the mortgage has a fixed rate or a floating rate, also called an *adjustable rate*.

A third major category of loans is the individual or consumer loan—for example, personal and auto loans. Commercial banks, finance companies, retailers, savings banks, and gas companies also provide consumer loan financing through credit cards such as Visa, MasterCard, and proprietary credit cards issued by companies such as Sears and AT&T. A typical credit card transaction is illustrated in Figure 13–1.

Other loans include a wide variety of borrowers and types such as loans to nonbank financial institutions, state and local governments, foreign banks, and sovereign governments. Each loan category entails a wide variety of characteristics that must be

---

6. Investment securities included in the bank's trading portfolio and designated as *trading securities* or *available-for-sale securities* are listed on the balance sheet at their *market value*. All other items on the balance sheet are listed at their *book values*.

Figure 13–1 Payment Flows in a Typical Credit Card Transaction

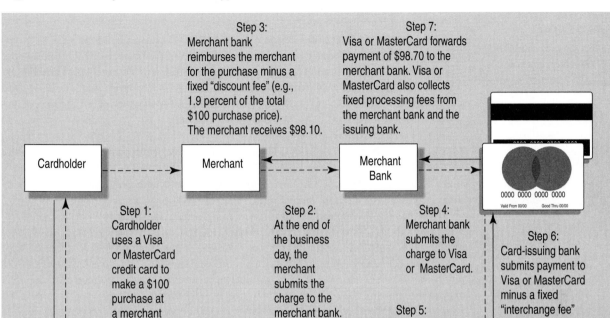

Step 3:
Merchant bank reimburses the merchant for the purchase minus a fixed "discount fee" (e.g., 1.9 percent of the total $100 purchase price). The merchant receives $98.10.

Step 7:
Visa or MasterCard forwards payment of $98.70 to the merchant bank. Visa or MasterCard also collects fixed processing fees from the merchant bank and the issuing bank.

Cardholder → Merchant ← Merchant Bank ←

0000 0000 0000 0000
Valid From 00/00   Good Thru 00/00

Step 1:
Cardholder uses a Visa or MasterCard credit card to make a $100 purchase at a merchant establishment.

Step 2:
At the end of the business day, the merchant submits the charge to the merchant bank.

Step 4:
Merchant bank submits the charge to Visa or MasterCard.

Step 5:
Visa or MasterCard forwards the charge to the bank that issued the credit card to the customer.

Step 6:
Card-issuing bank submits payment to Visa or MasterCard minus a fixed "interchange fee" (e.g., 1.3 percent of the total $100 purchase price). The total payment made is $98.70.

Step 8:
Card-issuing bank bills the cardholder for the $100 purchase.

Card-Issuing Bank

- - -► Charge
——► Payment

Step 9:
Cardholder pays the issuing bank the $100 or at least a minimum amount with the remaining balance paid over time.

Source: GAO, (GAO/GGD-94-23,1994), p. 57.

evaluated to determine the risk involved, whether the bank should grant the loan, and, if so, at what price. We discuss the evaluation methods in Chapter 21.

Unearned income (item 19) and the allowance (reserve) for loan and lease losses (item 20) are contra-asset accounts that are deducted from gross loans and leases on the balance sheet to create net loans and leases (item 21). Unearned income is the amount of income that the bank has received on a loan from a customer but has not yet recorded as income on the income statement. Over the life of the loan, the bank earns (or accrues) interest income and accordingly transfers it out of unearned income into interest income. The allowance for loan and lease losses is an estimate by the bank's management of the percentage of the gross loans (and leases) that will not be repaid to the bank. Although the maximum amount of the reserve is influenced by tax laws, the bank's management actually sets the level based on loan growth and recent loan loss experience. The allowance for loan losses is an accumulated reserve that is adjusted each period as management recognizes the possibility of additional bad loans and makes appropriate provisions for such losses. Actual losses are then deducted from, and recoveries are added to (referred to as **net write-offs**), their accumulated loan and lease loss reserve balance.

net write-offs

Actual loan losses less loan recoveries.

earning assets

Investment securities plus net loans and leases.

Investment securities plus net loans and leases are the **earning assets** of a depository institution. It is these items on the balance sheet that generate the most interest income and some of the noninterest income described below.

Other assets on the bank's balance sheet (item 27) consist of items such as premises and fixed assets (item 22), other real estate owned (collateral seized on defaulted loans—item 23), investments in unconsolidated subsidiaries (item 24), intangible assets (i.e., goodwill and mortgage servicing rights—item 25), and other (i.e., deferred taxes, prepaid expenses, and mortgage servicing fees receivable—item 26). These accounts are generally a small part of the bank's overall assets.

Liabilities.   A bank's liabilities consist of various types of deposit accounts and other borrowings used to fund the investments and loans on the asset side of the balance sheet. Liabilities vary in terms of their maturity, interest payments, check-writing privileges, and deposit insurance coverage.

Demand deposits (item 29) are transaction accounts held by individuals, corporations, partnerships, and governments that pay no explicit interest. Corporations are prohibited from using deposits other than demand deposits (e.g., NOW accounts) for transaction account purposes. This group therefore constitutes the major holders of demand deposits. Since 1980, all banks in the United States have been able to offer checkable deposits that pay interest and are withdrawable on demand; they are called *negotiable order of withdrawal accounts* or **NOW accounts**[7] (item 30). The major distinction between these instruments and traditional demand deposits is that these instruments require the depositor to maintain a minimum account balance to earn interest. If the minimum balance falls below some level, such as $500, the account formally converts to a status equivalent to a demand deposit and earns no interest. Also, there are restrictions on corporations holding NOW accounts.

NOW account

Negotiable order of withdrawal account is similar to a demand deposit but pays interest when a minimum balance is maintained.

MMDAs

Money market deposit accounts with retail savings accounts and some limited checking account features.

Money market deposit accounts or **MMDAs** (item 31) are an additional liability instrument that banks can use. To make banks competitive with the money market mutual funds offered by groups such as Vanguard and Fidelity, the MMDAs they offer must be liquid. In the United States, MMDAs are checkable but subject to restrictions on the number of checks written on each account per month, the number of preauthorized automatic transfers per month, and the minimum denomination of the amount of each check. In addition, MMDAs impose minimum balance requirements on depositors. The Federal Reserve does not require banks to hold cash reserves against MMDAs. Accordingly, banks generally pay higher rates on MMDAs than on NOW accounts. **Other savings deposits** (item 32) are all savings accounts other than MMDAs (i.e., regular passbook accounts) with no set maturity and no check-writing privileges. Like MMDAs, savings accounts currently carry zero reserve requirements.

other savings deposits

All savings accounts other than MMDAs.

retail CDs

Time deposits with a face value below $100,000.

The major categories of time deposits are retail certificates of deposit (CDs) and wholesale CDs. **Retail CDs** (item 33) are fixed-maturity instruments with face values under $100,000. Although the size, maturity, and rates on these CDs are negotiable, most banks issue standardized retail CDs. **Wholesale CDs** (item 35) (discussed also in Chapter 5) were created by banks in the early 1960s as a contractual mechanism to allow depositors to liquidate their position in these CDs by selling them in the secondary market rather than having to hold them to maturity or requesting that the bank cash in the deposit early (which involves a penalty cost for the depositor). Thus, a depositor can sell a relatively liquid instrument without causing adverse liquidity risk exposure for the bank. Consequently, the unique feature of wholesale CDs is not so much their large minimum denomination size of $100,000 or more but the fact that they are **negotiable instruments**. That is, they can be resold by title assignment in a secondary market to other investors. This means, for example, that if IBM had bought a $1

wholesale CDs

Time deposits with a face value of $100,000 or more.

negotiable instrument

An instrument whose ownership can be transferred in the secondary market.

---

7. Super-NOW accounts have very similar features to NOW accounts but require a larger minimum balance.

million three-month CD from Chase, but for unexpected liquidity reasons needed funds after only one month passed, it could sell this CD to another outside investor in the secondary market. This does not impose any obligation on Chase in terms of an early funds withdrawal request. Wholesale CDs obtained through a brokerage or investment house rather than directly from a customer are referred to as **brokered deposits.**[8] CDs held in foreign offices and denominated in dollars are referred to as *Eurodollar deposits* (see Chapter 5).

brokered deposits

Wholesale CDs obtained through a brokerage house.

Some banks separate foreign from domestic deposits on the balance sheet. Foreign deposits are not explicitly covered by FDIC-provided deposit insurance guarantees (see Chapter 14). These deposits are generally large and held by corporations with a high level of international transactions and activities.

The liabilities described above are all deposit liabilities, reflecting deposit contracts issued by banks in return for cash. However, banks not only fund their assets by issuing deposits but borrow in various markets for purchased funds. Since the funds generated from these purchases are not deposits, they are subject to neither reserve requirements (as with demand deposits and NOW accounts) nor deposit insurance premium payments to the FDIC (as with all the domestic deposits described earlier).[9] The largest market available for purchased funds is the federal funds market (item 37). As we discussed earlier, a bank with excess reserves can sell them in the fed funds market, recording them as an asset on the balance sheet. The bank that purchases fed funds shows them as a liability on its balance sheet. As with the fed funds market, the RP market (item 37) is a highly liquid and flexible source of funds for banks needing to increase their liabilities and to offset deposit withdrawals. Moreover, like fed funds, these transactions can be rolled over each day if the counterparty is willing. The major difference in flexibility of liability management for fed funds and RPs is that a fed funds transaction can be entered into at virtually any time in the banking day. In general, it is difficult to transact an RP borrowing late in the day since the bank sending the fed funds must be satisfied with the type and quality of the securities' collateral proposed by the borrowing bank. Although this collateral is normally T-bills, T-notes, T-bonds, and mortgage-backed securities, the maturities and other features, such as callability or coupons, may be unattractive to the fund seller.

Fed funds and RPs have been the major sources of borrowed funds, but banks have utilized other borrowing (item 38) sources to supplement their flexibility in liability management. Four of these sources are banker's acceptances (BAs), commercial paper, medium-term notes, and discount window loans. Banks often convert off-balance-sheet letters of credit into on-balance-sheet BAs by discounting the letter of credit when the holder presents it for acceptance (see Chapter 5). In addition, these BAs may be resold to money market investors. As a result, BA sales to the secondary market are an additional funding source. Although a bank subsidiary itself cannot issue commercial paper, its parent holding company can—that is, Citigroup can issue commercial paper but Citibank cannot. This provides banks owned by holding companies—most of the largest banks in the United States—with an additional funding source, since the holding company can "downstream" funds generated from its commercial paper sales to its bank subsidiary.

A number of banks in search of stable sources of funds with low withdrawal risk have begun to issue subordinated notes and debentures (item 39), often in the five- to seven-year range. These notes are especially attractive because they are subject to

8. These are often purchased in $100,000 increments. For example, a broker may receive $1 million from an investor and break this up into 10 lots of $100,000 CDs that are placed (brokered out) at 10 different banks. Thus, effectively, the full $1 million is covered by FDIC deposit insurance.

9. Foreign deposits are not subject to deposit insurance premiums. However, in the exceptional event of a very large failure in which all deposits are protected, under the 1991 FDICIA, the FDIC is required to levy a charge on surviving large banks proportional to their total asset size. To the extent that assets are partially funded by foreign liabilities, this is an implied premium on foreign deposits.

neither reserve requirements nor deposit insurance premiums, and some can serve as (Tier 2) capital for the bank to satisfy Federal Reserve regulations regarding minimum capital requirements (see Chapter 14).

Finally, banks facing temporary liquidity crunches can borrow from the central bank's discount window at the discount rate. Since this rate is not market determined and usually lies below fed funds and government security rates, it offers a very attractive borrowing opportunity to a bank with deficient reserves as the reserve maintenance period comes to an end (see Chapter 14).[10]

core deposits

Deposits of the bank that are stable over short periods of time and thus provide a long-term funding source to a bank.

purchased funds

Rate-sensitive funding sources of the bank.

Some banks separate core deposits from purchased funds on their balance sheets. The stable deposits of the bank are referred to as **core deposits** (item 34). These deposits are not expected to be withdrawn over short periods of time and are therefore a more permanent source of funding for the bank. Core deposits generally are defined as demand deposits, NOW accounts, MMDAs, other saving accounts, and retail CDs. **Purchased funds** are more expensive and/or volatile sources of funds because they are highly rate sensitive—these funds are more likely to be immediately withdrawn or replaced as rates on competitive instruments change. Further, interest rates on these funds, at any point in time, are generally higher than rates on core deposits. Purchased funds are generally defined as brokered deposits, wholesale CDs, deposits at foreign offices, fed funds purchased, RPs, and subordinated notes and debentures.

Banks also list other liabilities (item 40) that do not require interest to be paid. These items consist of accrued interest, deferred taxes, dividends payable, minority interests in consolidated subsidies, and other miscellaneous claims.

Equity Capital.   The bank's equity capital (item 46) consists mainly of preferred (item 42) and common (item 43) stock (listed at par value), surplus or additional paid-in capital (item 44), and retained earnings (item 45). Regulations require banks to hold a minimum level of equity capital to act as a buffer against losses from their on- and off-balance-sheet assets (see Chapter 14).

Off-Balance-Sheet Assets and Liabilities

Off-balance-sheet (OBS) items are *contingent* assets and liabilities that *may* affect the future status of a financial institution's balance sheet. OBS activities are less obvious and often invisible to financial statement readers because they usually appear "below the bottom line," frequently as footnotes to accounts. As part of the quarterly financial reports submitted to regulators, schedule L lists the notional dollar size of OBS activities of banks. We briefly summarized the OBS activities of commercial banks in Chapter 11. In this chapter, we introduce the items as they appear off the FI's balance sheet.

Although OBS activities are now an important source of fee income for many FIs, they have the potential to produce positive as well as negative *future* cash flows. Some OBS activities can involve risks that add to the institution's overall risk exposure; others can hedge or reduce their interest rate, credit, and foreign exchange risks. A depository institution's performance and solvency are also affected by the management of these items. Off-balance-sheet activities can be grouped into five major categories: loan commitments, letters of credit, when-issued securities, loans sold, and derivative securities. The OBS activities for North Fork Bancorp and Bank One Corporation are reported in Table 13–2.

---

10. Although the low rate makes the discount window an attractive place to borrow, banks do not use it very often because such borrowings are intended for use only as a last resort (see Chapter 4).

Table 13–2   Off-Balance-Sheet Activities for Two Commercial Banks on December 31, 1997

(in millions of dollars)

	North Fork Bancorp[*]	Bank One Corporation[†]
Commitments and Contingencies		
1. Loan commitments	$428.34	$ 96,674.61
2. Commercial letters of credit	4.72	37.16
3. Standby letters of credit	21.03	409.56
4. When-issued securities	0.00	0.00
5. Loans sold	0.00	2,064.90
Notional Amounts for Derivatives[†]		
6. Interest rate swaps	0.00	5,943.38
7. Total	$454.09	$105,129.61

[*]Values are taken from the 1997 FDIC report of condition data tapes and annual reports.

[†]Notional amounts reflect the face value of the contracts entered into.

loan commitment

Contractual commitment to loan to a firm a certain maximum amount at given interest rate terms.

up-front fee

The fee charged for making funds available through a loan commitment.

back-end fee

The fee charged on the unused component of a loan commitment.

letters of credit

Contingent guarantees sold by an FI to underwrite the trade or commercial performance of the buyers of the guarantees.

standby letters of credit

Guarantees issued to cover contingencies that are potentially more severe and less predictable than contingencies covered under trade-related or commercial letters of credit.

Loan Commitments.   These days, most commercial and industrial loans are made by firms that take down (or borrow against) prenegotiated lines of credit or loan commitments rather than borrow cash immediately in the form of spot loans. A **loan commitment** agreement (item 1 in Table 13–2) is a contractual commitment by a bank or another FI (such as an insurance company) to loan to a customer a certain maximum amount (say, $10 million) at given interest rate terms (say, 12 percent). The loan commitment agreement also defines the length of time over which the borrower has the option to take down this loan. In return for making this loan commitment, the bank may charge an **up-front fee** (or facility fee) of, say, ⅛ percent of the commitment size, or $12,500 in this example. In addition, the bank must stand ready to supply the full $10 million at any time over the commitment period—for example, one year. Meanwhile, the borrower has a valuable option to take down any amount between $0 and $10 million over the commitment period. The bank may also charge the borrower a **back-end fee** (or commitment fee) on any unused commitment balances at the end of the period. In this example, if the borrower takes down only $8 million over the year and the fee on *unused* commitments is ¼ percent, the bank generates additional revenue of ¼ percent times $2 million, or $5,000.

Note that only when the borrower actually draws on the commitment do the loans made under the commitment appear on the balance sheet. Thus, only when the $8 million loan is taken down exactly halfway through the one-year commitment period (i.e., six months later) does the balance sheet show the creation of a new $8 million loan. We illustrate the transaction in Figure 13–2. When the $10 million commitment is made at time 0, nothing shows on the balance sheet. Nevertheless, the bank must stand ready to supply the full $10 million in loans on any day within the one-year commitment period—at time 0 a new contingent claim on the resources of the bank was created. At time 6 months, when the $8 million is drawn down, the balance sheet will reflect this as an $8 million loan.

Commercial Letters of Credit and Standby Letters of Credit.   In selling commercial **letters of credit** (LCs—item 2 in Table 13–2) and **standby letters of credit** (SLCs—item 3) for fees, depository institutions add to their contingent future liabilities. Both LCs and SLCs are essentially *guarantees* to underwrite performance that a depository institution sells to the buyers of the guarantees (such as a corporation). In economic terms, the depository institution that sells LCs and SLCs is selling insurance

Figure 13–2 Loan Commitment Transaction

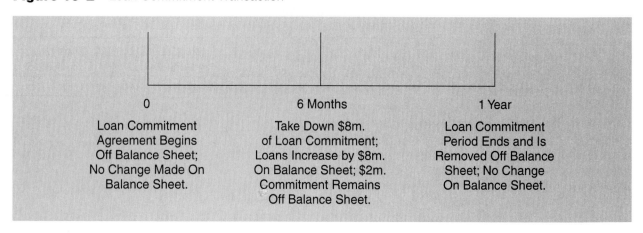

against the frequency or severity of some particular future event occurring. Further, similar to the different lines of insurance sold by property-casualty insurers, LC and SLC contracts differ as to the severity and frequency of their risk exposures. We look next at the risk exposure from engaging in LC and SLC activities off the balance sheet.

Commercial Letters of Credit. Commercial letters of credit are widely used in both domestic and international trade. For example, they ease the shipment of grain between a farmer in Iowa and a purchaser in New Orleans or the shipment of goods between a U.S. importer and a foreign exporter. The bank's role is to provide a formal guarantee that payment for goods shipped or sold will be forthcoming regardless of whether the buyer of the goods defaults on payment. We show a very simple LC example in Figure 13–3 for an international transaction between a U.S. importer and a German exporter.

Suppose that the U.S. importer sent an order for $10 million worth of machinery to a German exporter, as shown in step 1 of Figure 13–3. However, the German exporter may be reluctant to send the goods without some assurance or guarantee of being paid once the goods are shipped. The U.S. importer may promise to pay for the goods in 90 days, but the German exporter may feel insecure either because it knows little about the creditworthiness of the U.S. importer or because the U.S. importer has a low credit rating (i.e., B or BB). To persuade the German exporter to ship the goods, the U.S. importer may have to turn to a large U.S. bank with which it has developed a long-term customer relationship. In its role as a lender and monitor, the U.S. bank can better appraise the U.S. importer's creditworthiness. The U.S. bank can issue a contingent payment guarantee—that is, an LC to the German exporter on the importer's behalf—in return for an LC fee paid by the U.S. importer. In our example, the bank would send the German exporter an LC guaranteeing payment for the goods in 90 days regardless of whether the importer defaults on its obligation to the German exporter (step 2 in Figure 13–3). Implicitly, the bank is replacing the U.S. importer's credit risk with its own credit risk guarantee. For this substitution to work effectively, the bank, in guaranteeing payment, must have a higher credit standing or better credit quality reputation than the U.S. importer. Once the bank issues the LC and sends it to the German exporter, the exporter ships the goods to the U.S. importer (step 3 in Figure 13–3).[11] The probability is very high that in 90 days' time the U.S. importer will pay the German exporter for the goods sent and the bank keeps the LC fee as profit. The fee is perhaps 10 basis points of the face value of the letter of credit, or $10,000 in this example.

---

11. As discussed in Chapter 5, the German exporter may also receive a banker's acceptance written against the letter of credit.

Figure 13–3 Simple Letter of Credit Transaction

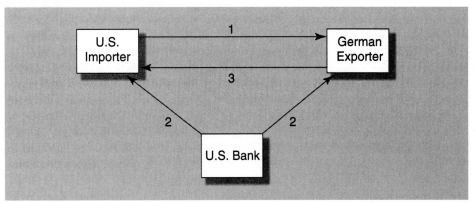

A small probability exists, however, that the U.S. importer will be unable to pay the $10 million in 90 days and will default. Then the bank is obliged to make good on its guarantee. The cost of such a default could mean that the bank must pay $10 million, although it would have a creditor's claim against the importer's assets to offset this loss. Clearly, the fee should exceed the expected default risk on the LC, which equals the probability of default times the expected payout on the LC after adjusting for the bank's ability to reclaim assets from the defaulting importer and any monitoring costs.

Standby Letters of Credit. Standby letters of credit perform an insurance function similar to commercial and trade letters of credit. The structure and type of risk covered differ, however. FIs may issue SLCs to cover contingencies that are potentially more *severe*, less *predictable* or frequent, and not necessarily trade related. These contingencies include performance bond guarantees by which an FI may guarantee that a real estate development will be completed in some interval of time. Alternatively, the FI may offer default guarantees to back an issue of commercial paper or municipal revenue bonds to allow issuers to achieve a higher credit rating and a lower funding cost than otherwise.

Without credit enhancements, for example, many firms would be unable to borrow in the commercial paper market (see Chapter 5) or would have to borrow at a higher funding cost. P1 borrowers, who offer the highest quality commercial paper, normally pay 40 basis points less than P2 borrowers, the next quality grade. By paying a fee of perhaps 25 basis points to a bank, an FI guarantees to pay commercial paper purchasers' principal and interest on maturity should the issuing firm itself be unable to pay. The SLC backing of commercial paper issues normally results in the paper's placement in the lowest default risk class (P1) and the issuer's savings of up to 15 basis points on issuing costs—40 basis points (the P2 − P1 spread) minus the 25-basis-point SLC fee equals 15 basis points.

Note that in selling the SLCs, banks are competing directly with another of their OBS products, loan commitments. Rather than buying an SLC from a bank to back a commercial paper issue, the issuing firm might pay a fee to a bank to supply a loan commitment. This loan commitment would match the size and maturity of the commercial paper issue—for example, a $100 million ceiling and 45-day maturity. If, on maturity, the commercial paper issuer had insufficient funds to repay the commercial paper holders, the issuer has the right to take down the $100 million loan commitment and to use these funds to meet repayments on the commercial paper. Often, the up-front fees on such loan commitments are less than those on SLCs; therefore, many firms issuing commercial paper prefer to use loan commitments.

Finally, remember that U.S. banks are not the only issuers of SLCs. Not surprising, property-casualty insurers have an increasingly important business line of performance bonds and financial guarantees. The growth in these lines for property-casualty insurers has come at the expense of U.S. banks. Moreover, foreign banks increasingly are taking a share of the U.S. market in SLCs. The reason for the loss in this business line by U.S. banks is that to sell guarantees such as SLCs credibly, the seller must have a better credit rating than the customer. In recent years, few U.S. FIs or their parent holding companies have had AA ratings or better. Other domestic FIs and foreign banks, on the other hand, have more often had AA ratings or better. High credit ratings not only make the guarantor more attractive from the buyer's perspective but also make the guarantor more competitive because its cost of funds is lower than that of less creditworthy FIs.

when-issued securities

Commitments to buy or sell securities before they are issued.

Forward Purchases and Sales of When-Issued Securities.　Very often, banks and other FIs—especially investment banks—enter into forward or future commitments to buy or sell securities before issue. This is called *when-issued (WI) trading* (item 4 in Table 13–2). These OBS commitments can expose an FI to future or contingent interest rate risk.

Good examples of WI commitments are those taken on with new T-bills in the week prior to the announcement of the T-bill auction results. Every Tuesday, the Federal Reserve, on behalf of the Treasury, announces the auction size of new three- and six-month bills to be allotted the following Monday. Between the announcement of the total auction size on Tuesday and the announcement of winning bill allotments on the following Monday, primary dealers sell WI contracts. Large investment banks and commercial banks (currently approximately 40 in number) normally are primary dealers. They sell the yet-to-be-issued T-bills for forward delivery to customers in the secondary market at a small margin above the price they expect to pay at the primary auction. This can be profitable if the primary dealer obtains all the bills needed at the auction at the expected price or interest rate to fulfill these forward WI contracts. A primary dealer that makes a mistake regarding the tenor of the auction (i.e., level of interest rates) faces the risk that the commitments entered into to deliver T-bills in the WI market can be met only at a loss. For example, an overcommitted dealer (resulting from a miscalculation of interest rate changes) may have to buy T-bills from other dealers at a loss right after the auction results are announced to meet the WI T-bill delivery commitments that the dealer made to its customers. This type of problem occurred for many commercial and investment bank primary dealers when Salomon Brothers cornered (or squeezed) the market for new two-year Treasury bonds in 1990. As a result, the Treasury instituted a wholesale reform program to change the way bills and bonds are auctioned.[12]

loans sold

Loans originated by the bank and then sold to other investors that can be returned to the originating institution.

recourse

The ability to put an asset or loan back to the seller should the credit quality of that asset deteriorate.

Loans Sold.　**Loans sold** (item 5 in Table 13–2) are loans that a bank originated and then sold to other investors that may be returned (sold with **recourse**) to the originating institution in the future if the credit quality of the loans deteriorates. We discuss the types of loans that FIs sell, their incentives to sell, and the way in which they can sell them in more detail in Chapter 25. Banks and other FIs increasingly originate loans on their balance sheets, but rather than holding the loans to maturity, they quickly sell them to outside investors. These outside investors include other banks, insurance companies, mutual funds, or even corporations. In acting as loan originators and loan sellers, FIs are operating more as loan brokers than as traditional asset transformers (see Chapters 1 and 11).

---

12. Under the auction rules, no bidder could bid for or attain more than 35 percent of an issue. By bidding using customers' names (without their knowledge) in addition to bidding under its own name, however, Salomon Brothers vastly exceeded the 35 percent limit and thus created a shortage in the availability of newly issued securities for other dealers.

When an outside party buys a loan with absolutely no recourse to the seller of the loan should the loan eventually go bad, loan sales have no OBS contingent liability implications for FIs. Specifically, *no recourse* means that if the loan the FI sells should go bad, the buyer of the loan must bear the full risk of loss. In particular, the buyer cannot go back to the seller or originating FI to seek payment on the bad loan. Suppose that the loan is sold with recourse. Then, loan sales present a long-term off-balance-sheet or contingent credit risk to the seller. Essentially, the buyer of the loan holds an option to put the loan back to the seller, which the buyer can exercise should the credit quality of the purchased loan materially deteriorate. In reality, the recourse or nonrecourse nature of loan sales is often ambiguous. For example, some have argued that banks generally are willing to repurchase bad no recourse loans to preserve their reputations with their customers. Obviously, reputation concerns may extend the size of a selling bank's contingent liabilities from OBS activities.

derivative securities

Futures, forward, swap, and option positions taken by the FI for hedging or other purposes.

Derivative Contracts. **Derivative securities** (item 6 in Table 13–2) are the futures, forward, swap, and option positions taken by a bank for hedging and other purposes (see Chapters 10 and 24). We discussed the tremendous growth of derivative securities activity in Chapter 11. Banks can be either users of derivative contracts for hedging (see Chapter 10 and 24) and other purposes or dealers that act as counterparties in trades with customers for a fee. It has been estimated that only 600 U.S. banks use derivatives and that five large dealer banks—Bank of America, Bank One, Chase Manhattan, Citigroup, and Morgan Guaranty—account for some 70 percent of the derivatives that user banks hold.[13]

Contingent credit risk is likely to be present when banks expand their positions in futures, forward, swap, and option contracts. This risk relates to the fact that the counterparty to one of these contracts may default on payment obligations, leaving the bank unhedged and having to replace the contract at today's interest rates, prices, or exchange rates, which may be relatively unfavorable. In addition, such defaults are most likely to occur when the counterparty is losing heavily on the contract and the bank is in the money on the contract. This type of default risk is much more serious for forward contracts than for futures contracts. This is because forward contracts are nonstandard contracts entered into bilaterally by negotiating parties, such as two banks, and all cash flows are required to be paid at one time (on contract maturity). Thus, they are essentially over-the-counter (OTC) arrangements with no external guarantees should one or the other party default on the contract (see Chapter 10). By contrast, futures contracts are standardized contracts guaranteed by organized exchanges such as the New York Futures Exchange (NYFE). Futures contracts, like forward contracts, make commitments to deliver foreign exchange (or some other asset) at some future date. If a counterparty were to default on a futures contract, however, the exchange would assume the defaulting party's position and payment obligations.

Option contracts can also be traded over the counter (OTC) or bought/sold on organized exchanges. If the options are standardized options traded on exchanges, such as bond options, they are virtually default risk free.[14] If they are specialized options purchased OTC, such as interest rate caps (see Chapter 10), some elements of default risk exist.[15] Similarly, swaps are OTC instruments normally susceptible to default risk (see Chapter 10).[16] In general, default risk on OTC contracts increases with the time to

---

[13]See OCC Bank Derivative Report, Second Quarter 1999; and Chapter 11.

[14]Note that the options still can be subject to interest rate risk; see the discussion in Chapter 24.

[15]Under an interest rate cap, the seller, in return for a fee, promises to compensate the buyer should interest rates rise above a certain level. If rates rise much more than expected, the cap seller may have an incentive to default to truncate the losses. Thus, selling a cap is similar to a bank's selling interest rate risk insurance (see Chapter 10 for more details).

[16]In a swap, two parties contract to exchange interest rate payments or foreign exchange payments. If interest rates (or foreign exchange rates) move a good deal, one party can face considerable future loss exposure, creating incentives to default.

maturity of the contract and the fluctuation of underlying prices, interest rates, or exchange rates.[17]

Income Statement

4 See Table 13–3 for the report of income or income statement for North Fork Bancorp and Bank One Corporation for the 1997 calendar year. The report of income identifies the interest income and expenses, net interest income, provision for loan losses, noninterest income and expenses, income before taxes and extraordinary items, and net income for the *year* for the banks earned from the on- and off-balance-sheet activities described above. Specifically, as we discuss the income statement, notice the direct relationship between it and the balance sheet (both on- and off-). The composition of an FI's assets and liabilities, combined with the interest rates earned or paid on them, directly determines the interest income and expense on the income statement. In addition, because the assets and liabilities of FIs are mainly financial, most of the income and expense reported on the income statement is interest rate related (rather than reflecting sales prices and cost of goods sold, as seen with manufacturing corporations).

Interest Income. The income statement for a commercial bank first shows the sources of interest income (item 13). Interest and fee income on loans and leases (item 6 in Table 13–3) is the largest interest income-producing category. Subcategories are often listed on the income statement (items 1–4) for each category of loan listed earlier. Most banks also list income from leases (item 5) as a separate item. Interest from investment securities held (item 12) is also included as interest income. These too may be listed by subcategories (items 7–11) described earlier. Interest income is recorded on an accrued basis (see earlier discussion). Thus, loans on which interest payments are past due can still be recorded as generating income for a bank.[18] Interest income is taxable, except for that on municipal securities and tax-exempt income from direct lease financing. Tax-exempt interest can be converted to a taxable equivalent basis as follows:

$$\text{Taxable equivalent interest income} = \frac{\text{Interest income}}{1 - \text{Bank's tax rate}}$$

Interest Expenses. Interest expense (item 23) is the second major category on a bank's income statement. Items listed here come directly from the liability section of the balance sheet: interest on deposits (item 19) [NOW accounts (item 14), MMDAs (item 15), other savings (item 16), retail CDs (item 17), and wholesale CDs (item 18)], and interest on fed funds (item 20), RPs (item 20), and other borrowed funds (item 21). Interest on subordinated notes and debentures is generally reported as a separate item.

Net Interest Income. Total interest income minus total interest expense is listed next on the income statement as net interest income (item 24). Net interest income is an important tool in assessing the bank's ability to generate profits and control interest rate risk (see Chapter 20).

Provision for Loan Losses. The provision for loan losses (item 25) is a noncash, tax-deductible expense. The provision for loan losses is the current period's allocation

---

17. Reputational considerations and the need for future access to markets for hedging deter the incentive to default (see Chapter 24 as well). However, most empirical evidence suggests that derivative contracts have reduced FI risk. See for example, G. Gorton and R. Rosen, "Banks and Derivatives," University of Pennsylvania Wharton School, working paper, February 1995. Gorton and Rosen find that swap contracts have generally reduced the systematic risk of the U.S. banking system.

18. A bank can recognize income for at least 90 days after the due date of the interest payment.

Table 13–3 Income Statement for Two Commercial Banks for 1997
(in millions of dollars)

	North Fork Bancorp*	Bank One Corporation*
Interest Income		
1. Income on C&I loans	$ 33.47	$1,555.24
2. Income on real estate loans	251.83	2,207.04
3. Income on consumer loans	17.80	3,345.92
4. Income on other loans	1.67	164.82
5. Income on leases	4.27	630.92
6. Interest and fees on loans and leases	$309.04	$7,903.94
7. Interest on deposits at other institutions	0.00	166.13
8. Interest on fed funds and RPs	1.54	185.20
9. Interest on U.S. Treasury and agency securities	94.20	726.10
10. Interest on municipals	5.36	91.76
11. Interest on other debt and equity securities	80.23	123.29
12. Interest income on investment securities	$181.33	$1,292.48
13. Total interest income	$490.37	$9,196.42
Interest Expense		
14. Interest on NOW accounts	1.60	26.67
15. Interest on MMDA accounts	9.68	837.76
16. Interest on other savings	32.68	279.95
17. Interest on retail CDs	70.00	981.10
18. Interest on wholesale CDs	19.76	439.60
19. Interest on deposit accounts	$133.72	$2,565.08
20. Interest on fed funds and RPs	72.67	778.19
21. Interest on other borrowed funds	6.33	260.37
22. Interest on subordinated notes and debentures	0.00	326.53
23. Total interest expense	$212.72	$3,930.17
24. Net interest income	277.65	5,266.25
25. Provision for loan losses	6.27	1,152.12
Noninterest Income		
26. Income from fiduciary activities	2.18	506.20
27. Service charges on deposit accounts	19.36	676.41
28. Gains from trading assets and liabilities	0.01	10.87
29. Other noninterest income	8.46	2,662.54
30. Total noninterest income	$ 30.01	$3,856.02
Noninterest Expense		
31. Salaries and employee benefits	60.50	1,328.01
32. Expenses of premises and fixed assets	21.00	440.07
33. Other noninterest expense	35.87	4,029.73
34. Total noninterest expense	$117.37	$5,797.81
35. Income before taxes and extraordinary items	$184.02	$2,172.34
36. Applicable income taxes	68.98	653.02
37. Extraordinary items	0.00	0.00
38. Net income	$115.04	$1,519.32

*Values are taken from the 1997 FDIC report of income data tapes and annual reports.

to the allowance for loan losses listed on the balance sheet. This item represents the bank management's prediction of loans at risk of default for the period. As mentioned earlier, the size of the provision is determined by management, and in the United States it is subject to a maximum allowable tax deductible amount set by the Internal Revenue Service.

Noninterest Income.   Noninterest income (item 30) includes all other income received by the bank as a result of its on- and off-balance sheet activities and is becoming increasingly important as the ability to attract core deposits and high-quality loan applicants becomes more difficult. Included in these categories are income from fiduciary activities (for example, earnings from operating a trust department—item 26), service charges on deposit accounts (generally the largest source of noninterest income—item 27), other gains (losses) and fees from trading assets and liabilities (from marketable instruments and OBS derivative instruments—item 28), and other noninterest income (fee income from OBS loan commitments and letters of credit, and revenue from one-time transactions such as sales of real estate owned, loans, premises, and fixed assets—item 29).

total operating income

The sum of the interest income and noninterest income.

The sum of interest income and noninterest income is referred to as the bank's *total operating income* or *total revenue*. **Total operating income** for a bank is equivalent to total sales in a manufacturing firm and represents the bank's income received from all sources.

Noninterest Expense.   Noninterest expense (item 34) items consist mainly of personnel expenses and are generally large relative to noninterest income. Items in this category include salaries and employee benefits (item 31), expenses of premises and fixed assets (i.e., utilities, depreciation, and deposit insurance—item 32), and other (expenses of one-time transactions such as losses on sale of real estate, loans, and premises—item 33).

Income before Taxes and Extraordinary Items.   Net interest income minus provisions for loan losses plus noninterest income minus noninterest expense produces the operating profit or income before taxes and extraordinary items for the bank (item 35).

Income Taxes.   All federal, state, local, and foreign income taxes due from the bank are listed next on the income statement (item 36). Some of this amount may have been paid to the Internal Revenue Service (IRS) and the remainder is recorded as a liability (deferred taxes) to be paid to the IRS later.

Extraordinary Items.   Extraordinary items and other adjustments (item 37) are events or transactions that are both unusual and infrequent. This includes such things as effects of changes in accounting rules, corrections of accounting errors made in previous years, and equity capital adjustments (losses from a major disaster such as an earthquake in an area where earthquakes are not expected to occur in the foreseeable future).

Net Income.   Income before taxes and extraordinary items minus income taxes plus (or minus) extraordinary items results in the net income for the bank (item 38). Net income is the *bottom line* on the income statement.

Direct Relationship between the Income Statement and the Balance Sheet

As mentioned earlier, banks' financial statements are directly related (more so than for nonfinancial companies). That is, the items on the income statement are determined by the balance sheet assets and liabilities along with the interest rates on each item. This direct relationship between the two financial statements can be seen by depicting the income statement as follows:

$$NI = \sum_{n=1}^{N} r_n A_n - \sum_{m=1}^{M} r_m L_m - P + NII - NIE - T$$

where

NI = Bank's net income
A_n = Dollar value of the bank's nth asset
L_m = Dollar value of the bank's mth liability
r_n = Rate earned on the bank's nth asset
r_m = Rate paid on the bank's mth liability
P = Provision for loan losses
NII = Noninterest income earned by the bank, including income from off-balance-sheet activities
NIE = Noninterest expenses incurred by the bank
T = Bank's taxes and extraordinary items
N = Number of assets the bank holds
M = Number of liabilities the bank holds

Net income is the direct result of (1) the amount and mix of assets and liabilities held by the bank taken from the balance sheet and (2) the interest rate on each of them. For example, increasing the dollar value of an asset, all else constant, results in a direct increase in the bank's net income equal to the size of the increase times the rate of interest on the asset. Likewise, decreasing the rate paid on a liability, all else constant, directly increases net income by the size of the rate decrease times the dollar value of the liability on the balance sheet. Finally, changing the mix of assets or liabilities on the balance sheet has a direct effect on net income equal to the size of the rate difference times the dollar value of the asset or liability being changed. For example, suppose that a bank replaces $100,000 of assets currently yielding 8 percent with assets yielding 10 percent. Net income increases by $2,000 ((10% − 8%) × $100,000).

Do You Understand?

1. The difference between a wholesale bank and a retail bank?
2. What the trade-offs are in holding a large proportion of short-term securities, such as T-bills, versus long-term securities, such as loans?
3. What the trade-offs are in issuing short-term deposit accounts such as demand deposits and retail CDs, versus long-term deposits and other funding sources, such as wholesale CDs and long-term debt?
4. What the major difference is between a commercial letter of credit and a standby letter of credit?
5. What counterparty risk in a forward contract means?
6. Which is riskier for a bank, loan sales with recourse or loan sales without recourse?
7. What the nature of the relationship is between balance sheet and income statement items?
8. How paying a lower rate for new deposits than for other liabilities impacts a bank's income statement?

Financial Statement Analysis Using a Return on Equity Framework

Do You Understand?

1. What factors caused the drop in BankBoston's profit in 1998?

time series analysis

Analysis of financial statements over a period of time.

cross-sectional analysis

Analysis of financial statements comparing one firm with others.

www.ffiec.gov/ UBPR.htm

In recent years, the commercial banking industry has experienced a period of record profits, quite a change from the late 1980s and early 1990s, when banks were failing in record numbers. Despite record profits, many banks have weak and inefficient areas that still need to be addressed. For example, In the News box 13–2 shows how trading account losses at BankBoston was the major cause for a 53 percent drop in its net income in the third quarter of 1998. One way to identify weaknesses and problem areas is by analyzing financial statements. In particular, an analysis of selected accounting ratios—ratio analysis—allows a bank manager to evaluate the bank's current performance, the change in its performance over time (**time series analysis** of ratios over a period of time), and its performance relative to that of competitor banks (**cross-sectional analysis** of ratios across a group of firms). A tool available to assist in cross-sectional analysis is the Uniform Bank Performance Report (UBPR) maintained by the Federal Financial Institutions Examination Council. The UBPR summarizes performance of banks for various peer groups (banks similar in size and economic environment), for various size groups, and by state.

In the News

13-2

BankBoston's net income dropped 53% to $105 million, or 35 cents a diluted share, a penny ahead of analysts' expectations, as measured by first call. Net income for the just-ended quarter was after $90 million in after-tax charges to cover costs related to the

BankBoston Net Slides 53%

acquisition of Robertson & Co. and the realignment of BankBoston business units, primarily in Asia.

BankBoston blamed the plunge of trading account losses of $72 million, or 15 cents a share, on global financial markets and the domestic high-yield bond market. Total non-interest income fell 14% to $385.1 million from $448.2 million.

Offsetting the losses was an 11% rise in interest income to $1.4 billion, as total assets grew 10% to $72.5 billion and the net interest margin edged up to 3.97% from 3.96% a year earlier. But efficiency ratios sagged, as return on assets plummeted to 0.57% from 1.36%, and return on equity sank to 8.75%.

On the positive side, BankBoston said operating income at businesses in Argentina and Brazil increased by more than 50%.

Source: *The Wall Street Journal*, October 16, 1998, p. B4, by Joseph B. Cahill. Reprinted by permission of *The Wall Street Journal.* © 2000 Dow Jones & Company, Inc. All Rights Reserved Worldwide.

www.wsj.com/

Figure 13–4 summarizes the return on equity (ROE) framework.[19] The ROE framework starts with the most frequently used measure of profitability, ROE, and then breaks it down to identify strengths and weaknesses in a bank's performance. The resulting breakdown provides a convenient and systematic method to identify strengths and weaknesses of a bank's profitability. Identification of strengths and weaknesses, and the reasons for them, provides an excellent tool for bank managers as they look for ways to improve profitability. Table 13–4 summarizes the role of ROE and the first two levels of the ROE framework (from Figure 13–4) in analyzing an FI's performance.

The remainder of this chapter applies the ROE framework to our two banks: North Fork Bancorp and Bank One Corporation. All of the ratios discussed as part of the ROE breakdown are reported in Table 13–5. We refer to these ratios by number (1 through 117). In addition, Figure 13–5 presents these ratios (by ratio number) as they fit into the ROE framework shown in Figure 13–4.

Return on Equity and Its Components

ROE (ratio 1 in Table 13–5) is defined as:

$$\text{ROE} = \frac{\text{Net income}}{\text{Total equity capital}}$$

19. The ROE framework is similar to the DuPont analysis that managers of nonfinancial institutions frequently use.

Figure 13–4   Breakdown of ROE into Various Financial Ratios

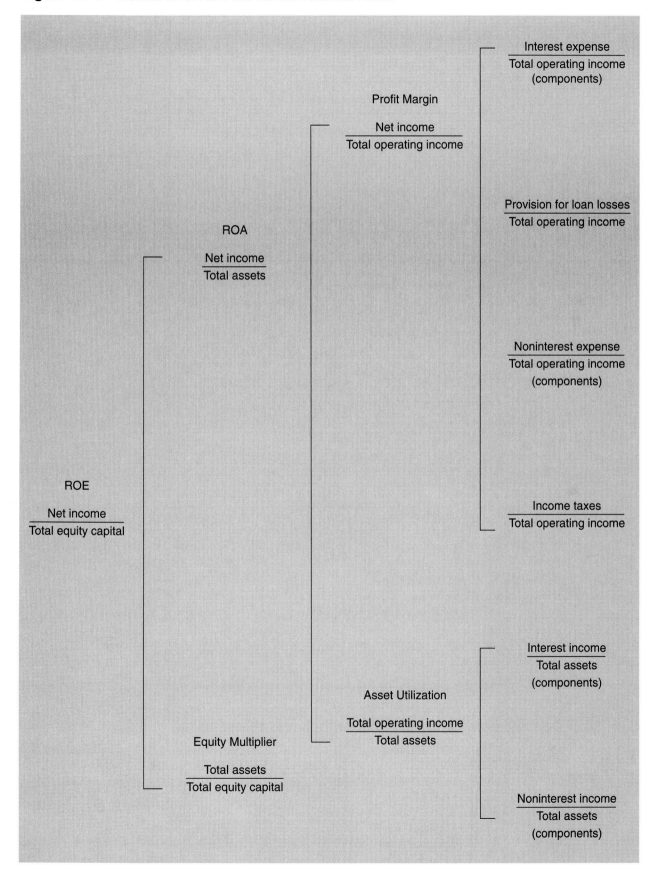

Table 13–4   Role of ROE, ROA, EM, PM, and AU in Analyzing Financial Institution Performance

Return on Equity (ROE)—measures overall profitability of the FI per dollar of equity.

Return on Assets (ROA)—measures profit generated relative to the FI's assets.

Equity Multiplier (EM)—measures the extent to which assets of the FI are funded with equity relative to debt.

Profit Margin (PM)—measures the ability to pay expenses and generate net income from interest and noninterest income.

Asset Utilization (AU)—measures the amount of interest and noninterest income generated per dollar of total assets.

Table 13–5   Financial Ratios for Two Commercial Banks for 1997

Ratio	North Fork Bancorp	Bank One Corporation
1. ROE	20.90%	14.64%
2. ROA	1.72%	1.29%
3. Equity multiplier	12.18X	11.36X
4. Profit margin	22.11%	11.64%
5. Asset utilization	7.72%	11.07%
6. Net interest margin	4.38%	4.94%
7. Spread	4.07%	4.05%
8. Overhead efficiency	25.57%	66.51%
Profit Margin Components		
9. Interest expense ratio	40.88%	30.11%
10. Provision for loan loss ratio	1.20%	8.83%
11. Noninterest expense ratio	22.55%	86.48%
12. Tax ratio	13.26%	5.00%
Interest Expenses as a Percentage of Total Operating Income		
13. NOW accounts	0.31%	0.20%
14. MMDAs	1.86%	6.42%
15. Other savings	6.28%	2.14%
16. Retail CDs	13.45%	7.52%
17. Wholesale CDs	3.80%	3.37%
18. Fed funds and RPs	13.96%	5.96%
19. Other borrowed funds	0.12%	1.99%
20. Subordinated notes and debentures	0.00%	2.50%
Noninterest Expense as a Percentage of Total Operating Income		
21. Salaries and employee benefits	11.63%	10.17%
22. Expenses of premises and fixed assets	4.04%	3.37%
23. Other noninterest expenses	6.89%	30.87%
Liability Yields		
24. NOW accounts	4.54%	1.42%
25. MMDAs	0.85%	3.42%
26. Other savings	2.29%	3.38%
27. Retail CDs	5.08%	5.79%
28. Wholesale CDs	5.74%	7.79%
29. Fed funds and RPs	5.14%	6.10%
30. Other borrowed funds	9.27%	5.51%
31. Subordinated notes and debentures	0.00%	2.95%

Table 13–5 *continued*

Ratio	North Fork Bancorp	Bank One Corporation
Liability Accounts as a Percentage of Total Assets		
32. Demand deposits	4.86%	16.87%
33. NOW accounts	0.52%	1.59%
34. MMDAs	16.94%	20.78%
35. Other savings	21.29%	7.02%
36. Retail CDs	20.56%	14.36%
37. Core deposits	64.11%	60.62%
38. Wholesale CDs	5.14%	4.78%
39. Fed funds and RPs	21.09%	10.82%
40. Other borrowed funds	1.02%	4.01%
41. Subordinated notes and debentures	0.00%	9.39%
42. Purchased funds	27.25%	29.00%
43. Other liabilities	0.43%	1.58%
Liability Items as a Percentage of Interest-Bearing Liabilities		
44. NOW accounts	0.61%	2.19%
45. MMDAs	19.57%	28.56%
46. Other savings	24.60%	9.66%
47. Retail CDs	23.75%	19.74%
48. Wholesale CDs	5.94%	6.58%
49. Fed funds and RPs	24.36%	14.87%
50. Other borrowed funds	1.17%	5.50%
51. Subordinated notes and debentures	0.00%	12.90%
Noninterest Expense as a Percentage of Noninterest Income		
52. Salaries and employee benefits	201.60%	34.44%
53. Expenses of premises and equipment	69.98%	11.41%
54. Other noninterest income	119.53%	104.50%
Noninterest Expense as a Percentage of Total Assets		
55. Salaries and employee benefits	0.90%	1.13%
56. Expenses of premises and equipment	0.31%	0.37%
57. Other noninterest income	0.54%	3.42%
Asset Utilization Breakdown		
58. Interest income ratio	7.31%	7.80%
59. Noninterest income ratio	0.45%	3.27%
Interest Income as a Percentage of Total Assets		
60. C&I loans	0.50%	1.32%
61. Real estate loans	3.76%	1.87%
62. Consumer loans	0.27%	2.84%
63. Other loans	0.02%	0.14%
64. Leases	0.06%	0.54%
65. Deposits at other institutions	0.00%	0.14%
66. Fed funds and RPs	0.02%	0.16%
67. U.S. Treasury and agencies	1.40%	0.62%
68. Municipals	0.08%	0.08%
69. Other debt and equity securities	1.20%	0.10%
Asset Yields		
70. C&I loans	8.43%	8.61%
71. Real estate loans	8.47%	8.34%
72. Consumer loans	6.72%	13.19%

continued

Table 13–5   *concluded*

Ratio	North Fork Bancorp	Bank One Corporation
73. Other loans	4.58%	5.74%
74. Leases	9.07%	7.21%
75. Fed funds and RPs	2.61%	5.00%
76. U.S. Treasury and agencies	54.38%	18.57%
77. Municipals	4.68%	4.08%
78. Other debt and equity securities	3.41%	1.00%
Asset Items as a Percentage of Total Assets		
79. Cash and balances due from institutions	2.28%	7.17%
80. C&I loans	5.88%	15.32%
81. Real estate loans	44.55%	22.45%
82. Consumer loans	3.95%	21.51%
83. Other loans	0.54%	2.43%
84. Leases	0.70%	7.42%
85. Net loans and leases	54.14%	68.01%
86. Deposits at other institutions	0.13%	3.55%
87. Fed funds and RPs	0.88%	3.14%
88. U.S. Treasury and agencies	2.58%	3.32%
89. Municipals	1.71%	1.91%
90. Other debt and equity securities	35.04%	10.44%
91. Total investment securities	40.35%	22.36%
92. Other assets	3.23%	2.46%
Asset Items as a Percentage of Earning Assets		
93. C&I loans	6.21%	16.96%
94. Real estate loans	47.15%	24.84%
95. Consumer loans	4.18%	23.81%
96. Other loans	0.58%	2.69%
97. Leases	0.74%	8.21%
98. Deposits at other institutions	0.14%	3.92%
99. Fed funds and RPs	0.93%	3.48%
100. U.S. Treasury and agencies	2.73%	3.67%
101. Municipals	1.81%	2.11%
102. Other debt and equity securities	37.09%	11.55%
Off-Balance-Sheet Items as a Percentage of Total Assets		
103. Loan commitments	6.39%	82.00%
104. Standby letters of credit	0.07%	0.03%
105. Commercial letters of credit	0.31%	0.35%
106. When-issued securities	0.00%	0.00%
107. Loans sold	0.00%	1.75%
108. Interest rate swaps	0.00%	5.04%
109. Total off-balance-sheet items	6.77%	89.17%
Noninterest Income as a Percentage of Total Assets		
110. Fiduciary accounts	0.03%	0.43%
111. Service charges	0.29%	0.57%
112. Trading gains	0.00%	0.01%
113. Other noninterest income	0.13%	2.26%
Noninterest Income as a Percentage of Total Noninterest Income		
114. Fiduciary accounts	7.27%	13.13%
115. Service charges	64.51%	17.54%
116. Trading gains	0.03%	0.28%
117. Other noninterest income	28.19%	69.05%

Figure 13–5 Classification of Ratios Listed in Table 13-5 in ROE Breakdown

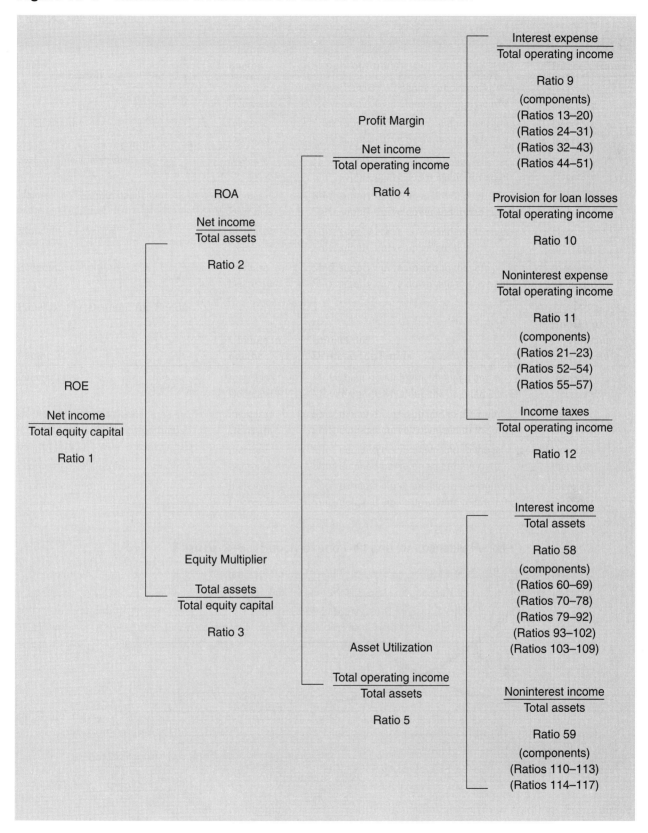

It measures the amount of net income after taxes earned for each dollar of equity capital contributed by the bank's stockholders. Taking these data from the financial statements for North Fork Bancorp and Bank One Corporation, the following ROEs for 1997 were:[20]

	North Fork Bancorp	Bank One Corporation
ROE	$\dfrac{115.04}{550.46} = 20.90\%$	$\dfrac{1,519.32}{10,376.00} = 14.64\%$

Generally, bank stockholders prefer ROE to be high. It is possible, however, that an increase in ROE indicates increased risk. For example, ROE increases if total equity capital decreases relative to net income. A large drop in equity capital may result in a violation of minimum regulatory capital standards and an increased risk of insolvency for the bank (see Chapter 20). An increase in ROE may simply result from an increase in a bank's leverage—an increase in its debt-to-equity ratio.

To identify potential problems, ROE (ratio 1) can be decomposed into two component parts, as follows:

$$\text{ROE} = \frac{\text{Net income}}{\text{Total assets}} \times \frac{\text{Total assets}}{\text{Total equity capital}}$$

$$= \text{ROA} \times \text{EM}$$

where

ROA ratio 2) = Return on assets
EM (ratio 3) = Equity multiplier (a measure of leverage)

ROA determines the net income produced per dollar of assets; EM measures the dollar value of assets funded with each dollar of equity capital (the higher this ratio, the more leverage or debt the bank is using to fund its assets). The values of these ratios for our two banks in 1997 were:

	North Fork Bancorp	Bank One Corporation
ROA	$\dfrac{115.04}{6,704.37} = 1.72\%$	$\dfrac{1,519.32}{117,891.48} = 1.29\%$
EM	$\dfrac{6,704.37}{550.46} = 12.18$ times	$\dfrac{117,891.48}{10,376.00} = 11.36$ times

High values for these ratios produce high ROEs, but, as noted, managers should be concerned about the source of high ROEs. For example, an increase in ROE due to an increase in the EM means that the bank's leverage, and therefore its solvency risk, has increased.

Return on Assets and Its Components

A further breakdown of a bank's profitability is that of dividing ROA (ratio 2 in Table 13–5) into its profit margin (PM) and asset utilization (AU) ratio components:

$$\text{ROA} = \frac{\text{Net income}}{\text{Total operating income}} \times \frac{\text{Total operating income}}{\text{Total assets}}$$

$$= \text{PM} \times \text{AU}$$

---

20. We are using year-end balance sheet data to calculate ratios. The use of these data may bias ratios in that they are data for one day in the year, whereas income statement data cover the full year. To avoid this bias, the use of average values for balance sheet data are often used to calculate ratios.

where

PM (ratio 4) = Net income generated per dollar of total operating (interest and noninterest) income

AU (ratio 5) = Amount of interest and noninterest income generated per dollar of total assets

For our two banks, these are as follows:

	North Fork Bancorp	Bank One Corporation
PM	$\dfrac{115.04}{490.37 + 30.01} = 22.11\%$	$\dfrac{1,519.32}{9,196.42 + 3,856.02} = 11.64\%$
AU	$\dfrac{490.37 + 30.01}{6,704.37} = 7.76\%$	$\dfrac{9,196.42 + 3,856.02}{117,891.48} = 11.07\%$

Again, high values for these ratios produce high ROAs and ROEs. PM measures the bank's ability to control expenses. The better the expense control, the more profitable the bank. AU measures the bank's ability to generate income from its assets. The more income generated per dollar of assets, the more profitable the bank. Again, bank managers should be aware that high values of these ratios may indicate underlying problems. For example, PM increases if the bank experiences a drop in salaries and benefits. However, if this expense decreases because the most highly skilled employees are leaving the bank, the increase in PM and in ROA is associated with a potential "labor quality" problem. Thus, it is often prudent to break these ratios down further.

Profit Margin.   As stated, PM measures a bank's ability to control expenses and thus its ability to produce net income from its operating income (or revenue). A breakdown of PM, therefore, can isolate the various expense items listed on the income statement as follows:

$$\text{Interest expense ratio (ratio 9)} = \frac{\text{Interest expense}}{\text{Total operating income}}$$

$$\text{Provision for loan loss ratio (ratio 10)} = \frac{\text{Provision for loan losses}}{\text{Total operating income}}$$

$$\text{Noninterest expense ratio (ratio 11)} = \frac{\text{Noninterest expense}}{\text{Total operating income}}$$

$$\text{Tax ratio (ratio 12)} = \frac{\text{Income taxes}}{\text{Total operating income}}$$

These ratios measure the proportion of total operating income that goes to pay the particular expense item. The values of these ratios for North Fork Bancorp and Bank One Corporation are as follows:

	North Fork Bancorp	Bank One Corporation
Interest expense ratio	$\dfrac{212.72}{490.37 + 30.01} = 40.88\%$	$\dfrac{3,930.17}{9,196.42 + 3,856.02} = 30.11\%$
Provision for loan loss ratio	$\dfrac{6.27}{490.37 + 30.01} = 1.20\%$	$\dfrac{1,152.12}{9,196.42 + 3,856.02} = 8.83\%$
Noninterest expense ratio	$\dfrac{117.37}{490.37 + 30.01} = 22.55\%$	$\dfrac{5,797.81}{9,196.42 + 3,856.02} = 86.48\%$

	North Fork Bancorp	**Bank One Corporation**
Tax ratio	$\dfrac{68.98}{490.37 + 30.01} = 13.26\%$	$\dfrac{653.02}{9,196.42 + 3,856.02} = 5.00\%$

The sum of the numerators of these four ratios subtracted from the denominator (total operating income) is the bank's net income.[21] Thus, the lower any of these ratios, the higher the bank's profitability (PM). As mentioned, however, although a low value for any of these ratios produces an increase in the bank's profit, it may be indicative of a problem situation in the bank. Thus, an even more detailed breakdown of these ratios may be warranted. For example, the interest expense ratio can be broken down according to the various interest expense-generating liabilities (ratios 13–20 in Table 13–5; e.g., interest on NOW accounts/total operating income). Additionally, the noninterest expense ratio may be broken down according to its components (ratios 21-23—e.g., salaries and benefits/total operating income). These ratios allow for a more detailed examination of the generation of the bank's expenses.

A different method to evaluate the bank's expense management is to calculate such ratios as deposit yields (ratios 24–31; e.g., interest expense on NOW accounts/dollar value of NOW accounts) or size of investment (e.g., dollar value of NOW accounts/total assets—ratios 32–43—or dollar value of NOW accounts/total interest bearing liabilities—ratios 44-51). The noninterest expense items can be evaluated using component percentages (ratios 52–54; e.g., salaries and benefits/noninterest income) or size of expense (ratios 55–57; e.g., salaries and benefits/total assets).

Asset Utilization.   The AU ratio measures the extent to which the bank's assets generate revenue. The breakdown of the AU ratio separates the total revenue generated into interest income and noninterest income as follows:

$$\text{Asset utilization ratio} = \frac{\text{Total operating income}}{\text{Total assets}} = \frac{\text{Interest}}{\text{income ratio}} + \frac{\text{Noninterest}}{\text{income ratio}}$$

where

$$\text{Interest income ratio (ratio 58)} = \frac{\text{Interest income}}{\text{Total assets}}$$

$$\text{Noninterest income ratio (ratio 59)} = \frac{\text{Noninterest income}}{\text{Total assets}}$$

which measure the bank's ability to generate interest income and noninterest income, respectively. For the banks represented in Tables 13–1 and 13–3, the value of these ratios are as follows:

	North Fork Bancorp	**Bank One Corporation**
Interest income ratio	$\dfrac{490.37}{6,704.37} = 7.31\%$	$\dfrac{9,196.42}{117,891.48} = 7.80\%$
Noninterest income ratio	$\dfrac{30.01}{6,704.37} = 0.45\%$	$\dfrac{3,856.02}{117,891.48} = 3.27\%$

The interest income and noninterest income ratios are not necessarily independent. For example, the bank's ability to generate loans affects both interest income and, through fees and service charges, noninterest income. High values for these ratios signify the

21. For example, for Bank One, the denominator of each of the four ratios ($9,196.42 + $3,856.02 = $13,052.44) less the sum of the numerators of the four ratios ($3,930.17 + $1,152.12 + $5,797.81 + $653.02 = $11,533.12) is $1,519.32, which is the net income reported for Bank One Corporation in Table 13–3.

efficient use of bank resources to generate income and are thus generally positive for the bank. But some problematic situations that result in high ratio values could exist; for example, a bank that replaces low-risk, low-return loans with high-risk, high-return loans will experience an increase in its interest income ratio. However, high-risk loans have a higher default probability, which could result in the ultimate loss of both interest and principal payments. Further breakdown of these ratios is therefore a valuable tool in the financial performance evaluation process.

The interest income ratio can be broken down using the various components of interest income (ratios 60–69; e.g., income on C&I loans/total assets); or by using asset yield (ratios 70–78; e.g., income on C&I loans/dollar value of C&I loans); or by using size of investment (e.g., dollar value of C&I loans/total assets—ratios 79–92—or dollar value of C&I loans/total earning assets—ratios 93–102). Off-balance-sheet activities can also be measured in terms of the size of the notional values they create in relation to bank assets (ratios 103–109—e.g., loan commitments/total assets). The noninterest income ratio can also be subdivided into the various subcategories (e.g., income from fiduciary activities/total assets—ratios 110–113—or income from fiduciary activities/noninterest income—ratios 114–117).

Other Ratios

A number of other profit measures are commonly used to evaluate bank performance. Three of these are (1) the net interest margin, (2) the spread (ratio), and (3) overhead efficiency.

net interest margin

Interest income minus interest expense divided by earning assets.

Net Interest Margin. **Net interest margin** (ratio 6 in Table 13–5) measures the net return on the bank's earning assets (investment securities and loans and leases) and is defined as follows:

$$\text{Net interest margin} = \frac{\text{Net interest income}}{\text{Earning assets}} = \frac{\text{Interest income} - \text{Interest expense}}{\text{Investments securities} + \text{Net loans and leases}}$$

Generally, the higher this ratio, the better. Suppose, however, that a preceding scenario (replacement of low-risk, low-return loans with high-risk, high-return loans) is the reason for the increase. This situation can increase risk for the bank. It highlights the fact that looking at returns without looking at risk can be misleading and potentially dangerous in terms of bank solvency and long-run profitability.

spread

The difference between lending and borrowing rates.

The Spread. The **spread** (ratio 7) measures the difference between the average yield of earning assets and average cost of interest-bearing liabilities and is thus another measure of return on the bank's assets. The spread is defined as:

$$\text{Spread} = \frac{\text{Interest income}}{\text{Earning assets}} - \frac{\text{Interest expense}}{\text{Interest-bearing liabilities}}$$

The higher the spread, the more profitable the bank, but again, the source of a high spread and the potential risk implications should be considered.

overhead efficiency

A bank's ability to generate noninterest income to cover noninterest expense.

Overhead Efficiency. **Overhead efficiency** (ratio 8) measures the bank's ability to generate noninterest income to cover noninterest expenses. It is represented as:

$$\text{Overhead efficiency} = \frac{\text{Noninterest income}}{\text{Noninterest expense}}$$

The higher this ratio, the better, but, because of the high levels of noninterest expense relative to noninterest income, it is rarely higher than

Do You Understand?

1. Two scenarios in which a high value of ROE may signal a risk problem for a bank?
2. What ratios ROA can be broken down into?
3. What the *spread* measure means?

1 (or in percentage terms, than 100 percent). The values of these ratios for the two banks are as follows:

	North Fork Bancorp	**Bank One Corporation**
Net interest margin	$\dfrac{277.65}{6,334.58} = 4.38\%$	$\dfrac{5,266.25}{106,537.09} = 4.94\%$
Spread	$\dfrac{490.37}{6,334.58} - \dfrac{212.72}{5,803.26} = 4.08\%$	$\dfrac{9,196.42}{106,537.09} - \dfrac{3,930.17}{85,770.36} = 4.05\%$
Overhead efficiency	$\dfrac{30.01}{117.37} = 25.57\%$	$\dfrac{3,856.02}{5,797.81} = 66.51\%$

Impact of Market Niche and Bank Size on Financial Statement Analysis

Impact of a Bank's Market Niche

As mentioned earlier, in 1997, North Fork Bancorp was a profitable and efficient bank that specialized in real estate loans and low-cost funding methods. Bank One, on the other hand, operated with a larger and more balanced portfolio of assets and liabilities across both wholesale and retail banking. Keeping the more specialized market niche of North Fork Bancorp in mind, let us make a comparative financial analysis using the ROE framework and the banks' 1997 financial statements.

ROE and Its Components.   As stated, the ROE (ratio 1) of 20.90 percent for North Fork Bancorp (NFB) was significantly higher than the 14.64 percent ROE reported for Bank One (BOC). NFB was paying less on many of its liabilities relative to BOC (ratios 24–31) and earning an overall higher rate on many of its assets relative to BOC (ratios 70–78). The breakdown of ROE indicates that NFB's higher profitability was due to its ROA of 1.72 percent compared with that of 1.29 percent for BOC (ratio 2). NFB's equity multiplier or leverage (ratio 3) was higher than that of BOC. NFB's EM of 12.18X translated to an equity-to-asset ratio (= 1/EM) of 8.21 percent, and BOC's EM of 11.36X translated to an equity-to-asset ratio of 8.80 percent. Thus, although both banks appeared to be well capitalized, NFB had more leverage. (As we see in the next section, these may be attributed to differences in bank size as well as market niche.)

The more focused orientation of NFB relative to BOC can best be seen by looking at the composition of the asset, and particularly the loan, portfolios (ratios 79 through 91) and the liabilities (ratios 32 through 42) of the two banks. NFB held 44.55 percent of its total assets in the form of real asset loans and 35.04 percent in other debt and equity securities (mainly mortgage-backed securities). Thus, consistent with its niche, a large majority of NFB's assets were tied up in real estate related assets. BOC, on the other hand, had its asset investments more evenly distributed: 15.32 percent in C&I loans, 22.45 percent in real estate loans, 21.52 percent in consumer loans, and 22.36 percent other debt and equity securities.

On the liability side of the balance sheet, NFB issued mainly retail-oriented deposits: MMDAs were 16.94 percent of total assets, other savings were 21.29 percent, and retail CDs were 20.56 percent. BOC again used a broader array of deposits: demand deposits were 16.87 percent, MMDAs were 20.78 percent, other savings were 7.02 percent, and retail CDs were 14.36 percent of total assets. Further, the deposits issued by NFB paid less than the same accounts at BOC (ratios 25 through 28). MMDAs at NFB yielded 0.85 in 1997 compared to 3.42 percent at BOC; other savings yielded 2.29 percent at NFB and 3.38 percent at BOC; retail CDs yielded 5.08 percent at NFB and 5.79 percent at BOC.

Clearly, NFB has decided to specialize its services in the retail area, while BOC offered the broader spectrum of financial services. The profit ratios in Table 13–5 show NFB's niche strategy has resulted in a highly profitable bank.

Impact of Size on Financial Statement Analysis

Bank size has traditionally affected the financial ratios of commercial banks, resulting in significant differences across size groups. Large banks' relatively easy access to purchased funds and capital markets compared to small banks' access is a reason for many of these differences. For example, large banks with easier access to capital markets operate with lower amounts of equity capital than do small banks. Also, large banks tend to use more purchased funds (such as fed funds and RPs) and fewer core deposits than do small banks. Large banks tend to put more into salaries, premises, and other expenses than small banks do, and they tend to diversify their operations and services more than small banks do. Large banks also generate more noninterest income (i.e., trading account, derivative security, and foreign trading income) than small banks do and when risky loans pay off, they earn more interest income. As a result, although large banks tend to hold less equity than small banks do, large banks do not necessarily return more on their assets. A study by the Federal Reserve Bank of St. Louis[22] reported that ROA consistently increased for banks grouped by size up to $15 billion in total assets but decreased for banks with more than $15 billion.

Examining ratios for the relatively large Bank One Corporation (BOC) compared to the smaller NFB, we see many of these size-related effects on accounting ratios. Looking at ROA (ratio 2), BOC is the less profitable of the two banks. Notice that BOC is producing the lower income per dollar of total operating income (ratio 4; PM for BOC = 11.64 percent and for NFB = 22.11 percent), but is producing much more operating income per dollar of assets (AU for BOC = 11.07 percent and for NFB = 7.72 percent). The generation of total operating income in the form of interest income (ratio 58) is larger for BOC (interest income ratio for BOC = 7.80 percent and for NFB = 7.31 percent). Further, BOC generates more noninterest income (3.27 percent of total assets) than NFB (0.45 percent of total assets; see ratio 59). This is likely due to BOC's relatively large amount of OBS activities (which is typical of large banks compared with small banks). BOC is using fewer core deposit and more purchased funds to total assets than NFB (see ratios 37 and 42). Notice, too, that BOC's net loans and leases (ratio 85) are 68.01 percent of total assets, compared with 54.14 percent for NFB. BOC generates much more noninterest income, 3.27 percent, than NFB, 0.45 percent (see ratio 59), and the addition of ratios 21 through 23 indicates that noninterest expenses are much higher for BOC (44.41 percent of total operating income) than for NFB (22.56 percent). Uncharacteristically, despite the size-related differences across the two banks, BOC's ROE (ratio 1) is well below that of NFB. In addition, EM (ratio 3) shows that BOC (EM = 11.36X) uses more equity funding than NFB (EM = 12.18X). Finally, BOC's other assets (i.e., premises and equipment) are 2.46 percent of total assets compared to 3.23 percent for NFB (ratio 92).

> **Do You Understand?**
>
> 1. How a bank's choice of market niche affects its financial ratios?
> 2. How a bank's asset size affects its financial ratios?

[22]See D. C. Wheelock, "A Changing Relationship between Bank Size and Profitability," in *Monetary Trends*, Federal Reserve Bank of St. Louis, September 1996, p. 1.

Summary

This chapter analyzed the financial statements of commercial banks. The assets, liabilities, and equity capital were described as they appear in the balance sheet. The financial statements of other DIs such as savings banks and credit unions take a similar form. The income and expenses were described as they appear in the income statement. From the items on the financial statements, the profitability of two banks was analyzed using a return on equity (ROE) framework. What might appear as a favorable sign of profitability and performance can sometimes, in fact, indicate risk problems that management should address. Many problems and areas of managerial concern can be identified by performing a detailed breakdown of the financial ratios of FIs. Thus, both profitability and risk management are interlinked and should be of concern to managers. The various risks to which FIs are exposed are examined in more detail in the next several chapters.

End of Chapter Questions

1. How does a bank's report of condition differ from its report of income?

2. Match these three types of cash balances with the functions that they serve:

   a. Vault cash   **(1)** Meet legal reserve requirements
   b. Deposits at   **(2)** Used to purchase services
   the Federal   **(3)** Meet customer withdrawals
   Reserve
   c. Deposits at
   other FIs

3. Classify the following accounts into one of the following categories:

   a. assets
   b. liabilities
   c. equity
   d. revenue
   e. expense
   f. off-balance-sheet activities

   (1) Services charged on deposit accounts
   (2) Retail CDs
   (3) Surplus and paid-in capital
   (4) Loan commitments
   (5) Consumer loans
   (6) Federal funds sold
   (7) Swaps
   (8) Interest on municipals
   (9) Interest on NOW accounts
   (10) NOW accounts
   (11) Commercial letters of credit
   (12) Leases
   (13) Retained earnings
   (14) Provision for loan losses
   (15) Interest on U.S. Treasury securities

4. If we examine a typical bank's asset portion of the balance sheet, how are the assets arranged in terms of expected return and liquidity?

5. Repurchase agreements are listed as both assets and liabilities in Table 13–1. How can an account be both an asset and a liability?

6. How does a NOW account differ from a demand deposit?

7. How does a retail CD differ from a wholesale CD?

8. How do core deposits differ from purchased funds?

9. What are the major categories of off-balance-sheet activities?

10. A bank is considering two securities: a 30-year Treasury bond yielding 7 percent and a 30-year municipal bond yielding 5 percent. If the bank's tax rate is 30 percent, which bond offers the higher tax equivalent yield?

11. A bank is considering an investment in a municipal security that offers a yield of 6 percent. What is this security's tax equivalent yield if the bank's tax rate is 35 percent?

12. How does a bank's annual net income compare with its annual cash flow?

13. How might the use of an end-of-the-year balance sheet bias the calculation of certain ratios?

14. How does the asset utilization ratio for a bank compare to that of a retail company? How do the equity multipliers compare?

15. Smallville Bank has the following balance sheet, rates earned on their assets, and rates paid on their liabilities.

Balance Sheet (in thousands)

Assets		Rate Earned (%)
Cash and due from banks	$ 6,000	4
Investment securities	22,000	8
Repurchase agreements	12,000	6
Loans less allowance		
for losses	80,000	10
Fixed Assets	10,000	0
Other assets	4,000	9
Total assets	134,000	

Liabilities and Equity		Rate Paid (%)
Demand deposits	$ 9,000	0
NOW accounts	69,000	5
Retail CDs	18,000	7
Subordinated debentures	14,000	8
Total liabilities	110,000	
Common stock	10,000	
Paid in capital surplus	13,000	
Retained earnings	11,000	
Total liabilities and equity	134,000	

If the bank earns $120,000 in noninterest income, incurs $80,000 in noninterest expenses, and pays $2,500,000 in taxes, what is its net income?

16. Megalopolis Bank has the following balance sheet and income statement.

Balance Sheet (in millions)

Assets		Liabilities and Equity	
Cash and due from banks	$ 9,000	Demand deposits	$ 19,000
Investment securities	23,000	NOW accounts	89,000
Repurchase agreements	42,000	Retail CDs	28,000
Loans	90,000	Debentures	19,000
Fixed assets	15,000	Total liabilities	$155,000
Other assets	4,000	Common stock	12,000
Total assets	$183,000	Paid in capital	4,000
		Retained earnings	12,000
		Total liabilities and equity	$183,000

Income Statement

Interest on fees and loans	$ 9,000
Interest on investment securities	4,000
Interest on repurchase agreements	6,000
Interest on deposits in banks	1,000
Total interest income	$20,000
Interest on deposits	$ 9,000
Interest on debentures	2,000
Total interest expense	$11,000
Operating income	$ 9,000
Provision for loan losses	2,000
Other income	2,000
Other expenses	1,000
Income before taxes	$ 8,000
Taxes	3,000
Net income	$ 5,000

For Megalopolis, calculate:
a. Return on equity
b. Return on assets
c. Asset utilization
d. Equity multiplier
e. Profit margin
f. Interest expense ratio
g. Provision for loan loss ratio
h. Noninterest expense ratio
i. Tax ratio

17. What is the likely relationship between the interest income ratio and the noninterest income ratio?

18. Anytown bank has the following ratios:
a. Profit margin: 21%
b. Asset utilization: 11%
c. Equity multiplier: 12X
Calculate Anytown's ROE and ROA.

19. A security analyst calculates the following ratios for two banks. How should the analyst evaluate the financial health of the two banks?

	Bank A	Bank B
Return on equity	22%	24%
Return on assets	2%	1.5%
Equity multiplier	11X	16X
Profit margin	15%	14%
Asset utilization	13%	11%
Spread	3%	3%
Interest expense ratio	35%	40%
Provision for loan loss ratio	1%	4%

20. What sort of problems or opportunities might ratio analysis fail to identify?

21. Go to the FDIC website and find the total number of deposits for the Fleet National Bank in Providence, Rhode Island.

chapter fourteen

Regulation *of* Depository Institutions

Chapter Navigator

1. What types of regulations are depository institutions subject to?

2. What major bank regulations have been passed in the last twenty years?

3. How has commercial banks' reentry into the investment banking business evolved?

4. Why did the FSLIC fail?

5. How do U.S. regulations on depository institutions compare with those of other countries?

6. Why are depository institutions subject to reserve requirements?

7. What capital regulations must depository institutions meet?

Specialness and Regulation: Chapter Overview

Chapter 1 showed that FIs are special because they provide vital services to various important sectors of the economy. The general areas of FI specialness include the following: information services; liquidity services; price-risk reduction services; transaction cost services; maturity intermediation services; money supply transmission; credit allocation; intergenerational wealth transfers; payment services; and denomination intermediation.

    Failure to provide these services or a breakdown in their efficient provision can be costly to both the ultimate providers (households) and users (firms) of savings. Because of the vital nature of the services they provide, depository institutions (DIs) are

Table 14–1   Areas of DI Specialness in Regulation

Safety and Soundness Regulation—layers of regulation have been imposed on DIs to protect depositors and borrowers against the risk of failure.

Monetary Policy Regulation—regulators control and implement monetary policy by requiring minimum levels of cash reserves to be held against depository institution deposits.

Credit Allocation Regulation—regulations support the DI's lending to socially important sectors such as housing and farming.

Consumer Protection Regulation—regulations are imposed to prevent the DI from discriminating unfairly in lending.

Investor Protection Regulation—laws protect investors who directly purchase securities and/or indirectly purchase securities by investing in mutual or pension funds.

Entry and Chartering Regulation—entry and activity regulations limit the number of DIs in any given financial services sector, thus impacting the charter values of DIs operating in that sector.

regulated to protect against a disruption in the provision of these services and the cost this would impose on the economy and society at large. In this chapter, we provide an overview of the regulations imposed on DIs. We first discuss the history of depository institutions' regulation and then review the specific on- and off-balance-sheet regulations under which depository institutions operate. We also highlight the differences in regulations imposed on domestic versus international depository institutions.

Types of Regulations and the Regulators

Six types of regulations seek to enhance the net social benefits of depository institutions'services to the economy: (1) safety and soundness regulation, (2) monetary policy regulation, (3) credit allocation regulation, (4) consumer protection regulation, (5) investor protection regulation, and (6) entry and chartering regulation. These regulations are summarized in Table 14–1. Regulation can be imposed at the federal or the state level and occasionally at the international level, as in the case of bank capital requirements.

Safety and Soundness Regulation

To protect depositors and borrowers against the risk of DI failure—for example, due to a lack of diversification in asset portfolios—regulators have developed layers of protective mechanisms, illustrated in Figure 14–1. Included in these mechanisms are requirements encouraging DIs to diversify their assets (the first layer of protection). The most obvious way to prevent DI failure is to prevent DIs from investing in an asset portfolio that produces cash flows that are insufficient to make the promised payments to the DI's liability holders. Thus, banks are prohibited from making loans exceeding more than 15 percent of their own equity capital funds to any one company or borrower. A bank that has 6 percent of its assets funded by its own capital (and therefore 94 percent by liabilities) can lend no more than 0.9 percent of its assets to any one borrower (i.e., 15 percent of 6 percent).

The second layer of protection concerns the minimum level of stockholder capital or equity funds that the owners of a DI need to contribute to the funding of its operations. For example, bank and thrift regulators are concerned with the minimum ratio of capital to (risk) assets. The higher the proportion of capital contributed by owners, the greater the protection against insolvency risk for liability claimholders such as depositors. This occurs because losses on the asset portfolio due, for example, to loan defaults are legally borne by the stockholders first and then, only after the equity holders'

Figure 14–1 Layers of Regulation

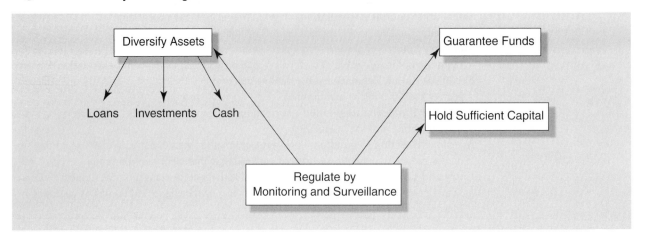

claims are totally wiped out, by outside liability holders.[1] Consequently, DI regulators can directly affect the degree of risk exposure faced by nonequity claim holders in DIs (such as depositors) by varying the minimum amount of equity capital required to operate and keep a bank open (see discussions below).

The third layer of protection is the provision of guarantee funds such as the Bank Insurance Fund (BIF) for banks and the Savings Association Insurance Fund (SAIF) for savings associations. Deposit insurance mitigates a rational incentive depositors otherwise have to withdraw their funds at the first hint of trouble. By protecting DI depositors when a DI collapses and owners' equity or net worth is wiped out, a demand for regulation of insured institutions is created so as to protect the funds' (and taxpayers') resources. For example, the Federal Deposit Insurance Corporation (FDIC) monitors and regulates participants in both BIF and SAIF in return for providing explicit deposit guarantees of up to $100,000 per depositor per bank.

The fourth layer of regulation involves monitoring and surveillance. Regulators subject all DIs—whether banks, savings institutions, or credit unions—to varying degrees of monitoring and surveillance. This involves on-site examination of the DI by regulators as well as the DI's production of accounting statements and reports on a timely basis for off-site evaluation. Just as savers appoint DIs as delegated monitors to evaluate the behavior and actions of ultimate borrowers, society appoints regulators to monitor the behavior and performance of DIs.

Finally, note that regulation is not without costs for those regulated. For example, regulators may require DIs to have more equity capital than private owners believe is in their own best interests. Similarly, producing the information requested by regulators is costly for DIs because it involves the time of managers, lawyers, and accountants. Again, the socially optimal amount of information may differ from a DI's privately optimal amount.

Although regulation may be socially beneficial, it imposes private costs, or a regulatory burden, on individual DI owners and managers. Consequently, regulation attempts to enhance the social welfare benefits and mitigate the social costs of providing DI services. The difference between the private benefits to a DI from being regulated—such as insurance fund guarantees—and the private costs it faces from adhering to regulation—such as examinations—is called its **net regulatory burden.**[2] The

www.fdic.gov/

net regulatory burden

The difference between the private costs of regulations and the private benefits for the producers of financial services.

---

1. Thus, equity holders are junior claimants and debt holders senior claimants to a DI's assets.

2. Other regulated firms such as gas and electric utilities also face a complex set of regulations imposing a net regulatory burden on their operations.

higher the net regulatory burden on DIs, the smaller are the benefits of being regulated compared to the costs of adhering to them from a private (DI) owner's perspective.

Monetary Policy Regulation

www.bog.frb.fed.us/

outside money

That part of the money supply directly produced by the government or central bank, such as notes and coin.

inside money

That part of the money supply produced by the private banking system.

Another motivation for regulation concerns the special role that banks play in the transmission of monetary policy from the Federal Reserve (the central bank) to the rest of the economy. The central bank directly controls only the quantity of notes and coin in the economy—called **outside money**—whereas the bulk of the money supply is bank deposits—called **inside money.** In theory, a central bank can vary the amount of cash or outside money and directly affect a bank's reserve position as well as the amount of loans and deposits it can create without formally regulating the bank's portfolio. In practice, regulators have chosen to impose formal controls.[3] In most countries, regulators commonly impose a minimum level of required cash reserves to be held against deposits (discussed below). Some argue that imposing such reserve requirements makes the control of the money supply and its transmission more predictable. Such reserves add to a DI's net regulatory burden if they are more than the institution believes are necessary for its own liquidity purposes. In general, all DIs would choose to hold some cash reserves—even noninterest bearing—to meet the liquidity and transaction needs of their customers directly. For well-managed DIs, however, this optimal level is normally low, especially if the central bank (or other regulatory body) does not pay interest on required reserves. As a result, DIs often view required reserves as similar to a tax and as a positive cost of undertaking financial intermediation.[4]

Credit Allocation Regulation

Credit allocation regulation supports the DI's lending to socially important sectors such as housing and farming. These regulations may require a DI to hold a minimum amount of assets in one particular sector of the economy or to set maximum interest rates, prices, or fees to subsidize certain sectors. An example of asset restrictions includes the qualified thrift lender (QTL) test, which requires savings institutions to hold 65 percent of their assets in residential mortgage-related assets to retain a thrift charter. Examples of interest rate restrictions are the usury laws that many states set on the maximum rates that can be charged on mortgages and/or consumer loans, and regulations (now abolished) such as the Federal Reserve Bank's Regulation Q maximums on time and savings deposit interest rates.

Such price and quantity restrictions may be justified for social welfare reasons—especially if society prefers strong (and subsidized) housing and farming sectors. However, they can also be harmful to DIs that must bear the private costs of meeting many of these regulations.

Consumer Protection Regulation

Congress passed the Community Reinvestment Act (CRA) in 1977 and the Home Mortgage Disclosure Act (HMDA) in 1975 to prevent discrimination by lending institutions. For example, since 1975, the HMDA has assisted the public in determining whether banks and other mortgage-lending institutions were meeting the needs of their local communities. HMDA is especially concerned about discrimination on the basis

---

3. We discussed these controls in Chapter 4.

4. In the United States, bank reserves held with the Central Bank (the Federal Reserve Bank, or the Fed) are noninterest bearing. In some other countries, interest is paid on bank reserves—thereby lowering the "regulatory tax" effect. The size of the tax, therefore, depends on the level of interest rates.

www.ffiec.gov/

www.bog.frb.fed.us/

www.fdic.gov/

www.occ.treas.gov/

of age, race, sex, or income. Since 1990, depository institutions have used a standard-ized form to report to their chief federal regulator the reasons that they granted or de-nied credit. To get some idea of the information production cost of regulatory compliance in this area, the Federal Financial Institutions Examination Council processes information on as many as 6 million mortgage transactions from more than 9,300 institutions each quarter. (The council is a federal supervisory body comprising the members of the Federal Reserve, the Federal Deposit Insurance Corporation, and the Office of the Comptroller of the Currency.) Many analysts believe that community and consumer protection laws are imposing a considerable net regulatory burden on DIs without offsetting social benefits that enhance equal access to mortgage and lend-ing markets.

Investor Protection Regulation

A considerable number of laws protect investors who use depository institutions directly to purchase securities and/or indirectly to access securities markets through investing in mutual or pension funds. Various laws protect investors against abuses such as insider trading, lack of disclosure, outright malfeasance, and breach of fiduciary responsibili-ties. Important legislation affecting investment banks and mutual funds includes the Se-curities Acts of 1933 and 1934 and the Investment Company Act of 1940. Since DIs are increasingly moving into offering investment banking and mutual fund services, these restrictions will increasingly impact their profits. As with consumer protection legisla-tion, compliance with these acts can impose a net regulatory burden on DIs.

Entry and Chartering Regulation

The entry of DIs is regulated, as are their activities once they have been established. In-creasing or decreasing the cost of entry into a financial sector affects the profitability of firms already competing in that industry. Thus, the industries heavily protected against new entrants by high direct costs (e.g., through capital requirements) and high indirect costs (e.g., by restricting the type of individuals who can establish DIs) of en-try produce larger profits for existing firms than those in which entry is relatively easy. In addition, regulations define the scope of permitted activities under a given charter. The broader the set of financial service activities permitted under a charter, the more valuable that charter is likely to be. Thus, barriers to entry and regulations pertaining to the scope of permitted activities affect a DI's *charter value* and the size of its net regulatory burden.

www.fdic.gov/

www.occ.treas.gov/

www.bog.frb.fed.us/

www.ftc.gov/

www.ots.treas.gov/

www.ncua.org/

Regulators

Unlike other countries that have one or sometimes two regulators, U.S. depository in-stitutions may be subject to the supervision and regulations of as many as four separate regulators. The key regulators for each type of depository institution were discussed in Chapters 11 and 12. They include the Federal Deposit Insurance Corporation (FDIC), the Office of the Comptroller of the Currency (OCC), the Federal Reserve System (FRS), state bank regu-lators, the Federal Trade Commission (FTC), the Office of Thrift Su-pervision (OTS), and the National Credit Union Administration (NCUA). Appendix A to this chapter lists the regulators that oversee the various activities of depository institutions.

In the sections that follow, we describe different facets of the regu-latory structure, including (1) regulation of product and geographic expansion, (2) the provision and regulation of deposit insurance, (3) balance sheet regulations (reserve requirements and capital regula-tions), and (4) regulations pertaining to off-balance-sheet activities.

Do You Understand?

1. The six major types of regulation DIs face?
2. What the layers of protection provided by safety and soundness regulations are? Describe each.
3. What the difference is between inside and outside money?
4. Who the key regulators of depository institutions are?

2 Regulation of Product and Geographic Expansion

Historically, commercial banks have been among the most regulated firms in the U.S. economy. Because of the inherent special nature of banking and banking contracts, regulators have imposed numerous restrictions on their products and geographic activities over the last 75 years. Table 14–2 lists the major laws beginning with the McFadden Act of 1927 to the Financial Services Modernization Act of 1999 and briefly describes the key features of each.

Table 14–2   Major Features of Major Bank Laws

1927—The McFadden Act

1. Subjected branching of nationally chartered banks to the same branching regulations as state-chartered banks.
2. Liberalized national banks' securities underwriting activities, which previously had to be conducted through state-chartered affiliates.

1933—The Banking Act of 1933 (The Glass-Steagall Act)

1. Generally prohibited commercial banks from underwriting securities with four exceptions:
   a. Municipal general obligation bonds.
   b. U.S. government bonds.
   c. Private placements.
   d. Real estate loans.
2. In addition, established the FDIC to insure bank deposits.

1956—The Bank Holding Company Act

1. Restricted the banking and nonbanking acquisition activities of multibank holding companies.
2. Empowered the Federal Reserve to regulate multibank holding companies by:
   a. Determining permissible activities.
   b. Exercising supervisory authority.
   c. Exercising chartering authority.
   d. Conducting bank examinations.

1970—Amendments to the Bank Holding Company Act of 1956

1. Extended the BHC Act of 1956 to one-bank holding companies.
2. Restricted permissible BHC activities to those "closely related to banking."

1978—International Banking Act

1. Regulated foreign bank branches and agencies in the United States.
2. Subjected foreign banks to the McFadden and Glass-Steagall Acts.
3. Gave foreign banks access to Fedwire, the discount window, and deposit insurance.

1980—Depository Institutions Deregulation and Monetary Control Act (DIDMCA)

1. Set a six-year phaseout for Regulation Q interest rate ceilings on small time and savings deposits.
2. Authorized NOW accounts nationwide.
3. Introduced uniform reserve requirements for state and nationally chartered banks.
4. Increased the ceiling on deposit insurance coverage from $40,000 to $100,000.
5. Allowed federally chartered savings institutions to make consumer and commercial loans (subject to size restrictions).

1982—Garn-St. Germain Depository Institutions Act (DIA)

1. Introduced money market deposit accounts (MMDAs) and super NOW accounts as interest rate–bearing savings accounts with limited check-writing features.

continues

Table 14–2 *concluded*

2. Allowed federally chartered savings institutions more extensive lending powers and demand deposit–taking powers.
3. Allowed sound commercial banks to acquire failed savings banks.
4. Reaffirmed limitations on banks' ability to underwrite and distribute insurance.

1987—Competitive Equality in Banking Act (CEBA)

1. Redefined the definition of *bank* to limit the growth of nonbank banks.
2. Sought to recapitalize the Federal Savings and Loan Insurance Corporation (FSLIC).

1989—Financial Institutions Reform, Recovery, and Enforcement Act (FIRREA)

1. Limited savings banks' investments in nonresidential real estate, required divestiture of junk bond holdings (by 1994), and imposed a restrictive asset test to qualify as a savings bank (the qualified thrift lender test, or QTL).
2. Equalized the capital requirements of savings institutions and banks.
3. Replaced FSLIC with FDIC-SAIF.
4. Replaced the Federal Home Loan Bank Board as the charterer of federal savings institutions with the Office of Thrift Supervision (OTS), an agency of the Treasury.
5. Created the Resolution Trust Corporation (RTC) to resolve failed and failing savings institutions.

1991—Federal Deposit Insurance Corporation Improvement Act (FDICIA)

1. Introduced prompt corrective action (PCA), requiring mandatory interventions by regulators whenever a bank's capital falls.
2. Introduced risk-based deposit insurance premiums beginning in 1993.
3. Limited the use of "too big to fail" bailouts by federal regulators for large banks.
4. Extended federal regulation over foreign bank branches and agencies in the Foreign Bank Supervision and Enhancement Act (FBSEA).

1994—Riegle-Neal Interstate Banking and Branching Efficiency Act

1. Permitted bank holding companies to acquire banks in other states, starting September 1995.
2. Invalidated the laws of states that allow interstate banking only on a regional or reciprocal basis.
3. Beginning June 1997, permitted bank holding companies to convert out-of-state subsidiary banks into branches of a single interstate bank.
4. Also permitted newly chartered branches within a state if state law allows.

1999—Financial Services Modernization Act

1. Eliminated restrictions on banks, insurance companies, and securities firms entering into each others' areas of business.
2. Provided for state regulation of insurance.
3. Streamlined bank holding company supervision, with the Federal Reserve as the umbrella holding company supervisor.
4. Prohibited FDIC assistance to affiliates and subsidiaries of banks and savings institutions.
5. Provided for national treatment of foreign banks engaging in activities authorized under the act.

Product Segmentation in the U.S. Depository Institutions Industry

The U.S. financial system has traditionally been segmented along product lines. Regulatory barriers and restrictions have often inhibited a depository institution's ability to operate in some areas of the financial services industry and expand its product set beyond some limited range. Depository institutions operating in the United States can be compared with those operating in Germany, Switzerland, and the United Kingdom, where a more **universal FI** structure allows individual financial services organizations to offer a far broader range of banking, insurance, securities, and other financial services products.[5]

universal FI

An FI that can engage in a broad range of financial service activities.

5. For a thorough analysis of universal banking systems overseas, see A. Saunders and I. Walter, *Universal Banking in the U.S.?* (New York: Oxford University Press, 1994); and A. Saunders and I. Walter, eds., *Financial System Design: Universal Banking Considered* (Burr Ridge, IL: Irwin/McGraw-Hill Professional Publishing, 1996).

commercial banking

Banking activity of deposit taking and lending.

investment banking

Banking activity of underwriting, issuing, and distributing securities.

Commercial and Investment Banking Activities.   Since 1863, the United States has experienced several phases of regulating the links between the commercial and investment banking industries. Simply defined, **commercial banking** is the activity of deposit taking and commercial lending; **investment banking** is the activity of underwriting, issuing, and distributing (via public or private placement) securities. Early legislation, such as the 1863 National Bank Act, prohibited nationally chartered commercial banks from engaging in corporate securities activities such as underwriting and distributing of corporate bonds and equities. As the United States industrialized and the demand for corporate finance increased, however, the largest banks such as National City Bank (a part of today's Citigroup) found ways around this restriction by establishing state-chartered affiliates to do the underwriting. In 1927, the Comptroller of the Currency formally recognized such affiliates as legitimate banking activities.

After the 1929 stock market crash, the United States entered a major recession, and approximately 10,000 banks failed between 1930 and 1933. A commission of inquiry (the Pecora Commission) established in 1931 began investigating the causes of the crash. Its findings included concerns about the riskiness and conflicts of interest that arise when commercial and investment banking activities are linked (affiliated) in one organization. This resulted in new legislation, the 1933 Banking Act, or the Glass-Steagall Act (summarized in Table 14–3). The Glass-Steagall Act sought to impose a rigid separation (or nonaffiliation) between commercial banking—taking deposits and making commercial loans—and investment banking—underwriting, issuing, and distributing stocks, bonds, and other securities. The act defined three major exemptions to this separation. First, banks were allowed to continue to underwrite new issues of Treasury bills, notes, and bonds. Second, banks were allowed to continue underwriting municipal general obligation (GO) bonds.[6] Third, banks were allowed to continue engaging in private placements (see Chapter 8) of all types of bonds and equities, corporate and noncorporate.

For most of the 1933–1963 period, commercial banks and investment banks generally appeared to be willing to abide by both the letter and spirit of the Glass-Steagall Act. Between 1963 and 1987, however, banks challenged restrictions on their municipal *revenue* bond underwriting activities, commercial paper underwriting activities, discount brokerage activities, and advising activities, including open- and closed-end mutual funds, the underwriting of mortgage-backed securities, and selling annuities.[7] In most cases, the courts eventually permitted these activities for commercial banks.[8]

With this onslaught, and the de facto erosion of the Glass-Steagall Act by legal interpretation, the Federal Reserve Board in April 1987 allowed commercial bank holding companies such as J.P. Morgan & Company, the parent of Morgan Guarantee Trust Company (a commercial bank) to establish separate **Section 20** securities **affiliates** as investment banks. Currently, approximately 40 Section 20 subsidiaries have been established by bank holding companies and foreign banks, most representing the largest

Section 20 affiliate

A securities subsidiary of a bank holding company through which a banking organization can engage in investment banking activities.

---

6. A municipal general obligation bond is a bond issued by a state, city, or local government whose interest and principal payments are backed by the full faith and credit of that local government—that is, its full tax and revenue base (see Chapter 6).

7. Municipal revenue bonds are riskier than municipal GO bonds since their interest and principal are guaranteed only by the revenue from the project they finance. One example is the revenue from road tolls of a bond funding the construction of a new section of highway.

8. Of the type of issues involved, *discount brokerage* was held to be legal, since it was not viewed as being the same as *full-service brokerage* supplied by securities firms. In particular, a full-service brokerage combines both the agency function of securities purchase along with investment advice (e.g., hot tips). By contrast, discount brokers only carry out the agency function of buying and selling securities for clients; they do not give investment advice. For further discussion of these issues, see M. Clark and A. Saunders, "Judicial Interpretation of Glass-Steagall: The Need for Legislative Action," *The Banking Law Journal* 97 (1980), pp. 721–40; and "Glass-Steagall Revisited: The Impact on Banks, Capital Markets, and the Small Investor," *The Banking Law Journal* 97 (1980), pp. 811–40.

Table 14–3   Provisions of Glass-Steagall Act (1933 Banking Act)

The 1933 Glass-Steagall Act imposed rigid separation between commercial banking and investment banking with three exemptions:

  1. The underwriting of new issues of Treasury securities.
  2. The underwriting of municipal general obligations bonds.
  3. The private placements of corporate debt and equity securities.

Figure 14–2   Bank Holding Company and Its Bank and Section 20 Subsidiary

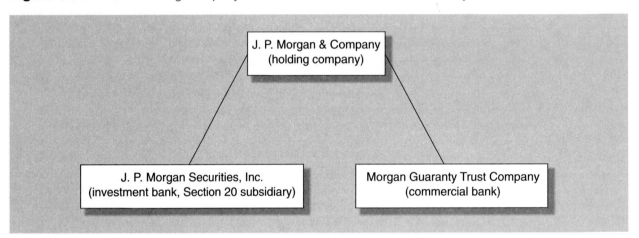

U.S. and international banking organizations in the world. Through these Section 20 affiliates, banks began to conduct all their "ineligible" or "gray area" securities activities, such as commercial paper underwriting, mortgage-backed securities underwriting, and municipal revenue bond underwriting.[9] Note the organizational structure of J.P. Morgan & Company, its bank, and its Section 20 subsidiary (or investment bank) in Figure 14–2. These Section 20 subsidiaries did not violate Section 20 of the Glass-Steagall Act, which restricted affiliations of commercial banks and investment banks, since the revenue generated from securities underwriting activities amounted to less than 5 percent (increased later to 10 percent and then 25 percent) of the total revenues generated.[10]

Significant changes occurred in 1997 as the Federal Reserve and the Office of the Comptroller of the Currency (OCC) took actions to expand bank holding companies' permitted activities. In particular, the Federal Reserve allowed commercial banks to acquire directly existing investment banks rather than establish completely new Section 20 investment banking subsidiaries.

The result was a number of mergers and acquisitions between commercial and investment banks in 1997 and 1998. Some of the largest mergers included Deutsche Bank's $9.7 billion purchase of Banker's Trust in 1999, Citicorp's $83 billion merger with Travelers Group in April 1998, Bankers Trust's April 1997 acquisition of Alex Brown for $1.7 billion, NationsBank's June 1997 $1 billion plus purchase of Montgomery Securities, U.S. Bancorp's December 1997 acquisition of Piper Jaffray for $730 million, and Bank of America's June 1997 purchase of Robert Stephens for $540

---

9. In 1989 corporate bonds and in 1990 corporate equities were added to the permitted list.

10. Legally, as long as less than 50 percent of the affiliate's revenues could be attributable to "ineligible activities," it could not be argued that the affiliate was "principally engaged in such activities"; therefore, an affiliate could not be viewed as violating Section 20 of the Glass-Steagall Act of 1933.

million. In each case, the banks stated that one motivation for their acquisition was the desire to establish a presence in the securities business since laws separating investment and commercial banking were changing. Also noted as a motivation in these acquisitions was the opportunity to expand business lines, taking advantage of economies of scale and scope to reduce overall costs and merge the customer bases of the respective commercial and investment banks involved in the acquisition.[11]

Finally, in 1999, after years of "homemade" deregulation by banks and securities firms, the U.S. Congress passed the Financial Services Modernization Act, which repealed the Glass-Steagall barriers between commercial banking and investment banking.[12] The bill, touted as the biggest change in the regulation of financial institutions in nearly 70 years, allowed for the creation of a "financial services holding company" that could engage in banking activities *and* securities underwriting. The bill also allowed large national banks to place certain activities, including some securities underwritings, in direct bank subsidiaries regulated by the Office of the Comptroller of the Currency. Thus, after nearly 70 years of partial or complete separation between investment banking and commercial banking, the Financial Services Modernization Act of 1999 opened the door for the creation of full-service financial institutions in the United States similar to those that existed in the United States pre-1933 and that exist in many other countries today. A summary of the act is provided in Appendix B to this chapter.

www.occ.treas.gov/

Banking and Insurance.   Prior to the passage of the Financial Services Modernization Act in 1999, very strong barriers restricted the entry of banks into insurance, and vice versa. One notable exception was Travelers Corp.'s acquisition of Citicorp to form Citigroup in 1998, which to some extent proved a catalyst for the eventual passage of the 1999 act. Insurance activities can be either of the property-casualty type (e.g., homeowners insurance, auto insurance) or the life/health type (e.g., term life insurance). Moreover, a distinction should be made between a bank selling insurance as an agent by selling other FIs' policies for a fee and a bank acting as an insurance underwriter and bearing the direct risk of underwriting losses itself. In general, the risks of insurance agency activities are quite low in loss potential when compared to insurance underwriting. It might also be noted that certain insurance products—for example, credit life insurance, mortgage insurance, and auto insurance—tend to have natural synergistic links to bank lending.[13]

Prior to the Financial Services Modernization Act of 1999, banks were under stringent restrictions when selling and underwriting almost every type of insurance. For example, national banks were restricted to offering credit-related life, accident, health, or unemployment insurance. Moreover, national banks could act as insurance agents only in towns of less than 5,000 people (although they could sell insurance from these offices anywhere in the United States). In addition, the Bank Holding Company Act of 1956 (and its 1970 amendments) and the Garn-St. Germain Depository Institutions Act of 1982 severely restricted bank holding companies from establishing separately capitalized insurance affiliates. Most states also took quite restrictive actions regarding the insurance activities of state-chartered banks. A few states, most notably Delaware, passed liberal laws allowing state-chartered banks to underwrite and broker various

---

11. The erosion of the product barriers between the commercial and investment banking industries has not been all one way. Large investment banks such as Merrill Lynch have increasingly sought to offer banking products. For example, in the late 1970s, Merrill Lynch created the cash management account (CMA), which allowed investors to own a money market mutual fund with check-writing privileges into which bond and stock sale proceeds could be swept on a daily basis. This account allows the investor to earn interest on cash held in a brokerage account. In addition, investment banks have been major participants as traders and investors in the secondary market for loans to less-developed countries and other loans.

12. The Financial Services Modernization Act also reduced the barriers between commercial banking, investment banking, and insurance.

13. See A. Saunders and I. Walter, *Universal Banking in the U.S.?,* for an elaboration of these arguments.

types of property-casualty and life insurance. This encouraged large bank holding companies such as Citigroup and Chase to enter Delaware and establish state-chartered banking subsidiaries with their own insurance affiliates.

One "insurance" area in which banks successfully survived legal challenges was the sale of annuities.[14] In 1986, NationsBank (which merged with BankAmerica in 1997) began selling annuities and was aggressively challenged in court by the insurance industry. In the meantime, a large number of other banks also began selling annuities. At the end of 1995, the Supreme Court upheld the legality of banks' rights to sell annuities. In its decision, the Supreme Court argued that annuities should be viewed more as investment products than insurance products. Such sales are estimated to add nearly $1 billion a year to bank profits.

Unlike banks, insurance companies are regulated solely at the state level.[15] Although few states explicitly restricted insurance companies from acquiring banks and, therefore, pursuing banking activities, banking laws have historically restricted such expansions. In particular, the Bank Holding Company Act of 1956 severely restricted insurance companies' ability to own, or to be affiliated with, full-service banks. However, as shown in In the News box 14–1, insurance companies have opened federally chartered thrifts to get around the laws restricting bank activities.

The Financial Services Modernization Act of 1999 completely changed the landscape for insurance activities as it allowed bank holding companies to open insurance underwriting affiliates and insurance companies to open commercial bank as well as securities firm affiliates through the creation of a financial service holding company. With the passage of this act banks no longer have to fight legal battles in states such as Texas and Rhode Island to overcome restrictions on their ability to sell insurance in these states. The insurance industry also applauded the act, as it forced banks that underwrite and sell insurance to operate under the same set of state regulations (pertaining to their insurance lines) as insurance companies operating in that state. Under the new act, a financial services holding company that engages in commercial banking, investment banking, and insurance activities will be functionally regulated. This means that the holding company's banking activities will be regulated by bank regulators (such as the Federal Reserve, FDIC, OCC), its securities activities will be regulated by the SEC, and its insurance activities will be regulated by up to 50 state insurance regulators.

Commercial Banking and Commerce. Although the direct holdings of other firms' equity by national banks has been constrained since 1863, the restrictions on the commercial activities of bank holding companies are a more recent phenomena. In particular, the 1970 amendments to the 1956 Bank Holding Company Act required bank holding companies to divest themselves of nonbank-related subsidiaries over a 10-year period following the amendment. When Congress passed the amendments, bank holding companies owned approximately 3,500 commercial sector subsidiaries ranging from public utilities to transportation and manufacturing firms. Nevertheless, bank holding companies today can still hold up to 4.9 percent of the voting shares in any commercial firm without regulatory approval.[16]

The 1956 Bank Holding Company Act has also effectively restricted acquisitions of banks by commercial firms (as was true for insurance companies before 1999). The

---

14. An annuity is a life insurance contract that provides a stated periodic payment to the annuity holder until death in exchange for a sum of money paid prior to the start of the annuity period.

15. This state level of regulation was reaffirmed by the McCarran-Ferguson Act of 1945. For an excellent discussion of the background to this act, see K. J. Meier. *The Political Economy of Regulation: The Case of Insurance* (Albany, NY: State University of New York Press, 1988).

16. The Bank Holding Company Act defines *control* as a holding company's equity stake in a subsidiary bank or affiliate that exceeds 25 percent.

In the News

14-1

Banks See 16,000-Branch Rival As State Farm Gets Thrift Charter

With plans to become a retail banking powerhouse, State Farm Mutual Automobile Insurance Co. won government approval Thursday to charter a federal thrift. The decision has the potential to reshape the banking industry's competitive landscape and affect congressional debate over financial reform.

"There is a danger of creating a parallel banking system that would be less regulated," said James D. Mclaughlin, director of regulatory and trust affairs at the American Bankers Association. "This more prosperous, less regulated part of the banking system will thrive and flourish and eventually starve out the more regulated traditional banking system."

Jeff Rodman, executive vice president of the Illinois Bankers Association, said, "Congress is going to have to decide quickly what it wants the financial services industry to look like because, while they debate, it is changing without them." Community bankers have been bracing for this ap-

Source: *American Banker,* November 13, 1998, p. 1, by David Harrison.

proval since July 1997, when State Farm filed its charter application with the Office of Thrift Supervision. Though many other insurance companies are seeking thrift charters, State Farm is the biggest and the first to pursue a retail strategy.

State Farm—the nation's largest property and casualty insurer, with 66.2 million policies outstanding—plans to offer the gamut of consumer deposit and loan products, from market accounts and certificates of deposit to auto loans and mortgages. State Farm Financial Services, the newly chartered thrift, plans to market these products through the insurer's network of 16,000 sales offices, which would become the functional equivalent of banking branch offices . . .

James P. Ghiglieri, president of $125 million-asset Alpha Community Bank, Toluca, Ill., will go head-to-head with State Farm. Operating about 30 miles north of Bloomington, Mr.

Ghiglieri said he expects the competition to be tough. But he is more worried about how the new thrift will be regulated. "I have a hard time believing the OTS can possibly regulate something as large as State Farm, with literally tens of thousands of what amounts to branches out there. "Agents do not have experience dealing with issues such as Truth-in-Lending and Truth-in-Savings," he said. "It all sounds good on paper, but what is going to happen when something goes wrong?"

James T. Ashworth, President and chief executive officer of $250 million-asset Carlinville (Ill.) National Bank Shares, operates about 90 miles from Bloomington. "We have a big problem with this," he said. The OTS decision could push Congress to enact financial reform—or not.

Jeffrey A. Myers, assistant vice president for public affairs at the Independent Insurance Agents of America, said he expects the ruling to encourage Congress to pass reform before more non-banks get charters. "This will put more pressure on Congress to enact and

(continues)

In the News continued

lay out the framework for an integrated financial services industry," he said.

But Marty Farmer, a lobbyist for the Independent

Bankers Association of America, said insurers will be less likely to support financial reform. "This diminishes the prospect for

financial reform because it lets an insurance company into the banking business without the need for a bill," he said.

nonbank bank

A bank divested of its commercial loans and/or its demand deposits.

major vehicle for a commercial firm's entry into commercial banking has been through **nonbank banks** or nonbank financial service firms that offer banking-type services by divesting a subsidiary "bank" of its commercial loans and/or its demand deposits (as well as any deposit insurance coverage).

Nonbank Financial Service Firms and Commerce. In comparison with the barriers separating banking and either securities, insurance, or commercial sector activities, the barriers among nonbank financial service firms and commercial firms have traditionally been less stringent. For example, in recent years, nonbank financial service firms and commercial firms have faced fewer barriers to entering into and exiting from various areas of nonbank finance service activity. For example, as the initial loopholes were opened, and in anticipation of a complete breakdown of Glass-Steagall barriers to the underwriting of securities, Travelers Group undertook a $9 billion acquisition of Salomon Brothers in 1997, one year after acquiring Smith Barney. Various major nonbank financial service acquisitions and divestitures since 1990 have occurred, many involving commercial firms such as Sears Roebuck, Xerox, and Gulf and Western. Table 14–4 shows some of the major acquisitions and divestitures.

Finally, the passage of the Financial Services Modernization Act of 1999 has standardized the relationship between financial services sectors (commercial banking, insurance, investment banking) and commerce. Specifically, a financial services holding company is now defined as holding a minimum of 85 percent of its assets in financial assets (i.e., a maximum of 15 percent in commercial sector or real assets). Any nonfinancial assets (activities) exceeding the maximum are grandfathered for at least 10 years (with a possible additional 5-year extension). Eventually, however, many financial service firms may have to sell off (divest) real sector assets and activities.

Geographic Expansion in the U.S. Depository Institutions Industry

Geographic expansions can have a number of dimensions. In particular, they can be (1) domestic, (2) within a state or region, or (3) international (participating in a foreign market). Expansions can also be carried out by opening a new office or branch or by acquiring another

Do You Understand?

1. The rationale for the passage of the Glass-Steagall Act in 1933? What permissible underwriting activities did it identify for commercial banks?

2. Why a 5 percent rather than a 50 percent maximum ceiling was originally imposed on the revenues earned from the eligible underwriting activities of a Section 20 subsidiary?

3. Why a bank that currently specializes in making consumer loans but makes no commercial loans qualifies as a nonbank bank?

4. How the provisions of the National Bank Act of 1863 affected the participation of national banks in establishing nonbank subsidiaries?

5. How the Financial Services Modernization Act of 1999 has opened the doors for the establishment of full-service financial institutions in the United States?

6. How the range of product activities permitted U.S. commercial banks compares to that of banks in other major industrialized countries?

Table 14–4 Selected Nonbank Financial Service Industry Divestitures and Acquisitions Since 1990

Insurance Services

National Organization of Life, Health Guarantee Associations acquires Executive Life
Primerica acquires 27 percent of Travelers
Sears divests itself of Allstate
American Express divests itself of American Express Life
Prudential divests itself of Prudential Reinsurance
Transamerica divests itself (through an IPO) of Transamerica Insurance Group
Aetna divests itself of Aetna Life & Casualty
AXA acquires Equitable Insurance
Unum acquires Colonial
Penn Central acquires National
Met Life acquires United Mutual
Reliance Life acquires GECC
American International Group of New York merges with SunAmerica

Consumer Finance Services

Gulf & Western Finance acquires Capitol Finance
Associates acquires First Family
Associates acquires Allied
Beneficial Mortgage closed
Sears divests itself of Coldwell Banker
Paine Webber divests itself of Paine Webber Mortgage
Primerica acquires Landmark
Primerica sells Margaretten
Household International acquires Beneficial Corp.
Citicorp acquires AT&T Universal Card
First Union acquires The Money Store

Investment Services

Gregg Mason acquires Fairchild
Franklin merges with Templeton
Kemper sells its Securities Division
Primerica acquires Shearson
Sears divests itself of Dean Witter
Weyerhauser sells its Annuities Division
Dun & Bradstreet acquires Gratner Group
Mellon Bank acquires Dreyfus
American Express spins off Lehman Brothers
Dean Witter merges with Morgan Stanley
BankAmerica acquires Robertson Stephens
NationsBank acquires Montgomery Securities
Bankers Trust NY acquires Alex Brown
U.S. Bancorp acquires Piper Jaffray
Travelers Group acquires Smith Barney
Travelers Group acquires Salomon Brothers
KeyCorp acquires McDonald & Company Investments
BankAmerica divests itself of Robertson Stephens
Bank of Boston acquires Robertson Stephens
Citicorp merges with Travelers Group

de novo office

A newly established office.

depository institution. Historically, in the United States, the ability of depository institutions to expand domestically has been constrained by regulation. By comparison, no special regulations inhibit the ability of commercial firms such as General Motors, IBM, or Sears from establishing new or **de novo offices,** factories, or branches anywhere in the country. Nor are such companies generally prohibited from acquiring other firms—as long as they are not banks. Depository institutions have faced a complex and changing network of rules and regulations covering geographic expansions. Such regulations may inhibit expansions, but they may also create potential opportunities to increase a depository institution's returns. In particular, regulations may create locally uncompetitive markets with high economic rents that new entrants can potentially exploit. Thus, for the most innovative depository institutions, regulation can provide profit opportunities as well as costs. As a result, regulation acts both as an inhibitor and an incentive to engage in geographic expansions.

Regulatory Factors Impacting Geographic Expansion

unit bank

A bank with a single office.

Restrictions on Intrastate Banking by Commercial Banks.   At the beginning of the 20th century, most U.S. banks were **unit banks** with a single office. Improving communications and customer needs resulted in a rush to branching in the first two decades of the 20th century. This movement ran into increasing opposition from the smallest unit banks and the largest money center banks. The smallest unit banks perceived a competitive threat to their retail business from the larger branching banks; money center banks feared a loss of valuable correspondent business such as check-clearing and other payment services. As a result, several states restricted banks' ability to branch within the state. Indeed, some states prohibited intrastate (or within state) branching per se, effectively constraining a bank to unit bank status. Over the years and in a very piecemeal fashion, states have liberalized their restrictions on within-state branching. As of 1997, only six states had laws that restricted *intrastate* banking, usually limiting banks to setting up branches in counties bordering the county in which the bank's head office is established.

Restrictions on Interstate Banking by Commercial Banks.   Historically, the defining piece of legislation affecting interstate branching was the McFadden Act, passed in 1927 and amended in 1933. The McFadden Act and its amendments restricted nationally chartered banks' branching abilities to the same extent allowed to state chartered banks, which essentially prevented all U.S. banks from branching across state lines. Given the McFadden prohibition on interstate branching, bank organizations expanding across state lines between 1927 and 1956 relied on establishing subsidiaries rather than branches. Some of the largest banking organizations established **multibank holding companies** for this purpose. A multibank holding company (MBHC) is a parent company that acquires more than one bank as a direct subsidiary (e.g., First Interstate).

multibank holding company (MBHC)

A parent banking organization that owns a number of individual bank subsidiaries.

grandfathered subsidiaries

Subsidiaries established prior to the passage of a restrictive law and not subject to that law.

one-bank holding company

A parent banking organization that owns one bank subsidiary and nonbank subsidiaries.

In 1956, Congress recognized the potential loophole to interstate banking posed by the MBHC movement and passed the Douglas Amendment to the Bank Holding Company Act. This act permitted MBHCs to acquire bank subsidiaries only to the extent allowed by the laws of the state in which the proposed bank target resided. Any MBHCs with out-of-state subsidiaries established prior to 1956 were **grandfathered subsidiaries**; that is, MBHCs were allowed to keep them. (One such example was First Interstate.) The passage of the 1956 Douglas Amendment did not close all potential interstate banking loopholes. Because the amendment pertained to MBHC acquisitions, it still left open the potential for **one-bank holding company** (OBHC) geographic extensions. An OBHC is a parent bank holding company that has a single bank subsidiary and a number of other nonbank financial subsidiaries. By creating an OBHC and establishing across state lines various nonbank subsidiaries that sell financial services such as consumer finance, leasing, and data processing, a bank could almost replicate an out-of-state banking presence.

In 1970, Congress again acted, recognizing that bankers had creatively innovated yet another loophole to interstate banking restrictions. The 1970 Bank Holding Company Act Amendments effectively restricted the nonbank activities that an OBHC could engage in to those "closely related to banking," as defined by the Federal Reserve under Section 4(c)(8) of the act. Thus, the year 1970 and the passage of the Bank Holding Company Act Amendments were probably the low point of interstate banking in the United States.

Riegle-Neal Interstate Banking and Branching Efficiency Act of 1994. It has long been recognized that the expansion of nationwide banking through multibank holding companies is potentially far more expensive than through branching. Separate corporations and boards of directors must be established for each bank in an MBHC, and it is hard to achieve the same level of economic and financial integration and synergies as is possible with branches. Moreover, most major banking competitor countries outside of the United States such as Japan, Germany, France, and the United Kingdom, have nationwide branching.

In the fall of 1994, the U.S. Congress passed an interstate banking law that allowed U.S. and foreign banks to branch interstate by consolidating out-of-state bank subsidiaries into a branch network and/or by acquiring banks or individual branches of banks through acquisition or merger. (The effective beginning date for these new branching powers was June 1, 1997.) Although the act was silent on the ability of banks to establish de novo branches in other states—essentially leaving it to individual states to pass laws allowing de novo branching—it is possible under the Riegle-Neal Act for a New York bank such as Chase to purchase, as an example, a single branch of Bank of America in San Francisco. To date, the most common approach to interstate branching has been to allow branching through acquisition and merger. Many states have barred de novo interstate branching by out-of-state banks.[17] States that bar de novo branching also have tended to prohibit the acquisition of individual in-state branches, preferring to require the out-of-state institutions to acquire an entire bank (and hence branch network). States were also given the opportunity to "opt out" of interstate banking. Only Montana (until 2001) has decided to opt out. Many other states opted to adopt interstate banking even before the June 1997 date. The passage of the Riegle-Neal Act is a major reason for the current merger wave (and increased consolidation) in U.S. banking. The result of the Riegle-Neal Act is that full interstate banking is becoming a reality in the United States.

www.ots.treas.gov/

Savings Institutions. A savings institution's ability to branch or expand geographically—whether intrastate (within a state) or interstate (between states)—was under the power of the Federal Home Loan Bank Board until 1989. Since 1989, the Office of Thrift Supervision has regulated the ability to branch as part of the 1989 Financial Institutions Reform, Recovery, and Enforcement Act (FIRREA) legislation. Generally, the policy historically had prohibited a federally chartered savings institution from branching across state lines. In the 1980s, a considerable loosening of these restrictions occurred. Both the Garn-St. Germain Act of 1982 and FIRREA allowed sound banks and savings institutions to acquire failing savings institutions across state lines and to run them either as separate subsidiaries or convert them into branches. For example, the Resolution Trust Corporation (RTC), which was established under FIRREA to resolve failing savings institutions (it finished its job in 1995), had wide-ranging powers to enable out-of-state acquisitions of failing

Do You Understand?

1. The difference between the interstate banking restrictions imposed under the 1956 Bank Holding Company Act and those passed under the 1970 Amendments to the Bank Holding Company Act?
2. How the Riegle-Neal Act affected geographic expansion opportunities of banks?

17. The reason for the restriction on de novo branching is to protect small community banks' franchise values. If branching can be accomplished only by acquisition, the franchise values of small banks will be higher than when larger banks have the option to branch de novo.

savings institutions to lower the costs of failure resolution. Thus, the RTC allowed banks to acquire savings institutions and convert them into branches, overriding state laws in Colorado, New Mexico, and Arkansas. The RTC also allowed banks to acquire a savings institution in another state, eroding barriers to geographic expansion for this class of DIs.

History of Bank and Savings Institution <u>Guarantee Funds</u>

A key component of the regulatory structure of DIs is deposit insurance and financial guarantees provided to depositors of DIs by regulators. This section describes the history of such insurance guarantees, as well as their current structure.

FDIC

www.fdic.gov/

The FDIC was created in 1933 in the wake of the banking panics of 1930–1933 to maintain the stability of, and public confidence in, the U.S. financial system. Over the period 1933–1979, the FDIC insurance system seemed to work well, failures were few (see Figure 14–3), and the FDIC insurance fund grew in size. Beginning in 1980, however, the number of bank failures increased, with more than 1,039 in the decade ending in 1990 (peaking at 221 in 1988). This number of failures was actually higher than that in the entire 1933–1979 period. Moreover, the costs of each of these failures were often larger than those of the mainly small bank failures that occurred in the 1933–1979 period. As the number and costs of these failures mounted in the 1980s, the FDIC fund was rapidly drained. In response to this crisis, Congress passed the FDIC Improvement Act (FDICIA) in December 1991 to restructure the bank insurance fund and to prevent its potential insolvency.

Since 1991, the fund's finances have dramatically improved and bank failures have decreased significantly, partially in response to record bank profit levels as a result of a very strong U.S. economy (see Chapter 11). Specifically, in 1999, the FDIC's Bank Insurance Fund (BIF) had reserves of $29.8 billion, and there was only one bank

Figure 14–3   Number of Failed Banks by Year, 1934–1999

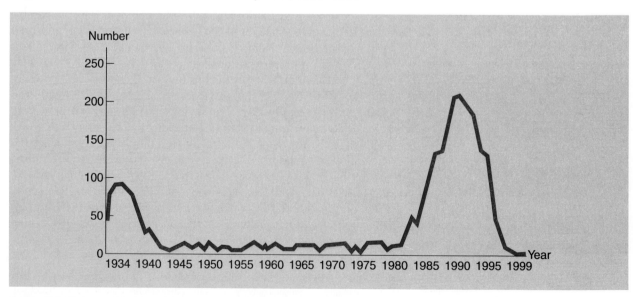

Source: "BIF Closings and Assistance Transactions," various years, FDIC. *www.fdic.gov/*

failure in 1997, three in 1998, and five in 1999. The fund's reserves now stand at a record high and exceed 1.40 percent of insured bank deposits.[18] As a result of the burgeoning size of the insurance fund, the industry's excellent health, and the economy's strength, the FDIC has assigned a 0 percent annual insurance premium to the nation's safest BIF insured banks (over 90 percent of all banks).[19]

The Federal Savings and Loan Insurance Corporation and Its Demise

The Federal Savings and Loan Insurance Corporation (FSLIC) insured the deposits of savings institutions from 1934 to 1989. Like the FDIC, this insurance fund was in relatively good shape until the end of the 1970s. Beginning in 1980, its resources began to be depleted as more and more savings institutions failed. Between 1980 and 1988, 514 savings institutions failed, at an estimated cost of $42.3 billion. By 1989, the FSLIC fund had been depleted and the present value of its liabilities exceeded that of its assets. Lacking the resources to close or resolve failing savings institutions, the FSLIC followed a policy of forbearance (or leniency) toward remaining weak and failing savings institutions. This meant that it allowed many badly run savings institutions to stay open and continue to accumulate losses.

In August 1989, Congress passed the Financial Institutions Reform, Recovery, and Enforcement Act (FIRREA), largely in response to the deepening crisis in the savings institution industry and the growing insolvency of the FSLIC. This act restructured the savings bank fund and transferred its management to the FDIC.[20] At the same time, the restructured savings bank insurance fund was renamed the Savings Association Insurance Fund (SAIF). Currently, the FDIC manages the SAIF separately from the commercial bank fund, which is now called the Bank Insurance Fund (BIF). At the end of 1999, SAIF had $9.1 billion in reserves, representing 1.29 percent of insured deposits, and no savings institution has failed in the four-year period 1996–1999. Like BIF-insured banks, the safest SAIF-insured institutions currently pay no insurance premiums. See Figure 14–4 for the organizational structure of FDIC and the number of depository institutions insured by the BIF and SAIF funds. As discussed in In the News box 14–2, it is highly likely that the two insurance funds will soon be combined into one.

Do You Understand?

1. What the arguments in favor of the merger of the BIF and SAIF are?

Causes of the Depository Fund Insolvencies

There are at least two views as to why depository institution insurance funds experienced extreme financial problems in the 1980s. In addition, some factors offer better explanations of the FSLIC insolvency than the FDIC near-insolvency, especially because the FSLIC insolvency was far worse than the financial problems of the FDIC fund.

The Financial Environment. One view is that a number of external events or shocks adversely impacted U.S. banks and savings institutions in the 1980s. The first of these was the dramatic rise in interest rates during the period 1979–1982. This rise in rates had a major negative effect on those savings institutions funding long-term, fixed-rate mortgages with short-term deposits (see Chapter 12). The second event was the collapse in oil, real estate, and other commodity prices, which particularly harmed oil, gas, and agricultural loans in the southwestern United States. The third event was

---

18. The target size for the fund's reserves has been 1.25 percent of insured deposits.

19. The 1999 failure of First National Bank of Keystone, however, created the biggest loss to the BIF ($700 million) since the early 1990s.

20. At that time, the FSLIC ceased to exist.

Figure 14–4   The Structure of FDIC, BIF, and SAIF in 1999

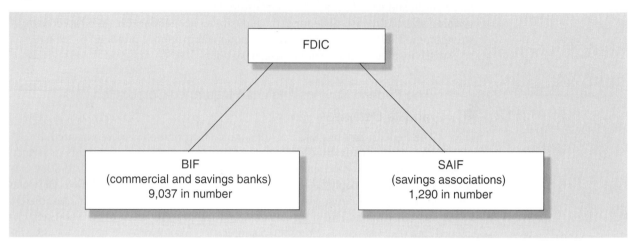

Source: FDIC, *Statistics on Banking,* Second Quarter 1999. *www.fdic.gov/*

the increased financial service firm competition at home and abroad, which eroded the value of bank and savings institution charters during the 1980s. We discussed these events in detail in Chapters 11 and 12.

Moral Hazard.   An alternative view is that these financial environment effects were catalysts for, rather than the causes of, the crisis. At the heart of the crisis was deposit insurance itself, especially some of its contractual features. Although deposit insurance had deterred depositors and other liability holders from engaging in major withdrawals of deposits or "deposit runs" over the 1933–1980 period, in so doing it had also removed or reduced depositor discipline. By guaranteeing or insuring depositors against losses on bank failure, deposit insurance allowed banks to borrow at rates close to the risk-free rate and, if they chose, to undertake high-risk, high-return asset investments. Bank owners, willing to incur the risk, reaped the higher returns if these investments paid off as expected. Bank owners and managers knew that insured depositors had little incentive to restrict such risky behavior, either by withdrawing funds or by requiring risk premia on deposit rates, since they were fully insured by the FDIC if the bank failed. Moreover, uninsured depositors were protected by the fact that failing banks were usually bailed out or merged (purchased and assumed) with a safe bank.[21] Given this scenario, losses on oil, gas, and real estate loans in the 1980s are viewed as the outcome of bankers' exploiting underpriced or mispriced risk under the deposit insurance contract. The provision of insurance that encourages rather than discourages risk taking is called **moral hazard.** This is because with deposit insurance a highly levered bank, whose creditors need not monitor the bank's (borrower's) actions, has a tremendous incentive to take excessive risks in its investment (e.g., loan granting) activities.[22]

In the absence of depositor discipline, regulators could have controlled bankers' risk taking by charging either explicit deposit insurance premiums linked to bank risk

moral hazard

The loss exposure an insurer faces when providing insurance encourages the insured to take more risks.

---

21. Specifically, the FDIC guaranteed small deposits up to $100,000 while large depositors often were protected as well by the FDIC policy of merging failing banks with safe banks. The latter policy was particularly evident for the largest troubled banks and has been called a "too big to fail" or TBTF policy.

22. The precise definition of *moral hazard* is the loss exposure of an insurer (the FDIC) that results from the behavioral incentive created for the insured (here, the bank).

In the News

14-2

OTS Backs Merger of Bank and Thrift Insurance Funds

Supporters of merging the Bank Insurance Fund and the Savings Association Insurance Fund have a strong ally in the Office of Thrift Supervision (OTS), which oversees the majority of institutions insured by the SAIF. A congressional subcommittee will hear testimony on the subject next week, and OTS Director Ellen S. Seidman says her agency will file a written statement in favor of merging the funds. "It is time," she said in an interview last week. "At this point, the SAIF no longer has any real independent identity."

The thrift fund was established in 1989 to insure the assets of thrifts that survived the S&L crisis of the late 1980s. But mergers among banks and thrifts accelerated in the 1990s, and the thrift fund's mission became less clear. Thrift deposits bought by banks continue to be insured by the fund, even if the institution that originally accepted the deposit ceased to exist.

Just over half of the deposits insured by the thrift fund are held by institutions regulated by the OTS, Ms. Seidman said. National banks hold 22% of SAIF-insured deposits, state-chartered banks hold 16%, and FDIC-supervised state savings banks hold 8%. Roughly 15% of the deposits insured by the Bank Insurance Fund are held by thrifts. "There is no longer any meaningful differentiation between the funds," Ms. Seidman said.

A merger also makes sense from a risk management perspective, she argued. "If there is anything insurers hate, it's a concentration of risk." For instance, Bank of America Corp. holds approximately 8.67% of all deposits insured by the bank fund, while Washington Mutual Inc. holds a similar percentage of deposits insured by the thrift fund. Merging the funds would reduce Bank of America's stake to about 6%. Washington Mutual's share would fall to 2%.

Source: *American Banker*, February 7, 2000, p. 4, by Rob Garver.

www.americanbanker.com/

---

implicit premiums

Deposit insurance premiums or costs imposed on a bank through activity constraints rather than direct monetary changes.

taking or **implicit premiums** through increased monitoring and restrictions on the risky activities of banks. This potentially could have substituted for depositor discipline (i.e., those banks that took more risk would have paid directly or indirectly for this risk-taking behavior). However, from 1933 until January 1, 1993, regulators based deposit insurance premiums on the amount or size of (domestic) deposits that a bank held rather than the risk of loss on its assets. The decade of the 1980s was also a period of deregulation, and the number of bank and savings institution examiners actually fell.[23] Finally, prompt corrective action and closure for undercapitalized banks did not begin until the end of 1992 (see below).

23. For example, L. J. White points to a general weakness of savings institution supervision and examination in the 1980s. The number of examinations fell from 3,210 in 1980 to 2,347 in 1984 and examinations per billion dollars of assets from 5.41 in 1980 to 2.4 in 1984. See L. J. White, The S and L Debacle (New York: Oxford University Press, 1991), p. 89.

Non-U.S. Deposit Insurance Systems

Most European countries have historically operated without explicit deposit insurance programs. Despite this, European countries have not seen the 1930s type of bank run and panic experienced in the United States. In respect to our earlier discussion of the moral hazard problem, the question of how this can happen arises. The answer is that European governments have often given implicit deposit guarantees at no cost to the largest banks in their countries. This has been possible as the result of the higher degree of concentration of deposits among the largest banks in European countries. However, deposit insurance systems are being increasingly adopted worldwide. One view of this trend toward implementation of explicit deposit programs is that governments are now simply collecting premiums as a fee to offset an obligation (implicit deposit insurance) that they previously offered for free.

Many of these systems offer quite different degrees of protection to depositors compared to the U.S. system. For example, in response to the single banking and capital market in Europe, the European Union (EU) has established a single deposit insurance system covering all EU-located banks. This insures deposit accounts up to 20,000 euros (approximately $20,000). However, depositors are subject to a 10 percent deductible (loss) to create incentives for them to monitor banks. The idea underlying the EU plan is to create a level playing field for banks across all European Union countries.

> **Do You Understand?**
>
> 1. What events led Congress to pass the FDICIA?
> 2. What events brought about the demise of the FSLIC?
> 3. The two basic views offered to explain the financial problems of depository institution insurance funds during the 1980s?
> 4. Why interest rate risk was less of a problem for banks than for savings institutions in the early 1980s?

Balance Sheet Regulations

A further form of regulation of DIs pertains to various assets and liabilities on their balance sheets.

Regulations on Depository Institution Liquidity

Holding relatively small amounts of liquid assets exposes a DI to increased illiquidity and insolvency risk. Excessive illiquidity can result in a DI's inability to meet required payments on liability claims (such as deposit withdrawals) and, at the extreme, its insolvency. Moreover, it can even lead to contagious effects that negatively impact other DIs. Consequently, regulators have often imposed minimum liquid asset reserve requirements on DIs. In general, these requirements differ in nature and scope for various DIs and even according to country. The requirements depend on the illiquidity risk exposure perceived for the DI's type and other regulatory objectives that relate to minimum liquid asset requirements (see Chapter 4). Currently, in accordance with Federal Reserve Regulation D, banks in the United States are required to hold the following "target" minimum reserves against net transaction accounts (transaction accounts minus demand deposit balances due from U.S. depository institutions and cash items in process of collection):[24]

Less than $5.0 million	0%
$5.0 million–$44.3 million	3
More than $44.3 million	10

---

24. The Garn-St. Germain Depository Institutions Act of 1982 (Public Law 97–320) requires that $2 million of reservable liabilities of each depository institution be subject to a zero percent reserve requirement. Each year, the Federal Reserve adjusts the amount of reservable liabilities subject to this zero percent reserve requirement for the succeeding calendar year by 80 percent of the percentage increase in the total reservable liabilities of all depository institutions, measured on an annual basis as of June 30. In 1999, this figure was $4.9 million. As of 2000 these were the requirements. The reserve was also reduced from 12 to 10 percent for transaction accounts in April 1992.

In Appendix C, we discuss the details of how to calculate the minimum reserve requirement for a bank.

Regulations on Capital Adequacy (Leverage)

The FDICIA of 1991 requires banks and thrifts to adopt essentially the same (minimum) capital requirements relative to their assets. Some minor differences exist, but the capital requirements for the two industries have essentially converged.[25] A minimum capital ratio effectively constrains the leverage of a DI—since highly leveraged DIs may be more prone to credit, interest rate, and other shocks, and thus, to the risk of failure. Given this, we concentrate on the recent evolution of capital requirements in commercial banking. Since 1987, U.S. commercial banks have faced two different capital requirements: a capital-to-assets ratio and a risk–based capital ratio that is subdivided into a Tier I capital risk–based ratio and a total capital (Tier I plus Tier II capital) risk–based ratio.

The Capital-to-Assets Ratio.   The **capital-to-assets ratio** measures the ratio of a bank's book value of primary or core capital to the book value of its assets. The lower this ratio, the more highly leveraged the bank is. Primary or core capital is a bank's common equity (book value) plus qualifying cumulative perpetual preferred stock plus minority interests in equity accounts of consolidated subsidiaries.

With the passage of the FDICIA of 1991, a bank's capital adequacy is assessed according to where its capital-to-assets (C), or leverage ratio, places it in one of five target zones listed in the Leverage Ratio column of Table 14–5. The capital-to-assets or leverage ratio is:

$$C = \frac{\text{Core capital}}{\text{Assets}}$$

If a bank's capital-to-assets ratio is 5 percent or higher, it is well capitalized. At 4 percent or more, it is adequately capitalized; at less than 4 percent, it is undercapitalized; at less than 3 percent, it is significantly undercapitalized; and at 2 percent or less, it is critically undercapitalized. Since 1995, less than 0.5 percent of the banking industry assets have been classified as undercapitalized. This compares to 31.3 percent undercapitalized in the fourth quarter of 1990 (i.e., during the 1989–1991 recession). Associated with each zone is a mandatory set of actions as well as a set of discretionary actions for regulators to take. Collectively, these are called "prompt corrective action," or PCA. The idea here is to enforce minimum capital requirements and to limit a regulator's ability to show forbearance to the worst capitalized banks.

Since December 18, 1992, under the FDICIA legislation, regulators must take specific actions—**prompt corrective action** (PCA)—when a bank falls outside zone 1, or the well-capitalized category. If prompt corrective actions are insufficient to save the bank, a receiver must be appointed when a bank's book value of capital-to-assets (leverage) ratio falls to 2 percent or lower.[26] Thus, receivership is mandatory even before the book value ratio falls to 0 percent.

Unfortunately, the leverage ratio as a measure of capital "adequacy" has three problems:

1. **Market Value**—Even if a bank is closed when its leverage ratio falls to 2 percent or less, a 2 percent book capital-to-assets ratio could be consistent with a massive negative market value net worth (i.e., the liquidation value of the bank's assets is

---

capital-to-assets ratio

Ratio of an FI's core capital to its assets.

---

prompt corrective action

Mandatory action that regulators must take as a bank's capital ratio falls.

---

25. Credit Unions are subject to capital adequacy requirements similar to commercial banks, as required by the National Credit Union Administration (NCUA).

26. Admittedly, managers and stockholders might exploit a number of loopholes and delaying tactics, especially through the courts

Table 14–5   Specifications of Capital Categories for Prompt Corrective Action

Zone	(1) Leverage Ratio		(2) Total Risk-Based Ratio		(3) Tier I Risk-Based Ratio		Capital Directive/ Other
1. Well capitalized	5% or above	and	10% or above	and	6% or above	and	Not subject to a capital directive to meet a specific level for any capital measure
2. Adequately capitalized	4% or above*	and	8% or above	and	4% or above	and	Does not meet the definition of well capitalized
3. Undercapitalized	Under 4%†	or	Under 8%	or	Under 4%		
4. Significantly undercapitalized	Under 3%	or	Under 6%	or	Under 4%		
5. Critically undercapitalized	2% or less	or	2% or less	or	2% or less		

*3 percent or higher for banks and savings associations that are not experiencing or anticipating significant growth.

†Under 3 percent for composite one-rated banks and savings associations that are not experiencing or anticipating significant growth.

Source: Federal Reserve Board of Governors, September 10, 1993. *www.bog.frb.fed.us/*

less than the market value of its liabilities). There is no assurance that depositors and regulators (including taxpayers) are adequately protected against losses.[27]

2. **Asset Risk**—by taking total assets as the denominator of the leverage or capital-to-assets ratio, it fails to consider, even partially, the different credit and interest rate risks of the assets that comprise total assets.

3. **Off-Balance-Sheet Activities**—despite the massive growth in banks' off-balance-sheet activities and their associated risks (see Chapters 11 and 20), the leverage or capital-to-assets ratio does not consider these activities.

Risk-Based Capital Ratios.   Considering the weaknesses of the simple capital-to-assets ratio just described above, in 1988 U.S. bank regulators formally agreed with other member countries of the Bank for International Settlements (BIS) to implement two new risk-based capital ratios for all commercial banks under their jurisdiction. The BIS phased in and fully implemented these risk-based capital ratios on January 1, 1993, under what has become known as the **Basel** (or **Basle**) **Accord.**

Regulators currently enforce the Basel Accord's risk-based capital ratios as well as the traditional capital-to-assets ratio. Unlike the simple capital-to-assets ratio, the calculation of the two risk-based capital adequacy measures is quite complex. Their major innovation is to distinguish among the size of the different credit risks of assets on the balance sheet and to identify the credit risk inherent in instruments off the balance sheet by using a risk-adjusted assets denominator in these capital adequacy ratios. In a very rough fashion, these capital ratios mark to market a bank's on- and off-balance-sheet positions to reflect its credit risk exposure.

Capital.   A bank's capital is divided into Tier I and Tier II. Tier I capital is primary or core capital; Tier II capital is supplementary capital. The total capital that the bank holds is defined as the sum of Tier I and Tier II capital. The definitions of Tier I core capital and Tier II supplementary capital are shown in Table 14–6.

www.bis.org/

Basel (or Basle) Accord

An agreement that requires the imposition of risk-based capital ratios on banks in major industrialized countries.

[27]Many savings institutions that were closed with low book capital values in the 1980s had negative net worths on a market value basis exceeding 30 percent.

Table 14–6   Summary Definition of Qualifying Capital for Bank Holding Companies Using Year-End 1992 Standards

Components	Minimum Requirements after Transition Period
Core-capital (Tier I)	Must equal or exceed 4 percent of weighted-risk assets
Common stockholders' equity	No limit
Qualifying cumulative and noncumulative perpetual preferred stock	Limited to 25 percent of the sum of common stock, minority interests, and qualifying perpetual preferred stock
Minority interest in equity accounts of consolidated subsidiaries	Organizations should avoid using minority interests to introduce elements not otherwise qualifying for Tier I capital
Less: Goodwill[*]	
Supplementary capital (Tier II)	Total of Tier II limited to 100 percent of Tier I[†]
Allowance for loan and lease losses	Limited to 1.25 percent of weighted-risk assets
Perpetual preferred stock	No limit within Tier II
Hybrid capital instruments, perpetual debt, and mandatory convertible securities	No limit within Tier II
Subordinated debt and intermediate-term preferred stock (original weighted-average maturity of five years or more)	Subordinated debt and intermediate-term preferred stock are limited to 50 percent of Tier I; amortized for capital purposes as they approach maturity[†]
Revaluation reserves (equity and buildings)	Not included; organizations encouraged to disclose; may be evaluated on a case-by-case basis for international comparisons; considered in making an overall assessment of capitalization
Deductions (from sum of Tier I and Tier II)	
Investments in unconsolidated subsidiaries	
Reciprocal holdings of banking organizations' capital securities	As a general rule, one-half of the aggregate investments would be deducted from Tier I capital and one-half from Tier II capital[‡]
Other deductions (such as other subsidiaries or joint ventures) as determined by supervisory authority	On a case-by-case basis or as a matter of policy after formal rule making
Total capital (Tier I + Tier II − deductions)	Must equal or exceed 8 percent of weighted-risk assets

[*]Goodwill on the books of bank holding companies before March 12, 1988, would be grandfathered for the transition period.

[†]Amounts in excess of limitations are permitted but do not qualify as capital.

[‡]A proportionately larger amount may be deducted from Tier I capital if the risks associated with the subsidiary so warrant.

Source: Federal Reserve Board of Governors, Press Release, January 1989, Attachment II. *www.bog.frb.fed.us/*

Tier I Capital.   Tier I capital is closely linked to a bank's book value of equity reflecting the concept of the core capital contribution of a bank's owners.[28] Basically, it includes the book value of common equity plus an amount of perpetual (nonmaturing) preferred stock plus minority equity interests held by the bank in subsidiaries minus goodwill. Goodwill is an accounting item that reflects the amount a bank pays above market value when it purchases or acquires other banks or subsidiaries.

Tier II Capital.   Tier II capital is a broad array of secondary capital resources. It includes a bank's loan loss reserves up to a maximum of 1.25 percent of risk-adjusted assets plus various convertible and subordinated debt instruments with maximum caps.

Risk-Adjusted Assets.   Risk-adjusted assets represent the denominator of the risk-based capital ratio. Two components comprise **risk-adjusted assets**: (1) risk adjusted on-balance-sheet assets, and (2) risk adjusted off-balance-sheet assets.

risk-adjusted assets

On- and off-balance-sheet assets whose value is adjusted for approximate credit risk.

28. However, loan loss reserves are assigned to Tier II capital because they often reflect losses that have already occurred rather than losses or insolvency risks that may occur in the future.

total risk-based capital ratio

The ratio of a DI's total capital to its risk-adjusted assets.

tier I (core) capital ratio

The ratio of a DI's core capital to its risk-adjusted assets.

To be adequately capitalized, a bank must hold a minimum total capital (Tier I core capital plus Tier II supplementary capital) to risk-adjusted assets ratio of 8 percent—that is, its **total risk-based capital ratio** is calculated as:

$$\text{Total risk-based capital ratio} = \frac{\text{Total capital (Tier I plus Tier II)}}{\text{Risk-adjusted assets}} \geq 8\%$$

In addition, the Tier I core capital component of total capital has its own minimum guideline. The **Tier I (core) capital ratio** is calculated as follows:

$$\text{Tier I (core) capital ratio} = \frac{\text{Core capital (Tier I)}}{\text{Risk-adjusted assets}} \geq 4\%$$

That is, of the 8 percent total risk-based capital ratio, a bank must hold a minimum of 4 percent in core or primary capital. Savings institutions also must operate according to these ratios. Capital ratios for credit unions vary by state, but they must maintain appropriate minimums.

In addition to their use to define adequately capitalized banks, risk-based capital ratios—along with the traditional capital-to-assets ratio—also define well-capitalized, undercapitalized, significantly undercapitalized, and critically undercapitalized banks as part of the prompt corrective action program under FDICIA. As with the simple leverage ratio for both the total risk-based capital ratio and the Tier I risk-based capital ratios, these five zones—specified in columns (2) and (3) of Table 14–5—assess capital adequacy and the actions regulators are mandated to take as well as those that regulators have the discretion to take.[29] Table 14–7 summarizes these regulatory actions. In Appendix D to this chapter, we discuss the details of how to calculate a bank's or a savings institution's risk-based capital ratio.

www.bis.org/

In 1999, the Basle Committee proposed changes to the 1988 Basle Accord. With respect to credit risk, the proposed new requirements will change the risk weights applied to government, bank, and corporate loans and other credits (see Table 14–8) such that the weight assigned will be based on external assessments by rating agencies (e.g., Moody's and S&P). The result is that risk weights are reduced (to as low as 0 percent) for high-quality borrowers and increased (a new risk weight, 150 percent, will be used) for low-quality borrowers. Eventually, it is proposed that regulators should use the bank's own internal rating system (e.g., one that categorizes loans into different internal rating classes, such as 1 to 10) to calculate capital requirements. Finally, given appropriate model and data development, capital requirements could be calculated taking into account diversification among the assets in a bank's portfolio as well (i.e., the default correlations among the assets in the portfolio as well as their individual risks could be utilized to assess credit risk exposure).

Do You Understand?

1. Why regulators impose reserve requirements on depository institutions?
2. The difference between a bank's leverage ratio and its risk-based capital ratio?
3. What actions regulators must take under prompt corrective action (PCA)?

Off-Balance-Sheet Regulations

In the 1980s, increasing losses on loans to less-developed and Eastern European countries, increased interest rate volatility, and squeezed interest margins for on-balance-sheet lending (as the result of nonbank competition) led many large commercial banks to seek profitable activities off the balance sheet (OBS). By moving activities off the balance sheet, banks hoped to earn more fee income to offset declining margins or spreads on their traditional lending business. At the same time, they could avoid regulatory costs or

---

29. Most commercial banks keep their capital ratios well above the minimums. One reason for this is that banks have become very dependent on large (greater than $100,000) deposits of commercial firms. Since these deposits are beyond the FDIC insurance limit, banks can attract and retain such deposits only to the extent they can show they are financially sound (i.e., having more than the minimum equity ratio).

Table 14–7 Summary of Prompt Corrective Action Provisions of the Federal Deposit Insurance Corporation Improvement Act of 1991

Zone	Mandatory Provisions	Discretionary Provisions
1. Well capitalized		
2. Adequately capitalized	1. Prohibit brokered deposits, except with FDIC approval	
3. Undercapitalized	1. Suspend dividends and management fees 2. Require capital restoration plan 3. Restrict asset growth 4. Require approval for acquisitions 5. Prohibit brokered deposits	1. Order recapitalization 2. Restrict interaffiliate transactions 3. Restrict deposit interest rates 4. Restrict certain other activities 5. Allow any other action that would better carry out prompt corrective action
4. Significantly undercapitalized	1. Same as for Zone 3 2. Order recapitalization* 3. Restrict interaffiliate transactions* 4. Restrict deposit interest rates* 5. Restrict pay of officers	1. Enforce any Zone 3 discretionary actions 2. Appoint conservatorship or receivership if fails to submit or implement plan or recapitalize pursuant to order 3. Enforce any other Zone 5 provision, if such action is necessary to carry out prompt corrective action
5. Critically undercapitalized	1. Same as for Zone 4 2. Appoint receiver/conservator within 90 days* 3. Appoint receiver if still in Zone 5 four quarters after becoming critically undercapitalized 4. Suspend payments on subordinated debt* 5. Restrict certain other activities	

*Not required if primary supervisor determines action would not serve purpose of prompt corrective action or if certain other conditions are met.
Source: Federal Reserve Board of Governors, Press Release, September 10, 1993. *www.bog.frb.fed.us/*

Table 14–8 Risk Weights Under Revised Basle Accord Plan

| Credit Instrument | Credit Weighting | | | | | |
	AAA to AA−	A+ to A−	BBB+ to BBB−	BB+ to B−	Below B−	Unrated
Government securities	0%	20%	50%	100%	150%	100%
Banks—Option 1*	20%	50%	100%	100%	150%	100%
Option 2†	20%	50%	50%	100%	150%	50%
Corporates	20%	100%	100%	100%	150%	100%

*Risk weighting based on risk weighting of country in which the bank is corporated.
†Risk weighting based on the assessment of the individual bank. *www.bis.org/*

taxes since reserve requirements, deposit insurance premiums, and capital adequacy requirements were not levied on off-balance-sheet activities. Thus, banks had both earnings and regulatory "tax-avoidance" incentives to move activities off their balance sheets.

The dramatic increase in OBS activities caused the Federal Reserve to introduce an OBS activity tracking plan in 1983. As part of the quarterly financial reports they file, banks began submitting schedule L, on which they listed the notional dollar size and variety of their OBS activities. In Chapter 13, we discussed five different OBS activities that banks must report to the Federal Reserve each quarter as part of their schedule L section of the financial report (loan commitments, letters of credit, derivative contracts, when-issued securities, and loans sold).

5 Foreign versus Domestic Regulation of Depository Institutions

As discussed earlier in this chapter, many of the product and geographic expansion barriers on U.S. depository institutions have recently been lowered. Despite the loosening of regulations, however, U.S. DIs are still subject to stricter regulations than DIs in foreign countries.

Product Diversification Activities

With the passage of the Financial Services Modernization Act of 1999, the range of nonbank product activities that U.S. banks are permitted to engage in is now more comparable to bank activities allowed in the major industrialized countries.[30]

Global or International Expansion Activities

U.S. DIs have expanded into foreign countries through branches and subsidiaries; this has been reciprocated by the increased entrance of foreign DIs into U.S. financial service markets.

Regulations of U.S. Banks in Foreign Countries. Although some U.S. banking organizations such as Citigroup and J. P. Morgan have had foreign offices since the beginning of the 20th century, the major phase of expansion began in the early 1960s following passage of the Overseas Direct Investment Control Act of 1964. This law restricted U.S. banks' ability to lend to U.S. corporations that wanted to make foreign investments. This law was eventually repealed, but it created incentives for U.S. banks to establish foreign offices to service the funding and other business needs of their U.S. clients in other countries. In addition, with certain exceptions, Federal Reserve Regulation K has allowed U.S. banking offices in other countries to engage in the foreign country's permitted banking activities, even if the United States did not permit such activities. For example, U.S. banks setting up foreign subsidiaries can lease real property, act as general insurance agents, and underwrite and deal in foreign corporate securities (up to a maximum commitment of $2 million).

NAFTA

North American Free Trade Agreement.

The 1994, **NAFTA** (North American Free Trade Agreement) enabled U.S. (and Canadian) banks to expand into Mexico, and the December 1997 agreement by 100 countries, reached under the auspices of the World Trade Organization (WTO), heralds an important step toward dismantling barriers inhibiting the entry of foreign banks, insurance companies, and securities firms into emerging market countries.[31]

---

30. Many of Japan's postwar regulations were modeled on those of the United States. Thus, Article 65 in Japan separates commercial banking from investment banking in a fashion similar to the Glass-Steagall Act. Japan recently passed a major deregulation, however, that will considerably weaken the historic barriers between commercial and investment banking in that country. Specifically, under the 1992 Comprehensive Financial Reform Law, Japanese banks are permitted to establish subsidiaries to engage in a full range of securities activities. To protect small brokers, however, the law withholds permission to engage in retail equities brokerage.

31. See "Accord Is Reached to Lower Barriers in Global Finance," *New York Times*, December 12, 1997, pp. A1.

Table 14–9   U.S. Bank Claims Held Outside the United States*

	1990	1991	1992	1993	1994	1995	1996	1997	1998	March 1999
Total	$320.1	$343.6	$346.5	$403.7	$496.6	$551.7	$645.0	$719.3	$714.1	$678.3
United Kingdom	60.9	68.5	60.8	84.5	90.1	82.4	104.6	113.4	121.5	110.6
Offshore banking centers†	44.7	54.2	58.5	72.5	71.4	99.0	134.9	139.0	94.1	83.0

*Billions of dollars held by U.S. offices and foreign branches of U.S. banks (including U.S. banks that are subsidiaries of foreign banks).
†Includes Bahamas, Bermuda, and Cayman Islands.
Source: *Federal Reserve Bulletin,* October 1999, Table 3.21, and earlier issues. *www.bog.frb.fed.us/*

As a result of these regulatory changes, U.S. banks have been accelerating their foreign business in recent years. U.S. bank claims held outside the country have risen from $320.1 billion in 1990 to $678.3 billion in March 1999 (Table 14–9). Interestingly, the fastest-growing segment has been "offshore banking"—issuing loans and accepting deposits. The U.S. bank claims held in the United Kingdom reflect its importance as the center of the Eurodollar market, which is the market for dollar loans and deposits made and held outside the United States.

Regulation of Foreign Banks in the United States.   Prior to 1978, foreign branches and agencies entering the United States were primarily licensed at the state level. As such, their entry, regulation, and oversight were almost totally confined to the state level. Beginning in 1978 with the passage of the International Banking Act (IBA) and the more recent passage of the Foreign Bank Supervision and Enforcement Act (FBSEA), federal regulators have exerted increasing control over foreign banks operating in the United States.

Pre-IBA.   Before the passage in 1978 of the IBA, foreign agencies and branches entering the United States with state licenses had some competitive advantages and disadvantages relative to most domestic banks. On the one hand, as state-licensed organizations, they were not subject to the Federal Reserve's reserve requirements, audits, and exams; interstate branching restrictions (the McFadden Act); or restrictions on corporate securities underwriting activities (the Glass-Steagall Act). However, they had no access to the Federal Reserve's discount window (i.e., lender of last resort); no direct access to Fedwire, and, thus, the fed funds market; and no access to FDIC deposit insurance.

Their inability to gain access to deposit insurance effectively precluded them from the U.S. retail banking market and its deposit base. As a result, prior to 1978, foreign banks in the United States largely concentrated on wholesale banking.

Post-IBA.   The unequal treatment of domestic and foreign banks regarding federal regulation and the lobbying by domestic banks regarding the unfairness of this situation provided the impetus for Congress to pass the IBA in 1978. The fundamental regulatory philosophy underlying the IBA was one of **national treatment,** a philosophy that attempted to create a level playing field for domestic and foreign banks in U.S. banking markets. As a result of this act, foreign banks were required to hold Federal Reserve–specified reserve requirements if their worldwide assets exceeded $1 billion, and they became subject to Federal Reserve examinations and to both the McFadden and Glass-Steagall Acts. With respect to the latter, an important grandfather provision in the act allowed foreign banks established in the United States prior to 1978 to keep

national treatment

Regulation of foreign banks in the same fashion as domestic banks, or the creation of a level playing field.

their "illegal" interstate branches and securities-activity operations—that is, interstate and security activity restrictions were applied only to foreign banks entering the United States after 1978.[32]

If anything, the passage of the IBA accelerated the expansion of foreign bank activities in the United States. A major reason for this was that for the first time, the IBA gave foreign banks access to the Federal Reserve's discount window, Fedwire, and FDIC insurance. In particular, access to FDIC insurance allowed access to retail banking. In 1979 alone, foreign banks acquired four large U.S. banks (Crocker, National Bank of North America, Union Planters, and Marine Midland). In addition, in the early 1980s, the Bank of Tokyo, Mitsubishi Bank, and Sanwa Bank invested $1.3 billion in California bank acquisitions.[33] Overall, Japanese banks owned more than 25 percent of California bank assets at the end of the 1980s.

The Foreign Bank Supervision Enhancement Act (FBSEA) of 1991.   Along with the growth of foreign bank assets in the United States came concerns about foreign banks' rapidly increasing share of U.S. banking markets and about the weakness of regulatory oversight of many of these institutions. Three events focused attention on the weaknesses of foreign bank regulation. The first event was the collapse of the Bank of Credit and Commerce International (BCCI), which had a highly complex international organization structure based in the Middle East, the Cayman Islands, and Luxembourg and had undisclosed ownership stakes in two large U.S. banks. BCCI was not subject to any consolidated supervision by a home country regulator; this quickly became apparent after its collapse, when massive fraud, insider lending abuses, and money-laundering operations were discovered. The second event was the issuance of more than $1 billion in unauthorized letters of credit to Saddam Hussein's Iraq by the Atlanta agency of the Italian bank, Banca Nazionale del Lavoro. The third event was the unauthorized taking of deposit funds by the U.S. representative office of the Greek National Mortgage Bank of New York.

These events and related concerns led to the passage of the FBSEA in 1991. The objective of this act was to extend federal regulatory authority over foreign banking organizations in the United States, especially when these organizations had entered using state licenses. The act's five main features have significantly enhanced the powers of federal bank regulators over foreign banks in the United States:

1. **Entry**—under FBSEA, a foreign banking organization must now have the Fed's approval to establish a subsidiary, branch, agency, or representative office in the United States. The approval applies to both a new entry and an entry by acquisition. To secure Fed approval, the organization must meet a number of standards, two of which are mandatory. First, the foreign bank must be subject to comprehensive supervision on a consolidated basis by a home country regulator. Second, that regulator must furnish all the information that the Federal Reserve requires to evaluate the application. Both standards attempt to avoid the lack of disclosure and lack of centralized supervision associated with BCCI's failure.

2. **Closure**—FBSEA also gives the Federal Reserve authority to close a foreign bank if its home country supervision is inadequate, if it violates U.S. laws, or if it engages in unsound and unsafe banking practices.

3. **Examination**—the Federal Reserve has the power to examine each office of a foreign bank, including its representative offices. Further, each branch or agency must be examined at least once a year.

---

32. For example, in 1978, approximately 60 foreign banks had branches in at least three states. As noted earlier, the McFadden Act prevented domestic banks from interstate branching.

33. Thus, the newly formed bank—as a result of the 1996 Bank of Tokyo—Mitsubishi Bank merger—controls 70 percent of the Union Bank of San Francisco (a $17 billion bank with 200 branches) and 100 percent of the Bank of California (a $7 billion bank with 50 branches).

4. **Deposit Taking**—only foreign subsidiaries with access to FDIC insurance can take retail deposits under $100,000. This effectively rolls back the provision of the IBA that gave foreign branches and agencies access to FDIC insurance.

5. **Activity Powers**—beginning December 19, 1992, state-licensed branches and agencies of foreign banks were not allowed to engage in any activity that was not permitted to a federal branch.

Overall, then, the FBSEA considerably increased the Federal Reserve's authority over foreign banks and added to the regulatory burden or costs of entry into the United States for foreign banks. This has made the post-FBSEA U.S. banking market much less attractive to foreign banks than it had been over the period 1980–1992. Perhaps the strongest punitive action taken so far against a foreign bank was the Federal Reserve's closure of all operations of Daiwa Bank in the United States for six weeks in 1995 for not reporting a bond trader's losses of nearly $1 billion and the resulting four-year prison sentence and $2.57 million fine imposed on the offending trader by a New York court. This closure signaled a willingness of the U.S. banking authorities to be much tougher on foreign banks in the United States in the future.

Do You Understand?

1. What regulatory changes have encouraged the growth of U.S. offshore banking? What factors have deterred U.S. offshore banking?
2. The impact the passage of the International Banking Act of 1978 had on foreign bank activities in the United States?
3. What the five main features of the Foreign Bank Supervision Enforcement Act of 1991 are?

Summary

Depository institutions provide services that are vital to all sectors of the economy. Failure to efficiently provide these services can be costly to both the suppliers and users of funds. Consequently, DIs are regulated to protect against a breakdown in the provision of DI services. In this chapter, we reviewed the regulations imposed on DIs. We provided an overview of historical and current regulations on DIs' product offerings and geographic expansion opportunities. The recent loosening of regulations in these areas is likely to result in the emergence of many large U.S. DIs as globally oriented universal banks. We also described regulations on the asset and liability portfolios of DIs. The chapter concluded with a look at foreign DI regulations and the regulation of foreign DIs in the United States.

Questions

1. What forms of protection and regulation are imposed by regulators of DIs to ensure their safety and soundness?
2. How has the separation of commercial banking and investment banking activities evolved through time? How does this differ from banking activities in other countries?
3. A Section 20 subsidiary of a major U.S. bank is planning to underwrite corporate securities and expects to generate $5 million in revenues. It currently underwrites U.S. Treasury securities and general obligation municipal bonds, and earns annual fees of $40 million.
   a. Is the bank in compliance with the laws regulating the turnover of Section 20 subsidiaries?
   b. If it plans to increase underwriting of corporate securities and generate $11 million in revenues, is it in compliance? Would it have been in compliance prior to passage of the Financial Services Modernization Act of 1999?

4. What insurance activities are permitted for U.S. commercial bank holding companies?
5. How did the absence of any U.S. commercial banks from the top 20 world banks likely affect bank industry reform in Congress?
6. What are the new provisions on interstate banking in the Riegle-Neal Interstate Banking and Branching Efficiency Act of 1994?
7. What is the difference between an MBHC and an OBHC? What are the implications of the difference for bank expansion?
8. Compared to banks, to what extent are other DIs subject to contagious runs?
9. How did the fixed-rate deposit insurance program of the FDIC contribute to the savings institutions crisis?
10. How does federal deposit insurance help mitigate the problem of bank runs? What are some other elements of the safety net available to banks in the United States?

11. Contrast the two views of the reasons that depository institution insurance funds had financial problems in the 1980s.

12. How has the International Banking Act of 1978 and FDICIA of 1991 been detrimental to foreign banks in the United States?

13. What are some of the main features of the Foreign Bank Supervision Enhancement Act of 1991?

The following questions are related to Appendix C and D material.

14. If the reserve computation period extends from May 18 through May 31, what is the corresponding reserve maintenance period? What accounts for the difference?

15. The average demand deposits of a bank during the most recent reserve computation period has been estimated at $225 million over a 14-day period (Tuesday to Monday). The average daily reserves at the Fed during the 14-day reserve maintenance period has been $16 million and the corresponding daily vault cash during this period was $4 million.
    a. What are the average daily required reserves to be held by the bank during the maintenance period?
    b. Is the bank in compliance with the requirements?

16. The following demand deposits and reserve deposits at the Fed have been documented by a bank for the computation of its reserve requirements (in millions).

	Tuesday 11th	Wednesday 12th	Thursday 13th	Friday 14th	Monday 17th
Demand Deposits	$300	$250	$280	$260	$280

	Tuesday 18th	Wednesday 19th	Thursday 20th	Friday 21st	Monday 24th
Demand Deposits	$300	$270	$260	$250	$240

The average daily reserves at the Fed for the 14-day reserve maintenance period have been $22.7 million per day and the average vault cash for the computation period has been estimated to be $2 million per day.
    a. What is the amount of the average daily required reserves to be held by the bank during the maintenance period?
    b. Is the bank in compliance with the requirements?

17. What is the contribution to the asset base of the following items under the Basle requirements? Under the U.S. capital-to-assets rule?
    a. $10 million cash reserves.
    b. $50 million 91-day U.S. Treasury bills.
    c. $25 million cash items in the process of collection.

d. $5 million U.K. government bonds.
e. $5 million Australian short-term government bonds.
f. $1 million general obligation municipal bonds.
g. $40 million repurchase agreements (against U.S. Treasuries).
h. $500 million 1- to 4-family home mortgages.
i. $500 million commercial and industrial loans
j. $100,000 performance-related standby letters of credit to a blue chip corporation.
k. $100,000 performance-related standby letters of credit to a municipality issuing general obligation bonds.
l. $7 million commercial letter of credit to a foreign corporation.
m. $3 million 5-year loan commitment to an OECD government.
n. $8 million bankers acceptance conveyed to a U.S. corporation.
o. $17 million 3-year loan commitment to a private agent.
p. $17 million 3-month loan commitment to a private agent.
q. $30 million standby letter of credit to back a corporate issue of commercial paper.
r. $4 million 5-year interest rate swap with no current exposure (the counterparty is a private agent).
s. $4 million 5-year interest rate swap with no current exposure (the counterparty is a municipality).
t. $6 million 2-year currency swap with $500,000 current exposure (the counterparty is a private agent).

The following information is for questions 18–21. Consider a bank's balance sheet as follows.

On-Balance-Sheet Items	Category	Face Value
Cash	1	$121,600
Short-term government securities (<92 days)	1	5,400
Long-term government securities (>92 days)	1	414,400
Federal reserve stock	1	9,800
Repos secured by federal agencies	2	159,000
Claims on U.S. depository institutions	2	937,900
Short-term (< 1 year) claims on foreign banks	2	1,640,000
General obligations municipals	2	170,000
Claims on or guaranteed by federal agencies	2	26,500
Municipal revenue bonds	3	112,900
Loans	4	6,645,700
Claims on foreign banks (>1 year)	4	5,800

Off-Balance-Sheet Items	Conversion Factor	Face Value
Guaranteed by U.S. Government: (Risk Weight Category 2)		
Loan Commitments:		
< 1 year	0%	300
1–5 year	50%	1,140
Standby letters of credit		
Performance related	50%	200
Other	100%	100

Off-Balance-Sheet Items	Conversion Factor	Face Value
Backed by Domestic Depository Institution: (Risk Weight Category 2)		
Loan Commitments:		
< 1 year	0%	$ 1,000
> 1 year	50%	3,000
Standby letters of credit		
Performance related	50%	200
Other	100%	56,400
Commercial letters of credit	20%	400

Off-Balance-Sheet Items	Conversion Factor	Face Value
Backed by State or Local Government Revenues: (Risk Weight Category 3)		
Loan Commitments:		
> 1 year	50%	$ 100
Standby letters of credit		
Non-performance related	50%	135,400

Extended to Corporate Customers: (Risk Weight Category 4)		
Loan Commitments:		
< 1 year	0%	$2,980,000
> 1 year	50%	3,046,278
Standby letters of credit		
Performance related	50%	101,543
Other	100%	485,000
Commercial letters of credit	20%	78,978
Note issuance facilities	50%	20,154
Forward agreements	100%	5,900

Category II Interest Rate Market Contracts: (current exposure assumed to be zero.)		
< 1 year (notional amount)	0%	2,000
> 1–5 year (notional amount)	.5%	5,000

18. What is the bank's risk-adjusted asset base?
19. What are the bank's Tier I and total risk-based capital requirements?
20. Using the leverage-ratio requirement, what is the U.S. bank's minimum regulatory capital requirement to keep it in the well-capitalized zone?
21. What is the bank's capital level if the par value of its equity is $150,000; surplus value of equity is $200,000; and qualifying perpetual preferred stock is $50,000? Does the bank meet Basle (Tier I) capital standards? Does the bank comply with the well-capitalized leverage-ratio requirement?

Appendix A   Depository Institutions and Their Regulators

Legend

FDIC	Federal Deposit Insurance Corporation
FTC	Federal Trade Commission
Federal Reserve	Board of Governors of the Federal Reserve System/Federal Reserve Banks
NCUA	National Credit Union Administration
OCC	Office of the Comptroller of the Currency
OTS	Office of Thrift Supervision

A. National banks	Federal Reserve, FDIC, OCC
B. State member banks	State authority, Federal Reserve, FDIC
C. State nonmember banks insured	State authority, Federal Reserve, FDIC
D. Noninsured state banks	State authority, Federal Reserve, FTC
E. Insured savings associations, federal[*]	OTS, Federal Reserve, FDIC
Insured savings associations, state[†]	State authority, OTS, Federal Reserve, FDIC
F. Uninsured savings associations, state	State authority, Federal Reserve, FTC
G. Credit unions, federal	NCUA, Federal Reserve, state authority
Credit unions, state	State authority, NCUA, Federal Reserve, FTC
H. Bank holding companies	Federal Reserve, state authority, FTC
I. Savings association holding companies	OTS, state authority, Federal Reserve, FTC
J. Foreign branches of U.S. banks, national and state members	Federal Reserve, state authority, OCC

Foreign branches of U.S. banks, insured state nonmembers	State authority, FDIC
K. Edge Act corporations	Federal Reserve
Agreement corporations	State authority, Federal Reserve
L. U.S. branches and agencies of foreign banks, federal U.S. branches and agencies of foreign banks, state	OCC, Federal Reserve, FDIC, FTC, state authority State authority, Federal Reserve, FDIC, OCC, FTC

The appendix provides an overview of primary regulators of depository institutions as of April 1998. It is not intended to cover each area of regulatory responsibility in detail. Further, the appendix and accompanying footnotes should not be considered either a substitute for or an interpretation of the regulations. Regulatory agencies should be consulted for answers to specific questions.

*Federal savings associations include any thrift institution such as federal savings banks, federally chartered under Section 5 of the Home Owners' Act.

†State savings associations include any state-chartered savings bank, savings and loan association, building and loan association, homestead association, or cooperative bank.

Source: Public Information Department, Federal Reserve Bank of New York, 33 Liberty Street, New York, NY 10045. *www.bog.frb.fed.us/*

Appendix B Financial Services Modernization Act of 1999: Summary of Provisions

Title I—Facilitating Affiliation among Banks, Securities Firms, and Insurance Companies

- Repeals the restrictions on banks affiliating with securities firms contained in Sections 20 and 32 of the Glass-Steagall Act.
- Creates a new "financial holding company" under section 4 of the Bank Holding Company Act. Such holding company can engage in a statutorily provided list of financial activities, including insurance and securities underwriting and agency activities, merchant banking, and insurance company portfolio investment activities. Activities that are "complementary" to financial activities also are authorized. The nonfinancial activities of firms predominantly engaged in financial activities (at least 85% financial) are grandfathered for at least 10 years, with a possibility of a five-year extension.
- The Federal Reserve may not permit a company to form a financial holding company if any of its insured depository institution subsidiaries are not well capitalized and well managed, or did not receive at least a satisfactory rating in its most recent CRA exam.
- If any insured depository institutions or insured depository institution affiliate of a financial holding company received less than a satisfactory rating in its most recent CRA exam, the appropriate Federal banking agency may not approve any additional new activities or acquisitions under the authorities granted under the Act.
- Provides for State regulation of insurance, subject to a standard that no State may discriminate against persons affiliated with a bank.
- Provides that bank holding companies organized as a mutual holding company will be regulated on terms comparable to other bank holding companies.
- Lifts some restrictions governing nonbank banks.
- Provides for a study of the use of subordinated debt to protect the financial system and deposit funds from "too big to fail" institutions and a study on the effect of financial modernization on the accessibility of small business and farm loans.
- Streamlines bank holding company supervision by clarifying the regulatory roles of the Federal Reserve as the umbrella holding company supervisor, and the State and other Federal financial regulators which "functionally" regulate various affiliates.
- Provides for Federal bank regulators to prescribe prudential safeguards for bank organizations engaging in new financial activities.

- Prohibits FDIC assistance to affiliates and subsidiaries of banks and savings institutions.
- Allows a national bank to engage in new financial activities in a financial subsidiary, except for insurance underwriting, merchant banking, insurance company portfolio investments, real estate development and real estate investment, so long as the aggregate assets of all financial subsidiaries do not exceed 45 percent of the parent bank's assets or $50 billion, whichever is less. To take advantage of the new activities through a financial subsidiary, the national bank must be well capitalized and well managed. In addition, the top 100 banks are required to have an issue of outstanding subordinated debt. Merchant banking activities may be approved as a permissible activity beginning 5 years after the date of enactment of the Act.
- Ensures that appropriate anti-trust review is conducted for new financial combinations allowed under the Act.
- Provides for national treatment for foreign banks wanting to engage in the new financial activities authorized under the Act.

Title II—Functional Regulation

- Amends the Federal Securities laws to incorporate functional regulation of bank securities activities.
- The broad exemptions banks have from broker-dealer regulation would be replaced by more limited exemptions designed to permit banks to continue their current activities and to develop new products.
- Provides for limited exemptions from broker-dealer registration for transactions in the following areas: trust, safekeeping, custodian, shareholder and employee benefit plans, sweep accounts, private placements (under certain conditions), and third party networking arrangements to offer brokerage services to bank customers, among others.
- Allows banks to continue to be active participants in the derivatives business for all credit and equity swaps (other than equity swaps to retail customers).
- Provides for a "jump ball" rulemaking and resolution process between the SEC and the Federal Reserve regarding new hybrid products.
- Amends the Investment Company act to address potential conflicts of interest in the mutual fund business and amendments to the Investment Advisers Act to require banks that advise mutual funds to register as investment advisers.

Title III—Insurance

- Provides for the functional regulation of insurance activities.
- Establishes which insurance products banks and bank subsidiaries may provide as principal.
- Prohibits national banks not currently engaged in underwriting or sale of title insurance from commencing that activity. However, sales activities by banks are permitted in States that specifically authorize such sales for State banks, but only on the same conditions. National bank subsidiaries are permitted to sell all types of insurance including title insurance. Affiliates may underwrite or sell all types of insurance including title insurance.
- State insurance and Federal regulators may seek an expedited judicial review of disputes with equalized deference.
- The Federal banking agencies are directed to establish consumer protections governing bank insurance sales.
- Preempts state laws interfering with affiliations.
- Provides for interagency consultation and confidential sharing of information between the Federal Reserve Board and State insurance regulators.
- Allows mutual insurance companies to re-domesticate.
- Allows multi-state insurance agency licensing.

Part 3   Depository Institutions

Title IV—Unitary Savings Institution Holding Companies

- De novo unitary thrift holding company application received by the Office of Thrift Supervision after May 4, 1999, shall not be approved.
- Existing unitary thrift holding companies may only be sold to financial companies.

Title V—Privacy

- Requires clear disclosures by all financial institutions of their privacy policy regarding the sharing of nonpublic personal information with both affiliates and third parties.
- Requires a notice to consumers and an opportunity to "opt-out" of sharing on nonpublic personal information with nonaffiliated third parties subject to certain limited exceptions.
- Addresses a potential imbalance between the treatment of large financial services conglomerates and small banks by including an exception.
- Clarifies that the disclosure of a financial institution's privacy policy is required to take place at the time of establishing a customer relationship with a consumer and not less than annually during the continuation of such relationship.
- Provides for a separate rather than joint rulemaking to carry out the purposes of the subtitle; the relevant agencies are directed, however, to consult and coordinate with one another for purposes of assuring to the maximum extent possible that the regulations that each prescribes are consistent and comparable with those prescribed by the other agencies.
- Allows the functional regulators sufficient flexibility to prescribe necessary exceptions and clarifications to the prohibitions and requirements of Section 502.
- Clarifies that the remedies described in Section 505 are the exclusive remedies for violations of the subtitle.
- Clarifies that nothing in this title is intended to modify, limit, or supersede the operation of the Fair Credit Reporting Act.
- Extends the time period for completion of a study on financial institutions' information-sharing practices from 6 to 18 months from date of enactment.
- Provides for an effective date of 18 months after the date on which the rulemaking pursuant to section 504 is completed, to allow sufficient time for state legislatures to empower state insurance regulators to comply with this subtitle.
- Assigns authority for enforcing the subtitle's provisions to the Federal Trade Commission and the Federal banking agencies, the National Credit Union Administration, the Securities and Exchange Commission, according to their respective jurisdictions, and provides for enforcement of the subtitle by the States.

Title VI—Federal Home Loan Bank System Modernization

- Banks with less than $500 million in assets may use long-term advances for loans to small businesses, small farms and small agri-businesses.
- A new, permanent capital structure for the Federal Home Loan Banks is established. Two classes of stock are authorized, redeemable on 6-months and 5-years notice. Federal Home Loan Banks must meet a 5 percent leverage minimum tied to total capital and a risk-based requirement tied to permanent capital.
- Equalizes the stock purchase requirements for banks and savings institutions.
- Voluntary membership for Federal savings associations takes effect six months after enactment.
- The current annual $300 million funding formula for the REFCORP obligations of the Federal Home Loan Banks is changed to 20 percent of annual net earnings.
- Governance of the Federal Home Loan Banks is decentralized from the Federal Housing Finance Board to the individual Federal Home Loan Banks. Changes include the election of chairperson and vice chairperson of each Federal Home Loan

Bank by its directors rather than the Finance Board, and a statutory limit on Federal Home Loan Bank directors' compensation.

Title VII—Other Provisions

- Requires ATM operators who impose a fee for use of an ATM by a noncustomer to post a notice on the machine that a fee will be charged and on the screen that a fee will be charged and the amount of the fee. This notice must be posted before the consumer is irrevocably committed to completing the transaction. A paper notice issued from the machine may be used in lieu of a posting on the screen.
- No surcharge may be imposed unless the notices are made and the consumer elects to proceed with the transaction. Provision is made for those older machines that are unable to provide the notices required. Requires a notice when ATM cards are issued that surcharges may be imposed by other parties when transactions are initiated from ATMs not operated by the card issuer. Exempts ATM operators for liability if properly placed notices on the machines are subsequently removed, damaged, or altered by anyone other than the ATM operator.
- Clarifies that nothing in the act repeals any provision of the CRA.
- Requires full public disclosure of all CRA agreements.
- Requires each bank and each nonbank party to a CRA agreement to make a public report each year on how the money and other resources involved in the agreement were used.
- Grants regulatory relief regarding the frequency of CRA exams to small banks and savings institutions (those with no more than $250 million in assets). Small institutions having received an outstanding rating at their most recent CRA exam shall not receive a routine CRA exam more often than once each 5 years. Small institutions having received a satisfactory rating at their most recent CRA exam shall not receive a routine CRA exam more often than once each 4 years.
- Directs the Federal Reserve Board to conduct a study of the default rates, delinquency rates, and profitability of CRA loans.
- Directs the Treasury, in consultation with the bank regulators, to study the extent to which adequate services are being provided as intended by the CRA.
- Requires a GAO study of possible revisions to S corporation rules that may be helpful to small banks.
- Requires Federal banking regulators to use plain language in their rules published after January 1, 2000.
- Allows Federal savings associations converting to national or State bank charters to retain the term "Federal" in their names.
- Allows one or more savings institutions to own a banker's bank.
- Provides for technical assistance to microenterprises (meaning businesses with fewer than 5 employees that lack access to conventional loans, equity, or other banking services). This program will be administered by the Small Business Administration.
- Requires annual independent audits of the financial statements of each Federal Reserve bank and the Board of Governors of the Federal Reserve System.
- Authorizes information sharing among the Federal Reserve Board and Federal or State authorities.
- Requires a GAO study analyzing the conflict of interest faced by the Board of Governors of the Federal Reserve System between its role as a primary regulator of the banking industry and its role as a vendor of services to the banking and financial services industry.
- Requires the Federal banking agencies to conduct a study of banking regulations regarding the delivery of financial services, and recommendations on adapting those rules to online banking and lending activities.
- Protects FDIC resources by restricting claims for the return of assets transferred from a holding company to an insolvent subsidiary bank.

- Provides relief to out-of-state banks generally by allowing them to charge interest rates in certain host states that are no higher than rates in their home states.
- Allows foreign banks generally to establish and operate Federal branches or agencies with the approval of the Federal Reserve Board and the appropriate banking regulator if the branch has been in operation since September 29, 1994 or the applicable period under appropriate state law.
- Expresses the sense of the Congress that individuals offering financial advice and products should offer such services and products in a nondiscriminatory, nongender-specific manner.
- Permits the Chairman of the Federal Reserve Board and the Chairman of the Securities and Exchange Commission to substitute designees to serve on the Emergency Oil and Gas Guarantee, Loan Guarantee Board and the Emergency Steel Loan Guarantee Board.
- Repeals section 11(m) of the Federal Reserve Act, removing the stock collateral restriction on the amount of a loan made by a state banks member of the Federal Reserve System.
- Allows the FDIC to reverse an accounting entry designating about $1 billion of SAIF dollars to a SAIF special reserve, which would not otherwise be available to the FDIC unless the SAIF designated reserve ratio declines by about 50 percent and would be expected to remain at that level for more than one year.
- Allows directors serving on the boards of public utility companies to also serve on the boards of banks.

Source: U.S. Senate website, November 1999. *www.senate.gov/~banking/conf/grmleach.htm*

Appendix C: Calculating Minimum Required Reserves at U.S. Depository Institutions

This appendix presents a detailed example of U.S. bank liquidity management under the current minimum reserve requirements imposed by the Federal Reserve. Many of the issues and trade-offs are readily generalizable, however, to any FI facing liability withdrawal risk under conditions in which regulators impose minimum liquid asset reserve ratios.

The issues involved in the optimal management of a liquid asset portfolio are illustrated by the problems faced by the money desk manager in charge of a U.S. bank's cash reserve position. In the context of U.S. bank regulation, we concentrate on a bank's management of its **cash reserves,** defined as vault cash and cash deposits held by the bank at the Federal Reserve.[34]

cash reserves

Vault cash and cash deposits held at the Federal Reserve.

transaction accounts

Deposits that permit the account holders to make multiple withdrawals.

Transaction accounts include all deposits on which an account holder may make withdrawals by negotiable or transferrable instruments and may make more than three monthly telephone or preauthorized fund transfers for the purpose of making payments to third parties (for example, demand deposits, NOW accounts, and share draft accounts—offered by credit unions). Historically, U.S. banks also had to hold reserves against time deposits and personal savings deposits (including money market deposit accounts—MMDAs). However, this was reduced from 3 to 0 percent at the beginning of 1991. Transaction account balances are reduced by demand balances due from U.S. depository institutions and cash items in process of collection to obtain net transaction accounts.

To calculate the target amount of reserves and to determine whether it is holding too many or too few reserves, the bank reserve manager requires two additional pieces

---

34. However, banks that are not members of the Federal Reserve System, mostly very small banks, may maintain reserve balances with a Federal Reserve Bank indirectly (on a pass-through basis) with certain approved institutions such as correspondent banks.

of information to manage the position. First, which period's deposits does the manager use to compute the bank's reserve requirement? Second, over which period or periods must the bank maintain the target reserve requirement just computed?

The U.S. system is complicated by the fact that the period for which the bank manager computes the required reserve target differs from the period during which the reserve target is maintained or achieved. We describe the computation and maintenance periods for bank reserves next.

reserve computation period

Period over which required reserves are calculated.

Computation Period

For the purposes of bank reserve management, a U.S. bank reserve manager must think of the year as being divided into two-week periods. The **reserve computation period** always begins on a Tuesday and ends on a Monday 14 days later.

Example 14–1 Computation of Daily Average Required Reserves

Consider ABC Bank's reserve manager, who wants to assess the bank's minimum cash reserve requirement target. The manager knows the bank's net transaction accounts balance at the close of the banking day on each of the 14 days over the period Tuesday, June 30, to Monday, July 13. Consider the realized net transaction account positions of ABC Bank in Table 14–C1.

The minimum daily average reserves that a bank must maintain is computed as a percentage of the daily average net transaction accounts held by the bank over the two-week computation period, where Friday's balances are carried over for Saturday and Sunday. The minimum daily average for ABC Bank to hold against the daily average of $1,350.70 million in net transaction accounts is calculated as follows (amounts in millions):

Daily Average Net Transaction Accounts	× Reserve Percentage =	Daily Average Reserves Required
$5.0	0%	$ 0.000
$44.3–$5.0	3	1.179
$1,350.7–$44.3	10	130.640
Minimum average reserves to be held		$131.819

Note that the daily average target in Example 14–1 is calculated by taking a 14-day average of net transaction accounts even though the bank is closed for 4 of the 14 days (two Saturdays and two Sundays). Effectively, Friday's deposit figures count three times compared to those of other days in the business week. This means that the bank manager who can engage in a strategy in which deposits are lower on Fridays can, on average, lower the bank's reserve requirements. This may be important if required liquid asset reserve holdings are above the optimal level from the bank's perspective to handle liquidity drains due to expected and unexpected deposit withdrawals.

weekend game

Name given to the policy of lowering deposit balances on Fridays, since that day's figures count three times for reserve accounting purposes.

One strategy employed in the past was for a bank to send deposits out of the country (e.g., transfer them to a foreign subsidiary) on a Friday, when a reduction in deposits effectively counts for 3/14ths of the two-week period, and to bring them back on the following Monday, when an increase counts for only 1/14th of the two-week period. This action effectively reduced the average demand deposits in the balance sheet of the bank over the 14-day period by 2/14th times the amount sent out of the country and, thus, reduced the amount of reserves it needed to hold. Analysts term this the **weekend game.**[35]

35. In fact, the weekend game is a special case of bank window dressing, in which transactions are undertaken to reduce reported deposits below their true or actual figures. For a discussion of window dressing in banking and the incentives for bankers to window dress, see L. Allen and A. Saunders, "Bank Window Dressing: Theory and Evidence," *Journal of Banking and Finance,* 1992, pp. 585–624.

Table 14–C1   Net Transaction Accounts and Vault Cash Balances of ABC Bank (in millions of dollars)

	Transaction Accounts	Less Demand Balances Due from U.S. Depository Institutions	Less Cash Items in Process of Collection	Net Transaction Accounts	Vault Cash
Tuesday, June 30	$ 1,850	$ 240	$ 140	$ 1,470	$ 30
Wednesday, July 1	1,820	235	135	1,450	21
Thursday, July 2	1,770	250	120	1,400	21
Friday, July 3	1,610	260	100	1,250	21
Saturday, July 4	1,610	260	100	1,250	28
Sunday, July 5	1,610	260	100	1,250	24
Monday, July 6	1,655	250	125	1,280	24
Tuesday, July 7	1,650	230	130	1,290	26
Wednesday, July 8	1,690	240	130	1,320	27
Thursday, July 9	1,770	275	135	1,360	27
Friday, July 10	1,820	280	140	1,400	27
Saturday, July 11	1,820	280	140	1,400	25
Sunday, July 12	1,820	280	140	1,400	25
Monday, July 13	1,785	260	135	1,390	29
Total	$24,280	$3,600	$1,770	$18,910	$355
Daily average net transaction accounts				$1,350.7	$25.357

Note that the $131.819 million figure is a minimum reserve target. The bank manager may hold excess cash reserves above this minimum level if the privately optimal or prudent level for the bank exceeds the regulatory specified minimum level because this bank is especially exposed to deposit withdrawal risk. In addition, the bank manager may hold some buffer reserves in the form of government securities that can quickly be turned into cash if deposit withdrawals are unusually high or to preempt the early stages of a bank run.

Maintenance Period

We have computed a daily average minimum cash reserve requirement for ABC Bank but have yet to delineate the exact period over which the bank manager must maintain this $131.819 million daily average reserve target. Reserves may be held either as vault cash or as deposits held by the bank at the Federal Reserve. Under the current set of regulations, the average daily vault cash held during the reserve computation period (June 30 through July 13 in our example) is deducted from the institution's required reserves to determine the reserve balance to be maintained at the Federal Reserve. In addition, a lag of 30 days exists between the beginning of the reserve computation period

reserve maintenance period

Period over which deposits at the Federal Reserve Bank must meet or exceed the required reserve target.

and the beginning of the **reserve maintenance period** (over which deposits at the Federal Reserve Bank must meet or exceed the required reserve target). For ABC Bank, this reserve maintenance period is from July 30 through August 12 (see Figure 14–C1). Thus, the bank's reserve manager knows the value of its target reserves with perfect certainty throughout the reserve maintenance period. However, the reserve manager still has a challenge in maintaining sufficient reserves at the Fed to hit the reserve target, while still minimizing these non-interest bearing balances and maintaining the liquidity position of the bank.

The reserve manager also knows the vault cash component of the reserve target, since this is based on the average vault cash held by the bank over the reserve computation period, as reported in Table 14–C1. The daily balances in vault cash and deposits at the Federal Reserve for ABC Bank for the 14-day reserve maintenance period from July 30 through August 12 are shown in Table 14–C2. Since the average daily balance in vault cash for this period is shown (in Table 14–C1) at $25.357 million, the average

Figure 14–C1 Lagged Reserve Requirements

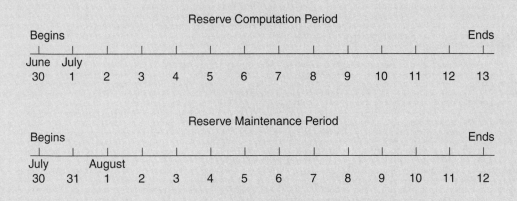

Table 14–C2 ABC Bank's Daily Reserve Position over the July 30–August 12
Reserve Maintenance Period
(in millions of dollars)

Date	Vault cash	Deposits at the Federal Reserve
Thursday, July 30	$ 30	$ 98
Friday, July 31	21	100
Saturday, August 1	21	100
Sunday, August 2	21	100
Monday, August 3	28	98
Tuesday, August 4	24	91
Wednesday, August 5	24	102
Thursday, August 6	26	101
Friday, August 7	27	99
Saturday, August 8	27	99
Sunday, August 9	27	99
Monday, August 10	25	107
Tuesday, August 11	25	154
Wednesday, August 12	29	142.468
Total	$355	$1,490.468
Daily average	$25.357	106.462

lagged reserve accounting system

An accounting system in which the reserve computation and reserve maintenance period do not overlap.

contemporaneous reserve accounting system

An accounting system in which the reserve computation and reserve maintenance periods overlap.

daily target balance for deposits at the Federal Reserve are $106.462 million (i.e., $25.357 million + $106.462 million = $131.819 million). Essentially, since the vault cash component of the reserve target is based on vault cash held over the reserve computation period, the bank's active target during the maintenance period itself is its reserve position at the Fed (in this case, it seeks to hold an average of $106.462 million per day over the 14-day maintenance period).

As discussed above, currently the reserve maintenance period for meeting the reserve target begins 30 days after the start of the reserve computation period—the reserve maintenance period does not begin until 17 days after the end of the computation period. Regulators introduced this **lagged reserve accounting system** to make it easier for bank reserve managers to calculate their required reserve balances and to increase the accuracy of information on aggregate required reserve balances. Prior to July 1998, regulators used a **contemporaneous reserve accounting system** in which the two-week reserve maintenance period for meeting the reserve target began only two days (as opposed to the current 17 days) after the start of the reserve computation period. This contemporaneous reserve system resulted in only a two-day window during which required reserves were known with certainty—in the above example, the reserve maintenance period would have been from Thursday, July 2, through Wednesday, July 15, for a reserve computation period beginning Tuesday, June 30, and ending Monday, July 13.

Appendix D   Calculating Risk-Based Capital Ratios

Risk-Adjusted On-Balance-Sheet Assets

Under the risk-based capital plan, each bank assigns its assets to one of four categories of credit risk exposure: 0 percent, 20 percent, 50 percent, or 100 percent.[36] Table 14–D1 lists the key categories and assets in these categories. The risk-adjusted value of the bank's on-balance-sheet assets are:

$$\sum_{i=1}^{n} w_i a_i$$

where

w_i = risk weight of the ith asset
a_i = dollar (book) value of the ith asset on the balance sheet

Risk-Adjusted Off-Balance-Sheet Activities

The calculation of the risk-adjusted values of the off-balance-sheet (OBS) activities involves some initial segregation of these activities. In particular, the calculation of the credit risk exposure or the risk-adjusted asset amount of contingent liability or guarantee

Table 14–D1   Summary of the Risk-Based Capital Standards for On-Balance Sheet Items

Risk Categories

Category 1 (0% weight)—cash; Federal Reserve Bank balances; U.S. Treasury securities; OECD* governments; and some U.S. agencies (e.g., GNMAs)

Category 2 (20% weight)—cash items in the process of collection; U.S. and OECD interbank deposits and guaranteed claims; some non-OECD bank and government deposits and securities; general obligation municipal bonds; some mortgage-backed securities; claims collateralized by the U.S. Treasury and some other government securities

Category 3 (50% weight)—loans fully secured by first liens on one- to four-family residential properties; other (revenue) municipal bonds; credit-equivalent amounts of interest rate and foreign exchange-related contracts except those assigned to a lower risk category

Category 4 (100% weight)—all other on-balance-sheet assets not listed above, including loans to private entities and individuals, some claims on non-OECD governments and banks, real assets, and investments in subsidiaries, contingent or guarantee contracts (e.g., loan commitments, letters of credit) except those assigned to a lower risk category

*Organization for Economic Cooperation and Development
Source: Federal Reserve Board of Governors, Press Release, January 1989, Attachment III. *www.bog.frb.fed.us/*

36. Under the revised capital requirements, a fifth category will be added at 150 percent (see Table 14–8).

Table 14–D2   Conversion Factors for Off-Balance-Sheet Contingent or Guarantee Contracts

Direct credit substitute standby letters of credit (100%)
Performance-related standby letters of credit (50%)
Unused portion of loan commitments with original maturity of more than one year (50%)
Commercial letters of credit (20%)
Bankers acceptances conveyed (20%)
Other loan commitments (0%)

Source: Federal Reserve Board of Governors, Press Release, January 1989, Attachment IV. *www.bog.frb.fed.us/*

contracts such as letters of credit or loan commitments differs from the calculation of the risk-adjusted asset amounts for derivative contracts such as foreign exchange and interest rate forward, option, and swap contracts. We next consider the risk-adjusted asset value of off-balance-sheet guarantee-type contracts and contingent contracts and then for derivative (or market) contracts.

The Risk-Adjusted Asset Value of Off-Balance-Sheet Contingent Guarantee Contracts

The beginning step in calculating the risk-adjusted asset values of these off-balance-sheet items is to convert them into credit equivalent amounts—amounts equivalent to the credit risk exposure of an on-balance-sheet item or asset. The conversion factors are listed in Table 14–D2.

credit equivalent amount

The amount of credit risk exposure of an off-balance-sheet item calculated by multiplying the face value of an off-balance-sheet instrument by a conversion factor.

To find the risk-adjusted asset value for off-balance-sheet items, we follow a two-step process. In the first step, we multiply the dollar amount outstanding of these items by the conversion factors listed in Table 14–D2 to derive the **credit equivalent amounts.** These conversion factors convert an off-balance-sheet item into an equivalent credit or on-balance-sheet item. In the second step, we multiply these credit equivalent amounts by their appropriate risk weights as listed in Table 14–D1. The appropriate risk weight in each case depends on the underlying counterparty—such as a municipality, a government, or a corporation—to the off-balance-sheet activity. If the underlying party being guaranteed were a municipality issuing general obligation (GO) bonds and a bank issued an off-balance-sheet standby letter of credit backing the credit risk of the municipal GO issue, the risk weight is 0.2. If, on the other hand, the counterparty being guaranteed is a *private entity,* the appropriate risk weight is 1. Note that if the counterparty had been the central government, the risk weight is zero.

The Risk-Adjusted Asset Value of Off-Balance-Sheet Derivative Instruments or Market Contracts

counterparty credit risk

The risk that the other party to a contract will default on payment obligations.

Modern DIs engage heavily in originating, buying, and selling OBS futures, options, forwards, swaps, caps, and other derivative securities contracts on their own account and on behalf of their customers (see Chapter 10). Each of these positions potentially exposes banks to **counterparty credit risk**—the risk that the counterparty (or other side of a contract) will default if it suffers large actual or potential (future) losses on its position. Such defaults mean that a bank must go back to the market to replace such contracts at (potentially) less favorable terms. To calculate the current and future replacement cost or risk of such contracts requires a two-step approach.

Specifically, we convert the notional or face values of all *non*exchange-traded swap, forward, and other derivative contracts into credit equivalent amounts.[37] The

---

37. The credit risk of exchange-traded contracts is viewed as being equal to zero, since such contracts are guaranteed by the exchange.

Table 14–D3   Credit Conversion Factors for Interest Rate and Foreign
Exchange Contracts in Calculating Potential Exposure

Remaining Maturity	(1) Interest Rate Contracts	(2) Exchange Rate Contracts
1. Less than 1 year	0.0%	1.0%
2. 1–5 years	0.5	5.0
3. More than 5 years	1.5	7.5

Source: Federal Reserve Board of Governors, Press Release, August 1995, Section II. *www.bog.frb.fed.us/*

credit equivalent amount itself is divided into a *potential exposure* element and a *current exposure* element. That is:

$$\text{Credit equivalent amount of OBS derivative security items (\$)} = \text{Potential exposure (\$)} + \text{Current exposure (\$)}$$

potential exposure

The risk that a counterparty to a derivative securities contract will default in the future.

The **potential exposure** component reflects the credit risk if the counterparty to the contract defaults in the *future*. The probability of such an occurrence depends on future volatility of either interest rates for an interest rate contract or exchange rates for an exchange rate contract. FX rates are generally more volatile than interest rates; thus, the potential exposure conversion factors in Table 14–D3 are larger for foreign exchange contracts than for interest rate contracts. Also note the larger potential credit risk exposure for longer-term contracts of both types.

current exposure

The cost of replacing a derivative securities contract at today's prices.

In addition to calculating the potential exposure of an OBS market instrument, a bank also must calculate its **current exposure** with the instrument. This reflects the cost of replacing a contract should a counterparty default *today*. The bank calculates this *replacement cost* or *current exposure* by replacing the rate or price initially in the contract with the current rate or price for a similar contract and recalculates all the current and future cash flows using the current rate or price.[38] The bank then compares the net present value of the old contract with the new contract to give a current net present value measure of the contract's replacement cost. If the contract's replacement cost is negative (i.e., the bank profits if the counterparty defaults), regulations require the replacement cost (current exposure) to be set to zero. If the replacement cost is positive (i.e., the old contract is more profitable to the bank than a new contract should the counterparty default), this value is used as the measure of current exposure. Since each swap or forward is in some sense unique, calculating current exposure involves a considerable task for the DI's management information systems. Indeed, specialized service firms are likely to perform this task for small banks.[39]

Once we total the current and potential exposure amounts to produce the credit equivalent amount for each contract, we multiply this dollar number by a risk weight to produce the final risk-adjusted asset amount for OBS market contracts. In general, the appropriate risk weight is .5, or 50 percent; that is:

$$\text{Risk-adjusted asset value of OBS market contracts} = \text{Total credit equivalent amount} \times \text{Risk weight}$$

38. For example, suppose that a two-year forward foreign exchange contract was entered into in January 2000 at \$1.55/£. In January 2001, the bank must evaluate the contract's credit risk, which now has one year remaining. To do this, the bank replaces the agreed forward rate, \$1.55/£, with the forward rate on a current one-year forward contract, \$1.65/£. It then recalculates its net gain or loss on the contract if it had to be replaced at this price. This is the contract's *replacement cost.*

39. One large New York money center bank calculates, on average, the replacement cost of more than 6,000 different forward contracts at any given point in time.

Example 14–2 Calculation of Risk-Adjusted Value of Assets

This example highlights six steps in calculating the risk-adjusted value of assets for a hypothetical bank balance sheet shown in Table 14–D4.

Step 1: The risk-adjusted value of the bank's on-balance-sheet assets are calculated as the book value of each asset times the percentage (credit) risk weight assigned to it.

$$\text{Risk-adjusted on-balance-sheet assets} = 0(8m. + 13m. + 60m. + 50m. + 42m.) + \\ .2 (10m. + 10m. + 20m.) + .5 (34m. + \\ 308m.) + 1 (530m. + 118m. + 22m.) = \\ \$849 \text{ million}$$

Although the simple book value of on-balance-sheet assets is $1,215 million, the risk-adjusted asset value is $849 million.

Step 2: To find the risk-adjusted asset value for off-balance-sheet contingent or guarantee contracts, we first multiply the dollar amount outstanding of these items by the conversion factors listed in Table 14–D2 to derive the credit equivalent amounts.

OBS Item	Fact Value (in millions)		Conversion Factor		Credit Equivalent Amount (in millions)
Two-year loan commitment	$80	×	.5	=	$40
Standby letter of credit	10	×	1.0	=	10
Commercial letter of credit	50	×	.2	=	10

Table 14–D4 Bank's Balance Sheet
(in millions of dollars)

Weight	Assets			Liabilities/Equity	Capital	Class
0%	Cash	$	8	Demand deposits	$ 150	
	Balances due from Fed		13	Time deposits	500	
	Treasury bills		60	CDs	400	
	Long-term Treasury securities		50	Fed funds purchased	80	
	Long-term government agencies (GNMAs)		42	Convertible bonds	15	Tier II
20	Items in process of collection		10	Subordinated bonds	15	Tier II
	Long-term government agencies (FNMAs)		10	Nonqualifying perpetual		
	Munis (general obligation)		20	preferred stock	5	Tier II
50	University dorm bonds (revenue)		34	Retained earnings	28	Tier I
	Residential 1- to 4-family mortgages		308	Common stock	12	Tier I
100	Commercial loans		530	Surplus	10	Tier I
	Third World loans		118		$1,215	
	Premises, equipment		22			
N/A	Reserve for loan losses		(10)			Tier II
	Total Assets	$	1,215			

Off-Balance-Sheet Items

100% $80m. in 2-year loan commitments to a large U.S. corporation
$10m. in standby letters of credit backing an issue of commercial paper
$50m. in commercial letters of credit
50% One fixed-floating interest rate swap for 4 years with notional dollar value of $100m. and replacement cost of $3m.
One two-year Euro$ forward contract for $40m. with a replacement cost of −$1m.

Step 3: Next we multiply the credit equivalent amounts calculated in step 2 by their appropriate risk weight. Since the counterparty for each of these contracts is a private agent, the appropriate weight is 1 (see Table 14–D1).

OBS Item	Credit Equivalent Amount (in millions)		Risk Weight (w_i)		Risk-Adjusted Asset Amount (in millions)
Two-year loan commitment	$40	×	1.0	=	$40
Standby letter of credit	10	×	1.0	=	10
Commercial letter of credit	10	×	1.0	=	10
					$60

The bank's risk-adjusted asset value of its OBS contingencies and guarantees is $60 million.

Step 4: To determine the risk-based asset value for off-balance-sheet interest rate and foreign exchange contracts, we first calculate the credit equivalent amount for each item or contract using the conversion factors listed in Table 14–D3 to find the potential exposure and add the current exposure or replacement cost should the counterparty default.

Type of Contract (remaining maturity)	Notional Principal	×	Potential Exposure Conversion Factor	=	Potential Exposure ($)	Replacement Cost	Current Exposure	=	Credit Equivalent Amount
Four-year fixed-floating interest rate swap	$100m.	×	.005	=	$.5m.	3m.	3m.	=	3.5m.
Two-year forward foreign exchange contract	$ 40m.	×	.05	=	2m.	−1m.	0m.	=	2m.

Potential Exposure + Current Exposure

Note that the replacement cost for the two-year forward contract is *minus* $1 million. In this example, our bank actually stands to *gain* if the counterparty were to default. Exactly why the counterparty would do this when it is "in the money" is unclear. Regulators cannot permit a bank to gain from a default by a counterparty, however, because this might produce all types of risk-taking incentives. Consequently, the current exposure must be set equal to zero (as shown). Thus, the sum of potential exposure ($2 million) and current exposure ($0) produces a total credit equivalent amount of $2 million for this contract.

Step 5: Since the bank has only two OBS derivative contracts, summing the two credit equivalent amounts produces a total credit equivalent amount of $5.5 million ($3.5m. + $2m.) for the bank's OBS market contracts.[40] Next, we multiply this credit equivalent amount by the appropriate risk weight. Specifically, to calculate the risk-adjusted asset

---

40. It might be noted that since 1995, regulators have allowed for a netting of the risk of OBS contracts with the same counterparty. By some estimates, this has reduced OBS risk exposure measures by approximately 40 percent.

value for the bank's OBS derivative or market contracts, we multiply the credit equivalent amount by the appropriate risk weight, which for virtually all over-the-counter derivative security products is .5, or 50 percent:

$$\begin{matrix} \text{Risk-adjusted asset value} \\ \text{of OBS derivatives} \end{matrix} = \begin{matrix} \$5.5 \text{ million (credit} \\ \text{equivalent amount)} \end{matrix} \times \begin{matrix} 0.5 \\ \text{(risk weight)} \end{matrix} = \$2.75 \text{ million}$$

Step 6: According to these calculations, the total risk-adjusted assets for the bank are the sum of the risk-adjusted assets on the balance sheet ($849 million), the risk-adjusted value of the OBS contingencies and guarantees ($60 million), and the risk-adjusted value of OBS derivatives ($2.75 million), or $911.75 million.

From Table 14–D4, the bank's Tier I capital (retained earnings, common stock, and surplus) totals $50 million; Tier II capital (convertible bonds, subordinate bonds, nonqualifying perpetual preferred stock, and reserve for loan losses) totals $45 million. The resulting total capital is therefore $95 million.

We can now calculate our bank's overall capital adequacy in light of the risk-based capital requirements:

$$\text{Tier I (core) capital} = \frac{\$50m}{\$911.75m} = 5.48\%$$

and

$$\text{Total risk-based capital ratio} = \frac{\$95m}{\$911.75m} = 10.42\%$$

Since the minimum Tier I capital ratio required is 4 percent and the minimum total risk-based capital ratio required is 8 percent, this bank has more than adequate capital, exceeding the required minimums by 1.48 percent and 2.42 percent, respectively.

Other Financial Institutions

P art four of the text provides an overview of key characteristics and regulatory features of the other major sectors of the U.S. financial services industry. We discuss insurance companies in Chapter 15, securities firms and investment banks in Chapter 16, finance companies in Chapter 17, mutual funds in Chapter 18, and pension funds in Chapter 19.

chapter fifteen

Insurance Companies

Chapter Navigator

1. What are the two types of insurance companies?

2. What are the four basic lines of business performed by life insurance companies?

3. What are the major assets and liabilities of life insurance companies?

4. What are the major regulations governing life insurance companies?

5. What are the major lines of business performed by property-casualty insurance companies?

6. What are the main asset and liability items on property-casualty insurance company balance sheets?

7. Who are the main regulators of property-casualty insurance companies?

1 Two Categories of Insurance Companies: Chapter Overview

The primary function of insurance companies is to protect individuals and corporations (policyholders) from adverse events. By accepting premiums, insurance companies promise to compensate policyholders if certain prespecified events occur. The insurance industry is classified into two major groups: (1) life and (2) property-casualty. Life insurance provides protection in the event of untimely death, illnesses, and retirement. Property insurance protects against personal injury and liability due to accidents, theft, fire, and other catastrophes.

This chapter discusses the main features of insurance companies by concentrating on (1) the size, structure, and composition of the industry in which they operate, (2) their balance sheets and recent trends, and (3) regulations.

Life Insurance Companies

Size, Structure, and Composition of the Industry

In the late 1990s, the United States had 1,563 life insurance companies, compared to 2,343 in 1988. The aggregate assets of life insurance companies were $2.82 trillion at the end of 1998, compared to $1.12 trillion in 1988. The two biggest life insurers in terms of premiums written (Metropolitan Life Insurance Co. and Prudential Insurance Co. of America) wrote 8.4 percent of the industry's $459.7 billion premiums in 1998.

The life insurance industry has experienced major mergers in recent years as competition within the industry and with other FIs has increased (see In the News box 15–1). Like consolidation in commercial banking, the consolidation of the insurance industry has mainly occurred to take advantage of economies of scale and scope, and other synergies (see Chapter 11).

Do You Understand?

1. What the volume of mergers in the insurance industry in 1997 and 1998 was?
2. What the reasons for such a large volume of insurance company mergers are?

Life insurance allows individuals to protect themselves and their beneficiaries against the risk of loss of income in the event of death or retirement. By pooling risks of individual customers, life insurance companies can diversify away some of the customer specific risk and offer insurance services at a cost (premium) lower than any individual could achieve saving funds on his or her own. Thus, life insurance companies transfer income-related uncertainties such as retirement from the individual to a group. Although life insurance may be their core activity area, modern life insurance companies also sell annuity contracts, manage pension plans, and provide accident and health insurance.

One problem that naturally faces life insurance companies (as well as property-casualty insurers) is the adverse selection problem. Adverse selection is the problem that customers who apply for insurance policies are more likely to be those most in need of insurance (i.e., someone with chronic health problems is more likely to purchase a life insurance policy than someone in perfect health). Thus, in calculating the probability of having to pay out on an insurance contract and, in turn, determining the insurance premium to charge, insurance companies' use of health (and other) statistics representing the overall population may not be appropriate (since the insurance company's pool of customers is more prone to health problems than the overall population). Insurance companies deal with the adverse selection problem by establishing different pools of the population based on health and related characteristics (such as income). By altering the pool used to determine the probability of losses to a particular customer's health characteristics, the insurance company can more accurately determine the probability of having to pay out on a policy and can adjust the insurance premium accordingly.

As the various types of insurance policies and services offered are described below, notice that some policies (such as universal life policies and annuities) provide not only insurance features but also savings components. For example, universal life policy payouts are a function of the interest earned on the investment of the policyholder's premiums. Similarly, annuities offer the policyholder a fixed or variable payment each period (generally monthly) for life or over some predetermined future horizon.

Life Insurance.   The four basic classes or lines of life insurance are distinguished by the manner in which they are sold or marketed to purchasers. These classes are (1) ordinary life, (2) group life, (3) industrial life, and (4) credit life. Of the life insurance policies in force in the United States, ordinary life accounts for approximately 60 percent, group life for less than 40 percent, industrial life for

In the News

15-1

Megadeals Shook Industry Last Year

While the number of insurance-related mergers and acquisitions was up only slightly during 1998 from the year before, their dollar values left mouths agape on Wall Street throughout the year. Even with a few lulls after midyear caused by a briefly bearish stock market, M&A activity at the end of 1998, measured in dollars, was at a record high for the industry.

By mid-December, 299 deals had been announced, valued at more than $81 billion, compared to 281 deals valued at a relatively meek $31.4 billion in 1997, according to an analysis by SNL Securities, a financial research firm in Charlottesville, Va. SNL's analysis covered the life/health, property/casualty, managed care and broker/agency businesses and included the late-breaking deals between Aetna and Prudential Healthcare, valued at $1 billion, and Unum and Provident's $5 billion merger . . .

"For the last three years, insurance M&A activity has

been sizzling, but this year it kept boiling over," said Nancy Carini, a vice president at Conning. Unless there's a downturn next year, Ms. Carini said, M&A deals will probably continue at high levels, driven by such factors as conversion of mutual insurers to public companies and continued competitive pressure to consolidate financial and insurance services.

Major deals began in January, with the announcement of St. Paul Insurance's merger with USF&G, in Baltimore, valued at $3.7 billion. Other blockbuster deals included Commercial Union, in Boston, and General Accident, in Philadelphia, announced in June and valued at $11 billion; and the August announcement that AIG, in New York, was going to buy SunAmerica in Los Angeles, valued at $18 billion.

"The increase in the size of the deals is the big story in 1998," said Mark Kilduff, an analyst with SNL. Con-

solidations were motivated by a maturing of insurance markets in general, forcing companies to look at M&A deals as the only practical way to grow. "Mergers and acquisitions are a sure way to grow revenues and cut costs," Mr. Kilduff said. Aetna, for example, is expected to achieve $150 million in savings from its purchase of Prudential Healthcare, he observed . . .

Feeding the merger frenzy will be the expected demutualizations of giants like John Hancock, Metropolitan and Prudential. Once public and flush with cash, they could start looking for firms to augment their product offerings, Mr. Riegel said. "Consolidation is good from a credit perspective and eliminates the weaker players, as long as the deal is financed in a prudent manner," he added. He noted, too, that acquisitions within the insurance industry tend to be more financially sound than in other industries. "If you step outside of insurance, a lot of deals are financed with stock rather than debt," he said. "But in this market, stock is a currency that is often inflated". . .

continues

Source: *National Underwriter,* December 21, 1998, p. 10, by Trevor Thomas.

In the News continued

"In the case of Unum and Provident, you see two firms that already have a dominant market position, yet they felt driven to do a transaction," Charles Carroll (director of Ernst & Young's M&A practice) said. "It just emphasizes that no company is so big it can't see the possibility of creating value by acquiring other firms" . . . , Ultimately, "Cigna and Aetna may be the only survivors from the life insurance industry that are still in health care," he added.

less than 1 percent, and credit life for less than 2 percent of the almost $20 trillion contract value outstanding.

Ordinary Life. Ordinary life insurance policies are marketed on an individual basis, usually in units of $1,000; policyholders make periodic premium payments. Despite the enormous variety of contractual forms, there are essentially five basic contractual types. The first three are traditional forms of ordinary life insurance, and the last two are newer contracts that originated in the 1970s and 1980s due to increased competition for savings from other segments of the financial services industry, such as mutual funds. The three traditional contractual forms are term life, whole life, and endowment life. The two newer forms are variable life and universal life. The key features of each of these contractual forms are identified as follows:

· **Term Life.** This policy is the closest to pure life insurance; it has no savings element attached. Essentially, an individual's beneficiary receives a payout at the time of the individual's death during the coverage period. The term of coverage can vary from as little as 1 year to 40 years or more.
· **Whole Life.** This policy protects the individual over an entire lifetime rather than for a specified coverage period. In return for periodic or level premiums, the individual's beneficiaries receive the face value of the life insurance contract on death. Thus, if the policyholder continues premium payments, the insurance company is certain to make a payment—unlike term insurance, where a payment is made only if death occurs during the coverage period.
· **Endowment Life.** This type of policy combines both a pure (term) insurance element with a savings element. It guarantees a payout to the beneficiaries of the policy if death occurs during some endowment period (e.g., prior to reaching retirement age). An insured person who lives to the endowment date receives the face amount of the policy.
· **Variable Life.** Unlike traditional policies that promise to pay the insured the fixed or face amount of a policy should a contingency arise, variable life insurance invests fixed premium payments in mutual funds of stocks, bonds, and money market instruments. Usually, policyholders can choose mutual fund investments to reflect their risk preferences. Thus, variable life provides an alternative way to build savings compared to the more traditional policies such as whole life because the value of the policy increases (or decreases) with the asset returns of the mutual fund in which premiums are invested.
· **Universal Life and Variable Universal Life.** A universal life policy allows the insured to change both the premium amounts and the maturity of the life contract, unlike traditional policies that maintain premiums at a given level over a fixed

contract period. In addition, for some contracts, insurers invest premiums in money, equity, or bond mutual funds—as in variable life insurance—so that the savings or investment component of the contract reflects market returns. In this case, the policy is called *variable universal life.*

Group Life Insurance. This insurance covers a large number of insured persons under a single policy. Usually issued to corporate employers, these policies may be either *contributory* (where the employer covers a share of the employee's cost of the insurance) or *noncontributory* (where the employer does not contribute to the employee's cost of the insurance) for the employees themselves. The principal advantage of group life over ordinary life policies involves cost economies. These occur as the result of mass administration of plans, lower costs for evaluating individuals through medical screening and other rating systems, and reduced selling and commission costs.

Industrial Life. This type of life insurance currently represents a very small area of coverage. Industrial life usually involves weekly payments collected directly by representatives of the companies. To a large extent, the growth of group life insurance has led to the demise of industrial life as a major activity class.

Credit Life. This insurance protects lenders against a borrower's death prior to the repayment of a debt contract such as a mortgage or car loan. Usually, the face amount of the insurance policy reflects the outstanding principal and interest on the loan.

Other Life Insurer Activities. Three other major activities of life insurance companies are the sale of annuities, private pension plans, and accident and health insurance.

Annuities. Annuities represent the reverse of life insurance principles. While life insurance involves different contractual methods to *build up* a fund and the eventual payout of a *lump sum* to the beneficiary, annuities involve different methods of *liquidating* a fund over a *long period* of time, such as paying out a fund's proceeds to the beneficiary. As with life insurance contracts, many different types of annuity contracts have been developed. Specifically, they can be sold to an individual or group and on either a fixed or variable basis by being linked to the return on some underlying investment portfolio. Individuals can purchase annuities with a single payment or payments spread over a number of years. Payments may be structured to begin immediately, or they can be *deferred* (for example, to start at retirement). These payments may cease at death or continue to be paid to beneficiaries for a number of years after death. Any interest earned on annuities is tax deferred (i.e., taxes are not paid until the annuity payments are actually made to the beneficiary). In contrast to Individual Retirement Accounts, or IRAs (see Chapter 19), the tax-deferred status of annual annuity contributions are not capped and are not affected by the policyholder's income level. Thus, annuities have become popular with individuals as a mechanism used to save for retirement. Annuity sales in 1998 were $120.1 billion ($91.4 billion of which were variable annuities), compared to $26.1 billion in 1996.[1]

Example 15–1 Calculation of the Fair Value of an Annuity Policy

Suppose that a person wants to purchase an annuity today that would pay $15,000 per year until the end of that person's life. The insurance company expects the person to live for 25 more years and can invest the amount received for the annuity at a guaranteed interest rate of 5 percent.[2] The fair price for the annuity policy today can be calculated

---

1. As discussed in Chapter 14, life insurers are facing increasingly intense competition from banks in the annuity product market.

as follows:

$$\text{Fair Value} = \frac{15,000}{1+r} + \frac{15,000}{(1+r)^2} + \ldots + \frac{15,000}{(1+r)^{25}}$$

$$= 15,000 \left[\frac{1}{1+r} + \frac{1}{(1+r)^2} + \ldots + \frac{1}{(1+r)^{25}} \right]$$

$$= 15,000 \, [PVIFA_{r=5\%, \, n=25}]$$

$$= 15,000 \, [14.0939]$$

$$= \$211,409$$

where $PVIFA_{r=5\%, n=25}$ = Present value annuity factor reflecting the present value of \$1 invested at 5 percent over 25 years.

Thus, the cost of purchasing this annuity today would be \$211,409.[3]

Private Pension Funds.   Insurance companies offer many alternative pension plans to private employers in an effort to attract this business away from other financial service companies such as commercial banks and securities firms. Some of their innovative pension plans are based on guaranteed investment contracts (GICs). With such plans, the insurer guarantees not only the rate of interest credited to a pension plan over some given period—for example, five years—but also the annuity rates on beneficiaries' contracts. Other plans include immediate participation and separate account plans that follow more aggressive investment strategies than does traditional life insurance, such as investing premiums in special-purpose equity mutual funds. As of June 1999, life insurance companies were managing \$1.46 trillion in pension fund assets, equal to 31.5 percent of all private pension plans.

Accident and Health Insurance.   While life insurance protects against mortality risk, accident and health insurance protect against morbidity or ill health risk. More than \$100 billion in premiums were written annually by life and health companies in the accident-health area in the late 1990s. The major activity line is group insurance, which provides health insurance coverage to corporate employees. Life insurance companies write more than 50 percent of all health insurance premiums. However, the growth in health maintenance organizations (HMOs) (nonregulated providers of health insurance) in the late 1990s has cut into this line of business. For example, in a 1998 survey of 11 major life insurance companies conducted by A.M. Best,[4] it was reported that from 1996 to 1997 the number of enrollees through life insurance company sponsored health insurance plans dropped by more than 8 percent, more than 25 percent of the companies' existing policies were dropped, and premiums dropped nearly 7 percent. In contrast, HMO enrollment increased more than 7 percent from 1996 to 1997.[5] Other coverages include credit health plans, whereby individuals have their debt repayments insured against unexpected health contingencies and various types of renewable, non-renewable, and guaranteed health and accident plans for individuals. In many respects, insurers in accident and health lines face loss exposures that are more similar to those

www.ambest.com/

2. One possible way to do this would be for the insurer to buy a 25-year maturity zero coupon Treasury bond that has an annual discount yield of 5 percent.

3. Tables listing $PVIFA_{r,n}$ are provided in the appendix in the back of the text.

4. A.M. Best is a leading source of information on the insurance industry. The company provides quantitative and qualitative data on the performance of individual insurance companies as well as the industry as a whole.

5. A.M. Best's Supplemental Rating Questionnaire, 1998.

Table 15–1   Life Insurance Company Assets
(*distribution of assets of U.S. life insurance companies*)

			Corporate Securities				
Year	Total Assets (in millions)	Government Securities	Bonds	Stocks	Mortgages	Policy Loans	Miscellaneous Assets*
1917	$ 5,941	9.6%	33.2%	1.4%	34.0%	13.6%	5.2%
1920	7,320	18.4	26.7	1.0	33.4	11.7	6.5
1925	11,538	11.3	26.2	0.7	41.7	12.5	5.3
1930	18,880	8.0	26.0	2.8	40.2	14.9	5.2
1935	23,216	20.4	22.9	2.5	23.1	15.2	7.3
1940	30,802	27.5	28.1	2.0	19.4	10.0	6.3
1945	44,797	50.3	22.5	2.2	14.8	4.4	3.9
1950	64,020	25.2	36.3	3.3	25.1	3.8	4.1
1955	90,432	13.1	39.7	4.0	32.6	3.6	4.1
1960	119,576	9.9	39.1	4.2	34.9	4.4	4.4
1965	158,884	7.5	36.7	5.7	37.8	4.8	4.5
1970	207,254	5.3	35.3	7.4	35.9	7.8	5.3
1975	289,304	5.2	36.6	9.7	30.8	8.5	5.9
1980	479,210	6.9	37.5	9.9	27.4	8.6	6.6
1985	825,901	15.0	36.0	9.4	20.8	6.6	8.7
1990	1,408,208	15.0	41.4	9.1	19.2	4.4	7.8
1991	1,551,201	17.4	40.2	10.6	17.1	4.3	7.4
1992	1,664,531	19.2	40.3	11.5	14.8	4.3	6.8
1993	1,839,127	20.9	39.7	13.7	12.5	4.2	6.1
1994	1,930,500	20.4	41.0	14.6	11.2	4.4	6.2
1995	2,131,900	18.6	41.4	17.4	9.9	4.5	6.3
1996	2,271,700	17.0	42.4	21.0	9.0	4.4	4.5
1997	2,510,400	15.9	41.5	23.8	8.3	4.2	4.7
1998	2,769,500	11.1	40.8	26.8	7.7	3.7	9.9
1999†	2,926,400	10.4	40.3	28.8	7.7	3.4	9.4

*Includes cash, checkable deposits, and money market funds.
†Second quarter 1999.
Note: Beginning with 1962, these data include the assets of separate accounts.
Source: *Federal Reserve Bulletin,* various issues. *www.bog.frb.fed.us/*

that property-casualty insurers face than those that traditional life insurers face (see the section on property-casualty insurance, which follows shortly).

Balance Sheets and Recent Trends

Assets.   Because of the long-term nature of their liabilities (resulting from the long-term nature of life insurance policyholders' claims) and the need to generate competitive returns on the savings elements of life insurance products, life insurance companies concentrate their asset investments at the longer end of the maturity spectrum (e.g., corporate bonds, equities, and government securities). Table 15–1 shows the distribution of life insurance assets. As you can see, in 1999 10.4 percent of assets were invested in government securities, 69.1 percent in corporate bonds and stocks, and 7.7 percent in mortgages, with other loans—including **policy loans** (i.e., loans made to policyholders using their policies as collateral)—and miscellaneous assets comprising the remaining assets. The major trend has been a long-term increase

policy loans

Loans made by an insurance company to its policyholders using their policies as collateral.

Table 15–2 Life Insurance Industry Balance Sheet as of December 31, 1998
(in millions of dollars)

Assets		Percent of Total
Bonds	$1,311,861	46.5%
Preferred stock	16,211	0.6
Common stock	69,353	2.5
Mortgage loans	211,113	7.5
Real estate	27,679	1.0
Policy loans	102,161	3.6
Cash and short-term investments	61,119	2.2
Other invested assets	33,856	1.0
Life and annuity premium due	11,880	0.4
Accident and health premium due	5,516	0.2
Accrued investment income	24,928	0.9
Separate account assets	922,242	32.7
Other assets	26,061	0.9
Total assets	$2,823,980	100.0%

Liabilities and Capital/Surplus			
Net policy reserves		$1,309,176	46.4%
Policy claims		30,008	1.1
Policy dividend accumulations		20,587	0.7
Dividend reserve		15,997	0.6
Premium and deposit funds		205,502	7.3
Interest maintenance reserve		14,462	0.5
Commissions, taxes, expenses		20,267	0.7
Securities valuation reserve		37,727	1.3
Other liabilities		86,720	3.1
Separate account business		919,295	32.5
Total capital and surplus		164,239	5.8
Capital	$4,088		0.1
Treasury stock	(341)		0.0
Paid-in and contributed surplus	67,980		2.4
Surplus notes	14,527		0.5
Unassigned surplus	61,897		2.2
Other surplus	1,768		0.1
Other reserves	14,320		0.5
Total liabilities and capital/surplus		$2,823,980	100.0%

Source: *Best's Aggregates & Averages, Life-Health* (Oldwick, NJ: A.M. Best Company, 1999), p. 3. Copyrighted by A.M. Best Company. Used with permission. *www.ambest.com/*

in the proportion of bonds and equities[6] and a decline in the proportion of mortgages on life insurer's balance sheets.

Liabilities. The aggregate balance sheet for the life insurance industry at the end of 1998 is presented in Table 15–2. Looking at the liability side of the balance sheet, we see that $1.309 trillion, or 46.4 percent, of total liabilities and

---

[6] The bull market of the 1980s and 1990s is likely a major reason for the large percentage of assets invested in equities. The need for a more certain stream of cash flows to pay off policies is a major reason for the investment in bonds.

policy reserves

A liability item for insurers that reflects their expected payment commitments on existing policy contracts.

surrender value of a policy

The cash value of a policy received from the insurer if a policyholder surrenders the policy prior to maturity; normally, only a portion of the contract's face value.

separate account

Annuity program sponsored by life insurance companies in which the payoff on the policy is linked to the assets in which policy premiums are invested.

capital reflect net **policy reserves.** These reserves are based on actuarial assumptions regarding an insurer's expected future liability or commitment to pay out on present contracts, including death benefits, maturing endowment policies (lump sum or otherwise), as well as the cash **surrender value of policies** (i.e., the cash value paid to the policyholder if the policy is "surrendered" by the policyholder before it matures). Even though the actuarial assumptions underlying policy reserves are normally very conservative, unexpected fluctuations in future payouts can occur; that is, life insurance underwriting is risky. For example, mortality rates—and life insurance payouts—might unexpectedly increase over those defined by historically based mortality tables due to a catastrophic epidemic as was the case with AIDS in the 1980s. To meet unexpected future losses, a life insurer holds a capital and surplus reserve fund with which to meet such losses. The capital and surplus reserves of life insurers in 1998 totaled $164 billion, or 5.8 percent of their total liabilities and capital.[7] **Separate account** business was 32.5 percent of total liabilities and capital in 1998. Legally, separate account funds are invested and held separately from the insurance company's other assets. In particular, these funds may be invested without regard to the usual restrictions (e.g., they may be invested in all stocks, or all bonds). The returns on life insurance policies written as part of separate account business depend, then, on the return on the funds invested in separate account assets. Another important life insurer liability, guaranteed investment contracts or GICs (7.3 percent of total liabilities and capital), are short- and medium-term debt instruments sold by insurance companies to fund their pension plan business (see premium and deposit funds in Table 15–2).

McCarran-Ferguson Act of 1945

Regulation confirming the primacy of state over federal regulation of insurance companies.

www.naic.org/

Regulation

The most important legislation affecting the regulation of life insurance companies is the **McCarran-Ferguson Act of 1945,** which confirms the primacy of state over federal regulation of insurance companies. Thus, unlike the depository institutions we discussed in Chapter 3, which can be chartered at either the federal or state levels, a life insurer is chartered entirely at the state level. In addition to chartering, state insurance commissions supervise and examine insurance companies using a coordinated examination system developed by the National Association of Insurance Commissioners (NAIC). An example of state insurance regulatory actions is the 1997 case of Prudential Insurance Company. Prudential's policyholders filed and settled (for $410 million) a class action lawsuit claiming that Prudential's sales representatives defrauded customers by talking them into using the built-up cash values held in older life insurance policies to buy newer, costlier policies. A task force of state insurance regulators from 45 states conducted an 18-month "deceptive sales practices" investigation. The report resulting from this investigation was instrumental in determining the legal settlement.

insurance guarantee fund

A fund of required contributions from within-state insurance companies to compensate insurance company policyholders in the event of failure.

www.ins.state.ny.us/

Other than supervision and examination, states also promote life **insurance guarantee funds.** Unlike banks and thrifts, life insurers have no access to a federal guarantee fund. These state guarantee funds differ in a number of important ways from deposit insurance. First, although these programs are sponsored by state insurance regulators, they are actually run and administered by the private insurance companies themselves.

Second, unlike SAIF or BIF, in which the FDIC has established a permanent reserve fund by requiring banks to pay annual premiums in excess of payouts to resolve failures (see Chapter 14), no such permanent guarantee fund exists for the insurance industry—with the sole exception of the P&C and life guarantee funds in the state of New York. This means that contributions are paid into the guarantee fund by surviving firms in a state only after an insurance company has actually failed.

---

[7] An additional line of defense against unexpected underwriting losses is the insurer's investment income from its asset portfolio plus any new premium income flows.

Do You Understand?

1. What the major consequences of the Financial Services Modernization Act on the insurance industry will be?

Do You Understand?

1. The difference between a life insurance contract and an annuity contract?

2. What the different forms of ordinary life insurance are?

3. Why life insurance companies invest in long-term assets?

4. What the major source of life insurance underwriting risk is?

5. Who the main regulators of the life insurance industry are?

Third, the size of the required contributions that surviving insurers make to protect policyholders in failed insurance companies differs widely from state to state. In those states that have guarantee funds, each surviving insurer is normally levied a pro rata amount, according to the size of its statewide premium income. This amount either helps pay off small policyholders after the assets of the failed insurer have been liquidated or acts as a cash injection to make the acquisition of a failed insurer attractive. The definition of small policyholders varies among states in the range from $100,000 to $500,000.

Finally, because no permanent fund exists, and the annual pro rata payments to meet payouts to failed insurer policyholders are often legally capped, a delay usually occurs before small policyholders receive the cash surrender values of their policies or other payment obligations from the guarantee fund. This contrasts with deposit insurance, which normally provides insured depositors immediate coverage of their claims up to $100,000.

As discussed in Chapter 14, a piece of legislation that will have a major impact on the insurance (both life insurance and property-casualty insurance) industry in the future is the Financial Services Modernization Act of 1999. This legislation allows insurance companies, commercial banks, and investment banks to engage in each other's business. In addition to the new opportunities this bill has brought to the insurance industry (see In the News box 15–2), industry leaders praised the legislation for its requirement that commercial banks and investment banks entering the insurance business would be subject to insurance regulations of the state in which they operate. This creates a level playing field for the regulation of the insurance activities of insurance companies, banks, and securities firms.

Property-Casualty Insurance Companies

Size, Structure, and Composition of the Industry

Currently, some 2,500 companies sell property-casualty (P&C) insurance, and approximately 1,200 firms write P&C business in all or most of the United States. The U.S. P&C insurance industry is quite concentrated. Collectively, the top 10 firms have a 43.5 percent share of the overall P&C market measured by premiums written, and the top 250 firms made up 95.1 percent of the industry premiums written.[8] In 1998, the top firm (State Farm) wrote 11.8 percent of all P&C insurance premiums, nearly twice as much as the second-ranked insurer, Allstate, which wrote 6.7 percent of all premiums (i.e., a joint total of 18.5 percent of premiums). In contrast, in 1985, these top two firms wrote 14.5 percent of the total industry insurance premiums. Thus, the industry leaders appear to be increasing their domination of this financial services sector. The total assets of the P&C industry as of December 1998 were $909 billion, or approximately 32 percent of the life insurance industry's assets.

P&C Insurance. Property insurance involves insurance coverages related to the loss of real and personal property. Casualty—or perhaps more accurately, liability—insurance offers protection against legal liability exposures. However, distinctions between the two broad areas of property and liability insurance are becoming increasingly blurred. This is due to the tendency of P&C insurers to offer multiple activity line coverages combining features of property and liability insurance into single policy packages—for example, homeowners multiple peril insurance. The following describes the

8. *Best's Review,* July 1999, p. 90.

In the News

Reform Could Trigger Some Novel Affiliations

Financial services deregulation could set off a flurry of mergers among a handful of banks, insurers, and brokers. But over the long term it's more likely to change how those businesses do business, industry leaders say. As Congress comes closer to repealing the nation's Depression-era financial-services laws, industry watchers expect a variety of results from deregulation. Many say banks—the best-capitalized businesses in the industry—could be better poised to buy insurance companies and brokers. "There are going to be some very aggressive banks who have not been in the insurance underwriting business who are going to try and define themselves by an acquisition," said Mark Olson, a Washington, D.C.-area financial consultant who recently retired from Ernst & Young. "I think

there will be a hyper market for a brief period."

Banks that could be scouting insurers include heavyweights like First Union, Bank of America, Key Bank, Wells Fargo, and Chase Manhattan, Olson said. Adam Klauber, an insurance industry analyst for Cochran, Caronia & Co., agrees that in the near term, financial-services reform could quicken the pace of consolidation. On the insurance industry side, Klauber said property/casualty insurers such as Allstate Corp., Mercury General Corp., Safeco Corp., and Progressive Corp. could be among the targets or acquirers in a new financial era. On the life side, Klauber named American General, Conseco Inc., Jefferson Pilot, Lincoln National, and ReliaStar. Klauber also said brokers could be in the hunt

to expand, including A.J. Gallagher, Aon Corp., Brown & Brown, and Marsh & McLennan.

Over the long term, Klauber said the reform could allow for a financial services industry that can better compete globally. "The previous restriction on commingling of banking, insurance, and brokerage has resulted in the most fragmented financial system in the world," Klauber said. The reform could also provide for some market shifts. Banks, for example, could gain a large portion of the asset-accumulation sector, while insurers could gain consumer-lending market share. Rodger Lawson, president of the Alliance of American Insurers, said he expects any sweeping changes to be market-driven. Consumers, for example, may not buy into the one-stop shopping that banks and insurers promise will come. "We're in a state of transition between the way people do business today and the wave of the future, which might be quite

continues

Source: *Best Week*, November 1, 1999, by Theresa Miller. Copyrighted by A.M. Best Company. Used with permission.

In the News continued

different." Lawson agrees that some banks may try to follow the Travelers-Citicorp model that formed Citigroup, but he added, "I don't suspect that the numbers will necessarily be huge."

More likely than mergers that mimic Citigroup will be partnerships between banks and insurance companies that create new products, Lawson said. Combinations between banks and insurers, for example, could give insurers access to a vast database of customer information banks maintain. That information could help companies target products to certain customers. "Information and the availability of information about customers is absolutely critical in this," Lawson said.

Joyce Kraeger, also of the Alliance, said banks and insurers could form affiliations before they buy each other. A large property/casualty company could form a partnership with a large bank that would sell its products, for example. Kraeger said the bill would also provide for more finan-

cial flexibility, and cited provisions in the bill pending before Congress that would allow mutual companies to move to new states if their states won't allow them to convert to stock-owned or mutual holding companies.

Michael White, president of Michael White Associates, a bank-insurance consulting firm in Radnor, Pa., agrees that a few large banks could buy insurers. "I don't think there's going to be a rush of these," he said. "I do think there's going to be some noteworthy ones." He said it's more likely that banks will look to acquire broker-dealers, investment bankers, asset managers and mutual funds. "I don't see the vast majority of banks going out and making acquisitions of insurance underwriters," White said. "You'd have to wonder why a bank with a 20% return on equity, would buy a business with an 11% return-on-equity."

Insurers, meanwhile, could become more active in banking. "We've already seen in the insurance industry a great interest in thrift

charters," Kraeger said. Lawson agreed, citing companies' interest in providing trust services. Ace Ltd., for example, recently won approval to organize a federal savings bank so it could offer those kinds of services. Ace has joined an increasing number of insurers that are applying for thrift charters in order to offer trust services. Northwestern Mutual Insurance Co., for example, applied for trust powers last month, according to the Office of Thrift Supervision. The OTS expects to render a decision on that application by January. Phoenix Home Mutual Life Insurance Co., New York Life, Hartford, American General, Guardian Life and TIAA-CREF are among the insurers that have either begun offering or plan to offer trust services. "We're going to see a lot more clutter in the financial-services market," Lawson said. "And it's going to take time for that market to reshape itself before you can tell who the winners and losers are going to be."

Table 15–3   Property and Casualty Insurance
(industry underwriting by lines, 1998)

	Net Premiums Written*	Losses Incurred†
Fire	$ 4,738,634	63.1%
Allied lines	2,930,158	75.2
Multiple peril (MP) crop	712,917	77.5
Farm owners MP	1,434,441	72.3
Homeowners MP	28,982,711	65.3
Commercial MP—nonliability	10,246,636	67.8
Commercial MP—liability	8,726,738	63.2
Mortgage guarantee	2,283,979	42.2
Ocean marine	1,833,240	67.2
Inland marine	5,765,993	54.4
Financial guarantee	1,260,329	6.4
Medical malpractice	5,145,066	57.7
Earthquake	628,193	14.7
Federal flood	27,639	148.9
Group accident and health	6,828,983	80.4
Other accident and health	2,621,986	63.6
Credit accident and health	391,212	22.3
Workers' compensation**	23,184,061	60.2
Other liability	17,410,294	61.6
Products liability	1,607,661	67.1
Private passenger auto liability	70,654,316	61.6
Commercial auto liability	12,978,989	72.1
Private passenger auto PD	46,636,351	63.7
Commercial auto PD	5,119,953	69.4
Aircraft	843,638	86.0
Fidelity	772,002	66.5
Surety	2,880,490	22.8
Burglary and theft	107,966	24.9
Boiler and machinery	774,283	52.5
Credit	607,902	36.1
International	435,611	76.5
Reinsurance	10,979,415	67.0
Other lines	1,957,487	66.6
Totals**	$281,508,998	63.1%

*In thousands.

†To premiums earned.

**Excludes state funds.

Source: *Best's Aggregates & Averages, Property–Casualty* (Oldwick, NJ: A.M. Best Company, 1999), p. 284. Copyrighted by A.M. Best Company. Used with permission. *www.ambest.com/*

key features of the main P&C lines. Note, however, that some P&C activity lines (e.g., auto insurance) are marketed as one product to individuals and another to commercial firms, while other lines (e.g., boiler and machinery insurance targeted at commercial purchasers) are marketed to one specific group. To understand the importance of each line in premium income and losses incurred in 1998, review Table 15–3. The changing composition in **net premiums written** (NPW)—the entire amount of premiums on insurance contracts written (these are the gross cash inflows or sales from the insurance

net premiums written

The entire amount of premiums on insurance contracts written.

Figure 15–1 Industry Net Premiums Written by Product Lines, 1960–1998

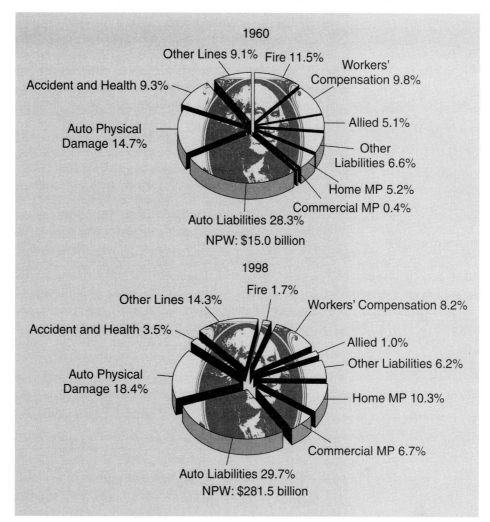

Source: *Best's Aggregates & Averages, Property-Casualty* (Oldwick, NJ: A.M. Best Company, 1994) p. 183; and *Best's Review*, July 1998, p. 41. Copyrighted by A.M. Best Company. Used with permission. *www.ambest.com/*

contracts)—for major P&C lines during the 1960–1998 period is shown in Figure 15–1. Important P&C lines include the following:

- **Fire Insurance and Allied Lines** protect against the perils of fire, lightning, and removal of property damaged in a fire (2.7 percent of all premiums written in 1998; 16.6 percent in 1960).
- **Homeowners Multiple Peril (MP) insurance** protects against multiple perils of damage to a personal dwelling and personal property as well as liability coverage against the financial consequences of legal liability resulting from injury to others. Thus, it combines features of both property and liability insurance (10.3 percent of all premiums written in 1998; 5.2 percent in 1960).
- **Commercial Multiple Peril Insurance** protects commercial firms against perils similar to homeowners multiple peril insurance (6.7 percent of all premiums written in 1998; 0.4 percent in 1960).
- **Automobile Liability and Physical Damage (PD) insurance** provides protection against (1) losses resulting from legal liability due to the ownership or use of the

vehicle (auto liability) and (2) theft or damage to vehicles (auto physical damage) (48.1 percent of all premiums written in 1998; 43.0 percent in 1960).

· **Liability Insurance (other than auto)** provides protection to either individuals or commercial firms against nonautomobile-related legal liability. For commercial firms, this includes protection against liabilities relating to their business operations (other than personal injury to employees covered by workers' compensation insurance) and product liability hazards (6.2 percent of all premiums written in 1998; 6.6 percent in 1960).

Balance Sheets and Recent Trends

6

The Balance Sheet and Underwriting Risk.   The balance sheet of P&C firms at the end of 1998 is shown in Table 15–4. Similar to life insurance companies, P&C insurers invest the majority of their assets in long-term securities. Bonds ($518.9 billion), preferred stock ($11.5 billion), and common stock ($146.6 billion) represented 74.5 percent of total assets in 1998. Looking at their liabilities, we can see that major components are the loss reserves set aside to meet expected losses ($301.3 billion) from *underwriting* the P&C lines described above and the loss adjustment expense ($63.9 billion) item, which relates to expected administrative and related costs of adjusting (settling) these claims. The two items combined represent 40.1 percent of total liabilities and capital. **Unearned premiums** (a set-aside reserve that contains the portion of a premium that has been paid at the start of the coverage period and

unearned premium

Reserves set aside that contain the portion of a premium that has been paid before insurance coverage has been provided.

Table 15–4   Balance Sheet Property-Casualty Industry as of December 31, 1998*

(in millions of dollars)

		Percent of Total
Assets		
Unaffiliated investments	$744,670	81.9%
Bonds	$518,928	57.1%
Preferred stocks	11,500	1.3
Common stocks.	146,567	16.1
Mortgage loans	1,787	0.2
Real estate investment	1,004	0.1
Cash and short-term investments	45,871	5.0
Other invested asset	19,013	2.1
Investments in affiliates.	44,243	4.9
Real estate, office.	7,868	0.9
Premium balance	61,270	6.8
Reinsurance funds	4,836	0.5
Reinsurance recoverable	12,038	1.3
Federal income taxes recoverable	2,010	0.2
Guarantee funds receivable	164	0.0
Electronic data processing equipment	2,576	0.3
Accrued interest.	8,654	1.0
Receivables from affiliates	8,934	1.0
Association accounts	2,138	0.2
Receivable uninsured accident and health plans . .	67	0.0
Future investment income on loss reserves	215	0.0
Other assets	9,084	1.0
Total assets.	$908,767	100.0%

Table 15–4 *concluded*

		Percent of Total
Liabilities and Capital/Surplus		
Losses	$301,265	33.1%
Loss adjustment expenses	63,930	7.0
Reinsurance payable on paid losses.	3,643	0.4
Commissions, taxes, expenses.	14,396	1.6
Federal income taxes	2,613	0.3
Borrowed money	1,676	0.2
Interest on borrowed money	57	0.0
Unearned premiums.	116,668	12.8
Dividends to stockholders	338	0.0
Dividends to policyholders	1,925	0.3
Reinsurance funds	10,116	1.1
Loss portfolio transfer (assumed)	2,373	0.3
Loss portfolio transfer (ceded).	(3,074)	−0.3
Amounts retained for others	5,604	0.6
Remittances not allocated	1,660	0.2
Foreign exchange rate adjustments	721	0.1
Drafts outstanding	4,791	0.5
Payable to affiliates	8,006	0.9
Payable for securities.	2,352	0.3
Amounts held for uninsured A&H plans	10	0.0
Capital notes	1	0.0
Discount on loss reserve	(281)	−0.0
Other liabilities	24,670	2.7
Conditional reserves	11,980	1.3
Policyholders' surplus	333,327	36.6
Capital paid-up $8,472		0.9
Guarantee funds 257		0.0
Surplus notes. 5,349		0.6
Assigned funds 145,609		16.0
Unassigned funds 173,640		19.1
Total liabilities and capital/surplus.	$908,767	100.0%

*Excludes state funds.

Source: *Best's Aggregates & Averages, Property-Casualty* (Oldwick, NJ: A.M. Best Company, 1999), p. 4.
Copyrighted by A.M. Best Company. Used with permission. *www.ambest.com/*

therefore before insurance coverage has been provided) are also a major liability and are equal to 12.8 percent of total liabilities and capital.

To understand how and why the loss reserve—which is the largest liability component—on the balance sheet is established, we need to understand the risks of underwriting P&C insurance. In particular, P&C underwriting risk results when the premiums generated on a given insurance line are insufficient to cover (1) the claims (losses) incurred insuring the risk and (2) the administrative expenses of providing that insurance coverage (legal expenses, commissions, taxes, etc.) after taking into account (3) the investment income generated between the time when the premiums are received to the time when losses are covered. Thus, underwriting risk may result from (1) unexpected increases in loss rates (or loss risk), (2) unexpected increases in expenses (or expense risk), and/or (3) unexpected decreases in investment yields or returns (investment yield/return risk). Next, we look more carefully at each of these three areas of P&C underwriting risk.

Loss Risk.   The key feature of claims loss risk is the actuarial *predictability* of losses relative to premiums earned. This predictability depends on a number of characteristics or features of the perils insured, specifically:

- **Property versus Liability.**   In general, the maximum levels of losses are more predictable for property lines than for liability lines. For example, the monetary value of the loss or damage to an auto is relatively easy to calculate, but the upper limit to the losses to which an insurer might be exposed in a product liability line—for example, asbestos damage to workers' health under other liability insurance—might be difficult if not impossible to estimate.

- **Severity versus Frequency.**   In general, loss rates are more predictable on low-severity, high-frequency lines than on high-severity, low-frequency lines. For example, losses in fire, auto, and homeowners peril lines tend to be expected to occur with high frequency and to be independently distributed across any pool of insured customers. Thus, only a limited number of customers are affected by any single event. Furthermore, the dollar loss of each event in the insured pool tends to be relatively small. Applying the law of large numbers, the expected loss potential of such lines—the **frequency of loss** times the extent of the damage (**severity of loss**)—may be estimable within quite small probability bounds. Other lines, such as earthquake, hurricane, and financial guarantee insurance, tend to insure very low-probability (frequency) events. Here, many policyholders in the insured pool are affected by any single event (i.e., their risks are correlated) and the severity of the loss could be potentially enormous. This means that estimating expected loss rates (frequency times severity) is extremely difficult in these coverage areas. This higher uncertainty of losses forces P&C firms to invest in more short-term assets and hold a larger percentage of capital and reserves than life insurance firms do.

- **Long Tail versus Short Tail.**   Some liability lines suffer from a long-tail risk exposure phenomenon that makes estimation of expected losses difficult. This **long-tail loss** arises in policies for which the insured event occurs during a coverage period but a claim is not filed or made until many years later. The delay in the filing of a claim is in accordance with the terms of the insurance contract and often occurs because the detrimental consequences of the event are not known for a period of time after the event actually occurs. Losses incurred but not reported have caused insurers significant problems in lines such as medical malpractice and other liability insurance where product damage suits (e.g., the Dalkon shield case and asbestos cases) have been filed many years after the event occurred and the coverage period expired.[9]

- **Product Inflation versus Social Inflation.**   Loss rates on all P&C property policies are adversely affected by unexpected increases in inflation. Such increases were triggered, for example, by the oil price shocks of 1973 and 1978. However, in addition to a systematic unexpected inflation risk in each line, line-specific inflation risks may also exist. The inflation risk of property lines is likely to reflect the approximate underlying inflation risk of the economy. Liability lines, however, may be subject to social inflation, as reflected by juries' willingness to award punitive and other damages at rates far above the underlying rate of inflation. Such social inflation has been particularly prevalent in commercial liability and medical malpractice insurance and has been directly attributed by some analysts to faults in the U.S. civil litigation system.

The **loss ratio** measures the actual losses incurred on a specific policy line. It measures the ratio of losses incurred to **premiums earned** (premiums received and earned on insurance contracts because time has passed without a claim being filed).

---

frequency of loss

The probability that a loss will occur.

severity of loss

The size of a loss.

long-tail loss

A loss for which a claim is made some time after a policy was written.

loss ratio

A measure of pure losses incurred to premiums earned.

premiums earned

Premiums received and earned on insurance contracts because time has passed with no claim filed.

---

9. In some product liability cases, such as those involving asbestos, the nature of the risk being covered was not fully understood at the time many of the policies were written.

Thus, a loss ratio of less than 100 means that premiums earned were sufficient to cover losses incurred on that line. Aggregate loss ratios for the period 1951–1998 are shown in Table 15–5. Notice the steady increase in industry loss ratios over the period, increasing from the 60 percent range in the 1950s to the 70 and 80 percent range in the 1980s and 1990s. For example, in 1998 the aggregate loss ratio on all P&C lines was 76.2. This includes, however, loss adjustment expenses (LAE)—see below—as well as "pure" losses. The (pure) loss ratio, net of LAE, in 1998 was 63.1 (see Table 15–3).

Expense Risk. The two major sources of expense risk to P&C insurers are (1) loss adjustment expenses (LAE) and (2) commissions and other expenses. LAE relate to the costs surrounding the loss settlement process; for example, many P&C insurers employ adjusters who determine the liability of an insurer and the size of an adjustment or settlement to make. The other major area of expense involves the commission costs paid to insurance brokers and sales agents and other operating expenses related to the acquisition of business. As mentioned above, the loss ratio reported in Table 15–5 includes LAE. The expense ratio reported in Table 15–5 includes the commission and other expenses for P&C insurers during the 1951–1998 period. Notice in this table that, in contrast to the increasing trend in the loss ratio, the expense ratio decreased over the period shown. Despite this trend, expenses continue to account for a significant portion of the overall costs of operations. In 1998, for example, commission and other expenses amounted to 27.7 percent of premiums written. Clearly, sharp rises in commissions and other operating costs can rapidly render an insurance line unprofitable.

combined ratio

A measure of the overall underwriting profitability of a line; equals the loss ratio plus the ratios of loss-adjusted expenses to premiums earned as well as commission and other acquisition costs to premiums written minus any dividends paid to policyholders as a proportion of premiums earned.

A common measure of the overall underwriting profitability of a line, which includes the loss, loss-adjusted expenses, and expense ratios, is the **combined ratio.** Technically, the combined ratio is equal to the loss ratio plus the ratios of LAE to premiums written, and commissions and other expenses to premiums written. The combined ratio after dividends adds dividends paid to policyholders as a portion of premiums earned to the combined ratio. If the combined ratio is less than 100, premiums alone are sufficient to cover both losses and expenses related to the line.

If premiums are insufficient and the combined ratio exceeds 100, the P&C insurer must rely on investment income on premiums for overall profitability. For example, in 1996, the combined ratio before dividend payments was 104.7, indicating that premiums alone were insufficient to cover the costs of both losses and expenses related to writing P&C insurance. Conversely, in 1997 an 8.6 percent drop in losses incurred on premiums written resulted in a combined ratio of 99.9, the first time premiums covered losses since 1979. Table 15–5 presents the combined ratio and its components for the P&C industry for the years 1951–1998. We see that the trend over this period is toward decreased profitability. The industry's premiums generally covered losses and expenses until the 1980s. Since then, premiums have generally been unable to cover losses and expenses (i.e., combined ratios have been consistently higher than 100).

Investment Yield/Return Risk. As discussed above, when the combined ratio is higher than 100, overall profitability can be ensured only by a sufficient investment return on premiums earned. That is, P&C firms invest premiums in assets between the time they receive the premiums and the time they make payments to meet claims. For example, in 1998, net investment income to premiums earned (or the P&C insurers' investment yield) was 10.4 percent. As a result, the overall average profitability (or **operating ratio**) of P&C insurers was 95.2. It was equal to the combined ratio after dividends (105.6, see Table 15–5) minus the investment yield (10.4). Since the operating ratio was less than 100, P&C insurers were profitable overall in 1998. However, lower net returns on investments (e.g., 1.5 percent rather than 10.4 percent) would have meant that underwriting P&C insurance would have been marginally unprofitable. Thus, the behavior of interest rates and default rates on P&C insurers' investments is crucial to the P&C insurers' overall profitability. That is, measuring and managing credit and interest rate risk are key concerns of P&C managers, as they are for all FI managers.

operating ratio

A measure of the overall profitability of a P&C insurer; equals the combined ratio minus the investment yield.

Table 15–5 Property-Casualty Industry Underwriting Ratios

Year	Loss Ratio*	Expense Ratio†	Combined Ratio	Dividends to Policyholders‡	Combined Ratio after Dividends
1951	60.3	34.0	94.3	2.6	96.9
1952	59.0	33.2	92.2	2.4	94.6
1953	57.9	32.9	90.9	2.6	93.4
1954	57.5	33.7	91.2	2.7	93.9
1955	58.9	33.9	92.9	2.7	95.6
1956	63.8	34.2	98.0	2.7	100.7
1957	66.1	33.7	99.8	2.4	102.3
1958	64.0	33.3	97.3	2.3	99.6
1959	63.0	32.5	95.5	2.2	97.7
1960	63.8	32.2	96.0	2.2	98.1
1961	64.2	32.3	96.5	2.1	98.6
1962	65.1	32.1	97.2	1.9	99.0
1963	67.7	32.2	99.9	2.1	102.0
1964	69.5	31.5	101.0	2.0	103.0
1965	70.3	30.4	100.7	1.9	102.6
1966	67.5	29.6	97.1	1.9	99.0
1967	68.7	29.5	98.2	2.0	100.2
1968	70.4	29.1	99.5	2.0	101.5
1969	72.2	28.4	100.6	1.9	102.5
1970	70.8	27.6	98.4	1.7	100.1
1971	67.5	27.2	94.7	1.7	96.4
1972	66.6	27.7	94.3	1.9	96.2
1973	69.3	28.0	97.3	1.9	99.2
1974	75.5	28.2	103.7	1.7	105.4
1975	79.3	27.3	106.6	1.3	107.9
1976	75.4	25.9	101.3	1.1	102.4
1977	70.7	25.3	96.0	1.2	97.2
1978	70.1	25.8	95.9	1.6	97.5
1979	73.1	26.0	99.1	1.5	100.6
1980	74.9	26.5	101.4	1.7	103.1
1981	76.8	27.4	104.1	1.9	106.0
1982	79.8	27.9	107.7	1.9	109.6
1983	81.5	28.4	109.9	2.1	112.0
1984	88.2	27.9	116.1	1.8	118.0
1985	88.7	25.9	114.6	1.6	116.3
1986	81.6	25.1	106.7	1.3	108.0
1987	77.9	25.3	103.3	1.3	104.6
1988	78.3	25.7	104.0	1.4	105.4
1989	82.0	26.0	107.9	1.3	109.2
1990	82.3	26.0	108.3	1.2	109.6
1991	81.1	26.4	107.6	1.3	108.8
1992	88.1	26.5	114.6	1.2	115.7
1993	79.5	26.2	105.7	1.1	106.9
1994	81.1	26.0	107.1	1.3	108.4
1995	78.9	26.1	105.0	1.4	106.4
1996	78.4	26.3	104.7	1.1	105.8

Table 15–5   *concluded*

Year	Loss Ratio*	Expense Ratio[†]	Combined Ratio	Dividends to Policyholders[‡]	Combined Ratio after Dividends
1997	72.8	27.1	99.9	1.7	101.6
1998	76.2	27.7	103.9	1.7	105.6

*Losses and adjustment expenses incurred to premiums earned.

[†]Expenses incurred (before federal income taxes) to premiums written.

[‡]Dividends to policyholders to premiums earned.

Source: *Best's Aggregates & Averages, Property-Casualty,* (Oldwick, NJ: A.M. Best Company, 1994), p. 158; *Best's Review,* May 1995–1999; and *Best's Aggregates & Averages, Property-Casualty,* (Oldwick, NJ: A.M. Best Company, 1998), p. 256. Copyrighted by A.M. Best Company. Used with permission. www.ambest.com/

Example 15–2   Calculation of P&C Company Profitability

Suppose that an insurance company's loss ratio is 79.8 percent, its expense ratio is 27.9 percent, and the company pays 2 percent of its premiums earned to policyholders as dividends. The combined ratio (after dividends) for this insurance company is equal to:

Loss ratio + Expense ratio + Dividend ratio = Combined ratio after dividends

79.8   +   27.9   +   2.0   =   109.7

Thus, expected losses on all P&C lines, expenses, and dividends exceeded premiums earned by 9.7 percent. As a result, without considering investment income, the P&C insurer is not profitable.

Suppose, however, that the company's investment portfolio yielded 12 percent; the operating ratio and overall profitability of the P&C insurer would then be:

Operating ratio = Combined ratio after dividends − Investment yield
= 109.7 percent   − 12.0 percent
= 97.7 percent

and:

Overall profitability = 100 percent − Operating ratio
= 100 percent − 97.7 percent
= 2.3 percent

As can be seen, the high investment returns (12 percent) make the P&C insurer profitable overall.

Given the importance of investment returns to P&C insurers' profitability, combined with the need for a predictable stream of cash flows to meet required payouts on their insurance policies, the balance sheet in Table 15–4 indicates that bonds—both treasury and corporate—dominate the asset portfolios of P&C insurers. For example, bonds represented 57.1 percent of total assets and 69.7 percent ($518,928m./ $744,670m.) of financial assets (unaffiliated investments) in 1998.

Finally, if losses, LAE, and other expenses are higher and investment yields are lower than expected, resulting in operating losses, P&C insurers carry a significant amount of surplus reserves (policyholder surplus) to reduce the risk of insolvency. In 1998, the ratio of policyholder surplus to assets was 36.6 percent.

Recent Trends.   The period 1987–1998 was not very profitable for the P&C industry. In particular, the combined ratio (the measure of loss plus expense risk) increased

Figure 15–2 The P&C Insurers' Combined Ratio, 1980–1998

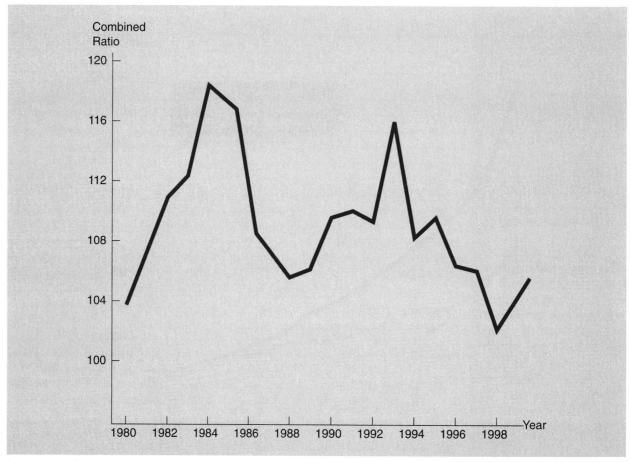

Source: *Best's Review,* various issues. *www.ambest.com/*

underwriting cycle

A pattern that the profits in the P&C industry tend to follow.

from 104.6 in 1987 to 115.7 in 1992 (see Figure 15–2), which was the highest ratio since 1985. (Remember that a combined ratio higher than 100 is bad in that it means that losses, expenses, and dividends totaled *more* than premiums earned.) The major reason for this rise was a succession of catastrophes from Hurricane Hugo in 1989, the San Francisco earthquake in 1991, the Oakland fires of 1991, to the losses (of more than $15 billion) incurred in Florida as a result of Hurricane Andrew in 1991. In the terminology of P&C insurers, the industry was in the trough of an **underwriting cycle**—that is, underwriting conditions were difficult. An example of how bad things were in this industry was that Lloyd's of London (arguably one of the world's most well-known and respected insurers) posted a £510 million loss in 1991.[10]

In 1993, the industry showed signs of improvement, with the combined ratio falling to 106.9. In 1994, however, the ratio rose again to 108.4, partly as a result of the Northridge earthquake with estimated losses of $7 billion to $10 billion. A drop in disaster related losses caused the industry ratio to fall back to 101.6 in 1997. However, major losses associated with El Nino (e.g., Hurricane Georges and Midwest storms) drove the combined ratio back to 105.6 in 1998. Overall, a number of catastrophes of historically high severity have impacted P&C insurers over the 1984–1999 period compared to other post-war periods. This is shown in Figure 15–3.

10. As Lloyd's management explained, the loss was a result of four years of unprecedented disaster claims. As a result of their losses, a group of Lloyd's investors sued the company for negligence in their business operations (some of which in the late 1990s were still working their way through the legal system).

Figure 15–3 U.S. Catastrophes, 1949–1999

Catastrophe	Year	Inflation Adjusted Amount U.S. $(millions)
Hurricane Andrew	1992	$15,900
Northridge earthquake	1994	7,200
Hurricane Hugo	1989	4,939
Hurricane Georges	1998	2,900
Hurricane Betsy	1965	2,346
Hurricane Opal	1995	2,100
Blizzard of '96	1996	2,000
Hurricane Iniki	1992	1,646
Blizzard of '93	1993	1,625
Hurricane Floyd	1999	1,600
Hurricane Fran	1995	1,600
Hurricane Frederic	1979	1,575
Wind; hail; tornadoes	1974	1,395
Minnesota storms	1998	1,300
Freeze	1983	1,280
Oakland fire	1991	1,273
Hurricane Cecelia	1970	1,169
Wind	1950	1,136
California earthquake	1989	1,130
Texas hailstorm	1995	1,100
Midwest storms	1998	1,000
Hurricane Alicia	1983	983
L.A. riots	1992	797

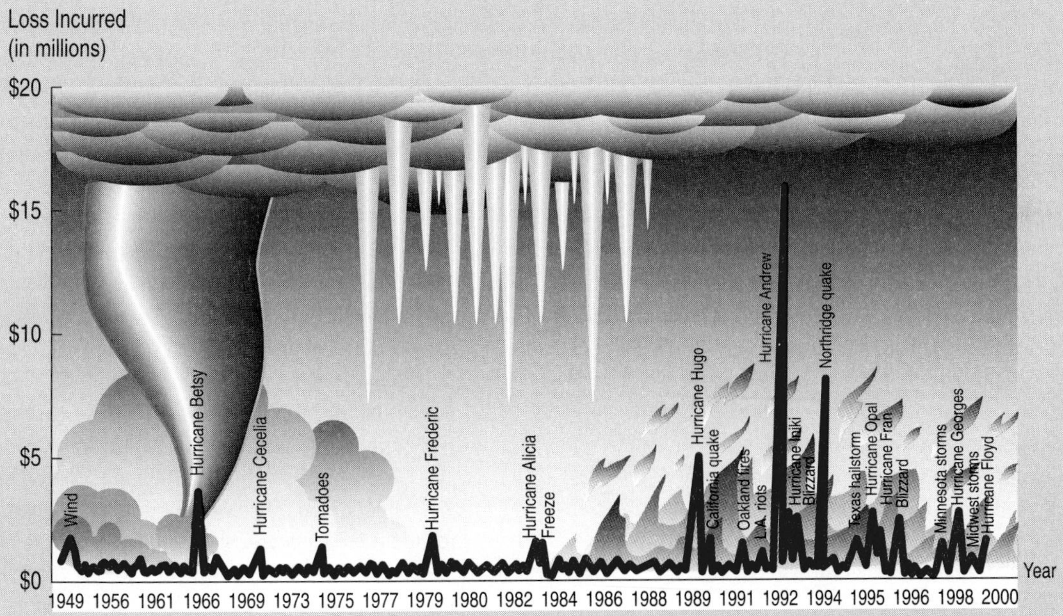

Loss Incurred
(in millions)

[Graph: A chart titled with a y-axis labeled from $0 to $20 in $5 increments, and an x-axis labeled Year from 1949 to 2000 (1949 1956 1961 1966 1969 1973 1975 1977 1979 1980 1982 1984 1986 1988 1989 1991 1992 1994 1995 1996 1998 2000). Peaks are labeled: Wind, Hurricane Betsy, Hurricane Cecelia, Tornadoes, Hurricane Frederic, Hurricane Alicia, Freeze, Hurricane Hugo, California quake, Oakland fires, L.A. riots, Hurricane Iniki, Blizzard, Hurricane Andrew, Northridge quake, Texas hailstorm, Hurricane Opal, Hurricane Fran, Blizzard, Minnesota storms, Hurricane Georges, Midwest storms, Hurricane Floyd.]

Source: Richard L. Sandor, Centre Financial Products, 1949–1994; author's research, 1995–1999.

Regulation

Similar to life insurance companies, P&C insurers are chartered at the state level and regulated by state commissions. In addition, state guarantee funds provide (some) protection to policyholders, in a manner similar to that described

www.naic.org/

earlier for life insurance companies, should a P&C insurance company fail. The National Association of Insurance Commissioners (NAIC) provides various services to state regulatory commissions. These include a standardized examination system, the Insurance Regulatory Information System (IRIS) to identify insurers with loss, combined, and other ratios operating outside normal ranges.

An additional burden that P&C insurers face in some activity lines—especially auto insurance and workers' compensation insurance—is rate regulation. Given the social welfare importance of these lines, state commissioners often set ceilings on the premiums and premium increases in these lines (usually based on specific cost of capital and line risk exposure formulas for the insurance supplier). This has led some insurers to leave states such as New Jersey, Florida, and California, which have the most restrictive regulations.

Do You Understand?

1. Why P&C insurers hold more capital and reserves than life insurers do?
2. Why life insurers' assets are, on average, longer in maturity than P&C insurers' assets?
3. What the main lines of insurance offered by P&C insurers are?
4. What the components of the combined ratio are?
5. How the operating ratio differs from the combined ratio?
6. Why the combined ratio tends to behave cyclically?

Summary

This chapter examined the activities and regulation of insurance companies. The first part of the chapter described the various classes of life insurance and recent trends in this sector. The second part discussed property-casualty companies. The various lines that comprise property-casualty insurance are becoming increasingly blurred as multiple activity line coverages are offered. Both life and property-casualty insurance companies are regulated at the state rather than the federal level.

Questions

1. How does the primary function of an insurance company compare with that of a depository institution?
2. Contrast the balance sheet of depository institutions with those of life insurance firms.
3. How has the composition of the assets of U.S. life insurance companies changed over time?
4. What are the similarities and differences among the four basic lines of life insurance products?
5. Explain how annuities represent the reverse of life insurance activities.
6. How can you use life insurance and annuity products to create a steady stream of cash disbursements and payments so as to avoid either the payment or receipt of a single lump sum cash amount?
7. If an insurance company decides to offer a corporate customer a private pension fund, how would this change the balance sheet of the insurance company?
8. How does the regulation of insurance companies compare with that of depository institutions?
9. a. Calculate the annual cash flows (annuity payments) from a fixed-payment annuity if the present value

of the 20-year annuity is $1 million and the annuity earns a guaranteed annual return of 10 percent. The payments are to begin at the end of the current year.

    b. Calculate the annual cash flows (annuity payments) from a fixed-payment annuity if the present value of the 20-year annuity is $1 million and the annuity earns a guaranteed annual return of 10 percent. The payments are to begin at the end of five years.

10. You deposit $10,000 annually into a life insurance fund for the next 10 years, at which time you plan to retire. Instead of a lump sum, you wish to receive annuities for the next 20 years. What is the annual payment you expect to receive beginning in year 11 if you assume an interest rate of 8 percent for the whole time period?

11. Suppose a 65-year-old person wanted to purchase an annuity from an insurance company that would pay $20,000 until the end of that person's life. The insurance company expected that this person would live for 15 more years and it would be willing to pay 6 percent on the annuity. How much should the insurance company ask this person to pay for the annuity? A second

65-year-old person wants the same $20,000 annuity, but this person is much healthier and is expected to live for 20 years. If the same 6 percent interest rate applies, how much should this healthier person be charged for the annuity?

12. How do life insurance companies earn profits? How does investment in junk bonds increase their returns and what are the drawbacks?

13. How have the product lines based on net premiums written by insurance companies changed over time?

14. What are the two major lines of property-casualty (P&C) insurance firms?

15. What are the three sources of underwriting risk in the P&C industry?

16. How do increases in unexpected inflation affect P&C insurers?

17. **a.** If the simple loss ratio on a line of property insurance is 73 percent, the loss adjustment expense is 12.5 percent, and the ratio of commissions and other acquisitions expenses is 18 percent, is this line profitable?

b. How does your answer to part (a) change if investment yields of 8 percent are added?

18. An insurance company's projected loss ratio is 77.5 percent and its loss adjustment expense ratio is 12.9 percent. It estimates that commission payments and dividends to policyholders will add another 16 percent. What is the minimum yield on investments required in order to maintain a positive operating ratio?

19. Which of the insurance lines listed below will be charged a higher premium by insurance companies and why?

a. Low-severity, high-frequency lines versus high-severity, low-frequency lines.

b. Long-tail versus short-tail lines.

20. An insurance company collected $3.6 million in premiums and disbursed $1.96 million in losses. Loss adjustment expenses amounted to 6.6 percent and dividends paid to policyholders totaled 1.2 percent. The total income generated from their investments was $170,000 after all expenses were paid. What is the net profitability in dollars?

Securities Firms *and* Investment Banks

Chapter Navigator

1. What are the different types of securities firms and investment banks?

2. What are the major activity areas in which securities firms and investment banks engage?

3. What are the major assets and liabilities held by securities firms?

4. Who are the main regulators of securities firms and investment banks?

Services Offered by Securities Firms versus Investment Banks: Chapter Overview

Investment banking involves the raising of debt and equity securities for corporations or governments. This includes the origination, underwriting, and placement of securities in money and capital markets for corporate or government issuers. Securities services involve assistance in the trading of securities in the secondary markets (brokerage services or market making). Together these services are performed by the securities firms and investment banking industry. The largest companies in this industry perform multiple services (e.g., underwriting and brokerage services). These full-line firms are generally called investment banks. Many other firms concentrate their services in one area only (either securities trading or securities underwriting)—that is, some firms in the industry specialize in the purchase, sale, and brokerage of existing securities (the retail side of the business) and are called securities firms, while other firms specialize in originating, underwriting, and distributing issues of new securities (the commercial side of the business) and are called investment banks.

Investment banking also includes corporate finance activities such as advising on mergers and acquisitions (M&As), as well as advising on the restructuring of existing

Figure 16–1 Merger Activity 1990–1998

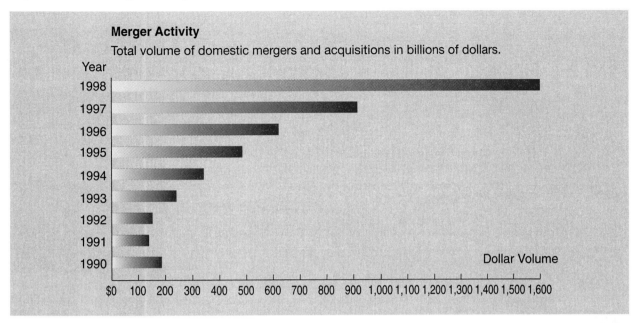

Merger Activity

Total volume of domestic mergers and acquisitions in billions of dollars.

Source: Securities Data Company, 1998. *www.securitiesdata.com/*

corporations. Figure 16–1 reports merger activity for the period 1990–1998, a boom period for this line of business. Total dollar volume (measured by transaction value) of domestic M&As has increased from less than $200 billion in 1990 to $1.62 trillion in 1998 and $1.49 trillion through the first nine months of 1999.[1] The investment bank Goldman Sachs alone managed over $597 billion worth of these mergers in 1998, followed by Merrill Lynch with $537 billion and Morgan Stanley, Dean Witter with $533 billion. This chapter presents an overview of (1) the size, structure, and composition of the industry; (2) the key activities of securities firms and investment banks; (3) the industry's balance sheet and recent trends; and (4) its regulation.

Size, Structure, and Composition of the Industry

Because of the emphasis on securities trading and underwriting, the size of the industry is usually measured by the equity capital of the firms participating in the industry. Securities trading and underwriting is a financial service that requires no investment in assets or liability funding (such as the issuance of loans funded through deposits or payments on insurance contracts funded through insurance premiums). Rather, securities trading and underwriting is a profit (equity) generating activity that does not require that FIs actually hold or invest in the securities they trade or issue for their customers. Accordingly, asset value is not traditionally a measure of the size of a firm in this industry. Equity capital in this industry amounted to $96.0 billion at the end of 1998, supporting total assets of $2.11 trillion.

Beginning in 1980 and until the stock market crash of October 19, 1987, the number of firms in the industry expanded dramatically, from 5,248 in 1980 to 9,515 in 1987. The aftermath of the crash included a major shakeout, with the number of firms declining to 7,785 by 1998, or by 18 percent since 1987. Concentration of business among the largest firms over this period has increased dramatically. According to data in Table 16–1, the largest investment bank in 1987, Salomon Brothers, held capital of $3.21 bil-

---

1. This reflected more than 11,400 deals in 1998 and 16,440 for the first nine months of 1999.

Table 16–1 Largest Investment Companies Ranked by Capital, 1987–1999

1999			1987		
Rank	Company	Capital (in billions of dollars)	Rank	Company	Capital (in billions of dollars)
1.	Morgan Stanley, Dean Witter	$15.40	1.	Salomon Brothers	$3.21
2.	Merrill Lynch	11.02	2.	Shearson Lehman Brothers*	3.12
3.	Goldman Sachs Group	7.86	3.	Merrill Lynch	2.88
4.	Lehman Brothers Holdings	5.95	4.	Goldman Sachs	1.95
5.	Bear Stearns	4.96	5.	Drexel Burnham Lambert†	1.85
6.	Donaldson, Lufkin & Jenrette	3.61	6.	First Boston Corp.	1.36
7.	Paine Webber Group**	3.28	7.	Prudential-Bache Securities	1.29
			8.	Dean Witter Reynolds‡	1.21
			9.	Bear Stearns	1.06
			10.	E.F. Hutton†	0.99
			11.	Morgan Stanley‡	0.99

* Shearson Lehman Brothers and E. F. Hutton merged in 1988.

† Now defunct.

‡ Morgan Stanley and Dean Witter merged in 1997.

** UBS acquired Paine Webber Group in July 2000.

Source: Securities Industry Association annual yearbooks, 1987; and Securities and Exchange Commission, *10-K Reports,* 1999. *www.sia.com/, www.sec.gov/*

lion. In 1999, the largest independent investment bank, Morgan Stanley, Dean Witter, held capital of $15.40 billion—almost five times as much. Some of the significant growth in size has come through M&A among the top-ranked firms in the industry. Table 16–2 lists major U.S. securities industry M&A transactions, many of which involve repeated ownership changes. Notice from this table that 12 of the largest 21 mergers in the industry occurred in 1997 through 1999. Notice, too, how many recent M&As are interindustry mergers among financial service firms (e.g., among insurance companies and investment banks). Figure 16–2 illustrates, for example, the many inter- and intraindustry transactions undertaken by Travelers Group and its subsidiaries prior to its merger with Citicorp in 1998. Historical and recent deregulatory changes such as the Financial Services Modernization Act of 1999 (discussed briefly here and in detail in Chapter 14) have been the major cause of such mergers.

broker-dealers

Firms that assist in the trading of existing securities.

underwriting

Assisting in the issue of new securities.

The firms in the industry can be categorized into three major types. The first type involves the largest firms, the national full-line investment banks that service both retail customers (especially by acting as **broker-dealers**—assisting in the trading of existing securities) and corporate customers (by securities **underwriting**—assisting in the issue of new securities). The major national full-line firms (ranked by capital) are Merrill Lynch and Morgan Stanley, Dean Witter, Discover. In 1997, Morgan Stanley, ranked sixth in capital size, and Dean Witter, Discover, ranked fifth in capital size, merged to create the then largest securities firm in the world. In the News box 16–1 discusses this merger and the way that it revolutionized this industry's provision of underwriting and brokerage services. The second type involves national full-line firms that specialize more in corporate finance. Perhaps the best example of this is Goldman Sachs. The third type involves the remainder of the industry and includes four classes:

Do You Understand?

1. Why the merger of Morgan Stanley and Dean Witter is a merger of "brains" and "brawn"? What does this statement mean?
2. How the Morgan Stanley-Dean Witter merger will affect Morgan Stanley's strategy in the type of clients served?

1. Specialized investment bank subsidiaries of commercial bank holding companies (such as J. P. Morgan).

Table 16–2   Major U.S. Securities Industry Merger and Acquisition Transactions

Rank	Deal	Price (in billions of dollars)	Year
1.	Travelers Group merges with Citicorp	$83.0	1998
2.	Dean Witter merges with Morgan Stanley*	10.2	1997
3.	Travelers Group acquires Salomon Inc.	9.0	1997
4.	Sears spins off Dean Witter, Discover	5.0	1993
5.	Mellon Bank acquires Dreyfus	1.8	1993
6.	Bankers Trust acquires Alex Brown	1.7	1997
7.	American Express spins off Lehman Bros. Holdings	1.6	1994
8.	Fleet Financial acquires Quick and Reilly	1.6	1997
9.	Primerica acquires Shearson	1.2	1993
10.	NationsBank acquires Montgomery Securities	1.2	1997
11.	Credit Suisse acquires First Boston	1.1	1988
12.	Shearson Lehman acquires E. F. Hutton	1.0	1987
13.	First Union acquires EverenCapital	1.0	1999
14.	American Express acquires Shearson	0.9	1981
15.	Bank of Boston acquires Montgomery Securities	0.8	1998
16.	Primerica acquires Smith Barney	0.8	1987
17.	Paine Webber acquires Kidder Peabody	0.7	1994
18.	U.S. Bancorp acquires Piper Jaffray	0.7	1997
19.	ING Group acquires Furman Selz	0.6	1997
20.	BankAmerica acquires Robertson Stephens	0.5	1997
21.	First Union acquires Wheat First Butcher & Singer	0.5	1997

* Value of Dean Witter, Discover shares to be exchanged for Morgan Stanley stock, based on closing price of $40.625 on February 5, 1997.

Source: Securities Data Company and *The Wall Street Journal,* various issues. *www.securitiesdata.com/*

Do You Understand?

1. The trend in the number of securities firms and investment banks since 1980?

2. What categories of firms exist in the securities firm and investment banking industry?

3. What the difference is between brokerage services and underwriting services?

2. Specialized **discount brokers** (such as Charles Schwab) that effect trades for customers without offering investment advice or tips.[2]

3. Regional securities firms that are often classified as large, medium, and small and concentrate on servicing customers in a particular region such as New York or California.

4. Specialized electronic trading securities firms (such as E*Trade) that provide a platform for customers to trade without the use of a broker. Rather, trades are enacted on a computer via the internet.

discount broker

A stockbroker that conducts trades for customers but does not offer investment advice.

Securities Firm and Investment Bank Activity Areas

Securities firms and investment banks engage in as many as seven key activity areas.[3] Note that while each activity is available to a firm's customers independently, many of the activities can be and are conducted simultaneously (such as mergers and acquisitions, issuing debt and equity, and advisory services) for a firm's customers.

2. Discount brokers usually charge lower commissions than do full-service brokers such as Merrill Lynch.

3. See Ernest Bloch, *Inside Investment Banking,* 2nd ed. (Burr Ridge, IL: McGraw-Hill/Irwin, 1989) for a similar list.

Figure 16–2 Interindustry Mergers and Acquisitions by Travelers Group Prior to Merger with Citicorp

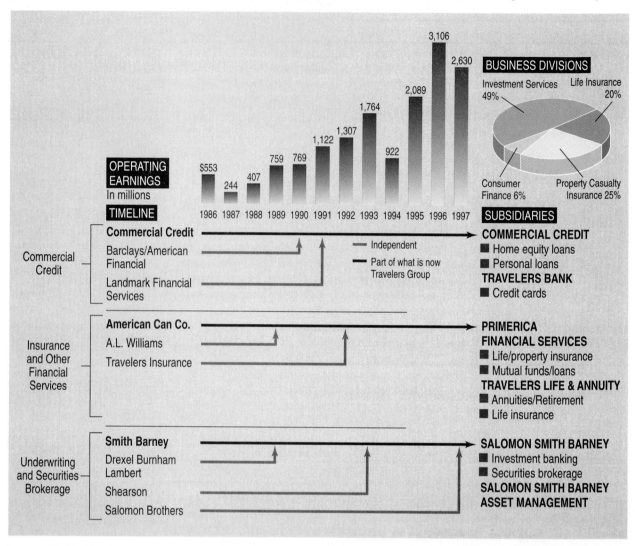

Source: *The New York Times*, January 2, 1998, p. D5. Copyright © 1998 by The New York Times Co. Reprinted by Permission. *www.nyt.com/*

Investing

Investing involves managing pools of assets such as closed- and open-end mutual funds (in competition with commercial banks, life insurance companies, and pension funds). Securities firms can manage such funds either as agents for other investors or as principals for themselves and their stockholders. The objective in funds management is to select asset portfolios to beat some return-risk performance benchmark such as the S&P 500 index.

Investment Banking

Investment banking refers to activities related to underwriting and distributing new issues of debt and equity securities. New issues can be either first-time issues of a company's debt or equity securities or the new issues of a firm whose debt or equity is already trading—seasoned issues (see Chapter 8 for a detailed discussion). Table 16–3 lists the top 10 underwriters through September 1999 based on the dollar value of issues underwritten. The top 10 underwriters represented 80.6 percent of the industry

In the News

16-1

For years, most Wall Street franchises were cleanly divided into blue-chip investment banks catering to institutional clients and brokerage houses serving individual investors. That landscape will soon change profoundly with the marriage of two Wall Street firms that personify those two cultural camps. Morgan Stanley Group Inc. and Dean Witter, Discover & Co. plan to announce a merger as early as today. It would create the largest securities firm in the world, people familiar with the transaction say.

With Morgan Stanley's market capitalization of $8.8 billion and Dean Witter valued in the market at $13 billion, the new firm would have a market capitalization topping $20 billion. The $8.8 billion merger—the biggest combination ever in the securities business—promises to usher in a new round of consolidation as securities firms scramble to find part-

Morgan Stanley Group and Dean Witter Plan an $8.8 Billion Merger

They Face Challenge Melding Elite Institutional Firm with Large Retail Broker

ners to compete with the new Wall Street giant.

Morgan Stanley and Dean Witter are making a bold bet that the future of the business lies in melding two camps that are called the "brains" and "brawn." The brains are blue-chip investment banks such as Morgan Stanley and Goldman, Sachs & Co. that provide strategic advice and underwrite stocks and bonds for corporate clients. The brawn encompasses big brokerage houses selling stocks, bonds and mutual funds to millions of small investors nationwide. These primarily "retail" operations include Dean Witter, which boasts the nation's third largest army of brokers, with more than 8,500. The merger is directly aimed at competing more effectively with Merrill

Lynch & Co., the only Wall Street firm ever to successfully bridge the two camps. But Merrill has accomplished this through internal growth; no Wall Street firm has been able to pull it off through a merger. By becoming the nation's biggest securities firm in terms of capital, the combination of Morgan and Dean Witter will eclipse Merrill, which in 1996 led all other securities firms. It had 1996 net income of $1.6 billion. Morgan Stanley had 1996 net of $1 billion; Dean Witter posted net of $951.4 million . . .

The stunning move marks a remarkable change in strategy for white-shoe Morgan Stanley. Unlike Dean Witter, which serves small investors, Morgan Stanley has long catered to Wall Street's biggest blue-chip clients. It dates back to when the firm was the investment-banking arm of J.P. Morgan & Co., before the two giant institutions were split up during the Depression. After the stock-market crash of 1929, the Glass-Steagall act mandated the separation of commercial banks and securities firms. . . The

(continues)

In the News continued

merger would give Morgan Stanley, with its risky investment-banking and trading businesses, a portfolio of stable franchises such as asset management and credit card. Many Wall Street firms have been trying to smooth out earnings bumps through more recurring streams of revenue. As of the end of last year, Dean Witter had $90 billion in assets under management and administration while Morgan Stanley had $171 billion in assets under management as of Nov. 30. The merger would make Morgan Stanley-Dean Witter the biggest asset-management company on Wall Street, after Merrill's $234 billion.

Meanwhile, Dean Witter's credit-card business has been the real cash cow over the past decade. Discover Card was one of the great success stories of the 1980s in the card business. . . . For Dean Witter, the merger would give it access to a vast array of investment-banking products, including hot initial public offerings and bond deals to hawk to small investors.

Table 16–3   Ten Largest Underwriting Firms Ranked by All Issues, 1999*
(in billions of dollars)

Rank	Underwriter	Value	Number of Issues	Market Share[†]
1.	Merrill Lynch	$ 257.1	1,587	15.2%
2.	Salomon Smith Barney	219.1	1,241	12.9
3.	Goldman Sachs	157.3	886	9.3
4.	Morgan Stanley, Dean Witter	155.1	1,614	9.2
5.	Credit Suisse First Boston	149.5	899	8.8
6.	Lehman Brothers	130.7	728	7.7
7.	Chase Manhattan	97.3	892	5.7
8.	Bear, Stearns	68.8	416	4.1
9.	J.P. Morgan	67.7	452	4.0
10.	Bank of America Securities	62.1	523	3.7
Top 10		$1,364.7	12,876	80.6%
Industry total		$1,692.7	13,537	100.0%

*Through September.

[†] Based on value of issues underwritten.

Source: Thompson Financial Securities Data, 1999. *www.tfsd.com/*

total. Obviously, the industry is dominated by a small number of underwriting firms. Reputation has a huge effect in this business. At times, investment banks have refused to participate in an issue because their name would not be placed where they desired it on the "tombstone" advertisement announcing an issue (see Chapter 1).

Securities underwriting can be undertaken through either public or private offerings. In a private offering, an investment banker acts as a **private placement** agent for a fee, placing the securities with one or a few large institutional investors such as life insurance companies.[4] In a public offering, the securities may be underwritten, either

private placement

A securities issue placed with one or a few large institutional investors.

4. See *Federal Reserve Bulletin,* February 1993, for an excellent description of the private placement market. Issuers of privately placed securities are not required to register with the SEC since the placements (sales of securities) are made only to large sophisticated investors.

on a best efforts or a firm commitment basis, and offered to the public at large. With best efforts underwriting, investment bankers act as *agents* on a fee basis related to their success in placing the issue with investors. In firm commitment underwriting, the investment banker acts as a *principal,* purchasing the securities from the issuer at one price and seeking to place them with public investors at a slightly higher price. Finally, in addition to investment banking operations in the corporate securities markets, the investment banker may participate as an underwriter (primary dealer) in government, municipal, and mortgage-backed securities. See Chapters 6 through 8 for a detailed discussion of these services.

Example 16–1 Calculating the Risk of Underwriting

best efforts underwriting

An underwriting in which the investment banker acts as an agent rather than as a principal that bears risk.

firm commitment underwriting

Securities offered from the issuing firm purchased by an underwriter.

An understanding of the returns and risks of securities underwriting by an investment bank must include an understanding of the mechanics of firm commitment securities offerings. Some corporate securities are offered on a **best efforts underwriting** basis in which the underwriter does not guarantee a price to the corporate issuer and acts more as a placing or distribution agent. The dominant form of underwriting in the United States, however, is firm commitment underwriting. A **firm commitment underwriting** involves securities being purchased by an underwriter directly from an issuing firm (say, at $99 per share), who then reoffers them for sale to the public or the market at large at a slightly higher price—say, $99.50. The difference between the underwriter's buy price ($99) and the public offer price ($99.50) is called the underwriting spread, which compensates the underwriter for accepting the risk of being unable to place the securities with outside investors as well as any administrative and distribution costs associated with the underwriting. In our simple example of a $0.50 spread, the maximum gross revenue the underwriter can gain from underwriting the issue is $0.50 times the number of shares issued. Thus, if 1 million shares were offered, the maximum gross revenue for the underwriting would be $0.50 \times 1,000,000 = $500,000. Note that once the public offering has been made and the price specified in the prospectus, the underwriter cannot raise the price during the offering period. In this example, the underwriter could not raise the price above $99.50, even if it were later determined that the market valued the shares more highly.[5]

As a result, the upside return from underwriting is normally capped. By contrast, downside return risk is not capped and can be very large. Downside risk arises if the underwriter overprices the public offering, setting the public offer price higher than outside investors' private valuations. As a result, the underwriter would be unable to sell the shares during the public offering period and would have to lower the price to get rid of the inventory of unsold shares, especially because this inventory is often financed by issuing short-term commercial paper or through repurchase agreements (see Chapter 5). In our example, if the underwriter has to lower the offering price to $99, the gross revenue from the underwriting would be zero, since this is the price paid to the issuing firm. Any price less than $99 generates a loss. For example, suppose that the issue could be placed only at $97. The underwriter's losses would be ($99 − $97) \times 1,000,000 shares = $2 million.

An underwriter may take a big loss or big hit on an underwriting for a number of reasons. The first is simply overestimating the investor's demand for the shares—especially the price they are willing to pay (i.e., the underwriter overprices the issue). The second is that in the short period between setting the public offering price and seeking to sell the securities to the public, security values may experience a major drop due to underlying stock market conditions. In efficient markets, however, the fees and spreads, together with the expected level of underpricing on the issue, would be set to adequately compensate the investment bank for bearing this risk.

---

5. The offering period is usually a maximum of 10 business days.

Figure 16–3   Profit-Loss Function for British Petroleum Share Underwriting

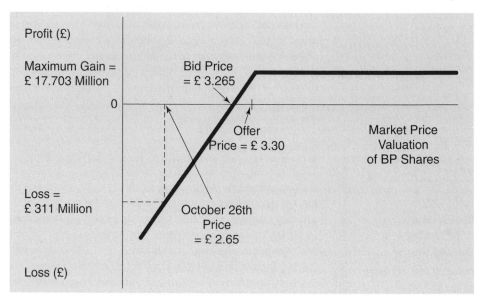

A classic example of this second type of underwriting risk was the sale of British Petroleum (BP) shares in October 1987 in the period surrounding the October 19, 1987, stock market crash. Underwriters set the bid (buy) price of the shares at £3.265 and the offer (sell) price at £3.30 on October 15, 1987, four days before the crash, and four large U.S. investment banks (including Goldman Sachs) agreed to underwrite 22 percent of the issue, or 505,800,000 shares. In the week following the October 19, 1987 crash, however, BP's share price fell to a low of £2.65, so that the underwriters faced a loss of as much as £0.615 per share (£3.265 − £2.65), or a total loss of £311 million. Note that the maximum gross revenue that U.S. underwriters could have made, if they had sold all shares at the originally planned offer price of £3.30, was [(£3.30 − £3.265) × 505.8 million], or £17,703,000. We show this profit and loss trade-off in Figure 16–3. As you can see, firm commitment underwriting involves a potential payoff with a limited potential upside gain (£17,703,000) and a very large downside loss risk.

Of course, the big hit described in the BP case is unusual for three reasons. First, to ensure that all shares are indeed sold upon issue, new issues tend to be underpriced rather than overpriced. Second, in the United States, the offer period is usually much shorter than in the BP example, and third, stock market crashes are fortunately rare.

Market Making

Market making involves the creation of a secondary market in an asset by a securities firm or investment bank. Market making can involve either agency or principal transactions. *Agency transactions* are two-way transactions on behalf of *customers*—for example, acting as a *stockbroker* or dealer for a fee or commission (as discussed in Chapter 8). On the NYSE, a market maker in a stock such as IBM may, upon the placement of orders by its customers, buy the stock at $185 from one customer and immediately resell it at $186 to another customer. The $1 difference between the buy and sell price is usually called the bid-offer spread and represents a large proportion of the market maker's profit. In *principal transactions,* the market maker seeks to profit on the price movements of securities and takes either long or short inventory positions for its own account. (Or, the market maker may take an inventory position to stabilize the market in the securities.[6]) In the example above, the market maker would buy the IBM stock at $185 and hold it in its own portfolio in expectation of a price increase.

Trading

Trading is closely related to the market-making activities performed by securities firms and investment banks just described; a trader takes an active net position in an underlying instrument or asset. There are at least six types of trading activities:

1. *Position Trading*—involves purchases of large blocks of securities on the expectation of a favorable price move. Such positions also facilitate the smooth functioning of the secondary markets in such securities.

2. *Pure Arbitrage*—entails buying an asset in one market at one price and selling it immediately in another market at a higher price.

3. *Risk Arbitrage*—involves buying securities in anticipation of some information release—such as a merger or takeover announcement or a Federal Reserve interest rate announcement.[7]

4. *Program Trading*—defined by the NYSE as the simultaneous buying and selling of a portfolio of at least 15 different stocks valued at more than $1 million, using computer programs to initiate such trades. Program trading is often associated with seeking to profit from differences between the cash market price (e.g., the Standard & Poor's 500 Stock Market Index) and the *futures* market price of a particular instrument.[8]

5. *Stock Brokerage*—involves the trading of securities on behalf of individuals who want to transact in the money or capital markets. To conduct such transactions, individuals contact their broker (such as Merrill Lynch), who then sends the orders to its representative at the exchange to conduct the trades (see Chapter 8).

6. *Electronic Brokerage*—offered by major brokers, involves direct access, via the Internet, to the trading floor (at low cost), therefore bypassing traditional brokers.

Securities trading can be conducted on behalf of a customer as an agent or on behalf of the firm as a principal. When trading at the retail level occurs on behalf of customers, it is often called brokerage (or stock brokering). Further, as noted above, many securities firms and investment banks offer on-line trading services to their customers as well as direct access to a client representative (stockbroker). Thus, customers may now conduct trading activities from their homes and offices through their account at a securities firm, at a lower cost in terms of fees and commissions. In 1999, there were also more than 100 purely electronic securities trading firms in existence. These firms, which generally require at least $5,000 to open an account, offer investors (day traders) a desk and a computer with high-speed access to the stock markets. An estimated 5 million people used the facilities offered by electronic trading firms in 1999. Figures 16–4 and 16–5 illustrate the tremendous growth in on-line trading based on the number of internet dealers and the amount of on-line trading. In the News box 16–2 also discusses the tremendous impact on-line is having on the industry.

Do You Understand?

1. Why electronic trading of stocks will not go the way of many fads and die out?

---

6. In general, full-service investment banks can become market makers in stocks on the National Association of Securities Dealers Automated Quotation (NASDAQ), but they have been prevented until recently from acting as market-making specialists on the NYSE.

7. It is termed *risk arbitrage* because if the event does not actually occur—for example, if a merger does not take place or the Federal Reserve does not change interest rates—the trader stands to lose money. A good example of heavy losses from such activities were those sustained by the hedge fund Long-Term Capital Management (LTCM) in 1998 with reported losses close to $4 billion.

8. An example is investing cash in the S&P index and selling futures contracts on the S&P index. Since stocks and futures contracts trade in different markets, their prices are not always equal. Moreover, program trading can occur between cash markets in other assets—for example, commodities.

Figure 16–4   Number of Internet Dealers Offering On-Line Trading

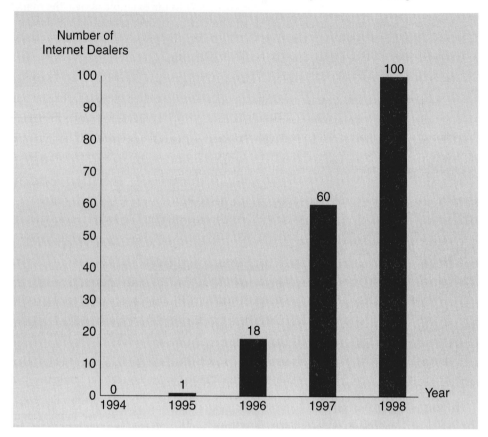

Source: Securities Industry Association, 1998. *www.sia.com/*

Figure 16–5   On-Line Trading: A Meteoric Rise in On-Line Accounts, Dollars

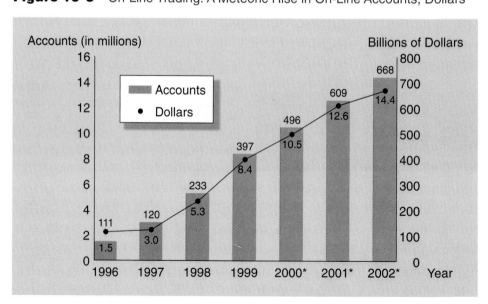

*Projected.

Source: Securities Industry Association, 1998. *www.sia.com/*

In the News

16-2

Internet Trading Turns Brokerage World Upside Down

Ever wonder why so many shares trade on the stock exchanges and over the NASDAQ? One of the reasons is the emergence of Internet brokerage firms. Today, before our very eyes, we're witnessing a revolution in the stock brokerage industry. And the companies dominating it are not—with the possible exception of Charles Schwab, which in reality is still a relative newcomer—any of the old-line brokerage firms. The Internet brokers are not called Merrill Lynch, Paine Webber or Morgan Stanley, but have names like Suretrade, E*Trade, Ameritrade, DATEK and so forth.

The brokerage business may very well go the way of the computer business. Just ask yourself, who are today's major computer companies? About the only one that remains from a decade ago is IBM. Companies like Burroughs, Sperry Rand, Control Data and Digital Equipment are either distant memories or have been folded into today's survivors.

The current giants are the newcomers of not that

Source: *Capital Times*, January 19, 1999, p. 2C, by Ray Unger.

many years ago. Companies like Compaq, Dell and Gateway. So who's to say Merrill Lynch will forever be the giant of the brokerage business? Only time will tell.

One thing is for sure. Internet brokerage firms are not a fad. I've researched a number of them and I can tell you that they offer to the general public what institutional investors used to pay hundreds of thousands of dollars for in terms of technical and fundamental research, not to mention incredible trading capability. And this is just the beginning.

Internet brokerage firm E*Trade is also entering the lucrative underwriting business, which could bring attractive IPOs (Initial Public Offerings) to the general public—something that heretofore was the domain of and the source of huge profits for both traditional brokerage firms and large institutions.

For the most part, IPOs—especially hot IPOs—are reserved for institutional investors.

Thus, when a hot new stock is offered to the public, most of the stock generally is swallowed up by the institutions that have paid the traditional underwriters the most in commissions.

This means that when the underwriting brokerage firm gives an institution first shot at buying the IPO at $15 per share and the first shares trade in public markets at $25, the institution makes an instant profit. The few shares that the general public receives are only a token and most times those tokens are reserved for individual investors who have also paid dearly in commission business. With E*Trade entering the IPO business, this cozy relationship may end . . .

E*Trade is expected to lower the cost and increase the speed of the IPO process. Will E*Trade allow individual investors to buy into these hot new issues at the issue price? You bet. The genius behind E*Trade's marketing strategy is to greatly expand its already huge customer base. And IPOs are an attractive lure. With an ever enlarging base of clients, E*Trade wants to offer smaller IPOs (in the $25 *(continues)*

In the News continued

million range) along with private placements, convertible debt and straight debt . . .

This is not, I repeat, an endorsement of E*Trade as a stock idea for investors.

This is simply a comment on the rapidly changing brokerage industry. Without question, the Internet brokers are here to stay because they offer an incredible array of research

and trading capability and a growing venue of other financial services. But I'm also reserving judgement on the advisability of using all those services.

Cash Management

cash management account

Money market mutual fund sold by investment banks that offer check-writing privileges.

Securities firms and investment banks offer bank deposit–like **cash management accounts** (CMAs) to individual investors and, since the 1999 Financial Services Modernization Act, deposit accounts themselves (Merrill Lynch being the first to offer a direct deposit account in June 2000 via the two banks it owns). Most of these accounts allow customers the ability to write checks against some type of mutual fund account (e.g., money market mutual fund). These accounts can even be covered directly or indirectly by federal deposit insurance from the FDIC. CMAs have been instrumental in this industry's efforts to provide deposit-type services.

Mergers and Acquisitions

Investment banks frequently provide advice on, and assistance in, mergers and acquisitions. For example, they assist in finding merger partners, underwrite any new securities to be issued by the merged firms, assess the value of target firms, recommend terms of the merger agreement, and even assist target firms in preventing a merger (for example, writing poison-pill provisions into a potential target firms's securities contracts). As mentioned in the chapter overview, mergers and acquisitions activity topped $1.62 trillion in 1998, the fifth consecutive annual record for domestic merger activity, and was $1.17 trillion through the first nine months of 1999. Table 16–4 lists the top 10 investment bank merger advisers ranked by dollar volume of the mergers in which they were involved.

Worldwide M&A activity boomed during this period as well. The volume of worldwide M&A activity exceeded $2.20 trillion through the third quarter of 1999, compared to $1.63 trillion over the same period in 1998. European M&As have represented a growing portion of the activity. Deals involving European targets accounted for approximately 36 percent of the total activity in 1999 (U.S. activity accounted for 52 percent). This is up from 21 percent of the volume in 1998 (U.S. activity in 1998 accounted for 67 percent). Table 16–5 lists the top 10 investment banks ranked by dollar volume of worldwide M&A activity. Notice that many of the top U.S. ranked investment banks reported in Table 16–4 are also top ranked for worldwide activity in Table 16–5.

Other Service Functions

Other service functions include custody and escrow services, clearance and settlement services, and research and advisory services—for example, giving advice on divestitures and asset sales. In performing these

Do You Understand?

1. What the key areas of activities for securities firms are?
2. What the difference is between a best efforts and a firm commitment offering?
3. What the six trading activities performed by securities firms are?

Table 16–4   Ten Largest U.S. Mergers and Acquisition Firms Ranked by Value of Mergers, 1999*

Rank	Investment Bank	Value (billions of dollars)	Number of Deals
1.	Goldman Sachs	$ 464.6	174
2.	Morgan Stanley, Dean Witter	405.8	177
3.	Merrill Lynch	361.1	150
4.	Credit Suisse First Boston	211.5	109
5.	Salomon Smith Barney	194.8	137
6.	Donaldson, Lufkin, and Jenrette	194.7	180
7.	Lehman Brothers	176.6	92
8.	Chase Manhattan	125.5	52
9.	J.P. Morgan	89.4	66
10.	Allen & Co.	71.2	7
Industry total		$1,166.1	8,199

*Through September

Source: Thomson Financial Securities Data, 1999. *www.tfsd.com/*

Table 16–5   Ten Largest Worldwide Mergers and Acquisition Firms Ranked by Total Credit Lent, 1999*

Rank	Investment Bank	Credit Lent (billions of dollars)	Number of Deals
1.	Goldman Sachs	$ 539.1	235
2.	Morgan Stanley, Dean Witter	411.7	238
3.	Merrill Lynch	357.6	233
4.	Credit Suisse First Boston	297.7	197
5.	Donaldson, Lufkin, and Jenrette	247.7	210
6.	J.P. Morgan	195.0	152
7.	Salomon Smith Barney	163.6	173
8.	Lehman Brothers	135.9	188
9.	Lazard Houses	102.1	106
10.	Deustche Bank	99.0	163
Industry total		$1,493.5	16,440

*Through September.

Source: Thomson Financial Securities Data, 1999. *www.tfsd.com/*

functions, investment banks normally act as agents for a fee. In addition, investment banks are making increasing inroads into traditional bank service areas such as small-business lending and the trading of loans (see Chapter 7).

Recent Trends and Balance Sheets

Recent Trends

In this section, we look at the balance sheet and trends in the securities firm and investment banking industry since the 1987 stock market crash. Trends in this industry depend heavily on the state of the stock market. For example, a major effect of the 1987 stock market crash was a sharp decline in stock market trading volume and, thus,

Figure 16–6 Commission Income as a Percentage of Total Revenues

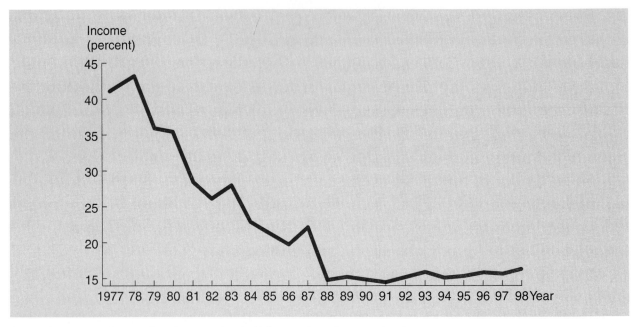

Source: Securities and Exchange Commission and Standard & Poor's *Industry Surveys,* various issues.

in the brokerage commissions earned by securities firms over the 1987–1991 period.[9] These commissions only began to recover in 1992 (see Figure 16–6), with record stock market trading volumes being achieved in 1995 through 1999 (when the Dow Jones and S&P indexes hit new highs—see Chapter 8.)[10] In addition to commissions from stock market trading, between 1987 and 1999, securities firms and investment banks in the aggregate nearly tripled their holdings of fixed-income securities (corporate bonds, foreign bonds, mortgage-backed bonds, and Treasury bonds) in a strategic move to enhance trading profits. A heavy reliance on fixed-income trading, however, can also produce losses if interest rates (and other asset prices) move in a direction other than expected. For example, Salomon Brothers and a number of other securities firms and investment banks announced record trading losses on their bond trading activities in 1994. Thus, interest rate risk is now a focal area of securities firm and investment bank risk exposure.

Also affecting the profitability of the investment banking industry was the decline in bond and equity underwriting during the 1987–1990 period. This was partly a result of the stock market crash, partly a result of a decline in M&As, and partly a reflection of investor concerns about junk bonds[11] following the Drexel Burnham Lambert scandal

9. The decline in brokerage commissions actually began as early as 1977 following the abolition of fixed commissions on securities trades by the Securities and Exchange Commission (SEC) in May 1975 and the fierce competition for wholesale commissions and trades that followed. Although a sharply increased volume of equities trading in 1992 returned commissions to 1987 levels, this may be a temporary phenomenon.

10. The Dow Jones Industrial Average crossed the 5000 mark on November 21, 1995, when it closed at 5023.55. Less than 18 months later, the Dow topped 7000 when it closed at 7022.44 on February 14, 1997. In another five months, on July 17, 1997, it topped 8000, closing at 8038.88; and just nine months later, on April 6, 1998, it topped 9000, closing at 9033.23. The Dow closed over 10,000 at 10,006.78 on March 29, 1999, and topped 11,000, closing at 11,014.69 just 24 days later on May 3, 1999.

11. A junk bond is a bond that rating agencies such as Standard and Poors (S&P) and Moody's classify as being excessively risky, having below investment grade quality.

Table 16–6   U.S. Corporate Underwriting Activity
(in billions of dollars)

	Straight Corporate Debt	Convertible Debt	Asset-Backed Debt	Total Debt	High-Yield Bonds	Common Stock	Preferred Stock	Total Equity	All IPOs	Total Underwriting
1990	$ 106.9	$4.8	$178.9	$ 290.6	$ 1.4	$ 19.2	$ 4.7	$ 23.9	$10.2	$ 314.4
1991	200.6	7.5	299.0	507.1	10.0	56.0	20.0	76.0	25.1	583.1
1992	309.7	7.0	427.8	744.5	38.2	72.4	29.2	101.6	39.4	871.6
1993	432.5	9.3	479.3	921.1	54.3	102.3	28.4	130.6	57.4	1,051.8
1994	367.4	4.7	253.4	625.5	31.6	61.6	15.5	177.1	34.0	745.5
1995	442.9	5.4	154.6	602.9	28.3	81.9	16.3	98.3	30.3	701.1
1996	544.2	8.4	248.5	801.1	34.1	115.1	37.4	152.5	50.0	953.6
1997	749.9	8.4	381.1	1,139.4	28.0	118.4	33.6	152.0	43.9	1,291.5
1998	1,089.0	6.2	560.9	1,656.0	35.5	114.8	37.6	152.4	43.7	1,808.4
1998*	872.0	5.0	424.6	1,301.6	30.2	87.7	32.3	120.0	31.0	1,421.7
1999*	916.6	7.7	401.0	1,325.3	21.7	110.4	22.2	132.6	41.9	1,457.9
% change	5.1%	54.0%	−5.6%	1.8%	−28.1%	25.9%	−31.3	10.5%	35.2%	2.5%

(1998 through September to 1999 through September)

*Through September.

Note: High-yield bonds represent a subset of straight corporate debt. IPOs is a subset of common stock; true and closed-end fund IPOs are subsets of all IPOs.

Source: Securities Industry Association, Industry Statistics, various issues. *www.sia.com/*

and that firm's failure in 1989.[12] Between 1991 and 1999, however, there was a resurgence in underwriting activity.[13] The growth in underwriting activity during this period is evident from the fact that the total dollar value of underwriting activity increased from $314 billion in 1990 to $1,808.4 billion in 1998 (and $1,457.9 billion through the *first nine months* of 1999—see Table 16–6).

Despite this resurgence of underwriting activity, the 1990s presented a new challenge for investment bank underwriters. Specifically, in 1987 the Federal Reserve allowed bank holding companies to expand their activities in securities underwriting (activities that had been prohibited since the Glass-Steagall Act was passed in 1933) through special subsidiaries of bank holding companies called Section 20 subsidiaries (see Chapter 14 for details). Indeed, among the top investment banks listed in Table 16–3 are Section 20 subsidiaries of commercial banks (such as J.P. Morgan's Section 20 subsidiary). By the late 1990s, these special investment bank subsidiaries (Section 20 subsidiaries) of commercial banks had captured 20 percent of the corporate debt underwriting market. In 1999, the Financial Services Modernization Act removed all Glass-Steagall barriers and restrictions between commercial banks and investment banks. This should produce even more competition for underwriting services in the future.[14]

12. Drexel was once the most influential firm on Wall Street because of its pioneering work under Michael Milken in the junk bond market. Drexel went bankrupt, however, after its corporate officials pleaded guilty to six felony counts of federal securities fraud. Drexel and Milken were found to have "plundered" the S&L industry by manipulating the market for junk bonds. The essence of the legal action involved the fact that Milken, working for Drexel, used S&Ls to create a web of buyers that helped give the appearance of a market for junk bonds. The fraudulent market allowed Drexel to sell junk bonds at prices above their fair market values; S&Ls held almost 20 percent of junk bonds outstanding, and when the junk bond market collapsed, many S&Ls, especially those in California, suffered large losses.

13. Pretax profit for the securities industry rose from $162 million in 1990 to $10.0 billion in 1998 and $6.7 billion in the first half of 1999.

14. See, A. Gande, M. Puri, and A. Saunders, "Bank Entry, Competition and the Market for Corporate Securities Underwriting," *Journal of Financial Economics* 54, no. 2 (October 1999), pp. 165–96.

Figure 16–7 Securities Industry Pretax Profits, 1990–1998

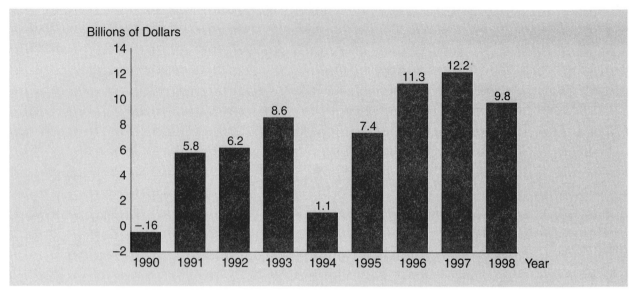

Source: Securities Industry Association, 1999. *www.sia.com/*

As a result of the resurgence of the stock markets, enhanced trading profits, and growth in new issues underwriting, pretax net income for the industry has topped $10 billion in recent years: $11.27 billion in 1996; $12.2 billion in 1997; and $9.8 billion in 1998 (see Figure 16–7).[15] This is despite the collapse of Russian ruble and bond markets, economic turmoil in Asia, and political uncertainty in Washington over much of this period. Such trends should continue as long as the U.S. economy continues to experience strong growth and low inflation.

Balance Sheet

The consolidated balance sheet for the industry is shown in Table 16–7. Looking at the asset portfolio, long positions in securities and commodities accounted for 23.33 percent of assets; reverse repurchase agreements—securities purchased under agreements to resell (i.e., the broker gives a short-term loan to the repurchase agreement seller, see Chapter 5)—accounted for 29.33 percent of assets.

With respect to liabilities, repurchase agreements—securities sold under agreement to repurchase—were the major source of funds (these are securities temporarily lent in exchange for cash received). Repurchase agreements amounted to 42.28 percent of total liabilities and equity. The other major sources of funds were securities and commodities sold short for future delivery and broker-call loans from banks. Equity capital amounted to only 4.35 percent of total assets. These levels are generally below the levels held by commercial banks (8.51 percent in 1999). One reason for their lower equity capital levels is that securities firm and investment bank balance sheets contain mostly tradable (liquid) securities compared to the relatively illiquid loans that represent a significant portion of banks' asset portfolios. Firms in this industry are

Do You Understand?

1. What the trend in profitability in the securities industry has been over the last 10 years?
2. What the major assets held by broker-dealers are?
3. Why broker-dealers tend to hold less equity capital than do commercial banks and thrifts?

15. This information is from the Securities Industry Association. The dip in pretax profits in 1994 coincides with the increase in interest rates and the resulting drop in new securities issues during this year.

Table 16–7   Assets and Liabilities of Broker-Dealers As of Year-End 1998
(in millions of dollars)

		Percent of Total Assets
Assets		
Cash	$ 27,780.4	1.26%
Receivables from other broker-dealers	766,399.7	34.72
Receivables from customers	135,723.3	6.15
Receivables from noncustomers	19,296.1	0.87
Long positions in securities and commodities	514,949.9	23.33
Securities and investments not readily marketable	8,833.8	0.40
Securities purchased under agreements to resell	647,360.8	29.33
Exchange membership	933.0	0.04
Other assets	85,964.0	3.90
Total assets	$2,207,241.0	100.00
Liabilities		
Bank loans payable	$ 47,363.2	2.15
Payables to other broker-dealers	361,774.7	16.39
Payables to noncustomers	39,604.9	1.79
Payables to customers	239,797.3	10.86
Short positions in securities and commodities	263,219.8	11.93
Securities sold under repurchase agreements	933,214.3	42.28
Other nonsubordinated liabilities	170,715.5	7.73
Subordinated liabilities	55,501.5	2.52
Total liabilities	$2,111,191.2	95.65
Capital		
Equity capital	$ 96,049.8	4.35
Number of firms	7,785	

Source: *Focus Report,* Office of Economic Analysis, U.S. Securities and Exchange Commission, 1998, Washington, D.C. *www.sec.gov/*

required by the SEC to maintain a minimum net worth (capital) to assets ratio of 2 percent.

Regulation

www.sec.gov/

The primary regulator of the securities industry is the Securities and Exchange Commission (SEC), established in 1934. Indeed, the National Securities Markets Improvement Act (NSMIA) of 1996 reiterated the primacy of the SEC in this capacity. Prior to NSMIA, most securities firms were subject to regulation from both the SEC and the state in which they operated. NSMIA provides that states may still require securities firms to pay fees and file documents submitted to the SEC, but most of the regulatory burden imposed by states has been removed. States are also now prohibited from requiring registration of securities firms' transactions. Thus, NSMIA effectively gives the SEC exclusive regulatory jurisdiction over securities firms.

The SEC mainly sets rules governing securities firms' underwriting and trading activities. For example, SEC Rule 144A defines the boundaries between the public offering of securities and the private placement of securities (see Chapter 8). SEC Rule

shelf registration

Allows firms that plan to offer multiple issues of stock over a two-year period to submit one registration statement summarizing the firm's financing plans for the period.

www.nyse.com/
www.nasd.com/
www.sipc.org/

Do You Understand?

1. What the major result of NSMIA is?
2. What two organizations monitor trading abuses?

---

415 on **shelf registrations** allows large corporations to register their new issues with the SEC up to two years in advance.[16]

While the SEC sets the overall regulatory standards for the industry, two self-regulatory organizations are involved in the day-to-day regulation of trading practices. These are the New York Stock Exchange (NYSE) and the National Association of Securities Dealers (NASD)—the latter responsible for trading in the over-the-counter markets such as NASDAQ. They monitor trading abuses (such as insider trading) and securities firms' capital (solvency positions)—such as the 2 percent net worth to assets minimum capital ratio (see above).

Finally, the Securities Investor Protection Corporation (SIPC) protects investors against losses of up to $500,000 on securities firm failures. This guarantee fund was created following the passage of the Securities Investor Protection Act in 1970 and is financed by premium contributions from member firms. The fund protects investor accounts in the event that a member firm cannot meet its financial obligations to customers. The fund does not, however, protect against losses on customers' accounts due to poor investment choices that reduce the value of their portfolio.

---

16. They are called *shelf* offerings because after registering the issue with the SEC, the firm can take the issue "off the shelf" and sell it to the market when conditions are the most favorable—for example, in the case of debt issues, when interest rates are low. In late 1998, the SEC proposed a fundamental overhaul of the registration process for public offerings, rejecting the short-form registration for companies selling new issues of seasoned securities and the shelf registration process. The proposal requires preliminary prospectuses to be delivered to all investors and all transactional information to be filed with the SEC prior to, or contemporaneous with, any sale of securities. Thus, delayed shelf offerings would be a thing of the past.

Summary

This chapter presented an overview of security firms, which primarily offer retail services to investors, and investment banking firms, which primarily offer activities and services related to corporate customers. Firms in this industry help bring new issues of debt and equity to the financial markets. In addition, this industry facilitates the trading and market making of securities after they are issued. The chapter discussed the structure of the industry and changes in the degree of concentration in firm size in the industry over the last decade. Balance sheet information that highlighted the major assets and liabilities of the firms was also analyzed.

Questions

1. In what ways are securities firms and investment banks financial intermediaries?
2. How has the size of the securities firm and investment banking industry changed since the late 1980s?
3. What are the different firms in the securities industry and how do they differ from each other?
4. Contrast the activities of securities firms with depository institutions and insurance firms.
5. What are the seven key activity areas of security firms and how were they impacted by the stock market crash of 1987?
6. What is the difference between pure arbitrage and risk arbitrage? If an investor observes the price of a stock trading in one exchange to be different from another exchange, what form of arbitrage is applicable and how could the investor participate in that arbitrage?
7. What three factors accounted for the resurgence in profits for securities firms from 1991–1999? Are firms that trade in fixed-income securities more or less likely to have volatile profits? Why or why not?
8. Explain the difference between the investing and investment banking activities performed by securities firms and investment banks.

9. How does a public offering differ from a private placement?

10. How does a best efforts underwriting differ from a firm commitment underwriting? If you operated a company issuing stock for the first time, which type of underwriting would you prefer? Why might you still choose the alternative?

11. How do agency transactions differ from principal transactions for market makers?

12. Why have brokerage commissions earned by securities firms fallen since 1977?

13. What was the largest single asset and largest single liability of securities firms in 1998?

14. What benefits could a commercial banker obtain by getting into the investment banking business?

15. An investor notices that an ounce of gold is priced at $318 in London and $325 in New York. What action could the investor take to try to profit from the price discrepancy? Which of the six trading activities would this be? What might be some impediments to the success of the transaction?

16. An investment banker agrees to underwrite a $5,000,000 bond issue for the JCN corporation on a firm commitment basis. The investment banker pays JCN on Thursday and plans to begin a public sale on Friday. What type of interest rate movement does the investment bank fear while holding these securities?

17. An investment banker pays $23.50 per share for 3,000,000 shares of the KDO company. It then sells these shares to the public for $25. How much money does KDO receive? What is the investment banker's profit? What is the stock price of KDO?

18. The MEP company has issued 5,000,000 new shares. Its investment banker agrees to underwrite these shares on a best efforts basis. The investment banker is able to sell 4,200,000 shares for $54 per share. It charges MEP $1.25 per shares sold. How much money does MEP receive? What is the investment banker's profit. What is the stock price of MEP?

19. Which type of security accounts for the most underwritings in the United States?

20. What was the significance of the National Securities Markets Improvement Act of 1996?

Finance Companies

Chapter Navigator

1. How do finance companies differ from commercial banks?

2. What are the major types of finance companies?

3. What are the major assets and liabilities held by finance companies?

4. To what extent are finance companies regulated?

1 Finance Company Functions: Chapter Overview

The primary function of finance companies is to make loans to both individuals and businesses. Finance companies provide such services as consumer lending, business lending, and mortgage financing. Some finance company loans are similar to commercial bank loans such as commercial and auto loans, but others are aimed at relatively specialized areas such as high-risk (low credit quality) loans to small businesses and consumers. Unlike banks, finance companies do not accept deposits; instead, they rely on short- and long-term debt for funding. This chapter discusses the size, structure, and composition of this industry, the services it provides, its competitive and financial position, and its regulation.

Size, Structure, and Composition of the Industry

The first major finance company was originated during the Depression when General Electric Corp. created General Electric Capital Corp. (GECC) to finance appliance sales to cash-strapped customers unable to obtain installment credit from banks. Installment credit is a loan that is paid back to the lender with periodic payments

Table 17–1 Assets and Liabilities of U.S. Finance Companies
(*June 30, 1999*)

	Billions of Dollars	Percent of Total Assets
Assets		
Accounts receivable gross	$ 756.5	71.2%
Consumer	269.2	25.3
Business	373.7	35.2
Real estate.	113.5	10.7
Less reserves for unearned income	(53.4)	(5.0)
Less reserves for losses	(13.4)	(1.3)
Accounts receivable net	$ 689.7	64.9%
All other	373.2	35.1
Total assets	$1,062.9	100.0%
Liabilities and Capital		
Bank loans	$ 25.1	2.4%
Commercial paper	231.0	21.7
Debt due to parent	65.4	6.2
Debt not elsewhere classified.	383.1	36.0
All other liabilities	226.1	21.3
Capital, surplus, and undivided profits. . . .	132.2	12.4
Total liabilities and capital	$1,062.9	100.0%

Source: *Federal Reserve Bulletin,* October 1999, p. A32. *www.bog.frb.fed.us/*

www.ge.com/gec/

(installments) consisting of varying amounts of interest and principal (e.g., auto loans, home mortgages, and student loans). Suppose a finance company lent $1,000 to a customer to be repaid in 36 equal installments at the end of each month over the next three years, and the finance company charges the borrower 8 percent interest on the balance of the loan outstanding at the beginning of each month. Accordingly, the borrower must pay the finance company an installment of $31.34 at the end of each month over the next three years to pay off principal and interest on the loan.[1]

By the late 1950s, banks had become more willing to make installment loans, so finance companies began looking outside their parent companies for business. GECC's loan and lease portfolio today includes leases for more than 182,000 rail cars, 200 commercial airlines, more than $1 billion in leveraged buyout financing (where the borrower is a firm with an unusually high leverage ratio, often up to 90 percent), and a $100 billion mortgage servicing portfolio,[2] along with more than $350 million in loans to General Electric customers.[3]

Because of the attractive rates they offer on some loans (such as new car loans, see below), their willingness to lend to riskier borrowers than commercial banks, their often direct affiliation with manufacturing firms, and the relatively limited amount of regulation imposed on these firms, finance companies have been among the fastest growing financial intermediary (FI) groups in recent years. As of the second quarter of 1999, their assets stood at $1,062.9 billion (see Table 17–1). Comparing this to assets

1. The installment amount is determined using the following equation as outlined in Chapter 2:
$$\$1,000 = PMT\,(PVIFA_{8\%/12,\ 3(12)}).$$

2. Mortgage servicing is a fee-related business whereby, after mortgages are securitized, the flow of mortgage repayments (interest and principal) has to be collected and passed on (by the mortgage servicer) to investors in either whole mortgage loan packages or securitization vehicles such as pass-through securities (see Chapters 7 and 25). In undertaking this intermediation activity, the servicer charges a fee.

3. See GECC's website, 1999.

Table 17–2   Assets and Liabilities of U.S. Finance Companies
(December 31, 1975)

	Billions of Dollars	Percent of Total Assets
Assets		
Accounts receivable gross	$75.3	92.3%
Consumer	36.0	44.1
Business	39.3	48.2
Less reserves for unearned income		
and losses	(9.4)	(11.5)
Accounts receivable net	$65.9	80.8%
Cash and bank deposit	2.9	3.5
Securities	1.0	1.2
All others	11.8	14.5
Total assets	$81.6	100.0%
Liabilities and Capital		
Bank loans	$ 8.0	9.8%
Commercial paper	22.2	27.2
Debt:		
Short-term.	4.5	5.5
Long-term.	27.6	33.8
Other.	6.8	8.4
Capital, surplus, and undivided profits. . . .	12.5	15.3
Total liabilities and capital	$81.6	100.0%

Source: *Federal Reserve Bulletin*, June 1976, p. A39. *www.bog.frb.fed.us/*

www.gmacfs.com/

www.fordcredit.com/

www.household.com/

www.americangeneral.com/

www.citgroup.com/

sales finance institutions

Finance companies specializing in loans to customers of a particular retailer or manufacturer.

personal credit institutions

Finance companies specializing in installment and other loans to consumers.

business credit institutions

Finance companies specializing in business loans.

factoring

The process of purchasing accounts receivable from corporations (often at a discount), usually with no recourse to the seller should the receivables go bad.

Do You Understand?

1. What the reason was for the strong reported 1998 earnings for some of the major finance companies?

of $81.6 billion at the end of 1975 (Table 17–2), this industry has experienced growth of more than 1,200 percent in the last 24 years. GMAC Commercial Mortgage Corp. (GMACCM), a subsidiary of General Motors Acceptance Corp. (GMAC), is in fact the largest commercial mortgage lender in the United States, with a mortgage portfolio of more than $40 billion in place. The company announced in the late 1990s that it had plans to expand its product mix to create one of the world's leading commercial finance companies.

The three major types of finance companies are (1) sales finance institutions, (2) personal credit institutions, and (3) business credit institutions. **Sales finance institutions** (e.g., Ford Motor Credit and Sears Roebuck Acceptance Corp.) specialize in making loans to customers of a specific retailer or manufacturer. **Personal credit institutions** (e.g., Household Finance Corp. and American General Finance) specialize in making installment and other loans to consumers. **Business credit institutions** (e.g., CIT Group and Heller Financial) provide financing to corporations, especially through equipment leasing and **factoring**, in which the finance company purchases accounts receivable from corporate customers at a discount from face value and the finance company assumes the responsibility for collecting the accounts receivable. Many large finance companies (e.g., GMAC) perform all three services.

The industry is quite concentrated; the 20 largest firms account for more than 80 percent of its assets. In addition, many of the largest finance companies such as GMAC tend to be wholly owned or captive

Do You Understand?

1. What the three major types of finance companies are? What types of customers does each serve?
2. What a captive finance company is?

captive finance company

A finance company wholly owned by a parent corporation.

subsidiaries of major manufacturing companies. A major role of a **captive finance company** is to provide financing for the purchase of products manufactured by the parent, as GMAC does for GM cars. In the News box 17–1 presents information on four of the largest finance companies.

In the News

17–1

Strong Profit Growth Reported at Biggest Finance Companies

Amid mixed year end reports by commercial banks, some of the largest finance companies are posting record-breaking growth. Household International, GE Capital Corp., Metris, and Associates First Capital Corp., four of the top nonbank lenders in the country, all reported strong earnings this week. These companies' focus on the healthy consumer loan market, a lack of risky trading activities, and the recent demise of several of the smaller consumer finance shops all work in their favor, analysts said. And they are making successful forays into overseas markets.

Household on Wednesday reported a 71% increase in net income for the fourth quarter, to $349.9 million. The Prospect Heights, Ill., company closed its merger with Beneficial Corp. in June, result-

ing in cost savings and increased originations, analysts said. Household also benefited from strong performances from its U.S. and U.K. consumer finance business, said chief executive William F. Aldinger.

Household, which sold nearly $2 billion of credit card receivables in the second half, said it is going to "focus on fewer, stronger MasterCard and Visa programs." Household pointed to a new alliance with Renaissance Holdings, a nonprime credit issuer. "Historically, Household branch customers and credit card customers are very separate," said BT Alex Brown analyst Mark Alpert. "They missed an opportunity to offer cards to non-prime customers." In

addition, Household is expected to announce initiatives with existing credit card partners General Motors and AFL-CIO next week, said Fox-Pitt Kelton analyst Dennis LaPlante. Analysts praised Household for building up its core portfolio this year. "Before, this had been a cost savings story," said Mr. LaPlante, referring to Household's long-standing strategy of making acquisitions and cutting costs to boost earnings.

General Electric Co.'s finance unit, GE Capital Services, is producing an increasingly significant portion of the company's profits. Its earnings were up 17%, to $3.796 billion. General Electric as a whole earned $9.296 billion for the year, up 13%. During the year, the unit purchased a U.K. reinsurance company, a Japanese consumer loan corporation, and a German equipment lender. GE also recast GE Capital's top management in early

(continues)

Source: *American Banker*, January 21, 1999, p. 4, by Heather Timmons.

www.americanbanker.com/

In the News continued

December, ousting chief executive Gary Wendt.

Metris Cos., a subprime credit card specialist, said Wednesday that its net income increased 51% for the year, to $57.3 million. Credit card loans under management by the St. Louis Park, Minn., company which was spun off by catalogue retailer Fingerhut Inc. increased $1.1 billion during the fourth quarter, to $5.3 billion.

Associates First Capital Corp. on Tuesday reported 19% increases in fourth-quarter and annual earnings, to $332 million and $1.22 billion, respectively. Associates First, based in Dallas, has its "strongest balance sheet, largest receivables base, and greatest number of customers ever," said chief executive Keith Hughes. The company's strong overseas operations—including a Japanese consumer finance company—and an overall shift to unsecured lending contributed to the growth, said chief financial officer Roy Guthrie. Despite Associates' earnings growth, its stock fell $1.125 the day of the announcement, in part because of an uptick in losses, analysts said. The percentage of Associates' loans that were 60 days or more delinquent rose 42 basis points in 1998, to 2.57%. Mr. Guthrie attributes the rise to a centralization of the company's manufactured housing servicing.

Balance Sheet and Recent Trends

Assets

Finance companies provide three basic types of loans: real estate, consumer, and business. The assets and liabilities of finance companies, as of the second quarter of 1999, are presented in Table 17–1. Business and consumer loans (called *accounts receivable*) are the major assets held by finance companies; they represent 60.5 percent of total assets. In 1975, 92.3 percent of total assets were consumer and business loans. Thus, compared to depository institutions, which hold a large percentage of longer term real estate loans, finance companies hold shorter term consumer and business loans. Over the last 25 years, however, finance companies have replaced consumer and business loans with increasing amounts of real estate loans and other assets, although these loans have not become dominant, as is the case with many depository institutions.

Table 17–3 presents information concerning the industry's loans from 1994 through June 1999 for consumer, real estate, and business lending. In recent years, the fastest growing areas of asset activity have been in the nonconsumer finance areas, especially leasing and business lending. In June 1999, consumer loans constituted 39.73 percent of all finance company loans, mortgages represented 14.97 percent, and business loans comprised 45.30 percent.

Consumer Loans. Consumer loans include motor vehicle loans and leases and other consumer loans. Motor vehicle loans and leases are traditionally the major type of consumer loan (75.0 percent of the consumer loan portfolio in June 1999). Table 17–4 data indicate that finance companies generally charge higher rates for automobile loans than do commercial banks. From 1994 through 1996, auto finance companies charged interest rates that were from 0.79 to 1.67 percent higher than those of commercial

Table 17–3 Finance Company Loans Outstanding from 1994 through June 1999

(in billions of dollars)

	1994	1995	1996	1997	1998	June 1999	Percent of Total, 1999
Consumer..................	$248.0	$285.8	$310.6	$330.9	$356.1	$374.6	39.73%
Motor vehicle loans........	70.2	81.1	86.7	87.0	103.1	108.6	11.52
Motor vehicle leases.......	67.5	80.8	92.5	96.8	93.3	95.6	10.14
Revolving*..............	25.9	28.5	32.5	38.6	32.3	32.4	3.44
Other†..................	38.4	42.6	33.2	34.4	33.1	32.6	3.46
Securitized assets							
Motor vehicle loans......	32.8	34.8	36.8	44.3	54.8	65.3	6.93
Motor vehicle leases.....	2.2	3.5	8.7	10.8	12.7	11.3	1.20
Revolving.............	N/A	N/A	0.0	0.0	8.7	9.7	1.03
Other	11.2	14.7	20.1	19.0	18.1	19.0	2.01
Real estate	66.9	72.4	111.9	121.1	131.4	141.2	14.97
One- to four-family........	N/A	N/A	52.1	59.0	75.7	80.5	8.54
Other	N/A	N/A	30.5	28.9	26.6	33.0	3.50
Securitized real estate assets‡							
One- to four-family	N/A	N/A	28.9	33.0	29.0	27.5	2.91
Other	N/A	N/A	0.4	0.2	0.1	0.2	0.02
Business..................	298.6	331.2	347.2	366.1	396.5	427.1	45.30
Motor vehicles	62.0	66.5	67.1	63.5	79.6	82.8	8.78
Retail loans............	18.5	21.8	25.1	25.6	28.1	30.9	3.28
Wholesale loans§........	35.2	36.6	33.0	27.7	32.8	32.7	3.47
Leases.................	8.3	8.0	9.0	10.2	18.7	19.2	2.03
Equipment	166.7	188.0	194.8	203.9	198.0	208.3	22.10
Loans	48.9	58.6	59.9	51.5	50.4	53.3	5.65
Leases.................	117.8	129.4	134.9	152.3	147.6	155.1	16.45
Other business receivables‖ ..	46.2	47.2	47.6	51.1	69.9	82.6	8.76
Securitized assets‡							
Motor vehicles	14.3	20.6	24.0	33.0	29.2	32.1	3.40
Retail loans...........	1.5	1.8	2.7	2.4	2.6	2.9	0.31
Wholesale loans.......	12.8	18.8	21.3	30.5	24.7	27.2	2.88
Leases..............	N/A	N/A	0.0	0.0	1.9	2.0	0.21
Equipment	8.9	8.1	11.3	10.7	13.0	13.3	1.41
Loans	4.7	5.3	4.7	4.2	6.6	6.7	0.71
Leases..............	4.2	2.8	6.6	6.5	6.4	6.6	0.70
Other business receivables‖	0.5	0.8	2.4	4.0	6.8	8.0	0.85
Total....................	$613.5	$689.5	$769.7	$818.1	$884.0	$942.9	100.0%

*Excludes revolving credit reported as held by depository institutions that are subsidiaries of finance companies.

†Includes personal cash loans, mobile home loans, and loans to purchase other types of consumer goods such as appliances, apparel, boats, and recreation vehicles.

‡Outstanding balances of pools on which securities have been issued; these balances are no longer carried on the balance sheets of the loan originator.

§Credit arising from transactions between manufacturers and dealers—that is, floor plan financing.

‖Includes loans on commercial accounts receivable, factored commercial accounts, and receivable dealer capital; small loans used primarily for business or farm purposes; and wholesale and lease paper for mobile homes, campers, and travel trailers.

Source: *Federal Reserve Bulletin,* September, 1999, p. A33. *www.bog.frb.fed.us/*

banks. Because new car sales by U.S. firms in 1997 through 1999 were lower than normal, finance companies owned by the major auto manufacturers slashed the interest rates charged on new car loans (some as low as 3.9 percent) over this period. However, other than for new auto loans, these types of low rates are fairly rare.

Table 17–4   Consumer Credit Interest Rates for 1994 through June 1999

Type	1994	1995	1996	1997	1998	May 1999
Commercial bank new car	8.12%	9.57%	9.05%	9.02%	8.72%	8.30%
Auto finance company new car	9.79	11.19	9.84	7.12	6.30	6.57
Difference in commercial bank versus finance company rate	1.67	1.62	0.79	−1.90	−2.42	−1.73

Source: *Federal Reserve Bulletin,* October 1999, p. A36. *www.bog.frb.fed.us/*

The higher rates that finance companies generally charge for consumer loans is due to the fact that they generally attract riskier customers than commercial banks. In fact, customers that seek individual (or business) loans from finance companies are often those who have been refused loans at banks or thrifts.[4] It is, in fact, possible for individuals to obtain a mortgage from a **subprime lender** finance company (a finance company that lends to high-risk customers) even with a bankruptcy in their credit records. Banks rarely make such loans. Most finance companies that offer these mortgages, however, charge rates commensurate with the higher risk, and a few **loan shark** companies prey on desperate consumers, charging exorbitant rates as high as 30 percent or more per annum. In the News box 17–2 points out that such subprime lending by finance companies often involves surprisingly high fees as well.

Other consumer loans include personal cash loans, mobile home loans, and loans to purchase other types of consumer goods such as appliances, apparel, general merchandise, and recreation vehicles. In June 1999, other consumer loans made up 25.0 percent of the consumer loan portfolios of finance companies.

Mortgages. Residential and commercial mortgages have become a major component in finance companies' asset portfolios, although they did not generally offer mortgages prior to 1979 (see Table 17–2). As explained in Chapter 7, finance companies, which are not subject to as extensive a set of regulations as are banks, are often willing to issue mortgages to riskier borrowers than commercial banks. They compensate for the additional risk by charging higher interest rates. Mortgages include all loans secured by liens on any type of real estate (see Chapter 7), either by directly lending to the mortgage customer or as a result of **securitizing mortgage assets** (e.g., mortgages packaged and used as assets backing secondary market securities).[5] The mortgages in the loan portfolio can be first mortgages, or second mortgages in the form of home equity loans. The bad debt expense and administrative costs of home equity loans are lower than on other finance company loans, and as a result they have become a very attractive product to finance companies.[6]

Business Loans. Business loans represent the largest portion of the loan portfolio of finance companies. Finance companies have several advantages over commercial banks in offering loan services to small-business customers. First, they are not subject to regulations that restrict the type of products and services they can offer (discussed later). Second, because finance companies do not accept deposits, they have no bank-type

subprime lender

A finance company that lends to high-risk customers.

loan sharks

Subprime lenders that charge unfairly exorbitant rates to desperate, subprime borrowers.

Do You Understand?

1. Why individuals borrow from subprime lenders?
2. What some of the strategies for finding the best deals among subprime lenders are?

securitized mortgage assets

Mortgages packaged and used as assets backing secondary market securities.

---

4. We look at the analysis of borrower (credit) risk in Chapter 21.

5. Chapter 25 discusses the securitization of mortgages in more detail.

6. A home equity loan is where a house-owner uses his or her house as collateral to borrow money. Should the borrower default, the finance company can seize the house. As a result, home equity finance is among the least risky of the loan products offered by finance companies.

In the News

17-2

In The Wild West of Subprime Lending, Borrowers Have to Dodge Many Bullets

I magine paying credit-card fees higher than your credit line. Or getting a mortgage loan with an interest rate twice the national average. Sound outrageous? Maybe so. But when it comes to the exploding "subprime" lending market—the wild west of consumer lending—almost anything goes. Just look at the newest credit card being touted to high-risk borrowers by First Alliance Mortgage Co., Irvine, Calif. In addition to annual interest of up to 24.8%, borrowers pay a $179.50 sign up fee and a $38.50 annual fee. Worse, their credit is tied to equity in their home. The penalty for nonpayment: foreclosure. ("This is for borrowers who otherwise wouldn't have access to this kind of credit," says Mark Mason, executive vice president of First Alliance.) . . .

Thousands of consumers are signing up for high-priced deals with subprime lenders; they aren't just people with low incomes and dismal credit

histories. "It is increasingly a broader spectrum of American households that qualify as subprime," says Mark Zandi, chief economist of Regional Financial Associates Inc., a West Chester, Pa., consulting firm. "Some have bad credit and others may just be over indebted."

To be sure, most people with troubled credit histories or heavy debt burdens are happy to get a loan or credit at all. But financial advisers and other experts say that in many cases borrowers are paying more than they have to, sometimes far more. Worse, some lenders in this market use pricing techniques that consumer advocates say are designed to veil the true cost of a loan or credit lines . . .

Dallas-based Associates says it is concerned about abusive lending practices and urges customers to educate themselves when considering a loan, according to a statement Monday

in response to the Senate hearings. "Loans should make economic sense for our customers and our company," it said . . .

"The subprime market provides a lot of flexibility for the consumer and the lender, but it's those same attributes that provide the opportunity for abuses," says William Anderson, President of Bank Rate Monitor in North Beach, Fla. . . .

The pitfalls of subprime lending can be more difficult to detect when it comes to used car loans, which can have interest rates of up to 30%. "Many times the true price of the financing is disguised by the increases to the price of the car," says Mr. Anderson. "So a dealer can do a loan at what appears to be a market rate, but inflate the price of the car." . . .

Meanwhile, here are some tips from experts to help you find the best deal:

First, check your credit report for accuracy. According to a study released last week by U.S. Public Interest Research Group, a consumer advocacy group in Washington, a third of credit reports contain errors. This suggests many

(continues)

In the News continued

people are classified as high-risk borrowers when they shouldn't be.

Don't assume you'll get shut out by a traditional lender. Indeed, according to Freddie Mac, 35% of borrowers who have obtained mortgages in the subprime market could have qualified for a conventional loan at a lower rate.

Request a list of all fees and expenses. A lender may advertise no "application fee" but charge a hefty fee by a different name.

Ask what the annual percentage rate will be on your loan. The APR, as it is known, is your interest rate, after all fees and other expenses have been included.

Do your research. "Don't take the loan from someone who calls you on the phone," says Norma Garcia, a staff attorney at the Consumers Union in San Francisco. "Compare the rates of at least three lenders."

regulators looking directly over their shoulders.[7] Third, being (in many cases) subsidiaries of corporate-sector holding companies, finance companies often have substantial industry and product expertise. Fourth—as mentioned with consumer loans—finance companies are more willing to accept risky customers than are commercial banks. Fifth, finance companies generally have lower overheads than banks (e.g., they do not need expensive tellers/branches for deposit taking.)

The major subcategories of business loans are retail and wholesale motor vehicle loans and leases (19.4 percent of all business loans in June 1999), equipment loans (48.8 percent), other business loans (19.3 percent), and securitized business assets (12.5 percent). Motor vehicle loans consist of retail loans that assist in transactions between the retail seller of the good and the ultimate consumer (i.e., cars purchased by individuals and passenger car fleets purchased by a business for use by its employees). Wholesale loans are loan agreements between parties other than the companies' consumers. For example, GMAC provides wholesale financing to GM dealers for inventory floor plans in which GMAC pays for GM dealers' auto inventories received from GM. GMAC puts a lien on each car on the showroom floor. While the dealer pays periodic interest on the floor plan loan, it is not until the car is sold that the dealer pays for the car.

Business-lending activities of finance companies also include equipment loans, with the finance company either owning or leasing the equipment directly to its industrial customer or providing the financial backing for a working capital loan or a loan to purchase or remodel the customer's facility. Finance companies often prefer to lease equipment rather then sell and finance the purchase of equipment. One reason for this is that repossession of the equipment in the event of default is less complicated when the finance company retains its title (by leasing). Further, a lease agreement generally requires no down payment, making a lease more attractive to the business customer. Finally, when the finance company retains ownership of the equipment (by leasing), it receives a tax deduction in the form of depreciation expense on the equipment. Other business loans include loans to businesses to finance or purchase accounts receivable at a discount (factoring), small farm loans, and wholesale loans and leases for mobile homes, campers, and trailers.

---

7. Finance companies do, of course, have market participants observing their work and monitoring their activities.

Liabilities and Equity

To finance asset growth, finance companies have relied primarily on short-term commercial paper and other debt (longer-term notes and bonds). As data in Table 17–1 indicate, in June 1999 commercial paper amounted to $231.0 billion (21.7 percent of total assets); other debt (due to parent holding companies and not elsewhere classified) totaled $448.5 billion (42.2 percent of total assets). Total capital comprised $132.2 billion (12.4 percent of total assets), and loans from banks totaled $25.1 billion (2.4 percent of total assets). A comparison of these figures with those for 1975 (in Table 17–2) indicates that commercial paper was used more in 1975 (27.2 percent of total assets), while other debt (short- and long-term) was less significant as a source of financing (39.3 percent). Finance companies also now rely less heavily on bank loans for financing and hold less capital. In 1975, bank loans were 9.8 percent of total assets, and capital was 15.3 percent of the total. Much of the change in funding sources is due to the strong economy and low interest rates in the U.S. economy in the late 1990s relative to that in the mid-1970s. The strong economy means that cheap, long-term financing is available through public debt markets. Accordingly, finance companies have increased their use of this type of funding.

As mentioned earlier, unlike banks and thrifts, finance companies cannot accept deposits. Rather, to finance assets, finance companies rely heavily on short-term commercial paper, with many having programs in which they sell commercial paper directly to mutual funds and other institutional investors on a continuous day-by-day basis. Finance companies are now the largest issuers in the short-term commercial paper market. Most commercial paper issues have maturities of 30 days or less, although they can be issued with maturities of up to 270 days (see Chapter 5).[8]

The outlook for the industry as a whole is currently quite bright. Loan demand among lower- and middle-income consumers is especially strong, because many of these consumers have little savings. Nevertheless, problems for industry participants specializing in loans to relatively lower quality customers have been well publicized. For example, Jayhawk Acceptance Corporation, which finances car loans to some of the nation's riskiest buyers, filed for bankruptcy in 1997. Indeed, some analysts predicted a shakeout in the market for subprime mortgages as well. For example, Cityscape Financial Corp. of Elmsford, New York, was close to bankruptcy in the late 1990s, as were some of this sector's biggest firms (e.g., Aames Financial Corp., Advanta, and FirstPlus Financial Group). Other leading subprime lenders (e.g., The Money Store, Beneficial Finance, and Green Tree Financial) ceased trading as they were merged into larger financial institutions. A major problem stems from finance companies' accounting practices, which let them record fees and profits on mortgages up front when, in fact, earnings on mortgages come in gradually, if at all.

www.aames.net/afc/
index.cgi/

www.advanta.com/

www.firstplus.com/

www.themoneystore.
com/

www.conseco.com/

Do You Understand?

1. How the major assets held by finance companies have changed in the last 25 years?
2. How subprime lender finance company customers differ from consumer loan customers at commercial banks?
3. What advantages finance companies offer over commercial banks to small-business customers?

Regulation

The Federal Reserve defines a *finance company* as a firm whose primary assets are loans to individuals and businesses.[9] Finance companies, like depository institutions, are financial intermediaries that borrow funds so as to profit on the difference between the rates paid on borrowed funds and charged on loans. Also like depository institutions, finance companies may be subject to state-imposed usury ceilings on the maximum loan rates assigned to individual customers. Because finance

---

8. Commercial paper issued with a maturity longer than 270 days must be registered with the SEC (i.e., it is treated the same as publicly placed bonds).

9. Whereas a bank is defined as an institution that *both* accepts deposits and makes loans.

companies do not accept deposits, they are not subject to the extensive oversight by federal and state regulators as are banks or thrifts—even though they offer services that compete directly with those of depository institutions (e.g., consumer installment loans and mortgages—see Table 17–3). The lack of regulatory oversight for these companies enables them to offer banklike services and yet avoid the expense of regulatory compliance and the same "net regulatory burden" imposed on banks and thrifts (see Chapter 14).

Nevertheless, since finance companies are heavy borrowers in the capital markets, they need to signal their safety and solvency to investors. Such signals are usually sent by holding much higher equity or capital-to-assets ratios—and therefore, lower leverage ratios—than banks. For example, their aggregate balance sheet for the second quarter of 1999 (Table 17–1) shows a capital-assets ratio of 12.4 percent for finance companies. This compares to the capital-to-assets ratio of 8.51 percent reported in Table 11–2 for commercial banks. Larger finance companies also use default protection guarantees from their parent companies and/or other guarantees, such as letters of credit or lines of credit purchased for a fee from high-quality commercial or investment banks, as additional protection against insolvency risk and as a device to increase their ability to raise additional funds in the capital and money markets. Thus, this group will tend to operate with lower capital-to-assets ratios than smaller finance companies. Given that there is relatively little regulatory oversight of this industry, having sufficient capital and access to financial guarantees are critical to their continued ability to raise funds. Thus, finance companies operate more like nonfinancial, nonregulated companies than the other types of financial institutions examined in this text.

Do You Understand?

1. Why finance companies are not subject to the same regulations as banks even though they seem to compete in the same lending markets as banks?
2. How finance companies signal solvency and safety to investors?

Summary

This chapter presented an overview of the finance company industry. This industry competes directly with depository institutions for high-quality (prime) loan customers by specializing in consumer, real estate, and business loans. The industry also services those subprime (high-risk) borrowers deemed too risky for depository institutions. Because firms in this industry do not accept deposits, however, they are not subject to the same (net) regulatory burden as depository institutions. Moreover, because they have no access to deposits, finance companies rely heavily on the short- and long-term debt markets for funding, especially the market for commercial paper. The industry is growing and is generally profitable, but some sectors of the industry—especially those specializing in subprime lending—are experiencing financial problems.

Questions

1. What are the three types of finance companies and how do they differ from commercial banks?
2. Why do you think finance companies have been among the fastest growing FI groups in recent years?
3. What are the three types of lending services offered by finance companies?
4. Compare Tables 16–7 and 17–1. Which firms have higher capital ratios (as a percentage of total assets), securities firms or finance companies? What does this indicate about the relative strengths of these two firms?
5. How does the amount of equity as a percentage of assets compare for finance companies and commercial banks? What accounts for the difference?
6. What are the major assets and liabilities held by finance companies?
7. What has been the fastest growing area of asset business for finance companies?
8. Why was the reported rate on motor vehicle loans historically higher for a finance company than a commercial bank? Why did this change in 1997?

9. What advantages do finance companies have over banks in offering services to small-business customers?

10. Why are finance companies less regulated than commercial banks?

11. Why have finance companies begun to offer more mortgage and home equity loans?

12. What is a wholesale motor vehicle loan?

13. What signal does a low debt-to-assets ratio for a finance company send to the capital markets?

14. Go to the GMAC website, www.gmacfs.com/, and use the calculator function to find out how much the monthly payment would be on a $25,000 car with a $2,000 trade-in, a $1,500 down payment, and a 12 percent annual financing rate payable monthly for 36 months.

Mutual Funds

Chapter Navigator

1. How has the mutual fund industry grown through time?

2. What is the difference in long-term mutual funds and money market mutual funds?

3. What is a mutual fund prospectus?

4. How is the net asset value of a mutual fund investment calculated?

5. Who are the main regulators of mutual funds?

Mutual Funds: Chapter Overview

Mutual funds are financial intermediaries that pool the financial resources of investors and invest those resources in (diversified) portfolios of assets. Open-end mutual funds (the majority of mutual funds) sell new shares to investors and redeem outstanding shares on demand at their fair market values. Thus, they provide opportunities for small investors to invest in financial securities and to diversify risk. Mutual funds are also able to enjoy economies of scale by incurring lower transaction costs and commissions. The tremendous increase in the market value of financial assets such as equities in the 1990s[1] and the relatively low transaction cost opportunity that mutual funds provide to investors (particularly small investors) who want to hold such assets (through either direct mutual fund purchases or contributions to retirement funds sponsored by employers and managed by mutual funds—see Chapter 19), have caused the mutual fund industry to boom. Shareholder services offered by mutual funds include

---

1. For example, the S&P index reported a return of more than 28 percent in 1998.

Table 18–1 Growth of Mutual Funds for Various Years from 1940 to 1998*

Year	Total Net Assets (in billions)	Gross Sales (in billions)	Redemptions (in billions)	Net Sales (in billions)	Shareholders (in thousands)	Number of Companies
1998	$3,791.4	$1,057.8	$747.7	$310.1	155,007	6,288
1997	3,430.8	874.3	542.8	331.5	135,689	5,765
1996	2,637.4	684.8	398.7	286.1	118,752	5,305
1995	2,070.5	477.2	313.6	168.7	101,597	4,764
1994	1,550.5	474.0	329.7	144.2	89,484	4,394
1993	1,510.0	511.6	231.4	280.2	70,049	3,638
1992	1,100.1	364.4	165.5	198.9	53,975	2,985
1991	853.1	236.6	116.3	120.3	45,030	2,606
1990	568.5	149.5	98.3	51.3	39,614	2,362
1980	58.4	10.0	8.2	1.8	7,325	458
1970	47.6	4.6	3.0	1.6	10,690	356
1960	17.0	2.1	0.8	1.3	4,898	161
1950	2.5	0.5	0.3	0.2	939	98
1940	0.4	N/A	N/A	N/A	296	68

*Data pertain to conventional fund members of the Investment Company Institute; money market funds not included. Institute "gross sales" figures include the proceeds of initial fund underwritings prior to 1970.

Source: *Mutual Fund Fact Book*, (Washington, D.C.: Investment Company Institute, 1999). Reprinted by permission of the Investment Company Institute. *www.ici.org/*

free exchanges of investments between a mutual fund company's funds, automatic investing, check-writing privileges on many money market funds and some bond funds, automatic reinvestment of dividends, and automatic withdrawals. As of January 2000, more than 7,800 different mutual funds held total assets of $6.8 trillion. This chapter presents an overview of the services offered by mutual funds and highlights their rapid growth in the last decade.

Size, Structure, and Composition of the Industry

Historical Trends

The first mutual fund was established in Boston in 1924. The industry grew very slowly at first; so that by 1970, 360 funds held about $50 billion in assets. Since then, the number of funds and the asset size of the industry have increased dramatically. This growth is attributed to the advent of money market mutual funds in 1972 (as investors looked for ways to earn market rates on short-term funds when regulatory ceilings constrained the interest rates they earned on bank deposits), to tax-exempt money market mutual funds first established in 1979, and to an explosion of special-purpose equity, bond, emerging market, and derivative funds (as capital market values soared in the 1990s). Money market mutual funds invest in securities with an original maturity under one year, while bond and equity funds invest in securities with an original maturity generally over one year. Table 18–1 documents this tremendous increase in mutual funds for various years from 1940 though 1998. For example, total assets invested in mutual funds (other than money market mutual funds) increased from $0.4 billion in 1940 to $3,791.4 billion in 1998. In addition, the number of companies offering mutual funds increased from 68 in 1940 to 6,288 in 1998.[2] The majority of this increase occurred during the bull market run in the 1990s (total mutual fund assets in 1990 were

2. Most mutual fund companies offer more than one type of fund.

Table 18–2 Net New Cash Flows to Long-Term Mutual Funds versus Annual Returns on the NYSE Composite Index

	Net New Cash Flows to Long-Term Mutual Funds*	Return on NYSE Composite Index
1984	$ 19.3	0.75%
1985	73.7	26.80
1986	130.5	13.97
1987	30.0	−0.25
1988	−23.1	13.00
1989	8.9	24.82
1990	21.3	−7.46
1991	106.7	27.12
1992	172.9	4.69
1993	243.3	7.86
1994	75.9	−3.14
1995	123.3	31.31
1996	232.0	19.06
1997	272.0	30.31
1998	243.7	16.55

*In billions of dollars.

Source: Investment Company Institute, *Perspectives*, February 1999. Reprinted by permission of the Investment Company Institute. *www.ici.org/*

$568.5 billion). Table 18–2 lists the net new investment in long-term mutual funds and the return on the New York Stock Exchange (NYSE) composite index from 1984 through 1998. Notice that net new cash flows into long-term mutual funds is highly correlated with the return on the NYSE stock index.

As Figure 18–1 illustrates, in terms of asset size, the mutual fund (money market and long-term mutual funds) industry is larger than the insurance industry but smaller than the commercial banking industry. This makes mutual funds the second most important FI group in the United States as measured by asset size. Worldwide investment in mutual funds is shown in Table 18–3. While not as striking as the growth in U.S. funds, worldwide (other than in the United States) investments in mutual funds have increased from $1.626 trillion in 1992 to $2.762 trillion in 1998.

Commercial banks have noticed the tremendous growth in this area of FI services (see In the News box 18–1) and have sought to directly compete by either buying existing mutual fund groups or managing mutual fund assets for a fee. Banks' share of all mutual fund assets managed had grown to 17 percent in 1998. See Table 18–4 for a list of the mutual fund assets managed by the top 10 banks and bank-owned companies participating in the industry in 1999. The percentage of total industry assets managed by each is also listed. Dreyfus (owned by Mellon Bank) is the top bank-owned mutual fund, managing almost 2 percent of the industry's assets.

Different Types of Mutual Funds

The mutual fund industry is usually considered to have two sectors: short-term funds and long-term funds. Long-term funds comprise **equity funds** (composed of common and preferred stock securities), **bond funds** (composed of fixed-income securities with a maturity of over one year), and **hybrid funds** (composed of both stock and bond

---

Do You Understand?

1. How bank management of mutual funds has increased in the 1990s?
2. Who the major banks involved in mutual fund sales are?

---

equity funds

Funds consisting of common and preferred stock securities.

bond funds

Funds consisting of fixed-income capital market debt securities.

hybrid funds

Funds consisting of stock and bond securities.

Figure 18–1 Financial Assets of Major Financial Intermediaries, 1990 and 1999
(in trillions of dollars)

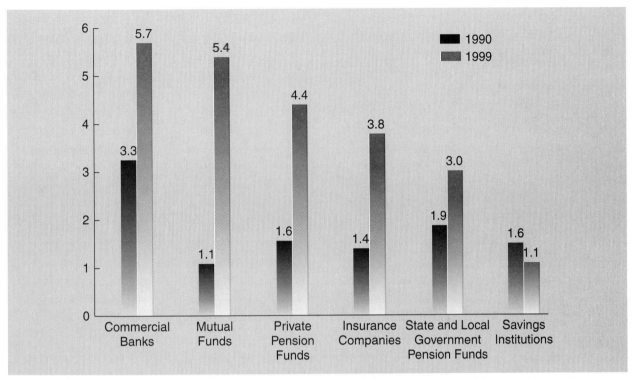

Note: Data for 1990 are at year end; data for 1999 are at the end of the second quarter. Commercial banks include U.S.-chartered commercial banks, foreign banking offices in the United States, bank holding companies, and banks in U.S.-affiliated areas.

Source: Federal Reserve Board, Statistical Releases, "Flow of Fund Accounts," March 1991 and September 1999. *www.bog.frb.fed.us/*

In the News

Banks Enter Fund Management Big Leagues

After struggling for years, banks are starting to make a big mark in mutual funds management. At the end of 1998 banking companies were managing 17% of all mutual fund assets in the United States, up from 10% just five years ago. Equally telling, 47 banks were each managing more than $20 billion of assets, up from

Source: *American Banker,* Friday, February 12, 1999, by Niamh Ring.

just one bank in 1993, according to data from Lipper Analytical Services. The $20 billion mark is considered a sign of serious commitment.

Many banks say they are already reaping the rewards that come with size. And few are planning to let up. "The growth is just be-

ginning," said Sarah E. Jones, managing director in Chase Manhattan Corp.'s global asset management and mutual fund group. "Banks have the self-confidence to feel that we're credible players." Chase's fund family ended the year with $43 billion under management, up from $5 billion five years ago. And Ms. Jones predicts the total will hit $100 billion by 2000.

Plenty of others are also *(continues)*

In the News continued

shooting high. KeyCorp, which closed the year with $16.5 billion under management, plans to hit $50 billion within five years, said Kathleen A. Dennis, a senior managing director with Key Asset Management. Just five years ago, the Cleveland banking company barely managed $1 billion. To be sure, these banks and others are still a long way from the upper echelons of the fund industry. Fidelity Investments, the industry leader, managed some $691 billion of fund assets as of Dec. 31, according to the Investment Company Institute. Vanguard Group was the No. 2 U.S. asset manager with $435 billion under management.

But banks have unquestionably made big strides since the early 1990s. Back then, most were dismissed as bit players that lacked the commitment, skills, and culture needed to succeed in the burgeoning funds industry. Gradually, those doubts have faded. "What's changed is our need to have to justify our existence," said Ms. Dennis of Key-Corp. Five years ago the fund group had to fight for the attention of the company's distribution channels, such as branches and retirement management units. "They said, Tell me

why you're better than Fidelity, better than Putman," Ms. Dennis recalled. "Now that we have the performance, it's easier."

Increased size also makes it easier for fund management units to reinvest profits and expand beyond their geographic markets, said W. Christopher Maxwell, a principal and investment consultant with Maxwell Associates, Rock Hall, Md. "It is extremely expensive to compete outside your footprint," Mr. Maxwell said.

Some banking companies, like Mellon Bank Corp. and Citigroup, already are in the mutual fund major leagues, with well over $100 billion under management. Others are clearly on the way, propelled by the acquisitions, growth of sales forces, and programs to distribute funds through third parties. "Banks that are north of $20 billion are the ones that have made the decision they want to be players in the fund business," Mr. Maxwell said.

The future is less clear for banks that have $3 billion to $10 billion under management, Mr. Maxwell said. But it is by no means hopeless. For example, he said, these banks could forge strategic alliances with one another to market

funds. "The more intelligent banks will take a creative way to go after this business," Mr. Maxwell predicts.

Certainly, many banking companies have set their sights on asset management. "Banks are still banks and the drivers of banks are still deposit products and loan products," said Robert L. Ash, a managing director at Fleet Investment Management. "But right underneath that is an emerging recognition at most large banks of the importance of asset management and the revenues stream it provides." Fleet acquired Columbia Asset Management in 1997 and has aggressively marketed its proprietary fund family, the Galaxy Funds. Chase, in its growth plans, is betting partly on its extensive U.S. distribution network, which gives the company access to 80,000 brokers. The bank will also look to the developing investment markets of Japan and Europe, Ms. Jones said. KeyCorp, meanwhile, plans to leverage its October acquisition of neighboring brokerage firm McDonald Investments. That has doubled Key's brokerage force, to roughly 700 representatives. The banking company is also forging external distribution relationships.

Table 18–3 Worldwide Assets of Open-End Investment Companies
(in million of dollars)

Non-USA Countries	1992	1993	1994	1995	1996	1997	1998[a]
Argentina	$ 184	$ 235	$ 389	$ 631	$ 1,869	$ 5,247	$ 5,610
Australia	19,280	24,556	44,036	36,505	47,761	50,627	44,124
Austria[b]	15,029	18,174	23,492	33,452	39,543	44,930	57,195
Belgium	8,954	15,149	18,877	25,553	29,247	35,748	49,264
Brazil	18,862	24,007	54,426	63,637	103,786	108,606	113,441
Canada[b]	52,921	86,567	90,349	107,812	154,529	197,984	189,210
Chile	N/A	1,592	2,503	2,843	2,934	4,549	2,502
Czech Republic	N/A	N/A	N/A	N/A	N/A	361	456
Denmark	3,658	4,401	5,448	6,455	9,338	13,037	17,023
Finland	110	618	1,089	1,211	2,510	3,534	4,974
France	447,338	483,327	496,743	519,376	534,145	499,881	604,381
Germany: Public	70,196	78,552	112,697	134,543	137,860	146,889	175,375
Special	101,405	133,734	160,335	213,047	241,642[c]	N/A	N/A
Greece	1,018	3,465	6,111	10,303	15,788	25,759	30,760
Hong Kong	16,351	31,135	29,522	33,695	41,017	58,456	75,760
Hungary	N/A	N/A	N/A	N/A	N/A	713	1,277
India	5,835	7,925	11,669	10,107	9,717[d]	9,353	9,726
Ireland[e]	5,905	5,244	7,806	8,461	7,735	22,729	22,520[f]
Italy	41,036	64,272	79,402	79,878	129,755	209,410	394,486
Japan	346,924	454,608	435,603	469,980	420,103	311,335	310,810
Korea	49,183	69,988	81,304	92,405	N/A	N/A	N/A
Luxembourg	182,244	247,804	283,020	285,448	338,236	390,623	N/A
Mexico	N/A	N/A	N/A	9,025	N/A	N/A	N/A
Netherlands[b]	34,797	48,530	62,100	62,128	64,147	70,373	N/A
New Zealand[b]	1,062	1,833	2,471	6,868	7,686	7,519	6,448
Norway	2,722	4,737	5,119	6,834	9,930	13,058	11,086
Russia	N/A	N/A	N/A	N/A	6	41	29
Poland	N/A	N/A	N/A	N/A	N/A	N/A	574[f]
Portugal	7,925	9,319	12,854	14,233	17,087	21,392	21,969
South Africa	4,524	4,647	7,421	9,226	9,354	12,688	10,433
Spain	54,699	72,058	84,877	99,923	144,134	177,192	223,507
Sweden	18,108	24,356	20,208	27,388	34,981	45,452	48,411
Switzerland	24,304	34,094	38,864	44,638	48,166	53,444	63,507
Taiwan	N/A	N/A	3,616	4,388	8,351[g]	12,365	17,850
United Kingdom[h]	91,153	131,455	133,092	154,452	201,304	235,683	249,030
Total Non-USA	$1,625,543	$2,086,147	$2,315,054	$2,573,814	$2,813,786	$2,788,978	$2,761,738
USA: (Long-term)	$1,100,065	$1,510,047	$1,550,490	$2,067,337	$2,637,398	$3,409,315	$3,622,978
(Short-term)	546,195	565,319	611,005	753,018	901,807	1,058,886	1,266,902
Total USA	$1,646,259	$2,075,366	$2,161,495	$2,820,355	$3,539,205	$4,468,201	$4,889,880
Total World	$3,271,802	$4,161,513	$4,476,549	$5,394,169	$6,352,991	$7,257,179	$7,651,618

Note: Comparison of annual total assets across countries is not recommended because reporting coverage, dates, and definitions are not consistent.

[a]As of September 30, 1998.

[b]Includes real estate funds.

[c]As of September 30, 1996.

[d]As of March 31, 1996.

[e]Approximately 95 percent relates to life assurance–linked funds; the other 5 percent are unit investment trusts. International Financial Source Control funds are not included.

[f]As of March 31, 1998.

[g]As of June 30, 1996.

[h]Fund-of-fund assets not included.

Source: Investment Company Institute, *Mutual Fund Fact Book,* 1998 and 1999. Reprinted by permission of the Investment Company Institute. www.ici.org/

Table 18–4   Top Commercial Bank Involvement in Mutual Fund Business

Rank	Company	Assets (in billions)	Percent of Industry Assets Managed
1	Dreyfus Corp. (Mellon Bank)	$109.7	1.98
2	Evergreen Keystone		
	Investment Sec. (First Union)	68.2	1.23
3	BankAmerica	66.0	1.19
4	Bank One Corp.	55.1	1.00
5	PNC Asset Management Group	52.6	0.95
6	Wells Fargo	46.1	0.93
7	Chase Manhattan Bank	42.6	0.77
8	U.S. Bancorp	30.3	0.55
9	Bankers Trust	27.7	0.50
10	Northern Trust	20.9	0.38
Top 100 commercial banks		$835.6	15.11

Source: Lipper Analytical Services, Inc., press release, February 1999, Summit, NJ. *www.lipperweb.com/*

money market mutual funds

Funds consisting of various mixtures of money market securities.

securities). Short-term funds comprise taxable **money market mutual funds** (MMMFs) and tax-exempt money market mutual funds (containing various mixes of the money market securities with an original maturity of less than 1 year, discussed in Chapter 5). Tables 18–5 and 18–6 report the growth of bond and equity as well as hybrid mutual funds relative to money market mutual funds. Table 18–5 presents the dollar values invested in various funds from 1991 through 1999.

As of June 1999, 74.2 percent of all mutual fund assets were in long-term funds; the remaining funds, or 25.8 percent, were in money market mutual funds. From Table 18–5, the percentage invested in long-term versus short-term funds can, and has, varied considerably over time. For example, the share of money market funds was 41.0 percent in 1991 compared to 25.8 percent in 1999. The decline in the growth rate of short-term funds and increase in the growth rate of long-term funds reflects the increase in equity returns during the period 1992–1999 and the generally low level of short-term interest rates over the period.

Money market mutual funds provide an alternative investment opportunity to interest-bearing deposits at commercial banks, which may explain the increase in MMMFs in the 1980s. Figure 18–2 illustrates the net cash flows invested in taxable money market mutual funds and the interest rate spread between MMMFs and the average rate on savings deposits from 1985 through 1998. Both investments are relatively safe and earn short-term returns. The major difference between the two is that interest-bearing deposits (below $100,000) are fully insured by the FDIC but, because of bank regulatory costs (such as Federal Reserve–imposed reserve requirements, capital adequacy requirements, and FDIC deposit insurance premiums), offer lower returns than noninsured MMMFs.[3] Thus, the net gain in switching to MMMFs is a higher return in exchange for the loss of FDIC deposit insurance coverage. Many investors appear willing to give up FDIC insurance coverage to obtain additional returns.

Table 18–6 reports the growth in this industry based on the number of mutual funds in 1980, 1990, and 1999. All categories of funds have increased in number in the 1980s and 1990s, from a total of 564 in 1980 to 7,621 in 1999. *Tax-exempt* money market funds first became available in 1980. This was the major reason for their relatively

---

3. Some mutual funds are covered by private insurance and/or by implicit or explicit guarantees from mutual fund management companies.

Table 18–5   Growth in Long-Term versus Short-Term Mutual Funds from 1991 through June 1999
(in billions of dollars)

	1991	1992	1993	1994	1995	1996	1997	1998	1999 (Q2)
A. Equity, Hybrid, and Bond Mutual Funds									
Holdings at market value	$769.5	$992.5	$1,375.4	$1,477.3	$1,852.8	$2,342.4	$2,989.4	$3,610.5	$4,029.9
Household sector	586.6	727.9	990.9	1,047.4	1,247.8	1,582.9	1,996.7	2,500.6	2,787.1
Nonfinancial corporate business	14.8	21.1	29.8	31.1	45.7	58.6	81.8	91.0	98.1
State and local governments	9.4	14.9	21.3	29.1	35.0	41.0	44.6	26.3	27.4
Commercial banking	3.7	3.4	3.9	2.0	2.3	2.6	8.1	9.2	10.0
Credit unions	2.6	4.1	4.2	2.6	2.8	2.6	2.4	3.6	3.9
Bank personal trusts and estates	93.6	128.1	183.5	200.4	253.5	293.6	342.2	397.1	439.3
Life insurance companies	8.6	18.2	25.9	9.6	27.7	40.0	57.6	18.6	16.5
Private pension funds	50.2	74.9	116.0	155.1	228.5	332.6	456.0	564.0	647.6
B. Money Market Mutual Funds									
Total assets	$535.0	$539.5	$559.6	$602.9	$745.3	$891.1	$1,048.7	$1,334.2	$1,398.1
Household sector	379.5	338.6	338.9	351.3	451.6	530.8	639.0	739.7	753.3
Nonfinancial corporate business	35.1	50.9	48.7	56.2	83.0	88.5	105.0	163.9	176.8
Bank personal trusts and estates	29.6	29.2	29.3	29.9	30.2	41.4	43.0	44.9	45.9
Life insurance companies	19.6	25.0	31.5	16.2	22.8	40.7	56.5	111.5	125.9
Private pension funds	18.8	19.8	26.3	31.6	37.5	42.2	47.3	58.4	64.4
Funding corporations	52.4	75.9	86.0	117.8	120.2	147.5	157.9	215.8	231.8

Source: Federal Reserve Bulletin, "Flow of Fund Accounts," September 1999. *www.bog.frb.fed.us/*

Table 18–6   Number of Mutual Funds, 1980, 1990, and 1999

Year	Equity	Hybrid	Bond	Taxable Money Market	Tax-Exempt Money Market	Total
1980	288	N/A	170	96	10	564
1990	1,116	203	1,024	508	235	3,086
1999	3,810	522	2,253	696	340	7,621

Source: *Mutual Fund Fact Book,* 1998; and Current Statistical Release, September 1999 (Washington, D.C.: Investment Company Institute). Repritned by permission of the Investment Company Institute. *www.ici.org/*

small number (10 funds) in 1980. Also, the number of equity funds has boomed in the 1990s: equity funds numbered 3,810 in 1999, up from 1,116 in 1990, while bond funds numbered 2,253 in 1999, up from 1,024 in 1990.

Notice that in Table 18–5, households (i.e., small investors) own the majority of both long- and short-term funds, 69.2 percent for long-term mutual funds and 53.9 percent for short-term mutual funds in June 1999. This is to be expected, given that the rationale for the existence of mutual funds is to achieve superior diversification through fund and risk pooling compared to what individual small investors can achieve on their

Figure 18–2   Interest Rate Spread and Net New Cash Flow to Retail Money Market Funds*

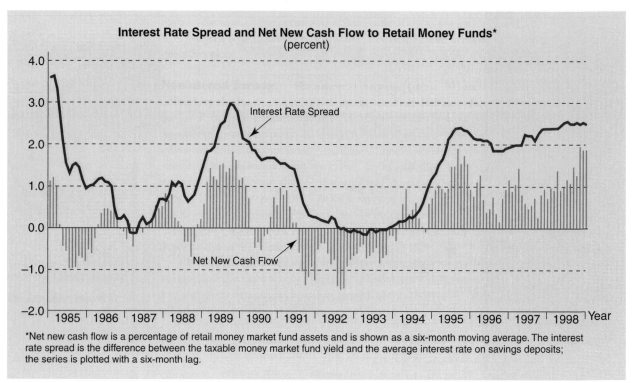

*Net new cash flow is a percentage of retail money market fund assets and is shown as a six-month moving average. The interest rate spread is the difference between the taxable money market fund yield and the average interest rate on savings deposits; the series is plotted with a six-month lag.

Source: IBC Financial Data Inc., Federal Reserve Board and Investment Company Institute.

own. Consider that wholesale CDs sell in minimum denominations of $100,000 each and often pay higher interest rates than passbook savings accounts or small time deposits offered by depository institutions. By pooling funds in a money market mutual fund, small investors can gain access to wholesale money markets and instruments and, therefore, to potentially higher interest rates and returns.

Indeed, 48.4 million households (47.4 percent of all 102.1 million U.S. households) owned mutual funds in 1999. Most are long-term owners, with 64 percent making their first purchases after 1990. As can be seen from In the News box 18–2, "Generation X'ers" (those born after 1970) are already a dominant group in this industry. Table 18–7 compares those who made their first purchase before 1990, those who made their first purchase between 1990 and 1995, and those who made their first purchase after 1995. Comparing those who first purchased mutual funds shares in the most recent period (since 1995) to those who first purchased mutual funds before 1990, we find that the most recent purchasers are younger (33 versus 49 years old), are less likely to be married (56 percent versus 77 percent), earn less per annum ($40,000 versus $60,000), have fewer financial assets ($17,000 versus $140,000), and invest smaller amounts in mutual funds ($4,000 versus $50,000).

> **Do You Understand?**
>
> 1. What the percentage of mutual fund ownership owned by Generation X'ers is?
> 2. What the distribution of investments made by the average Generation X'er is?

Most household owners use mutual funds as vehicles for retirement savings (ranging from 68 to 79 percent of investors across the three groups). Interestingly, the number of families with less than a college degree investing in mutual funds is increasing (45 percent for first purchasers before 1990, 52 percent for first purchasers between 1990 and 1995, and 59 percent for first purchasers after 1995). The bull markets of the 1990s, the low transaction costs of purchasing mutual funds shares, and the diversification benefits achievable through mutual fund investments are again the likely reasons for these changes.

In the News

18-2

T he so-called slackers of Generation X have been getting a bad rap—at least when it comes to investing for their future. A new study by the Investment Company Institute, "Mutual Fund Shareholders: The People Behind the Growth," shows Americans aged 18 to 30 are already accumulating sizeable assets which they have earmarked for retirement rather than Roller Blades.

The study, which looked at the characteristics of mutual fund owning households nationwide, found that Generation X accounts for 12% of fund shareholders. A large majority of these young Americans say saving for retirement is their primary reason for investing (76%), and nearly two-thirds of them (61%) have an Individual Retirement Account.

Source: Investment Company Institute, Shareholder Demographic Information, October 1996. Reprinted by permission of the Investment Company Institute.

Generation X Takes Control of Financial Future, New Study Shows

Generation X'ers also have more of their assets in mutual funds than the previous generation, the Baby Boomers; the average 20-Something surveyed has $6,000 or 38% of his or her total assets in mutual funds, compared with Baby Boomers who have only 27%. In addition, 45% of Generation X'ers own individual stocks and 18% own individual bonds.

When it comes to risk and reward, these young investors take a sophisticated approach. Since a long term goal such as retirement is 40 years down the road, Generation X'ers can tolerate a greater amount of risk in their investment strategy, and in fact 53% of them said they were willing to assume above average risk for above average gain, compared to 41% of Baby

Boomers who said the same.

Fund-owning Generation X households typically own shares of three different mutual funds and divide their investments almost evenly among stock (37%), bond (29%), and money market funds (31%). Such diversity shows these 20-Somethings are savvy, serious investors, most of whom are not new on the fund scene. Three-fourths of them bought their fund shares before 1993, and 36% made their first fund purchase before 1990.

On average, the members of Generation X surveyed have a household income of $50,000, liquid assets of $16,000, and are more likely than the Baby Boomers surveyed to have a four-year college degree. More than one-half are married and 95% are employed. This information is part of a larger survey of more than 1,000 households that own mutual funds outside of employer-sponsored retirement plans. The full results of the survey are detailed in the report.

www.ici.org/

3

Mutual Fund Prospectuses and Objectives

Regulations require that mutual fund managers specify the investment objectives of their funds in a prospectus available to potential investors. This

Table 18–7 Selected Characteristics of Household Owners of Mutual Funds*

	First Purchase before 1990	First Purchase between 1990 and 1995	First Purchase after 1995
Demographic characteristics			
Median age	49	39	33
Percent of households			
Married	77	66	56
Employed, full- or part-time	76	90	90
Four-year college degree or more	55	48	41
Retired from lifetime occupation	26	8	9
Median household income	$ 60,000	$56,000	$40,000
Median household financial assets†	$140,000	$60,000	$17,000
Percent of households owning			
Individual stocks, bonds, or annuities	82	75	80
IRA	70	44	33
401 (k)	58	63	63
Mutual fund ownership characteristics			
Median mutual fund assets	$ 50,000	$14,700	$ 4,000
Medium number of funds owned	4	3	2
Percent			
Household assets in mutual funds	36	25	24
Fund types owned			
Equity	92	86	79
Bond	47	37	34
Hybrid	41	31	26
Money market	42	52	40
Investment goal			
Retirement	79	78	68
Education	9	12	13
Other	12	10	19
Risk tolerance to profile			
Willing to take:			
Substantial risk with expectation of substantial gain	8	12	11
Above-average risk with expectation of above-average gain	31	29	25
Average-risk with expectation of average gain	46	51	46
Below-average risk with expectation of below-average gain	9	4	9
No risk	6	5	9

*Characteristics of primary financial decision maker in the household.

†Excludes primary residence but includes assets in employer-sponsored retirement plans.

Source: *Mutual Fund Fact Book*, (Washington, D.C.: Investment Company Institute, 1999). Reprinted by permission of the Investment Company Institute. *www.ici.org/*

prospectus includes a list of the securities that the fund holds. Many "large" company funds, aiming to diversify across company size, held stocks of relatively "small" companies in the late 1990s, contrary to their stated objectives. Some fund managers justified the inclusion of seemingly "smaller" companies by changing their definition of what a large company is. For example, one fund manager stated that the definition of a small company he used is one that has less than $1 billion in equity capital versus a large company that has more than $1 billion (the median size of equity capital of firms in the S&P 500 index is $28 billion). The point here is that investors need to read a prospectus carefully before making an investment.

Table 18–8 Total Net Asset Value of Equity, Hybrid, and Bond Funds by Investment Objective, December 31, 1998

Objective of Fund	Combined Assets (in millions of dollars)	Percent of Total
Total net assets	**$4,173,531.1**	**100.0%**
Aggressive growth	394,175.3	9.4%
Growth	890,077.5	21.3
Sector	120,742.2	2.9
World equity—emerging markets	12,674.8	0.3
World equity—global	159,774.7	3.8
World equity—international	187,185.6	4.5
World equity—regional	32,002.4	0.8
Growth and income	1,032,842.7	24.8
Income equity	148,751.4	3.6
Total equity funds	**$2,978,226.6**	**71.4%**
Asset allocation	40,113.6	1.0%
Balanced	168,368.8	4.0
Flexible portfolio	85,785.6	1.7
Income—mixed	70,446.2	1.7
Total hybrid funds	**$364,714.2**	**8.7%**
Corporate bond—general	37,326.3	0.9%
Corporate bond—intermediate term	69,035.1	1.6
Corporate bond—short term	37,147.6	0.9
High-yield bond	117,443.5	2.8
World bond—global general	15,922.1	0.4
World bond—global short-term	5,674.3	0.1
World bond—other	3,323.7	0.1
Government bond—general	38,338.4	0.9
Government bond—intermediate term	25,389.8	0.6
Government bond—short term	19,735.0	0.5
Government bond—mortgage-backed	60,890.9	1.5
Strategic income	101,769.1	2.4
State municipal—general	129,648.0	3.1
State municipal—short term	10,311.9	0.3
National municipal bond—general	126,756.0	3.0
National municipal bond—short term	31,878.6	0.8
Total bond funds	**$830,590.3**	**19.9%**

Source: *Mutual Fund Fact Book*, (Washington, D.C.: Investment Company Institute, 1999). Reprinted by permission of the Investment Company Institute. *www.ici.org/*

The aggregate figures for long-term funds tend to obscure the fact that many different funds fall into this group of funds. Table 18–8 classifies 29 major categories of investment objectives for mutual funds, with the assets allocated to each of these major categories in 1998. The fund objective provides general information about the types of securities the mutual fund holds as assets. For example, aggressive growth funds hold securities (mainly equities) of the highest growth and highest-risk firms; growth funds also hold high-growth and high-risk securities, but neither the growth nor the risk of these funds is as high as that of the aggressive growth funds.

See Table 18–9 for the largest 20 mutual funds in total assets held in November 1999, including the fund objective, 12-month and five-year returns, and net asset value

Table 18–9   The Largest Mutual Funds in Assets Held

Name of Fund	Objective	Total Assets (in millions)	Total Return 12 month	Total Return 5 year	NAV
Fidelity Magellan	Growth	$92,187	34.5%	197.0%	132.86
Vanguard Index:500	Growth/Income	89,364	26.5	231.1	129.20
American Funds: WshMut	Growth/Income	53,537	12.1	185.1	34.29
American Funds: InvCoA	Growth/Income	51,071	21.3	175.6	34.04
Fidelity Invest: Grw/Inc	Growth/Income	45,985	18.1	188.9	46.19
Fidelity Invest: Contra	Growth	41,035	33.9	201.9	64.24
American Century: Ultra	Growth	33,051	45.7	223.9	41.59
Janus Fund	Capital appreciation	32,695	63.7	253.3	45.27
Vanguard: WndsII	Growth/Income	30,315	4.3	155.6	29.11
Janus: Twenty	Capital appreciation	26,170	69.8	421.5	73.59
American Funds: Eupac	International	25,954	44.6	120.3	37.80
American Funds: NewPer	Growth/Income	25,752	37.4	157.3	28.60
Vanguard: Welltn	Balanced	25,701	7.9	126.0	30.07
Vanguard: Indstl. Indx	Growth/Income	25,249	26.6	233.1	127.94
Fidelity Invest: Puritan	Balanced	24,419	9.2	101.5	19.23
Fidelity Advisor: Grw Opp	Growth	24,122	13.4	157.1	52.01
PIMCO Funds: Total Returns	Investment grade bonds	23,328	2.3	53.8	10.10
Fidelity: Blue Chip	Growth	23,298	29.0	187.7	55.40
Fidelity Invest: Eq/Inc	Equity/Income	22,848	15.6	148.8	58.58
American Funds: Income	Equity/Income	21,891	5.2	100.2	16.91

Source: *Associated Press,* November 12,1999. *www.associatedpress.com/*

www300.fidelity.com/

www.vanguard.com/

(NAV—see later). Fidelity's Magellan Fund was the largest fund in 1999 (despite having been closed to new investors since 1997). Fidelity and Vanguard, the two major U.S. mutual fund management companies, offered 11 of the top 20 funds. Many of the top funds list either growth or growth and income as the fund's objective, and all of the top 20 funds performed well, in terms of return, in the bull market of the 1990s. Five-year returns ranged from a low of 53.8 percent for PIMCO Fund's Total Return Fund to 421.5 percent for Janus's Twenty Fund. The return for the S&P 500 Index over the same five-year period was 130.1 percent. All funds except PIMCO Fund's Total Return Fund reported a five-year return exceeding 100 percent. It should be noted, however, that prospectuses rarely mention the risk of returns (e.g., the fund's total return risk or, alternatively, its systematic risk or "beta"[4]). Currently, the SEC is proposing an initiative to require mutual funds to disclose more information about their return risk as well as the returns themselves. The results of the SEC's proposal would better enable investors to compare return-risk trade-offs from investing in different mutual funds.[5]

Size and Mutual Fund Performance: The Case of the Magellan Fund

www300.fidelity.com/

Fidelity's Magellan Fund has been a unique fund in the history of the industry. The Magellan Fund began in the 1970s, and under the management of Peter Lynch (from

4. Beta measures covariability of the returns on a specific investment (e.g., a mutual fund) with the returns on the market portfolio (e.g., the S&P 500 Index).

5. See GAO/GGD-97-67, Letter Report, Mutual Funds: SEC Adjusted Its Oversight in Response to Rapid Industry Growth, May 28, 1997.

1977 through 1990) and Jeffrey Vinik (from 1992 to 1995), it became the country's largest mutual fund. In the 13 years Peter Lynch managed the fund, Magellan reported average returns of 29.2 percent per year (almost double the 15.9 percent average return on the S&P 500 Index). From July 1992 to August 1995, when Vinik managed the fund, Magellan returned a total of 78.85 percent (the average growth fund earned 52.86 percent over this period). Obviously, these tremendous returns resulted in a large increase in investor interest. Specifically, the fund grew from $20 million when Lynch took control to more than $56 billion when Vinik left in 1995. By 1996, the Magellan Fund alone was larger in asset size than the whole mutual fund industry had been in 1978, and it was also twice the size of the second largest fund and larger than the third, fourth, and fifth largest funds combined. However, with size comes problems. In particular, the fund became too large to exploit profitably numerous investment opportunities, and changes in the fund's portfolio composition were so large as to adversely affect security prices. For example, a major purchase of shares in a certain company by Magellan often drove the price of those shares up—making the stock more expensive and less attractive to hold.

In late 1995, expecting a slowdown in the profitability of technology companies, Magellan switched to holding more long-term bonds. As it turned out, from September 1995 through April 1996, the fund earned only a 2.78 percent return while the average growth fund earned 15.02 percent. Largely as a result of these poor returns, Vinik resigned in May 1996, and Bob Stansky assumed the fund's management. Following strategies that mimicked indexes such as the S&P 500, Stansky brought Magellan back to earning above 20 percent returns in the late 1990s, but these returns were still not comparable to those of other growth funds. For example, the 33.6 percent return earned by Magellan in 1998 ranked 303 of over 660 funds tracked by Bloomberg Fund Performance. Despite this, Magellan's assets continued to grow to more than $83.5 billion, and, citing an inability to produce above average returns with such a large fund, Magellan closed its doors to new investors in September 1997.

Investor Returns from Mutual Fund Ownership

marked to market

Asset and balance sheet values adjusted to reflect current market prices.

NAV

The net asset value of a mutual fund—equal to the market value of the assets in the mutual fund portfolio divided by the number of shares outstanding.

The return for the investor from investing in mutual fund shares reflects three aspects of the underlying portfolio of mutual fund assets. First, the portfolio earns income and dividends on those assets. Second, it experiences capital gains when the mutual fund sells an asset at prices higher than the original purchase price of the asset. Third, capital appreciation in the underlying values of its existing assets adds to the value of mutual fund shares. With respect to capital appreciation, mutual fund assets are normally **marked to market** daily. This means that the managers of the fund calculate the current value of each mutual fund share by computing the daily market value of the fund's total asset portfolio and then dividing this amount by the number of mutual fund shares outstanding. The resulting value is called the net asset value (**NAV**) of the fund. This is the price that investors obtain when they sell shares back to the fund that day or the price they pay to buy new shares in the fund on that day.

Example 18–1 Calculation of NAV on an Open-End Mutual Fund

Suppose today a mutual fund contains 1,000 shares of Sears, Roebuck currently trading at $40.50, 2,000 shares of Mobil Oil currently trading at $86.50, and 4,500 shares of Household International currently trading at $42.25. The mutual fund has 15,000 shares outstanding held by investors. Thus, today, the fund's NAV[6] is calculated as:

---

6. We omit any fees that the mutual fund company charges for managing the mutual fund. These fees and their impact on returns are discussed later in the chapter.

$$NAV = \frac{\text{Total market value of assets under management}}{\text{Number of mutual fund shares outstanding}}$$

$$= (1,000 \times \$40.50 + 2,000 \times \$86.50 + 4,500 \times \$42.25) \div 15,000 = \$26.908$$

If tomorrow Sears' shares increase to \$45, Mobil shares increase to \$92, and Household International's shares increase to \$47, the NAV (assuming the number of shares outstanding remains the same) would increase to:

$$NAV = (1,000 \times \$45 + 2,000 \times \$92 + 4,500 \times \$47) \div 15,000 = \$29.367$$

open-end mutual fund

A fund for which the supply of shares is not fixed but can increase or decrease daily with purchases and redemptions of shares.

Mutual funds are **open end** in that the number of shares outstanding fluctuates daily with the amount of share redemptions and new purchases. With open-end funds, investors buy and sell shares from and to the mutual fund company. Thus, the demand for shares determines the number of shares outstanding, and the market value of the underlying securities held in the mutual fund divided by the number of shareholders outstanding determines the NAV of shares.

Example 18–2 Calculation of NAV of an Open-End Mutual Fund When the Number of Shares Increases

Consider the mutual fund in Example 18–1, but suppose that today 1,000 additional investors buy 1 share each of the mutual fund at the NAV of \$26.908. This means that the fund manager has \$26,908 additional funds to invest. Suppose that the fund manager decides to use these additional funds to buy additional shares in Household International. At today's market price, the manager could buy 637 additional shares (\$26,908/\$42.25) of Household International. Thus, its new portfolio of shares has 1,000 in Sears, 2,000 in Mobil, and 5,137 in Household International. Given the same rise in share values as assumed in Example 18–1, tomorrow's NAV will now be:

$$NAV = (1,000 \times \$45 + 2,000 \times \$92 + 5,137 \times \$47) \div 16,000 = \$29.402$$

A comparison of the NAV in Example 18–1 with the one in this example indicates that the additional shares alone enabled the fund to gain a slightly higher NAV than had the number of shares remained static (\$29.402 versus \$29.367).

closed-end investment companies

Specialized investment companies that have a fixed supply of outstanding shares but invest in the securities and assets of other firms.

REIT

A real estate investment trust; a closed-end investment company that specializes in investing in mortgages, property, or real estate company shares.

Open-end mutual funds can be compared with regular corporations traded on stock exchanges and to **closed-end investment companies**, both of which have a fixed number of shares outstanding at any given time. For example, real estate investment trusts (**REITs**) are closed-end investment companies that specialize in investment in real estate company shares and/or in buying mortgages.[7] For most closed-end company funds, investors generally buy and sell the company's shares on a stock exchange as they do for corporate stocks. Since the number of shares available for purchase, at any moment in time, is fixed, the NAV of the fund's shares is determined by the value of the underlying shares as well as by the demand for the investment company's shares themselves. When demand for the investment company's shares is high, the shares can trade for more than the NAV of the securities held in the fund's asset portfolio. In this case, the fund is said to be *trading at a premium* (i.e., more than the fair market value of the securities held). When the value of the closed-end fund's shares are less than the

---

7. Many closed-end funds are specialized funds investing in shares in countries such as Argentina, Brazil, or Mexico. The shares of these closed-end funds are traded on the NYSE or in the over-the-counter market. The total market value of funds invested in closed-end funds was \$147.7 billion at the end of the second quarter of 1999. This compares to \$5,428.0 billion invested in open-end funds at that time.

NAV of its assets, its shares are said to be *trading at a discount* (i.e., less than the fair market value of the securities held).

Example 18–3   Market Value of Closed-End Mutual Fund Shares

Because of high demand for a closed-end investment company's shares, the 50 shares (N_S) are trading at $20 per share ($P_S$). The market value of the equity-type securities in the fund's asset portfolio, however, is $800, or $16 ($800 ÷ 50) per share. The market value balance sheet of the fund is shown below:

Assets		Liabilities and Equity	
Market value of asset portfolio	$800	Market value of closed-end fund shares ($P_S \times N_S$)	$1,000
Premium	$200		

The fund's shares are trading at a premium of $4 (200 ÷ 50) per share.

Because of low demand for a *second* closed-end fund, the 100 shares outstanding are trading at $25 per share. The market value of the securities in this fund's portfolio is $3,000, or each share has a NAV of $30 per share. The market value balance sheet of this fund is:

Assets		Liabilities and Equity	
Market value of asset portfolio	$3,000	Market value of closed-end fund shares (100 × $25)	$2,500
Discount	−$500		

Mutual Fund Costs

Mutual funds charge shareholders a price or fee for the services they provide (i.e., management of a diversified portfolio of financial securities). Two types of fees are incurred by investors: sales loads and fund operating expenses. We discuss these next. The total cost to the shareholder of investing in a mutual fund is the sum of the annualized sales load and other fees charged.

Load versus No-Load Funds.   An investor who buys a mutual fund share from a registered representative of a brokerage firm may be subject to a one-time sales or commission charge, sometimes as high as 8.5 percent. In this case, the fund is called a **load fund**.[8] Funds that market shares directly to investors and do not use sales agents working for commissions (and have no up-front commission charges) are called **no-load funds**.

> **load fund**
>
> A mutual fund with an up-front sales or commission charge that the investor must pay.
>
> **no-load fund**
>
> A mutual fund that does not charge up-front sales or commission charges on the sale of mutual fund shares to investors.

The argument in favor of load funds is that they provide the investor with more personal attention and advice than no-load funds. The cost of increased personal attention may not be worthwhile, however. For example, Table 18–10 shows the top 10 performing U.S. stock funds in 1998 before and after adjusting returns for any load fees. Notice that the ranking of all but the top two load funds is reduced by at least 1 position and as many as 10 positions when the return is adjusted for load fees. As Figure 18–3 indicates, the rising share of no-load funds indicates that investors are increasingly recognizing that this cost disadvantage outweighs any perceived benefits of more active management attention. In 1985, load funds represented almost 70 percent of mutual fund sales, and no-load funds represented just over 30 percent. By 1998, however,

---

8. Another kind of load, called a *back-end load,* is sometimes charged when mutual fund shares are sold by investors. Back-end loads, also referred to as deferred sales charges, are an alternative way to compensate the fund managers or sales force for their services.

Table 18–10   Impact of Load Charges on Mutual Fund Returns

Fund	Total Return	Rank	Load	Adjusted Return	Adjusted Rank
Fidelity Sel Computer	96.37%	1	3.00%	93.37%	1
Flag Inv Comm; A	81.72	2	4.50	77.22	2
Fidelity Sel Technology	74.16	3	3.00	71.16	4
Janus Twenty	73.39	4	None	73.39	3
Fidelity Select Dvlp Comm	67.67	5	3.00	64.67	5
IDEX: Growth; A	64.00	6	5.50	58.50	8
Alger Ret: Cap Apprec	63.44	7	None	63.44	6
Alliance Technology; B	61.98	8	4.25	57.73	10
United; Science & Tech	59.31	9	5.75	53.56	19
Reynolds: Opportunity	59.14	10	None	59.14	7

Source: Author's research.

Figure 18–3   Load versus No-Load Sales

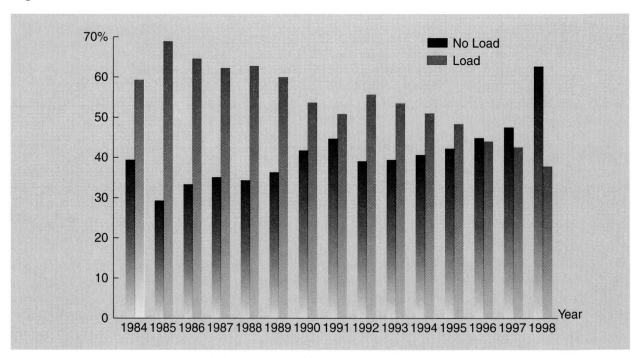

Source: *Perspective* 3, no.1 (March 1997); and *Mutual Funds Fees and Expenses* (Washington, D.C.: Investment Company Institute, November 1998). Reprinted by permission of the Investment Company Institute. *www.ici.org/*

no-load fund sales led load fund sales by 63 to 37 percent. Given the comparable returns available on no-load funds relative to load funds, the decreased investment in load funds is likely to continue.

Fund Operating Expenses.   In contrast to one-time up-front load charges on the initial investment in a mutual fund, annual fees are charged to cover all fund level expenses experienced as a percent of the fund assets. One type of fee (called a management fee) is charged to meet operating costs (such as administration and shareholder services). In addition, no-load funds generally require a small percentage (or

12b-1 fees

Fees relating to the distribution costs of mutual fund shares.

fee) of investable funds to meet fund level marketing and distribution costs. Such annual fees are known as **12b-1 fees** after the SEC rule covering such charges.[9] Because these fees, charged to cover fund operating expenses, are paid out of the fund's assets, investors indirectly bear these expenses.

Example 18–4 Calculation of Mutual Fund Costs

The cost of mutual fund investing to the shareholder includes both the one-time sales load and any annual fees charged. Because the sales load is a one-time charge, it must be converted to an annualized payment incurred by the shareholder over the life of his or her investment. With this conversion, the total shareholder cost of investing in a fund is the sum of the annualized sales load plus any annual fees.

For example, suppose an investor purchases fund shares with a 4 percent front-end load and expects to hold the shares for 10 years. The annualized sales load[10] incurred by the investor is:

$$4 \text{ percent} / 10 \text{ years} = .4 \text{ percent per year}$$

Further, suppose the fund has a total fund expense ratio (including 12b-1 fees) of 1 percent per year. The annual total shareholder cost for this fund is calculated as:

$$.4 \text{ percent} + 1 \text{ percent} = 1.4 \text{ percent per year}$$

Figure 18–4 shows the total shareholder cost, measured as the sum of fund operating expenses (12b-1 fees) and the annualized sales load as a percent of sales, for equity mutual funds from 1980 through 1998. Notice that total costs have declined from 2.26 percent in 1980 to 1.35 percent in 1998, a drop of over 40 percent. The average shareholder cost for load funds was 2 percent in 1998, while for no-load funds it was 0.83 percent in 1998.

Figure 18–4 Total Shareholder Cost for Equity Mutual Funds

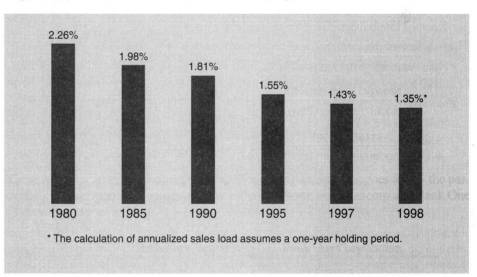

* The calculation of annualized sales load assumes a one-year holding period.

Source: Investment Company Institute, *Perspective*, February 1999. Reprinted by permission of the Investment Company Institute. *www.ici.org/*

9. 12b-1 fees are limited to a maximum of 0.25 percent.

10. Convention in the industry is to annualize the sales load without adjusting for the time value of money.

Table 18–11 Mutual Fund Quote

Fund Name	Objective	Min $ Inv	Assets ($ Mil)	Max. Sales Charge Initial	Max. Sales Charge Exit	Annual Exp As %	NAV $ 12/31	Dividends From Income	Dividends Capital Distrib	Performance & Rank Fourth Quarter	One Year	Annualized Three Years	Annualized Five Years
VANGUARD INDEX FDS			☎ 800-662-7447										
500 Index	GI	3K	69,545	No	No	0.19	113.95	1.33	0.42	21.4	28.6-A	28.2-A	24.0-A
Balanced Index	BL	3K	1,901	No	No	0.20	18.48	0.54	0.14	12.7	17.9-B	18.0-B	15.8-A
Em Mkts Stk	EM	3K	612	No	1.00	0.57	7.91	0.26	0.02	19.2	−18.1-A	−7.5-B	NS
Euro Stk Idx	EU	3K	4,021	No	No	0.31	25.28	0.52	0.14	18.4	28.9-A	24.7-A	19.3-A
Extnd Mkt Idx	MC	3K	2,774	No	No	0.23	30.62	0.37	2.17	22.1	8.3-C	17.3-C	16.2-B
Ext Mkt Idx;Inst	MC	10M	412	No	No	NA	30.62	0.41	2.17	22.1	8.5-C	NS	NS
Growth Index	GR	3K	5,721	No	No	0.20	31.67	0.22	0.12	24.6	42.2-A	33.9-A	27.8-A
Growth Index;Inst	GR	10M	209	No	No	NA	31.67	u0.19	0.12	24.6	NS	NS	NS
Instl Index Fd	GI	10M	20,806	No	No	0.06	112.85	1.42	0.90	21.4	28.8-A	28.3-A	24.1-A
Instl Index;Instl pl	GI	200M	4,695	No	No	NA	112.85	1.45	0.90	21.4	28.8-A	NS	NS
Int-Tm Bd Idx	IG	3K	1,061	No	No	0.20	10.49	0.65	0.07	−0.2	10.2-A	7.3-A	NS
Long-Tm Bd Idx	LG	3K	197	No	No	0.20	11.32	0.67	0.05	−0.3	12.0-A	8.5-A	NS
Mid Cap Index	MC	3K	166	No	No	NA	10.77	u0.05	0.05	28.4	NS	NS	NS
Mid Cap Idx;Inst	MC	10M	35	No	No	NA	10.78	u0.06	0.05	28.5	NS	NS	NS
Pac Stk Idx	PR	3K	990	No	No	0.35	7.84	0.07	0.00	26.5	2.4-A	−11.1-C	−4.0-B
Small Cap Index	SC	3K	2,644	No	No	0.23	21.20	0.30	1.55	16.6	−2.6-C	12.7-C	12.9-C
Small Cap Idx;Inst	SC	10M	207	No	No	0.12	21.20	0.33	1.55	16.6	−2.5-C	NS	NS
Small Cap Growth Idx	SC	3K	NA	No	No	NA	9.53	u0.03	0.00	22.3	NS	NS	NS
Small Cap Value Idx	SC	3K	106	No	No	NA	8.74	u0.06	0.00	13.7	NS	NS	NS
Sht-Tm Bd Idx	SG	3K	685	No	No	0.20	10.10	0.57	0.07	0.6	7.6-A	6.4-A	NS
Tot Bd Mkt	IG	3K	7,510	No	No	0.20	10.27	0.62	0.04	0.3	8.6-B	7.2-A	7.2-A
Tot Bd Mkt;Inst	IG	10M	2,183	No	No	0.10	10.27	0.63	0.04	0.3	8.7-B	7.3-A	NS
Tot Intl Stock	IL	3K	1,310	No	No	0.00	11.19	0.21	0.01	20.5	15.6-B	NS	NS
Tot Stock Mkt Idx	GR	3K	8,549	No	No	0.20	27.42	0.33	0.13	21.5	23.3-C	25.0-C	21.5-B
Tot Stock Mkt Idx;Inst	GR	10M	2,248	No	No	0.10	27.42	0.35	0.13	21.5	23.4-C	NS	NS
Value Index	GI	3K	2,329	No	No	0.20	22.51	0.36	0.99	17.5	14.6-D	21.9-C	19.8-C

Notes: GI= growth & income fund; BL= balanced fund; EM= emerging market fund; EU= European region fund; MC= middle-sized company fund; GR= growth fund; IG= intermediate maturity Treasury and government agency bond fund; LG= long term Treasury and government agency bond fund; SG=short-term Treasury and government agency bond fund; IL=Canadian and International small cap fund; PR= Pacific region fund; and SC= small company fund.

Source: *The Wall Street Journal*, January 7, 2000, p. R39. Reprinted by permission of *The Wall Street Journal* © 2000 Dow Jones & Company, Inc. All Rights Reserved Worldwide. *www.wsj.com/*

www.vanguard.com/

Do You Understand?

1. Where mutual funds rank in terms of asset size of all FI industries?
2. What the difference is between short-term and long-term mutual funds?
3. What the trends as to the number of mutual funds have been since 1980?
4. What the two largest mutual fund companies are? How have their funds performed in recent years?
5. What the difference is between open-end and closed-end mutual funds?

Mutual Fund Share Quotes

Year-end mutual fund quotes for Vanguard Index Funds from *The Wall Street Journal* are presented in Table 18–11. Each quote includes information on each fund's name; its objective; the minimum investment allowed; the fund's asset size; its maximum initial and exit sales charges; annual expenses; NAV; its dividends from income and capital distributions; and its fourth quarter 1998, and one- through five-year return and rating (A through E).[11] The maximum initial charge is listed as "No" for each of the Vanguard Index Funds, meaning that they are all no-load funds.

11. Funds are ranked by total return within each investment objective defined by *The Wall Street Journal*: A = top 20 percent; B = next 20 percent; C = middle 20 percent; D = next 20 percent; and E = bottom 20 percent.

Table 18–12 Distribution of Assets in Money Market Mutual Funds from 1991 through June 1999
(in billions of dollars)

	1991	1992	1993	1994	1995	1996	1997	1998	1999 (Q2)
Total financial assets	$535.0	$539.5	$559.6	$602.9	$745.3	$ 891.1	$1,048.7	$1,334.2	$1,398.1
Foreign deposits	21.4	20.3	10.0	15.7	19.7	23.1	23.2	30.6	45.1
Checkable deposits and currency	−0.2	−2.7	−1.2	−2.5	−3.5	−1.1	1.5	−1.0	−1.8
Time and savings deposits	35.1	34.6	31.9	31.4	52.3	82.7	111.3	127.0	137.5
Security RPs	67.0	65.9	66.4	68.8	87.8	103.8	126.6	139.5	139.3
Credit market instruments	403.9	408.6	429.0	459.0	545.5	634.3	721.9	965.9	1,002.1
Open-market paper	190.6	173.6	164.4	187.2	235.5	273.9	336.0	414.2	468.9
U.S. government securities	118.9	132.7	147.2	143.3	160.8	192.0	182.5	277.5	240.9
Treasury	78.3	78.4	79.4	66.1	70.0	90.2	86.2	103.6	84.0
Agency	40.6	54.3	67.8	77.2	90.8	101.8	96.3	173.8	156.9
Municipal securities	90.6	96.0	105.6	113.4	127.7	144.5	167.0	193.0	196.4
Corporate and foreign bonds	3.8	6.3	11.7	15.2	21.5	23.9	36.4	81.2	95.9
Miscellaneous assets	7.7	12.7	23.7	30.6	43.4	48.3	64.3	72.2	75.9

Source: Federal Reserve Bulletin, "Flow of Fund Accounts," September 15, 1999. *www.bog.frb.fed.us/*

Balance Sheets and Recent Trends

Money Market Funds

Consider the distribution of assets of money market mutual funds from 1991 through June 1999 in Table 18–12. In the second quarter of 1999, $1,029.9 billion (73.7 percent of total assets) were invested in short-term (under one year to maturity) financial securities—such as foreign deposits, domestic checkable deposits and currency, time and savings deposits, repurchase agreements (RPs or repos), open-market paper (mostly commercial paper), and U.S. government securities. Short-maturity asset holdings reflect the objective of these funds to retain the depositlike nature of the share liabilities they issue. In fact, most money market mutual fund shares have their values fixed at $1. Asset value fluctuations due to interest rate changes and any small default risk and capital gains or losses are adjusted for by increasing or reducing the number of $1 shares owned by the investor.

Example 18–5 Calculation of Number of Shares Outstanding in a Money Market Mutual Fund

Due to a drop in interest rates, the market value of the assets held by a particular MMMF increases from $100 to $110.[12] The market value balance sheet for the mutual fund before and after the drop in interest rates is:

(a) Before interest rate drop:

Assets		Liabilities and Equity	
Market value of MMMF assets	$100	Market value of MMMF fund shares (100 shares × $1)	$100

12. As discussed in Chapter 2, the value of fixed-income securities such as T-bills, CDs, and so on will rise in value whenever yields (interest rates) fall. That is, there is an inverse relationship between market value and interest rates for most MMMFs since they specialize in holding (short-term) fixed-income securities.

(b) After interest rate drop:

Assets		Liabilities and Equity	
Market value of MMMF assets	$110	Market value of MMMF fund shares (110 shares × $1)	$110

The interest rate drop results in 10 (110 − 100) new equity-type shares that are held by investors in the MMMF, reflecting the increase in the market value of the MMMF's assets of $10 (i.e., 10 new shares of $1 each).

Long-Term Funds

Note the asset distribution of long-term mutual funds in Table 18–13. As might be expected, it reflects the relative popularity of bonds and equities at various times. Underscoring the attractiveness of equities in 1999 was the fact that corporate equities represented more than 70.9 percent of total long-term mutual fund asset portfolios, while U.S. government bonds and municipal bonds were the next most popular assets (15.8 percent of the asset portfolio). In contrast, consider the distribution of assets in 1991 when the equity markets were not doing well and the economy was in recession. Corporate equities made up only 40.1 percent of long-term mutual fund portfolios, with U.S. government securities and municipals comprising the largest asset group at 44.2 percent of total assets.

Do You Understand?

1. What the major assets held by mutual funds have been in the 1990s?
2. How the asset distribution for money market mutual funds and long-term mutual funds differs?

Table 18–13   Distribution of Assets in Long-Term Bond, Income, and Equity Mutual Funds from 1991 through June, 1999
(in billions of dollars)

	1991	1992	1993	1994	1995	1996	1997	1998	1999 (Q2)
Total financial assets	$769.5	$992.5	$1,375.4	$1,477.3	$1,852.8	$2,342.4	$2,989.4	$3,610.5	$4,029.9
Security RPs	12.2	21.9	38.7	43.1	50.2	47.5	57.8	68.2	80.1
Credit market instruments	440.2	566.4	725.9	718.8	771.3	820.2	901.1	1,025.9	1,078.1
Open market paper	12.2	21.9	38.7	43.1	50.2	47.2	57.8	68.2	80.1
U.S. government securities	200.6	257.4	306.6	296.2	315.1	330.2	349.7	375.8	385.4
Treasury	133.5	169.5	200.9	194.1	205.3	214.1	225.2	230.4	235.3
Agency	67.1	87.9	105.7	102.1	109.9	116.1	124.5	145.5	150.1
Municipal securities	139.7	168.4	211.3	207.0	210.2	213.3	219.8	242.6	250.7
Corporate and foreign bonds	87.7	118.7	169.3	172.4	195.7	229.5	273.8	320.5	361.9
Corporate equities	308.9	401.3	607.4	709.6	1,024.9	1,470.0	2,081.7	2,029.1	2,857.4
Miscellaneous assets	8.2	3.0	3.3	5.9	6.3	4.7	11.5	8.0	14.3

Source: Federal Reserve Bulletin, "Flow of Fund Accounts," September 15, 1999. *www.bog.frb.fed.us/*

5 Regulation

Because mutual funds manage and invest small investors' savings, this industry is heavily regulated. Indeed, many regulations have been enacted to protect investors against possible abuses by mutual fund managers. The SEC is the primary regulator of mutual funds. Specifically, the Securities Act of 1933 requires a mutual fund to file a registration statement with the SEC and sets rules and procedures regarding a fund's prospectus that it sends to investors. In addition, the Securities Exchange Act of 1934 makes the purchase and sale of mutual fund shares subject to various antifraud provisions. This act requires mutual funds to furnish full and accurate information on all financial and corporate matters to prospective fund purchasers. The 1934 Act also appointed the National Association of Securities Dealers (NASD) to supervise mutual fund share distributions. In 1940, Congress passed the Investment Advisers Act and Investment Company Act. The Investment Company Act established rules to prevent conflicts of interest, fraud, and excessive fees or charges for fund shares.

In recent years, the Insider Trading and Securities Fraud Enforcement Act, passed in 1988, has required mutual funds to develop mechanisms and procedures to avoid insider trading abuses. In addition, the Market Reform Act of 1990, passed in the wake of the 1987 stock market crash, allows the SEC to introduce circuit breakers to halt trading on exchanges and to restrict program trading when it deems necessary. Finally, the National Securities Markets Improvement Act (NSMIA) of 1996 (discussed in Chapter 16) also applies to mutual fund companies. Specifically, the NSMIA exempts mutual fund sellers from oversight by state securities regulators, thus reducing their regulatory burden.

Do You Understand?

1. Who the primary regulator of mutual fund companies is?
2. How the NSMIA affected mutual funds?

Summary

This chapter presented an overview of the mutual fund industry. Mutual funds pool funds from individuals and corporations and invest in diversified asset portfolios. Due to the tremendous increase in the value of financial assets such as equities in the 1990s and the cost-effective opportunity that mutual funds offer for small investors to participate in these markets, mutual funds have increased tremendously in size, number of funds, and number of shareholders. The chapter also discussed the two major categories of mutual funds—short-term and long-term open-end funds—highlighting the differences in their growth rates and the composition of their assets. The chapter also illustrated the calculation of the net asset values (NAV) of mutual fund shares.

Questions

1. What is a mutual fund? In what sense is it a financial intermediary?
2. What is the NAV of a mutual fund? What three sources of gains and losses affect the NAV?
3. What benefits do mutual funds have for individual investors?
4. What are the economic reasons for the existence of mutual funds?
5. What is the difference between open-end and closed-end mutual funds? Which of them tend to be more specialized?
6. How do the composition and size of short-term funds differ from long-term funds?
7. What appears to be the reason for the change in the composition of mutual funds over time?
8. How does the risk of short-term funds differ from that of long-term funds?
9. Who are the major holders of mutual fund shares?
10. What are the three components of the return that an investor receives from a mutual fund?
11. Open-end Fund A has 100 shares of ATT valued at $100 each and 50 shares of Toro valued at $50 each.

Closed-end Fund B has 75 shares of ATT and 100 shares of Toro. Both funds have 100 shares outstanding.

a. What is the NAV of each fund using these prices?

b. Assume that another 100 shares of ATT valued at $100 are added to Fund A. What is the effect on Fund A's NAV if the prices remain unchanged?

c. If the price of ATT stock increases to $105 and the price of Toro stock declines to $45, how does that impact the NAV of both funds? Assume that Fund A has only 100 shares of ATT.

12. A mutual fund has 200 shares of Fiat, Inc., currently trading at $14, and 200 shares of Microsoft, Inc., currently trading at $140. The fund has 100 shares outstanding.

a. What is the NAV of the fund?

b. If investors expect the price of Fiat shares to increase to $18 and the price of Microsoft to decline to $110 by the end of the year, what is the expected NAV at the end of the year?

c. What is the maximum that the price of Microsoft can decline to maintain the NAV as estimated in (a)?

13. How does the regulation of mutual funds differ from that of other financial institutions?

14. Why do mutual funds require regulations?

15. How might an individual's preference for a mutual fund's objective change over time?

16. An investor purchases a mutual fund for $100. The fund pays dividends of $3, distributes a capital gain of $4, and charges a fee of $2 when the fund is sold one year later for $105. What is the net rate of return from this investment?

17. Suppose that you have a choice between two mutual funds, one a load fund with no annual 12b-1 fees, and the other a no-load fund with a maximum 12b-1 fee. How would the length of your expected holding period influence your choice between these two funds?

18. How has the growth in mutual funds affected the growth in other types of financial intermediaries?

19. What is a REIT? What type of interest rate risks would it face?

20. Go to the Fidelity Investments website and look up the annual 1-, 5-, and 10-year returns for the Fidelity Select Biotechnology Fund.

Pension Funds

Chapter Navigator

1. What is the difference between a private pension fund and a public pension fund?

2. What is the difference between a defined benefit and defined contribution pension fund?

3. What are the different types of private pension funds?

4. What are the different types of public pension funds?

5. What are the main regulations governing pension funds?

Pension Funds Defined: Chapter Overview

Pension funds offer savings plans through which fund participants accumulate tax-deferred savings during their working years before withdrawing them during their retirement years. Funds originally invested in and accumulated in a pension plan are exempted from current taxation. Rather, tax payments are not made until funds are actually distributed to the fund participant, often later in his or her life.

Pension funds were first established in the United States in 1759 to benefit the widows and children of church ministers. It was not until 1875 that the American Express Company established the first corporate pension fund. By 1940, only 400 pension funds were in existence, mainly for employees in the railroad, banking, and public utilities industries. Since then, the industry has boomed, so that currently over 700,000 pension funds now exist. In 1998, U.S. households had 31.6 percent of their financial assets invested in pension funds, compared to just over 5 percent in 1950.

Table 19–1   Pension Fund Reserves, 1993–1999
(in billions of dollars)

	1993	1994	1995	1996	1997	1998	1999*
Federal government	$ 331.1	$ 358.9	$ 374.8	$ 419.2	$ 450.5	$ 642.9	$ 642.7
Private pension funds							
Life insurance companies	836.4	884.5	997.3	1,088.9	1,226.7	1,356.2	1,479.6
Other private pension funds	2,216.3	2,317.2	2,681.4	3,072.6	3,604.2	4,354.7	4,624.1
State and local government							
retirement funds	1,268.7	1,309.9	1,535.9	1,734.7	2,117.6	2,806.9	3,023.7
Total	$4,625.5	$4,870.5	$5,589.4	$6,315.4	$7,399.0	$9,160.7	$9,770.1

*Through second quarter.

Source: Federal Reserve Board, "Flow of Fund Accounts," September 15, 1999. *www.bog.frb.fed.us/*

private pension funds

Funds administered by a private corporation.

public pension funds

Funds administered by a federal, state, or local government.

The pension fund industry comprises two distinct sectors. **Private pension funds** are those funds administered by a private corporation (e.g., insurance company, mutual fund). Because pension funds are such a large percentage of the insurance industry's business (see below), they are often listed separately from other private pension funds. **Public pension funds** are those funds administered by a federal, state, or local government (e.g., Social Security). In 1999, total financial assets invested in pension funds were $9,770.1 billion: $6,103.7 billion in private funds (including life insurance companies), $3,023.7 billion in state and local government funds, and $642.7 billion in federal government funds (see Table 19–1). Growth of private funds was particularly significant in the 1990s as the long-term viability of the major public pension fund, Social Security, came into question.

This chapter provides an overview of the pension fund industry. In particular, we examine the size, structure, and composition of the industry. We also describe recent trends in private and public pension fund growth as well as the differences between these two major types of funds. Finally, we describe the major regulations under which the industry operates.

Size, Structure, and Composition of the Industry

In this section, we describe the various characteristics of pension funds, including insured versus noninsured pension funds and defined benefit versus defined contribution pension funds. We then present an overview of the private pension funds and public pension funds that comprise this industry.

Insured versus Noninsured Pension Funds

pension plan

Document that governs the operations of a pension fund.

insured pension fund

A pension fund administered by a life insurance company.

A **pension plan** governs the operations of a pension fund. Pension funds administered by life insurance companies (about 15 percent of the industry's assets) are termed **insured pension funds.** The designation as an insured pension fund is not necessarily due to the type of administrator but to the classification of assets in which pension fund contributions are invested. Specifically, there is no separate pool of assets backing the pension plan. Rather, pension plan funds are pooled and invested in the general assets of the insurance company. The amount of the insurance company's assets devoted to pension funds is reported on the liability side of the balance sheet under "pension fund reserves." For example, in June 1999 (see Table 19–2), life insurance companies managed a total of $1,456.7 billion in pension fund assets (reported in the liability account as "pension fund reserves"). These reserves represented almost half of the industry's

Table 19–2 Life Insurance Company Balance Sheet, June 1999

(in billions of dollars)

Total Assets	$2,926.4	100.0%
Checkable deposits and currency	4.0	0.1
Money market fund shares	125.9	4.3
Credit market instruments	1,876.0	64.1
Open market paper	69.0	2.4
U.S. government securities	286.1	9.7
Treasury	68.7	2.3
Agency	217.4	7.4
Municipal securities	18.1	0.6
Corporate and foreign bonds	1,179.3	40.3
Policy loans	98.8	3.4
Mortgages	224.7	7.7
Corporate equities	825.9	28.2
Mutual fund shares	16.5	0.6
Miscellaneous assets	78.1	2.7
Total Liabilities	$2,746.1	93.8%
Other loans and advances	4.0	0.1
Life insurance reserves	713.0	24.4
Pension fund reserves	**1,456.7**	**49.8**
Taxes payable	17.6	0.6
Miscellaneous liabilities	554.7	18.9

Source: Federal Reserve Board, "Flow of Fund Accounts," September 15, 1999. *www.bog.frb.fed.us/*

noninsured pension fund

A pension fund administered by a financial institution other than a life insurance company.

total liabilities and equity. Pension fund assets were distributed among various assets on life insurance companies' balance sheets (e.g., U.S. government securities, corporate and foreign bonds, corporate equities), rather than being reported as a separate pool of pension fund assets segregated from other life insurance assets.

Noninsured pension funds are managed by a trust department of a financial institution appointed by the sponsoring business, participant, or union. Trustees invest the contributions and pay the retirement benefits in accordance with the terms of the pension fund. In contrast to insured pension funds, assets managed in noninsured pension funds are owned by the sponsor and are thus segregated and listed as separate pools of assets on the trustees' balance sheet. While the day-to-day investment decisions for a noninsured pension fund are controlled by the trustee, the sponsor of the pension fund normally specifies general guidelines the trustee should follow.

Premiums paid into insured pension funds, and the assets purchased with these premiums, become the legal property of the insurance company managing the pension funds. In contrast, premiums paid into noninsured pension funds, and the assets purchased with these premiums, are the legal property of the sponsoring corporation. Because insurance companies, as the asset owners (of insured pension funds), incur the risk associated with value fluctuations in their pension fund assets, they generally concentrate their asset investments in less risky securities (bonds and mortgages). Noninsured pension fund managers, by contrast, do not incur the risk associated with asset value fluctuations. Thus, the trustees overseeing these pension funds generally invest pension premiums received in more risky securities (e.g., equities). As a result, noninsured pension funds generally offer the potential for higher rates of return but are also more risky than insured pension funds.

2 Defined Benefit versus Defined Contribution Pension Funds

Pension funds can also be distinguished by the way contributions are made and benefits are paid. A pension fund is either a defined benefit fund or a defined contribution fund. In a **defined benefit pension fund,** the corporate employer (or fund sponsor) agrees to provide the employee a specific cash benefit upon retirement, based on a formula that considers such factors as years of employment and salary during employment. The formula is generally one of three types: flat benefit, career average, or final pay formula. These three types of defined benefit funds are discussed in more detail next.

defined benefit pension fund

Pension fund in which the employer agrees to provide the employee with a specific cash benefit upon retirement.

flat benefit formula

Pension fund that pays a flat amount for every year of employment.

Flat Benefit Formula.   A **flat benefit formula** pays a flat amount for every year of employment.

Example 19–1   Calculation of Retirement Benefit for a Defined Benefit Fund under a Flat Benefit Formula

An employee with 20 years of service at a company is considering retirement at some point in the next 10 years. The employer uses a flat benefit formula by which the employee receives an annual benefit payment of $2,000 times the number of years of service. For retirement now, in 5 years, and in 10 years, the employee's annual retirement benefit payment is:

	Retirement Benefit
Retire now	$2,000 × 20 = $40,000
Retire in 5 years	$2,000 × 25 = $50,000
Retire in 10 years	$2,000 × 30 = $60,000

career average formula

Pension fund pays retirement benefits based on the employee's average salary over the entire period of employment.

Career Average Formula.   Two variations of **career average formulas** exist; both base retirement benefits on the average salary over the entire period of employment. Under one formula, retirees earn benefits based on a percentage of their average salary during the entire period they belonged to the pension fund. Under the alternative formula, the retirement benefit is equal to a percentage of the average salary times the number of years employed.

Example 19–2   Calculation of Retirement Benefit under a Defined Benefit Fund Using a Career Average Formula

An employee with 20 years of service at a company is considering retirement some time in the next 10 years. The employer uses a career average benefit formula by which the employee receives an annual benefit payment of 4 percent of his career average salary times the number of years of service. For retirement now, in 5 years, and in 10 years, the employee's annual retirement benefit payment is:

	Average Salary	Retirement Benefit
Retire now	$48,000	$48,000 × .04 × 20 = $38,400
Retire in 5 years	$50,000	$50,000 × .04 × 25 = $50,000
Retire in 10 years	$52,000	$52,000 × .04 × 30 = $62,400

final pay formula

Pension fund pays retirement benefits based on a percentage of the average salary during a specified number of years at the end of the employee's career times the number of years of service.

Final Pay Formula. A **final pay formula** pays a retirement benefit based on a percentage of the average salary during a specified number of years at the end of the employee's career times the number of years of service.

Example 19–3 Calculation of Retirement Benefit under a Defined Benefit Fund Using a Final Pay Formula

An employee with 20 years of service at a company is considering retirement at some time in the next 10 years. The employer uses a final pay benefit formula by which the employee receives an annual benefit payment of 2.5 percent of her average salary during her last five years of service times her total years employed. For retirement now, in 5 years, and in 10 years, the employee's (estimated) annual retirement benefit payment is:

	Average Salary during Last Five Years of Service	Retirement Benefit
Retire now	$75,000	$75,000 × .025 × 20 = $37,500
Retire in 5 years	$80,000*	$80,000 × .025 × 25 = $50,000
Retire in 10 years	$85,000*	$85,000 × .025 × 30 = $63,750

*These are based on estimates of the employee's future salary.

fully funded

A pension fund that has sufficient funds available to meet all future payment obligations.

underfunded

A pension fund that does not have sufficient funds available to meet all future promised payments.

overfunded

A pension fund that has more than enough funds available to meet the required future payouts.

defined contribution benefit fund

Pension fund in which the employer agrees to make a specified contribution to the pension fund during the employee's working years.

Notice that of the three benefit formulas, the final pay formula usually produces the biggest retirement benefit increases as years of service increase. This formula generally provides better protection against erosion of pension income by inflation; benefit payments are based on the employee's career-end salary, which is generally the highest and often reflects current levels of price and wage inflation. This type of plan is also generally more costly to the employer.

Under defined benefit pension funds, the employer should set aside sufficient funds to ensure that it can meet the promised payments. When sufficient funds are available, the pension fund is said to be **fully funded**. Frequently, pension funds do not have sufficient funds available to meet all future promised payments, in which case the fund is said to be **underfunded**. While underfunding is not illegal, the pension fund is required by law to meet all of its payment obligations (see discussion below). Occasionally, pension funds have more than enough funds available to meet the required future payouts. In this case, the fund is said to be **overfunded**.

With a **defined contribution pension fund,** the employer (or plan sponsor) does not precommit to providing a specified retirement income. Rather, the employer contributes a specified amount to the pension fund during the employee's working years. The final retirement benefit is then based on total employer contributions, any additional employee contributions, and any gains or losses on the investments purchased by the fund with these contributions. For *fixed-income funds,* a minimum rate of return is often guaranteed, with the possibility of higher returns if fund assets earn above minimum rates of return. For *variable-income funds,* all investment profits and losses are passed through to fund participants. Thus, defined contribution funds provide benefits to employees in the form of higher potential returns than offered by defined benefit funds, but employees also must accept the increased risk of uncertain pension fund payouts.

Private Pension Funds

Private pension funds are created by private entities (e.g., manufacturing, mining, or transportation firms) and are administered by private corporations (financial institutions). Of the $6,103.7 billion of financial assets in private pension funds in 1999, life insurance companies administered $1,479.6 billion, mutual funds

Figure 19–1 Pension Fund Assets, 1975–1998*

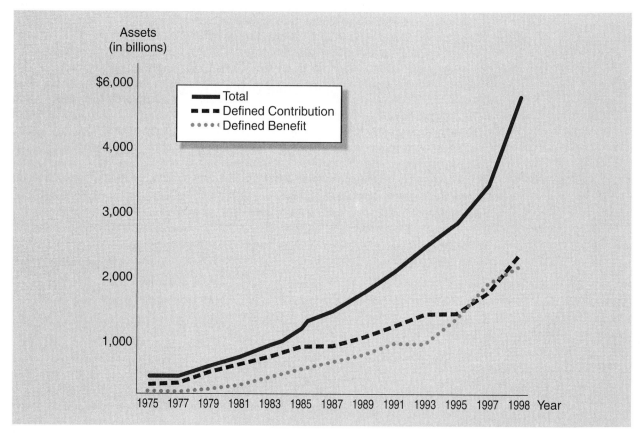

*Through second quarter.

Source: Department of Labor, Pension and Welfare Benefits Administration, *Private Pension Plan Bulletin*, Spring 1999. *www.dol.gov/dol/pwba/*

administered $1,860.0 billion, and other financial institutions such as banks administered $2,764.1 billion. Private fund contributions come from fund participants and/or their employers.

Defined contribution funds are increasingly dominating the private pension fund market. Indeed, many defined benefit funds are converting to defined contribution funds. Figures 19–1, 19–2, and 19–3 show private pension fund assets, the number of private pension funds, and the number of private pension fund participants, respectively. In all three figures, defined contribution funds are increasing in importance relative to defined benefit funds. Table 19–3 shows the net acquisition of financial assets in defined benefit and defined contribution funds from 1987 through 1998. In four of the years, defined benefit funds actually experienced a reduction in assets held, while the industry as a whole was growing at an average rate of over 10 percent per annum. One reason for this shift is that defined contribution funds do not require the employer to guarantee retirement benefits, and thus corporate stockholders and managers do not need to monitor the pension fund's performance once the required contribution are made. As noted in In the News box 19–1, not everyone sees this trend as a good thing.

Do You Understand?

1. How did the growth in defined benefit pension funds improve the efficiency of the U.S. economy?

Types of Private Pension Funds. Private defined benefit and defined contribution pension funds come in various types. Employees may participate in 401(k) plans, individual retirement accounts (IRAs), and Keogh accounts.

Figure 19–2 Number of Pension Funds

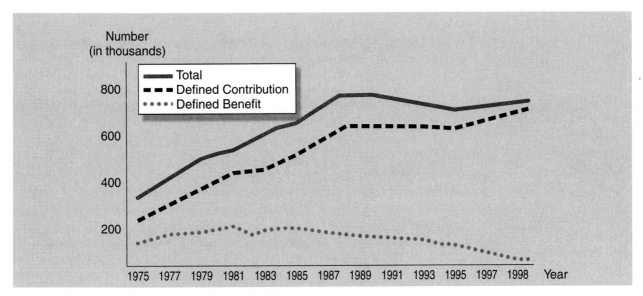

Source: Department of Labor, Pension and Welfare Benefits Administration, *Private Pension Plan Bulletin*, Spring 1999. *www.dol.gov/dol/pwba/*

Figure 19–3 Pension Fund Active Participants

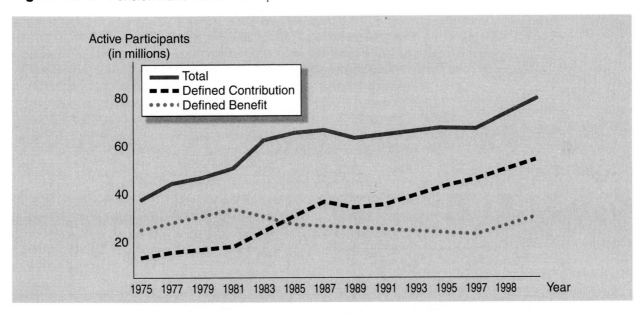

Source: Department of Labor, Pension and Welfare Benefits Administration, *Private Pension Plan Bulletin*, Spring 1999. *www.dol.gov/dol/pwba/*

Table 19–3 Net Acquisition of Financial Assets, Defined Benefit and Defined Contribution Pension Funds, 1987–1998
(in billions of dollars)

	1987	**1988**	**1989**	**1990**	**1991**	**1992**	**1993**	**1994**	**1995**	**1996**	**1997**	**1998***
Defined benefit funds	−6.0	13.2	−0.8	2.9	1.5	4.0	18.5	−1.1	10.6	4.1	−2.3	6.5
Defined contribution funds	40.1	44.3	40.7	56.2	66.7	73.9	81.5	82.0	80.0	83.1	90.9	102.7

*Through June.

Source: Federal Reserve Board, "Flow of Fund Accounts," September 15, 1999. *www.bog.frb.fed.us/*

In the News

Killing the Golden Goose of Defined Benefit Plans

According to the Federal Reserve Board's flow-of-funds statistics, the assets held by private defined contribution plans now exceed those held by private defined benefit plans. Since 1988, defined contribution assets have grown at a 12.6 percent compound annual rate. Defined benefit assets, in the same period grew at a 9.1 percent rate. That is, defined contribution assets have grown 38 percent faster. By all appearances, this trend will continue. Defined contribution plans will continue to dominate the pension scene. No rival of defined contribution plans is in sight.

No problem, right? We're just swapping an old, less-flexible form of pension provision for a more flexible one that employees (and employers) seem to prefer. Wrong. There will be hidden costs to the economy as a whole from the switch to defined contribution plans—arising from differences in the way they

are invested. We've probably killed the defined benefit goose that helped lay the golden eggs we are now harvesting in our economy.

Since 1980, defined benefit pension funds have invested in a wide range of (fixed-income) investment vehicles, most of which helped the economy in numerous, non-obvious ways. Defined benefit funds and their money managers have, through the capital markets, allocated capital to the areas expected to generate the highest expected returns. The competing investment ideas of the money managers have helped make the capital markets more efficient, and through them, improved the efficiency of the economy. For example, the rise of Silicon Valley and the technological revolution it has generated coincided almost exactly with the first serious forays by defined benefit funds into venture capital investing beginning in the early 1980s.

Pension funds did not spark the Silicon Valley rev-

olution, but they provided a significant amount of (fixed-income) financing to the venture capital industry at a critical time. They at least provided the marginal dollars that made the difference in many cases. Likewise, pension fund participation in leveraged buyouts helped improve the performance of many corporations. Though not every significant LBO worked, the existence of buyout groups, amply financed by major pension funds, prodded corporate CEOs all over the country to manage their company's assets more aggressively and efficiently. If they didn't, they risked being takeover targets. Would the corporate restructuring that has occurred over the past decade have taken place anywhere near as rapidly or completely without the LBO threat? Unlikely. And it further was stimulated by the corporate governance movement, again driven by defined benefit pension funds.

As growth of defined benefit plan assets continues to slow, what will take up the slack in these areas? Few, if any, defined contribution plan sponsors are likely to offer venture capital

Source: *Pensions & Investments*, May 3, 1999, by Mike Clowes. Reprinted with permission *Pension & Investments*, May 3, 1999. Copyright Crain Communications, Inc.

In the News continued

or LBO funds as options. There will still be some flow into venture capital and LBO funds trickling down from the surviving defined benefit funds and individual investors seeking higher returns. But it will be nothing like the flows of the past 15 years, and financial costs will be higher. If America's economic vitality begins to wane in the next decade you'll know who deserves some of the blame—those in Congress who fatally weakened the defined benefit system.

401(k) plans

Employer-sponsored plans that supplement a firm's basic retirement plan.

401(k) Plans. **401(k) plans** are employer-sponsored plans that supplement a firm's basic retirement plan, allowing for both employee and employer contributions (e.g., Supplementary Retirement Accounts offered by TIAA-CREF). Figure 19-4 shows the growth in 401(k) plans in the 1990s: from $385 billion in 1990, to $1,407 billion in 1998. In 1998, there were over 300,000 401(k) plans and over 37 million participants.

Participants in 401(k) plans generally have some discretion over the allocation of assets from both employee and employer contributions (e.g., the choice among investing in equity, bonds, and money market securities). Table 19–4 shows the allocation of assets by age of participants in 401(k) plans in 1997. Younger participants invest the majority of their contributions in equities, while older participants invest more heavily in fixed-income bond and guaranteed investment contract (GIC) funds.[1] The choice of asset allocation affects the fund's payout during retirement, similar to defined contribution funds.

Example 19–4 Calculating the Return on a 401(k) Plan

An employee contributes 10 percent of his $75,000 salary into the company's 401(k) plan. The company matches 40 percent of the first 6 percent of the employee's contributions. The employee is in the 31 percent tax bracket and the 401(k) plan expects to yield an 8 percent rate of return. The employee's own contribution and his plan return for one year are calculated as follows.

1. Employee's gross contribution = $75,000 × .10 = $ 7,500
2. Tax savings = $7,500 × .31 = $ 2,325
3. Employee's net of tax contribution $ 5,175
4. Employer's contribution = $75,000 × .40 × .06 = $ 1,800
5. Total 401(k) plan investment at year's start $ 9,300
6. 1-year earnings = $9,300 x .08 = $ 744
7. Total 401(k) investment at year-end $10,044   (= (1) + (4) + (6))
   Employee's 1-year return = ($10,044 − $5,175)/$5,175 = 94.09%

Assuming the employee's salary, tax rate, and 401(k) yield remain constant over a 20-year career, when the employee retires, the 401(k) will be worth:

$$\$9,300(FVIFA_{8\%, 20}) = \$425,586$$

The employee's net of tax contributions over the period are $5,175 × 20 = $103,500.

---

[1] A GIC is a long-term liability issued by insurance companies. A GIC guarantees not only a rate of interest over some given period but also the annuity rate on beneficiary's contracts, (see Chapter 15).

Figure 19–4   Assets in 401(k) Plans

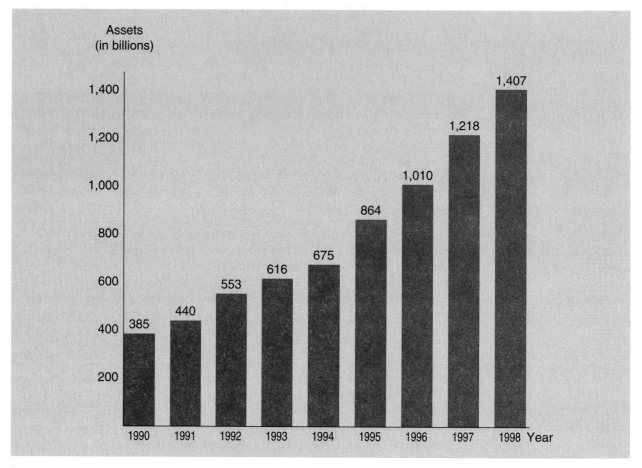

Source: Investment Company Institute, website data, 1999. Reprinted by permission of the Investment Company Institute. *www.ici.org/*

Table 19–4   401(k) Asset Allocation by Age

Age Cohort	Equity Funds	Bond Funds	Company Stock	Money Funds	Balanced Funds	GICs	Other
20s	55.1%	5.8%	16.7%	5.2%	8.3%	7.8%	1.2%
30s	51.2	5.6	19.6	4.8	8.1	9.0	1.6
40s	46.2	6.0	21.1	5.2	8.0	12.0	1.7
50s	42.5	7.0	19.5	5.3	7.8	16.1	1.9
60s	33.9	9.2	15.0	6.1	7.2	26.1	2.5
All	44.0	6.8	19.1	5.4	7.8	15.1	1.8

Source: Investment Company Institute and Employee Benefit Research Institute, *401(k) Plan Asset Allocation, Account Balances, and Loan Activity*, January 1999. Reprinted by permission of the Investment Company Institute. *www.ici.org/*

The allocation of a fund's assets across different types of securities can have a significant effect on the fund's returns and risks.

Example 19–5   Impact of Asset Allocation on a 401(k) Plan Return

An employee contributes $10,000 to a 401(k) plan each year, and the company matches 20 percent of this annually, or $2,000. The employee can allocate the contributions among equities (earning 10 percent annually), bonds (earning 6 percent annually), and money market securities (earning 4 percent annually). The employee expects to work at the company 30 years. The employee can contribute annually along one of the three following patterns:[2]

	Option 1	Option 2	Option 3
Equities	60%	50%	40%
Bonds	40%	30%	50%
Money market securities	0%	20%	10%
	100%	100%	100%

The terminal value of the 401(k) plan, assuming all returns and contributions remain constant (at \$12,000) over the 30 years,[3] will be:

Option 1:

$$12,000(.6)(FVIFA_{10\%,\ 30}) + 12,000(.4)(FVIFA_{6\%,\ 30}) = \$1,563,836$$

Option 2:

$$12,000(.5)(FVIFA_{10\%,\ 30}) + 12,000(.3)(FVIFA_{6\%,\ 30}) + 12,000(.2)(FVIFA_{4\%,\ 30})$$
$$= \$1,406,177$$

Option 3:

$$12,000(.4)(FVIFA_{10\%,\ 30}) + 12,000(.5)(FVIFA_{6\%,\ 30}) + 12,000(.1)(FVIFA_{4\%,\ 30})$$
$$= \$1,331,222$$

Notice that Option 1, which includes the largest investment in equities, produces the largest terminal value for the 401(k) plan, while Option 3, with the smallest investment in equities, produces the smallest terminal value. However, as discussed in Chapter 3, equity investments are riskier than bond and money market investments. Thus, the larger the portion of funds invested in equities, the higher the return risk of the pension plan—that is, the more uncertain the final (terminal) value of the plan. For example, suppose the economy slumped and equity investments only earned a 3 percent annual return over the 30 years the employee worked. In this case, the terminal value of the 401(k) plan would be:

Option 1:

$$12,000(.6)(FVIFA_{3\%,\ 30}) + 12,000(.4)(FVIFA_{6\%,\ 30}) = \$722,022$$

Option 2:

$$12,000(.5)(FVIFA_{3\%,\ 30}) + 12,000(.3)(FVIFA_{6\%,\ 30}) + 12,000(.2)(FVIFA_{4\%,\ 30})$$
$$= \$704,666$$

Option 3:

$$12,000(.4)(FVIFA_{3\%,\ 30}) + 12,000(.5)(FVIFA_{6\%,\ 30}) + 12,000(.1)(FVIFA_{4\%,\ 30})$$
$$= \$770,013$$

In this case, Option 3, which involves the smallest investment in risky equities, produces the largest terminal value for the 401(k) plan.

---

2. In reality, the employee has a larger number of possible choices in terms of fund asset allocation.

3. For simplicity, we assume that the employee's contribution remains constant over the 30 years. Realistically, as an employee's salary increases over his or her working years, contributions to the retirement funds increase as well.

Table 19–5   Differences Between a Roth IRA and Traditional IRA

Terms	Roth IRA	Traditional IRA
Eligibility	Adjusted gross income (AGI) under: Single: $110,000. Married (filing jointly): $160,000.	Anyone under the age of 70½ with earned income.
Annual contributions	Maximum $2,000 for single with AGI of $95,000 or less. Maximum $4,000 for married, filing jointly, with AGI of $150,000 or less.	The lessor of $2,000 or 100% of earned income.
Withdrawals and distributions	No mandatory withdrawal age. Cannot make withdrawals until age 59½. No income tax on withdrawals after age 59½. Take a lump sum or withdraw in installments.	Must begin to withdraw required minimum distribution (RMD) amount of your account no later than when you turn 70½. Cannot make withdrawals until age 59½. Take a lump sum or withdraw in installments.
Deductions	No deductions allowed.	Contribution is fully deductible under specified conditions.
Taxes and limitations	Cannot make withdrawals until age 59½. No income tax on withdrawals after age 59½.	Cannot make withdrawals until age 59½. Must start withdrawing by age 70½ to avoid penalties. Pay regular income tax on withdrawals of all earnings and pretax dollars you contributed.
Conversions	Conversion from traditional IRA allowed if AGI is $100,000 or less. Direct rollovers from qualified retirement plan to a Roth IRA prohibited.	Direct rollovers from qualified retirement plans to IRAs are tax free.

individual retirement accounts (IRAs)

Self-directed retirement accounts set up by employees who may also be covered by employer-sponsored pension plans.

Individual Retirement Accounts.   **Individual retirement accounts (IRAs)** are self-directed retirement accounts set up by employees who may also be covered by employer-sponsored pension plans as well as self-employed individuals. Contributions to IRAs are made strictly by the employee. IRAs were first allowed in 1981 as a method of creating a tax-deferred retirement account to supplement an employer-sponsored plan. A maximum of $2,000 may be contributed to an IRA per year, and nonworking spouses may contribute an additional $2,000 as long as the couple's adjusted gross income is less than $150,000 and neither person is covered by an employer-sponsored pension plan. IRAs may also be used by employees changing jobs. Any funds held by an employee in the old employer's pension fund may be invested in a tax-qualified IRA to maintain the tax-deferred status. In 1998, IRA account assets were greater than $2.1 trillion.

In 1998, a new type of IRA, a Roth IRA, was established. Like a regular IRA, Roth IRAs allow a maximum of $2,000 after-tax contribution per individual ($4,000 per household). Unlike a regular IRA, contributions to a Roth IRA are taxed in the year of contribution and withdrawals from the account are tax free (provided funds have been invested for at least five years and the account holder is at least 59½ years old). Roth IRAs are available only to individuals earning less than $95,000 or households earning less than $150,000. Table 19–5 summarizes the main differences between a Roth IRA and a traditional IRA.

Keogh accounts.   A Keogh account is a retirement account available to self-employed individuals. Contributions by the individual may be deposited in a tax-deferred account administered by a life insurance company, a bank, or other financial institution. Similar to 401(k) plans, the participant in a Keogh account is given some discretion as to how the funds are to be invested.

Public Pension Funds

Pension funds sponsored by the federal or state and local governments are referred to as public pension funds. In 1999, these funds managed assets of more than $3 trillion.

State or Local Government Pension Funds. Employees of state or local governments may contribute to pension funds sponsored by these employers. Most of these are funded on a "pay as you go" basis, meaning that contributions collected from current employees are the source of payments to the current retirees. As a result of the increasing number of retirees relative to workers, some of these pension funds (e.g., New York City) have experienced a situation in which contributions have not been high enough to cover the increases in required benefit payments (or the pension funds are what we called earlier "underfunded"). Some state and local governments have proposed tax increases to address this underfunding. Others have considered modifying the "pay as you go" method of funding contributions to operate their funds more like private pension funds. Without some modifications, many of the state and local government funds will increasingly be unable to maintain their promised payments to retirees, especially as the longevity of the population increases.

Federal Government Pension Funds. The federal government sponsors two types of pension funds. The *first type* are funds for federal government employees: civil service employees, military personnel, and railroad employees. Civil service funds cover all federal employees who are not members of the armed forces. This group is not covered by Social Security. Similar to private pension funds, the federal government is the main contributor to the fund, but participants may contribute as well. In addition to Social Security, career military personnel receive retirement benefits from a federal government-sponsored military pension fund. Contributions to the fund are made by the federal government, and participants are eligible for benefits after 20 years of military service. Employees of the nation's railroad system are eligible to participate in the federal railroad pension system. Originated in the 1930s, contributions are made by railroad employers, employees, and the federal government.

The *second type* of fund, and the largest federal government pension fund, is Social Security. Also known as the Old Age and Survivors Insurance Fund, Social Security provides retirement benefits to almost all employees and self-employed individuals in the United States. Social Security was established in 1935 with the objective of providing minimum retirement income to all retirees. Social Security is funded on a pay as you go basis; current employer and employee Social Security taxes are used to pay benefits to current retirees. Historically, Social Security tax contributions have generally exceeded disbursements to retirees. Any surpluses are held in a trust fund that can be used to cover required disbursements in years when contributions are insufficient to cover promised disbursements. Contributions are a specified percentage of an individual's gross income—currently 6.2 percent of the first $72,600 earned—and are matched with equivalent employer contributions.

As the percent of the population that is retired has increased, and the percent of the population that is working has decreased, Social Security tax revenue has dropped relative to benefits being paid out (i.e., Social Security is an underfunded pension fund). Based on current trends, Social Security payouts are expected to exceed revenues by 2022, and the Social Security system will be bankrupt (annual contributions and trust fund assets will be insufficient to cover required disbursements to retirees) by 2055. As a result, the federal government is

Do You Understand?

1. What the difference is between an insured and a noninsured pension fund?
2. What the differences are between a flat benefit and final pay benefit formula for a defined benefit pension fund?
3. What a defined contribution pension fund is?
4. What the major federally sponsored pension funds are?

Table 19–6   Financial Assets Held by Private Pension Funds, 1975 and 1999[*]
(in billions)

	1975		1999	
Total financial assets	$244.3	100.00%	$4,624.1	100.00%
Checkable deposits and currency	4.4	1.77	3.6	0.08
Time and savings deposits	14.5	5.84	29.8	0.64
Money market mutual shares	0.0	0.00	64.4	1.39
Security RPs	4.3	1.73	58.3	1.26
Credit market instruments	71.3	28.70	1,006.0	21.76
Open market paper	9.1	3.66	67.0	1.45
U.S. government securities	17.9	7.21	587.0	12.70
Treasury	12.4	4.99	226.6	4.90
Agency	5.5	2.22	360.4	7.79
Municipal securities	0.0	0.00	1.3	0.03
Corporate and foreign bonds	41.9	16.87	321.9	6.96
Mortgages	2.4	0.96	28.8	0.62
Corporate equities	108.0	43.48	2,344.4	50.70
Mutual fund shares	2.8	1.13	647.6	14.01
Miscellaneous assets	43.1	17.35	470.0	10.16
Unallocated insurance contracts	0.0	0.00	266.0	5.75
Contributions receivable	3.7	1.49	39.0	0.84
Other	39.4	15.86	165.0	3.57

[*]Through June.

Source: Federal Reserve Board, "Flow of Fund Accounts," September 15, 1999. *www.bog.frb.fed.us/*

currently considering new methods and ideas (discussed later) for fully funding the Social Security system.

Financial Asset Investments and Recent Trends

Employer and employee contributions made to pension funds are invested in financial assets. These investments are tracked by the Federal Reserve because of the increasing importance of pension funds as participants in national and international security markets.

Private Pension Funds

Financial assets (pension fund reserves) held by private pension funds in 1975 and 1999 are reported in Table 19–6. Financial assets held by pension funds totaled $244.3 billion in 1975 and $4,624.1 billion in 1999 (a 1,793 percent increase in 24 years). In 1999, 64.71 percent of pension fund contributions were in corporate equities or equity mutual funds shares. This compares to 44.61 percent in 1975. In fact, pension funds are the largest institutional investor in the U.S. stock market. Certainly the booming stock market was a major reason for the increased investment in equities by pension funds in the 1990s. For example, corporate equities represented over 50 percent ($2,344.4 billion) of the financial assets held by private pension funds.

Figure 19–5 shows differences between defined benefit and defined contribution fund investment portfolio allocations. In 1999, defined benefit funds had 24.47 percent of their funds invested in U.S. governments securities and bonds compared to 15.55 percent for defined contributions funds. Also, defined benefit funds had 55.20 percent

Figure 19–5 Financial Assets in Defined Benefit and Defined Contribution Pension Funds

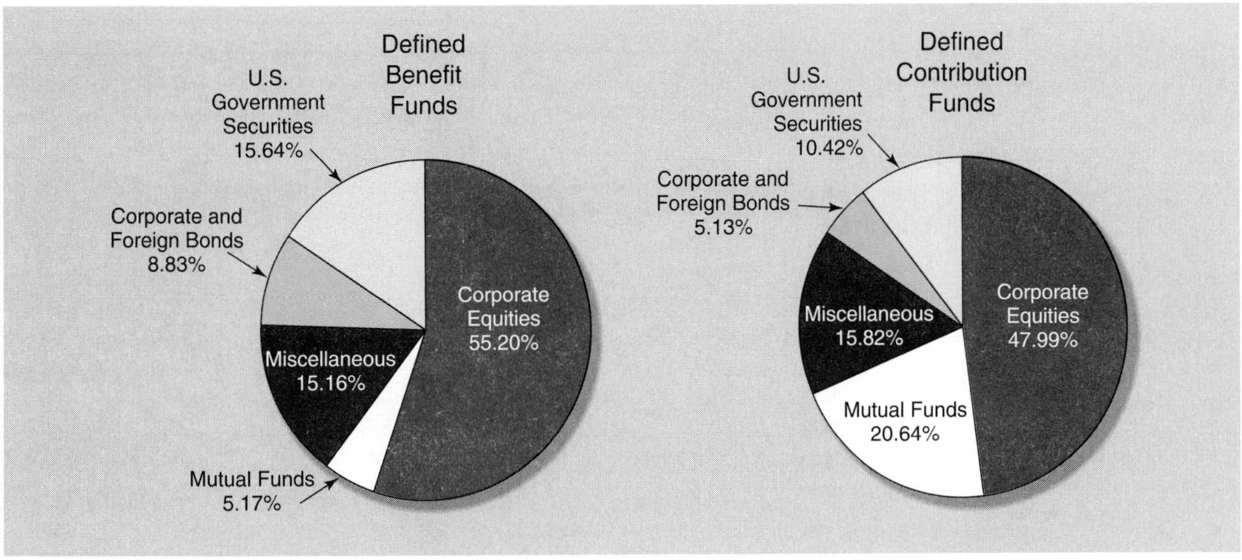

Source: Federal Reserve Board, "Flow of Fund Accounts," September 15, 1999. *www.bog.frb.fed.us/*

of their assets invested in corporate equities compared to 47.99 percent by defined contribution funds. In contrast, defined contribution funds had 20.64 percent of their funds invested in mutual fund shares compared to 5.17 percent for defined benefit funds.

Defined benefit pension funds offer employees a guaranteed payout, while defined contribution funds do not. The promise made of a guaranteed retirement payment is likely a major reason for the larger percentage of investments in fixed-income securities made by defined benefit funds. Defined contribution funds do not offer a guaranteed retirement payout—thus, defined contribution fund administrators are more likely to invest in risky equities and equity mutual fund shares. The introduction of equities into these funds helps to reduce the funding contributions required of the plan sponsor.

Public Pension Funds

Financial assets held by state and local government pension funds in 1975 and 1999 are reported in Table 19–7. Similar to private pension funds, state and local pension funds held most of their assets in corporate equities (64.69 percent in 1999). Second in importance were U.S. government securities and bonds (22.18 percent in 1999). In 1975, only 23.32 percent of pension fund assets were in equities and 66.03 percent were in U.S. government securities and bonds.

Social Security contributions are invested in relatively low-risk, low-return Treasury securities. This, along with the fact that the growth of the population is slowing, and the percentage of the population in retirement is increasing, has led to questions regarding the long-term viability of the Social Security fund (and the Social Security system in general). To bolster public confidence, the Social Security system was restructured in the mid-1990s by raising contributions and reducing retirees' benefits. In the late 1990s, several proposals were also introduced as possible ways of bolstering the Social Security fund's resources. Many politicians proposed that all, or a portion, of any U.S. government budget surplus[4] be transferred to

Do You Understand?

1. What the major financial assets held by private pension funds are?
2. What the major financial assets held by public pension funds are?

4. That is, the difference between federal revenues and expenditures.

Table 19–7   Financial Assets Held by State and Local Government Pension Funds, 1975 and 1999*

(in billions)

	1975		1999	
Total financial assets	$104.0	100.00%	$2,994.5	100.00%
Checkable deposits and currency	0.3	0.29	9.6	0.32
Time and savings deposits	1.2	1.15	0.4	0.01
Security RPs	0.0	0.00	39.7	1.33
Credit market instruments	78.2	75.05	724.9	24.21
Open market paper	0.0	0.00	39.7	1.33
U.S. government securities	7.8	7.49	370.7	12.38
Treasury	2.5	2.40	212.9	7.11
Agency	5.3	5.09	157.8	5.27
Municipal securities	1.9	1.82	2.0	0.06
Corporate and foreign bonds	61.0	58.54	293.4	9.80
Mortgages	7.5	7.20	19.1	0.64
Corporate equities	24.3	23.32	1,937.1	64.69
Miscellaneous assets	0.2	0.19	282.7	9.44

*Through June.

Source: Federal Reserve Board, "Flow of Fund Accounts," September 15, 1999. *www.bog.frb.fed.us/*

Do You Understand?

1. How President Clinton proposed to shore up the Social Security fund in 1999?
2. When, if no changes are made to Social Security funding, the fund is expected to be depleted?

Social Security. In addition, investing in securities issued by private companies was proposed (see In the News box 19–2). Such funding was touted as keeping the Social Security fund solvent through 2055. Other proposals suggested federally sponsored alternatives to Social Security (e.g., bumping up IRA and 401(k) limits or introducing Personal Savings Accounts), hoping to take some of the pressure off having to maintain "minimum" levels of Social Security retirement income.

5   Regulation of Pension Funds

The major piece of regulation governing private pension plans is the Employee Retirement Income Security Act (ERISA) of 1974 (also called the Pension Reform Act). While ERISA does not mandate that employers establish pension funds for their employees, it does require them to meet certain standards if a fund is to be eligible for tax-deferred status. ERISA was passed when many workers, who had contributed to pension funds for years, were failing to receive their pension benefits in a timely fashion. ERISA charged the Department of Labor with the task of overseeing pension funds. The principal features of ERISA involve pension plan funding, vesting of benefits, fiduciary responsibility, pension plan transferability, and pension plan insurance.

www.dol.gov/

Funding.   Prior to ERISA, there were no statutory requirements forcing defined benefit fund administrators to adequately fund their pension funds. Specifically, funds sometimes operated such that employees' annual contributions to pension funds were insufficient to meet promised annual pension obligations. ERISA established guidelines for funding and set penalties for fund deficiencies. Contributions to pension funds must be sufficient to meet all annual costs and expenses and to fund any unfunded historical liabilities over a 30-year period. Further, any new underfunding arising from low investment returns or other losses had to be funded over a 15-year period.

In the News

19-2

President Wants to Use Surplus to Preserve Social Security System

Proposal Puts $700 Billion into Stock Market, Sets Up New Retirement Accounts

President Clinton yesterday proposed to use nearly all of the federal government's burgeoning budget surplus to shore up Social Security and create new individual retirement savings accounts for most American workers. Following up on last year's pledge to "save Social Security first," Clinton again made the popular retirement security program the centerpiece of his State of the Union address, with a dramatic proposal that is sure to irk Republicans and Democrats alike.

The plan, which calls for investing up to $700 billion in federal budget surpluses in the stock market, would be the most far-reaching change in Social Security financing since the system was created 64 years ago. "You really have a fundamental choice," said Gene Sperling, chairman of the president's National Economic Council. "We have over $4 trillion in budget surpluses over the next 15 years. We could consume that now and let our children figure out what to do with Social Security and

Medicare, or we can use this moment, when the sun is shining, to lift the burden off future generations." . . .

Under the plan, about 62 percent of the surplus—or $2.7 trillion—would go directly to bolster Social Security's cash reserves, which are expected to dwindle rapidly once the baby boomer generation begins to retire around 2010. Another 11 percent, or $500 billion, would go to new, government-subsidized retirement savings accounts. Some 15 percent of the surplus would be dedicated to strengthening Medicare, the federal medical program for disabled and senior citizens that faces the most immediate cash crunch. The rest—about 11 percent—would be spent on military and domestic programs.

Sperling estimated yesterday that the proposal

would keep Social Security solvent until 2055, 23 years past the date that the program is now expected to go broke. Medicare would be kept afloat through 2020. Other structural changes may be needed, such as raising the retirement age, taxing more of the income of the rich, or subjecting more taxpayers, including some government workers, to the Social Security payroll tax. But White House aides say those tough decisions will have to be negotiated with Congress . . .

Almost all the money going into the stock market would be controlled by fund managers under contract with the federal government, a proposal that key Republicans vehemently oppose. The $700 billion in federal money that would flow into the markets over the next 15 years would represent just 4 percent of the total money currently in the nation's stock markets, Sperling said, about the same amount controlled by mutual fund giant Fidelity Investments. And the funds would be channeled mainly into mutual funds tied to the performance of the broad stock market and not

Source: *The Baltimore Sun*, January 20, 1999, p. 8A, by Jonathan Weisman.

(continues)

In the News continued

to the stocks of individual companies.

The proposal prompted a sharp response from Rep. Bill Archer, chairman of the powerful House Ways and Means Committee, which has jurisdiction over Social Security reform. "No, no, a thousand times no," Archer declared. "If you thought a government takeover of health care was bad, just wait until the government becomes an owner in America's private sector companies. Government-controlled investment in markets is contrary to free enterprise, and it will open the doors to all kinds of mischief."

The individual accounts—or Universal Savings Accounts—would be similarly conservative, working something like the 401(k) savings plans many companies offer. Under the proposal, the federal government would match workers' contributions up to a limit and in some cases make a modest lump sum contribution.

Vesting of Benefits. Frequently, while employers start contributing to an employee's pension fund as soon as the employee is eligible to participate, benefits may not be paid to the employee until he or she has worked for the employer for a stated period of time (or until the employee is **vested**). For example, prior to ERISA, some plans required their employees to work 15 and even 25 years before they were eligible to receive pension benefits. ERISA requires that a plan must have a minimum vesting requirement, and sets a maximum vesting period of 10 years.

vested

The period of time an employee must work before he or she is eligible to receive pension benefits.

Fiduciary Responsibilities. A pension plan fiduciary is a trustee or investment adviser charged with management of the pension fund. ERISA set standards governing the pension fund management. Specifically, ERISA required that pension fund contributions be invested with the same diligence, skill, and care as a "prudent person" in like circumstances (the *prudent-person rule*). Fund assets are required to be managed with the sole objective of providing the promised benefits to participants. To ensure that a fund operates in this manner, ERISA requires pension funds to report on the current status (e.g., market value of assets held, income and expenses of the fund) of the pension fund.

Transferability. ERISA allowed employees to transfer pension credits from one employer's fund to another's when switching jobs.

www.pbgc.gov/

Insurance. ERISA established the Pension Benefit Guarantee Corporation (PBGC), an insurance fund for pension fund participants similar to the FDIC. The PBGC insures participants of defined benefit funds if the proceeds from the fund are unable to meet its promised pension obligations (e.g., in 1991 and 1992 Pan American World Airways pension fund failures resulted in payouts of $688 million incurred by the PBGC).

When PBGC was created in 1974, the single-employer premium was a flat-rate $1 per plan participant. Congress raised the premium to $2.60 in 1979 and to $8.50 in 1986. In 1987, the basic premium was raised to $16 and an additional variable-rate premium was imposed on underfunded plans up to a maximum of $50. In 1991, Congress set the maximum at $72 per participant for underfunded plans and $19 per participant for fully funded plans.

Despite these premium increases, however, PBGC has generally operated at a deficit since its inception. This reflects the fact that unlike the FDIC, the PBGC has little regulatory power over the pension funds it insures. Thus, it cannot use portfolio restrictions or on-site supervision to restrict the risk taking of fund managers.[5] Partly in response to the growing PBGC deficit, the 1994 Retirement Protection Act was passed. Under the act (in 1997), the $72 premium cap was phased out (80 percent of underfunded plans were at the cap in 1997). Thus, underfunded programs are now subjected to even higher premiums (some as high as several hundred dollars per participant).[6] As a result of these changes, as of 1999 the PBGC's insurance fund operated at a record surplus of $5 billion. Thus, like the FDIC in 1993, the PBGC has changed to a more overtly risk-based premium plan.

In 1999, the operations of the PBGC came into question in a series of audits by the agency's inspector general, and Senate Hearings on the audits, held in September 1999, investigated how well the agency was run. The audits and hearings investigated, for example, why nearly half of the 472,000 people covered by failed pension funds the PBGC had taken over have not been told how much they are due each month. About 19,000 of these people have been waiting for more than 13 years and some have been waiting for as long as 18 years (estimated payments are being sent until the actual amount is determined). Audits also found that there were no monitoring controls in place to detect potential unauthorized data modification, such as creating and sending pension checks to "ghost" retirees with no record of ever working for the firm.[7]

Do You Understand?

1. Why ERISA was passed?
2. What the major features introduced by ERISA are?

---

5. To the extent that regulation restricts the asset and liability activities of a firm or FI, these restrictions are similar to imposing an "implicit" premium or tax on the activities of the firm.

6. Underfunded plans pay a surcharge of $9 per participant per $1,000 of underfunding.

7. This has caused proposals for more direct (on-site) audits of pension funds and their sponsors/administrators.

Summary

This chapter provided an overview of the pension fund industry. Pension funds provide a way of accumulating retirement funds similar to life insurance contracts and mutual funds. Pension funds, however, have a tax advantage in that an employee's contributions to pension funds are exempt from current taxation. The chapter reviewed the types of funds offered by private companies (financial institutions) and by federal and state or local governments. Given the problems with the funding of public pension funds and the phenomenal increase in stock market values, growth in private pension funds has been larger than any other type of financial institution in the 1990s. We looked at the distribution of asset investments for both private and public pension funds and highlighted their differences. The chapter also reviewed the major piece of regulation governing the industry, ERISA, and the role played by the Pension Benefit Guarantee Corporation (PBGC).

Questions

1. Describe the difference between a private pension fund and a public pension fund.
2. Describe the difference between an insured pension fund and a noninsured pension fund. What type of financial institutions would administer each of these?
3. Describe the difference between a defined benefit pension fund and a defined contribution pension fund.
4. What are the three types of formulas used to determine pension benefits for defined benefit pension funds? Describe each.

5. Your employer uses a flat benefit formula to determine retirement payments to its employees. The fund pays an annual benefit of $2,500 per year of service. Calculate your annual benefit payments for 25, 28, and 30 years of service.

6. Your employer uses a career average formula to determine retirement payments to its employees. The annual retirement payout is 5 percent of the employees' career average salary times the number of years of service. Calculate your annual benefit payment under the following scenarios.

Years Worked	Career Average Salary
30	$60,000
33	$62,500
35	$64,000

7. Your employer uses a final pay formula to determine retirement payouts to its employees. The annual payout is 3 percent of the average salary over the employees' last three years of service times the total years employed. Calculate your annual benefit under the following scenarios.

Years Worked	Average Salary during Last Three Years of Service
17	$40,000
20	$47,000
22	$50,000

8. What have the trends been for assets invested, number of funds, and number of participants in defined benefit versus defined contribution pension funds in the last two decades?

9. Describe the trend in assets invested in 401(k) plans in the 1990s.

10. Your company sponsors a 401(k) plan into which you deposit 12 percent of your $60,000 annual income. Your company matches 50 percent of the first 5 percent of your contributions. You expect the fund to yield 10 percent next year. If you are currently in the 31 percent tax bracket, what is your annual investment in the 401(k) plan and your one-year return?

11. Using the information in Question 10, and assuming all variables remain constant over the next 25 years, what will your 401(k) fund value be in 25 years (when you expect to retire)?

12. What is the difference between an IRA and a Keogh account?

13. Describe the "pay as you go" funding method that is used by many federal and state or local government pension funds. What is the problem with this method that may damage the long-term viability of such funds?

14. Describe the different pension funds sponsored by the federal government.

15. What are the major assets held by private pension funds in 1975 versus 1999? Explain the differences.

16. How do the financial asset holdings of defined benefit pension funds differ from those of defined contribution pension funds? Explain the differences.

17. What was the motivation for the passage of ERISA?

18. Describe the major features of ERISA.

19. Go to the Department of Labor's Pension and Welfare Benefits Administration website and locate updated information on the assets held and number of participants in pension funds.

20. Go to the Federal Reserve Board's website and find the most recent pension reserve levels for the federal government, life insurance companies, private pension funds, and state and local government retirement funds.

Risk Management *in* Financial Institutions

P art Five concludes the text by examining risks facing a modern FI and FI managers, and the various strategies for managing these risks. In Chapter 20, we preview the risk measurement and management chapters that follow with an overview of the risks facing a modern FI. In Chapter 21, we look at credit risk on individual loans and bonds and how these risks adversely affect an FI's profit and value. Chapter 22 covers liquidity risk in FIs. In Chapter 23, we investigate the effects of interest rate risk and the mismatching of asset and liability maturities on FI risk exposure. At the core of FI risk insulation is the size and adequacy of the FI owners' capital stake, which is also a focus of Chapter 23. The management of risk off the balance sheet is examined in Chapter 24, which highlights various new markets and instruments that have emerged to allow FIs to better manage risk. Finally, Chapter 25 explores ways of removing credit risk from the loan portfolio through asset sales and securitization.

Types *of* Risks Incurred *by* Financial Institutions

Chapter Navigator

1. What are the major risks faced by financial institutions?

2. How is insolvency risk a consequence of the other types of risk?

3. How are the various risks faced by financial institutions related?

1   Why Financial Institutions Need to Manage Risk: Chapter Overview

As has been mentioned in previous chapters, a major objective of FI management is to increase the FI's returns for its owners. This often comes, however, at the cost of increased risk. This chapter overviews the various risks facing FIs: credit risk, liquidity risk, interest rate risk, market risk, off-balance-sheet risk, foreign exchange risk, country or sovereign risk, technology risk, operational risk, and insolvency risk. Table 20–1 presents a brief definition of each of these risks. As will become clear, the effective management of these risks is central to an FI's performance. Indeed, it can be argued that the main business of FIs is to manage these risks.

While over the last decade U.S. financial institution profitability has been robust, the risks of financial intermediation have increased as the U.S. and overseas economies have become more integrated. For example, weak economic conditions outside the United States—especially in Asia and South America—have presented great risks for those FIs that operate in and lend to foreign markets and customers. Even those FIs that do not have foreign customers can be exposed to foreign exchange and sovereign risk if their domestic customers have business dealings with foreign countries. As a result, FI managers must devote significant time to understanding and managing the various risks to which their FIs are exposed. By the end of this chapter, you will have a basic understanding of the variety and complexity of the risks facing managers of mod-

Table 20–1 Risks Faced by Financial Institutions

1. **Credit Risk**—the risk that promised cash flows from loans and securities held by FIs may not be paid in full.
2. **Liquidity Risk**—the risk that a sudden surge in liability withdrawals may require an FI to liquidate assets in a very short period of time and at low prices.
3. **Interest Rate Risk**—the risk incurred by an FI when the maturities of its assets and liabilities are mismatched.
4. **Market Risk**—the risk incurred in trading assets and liabilities due to changes in interest rates, exchange rates, and other asset prices.
5. **Off-Balance-Sheet Risk**—the risk incurred by an FI as the result of activities related to contingent assets and liabilities.
6. **Foreign Exchange Risk**—the risk that exchange rate changes can affect the value of an FI's assets and liabilities denominated in foreign currencies.
7. **Country or Sovereign Risk**—the risk that repayments by foreign borrowers may be interrupted because of interference from foreign governments.
8. **Technology Risk**—the risk incurred by an FI when its technological investments do not produce anticipated cost savings.
9. **Operational Risk**—the risk that existing technology or support systems may malfunction or break down.
10. **Insolvency Risk**—the risk that an FI may not have enough capital to offset a sudden decline in the value of its assets.

ern FIs. In the remaining chapters of the text, we look at the management of the most important of these risks in more detail.

Credit Risk

credit risk

The risk that the promised cash flows from loans and securities held by FIs may not be paid in full.

Credit risk arises because of the possibility that promised cash flows on financial claims held by FIs, such as loans and bonds, will not be paid in full. If the principal on all financial claims held by FIs were paid in full on maturity and interest payments were made on their promised payment dates, FIs would always receive back the original principal lent plus an interest return—that is, they would face no credit risk. Should a borrower default, however, both the principal loaned and the interest payments expected to be received are at risk. Many financial claims issued by individuals or corporations and held by FIs promise a limited or fixed upside return (principal and interest payments to the lender) with a high probability, but they also may result in a large downside risk (loss of loan principal and promised interest) with a much smaller probability. Some examples of financial claims issued with these return-risk trade-offs are fixed-coupon bonds issued by corporations and bank loans. In both cases, an FI holding these claims as assets earns the coupon on the bond or the interest promised on the loan if no borrower default occurs. In the event of default, however, the FI earns zero interest on the asset and may well lose all or part of the principal lent, depending on its ability to lay claim to some of the borrower's assets through legal bankruptcy and insolvency proceedings. Accordingly, a key role of FIs involves screening and monitoring loan applicants to ensure that FI managers fund the most creditworthy loans (see Chapter 21).

The effects of credit risk are evident in Figures 20–1 and 20–2, which show commercial bank charge-off (or write-off) rates for various types of loans. Notice, in particular, the high rate of charge-offs experienced on credit card loans in the 1980s and most of the 1990s. Indeed, credit card charge-offs by commercial banks increased persistently from the mid 1980s until late 1991 and again from 1995 through early 1997. By February 1997, charge-offs leveled off, and they even declined after 1998. Despite

Figure 20–1 Charge-Off Rates for Commercial Bank Lending Activities, 1984–1999[*]

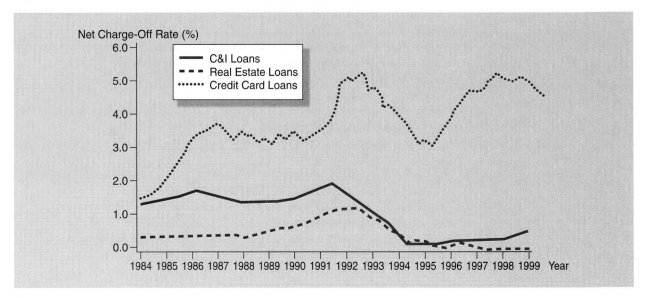

[*]Through June.
Source: FDIC, *Quarterly Banking Profile,* Second Quarter 1999. *www.fdic.gov/*

Figure 20–2 Credit Card Loss Rates, 1984–1999[*]

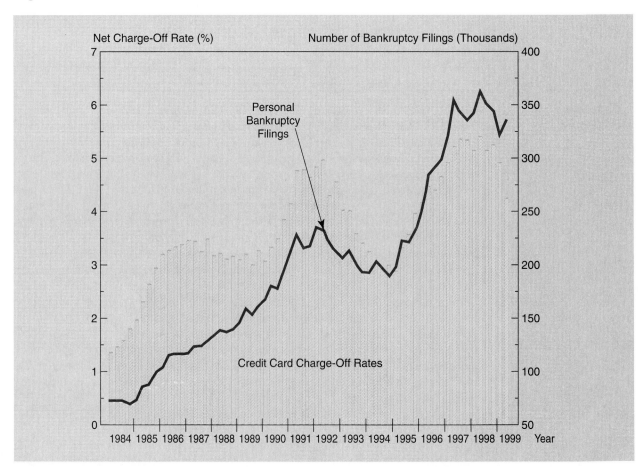

[*]Through June.
Source: FDIC, *Quarterly Banking Profile,* Second Quarter 1999. *www.fdic.gov/*

Figure 20–3 Expansion of Credit Card Lines, 1997–1999*

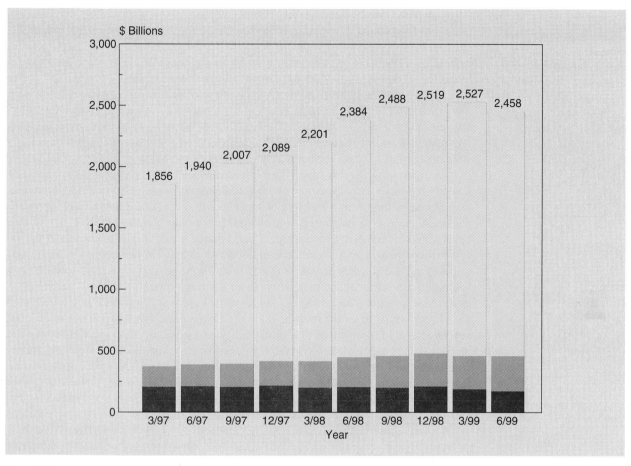

*Through June.

Source: FDIC, *Quarterly Banking Profile,* Second Quarter 1999. *www.fdic.gov/*

these losses, credit card loans extended by commercial banks continue to grow, from $1.856 trillion in March 1997 to $2.458 trillion in June 1999 (see Figure 20–3).

The potential loss an FI can experience from lending suggests that FIs need to collect information about borrowers whose assets are in their portfolios and to monitor those borrowers over time. Thus, managerial (monitoring) efficiency and credit risk management strategies directly affect the returns and risks of the loan portfolio. Moreover, one of the advantages that FIs have over individual investors is their ability to diversify credit risk exposures by exploiting the law of large numbers in their asset investment portfolios. Diversification across assets, such as loans exposed to credit risk, reduces the overall credit risk in the asset portfolio and thus increases the probability of partial or full repayment of principal and/or interest. In particular, diversification reduces individual **firm-specific credit risks**, such as the risk specific to holding the bonds or loans of General Motors or IBM, while still leaving the FI exposed to **systematic credit risk,** such as factors that simultaneously increase the default risk of all firms in the economy (e.g., an economic recession).

Chapter 21 describes methods to measure the default risk of individual bonds and loans and investigates methods to measure the risk of portfolios of such claims. Chapter 25 discusses various methods—for example, loan sales and loan reschedulings—to manage and control credit risk exposures better.

firm-specific credit risk

The risk of default for the borrowing firm associated with the specific types of project risk taken by that firm.

systematic credit risk

The risk of default associated with general economywide or macroconditions affecting all borrowers.

Do You Understand?

1. Why credit risk exists for FIs?
2. How diversification affects an FI's credit risk exposure?

Liquidity Risk

Liquidity risk arises when an FI's liability holders, such as depositors or insurance policyholders, demand immediate cash for the financial claims they hold with an FI. When liability holders demand cash immediately—that is, "put" their financial claim back to the FI—the FI must either borrow additional funds or sell assets to meet the demand for the withdrawal of funds. The most liquid asset of all is cash, which FIs can use directly to meet liability holders' demands to withdraw funds. Although FIs limit their cash asset holdings because cash earns no interest, low cash holdings are generally not a problem. Day-to-day withdrawals by liability holders are generally predictable, and large FIs can normally expect to borrow additional funds to meet any sudden shortfalls of cash on the money and financial markets (see Chapter 22).

At times, however, FIs face a liquidity crisis. Due to either a lack of confidence by liability holders in an FI or some unexpected need for cash, liability holders may demand larger withdrawals than usual. When all, or many, FIs face abnormally large cash demands, the cost of purchased or borrowed funds rises and the supply of such funds becomes restricted. As a consequence, FIs may have to sell some of their less liquid assets to meet the withdrawal demands of liability holders. This results in a more serious liquidity risk, especially as some assets with "thin" markets generate lower prices when the sale is immediate than when an FI has more time to negotiate the sale of an asset. As a result, the liquidation of some assets at low or "fire-sale" prices (the price the FI receives if the assets must be liquidated immediately at less than their fair market value) could threaten an FI's profitability and solvency. Good examples of such illiquid assets are bank loans to small firms. Serious liquidity problems may eventually result in a "run" in which all liability claimholders seek to withdraw their funds simultaneously from an FI because they fear that it will be unable to meet their demands for cash in the near future. This turns the FI's liquidity problem into a solvency problem and can cause it to fail.

The situation of several Ohio savings institutions in 1985 is an extreme example of liquidity risk. A group of 70 Ohio savings institutions were insured by a private fund, the Ohio Deposit Guarantee Fund (ODGF). One of these savings banks, Home State Savings Bank (HSSB), had invested heavily in a Florida-based government securities dealer, EMS Government Securities, Inc., which eventually defaulted on its debts to HSSB (note the interaction between credit risk and liquidity risk). This in turn made it difficult for HSSB to meet deposit withdrawals of its customers. HSSB's losses from the ESM default were, in fact, so large that the ODGF could not cover them. Not only was HSSB unable to cover the deposit withdrawals, but also other Ohio savings institutions insured by ODGF were inundated with deposit withdrawals to the extent that they could not cover them as well. As a result, ODGF-insured institutions were temporarily closed and the Ohio state legislature had to step in to cover depositors' claims.

Chapter 22 examines the nature of normal, abnormal, and run-type liquidity risks and their impact on banks, thrifts, insurance companies, and other FIs in more detail. In addition, it looks at ways in which an FI can better manage liquidity and liability risk exposures. Finally, Chapter 14 discusses the roles of deposit insurance and other liability guarantees in deterring deposit or other liability runs in depository institutions.

Do You Understand?

1. Why an FI might face a sudden liquidity crisis?
2. What circumstances might lead an FI to liquidate assets at fire-sale prices?

Interest Rate Risk

The Federal Reserve and Interest Rate Risk

The central bank's monetary policy strategy (see Chapter 4) underlies the movement of interest rates that affect an FI's cost of funds and return on assets. The central bank

Figure 20–4 Yields of 91-Day U.S. Treasury Bills

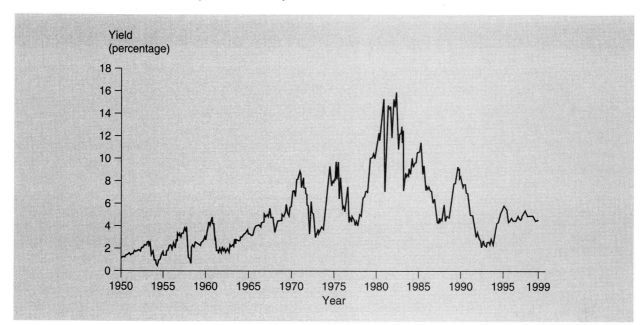

Source: *Federal Reserve Bulletin,* Table A26, various issues. *www.bog.frb.fed.us/*

www.bog.frb.fed.us/

in the United States is the Federal Reserve (the Fed). Through its daily open-market operations such as buying and selling Treasury bonds and Treasury bills, the Fed seeks to influence the money supply, inflation, and the level of interest rates (particularly short-term interest rates). In turn, changing interest rates impact economic decisions, such as whether to consume or save.

Furthermore, if the Fed smooths or targets the level of interest rates, unexpected interest rate movements or shocks over time (interest rate volatility) tend to be small. Accordingly, in a low interest rate volatility environment, the risk exposure to an FI from mismatching the maturities of its assets and liabilities tends to be small. On the other hand, to the extent that the Fed is willing to let interest rates find their own levels, the volatility of interest rates can be very high. Figure 20–4 shows the yields of U.S. 91-day T-bills for the period 1950–1999. As can be seen, there have been periods of relatively low interest rate volatility (e.g., 1995–1999) and periods of relatively high interest rate volatility (e.g., 1975–1985).

In addition to the Fed's impact on interest rates via its monetary policy strategy, the increased level of financial market integration over the last decade also affects interest rates. Financial market integration increases the speed with which interest rate changes and associated volatility are transmitted among countries, making the control of U.S. interest rates by the Federal Reserve more difficult and less certain than before. The increased globalization of financial market flows in recent years has made the measurement and management of interest rate risk a prominent concern facing many modern FI managers. For example, investors across the world carefully evaluate the statements by Alan Greenspan (chairman of the Federal Reserve Board of Governors) before Congress. Even hints of increased U.S. interest rates may have a major effect on world interest rates (as well as foreign exchange rates and stock prices).

Maturity Mismatching and Interest Rate Risk

Chapter 1 discussed asset transformation as a special or key function of FIs. *Asset transformation* involves an FI buying primary securities or assets and issuing secondary

interest rate risk

The risk incurred by an FI when the maturities of its assets and liabilities are mismatched.

securities or liabilities to fund the assets. The primary securities that FIs purchase often have maturity characteristics different from the secondary securities that FIs sell. In mismatching the maturities of its assets and liabilities as part of its asset transformation function, an FI potentially exposes itself to **interest rate risk**.

Example 20–1   Impact of an Interest Rate Increase on an FI's Profit When the Maturity of Assets Exceeds the Maturity of Liabilities

Consider an FI that issues $100 million of liabilities with one year to maturity to finance the purchase of $100 million of assets with a two-year maturity. We show this in the following time lines:

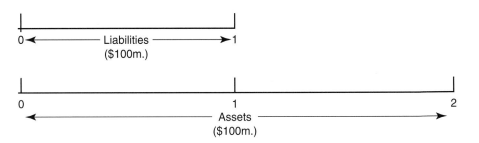

Suppose that the cost of funds (liabilities) for an FI is 9 percent per year and the interest return on the assets is 10 percent per year. Over the first year, the FI can lock in a profit spread of 1 percent (10 percent − 9 percent) times $100 million by borrowing short term (for one year) and lending long term (for two years). Thus, its profit is $1 million (.01 × 100m.).

Its profit for the second year, however, is uncertain. If the level of interest rates does not change, the FI can *refinance* its liabilities at 9 percent and lock in a 1 percent or $1 million profit for the second year as well. The risk always exists, however, that interest rates will change between years 1 and 2. If interest rates rise and the FI can borrow only new one-year liabilities at 11 percent in the second year, its profit spread in the second year is actually negative; that is, 10 percent − 11 percent = −1 percent or the FI loses $1 million (−.01 × 100m.). The positive spread earned in the first year by the FI from holding assets with a longer maturity than its liabilities is offset by a negative spread in the second year. Note that if interest rates were to rise by more than 1 percent in the second period, the FI would stand to make losses over the two-year period as a whole. As a result, when an FI holds longer-term assets relative to liabilities, it potentially exposes itself to the interest rate risk that the cost of refinancing can be more than the return earned on asset investments. The classic example of this mismatch in recent years was demonstrated by U.S. savings institutions in the 1980s (see Chapter 12).

Example 20–2   Impact of an Interest Rate Decrease When the Maturity of an FI's Liabilities Exceeds the Maturity of Assets

An alternative balance sheet structure would have the FI borrowing $100 million for a longer term than the $100 million of assets in which it invests. This is shown as follows:

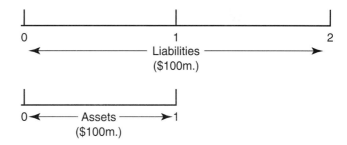

In this case, the FI is also exposed to an interest rate risk; by holding shorter term assets relative to liabilities, it faces uncertainty about the interest rate at which it can *reinvest* funds in the second period. As before, suppose that the cost of funds for the FI is 9 percent per year over the two years and the interest rate on assets is 10 percent in the first year. Over the first year, the FI can lock in a profit spread of 1 percent or $1 million. If in the second year interest rates on $100 million invested in new one-year assets decreases to 8 percent, the FI's profit spread is negative 1 percent (8 percent − 9 percent), or the FI loses $1 million (−.01 × $100m.). The positive spread earned in the first year by the FI from holding assets with a shorter maturity than its liabilities is offset by a negative spread in the second year. As a result, when an FI holds longer term liabilities relative to assets, it potentially exposes itself to the interest rate risk that borrowed funds can only be reinvested at a rate lower than their cost. In recent years, good examples of this exposure are banks operating in the Euromarkets that have borrowed fixed-rate deposits while investing in floating-rate loans—loans whose interest rates are changed or adjusted frequently.

In addition to a potential refinancing or reinvestment affect, an FI faces *economic* or *present-value* uncertainty as well when interest rates change. Remember that the economic or fair market value of an asset or liability is conceptually equal to the present value of the current and future cash flows on that asset or liability. Therefore, rising interest rates increase the discount rate on future asset (liability) cash flows and reduce the market price or present value of that asset or liability. Conversely, falling interest rates increase the present value of the cash flows from assets and liabilities. Moreover, mismatching maturities by holding longer term assets than liabilities means that when interest rates rise, the economic or present value of the FI's assets fall by a larger amount than do its liabilities.[1] This exposes the FI to the risk of economic loss and potentially to the risk of insolvency.

If holding assets and liabilities with mismatched maturities exposes FIs to interest rate risk, the FIs can seek to hedge or protect themselves against interest rate risk by matching the maturity of their assets and liabilities. This has resulted in the general philosophy that matching maturities is somehow the best policy for FIs averse to risk. Note, however, that matching maturities is not necessarily consistent with an active asset transformation function for FIs. That is, FIs cannot be asset transformers (i.e., transforming short-term deposits into long-term loans) and direct balance sheet matchers or hedgers at the same time. Although it does reduce exposure to interest rate risk, matching maturities may reduce the FI's profitability because returns from acting as specialized risk-bearing asset transformers are reduced. We discuss the *causes* of interest rate risk and methods used to *measure* interest rate risk in detail in Chapter 23. We discuss the instruments and methods to *hedge* interest rate risk in Chapters 10 and 24.

Do You Understand?

1. What refinancing risk is? What type of FI best illustrates this concept in the 1980s?
2. Why a rise in the level of interest rates adversely affects the market value of both assets and liabilities?
3. What the concept of maturity matching means?

---

1. As discussed in Chapter 3, this is because this discounting affect is more powerful the more future cash flows there are (i.e., the longer the maturity of the asset or liability).

Market Risk

market risk

The risk incurred in trading assets and liabilities due to changes in interest rates, exchange rates, and other asset prices.

Market risk arises when FIs actively trade assets and liabilities (and derivatives) rather than holding them for longer term investment, funding, or hedging purposes. Market risk is closely related to interest rate and foreign exchange risk in that as these risks increase or decrease, the overall risk of the FI is affected. However, market risk adds another dimension of risk: trading activity. Market risk is the incremental risk incurred by an FI when interest rate and foreign exchange risks are combined with an active trading strategy. As discussed in Chapters 11 through 19, the traditional roles of many financial institutions have changed in recent years. For example, for large commercial banks such as money center banks, the decline in income from traditional deposit taking and lending activities has been matched by an increased reliance on income from trading. Similarly, the decline in underwriting and brokerage income for large investment banks has also been met by more active and aggressive trading in securities, derivatives, and other assets.

Trading or market risk is the risk that when an FI takes an open or unhedged long (buy) or short (sell) position in bonds, equities, commodities, and derivatives, prices may change in a direction opposite to that expected. As a result, as the volatility of asset prices increases, the market risks faced by FIs that adopt open trading positions increase. This requires FI management (and regulators) to establish controls or limits on positions taken by traders as well as to develop models to measure the market risk exposure of an FI on a day-to-day basis.

Do You Understand?

1. What trading or market risk is?
2. What modern conditions have led to an increase in market risk for FIs?

Off-Balance-Sheet Risk

off-balance-sheet risk

The risk incurred by an FI as the result of activities related to contingent assets and liabilities.

One of the most striking trends involving modern FIs has been the growth in their off-balance-sheet activities and thus, their **off-balance-sheet risks.** An off-balance-sheet activity, by definition, does not appear on an FI's current balance sheet since it does not involve holding a current primary claim (asset) or the issuance of a current secondary claim (liability). Instead, off-balance-sheet activities affect the *future shape* of an FI's balance sheet since they involve the creation of contingent assets and liabilities that give rise to their potential placement in the future on the balance sheet. As such, accountants place them "below the bottom line" on an FI's balance sheet. A good example of an off-balance-sheet activity is the issuance of standby **letter of credit** guarantees by insurance companies and banks to back the issuance of municipal bonds. Many state and local governments could not issue such securities without bank or insurance company letter of credit guarantees that promise principal and interest payments to investors should the municipality default on its obligations in the future. Thus, the letter of credit guarantees payment should a municipal government (e.g., New York state) face financial problems in paying either the promised interest and/or principal payments on the bonds it issues. If a municipal government's cash flow is sufficiently strong so as to pay off the principal and interest on the debt it issues, the letter of credit guarantee issued by the FI expires unused. Nothing appears on the FI's balance sheet today or in the future. The fee earned for issuing the letter of credit guarantee appears on the FI's income statement (see Chapter 13). However, if the municipal government defaults on its bond payments, the FI stands ready to compensate the bond holders and the contingent liability becomes an *actual* liability that appears on the FI's balance sheet.

letter of credit

A credit guarantee issued by an FI for a fee on which payment is contingent on some future event occurring, most notably default of the agent that purchases the letter of credit.

A letter of credit is just one example of off-balance-sheet activities. Others include loan commitments by banks, mortgage servicing contracts by thrifts, and positions in forwards, futures, swaps, options, and other derivative securities by virtually all large FIs. Some of these activities are structured so as to reduce an FI's exposure to credit, interest rate, or foreign exchange risks, but mismanagement or speculative use of these instruments can result in major losses for the FI. We detail the

Do You Understand?

1. Why FIs are motivated to pursue off-balance-sheet business? What are the risks?
2. Why letter of credit guarantees are an off-balance-sheet item?

specific nature of the risks of off-balance-sheet activities and instruments more fully in Chapter 13. We also look at how some of these instruments (forwards, futures, swaps, and options) can be used to manage risk in Chapter 24.

Foreign Exchange Risk

FIs have increasingly recognized that both direct foreign investment and foreign portfolio investment can extend the operational and financial benefits available from purely domestic investments. To the extent that the returns on domestic and foreign investments are imperfectly correlated, FIs can reduce risk through domestic-foreign activity/investment diversification.

The returns on domestic and foreign direct investments and portfolio investments are not perfectly correlated for two reasons. The first is that the underlying technologies of various economies differ, as do the firms in those economies. For example, one economy may be agriculturally based and another industry based. Given different economic infrastructures, one economy could be expanding while another is contracting—in the late 1990s, for example, the U.S. economy was rapidly expanding while the Japanese economy was contracting. The second reason is that exchange rate changes are not perfectly correlated across countries—the dollar–euro exchange rate may be appreciating while the dollar–yen exchange rate may be falling.

foreign exchange risk

The risk that exchange rate changes can affect the value of an FI's assets and liabilities denominated in foreign currencies.

One potential benefit to an FI from becoming increasingly global in its outlook is an ability to expand abroad directly through branching or acquisitions or by developing a financial asset portfolio that includes foreign as well as domestic securities. Even so, foreign investment activities expose an FI to **foreign exchange risk**. Foreign exchange risk is the risk that exchange rate changes can adversely affect the value of an FI's assets and liabilities denominated in foreign currencies.

Chapter 9 introduced the basics of FX markets and risks by discussing how events in other countries affect an FI's return-risk opportunities. Foreign exchange risks can occur either directly as the result of trading in foreign currencies, making foreign currency loans (a loan in British pounds to a corporation), buying foreign-issued securities (British pound–denominated bonds or euro-denominated government bonds), or issuing foreign currency–denominated debt (British pound–denominated certificates of deposit) as a source of funds.

Extreme foreign exchange risk was evident in 1997 when a currency crisis occurred in Asia. The crisis began on July 2, when an economic crisis in Thailand resulted in a nearly 50 percent drop in the value of the Thai baht relative to the U.S. dollar. This drop led to contagious falls in the value of other Asian currencies and eventually affected currencies outside of Asia (e.g., the Brazilian real and Russian ruble). See Figure 20–5 for the fall in the value of several currencies experienced in late 1997

Figure 20–5   1997 Currency Devaluation in Southeast Asian Countries

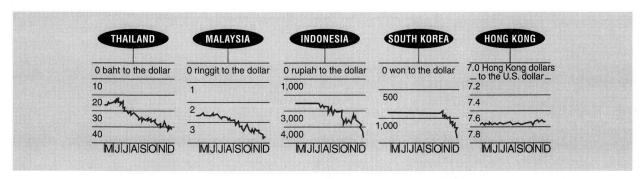

Source: *New York Times*, December 10, 1997, p. D1. Copyright © 1997 by The New York Times Co. Reprinted by Permission. *www.nyt.com/*

In the News

Emerging Markets Battered, but a Few Prove Resilient

Emerging markets started 1997 at a healthy gait. At the time, it looked as if the year would bring a race among players for the biggest gains. It seemed hard for investors to make a mistake. Then came the Asian contagion. It started in Thailand, where foreign investors fell over each other on the way for the exits. They were concerned that big government deficits—primarily funded by foreigners—and some troubling economic signals such as higher inflation and slowing growth spelled trouble for the Asian tiger.

On July 2, after doing its best to maintain the Thai baht's value, Thailand's central bank had to step back.

Source: *Investor's Business Daily,* January 5, 1998, p. A7, by Donald H. Gold.

The baht began what so far has been a six month 43% plunge against the dollar . . . At first, the trouble was confined to Thailand. But not for long. Just two weeks after the Thai baht began its meltdown, the same problem began showing up in other Asian tigers: the Indonesian rupiah and the Malaysian ringgit started to unravel. To date, the ringgit has fallen 36% against the dollar, and the rupiah has plunged an ugly 53%. The two countries' stock markets also suffered badly. Suddenly, emerging markets on every continent started to show signs of a meltdown . . .

South Korea, the 11th-biggest economy in the world, . . . began to fall apart at the seams Oct. 23, when it took only 918 Korean won to buy a dollar. Put the other way, a won was worth 0.1089 of a U.S. cent . . . the dollar soared to 1,960 won by Dec. 23. So in two months, the dollar doubled in terms of won. Or the won, which fell to 0.05102 cents, lost half its value . . .

Mexico didn't escape the emerging markets' rout . . . On Oct. 22, the dollar fetched a comfortable 7.7170 Mexican pesos. Four trading days later, the dollar soared to 9.15 pesos, an 18.6% climb. In that time, the IPC, Mexico's benchmark stock index, plunged from 5299—less than 100 points from its all-time high—to 3858.

www.investors.com/

Do You Understand?

1. What happened to the value of the Thai baht at the beginning of the Asian crisis?
2. How the value of other Asian currencies were subsequently affected at the start of the Asian crisis?

and In the News box 20–1, which describes the decline in various currency values. As a result of these currency devaluations, the earnings of some major U.S. FIs were adversely impacted. For example, in November 1997, Chase Manhattan Corp. announced a $160 million loss for October 1997 from foreign currency trading and holdings of foreign currency bonds. Similarly, in 1998, J.P. Morgan was forced to discharge about 700 employees (nearly 5 percent of its work force) partly as a result of losses experienced when Asian currency values dropped in 1997 and 1998. In addition, the stability of the Japanese banking system has been questioned, given its foreign currency loan and investment exposures in troubled Asian countries, including Indonesia, South Korea, and Thailand.

country or sovereign risk

The risk that repayments from foreign borrowers may be interrupted because of interference from foreign governments.

Country or Sovereign Risk

A globally oriented FI that mismatches the size and maturities of its foreign assets and liabilities is exposed to foreign currency risk. Even beyond this risk, and even when investing in dollars, holding assets in a foreign country can expose an FI to an additional type of foreign investment risk called **country** or **sovereign risk**. Country or sovereign risk is different from the type of credit risk that is faced by an FI that purchases domestic assets such as the bonds and loans of domestic corporations. For example, when a domestic corporation is unable or unwilling to repay a loan, an FI usually has recourse to the domestic bankruptcy court and eventually may recoup at least a portion of its original investment when the assets of the defaulted firm are liquidated or restructured. By comparison, a foreign corporation may be unable to repay the principal or interest on a loan even if it would like to do so. The government of the country in which the corporation is headquartered may prohibit or limit debt repayments due to foreign currency shortages and adverse political events. For example, in 1982, the Mexican and Brazilian governments announced a debt moratorium (i.e., a delay in their debt repayments) to Western creditors. The largest U.S. banks had made substantial loans to these countries and their government-owned corporations (such as Pemex, the Mexican state-run oil company). As a result, banks such as Citicorp (now Citigroup) eventually had to make additions to their loan loss reserves to meet expected losses on these loans. In 1987 alone, Citicorp set aside more than $3 billion to cover expected losses (again, note the interaction between credit risk and country risk) on South American loans made in 1982 or earlier. More recently, in the late 1990s, U.S., European, and Japanese banks had enhanced sovereign risk exposures to countries such as Russia, Thailand, South Korea, Malaysia, and Indonesia. Financial support given to these countries by the International Monetary Fund (IMF) and the U.S., Japanese, and European governments enabled the banks largely to avoid the full extent of the losses that were possible. Nevertheless, Indonesia had to declare a moratorium on some of its debt repayments, while Russia defaulted on payments on its short-term government bonds. In 1999, some banks agreed to settle their claims with the Russian government, receiving less than 5 cents for every dollar owed (see In the News box 20–2).

In the event of restrictions or outright prohibitions on the payment of debt obligations by sovereign governments, the FI claimholder has little if any recourse to local bankruptcy courts or to an international civil claims court. The major leverage available to an FI, so as to ensure or increase repayment probabilities, is its control over the future supply of loans or funds to the country concerned. Such leverage may be very weak, however, in the face of a country's collapsing currency and government.

Technology and Operational Risk

Central to an FI's day-to-day operations is the cost of the inputs used to produce bank services both on and off the balance sheet. Two important inputs are labor (tellers, credit officers) and capital (buildings, machinery, furniture). Crucial to the efficient management and combination of these inputs (which result in financial outputs at the lowest possible cost) is technology. Technological innovation has been a major concern of FIs in recent years. In the 1980s and 1990s, banks, insurance companies, and investment companies have sought to improve their operational efficiency with major

In the News

The Russian government Wednesday extended to April 30 its deadline to foreign creditors for accepting its terms to restructure billions of dollars of defaulted debt. The extension came as commercial and investment banks continued to clash over the terms of Russia's restructuring offer, which had originally been scheduled to expire March 5. Among foreign creditors, most U.S. and European commercial banks are prepared to accept a payoff of less than 5 cents on the dollar for the Russian securities they hold, banking sources said. "The cupboard is bare in Russia, so we might as well take what we can get," one commercial banking source said . . .

Russia unilaterally defaulted last August on about

Commercial, Investment Banks Diverge As Russia Extends Debt Deal Deadline

$12 billion of short-term, ruble-denominated government securities, also known as GKOs. Around half the securities are held by foreign commercial and investment banks, foreign investors, and what is thought to be Russian investors operating through offshore accounts. The default forced big banks like BankAmerica Corp., Republic New York Corp., and Chase Manhattan Corp. to write off hundreds of millions in losses on their holdings of Russian government securities.

Late last week Deutsche Bank and Chase Manhattan Corp. agreed to accept an offer by Russia to restructure its debt, triggering protests from investment banks opposed to the terms. The protests forced Deutsche Bank to relinquish chairmanship of the 19-member committee responsible for negotiating with the Russian government, creating a leadership vacuum among creditors.

Banking sources said commercial banks believed they had no other option than to accept the Russian offer. "The Russians have been willing to come to the negotiating table but have few financial resources at their disposal," said Arnab Das, an emerging market analyst at J.P. Morgan. . . . "It's clear that the Russians don't have enough dollars to go around for all sets of debt," said Richard Gray, an economist with BankAmerica Corp. in London. "That means all of Russia's creditors are in competition for a finite amount of dollars."

Source: *American Banker,* March 3, 1999, p. 1, by James R. Kraus.

www.americanbanker.
com/

www.bankofny.com/

investments in internal and external communications, computers, and an expanded technological infrastructure.[2]

For example, the Bank of New York provides depositors with the capabilities to check account balances, transfer funds between accounts, manage finances, pay bills, and more from their home personal computer. At the wholesale level, electronic transfers of funds through the automated clearing houses (ACH) and wire transfer payment networks such as the Clearing House Interbank Payments Systems (CHIPS) have been

[2]A comprehensive list of banks on the World Wide Web can be found at the website *www. mybank.com/.*

developed. Indeed, a global financial service firm such as Citigroup has operations in more than 100 countries connected in real time by a proprietary satellite system.

The major objectives of technological expansion are to lower operating costs, increase profits, and to capture new markets for an FI. In current terminology, the object is to allow the FI to exploit, to the fullest extent possible, potential economies of scale and economies of scope in selling its products (see Chapter 11). For example, an FI could use the same information on the quality of customers stored in its computers to expand the sale of both loan products and insurance products—the same information (e.g., age, job, size of family, or income) can identify both potential loan and life insurance customers.

technology risk

The risk incurred by an FI when its technological investments do not produce anticipated cost savings.

Technology risk occurs when technological investments do not produce the anticipated cost savings in the form of either economies of scale or economies of scope. Diseconomies of scale, for example, arise because of excess capacity, redundant technology, and/or organizational and bureaucratic inefficiencies (red tape) that become worse as an FI grows in size. Diseconomies of scope arise when an FI fails to generate perceived synergies or cost savings through major new technology investments. Technological risk can result in major losses in an FI's competitive efficiency and ultimately result in its long-term failure. Similarly, gains from technological investments can produce performance superior to an FI's rivals as well as allow it to develop new and innovative products enhancing its long-term survival chances.

operational risk

The risk that existing technology or support systems may malfunction or break down.

Operational risk is partly related to technology risk and can arise when existing technology malfunctions or "back-office" support systems break down. For example, major banks use the federal funds market both to sell to and buy funds from other banks for periods as short as a day. Their payment messages travel along a wire transfer network called Fedwire. Suppose that the Bank of New York wished to lend federal funds to Bank of America. The Bank of New York transmits an electronic message instructing its Federal Reserve Bank (in New York) to deduct reserves from its account at the Fed at the end of the day and sends a message by Fedwire to credit Bank of America's account at its own Federal Reserve Bank (in San Francisco) by this reserve amount at the end of the day (see Chapter 5). Normally, this system functions highly efficiently. Occasionally, however, risk exposures such as that actually faced by the Bank of New York in 1985 can arise. Specifically, the Bank of New York's computer system failed to register incoming payment (funds borrowed) messages on Fedwire but continued to process outbound (funds lent) messages similar to the one described above. As a result, at the end of the day, the bank faced a huge funds deficit position that it had to settle with other banks. The Bank of New York could do this only by arranging emergency loans from the Federal Reserve. Even though such computer glitches are rare, their occurrence can cause major problems for the FIs involved and potentially disrupt the financial system in general.

Back-office systems combine labor and technology to provide clearance, settlement, custodial, and other services to support FIs' underlying on- and off-balance-sheet transactions. Prior to 1975, most transactions in equities among securities firms and their customers were paper based. As the market volume of trades rose, severe backlogs in settling and clearing transactions occurred because of the general inefficiency of decentralized paper-based systems. Such problems have stimulated the development of centralized depositories for equities and other securities as well as computerized trading and settlement in the securities industry (e.g., electronic exchanges).

A failure of a back-office system, as well as the downside of operational risk, was evident in the Wells Fargo/First Interstate merger in 1996. Wells Fargo wanted to make the merger process easy for First Interstate customers by allowing them to use up their old checks and deposit forms. Unfortunately, due to the merger, customer account numbers had been changed. As a result, some deposits were not posted to the proper account and there was a deluge of improperly bounced checks. Further, Wells Fargo's back-office operations were thinly

Do You Understand?

1. How operational risk is related to technology risk?
2. How technological expansion can help an FI better exploit economies of scale and economies of scope?

staffed and unable to find where all the misplaced deposits had gone. Promising to reimburse all customers for its accounting mistakes, Wells Fargo eventually corrected the problem, incurring an operating loss of some $180 million.

2 Insolvency Risk

insolvency risk

The risk that an FI may not have enough capital to offset a sudden decline in the value of its assets relative to its liabilities.

Insolvency risk is a consequence or an outcome of one or more of the risks described above: interest rate, market, credit, off-balance-sheet, technological, foreign exchange, sovereign, and liquidity. Technically, insolvency occurs when the capital or equity resources of an FI's owners are driven to, or near to, zero due to losses incurred as the result of one or more of the risks described above. Consider the case of the 1984 failure of Continental Illinois National Bank and Trust. Continental's strategy in the late 1970s and early 1980s had been to pursue asset growth through aggressive lending. Continental's loan portfolio grew at an average rate of 19.8 percent per year from 1977 to 1981. The downturn in the U.S. economy at the beginning of the 1980s resulted in the default of many of these loans (credit risk). In addition, Continental had a very small core deposit base, relying instead on purchased and borrowed funds such as fed funds, RPs, and Eurodollar deposits. The increasing number of defaults in Continental's loan portfolio fueled concerns about the bank's ability to meet its liability payments, resulting in the refusal by a number of major lenders to renew or rollover the short-term funds they had lent to Continental (liquidity risk). The substantial defaults on Continental's loans combined with its inability to obtain new, or retain existing, funds resulted in the rapid deterioration of Continental's capital position (insolvency risk). Continental was unable to survive, and the FDIC assumed control in 1984.

In general, the more equity capital to borrowed funds an FI has—that is, the lower its leverage—the better able it is to withstand losses due to risk exposures such as adverse liquidity changes, unexpected credit losses, and so on. Thus, both the management and regulators of FIs focus on an FI's capital (and its "adequacy") as a key measure of its ability to remain solvent and grow in the face of a multitude of risk exposures. Chapter 14 discusses the issue of what is considered to be an adequate level of capital to manage an FI's overall risk exposure.

> ### Do You Understand?
>
> 1. When insolvency risk occurs?
> 2. How insolvency risk is related to credit risk and liquidity risk?

3 Interaction among Risks

This overview chapter concentrated on 10 major risks continuously impacting an FI manager's decision-making process and risk management strategy. These risks were interest rate risk, foreign exchange risk, market risk, credit risk, liquidity risk, off-balance-sheet risk, technology risk, operational risk, country or sovereign risk, and insolvency risk. Even though the discussion generally described each independently, in reality these risks are interdependent. For example, when interest rates rise, corporations and consumers find maintaining promised payments on their debt more difficult. Thus, over some range of interest rate movements, credit and interest rate risks are positively correlated. Furthermore, the FI may have been counting on the funds from promised payments on its loans for liquidity management purposes. Thus, liquidity risk is also correlated with interest rate and credit risks. The inability of a customer to make promised payments also affects the FI's income and profits and, consequently, its equity or capital position. Thus, each risk and its interaction with other risks ultimately affects solvency risk. The interaction of the various risks also means that FI managers face making complicated trade-offs. In particular, as they take actions to manage one type of risk, FI managers must consider the possible impact of such actions on other risks.

Various other risks, often of a more discrete or event-type, also impact an FI's profitability and risk exposure. Discrete risks include a sudden change in taxation, such as the Tax Reform Act of 1986, which subjected banks to a minimum corporate tax rate of 20 percent (the alternative minimum tax) and limited their ability to expense the cost of funds used to purchase tax-free municipal bonds. Such changes can affect the attractiveness of some types of assets over others, as well as the liquidity of an FI's balance sheet. For example, banks' demand for municipal bonds fell quite dramatically following the 1986 tax law change. As a result, the municipal bond market became quite illiquid for a time.

Changes in regulatory policy constitute another type of discrete or event-type risk. These include lifting the regulatory barriers to lending or to entry or on products offered (see Chapter 14). The 1994 regulatory change allowing interstate banking after 1997 is one example.

Other discrete or event risks involve sudden and unexpected changes in financial market conditions due to war, revolution, or sudden market collapse, such as the 1929 and 1987 stock market crashes. These can have a major impact on an FI's risk exposure. Other event risks include theft, malfeasance, and breach of fiduciary trust; all of these can ultimately cause an FI to fail or be severely harmed. Yet, each is difficult to model and predict.

Finally, more general macroeconomic risks such as increased inflation, inflation volatility, and unemployment can directly and indirectly impact an FI's level of interest rate, credit, and liquidity risk exposure. For example, inflation was very volatile during the period 1979–1982 in the United States and interest rates reflected this volatility. During periods in which an FI faces high and volatile inflation and interest rates, its interest rate risk exposure from mismatching its balance sheet maturities tends to rise. Its credit risk exposure also rises because borrowing firms with fixed price product contracts often find it difficult to keep up their loan interest payments when inflation and interest rates rise abruptly.

Do You Understand?

1. What the term *event risk* means?
2. What some examples of event and general macroeconomic risks that impact FIs are?

Summary

This chapter provided an overview of the major risks that modern FIs face. FIs face *interest rate risk* when the maturities of their assets and liabilities are mismatched. They incur *market risk* for their trading portfolios of assets and liabilities if adverse movements in the prices of these assets or liabilities occur. They face *credit risk* or default risk if their clients default on their loans and other obligations. They encounter *liquidity risk* as a result of excessive withdrawals of liabilities by customers. Modern-day FIs also engage in significant amount of off-balance-sheet activities, thereby exposing them to *off-balance-sheet risks*—changing values of their contingent assets and liabilities. If FIs conduct foreign business, they are subject to *foreign exchange risk*. Business dealings in foreign countries or with foreign companies also subject FIs to *sovereign risk*. The advent of sophisticated technology and automation increasingly exposes FIs to both *technological* and *operational risks*. FIs face *insolvency risk* when their overall equity capital is insufficient to withstand the losses that they incur as a result of such risk exposures. The effective management of these risks—including the interaction among them—determines the ability of a modern FI to survive and prosper over the long run. The chapters that follow analyze these risks in greater detail, beginning with those risks incurred on the balance sheet.

Questions

1. What is the difference between firm-specific credit risk and systematic credit risk? How can an FI alleviate firm-specific credit risk?

2. In the 1980s, many thrifts that failed had made loans to oil companies located in Louisiana, Texas, and Oklahoma. When oil prices fell, these companies, the regional economy, and the thrifts all experienced financial problems. What types of risk were inherent in the loans that these thrifts had made?

3. What is the difference between refinancing risk and reinvestment risk? If an FI funds long-term assets with short-term liabilities, what will be the impact of an interest rate increase on earnings?

4. The sales literature of a mutual fund claims that the fund has no risk exposure since it invests exclusively in default risk free federal government securities. Is this claim true? Why or why not?

5. What does the term *economic value risk* mean?

6. Consider two bonds; a 10-year premium bond with a coupon rate higher than its required rate of return and a zero coupon bond that pays only a lump sum payment after 10 years with no interest over its life. Which do you think would have more interest rate risk—that is, which bond's price would change by a larger amount for a given change in interest rates? Explain your answer.

7. Consider the following income statement for WatchoverU Savings Inc. (in millions):

Assets		Liabilities	
Floating-rate		NOW accounts	$ 70
mortgages	$ 50	(currently 6%	
(currently		annually)	
10% annually)			
30-year fixed-rate		Time deposits	20
loans	50	(currently 6%	
(currently 7%		annually)	
annually)			
		Equity	10
Total	$100		$100

   a. What is WatchoverU's expected net interest income at year end?

   b. What will be the net interest income at year end if interest rates rise by 2%?

8. If a bank invested $50 million in a two-year asset paying 10 percent interest per annum and simultaneously issued a $50 million one-year liability paying 8 percent interest per annum, what would be the impact on the bank's net interest income if, at the end of the first year, all interest rates increased by 1 percentage point?

9. A money market mutual fund bought $1,000,000 of two-year Treasury notes six months ago. During this time, the value of the securities has increased, but for tax reasons the mutual fund wants to postpone any sale for two more months. What type of risk does the mutual fund face for the next two months?

10. Corporate bonds usually pay interest semiannually. If a company decided to change from semiannual to annual interest payments, how would this affect the bond's interest rate risk?

11. Off-balance-sheet risk encompasses several of the other nine sources of risk exposure (e.g., interest rate risk, credit risk, and foreign exchange rate risk). Discuss.

12. If international capital markets are well integrated and operate efficiently, will banks be exposed to foreign exchange risk? What are the sources of foreign exchange risk for FIs?

13. A U.S. insurance company invests $1,000,000 in a private placement of German bonds. Each bond pays DM300 in interest per year for 20 years. If the current exchange rate is DM1.7612 for U.S. dollars, what is the nature of the insurance company's exchange rate risk? Specifically, what type of exchange rate movement concerns this insurance company?

14. If you expect the French franc to depreciate in the near future, would a U.S.-based FI in Paris prefer to be net long or net short in its asset positions? Discuss.

15. Assume that a bank has assets located in Germany worth DM150 million earning an average of 8 percent on its assets. It also holds DM100 in liabilities and pays an average of 6 percent per year. The current spot rate is DM1.50 for U.S. dollars. If the exchange rate at the end of the year is DM2.00 for U.S. dollars,

   a. What happened to the dollar? Did it appreciate or depreciate against the mark?

   b. What is the effect of the exchange rate change on the net interest margin (interest received minus interest paid) in dollars from its foreign assets and liabilities?

   c. What is the effect of the exchange rate change on the value of the assets and liabilities in dollars?

16. Six months ago, Qualitybank, Ltd., issued a $100 million, one-year maturity CD, denominated in German deutsche mark (Euromark CD). On the same date, $60 million was invested in a DM-denominated loan and $40 million in a U.S. Treasury bill. The exchange rate on this date was DM1.7382 for U.S. dollars. If you assume no repayment of principal and if today's exchange rate is DM1.3905 for U.S. dollars:

   a. What is the current value of the Euromark CD principal in dollars and DM?

   b. What is the current value of the German loan principal in dollars and DM?

   c. What is the current value of the U.S. Treasury bill in dollars and DM?

   d. What is Qualitybank's profit/loss from this transaction in dollars and DM?

17. Suppose you purchase a 10-year AAA-rated Swiss bond for par that is paying an annual coupon of 8 percent and has a face value of 1,000 Swiss francs (SF). The spot rate is .66667 U.S. dollars for SF. At the end of the year, the bond is downgraded to AA and the yield increases to 10 percent. In addition, the SF depreciates to .74074 U.S. dollars for SF.
    a. What is the loss or gain to a Swiss investor who holds this bond for a year?
    b. What is the loss or gain to a U.S. investor who holds this bond for a year?

18. What is the difference between technology risk and operational risk? How does internationalizing the payments system among banks increase operational risk?

19. Bank 1, with $130 million in assets and $20 million in costs, acquires Bank 2 which has $50 million in assets and $10 million in costs. After the acquisition, the bank has $180 million in assets and $35 million in costs. Did this acquisition produce economies of scale or economies of scope?

20. Characterize the risk exposure(s) of the following FI transactions by choosing one or more of the following:
    a. Credit risk
    b. Interest rate risk
    c. Off-balance-sheet risk
    d. Foreign exchange rate risk
    e. Country/sovereign risk
    f. Technology risk
    (1) A bank finances a $10 million, six-year fixed-rate commercial loan by selling one-year certificates of deposit.
    (2) An insurance company invests its policy premiums in a long-term municipal bond portfolio.
    (3) A French bank sells two-year fixed-rate notes to finance a two-year fixed-rate loan to a British entrepreneur.
    (4) A Japanese bank acquires an Austrian bank to facilitate clearing operations.
    (5) A mutual fund completely hedges its interest rate risk exposure using forward contingent contracts.
    (6) A bond dealer uses his own equity to buy Mexican debt on the less developed countries (LDC) bond market.
    (7) A securities firm sells a package of mortgage loans as mortgage-backed securities.

21. Discuss the interrelationships among the different sources of FI risk exposure.

Managing Risk on *the* Balance Sheet I: Credit Risk

Chapter Navigator

1. What has been the trend in nonperforming loans at commercial banks?

2. How does a financial institution evaluate a loan application?

3. What is a credit-scoring model?

4. What type of analysis is involved in mid-market commercial and industrial lending?

5. How are large commercial and industrial loans analyzed?

6. How do you calculate the return on a loan?

Credit Risk Management: Chapter Overview

In Chapter 20, we provided a basic description of the risks that emanate from financial markets as well as from the traditional activities of financial institutions. In the next three chapters, we provide a more detailed analysis of four of these risks. We also discuss how these risks can be managed. Specifically, we look at the measurement and management of credit risk, liquidity risk, interest rate risk, and insolvency risk. We start our analysis with credit risk.

    As discussed in Chapter 1, financial institutions (FIs) are special because of their ability to transform financial claims of household savers efficiently into claims issued to corporations, individuals, and governments. An FI's ability to evaluate information and control and monitor borrowers allows them to transform these claims at the lowest possible cost to all parties. One of the specific types of financial claim transformation discussed in Chapter 1 was credit allocation. FIs transform claims of household savers (in the form of deposits) into loans issued to corporations, individuals, and governments. The FI accepts the credit risk on these loans in exchange for a fair return sufficient to cover the cost of funding paid (e.g., covering the cost of borrowing, or issuing deposits) to household savers and the credit risk involved in lending.

Over the past two decades, the credit quality of many FIs' lending and investment decisions has attracted a great deal of attention. For most of the 1980s, tremendous problems occurred with bank and thrift residential and farm mortgage loans. In the late 1980s and early 1990s, attention shifted to the problems relating to commercial real estate loans (to which banks, thrifts, and insurance companies were all exposed) and to **junk bonds** (bonds rated as speculative or less than investment-grade securities by rating agencies such as Moody's or S&P—see Chapter 6 for the assignment and meaning of bond ratings). In the late 1990s, concern shifted to the rapid increase in auto loans and credit cards as well as the declining quality in commercial lending standards as high-yield business loan delinquencies started to increase (see In the News box 21–1). Most recently, attention has focused on the risk of lending to borrowers in Southeast Asian countries such as Thailand, Indonesia, South Korea, and Malaysia as well as to Russia, which defaulted on its ruble-denominated bonds in 1998.

junk bond

A bond rated as speculative or less than investment grade (below Baa by Moody's and BBB by S&P) by bond-rating agencies such as Moody's.

Do You Understand?

1. What sectors of the U.S. economy experienced increased loan default rates in the late 1990s?
2. Why this trend is of concern to economists?

Nevertheless, the credit quality of most FIs has improved throughout the last decade. For example, for FDIC-insured commercial banks, the ratio of nonperforming loans to assets has declined significantly since 1990 (see Figure 21–1).[1] Nonperforming loan ratios are also shown in Table 21–1.[2] Notice that nonperforming business loans are larger in smaller banks (with assets less than $1 billion), while nonperforming loans to individuals are larger in those banks with more than $1 billion in assets.

A credit quality problem, in the worst case, can cause an FI to become insolvent, or it can result in such a significant drain on earnings and net worth that it can adversely affect the FI's profitability and its ability to compete with other domestic and international FIs. For example, consider an FI with the following balance sheet:

Cash	$ 20m.	Deposits	$ 90m.
Gross loans	80m.	Equity (net worth)	10m.
	$100m.		$100m.

Suppose that the managers of the FI recognize that $10 million of its $80 million in loans are unlikely to be repaid due to an increase in credit repayment difficulties of its borrowers. Eventually, the FI's managers must respond by charging off or writing down the value of these loans on the FI's balance sheet. This means that the value of loans falls from $80 million to $70 million, an economic loss that must be charged off against the stockholder's equity capital or net worth (i.e., equity capital falls from $10 million to zero). Thus, both sides of the balance sheet shrink by the amount of the loss:

Cash		$20m.	Deposits	$90m.
Gross loans	80m.		Equity after charge-off	0m.
Less: Loan loss	−10m.			
Loans after charge-off		70m.		
		$90m.		$90m.

---

1. In addition, the increased securitization or sale of loans (see Chapter 25) has caused banks to hold loans for shorter periods of time, thus reducing the potential for credit quality problems.

2. *Nonperforming loans* are defined as loans past due 90 days or more and loans that are not accruing interest due to problems of the borrower.

In the News

21-1

Under Boom Economy, Strain over Debt

American companies and individual consumers alike are struggling to meet their debt payments, even as the economy's expansion enters record territory. The difficulties, the worst since the U.S. economy emerged from recession in the early 1990s, suggest to some analysts that below the economy's rosy surface are growing difficulties. If companies and individuals can't keep up with their debt now, amid a robust economy, there could be wider-spread difficulties in any downturn, those analysts say.

Some optimists insist that it is the economy's exuberance itself that has lured companies and individuals to take on too much debt and that the increased problems won't cripple the economy. But everyone in the bond market concedes that the increases in bond defaults and personal bankruptcies are significant.

As many as 5.3% of U.S. companies with outstanding junk bonds defaulted on interest payments in the past 12 months, up from 4.1% in calendar year 1998 and 2.1% in 1997, and the fastest pace since 1992, according to Moody's Investors Service. "The trend quite frankly merits attention, and some would consider it alarming," says John Lonski, Moody's senior economist, who says defaults could reach 6% this year.

The man on the street is having the same problem as corporate America. About 1.35% of all U.S. households declared bankruptcy in the 12 months ending June 30, off a tad from the previous 12 months' 1.38% figure, but up sharply from 0.8% in 1995, according to the Administrative Office of the U.S. Courts. The continuing difficulties for individuals, in particular—coming as they do despite a puny unemployment rate and record stock-market

gains—have economists scratching their heads. "Given the job market's improvement and the fact that growth and income are above inflation, it stands to reason that personal bankruptcies would be coming down, and it's surprising they're at such a high level," Stuart Hoffman, chief economist at PNC Bank in Pittsburgh, says.

Overall 2.1% of companies with any kind of bonds defaulted in the past 12 months, up from 1.3% in calendar year 1998 and 0.7% in 1997 . . . The soaring number of corporate defaults continues a trend that started in 1998, says Leo Brand, a Standard & Poor's analyst who says a record $27 billion of debt has been defaulted upon this year, up from $11 billion in all of 1998. The debt troubles suggest to some that if the economy hits a speed bump, or the stock market slumps, both companies and consumers could quickly reign in spending, hurting the economy in the process. Such a scenario "could bring upon a credit crunch that would imperil the eight-year-long expansion," Mr. Lonski says.

Figure 21-1   Nonperforming Asset Ratio for U.S. Commercial Banks

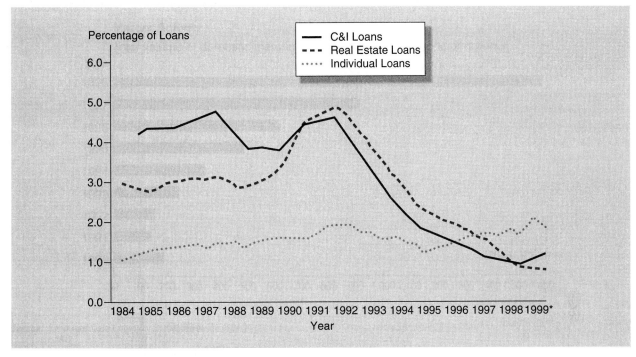

*As of June.

Source: Federal Deposit Insurance Corporation. *www.fdic.gov/*

Table 21-1   Nonperforming Loans as a Percentage of Total Loans
Insured Commercial Banks by Consolidated Assets

Quarter	All Banks	$0–$100 million	$100 million– $1 billion	$1 billion– $10 billion	$10 billion +
Commercial and Industrial					
December 1995	1.19%	1.32%	1.23%	0.98%	1.13%
December 1996	0.98	1.41	1.26	0.91	0.83
December 1997	0.86	1.26	1.19	0.84	0.71
December 1998	0.99	1.40	1.24	0.90	0.89
June 1999	1.11	1.58	1.24	1.03	1.02
Real Estate					
December 1995	1.39%	0.98%	1.06%	1.18%	1.78%
December 1996	1.23	0.94	0.92	1.28	1.40
December 1997	1.01	0.87	0.77	0.97	1.15
December 1998	0.91	0.87	0.71	0.84	1.02
June 1999	0.85	0.87	0.66	0.77	0.95
Loans to Individuals					
December 1995	1.22%	0.72%	0.64%	1.14%	1.56%
December 1996	1.36	0.84	0.79	1.42	1.50
December 1997	1.46	0.86	0.78	1.53	1.62
December 1998	1.52	0.92	0.81	1.54	1.69
June 1999	1.33	0.82	0.81	1.12	1.54

Source: Federal Deposit Insurance Corporation, various years. *www.fdic.gov/*

However, credit risk applies not only to traditional areas of lending and investing. As banks and other FIs have expanded into credit guarantees and other off-balance-sheet activities (such as options, swaps, and foreign exchange), new types of credit risk exposure have occurred, causing concern among managers and regulators. Thus, credit analysis by FI managers is now more important than ever before.[3] We discuss credit analysis next.

Credit Analysis

This section discusses credit analysis for real estate lending, consumer and small-business lending, mid-market commercial and industrial lending, and large commercial and industrial lending. It also provides insights into the credit risk evaluation process from the perspective of a credit officer (or an FI manager) evaluating a loan application.

Real Estate Lending

Because of the importance of residential mortgages to banks, savings institutions, credit unions, and insurance companies, residential mortgage loan applications are among the most standardized of all credit applications. In Chapter 7, we outlined the different types of characteristics of real estate loans (e.g, adjustable-rate versus fixed-rate mortgages, interest rate payments versus fee payments,[4] and down payments). In this chapter, we look at the evaluation process that FIs (such as commercial banks, savings institutions, and finance companies) use to determine whether a real estate loan application should be approved.

Two considerations dominate an FI's decision as to whether to approve a mortgage loan application or not: (1) the applicant's ability and willingness to make timely interest and principal repayments and (2) the value of the borrower's collateral.

Ability and willingness of the borrower to repay debt outstanding is usually established by application of qualitative and quantitative models. The character of the applicant is also extremely important. Stability of residence, occupation, family status (e.g., married, single), previous history of savings, and credit (or bill payment) history are frequently used in assessing character. The loan officer must also establish whether the applicant has sufficient income. In particular, the loan amortization (i.e., principal payments) should be reasonable when compared with the applicant's income and age. The loan officer should also consider the applicant's monthly expenditures. Family responsibilities and marital stability are also important. Monthly financial obligations relating to auto, personal, and credit card loans should be ascertained, and an applicant's personal balance sheet and income statement should be constructed.

GDS (gross debt service) ratio

Gross debt service ratio calculated as total accommodation expenses (mortgage, lease, condominium, management fees, real estate taxes, etc.) divided by gross income.

TDS (total debt service) ratio

Total debt ratio calculated as total accommodation expenses plus all other debt service payments divided by gross income.

Two ratios are very useful in determining a customer's ability to maintain mortgage payments: the **GDS (gross debt service)** and the **TDS (total debt service) ratios**. Gross debt service ratio is the customer's total annual accommodation expenses (mortgage, lease, condominium, management fees, real estate taxes, etc.) divided by annual gross income. Total debt service ratio is the customer's total annual accommodation expenses plus all other debt service payments divided by annual gross income. These can be represented as follows:

$$GDS = \frac{\text{Annual mortgage payments} + \text{Property taxes}}{\text{Annual gross income}}$$

$$TDS = \frac{\text{Annual total debt payments}}{\text{Annual gross income}}$$

3. This is one of the reasons for bank regulators' new approach to setting capital requirements against credit risk (see Chapter 14).

4. Often called "points" (see Chapter 7).

As a general rule, for an FI to consider an applicant, the GDS and TDS ratios must be less than an acceptable threshold. The threshold is commonly 25 to 30 percent for the GDS and 35 to 40 percent for the TDS ratios.[5]

Example 21–1 Calculation of the GDS and TDS Ratios

Consider two customers who have applied for a mortgage from an FI with a GDS threshold of 25 percent and a TDS threshold of 40 percent.

Customer	Gross Annual Income	Monthly Mortgage Payments	Annual Property Taxes	Monthly Other Debt Payments
1	$150,000	$3,000	$3,500	$2,000
2	60,000	500	1,500	200

The GDS and TDS ratios for the mortgage applicants are as follows:

Customer	GDS	TDS
1	$\dfrac{3,000(12) + 3,500}{150,000} = 26.33\%$	$\dfrac{3,000\,(12) + 3,500 + 2,000\,(12)}{150,000} = 42.33\%$
2	$\dfrac{500(12) + 1,500}{60,000} = 12.50\%$	$\dfrac{500(12) + 1,500 + 200(12)}{60,000} = 16.50\%$

Despite a higher level of gross income, Customer 1 does not meet the GDS or TDS thresholds because of relatively high mortgage, tax, and other debt payments. Customer 2, while earning less, has fewer required payments and meets both the FI's GDS and TDS thresholds.

credit scoring system

A mathematical model that uses observed loan applicant's characteristics to calculate a score that represents the applicant's probability of default.

3

FIs often combine the various factors affecting the ability and willingness to make loan repayments into a single credit score. A **credit-scoring system** (illustrated below) is a quantitative model that uses observed characteristics of the applicant to calculate a "score" representing the applicant's probability of default (versus repayment). The score may be computed on a paper scorecard or on the loan officer's computer terminal. Either way, the loan officer collects information concerning the applicant's assets, income, monthly expenses, dependents, other credit obligations, as well as credit history, and inputs this information into a scoring model. The applicant's total score must be above a certain threshold to be considered acceptable for a loan. The theory behind credit scoring is that by selecting and combining different economic and financial characteristics, an FI manager may be able to separate good from bad loan customers based on the characteristics of borrowers who have defaulted in the past.

If the FI uses a scoring system, the loan officer can give an immediate answer—yes, maybe, or no—and the reasons for that answer. A maybe occurs in borderline cases or when the loan officer is uncertain of the classification of certain input information. A credit scoring system allows an FI to reduce the ambiguity and turnaround time and increase the transparency of the credit approval process.

---

5. Other FIs may impose different thresholds. The numerator of the GDS is often increased to include home heating and property taxes. When the GDS ratio is used for consumer credit, rent is substituted for mortgage payments.

Example 21–2   Credit Scoring of a Real Estate Loan

An FI uses the following credit-scoring model to evaluate real estate loan applications:

Characteristic	Characteristic Values and Weights				
Annual gross income	<$10,000	$10,000–$25,000	$25,000–$50,000	$50,000–$100,000	>$100,000
Score	0	15	35	50	75
TDS	<50%	35%–50%	15%–35%	5%–15%	>5%
Score	0	10	20	35	50
Relations with FI	None	Checking account	Savings account	Both	
Score	0	30	30	60	
Major credit cards	None	1 or more			
Score	0	20			
Age	<25	25–60	>60		
Score	5	30	25		
Residence	Rent	Own with mortgage	Own outright		
Score	5	20	50		
Length of residence	<1 year	1–5 years	>5 years		
Score	0	20	45		
Job stability	<1 year	1–5 years	>5 years		
Score	0	25	50		
Credit history	No record	Missed a payment in last 5 years	Met all payments		
Score	0	−15	50		

The loan is automatically rejected if the applicant's *total* score is less than 120 (i.e., applicants with a score of 120 or less have, in the past, mainly defaulted on their loan); the loan is automatically approved if the total score is greater than 190 (i.e., applicants with a score of 190 or more have, in the past, mainly paid their loan in complete accordance with the loan agreement). A score between 120 and 190 is reviewed by a loan committee for a final decision.

A loan customer listing the following information on the loan application receives the following points:

Characteristic	Value	Score
Annual gross income	$67,000	50
TDS	12%	35
Relations with FI	None	0
Major credit cards	4	20
Age	37	30
Residence	Own/Mortgage	20
Length of residence	2½ years	20
Job stability	2½ years	20
Credit history	Met all payments	50
Total score		245

The real estate loan for this customer would be automatically approved.

perfecting collateral

The process of ensuring that collateral used to secure a loan is free and clear to the lender should the borrower default on the loan.

foreclosure

The process of taking possession of the mortgaged property in satisfaction of a defaulting borrower's indebtedness and forgoing claim to any deficiency.

power of sale

The process of taking the proceedings of the forced sale of a mortgage property in satisfaction of the indebtedness and returning to the mortgagor the excess over the indebtedness or claiming any shortfall as an unsecured creditor.

Verification of the borrower's financial statements is essential. If the answer is yes to a loan application, the loan officer states that the FI is prepared to grant the loan subject to a verification of his or her creditworthiness and obtains the applicant's permission to make all necessary inquiries. The collateral provided by the mortgage is normally considered only after the loan officer has established that the applicant can service the loan. If collateral secures a loan, the FI must make sure that its claim, should the borrower default, is free and clear from other claims. This process is referred to as **perfecting** a security interest in the **collateral**. Even if collateral secures the loan, no FI should become involved in a loan that is likely to go into default. In such a case, the FI would at best seize the property in a **foreclosure** (where the FI takes possession of the mortgaged property in satisfaction of the defaulting borrower's indebtedness, forgoing claim to any deficiency) or **power of sale** (where the FI takes the proceeds of the forced sale of a mortgaged property in satisfaction of the indebtedness and returns to the mortgagor the excess over the indebtedness or claims any shortfall as an unsecured creditor).

Before an FI accepts a mortgage, it must satisfy itself regarding the property involved in the loan by doing the following:

- Confirming the title and legal description of the property.
- Obtaining a surveyor's certificate confirming that the house is within the property boundaries.
- Checking with the tax office to confirm that no property taxes are unpaid.
- Requesting a land title search to determine that there are no other claims against the property.
- Obtaining an independent appraisal to confirm that the purchase price is in line with the market value.

Consumer (Individual) and Small-Business Lending

The techniques used for mortgage loan credit analysis are very similar to those applied to individual and small-business loans. Individual consumer loans are scored like mortgages, often without the borrower ever meeting the loan officer. Unlike mortgage loans for which the focus is on a property, however, nonmortgage consumer loans focus on the individual's ability to repay. Thus, credit-scoring models for such loans would put more weight on personal characteristics such as annual gross income, the TDS score, and so on.

Small-business loans are more complicated because the FI is frequently asked to assume the credit risk of an individual whose business cash flows require considerable analysis, often with incomplete accounting information available to the credit officer. The payoff for this analysis is also small, by definition, because loan principal amounts are usually small. A $50,000 loan with a 3 percent interest spread over the cost of funds provides only $1,500 of gross revenues before loan loss provisions, monitoring costs, and allocation of overheads. This low profitability has caused many FIs to build small-business scoring models similar to, but more sophisticated than, those used for mortgages and consumer credit. These models often combine computer-based financial analysis of borrower financial statements with behavioral analysis of the owner of the small business.

Mid-Market Commercial and Industrial Lending

In recent years, mid-market commercial and industrial lending has offered some of the most profitable opportunities for credit-granting FIs. Although definitions of mid-market corporates vary, they typically have sales revenues from $5 million to $100 million a year, have a recognizable corporate structure (unlike many small businesses), but do not have ready access to deep and liquid capital markets (as do large corporations).

Credit analysis of a mid-market corporate customer differs from that of a small business because, while still assessing the character of the firm's management, its main focus is on the business itself. The credit process begins with an account officer gathering information by meeting existing customers, checking referrals, and meeting with new business prospects. Having gathered information about the credit applicant, an account officer decides whether it is worthwhile to pursue the new business, given the applicant's needs, the FI's credit policies, the current economy, and the competitive lending environment. If it is, the account officer structures and prices the credit agreement with reference to the FI's credit granting policy. This includes several areas of analysis, including the five Cs of credit, cash flow analysis, ratio analysis, and financial statement comparisons (described below). At any time in this process, conditions could change or new information could be revealed, significantly changing the borrower's situation and forcing the account officer to begin the process again.

Once the applicant and an account officer tentatively agree on a loan, the account officer must obtain internal approval from the FI's credit risk management team. Generally, even for the smallest mid-market credit, at least two officers must approve a new loan customer. Larger credit requests must be presented formally (either in hard copy or through a computer network) to a credit approval officer and/or committee before they can be signed. This means that, during the negotiations, the account officer must be very well acquainted with the FI's overall credit philosophy and current strategy.

Five C's of Credit. To analyze the loan applicant's credit risk, the account officer must understand the customer's character, capacity, collateral, conditions, and capital (sometimes referred to as the *five Cs of credit*). Some important questions that provide information on the five Cs follows.

Production (measures of capacity and conditions)

- On what production inputs does the applicant depend?
- To what extent does this cause supply risk?
- How do input price risks affect the applicant?
- How do costs of production compare with those of the competition?
- How does the quality of goods and services produced compare with those of the competition?

Management (measures of character and conditions)

- Is management trustworthy?
- Is management skilled at production? Marketing? Finance? Building an effective organization?
- To what extent does the company depend on one or a few key players?
- Is there a successful plan?
- Are credible and sensible accounting, budgeting, and control systems in place?

Marketing (measures of conditions)

- How are the changing needs of the applicant's customers likely to affect the applicant?
- How creditworthy are the applicant's customers?
- At what stage of their life cycles are the applicant's products and services?
- What are the market share and share growth of the applicant's products and services?
- What is the applicant's marketing policy?
- Who are the applicant's competitors? What policies are they pursuing? Why are they able to remain in business?
- How is the applicant meeting changing market needs?

Capital (measures of capital and collateral)

- How much equity is currently funding the firm's assets?
- How much access does the firm have to equity and debt markets?
- Will the company back the loan with the firm's assets?

Cash Flow Analysis. FIs require corporate loan applicants to provide cash flow information, which provides the FI with relevant information about the applicant's cash receipts and disbursements that are compared with the principal and interest payments on the loan. *Cash receipts* include any transaction that results in an increase in cash assets (i.e., receipt of income, decrease in a noncash asset, increase in a liability, and increase in an equity account). *Cash disbursements* include any transaction that results in a decrease in cash assets (i.e., cash expenses, increase in a noncash asset, decrease in a liability, and decrease in equity).[6] The cash flow statement (or cash-based income statement) reconciles changes in the cash account over some period according to three cash flow activities: operations, investing, and financing.

Example 21–3   Computation of Cash Flow Statement

Consider the financial statement for the loan applicant presented in Table 21–2. The cash flow statement reconciles the change in the firm's cash account from 2000 to 2001 as equal to −$61 (see the first row of panel A). Construction of the cash flow statement begins with all cash flow items associated with the operations of the applicant. Panel A of Table 21–3 shows that the cash flows from operations total −$78. Next, cash flows from investment activities (i.e., fixed-asset investments and other nonoperating investments of the firm) are calculated in Table 21–3, Panel B as −$168. Finally, cash flows from financing activities are shown in Panel C as $185. The sum of these cash flow activities, reported in Panel D, −$61, equals the change in the cash account from 2000 to 2001 (Table 21–2, Panel A, first row).

Cash flows generated from operations, as in the preceding example, are the source of cash used to repay the loan to the FI, and thus they play a key role in the credit decision process.

Ratio Analysis. In addition to cash flow information, an applicant requesting specific levels of credit substantiates these business needs by presenting historical audited financial statements and projections of future needs. Historical financial statement analysis can be useful in determining whether cash flow and profit projections are plausible in quantifying many of the qualitative issues just discussed and in highlighting the applicant's risks.

Calculation of financial ratios is useful when performing financial statement analysis on a mid-market corporate applicant. Although stand-alone accounting ratios are used for determining the size of the credit facility, the analyst may find relative ratios more informative when determining how the applicant's business is changing over time. Ratios are particularly informative when they differ either from an industry average (or FI-determined standard of what is appropriate) or from the applicant's own past history. An optimal value is seldom given for any ratio because no two companies are identical. A ratio that differs from an industry average or an FI-determined standard, however, should raise a "flag" and cause the account officer to investigate

---

6. For example, if a firm issues new bonds (increasing liabilities), it will have a(n) (increased) cash flow from the purchasers of the newly issued bonds. Similarly, a sale of new equity (such as common stock) will create a positive cash inflow to the firm from purchasers of the equity.

Table 21–2 Financial Statements Used to Construct a Cash Flow Statement
(in thousands of dollars)

Panel A : Balance Sheets

Assets	2000	2001	Change from 2000 to 2001	Liabilities/Equity	2000	2001	Change from 2000 to 2001
Cash	$ 133	$ 72	$ **(61)**	Notes payable	$ 657	$ 967	$ 310
Accounts receivable	1,399	1,846	447	Accounts payable	908	1,282	374
Inventory	1,255	1,779	524	Accruals	320	427	107
Gross fixed assets	876	1,033	157	Long-term debt	375	300	(75)
Less: depreciation	(277)	(350)	(73)	Common stock	700	700	0
Net fixed assets	599	683	84	Retained earnings	465	754	298
Temporary investments	39	50	11	Total	$3,425	$4,430	$1,005
Total assets	$3,425	$4,430	$1,005				

Panel B: Income Statement

	2001
Net sales	$12,430
Cost of goods sold	(8,255)
Gross profit	4,175
Cash operating expenses	(3,418)
Depreciation	(73)
Operating profit	684
Interest expense	(157)
Taxes	(188)
Net income	339
Dividends	(50)
Change in retained earnings	$289

further. For example, a ratio that shifts radically from accounting period to accounting period may reveal a company's weakness.

Hundreds of ratios could be calculated from any set of accounting statements. The following are a few that credit analysts find useful.

Liquidity Ratios

$$\text{Current ratio} = \frac{\text{Current assets}}{\text{Current liabilities}}$$

$$\text{Quick ratio (acid-test ratio)} = \frac{\text{Cash} + \text{Cash equivalents} + \text{Receivables}}{\text{Current liabilities}}$$

Liquidity provides the defensive cash and near-cash resources for firms to meet claims for payment. Liquidity ratios express the variability of liquid resources relative to potential claims. As we will discuss in the next chapter, when considering the liquidity of FIs, high levels of liquidity effectively guard against liquidity crises but at the cost of lower returns on investment. Note that a company with a very predictable cash flow can maintain low levels of liquidity without much liquidity risk. Account officers frequently request detailed cash flows from an applicant that specify exactly when cash inflows and outflows are anticipated.

Table 21–3 Cash Flow Statement

(in thousands of dollars)

		Cash Flow Impact
Panel A: Cash Flow from Operations		
Net sales	$12,430	↑
Change in accounts receivable	(447)	↓
Cash receipts from sales	11,983	
Cost of goods sold	(8,255)	↓
Change in inventory	(524)	↓
Change in accounts payable	374	↑
Cash margin	3,578	
Cash operating expenses	(3,418)	↓
Change in accruals	107	↑
Cash before interest and taxes	267	
Interest expense	(157)	↓
Taxes	(188)	↓
Cash flows from operations	(78)	
Panel B: Cash Flow from Investing Activities		
Change in gross fixed assets	(157)	↓
Change in temporary investments	(11)	↓
Cash flows from investing activities	(168)	
Panel C: Cash Flows from Financing Activities		
Retirement of long-term debt	(75)	↓
Change in notes payable	310	↑
Change in common stock	0	—
Dividends paid	(50)	↓
Cash flow from financing activities	185	
Panel D: Net Increase (Decrease) in Cash		
	(61)*	

*This is equal to the change in cash for 2000–2001 reported in Panel A of Table 21–2.

Asset Management Ratios

$$\text{Number of days sales in receivables} = \frac{\text{Accounts receivable} \times 365}{\text{Credit sales}}$$

$$\text{Number of days in inventory} = \frac{\text{Inventory} \times 365}{\text{Cost of goods sold}}$$

$$\text{Sales to working capital} = \frac{\text{Sales}}{\text{Working capital}}$$

$$\text{Sales to fixed assets} = \frac{\text{Sales}}{\text{Fixed assets}}$$

$$\text{Sales to total assets (asset turnover)} = \frac{\text{Sales}}{\text{Total assets}}$$

The asset management ratios give the account officer clues to how well the applicant uses its assets relative to its past performance and the performance of the industry. For example, ratio analysis may reveal that the number of days that finished goods are in inventory is increasing. This suggests that finished goods inventories, relative to the sales they support, are not being as well as in the past. If this increase is the result of a deliberate policy to increase inventories to offer customers a wider choice and if it results in higher future sales volumes or increased margins that more than compensate for increased capital tied up in inventory, the increased relative size of finished goods inventories is good for the applicant and, thus, the FI. An FI should be concerned, on the other hand, if increased finished goods inventories are the result of declining sales but steady purchases of supplies and production. Inventory aging schedules give more information than single ratios and should be requested by the account officer concerned about deteriorating ratios.

What a loan applicant often describes in words differs substantially from what the ratio analysis reveals. For example, a company that claims to be a high-volume producer but has low sales-to-assets ratios relative to the industry bears further investigation. In discussing the analysis with the applicant, the account officer not only gains a better appreciation of the applicant's strategy and needs but also may help the applicant better understand the company relative to financial and industry norms.

Debt and Solvency Ratios

$$\text{Debt-asset ratio} = \frac{\text{Short-term liabilities} + \text{Long-term liabilities}}{\text{Total assets}}$$

$$\text{Fixed-charge coverage ratio} = \frac{\text{Earnings available to meet fixed charges}}{\text{Fixed charges}}$$

$$\text{Cash-flow-to-debt ratio} = \frac{\text{EBIT} + \text{Depreciation}}{\text{Debt}}$$

EBIT

Earnings before interest and taxes.

where **EBIT** represents earnings before interest and taxes.

Debt and solvency ratios give the account manager an idea of the extent to which the applicant finances its assets with debt versus equity. Specifically, the lower the debt-asset ratio, the less debt and more equity the applicant uses to finance its assets (i.e., the bigger the applicant's equity cushion). Similarly, the higher the fixed-charge coverage ratio and the cash-flow-to-debt, the more equity and less debt the applicant uses to finance its assets.

Adequate levels of equity capital are as critical to the health of a credit applicant as they are to the health of FIs. The account officer analyzing a credit application or renewal wishes to know whether a sufficient equity cushion exists to absorb fluctuations in the loan applicant's earnings and asset values and sufficient cash flow to make debt service payments. Clearly, the larger the fluctuations or variability of cash flows, the larger is the need for an equity cushion. Note that from a secured debtor's point of view, the unsecured creditors and subordinate lenders (such as subordinate bond holders) form part of the quasi-equity cushion in liquidation. The secured creditor must make sure, however, that it enjoys true seniority in cash payment so that the firm's assets are not liquidated in paying down the claims of the subordinate (junior) creditors and equity holders.

Whether a debt burden is too large can be analyzed with the help of a fixed-charge coverage ratio. This ratio measures the dollars available to meet fixed-charge obligations (earnings available to meet fixed charges). A value of 1 for this ratio means that $1 of earnings is available to meet each dollar of fixed-charge obligations. A value of less (greater) than 1 means that the applicants has less (more) than $1 of earnings available to pay each dollar of fixed-charge obligations. This ratio can be tailored to the applicant's situation, depending on what really constitutes fixed charges that must be paid. One version of it follows: (EBIT + Lease payments)/(Interest + Lease payments + Sinking fund/$(1 - T)$), where T is the marginal tax rate.[7] Here, it is assumed that

7. Another version adds to the denominator investments for replacing equipment that is needed for the applicant to remain in business.

sinking fund payments must be made.[8] They are adjusted by the division of $(1 - T)$ into a before-tax cash outflow so they can be added to other before-tax cash outflows. The variability of cash flows (the cash flow ratio) provides a clue as to how much higher than 1 a fixed-charge coverage ratio should be.

The cash-flow-to-debt ratio is a variant of the fixed-charge coverage ratio. It measures the cash flow available for debt service in proportion to the debt principal being serviced and can be compared to the interest rate on the debt. If this ratio is equal to the interest rate on the debt, the applicant's cash flows are just sufficient to pay the required interest on the debt principal. The more the ratio exceeds the interest rate on the debt, the larger is the debt-service cushion.

Profitability Ratios

$$\text{Gross margin} = \frac{\text{Gross profit}}{\text{Sales}}$$

$$\text{Operating profit margin} = \frac{\text{Operating profit}}{\text{Sales}}$$

$$\text{Income to sales} = \frac{\text{EBIT}}{\text{Sales}}$$

$$\text{Return on assets} = \frac{\text{EAT}}{\text{Average total assets}}$$

$$\text{Return on equity} = \frac{\text{EAT}}{\text{Total equity}}$$

$$\text{Dividend payout} = \frac{\text{Dividends}}{\text{EAT}}$$

EAT

Earnings after taxes.

where **EAT** represents earnings after taxes, or net income.

For all but the dividend payout ratio, the higher the value of the ratio, the higher the profitability of the firm. The dividend payout ratio measures how much of the profit is retained in the firm versus paid out to the stockholders as dividends. The lower the dividend payout ratio, the more profits are retained in the firm. A profitable firm that retains its earnings increases its level of equity capital as well as its creditworthiness. The analyst should be concerned about large swings in profitability as well as trends.[9]

Common Size Analysis and Growth Rates.   In addition to the ratios listed above, an analyst can compute sets of ratios by dividing all income statement amounts by total sales revenue and all balance sheet amounts by total assets. These calculations yield common-size financial statements that can be used to identify changes in corporate performance. Year-to-year growth rates also give useful ratios for identifying trends. Common-size financial statements may provide quantitative clues as to the direction that the firm is moving and that the analysis should take (see Chapter 13 on accounting ratios).

Having reviewed the financial and other conditions of the applicant, the FI can include loan covenants (similar to bond covenants discussed in Chapter 6) as a part of the

---

8. *Sinking funds* are required periodic payments into a fund that is used to retire the principal amounts on bonds outstanding.

9. *Market value ratios* such as the growth rate in the share price, price–earnings ratio, and dividend yield are also valuable indicators if they are available. For a mid-market corporation, however, they are probably unavailable since the debt and equity claims of most mid-market corporations are not publicly traded. The account officer may find it informative to substitute a similar listed firm (a comparability test).

loan agreement. Loan covenants reduce the risk of the loan to the lender. They can include a variety of conditions such as maintenance of various ratios at or within stated ranges, key-person insurance policies on employees critical to the success of the project funded by the loan, and so on.

Following Approval.   The credit process does not end when the applicant signs the loan agreement. As is the case for mortgage loans, before allowing a drawdown (the actual release of the funds to the borrower) of a mid-market credit, the account officer must make sure that **conditions precedent** have been cleared. Conditions precedent are those conditions specified in the credit agreement or terms sheet for a credit that must be fulfilled before drawdowns are permitted. These include various title searches, perfecting of collateral, and the like. Following drawdown, the credit must be monitored throughout the loan's life to ensure that the borrower is living up to its commitments and to detect any deterioration in the borrower's creditworthiness so as to protect the bank's interest in the loan being repaid in full with the promised interest return.

Typically, the borrower's credit needs will change from time to time. A growing company has an expanding need for credit. A company moving into the international arena needs foreign exchange. A contractor may have periodic guarantee requests. Even if the credit agreements being offered do not change, a corporation's credit needs are usually reviewed on an annual basis to ensure that they comply with the terms of the original credit agreement. FIs typically wish to maintain close contact with customers to meet their ongoing financial service requirements—both credit and noncredit—so that the relationship will develop into a permanent, mutually beneficial one (the customer relationship effect).

conditions precedent

Those conditions specified in the credit agreement or terms sheet for a credit that must be fulfilled before drawings are permitted.

Large Commercial and Industrial Lending

An FI's bargaining strength is severely diminished when it deals with large creditworthy corporate customers. Large corporations are able to issue debt and equity directly in the capital markets as well as to make private placements of securities.[10] Also, they typically maintain credit relationships with several FIs and have significant in-house financial expertise. They manage their cash positions through the money markets by issuing their own commercial paper to meet fund shortfalls and use excess funds to buy Treasury bills, banker's acceptances, and other companies' commercial paper. Moreover, large corporate clients are not seriously restricted by international borders but have operations and access to international capital markets and FIs in many parts of the world. Large corporate clients are very attractive to FIs because, although spreads and fees are small in percentage terms, the transactions are often large enough to make them very profitable as long as a default does not occur.

Moreover, the FI's relationship with large corporate clients goes beyond lending. The FI's role as broker, dealer, and adviser to a corporate client may rival or exceed the importance of its role as a lender. A large corporate client is likely to investigate several avenues for obtaining credit and to compare, for example, the flexibility and cost of a bond, a private placement, and borrowing from different FIs. The client may periodically poll FIs to determine opportune times to tap financial markets, even if this means inventorying funds.[11] The FI's loan account officer must often liaise with the FI's investment banker to obtain information and indicative pricing on new security issues. Clearly, the amount of time this involves means that an FI's senior corporate account officer manages far fewer accounts than colleagues providing mid-market credits.

---

10. This additional source of funds for large corporations is a major reason for some of the mergers between large commercial banks and investment banks in the late 1990s (e.g., U.S. Bancorp/Piper Jaffray). Such mergers offer commercial banks the opportunity to participate in new security issues of large corporations in addition to the traditional business of lending.

11. Or opening new lines of credit (loan commitments)—see below.

In providing a credit service to large corporations, credit management remains an important issue. Large corporations frequently use loan commitments (a contractual commitment to loan to a firm a certain maximum amount at a given interest rate), performance guarantees (such as letters of credit, see Chapter 5), and term loans, as do mid-market corporates. If the FI is contracting in spot and forward foreign exchange or swaps, or is engaging in other derivative activities with the corporate client as a counterparty, it must do so within the credit limits established by a regular credit review process.

An additional complicating factor is that large corporate accounts often consist of several related corporate entities under a common management. For example, a holding company may wholly own, control, or have substantial stakes in various operating subsidiaries. A subsidiary's credit risk may be better than, the same as, or worse than that of a holding company as a whole. An FI lending to a holding company with no assets other than its equity stake in its subsidiaries puts itself in a subordinate lending position relative to the lenders to the operating subsidiaries, which have direct claims over those subsidiaries' operating assets.

An account officer preparing a credit review for a large corporate customer often faces a complex task. The standard methods of analysis that we introduced when discussing mid-market corporates applies to large corporate clients but with additional complications. The corporate business often crosses more than one business activity and location. Hence, industry comparisons are difficult at best. Additional analytical aids are available to account officers. Specifically, large corporations are tracked by rating agencies and market analysts, who can provide account officers with a great deal of information to aid in their credit analysis. Also, because of these customers' additional complexities and large credit risk exposures, FIs can use sophisticated credit-scoring models in the credit review process based on accounting and/or financial market data. We discuss two such credit-scoring models below.

Credit-Scoring Models.   Credit-scoring models use data on observed borrower characteristics either to calculate the probability of default or to sort borrowers into different default risk classes. By selecting and combining different economic and financial borrower characteristics, an FI manager may be able to:

1. Numerically establish which factors are important in explaining default risk.
2. Evaluate the relative degree or importance of these factors.
3. Improve the pricing of default risk.
4. Screen high-risk loan applicants.
5. Calculate any reserves needed to meet expected future loan losses.

To employ credit-scoring models in this manner, the FI manager must identify objective economic and financial measures of risk for any particular class of borrower. For corporate debt, financial ratios such as the debt–equity ratio are usually key factors. After data are identified, a statistical technique quantifies or scores the default risk probability or default risk classification.

Altman's Z-Score.   E. I. Altman developed a Z-score model for analyzing publicly traded manufacturing firms in the United States. The indicator variable Z is an overall measure of the borrower's default risk classification. This classification, in turn, depends on the values of various financial ratios of the borrower (X_j) and the weighted importance of these ratios based on the observed experience of defaulting versus nondefaulting borrowers derived from a discriminant analysis model.[12]

Altman's credit-scoring model takes the following form:

---

12. E. I. Altman, "Managing the Commercial Lending Process," in *Handbook of Banking Strategy,* ed. R. C. Aspinwall and R. A. Eisenbeis (New York: John Wiley & Sons, 1985), pp. 473–510.

$$Z = 1.2X_1 + 1.4X_2 + 3.3X_3 + 0.6X_4 + 1.0X_5$$

where

X_1 = Working capital/Total assets ratio
X_2 = Retained earnings/Total assets ratio
X_3 = Earnings before interest and taxes/Total assets ratio
X_4 = Market value of equity/Book value of long-term debt ratio
X_5 = Sales/Total assets ratio.

The higher the value of Z, the lower the borrower's default risk classification.[13] Thus, low or negative Z values may be evidence that the borrower is a member of a relatively high default risk class.

Example 21–4 Calculation of Altman's Z-Score

Suppose that the financial ratios of a potential borrowing firm took the following values:

$$X_1 = .2$$
$$X_2 = 0$$
$$X_3 = -.20$$
$$X_4 = .10$$
$$X_5 = 2.0$$

The ratio X_2 is zero and X_3 is negative, indicating that the firm has had negative earnings or losses in recent periods. Also, X_4 indicates that the borrower is highly leveraged. However, the working capital ratio (X_1) and the sales/assets ratio (X_5) indicate that the firm is reasonably liquid and is maintaining its sales volume. The Z-score provides an overall score or indicator of the borrower's credit risk since it combines and weights these five factors according to their past importance in explaining borrower default. For the borrower in question:

$$Z = 1.2(.2) + 1.4(0) + 3.3(-.20) + 0.6(.10) + 1.0(2.0)$$
$$Z = 0.24 + 0 - .66 + 0.06 + 2.0$$
$$Z = 1.64$$

According to Altman's credit-scoring model, any firm with a Z-score of less than 1.81 should be considered to be a high default risk.[14] Thus, the FI should not lend to this borrower until it improves its earnings performance.

Use of the Z-score model to make credit risk evaluations has a number of problems. The first problem is that this model usually discriminates only between two extreme cases of borrower behavior: no default and default. As discussed in Chapter 20, in the real world various gradations of default exist, from nonpayment or delay of interest payments (nonperforming assets) to outright default on all promised interest and principal payments. This problem suggests that a more accurate or finely calibrated sorting among borrowers may require defining more classes in the scoring model.

The second problem is that there is no obvious economic reason to expect that the weights in the Z-score model—or, more generally, the weights in any credit-scoring model—will be constant over any but very short periods. The same concern also

---

13. Working capital is Current assets − Current liabilities.

14. This "critical value" is calculated by taking the average or the mean Z-score for firms that defaulted in the FI's sample and the mean Z-score for firms that did not default. Thus, if defaulting firms had a mean Z-score of 1.61 and nondefaulting firms a mean Z-score of 2.01, the critical Z-score is 1.81 (i.e., halfway between these two values).

applies to the scoring model's explanatory variables (X_j). Specifically, due to changing financial market conditions, other borrower-specific financial ratios may come to be increasingly relevant in explaining default risk probabilities.

The third problem is that these models ignore important, hard-to-quantify factors that may play a crucial role in the default or no-default decision. For example, the reputation of the borrower and the nature of long-term borrower-lender relationships could be important borrower-specific characteristics, as could macro factors such as the phase of the business cycle. Credit-scoring models often ignore these variables. Moreover, traditional credit-scoring models rarely use publicly available information, such as the prices of the outstanding public debt and equity of the borrower.[15]

A fourth problem relates to default records kept by FIs. Currently, no centralized, publicly available database on defaulted loans for proprietary or other reasons exists. Some task forces by consortiums of commercial banks and consulting firms are currently seeking to construct such databases, but it may well be many years before they are fully developed. This constrains the ability of many FIs to use credit-scoring models for larger business loans.

KMV Model.   In recent years, following the pioneering work on options by Merton, Black, and Scholes, we now recognize that when a firm raises funds either by issuing bonds or increasing its bank loans, it holds a very valuable default or repayment option.[16] That is, if a borrower's investments fail to pay off, so that it cannot repay its bond holders or the loan to the FI, it has the option to default on its debt repayments and turn any remaining assets over to the debtholder. Because of limited liability, the borrower's loss is limited, on the downside, by the amount of equity that is invested in the firm.[17] On the other hand, if things go well, the borrower can keep most of the upside returns on asset investments after the promised principal and interest on the debt have been paid. The KMV Corporation has turned this relatively simple idea into a credit-monitoring model. Many of the largest U.S. banks are now using this model to determine the expected default frequency (EDF) of large corporations.[18]

The KMV model uses the value of the equity in a firm (from a stockholder's perspective) as equivalent to holding a call option on the assets of the firm (with the amount of debt borrowed acting similar to the exercise price of the call option). From this approach, and the link between the volatility of the market value of a firm's equity and that of its assets, it is possible to derive the asset volatility (risk) of a given firm (σ) and the market value of the firm's assets (A). Using the derived values of σ and A, along with the amount of debt outstanding, the probability of the firm defaulting on its current debt obligations can be calculated.[19] The expected probability of default (EDF) that is calculated reflects the probability that the market value of the firm's assets (A) will fall below the promised repayments on debt liabilities in one year. If the value of a firm's assets falls below its debt liabilities, it can be viewed as being economically insolvent. Simulations by KMV have shown that this model outperforms both Z-score models and S&P rating changes as predictors of corporate failure and distress.[20] For example, Figure 21–2 illustrates the EDF for IBM in the early 1990s, when IBM was incurring

15. However, it might be noted that the X_4 variable in Altman's Z-score model includes a market value of equity measure (i.e., the price of the firm's shares times the number of its shares outstanding).

16. R. C. Merton, "On the Pricing of Corporate Debt: The Risk Structure of Interest Rates," *Journal of Finance* 29 (1974), pp. 449–70; and F. Black and M. Scholes, "The Pricing of Options and Corporate Liabilities," *Journal of Political Economy* 81 (1973), pp. 737–59.

17. Given limits to losses in personal bankruptcy, a similar analysis can be applied to retail and consumer loans.

18. See KMV Corporation, *Credit Monitor* (San Francisco: KMV Corporation, 1994).

19. See A. Saunders, *Credit Risk Measurement: New Approaches to Value at Risk and Other Paradigms* (New York: John Wiley & Sons, 1999).

20. KMV currently provides EDFs for more than 20,000 U.S. and foreign companies.

Figure 21–2 KMV versus S&P Ratings of IBM

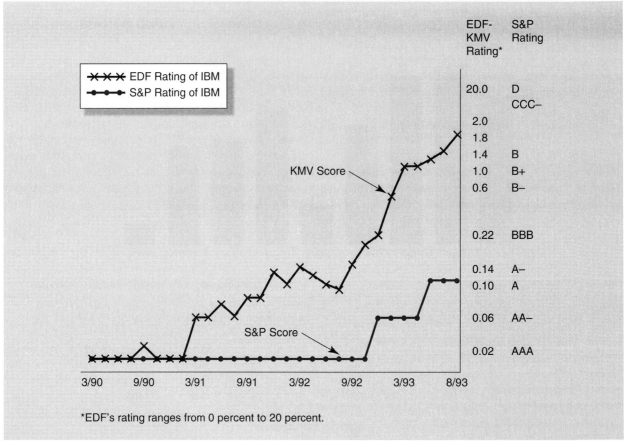

*EDF's rating ranges from 0 percent to 20 percent.

Source: KMV Corporation.

significant financial problems. IBM's EDF in this figure begins to rise more than two years before it suffered two credit rating downgrades by Standard & Poor's in the fall of 1992 and the spring of 1993.[21]

6 Calculating the Return on a Loan

An important element in the credit management process, once the decision to make a loan has been made, is its pricing. This includes adjustments for the perceived credit risk or default risk of the borrower. This section demonstrates two ways to calculate the return on a loan: the traditional *return on assets approach* and a newer approach called *risk-adjusted return on capital* (RAROC) that considers loan returns in the context of the risk of the loan to the FI. While we demonstrate the return calculations using examples of commercial and industrial loans, the techniques can be used to calculate the return on other loans (such as credit card or mortgage loans) as well. Indeed, In the News box 21–2 demonstrates how fierce competition for credit card customers has affected the return on this segment of the consumer loan market.

21. Note a KMV EDF score varies from a minimum of zero percent to a maximum of 20 percent per annum.

In the News

The Big Profit Squeeze

Caught between rate-surfing consumers and the imperative for growth, seemingly at any cost, credit card issuers face lower profitability on their core product than ever before. Relentless competition has eroded the industry's returns on assets for the past decade, despite greater operating efficiencies and lower cost of funds. Those forces show no sign of abating. Indeed, the profit pressure could get worse before it gets better. Consumers have a diminished appetite for borrowing, slowing the growth in receivables. And with delinquencies close to record levels and personal bankruptcies soaring to an all-time high, credit card issuers are likely to get clobbered if there is an economic downturn.

"Banks are stuck walking a very narrow tightrope," says Robert K. Hammer, chairman and chief executive of R. K. Hammer, Investment Bankers, an advisory ser-

Source: *U.S. Banker*, September 1998, by Miriam Leuchter.

vice based in Thousand Oaks, California. "On one end is the need to satisfy customers at a reasonable price—reasonable, that is, from the consumer's point of view—and on the other side are the financial obligations they have to shareholders." The trend is driving issuers out of the market altogether. In the past year, some of the most recognized names in the industry have abandoned the business. These include monoline pioneer Advanta Corp. and no-fee pacesetter AT&T Universal Card, which sold their huge credit card portfolios to Fleet Financial Group and Citicorp, respectively. But in spite of the industry's consolidation, there's still enough competition among commercial banks, specialty finance companies and the remaining monoline card banks to prevent the kinds of price hikes that would lift profitability significantly.

To be sure, lower profitability does not necessarily equal lower profits, since growth in volume can make up the difference. Earnings at credit card issuers such as Capital One Financial Corp. and MBNA Corp. set records in the most recent quarter. And a few companies either offer such unique products that they command premium prices or operate efficiently enough to maintain high margins. "This is still a great business," says equities analyst David Hochstim of Bear, Stearns & Co. "It's just not as good as it was—and certainly not for the average bank." . . .

The number of personal bankruptcies filed in federal court in the 12 months ended June 30 reached 1.37 million, a 9% increase from the year before. Says Hammer, "My worry is that however bad bankruptcies are—and they are bad—this is all in a great economy. What will happen when the economy heads south? They're nothing compared to what they'll be in 6 months or 18 months if the stock market keeps going down."

Return on Assets (ROA)

A number of factors impact the promised return that an FI achieves on any given dollar loan (asset) amount. These factors include the following:

1.   The interest rate on the loan.
2.   Any fees relating to the loan.
3.   The credit risk premium (m) on the loan.
4.   The collateral backing the loan.
5.   Other nonprice terms (such as compensating balances and reserve requirements).

In this section, we consider an example of how to calculate the promised return on a C&I loan. Suppose that a bank makes a spot one-year, $1 million loan. The loan rate is set at as follows:

$$\begin{aligned} \text{Base lending rate } (L) &= 12\% \\ + \text{ Risk premium } (m) &= \underline{2} \\ L + m &= 14\% \end{aligned}$$

LIBOR

The London Interbank Offered Rate, the rate for interbank dollar loans in the foreign or Eurodollar market of a given maturity.

The base lending rate (L) could reflect the bank's weighted average cost of capital or its marginal cost of funds, such as the commercial paper rate, the federal funds rate, or **LIBOR**—the London Interbank Offered Rate, which is the rate for interbank dollar loans in the foreign or Eurodollar market of a given maturity. Alternatively, it could reflect the **prime lending rate**. Traditionally, the prime rate has been the rate charged to the bank's lowest risk customers. Now it is more a rate to which positive or negative risk premiums can be added. In other words, banks now charge their best and largest borrowers below prime rate to compete with the commercial paper market.

prime lending rate

The base lending rate periodically set by banks.

Direct and indirect fees and charges relating to a loan generally fall into three categories:

1.   A loan origination fee (f) to the borrower charged for processing the application.
2.   A compensating balance requirement (b) to be held as noninterest-bearing demand deposits. **Compensating balances** represent a percentage of a loan that a borrower cannot actively use for expenditures. Instead, these balances must be kept on deposit at the FI. For example, a borrower facing a 10 percent compensating balance requirement on a $100 loan would have to place $10 on deposit (traditionally in a demand deposit) with the FI and could use only $90 of the $100 borrowed. This requirement raises the effective cost of loans for the borrower since less than the full loan amount ($90 in this case) can actually be used by the borrower and the deposit rate earned on compensating balances is less than the borrowing rate. Thus, compensating balance requirements act as an additional source of return on lending for an FI.[22] Consequently, although credit risk may be the most important factor ultimately affecting the return on a loan, FI managers should not ignore these other factors in evaluating loan profitability and risk. Indeed, FIs can compensate for high credit risk in a number of ways other than charging a higher explicit interest rate or risk premium on a loan or restricting the amount of credit available. In particular, higher fees, high compensating balances, and increased collateral backing offer implicit and indirect methods to compensate an FI for lending risk.

compensating balance

A proportion of a loan that a borrower is required to hold on deposit at the lending institution.

3.   A reserve requirement charge (R) imposed by the Federal Reserve on the bank's demand deposits, including any compensating balances (see Chapter 14).

---

22. They also create a more stable supply of deposits and, thus, mitigate liquidity problems.

The contractually promised gross return on the loan, k, per dollar lent—or ROA per dollar lent—equals:[23]

$$1 + k = \frac{1 + f + (L + m)}{1 - (b(1 - R))}$$

This formula may need some explanation. The numerator is the promised gross cash inflow to the FI per dollar lent, reflecting direct fees f plus the loan interest rate $(L + m)$ discussed above. In the denominator, for every $1 in loans that the FI lends, it retains b as noninterest-bearing compensating balances. Thus, $1 - b$ represents the net proceeds of each $1 of loans received by the borrower from the FI, ignoring reserve requirements. However, since b (compensating balances) are held by the borrower at the FI as demand deposits, the Federal Reserve requires the FI to hold noninterest-bearing reserves at the rate R against these compensating balances. Thus, the FI's net benefit from requiring compensating balances must consider the cost of holding higher noninterest-bearing reserves. The net outflow by the FI per $1 of loans is $1 - (b(1 - R))$, or 1 minus the reserve adjusted compensating balance requirement.

Example 21–5   Calculation of ROA on a Loan

Suppose a bank does the following:

1. Sets the loan rate on a prospective loan at 14 percent (where $L = 12\%$ and $m = 2\%$).
2. Charges a $\frac{1}{8}$ percent (or 0.125 percent) loan origination fee to the borrower.
3. Imposes a 10 percent compensating balance requirement to be held as noninterest-bearing demand deposits.
4. Sets aside reserves, at a rate of 10 percent of deposits, held at the Federal Reserve (i.e., the Fed's cash-to-deposit reserve ratio is 10 percent).

Placing the numbers from our example into this formula, we have:

$$1 + k = 1 + \frac{.00125 + (.12 + .02)}{1 - ((.10)(.9))}$$

$$1 + k = 1 + \frac{.14125}{.91}$$

$$1 + k = 1.1552, \text{ or } k = 15.52\%$$

This is, of course, larger than the simple promised interest return on the loan, $L + m = 14$ percent.

In the special case in which fees (f) are zero and the compensating balance (b) is zero:

$$f = 0$$
$$b = 0$$

the contractually promised return formula reduces to:

$$1 + k = 1 + (L + m)$$

That is, the credit risk premium is the fundamental factor driving the promised return on a loan, once the base rate on the loan has been set.

Note that as commercial lending markets have become more competitive, both origination fees (f) and compensating balances (b) have become less important. For

---

23. This formula ignores present value aspects that could easily be incorporated. For example, fees are earned in up-front undiscounted dollars, while interest payments and risk premiums are normally paid on loan maturity and, thus, should be discounted by the FI's cost of funds.

example, when compensating balances are still required, banks may now allow them to be held as time deposits and earn interest. As a result, borrowers' opportunity losses from compensating balances have been reduced to the difference between the loan rate and the compensating balance time-deposit rate. In addition, compensating balance requirements are very rare on international loans such as Eurodollar loans.[24]

RAROC Models

An increasingly popular model used to evaluate the return on a loan to a large customer is the risk-adjusted return on capital (RAROC) model. Bankers Trust (acquired by Deutsche Bank in 1998) pioneered RAROC, which has now been adopted by virtually all the large banks in the United States and Europe, although with some proprietary differences among them.

The essential idea behind RAROC is that rather than evaluating the actual or promised annual cash flow on a loan as a percentage of the amount lent (or ROA), as described in the last subsection, the lending officer balances the loan's expected income against the loan's expected risk.[25] Thus, rather than dividing expected annual loan income by assets lent, it is divided by some measure of asset (loan) risk or what is often called capital at risk, since loan losses have to be written against a bank's capital.

$$\text{RAROC} = \frac{\text{One-year income on a loan}}{\text{Loan (asset) risk or capital at risk}}$$

A loan is approved only if RAROC is sufficiently high relative to a benchmark return on equity capital (ROE) for the FI, where ROE measures the return stockholders require on their equity investment in the FI. The idea here is that a loan should be made only if the risk-adjusted return on the loan adds to the FI's equity value as measured by the ROE required by the FI's stockholders. Thus, for example, if an FI's ROE is 15 percent, a loan should be made only if the estimated RAROC is higher than the 15 percent required by the FI's stockholders as a reward for their investment. Alternatively, if the RAROC on an existing loan falls below an FI's RAROC benchmark, the lending officer should seek to adjust the loan's terms to make it "profitable" again.

One problem in estimating RAROC is the measurement of loan risk (the denominator in the RAROC equation). In calculating RAROC, most FIs divide one-year loan income (usually the spread between the loan rate—the ROA from above—and the cost of funds) by a loan risk measure calculated as the product of an "unexpected" default rate and the proportion of the loan that cannot be recaptured on a borrower's default—the loss given default. The denominator in the RAROC equation is, therefore, an estimate of the unexpected overall loss on the loan, which is the product of the unexpected default rate and the loss given default. For example, suppose a borrower of $100,000 has risk characteristics that put her in a risk class that has experienced an average historical default rate of 0.1 percent. However, one year in every 100 (or 1 percent of the time), such as in a major recession, the bank expects 2 percent of these types of loans to default. This 2 percent can be viewed as the unexpected default rate.[26] Moreover,

---

24. As mentioned above, the ROA model can also be applied to other than commercial and industrial loans. For example, a consumer loan could also be priced using a risk premium (m) over some base rate (L) and fees are generally charged on a consumer loan (e.g., annual fees for credit card provision). However, consumer loans do not require compensating balance requirements. Thus, the gross return on a consumer loan would be $1 + k = 1 + f + (L + m)$.

25. Since loan defaults are charged to the FI's capital or equity account, the loan's risk is also a measure of "risk capital," or capital at risk.

26. The extreme loss rate is usually calculated by taking the average annual loss rate over some historical period and estimating the annual standard deviation of loan loss rates around that mean. If the standard deviation is multiplied by 2.33, as long as loan loss rates are normally distributed, this reflects the 99th percentile worst-loss case scenario. In practice, loss rates are not normally distributed, so many FIs use higher multiples of σ. For example, BankAmerica uses a multiple of $6 \times \sigma$.

upon default, the FI has historically recovered 25 percent of the defaulted loans. As a result, the loss given default is 75 percent. Accordingly, for this borrower, the loan loss risk per dollar lent is 0.015 (0.02 × 0.75), or the capital at risk to the FI is $100,000(0.02 × 0.75) = $1,500.[27]

Thus:

$$RAROC = \frac{\text{One-year income per dollar loaned}}{\text{Unexpected default rate} \times \text{Loss given default}}$$

Example 21–6 Calculation of RAROC

Suppose the cost of funds for the FI is 15.20 percent and its loan rate is 16 percent. After adjusting for expected losses of 0.5 percent, the expected one-year income per dollar lent, or the numerator of the RAROC equation, is 0.3 cents per dollar lent, or .003. The 99th (extreme case) loss rate for borrowers of this type has historically run at 4 percent, and the dollar proportion of loans of this type that cannot be recaptured on default (loss given default) has historically been 80 percent. Then:

$$RAROC = \frac{.003}{(.04)(.8)} = \frac{.003}{(.032)} = 9.375\%$$

If the FI's ROE is less than 9.375 percent (e.g., it is 9 percent), the loan can be viewed as being profitable. If the ROE is higher than 9.375 percent (e.g., 15 percent), it should be rejected and/or the loan officer should seek higher spreads and fees on the loan.

---

[27]Again, unexpected losses are written off against the bank's capital. Traditionally, loan loss reserves have been viewed as the reserve against losses.

Summary

This chapter provided an in-depth look at the measurement and on-balance-sheet management of credit risks. The chapter then discussed the role of credit analysis and how it differs across different types of loans, especially mortgage loans, individual loans, mid-market corporate loans, and large corporate loans. Both qualitative and quantitative approaches to credit analysis were discussed, as well as methods to evaluate the risk of loan portfolios.

Questions

1. Why is credit risk analysis an important component of FI risk management?
2. How does an FI evaluate its credit risks with respect to consumer and commercial loans?
3. Jane Doe earns $30,000 per year and has applied for an $80,000, 30-year mortgage at 8 percent interest, paid monthly. Property taxes on the house are expected to be $1,200 per year. If her bank requires a gross debt service ratio of no more than 30 percent, will Jane be able to obtain the mortgage?
4. Suppose you are a loan officer at Carbondale Local Bank. Joan Doe listed the following information on her mortgage application:

Characteristic	Value
Annual gross income	$45,000
TDS	10%
Relations with FI	Checking account
Major credit cards	5
Age	27
Residence	Own/Mortgage
Length of residence	2½ years
Job stability	5½ years
Credit history	Missed 2 payments 1 year ago

Use the information below to determine whether or not Joan Doe should be approved for a mortgage from your bank.

Characteristic	Characteristic Values and Weights				
Annual gross income	<$10,000	$10,000–$25,000	$25,000–$50,000	$50,000–$100,000	>$100,000
Score	0	10	20	35	60
TDS	>50%	35%–50%	15%–35%	5%–15%	<5%
Score	−10	0	20	40	60
Relations with FI	None	Checking account	Savings account	Both	
Score	0	10	10	20	
Major credit cards	None	Between 1 and 4	5 or more		
Score	0	20	10		
Age	<25	25–60	>60		
Score	5	25	35		
Residence	Rent	Own with mortgage	Own outright		
Score	5	20	50		
Length of residence	<1 year	1–5 years	>5 years		
Score	0	25	40		
Job stability	<1 year	1–5 years	>5 years		
Score	0	25	50		
Credit history	No record	Missed a payment in last 5 years	Met all payments		
Score	0	−15	40		

The loan is automatically rejected if the applicant's *total* score is less than or equal to 120; the loan is automatically approved if the total score is greater than or equal to 190. A score between 120 and 190 (noninclusive) is reviewed by a loan committee for a final decision.

5. In what ways does the credit analysis of a mid-market borrower differ from that of a small-business borrower?

6. What are some of the special risks and considerations when lending to small businesses rather than large businesses?

7. How does ratio analysis help to answer questions about the production, management, and marketing capabilities of a prospective borrower?

8. Consider the following company's balance sheet and income statement.

Balance Sheet

Assets		Liabilities and Equity	
Cash	$ 4,000	Accounts payable	$ 30,000
Accounts receivable	52,000	Notes payable	12,000
Inventory	40,000		
Total current assets	96,000	Total current liabilities	42,000
Fixed assets	44,000	Long-term debt	36,000
		Equity	62,000
Total assets	$140,000	Total liabilities and equity	$140,000

Income Statement

Sales (all on credit)	$200,000
Cost of goods sold	130,000
Gross margin	70,000
Selling and administrative expenses	20,000
Depreciation	8,000
EBIT	42,000
Interest expense	4,800
Earnings before tax	37,200
Taxes	11,160
Net income	$ 26,040

For this company, calculate the following:
a. Current ratio.
b. Number of days' sales in receivables.
c. Sales to total assets.
d. Number of days in inventory.
e. Debt ratio.
f. Cash-flow debt ratio.
g. Return on assets.
h. Return on equity.

9. In Question 8, how might we determine whether these ratios reflect a well-managed, creditworthy company?

10. Industrial Corporation has an income-to-sales (profit margin) ratio of .03, a sales-to-assets (asset utilization) ratio of 1.5, and a debt-to-asset ratio of .66. What is Industrial's return on equity?

11. Consider the coefficients of Altman's Z-score. Can you tell by the size of the coefficients which ratio appears most important in assessing the creditworthiness of a loan applicant? Explain.

12. The following is ABC Inc's balance sheet (in thousands):

Assets		Liabilities	
Cash	$ 20	Accounts payable	$ 30
Accounts receivables	90	Notes payable	90
Inventory	90	Accruals	30
		Long-term debt	150
Plant and equipment	500	Equity	400
Total	$700		$700

Also assume that sales equal $500, cost of goods sold equals $360, interest payments equal $62, taxes equal $56, and net income equals $22. Assume the beginning retained earnings is $0, the market value of equity is equal to its book value, and the company pays no dividends.

a. Calculate Altman's Z-score for ABC Inc. if ABC has a 50% dividend payout ratio and the market value of equity is equal to its book value. Recall the following:

Net working capital = Current assets − Current liabilities

Current assets = Cash + Accounts receivable + Inventories

Current liabilities = Accounts payable + Accruals + Notes payable

EBIT = Revenues − Cost of goods sold − Depreciation

Taxes = (EBIT − Interest)(Tax rate)

Net income = EBIT − Interest − Taxes

Retained earnings = Net income (1 − Dividend payout ratio).

b. Should you approve ABC Inc.'s application to your bank for $500,000 for a capital expansion loan?

c. If ABC's sales were $450,000, taxes were $16,000, and the market value of equity fell to one-quarter of its book value (assume cost of goods sold and interest are unchanged), how would that change ABC's income statement? ABC's tax liability can be used to offset tax liabilities incurred by the other divisions of the firm. Would your credit decision change?

d. What are some of the shortcomings of using a discriminant function model to evaluate credit risk?

13. Why could a lender's expected return be lower when the risk premium is increased on a loan?

14. Countrybank offers one-year loans with a stated rate of 10 percent but requires a compensating balance of 10 percent. What is the true cost of this loan to the borrower?

15. Metrobank offers one-year loans with a 9 percent stated rate, charges a ¼ percent loan origination fee, imposes a 10 percent compensating balance requirement, and must pay a 6 percent reserve requirement to the Federal Reserve. What is the return to the bank on these loans?

16. An FI is planning a loan of $5,000,000 to a firm in the steel industry. It expects to charge an up-front fee of 0.10 percent and a service fee of 5 basis points. The loan has a maturity of 8 years. The cost of funds (and the RAROC benchmark) for the FI is 10 percent. Assume that the FI has estimated the risk premium on the steel manufacturing sector to be approximately 0.18 percent, based on two years of historical data. The current market interest rate for loans in this sector is 10.1 percent. The 99th (extreme case) loss rate for borrowers of this type has historically run at 3 percent, and the dollar proportion of loans of this type that cannot be recaptured on default has historically been 90 percent. Using the RAROC model, should the FI make the loan?

17. Go to the FDIC website and update Table 21–1.

The following questions are related to the appendix material.

18. How does loan portfolio risk differ from individual loan risk?

19. Explain how modern portfolio theory can be applied to lower the credit risk of an FI's portfolio.

20. A bank has two loans of equal size outstanding, A and B, and the bank has identified the returns they would earn in two different states of nature, 1 and 2, representing default and no default, respectively.

	State	
	1	2
Security A	.02	.14
Security B	.00	.18

If the probability of state 1 is .2 and the probability of state 2 is .8, calculate:

a. The expected return of each security.

b. The expected return on the portfolio in each state.

c. The expected return on the portfolio.

Appendix Loan Portfolio Risk and Management

In this chapter, we have evaluated the risk of a loan on a stand-alone basis. However, as is shown below, the credit risk of a portfolio of loans will be generally less than the sum of the risks of loans when viewed on a stand-alone basis. Let the expected return on a portfolio of loans be equal to R_P, where:

$$R_P = \sum_{i=1}^{N} X_i \bar{R}_i$$

The variance of returns or risk on a portfolio (σ_p^2) of loans can be calculated as:

$$\sigma_p^2 = \sum_{i=1}^{N} X_i^2 \sigma_i^2 + \sum_{i=1}^{N} \sum_{\substack{j=1 \\ i \neq j}}^{N} X_i X_j \sigma_{ij}$$

where

R_p = Expected or mean return on the loan portfolio
$\bar{R}_i$ = Mean return on the ith loan in the portfolio
X_i = Proportion of the loan portfolio invested in the ith loan
σ_i^2 = Variance of returns on the ith loan
σ_{ij} = Covariance of returns between the ith and jth loans (this reflects the correlation or covariance between the default risks of borrowers i and j)

The fundamental lesson of modern portfolio theory (MPT) is that by taking advantage of its size, an FI can diversify considerable amounts of credit risk as long as the returns on different loans are imperfectly correlated.[28]

Consider the equation for variance of returns, σ_p^2. If many loans have negative correlations or covariances of returns (σ_{ij} are negative)—that is, when one borrower's loan does badly, another's does well—the sum of the individual credit risks of loans viewed independently overestimates the risk of the whole portfolio. This is what we meant in Chapter 20 when we stated that by pooling funds, FIs can reduce risk by taking advantage of the law of large numbers in their investment decisions.[29]

Example 21–7   Calculation of Return and Risk on a Two-Asset Portfolio

Suppose that an FI holds two loans with the following characteristics:[30]

Loan i	X_i	$\bar{R}_i$	σ_i	σ_i^2	
1	.40	10%	9.80%	96.0%	$\sigma_{12} = -80\%$
2	.60	12	8.57	73.5	

The return on the loan portfolio is:

$$\bar{R}_p = .4\,(10\%) + .6\,(12\%) = 11.2\%$$

28. One objection to using MPT for loans is that the returns on individual loans are not normally or symmetrically distributed. In particular, most loans have limited upside returns and long-tail downside risks (see the discussion in Chapter 9). Nevertheless, default correlations in general are likely to be low. For example, the joint probability of two major companies such as General Motors and Ford defaulting on their loans at exactly the same time is quite small, even though they are both in the same industry.

Since loans are not publicly traded, assumptions have to be made about the returns, risks, and correlations among loans. For a full description of different approaches, see A. Saunders, *Credit Risk Measurement: New Approaches to Value at Risk and Other Paradigms* (New York: John Wiley & Sons, 1999).

29. CreditMetrics, released by J. P. Morgan and its co-sponsors (Bank of America, BZW, Deutsche Morgan Greenfell, Swiss Bank Corporation, Union Bank of Switzerland, and KMV Corporation) in 1997, is the first publicly available model that applies portfolio theory and value-at-risk methodology to evaluate credit risk across a broad range of instruments and portfolios of these instruments, including traditional loans, commitments, and letters of credit; fixed-income instruments; commercial contracts (such as trade credits and receivables); and derivative instruments (such as swaps, forwards, and futures). In general, CreditMetrics and other vendors have found that default correlations are low (in the zero to .3 range), suggesting considerable credit portfolio risk diversification possibilities.

30. Note that variance (σ^2) is measured in percent squared; standard deviation (σ) is measured in percent. Also, since the correlation coefficient, ρ_{12}, equals $\sigma_{12} / (\sigma_1 \times \sigma_2)$, then $\rho_{12} = -80/(9.8)(8.57) = -.95$.

while the risk of the portfolio is:

$$\sigma_p^2 = (.4)^2\,(96.0\%) + (.6)^2\,(73.5\%) + 2\,(.4)\,(.6)(-80\%) = 3.42\%$$

thus:

$$\sigma_p = \sqrt{3.42\%} = 1.85\%$$

Notice that the risk (or standard deviation of returns) of the portfolio, σ_p (1.85 percent), is less than the risk of either individual loan (9.8 percent and 8.57 percent, respectively). The negative covariance of the returns of the two loans (-80 percent) results in an overall reduction of risk when they are put together in an FI's portfolio.

Consider the advantages of diversification in Figure 21–1A. Note that A is an undiversified portfolio with heavy investment concentration in just a few loans. By fully exploiting diversification potential with loans whose returns are negatively correlated or that have a low positive correlation with those in the existing portfolio, the FI manager can lower the credit risk on the portfolio from σ_{pA} to σ_{pB} while earning the same expected return. That is, portfolio B is the "efficient" (lowest risk) portfolio associated with portfolio return level $\bar{R}_p$. By varying the required portfolio return level $\bar{R}_p$ up and down, the manager can identify an entire frontier of efficient portfolio mixes of loans. Each portfolio mix is efficient in the sense that it offers the lowest risk level to the FI manager at each possible level of portfolio returns. As Figure 21–1A indicates, however, of all possible efficient portfolios that can be generated, portfolio B produces the lowest possible risk level for the FI manager—that is, it maximizes the gains from diversifying across all available loans so that the manager cannot reduce the risk of the portfolio below σ_{pB}. For this reason, σ_{pB} is usually considered the **minimum risk portfolio**.

minimum risk portfolio

A portfolio for which a combination of assets reduces the variance of portfolio returns to the lowest feasible level.

Even though B is clearly the minimum *risk* portfolio, it does not generate the highest returns. Consequently, portfolio B may be chosen only by the most risk-averse FI managers, whose sole objective is to minimize portfolio risk regardless of the portfolio's return. Most portfolio managers have some desired return–risk trade-off in mind;

Figure 21–1A   FI Portfolio Diversification

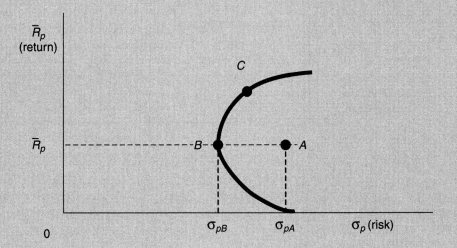

they are willing to accept more risk if they are compensated with higher expected returns.[31] One such possibility would be portfolio C in Figure 21–1A. This is an efficient portfolio because the FI manager has mixed loans to produce a portfolio risk level that is a minimum for that higher expected return level. This portfolio dominates all other portfolios that can produce the same expected return level.[32]

[31]The point that is chosen depends on the manager's risk aversion and the degree of separation of ownership from control. If the FI is managed by agents who perform the task of maximizing the value of the firm, they act as risk-neutral agents. They would know that stockholders who are well diversified could, through homemade diversification, hold the shares of many firms to eliminate borrower-specific risk. Thus, managers would seek to maximize expected return subject to any regulatory constraints on risk-taking behavior (i.e., they would likely pick a point in the region C in Figure 21–1A). However, if managers are risk averse because of their human capital invested in the FI and make lending decisions based on their own risk preferences rather than those of the stockholders, they are likely to choose a relatively low-risk portfolio, something closer to the minimum risk portfolio.

[32]For a detailed discussion of portfolio risk calculation, see R. A. Brealey, S. C. Myers, and A. J. Marcus, *Fundamentals of Corporate Finance* (New York: McGraw-Hill, 1999), pp. 225–29.

Managing Risk on *the* Balance Sheet II: Liquidity Risk

Chapter Navigator

1. What are the causes of liquidity risk?

2. What two methods do financial institutions use to manage liquidity risk?

3. How do banks measure liquidity risk?

4. What are the components of a liquidity plan?

5. Why do abnormal deposit drains occur?

6. To what extent are insurance companies exposed to liquidity risk?

7. To what extent are mutual funds exposed to liquidity risk?

Liquidity Risk Management: Chapter Overview

This chapter looks at the problems created by liquidity risk. Unlike other risks that threaten the very solvency of an FI, liquidity risk is a normal aspect of the everyday management of an FI. In extreme cases, liquidity risk problems develop into solvency risk problems (see In the News box 22–1). Moreover, some FIs are more exposed to liquidity risk than others. At one extreme, depository institutions are highly exposed; at the other extreme, mutual and pension funds and property-casualty insurance companies have relatively low liquidity risk exposure. We examine the reasons for these differences in this chapter.

Do You Understand?

1. What the main reasons were for the failure of Bank of New England?

In the News

Public's Confidence in Bank System Tested

The weekend run on Bank of New England (BNE) and its subsequent seizure by the government underscore the public's fragile confidence in the banking system. While the large increase in troubled loans announced last Friday apparently prompted large withdrawals, the insolvency of Rhode Island's private deposit insurance fund earlier in the week and large losses reported in the national deposit fund played a role as well. "The psychological atmosphere in New England following the Rhode Island debacle is not good," said William Isaac, head of the Secura Group, a Washington consulting firm. Bert Ely, a financial consultant based in Alexandria, VA, chalked it up to "jitteriness, uncertainty and confusion . . . I think we're

asking too much of people to worry about how sound their bank is," he said. Ely called the seizure a "terrible comment on the bank regulatory process."

To some extent, the run and seizure were unexpected, even though analysts noted that Bank of New England has been the nation's largest problem bank for the past year. The bank also had recently worked out a deal to swap some of its debt for equity. Yet, analysts said, failure may have been inevitable. "Failure was in the cards," said Gerard Cassidy, a banking analyst with Tucker Anthony based in Portland, Maine. "And the FDIC played them this weekend." "They were somewhat of an aberration in their

lending and the way they ran the institution," said Ely . . . "They were not representative of the New England banks, and New England is not representative of the rest of the country." After years as the region's most aggressive real estate lender, BNE was particularly hard hit when that market headed south, analysts said. The large increase in troubled loans BNE reported Friday was mainly due to real estate and effectively wiped out its capital . . .

All of BNE's depositors will be covered by deposit insurance, regardless of the amount. By contrast, the larger depositors at Freedom National Bank in Harlem, formerly the nation's largest minority-owned bank, got only 50 cents for each $1 above $100,000. But some of that money may be recovered after assets are sold, according to regulators.

Source: *Investor's Daily*, January 8, 1991, p. 1, Karen Padley.

www.investors.com/

1 Causes of Liquidity Risk

There are two types of liquidity risk. The first type arises when an FI's liability holders, such as depositors or insurance policyholders, seek to cash in or withdraw their financial claims. The second type arises when commitments made by the FI and recorded off the balance sheet, such as loan commitments, are exercised by the commitment holder. Upon exercise, the commitment becomes an asset on the FI's balance sheet.

Table 22–1 Adjusting to a Deposit Withdrawal Using Asset Sales
(in millions)

Before the Withdrawal				After the Withdrawal			
Assets		**Liabilities/Equity**		**Assets**		**Liabilities/Equity**	
Cash assets	$ 10	Deposit	$ 90	Cash assets	$ 0	Deposits	$70
Nonliquid assets	90	Equity	10	Nonliquid assets	70	Equity	0
	$100		$100		$70		$70

fire-sale price

The price received for an asset that has to be liquidated (sold) immediately.

With respect to the first type of liquidity risk, when liability holders withdraw their financial claims, the FI needs to meet these withdrawals by borrowing additional funds or selling assets so as to generate cash. Although most assets can be turned into cash eventually, for some assets this can only be done at high transaction costs. For example, the price that an asset holder must accept for the immediate sale of an asset may be far less than he or she would receive with a longer horizon over which to negotiate the sale. Thus, some assets may be liquidated only at low or **fire-sale prices**. If asset sale prices are insufficient to meet all the cash liquidity needs to meet liability withdrawals, the FI is effectively insolvent.

To understand the connection between liquidity risk and insolvency risk, consider the simple FI balance sheet in Table 22–1. Before deposit withdrawals, the FI has $10 million in cash assets and $90 million in nonliquid assets. These assets were funded with $90 million in deposits and $10 million in owner's equity. Suppose that depositors unexpectedly withdrew $20 million in deposits (perhaps due to the release of negative news about the profits of the FI) and the FI receives no new deposits to replace them. To meet these deposit withdrawals, the FI first uses the $10 million it has in cash assets and then seeks to sell some of its nonliquid assets to raise an additional $10 million in cash. Assume that the FI cannot borrow any more funds in the short-term money markets (see Chapter 5), and because it cannot wait to get better prices for its assets in the future (as it needs the cash now to meet immediate depositor withdrawals), the FI has to sell any nonliquid assets at 50 cents on the dollar. Thus, to cover the remaining $10 million in deposit withdrawals, the FI must sell $20 million in nonliquid assets, incurring a loss of $10 million from the face value of those assets. The FI must then write off any such losses against its capital or equity funds. Since its capital was only $10 million before the deposit withdrawal, the loss on the fire-sale of assets of $10 million leaves the FI economically insolvent (i.e., with zero equity capital or net worth).

The second type of liquidity risk arises directly from the effect on the asset side of the balance sheet of an exercise of off-balance-sheet loan commitments. As we described in Chapter 13, a loan commitment allows a customer to borrow (take down) funds on demand from an FI. When a borrower draws on its loan commitment, it creates a need for liquidity by the FI, since the FI is contractually obliged to supply (loanable) funds to the customer immediately. As was the case for liability withdrawals, an FI can meet such liquidity needs either by running down its cash assets, selling off other assets to raise cash, or borrowing additional funds in the money markets.

Do You Understand?

1. What the sources of liquidity risk are?
2. What the phrase "liquidating assets at fire-sale prices" means?

Liquidity Risk and Depository Institutions

Liability Side Liquidity Risk

As discussed in Chapter 11, a depository institution's balance sheet typically has a large amount of short-term liabilities, such as demand deposits and other transaction

Figure 22–1   Distribution of an FI's Net Deposit Drains (cash outflows)

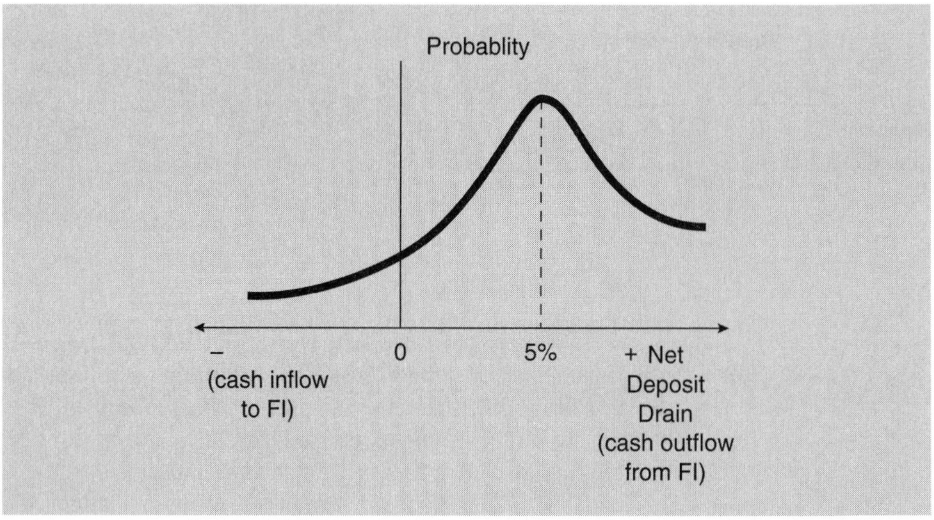

accounts (discussed in Chapter 13), which fund relatively long-term, relatively illiquid assets such as commercial loans and mortgages. Demand deposit accounts and other transaction accounts are contracts that give the holders the right to put their financial claims back to the depository institution on any given day and demand immediate repayment of the face value in cash.[1] Thus, an individual demand deposit account holder with a balance of $10,000 can demand cash to be repaid immediately in cash as can a corporation with $100 million in its demand deposit account. In theory, at least, a depository institution that has 20 percent of its liabilities in demand deposits and other transaction accounts must stand ready to pay out that amount by liquidating an equivalent amount of assets (or borrowing additional funds) on any given banking day.

In reality, a depository institution knows that *normally* only a small proportion of its demand deposits will be withdrawn on any given day. Most demand deposits remain with the FI, thus behaving as **core deposits** on a day-by-day basis, providing a relatively stable or long-term source of funding for the depository institution. Moreover, deposit withdrawals may in part be offset by the inflow of new deposits. The depository institution manager must monitor the resulting net deposit withdrawals or **net deposit drains**. Specifically, over time a depository institution manager can normally predict—with a good degree of accuracy—the probability of different-sized net deposit drains (the difference between deposit withdrawals and deposit additions) on any given banking day.

Consider the distribution of net deposit drains shown in Figure 22–1. This distribution is assumed to be strongly peaked at the 5 percent net (deposit) withdrawal level—this FI expects approximately 5 percent of its net deposit funds to be withdrawn on any given day with the highest probability. A net deposit drain means that an FI is receiving insufficient additional deposits (and other cash inflows) to offset deposit withdrawals, which means that the liability side of its balance sheet is contracting (see Table 22–2, which illustrates a 5 percent, equal to $5 million, net deposit drain).

core deposits

Deposits that provide a relatively stable, long-term funding source to a depository institution.

net deposit drain

The amount by which cash withdrawals exceed additions; a net cash outflow.

---

1. Accounts with this type of put option include demand deposits, NOW accounts (checking accounts with minimum balance requirements), and money market accounts (checking accounts with minimum balance and restrictions as to the number of checks written). We describe these accounts in more detail in Chapter 13. Banks typically liquidate savings account contracts immediately upon request of the customer. Many savings account contracts, however, give a bank some powers to delay withdrawals by requiring notification of withdrawal a certain number of days before withdrawal or by imposing penalty fees such as loss of interest.

Table 22–2 The Effect of Net Deposit Drains on the Balance Sheet
(in millions)

Before the Drain				After the Drain			
Assets		**Liabilities/Equity**		**Assets**		**Liabilities/Equity**	
Cash assets	$ 10	Deposits	$ 70	Cash assets	$ 10	Deposits	$65
Nonliquid assets	90	Borrowed funds	10	Nonliquid assets	90	Borrowed funds	10
		Equity	20			Equity	20
	$100		$100		$100		$95

Table 22–3 Adjusting to a Deposit Drain by Purchasing Funds
(in millions)

Assets		**Liabilities/Equity**	
Cash assets	$ 10	Deposits	$ 65
Nonliquid assets	90	Borrowed funds	15
		Equity	20
	$100		$100

An FI can manage a drain on deposits in two major ways: (1) purchased liquidity management, and/or (2) stored liquidity management. Traditionally, FI managers relied on *stored liquidity* as the primary mechanism of liquidity management. Today, many FIs—especially the largest banks with access to the money market and other nondeposit markets for funds—rely on *purchased liquidity*.

Purchased Liquidity. An FI manager who purchases liquidity to offset a deposit drain turns to the markets for purchased funds, such as the federal funds market and/or the repurchase (repo) agreement markets (discussed in Chapter 5),[2] which are interbank markets for short-term loans. Alternatively, an FI manager could issue additional fixed-maturity certificates of deposit (see Chapter 13) or additional notes and bonds.[3] In our example, as long as the total amount of the funds raised equals $5 million, the FI in Table 22–2 could fully fund its net deposit drain. This can be expensive for the FI, however, since it is paying *market rates* for funds to offset net drains on low interest-bearing deposits.[4] Thus, the higher the cost of purchased funds relative to the rates earned on assets, the less attractive this approach to liquidity management becomes. Further, since most of these funds are not covered by deposit insurance, their availability may be limited should the FI incur insolvency difficulties. Table 22–3 shows the FI's balance sheet if it responds to deposit drains by using purchased liquidity techniques.

Note that purchased liquidity has allowed the FI to maintain its overall balance sheet size of $100 million without disturbing the size and composition of the asset side of its balance sheet—that is, the complete adjustment to the deposit drain occurs on the liability side of the balance sheet. In other words, purchased liquidity management can

2. Securities companies and institutional investors use the repo market extensively for liquidity management purposes.

3. The *discount window* is also a source of funds, but in emergency situations only. See the section on Bank Runs, the Discount Window, and Deposit Insurance in this chapter for more discussion of the role of the discount window.

4. Although checking accounts pay no explicit interest, other transaction accounts such as NOW and money market accounts do. However, the rates paid are normally slow to adjust to changes in market interest rates and lie below purchased fund rates.

Table 22–4   Composition of an FI's Balance Sheet
  (in millions)

Assets		Liabilities/Equity	
Cash assets	$ 9	Deposits	$ 70
Nonliquid assets	91	Borrowed funds	10
		Equity	20
	$100		$100

Table 22–5   Reserve Asset Adjustment to Deposit Drain
  (in millions)

Assets		Liabilities/Equity	
Cash assets	$ 4	Deposits	$65
Nonliquid assets	91	Borrowed funds	10
		Equity	20
	$95		$95

insulate the asset side of the balance sheet from normal drains on the liability side of the balance sheet. This is one of the reasons for the enormous growth of FI-purchased liquidity techniques and associated purchased fund markets such as fed funds, repurchase agreements, and CDs. (We described and discussed these instruments and markets in Chapter 5.)

Stored Liquidity.   Instead of meeting the net deposit drain by purchasing liquidity in the money markets, the FI could use or sell off some of its assets (or utilize its stored liquidity). U.S. banks traditionally have held or "stored" cash reserves in their vaults and at the Federal Reserve for this very purpose. The Federal Reserve sets minimum requirements for the cash reserves that banks must hold (see Chapter 14).[5] Even so, banks still tend to hold cash reserves in excess of the minimum required amount to meet liquidity drains.

Suppose in our example that on the asset side of the balance sheet the FI normally holds $9 million of its assets in cash (of which $3 million are to meet Federal Reserve minimum reserve requirements and $6 million is an "excess" cash reserve). We depict the situation before the net drain in liabilities in Table 22–4. As depositors withdraw $5 million in deposits, the FI meets this by using the excess cash stored in its vaults or held on deposit at other FIs or at the Federal Reserve. If the reduction of $5 million in deposit liabilities is met by a $5 million reduction in cash assets held by the FI, its balance sheet is as shown in Table 22–5.

When the FI uses its cash as the liquidity adjustment mechanism, both sides of its balance sheet contract. In this example, both the FI's total assets and liabilities shrink from $100 to $95 million. The cost to the FI of using stored liquidity, apart from decreased asset size,[6] is that it must hold excess noninterest-bearing assets in the form of cash on its balance sheet.[7] Thus, the cost of using cash to meet liquidity needs is the

5. Currently, the Fed requires a minimum 3 percent cash reserve on the first $44.3 million and 10 percent on the rest of a bank's demand deposit and transaction account holdings. The $44.3 million figure is adjusted annually along with the increase or decrease in bank deposits. The first $5.0 million of the $44.3 million is not subject to reserve requirements. See Chapter 14.

6. There is no empirical evidence supporting a significant positive correlation between a bank's asset size and its profits.

7. FIs could hold highly liquid interest-bearing assets such as T-bills, but they are still less liquid than cash, and immediate liquidation may result in some small capital value losses.

Table 22–6   The Effects of a Loan Commitment Exercise
(in millions)

Before				After			
Cash assets	$ 9	Deposits	$ 70	Cash assets	$ 9	Deposits	$ 70
Nonliquid		Borrowed funds	10	Nonliquid		Borrowed funds	10
assets	91	Equity	20	assets	96	Equity	20
	$100		$100		$105		$100

Table 22–7   Adjusting the Balance Sheet to a Loan Commitment Exercise
(in millions)

Liability Management				Cash Reserve Asset Adjustment			
Cash assets	$ 9	Deposits	$ 70	Cash assets	$ 4	Deposits	$ 70
Nonliquid		Borrowed funds	15	Nonliquid		Borrowed funds	10
assets	96	Equity	20	assets	96	Equity	20
	$105		$105		$100		$100

forgone return (or opportunity cost) of being unable to invest these funds in loans and other higher income-earning assets.

Finally, note that although stored liquidity management and purchased liquidity management are alternative strategies for meeting deposit drains, an FI can combine the two methods by using some purchased liquidity management and some stored liquidity management to meet any given deposit drain. Moreover, an FI can sell off its noncash assets to generate additional cash reserves to meet liquidity needs.

Asset Side Liquidity Risk

Just as deposit drains can cause an FI liquidity problems, so can the exercise by borrowers of their loan commitments and other credit lines. Table 22–6 shows the effect of a $5 million exercise of a loan commitment by a borrower. As a result, the FI must fund $5 million in additional loans on the balance sheet. Consider the Before columns in Table 22–6 (the balance sheet before the commitment exercise) and the After columns (the balance sheet after the exercise). In particular, the exercise of the loan commitment means that the FI needs to provide $5 million immediately to the borrower (other assets increase from $91 to $96 million). This can be done by either purchased liquidity management (borrowing an additional $5 million in the money market and lending these funds to the borrower) or by stored liquidity management (decreasing the bank's excess cash assets from $9 million to $4 million). We present these two policies in Table 22–7. The next section illustrates several methods for measuring an FI's liquidity exposure that take into account its excess cash reserves and its ability to raise additional purchased funds.

Measuring a Bank's Liquidity Exposure

Sources and Uses of Liquidity.   As discussed above, a bank's liquidity risk can arise either from a drain on deposits or from new loan demands, and the subsequent need to meet these demands by liquidating assets or borrowing funds. Therefore, a bank manager must be able to measure its liquidity position on a daily basis, if possible. A useful tool is a *net liquidity statement*, which lists sources and uses

Table 22–8   Net Liquidity Position
(in millions)

Sources of Liquidity	
1. Total cash-type assets	$ 2,000
2. Maximum borrowed funds limit	12,000
3. Excess cash reserves	500
Total	$14,500
Uses of Liquidity	
1. Funds borrowed	$ 6,000
2. Federal Reserve borrowing	1,000
Total	7,000
Total net liquidity	$ 7,500

of liquidity and, thus, provides a measure of a bank's net liquidity position. Such a statement for a hypothetical U.S. money center bank is presented in Table 22–8.

The bank can obtain liquid funds in three ways. First, it can sell its liquid assets such as T-bills immediately with little price risk and low transaction costs. Second, it can borrow funds in the money/purchased funds market up to a maximum amount (this is an internal guideline based on the manager's assessment of the credit limits that the purchased or borrowed funds market is likely to impose on the bank). Third, it can use any excess cash reserves over and above the amount held to meet regulatory imposed reserve requirements. The bank's *sources* of liquidity total $14,500 million. Compare this to the bank's *uses* of liquidity—in particular, the amount of borrowed or purchased funds it has already utilized (e.g., fed funds, RPs borrowed) and the amount of cash it has already borrowed from the Federal Reserve through discount window loans. These total $7,000 million. As a result, the bank has a positive net liquidity position of $7,500 million. These liquidity sources and uses can be tracked easily on a day-by-day basis.

Peer Group Ratio Comparisons.   Another way to measure a bank's liquidity exposure is to compare certain of its key ratios and balance sheet features—such as loans-to-deposits, borrowed funds-to-total assets, and commitments to lend-to-assets ratios—with those for banks of a similar size and geographic location (see Chapter 13). A high ratio of loans to deposits and borrowed funds to total assets means that the bank relies heavily on the short-term money market rather than on core deposits to fund loans. This could mean future liquidity problems if the bank is at or near its borrowing limits in the purchased funds market. Similarly, a high ratio of loan commitments to assets indicates the need for a high degree of liquidity to fund any unexpected takedowns of these loans by customers—high-commitment banks often face more liquidity risk exposure than do low-commitment banks.

Table 22–9 lists the 1997 values of these ratios for the banks we reviewed in Chapter 13: North Fork Bancorp (NFB) and Bank One Corporation (BOC). Neither of these banks relied heavily on borrowed funds (short-term money market instruments) to fund loans. Their ratio of borrowed funds to total assets was 27.25 percent and 19.61 percent, respectively. Their ratio of core deposits (the stable deposits of the FI, such as demand deposits, NOW accounts, MMDAs, other savings accounts, and retail CDs) to total assets, on the other hand, was 64.11 percent and 60.62 percent, respectively. Furthermore, NFB had a ratio of loan commitments to total assets of only 6.77 percent, while BOC had a ratio of 82.38 percent. Thus, BOC was exposed to substantially greater liquidity risk from unexpected takedowns of these commitments.

Table 22–9 Liquidity Exposure Ratios for Two Banks, 1997 Values

	North Fork Bancorp	Bank One Corporation
Borrowed funds to total assets	27.25%	19.61%
Core deposits to total assets	64.11	60.62
Loans to deposits	80.32	105.71
Commitments to lend to total assets	6.77	82.38

Liquidity Index. A third way to measure liquidity risk is to use a liquidity index. This index measures the potential losses a bank could suffer from a sudden or fire-sale disposal of assets compared to the amount it would receive at a fair market value established under normal market conditions. The larger the differences between immediate fire-sale asset prices (P_i) and fair market prices (P_i^*), the less liquid is the bank's portfolio of assets. Define an index I such that:

$$I = \sum_{i=1}^{N} [(w_i)(P_i/P_i^*)]$$

where

w_i = Percentage of each asset in the FI's portfolio
$\Sigma w_i = 1$

Example 22–1 Calculation of the Liquidity Index

Suppose that a bank has two assets: 50 percent in one-month Treasury bills and 50 percent in real estate loans. If the bank must liquidate its T-bills today (P_1), it receives $99 per $100 of face value; if it can wait to liquidate them on maturity (in one month's time), it will receive $100 per $100 of face value ($P_1^*$). If the bank has to liquidate its real estate loans today, it receives $85 per $100 of face value ($P_2$); liquidation at the end of one month (closer to maturity) will produce $92 per $100 of face value ($P_2^*$). Thus, the one-month liquidity index value for this bank's asset portfolio is:

$$I = (\tfrac{1}{2})(.99/1.00) + (\tfrac{1}{2})(.85/.92)$$
$$= 0.495 + 0.462$$
$$= 0.957$$

Suppose alternatively that a slow or thin real estate market caused the bank to be able to liquidate the real estate loans at only $65 per $100 of face value ($P_2$). The one-month liquidity index for the bank's asset portfolio is:

$$I = (\tfrac{1}{2})(.99/1.00) + (\tfrac{1}{2})(.65/.92)$$
$$= 0.495 + 0.353$$
$$= 0.848$$

The value of the one-month liquidity index decreases due to the larger discount on the fire-sale price—from the fair (full value) market price of real estate—over the one-month period. The larger the discount from fair value, the smaller the liquidity index or higher the liquidity risk the bank faces.[8]

8. The liquidity index is always between 0 and 1. The liquidity index for this bank could be compared with similar indexes calculated for a group of similar banks.

financing gap

The difference between a bank's average loans and average (core) deposits.

financing requirement

The financing gap plus a bank's liquid assets.

Financing Gap and the Financing Requirement. A fourth way to measure liquidity risk exposure is to determine the bank's financing gap. As we discussed earlier, even though demand depositors can withdraw their funds immediately, they do not do so in normal circumstances. On average, most demand deposits stay at banks for quite long periods, often two years or more.[9] Thus, a banker often thinks of the average deposit base, including demand deposits, as a core source of funds that over time can fund a bank's average amount of loans. We define a **financing gap** as the difference between a bank's average loans and average (core) deposits, or:

$$\text{Financing gap} = \text{Average loans} - \text{Average deposits}$$

If this financing gap is positive, the bank must fund it by using its cash and liquid assets and/or borrowing funds in the money market. Thus:

$$\text{Financing gap} = -\text{Liquid assets} + \text{Borrowed funds}$$

We can write this relationship as:

$$\text{Financing gap} + \text{Liquid assets} = \text{Financing requirement (borrowed funds)}$$

As expressed in this fashion, the liquidity and managerial implications of the **financing requirement** (the financing gap plus a bank's liquid assets) are that the level of core deposits and loans as well as the amount of liquid assets determines the bank's borrowing or purchased fund needs.[10] In particular, the larger a bank's financing gap and liquid asset holdings, the higher the amount of funds it needs to borrow in the money markets and the greater is its exposure to liquidity problems from such a reliance.

The balance sheet in Table 22–10 indicates the relationship between the financing gap, liquid assets, and the borrowed funds financing requirement. See also the following equation:

$$\underset{(\$5 \text{ million})}{\text{Financing gap}} + \underset{(\$5 \text{ million})}{\text{Liquid assets}} = \underset{(\$10 \text{ million})}{\text{Financing requirement}}$$

A widening financing gap can warn of future liquidity problems for a bank since it may indicate increased deposit withdrawals (core deposits falling below $20 million in Table 22–10) and increasing loans due to more exercise of loan commitments (loans rising above $25 million). If the bank does not reduce its liquid assets—they stay at $5 million—the manager must resort to more money market borrowings. As these borrowings rise, sophisticated lenders in the money market may be concerned about the bank's creditworthiness. They may react by imposing higher risk premiums on borrowed funds or establishing stricter credit limits by not rolling over funds lent to the bank. If the bank's financing requirements dramatically exceed such limits, it may become insolvent. A good example of an excessive financing requirement resulting in bank insolvency is the failure of Continental Illinois in 1984 (see Chapter 20). This possibility of insolvency also highlights the need for bank managers to engage in active liquidity planning to avoid such crises.

Liquidity Planning. Liquidity planning is a key component in measuring (and being able to deal with) liquidity risk and its associated costs. Specifically, liquidity planning allows managers to make important borrowing priority decisions before liquidity problems arise. Such forward planning can lower the cost of funds (by determining an optimal funding mix) and can minimize the amount of excess reserves that a bank needs to hold.

---

9. See Federal Reserve Board of Governors, "Risk-Based Capital and Interest Rate Risk," press release, July 30, 1992.

10. The bank holds cash and liquid assets to meet day-to-day variations in the actual level of deposits and loans. On any given day, however, cash and liquid asset balances may exceed those needed to meet daily variations in deposits and loans. These excess balances may be run down to fund the financing gap.

Table 22–10 The Financing Requirement of a Bank
(in millions)

Assets		Liabilities	
Loans	$25	Core deposits	$20
Financing gap	**(5)**		
Liquid assets	5	Financing requirement (borrowed funds)	10
Total	$30	Total	$30

www.bog.frb.fed.us/

www.fdic.gov/

www.ots.treas.gov/

A liquidity plan has a number of components. The first component is the delineation of managerial details and responsibilities. Responsibilities are assigned to key management personnel should a liquidity crisis occur; the plan identifies those managers responsible for interacting with various regulatory agencies such as the Federal Reserve, the FDIC, and Office of Thrift Supervision (OTS). It also specifies areas of managerial responsibility in disclosing information to the public, including depositors. The second component of a liquidity plan is a detailed list of fund providers most likely to withdraw as well as the pattern of fund withdrawals. For example, in a crisis, financial institutions such as mutual funds and pension funds are more likely than correspondent banks and small business corporations to withdraw funds quickly from banks and thrifts. In turn, correspondent banks and small corporations are more likely than individual depositors to withdraw funds quickly. This makes liquidity exposure sensitive to the effects of future funding composition changes. In addition, FIs such as depository institutions face particularly heavy seasonal withdrawals of deposits in the quarter before Christmas. The third component of liquidity planning is the identification of the size of potential deposit and fund withdrawals over various time horizons in the future (one week, one month, one quarter, etc.) as well as alternative private market funding sources to meet such withdrawals (e.g., emergency loans from other FIs and the Federal Reserve). The fourth component of the plan sets internal limits on separate subsidiaries' and branches' borrowings as well as bounds for acceptable risk premiums to pay in each market (fed funds, RPs, CDs, etc.). In addition, the plan details a sequencing of assets for disposal in anticipation of various degrees or intensities of deposit/fund withdrawals. Such a plan may evolve from a bank's asset-liability management committee and may be relayed to various key departments of the bank (e.g., the money desk and the treasury department) that play vital day-to-day roles in liability funding.

Consider, for example, Table 22–11. The data are for a bank that holds $250 million in deposits from mutual funds, pension funds, correspondent banks, small businesses, and individuals. The table includes the average and maximum expected withdrawals over the next one-week, one-month, and one-quarter periods. The liquidity plan for the bank outlines how to cover expected deposit withdrawals should they materialize. In this case, the bank will seek to cover expected deposit withdrawals over the next three months first with new deposits, then with the liquidation of marketable securities in its investment portfolio, then with borrowings from other FIs, and finally, if necessary, with borrowings from the Federal Reserve.

Liquidity Risk, Unexpected Deposit Drains, and Bank Runs

Under normal banking conditions, and with appropriate management planning, neither net deposit withdrawals or the exercise of loan commitments pose significant liquidity problems for banks. For example, even in December and the summer vacation season,

Table 22–11 Deposit Distribution and Possible Withdrawals Involved in a Bank's Liquidity Plan

(in millions)

Deposits		$250	
From:			
Mutual funds		60	
Pension funds		50	
Correspondent banks		15	
Small businesses		70	
Individuals		55	

Expected withdrawals	Average		Maximum
One week	$40		$105
One month	55		140
Three months	75		200

The sequence of deposit withdrawal funding	One week	One month	Three months
1. New deposits	$10	$35	$75
2. Investment portfolio asset liquidation	50	60	75
3. Borrowings from other FIs	30	35	45
4. Borrowings from Fed	15	10	5

when net deposit withdrawals are high, banks anticipate these *seasonal* effects by holding larger than normal excess cash reserves or borrowing more than normal on the wholesale money markets.

 Major liquidity problems can arise, however, if deposit drains are abnormally large and unexpected. Abnormal deposit drains may occur for a number of reasons, including:

1. Concerns about a bank's solvency relative to that of other banks.
2. Failure of a related bank, leading to heightened depositor concerns about the solvency of surviving banks (a *contagion effect*).
3. Sudden changes in investor preferences regarding holding nonbank financial assets (such as T-bills or mutual fund shares) relative to bank deposits.

In such cases, sudden and unexpected surges in net deposit withdrawals risk triggering a **bank run**, which could force a bank into insolvency.

bank run

A sudden and unexpected increase in deposit withdrawals from a bank.

Deposit Drains and Bank Run Liquidity Risk. At the core of bank run liquidity risk is the fundamental and unique nature of the demand deposit contract. Specifically, demand deposit contracts are first-come, first-served contracts in the sense that a depositor's place in line determines the amount he or she will be able to withdraw from a bank. For example, suppose that a bank has 100 depositors, each of whom deposited $1. Suppose that each has a reason to believe—correctly or incorrectly—that the bank has assets worth only $90 on its balance sheet (see Table 22–12). A frequent reason for depositors to believe this is the announcement of trouble in the bank's loan portfolio (refer again to In the News box 22–1).

As a result, each depositor has an incentive to be the first to go to the bank and to withdraw his or her $1 deposit because the bank pays depositors sequentially as it liquidates its assets. If it has $90 in assets, it can pay in full only the first 90 depositors

Table 22–12 Bank Run Incentives

Assets		Liabilities	
Assets	$90	Deposits	$100
			(100 × $1 each)

bank panic

A systemic or contagious run on the deposits of the banking industry as a whole.

in the line. The 10 depositors at the end of the line get *nothing at all*.[11] Thus, demand deposits are in essence either full-pay or no-pay contracts.

Because demand deposit contracts pay in full only a certain proportion of depositors when a bank's assets are valued at less than its deposits—and because depositors realize this—any line outside a bank encourages other depositors to join the line immediately even if they do not need cash today for normal consumption purposes. Thus, even the bank's core depositors, who really do not need to withdraw deposits for current consumption needs, rationally seek to withdraw their funds immediately when they observe a sudden increase in the lines at their bank.

The incentives for depositors to run first and ask questions later creates a fundamental instability in the banking system, in that an otherwise sound bank can be pushed into insolvency and failure by unexpectedly large depositor drains and liquidity demands. This is especially so in periods of contagious runs or **bank panics** (such as the panic involving the Ohio savings banks in 1985 discussed in Chapter 20 and the Russian banking crisis of 1998 discussed in In the News box 22–2) when depositors lose faith in the banking system as a whole and engage in a run on all banks in a banking system.

Bank Runs, the Discount Window, and Deposit Insurance

Regulators have recognized the inherent instability of the banking system due to the all-or-nothing payoff features of deposit contracts. As a result, regulatory mechanisms are in place to ease banks' liquidity problems and to deter bank runs and panics. The two major liquidity risk insulation mechanisms are *deposit insurance* and the *discount window*.

Deposit Insurance. Because of the serious effects that a contagious run on banks could have on the economy (e.g., inability to transfer wealth from period to period, inability to implement monetary policy, inability to allocate credit to various sectors of the economy in special need of financing—see Chapter 1), government regulators of depository institutions have established guarantee programs offering deposit holders varying degrees of insurance protection to deter runs. Specifically, if a deposit holder believes his or her claim is totally secure, even if the bank is in trouble, the holder has no incentive to run. The deposit holder's place in line no longer affects his or her ability to retrieve funds deposited in the bank.

www.fdic.gov/

When the deposit insurance contract was introduced in 1933, the level of coverage per depositor was $2,500. This coverage cap gradually rose over the years to $100,000 in 1980. The $100,000 cap concerns a depositor's beneficial interest and ownership of deposited funds. In actuality, by structuring deposit funds in a bank or thrift in a particular fashion, a depositor can achieve many times the $100,000 coverage cap on deposits. To see this, consider the different categories of deposit fund ownership available to an individual shown in Table 22–13. Each of these categories represents a

11. We assume no deposit insurance exists that guarantees payment of deposits or no discount window borrowing is available to fund a temporary need for funds. The presence of deposit insurance and the discount window alters the incentive to engage in a bank run, as we describe later in this chapter.

In the News

22-2

Banking Crisis Impacts Expatriates in Russia

Expatriates in Russia who did their banking at Russian banks spent weeks in August and September trying to find ways to get their money out. ATM machines worked only sporadically and dispensed only devalued rubles. There were long lines at banks. One employee of a Western law firm told Russia & Commonwealth she was borrowing money from friends to get by. Another had friends returning to Russia bring in hard currency for her to use. Another method has been to have money wired into the country from abroad. This works best when the money is wired to branches of Western banks, which are faring better in the crisis.

The Russian banks were hard-hit by the Kiriyenko government's Aug. 17 devaluation of the ruble, which turned into a free-fall when President Yelstin fired Kiriyenko and could not get

a new prime minister confirmed by the parliament for a month. The simultaneous restructuring of the T-bill debts that were primarily owed to major Russian banks was a second blow. The thin reed offered to the banks was a three-month moratorium on paying their external debts. The huge loss of liquidity and the unstable ruble exchange rate have forced banks to close down ATM machines and severely restrict the access of depositors to their funds.

Many Russian banks are highly indebted to foreign creditors and what foreign currency they possess will be needed to pay these loans. Therefore, banks have been very unwilling to allow depositors to withdraw hard currency from their accounts. Instead, the banks have offered to convert the hard currency to rubles—at a rate set by the bank—which leaves the depositors with little choice but to take out their savings in devalued rubles. Many

have done so, fearing that the longer they waited the less the rubles would be worth. Another poor option would be to obtain a written refusal to release hard currency from the bank and to start a law suit.

The Central Bank complicated the situation by recommending that certain major commercial banks that had become unstable enter into agreements with the government's Sberbank to transfer their private accounts there where they would be guaranteed by the government. The Central Bank's Sept. 2 recommendation applied to SBS-Agro, Menatep, Inkombank, Promstroybank, Mosbiznesbank and Most Bank and was accompanied by a threat to block their transactions with such accounts as of Sept. 3. The Central Bank also recommended that all banks with deposits totaling more than 300 million rubles also consider transferring their private accounts to Sberbank. The banks were given until Sept.19 to conclude an agreement with Sberbank determining when and how the accounts would be transferred. The banks were

(continues)

Source: *Russia and Commonwealth Business Law Report,* September 23, 1998. Reprinted by permission of the Russia and Commonwealth Business Law Report, September 1998, pp. 34–35. Copyright 1998, BNA International, Inc.

In the News continued

to seek written permission from depositors to transfer their accounts. Until such time as the accounts were transferred, they would be frozen.

At best, said Jacobs, depositors will receive 50 cents on the dollar when their accounts are unfrozen in mid-November. "But there were no guarantees

on the deposits," she reminded. "Depositors will be lucky if they recover anything at all."

Table 22–13   Deposit Ownership Categories

- Individual ownership, such as a simple checking account.
- Joint ownership, such as the savings account of a husband and wife.
- Revocable trusts, in which the beneficiary is a qualified relative of the settlor, and the settlor has the ability to alter or eliminate the trust.
- Irrevocable trusts whose beneficial interest is not subject to being altered or eliminated.
- Employee benefit plans whose interests are vested and thus not subject to being altered or eliminated.
- Public units—accounts of federal, state, and municipal governments.
- Corporations and partnerships.
- Unincorporated businesses and associates.
- Individual retirement accounts (IRAs).
- Keogh accounts.
- Executor or administrator accounts.
- Accounts held by banks in an agency or fiduciary capacity.

Source: U.S. Department of the Treasury, "Modernizing the Financial System: Recommendations for Safer More Competitive Banks" (Washington, D.C.: Treasury Department, February 1991). *www.ustreas.gov/*

distinct accumulation of funds toward the $100,000 insurance cap; the coverage ceiling is *per bank*. We give an example of how depositors can raise the coverage level by adopting certain strategies.

Example 22–2   Calculation of Insured Deposits

A married couple with one child and with Individual Retirement Account (IRA) and Keogh private pension plans for both the husband and the wife at the bank could accrue a total coverage cap of $800,000 as a family: his individual deposit account, her individual deposit account, their joint deposit account, their child's deposit account held in trust, his IRA account, his Keogh account, her IRA account, and her Keogh account. By expanding the range of ownership in this fashion, the coverage cap for a family per bank can rapidly approach $1 million or more.

www.bog.frb.fed.us/

The Discount Window.   In addition to deposit insurance, central banks such as the Federal Reserve have traditionally provided a discount window facility to meet banks' short-term nonpermanent liquidity needs (see the discussion in Chapters 4 and 14). Suppose that a bank has an unexpected deposit drain near the end of a reserve requirement

Table 22–14 The Spread between the Discount Rate and the Fed Funds Rate

	1990	1991	1992	1993	1994	1995	1996	1997	1998	1999
Federal funds	8.10	5.69	3.52	3.02	4.21	5.83	5.30	5.50	4.68	5.25
Discount window	6.98	5.45	3.25	3.00	3.60	5.21	5.02	5.00	4.50	4.75

Source: *Federal Reserve Bulletin,* Table A26, various *www.bog.frb.fed.us/*

period but cannot meet its reserve target (see Chapter 14). It can seek to borrow from the central bank's discount window facility. Alternatively, discount window loans can also meet short-term seasonal liquidity needs due to crop-planting cycles. Normally, banks make such loans by discounting short-term high-quality securities such as Treasury bills and banker's acceptances with the central bank. Banks that borrow from the discount window receive increased monitoring from the Federal Reserve. This often acts as a disincentive to banks using the discount window for "cheap" funding. The interest rate at which such securities are discounted is called the *discount rate* and is set by the central bank. In the United States, the central bank has traditionally set the discount rate below market rates, such as the overnight bank-determined federal funds rates, shown in Table 22–14.[12]

For a number of reasons, bank access to the discount window is unlikely to deter bank runs and panics the way deposit insurance does. The first reason is that to borrow from the discount window, a bank is required to pledge high-quality liquid assets (generally Treasury securities or federal agency securities) as collateral. Failing, highly illiquid banks are by definition unlikely to have such assets available to discount. The second reason is that unlike deposit insurance coverage, discount window borrowing is not automatic. Specifically, banks gain access to the window only on a "need-to-borrow" basis. If the Federal Reserve (Fed) considers that a borrowing request is the result of a profit motive because the discount rate is set below bank-determined fed fund rates, the Fed would refuse the borrowing request. That is, the Fed at its discretion makes discount window loans. Third, discount window loans are meant to provide temporary liquidity for inherently solvent banks, not permanent long-term support for otherwise insolvent banks.[13]

This narrow role of the discount window was confirmed in the 1991 FDICIA, which limited the discretion of the Federal Reserve in making extended loans to troubled banks. Specifically, the discount window is intended to mitigate the consequences of bank runs by averting the need for fire-sale losses and not necessarily to mitigate depositors' incentives to run. For example, loans to troubled, undercapitalized banks are limited to no more than 60 days in any 120-day period unless both the FDIC and the institution's primary regulator certify that the bank is viable. Additional extensions of up to 60 days are allowed subject to regulator certification. Finally, any discount window advances to undercapitalized banks that eventually fail would require the Federal Reserve to compensate the FDIC for incremental losses caused by the delay in keeping the troubled bank open longer than necessary. Consequently, the discount window is a partial, but not a full, substitute for deposit insurance as a liquidity stabilizing mechanism.

> **Do You Understand?**
>
> 1. The benefits and costs of using
>   (*a*) liability management and
>   (*b*) reserve or cash assets to meet
>   a deposit drain?
> 2. What the major sources of FI
>   liquidity are? What the two major
>   uses are?
> 3. What factors determine a bank's
>   financing requirement?
> 4. How to measure liquidity risk?

---

12. As the level of market rates drops, however, fed fund rates can lie below the discount rate. This occurred in October 1992, when the fed funds rate was 2.96 percent and the discount rate was 3 percent.

13. Note that all three of these reasons are the result of regulations set by U.S. regulators. If regulators and politicians want to use the discount window as a substitute for deposit insurance, it is within their jurisdiction to remove these barriers.

Liquidity Risk and Insurance Companies

Life Insurance Companies

surrender value

The amount that an insurance policyholder receives when cashing in a policy early.

Like banks, life insurance companies hold cash reserves and other liquid assets in order to meet policy cancellations (surrenders) and other working capital needs that arise in the course of writing insurance. The early cancellation of an insurance policy results in the insurer having to pay the insured the **surrender value** of that policy.[14] In the normal course of business, premium income and returns on an insurer's asset portfolio are sufficient to meet the cash outflows required when policyholders surrender their policies early (see Chapter 15). When premium income is insufficient to meet surrenders, however, a life insurer can sell some of its relatively liquid assets, such as government bonds. In this case, bonds act as a buffer or reserve asset source of liquidity for the insurer.

www.naic.org/

Nevertheless, concerns about the solvency of an insurer can result in a run in which new premium income dries up and existing policyholders as a group seek to cancel their policies by cashing them in early. To meet exceptional demands for cash, a life insurer could be forced to liquidate other assets in its portfolio, such as commercial mortgage loans and other securities, potentially at fire-sale prices.[15] Forced asset liquidations can push an insurer, like a bank, into insolvency. An insurance company run occurred in 1991 on First Capital, an $8.5 billion California-based insurer. With more than 300,000 life policies and 167,000 annuity policies, First Capital held more than 40 percent of its assets in junk bonds. Losses on its junk bond portfolio (estimated to be worth 75 cents on the dollar in May 1991) raised regulator and policyholder concerns about the quality of its balance sheet. New policyholder premiums dried up, and existing policyholders engaged in a run by seeking to cash in their policies for whatever surrender values they could obtain. Policy surrenders rose to $100 million on May 10, 1991 and totaled $265 million in the first two weeks of May 1991. To deter the run, the California state insurance regulator placed limits on the ability of existing policyholders to surrender their policies.

Property-Casualty Insurance Companies

As discussed in Chapter 15, property-casualty (PC) insurers sell policies insuring against certain contingencies impacting either real property or individuals. These contingencies are relatively short term and unpredictable, unlike those covered by life insurers. With the help of mortality tables, claims on life insurance policies are generally predictable. PC claims (such as those associated with Hurricane Andrew) are virtually impossible to predict. Thus, PC insurers have a greater need for liquidity than life insurers. As a result, PC insurers tend to hold shorter term, more liquid assets than do life insurers. PC insurers' contracts and premium-setting intervals are usually relatively short term as well, so that problems caused by policy surrenders are less severe. PC insurers' greatest liquidity exposure occurs when policyholders cancel or fail to renew policies with an insurer because of pricing, competition, or safety and solvency

14. A *surrender value* is usually some proportion or percentage less than 100 percent of the face value of the insurance contract. The surrender value continues to grow as funds invested in the policy earn interest (returns). Earnings to the policyholder are taxed if and when the policy is actually surrendered or cashed in before the policy matures. Some insurance companies have faced run problems resulting from their sale of guaranteed investment contracts (GICs). A GIC, similar to a long-term, fixed-rate bank deposit, is a contract between an investor and an insurance company. As market interest rates rose, many investors withdrew their funds early and reinvested elsewhere in higher return investments. This created both liquidity and refinancing problems for life insurers that supplied such contracts and eventually led to restrictions on withdrawals.

15. Life insurers also provide a considerable amount of loan commitments, especially in the commercial property area. As a result, they face asset side loan commitment liquidity risk in a similar fashion to banks.

concerns. This may cause an insurer's premium cash inflow, when added to its investment returns, to be insufficient to meet its policyholders' claims. Alternatively, large unexpected claims may materialize as a result of disasters such as Hurricane Andrew in 1991 and the East Coast "blizzard of the century" in 1996.[16]

Guarantee Programs for Life and Property-Casualty Insurance Companies

Both life insurance and property-casualty (PC) insurance companies are regulated at the state level (see Chapter 15). Unlike banks and thrifts, neither life nor PC insurers have a federal guarantee fund. Beginning in the 1960s, most states began to sponsor state guarantee funds for firms selling insurance in that state.[17] These state guarantee funds differ in a number of important ways from deposit insurance. First, although these programs are sponsored by state insurance regulators, they are actually run and administered by the private insurance companies themselves.

Second, unlike SAIF or BIF, in which the FDIC established a permanent reserve fund by requiring banks to pay annual premiums in excess of payouts to resolve failures, no such permanent guarantee fund exists for the insurance industry, with the sole exception of the PC and life guarantee funds in the state of New York. This means that contributions are paid into the guarantee fund by surviving firms only after an insurance company has failed.

Third, the size of the required contributions that surviving insurers make to protect policyholders in failed insurance companies differs widely from state to state. In those states that have guarantee funds, each surviving insurer is normally levied a pro rata amount, according to the size of its statewide premium income. This amount either helps pay off small policyholders after the assets of the failed insurer have been liquidated or acts as a cash injection to make the acquisition of a failed insurer attractive. The definition of small policyholders generally varies among states from $100,000 to $500,000.

Finally, because no permanent fund exists and the annual pro rata contributions are often legally capped, a delay usually occurs before small policyholders receive the cash surrender values of their policies or other payment obligations from the guarantee fund. (This contrasts with deposit insurance, which normally provides insured depositors immediate coverage of their claims.) For example, the failure of Executive Life Insurance in 1991 left approximately $117.3 million in outstanding claims in Hawaii. But the Hawaii life insurance guarantee fund can raise only $13.1 million a year due to legal caps on surviving firms' contributions. This means that it took nine years for surviving firms to meet the claims of Executive Life policyholders in Hawaii. In the failure of Baldwin United in 1983, the insurers themselves raised additional funds, over and above the guarantee fund, to satisfy policyholders' claims.

Thus, the private nature of insurance industry guarantee funds, their lack of permanent reserves, and low caps on annual contributions mean that they provide less credible protection to claimants than do

16. Claims also may arise in long-tail lines when a contingency takes place during the policy period but a claim is not lodged until many years later. As mentioned in Chapter 15, the claims regarding damage caused by asbestos contacts are in this category.

17. However, Louisiana, New Jersey, and Washington, D.C. have no fund for life insurance industry failures, and Colorado has only recently established one. However, New York has a permanent fund into which insurers pay premiums regardless of the failure rate.

bank and thrift insurance funds. As a result, the incentives for insurance policyholders to engage in a run, should they perceive that an insurer has asset quality problems or insurance underwriting problems, is quite strong even in the presence of such guarantee funds.

www.sec.gov/

Liquidity Risk and Mutual Funds

Mutual funds sell shares as liabilities to investors and invest the proceeds in assets such as bonds and equities. Open-end mutual funds must stand ready to buy back issued shares from investors, at their current market price or net asset value (see Chapter 18). A mutual fund's willingness to provide instant liquidity to shareholders while it invests funds in equities, bonds, and other long-term instruments could expose it to liquidity problems similar to those depository institutions face when the number of withdrawals (or in this case, mutual fund shares redeemed) rise to abnormally high or unexpected levels. Indeed, mutual funds can be subject to dramatic liquidity needs if investors become nervous about the true value of a mutual fund's assets.[18] If the market value of the underlying assets falls and is expected to continue to fall, fund holders will want to liquidate their positions as fast as possible. The fundamental difference in the way that mutual fund contracts are valued compared to the valuation of bank deposit contracts, however, mitigates the incentives for mutual fund shareholders to engage in depositlike runs. Specifically, if a mutual fund were to be closed and liquidated, its assets would be distributed to fund shareholders on an equal or pro rata basis rather than on the first-come, first-served basis employed under deposit and insurance policy contracts. All mutual fund shareholders realize this and know that investors share asset losses equally. As a result, being first in line to withdraw mutual fund shares, on any given day, has no overall advantage.[19] Of course, rapidly falling asset values will result in a greater incentive for investors to cash in their shares as quickly as possible before values fall any further. However, this rush, or run, by investors is due to a drop in the underlying value of their investments and not the threat of receiving nothing because they are not first in line to cash in.

Do You Understand?

1. What the impact would be on a bank's liquidity needs if it offered deposit contracts of an open-end mutual fund type rather than the traditional all-or-nothing demand deposit contract?

2. How the incentives of a mutual fund's investors to engage in runs compare with the incentives of bank depositors?

---

18. For example, the value of assets held by mutual funds specializing in the equities of Asian countries such as Indonesia and Thailand as well as Russia during the emerging market crises of 1997–1998.

19. For example, in the case of a bank run discussed earlier in the chapter, rather than the first 90 claimholders receiving full payment ($1 each) and the last 10 nothing, in the case of a mutual fund liquidation each of the 100 shareholders would receive a payout of $0.90 (or 90 cents) in this example.

Summary

This chapter provided an in-depth look at the measurement and on-balance-sheet management of liquidity risks. Liquidity risk is a common problem that FI managers face. Well-developed policies for holding liquid assets or having access to markets for purchased funds are normally adequate to meet liability withdrawals. Very large withdrawals, however, can cause asset liquidity problems to be compounded by incentives for liability claimholders to engage in runs at the first sign of a liquidity problem. The incentives for depositors and life insurance policyholders to engage in runs can push normally sound FIs into insolvency.

End-of-Chapter Questions

1. How does the asset side reason for liquidity risk differ from the liability side reason?

2. The probability distribution of the net deposit drain of an FI has been estimated to have a mean of 2 percent and a standard deviation of 1 percent.

   a. Is this FI increasing or decreasing in size? Explain.

   b. If an FI has a net deposit drain, what are the two ways it can offset this drain of funds? How do the two methods differ?

3. How is asset side liquidity risk likely to be related to liability side liquidity risk?

4. Why would an FI be forced to sell assets at fire-sale prices?

5. The AllStarBank has the following balance sheet

Assets (in millions)		Liabilities	
Cash	$ 30	Deposits	$ 90
Other assets	140	Borrowed funds	40
	$170	Other liabilities	40
			$170

   Its largest customer decides to exercise a $15 million loan commitment. Show how the new balance sheet changes if AllStar uses (a) asset management, or (b) liability management.

6. Assume that an FI has assets of $10 million consisting of $1 million in cash and $9 million in loans. It has core deposits of $6 million. It also has $2 million in subordinated debt and $2 million in equity. Increases in interest rates are expected to result in a net drain of $2 million in core deposits over the year.

   a. The average cost of deposits is 6 percent and the average cost of loans is 8 percent. The FI decides to reduce its loan portfolio to offset this expected decline in deposits. What is the cost and what will be the total asset size of the firm from this strategy after the drain?

   b. If the cost of issuing new short-term debt is 7.5 percent, what is the cost of offsetting the expected drain if it increases its liabilities? What will be the total asset size of the FI from this strategy after the drain?

7. Consider the balance sheet for an FI listed below:

Balance Sheet ($ millions)

Cash	$10	Deposits	$68
Loans	50	Equity	7
Securities	15		

   The FI is expecting a $15 million net deposit drain. Show the FI's balance sheet if under these two conditions:

   a. The FI purchases liabilities to offset this expected drain.

   b. The stored liquidity method is used to meet the liquidity shortfall.

8. What are four measures of liquidity risk?

9. The Acme Corporation has been acquired by the Conglomerate Corporation. To help finance the takeover, Conglomerate is going to liquidate the overfunded portion of Acme's pension fund. The assets listed below are going to be liquidated. Listed are their face values, liquidation values today, and their anticipated liquidation values one year from now (their fair market values).

Asset	Face Value	Current Liquidation Value	One-Year Liquidation Value
IBM stock	$10,000	$ 9,900	$10,500
GE bonds	5,000	4,000	4,500
Treasury securities	15,000	13,000	14,000

   Calculate the one-year liquidity index for these securities.

10. An FI has the following assets in its portfolio: $20 million in cash reserves with the Fed, $20 million in T-Bills, $50 million in mortgage loans, and $10 million in fixed assets. If it needs to dispose of its assets at short notice, it will receive only 99 percent of the fair market value of the T-Bills, 90 percent of the fair market value of its mortgage loans, and 0 percent of the fair market value of the fixed assets. Calculate the liquidity index using the above information.

11. A bank has $10 million in T-bills, a $5 million line of credit to borrow in the repo market, and $5 million in cash reserves with the Fed in excess of its required reserve requirements. It has also borrowed $6 million in federal funds and $2 million from the Federal Reserve's discount window to meet seasonal demands.

    a. What is the bank's total available (sources of) liquidity?

    b. What are the bank's total uses of liquidity?

    c. What is the net liquidity of the bank and what conclusions can you derive from the result?

12. What are the several components of an FI's liquidity plan? How can the plan help an FI reduce liquidity shortages?

13. The Plainbank has $10 million in cash and equivalents, $30 million in loans, and $15 in core deposits. Calculate (a) the financing gap and (b) the financing requirement.

14. How does federal deposit insurance help mitigate the problem of bank runs? What are some other elements of the safety net available to banks in the United States?

15. Why is access to the discount window of the Federal Reserve less effective as a deterrent for bank runs than deposit insurance?

16. How is the liquidity problem faced by mutual funds different from those of banks and insurance companies?

17. A mutual fund has the following assets in its portfolio: $40 million in fixed-income securities and $40 million in stocks at current market values. In the event of a liquidity crisis, it can sell its assets at a 96 percent discount if they are disposed of in two days. It will receive 98 percent if disposed of in four days. Two shareholders, A and B, own 5 percent and 7 percent of equity (shares), respectively.

    a. Market uncertainty has caused shareholders to sell their shares back to the fund. What will the two shareholders receive if the mutual fund must sell all its assets in two days? In four days?

    b. How does this differ from a bank run? How have bank regulators mitigated the problem of bank runs?

18. A mutual fund has $1 million in cash and $9 million invested in securities. It currently has 1 million shares outstanding.

    a. What is the NAV of this fund?

    b. Assume that some of the shareholders decide to cash in their shares of the fund. How many shares, at its current NAV, can the fund take back without resorting to a sale of assets?

    c. As a result of anticipated heavy withdrawals, it sells 10,000 shares of IBM stock currently valued at $40. Unfortunately, it receives only $35 per share. What is the net asset value after the sale? What are the fund's cash assets after the sale?

    d. Assume after the sale of IBM shares, 100,000 shares are sold back to the fund. What is the current NAV? Is there a need to sell more stocks to meet this redemption?

19. What is the greatest cause of liquidity exposure that property-casualty insurers face?

20. Go to the website of the Board of Governors of the Federal Reserve and update Table 22–14.

Managing Risk on *the* Balance Sheet III: Interest Rate *and* Insolvency Risk

Chapter Navigator

1. What is the repricing gap model used to measure interest rate risk?

2. What is the duration gap model used to measure interest rate risk?

3. What are the weaknesses of the repricing gap and duration gap models?

4. How does capital protect against credit risk and interest rate risk?

5. What causes the discrepancies between the book value and market value of equity?

Interest Rate and Insolvency Risk Management: Chapter Overview

In this third chapter on managing risk on an FI's balance sheet, we provide a detailed analysis of interest rate risk and insolvency risk. Chapter 20 established the fact that while performing their asset-transformation functions, financial institutions (FIs) often mismatch the maturities of their assets and liabilities. In so doing, they expose themselves to interest rate risk. For example, in the 1980s, a large number of thrifts suffered economic insolvency (i.e., the net worth or equity of their owners was eradicated) when interest rates unexpectedly increased. As discussed in In the News box 23–1, in recent years many small banks have been increasingly exposed to interest rate risk.

This chapter analyzes two methods used to measure an FI's interest rate risk exposure: the repricing model and the duration model. The repricing model examines the impact of interest rate changes on an FI's net interest income (NII). However, as we explain later in the chapter, the FI's duration gap is a more comprehensive measure of interest

In the News

23-1

And Don't Forget about Interest Rate Risk

I n the world of risk management, interest rate exposure is often viewed as a distant second in urgency to the risk that enough borrowers will default to cause earnings and capital problems. But while credit risk may be king, one company has news that may make bankers take notice of their rate risk.

According to Sheshunoff Information Services, community-based financial institutions have generally taken on more interest rate exposure in recent years. A Sheshunoff survey of 200 banks and thrifts found that a two-percentage-point move in rates—either up or down—would have caused the median net interest income at small banks to decline by 7.19% as of June 1998, compared to a 6% hit a year earlier. Though these banks' rate exposures had fallen by September—a 200-basis-point rate shock then would have prompted a 6.37% decline in net interest income—community banks still appear to be taking on more rate risk over the long run, said Robert

Colvin, a Sheshunoff managing director. "I think that this trend of added interest rate exposure will continue," he said. "That's because margins have been squeezed and banks will have to take on more risk to expand that margin." . . .

According to Mr. Colvin, small banks—to a greater degree than in the recent past—have been "mismatching" the maturities of their assets and liabilities in pursuit of higher spreads at a time when the yield curve is relatively flat. For example, a bank might lend at longer average maturities than normal to gain a little extra profit, thereby increasing the maturity gap between loans and deposits. While the strategy is quite common, a sharp and unexpected rise in interest rates would squeeze margins, since the shorter-maturity deposits would reprice upward more quickly than the loans.

Mr. Colvin said he sees the falloff in interest rate exposure from June to Sep-

tember last year as an aberration rather than a reversal of the trend. Based on conversations with bankers, he said, it appears an unusual number of loan prepayments led to a shortening of average loan maturities.

What are small banks doing to get a grip on their rate exposure? According to the Robert Morris Associates' report "Beating the Odds: a Community Banker's Guide to Risk Management," two-thirds of the small banks surveyed use a consultant or vendor-derived asset/liability model to aid in measuring rate risk. Banks most commonly measure interest rate gap, net interest margin, liquidity, and trends in interest-sensitive assets and liabilities. Most respondents in the study stress-tested their investment portfolios, yet only one-third stress-tested their commercial and industrial loans and commercial real estate loans.

At Amarillo National Bancorp in Texas, officials subject their balance sheet to a mock 200-basis-point rate shock. The results are currently no cause for worry, said Bill Ware, an executive vice president. "We

(continues)

Source: *American Banker*, March 15, 1999, p. 11A, by John Kimelman.

In the News continued

are in a stable inflation environment, and we don't think that interest rates will fluctuate that much," he said. "I have a lot of confidence in" Federal Reserve Board Chairman Alan Greenspan. Still, Mr. Ware argued that bankers must take measurement of interest rate risk more seriously, if only because regulators are focusing more on it than in the past. Said Sheshunoff's Mr. Colvin: "To do this well, you need more detailed analysis, and most banks don't do that."

rate risk exposure than the repricing gap. We also discuss in this chapter the measurement and on-balance-sheet management of interest rate risk.[1]

Insolvency risk is the result or consequence or an outcome of excessive amounts of one or more of the risks taken by an FI (e.g., liquidity risk, credit risk, and interest rate risk). Technically, insolvency occurs when the internal capital or equity resources of an FI's owners are at or near to zero as a result of bad balance sheet outcomes due to one or more of these risks.

Do You Understand?

1. What the trend in interest rate risk exposure by community-based banks in the late 1990s was?

Interest Rate Risk Measurement and Management

In this section, we analyze two methods used to measure an FI's interest rate risk: the repricing model and the duration gap model. The repricing model, sometimes called the funding gap model, concentrates on the impact of interest rate changes on an FI's net interest income (NII), which is the difference between an FI's interest revenue and interest expense (see Chapter 13), and thus the FI's profits. This contrasts with the market value–based duration gap model, which incorporates the impact of interest rate changes on the overall market value of an FI's balance sheet and ultimately on its owners' equity or net worth. Until recently, U.S. bank regulators had been content to base their evaluations of bank interest rate risk exposures on the repricing model alone. As discussed later in this chapter, regulators and other analysts now recognize the serious weaknesses of the repricing gap model. As a result, while the repricing gap is still used to measure interest rate risk in most FIs, it is increasingly being used in conjunction with the duration gap model.

Repricing Model

repricing or **funding gap**

The difference between those assets whose interest rates will be repriced or changed over some future period (RSAs) and liabilities whose interest rates will be repriced or changed over some future period (RSLs).

The **repricing** or **funding gap** model is essentially a book value accounting cash flow analysis of the interest revenue earned on an FI's assets and the interest expense paid on its liabilities (or its net interest income) over some particular period. For example, until recently, the Fed required quarterly reporting by commercial banks of repricing gaps for assets and liabilities with these maturities:

1. One day.
2. More than 1 day to 3 months.
3. More than 3 months to 6 months.
4. More than 6 months to 12 months.
5. More than 1 year to 5 years.
6. More than 5 years.

1. In Chapter 24, we examine how derivative securities can be used to hedge interest rate risk.

Table 23–1   Repricing Gaps for an FI
(in millions of dollars)

	Assets	Liabilities	Gaps
1. 1 day	$ 20	$ 30	$−10
2. More than 1 day–3 months	30	40	−10
3. More than 3 months–6 months	70	85	−15
4. More than 6 months–12 months	90	70	+20
5. More than 1 year–5 years	40	30	+10
6. More than 5 years	10	5	+5
	$260	$260	0

rate sensitivity

The time to repricing of an asset or liability.

The gap in each maturity bucket (or bin) is calculated by estimating the difference between the rate-sensitive assets (RSAs) and rate-sensitive liabilities (RSLs) on its balance sheet. **Rate sensitivity** means that the asset or liability is repriced (either because it matures and the funds will be rolled into a new asset or liability, or because it is a financial instrument with a variable interest rate) at or near current market interest rates within the maturity horizon of the bucket under consideration.

Refer to Table 23–1 to see how the assets and liabilities of an FI might be categorized into each of the six buckets according to their time to repricing. Although the cumulative repricing gap over the whole balance sheet must be zero by definition, the advantage of the repricing model lies in its information value and its simplicity in pointing to an FI's net interest income exposure (or profit exposure) to interest rate changes in each different maturity bucket.[2]

For example, suppose that an FI's report indicates a negative $10 million difference between assets and liabilities being repriced in one day (or the one-day bucket). Assets and liabilities that are repriced each day are likely to be interbank borrowings on the federal funds or repurchase agreement markets (see Chapter 5). Thus, a negative gap (RSA < RSL) indicates that a rise in these short-term rates would lower the FI's net interest income since the FI has more rate-sensitive liabilities than assets in that bucket. In other words, assuming equal changes in interest rates on RSAs and RSLs, interest expense will increase by more than interest revenue. Specifically, let:

ΔNII_i = Change in net interest income in the ith maturity bucket
GAP_i = Dollar size of the gap between the book value of rate-sensitive assets and rate-sensitive liabilities in maturity bucket i
ΔR_i = Change in the level of interest rates impacting assets and liabilities in the ith maturity bucket

Then:

$$\Delta NII_i = (GAP_i) \, \Delta R_i = (RSA_i - RSL_i) \, \Delta R_i$$

In this first bucket, if the gap is negative $10 million and short-term interest rates (such as the fed funds and/or repo rates) rise by 1 percent, the annualized change in the FI's future net interest income is:

$$\Delta NII = (-\$10 \text{ million}) \times .01 = -\$100,000$$

This approach is very simple and intuitive. We will see later in this section, however, that market or present-value losses (and gains) also occur on assets and liabilities when interest rates change. These effects are not accounted for in the funding gap model because asset and liability values are reported at their *historic* book values

2. We include equity capital as a long-term (over five years) liability.

rather than on a market value basis. Thus, in this model, interest rate changes affect only the current interest income earned and interest paid on an asset or liability.[3]

The FI manager can also estimate cumulative gaps (CGAP) over various repricing categories or buckets. A common cumulative gap of interest is the one-year repricing gap estimated from Table 23–1 as:

$$CGAP = (-\$10m.) + (-\$10m.) + (-\$15m.) + \$20m. = -\$15 \text{ million}$$

If ΔR_i is the average interest rate change affecting assets and liabilities that can be repriced within a year, the cumulative effect on the bank's net interest income is:

$$\Delta NII = (\sum_{i=1\text{-day}}^{1\text{-year}} RSA_i - \sum_{i=1\text{-day}}^{1\text{-year}} RSL_i) \Delta R_i$$

$$= (CGAP) \Delta R_i$$

$$= (-\$15 \text{ million})(.01) = -\$150,000$$

We next look at an example of calculating the cumulative one-year gap using an FI in the form of a commercial bank. Remember that the manager considers whether each asset or liability will, or can, have its interest rate changed within the next year. If it will or can, it is a rate-sensitive asset or liability; if not, it is a rate-insensitive asset or liability.

Measuring and Managing Interest Rate Risk Using the Repricing Gap. Consider the simplified bank balance sheet in Table 23–2. Rather than the original maturities, the reported maturities are those remaining on different assets and liabilities at the time the repricing gap is estimated.

Rate-Sensitive Assets. Looking down the asset side of the balance sheet in Table 23–2, we see the following one-year rate-sensitive assets (RSAs):

1. *Short-term consumer loans: $50 million*, which are repriced at the end of the year and just make the one-year cutoff.
2. *Three-month T-bills: $30 million*, which are repriced on maturity (rollover) every three months.
3. *Six-month T-notes: $35 million*, which are repriced on maturity (rollover) every six months.
4. *30-year floating-rate mortgages: $40 million*, which are repriced (i.e., the mortgage rate is reset) every nine months. Thus, these long-term assets are RSAs in the context of the repricing model with a one-year repricing horizon.

Summing these four items produces total one-year RSAs of $155 million. The remaining $115 million of assets are not rate sensitive over the one-year repricing horizon—that is, a change in the level of interest rates will not affect the size of the interest revenue generated by these assets over the next year.[4] The $5 million in the cash and due from category and the $5 million in premises are nonearning assets. Although the $105 million in long-term consumer loans, three-year Treasury bonds, and 10-year, fixed-rate mortgages generate interest revenue, the size of revenue generated will not change over the next year, since the interest rates on these assets are not expected to change (i.e., they are fixed over the next year).

---

3. For example, a 30-year bond purchased 10 years ago when rates were 13 percent would be reported as having the same book (accounting) value as when rates were 7 percent. Using market values, capital gains and losses would be reflected on the balance sheet as rates change.

4. We are assuming that the assets are noncallable over the year and that there will be no prepayments (runoffs, see below) on the mortgages within a year.

Table 23–2 Simple Bank Balance Sheet and Repricing Gap

Assets ($ millions)		Liabilities ($ millions)	
1. Cash and due from	$ 5	1. Two-year time deposits	$ 40
2. Short-term consumer loans (one-year maturity)	50	2. Demand deposits	40
3. Long-term consumer loans (two-year maturity)	25	3. Passbook savings	30
4. Three-month T-bills	30	4. Three-month CDs	40
5. Six-month T-notes	35	5. Three-month banker's acceptances	20
6. Three-year T-bonds	60	6. Six-month commercial paper	60
7. 10-year, fixed-rate mortgages	20	7. One-year time deposits	20
8. 30-year, floating-rate mortgages	40	8. Equity capital (fixed)	20
9. Premises	5		
	$270		$270

Rate-Sensitive Liabilities.   Looking down the liability side of the balance sheet in Table 23–2, we see that the following liability items clearly fit the one-year rate or repricing sensitivity test:

1. *Three-month CDs: $40 million*, which mature in three months and are repriced on rollover.
2. *Three-month bankers acceptances: $20 million*, which mature in three months and are repriced on rollover.
3. *Six-month commercial paper: $60 million*, which mature and are repriced every six months.
4. *One-year time deposits: $20 million*, which are repriced at the end of the one-year gap horizon.

Summing these four items produces one-year rate-sensitive liabilities (RSLs) of $140 million. The remaining $130 million is not rate sensitive over the one-year period. The $20 million in equity capital and $40 million in demand deposits (see the following discussion) do not pay interest and are therefore classified as noninterest paying. The $30 million in passbook savings (see the following discussion) and $40 million in two-year time deposits generate interest expense over the next year, but the level of the interest expense generated will not change if the general level of interest rates change. Thus, we classify these items as rate-insensitive liabilities.

The four repriced liabilities ($40 + $20 + $60 + $20) sum to $140 million, and the four repriced assets ($50 + $30 + $35 + $40) sum to $155 million. Given this, the cumulative one-year repricing gap (CGAP) for the bank is:

$$CGAP = \text{(One-year RSA)} - \text{(One-year RSL)}$$
$$= RSA - RSL$$
$$= \$155 \text{ million} - \$140 \text{ million} = \$15 \text{ million}$$

Interest rate sensitivity can also be expressed as a percentage of assets (*A*) (typically called the gap ratio)

$$\frac{CGAP}{A} = \frac{\$15 \text{ million}}{\$270 \text{ million}} = .056 = 5.6\%$$

Expressing the repricing gap in this way is useful since it tells us (1) the direction of the interest rate exposure (positive or negative CGAP) and (2) the scale of that exposure as indicated by dividing the gap by the asset size of the institution. In our example, the bank has a CGAP equal to 5.6 percent of the value of its total assets.

Table 23–3 Impact of CGAP on the Relation between Changes in Interest Rates and Changes in Net Interest Income, Assuming Rate Changes for RSAs Equal Rate Changes for RSLs

Row	CGAP	Change in Interest Rates	Change in Interest Revenue		Change in Interest Expense	Change in NII
1	>0	↑	↑	>	↑	↑
2	>0	↓	↓	>	↓	↓
3	<0	↑	↑	<	↑	↓
4	<0	↓	↓	<	↓	↑

Equal Changes in Rates on RSAs and RSLs.   The CGAP provides a measure of a bank's interest rate sensitivity. Table 23–3 highlights the relation between CGAP and changes in NII when interest rate changes for RSAs are equal to interest rate changes for RSLs. For example, when CGAP (or the gap ratio) is positive (or the bank has more RSAs than RSLs), NII will rise when interest rates rise (row 1, Table 23–3), since interest revenue increases more than interest expense does.

Example 23–1   Impact of Rate Changes on Net Interest Income When CGAP Is Positive

Suppose that interest rates rise by 1 percent on both RSAs and RSLs. The CGAP would project the expected annual change in net interest income (ΔNII) of the bank as approximately:

$$\Delta NII = CGAP \times \Delta R$$
$$= (\$15 \text{ million}) \times .01$$
$$= \$150,000$$

Similarly, if interest rates fall equally for RSAs and RSLs (row 2, Table 23–3), NII will fall when CGAP is positive. As rates fall, interest revenue falls by more than interest expense. Thus, NII falls. Suppose that for our bank, rates fall by 1 percent. The CGAP predicts that NII will fall by approximately:

$$\Delta NII = CGAP \times \Delta R$$
$$= (\$15 \text{ million}) \times (-.01)$$
$$= -\$150,000$$

It is evident from this equation that the larger the absolute value of CGAP, the larger the expected change in NII (i.e., the larger the increase or decrease in the FI's interest revenue relative to interest expense). In general, when CGAP is positive, the change in NII is positively related to the change in interest rates. Conversely, when CGAP (or the gap ratio) is negative, if interest rates rise by equal amounts for RSAs and RSLs (row 3, Table 23–3), NII will fall (since the bank has more RSLs than RSAs). Thus, an FI would want its CGAP to be positive when interest rates are expected to rise.

Similarly, if interest rates fall equally for RSAs and RSLs (row 4, Table 23–3), NII will increase when CGAP is negative. As rates fall, interest expense decreases by more than interest revenue. In general then, when CGAP is negative, the change in NII is negatively related to the change in interest rates. Thus, an FI would want its CGAP to be negative when interest rates are expected to fall. We refer to these relationships as **CGAP effects**.

CGAP effect

The relation between changes in interest rates and changes in net interest income.

Figure 23–1   Three-Month CD Rates versus Prime Rate for 1990–1999

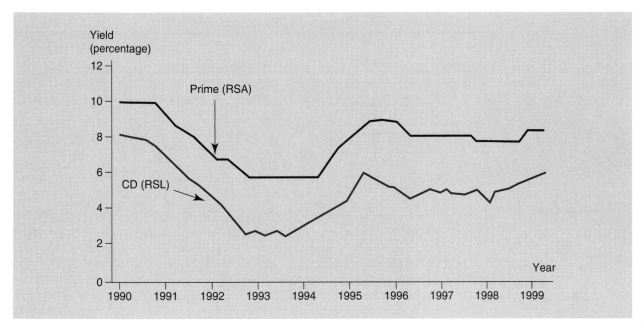

RSA = Rate-sensitive assets.
RSL = Rate-sensitive liabilities.
Source: *Federal Reserve Bulletin*, various issues. *www.bog.frb.fed.us*

Unequal Changes in Rates on RSAs and RSLs.   The previous section considered changes in net interest income as interest rates changed, assuming that the change in rates on RSAs was exactly equal to the change in rates on RSLs (in other words, assuming the interest rate spread between rates on RSAs and RSLs remained unchanged). This is not often the case; rather, rate changes on RSAs generally differ from those on RSLs (i.e., the spread between interest rates on assets and liabilities changes along with the levels of these rates). See Figure 23–1, which plots quarterly CD rates (liabilities) and prime lending rates (assets) for the period 1990–1999. Notice that although the rates generally move in the same direction, they are not perfectly correlated. In this case, as we consider the impact of rate changes on NII, we have a spread effect in addition to the CGAP effect.[5]

Example 23–2   Impact of Spread Effect on Net Interest Income

To understand spread effect, assume for a moment that RSAs equal RSLs equals $155 million. Suppose that rates rise by 1.2 percent on RSAs and by 1 percent on RSLs (i.e., the spread between the rate on RSAs and RSLs increases by 1.2 percent − 1 percent = 0.2 percent). The resulting change in NII is calculated as:

$$\Delta NII = (RSA \times \Delta R_{RSA}) - (RSL \times \Delta R_{RSL})$$
$$= \Delta\text{Interest revenue} - \Delta\text{Interest expense}$$
$$= (\$155 \text{ million} \times 1.2\%) - (\$155 \text{ million} \times 1.0\%)$$
$$= \$155 \text{ million} (1.2\% - 1.0\%)$$
$$= \$310{,}000$$

5. The spread effect therefore presents a type of basis risk for the FI. The FI's net interest income varies as the difference (basis) between interest rates on RSAs and interest rates on RSLs vary. We discuss basis risk in detail in Chapter 24.

Table 23–4   Impact of CGAP on the Relation between Changes in Interest Rates and Changes in Net Interest Income, Allowing for Different Rate Changes on RSAs and RSLs

Row	GAP	Change in Interest Rates	Change in Spread	Change in NII
1	>0	↑	↑	↑
2	>0	↑	↓	↑↓
3	>0	↓	↑	↑↓
4	>0	↓	↓	↓
5	<0	↑	↑	↑↓
6	<0	↑	↓	↓
7	<0	↓	↑	↑
8	<0	↓	↓	↑↓

spread effect

The effect that a change in the spread between rates on RSAs and RSLs has on net interest income (NII) as interest rates change.

If the spread between the rate on RSAs and RSLs increases, when interest rates rise (fall), interest revenue increases (decreases) by more (less) than interest expense. The result is an increase in NII. Conversely, if the spread between the rates on RSAs and RSLs decreases, when interest rates rise (fall), interest revenue increases (decreases) less (more) than interest expense, and NII decreases. In general, the **spread effect** is such that, regardless of the direction of the change in interest rates, a positive relation occurs between changes in the spread (between rates on RSAs and RSLs) and changes in NII. Whenever the spread increases (decreases), NII increases (decreases).

See Table 23–4 for various combinations of CGAP and spread changes and their effects on NII. The first four rows in Table 23–4 consider a bank with a positive CGAP; the last four rows consider a bank with a negative CGAP. Notice in Table 23–4 that the CGAP and spread effects can both have the same effect on NII. In these cases, bank managers can accurately predict the direction of the change in NII as interest rates change. When the two work in opposite directions, however, the change in NII cannot be predicted without knowing the size of the CGAP and expected change in the spread.

The repricing gap is the measure of interest rate risk most often used by FIs. The repricing gap model is conceptually easy to understand and can easily be used to forecast changes in profitability for a given change in interest rates. The repricing gap can be used to allow an FI to structure its assets and liabilities or to go off the balance sheet to take advantage of a projected interest rate change. However, the repricing gap model has some major weaknesses that have resulted in regulators calling for the use of more comprehensive models (e.g., the duration gap model) to measure interest rate risk. We next discuss some of the major weaknesses of the repricing model.

Weakness of the Repricing Model. The repricing model has four major weaknesses: (1) it ignores market value effects of interest rate changes, (2) it ignores cash flow patterns within a maturity bucket, (3) it fails to deal with the problem of rate-insensitive asset and liability cash flow runoffs and prepayments, and (4) it ignores cash flows from off-balance-sheet activities. This section discusses each of these weaknesses.

Market Value Effects. As discussed in the next section, interest rate changes have a market (or present) value effect in addition to an income effect on asset and liability values. That is, the present value of the cash flows on assets and liabilities changes, in addition to the immediate interest received or paid on them, as interest rates change. In fact, the present values (and, where relevant, the market prices) of virtually all assets and liabilities on an FI's balance sheet change as interest rates change. As such, the repricing gap is only a *partial* and near term measure of an FI's true overall interest rate risk exposure.

Cash Flow Patterns within a Maturity Bucket. The problem of defining buckets over a range of maturities ignores information regarding the distribution of assets and liabilities within that bucket. For example, the dollar values of RSAs and RSLs within any maturity bucket range may be equal; however, on average, liabilities may be repriced toward the end of the bucket's range, and assets may be repriced toward the beginning, in which case a change in interest rates will have an effect on asset and liability cash flows that will not be accurately measured by the repricing gap approach.

The Problem of Runoffs and Prepayments. Even if an asset or liability is rate insensitive, virtually all assets and liabilities pay some interest and/or principal back in any given year. As a result, the FI receives a cash flow or **runoff** from its rate insensitive portfolio that can be reinvested at current market rates; that is, the runoff cash flow component of a rate *in*sensitive asset and liability is itself rate *sensitive*. The FI manager can easily deal with this in the repricing gap model by identifying for each asset and liability item the estimated dollar cash flow that will be run off within the next year and adding these amounts to the value of rate-sensitive assets and liabilities.

Similarly, the repricing model assumes that there is no prepayment of RSAs and RSLs. In reality, however, cash flows from RSAs and RSLs do not act in such a predictable fashion. For example, a mortgage may be paid off early, either to buy a new house or to refinance the mortgage should interest rates fall. For a variety of reasons, mortgagees relocate or refinance their mortgages (especially when current mortgage rates are below mortgage coupon rates). This propensity to prepay means that realized cash flows on RSAs and RSLs can often deviate substantially from the stated or expected cash flows in a no-prepayment world. As with runoffs, the FI manager can deal with prepayments in the repricing gap model by identifying the possibility of prepayment on each asset and liability within the next year and adding these amounts to the values of RSAs and RSLs.

Cash Flows from Off-Balance-Sheet Activities. The RSAs and RSLs used in the repricing model generally include only assets and liabilities listed on the balance sheet. Changes in interest rates will affect the cash flows on many off-balance-sheet instruments as well. For example, an FI might have hedged its interest rate risk with an interest rate futures contract (see Chapter 24). As interest rates change, these futures contracts—as part of the marking-to-market process—produce a daily cash flow (either positive or negative) for the FI that may offset any on-balance-sheet gap exposure. These offsetting cash flows from futures contracts are ignored by the simple repricing model and should (and could) be included in the model.

Duration Model

2 In Chapter 3, we learned how to calculate duration and came to understand that the duration measure has economic meaning as the interest sensitivity of an asset or liability's value to small changes in interest rates. That is:

$$D = -\frac{\% \, \Delta \text{ in market value of a security}}{\Delta R / (1 + R)}$$

For FIs, the major relevance of duration is its use as a measure of interest rate risk exposure. The duration model can be used instead of the repricing model discussed above to evaluate an FI's overall interest rate exposure—to measure the FI's **duration gap**.

The Duration Gap for a Financial Institution. To estimate the overall duration gap of an FI, we first determine the duration of an FI's asset portfolio (*A*) and the duration of its liability portfolio (*L*). Specifically, the duration of a portfolio of assets

runoff

Periodic cash flow of interest and principal amortization payments on long-term assets such as conventional mortgages that can be reinvested at market rates.

duration gap

A measure of overall interest rate risk exposure for an FI.

or liabilities is the market value weighted average of the durations of the components of the portfolio. These can be calculated as:

$$D_A = X_{1A}D_1{}^A + X_{2A}D_2{}^A + \ldots + X_{nA}D_n{}^A$$

and:

$$D_L = X_{1L}D_1{}^L + X_{2L}D_2{}^L + \ldots + X_{nL}D_n{}^L$$

where

$$X_{1j} + X_{2j} \ldots + X_{nj} = 1$$
$$j = A, L$$

The X_{ij}'s in the equation represent the market value proportions of each asset or liability held in the respective asset and liability portfolios. Thus, if new 30-year Treasury bonds were 1 percent of a life insurer's portfolio and $D_1{}^A$, the duration of those bonds, was equal to 9.25 years, $X_{1A}D_1{}^A = .01(9.25) = 0.0925$. More simply, the duration of a portfolio of assets or liabilities is a market value weighted average of the individual durations of the assets or liabilities on the FI's balance sheet.[6]

Consider an FI's simplified market value balance sheet:

Assets ($)	Liabilities/Equity ($)	
Assets (A) = $100	Liabilities (L) = $ 90	
	Equity (E) =	10
$100	$100	

From the balance sheet

$$A = L + E$$

and:

$$\Delta A = \Delta L + \Delta E$$

or:

$$\Delta E = \Delta A - \Delta L$$

That is, when interest rates change, the change in the FI's equity or net worth (E) equals the difference between the change in the market values of assets and liabilities on each side of the balance sheet.

Since $\Delta E = \Delta A - \Delta L$, we need to determine how ΔA and ΔL—the changes in the market values of assets and liabilities on the balance sheet—are related to duration.[7] From the duration model (assuming annual compounding of interest):

$$\frac{\Delta A}{A} = -D_A \frac{\Delta R}{(1 + R)}$$

and:

$$\frac{\Delta L}{L} = -D_L \frac{\Delta R}{(1 + R)}$$

Here we have simply substituted $\Delta A/A$ or $\Delta L/L$, the percentage change in the market values of assets or liabilities, for $\Delta P/P$, the percentage change in any single bond's price, and D_A or D_L, the duration of the FI's asset or liability portfolio, for D_i, the duration on any given bond, deposit, or loan. The term $\Delta R/(1 + R)$ reflects the shock to interest rates as before.[8] To show dollar changes, these equations can be rewritten as:

---

6. This derivation of an FI's duration gap closely follows G. G. Kaufman, "Measuring and Managing Interest Rate Risk: A Primer," *Economic Perspective* (Chicago: Federal Reserve Bank of Chicago, 1984), pp. 16–29.

7. In what follows, we use the Δ (change) notation instead of d (derivative notation) to recognize that interest rate changes tend to be discrete rather than infinitesimally small. For example, in real-world financial markets, the smallest observed rate change is usually one basis point or 1/100th of 1 percent.

8. For simplicity, we assume that the interest rate changes are the same for both assets and liabilities. This assumption is standard in Macauley duration analysis (see Chapter 3).

$$\Delta A = A \times -D_A \times \frac{\Delta R}{(1 + R)}$$

and:

$$\Delta L = L \times -D_L \times \frac{\Delta R}{(1 + R)}$$

Since $\Delta E = \Delta A - \Delta L$, we can substitute these two expressions into this equation. Rearranging and combining these equations[9] results in a measure of the change in the market value of equity:

$$\Delta E = -(D_A - kD_L) \times A \times \frac{\Delta R}{(1 + R)}$$

where

$k = L/A =$ Measure of the FI's leverage—the amount of borrowed funds or liabilities rather than owners' equity used to fund its asset portfolio.

The effect of interest rate changes on the market value of an FI's equity or net worth (ΔE) breaks down into three effects:

1. *The leverage-adjusted duration gap* $= D_A - kD_L$. This gap is measured in years and reflects the degree of duration mismatch in an FI's balance sheet. Specifically, the larger this gap *in absolute terms*, the more exposed the FI is to interest rate risk.
2. *The size of the FI.* The term A measures the size of the FI's assets. The larger the scale of the FI, the larger the dollar size of the potential net worth exposure from any given interest rate shock.
3. *The size of the interest rate shock* $= \Delta R/(1 + R)$. The larger the shock, the greater the FI's exposure.[10]

Given this, we express the exposure of the net worth of the FI as:

$$\Delta E = -\text{Adjusted duration gap} \times \text{Asset size} \times \text{Interest rate shock}$$

9.

$$\Delta E = \left(A \times (-D_A) \times \frac{\Delta R}{(1 + R)}\right) - \left(L \times (-D_L) \times \frac{\Delta R}{(1 + R)}\right)$$

Assuming that the level of interest rates and expected shock to interest rates are the same for both assets and liabilities:

$$\Delta E = ((-D_A)A + (D_L)L) \frac{\Delta R}{(1 + R)}$$

or:

$$\Delta E = -(D_A A - D_L L) \frac{\Delta R}{(1 + R)}$$

To rearrange the equation in a slightly more intuitive fashion, we multiply and divide both the terms $D_A A$ and $D_L L$ by A (assets):

$$\Delta E = -((A/A)D_A - (L/A)D_L) \times A \times (\Delta R/(1 + R))$$

Therefore:

$$\Delta E = -(D_A - (L/A)D_L) \times A \times (\Delta R/(1 + R))$$

and thus:

$$\Delta E = -(D_A - kD_L) \times A \times (\Delta R/(1 + R))$$

where

$$k = L/A.$$

10. We assume that the level of rates and the expected shock to interest rates are the same for both assets and liabilities. This assumption is standard in Macauley duration analysis. Although restrictive, this assumption can be relaxed. Specifically, if ΔR_A is the shock to assets and ΔR_L is the shock to liabilities, we can express the duration gap model as:

$$\Delta E = -((D_A \times A \times \frac{\Delta R_A}{1 + R_A}) - (D_L \times L \times \frac{\Delta R_L}{1 + R_L}))$$

Interest rate shocks are largely external to the FI and often result from changes in the Federal Reserve's monetary policy or from international capital movements (as discussed in Chapter 20). The size of the duration gap and the size of the FI, however, are largely under the control of its management.

The next section uses an example to explain how a manager can utilize information on an FI's duration gap to restructure the balance sheet to immunize stockholders' net worth against interest rate risk (i.e., set the balance sheet up *before* a change in interest rates, so that ΔE is nonnegative for an expected change in interest rates). The general rules we illustrate are as follows. If the duration gap (DGAP) is negative, there is a positive relation between changes in interest rates and changes in the market value of the FI. Thus, if interest rates increase (decrease), the market value of the FI increases (decreases). If the DGAP is positive, there is a negative relation between changes in interest rates and changes in the market value of the FI. Thus, if interest rates decrease (increase), the market value of the FI increases (decreases).

Example 23–3   Duration Gap Measurement and Exposure

Suppose that the FI manager calculates that:

$$D_A = 5 \text{ years}$$
$$D_L = 3 \text{ years}$$

Then the manager learns from an economic forecasting unit that rates are expected to rise from 10 to 11 percent in the immediate future, that is:

$$\Delta R = 1\% = .01$$
$$1 + R = 1.10$$

The FI's initial balance sheet is assumed to be:

Assets ($ millions)	Liabilities ($ millions)
$A = \$100$	$L = \$\ 90$
	$E = \underline{\ \ \ 10}$
$\underline{\$100}$	$\underline{\$100}$

The FI manager calculates the potential loss to equity holders' net worth (E) if the forecast of rising rates proves true:

$$\Delta E = -(D_A - kD_L) \times A \times \frac{\Delta R}{(1 + R)}$$

$$= -(5 - (.9)(3)) \times \$100 \text{ million} \times \frac{.01}{1.1} = -\$2.09 \text{ million}$$

The bank could lose $2.09 million in net worth if rates rise by 1 percent. The FI started with $10 million in equity, so the loss of $2.09 million is almost 21 percent of its initial net worth. The market value balance sheet after the rise in rates by 1 percent then appears as follows:[11]

---

11. These values are calculated as follows:

$$\frac{\Delta A}{A} = -5\left(\frac{.01}{1.1}\right) = -.04545 = -4.545\%$$

$$100 + (-.04545)100 = 95.45$$

and:

$$\frac{\Delta L}{L} = -3\left(\frac{.01}{1.1}\right) = -.02727 = -2.727\%$$

$$90 + (-.02727)90 = 87.54$$

Assets ($ millions)	Liabilities ($ millions)
$A = \$95.45$	$L = \$87.54$
	$E = \quad 7.91$
$\$95.45$	$\$95.45$

Even though the rise in interest rates would not push the FI into economic insolvency, it reduces the FI's net worth-to-assets ratio from 10 (10/100) to 8.29 percent (7.91/95.45). To counter this effect, the manager might reduce the FI's adjusted duration gap. In an extreme case, the gap might be reduced to zero:

$$\Delta E = -(0) \times A \times \Delta R/(1 + R) = 0$$

To do this, the FI should not directly set $D_A = D_L$, which ignores the facts that the FI's assets (A) do not equal its borrowed liabilities (L) and that k (which reflects the ratio L/A) is not equal to 1. To see the importance of factoring in leverage (or L/A), suppose that the manager increases the duration of the FI's liabilities to five years, the same as D_A, then:

$$\Delta E = -(5 - (.9)(5)) \times \$100 \text{ million} \times (.01/1.1) = -\$0.45 \text{ million}$$

The FI is still exposed to a loss of $0.45 million if rates rise by 1 percent.

An appropriate strategy involves changing D_L until:

$$D_A = kD_L = 5 \text{ years}$$

For example:

$$\Delta E = -(5 - (.9)5.55) \times \$100 \text{ million} \times (.01/1.1) = 0$$

In this case, the FI manager sets $D_L = 5.55$ years, or slightly longer than $D_A = 5$ years, to compensate for the fact that only 90 percent of assets are funded by borrowed liabilities, with the other 10 percent funded by equity. Note that the FI manager has at least three other ways to reduce the adjusted duration gap to zero:

1. *Reduce D_A.* Reduce D_A from 5 years to 2.7 years (equal to kD_L or (.9)(3)) so that

$$(D_A - kD_L) = (2.7 - (.9)(3)) = 0$$

2. *Reduce D_A and increase D_L.* Shorten the duration of assets and lengthen the duration of liabilities at the same time. One possibility is to *reduce D_A* to 4 years and to *increase D_L* to 4.44 years so that

$$(D_A - kD_L) = (4 - (.9)(4.44)) = 0$$

3. *Change k and D_L.* Increase k (leverage) from .9 to .95 and increase D_L from 3 years to 5.26 years so that:

$$(D_A - kD_L) = (5 - (.95)(5.26)) = 0$$

The preceding example demonstrated how the duration model can be used to immunize an FI's entire balance sheet against interest rate risk.

Difficulties in Applying the Duration Model to Real-World FI Balance Sheets.

Critics of the duration model have often claimed that it is difficult to apply in real-world situations. However, duration measures and immunization strategies are useful in most real-world situations. In fact, the model recently proposed by the Federal Reserve and the Bank for International Settlements (BIS)[12]

---

12. In 1993, the BIS proposed a duration gap model to measure the interest rate risk of the whole balance sheet. This was reaffirmed in 1999 (see Basel Committee on Banking Supervision, A New Capital Adequacy Framework, Basel, June 1999, and Chapter 14). Since 1998, the Federal Reserve has been using a duration gap model as part of the standardized model to measure a bank's interest rate risk exposure in its trading (or market) portfolio—see Chapter 20.

to monitor bank interest rate risk taking is heavily based on the duration model. We next consider the various criticisms of the duration model and discuss ways in which a modern FI manager would deal with these criticisms in practice.

Duration Matching Can Be Costly.   Critics charge that although in principle an FI manager can change D_A and D_L to immunize the FI against interest rate risk, restructuring the balance sheet of a large and complex FI can be both time-consuming and costly. This argument may have been true historically, but the growth of purchased funds, asset securitization, and loan sales markets has considerably eased the speed and lowered the transaction costs of major balance sheet restructurings. (See Chapter 25 for a discussion of these strategies.) Moreover, an FI manager could still manage risk exposure using the duration model by employing techniques other than direct portfolio rebalancing to immunize against interest rate risk. Managers can obtain many of the same results of direct duration matching by taking offsetting (hedging) positions in the markets for derivative securities, such as futures, forwards, options, and swaps (Chapter 24).

Immunization Is a Dynamic Problem.   Even though assets and liabilities are duration matched today, the same assets and liabilities may not be matched tomorrow. This is because the duration of assets and liabilities change as they approach maturity, and, most importantly, the rate at which their durations change through time may not be the same on the asset and liability sides of the balance sheet. As long as the FI manager recognizes this problem, he or she can mitigate this effect by seeking to rebalance the FI's portfolio such that $D_A = kD_L$ through time.

Large Interest Rate Changes and Convexity.   Duration measures the price sensitivity of fixed-income securities for small changes in interest rates of the order of one basis point (or one-hundredth of 1 percent). But suppose that interest rate shocks are much larger, of the order of 2 percent or 200 basis points. In this case, duration becomes a less accurate predictor of how much the prices of securities will change and, therefore, a less accurate measure of the interest rate sensitivity and the interest rate gap of an FI. Figure 23–2 is a graphic representation of the reason for this. Note the change in an asset's or liability's price, such as that of a bond, due to yield (interest rate) changes according to the duration model and the "true relationship," as calculated directly, using the exact present value calculation for a bond.

Specifically, the duration model predicts that the relationship between an interest rate change (or shock) and a bond's price change will be proportional to the bond's D (duration). By precisely calculating the true change in the bond's price, however, we would find that for large interest rate increases, duration overpredicts the *fall* in the bond's price, and for large interest rate decreases, it underpredicts the *increase* in the bond's price. That is, the duration model predicts symmetric effects for rate increases and decreases on the bond's price. As Figure 23–2 shows, in actuality, the capital *loss* effect of rate increases tends to be smaller than the capital *gain* effect of rate decreases. This is the result of the bond's price-yield relationship exhibiting a property called **convexity** rather than linearity, as assumed by the basic duration model. Nevertheless, an FI manager sufficiently concerned about the impact of large rate changes on the FI's balance sheet can capture the convexity effect by directly measuring it and incorporating it into the duration gap model.[13]

convexity

The degree of curvature of the price-yield curve around some interest rate level.

Do You Understand?

1. How FIs can change the size and the direction of their repricing gap?
2. What four major weaknesses of the repricing model are?
3. What a runoff means?
4. Why critics argue that the duration model is difficult to apply in real-world situations? How these arguments can be countered?
5. What convexity is?

---

13. Technically speaking, convexity can be viewed as the *rate of change* of the bond's value with respect to any interest rate change, whereas duration measures the *change* in a bond's value with respect to a change in interest rates.

Figure 23–2   Duration Estimated versus True Bond Price

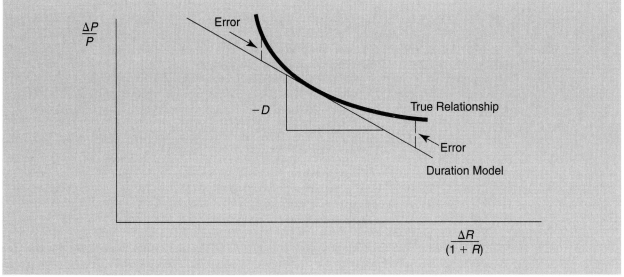

Example 23–4   The Impact of Convexity for Large Interest
Rate Changes

Consider a 4-year bond that pays 8 percent coupons annually and has a yield to maturity of 10 percent. Table 23–5 shows that the market value of this bond is $936.603 and the duration of this bond is 3.484 years. Suppose interest rates change such that the yield to maturity on the bond increases to 12 percent. The true market value of the bond decreases to:

$$V_b = 80 \, (PVIFA_{12\%,4}) + 1{,}000(PVIF_{12\%,4})$$
$$= 80 \, (3.03735) + 1{,}000 \, (0.63552) = \$878.508$$

This is a drop of $58.095. According to the duration model, however, the change in the bond's value is:

$$P = 936.603 \times (-3.484) \times (.02/1.10) = -\$59.330$$

or the new bond value is $877.273.

The difference in these two values, $1.235 ($878.508 − $877.273), is due to the convexity in the "true" market value calculation versus the linearity in the duration model. This linearity assumption leads to inaccuracies in the duration value calculations that increase with the size of the interest rate change.

Insolvency Risk Management

In the previous two chapters and in this chapter, we have examined three major areas of risk exposure facing a modern FI manager. To ensure survival, an FI manager needs to protect the institution against the risk of insolvency—to shield it from those risks that are sufficiently large to cause the institution to fail. The primary means of protection against the risk of insolvency and failure is an FI's equity capital. However, capital also serves as a source of funds and as a necessary requirement for growth under the existing minimum capital-to-assets ratios set by regulators. FI managers may often

Table 23–5   Duration of a Four-Year Bond with 8 Percent Coupon Paid Annually and a 10 Percent Yield

t	CF_t	$PVIF_{10\%,\,t}$	*PVIF* of *CF*	*PVIF* of $C \times t$
1	80	0.9091	72.727	72.727
2	80	0.8264	66.116	132.231
3	80	0.7513	60.105	180.316
4	1,080	0.6830	737.655	2,950.618
			$936.603	$3,263.165

$$D = \frac{3,263.165}{936.603} = 3.484 \text{ years}$$

prefer low levels of capital because they allow the institution to generate a higher return on equity for the firm's stockholders. The moral hazard problem of deposit insurance (see Chapter 14) exacerbates this tendency. However, this strategy results in a greater chance of insolvency. Since regulators are more concerned with the safety of the financial system than stockholder returns, there is a need for minimum capital requirements (Chapter 14 discussed the regulatory requirements on an FI's capital).

In this chapter, we focus on how various risks affect the level of an FI's capital. As discussed in In the News box 23–2, high capital levels and sound risk management by bank managers in the late 1990s significantly lowered the risk of bank failures.

Capital and Insolvency Risk

Capital. To understand how an FI's equity capital protects against insolvency risk, we must define *capital* more precisely. The problem is that equity capital has many definitions: an economist's definition of capital may differ from an accountant's definition, which in turn may differ from a regulator's definition. Specifically, the economist's definition of an FI's capital, or owners' equity stake, is the difference between the market values of its assets and its liabilities. This is also called an FI's **net worth** (see Chapter 13). This is the *economic* meaning of capital, but regulators and accountants have found it necessary to adopt definitions that depart by a greater or lesser degree from economic net worth. The concept of an FI's economic net worth is really a *market value accounting* concept. With the exception of the investment banking industry, regulatory- and accounting-defined capital and required leverage ratios are based in whole or in part on historical or **book value** accounting concepts.

net worth

A measure of an FI's capital that is equal to the difference between the market value of its assets and the market value of its liabilities.

book value

Value of assets and liabilities based on their historical costs.

We begin by looking at the role of economic capital or net worth as a device to protect against two of the major types of risk described in the previous chapters and in this chapter: credit risk and interest rate risk. We then compare this market value concept with the book value concept of capital. Because it can actually distort an FI's true solvency position, the book value of capital concept can be misleading to managers, owners, liability holders, and regulators alike. We also examine some possible reasons as to why FI regulators continue to rely on book value concepts when such economic value transparency problems exist.

 The Market Value of Capital. To understand how economic net worth insulates an FI against the risk of insolvency, consider the following example. Table 23–6 presents a simple balance sheet, where an FI's assets and liabilities

In the News

23-2

Chance of Banking Crisis Near Zero, Fed Official Says

Federal Reserve Board Governor Susan M. Phillips said Friday that the chance of another banking crisis is "virtually zero." Despite the increased complexity of bank risk-taking activities, the chances of a repeat of the banking crisis of the late 1980s have been reduced, Ms. Phillips told the Atlanta Society of Financial Analysts. "The bank's higher capital levels and the improvements in their risk measurement and management processes contribute to the safety and soundness of the system." Banks are

Source: *The American Banker*, February 18, 1997, p. 2, by Jaret Seiberg.

beginning to allocate capital to cover interest rate and market risk, she said. They also are using risk-based pricing, forcing corporate customers with less than stellar credit histories to pay higher rates. Large trading banks have even developed models that compute an institution's exposure to swings in securities prices, she said.

Ms. Phillips also called on banks to disclose publicly more information about the riskiness of their

portfolios. "We applaud recent efforts on the part of some managements to increase voluntary risk disclosures in footnotes to their financial statements," she said. "But still a lot more can and should be done."

Ms. Phillips noted that the industry wants new powers and fewer regulatory burdens for banks with "good management" and "adequate capital." "As a bank supervisor, I would not rely even partially on the market's assessment of the capital adequacy of a bank—unless I were assured that market analysts had the data necessary to reach informed judgments," she said.

www.americanbanker. com/

market value or **mark-to-market value basis**

Balance sheet values that reflect current rather than historical prices.

are valued in market value terms. On a **market value** or **mark-to-market value basis,** asset and liability values are adjusted each day to reflect current market conditions. Thus, the economic value of the FI's equity is $10 million, which is the difference between the market value of its assets and liabilities, and it is economically solvent. Let's consider the impact of two classic types of FI risk—credit and interest rate—on this FI's net worth.

Market Value of Capital and Credit Risk. The balance sheet in Table 23–6 indicates that the FI (such as a finance company) has $20 million in long-term loans. Suppose that as the result of a recession, a number of its borrowers have cash flow problems and are unable to keep up their promised loan repayment schedules. A decline in the current and expected future cash flows on loans lowers the market value of the FI's loan portfolio below $20 million. Suppose that loans are really worth only $12 million (the price the FI would receive if it could sell these loans in a secondary market). This means the market value of the loan portfolio has fallen from $20 million to $12 million. The revised market value balance sheet is presented in Table 23–7.

The loss of $8 million in the market value of loans appears on the liability side of the balance sheet as a loss of $8 million of the FI's net worth—the loss of asset value is directly charged against the equity owners' capital or net worth. As you can see, the

Table 23–6   An FI's Market Value Balance Sheet

(in millions of dollars)

Assets		Liabilities	
Long-term securities	$ 80	Liabilities (short-term,	
Long-term loans	20	floating-rate deposits)	$ 90
		Net worth	10
	$100		$100

Table 23–7   An FI's Market Value Balance Sheet after a Decline in the Value of Loans

(in millions of dollars)

Assets		Liabilities	
Long-term securities	$80	Liabilities	$90
Long-term loans	12	Net worth	2
	$92		$92

liability holders are fully protected because the total market value of their $90 million in liability claims is still $90 million. This is due to the fact that liability holders legally are senior claimants and equity holders are junior claimants to the FI's assets. Consequently, equity holders bear losses on the asset portfolio first. In fact, in this example, liability holders are hurt only when losses on the loan portfolio exceed $10 million (which was the FI's original net worth). Let's consider a larger credit risk shock in which the market value of the loan portfolio plummets from $20 million to $8 million, a loss of $12 million (see Table 23–8).

This larger loss renders the FI insolvent; the market value of its assets ($88 million) is now less than the value of its liabilities ($90 million). The owners' net worth stake has been completely wiped out—reduced from $10 million to −$2 million, resulting in a negative net worth. Therefore, this hurts liability holders, but only a bit. Specifically, the equity holders bear the first $10 million of the $12 million loss in value of the loan portfolio. Only after the equity holders are completely wiped out do the liability holders begin to lose. In this example, the economic value of their claims on the FI has fallen from $90 million to $88 million, or a loss of $2 million (a percentage loss of 2.22 percent). After insolvency, the remaining $88 million in assets is liquidated and distributed to deposit holders. Note here that we are ignoring insurance guarantees afforded to some FI (e.g., bank) liability holders.[14]

This example clearly demonstrates the concept of net worth or capital as a source of funds protecting liability holders against insolvency risk. The larger the FI's net worth relative to the size of its assets, the more insolvency protection its liability holders and, in some cases, liability guarantors such as the FDIC have. This is the reason that regulators focus on capital requirements such as the ratio of net worth to assets in assessing an FI's insolvency risk exposure and in setting insurance premiums (see Chapter 14).

Market Value of Capital and Interest Rate Risk.   Consider the market value balance sheet in Table 23–6 after interest rates rise. As we discussed earlier in the chapter, rising interest rates reduce the market value of the FI's long-term fixed-income assets and loans, while floating-rate instruments find their market values largely unaffected if

---

14. In the presence of deposit insurance, the insurer, such as the FDIC, bears some of the depositors' losses; for details, see Chapter 14.

Table 23–8   An FI's Market Value Balance Sheet after a Major Decline in the Value of the Loan Portfolio

(in millions of dollars)

Assets		Liabilities	
Long-term securities	$80	Liabilities	$90
Long-term loans	8	Net worth	−2
	$88		$88

Table 23–9   An FI's Market Value Balance Sheet after a Rise in Interest Rates

(in millions of dollars)

Assets		Liabilities	
Long-term securities	$75	Liabilities	$90
Long-term loans	17	Net worth	2
	$92		$92

interest rates are instantaneously reset.[15] Suppose that a rise in interest rates reduces the market value of the FI's long-term securities investments to $75 million from $80 million and the market value of its long-term loans to $17 million from $20 million. Because all deposit liabilities are assumed to be short-term floating-rate deposits, their market values are unchanged at $90 million.

After the shock to interest rates, the market value balance sheet is represented in Table 23–9. The loss of $8 million in the market value of the FI's assets is once again reflected on the liability side of the balance sheet by an $8 million decrease in net worth to $2 million. Thus, as for increased credit risk, the equity holders first bear losses in asset values due to adverse interest rate changes. Only if the fall in the market value of assets exceeds $10 million are the liability holders, as senior claimants to the FI's assets, adversely affected.

These examples show that market valuation of the balance sheet produces an economically accurate picture of net worth and, thus, an FI's solvency position. The equity holders directly bear the credit risk and interest rate risks that result in losses in the market value of assets and liabilities in the sense that such losses are charges against the value of their ownership claims in the FI. As long as the owners' capital or equity stake is adequate, or sufficiently large, liability holders (and implicitly regulators that back the claims of liability holders) are protected against insolvency risk. If regulators were to close an FI before its economic net worth became zero, neither liability holders, nor those regulators guaranteeing the claims of liability holders, would stand to lose. Thus, many academics and analysts advocate the use of market value accounting and market value of capital closure rules for all FIs, especially because the book value of capital rules are closely associated with the savings institutions disaster in the 1980s (discussed in Chapter 14).[16] To see why book value of capital rules may incorrectly measure insolvency risk,

---

15. This is because the interest rate increase is incorporated in the revised coupon rate on the floating-rate loan leaving the market value unchanged, while the coupon rate on the fixed-income loan cannot change. Rather, for the fixed-income loan, the interest rate increase can only be incorporated in the yield to maturity, which in turn affects the market value (see Chapter 3).

16. Three regulatory concerns expressed in the banking industry about market value accounting that slow this from happening are (1) market value accounting (MVA) is difficult to implement, especially for small commercial banks and thrifts; (2) MVA introduces an unnecessary degree of variability into an FI's earnings because paper capital gains and losses are passed through the income statement; and (3) FIs would be less willing to accept long-term asset exposure with MVA, since they are continually marked to market.

Table 23–10 An FI's Book Value Balance Sheet
(in millions of dollars)

Assets		Liabilities	
Long-term securities	$ 80	Short-term liabilities	$ 90
Long-term loans	20	Net worth	10
	$100		$100

consider the same credit and interest rate risk scenarios discussed above, but this time in a world where book value accounting and capital regulations hold sway.

4 **The Book Value of Capital.** Table 23–10 uses the same initial balance sheet as in Table 23–6 but assumes that assets and liabilities are now valued at their historical book values.

In Table 23–10, the $80 million in long-term securities and $20 million in long-term loans reflect the historic or original book values of those assets—that is, they reflect the (historic) values at the time the loans were made and bonds were purchased, which may have been many years ago when the economy was in a different stage of the business cycle and interest rates were at different levels. Similarly, on the liability side, the $90 million in liabilities also reflects their historic cost, so that net worth or equity of the FI is now the book value of the stockholders' claims rather than the market value of those claims. For example, the book value of capital—the difference between the book value of an FI's assets and the book value of its liabilities—usually comprises the following three components in banking:

1. Par Value of Shares—the face value of the common shares issued by the FI (the par value is usually $1 per share) times the number of shares outstanding.
2. Surplus Value of Shares—the difference between the price the public paid for common shares when originally offered (e.g., $5 per share) and their par values (e.g., $1) times the number of shares outstanding.
3. Retained Earnings—the accumulated value of past profits not yet paid in dividends to shareholders. Since these earnings could be paid in dividends, they are part of the equity owners' stake in the FI.

Consequently for an FI, Book value of its capital = Par value + Surplus + Retained earnings. As the example in Table 23–10 is constructed, the book value of capital equals $10 million. However, invariably, the book value of equity *does not equal* the market value of equity (the difference between the market value of assets and liabilities).

This inequality between the book and market values of equity can be best understood by examining the effects of the same credit and interest rate shocks on the FI, but assuming book value rather than market value accounting methods.

www.rutgers.edu/
Accounting/raw/fasb/

The Book Value of Capital and Credit Risk. Suppose that some of the $20 million in loans are in difficulty due to the inability of businesses to maintain their repayment schedules. We assumed in Table 23–7 that the revaluation of the promised cash flows of loans leads to an immediate downward adjustment of the loan portfolio's market value from $20 million to $12 million, and a market value loss of $8 million. By contrast, under historic book value accounting methods, such as generally accepted accounting principles (GAAP), FIs have more discretion in reflecting and timing the recognition of loan loss on their balance sheets, and thus of the impact of such losses on capital. Indeed, managers of FIs may well resist writing down the values of bad assets as long as possible to try to present a more favorable picture to depositors, shareholders, and regulators. Such resistance might be expected if managers believe that the recognition of such losses could threaten their careers. Similarly, FI managers can selectively sell assets to inflate their reported capital. For example, managers can sell assets that have market values above their book values, resulting in an increase in the book value of capital. Only pressure from auditors and regulators such as bank, thrift, and insurance examiners may force loss recognition and write-downs of the values of problem assets. In recent years, on-site examinations of property insurance companies have occurred as infrequently as once every three years, while insurance regulators analyze off-site balance sheet information as infrequently as once every 18 months. Although bank call report data and on-site examinations are now more frequent,[17] the tendency is still to delay writing down the book values of loans. In Japan, the financial crisis of the late 1990s resulted in the Finance Ministry calling for banks to discontinue their delay in writing off many of the nonperforming loans in their portfolios.

Book Value of Capital and Interest Rate Risk.   Although book value accounting systems recognize credit risk problems, albeit only partially and usually with a long and discretionary time lag, their failure to recognize the impact of interest rate risk is even more extreme.

In the market value accounting example in Table 23–9, a rise in interest rates lowered the market values of long-term securities and loans by $8 million and led to a fall in the market value of net worth from $10 million to $2 million. In a book value accounting world, when all assets and liabilities reflect their original cost of purchase, the rise in interest rates has no effect on the value of assets, liabilities, or the book value of equity—the balance sheet remains unchanged. Table 23–10 reflects the position both before and after the interest rate rise. Such was the case for those thrifts that continued to report long-term fixed-rate mortgages at historic book values even though interest rates rose dramatically in the early 1980s and, therefore, continued to record a positive book capital position. On a market value net worth basis, however, their mortgages were worth far less than the book values shown on their balance sheets.[18] Indeed, more than half of the firms in the industry were economically insolvent, many massively so.[19]

The Discrepancy between the Market and Book Values of Equity.   The degree to which the book value of an FI's capital deviates from its true economic market value depends on a number of factors, especially:

1. Interest Rate Volatility—the higher the interest rate volatility, the greater the discrepancy.
2. Examination and Enforcement—the more frequent are on-site and off-site examinations and the stiffer the examiner/regulator standards regarding charging off problem loans, the smaller the discrepancy.
3. Loan Trading—the more loans that are traded, the easier it is to assess the true market value of the loan portfolio.

In actual practice, we can get an idea of the discrepancy between book values (BV) and market values (MV) of equity for large publicly traded FIs even when the FI does not mark its balance sheet to market.

17. The FDIC Improvement Act of 1991 requires examinations at least annually for large and troubled banks and every 18 months for smaller, healthy banks. Banks produce call reports (balance sheet and income statement data) quarterly.

18. Note that although book values were not directly affected by changes in interest rates, the increase in interest rates resulted in shrinking spreads and accounting earnings. As a result, the rise in interest rates did not leave the book value accounting results entirely unaffected.

19. See L. J. White, *The S and L Debacle* (New York: Oxford University Press, 1991), p. 89

Table 23–11 Market-to-Book Value Ratios for U.S. Banks

Bank Name	Market-to-Book Ratio
AmSouth Bancorp	3.34X
Banc One Corp.	3.47
Bank of New York	4.70
BankAmerica	3.06
BankBoston Corp.	3.60
Bankers Trust	2.20
BB&T Corp.	3.93
Chase Manhattan	3.11
Citicorp	3.39
Comerica	4.02
Commerce Bancorp	2.78
First America	3.12
First Chicago	3.26
First Union	3.04
Fleet Financial	2.99
J.P. Morgan	1.91
KeyCorp	2.93
MBNA Corp.	8.27
Mellon Bank	4.44
PNC Bank Corp.	2.96
Republic New York Corp.	2.24
SunTrust Bank	2.99
U.S. Bancorp	5.21
Wachovia Corp.	3.33
Wells Fargo	2.51

Source: *American Banker,* August 19, 1998, p. 9. *www.americanbanker.com/*

market-to-book ratio

A ratio that shows the discrepancy between the stock market value of an FI's equity and the book value of its equity.

Do You Understand?

1. Why an FI can be economically insolvent when its book value of net worth is positive?
2. What the major components of an FI's book value of equity are?
3. Whether book value accounting for loan losses is backward or forward looking?
4. What a market-to-book ratio that is less than 1 implies about an FI's performance?

Specifically, in an efficient capital market, the FI's stock price reflects the market value of the FI's outstanding equity shares. This valuation is based on the FI's current and expected future net earnings or dividend flows. The market value (MV) of equity per share is therefore:

$$MV = \frac{\text{Market value of equity ownership in shares outstanding}}{\text{Number of shares}}$$

By contrast, the historical or book value of the FI's equity per share (BV) is equal to:

$$BV = \frac{\text{Par value of equity} + \text{Surplus value} + \text{Retained earnings}}{\text{Number of shares}}$$

The ratio MV/BV is often called the **market-to-book ratio** and shows the degree of discrepancy between the market value of an FI's equity capital as perceived by investors in the stock market and the book value of capital on its balance sheet. The higher the market-to-book ratio, the more the book value of capital understates an FI's true equity or economic net worth position as perceived by investors in the capital market. Table 23–11 lists the market-to-book ratios for selected U.S. banks. The values range from a low of 1.91 times for J.P. Morgan to 8.27 times for MBNA Corp. The high market-to-book ratio for MBNA may reflect its specialization in credit card lending. MBNA's specialization in this area has generated substantial intangible value in the form of customer knowledge and relationships that are valued highly by capital markets but do not show up directly on MBNA's balance sheet.

Summary

This chapter provided an in-depth look at the measurement and on-balance-sheet management of interest rate and insolvency risks. The chapter first introduced two methods to measure an FI's interest rate gap and thus its risk exposure: the repricing model and the duration model. The repricing model concentrates only on the net interest income effects of rate changes and ignores balance sheet or market value effects. As such it gives a partial, but potentially misleading, picture of an FI's interest rate risk exposure. The duration model is superior to the simple repricing model because it incorporates the effects of interest rate changes on the market values of assets and liabilities. The chapter concluded with an analysis of the role of an FI's capital in insulating it against credit, interest rate, and other risks. According to economic theory, shareholder equity capital or economic net worth should be measured on a market value basis as the difference between the market value of an FI's assets and liabilities. In actuality, regulators use a mixture of book value and market value accounting rules. For example, FIs are required to mark-to-market investment securities held as trading assets, while being able to carry most loans at their book values. This mix of book value and market value accounting for various assets and liabilities creates a potential distortion in the measured net worth of the FI.

End-of-Chapter Questions

1. Why is the length of time selected for repricing assets and liabilities important when using the repricing model?

2. Calculate the repricing gap and impact on net interest income of a 1 percent increase in interest rates for the following positions:
   a. Rate-sensitive assets = $100 million; Rate-sensitive liabilities = $50 million.
   b. Rate-sensitive assets = $50 million; Rate-sensitive liabilities = $150 million.
   c. Rate-sensitive assets = $75 million; Rate-sensitive liabilities = $70 million.
   d. What conclusions can you draw about the repricing model from the above results?

3. Consider the repricing model.
   a. What are some of its weaknesses?
   b. How have large banks solved the problem of choosing the optimal time period for repricing?

4. Which of the following assets or liabilities fit the one-year rate or repricing sensitivity test?
   a. 91-day U.S. Treasury bills.
   b. 1-year U.S. Treasury notes.
   c. 20-year U.S. Treasury bonds.
   d. 20-year floating-rate corporate bonds with annual repricing.
   e. 30-year floating-rate mortgages with repricing every two years.

   f. 30-year floating-rate mortgages with repricing every six months.
   g. Overnight fed funds.
   h. 9-month fixed-rate CDs.
   i. 1-year fixed-rate CDs.
   j. 5-year floating-rate CDs with annual repricing.
   k. Common stock.

5. If a bank manager was quite certain that interest rates were going to rise within the next six months, how should the bank manager adjust the bank's repricing gap to take advantage of this anticipated rise? What if the manager believed rates would fall?

6. What is the difference between book value accounting and market value accounting? How do interest rate changes affect the value of bank assets and liabilities under the two methods?

7. If you use duration only to immunize your portfolio, what three factors affect changes in an FI's net worth when interest rates change?

8. Consider the following.
   a. Calculate the leverage-adjusted duration gap of an FI that has assets of $1 million invested in 30-year, 10 percent semiannual coupon Treasury bonds selling at par and whose duration has been estimated at 9.94 years. It has liabilities of $900,000 financed through a two-year, 7.25 percent semiannual coupon note selling at par.

b. What is the impact on equity values if all interest rates fall 20 basis points—that is, $(\Delta R/2)(1 + R/2) = -0.0020$?

9. If interest rates rise and an investor holds a bond for a time longer than the duration, will the return earned exceed or fall short of the original required rate of return?

10. Use the data provided for Gotbucks Bank, Inc. to answer this question.

Gotbucks Bank, Inc. (in $ millions)

Assets		Liabilities	
Cash	$ 30	Core deposits	$ 20
Federal funds	20	Federal funds	50
Loans (floating)	105	Euro CDs	130
Loans (fixed)	65	Equity	20
Total assets	$220	Total liabilities and equity	$220

Notes to the balance sheet: Currently, the fed funds rate is 8.5 percent. Variable-rate loans are priced at 4 percent over LIBOR (currently at 11 percent). Fixed-rate loans are selling at par and have five-year maturities with 12 percent interest paid annually. Core deposits are all fixed rate for two years at 8 percent paid annually. Euros currently yield 9 percent.

a. What is the duration of Gotbucks Bank's (GBI) fixed-rate loan portfolio if the loans are priced at par?

b. If the average duration of GBI's floating-rate loans (including fed fund assets) is .36 years, what is the duration of the bank's assets? (Note that the duration of cash is zero.)

c. What is the duration of GBI's core deposits if they are priced at par?

d. If the duration of GBI's Euro CD and fed fund liabilities is .401 years, what is the duration of the bank's liabilities?

e. What is GBI's duration gap? What is its interest rate risk exposure? If *all* yields increase by 1 percent, what is the impact on the market value of GBI's equity? (That is, $\Delta R/1 + R = .01$ for all assets and liabilities.)

11. An insurance company issued a $90 million one-year, zero-coupon note at 8 percent add-on annual interest (paying one coupon at the end of the year) and used the proceeds to fund a $100 million face value, two-year commercial loan at 10 percent annual interest. Immediately after these transactions were (simultaneously) undertaken, all interest rates went up 1.5 percent.

a. What is the market value of the insurance company's loan investment after the changes in interest rates?

b. What is the duration of the loan investment when it was first issued?

c. Using duration, what is the expected change in the value of the loan if interest rates are predicted to increase to 11.5 percent from the initial 10 percent?

d. What is the market value of the insurance company's $90 million liability when interest rates rise by 1.5 percent?

e. What is the duration of the insurance company's liability when it is first issued?

12. Use the following balance sheet information to answer the questions.

Balance Sheet ($ thousands) and Duration (in years)

	Duration	Amount
T-bills	0.5	$ 90
T-notes	0.9	55
T-bonds	4.393	176
Loans	7	2,724
Deposits	1	2,092
Federal funds	.01	238
Equity		715

Notes: Treasury Bonds are five-year maturities paying 6% semiannually and selling at par.

a. What is the average duration of all the assets?

b. What is the average duration of all the liabilities?

c. What is the FI's leverage-adjusted duration gap? What is the FI's interest rate risk exposure?

d. If the entire yield curve shifted upward 0.5 percent (i.e., $\Delta R/1 + R = .0050$), what is the impact on the FI's market value of equity?

e. If the entire yield curve shifted downward 0.25 percent (i.e., $\Delta R/1 + R = -.0025$), what is the impact on the FI's market value of equity?

13. If a bank manager was quite certain that interest rates were going to rise within the next six months, how should the bank manager adjust the bank's duration gap to take advantage of this anticipated rise? What if the manager believed rates would fall?

14. What are the criticisms of using the duration model to immunize an FI's portfolio?

15. Consider the following.

a. What is the duration of a two-year bond that pays an annual coupon of 10 percent and whose current yield to maturity is 14 percent? Use $1,000 as the face value.

b. What is the expected change in the price of a bond if interest rates are expected to decline by 0.5 percent?

16. What are some of the arguments for and against the use of market value versus book value of capital?

17. Why is the market value of equity a better measure of a bank's ability to absorb losses than book value of equity?

18. Go to the FDIC website and look up the assets, deposits, liabilities, and equity capital of all insured banks for the five most recent years available. How has the ratio of equity to assets changed over this period?

19. Consider the following income statement for WatchoverU Savings Inc. (in millions):

Assets		Liabilities	
Floating-rate		Demand deposits	
mortgages	$ 60	(currently	$105
(currently 10% p.a.)		6% p.a.)	
30-year fixed-rate loans	90	Time deposits	$ 25
(currently		(currently	
7% p.a.)		6% p.a.)	
		Equity	20
Total	$150		$150

a. What is WatchoverU's expected net interest income
at year end?
b. What will be the net interest income at year end if
interest rates rise by 2 percent?
c. Using the 1-year cumulative repricing gap model,
what is the expected net interest income for a 2 percent increase in interest rates?
20. Use the following information about a hypothetical
government security dealer named J.P. Groman. (Market yields are in parentheses; amounts are in millions.)

J.P. Groman

Cash	$ 10	Overnight repos	$170
1 month T-bills (7.05%)	75	Subordinated debt	
3 month T-bills (7.25%)	75	7-year fixed (8.55%)	150
2-year T-notes (7.50%)	50		
8-year T-notes (8.96%)	100		
5-year munis			
(floating rate)			
(8.20% reset			
every six months)	25	Equity	15
Total	$335		$335

a. What is the repricing or funding gap if the planning
period is 30 days? 91 days? 2 years? (Recall that
cash is a noninterest-earning asset.)
b. What is the impact over the next 30 days on net interest income if all interest rates rise by 50 basis
points?
c. The following one-year runoffs are expected: $10
million for two-year T-notes, $20 million for the
eight-year T-notes. What is the one-year repricing
gap?
d. If runoffs are considered, what is the effect on net
interest income at year end if interest rates rise by
50 basis points?

chapter twenty-four

Managing Risk with Derivative Securities

Chapter Navigator

1. How can interest rate risk be hedged using forward contracts?

2. How can interest rate risk be hedged using future contracts?

3. What is the difference between a microhedge and a macrohedge?

4. How can interest rate risk be hedged using option contracts?

5. How can interest rate risk be hedged using swap contracts?

6. How do the different hedging methods compare?

Derivative Securities Used to Manage Risk: Chapter Overview

Chapters 21 through 23 described ways financial institutions (FIs) measure and manage various risks on the balance sheet. Rather than managing risk by making on-balance-sheet changes to hedge these risks, FIs are increasingly turning to off-balance-sheet instruments such as forwards, futures, options, and swaps. As the use of these derivatives has increased, so have the fees and revenues FIs have generated (see In the News box 24–1). We discussed the basic characteristics of derivative securities and derivative securities markets in Chapter 10. This chapter considers the role that derivative securities contracts play in managing an FI's interest rate risk, foreign exchange, and credit risk exposures. Although large banks and other FIs are responsible for a significant amount of derivatives trading activity, FIs of all sizes have used these instruments to hedge their asset-liability risk exposures.

In the News

24-1

Market Trends

Revenues from Trading Show Huge Improvements in Fourth Quarter

Bank revenues from derivatives rebounded sharply in last year's final quarter—a vast improvement from the previous quarter, when global and domestic market volatility saw growth recede, the Office of the Comptroller of Currency reported last week. Revenues from trading derivatives and other types of cash instruments rose to $2 billion after totaling only $614 million in the third quarter. But the fourth quarter level was still below the $2.6 billion total from the second quarter, OCC figures show. Trading revenue reached $7.9 billion for all of last year, nearly in line with the $8 billion racked up in 1997, said the

Source: *Bond Buyer*, March 29, 1999, p. 31, by Rachel Koning.

OCC, which oversees U.S. national banks.

"The fourth quarter marked a return to stability," said Michael Brosnan, the OCC's deputy comptroller for risk evaluation. "The previous three months were characterized by extreme volatility in both domestic and foreign markets, including the default in Russia. That volatility led to unexpected losses on trading positions at a number of banks." In particular, banks found interest rates returning in their favor in the final quarter of the year, the OCC noted. "Revenues from interest rate positions

bounced back to $669 million in the fourth quarter, compared to a loss of $284 million in the previous three months."

The notional volume of all outstanding derivative products was up for the thirteenth straight quarter, and wrapped up 1998 valued at $32.9 trillion, up from $32.5 trillion at the end of the third quarter, according to the OCC. The most popular contracts continue to be tied to interest rates and foreign exchange transactions. Moreover, "over-the-counter transactions, particularly swaps, continue to be the contract of choice for both banks and their customers," the OCC said in part of a press briefing to release its quarterly report. "Eighty-seven percent of derivatives are in (OTC) contracts, while 13% are exchange-traded."

www.americanbanker.com/

Do You Understand?

1. What the fourth quarter 1999 revenue from derivatives trading was?
2. What the most actively traded derivative contracts in 1999 were?

spot contract

An agreement to transact involving the immediate exchange of assets and funds.

Forward and Futures Contracts

To present the essential nature and characteristics of forward and futures contracts, we first review the comparison of these derivative contracts with spot contracts (see also Chapter 10).

Spot Contract. A **spot contract** is an agreement between a buyer and a seller at time 0, when the seller of the asset agrees to deliver it immediately for cash and the buyer agrees to pay in cash for that asset.[1] Thus,

---

1. Technically, physical settlement and delivery may take place one or two days after the contractual spot agreement in bond markets. In equity markets, delivery and cash settlement normally occur three business days after the spot contract agreement.

642

the unique feature of a spot market is the immediate and simultaneous exchange of cash for securities, or what is often called *delivery versus payment*. A spot bond quote of $97 for a 20-year maturity bond means that the buyer must pay the seller $97, per $100 of face value, for immediate delivery of the 20-year bond.[2]

forward contract

An agreement to transact involving the future exchange of a set amount of assets at a set price.

Forward Contract.   A **forward contract** is a contractual agreement between a buyer and a seller, at time 0, to exchange a prespecified asset for cash at some later date. For example, in a three-month forward contract to deliver 20-year bonds, the buyer and seller agree on a price and amount today (time 0), but the delivery (or exchange) of the 20-year bond for cash does not occur until three months hence. If the forward price agreed to at time 0 was $97 per $100 of face value, in three months' time the seller delivers $100 of 20-year bonds and receives $97 from the buyer. This is the price the buyer must pay and the seller must accept no matter what happens to the spot price of 20-year bonds during the three months between the time the contract was entered into and the time the bonds are delivered for payment.

Forward contracts often involve underlying assets that are nonstandardized (e.g., six-month pure discount bonds). As a result, the buyer and seller involved in a forward contract must locate and deal directly with each other to set the terms of the contract rather than transacting the sale in a centralized market. Accordingly, once a party has agreed to a forward position, canceling the deal prior to expiration is generally difficult (although an offsetting forward contract can normally be arranged).

futures contract

An agreement to transact involving the future exchange of a set amount of assets for a price that is settled daily.

marked to market

Describes the prices on outstanding futures contracts that are adjusted each day to reflect current futures market conditions.

Futures Contract.   A **futures contract** is usually arranged by an organized exchange. It is an agreement between a buyer and a seller at time 0 to exchange a standardized, prespecified asset for cash at some later date. As such, a futures contract is very similar to a forward contract. The difference relates to the price, which in a forward contract is fixed over the life of the contract ($97 per $100 of face value with payment in three months), but a futures contract is **marked to market** daily. This means that the contract's price is adjusted each day as the futures price for the contract changes. Therefore, actual daily cash settlements occur between the buyer and seller in response to this marking-to-market process. This can be compared to a forward contract for which cash payment from buyer to seller occurs only at the end of the contract period.[3]

naive hedge

A hedge of a cash asset on a direct dollar-for-dollar basis with a forward or futures contract.

Hedging with Forward Contracts

To understand the usefulness of forward contracts in hedging an FI's interest rate risk, consider a simple example of a **naive hedge** (a hedge of a cash asset on a direct dollar-for-dollar basis with a forward or futures contract). Suppose that an FI portfolio manager holds a 20-year, $1 million face value government bond on the balance sheet. At time 0, the market values these bonds at $97 per $100 of face value, or $970,000 in total. Assume that the manager receives a forecast that interest rates are expected to rise by 2 percent from their current level of 8 percent to 10 percent over the next three months. Knowing that if the predicted change in interest rates is correct, rising interest rates mean that bond prices will fall, the manager stands to make a capital loss on the bond portfolio. Having read Chapters 3 and 23, the manager is an expert on duration and has calculated the 20-year maturity bond's duration to be exactly nine years. Thus, the manager can predict a capital loss, or change in bond values (ΔP), from the duration equation of Chapter 3:[4]

---

2. Throughout this chapter, as we refer to the prices of various securities, we do not include the transaction fees charged by brokers and dealers for conducting trades for investors and hedgers (see Chapter 10).

3. Another difference between forwards and futures is that forward contracts are bilateral contracts subject to counterparty default risk, but the default risk on futures is significantly reduced by the futures exchange guaranteeing to indemnify counterparties against credit or default risk.

4. For simplicity, we ignore issues relating to convexity here.

$$\frac{\Delta P}{P} = -D \times \frac{\Delta R}{1 + R}$$

where

ΔP = Capital loss on bond = ?
P = Initial value of bond position = \$970,000
D = Duration of the bond = 9 years
ΔR = Change in forecast yield = .02
$1 + R$ = 1 plus the current yield on 20-year bond = 1.08

$$\frac{\Delta P}{\$970,000} = -9 \times \left(\frac{.02}{1.08}\right)$$

$$\Delta P = -9 \times \$970,000 \times \left(\frac{.02}{1.08}\right) = -\$161,667$$

As a result, the FI portfolio manager expects to incur a capital loss on the bond of \$161,667—as a percentage loss ($\Delta P/P$) = 16.67%—or a drop in price from \$97 per \$100 face value to \$80.833 per \$100 face value. To offset this loss—in fact, to reduce the risk of capital loss to zero—the manager may hedge this position by taking an off-balance-sheet hedge, such as selling \$1 million face value of 20-year bonds for forward delivery in three months' time.[5] Suppose that at time 0, the portfolio manager can find a buyer willing to pay \$97 for every \$100 of 20-year bonds delivered in three months' time.

Now consider what happens to the FI portfolio manager if the gloomy forecast of a 2 percent rise in interest rates is accurate. The portfolio manager's bond position has fallen in value by 16.67 percent, equal to a capital loss of \$161,667. After the rise in interest rates, however, the manager can buy \$1 million face value of 20-year bonds in the spot market at \$80.833 per \$100 of face value, a total cost of \$808,333, and deliver these bonds to the forward contract buyer. Remember that the forward contract buyer agreed to pay \$97 per \$100 of face value for the \$1 million of face value bonds delivered, or \$970,000. As a result, the portfolio manager makes a profit on the forward transaction of:

\$970,000	−	\$808,333	=	\$161,667
(price paid by forward buyer to forward seller)		(cost of purchasing bonds in the spot market at t = month 3 for delivery to the forward buyer)		

As you can see, the on-balance-sheet loss of \$161,667 is exactly offset by the off-balance-sheet gain of \$161,667 from selling the forward contract. In fact, for any change in interest rates, a loss (gain) on the balance sheet is offset by a partial or complete gain (loss) on the forward contract. Indeed, the success of a hedge does not hinge on the manager's ability to accurately forecast interest rates. Rather, the reason for the hedge is the lack of ability to perfectly predict interest rate changes. The hedge allows the FI manager to protect against interest rate changes even if they are not perfectly predicted. Thus, the FI's net interest rate exposure is zero, or, in the parlance of finance, it has **immunized** its assets against interest rate risk.

immunized

Describes an FI that is fully hedged or protected against adverse movements in interest rates (or asset prices).

Hedging with Futures Contracts

Even though some hedging of interest rate risk does take place using forward contracts—such as forward rate agreements commonly used by insurance

---

5. Since a forward contract involves the delivery of bonds at a future time period, it does not appear on the balance sheet, which records only current and past transactions. Thus, forwards are one example of off-balance-sheet items (see Chapter 13).

companies and banks prior to mortgage loan originations—most FIs hedge interest rate risk either at the micro level (called *microhedging*) or at the macro level (called *macrohedging*) using futures contracts. Before looking at futures contracts, we explain the difference between microhedging and macrohedging.

microhedging

Using a futures (forward) contract to hedge a specific asset or liability.

Microhedging. An FI is **microhedging** when it employs a futures or a forward contract to hedge a particular asset or liability risk. For example, we earlier considered a simple example of microhedging asset-side portfolio risk in which an FI manager wanted to insulate the value of the institution's bond portfolio fully against a rise in interest rates. An example of microhedging on the liability side of the balance sheet occurs when an FI, attempting to lock in a cost of funds to protect itself against a possible rise in short-term interest rates, takes a short (sell) position in futures contracts on CDs or T-bills. In microhedging, the FI manager often tries to pick a futures or forward contract whose underlying deliverable asset closely matches the asset (or liability) position being hedged. The earlier example of exactly matching the asset in the portfolio with the deliverable security underlying the forward contract (20-year bonds) was unrealistic. Because such exact matching often cannot be achieved, the usual situation produces a residual "unhedgeable" risk termed **basis risk**. This risk occurs mainly because the prices of the assets or liabilities that an FI wishes to hedge are imperfectly correlated over time with the prices on the futures or forward contract used to hedge risk.

basis risk

A residual risk that occurs because the movement in a spot (cash) asset's price is not perfectly correlated with the movement in the price of the asset delivered under a futures or forward contract.

macrohedging

Hedging the entire duration gap of an FI.

Macrohedging. **Macrohedging** occurs when an FI manager wishes to use futures or other derivative securities to hedge the entire balance sheet duration gap. This contrasts with microhedging in which an FI manager identifies specific assets and liabilities and seeks individual futures and other derivative contracts to hedge those individual risks. Note that macrohedging and microhedging can lead to quite different hedging strategies and results. In particular, a macrohedge takes a whole portfolio view and allows for individual asset and liability interest sensitivities or durations to net out each other. This can result in a very different aggregate futures position than when an FI manager disregards this netting or portfolio effect and hedges only individual asset and liability positions on a one-to-one basis.[6]

The Choice between Microhedging and Macrohedging. Several factors affect an FI's choice between microhedging and macrohedging interest rate risk. These include risk-return considerations, accounting rules, and for depository institutions, federal regulation.

Risk-Return Considerations. Ideally, an FI would like to reduce its interest rate or other risk exposures to their lowest possible level by buying or selling sufficient futures to offset the interest rate risk exposure of its whole balance sheet or cash positions in each asset and liability. For example, this reduction might be achieved by macrohedging the duration gap. However, since reducing risk also reduces expected return, not all FI managers seek to do this.

Rather than taking a fully hedged position, many FIs choose to bear some interest rate risk as well as credit and FX risks because of their comparative advantage as FIs (see Chapter 1). For example, an FI manager may generate expectations regarding future interest rates before deciding on a futures position. As a result, the manager may selectively hedge only a portion of its balance sheet position, or microhedge.

---

6. P. H. Munter, D. K. Clancy, and C. T. Moores found that macrohedges provided better hedge performance than microhedges in a number of different interest rate environments. See "Accounting for Financial Futures: A Question of Risk Reduction," in *Advances in Accounting* (1986), pp. 51–70. See also R. Stoebe, "Macrohedging Bank Investment Portfolios," *Bankers Magazine*, November–December 1994, pp. 45–48.

Alternatively, the FI manager may decide to remain unhedged or even to overhedge by selling more futures than the cash position requires, although regulators may view this as speculative. Thus, the fully hedged position becomes one of several choices depending, in part, on managerial interest rate expectations, managerial objectives, and the nature of the return-risk trade-off from hedging.

www.rutgers.edu/
Accounting/raw/fasb/

Accounting Rules and Hedging Strategies. The Financial Accounting Standards Board (FASB) has made a number of rulings regarding the accounting and tax treatment of futures transactions.[7] In hedge accounting, a futures position is a hedge transaction if it can be linked to a particular asset or liability. An example is using a T-bond futures contract to hedge an FI's holdings of long-term bonds as investments.

In 1997, the FASB required that all gains and losses on derivatives used to hedge assets and liabilities on the balance sheet be recognized *immediately* as earnings, together with the offsetting gain or loss on the hedged item. Thus, the 1997 ruling effectively requires derivatives to be marked to market. Additionally, U.S. companies that hold or issue derivatives must report their trading objectives and strategies in public document disclosures such as annual reports.[8]

www.bog.frb.fed.us/

www.fdic.gov/

www.occ.treas.gov/

Policies of Bank Regulators. The main bank regulators—the Federal Reserve, the FDIC, and the Comptroller of the Currency—have issued uniform guidelines for banks taking positions in futures and forwards. These guidelines require a bank to (1) establish internal guidelines regarding its hedging activity, (2) establish trading limits, and (3) disclose large contract positions that materially affect a bank's risk to shareholders and outside investors. Overall, regulatory policy is to encourage the use of futures for hedging and to discourage their use for speculation, although—as noted—on a practical basis, it is often difficult to distinguish between the two.

Finally, as Chapter 14 discusses, futures contracts are not subject to the risk-based capital requirements imposed by regulators on depository institutions; by contrast, over-the-counter forward contracts are potentially subject to capital requirements. Other things being equal, the risk-based capital requirements favor the use of futures over forwards. To the dismay of some legislators in Congress and regulators, the use of derivative securities in some nondepository FIs—especially hedge funds—remains virtually unregulated.[9]

Do You Understand?

1. The difference between a futures contract and a forward contract?
2. What the major differences between a spot contract and a forward contract are?
3. How a naive hedge works?
4. What is meant by the phrase "an FI has immunized its portfolio against a particular risk."
5. When a futures position is a hedge transaction according to FASB rules?

Microhedging with Futures. The number of futures contracts that an FI should buy or sell in a microhedge depends on the interest rate risk exposure created by a particular asset or liability on the balance sheet. The key is to take a position in the futures market to offset a loss on the balance sheet due to a move in interest rates with a gain in the futures market. Table 24–1 lists interest rate futures contracts that are currently available. In this list, a March 2000 Eurodollar futures contract can be bought (long) or sold (short) on January 18, 2000, for 93.77 percent of the face value of the Eurodollar CD contract, or the yield on the Eurodollar CD contract deliverable in March 2000 will be 6.23 percent (100% − 93.77%). The minimum contract size on one of these futures is $1,000,000, so a position in one contract can be taken at a price of $937,700.

The subsequent profit or loss from a position in March 2000 Eurodollar futures taken on January 18, 2000, is graphically described in

---

7. *FASB Statement No. 80,* "Accounting for Futures Contracts" (1984) is probably the most important.

8. See "Called to Account," *Risk Magazine,* August 1996, pp. 15–17.

9. See "Long-Term Capital Management: Regulators Need to Focus Greater Attention on Systematic Risk," GAO/GGD-00-3 (October 1999).

Table 24–1   Futures Contracts on Interest Rates, January 18, 2000

INTEREST RATE

TREASURY BONDS (CBT)-$100,000; pts. 32nds of 100%

	Open	High	Low	Settle	Change	Lifetime High	Lifetime Low	Open Interest
Mar	89-22	89-27	89-00	89-07	− 17	101-07	89-00	597,119
June	89-16	89-16	88-22	88-28	− 18	99-15	88-22	45,348
Sept	88-16	88-19	88-16	88-19	− 18	93-28	88-16	626

Est vol 260,000; vol Fri 475,394; open int 643,134, +16,738.

TREASURY BONDS (MCE)-$50,000; pts. 32nds of 100%

	Open	High	Low	Settle	Change	High	Low	Open Interest
Mar	89-16	89-19	89-00	89-08	− 17	96-01	89-00	8,706

Est vol 2,600; vol Fri 5,445; open int 8,714, +100.

TREASURY NOTES (CBT)-$100,000; pts. 32nds of 100%

	Open	High	Low	Settle	Change	High	Low	Open Interest
Mar	94-19	94-23	93-32	94-04	− 16	100-11	93-32	567,863
June	94-06	94-07	93-22	93-26	− 17	96-10	93-22	22,052

Est vol 170,000; vol Fri 177,212; open int 589,915, +13,495.

5 YR TREAS NOTES (CBT)-$100,000; pts. 32nds of 100%

	Open	High	Low	Settle	Change	High	Low	Open Interest
Mar	97-105	97-125	97-00	97-035	− 7.5	00-055	97-00	379,607

Est vol 65,000; vol Fri 77,308; open int 388,545, +1,878.

2 YR TREAS NOTES (CBT)-$200,000; pts. 32nds of 100%

	Open	High	Low	Settle	Change	High	Low	Open Interest
Mar	98-31	98-312	98-267	98-287	− 2.2	00-035	98-267	32,502

Est vol 3,000; vol Mon 1,943; open int 32,502, −32.

30-DAY FEDERAL FUNDS (CBT)-$5 million; pts. of 100%

	Open	High	Low	Settle	Change	High	Low	Open Interest
Jan	94.550	94.550	94.530	94.545	− .015	95.260	94.400	8,871
Feb	94.22	94.22	94.21	94.21	− .01	94.75	94.17	8,095
Mar	94.13	94.14	94.13	94.13	....	94.50	94.10	3,640
Apr	94.00	94.01	94.00	94.00	....	94.45	93.98	1,884
May	93.91	93.91	93.91	93.91	....	94.20	93.91	468

Est vol 2,100; vol Fri 5,826; open int 22,969, +913.

MUNI BOND INDEX (CBT)-$1,000; times Bond Buyer MBI

	Open	High	Low	Settle	Change	High	Low	Open Interest
Mar	90-25	90-30	90-17	90-18	− 14	97-00	90-17	21,237

Est vol 1,400; vol Fri 1,817; open int 21,318, −255.
Index: Close 91-07; Yield 6.69.

TREASURY BILLS (CME)-$1 mil.; pts. of 100%

	Open	High	Low	Settle	Chg	Discount Settle	Discount Chg	Open Interest
Mar	....	....	....	94.43	....	5.57	....	2,411

Est vol 0; vol Fri 3; open int 2,411, +3.

LIBOR-1 MO. (CME)-$3,000,000; points of 100%

	Open	High	Low	Settle	Chg	Discount Settle	Discount Chg	Open Interest
Feb	94.04	94.04	94.03	94.04	....	5.96	....	12,439
Mar	93.91	93.92	93.91	93.91	....	6.09	....	4,599
Apr	93.84	93.85	93.84	93.84	....	6.16	....	1,278
May	93.73	93.73	93.73	93.73	+ .01	6.27	− .01	134
June	....	....	....	93.56	....	6.44	....	138
July	....	....	....	93.47	....	6.53	....	447
Aug	....	....	....	93.40	....	6.60	....	334
Sept	....	....	....	93.32	− .01	6.68	+ .01	450
Oct	93.24	93.24	93.22	93.23	....	6.77	....	275
Nov	....	....	....	93.18	− .01	6.82	+ .01	400

Est vol 3,019; vol Fri 4,819; open int 34,586, +1,416.

EURODOLLAR (CME)-$1 million; pts of 100%

	Open	High	Low	Settle	Chg	Yield Settle	Yield Chg	Open Interest
Feb	93.85	93.86	93.85	93.85	....	6.15	....	17,431
Mar	93.76	93.77	93.76	93.77	....	6.23	....	496,047
Apr	93.65	93.65	93.65	93.65	....	6.35	....	454
May	93.52	93.53	93.52	93.52	....	6.48	....	185
June	93.41	93.43	93.39	93.41	....	6.59	....	462,186
Sept	93.16	93.17	93.12	93.16	− .01	6.84	+ .01	387,544
Dec	92.94	92.95	92.90	92.94	− .02	7.06	+ .02	287,625
Mr01	92.88	92.89	92.85	92.88	− .03	7.12	+ .03	236,869
June	92.80	92.81	92.76	92.78	− .04	7.22	+ .04	170,063
Sept	92.75	92.75	92.70	92.73	− .04	7.27	+ .04	121,621
Dec	92.66	92.67	92.61	92.64	− .05	7.36	+ .05	99,806
Mr02	92.69	92.70	92.65	92.67	− .05	7.33	+ .05	94,781
June	92.68	92.69	92.63	92.65	− .05	7.35	+ .05	67,739
Sept	92.67	92.67	92.61	92.63	− .05	7.37	+ .05	63,676
Dec	92.58	92.58	92.55	92.57	− .06	7.43	+ .06	62,115
Mr03	92.64	92.64	92.58	92.60	− .06	7.40	+ .06	57,411
June	92.61	92.62	92.55	92.57	− .06	7.43	+ .06	51,091
Sept	92.59	92.59	92.53	92.54	− .07	7.46	+ .07	56,405
Dec	92.50	92.51	92.44	92.45	− .07	7.55	+ .07	30,504
Mr04	92.49	92.49	92.44	92.46	− .07	7.54	+ .07	26,709
June	92.44	92.44	92.39	92.41	− .07	7.59	+ .07	22,829
Sept	92.40	92.40	92.35	92.36	− .07	7.64	+ .07	17,419
Dec	92.32	92.33	92.26	92.27	− .07	7.73	+ .07	17,664
Mr05	....	....	....	92.27	− .07	7.73	+ .07	12,384
June	92.23	92.24	92.22	92.23	− .07	7.77	+ .07	11,281
Sept	92.26	92.26	92.18	92.19	− .07	7.81	+ .07	10,702
Dec	....	....	....	92.10	− .07	7.90	+ .07	6,262
Mr06	92.17	92.17	92.09	92.11	− .07	7.89	+ .07	5,955
June	92.12	92.12	92.05	92.06	− .07	7.94	+ .07	5,047
Sept	92.09	92.09	92.01	92.03	− .07	7.97	+ .07	4,816
Dec	....	....	....	91.93	− .07	8.07	+ .07	3,938
Mr07	91.96	91.96	91.93	91.94	− .08	8.06	+ .08	3,929
June	....	....	....	91.89	− .08	8.11	+ .08	3,279
Sept	....	....	....	91.86	− .08	8.14	+ .08	3,455
Dec	....	....	....	91.76	− .08	8.24	+ .08	5,028
Mr08	....	....	....	91.77	− .08	8.23	+ .08	3,362
June	....	....	....	91.72	− .08	8.28	+ .08	4,084
Sept	....	....	....	91.69	− .08	8.31	+ .08	3,603
Dec	....	....	....	91.59	− .08	8.41	+ .08	2,934
Mr09	....	....	....	91.60	− .08	8.40	+ .08	2,187
June	....	....	....	91.55	− .08	8.45	+ .08	1,864
Sept	....	....	....	91.52	− .08	8.48	+ .08	1,582
Dec	....	....	....	91.42	− .08	8.58	+ .08	793

Est vol 262,109; vol Fri 524,222; open int 2,986,753, +4,953.

Source: *The Wall Street Journal*, January 19, 2000, p. C22. Reprinted by permission of *The Wall Street Journal*. © 2000 Dow Jones & Company, Inc. All Rights Reserved Worldwide. *www.cbot.com/; www.cme.com/; www.wsj.com/*

Figure 24–1. A short position in the futures will produce a profit when interest rates rise (meaning that the value of the underlying Eurodollar contract decreases). Therefore, a short position in the futures market is the appropriate hedge when the FI stands

Figure 24–1 Profit or Loss on a Futures Position in Eurodollar Futures Taken on January 18, 2000

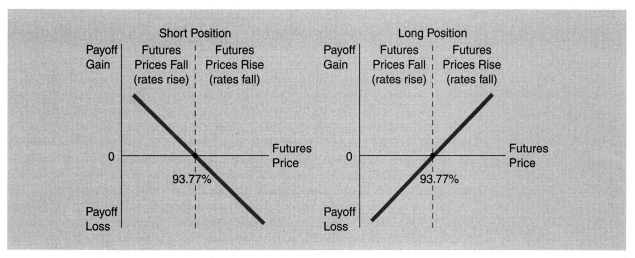

Figure 24–2 FI Value Change On and Off the Balance Sheet from a Perfect Short Hedge

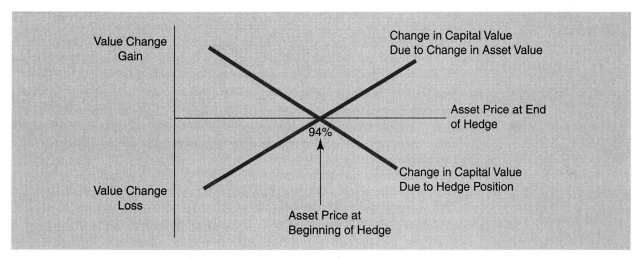

to lose on the balance sheet if interest rates are expected to rise (e.g., the FI holds Eurodollar CDs in its asset portfolio[10]). In fact, if the FI is perfectly hedged, any loss in value from a change in the yield on an asset on the balance sheet over the period of the hedge is exactly offset by a gain on the short position in the Eurodollar futures contract (see Figure 24–2). A long position in the futures market produces a profit when interest rates fall (meaning that the value of the underlying Eurodollar CD contract increases).[11] Therefore, a long position is the appropriate hedge when the FI stands to

10. We assume that the balance sheet has no liability of equal size and maturity (or duration) as the CD. If the FI has such a liability, any loss in value from the CD could be offset with an equivalent decrease in value from the liability. In this case, there is no interest rate risk exposure and thus there is no need to hedge.

11. Notice that if rates move in an opposite direction from that expected, losses are incurred on the futures position—that is, if rates rise and futures prices drop, the long hedger loses. Similarly, if rates fall and futures prices rise, the short hedger loses.

Table 24–2   Summary of Gains and Losses on Microhedges Using Futures Contracts

Type of Hedge	Change in Interest Rates	Cash Market	Futures Market
Long hedge (buy)	Decrease	Loss	Gain
Short hedge (sell)	Increase	Loss	Gain

lose on the balance sheet if interest rates are expected to fall.[12] Table 24–2 summarizes the long and short position.

Options

This section discusses the role of options in hedging interest rate risk. FIs have a wide variety of option products to use in hedging, including exchange-traded options, over-the-counter (OTC) options, options embedded in securities, and caps, collars, and floors (see Chapter 10). Not only have the types of option products increased in recent years but the use of options has increased as well. However, options can also lead to huge losses for FIs (see In the News box 24–2). We begin by reviewing the four basic option strategies: buying a call, writing (selling) a call, buying a put, and writing (selling) a put.[13]

Basic Features of Options

In describing the features of the four basic option strategies that FIs might employ to hedge interest rate risk, we review their return payoffs in terms of interest rate movements (see Chapter 10). Specifically, we consider bond options whose payoff values are inversely linked to interest rate movements in a manner similar to bond prices and interest rates in general (see Chapter 3).

call option

An option that gives a purchaser the right, but not the obligation, to buy the underlying security from the writer of the option at a prespecified exercise price on a prespecified date.

Buying a Call Option on a Bond.   The first strategy of buying (or taking a long position in) a call option on a bond is shown in Figure 24–3. A **call option** gives the purchaser the right (but not the obligation) to buy an underlying security—a bond—at a prespecified price called the *exercise* or *strike* price (X). In return, the buyer of the call option must pay the writer or seller an up-front fee known as a *call premium* (C). This premium is an immediate negative cash flow for the buyer of the call that potentially stands to make a profit should the underlying bond's price rise above the exercise price by an amount exceeding the premium. If the price of the bond never rises above X, the buyer of the call never exercises the option (i.e., buying the bond at X when its market value is less than X). In this case, the option matures unexercised. The call buyer incurs a cost C for the option, and no other cash flows result.

As Figure 24–3 shows, if the bond price rises to A (where A is the price at which $A - X = C$), the buyer of the call has broken even because the profit from exercising the call ($A - X$) just equals the premium payment for the call (C). If the price of the bond underlying the option rises to price B, the buyer makes a net profit of π, which is the difference between the bond price (B) and the exercise price of the option (X) minus the call premium ($\pi = B - X - C$).

---

12. This might be the case when the FI is financing itself with long-term, fixed-rate certificates of deposit.

13. The two basic option contracts are *puts* and *calls*. However, an FI could potentially be a buyer or seller (writer) of each.

In the News

Blind Faith

Full details about the derivatives losses at Union Bank of Switzerland (UBS) are still not known. But according to sources at UBS and at SBC Warburg Dillon Read, the investment-banking arm of Swiss Bank Corporation (SBC), two familiar factors may be at fault. One is that UBS traders may have fed incorrect data into the computer models that the bank used to price derivatives, particularly options. The other is that the bank had too much faith in its models.

Many of UBS's losses appear to have involved huge amounts of convertible preference shares, arcane securities issued last year in copious amounts by Japanese banks . . . Normally, a bank with such large positions protects itself against a drop in the value of its options. The best way, buying offsetting options in particular shares, is difficult and expensive, particularly in Japan. A second way for UBS to have

hedged its risk was to sell the banks' shares. UBS apparently did relatively little of this at the start: it thought that bank shares would not fall below the lowest price at which the preferred shares could be converted, so that its downside risks were limited.

Not so. Shares in Japanese banks fell precipitously when Yamaichi Securities, then Japan's fourth-largest securities firm, went bust in November. Share prices also became much more volatile, making it even more expensive for UBS to hedge its risk. UBS seems to have had a particularly large exposure to Fuji Bank, whose shares stopped trading altogether for three days.

UBS desperately tried to cut its losses by selling some of the Japanese banks' shares, to the point that in November and December it became the biggest seller of bank stocks. The result was to drive share prices down even more, magnifying the losses on its options. It also tried to sell futures contracts on the Nikkei 225

stock market average. But there were days when the Nikkei rose and bank shares fell. As a result, losses mounted alarmingly. UBS refuses to say whether it has incurred any losses on derivatives trading in Japan.

And why did UBS's global equity derivatives department sell so many options on Japanese banks' shares? The answer is that it seems to have systematically overestimated the value of these contracts. That value depends in part on the expected dividend yield on the underlying shares. Sources suggest that people in the global equity derivatives department may have fed inflated estimates of future dividends into the computers. To the bank's bosses, this would have made the positions in Japanese preference shares seem far more profitable than they were.

On top of that, the department seemingly had blind faith in the accuracy of the assumptions used to build price-setting models. This may be the best-known danger in derivatives dealing: everyone in the markets knows that if shares

Source: *The Economist*, January 31, 1998, p. 76. © 1998 The Economist Newspaper Group, Inc. Reprinted with permission. Further reproduction prohibited.

(continues)

Figure 24–3 Payoff Function for the Buyer of a Call Option on a Bond

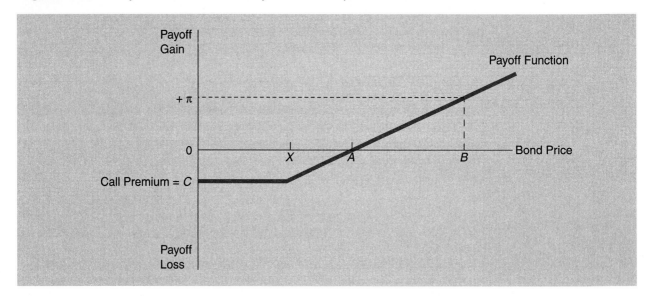

Notice two important things about bond call options in Figure 24–3:

1. As interest rates fall, bond prices rise, and the call option buyer has a large profit potential; the more rates fall (the higher bond prices rise), the larger the profit on the exercise of the option.
2. As interest rates rise, bond prices fall and the potential for a negative payoff (loss) for the buyer of the call option increases. If rates rise so that bond prices fall below the exercise price *X,* the call buyer is not obligated to exercise the option. Thus, the buyer's losses are truncated by the amount of the up-front premium payment (*C*) made to purchase the call option.

Thus, buying a call option is a strategy to take when interest rates are expected to fall. Notice that unlike interest rate futures, whose prices and payoffs move symmetrically with changes in the level of interest rates, the payoffs on bond call options move asymmetrically with changes in interest rates.[14] As we discuss below, this often results in options being the preferred hedging instruments over futures contracts.

14. This does not necessarily mean that options are less risky than spot or futures positions. Options can, in fact, be riskier than other investments since they exist for only a limited period of time and are leveraged investments (i.e., their value is only a fraction of the underlying security). To compare an option position to a spot position one must consider an equal dollar investment in the two positions over a common period of time.

Figure 24–4 Payoff Function for the Writer of a Call Option on a Bond

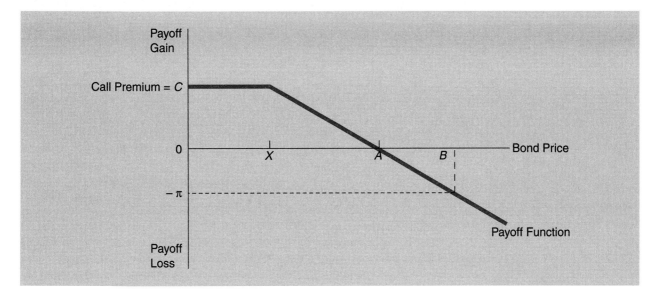

Writing a Call Option on a Bond. The second strategy is writing (or taking a short position in) a call option on a bond. In writing a call option on a bond, the writer or seller receives an up-front fee or premium (*C*) and must stand ready to sell the underlying bond to the purchaser of the option at the exercise price, *X*. Note the payoff from writing a call option on a bond in Figure 24–4.

Notice two important things about this payoff function:

1. When interest rates rise and bond prices fall, the potential for the writer of the call to receive a positive payoff or profit increases. The call buyer is less likely to exercise the option, which would force the option writer to sell the underlying bond at the exercise price. However, this profit has a maximum equal to the call premium (*C*) charged up front to the buyer of the option.
2. When interest rates fall and bond prices rise, the probability that the writer will take a loss increases. The call buyer will exercise the option, forcing the option writer to sell the underlying bonds. Since bond prices are theoretically unbounded in the upward direction, although they must return to par at maturity, these losses could be very large.

Thus, writing a call option is a strategy to take when interest rates are expected to rise. Caution is warranted, however, because profits are limited but losses are unlimited. A fall in interest rates and a rise in bond prices to *B* results in the writer of the option losing π (in Figure 24–4).

Buying a Put Option on a Bond. The third strategy is buying (or taking a long position in) a put option on a bond. The buyer of a **put option** on a bond has the right (but not the obligation) to sell the underlying bond to the writer of the option at the agreed exercise price (*X*). In return for this option, the buyer of the put option pays a premium (*P*) to the writer. We show the potential payoffs to the buyer of the put option in Figure 24–5. Note the following:

1. When interest rates rise and bond prices fall, the probability that the buyer of the put will make a profit from exercising the option increases. Thus, if bond prices fall to *D*, the buyer of the put option can purchase bonds in the bond market at that price and put them (sell them) back to the writer of the put at the higher exercise

put option

An option that gives a purchaser the right, but not the obligation, to sell the underlying security to the writer of the option at a prespecified exercise price on a prespecified date.

Figure 24–5 Payoff Function for the Buyer of a Put Option on a Bond

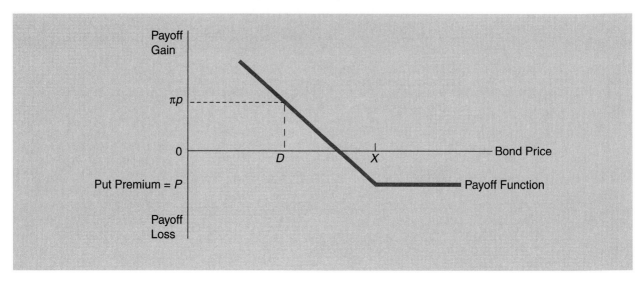

price X. As a result, after deducting the cost of the put premium, the buyer makes a profit of πp in Figure 24–5. The put option buyer has unlimited profit potential; the higher the rates rise, the more the bond prices fall and the larger the profit on the exercise of the option.

2. When interest rates fall and bond prices rise, the probability that the buyer of a put will lose increases. If rates fall so that bond prices rise above the exercise price X, the put buyer does not have to exercise the option. Thus, the maximum loss is limited to the size of the up-front put premium (P).

Thus, buying a put option is a strategy to take when interest rates are expected to rise.

Writing a Put Option on a Bond. The fourth strategy is writing (or taking a short position in) a put option on a bond. To do this, the writer or seller receives a fee or premium (P) in return for standing ready to buy bonds at the exercise price (X) should the buyer of the put choose to exercise the option to sell. See the payoff function for writing a put option on a bond in Figure 24–6. Note the following:

1. When interest rates fall and bond prices rise, the writer has an enhanced probability of making a profit. The put buyer is less likely to exercise the option, which would force the option writer to buy the underlying bond. However, the writer's maximum profit is constrained to equal the put premium (P).

2. When interest rates rise and bond prices fall, the writer of the put is exposed to potentially large losses (e.g., $-\pi p$ if bond prices fall to D in Figure 24–6). The put buyer will exercise the option, forcing the option writer to buy the underlying bond at the exercise price. Since bond prices are theoretically unbounded in the downward direction, these losses can be unlimited.

Thus, writing a put option is a strategy to take when interest rates are expected to fall. However, profits are limited and losses are potentially unlimited (i.e., the investor could potentially lose his or her entire investment in the option).

Actual Interest Rate Options

www.cboe.com/

www.cme.com/

www.liffe.com/

FIs have a wide variety of OTC and exchange-traded options available. Table 24–3, from *The Wall Street Journal*'s business section, reports exchange-traded interest rate futures options traded on the Chicago Board of Options Exchange (CBOE), the

Figure 24–6 Payoff Function for the Writer of a Put Option on a Bond

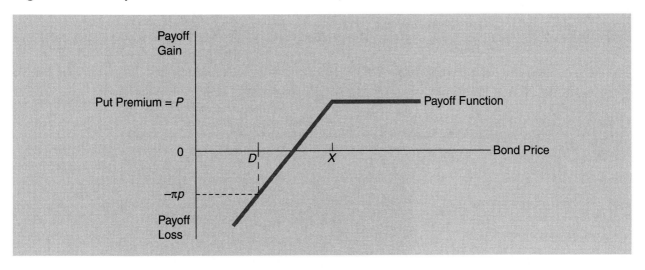

Table 24–3 Futures Options on Interest Rates, January 18, 2000

INTEREST RATE

T-BONDS (CBT)
$100,000; points and 64ths of 100%

Strike Price	Calls-Settle Feb	Mar	Jun	Puts-Settle Feb	Mar	Jun
87	2-16	2-34	....	0-02	0-21	
88	1-20	1-50	2-38	0-06	0-37	1-47
89	0-34	1-10	....	0-20	0-61	....
90	0-08	0-45	1-37	0-57	1-30	2-45
91	0-01	0-24	....	1-51	2-10	....
92	0-01	0-12	0-58	2-50	2-62	4-00

Est vol 100,000;
Fr vol 68,655 calls 74,913 puts
Op int Fri 473,764 calls 369,200 puts

T-NOTES (CBT)
$100,000; points and 64ths of 100%

Strike Price	Calls-Settle Feb	Mar	Jun	Puts-Settle Feb	Mar	Jun
92	....	....	....	....	0-11	0-53
93	....	....	....	0-03	0-23	1-11
94	0-23	0-54	1-27	0-16	0-46	1-40
95	0-03	0-26	1-00	0-59	1-18	2-12
96	0-01	0-11	0-44	1-56	2-02	2-55
97	0-01	0-04	0-29	2-56	2-59	....

Est vol 40,000 Fr 24,851 calls 31,369 puts
Op int Fri 266,081 calls 191,986 puts

5 YR TREAS NOTES (CBT)
$100,000; points and 64ths of 100%

Strike Price	Calls-Settle Feb	Mar	Jun	Puts-Settle Feb	Mar	Jun
9600	....	....	....	....	0-09	0-40
9650	....	0-55	....	0-02	0-16	....
9700	0-16	0-34	....	0-09	0-27	....
9750	0-03	0-18	....	0-28	0-43	....
9800	0-01	0-09	0-28	0-58	1-01	1-43
9850	0-01	0-04	....	1-25	1-28	....

Est vol 18,000 Fr 3,703 calls 2,478 puts
Op int Fri 91,380 calls 114,849 puts

MUNI BOND INDEX (CBT)
$1,000; times Bond Buyer MBI

Strike Price	Calls-Settle Mar	Puts-Settle Mar
89	....	....
90	....	....
91	2-09	....
92	....	....
93	....	....
94	....	....

Est vol 0 Fr 0 calls 0 puts
Op int Fri 0 calls 10 puts

EURODOLLAR (CME)
$ million; pts. of 100%

Strike Price	Calls-Settle Feb	Mar	Jun	Puts-Settle Feb	Mar	Jun
9325	....	....	2.60	....	0.05	1.05
9350	....	2.80	1.20	0.05	0.10	2.10
9375	0.55	0.75	0.45	0.35	0.55	3.80
9400	0.00	0.10	0.15	2.30	2.40	5.95
9425	0.00	0.05	0.10	4.80	4.85	8.40
9450	0.00	0.05	0.05	....	6.05	10.90

Est vol 68,142;
Fr vol 125,800 calls 88,415 puts
Op int Fri 2,154,330 calls 1,204,429 puts

1 YR. MID-CURVE EURODLR (CME)
$1,000,000 contract units; pts. of 100%

Strike Price	Calls-Settle Feb	Mar	Apr	Puts-Settle Feb	Mar	Apr
9250	....	....	....	0.20	0.55	....
9275	....	....	2.50	0.70	1.25	2.15
9300	0.70	1.20	....	1.90	2.40	....
9325	0.15	0.50	....	3.85	4.20	....
9350	0.05	0.20	....	6.25	6.35	....
9375	0.00	0.05	....	....	8.70	....

Est vol 17,354 Fr 9,052 calls 4,375 puts
Op int Fri 147,108 calls 117,051 puts

2 YR. MID-CURVE EURODLR (CME)
$1,000,000 contract units; pts. of 100%

Strike Price	Calls-Settle Mar	Jun	Puts-Settle Mar	Jun
9225	....	....	....	....
9250	....	....	....	....
9275	2.35	....	2.15	3.35
9300	0.55	....	3.85	....
9325	0.20	....	5.95	....
9350	0.10	....	8.35	....

Est vol 0 Fr 0 calls 0 puts
Op int Fri 13,972 calls 17,635 puts

EUROLIBOR (LIFFE)
Euro 1,000,000

Strike Price	Calls-Settle Feb	Mar	Apr	Puts-Settle Feb	Mar	Apr
9600	0.39	0.40	0.13	....	0.01	0.12
9625	0.16	0.17	0.04	0.01	0.02	0.28
9650	0.01	0.03	0.01	0.12	0.14	0.50
9675	....	0.00	....	0.35	0.36	0.74
9700	....	....	....	0.60	0.60	0.99
9725	....	....	....	0.85	0.85	1.24

Source: *The Wall Street Journal*, January 19, 2000, p. C23. Reprinted by permission of *The Wall Street Journal*. © 2000 Dow Jones & Company, Inc. All Rights Reserved Worldwide. *www.cbot.com/; www.cme.com/; www.liffe.com/; www.wsj.com/*

Chicago Mercantile Exchange (CME), and the London International Financial Futures Exchange (LIFFE) on January 18, 2000. We discussed these contracts and the operations of the markets in detail in Chapter 10.

Figure 24–7 Buying a Put Option to Hedge the Interest Rate Risk on a Bond

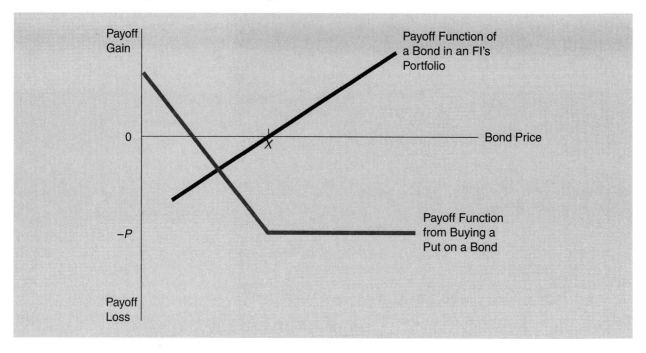

Hedging with Options

Figures 24–7 and 24–8 graphically describe the way that buying a put option on a bond can potentially hedge the interest rate risk exposure of an FI that holds bonds as part of its asset investment portfolio. Figure 24–7 shows the gross payoff of a bond and the payoff from buying a put option on it. In this case, any losses on the bond (as rates rise and bond values decrease) are offset with profits from the put option that was bought (points to the left of point X in Figure 24–7). If rates fall, the bond value increases, yet the accompanying losses on the purchased put option positions are limited to the option premiums paid (points to the right of point X). Figure 24–8 shows the net overall payoff from the bond investment combined with the put option hedge. Note in Figure 24–8 that buying a put option truncates the downside losses on the bond following interest rate rises to some maximum amount and scales down the upside profits by the cost of bond price risk insurance—the put premium—leaving some positive upside profit potential. Notice too that the combination of being long in the bond and buying a put option on a bond mimics the payoff function of buying a call option (compare Figures 24–3 and 24–7). Conversely, an FI can buy a call option on a bond to hedge interest rate risk exposure from a bond that is part of the FI's liability portfolio. Option contracts can also be used to hedge the aggregate duration gap exposure (macrohedge), foreign exchange risk, and credit risk of an FI as well.

Do You Understand?

1. How interest rate increases affect the payoff from buying a call option on a bond? How they affect the payoff from writing a call option on a bond?
2. How interest rate increases affect the payoff from buying a put option on a bond? How they affect the payoff from writing a put option on a bond?
3. Why bond or interest rate futures options are generally preferred to options on the underlying bond?
4. What the outcome is if an FI hedges by buying put options on futures and interest rates rise (i.e., bond prices fall)?

Swaps

The market for swaps has grown enormously in recent years—the value of swap contracts outstanding by U.S. commercial banks was $15.42 trillion in 1999. The five generic types of swaps, in order of their notional principal, are *interest rate swaps, currency swaps, credit risk*

Figure 24–8 Net Payoff of Buying a Bond Put and Investing in a Bond

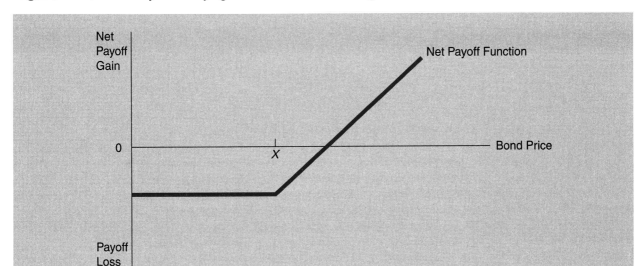

swaps, commodity swaps, and *equity swaps* (see Chapter 10).[15] The instrument underlying the swap may change, but the basic principle of a swap agreement is the same in that it involves the transacting parties restructuring asset or liability cash flows in a preferred direction. In this section, we review the basic swap terminology (see Chapter 10) and consider the role of the two major generic types of swaps—interest rate and currency—in hedging FI risk. We then examine the credit risk characteristics of these instruments.

Interest Rate Swaps

By far the largest segment of the U.S. commercial bank swap market comprises **interest rate swaps.** Conceptually, an interest rate swap is a succession of forward contracts on interest rates arranged by two parties.[16] As such, it allows a financial intermediary (FI) to put in place a long-term hedge (sometimes for as long as 20 years). This hedge reduces the need to roll over contracts if futures or forward contracts had been relied on to achieve such long-term hedges.

In a swap, the **swap buyer** agrees to make a number of fixed interest rate payments on periodic settlement dates to the **swap seller**. The swap seller, in turn, agrees to make floating-rate payments to the swap buyer on the same periodic settlement dates. In undertaking this transaction, the FI that is the fixed-rate payer is seeking to transform the variable-rate nature of its liabilities into fixed-rate liabilities to better match the fixed returns earned on its assets. Meanwhile, the FI that is the variable-rate payer seeks to turn its fixed-rate liabilities into variable-rate liabilities to better match the variable returns on its assets.

To explain the role of a swap transaction in hedging FI interest rate risk, we use a simple example. Consider two FIs: the first is a money center bank that has raised $100 million of its funds by issuing four-year, medium-term notes with 10 percent annual

interest rate swap

An exchange of fixed-interest payments for floating-interest payments by two counterparties.

swap buyer

By convention, a party that makes the fixed-rate payments in an interest rate swap transaction.

swap seller

By convention, a party that makes the floating-rate payments in an interest rate swap transaction.

---

15. There are also *swaptions,* which are options to enter into a swap agreement at some preagreed contract terms (e.g., a fixed rate of 10 percent) at some time in the future in return for the payment of an up-front premium.

16. For example, a four-year swap with annual swap dates involves four net cash flows between the parties to a swap. This is essentially similar to arranging four forward rate agreement (FRA) contracts: a one-year, a two-year, a three-year, and a four-year contract.

Table 24–4   Money Center Bank Balance Sheet

Assets		Liabilities	
C&I loans (rate indexed to LIBOR)	$100 million	Medium-term notes (coupons fixed at 10% annually)	$100 million

Table 24–5   Savings Bank Balance Sheet

Assets		Liabilities	
Fixed-rate mortgages	$100 million	Short-term CDs (one year)	$100 million

fixed coupons rather than relying on short-term deposits to raise funds (see Table 24–4). On the asset side of its portfolio, the bank makes commercial and industrial (C&I) loans whose rates are indexed to annual changes in the London Interbank Offered Rate (LIBOR). Banks often index most large commercial and industrial loans to either LIBOR or the federal funds rate in the money market.

As a result of having floating-rate loans and fixed-rate liabilities in its asset-liability structure, the money center bank has a negative duration gap; the duration of its assets is shorter than that of its liabilities.

$$D_A - kD_L < 0$$

One way for the bank to hedge this exposure is to shorten the duration or interest rate sensitivity of its liabilities by transforming them into short-term floating-rate liabilities that better match the rate sensitivity of its asset portfolio. The bank can make changes either on or off the balance sheet. On the balance sheet, the bank could attract an additional $100 million in short-term deposits that are indexed to the LIBOR rate (at, say, LIBOR plus 2.5 percent) in a manner similar to its loans. The proceeds of these deposits would used to pay off the medium-term notes. This reduces the duration gap between the bank's assets and liabilities. Alternatively, the bank could go off the balance sheet and sell an interest rate swap—that is, enter into a swap agreement to make the floating-rate payment side of a swap agreement.

The second party of the swap is a thrift institution (savings bank) that has invested $100 million in fixed-rate residential mortgages of long duration. To finance this residential mortgage portfolio, the savings bank had to rely on short-term certificates of deposit with an average duration of one year (see Table 24–5). On maturity, these CDs must be rolled over at the current market rate.

Consequently, the savings bank's asset-liability balance sheet structure is the reverse of the money center bank's:

$$D_A - kD_L > 0$$

The savings bank could hedge its interest rate risk exposure by transforming the short-term floating-rate nature of its liabilities into fixed-rate liabilities that better match the long-term maturity (duration) structure of its assets. On the balance sheet, the thrift could issue long-term notes with a maturity equal or close to that on the mortgages (at, say, 12 percent). The proceeds of the sale of the notes can be used to pay off the CDs and reduce the repricing gap. Alternatively, the thrift can buy a swap—that is, take the fixed-payment side of a swap agreement.

The opposing balance sheet and interest rate risk exposures of the money center bank and the savings bank provide the necessary conditions for an interest rate swap agreement between the two parties. This swap agreement can be arranged directly between the parties. However, it is likely that an FI—another bank or an investment bank—would act either as a broker or an agent, receiving a fee for bringing the two parties together or to intermediate fully by accepting the credit risk exposure and guaranteeing the cash flows underlying the swap contract. By acting as a principal as well as an agent, the FI can add a credit risk premium to the fee. However, the credit risk exposure of a swap to an FI is somewhat less than that on a loan (this is discussed later in this chapter). Conceptually, when a third-party FI fully intermediates the swap, that FI is really entering into two separate swap agreements, one with the money center bank and one with the savings bank.

plain vanilla

A standard agreement without any special features.

For simplicity, we consider an example below of a **plain vanilla** fixed-floating rate swap (a standard swap agreement without any special features) in which a third-party intermediary acts as a simple broker or agent by bringing together two banks with opposing interest rate risk exposures to enter into a swap agreement or contract.

Example 24–1   Expected Cash Flows on an Interest Rate Swap

In this example, the notional (or face) value of the swap is $100 million—equal to the assumed size of the money center bank's medium-term note issue—and the four-year maturity is equal to the maturity of it's note liabilities. The annual coupon cost of these note liabilities is 10 percent. The money center bank's problem is that the variable return on its assets may be insufficient to cover the cost of meeting these fixed coupon payments if market interest rates *fall*. By comparison, the fixed returns on the savings bank's mortgage asset portfolio may be insufficient to cover the interest cost of its CDs should market rates *rise*. As a result, the swap agreement might dictate that the savings bank send fixed payments of 10 percent per annum of the notional $100 million value of the swap to the money center bank to allow the money center bank to cover fully the coupon interest payments on its note issue. In return, the money center bank sends annual payments indexed to the one-year LIBOR to help the savings bank cover the cost of refinancing its one-year renewable CDs. Suppose that the money center bank agrees to send the saving bank annual payments at the end of each year equal to one-year LIBOR plus 2 percent.[17] We depict this fixed-floating rate swap transaction in Figure 24–9; the expected net financing costs for the FIs are listed in Table 24–6.

As a result of the swap, the money center bank has transformed its four-year, fixed-rate liability notes into a variable-rate liability matching the variability of returns on its C&I loans. Further, through the interest rate swap, the money center bank effectively pays LIBOR plus 2 percent for its financing. Had it gone to the debt market, the money center bank would pay LIBOR plus 2.5 percent (a savings of .5 percent with the swap). The savings bank also has transformed its variable-rate CDs into fixed-rate payments similar to those received on its fixed-rate mortgages—it has successfully microhedged.

Note in Example 24–1 that in the absence of default/credit risk, only the money center bank is really fully hedged. This happens because the annual 10 percent payments it receives from the savings bank at the end of each year allows it to meet the promised 10 percent coupon rate payments to its note holders regardless of the return it receives on its variable-rate assets. By contrast, the savings bank receives variable-rate payments based on LIBOR plus 2 percent. It is quite possible that the CD rate that the savings bank must pay on its deposit liabilities does not exactly track the LIBOR-indexed payments sent by the money center bank—that is, the savings bank is subject to basis risk exposure on the swap contract. This basis risk can come from two

---

17. These rates implicitly assume that this is the cheapest way each party can hedge its interest rate exposure. For example, LIBOR plus 2 percent is the lowest cost way that the money center bank can transform its fixed-rate liabilities into floating-rate liabilities.

Figure 24–9   Fixed-Floating Rate Swap

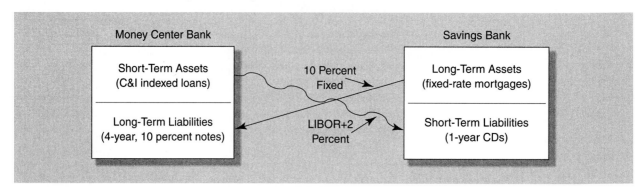

Table 24–6   Financing Cost Resulting from Interest Rate Swap
(in millions of dollars)

	Money Center Bank	**Savings Bank**
Cash outflows from balance sheet financing	$-10\% \times \$100$	$-(\text{CD Rate}) \times \$100$
Cash inflows from swap	$10\% \times \$100$	$(\text{LIBOR} + 2\%) \times \$100$
Cash outflows from swap	$-(\text{LIBOR} + 2\%) \times \$100$	$-10\% \times \$100$
Net cash flows	$-(\text{LIBOR} + 2\%) \times \$100$	$-(8\% + \text{CD Rate} - \text{LIBOR}) \times \$100$
Rate available on		
Variable-rate debt	LIBOR + 2½%	
Fixed-rate debt		12%

sources. First, CD rates do not exactly match the movements of LIBOR rates over time since the former are determined in the domestic money market and the latter in the Eurodollar market. Second, the credit/default risk premium on the savings bank's CDs may increase over time; thus, the plus 2 percent add-on to LIBOR may be insufficient to hedge the savings bank's cost of funds. The savings bank might be better hedged by requiring the money center bank to send it floating payments based on U.S. domestic CD rates rather than on LIBOR. To do this, the money center bank would probably require additional compensation since it would then bear basis risk. Its asset returns would be sensitive to LIBOR movements while its swap payments were indexed to U.S. CD rates.

Currency Swaps

Swaps are long-term contracts that can also be used to hedge an FI's exposure to currency risk. The following section considers a plain vanilla example of how **currency swaps** can immunize FIs against foreign exchange rate risk when they mismatch the currencies of their assets and liabilities.

> **currency swap**
>
> A swap used to hedge against foreign exchange rate risk from mismatched currencies on assets and liabilities.

Fixed-Fixed Currency Swaps.   Consider a U.S. FI with all of its fixed-rate assets denominated in dollars. It is financing part of its asset portfolio with a £50 million issue of four-year, medium-term British pound sterling notes that have a fixed annual coupon of 10 percent. By comparison, an FI in the United Kingdom has all its assets denominated in sterling; it is partly funding those assets with a $100 million issue of four-year, medium-term dollar notes with a fixed annual coupon of 10 percent.

Figure 24–10   Fixed-Fixed Pound/Dollar Currency Swap

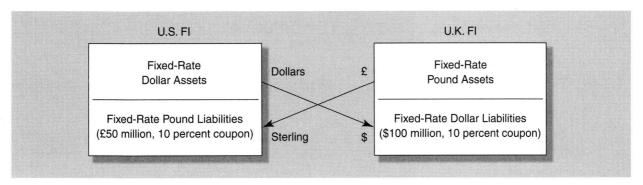

These two FIs are exposed to opposing currency risks. The U.S. FI is exposed to the risk that the dollar will depreciate against the pound over the next four years, which would make it more costly to cover the annual coupon interest payments and the principal repayment on its pound-denominated notes. On the other hand, the U.K. FI is exposed to the risk that the dollar will appreciate against the pound, making it more difficult to cover the dollar coupon and principal payments on its four-year, $100 million note issue from the sterling cash flows on its assets.

The FIs can hedge the exposures either on or off the balance sheet. Assume that the dollar/pound exchange rate is fixed at $2/£1. On the balance sheet, the U.S. FI can issue $100 million in four-year, medium-term dollar notes (at, say, 10.5 percent). The proceeds of the sale can be used to pay off the £50 million of four-year, medium-term sterling notes. Similarly, the U.K. FI can issue £50 million in four-year, medium-term sterling notes (at, say, 10.5 percent), using the proceeds to pay off the $100 million of four-year, medium-term dollar notes. Both FIs have taken actions on the balance sheet so that they are no longer exposed to movements in the exchange rate between the two currencies.

Example 24–2   Expected Cash Flows on Fixed-Fixed Currency Swap

Off the balance sheet, the U.K. and U.S. FIs can enter into a currency swap by which the U.K. FI sends annual payments in pounds to cover the coupon and principal repayments of the U.S. FI's pound sterling note issue, and the U.S. FI sends annual dollar payments to the U.K. FI to cover the interest and principal payments on its dollar note issue.[18] We summarize this currency swap in Figure 24–10 and Table 24–7. As a result of the swap, the U.K. FI transforms fixed-rate dollar liabilities into fixed-rate sterling liabilities that better match the sterling fixed-rate cash flows from its asset portfolio. Similarly, the U.S. FI transforms fixed-rate sterling liabilities into fixed-rate dollar liabilities that better match the fixed-rate dollar cash flows from its asset portfolio. Further, both FIs transform the pattern of their payments at a lower rate than had they made changes on the balance sheet. Both FIs effectively obtain financing at 10 percent while hedging against exchange rate risk. Had they gone to the market, they would have paid 10.5 percent to do this. In undertaking this exchange of cash flows, the two parties normally agree on a fixed exchange rate for the cash flows at the beginning of the period.[19] In this example, the fixed exchange rate is $2/£1.

18. In a currency swap, it is usual to include both principal and interest payments as part of the swap agreement. (For interest rate swaps, it is usual to include only interest rate payments.) The reason for this is that both principal and interest are exposed to foreign exchange risk.

19. As with interest rate swaps, this exchange rate reflects the contracting parties' expectations as to future exchange rate movements.

Table 24–7 Financing Costs Resulting from the Fixed-Fixed Currency Swap
Agreement

(in millions of dollars)

	U.S. FI	U.K. FI
Cash outflows from balance sheet financing	$-10\% \times £50$	$-10\% \times \$100$
Cash inflows from swap	$10\% \times £50$	$10\% \times \$100$
Cash outflows from swap	$-10\% \times \$100$	$-10\% \times £50$
Net cash flows	$-10\% \times \$100$	$-10\% \times £50$
Rate available on		
Dollar-denominated notes	10.5%	
Pound-denominated notes		10.5%

By combining an interest rate swap of the fixed-floating type described earlier with a currency swap, we can also produce a fixed-floating currency swap that is a hybrid of the two plain vanilla swaps we have considered so far.

Credit Risk Concerns with Swaps

www.bis.org/

www.isda.org/

The growth of the over-the-counter (OTC) swap market was one of the major factors underlying the imposition of the BIS risk-based capital requirements in January 1993 (see Chapter 14). The fear was that in a long-term OTC swap-type contract, the losing or out-of-the-money counterparty would have incentives to default on such contracts to deter current and future losses. Consequently, the BIS (with significant input and support from the global trade association the International Swaps and Derivatives Association (ISDA), which sets codes and standards for swap markets) imposed a risk-based capital requirement for banks to hold against their interest rate, currency, and other swaps.

This raises the following questions. What, exactly, is the default risk on swaps? Is it high or low? Is it the same as or different from the credit risk on loans? In fact, the credit risk on swaps and the credit risk on loans differ in three major ways, so that the credit risk on a swap is much less than that on a loan of equivalent dollar size.[20] We discuss these differences next.

Netting and Swaps.   One factor that mitigates the credit risk on swaps is the netting of swap payments. On each swap payment date, one party makes a fixed payment and the other makes a floating payment. In general, however, each party calculates the net difference between the two payments, and one party makes a single payment for the net difference to the other. This netting of payments implies that the default exposure of the in-the-money party is limited to the net payment rather than either the total fixed or floating payment itself.

Payment Flows Are Interest, not Principal.   Currency swaps involve swaps of interest and principal, but interest rate swaps involve swaps of interest payments only measured against some notional (or face) principal value. This suggests that the default risk on such interest rate swaps is less than on a regular loan, in which both interest and principal are exposed to credit risk.

20. As with loans, swap participants deal with the credit risk of counterparties by setting bilateral limits on the notional amount of swaps entered into (similar to credit rationing on loans) and adjusting the fixed and/or floating rates by including credit risk premiums. For example, a low credit–quality, fixed-rate payer may have to pay an additional spread to a high credit–quality, floating-rate payer.

Table 24–8 Comparison of Hedging Methods

Writing versus Buying Options

- Writing options truncates upside profit potential while downside loss potential is unlimited.
- Buying options truncates downside loss potential while upside profit potential is unlimited.
- Commercial banks are prohibited by regulators from writing options in certain areas of risk management.

Futures versus Options Hedging

- Futures hedging produces symmetric gains and losses when interest rates move against the on-balance-sheet securities, *as well as* when interest rates move in favor of on-balance-sheet securities.
- Options hedging protects the FI against value losses when interest rates move against the on-balance-sheet securities but, unlike with futures hedging, does not fully reduce value gains when interest rates move in favor of on-balance-sheet securities.

Swaps versus Forwards, Futures, and Options

- Futures, and most options, are standardized contracts with fixed principal amounts. Swaps (and forwards) are OTC contracts negotiated directly by the counterparties to the contract.
- Futures contracts are marked-to-market daily. Swaps and forwards require payments only at times specified in the swap or forward agreement.
- Swaps can be written for relatively long time horizons. Futures and option contracts do not trade for more than two or three years into the future and active trading in these contracts generally extends to contracts with a maturity of less than one year.
- Swap and forward contracts are subject to default risk. Most futures and option contracts are not subject to default risk.

Standby Letters of Credit.   When swaps are made between parties of different credit standings so that one party perceives a significant risk of default by the other party, the poor-quality credit risk party may be required to buy a standby letter of credit (or another form of performance guarantee) from a third-party high-quality (AAA-rated) FI so that should default occur, the standby letter of credit party would provide the swap payments in lieu of the defaulting party.[21]

Comparison of Hedging Methods

As described above, an FI has many alternative derivative instruments with which it can hedge a particular risk. In this section, we look at some general features of the different types of contracts that may lead to an FI preferring one derivative instrument over another. We summarize these in Table 24–8.

Writing versus Buying Options

Many FIs prefer to buy rather than write options. Of the two reasons for this, one is economic and the other is regulatory.

Economic Reasons for Not Writing Options.   In writing an option, the upside profit potential is truncated but the downside losses are not. On an *expected* basis, the writing of an appropriate call or put option would lead to a fair rate of return. However, the *actual* price or interest rate movement on the underlying asset may move against the

---

21. Another solution being considered by market participants (such as the ISDA) is to use collateral to mark to market a swap contract in a way similar to marking futures to market to prevent credit risk building up over time. Remember that a swap contract is like a succession of forward contracts. A 1994 survey by Arthur Andersen showed that approximately $6.9 billion was posted as collateral against a net replacement value of $77.9 billion of swaps. (See "A Question of Collateral," *Euromoney,* November 1995, pp. 46–49.)

Figure 24–11 Writing a Call Option to Hedge the Interest Rate Risk on a Bond

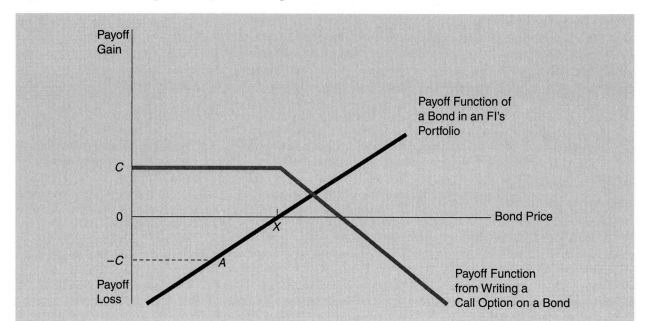

option writer. It is this actual price or rate change that leads to the possibility of unlimited losses. Although such risks may be offset by writing a large number of options at different exercise prices and/or hedging an underlying portfolio of bonds, the writer's downside risk exposure may still be significant. Figure 24–11 indicates this. An FI is long in a bond in its portfolio and seeks to hedge the interest rate risk on that bond by writing a bond call option. Note that writing the call may hedge the FI when rates fall and bond prices rise—that is, the increase in the value of the bond is offset by losses on the written call. When the reverse occurs and interest rates rise, the FI's profits from writing the call may be insufficient to offset the loss on its bonds. This occurs because the upside profit (per call written) is truncated and equals the premium income (C). If the decrease in the bond value is larger than the premium income (to the left of point A in Figure 24–11), the FI is unable to offset the associated capital value loss on the bond with profits from writing options.

By contrast, hedging the FI's risk by buying a put option on a bond generally offers the manager a more attractive alternative. Refer again to Figures 24–7 and 24–8. The net overall payoff from the bond investment combined with the put option hedge truncates the downside losses on the bond following interest rate rises to some maximum amount and scales down the upside profits by the put premium.

naked options

Option positions that do not identifiably hedge an underlying asset or liability.

Regulatory Reasons. Many FIs also buy options rather than write options for regulatory reasons. Regulators consider writing options, especially **naked options** that do not identifiably hedge an underlying asset or liability position, to be risky because of their unlimited loss potential. Indeed, bank regulators prohibit commercial banks from writing puts or calls in certain areas of risk management.

Futures versus Options Hedging

To understand the factors that impact the choice between using futures rather than options contracts to hedge, compare the payoff gains illustrated in Figure 24–12 (for futures contracts) with those in Figure 24–7 (for option contracts). A hedge with futures contracts produces symmetric gains and losses with interest rate increases and

Figure 24–12 Buying a Futures Contract to Hedge the Interest Rate Risk on a Bond

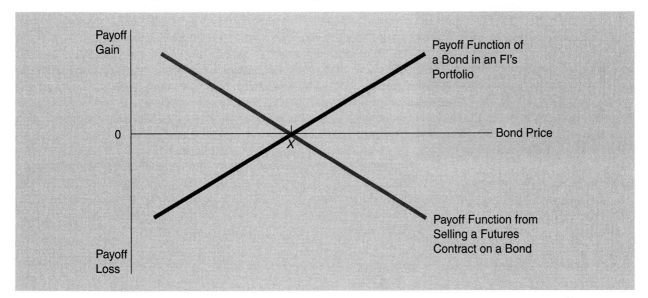

Payoff Gain

0

Bond Price

Payoff Loss

Payoff Function of a Bond in an FI's Portfolio

Payoff Function from Selling a Futures Contract on a Bond

X

decreases. That is, if the FI in Figure 24–12 loses value on the bond resulting from an interest rate increase (to the left of point *X*), it enjoys a gain on the futures contract to offset this loss. If the FI gains value on the bond due to an interest rate decrease (to the right of point *X*), a loss on the futures contract offsets this gain.

By comparison, a hedge with an option contract offsets losses but only partly offsets gains—gains and losses from hedging with options are no longer symmetric for interest rate increases and decreases. For example, in Figure 24–7, if the FI loses value on the bond due to an interest rate increase (to the left of point *X*), a gain on the options contract offsets the loss. However, if the FI gains value on the bond due to an interest rate decrease (to the right of point *X*), the gain is offset only to the extent that the FI loses the fixed option premium (because it never exercises the option). Thus, the option hedge protects the FI against value losses when interest rates move against the on-balance-sheet securities but, unlike futures hedging, does not fully reduce value gains when interest rates move in favor of on-balance-sheet securities. Thus, many FIs prefer option-type contracts to future/forward type contracts.

Swaps versus Forwards, Futures, and Options

We have shown in this chapter that swaps can be used to alter the cash flows of an FI from a particular asset and liability structure. In this respect, swaps are comparable to forwards, futures, and options. Indeed, conceptually a swap is just a succession of forward rate contracts. Further, all of the derivative instruments can be viewed as relatively low-cost hedging alternatives when compared to changing the overall composition of the FI's balance sheet of assets and liabilities.

There are, however, some significant contractual differences between swaps and forwards, futures, and option contracts that assist the FI manager in his or her choice of hedging method. First, futures and most options are standardized contracts with fixed principal amounts. Swaps (and forwards), on the other hand, are OTC contracts negotiated directly by the counterparties to the contract. This feature allows for flexibility in the principal amount of the swap contract. Second, futures contracts are marked to market daily, while swaps and forwards require payments only at times specified in the swap or forward agreement. Thus, hedging risk exposure with futures can result in large cash inflows and outflows for the FI if price movements result in margin calls at the end of the day as a result of this marking-to-market process. Third, swaps can be written for relatively long time horizons, sometimes as long as 20 years. Futures and option contracts do not trade for more than two or three years into the future and active trading in these contracts generally extends to contracts with a maturity of less than one year. Thus, swaps provide the FI with better long-term contractual protection against risk exposures than futures and options. Finally, swap and forward contracts are subject to default risk, while most futures and option contracts are not. Swap and forward contracts are negotiated between two counterparties, and should one party fail to abide by the terms of the contract the counterparty incurs this default risk. Futures and option contracts, however, are guaranteed by the exchange on which they trade. Thus, futures and (exchange-traded) options are only subject to default risk when the entire exchange has a default risk problem.

Summary

This chapter analyzed the risk-management role of forwards, futures, options, and swaps. These (off the balance sheet) derivative securities provide FIs with a low-cost alternative to managing risk exposure directly on the balance sheet. We first looked at the use of forwards and futures contracts as hedging instruments. We saw that while they are close substitutes, they are not perfect substitutes. A number of characteristics such as maturity, liquidity, flexibility, marking to market, and capital requirements differentiate these products and make one or the other more attractive to any particular FI manager. We next discussed the use of option-type contracts available to FI managers to hedge interest rate risk. In particular, we noted that the unique nature of the asymmetric payoff structure of option-type contracts often makes them more attractive to FIs than other hedging instruments such as forwards and futures. Finally, we evaluated the role of swaps as risk-management vehicles for FIs. We analyzed the major types of swaps, such as interest rate and currency swaps. Swaps have special features of long maturity, flexibility, and liquidity that make them attractive alternatives relative to shorter-term hedging vehicles such as futures, forwards, and options.

End-of-Chapter Questions

1. What are some of the major differences between futures and forward contracts?
2. In each of the following cases, indicate whether it would be appropriate for an FI to buy or sell a forward contract to hedge the appropriate risk.
   a. A commercial bank plans to issue CDs in three months.
   b. An insurance company plans to buy bonds in two months.
   c. A thrift is going to sell Treasury securities next month.
   d. A U.S. bank lends to a French company; the loan is payable in francs.
   e. A mutual fund plans to sell its holding of stock in a German company.
   f. A finance company has assets with a duration of 6 years and liabilities with a duration of 13 years.
3. Suppose that you purchase a Treasury bond futures contract at $95 per $100 of face value.
   a. What is your obligation when you purchase this futures contract?
   b. If an FI purchases this contract, in what kind of hedge is it engaged?
   c. Assume that the Treasury bond futures price falls to 94. What is your loss or gain?
   d. Assume that the Treasury bond futures price rises to 97. Mark your position to market.
4. Answer the following.
   a. What is the duration of a 20-year 8 percent coupon (paid semiannually) Treasury bond (deliverable

against the Treasury bond futures contract) selling at par?

b. What is the impact on the Treasury bond price if interest rates increase 50 basis points annually (25 basis points semiannually)?

c. What is the meaning of the following Treasury bond futures price quote: 101-13?

5. An FI holds a 15-year, par value, $10,000,000 bond that is priced at 104 and yields 7 percent. The FI plans to sell the bond but for tax purposes must wait two months. The bond has a duration of eight years. The FI's market analyst is predicting that the Federal Reserve will raise interest rates within the next two months and doing so will raise the yield on the bond to 8 percent. Most other analysts are predicting no change in interest rates, so presently plenty of two-month forward contracts for 15-year bonds are available at 104. The FI would like to hedge against this interest rate forecast with an appropriate position in a forward contract. What will this position be? Show that if rates rise by 1 percent as forecast, the hedge will protect the FI from loss.

6. Answer the following.

a. What are the two ways to use call and put options on T-bonds to generate positive cash flows when interest rates decline?

b. When and how can an FI use options on T-bonds to hedge its assets and liabilities against interest rate declines?

c. Is it more appropriate for FIs to hedge against a decline in interest rates with long calls or short puts?

7. In each of the following cases, indicate whether it is appropriate for an FI to buy a put or a call option in order to hedge the appropriate risk.

a. A commercial bank plans to issue CDs in three months.

b. An insurance company plans to buy bonds in two months.

c. A thrift plans to sell Treasury securities next month.

d. A U.S. bank lends to a French company; the loan is payable in francs.

e. A mutual fund plans to sell its holding of stock in a German company.

f. A finance company has assets with a duration of 6 years and liabilities with a duration of 13 years.

8. Consider Table 24–3. What are the prices paid for the following futures options:

a. March T-bond calls at 90.

b. March 5-year T-note puts at 9650.

c. June Eurodollar calls at 9350.

9. Consider Table 24–3 again.

a. What happens to the price of a call when:
   (1) The exercise price increases?
   (2) The time until expiration increases?

b. What happens to the price of the put when these two variables increase?

10. Suppose that an FI manager writes a call option on a T-bond futures contract with an exercise price of 114 at a quoted price of 0-55. What type of opportunities or obligations does the manager have?

11. Suppose that a pension fund manager anticipates the purchase of a 20-year 8 percent coupon T-bond at the end of two years. Interest rates are assumed to change only once every year at year end. At that time, it is equally probable that interest rates will increase or decrease 1 percent. When purchased in two years, the T-bond will pay interest semiannually. Currently, it is selling at par.

a. What is the pension fund manager's interest rate risk exposure?

b. How can the pension fund manager use options to hedge that interest rate risk exposure?

12. Distinguish between a swap *seller* and a swap *buyer*.

13. An insurance company owns $50 million of floating-rate bonds yielding LIBOR plus 1 percent. These loans are financed by $50 million of fixed-rate guaranteed investment contracts (GICs) costing 10 percent. A finance company has $50 million of auto loans with a fixed rate of 14 percent. They are financed by $50 million of CDs with a variable rate of LIBOR plus 4 percent. If the insurance company is going to be the swap buyer and the insurance company the swap seller, what is an example of a feasible swap?

14. A commercial bank has $200 million of floating-rate loans yielding the T-bill rate plus 2 percent. These loans are financed by $200 million of fixed-rate deposits costing 9 percent. A savings association has $200 million of mortgages with a fixed rate of 13 percent. They are financed by $200 million of CDs with a variable rate of T-bill plus 3 percent.

a. Discuss the type of interest rate risk each FI faces.

b. Propose a swap that would result in each FI having the same type of assets and liabilities (i.e., one has fixed assets and fixed liabilities, and the other has assets and liabilities all tied to some floating rate).

c. Show that this swap would be acceptable to both parties.

d. What are some practical difficulties in arranging this swap?

15. A German bank issues a $100 million, three-year Eurodollar CD at a fixed annual rate of 7 percent. The proceeds of the CD are lent to a German company for three years at a fixed rate of 9 percent. The spot exchange rate of Deutsche marks for U.S. dollars is DM1.50/US$.

a. Is this expected to be a profitable transaction ex ante? What are the cash flows if exchange rates are unchanged over the next three years? What is the risk exposure of the bank's underlying cash position? How can the German bank reduce that risk exposure?

b. If the U.S. dollar is expected to appreciate against the Deutsche mark to DM1.65/$, DM1.815/$, and

DM2.00/$ over the next three years, respectively, what will be the cash flows on this transaction?

c. If the German bank swaps U.S. dollar payments for DM payments at the current spot exchange rate, what are the cash flows on the swap? What are the cash flows on the entire hedged position? Assume that the U.S. dollar appreciates at the same rates as in part (b).

16. Bank 1 can issue five-year CDs at an annual rate of 11 percent fixed or at a variable rate of LIBOR + 2 percent. Bank 2 can issue five-year CDs at an annual fixed rate of 13 percent or at a variable rate of LIBOR + 3 percent.

a. Is a mutually beneficial swap possible between the two banks?

b. What is the comparative advantage of the two banks?

c. What is an example of a feasible swap?

17. How does hedging with options differ from hedging with forward or futures contracts?

18. Contrast the use of financial futures options with the use of options on cash instruments to construct interest rate hedges.

19. Consider the following FI's balance sheet:

Assets ($000)		Liabilities ($000)	
Duration =		Duration =	
10 years	$950	2 years	$860
		Equity	90

a. What is the FI's duration gap?

b. What is the FI's interest rate risk exposure?

c. How can the FI use futures and forward contracts to macrohedge?

20. A bank purchases a six-month $1 million Eurodollar deposit at an interest rate of 6.5 percent per year. It invests the funds in a six-month Swedish Krone bond paying 7.5 percent per year. The current spot rate of U.S. dollars for Swedish Krone is $0.18/SK.

a. The six-month forward rate on the Swedish Krone is being quoted at $0.1810/SK. What is the net spread earned on this investment if the bank covers its foreign exchange exposure using the forward market?

b. At what forward rate will the spread be only 1 percent per year?

chapter twenty . five

Loan Sales *and* Asset Securitization

Chapter Navigator

1. What characteristics describe the bank loan sale market?

2. What factors encourage and deter loan sales growth?

3. What are the major forms of asset securitization?

4. Can all assets be securitized?

Why Financial Institutions Securitize Assets: Chapter Overview

Loan sales and **asset securitization**—the packaging and selling of loans and other assets backed by loans or other securities issued by the FI—are one of the mechanisms that FIs have used to hedge their interest rate exposure and credit risks. In addition, loan sales and securitization have allowed FI asset portfolios to become more liquid, provided an important source of fee income (with FIs acting as servicing agents for the assets sold), and helped to reduce the adverse effects of regulatory "taxes" such as capital requirements, reserve requirements, and deposit insurance premiums on FI profitability. In Chapter 1, we discussed the role of FIs as both asset transformers and asset brokers. By increasingly relying on loan sales and securitization, depository institutions have begun moving away from being strictly asset transformers that originate and hold assets to maturity toward becoming more reliant on servicing and other fees. This makes depository institutions look increasingly similar to securities firms and investment banks in terms of the enhanced importance of asset brokerage over asset transformation functions.

In Chapter 7, we discussed the basics of asset sales and securitization and the markets in which these securities trade. This chapter investigates the role of loan sales and

Table 25–1 Basic Description of Loan Sales and Other Forms of Mortgage Securitization

---

Loan Sale—an FI originates a loan and subsequently sells it.

Pass-Through Securities—mortgages or other assets originated by an FI are pooled and investors are offered an interest in the pool in the form of pass-through certificates or securities. Examples of pass-through securities are Government National Mortgage Association (GNMA) or Federal National Mortgage Association (FNMA) securities.

Collateralized Mortgage Obligations (CMOs)—similar to pass-throughs, CMOs are securities backed by pools of mortgages or other assets originated by an FI. Pass-throughs give investors common rights in terms of risks and returns, but CMOs assign varying combinations of risk and return to different groups of investors in the CMO by repackaging the pool.

Mortgage-Backed Bonds (MBBs)—a bond issue backed by a group of mortgages on an FI's balance sheet. With MBBs, the mortgages remain on the FI's balance sheet, and funds used to pay the MBB holders' coupons and principal repayments may or may not come from the collateralized mortgages.

---

asset securitization

The packaging and selling of loans and other assets backed by securities issued by an FI.

other forms of asset securitization in improving the return-risk trade-off for FIs. It describes the process associated with loan sales and the major forms, or vehicles, of asset securitization and analyzes their unique characteristics. Table 25–1 presents a definition of the loan sale and securitization mechanisms that this chapter discusses.

Loan Sales

correspondent banking

A relationship between a small bank and a large bank in which the large bank provides a number of deposit, lending, and other services.

highly leveraged transaction (HLT) loan

A loan that finances a merger and acquisition; a leveraged buyout results in a high leverage ratio for the borrower.

Banks and other FIs have sold loans among themselves for more than 100 years. In fact, a large part of **correspondent banking** involves small banks making loans that are too big for them to hold on their balance sheets—either for lending concentration risk or capital adequacy reasons—and selling parts of these loans to large banks with whom they have had a long-term deposit-lending correspondent relationship. In turn, the large banks often sell parts of their loans called *participations* to smaller banks. Even though this market has existed for many years, it grew slowly until the early 1980s when it entered a period of spectacular growth, largely due to expansion in **highly leveraged transaction (HLT) loans** to finance leveraged buyouts (LBOs) and mergers and acquisitions (M&As). Specifically, the volume of loans sold by U.S. banks increased from less than $20 billion in 1980 to $285 billion in 1989. In the early 1990s, the volume of loan sales declined almost as dramatically, along with the decline in LBO and M&A activity. In 1995, the volume of loan sales had fallen to approximately $32 billion. In the last few years, however, the volume of loan sales has started to increase again as M&As have increased.[1] For example, secondary trading volume through the first three quarters of 1999 was over $70 billion.

Figure 25–1 shows recent trends in the loan sales market—in particular, the increasing number of loan sales during the period 1994–1998 and for the first nine months of 1999. Notice the increasing (relative) proportion of nondistressed (par loans) to distressed loans. The latter reflects the improving macroeconomic conditions that have moved many distressed firms out of Chapter 11 bankruptcy protection in recent years.

bank loan sale

Sale of loan originated by a bank with or without recourse to an outside buyer.

A **bank loan sale** occurs when an FI originates a loan and sells it with or without recourse to an outside buyer. As an extreme example, Westmark Group Holdings, Inc., of Delray Beach, Florida, one of the country's top 15 subprime lenders, issued in ex-

---

1. Also, the composition of loan sales is changing, with increasing amounts of commercial real estate loans being sold.

Figure 25–1 Recent Trends in the Loan Sales Market

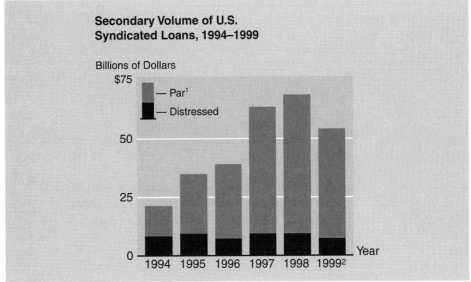

Secondary Volume of U.S.
Syndicated Loans, 1994–1999

[1]Loans trading near face value.
[2]Through September.
Source: Loan Pricing Corporation, *Goldsheets,* November, 1999. *www.loanpricing.com/*

cess of $290 million in subprime mortgage loans in 1998. By year end, Westmark had sold over $277 million of these loans to secondary market investors and recorded revenues of $17.3 million in 1998 from its mortgage division, a 107 percent increase over 1997.

If the loan is sold without recourse, the FI not only removes it from its balance sheet (purchasing new investments with the freed up funds) but also has no explicit liability if the loan eventually goes bad. Panel A of Table 25–2 shows an FI's balance sheet before and after a $20 million loan sale. The loan buyer (not the FI that originated the loan) bears all the credit risk. If, however, the loan is sold with **recourse,** under certain conditions the buyer can put the loan back to the selling bank; therefore, the FI retains a contingent (credit risk) liability. Panel B of Table 25–2 shows the FI's balance sheet, including the contingent liability from the loan sale held off the balance sheet. In practice, most loan sales are without recourse because a loan sale is technically removed from the balance sheet only when the buyer has no future credit risk claim on the bank. Loan sales usually involve no creation of new types of securities, such as those described later in the chapter when we consider securitization.

Types of Loan Sales Contracts

The two basic types of loan sales contracts are *participations* and *assignments*. Currently, assignments represent the bulk of loan sales.

Participations. The unique characteristics of **participations in loans** are:

- The holder (buyer) is not a party to the underlying credit agreement, so that the initial contract between loan seller and borrower remains in place after the sale.
- The loan buyer can exercise only partial control over changes in the loan contract's terms. The holder can vote on only material changes to the loan contract, such as the interest rate or collateral backing.

recourse

The ability of a loan buyer to sell the loan back to the originator should it go bad.

participation in a loan

The act of buying a share in a loan syndication with limited contractual control and rights over the borrower.

Table 25–2 FI Balance Sheet Before and After a $20 Million Loan Sale
(in millions)

Panel A: Loan Sale without Recourse

Before Loan Sale				After Loan Sale			
Assets		Liabilities/Equity		Assets		Liabilities/Equity	
Cash assets	$ 10	Deposit	$ 90	Cash assets	$ 10	Deposits	$ 90
				Loans	70		
Loans	90	Equity	10	New investments	20	Equity	10
	$100		$100		$100		$100

Panel B: Loan Sale with Recourse

Before Loan Sale				After Loan Sale			
Assets		Liabilities/Equity		Assets		Liabilities/Equity	
Cash assets	$ 10	Deposit	$ 90	Cash assets	$ 10	Deposits	$ 90
				Loans	70		
Loans	90	Equity	10	New investments	20	Equity	10
	$100		$100		$100		$100

Off balance sheet: Loan sale $20
(contingent liability)

The economic implication of these characteristics is that the buyer of the loan participation has a double-risk exposure—to the borrower as well as to the lender. Specifically, if the selling bank fails, the loan participation bought by an outside party may be characterized as an unsecured obligation of the bank rather than a true sale. Alternatively, the borrowers' claims against a failed selling bank may be netted against its loans, reducing the amount of loans outstanding and adversely impacting the buyer of a participation in those loans. As a result of these exposures, the buyer bears a double monitoring cost as well.

Assignments.   Because of the monitoring costs and the risks involved in participations, loans are sold on an assignment basis in more than 90 percent of the cases on the U.S. domestic market. The key features of an **assignment** are:

assignment

The purchase of a share in a loan syndication with some contractual control and rights over the borrower.

- The transfer of all rights on sale, meaning that the loan buyer holds a direct claim on the borrower.
- The transfer of U.S. domestic loans normally associated with a Uniform Commercial Code filing (as proof that a change of ownership has been completed).

Although ownership rights are generally much clearer in a loan sale by assignment, contractual terms frequently limit the seller's (e.g., a bank's) scope regarding to whom the loan can be sold. In particular, to protect the borrower (say, IBM), the original loan contract may require either the bank agent or the borrower (IBM) to agree to the sale.[2] The loan contract may also restrict the sale to a certain class of institutions, such as those that meet certain net worth/net asset size conditions (say, Allstate Insurance Company). Currently, the trend appears to be toward originating loan contracts with very limited assignment restrictions. This is true in both the

Do You Understand?

1. Some of the new innovations occurring in the loan trading market?

---

2. A bank agent is a bank that distributes interest and principal payments to lenders in loan syndications with multiple lenders.

U.S. domestic and less developed country (LDC) loan sales markets. The most tradable loans are those that can be assigned without buyer restrictions. In evaluating ownership rights, the buyer of the loan (Allstate) also needs to verify the original loan contract and to establish the full implications of the purchase regarding the buyer's (Allstate) rights to collateral if the borrower (IBM) defaults. Because of these contractual problems, trading frictions, and costs, some loan sales take as long as three months to complete, although for most loan sales the developing market standard is that loan sales should be completed within 10 days. In the News box 25–1 discusses some of the details of the loan sales process and changes that are underway.

In the News

Changes Are Afoot to Streamline Trading of Syndicated Loans

For veteran investment banker Kevin Meenan, trading in the $1 trillion syndicated-loan market brings back memories of the early 1980s, the Stone Age of bond trading. The bond market has developed enormously since then, and now there are signs that the huge loan market could be on the verge of its own renaissance.

When Mr. Meenan started working at Salomon Brothers in 1981, trunks holding billions of dollars of certificates for mortgage-backed bonds were lined up along Salomon's hallways each month and delivered to investors. Investors trading loans go through some-

Source: *The Wall Street Journal*, December 6, 1999, p. C1, by Paul M. Sherer. Reprinted by permission of *The Wall Street Journal.* © 1999 Dow Jones & Company, Inc. All Rights Reserved Worldwide.

thing similar today, using teams of overnight couriers to lug complex loan documents between lawyers and bankers. It typically takes 10 days to complete the trade of a single loan.

Loan trading is, "relative to other markets, an extraordinarily cumbersome, labor intensive process," says Mr. Meenan . . . But today the loan-trading market is beginning to incorporate many of the developments that helped spur efficient bond trading . . . The big loan players trying to develop the trading market "want people to be able to manage their loan portfolios in the same

way they manage their bond portfolios, with little resistance to taking a position," (says Michael H. Rushmore, head of syndicated finance research at Banc of America Securities LLC).

But loan trades still take days—as many as 30 days for a "distressed loan" for a company in financial trouble. Because the legal documentation varies from loan to loan and trade to trade, the process typically involves teams of lawyers. Forget about click and trade: it takes an average of three days just to negotiate the assignment agreement that transfers ownership of a loan, says Allison Taylor, executive director of Loan Syndications & Trading Association Inc., an industry group. Typically, a two-page to ten-page assignment agreement has to be physically transported to concerned parties, and

(continues)

In the News continued

designed by the buyer, the seller, the agent bank, and the borrower.

Moreover, in the loan market there is no public price reporting and thus no easy way to know how much a loan is worth. That is one of the things that is changing. The LSTA, together with Loan Pricing, recently launched a service to provide pricing information on more than 1,000 loans ... Ratings agencies such as Standard & Poor's Corp. and Fitch IBCA Inc. are now providing credit ratings on more than 1,000 loans. And to combat the problem of each company using different types of agreements for loan trading, the LSTA has developed a set of standardized documents, including confidentiality agreements and trade confirmations.

For loan trading to flourish, several other key changes need to be made, market participants say. One is a system for unique numbers that identify each loan, as exist for stocks and bonds, so that computers can track them. The LSTA is working on such a system ... Among the most ambitious of the new efforts to streamline trading: A number of firms are launching Internet sites for online loan trading of syndicated loans or distressed loans.

LDC loan

Loans made to a less developed country (LDC).

Bank Loan Sale Market

The U.S. bank loan sale market has three segments; two involve sales and trading of domestic loans, and the third involves sales of **LDC** (less developed country) **loans** (loans that have been made to certain Asian, African, and Latin American countries).

Traditional Short-Term Segment.   In the traditional short-term segment of the market, banks sell loans with short maturities, often one to three months. This market has characteristics similar to that of the market for commercial paper (see Chapter 5) in that loan sales have similar maturities and issue sizes. Loan sales, however, usually have yields that are 1 to 10 basis points above those of commercial paper of a similar rating and, unlike commercial paper, are secured by the assets of the borrowing firm. The key characteristics of the loans bought and sold in the short-term loan sale market are:

- The loans are secured by assets of the borrowing firm.
- They have been made to investment-grade borrowers or better.
- They are issued for a short term (90 days or less).
- They are sold in units of $1 million and up.
- Loan rates are closely tied to the commercial paper rate.

Traditional short-term loan sales dominated the market until 1984 and the emergence of the HLT and LDC loan markets. The growth of the commercial paper market (see Chapter 5) has also reduced the importance of this market segment.

HLT Loan Sales.   With the increase in M&As and LBOs financed via HLTs, especially from 1985 to 1989, a new segment in the loan sales market, HLT loan sales or leveraged loan market, appeared.[3] One measure of the increase in HLTs is that between

---

3. What constitutes an HLT loan has often caused dispute. In October 1989, however, the three U.S. federal bank regulators adopted a definition of an HLT as a loan that involves (1) a buyout, acquisition, or recapitalization and (2) either doubles the company's liabilities and results in a leverage ratio higher than 50 percent, results in a leverage ratio higher than 75 percent, or is designated as an HLT by a syndication agent.

www.loanpricing.com/

January 1987 and September 1994, the loan market research firm, Loan Pricing Corporation, reported 4,122 M&A deals with a combined dollar amount in new-issue HLT loans estimated at $593.5 billion. HLT loans mainly differ according to whether they are nondistressed (bid price exceeds 80 cents per $1 of loans) or distressed (bid price is less than 80 cents per $1 of loans or the borrower is in default).

Virtually all HLT loans have the following characteristics:

· The loans are term loans.
· They are secured by assets of the borrowing firm (usually given senior security status).
· They have long maturity (often three- to six-year maturities).
· They have floating rates tied to the London Interbank Offered Rate (LIBOR), the prime rate, or a CD rate (HLT rates are normally 200–275 basis points above these rates).
· They have strong covenant protection.

financial distress

The state when a borrower is unable to meet a payment obligation to lenders and other creditors.

Nevertheless, HLTs tend to be quite heterogeneous with respect to the size of the issue, the interest payment date, interest indexing, and prepayment features. After origination, some HLT borrowers such as Macy's and El Paso Electric suffered periods of **financial distress** in that they were unable to make timely payments on many of the bonds they had issued and loans they had outstanding. As a result, a distinction between the market for distressed and nondistressed HLTs is usually made.

The Buyers. Of the wide array of potential buyers, some are interested in only a certain segment of the market for regulatory and strategic reasons. In particular, an increasingly specialized group of buyers of distressed HLT loans includes investment banks and **vulture funds.** For the nondistressed HLT market and the traditional U.S. domestic loan sales market, the five major buyers are other domestic banks, foreign banks, insurance companies and pension funds, closed-end bank loan mutual funds, and nonfinancial corporations.

vulture fund

A specialized fund that invests in distressed loans.

Investment Banks. Investment banks are predominantly buyers of HLT loans because (1) analysis of these loans[4] utilizes investment skills similar to those required for junk bond trading and (2) investment banks were often closely associated with the HLT borrower in underwriting the original junk bond/HLT deals. As such, large investment banks—for example, First Boston, Merrill Lynch, and Goldman Sachs—are relatively more informed agents in this market, either by acting as market makers or in taking short-term positions on movements in the market prices of these loans.

Vulture Funds. Vulture funds are specialized investment funds established to invest in distressed loans. These investments can be active, especially for those seeking to use the loans purchased for bargaining in a restructuring deal, which generates restructuring returns that strongly favor the loan purchaser. Alternatively, such loans may be held as passive investments or high-yield securities in a well-diversified portfolio of distressed securities. Investment banks, in fact, manage many vulture funds. Most secondary market trading in U.S. loan sales occurs in this segment of the market.

Other Domestic Banks. Interbank loan sales are at the core of the traditional market and historically have revolved around correspondent banking and regional banking/branching restrictions. Restrictions on nationwide banking in the past led banks to originate regionally undiversified and borrower-undiversified loan portfolios. Small banks often sold loan participations to their large correspondents to improve regional/borrower diversification and to avoid regulatory imposed single-borrower loan concentration ceilings. (A loan to a single borrower should not exceed 10 percent of a

---

4. Junk bonds are noninvestment-grade bonds (i.e., those issued with a credit rating of BB or below by Standard & Poors or Ba1 or below by Moody's)—see Chapter 6.

bank's capital.) This arrangement also worked in the other direction, with the larger banks selling participations to smaller banks. The traditional interbank market, however, has been shrinking as a result of three factors. First, the traditional correspondent banking relationship is breaking down as markets become more competitive. Second, concerns about counterparty risk and moral hazard have increased. In particular, moral hazard is the risk that the selling bank will seek to offload its "bad" loans (via loan sales) keeping the "good" loans in its portfolio. An extreme example of this is Penn Square, a small Texas bank, which sold many risky (energy-based) loans to its larger correspondent bank, Continental Illinois, in the early 1980s. Not only did Penn Square fail, but in 1984 Continental Illinois, then the eighth largest bank in the United States, also failed as a result of losses on these loans. Third, the barriers to nationwide banking are being eroded, particularly with the full implementation of interstate banking in 1997 (following the passage of the Riegle-Neal Interstate Banking and Branching Efficiency Act in 1994) and the (continuing) contraction in the number of small banks (see Chapter 14).

Foreign Banks. Foreign banks remain the dominant buyer of domestic U.S. loans. Because of the cost of branching, the loan sales market allows foreign banks to achieve a well-diversified domestic U.S. loan portfolio without developing a nationwide banking network. However, renewed interest in asset **downsizing,** especially among Japanese banks, has caused this source of demand to begin to contract.

downsizing

Shrinking an FI's asset size.

Insurance Companies and Pension Funds. Subject to meeting liquidity and credit quality restrictions (such as buying only BBB-rated borrowers or above), insurance companies (such as Aetna) and pension funds are important buyers of long-term loans.

Closed-End Bank Loan Mutual Funds. First established in 1988, these leveraged mutual funds, such as Merrill Lynch Prime Fund, invest in domestic U.S. bank loans. Although they could purchase loans in the loan sales market, the largest funds have moved into primary loan syndications as well because of the attractive fee income available. These mutual funds increasingly participate in funding loans originated by commercial banks; indeed, some money center banks, such as Chase, have actively encouraged closed-end fund participation in primary loan syndications.

Nonfinancial Corporations. Some corporations—primarily the financial services arms of the very largest U.S. and European companies (e.g., GE Capital and ITT Finance)—buy loans. This activity amounts to no more than 5 percent of total U.S. domestic loan sales.

The Sellers. The sellers of domestic loans and HLT loans are major money center banks, small regional or community banks, foreign banks, and investment banks.

Major Money Center Banks. The largest money center banks have dominated loan selling. In recent years, market concentration in loan selling has been accentuated by the increase in HLTs (and the important role that major money center banks have played in originating loans in HLT deals) and in problem real estate loans as a result of the recession in the real estate market in the early 1990s.

Small Regional or Community Banks. As mentioned earlier, small banks sell loans and loan participations to larger FIs for diversification and regulatory purposes. Although they are not a major player in the loan sales market, small banks have found loan sales to be essential for diversifying their credit risk.

Foreign Banks. To the extent that foreign banks are sellers rather than buyers of loans, these loans come from branch networks such as the Japanese-owned banks in California or through selling loans originated in their home country in U.S. loan sales markets.

Investment Banks.   Investment banks such as Salomon Brothers Smith Barney (a subsidiary of Citigroup) act as loan sellers either as part of their loan origination function or as active traders. Again, these loan sales are generally confined to large HLT transactions.

Secondary Market for Less Developed Country Debt

Since the mid-1980s, a secondary market for trading less developed country (LDC) debt has developed among large commercial and investment banks in New York and London. For example, total trading in emerging market debt in 1998 was $4.2 trillion, down from the $5.9 trillion traded in 1997. As discussed in Chapter 20, many of these countries (such as Mexico and Brazil) had trouble paying off this debt in the mid- and late-1980s. The Asian crisis in 1997 and 1998 led to another round of delayed- and nonpayment. Like domestic loan sales, the removal of LDC loans from the balance sheet allows an FI to free up assets for other investments. Further, being able to sell these loans—even if at a price below the face value of the original loan—may signify that the bank's balance sheet is sufficiently strong to bear the loss. In fact, a number of studies have found that announcements of banks writing down the value of LDC loans—prior to their charge-off and sale—has a positive effect on bank stock prices.

The major cost of LDC loan sales is the loss itself (the tax-adjusted difference between the face value of the loan and its market value at the time of the sale). In addition, many banks engaged in LDC loan sales in 1987 and 1988 after taking big loan-loss reserve additions in May and June 1987. Beginning in 1988, and in particular in the period 1991–1993, the secondary market loan prices of many LDC countries rose in value. However, an economic crisis in southeast Asia, South America, and Russia in the late 1990s sent prices back down. This suggests an additional cost related to loan sales—the optimal timing of such sales (the point when FIs can minimize losses from such sales).

Trading in LDC loans often takes place in the high-yield (or junk bond) departments of participating banks. These reflect programs under which the U.S. and other banks have exchanged their dollar loans for dollar bonds issued by the relevant countries. These bonds have a much longer maturity than that promised on the original loans and a lower promised original coupon (yield) than the interest rate on the original loan. These loans for bond restructuring programs, also called *debt-for-debt swaps*, have developed under the auspices of the U.S. Treasury's Brady Plan and other international organizations such as the IMF. Once banks and other FIs have swapped loans for bonds, they can sell them on the secondary market. By converting loans into **Brady bonds** (a bond that is swapped for an outstanding loan to an LDC, see Chapter 6), LDCs' assets become more liquid[5] because these bonds are often partially collateralized. These bond-for-loan swap programs seek to restore LDCs' creditworthiness and thus the value of bank holdings of such debt by creating longer-term, lower fixed-interest but more liquid securities in place of shorter-term, floating-rate loans. In recent years, many of the more successful emerging market LDCs have repurchased collateralized Brady bonds and replaced them with dollar bonds with no collateral backing—the price of these bonds reflects the creditworthiness of the issuing country.

Brady bond

A bond that is swapped for an outstanding loan to an LDC.

Factors Encouraging Future Loan Sales Growth

The introduction to this chapter stated that one reason that FIs sell loans is to manage their credit risk better. Loan sales remove assets (and credit risk) from

---

5. The Brady bond is usually created on an interest rate rollover date. On that date, the floating-rate loans are usually converted into fixed-rate coupon bonds on the books of an agent bank. The agent bank is the bank that kept the records of loan ownership and distributed interest payments made by the LDC to individual bank creditors. Once converted, the bonds can start trading.

Table 25–3 Factors Influencing Loan Sales

Factors Encouraging Loan Sales

Remove credit risk associated with loans from the balance sheet

Generate fee income

Reduce liquidity risk

Alleviate the burden of capital adequacy requirements

Reduce regulatory requirements, such as noninterest-bearing reserve requirements

Factors Discouraging Loan Sales

Commercial paper underwriting is an acceptable substitute

Legal challenges are often incurred if the borrower incurs financial distress

---

the balance sheet and allow an FI to achieve better asset diversification. Other than credit risk management, however, FIs are encouraged to sell loans for a number of other economic and regulatory reasons. The factors encouraging loan sales are summarized in Table 25–3 and discussed in detail here.

Fee Income. A bank can often report any fee income earned from originating loans as current income, but interest earned on direct lending can be accrued (as income) only over time (see Chapter 13). As a result, originating and quickly selling loans can boost a bank's reported income under current accounting rules.

Liquidity Risk. In addition to credit risk, holding loans on the balance sheet can increase the overall illiquidity of a bank's assets. This illiquidity is a problem because bank liabilities tend to be highly liquid. Asset illiquidity can expose the bank to harmful liquidity problems when depositors unexpectedly withdraw their deposits. To mitigate a liquidity problem, a bank's management can sell some of its loans to outside investors (see Chapter 21). Thus, the bank loan market has created a secondary market that has significantly reduced the illiquidity of bank loans held as assets on the balance sheet.

Capital Costs. The capital adequacy requirements imposed on banks are a burden as long as required capital exceeds the amount the bank believes to be privately beneficial. Thus, banks struggling to meet a required capital (K)-to-assets (A) ratio can boost this ratio by reducing assets (A) rather than boosting capital (K)—see Chapter 14. One way to downsize or reduce A and boost the K/A ratio is through loan sales.

Reserve Requirements. Regulatory requirements, such as noninterest-bearing reserves that a bank must hold at the central bank, represent a form of tax that adds to the cost of funding the loan portfolio. Regulatory taxes such as reserve requirements create an incentive for banks to remove loans from the balance sheet by selling them without recourse to outside parties.[6] Such removal allows banks to shrink both their assets and deposits and, thus, the amount of reserves they have to hold against their deposits.

Factors Deterring Future Loan Sales Growth

The loan sales market has experienced a number of up-and-down phases in recent years. Notwithstanding the value of loan sales as a credit risk management

---

6. Under current reserve requirement regulations (Regulation D, amended May 1986), bank loan sales with recourse are regarded as a liability and hence are subject to reserve requirements. The reservability of loan sales extends to a bank issuing a credit guarantee and a recourse provision. Loans sold without recourse (or credit guarantees by the selling bank) are free of reserve requirements. With the elimination of reserve requirements on nontransaction accounts and the lowering of reserve requirements on transaction accounts in 1991, the reserve tax effect is likely to become a less important feature driving bank loan sales (as well as the recourse/nonrecourse mix) in the future.

fraudulent conveyance

A transaction such as a sale of securities or transference of assets to a particular party that is determined to be illegal.

www.bondmarkets.com/

tool and other reasons described above, there are a number of factors that may deter the market's growth and development in the future. We discuss these next and summarize them in Table 25–3.

Access to the Commercial Paper Market.   Since 1987, large banks have enjoyed much greater powers to underwrite commercial paper directly, without experiencing legal challenges by the securities industry claiming that underwriting by banks is contrary to the Glass-Steagall Act. These underwriting powers were expanded in 1999 with the passage of the Financial Services Modernization Act that eliminated Glass-Steagall restrictions on underwriting activities such as commercial paper underwriting (see Chapter 14). This means that the need to underwrite or sell short-term bank loans as an imperfect substitute for commercial paper underwriting has now become much less important. In addition, more and more smaller middle markets are gaining direct access to the commercial paper market. As a result, such firms have less need to rely on bank loans to finance their short-term expenditures, with fewer loan originations generally resulting in fewer loans being sold.

Legal Concerns.   A number of legal concerns are currently hampering the loan sale market's growth, especially for distressed HLT loans. In particular, although banks are normally secured creditors, other creditors may attack this status if the borrowing firm enters bankruptcy. For example, **fraudulent conveyance** proceedings have been brought against the secured lenders to firms such as Revco, Circle K, Allied Stores, and RJR Nabisco. In these cases, the sale of loans to a particular party were found to be illegal. As discussed above, contractual terms in loan contracts can limit the loan originator's scope regarding to whom the loan can be sold. Fraudulent conveyance proceedings are challenges of loan sales as defined in the original loan contract. Such lawsuits represent one of the factors that have slowed the growth of the distressed loan market.

Loan Securitization

Loan securitization is useful in improving the risk-return trade-off for FIs. This section discusses the three major forms of securitization—the pass-through security, collateralized mortgage obligation (CMO), and mortgage-backed bonds—and analyzes their unique characteristics. Although depository institutions mainly undertake loan securitization, the insurance industry has also entered into this area (see In the News box 25–2). In addition, although all three forms of securitization originated in the real estate lending market, these techniques are currently being applied to loans other than mortgages—for example, credit card loans, auto loans, student loans, and commercial and industrial (C&I) loans. The Bond Market Association, a bond industry trade group representing over 260 member and associate securities firms, banks, and government agencies, reported that over $572 billion of mortgage-backed securities were issued in just the first nine months of 1999.

Pass-Through Security

FIs frequently pool the mortgages and other assets they originate and offer investors an interest in the pool in the form of *pass-through certificates* or *securities*. Although many different types of loans and assets on FIs' balance sheets are currently being

In the News

Insurers Piling into CMBS Market

Life insurance companies, no longer content to be caterers, now want their place at the CMBS (Collateralized Mortgage Backed Securities) table. This summer, at least three insurers are offering deals in the commercial mortgage-backed securities market, said officials attending the Mortgage Bankers Association's commercial mortgage conference in Tampa, Fla., last week. Most will price through their recently formed conduits.

John Hancock Real Estate Finance Inc. plans to originate $400 million via its conduit and securitize up to $400 million this year, and hopes to push that figure to $750 million for both originations and securitizations in 1998. The Lutheran Brotherhood, which has offered two deals in the last two years, will come to market in June with a $200 million privately placed CMBS. Underwriters were not disclosed but one source said Morgan Stanley Dean Witter, which has shepherded previous Lutheran-backed deals, is a likely choice. Prudential

Source: *Mortgage-Backed Securities Letter,* April 27, 1998, p. 1.

Mortgage Capital Co. will conduct a securitization in June or July of about $400 million, and plans up to two more deals this year, with the goal being $1.2 billion in securitizations by year-end. And other life companies may be taking their places soon as well. Nationwide Insurance Enterprise, for one, "is taking a very hard look at and may be involved in securitization," said Robert McNaghten, vice president of real estate investments for the insurer.

Why the decision to create conduits and dive into CMBS securitization? Insurers have been blindsided by both mortgage conduits and real estate investment trusts in recent years, and are also on the prowl for new sources of funding, as traditional insurance lending has stagnated. "Conduits surpassed life companies in loan origination in 1997, " said Sam Davis, senior vice president at John Hancock . "We felt we needed to do something about it." Nationwide's Mc-Naghten noted that smaller

mortgage correspondents are increasingly being wooed by Wall Street conduits. "They've digressed from feeding products to life companies and I don't blame them," he said.

The common story for most of these companies is a step-by-step entry into the CMBS market, with many now ready to delve further into bigger-ticket deals. Take John Hancock. Where in 1995 the company was only originating $100 million in loans for J.P. Morgan conduit, it is now ready to start building a brand name for itself in the market. In the future, "we hope to be the lead contributor of collateral for deals we do and build more name recognition with rating agencies," Davis said. "We need to step up to the plate with our own capital."

Lutheran Brotherhood has taken a similar path. In 1995 it was selling home loans to other life insurance companies; in 1996 it priced its first securitization, a REMIC that was privately placed. Last September, the company offered a fully rated $183.0 million securitization led by Morgan Stanley. For the Minneapolis-based insurer,

(continues)

In the News continued

which has $20 billion in assets, the driving force behind its CMBS dealings has been the need to create liq-uidity, said Gary Kallasen, vice president for Lutheran Brotherhood. "If we ever intend to back variable products in mutual funds, we need to make sure dollars can be created if we need them."

securitized, the original use of securitization is a result of government-sponsored programs to enhance the liquidity of the residential mortgage market. These programs indirectly subsidize the growth of home ownership in the United States.

www.ginniemae.gov/

We begin by analyzing the government-sponsored securitization of residential mortgage loans. Three government agencies or government-sponsored enterprises (introduced in Chapter 7) are directly involved in the creation of mortgage-backed pass-through securities. Informally, they are known as Ginnie Mae (GNMA), Fannie Mae (FNMA), and Freddie Mac (FHLMC).

timing insurance

A service provided by a sponsor of pass-through securities (such as GNMA) guaranteeing the bond holder interest and principal payments at the calendar date promised.

GNMA.   The Government National Mortgage Association (GNMA), or Ginnie Mae, is a government-owned agency with two major functions: sponsoring mortgage-backed securities programs and acting as a guarantor to investors in mortgage-backed securities regarding the timely pass-through of principal and interest payments on their sponsored bonds. In other words, GNMA provides **timing insurance.**

www.fanniemae.com/

FNMA.   FNMA, or Fannie Mae, is a more active agency than GNMA in creating pass-through securities. GNMA merely sponsors such programs; FNMA actually helps create pass-throughs by buying and holding mortgages on its balance sheet, and it also issues bonds directly to finance those purchases. Specifically, FNMA creates mortgage-backed securities (MBSs) by purchasing packages of mortgage loans from banks and thrifts; it finances such purchases by selling MBSs to outside investors such as life insurers or pension funds. In addition, FNMA engages in swap transactions by which it swaps MBSs with an FI for original mortgages. Since FNMA guarantees securities as to the full and timely payment of interest and principal, the FI receiving the MBSs can then resell them on the capital market or can hold them in its portfolio. Unlike GNMA, FNMA securitizes conventional mortgage loans as well as FHA/VA insured loans, as long as the conventional loans have acceptable loan-to-value or collateral ratios not normally exceeding 80 percent. Conventional loans with high loan-to-value ratios usually require additional private sector credit insurance before they are accepted into FNMA securitization pools.

www.freddiemac.com/

FHLMC.   The Federal Home Loan Mortgage Corporation (FHLMC), or Freddie Mac, performs a similar function to that of FNMA except that its major securitization role has historically involved thrifts. Like FNMA, it buys mortgage loan pools from FIs and swaps MBSs for loans. FHLMC also sponsors conventional loan pools as well as FHA/VA mortgage pools and guarantees timely payment of interest and ultimate payment of principal on the securities it issues.

The Incentives and Mechanics of Pass-Through Security Creation. In beginning to analyze the securitization process, we trace the mechanics of a mortgage pool securitization to provide insights into the return-risk benefits of this process to the mortgage-originating FI, as well as the attractiveness of these securities to investors. Given that more than $2.55 trillion of mortgage-backed securities are outstanding—a large proportion sponsored by GNMA—we analyze an example of the creation of a GNMA pass-through security next.[7]

Example 25–1 Creation of a GNMA Pass-Through Security

Suppose that a bank has just originated 1,000 new residential mortgages in its local area. The average size of each mortgage is $100,000. Thus, the total size of the new mortgage pool is:

$$1,000 \times \$100,000 = \$100 \text{ million}$$

Each mortgage, because of its small size, receives credit risk insurance protection from the FHA. This insurance costs a small fee to the originating bank. In addition, each of these new mortgages has an initial stated maturity of 30 years and a mortgage rate—often called the *mortgage coupon*—of 9 percent per year. Suppose that the bank originating these loans relies mostly on liabilities such as demand deposits as well as its own capital or equity to finance its assets. Under current capital adequacy requirements, each $1 of new residential mortgage loans must be backed by some capital. Since residential mortgages fall into the 50 percent risk weight category under the risk-based capital standards and the risk-based capital requirement is 8 percent (see Chapter 14), the bank capital needed to back the $100 million mortgage portfolio is:

$$\text{Capital requirement} = \$100 \text{ million} \times .5 \times .08 = \$4 \text{ million}$$

We assume that the remaining $96 million needed to fund the mortgages comes from the issuance of demand deposits. Current regulations require that for every dollar of demand deposits held by the bank, a 10 percent cash reserve has to be held at the Federal Reserve Bank or in the vault (see Chapter 14). Assuming that the bank funds the cash reserves on the asset side of the balance sheet with demand deposits, the bank must issue $106.67 ($96/(1 − .1)) in demand deposits (i.e., $96 to fund mortgages and $10.67 to fund the required cash reserves on these demand deposits). The reserve requirement on demand deposits is essentially an additional tax, over and above the capital requirement, on funding the bank's residential mortgage portfolio. Note that since a 0 percent reserve requirement currently exists on CDs and time deposits, the FI needs to raise fewer funds if it uses CDs to fund its mortgage portfolio.

Given these considerations, the bank's initial postmortgage balance sheet may look like the one in Table 25–4. In addition to the capital and reserve requirement taxes, the bank also must pay an annual insurance premium to the FDIC based on the size of its deposits (see Chapter 14). Assuming a deposit insurance premium of 27 basis points,[8] the fee would be:

$$\$106.67 \text{ million} \times .0027 = \$288,000$$

Although the bank is earning a 9 percent mortgage coupon on its mortgage portfolio, it is facing three levels of regulatory taxes:

www.bog.frb.fed.us/

www.fdic.gov/

1. Capital requirements
2. Reserve requirements
3. FDIC insurance premiums

---

7. At the end of the second quarter 1999, outstanding mortgage pools were $2.861 trillion, with GNMA pools amounting to $553 billion; FNMA, $911 billion; and FHLMC, $718 billion.

8. As of 1999, this was the fee charged to the lowest-quality banks.

Table 25–4   Bank Balance Sheet
(in millions of dollars)

Assets		Liabilities	
Cash reserves	$ 10.67	Demand deposits	$106.67
Long-term mortgages	100.00	Capital	4.00
	$110.67		$110.67

Thus, one incentive to securitize is to reduce the regulatory "tax" burden on the FI to increase its after-tax return.

Another reason for securitization is increased geographic diversification of the loan portfolio. Specifically, many FIs originate mortgages from the local community; the ability to securitize facilitates replacing them with MBSs based on mortgages from other cities and regions. In addition to facing regulatory taxes on its residential mortgage portfolio earnings, the bank in Table 25–4 has three risk exposure problems:

1. *Interest Rate Risk Exposure.* The FI funds the 30-year mortgage portfolio from (short-term) demand deposits; thus, it has a maturity mismatch (see Chapters 20 and 23). This is true even if the mortgage assets have been funded with short-term CDs, time deposits, or other purchased funds.

2. *Liquidity Risk Exposure.* The bank is holding an illiquid asset portfolio of long-term mortgages and no excess reserves; as a result, it is exposed to the type of potential liquidity problems discussed in Chapter 22, including the risk of having to conduct mortgage asset "fire sales" to meet large unexpected demand deposit withdrawals.

One possible solution to these interest rate and liquidity risk problems is to lengthen the bank's on-balance-sheet liabilities by issuing longer-term deposits or other liability claims such as medium-term notes. Another solution is to engage in interest rate swaps to transform the bank's liabilities into those of a long-term, fixed-rate nature (see Chapter 24). These techniques do not resolve the problem of regulatory taxes and the burden they impose on the FI's returns.

In contrast, creating GNMA pass-through securities can largely resolve the interest rate and liquidity risk problems on the one hand and reduce the burden of regulatory taxes on the other. This requires the bank to securitize the $100 million in residential mortgages by issuing GNMA pass-through securities. In our example, the bank can do this since each of the 1,000 underlying mortgages has FHA/VA mortgage insurance, the same stated mortgage maturity of 30 years, and coupons of 9 percent. Therefore, they are eligible for securitization under the GNMA program if the bank is an approved lender (which we assume it is—see Chapter 7).

The bank begins the securitization process by packaging the $100 million in mortgage loans. The packaged mortgage loans are removed from the balance sheet by placing them with a third-party trustee off the balance sheet. This third-party trustee may be another bank of high creditworthiness or a legal trustee. Next, the bank determines that (1) GNMA will guarantee, for a fee, the timing of interest and principal payments on the bonds issued to back the mortgage pool and (2) the bank itself will continue to service the pool of mortgages for a fee, even after they are placed in trust. Then, GMNA issues pass-through securities backed by the underlying $100 million pool of mortgages. These GNMA securities or pass-through bonds are sold to outside investors in the capital market, and the proceeds (net of any underwriting fees) go to the originating bank. The steps followed in this securitization process are summarized in Figure 25–2.

3. *Prepayment Risk on GNMA Pass-Throughs.* Following the sale, each mortgagee makes a payment every month to the bank. The bank aggregates these payments and passes the funds through to GNMA bond investors via the trustee net of servicing fee

Figure 25–2   Summary of a GNMA Pass-Through

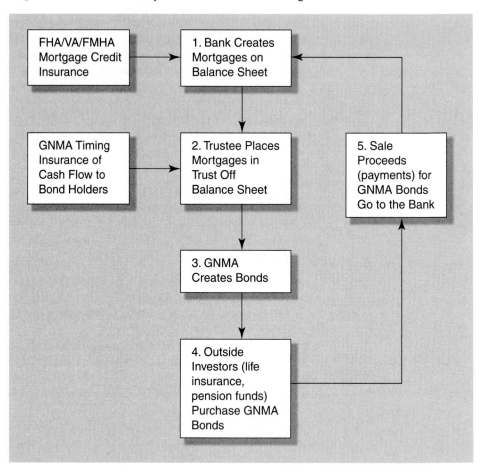

fully amortized

The equal, periodic repayment on a loan that reflects part interest and part principal over the life of the loan.

prepay

To pay back a loan before its maturity to the FI that originated the loan.

and insurance fee deductions. Most fixed-rate mortgages are **fully amortized** over the mortgage's life. This means that so long as the mortgagee does not seek to prepay the mortgage early within the 30-year period, either to buy a new house or to refinance the mortgage should interest rates fall, bond holders can expect to receive a constant stream of payments each month analogous to the stream of income on fixed-coupon, fixed-income bonds. In reality, however, mortgagees do not act in such a predictable fashion. For a variety of reasons, they relocate or refinance their mortgages (especially when current mortgage rates are below mortgage coupon rates). This propensity to **prepay** means that *realized* coupons/cash flows on pass-through securities can often deviate substantially from the stated or expected coupon flows in a no-prepayment world. This unique prepayment risk provides the attraction of pass-throughs to some (less risk-averse) GNMA pass-through investors but leads other more risk-averse investors to avoid these instruments. Collateralized mortgage obligations, discussed in the next section, provide a way to reduce this prepayment risk.

Assuming that a bank incurs no fees or underwriting costs in the securitization process, its balance sheet might be similar to the one in Table 25–5 immediately after the securitization has taken place. A dramatic change in the bank's balance sheet exposure has occurred. First, $100 million cash has replaced $100 million illiquid mortgage loans. Second, the maturity mismatch is reduced as long-term mortgages are replaced by cash (a short-term asset). Third, the bank has an enhanced ability to deal with and reduce its regulatory taxes. Specifically, it can reduce its capital, since capital standards require none be held against cash on the balance sheet compared to

Table 25–5 The Bank's Balance Sheet Postsecuritization
(in millions of dollars)

Assets		Liabilities	
Cash reserves	$ 10.67	Demand deposits	$106.67
Cash proceeds from mortgage securitization	100.00	Capital	4.00
	$110.67		$110.67

residential mortgages, which require 8 percent capital be held against 50 percent of the face value of the mortgage (i.e., on a $100,000 mortgage, a bank must hold $4,000 ($100,000 × .5 × .08) in capital—(see Chapter 14). The bank also reduced its reserve requirement and deposit insurance premiums if it uses part of the cash proceeds from the GNMA sale to pay off or retire demand deposits and downsize its balance sheet (as in Table 25–2).

Of course, keeping an all- or highly liquid asset portfolio and/or downsizing is a way to reduce regulatory taxes, but these strategies are hardly likely to enhance an FI's profits. The real logic of securitization is that the bank can use cash proceeds from the mortgage/GNMA sale to create or originate new mortgages, which in turn can be securitized. In so doing, the bank is acting more as an asset (mortgage) broker than a traditional asset transformer, as we discussed in Chapter 1. The advantage of being an asset broker is that the bank profits from mortgage pool servicing fees plus up-front points and fees from mortgage origination. At the same time, the bank no longer must bear the illiquidity and maturity mismatch risks and regulatory taxes that arise when it acts as an asset transformer and holds mortgages to maturity on its balance sheet. Put more simply, the bank's profitability becomes more fee dependent than interest rate spread dependent.

Collateralized Mortgage Obligation

www.freddiemac.com/

Although pass-throughs are still the primary mechanism for securitization, the collateralized mortgage obligation (CMO) is a second vehicle for securitizing FI assets that is used increasingly. Innovated in 1983 by FHLMC and First Boston, the CMO is a device for making mortgage-backed securities more attractive to investors. The CMO does this by repackaging the cash flows from mortgages and pass-through securities in a different fashion to attract different types of investors. A pass-through security gives each investor a pro rata share of any promised and prepaid cash flows on a mortgage pool; the CMO is a multiclass pass-through with a number of different bond holder classes or tranches differentiated by the order in which each class is paid off. Unlike a pass-through, each bond holder class has a different guaranteed coupon just as a regular T-bond has, but more importantly, the allocation of early cash flows due to mortgage prepayments is such that at any one time, all prepayments go to retire the principal outstanding of only one class of bond holders at a time, leaving the other classes' prepayment protected for a period of time. Thus, a CMO serves as a way to distribute or reduce prepayment risk.

collateralized mortgage obligation (CMO)

A mortgage-backed bond issued in multiple classes or tranches.

Creation of CMOs. CMOs can be created either by packaging and securitizing whole mortgage loans or, more usually, by placing existing pass-throughs in a trust off the balance sheet. The trust or third-party bank holds the GNMA pass-through as collateral against issues of new CMO securities. The trust issues these CMOs in three or more different classes. For example, the first CMO that Freddie Mac issued in 1983,

Figure 25–3   The Creation of a CMO

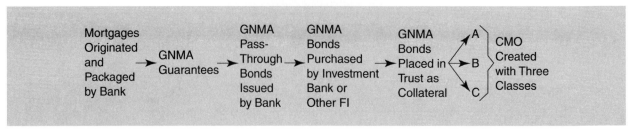

secured by 20,000 conventional home mortgages worth $1 billion, had three classes: A, $215 million; B, $350 million; and C, $435 million. We show a three-class or -tranche CMO in Figure 25–3.

Example 25–2   Calculation of Payments to Three Classes of CMO Bond Holders

Suppose that an investment bank buys a $150 million issue of GNMAs and places them in trust as collateral. It then issues a CMO with the following three classes:

Class A: Annual fixed coupon 7 percent, class size $50 million.
Class B: Annual fixed coupon 8 percent, class size $50 million.
Class C: Annual fixed coupon 9 percent, class size $50 million.

Suppose that in month 1 the promised amortized cash flows (R) on the mortgages underlying the GNMA pass-through collateral are $1 million, but an additional $1.5 million cash flow results from early mortgage prepayments. Thus, in the first month, the cash flows available to pay promised coupons to the three classes of bond holders is:

$$R + \text{Prepayments} = \$1 \text{ million} + \$1.5 \text{ million} = \$2.5 \text{ million}$$

This cash flow is available to the trustee, who uses it in the following fashion:

1. **Coupon Payments.** Each month (or more commonly, each quarter or half-year), the trustee pays the guaranteed coupons to the three classes of bond holders at annualized coupon rates of 7 percent, 8 percent, and 9 percent, respectively. Given the stated principal of $50 million for each class, the class A (7 percent annual coupon) bond holders receive approximately $291,667 in coupon payments in month 1; the class B (8 percent annual coupon) receives approximately $333,333 in month 1; and the class C (9 percent annual coupon) receives approximately $375,000 in month 1. Thus, the total promised coupon payments to the three classes amounts to $1,000,000 (equal to R, the no-prepayment principal and interest cash flows in the GNMA pool).

2. **Principal Payments.** The trustee has $2.5 million available to pay as a result of promised mortgage payments plus early prepayments, but the total payment of coupon interest amounts to only $1 million. For legal and tax reasons, the remaining $1.5 million must be paid to the CMO bond holders. The unique feature of the CMO is that the trustee pays this remaining $1.5 million to class A bond holders only. This retires early some of these bond holders' principal outstanding. At the end of month 1, only $48.5 million ($50 million–$1.5 million) of class A bonds remains outstanding, compared to $50 million of class B and $50 million of class C. These payment flows are shown graphically in Figure 25–4.

Let's suppose that the same thing happens in month 2. The cash flows from the mortgage/GNMA pool exceed the promised coupon payments to the three classes of

Figure 25–4   Allocation of Cash Flows to Owners of CMO Classes

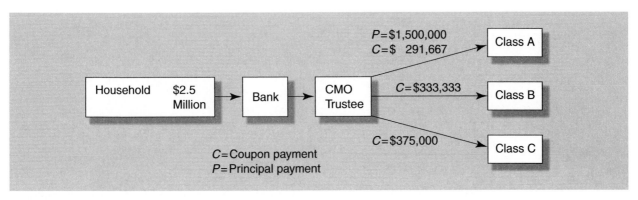

bond holders. Again, the trustee uses any excess cash flows to pay off or retire the principal of class A bond holders. If the excess cash flows again amount to $1.5 million, at the end of month 2 only $47 million ($48.5 million − $1.5 million) of class A bonds is outstanding. This continues until the full amount of the principal of class A bonds is paid off. Once this happens, any subsequent prepayments go to retire the principal outstanding to class B bond holders and, after they are paid off, to class C bond holders.

Clearly, issuing CMOs is often equivalent to engaging in double securitization. An FI packages mortgages and issues a GNMA pass-through. An investment bank such as Goldman Sachs or another CMO issuer such as FHLMC, a commercial bank, or a savings bank may buy this entire issue or a large part of it. Goldman Sachs, for example, then places these GNMA securities as collateral with a trust and issues three new classes of bonds backed by the GNMA securities as collateral. These trusts are sometimes called real estate mortgage investment conduits (REMICs). As a result, the investors in each CMO class have a claim to the GNMA collateral should the issuer fail. The investment bank or other issuer creates the CMO to make a profit by repackaging the cash flows from the single-class GNMA pass-through into cash flows more attractive to different groups of investors. The sum of the prices at which the three CMO bond classes can be sold normally exceeds that of the original pass-through:

$$\sum_{i=1}^{3} P_{iCMO} > P_{GNMA}$$

Gains from repackaging come from the way CMOs restructure prepayment risk to make it more attractive to different classes of investors. Specifically, under a CMO, each class has a guaranteed or fixed coupon.[9] By restructuring the GNMA as a CMO, a bank can offer investors who buy bond class C a high degree of mortgage prepayment protection compared to a pass-through. Those who buy class B receive an average degree of prepayment protection; those who buy class A have virtually no prepayment protection.

Each month mortgagees in the GNMA pool pay principal and interest on their mortgages (R) plus a prepayment of principal (some of the mortgage holders prepay principal either to refinance their mortgages or because they have sold their houses and are relocating). These cash flows are passed through to the owner of the GNMA pass-throughs. The CMO issuer uses the cash flows to pay promised coupon interest to the three classes of CMO bond holders.

9. Coupons may be paid monthly, quarterly, or semiannually.

Figure 25–5   Principal Balance Outstanding to Classes of Three-Class CMO

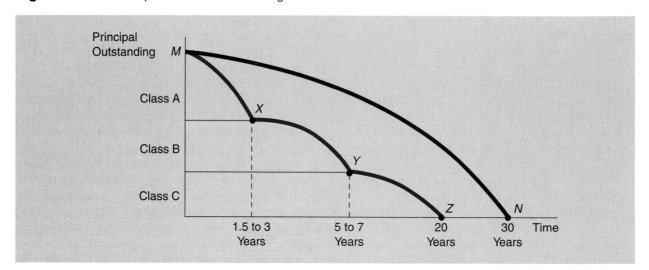

Figure 25–5 illustrates the typical pattern of outstanding principal balances for a three-tranche (class) CMO over time. With no prepayment, the outstanding principal balance is represented in Figure 25–5 by the curved line *MN*. Given any positive flow of prepayments, within a few years, the class A bonds clearly would be fully retired, point *X* in Figure 25–5. In practice, this often occurs between 1.5 and 3 years after issue. After the trustee retires class A, only classes B and C remain. As the months pass, the trustee uses any excess cash flows over and above the promised coupon payments to class B and C bond holders to retire bond class B's principal. Eventually, all of the principal on class B bonds is retired (point *Y* in Figure 25–5)—in practice, five to seven years after CMO issue. After class B bonds are retired, all remaining cash flows are dedicated to paying the promised coupon of class C bond holders and retiring the full amount of principal on class C bonds (point *Z* in Figure 25–5). In practice, class C bonds can have an average life of as long as 20 years.

Class A, B, and C Bond Buyers.   Class A bonds have the shortest average life with a minimum amount of prepayment protection. They are therefore of great interest to investors seeking short-duration mortgage-backed assets to reduce the duration of their mortgage-related asset portfolios. In recent years, savings banks and commercial banks have been large buyers of CMO class A securities.

Class B bonds have some prepayment protection and expected durations of five to seven years, depending on the level of interest rates. Pension funds and life insurance companies purchase these bonds, although some depository institutions also buy them.

Because of their long expected duration, class C bonds are highly attractive to insurance companies and pension funds seeking longer-term assets to match their long-term liabilities. Indeed, because of their failure to offer prepayment protection, regular GNMA pass-throughs may not have much attraction for these institutions. Class C CMOs, with their high but imperfect degree of prepayment protection, may be of more interest to the managers of these institutions.

In summary, by separating bond holders into different classes and by restructuring cash flows into forms more valued by different investor clienteles, the CMO issuer adds value to the securitization process.

mortgage- (asset-) backed bonds

Bonds collateralized by a pool of assets.

Mortgage-Backed Bond

As discussed in Chapter 7, **mortgage- (asset-) backed bonds** (MBBs) differ from pass-throughs and CMOs in two key dimensions. First, while pass-throughs and

Table 25–6 Balance Sheet of Potential MBB Issuer
(in millions of dollars)

Assets		Liabilities	
Long-term mortgages	$20	Insured deposits	$10
		Uninsured deposits	10
	$20		$20

CMOs help depository institutions remove mortgages from their balance sheets, MBBs normally remain on the balance sheet. Second, pass-throughs and CMOs have a direct link between the cash flows on the underlying mortgages and the cash flows on the bond instrument issued. By contrast, the relationship for MBBs is one of collateralization—the cash flows on the mortgages backing the bond are not necessarily directly connected to interest and principal payments on the MBB.

An FI issues an MBB to reduce risk to the MBB holders, who have a first claim to a segment of the FI's mortgage assets. The FI segregates a group of mortgage assets on its balance sheet and pledges this group of assets as collateral against the MBB issue. A trustee normally monitors the segregation of assets and ensures that the market value of the collateral exceeds the principal owed to MBB holders. That is, FIs back most MBB issues by excess collateral. This excess collateral backing of the bond, in addition to the priority rights of the bond holders, generally ensures the sale of these bonds with a high investment grade credit rating. In contrast, the FI, when evaluated as a whole, could be rated as BB or even lower. A high credit rating results in lower coupon payments than would be required if significant default risk had lowered the credit rating. To explain the potential benefits and the sources of any gains to an FI from issuing MBBs, we examine the following simple example.

Example 25–3 Gains to an FI from Issuing MBBs

Consider an FI with $20 million in long-term mortgages as assets. It is financing these mortgages with $10 million in short-term uninsured deposits (e.g., wholesale deposits over $100,000) and $10 million in insured deposits (e.g., retail deposits of $100,000 or less). In this example, we ignore the issues of capital and reserve requirements. Look at the balance sheet structure shown in Table 25–6.

This balance sheet poses problems for the FI manager. First, the FI has significant interest rate risk exposure due to the mismatch of the maturities of its assets and liabilities. Second, because of this interest rate risk and the potential default and prepayment risk on the FI's mortgage assets, uninsured depositors are likely to require a positive and potentially significant risk premium to be paid on their deposits. By contrast, the insured depositors may require approximately the risk-free rate on their deposits because they are fully insured by the FDIC (see Chapter 22).

To reduce its interest rate risk exposure and to lower its funding costs, the FI can segregate $12 million of the mortgages on the asset side of its balance sheet and pledge them as collateral backing a $10 million long-term MBB issue. Because the $10 million in MBBs is backed by mortgages worth $12 million, the mortgage-backed bond issued by the FI may cost less to issue, in terms of required yield, than uninsured deposit rates currently being paid—it may well be rated AA while uninsured deposits might be rated BB. The FI can then use the proceeds of the $10 million bond issue to replace the $10 million of uninsured deposits.

Consider the FI's balance sheet after the issue of the MBBs (Table 25–7). It might seem that the FI has miraculously engineered a restructuring of its balance sheet that has resulted in a better match of the maturities of its assets and liabilities and

Table 25–7   FI's Balance Sheet after MBB Issue
(in millions of dollars)

Assets		Liabilities	
Collateral (market value of segregated mortgages)	$12	MBB issue	$10
Other mortgages	8	Insured deposits	10
	$20		$20

a decrease in funding costs. The bond issue has lengthened the average maturity of liabilities by replacing short-term wholesale deposits with long-term MBBs and has lowered funding costs because AA-rated bond coupon rates are below BB-rated uninsured deposit rates. This outcome, however, occurs only because the insured depositors do not worry about risk exposure since they are 100 percent insured by the FDIC. The result of the MBB issue and the segregation of $12 million of assets as collateral backing the $10 million bond issue is that the insured deposits of $10 million are now backed by only $8 million in free or unpledged assets. If smaller depositors were not insured by the FDIC, they would surely demand very high risk premiums for holding these risky deposits. The implication of this is that the FI gains only because the FDIC is willing to bear enhanced credit risk through its insurance guarantees to depositors.[10] As a result, the FI is actually gaining at the expense of the FDIC. Consequently, it is not surprising that the FDIC is concerned about the growing use of this form of securitization by risky banks and thrifts.

Do You Understand?

1. What the three forms of asset securitization are? What are the major differences in the three forms?
2. How a simple bank balance sheet would change when a pass-through mortgage is securitized? Assume the mortgage is funded with demand deposits and capital and reserve regulations are in force.
3. Why an investor in a securitized asset who is concerned about prepayment risk would prefer a CMO over a pass-through security?
4. Why an AAA FI would ever issue mortgage-backed bonds? Explain your answer.

MBB issuance also has a number of costs. First, MBBs tie up mortgages on the FI's balance sheet for a long time, thus decreasing the asset portfolio's liquidity. Second, the balance sheet becomes more illiquid due to the need to collateralize MBBs to ensure a high-quality credit risk rating for the issue; in our example, the overcollateralization was $2 million. Third, the FI continues to be liable for capital adequacy and reserve requirement taxes by keeping the mortgages on the balance sheet. Because of these costs, MBBs are the least used of the three basic vehicles of securitization.

Securitization of Other Assets

The major use of the three securitization vehicles—pass-throughs, CMOs, and mortgage-backed bonds—has been to package fixed-rate residential mortgage assets. The standard features on mortgages have made the packaging and securitization of these securities relatively easy. But these techniques can and have been used for other assets, including the following:

- Automobile loans.
- Credit card receivables (CARDs).
- Small-business loans guaranteed by the Small Business Administration.
- Commercial and industrial loans.
- Student loans.

---

10. The FDIC does not make the risk-based deposit insurance premium to banks and thrifts sufficiently large to reflect this risk.

Table 25–8 Benefits versus Costs of Securitization

Benefits	Costs
1. New funding source (bonds versus deposits).	1. Public/private credit risk insurance and guarantees.
2. Increased liquidity of bank loans.	2. Overcollateralization.
3. Enhanced ability to manage the maturity gap and thus interest rate risk.	3. Valuation and packaging (the cost of asset heterogeneity).
4. A savings to the issuer, if off balance sheet, on reserve requirements, deposit insurance premiums, and capital adequacy requirements.	

- Mobile home loans.
- Junk bonds.
- Time share loans.
- Adjustable rate mortgages.[11]

Can All Assets Be Securitized?

The extension of securitization technology to assets other than fixed-rate residential mortgages raises questions about the limits of securitization and whether all assets and loans can eventually be securitized. Conceptually, the answer is that they can, so long as doing so is profitable or the benefits to the FI from securitization outweigh its costs. With heterogeneous loans, it is important to standardize the salient features of loans. Default risks, if significant, have to be reduced by diversification. Expected maturities have to be reasonably similar. As mechanisms are developed to overcome these difficulties, it is perfectly reasonable to expect securitization to grow. Table 25–8 summarizes the benefits versus the costs of securitization.

From Table 25–8, given any set of benefits, the more costly and difficult it is to find asset packages of sufficient size and homogeneity, the more difficult and expensive it is to securitize. For example, C&I loans have maturities running from a few months to eight years; in addition, they have varying interest rate terms (fixed, LIBOR floating, federal funds-rate floating) and fees. In addition, C&I loans contain different contractual covenants (covering items such as dividend payments by firms) and are made to firms in a wide variety of industries. Given this, it is difficult for investors, insurers, and bond rating agencies to value C&I loan pools.[12] The more difficult it is to value such asset pools, the higher are the costs of securitization. The potential boundary to securitization may well be defined by the relative degree of homogeneity of an asset type or group—the more homogeneous or similar are the assets in any pool, the easier they are to securitize. Thus, it is not surprising that 30-year fixed-rate residential mortgages were the first assets to be securitized, since they are the most homogeneous of all assets on bank balance sheets (i.e., have similar maturities and interest rates). Moreover, the existence of secondary markets for houses provides price information that allows for reasonably accurate market valuations of the underlying asset to be made by originators, insurers, and investors in the event of mortgage defaults.

Do You Understand?

1. Whether or not all assets and loans can be securitized? Explain your answer.

---

11. As of June 1999, securitized automobile loans totaled $109.9 billion, credit card receivables totaled $295.8 billion, and commercial and industrial loans totaled $94.2 billion.

12. Despite this, there has been some securitization of C&I loans. These are called collateralized loan obligations (CLOs). A CLO is modeled on the CMO. A bank collects a diversified pool of loans, places them in a trust, and usually issues three tranches of securities against the pool: usually a senior tranche, a subordinated tranche, and a tranche that has features similar to the residual tranche of CMOs. Most issues so far have involved securitizing highly leveraged loans to finance mergers and acquisitions.

Summary

Loan sales provide a simple alternative to the full securitization of loans through bond packages. In particular, they provide a valuable tool to an FI that wishes to manage its credit risk exposure better. Recently, by increasingly relying on securitization, banks and thrifts have begun to move away from being asset transformers to become asset brokers. Thus, over time, we can expect the traditional differences between commercial banking and investment banking to diminish as more and more loans and assets are securitized. This chapter discussed the increasing role of loan sales in addition to the legal and regulatory factors that are likely to affect the future growth of this market. The chapter also discussed three major forms of securitization—pass-through securities, collateralized mortgage obligations (CMOs), and mortgage-backed bonds— and described recent innovations in the securitization of other FI assets.

End-of-Chapter Questions

1. What is the difference between loans sold with recourse and without recourse from the perspective of both sellers and buyers?

2. What are some of the key features of short-term loan sales? How have banks used this sector of the loan market to circumvent Glass-Steagall limitations?

3. Why are yields higher on loan sales than they are for similar maturity and issue size commercial paper issues?

4. What is the difference between loan participations and loan assignments?

5. Why have FIs been very active in loan securitization issuance of pass-through securities while they have reduced their volume of loan sales? Under what circumstances would you expect loan sales to dominate loan securitization?

6. Who are the buyers and sellers of U.S. loans? Why do they participate in this activity?

7. A bank has made a 3-year $10 million dollar loan that pays annual interest of 8 percent. The principal is due at the end of the third year.
   a. The bank is willing to sell this loan with recourse at a 8.5 percent discount rate. What should it receive for this loan?
   b. The bank also has the option to sell this loan without recourse at a discount rate of 8.75 percent. What should it expect for selling this loan?
   c. If the bank expects a ½ percent probability of default on this loan over its three-year life, is it better off selling this loan with or without recourse? It expects to receive no interest payments or principal if the loan is defaulted.

8. City bank has made a 10-year, $2 million HLT loan that pays annual interest of 10 percent per year. The principal is expected at maturity.
   a. What should it expect to receive from the sale of this loan if the current market rate on loans is 12 percent?
   b. The prices of loans of this risk are currently being quoted in the secondary market at bid-offer prices of 88-89 cents (on each dollar). Translate these quotes into actual prices for the above loan.
   c. Do these prices reflect a distressed or nondistressed loan? Explain.

9. What role do reserve requirements play in the decision to sell a loan with or without recourse?

10. What are the three levels of regulatory taxes faced by FIs when making loans? How does securitization reduce the levels of taxation?

11. How will a move towards market value accounting affect the market for loan sales?

12. An FI is planning to issue $100 million in commercial loans. It will finance all of it by issuing demand deposits.
   a. What is the minimum capital required if there are no reserve requirements?
   b. What is the minimum demand deposits it needs to attract in order to fund this loan if you assume there is a 10 percent average reserve requirement on demand deposits, all reserves are held in the form of cash, and $8 million of funding is through equity?
   c. Show a simple balance sheet with total assets and total liabilities and equity if this is the only project funded by the bank.

13. How do loan sales and securitization help a bank manage its interest rate and liquidity risk exposures?

14. Go to the Ginnie Mae website and find the following for the most recent year available: new securities issued, cumulative issuances, and securities outstanding.

15. What are the differences between CMOs and MBBs?

16. Consider $200 million of 30-year mortgages with a coupon of 10 percent paid quarterly.
   a. What is the quarterly mortgage payment?
   b. What are the interest repayments over the first year of life of the mortgages? What are the principal repayments?

   Construct a 30-year CMO using this mortgage pool as collateral. There are three tranches (where A offers the least protection against prepayment and C offers the most). A $50 million tranche A makes quarterly payments of 9 percent; a $100 million tranche B makes quarterly payments of 10 percent; and a $50 million tranche C makes quarterly payments of 11 percent.

c.   Assuming no amortization of principal and no prepayments, what are the total promised coupon payments to the three classes? What are the principal payments to each of the three classes for the first year?

d.   If, over the first year, the trustee receives quarterly prepayments of $10 million on the mortgage pool, how are the funds distributed?

e.   How can the CMO issuer earn a positive spread on the CMO?

17.   Assume an FI originates a pool of short-term real estate loans worth $20 million with maturities of 5 years and paying interest rates of 9 percent (paid annually).

a.   What is the average payment received by the FI (both principal and interest) if no prepayment is expected over the life of the loans?

b.   If the loans are converted into real estate certificates and the FI charges 50 basis points servicing fee (including insurance), what are the payments expected by the holders of the securities, if no prepayment is expected?

18.   How do FIs use securitization to manage their interest rate, credit, and liquidity risks?

19.   Why do buyers of class C tranches of collateralized mortgage obligations (CMOs) demand a lower return than do purchasers of class A tranches?

20.   Go to the FHA website and locate the most recent information on net prices and averaged yields for HUD-insured new home mortgages.

Glossary

Accrued interest That portion of the coupon payment accrued between the last coupon payment and the settlement day.

Adjustable-rate mortgage A mortgage in which the interest rate is tied to some market interest rate. Thus, the required monthly payments can change over the life of the mortgage.

Adjustment credit Discount window loan offered for short-term liquidity problems that may result from a temporary deposit outflow.

American option An option that can be exercised at any time before the expiration date.

Amortization schedule Schedule showing how the monthly mortgage payments are split between principal and interest.

Amortized A mortgage is amortized when the fixed principal and interest payments fully pay off the mortgage by its maturity date.

Annuity A series of equal cash flows received at fixed intervals over the investment horizon.

Asset securitization The packaging and selling of loans and other assets backed by securities issued by an FI.

Asset transformer Financial claims issued by an FI that are more attractive to investors than are the claims directly issued by corporations.

Assignment The purchase of a share in a loan syndication with some contractual control and rights over the borrower.

Automatic rate-reduction mortgages Mortgages in which the lender automatically lowers the rate on an existing mortgage when prevailing rates fall.

Back-end fee The fee charged on the unused component of a loan commitment.

Balance of payment accounts Summary of all transactions between citizens of two countries.

Balloon payment mortgage Mortgage that requires a fixed monthly interest payment for a three- to five-year period. Full payment of the mortgage principal (the balloon payment) is then required at the end of the period.

Bank loan sale Sale of loan originated by a bank with or without recourse to an outside buyer.

Bank panic A systemic or contagious run on the deposits of the banking industry as a whole.

Bank run A sudden and unexpected increase in deposit withdrawals from a bank.

Banker's acceptance A time draft payable to a seller of goods, with payment guaranteed by a bank.

Basel (or Basle) Accord An agreement that requires the imposition of risk-based capital ratios on banks in major industrialized countries.

Basis risk A residual risk that occurs because the movement in a spot (cash) asset's price is not perfectly correlated with the movement in the price of the asset delivered under a futures or forward contract.

Bearer bonds Bonds with coupons attached to the bond. The holder presents the coupons to the issuer for payments of interest when they come due.

Bearer instrument An instrument in which the holder at maturity receives the principal and interest.

Best efforts underwriting An underwriting in which the investment banker acts as an agent rather than as a principal that bears risk. The underwriter does not guarantee a price to the issuer and acts more as a placing or distribution agent on a fee basis related to its success in placing the issue.

Bond and income funds Funds consisting of fixed-income capital market debt securities.

Bond indenture The legal contract that specifies the rights and obligations of the bond issuer and the bond holders.

Bond markets Markets in which bonds are issued and traded.

Bonds Long-term debt obligations issued by corporations and government units.

Book value Value of assets and liabilities based on their historical costs.

Brady bond A bond that is swapped for an outstanding loan to a less developed country (LDC).

Broker-dealers Firms that assist in the trading of existing securities.

Brokered deposits Wholesale CDs obtained through a brokerage house.

Business credit institutions Finance companies specializing in business loans.

Call option An option that gives a purchaser the right, but not the obligation, to buy the underlying security from the writer of the option at a prespecified exercise price on a prespecified date.

Call premium The difference between the call price and the face value on the bond.

Call provision A provision on a bond issue that allows the issuer to force the bond holder to sell the bond back to the issuer at a price above the par value (or at the call price).

Cap A call option on interest rates, often with multiple exercise dates.

Capital accounts The section of the balance of payment table that summarizes capital flows into and out of a country.

Capital markets Markets that trade debt (bonds) and equity (stock) instruments with maturities of more than one year.

Capital-to-assets ratio Ratio of an FI's core capital to its assets.

Captive finance company A finance company wholly owned by a parent corporation.

Career average formula Pension plan pays retirement benefits based on the employee's average salary over the entire period of employment.

Cash management account Money market mutual fund sold by investment banks that offer check-writing privileges.

Cash reserves Vault cash and cash deposits held at the Federal Reserve.

CGAP effect The relation between changes in interest rates and changes in net interest income.

Clearinghouse The unit that oversees trading on the exchange and guarantees all trades made by the exchange traders.

Closed-end investment companies Specialized investment companies that have a fixed supply of outstanding shares but invest in the securities and assets of other firms.

Collar A position taken simultaneously in a cap and a floor.

Collateralized mortgage obligation (CMO) A mortgage-backed bond issued in multiple classes or tranches.

Combined ratio A measure of the overall underwriting profitability of a line; equals the loss ratio plus the ratios of loss-adjustment expenses to premiums earned as well as commission and other acquisition costs to premiums written minus any dividends paid to policyholders as a proportion of premiums earned.

Commercial banking Banking activity of deposit taking and lending.

Commercial paper An unsecured short-term promissory note issued by a company to raise short-term cash, often to finance working capital requirements.

Common stock The fundamental ownership claim in a public corporation.

Community bank A bank that specializes in retail or consumer banking.

Compensating balance A proportion of a loan that a borrower is required to hold on deposit at the lending institution.

Compound interest Interest earned on an investment is reinvested.

Conditions precedent Those conditions specified in the credit agreement or terms sheet for a credit that must be fulfilled before drawings are permitted.

Consol bond A bond that pays a fixed coupon each year forever.

Contemporaneous reserve accounting system An accounting system in which the reserve computation and reserve maintenance periods overlap.

Conventional mortgages Mortgages issued by financial institutions that are not federally insured.

Convertible bonds Bonds that may be exchanged for another security of the issuing firm at the discretion of the bond holder.

Convexity The degree of curvature of the price–interest rate curve around some interest rate level.

Core deposits Deposits of the bank that are stable over short periods of time and thus provide a long-term funding source to a bank.

Corporate bonds Long-term bonds issued by corporations.

Correspondent bank A bank that provides services such as reciprocal accounts and agreements to another commercial bank.

Correspondent banking A relationship between a small bank and a large bank in which the large bank provides a number of deposit, lending, and other services.

Counterparty credit risk The risk that the other party to a contract will default on payment obligations.

Country or **sovereign risk** The risk that repayments from foreign borrowers may be interrupted because of interference from foreign governments.

Coupon bonds Bonds that pay interest based on a stated coupon rate. The interest or coupon payments per year is generally constant over the life of the bond.

Coupon interest rate Interest rate used to calculate the annual cash flow the bond issuer promises to pay the bond holder.

Credit equivalent amount The amount of credit risk exposure of an off-balance-sheet item calculated by multiplying the face value of an off-balance-sheet instrument by a conversion factor.

Credit risk The risk that the promised cash flows from loans and securities held by FIs may not be paid in full.

Credit-scoring system A mathematical model that uses observed loan applicant's characteristics to calculate a score that represents the applicant's probability of default.

Credit spread call option A call option whose payoff increases as a yield spread decreases below a stated spread.

Cross-sectional analysis Analysis of financial statements comparing one firm with others.

Cumulative preferred stock Preferred stock in which missed dividend payments go into arrears and must be made up before any common stock dividends can be paid.

Cumulative voting All directors up for election are voted on at the same time. The number of votes assigned to each stockholder equals the number of shares held multiplied by the number of directors to be elected.

Currency appreciation When a country's currency rises in value relative to other currencies, meaning that the country's goods are more expensive for foreign buyers and foreign goods are cheaper for foreign sellers (all else constant).

Currency depreciation When a country's currency falls in value relative to other currencies, meaning the country's goods become cheaper for foreign buyers and foreign goods become more expensive for foreign sellers.

Currency swap A swap used to hedge against foreign exchange rate risk from mismatched currencies on assets and liabilities.

Current accounts The section of the balance of payment table that summarizes foreign trade in goods and services, net investment income, and gifts, grants, or aid given to other countries.

Current exposure The cost of replacing a derivative securities contract at today's prices.

Day traders Exchange members who take a position within a day and liquidate it before day's end.

Debentures Bonds backed solely by the general credit of the issuing firm, unsecured by specific assets or collateral.

Default option An option that pays the par value of a loan in the event of a loan default.

Default risk The risk that a security's issuer will default on that security by being late on or missing an interest or principal payment.

Defined benefit pension plan Pension plan in which the employer agrees to provide the employee with a specific cash benefit upon retirement.

Defined contribution benefit plan Pension plan in which the employer agrees to make a specified contribution to the pension fund during the employee's working years.

Delegated monitor An economic agent appointed to act on behalf of smaller investors in collecting information and/or investing funds on their behalf.

De novo office A newly established office.

Derivative security An agreement such as a futures, forward, swap, or option contract between two parties to exchange a standard quantity of an asset at a predetermined price at a specified date in the future. The agreement is entered by an FI for hedging or other purposes.

Derivative securities markets The markets in which derivative securities trade.

Direct transfer A corporation sells its stock of debt directly to investors without going through a financial institution.

Discount bond A bond in which the present value of the bond is less than its face value.

Discount broker A stockbroker that conducts trades for customers but does not offer investment advice.

Discount points Interest payments made when the loan is issued (at closing). One discount point paid up front is equal to 1 percent of the principal value of the mortgage.

Discount rate The interest rate on loans made by Federal Reserve Banks to depository institutions.

Discount window The facility through which Federal Reserve Banks issue loans to depository institutions.

Disintermediation Withdrawal of deposits from depository institutions to be reinvested elsewhere—for example, in money market mutual funds.

Diversify The ability of an economic agent to reduce risk by holding a number of securities in a portfolio.

Down payment A portion of the purchase price of the property a financial institution requires the mortgage borrower to pay up front.

Downsizing Shrinking an FI's asset size.

Dual banking system The coexistence of both nationally and state-chartered banks, as in the United States.

Dual-class firms Two classes of common stock are outstanding, with differential voting rights assigned to each class.

Duration The weighted-average time to maturity on an investment.

Duration gap A measure of overall interest rate risk exposure for an FI.

Earning assets Investment securities plus net loans and leases.

EAT Earnings after taxes.

EBIT Earnings before interest and taxes.

Economies of scale The concept that cost reduction in trading and other transaction services results from increased efficiency when FIs perform these services. It is measured as the degree to which an FI's average unit costs of producing financial services fall as its output of services increases. For example, cost reduction in trading and other transaction services resulting from increased efficiency when these services are performed by FIs.

Economies of scope The degree to which an FI can generate cost synergies by producing multiple financial service products.

Elasticity The percentage change in the price of a bond for any given change in interest rates.

Equity funds Funds consisting of common and preferred stock securities.

Equity-participation mortgage A mortgage that is similar to a SAM except that an outside investor shares in the appreciation of the property rather than the financial institution.

Equivalent annual return Rate earned over a 12-month period taking the compounding of interest into account.

Etrade Buying and selling shares on the Internet.

Eurocommercial paper Eurosecurities issued by dealers of commercial paper without involving a bank.

Eurodollar bond Dollar-denominated bonds issued mainly in London and other European centers such as Luxembourg.

Eurodollar deposit Dollar-denominated deposits in non-U.S. banks.

Eurodollar market The market in which Eurodollars trade.

Euronotes Short-term notes similar to commercial paper. These instruments are most frequently used by European banks that deal in commercial paper.

European option An option that can be exercised only on the expiration date.

Excess reserves Additional reserves banks choose to hold.

Expected rate of return The interest rate an investor would earn on a security if he or she buys the security at its current market price, receives all promised or expected payments on the security, and sells the security at the end of his or her investment horizon.

Extended credit Discount window loan offered to banks with severe liquidity problems due to deposit outflows that will not be resolved in the foreseeable future.

Factoring The process of purchasing accounts receivable from corporations (often at a discount), usually with no recourse to the seller should the receivables go bad.

Fed funds rate The interest rate on short-term funds transferred between financial institutions, usually for a period of one day.

Federal funds Short-term funds transferred between financial institutions, usually for a period of one day.

Federal funds market An interbank market for short-term borrowing and lending of bank reserves.

Federal Open Market Committee (FOMC) The major monetary policy-making body of the Federal Reserve System.

Federal Reserve Board Trading Desk Unit of the Federal Reserve Bank of New York through which open market transactions are conducted.

Federally insured mortgages Mortgages originated by financial institutions, with repayment guaranteed by either the Federal Housing Administration (FHA) or the Veterans Administration (VA).

Final pay formula Pension plan pays retirement benefits based on a percentage of the average salary during a specified number of years at the end of the employee's career times the number of years of service.

Financial distress The state when a borrower is unable to meet a payment obligation to lenders and other creditors.

Financial institutions Institutions that perform the essential function of channeling funds from those with surplus funds to those with shortages of funds.

Financial markets The arenas through which funds flow.

Financing gap The difference between a bank's average loans and average (core) deposits.

Financing requirement The financing gap plus a bank's liquid assets.

Fire-sale price The price received for an asset that has to be liquidated (sold) immediately.

Firm commitment offering Securities offered from the issuing firm purchased by an underwriter.

Firm commitment underwriting The issue of financial instruments by an investment bank in which the investment bank guarantees the corporation a price for newly issued instruments by buying the whole issue at a fixed price from the corporate issuer. It then seeks to resell these instruments to suppliers of funds (investors) at a higher price.

Firm-specific credit risk The risk of default for the borrowing firm associated with the specific types of project risk taken by that firm.

Fixed-rate mortgage A mortgage that locks in the borrower's interest rate and thus the required monthly payment over the life of the mortgage, regardless of how market rates change.

Flat benefit formula Pension plan that pays a flat amount for every year of employment.

Floor A put option on interest rates, often with multiple exercise dates.

Floor broker Exchange members who place trades from the public.

Foreclosure The process of taking possession of the mortgaged property in satisfaction of a defaulting borrower's indebtedness and forgoing claim to any deficiency.

Foreign exchange intervention Commitments between countries about the institutional aspects of their intervention in the foreign exchange markets.

Foreign exchange markets Markets in which cash flows from the sale of products or assets denominated in a foreign currency are transacted.

Foreign exchange rate The price at which one currency can be exchanged for another currency.

Foreign exchange risk Risk that cash flows will vary as the actual amount of U.S. dollars received on a foreign investment changes due to a change in foreign exchange rates.

Foreign exchange risk The risk that exchange rate changes can affect the value of an FI's assets and liabilities located abroad.

Forward contract An agreement to transact involving the future exchange of a set amount of assets at a set price.

Forward foreign exchange transaction The exchange of currencies at a specified exchange rate (or forward exchange rate) at some specified date in the future.

Forward rate An expected rate (quoted today) on a security that originates at some point in the future.

401(k) plans Employer-sponsored plans that supplement a firm's basic retirement plan.

Fraudulent conveyance A transaction such as a sale of securities or transference of assets to a particular party that is determined to be illegal.

Frequency of loss The probability that a loss will occur.

Fully amortized The equal, periodic repayment on a loan that reflects part interest and part principal over the life of the loan.

Futures contract An agreement to transact involving the future exchange of a set amount of assets for a price that is settled daily.

Futures option An option contract that, when exercised, results in the delivery of a futures contract as the underlying asset.

GDS (gross debt service) ratio Gross debt service ratio calculated as total annual accommodation expenses divided by annual gross income.

General obligation bonds Bonds backed by the full faith and credit of the issuer.

Graduated-payment mortgages Mortgages in which borrowers make small payments early in the life of the mortgage. Payments then increase over the first 5 to 10 years, and finally payments level off at the end of the mortgage period.

Grandfathered subsidiaries Subsidiaries established prior to the passage of a restrictive law and not subject to that law.

Gross proceeds The price at which the investment bank resells the stock to investors.

Growing-equity mortgages Mortgages in which the initial payments are the same as on a conventional mortgage, but they increase over a portion or the entire life of the mortgage. In contrast to GPMs, which do not affect the time until the mortgage is paid off, the incremental increase in monthly payments on GEMs reduces the principal on the mortgage more quickly. This reduces the actual life of the mortgage.

Hedging selectively Only partially hedging the gap on individual assets and liabilities.

Highly leveraged transaction (HLT) loan A loan that finances a merger and acquisition; a leveraged buyout results in a high leverage ratio for the borrower.

Holding company A parent company that owns a controlling interest in a subsidiary bank or other FI.

Home equity loan Loans that let customers borrow on a line of credit secured with a second mortgage on their homes.

Hybrid funds Funds consisting of stock and bond securities.

Immunized Describes an FI that is fully hedged or protected against adverse movements in interest rates (or asset prices).

Implicit premiums Deposit insurance premiums or costs imposed on a bank through activity constraints rather than direct monetary charges.

Indirect transfer A transfer of funds between suppliers and users of funds through a financial intermediary.

Individual retirement accounts (IRAs) Self-directed retirement accounts set up by employees who may also be covered by employer-sponsored pension plans.

Inflation The continual increase in the price level of a basket of goods and services.

Initial margin A deposit required on futures trades to ensure that the terms of any futures contract will be met.

Initial public offerings (IPOs) The first public issue of financial instruments by a firm.

Inside money That part of the money supply produced by the private banking system.

Insolvency risk The risk that an FI may not have enough capital to offset a sudden decline in the value of its assets relative to its liabilities.

Insurance guarantee fund A fund of required contributions from within-state insurance companies to compensate insurance company policyholders in the event of a failure.

Insured pension plan A pension fund administered by a life insurance company.

Interest rate parity theorem (IRPT) The theory that the domestic interest rate should equal the foreign interest rate minus the expected appreciation of the domestic currency.

Interest rate risk The risk incurred by an FI when the maturities of its assets and liabilities are mismatched.

Interest rate spread The difference between lending and deposit rates.

Interest rate swap An exchange of fixed-interest payments for floating-interest payments by two counterparties.

Intrinsic value of an option The difference between an option's exercise price and the underlying asset's price.

Investment banking Banking activity of underwriting, issuing, and distributing securities.

IO strips The owner of an IO strip has a claim to the present value of interest payments by the mortgagees in the GNMA pool.

IPO A corporation's initial or first-time public offering of debt or equity.

Junk bond A bond rated as speculative or less than investment grade (below Baa by Moody's and BBB by S&P) by bond-rating agencies.

Lagged reserve accounting system An accounting system in which the reserve computation and reserve maintenance period do not overlap.

LDC loan Loans made to a less developed country (LDC).

Letter of credit A credit guarantee issued by an FI for a fee on which payment is contingent on some future event occurring, most notably default of the agent that purchases the letter of credit. For example, contingent guarantees sold by an FI to underwrite the trade or commercial performance of the buyer of the guarantee.

Lien A public record attached to the title of the property that gives the financial institution the right to sell the property if the mortgage borrower defaults.

Limit order An order to transact at a specified price.

Limited liability No matter what financial difficulties the issuing corporation encounters, neither it nor its creditors can seek repayment from the firm's common stockholders. This implies that common stockholder losses are limited to the original amount of their investment.

Liquidity The ease with which an asset can be converted into cash.

Liquidity risk The risk that a sudden surge in liability withdrawals may require an FI to liquidate assets in a very short period of time and at low prices.

Load fund A mutual fund with an up-front sales or commission charge that the investor must pay.

Loan commitment agreement Contractual commitment to loan to a firm a certain maximum amount at given interest rate terms.

Loan sharks Subprime lenders that charge unfairly exorbitant rates to desperate, subprime borrowers.

Loanable funds theory A theory of interest rate determination that views equilibrium interest rates in financial markets as a result of the supply and demand for loanable funds.

Loans sold Loans originated by the FI and then sold to other investors that can be returned to the originating institution.

London Interbank Offered Rate (LIBOR) A base rate for prime interbank dollar loans in the Eurodollar market of a given maturity. FIs use LIBOR as an index for annual changes on variable rate loans.

Long position A purchase of a futures contract.

Long-tail loss A loss for which a claim is made some time after a policy was written.

Loss ratio A measure of pure losses incurred to premiums earned.

Lump sum payment A single cash flow occurs at the beginning and end of the investment horizon with no other cash flows exchanged.

Macrohedging Hedging the entire duration gap of an FI.

Maintenance margin The margin a futures trader must maintain once a futures position is taken. If losses on the customer's futures position occur and the level of the funds in the margin account drop below the maintenance margin, the customer is required to deposit additional funds into his or her margin account, bringing the balance back up to the initial margin.

Marked to market Describes the prices on outstanding assets and liabilities that are adjusted each day to reflect current market conditions. For example, asset and balance sheet values are marked to market when their values are adjusted to reflect current market prices.

Market efficiency The process by which financial security prices move to a new equilibrium when interest rates or a security-specific characteristic changes. Measured as the speed with which financial security prices adjust to unexpected news pertaining to interest rates or a stock-specific characteristic.

Market order An order to transact at the best price available when the order reaches the post.

Market risk The risk incurred in trading assets and liabilities due to changes in interest rates, exchange rates, and other asset prices.

Market-to-book ratio A ratio that shows the discrepancy between the stock market value of an FI's equity and the book value of its equity.

Market value or **mark to market value basis** Balance sheet values that reflect current rather than historical prices.

McCarran-Ferguson Act of 1945 Regulation confirming the primacy of state over federal regulation of insurance companies.

Megamerger The merger of banks with assets of $1 billion or more.

Microhedging Using a futures (forward) contract to hedge a specific asset or liability.

Minimum risk portfolio A portfolio for which a combination of assets reduces the variance of portfolio returns to the lowest feasible level.

MMDAs Money market deposit accounts with retail savings accounts and some limited checking account features.

Modified duration Duration divided by 1 plus the interest rate.

Monetary base Currency in circulation and reserves (depository institution reserves and vault cash of commercial banks) held by the Federal Reserve.

Money center bank A bank that relies heavily on nondeposit or borrowed sources of funds.

Money market mutual fund Specialized mutual funds that offer depositlike interest-bearing claims to savers. These funds consist of various mixtures of money market securities.

Money markets Markets that trade debt securities or instruments with maturities of less than one year.

Moral hazard The loss exposure an insurer faces when providing insurance encourages the insured to take more risks.

Mortgage (asset)-backed bonds Bonds collateralized by a pool of assets.

Mortgage bonds Bonds issued to finance specific projects, which are pledged as collateral for the bond issue.

Mortgage sale Sale of a mortgage originated by a bank with or without recourse to an outside buyer.

Mortgages Loans to individuals or businesses to purchase a home, land, or other real property.

Multibank holding company (MBHC) A parent banking organization that owns a number of individual bank subsidiaries.

Municipal bonds Securities issued by state and local (e.g., county, city, school) governments.

Mutual organization An institution in which the liability holders are also the owners—for example, in a mutual savings bank, depositors also own the bank.

NAFTA   North American Free Trade Agreement.

Naive hedge   A hedge of a cash asset on a direct dollar-for-dollar basis with a forward or futures contract.

Naked options   Option positions that do not identifiably hedge an underlying asset or liability.

National treatment   Regulation of foreign banks in the same fashion as domestic banks, or the creation of a level playing field.

NAV   The net asset value of a mutual fund—equal to the market value of the assets in the mutual fund portfolio divided by the number of shares outstanding.

Negotiable certificates of deposit (CDs)   Bank-issued, fixed maturity, interest-bearing time deposits with face values of $100,000 or more that specify an interest rate and maturity date and are negotiable. They can be resold in the secondary market.

Negotiable instrument   An instrument whose ownership can be transferred in the secondary market.

Net charge-offs   Actual losses on loans and leases.

Net deposit drain   The amount by which cash withdrawals exceed additions; a net cash outflow.

Net exposure   A financial institution's overall foreign exchange exposure in any given currency.

Net interest margin   Interest income minus interest expense divided by earning assets.

Net long (short) in a currency   A position of holding more (fewer) assets than liabilities in a given currency.

Net operating income   Income before taxes and extraordinary items.

Net premiums written   The entire amount of premiums on insurance contracts written.

Net proceeds   The guaranteed price at which the investment bank purchases the stock from the issuer.

Net regulatory burden   The difference between the private costs of regulations and the private benefits for the producers of financial services.

Net worth   A measure of an FI's capital that is equal to the difference between the market value of its assets and the market value of its liabilities.

Net write-offs   Actual loan losses less loan recoveries.

No-load fund   A mutual fund that does not charge up-front sales or commission charges on the sale of mutual fund shares to investors.

Nominal interest rates   The interest rates actually observed in financial markets.

Nonbank bank   A bank divested of its commercial loans and/or its demand deposits.

Noncumulative preferred stock   Preferred stock in which dividend payments do not go into arrears and are never paid.

Noninsured pension plan   A pension fund administered by a financial institution other than a life insurance company.

Nonparticipating preferred stock   Preferred stock in which the dividend is fixed regardless of any increase or decrease in the issuing firm's profits.

Notional principal   The principal amount involved in a swap.

NOW account   Negotiable order of withdrawal account is similar to a demand deposit but pays interest when a minimum balance is maintained—that is, an interest-bearing checking account.

Off-balance-sheet (OBS) asset   When an event occurs, this item moves onto the asset side of the balance sheet or income is realized on the income statement.

Off-balance-sheet liability   When an event occurs, this item moves onto the liability side of the balance sheet or an expense is realized on the income statement.

Off-balance-sheet risk   The risk incurred by an FI as the result of activities related to contingent assets and liabilities.

One-bank holding company   A parent banking organization that owns one bank subsidiary and nonbank subsidiaries.

Open-end mutual fund   A fund for which the supply of shares is not fixed but can increase or decrease daily with purchases and redemptions of shares.

Open interest   The total number of the futures, put option, or call option contracts outstanding at the beginning of the day. For example, the outstanding stock of put or call contracts.

Open market operations   Purchases and sales of U.S. government and federal agency securities by the Federal Reserve.

Open-outcry auction   Method of futures trading where traders face each other and "cry out" their offer to buy or sell a stated number of futures contracts at a stated price.

Open position   An unhedged position in a particular currency.

Operating ratio   A measure of the overall profitability of a P&C insurer; equals

the combined ratio minus the investment yield.

Operational risk   The risk that existing technology or support systems may malfunction or break down.

Opportunity cost   The forgone interest cost from the holding of cash balances when they are received.

Option   A contract that gives the holder the right, but not the obligation, to buy or sell the underlying asset at a specified price within a specified period of time.

Originating house   The lead bank in the syndicate negotiates with the issuing company on behalf of the syndicate.

Other savings deposits   All savings accounts other than MMDAs.

Outside money   That part of the money supply directly produced by the government or central bank, such as notes and coin.

Overfunded   A pension plan that has more than enough funds to meet the required future payments.

Overhead efficiency   A bank's ability to generate noninterest income to cover noninterest expense.

Over-the-counter market   Markets that do not operate in a specific fixed location—rather, transactions occur via telephones, wire transfers, and computer trading.

Par bond   A bond in which the present value of the bond is equal to its face value.

Participating preferred stock   Preferred stock in which actual dividends paid in any year may be greater than the promised dividends.

Participation in a loan   The act of buying a share in a loan syndication with limited contractual control and rights over the borrower.

Pass-through mortgage securities   Mortgage-backed securities that "pass through" promised payments of principal and interest on pools of mortgages created by financial institutions to secondary market participants holding interests in the pools.

Pension plan   Document that governs the operations of a pension fund.

Perfecting collateral   The process of ensuring that collateral used to secure a loan is free and clear to the lender should the borrower default on the loan.

Personal credit institutions   Finance companies specializing in installment and other loans to consumers.

Plain vanilla   A standard agreement without any special features.

PO strips Represent the mortgage principal components in each monthly payment by the mortgagee.

Policy directive Statement sent to the Federal Reserve Board Trading Desk from the FOMC that specifies the money supply target.

Policy loans Loans made by an insurance company to its policyholders using their policies as collateral.

Policy reserves A liability item for insurers that reflects their expected payment commitments on existing policy contracts.

Position traders Exchange members who take a position in the futures market based on their expectations about the future direction of the prices of the underlying assets.

Potential exposure The risk that a counter-party to a derivative securities contract will default in the future.

Power of sale The process of taking the proceeds of the forced sale of a mortgaged property in satisfaction of the indebtedness and returning to the mortgagor the excess over the indebtedness or claiming any shortfall as an unsecured creditor.

Preemptive rights A right of existing stockholders in which new shares must be offered to existing shareholders first in such a way that they can maintain their proportional ownership in the corporation.

Preferred stock A hybrid security that has characteristics of both bonds and common stock.

Premium bond A bond in which the present value of the bond is greater than its face value.

Premiums earned Premiums received and earned on insurance contracts because time has passed with no claim filed.

Prepay To pay back a loan before its maturity to the FI that originated the loan.

Price risk The risk that an asset's sale price will be lower than its purchase price.

Price sensitivity The percentage change in a bond's present value for a given change in interest rates.

Primary markets Markets in which corporations raise funds through new issues of securities.

Prime lending rate The base lending rate periodically set by banks.

Private mortgage insurance Insurance contract purchased by a mortgage borrower guaranteeing to pay the financial institution the difference between the value of the property and the balance remaining on the mortgage.

Private pension funds Funds administered by a private corporation.

Private placement A securities issue placed with one or a few large institutional investors.

Professional traders Exchange members who trade for their own account.

Prompt corrective action Mandatory action that regulators must take as a bank's capital ratio falls.

Provision for loan losses Bank management's recognition of expected bad loans for the period.

Proxy A voting ballot sent by a corporation to its stockholders. When returned to the issuing firm, a proxy allows stockholders to vote by absentee ballot or authorizes representatives of the stockholders to vote on their behalf.

Public pension funds Funds administered by a federal, state, or local government.

Purchased funds Rate-sensitive funding sources of the firm.

Purchasing power parity The theory explaining the change in foreign currency exchange rates as inflation rates in the countries change.

Put option An option that gives a purchaser the right, but not the obligation, to sell the underlying security to the writer of the option at a prespecified exercise price on a prespecified date.

QTL test Qualified thrift lender test that sets a floor on the mortgage-related assets that thrifts can hold (currently, 65 percent).

Random walk hypothesis The theory that historical prices on a financial claim cannot help in predicting future prices.

Rate sensitivity The time to repricing of an asset or liability.

Real interest rate The interest rate that would exist on a default free security if no inflation were expected.

Realized rate of return The actual interest rate earned on an investment in a financial security.

Recourse The ability to put an asset or loan back to the seller or originator should the credit quality of that asset deteriorate.

Red herring proxy A preliminary version of the prospectus describing a new security issue distributed to potential buyers prior to the security's registration.

Regional or superregional bank A bank that engages in a complete array of wholesale commercial banking activities.

Registered bond A bond in which the owner is recorded by the issuer and the coupon payments are mailed to the registered owner.

Regulation Q ceiling An interest ceiling imposed on small savings and time deposits at banks and thrifts until 1986.

Regulator forbearance A policy not to close economically insolvent FIs, allowing them to continue in operation.

REIT A real estate investment trust; a closed-end investment company that specializes in investing in mortgages, property, or real estate company shares.

Report of condition Balance sheet of a commercial bank reporting information at a single point in time.

Report of income Income statement of a commercial bank reporting revenues, expenses, net profit or loss, and cash dividends over a period of time.

Repricing or **funding gap** The difference between those assets whose interest rates will be repriced or changed over some future period (RSAs) and liabilities whose interest rates will be repriced or changed over some future period (RSLs).

Repurchase agreement An agreement involving the sale of securities by one party to another with a promise to repurchase the securities at a specified price and on a specified date. For example, open market transactions in which the Trading Desk purchases government securities with an agreement that the seller will repurchase them within a stated period of time.

Required rate of return The interest rate an investor should receive on a security given its risk.

Required reserves Reserves the Federal Reserve requires banks to hold.

Reserve computation period Period over which required reserves are calculated.

Reserve maintenance period Period over which deposits at the Federal Reserve Bank must meet or exceed the required reserve target.

Reserves Depository institution's vault cash plus reserves deposited at Federal Reserve Banks.

Residual claim In the event of liquidation, common stockholders have the lowest priority in terms of any cash distribution.

Retail bank A bank that focuses its business activities on consumer banking relationships.

Retail CDs Time deposits with a face value below $100,000.

Revenue bonds Bonds sold to finance a specific revenue-generating project; they are backed by cash flows from that project.

Reverse-annuity mortgage A mortgage for which a mortgage borrower receives regular monthly payments from a financial institution rather than making them. When the RAM matures (or the borrower dies), the borrower (or the estate of the borrower) sells the property to retire the debt.

Reverse repurchase agreement An agreement involving the purchase of securities by one party from another with the promise to sell them back.

Risk-adjusted assets On- and off-balance-sheet assets whose value is adjusted for approximate credit risk.

Routine hedging Hedging all interest rate risk exposure.

Runoff Periodic cash flow of interest and principal amortization payments on long-term assets such as conventional mortgages that can be reinvested at market rates.

Sales finance institutions Finance companies specializing in loans to customers of a particular retailer or manufacturer.

Saving institutions Savings associations and savings banks combined.

Scalpers Exchange members who take positions for very short periods of time, sometimes only minutes, in an attempt to profit from this active trading.

Seasonal credit Discount window loan offered to banks for seasonal liquidity squeezes.

Second mortgages Loans secured by a piece of real estate already used to secure a first mortgage.

Secondary market A market that trades financial instruments once they are issued.

Secondary stock markets The markets in which stocks, once issued, are traded—rebought and resold.

Section 20 affiliate A securities subsidiary of a bank holding company through which a banking organization can engage in investment banking activities.

Securitized Securities are packaged and sold as assets backing a publicly traded or privately held debt instrument.

Securitized mortgage assets Mortgages packaged and used as assets backing secondary market securities.

Separate account Annuity program sponsored by life insurance companies in which the payoff on the policy is linked to the assets in which policy premiums are invested.

Serial bonds Bonds that mature on a series of dates, with a portion of the issue paid off on each.

Severity of loss The size of a loss.

Shared-appreciation mortgage Allows a home buyer to obtain a mortgage at an interest rate below current market rates in exchange for a share in any appreciation in the property value. If the property is eventually sold for more than the original purchase price, the financial institution is entitled to a portion of the gain.

Shelf registration Allows firms that plan to offer multiple issues of stock over a two-year period to submit one registration statement summarizing the firm's financing plans for the period.

Short position A sale of a futures contract.

Simple interest Interest earned on an investment is not reinvested.

Sinking fund provision A requirement that the issuer retire a certain amount of the bond issue each year.

Sovereign bonds A bond that is swapped for an outstanding loan to a less developed country, in which the U.S. Treasury secondary collateral backing is removed and the creditworthiness of the country is substituted instead.

Specialists Exchange members who have an obligation to keep the market going, maintaining liquidity in their assigned stock at all times.

Spot contract An agreement to transact involving the immediate exchange of assets and funds.

Spot foreign exchange transactions Foreign exchange transactions involving the immediate exchange of currencies at the current (or spot) exchange rate.

Spread The difference between lending and deposit rates.

Spread effect The effect that a change in the spread between rates on RSAs and RSLs has on net interest income (NII) as interest rates change.

Standby letters of credit Guarantees issued to cover contingencies that are potentially more severe and less predictable than contingencies covered under trade-related or commercial letters of credit.

Stock warrants Bonds issued with stock warrants attached giving the bond holder an opportunity to purchase common stock at a specified price up to a specified date.

STRIP A Treasury security in which the periodic interest payment is separated from the final principal payment.

Subordinated debentures Bonds that are unsecured and are junior in their rights to mortgage bonds and regular debentures.

Subprime lender A finance company that lends to high-risk customers.

Surrender value of a policy The cash value of a policy received from the insurer if a policyholder surrenders the policy prior to maturity; normally, only a portion of the contract's face value.

Swap An agreement between two parties to exchange assets or a series of cash flows for a specified period of time at a specified price.

Swap buyer By convention, a party that makes the fixed-rate payments in an interest rate swap transaction.

Swap seller By convention, a party that makes the floating-rate payments in an interest rate swap transaction.

Syndicate The process of distributing securities through a group of investment banks.

Systematic credit risk The risk of default associated with general economywide or macroconditions affecting all borrowers.

TDS (total debt service) ratio Total debt ratio calculated as total annual accommodation expenses plus all other debt service payments divided by annual gross income.

Technology risk The risk incurred by an FI when its technological investments do not produce anticipated cost savings.

Term bonds Bonds in which the entire issue matures on a single date.

Term structure of interest rates A comparison of market yields on securities, assuming all characteristics except maturity are the same.

Tier I (core) capital ratio The ratio of an FI's core capital to its risk-adjusted assets.

Time series analysis Analysis of financial statements over a period of time.

Time value of an option The difference between an option's price (or premium) and its intrinsic value.

Timing insurance A service provided by a sponsor of pass-through securities (such as GNMA) guaranteeing the bond holder interest and principal payments at the calendar date promised.

Tombstone A public announcement of a new issue of financial instruments in the financial press.

Total operating income The sum of the interest income and noninterest income.

Total risk-based capital ratio The ratio of an FI's total capital to its risk-adjusted assets.

Trading post A specific place on the floor of the exchange where transactions on the NYSE occur.

Tranches A bond holder class associated with a CMO.

Transaction accounts Deposits that permit the account holders to make multiple withdrawals. Measured as the sum of noninterest-bearing demand deposits and interest-bearing checking accounts.

Treasury bills Short-term obligations of the U.S. government issued to cover government budget deficits and to refinance maturing government debt.

Treasury bill auction The formal process by which the U.S. Treasury sells new issues of Treasury bills.

Treasury notes and bonds Long-term bonds issued by the U.S. Treasury to finance the national debt and other federal government expenditures.

12b-1 fees Fees relating to the distribution costs of mutual funds shares.

Underfunded A pension plan that does not have sufficient funds available to meet all future promised payments.

Underwriter's spread The difference between the gross proceeds and the net proceeds.

Underwriting Assisting in the issue of new securities.

Underwriting cycle A pattern that the profits in the P&C industry tend to follow.

Unearned premiums Reserves set aside that contain the portion of a premium that has been paid before insurance coverage has been provided.

Unit bank A bank with a single office.

Universal FI An FI that can engage in a broad range of financial service activities.

Up-front fee The fee charged for making funds available through a loan commitment.

Vested The period of time an employee must work before he or she is eligible to receive pension benefits.

Vulture fund A specialized fund that invests in distressed loans.

Weekend game Name given to the policy of lowering deposit balances on Fridays, since that day's figures count three times for reserve accounting purposes.

When-issued securities Commitments to buy or sell securities before they are issued.

Wholesale bank A bank that focuses its business activities on commercial banking relationships.

Wholesale CDs Time deposits with a face value of $100,000 or more.

X efficiencies Cost savings due to the greater managerial efficiency of the acquiring bank.

Yield to maturity The return or yield the bond holder will earn on the bond if he or she buys it at its current market price, receives all coupon and principal payments as promised, and holds the bond until maturity.

Zero-coupon bonds Bonds that do not pay interest.

Appendix

Table A–1   Future Value of $1 at the End of t Periods $= (1 + r)^t$

Period	1%	2%	3%	4%	5%	6%	7%	8%	9%
					Interest Rate				
1	1.0100	1.0200	1.0300	1.0400	1.0500	1.0600	1.0700	1.0800	1.0900
2	1.0201	1.0404	1.0609	1.0816	1.1025	1.1236	1.1449	1.1664	1.1881
3	1.0303	1.0612	1.0927	1.1249	1.1576	1.1910	1.2250	1.2597	1.2950
4	1.0406	1.0824	1.1255	1.1699	1.2155	1.2625	1.3108	1.3605	1.4116
5	1.0510	1.1041	1.1593	1.2167	1.2763	1.3382	1.4026	1.4693	1.5386
6	1.0615	1.1262	1.1941	1.2653	1.3401	1.4185	1.5007	1.5869	1.6771
7	1.0721	1.1487	1.2299	1.3159	1.4071	1.5036	1.6058	1.7138	1.8280
8	1.0829	1.1717	1.2668	1.3686	1.4775	1.5938	1.7182	1.8509	1.9926
9	1.0937	1.1951	1.3048	1.4233	1.5513	1.6895	1.8385	1.9990	2.1719
10	1.1046	1.2190	1.3439	1.4802	1.6289	1.7908	1.9672	2.1589	2.3674
11	1.1157	1.2434	1.3842	1.5395	1.7103	1.8983	2.1049	2.3316	2.5804
12	1.1268	1.2682	1.4258	1.6010	1.7959	2.0122	2.2522	2.5182	2.8127
13	1.1381	1.2936	1.4685	1.6651	1.8856	2.1329	2.4098	2.7196	3.0658
14	1.1495	1.3195	1.5126	1.7317	1.9799	2.2609	2.5785	2.9372	3.3417
15	1.1610	1.3459	1.5580	1.8009	2.0789	2.3966	2.7590	3.1722	3.6425
16	1.1726	1.3728	1.6047	1.8730	2.1829	2.5404	2.9522	3.4259	3.9703
17	1.1843	1.4002	1.6528	1.9479	2.2920	2.6928	3.1588	3.7000	4.3276
18	1.1961	1.4282	1.7024	2.0258	2.4066	2.8543	3.3799	3.9960	4.7171
19	1.2081	1.4568	1.7535	2.1068	2.5270	3.0256	3.6165	4.3157	5.1417
20	1.2202	1.4859	1.8061	2.1911	2.6533	3.2071	3.8697	4.6610	5.6044
21	1.2324	1.5157	1.8603	2.2788	2.7860	3.3996	4.1406	5.0338	6.1088
22	1.2447	1.5460	1.9161	2.3699	2.9253	3.6035	4.4304	5.4365	6.6586
23	1.2572	1.5769	1.9736	2.4647	3.0715	3.8197	4.7405	5.8715	7.2579
24	1.2697	1.6084	2.0328	2.5633	3.2251	4.0489	5.0724	6.3412	7.9111
25	1.2824	1.6406	2.0938	2.6658	3.3864	4.2919	5.4274	6.8485	8.6231
30	1.3478	1.8114	2.4273	3.2434	4.3219	5.7435	7.6123	10.063	13.268
40	1.4889	2.2080	3.2620	4.8010	7.0400	10.286	14.974	21.725	31.409
50	1.6446	2.6916	4.3839	7.1067	11.467	18.420	29.457	46.902	74.358
60	1.8167	3.2810	5.8916	10.520	18.679	32.988	57.946	101.26	176.03

(continued)

Table A–1   *(concluded)*

					Interest Rate					
10%	**12%**	**14%**	**15%**	**16%**	**18%**	**20%**	**24%**	**28%**	**32%**	**36%**
1.1000	1.1200	1.1400	1.1500	1.1600	1.1800	1.2000	1.2400	1.2800	1.3200	1.3600
1.2100	1.2544	1.2996	1.3225	1.3456	1.3924	1.4400	1.5376	1.6384	1.7424	1.8496
1.3310	1.4049	1.4815	1.5209	1.5609	1.6430	1.7280	1.9066	2.0972	2.3000	2.5155
1.4641	1.5735	1.6890	1.7490	1.8106	1.9388	2.0736	2.3642	2.6844	3.0360	3.4210
1.6105	1.7623	1.9254	2.0114	2.1003	2.2878	2.4883	2.9316	3.4360	4.0075	4.6526
1.7716	1.9738	2.1950	2.3131	2.4364	2.6996	2.9860	3.6352	4.3980	5.2899	6.3275
1.9487	2.2107	2.5023	2.6600	2.8262	3.1855	3.5832	4.5077	5.6295	6.9826	8.6054
2.1436	2.4760	2.8526	3.0590	3.2784	3.7589	4.2998	5.5895	7.2058	9.2170	11.703
2.3579	2.7731	3.2519	3.5179	3.8030	4.4355	5.1598	6.9310	9.2234	12.166	15.917
2.5937	3.1058	3.7072	4.0456	4.4114	5.2338	6.1917	8.5944	11.806	16.060	21.647
2.8531	3.4785	4.2262	4.6524	5.1173	6.1759	7.4301	10.657	15.112	21.199	29.439
3.1384	3.8960	4.8179	5.3503	5.9360	7.2876	8.9161	13.215	19.343	27.983	40.037
3.4523	4.3635	5.4924	6.1528	6.8858	8.5994	10.699	16.386	24.759	36.937	54.451
3.7975	4.8871	6.2613	7.0757	7.9875	10.147	12.839	20.319	31.691	48.757	74.053
4.1772	5.4736	7.1379	8.1371	9.2655	11.974	15.407	25.196	40.565	64.359	100.71
4.5950	6.1304	8.1372	9.3576	10.748	14.129	18.488	31.243	51.923	84.954	136.97
5.0545	6.8660	9.2765	10.761	12.468	16.672	22.186	38.741	66.461	112.14	186.28
5.5599	7.6900	10.575	12.375	14.463	19.673	26.623	48.039	85.071	148.02	253.34
6.1159	8.6128	12.056	14.232	16.777	23.214	31.948	59.568	108.89	195.39	344.54
6.7275	9.6463	13.743	16.367	19.461	27.393	38.338	73.864	139.38	257.92	468.57
7.4002	10.804	15.668	18.822	22.574	32.324	46.005	91.592	178.41	340.45	637.26
8.1403	12.100	17.861	21.645	26.186	38.142	55.206	113.57	228.36	449.39	866.67
8.9543	13.552	20.362	24.891	30.376	45.008	66.247	140.83	292.30	593.20	1178.7
9.8497	15.179	23.212	28.625	35.236	53.109	79.497	174.63	374.14	783.02	1603.0
10.835	17.000	26.462	32.919	40.874	62.669	95.396	216.54	478.90	1033.6	2180.1
17.449	29.960	50.950	66.212	85.850	143.37	237.38	634.82	1645.5	4142.1	10143.
45.259	93.051	188.88	267.86	378.72	750.38	1469.8	5455.9	19427.	66521.	*
117.39	289.00	700.23	1083.7	1670.7	3927.4	9100.4	46890.	*	*	*
304.48	897.60	2595.9	4384.0	7370.2	20555.	56348.	*	*	*	*

*The factor is greater than 99,999.

Table A–2 Present Value of $1 to Be Received after t Periods $= 1/(1 + r)^t$

Period	1%	2%	3%	4%	5%	6%	7%	8%	9%
					Interest Rate				
1	0.9901	0.9804	0.9709	0.9615	0.9524	0.9434	0.9346	0.9259	0.9174
2	0.9803	0.9612	0.9426	0.9246	0.9070	0.8900	0.8734	0.8573	0.8417
3	0.9706	0.9423	0.9151	0.8890	0.8638	0.8396	0.8163	0.7938	0.7722
4	0.9610	0.9238	0.8885	0.8548	0.8227	0.7921	0.7629	0.7350	0.7084
5	0.9515	0.9057	0.8626	0.8219	0.7835	0.7473	0.7130	0.6806	0.6499
6	0.9420	0.8880	0.8375	0.7903	0.7462	0.7050	0.6663	0.6302	0.5963
7	0.9327	0.8706	0.8131	0.7599	0.7107	0.6651	0.6227	0.5835	0.5470
8	0.9235	0.8535	0.7894	0.7307	0.6768	0.6274	0.5820	0.5403	0.5019
9	0.9143	0.8368	0.7664	0.7026	0.6446	0.5919	0.5439	0.5002	0.4604
10	0.9053	0.8203	0.7441	0.6756	0.6139	0.5584	0.5083	0.4632	0.4224
11	0.8963	0.8043	0.7224	0.6496	0.5847	0.5268	0.4751	0.4289	0.3875
12	0.8874	0.7885	0.7014	0.6246	0.5568	0.4970	0.4440	0.3971	0.3555
13	0.8787	0.7730	0.6810	0.6006	0.5303	0.4688	0.4150	0.3677	0.3262
14	0.8700	0.7579	0.6611	0.5775	0.5051	0.4423	0.3878	0.3405	0.2992
15	0.8613	0.7430	0.6419	0.5553	0.4810	0.4173	0.3624	0.3152	0.2745
16	0.8528	0.7284	0.6232	0.5339	0.4581	0.3936	0.3387	0.2919	0.2519
17	0.8444	0.7142	0.6050	0.5134	0.4363	0.3714	0.3166	0.2703	0.2311
18	0.8360	0.7002	0.5874	0.4936	0.4155	0.3503	0.2959	0.2502	0.2120
19	0.8277	0.6864	0.5703	0.4746	0.3957	0.3305	0.2765	0.2317	0.1945
20	0.8195	0.6730	0.5537	0.4564	0.3769	0.3118	0.2584	0.2145	0.1784
21	0.8114	0.6598	0.5375	0.4388	0.3589	0.2942	0.2415	0.1987	0.1637
22	0.8034	0.6468	0.5219	0.4220	0.3418	0.2775	0.2257	0.1839	0.1502
23	0.7954	0.6342	0.5067	0.4057	0.3256	0.2618	0.2109	0.1703	0.1378
24	0.7876	0.6217	0.4919	0.3901	0.3101	0.2470	0.1971	0.1577	0.1264
25	0.7798	0.6095	0.4776	0.3751	0.2953	0.2330	0.1842	0.1460	0.1160
30	0.7419	0.5521	0.4120	0.3083	0.2314	0.1741	0.1314	0.0994	0.0754
40	0.6717	0.4529	0.3066	0.2083	0.1420	0.0972	0.0668	0.0460	0.0318
50	0.6080	0.3715	0.2281	0.1407	0.0872	0.0543	0.0339	0.0213	0.0134

(continued)

Table A–2   *(concluded)*

					Interest Rate					
10%	12%	14%	15%	16%	18%	20%	24%	28%	32%	36%
0.9091	0.8929	0.8772	0.8696	0.8621	0.8475	0.8333	0.8065	0.7813	0.7576	0.7353
0.8264	0.7972	0.7695	0.7561	0.7432	0.7182	0.6944	0.6504	0.6104	0.5739	0.5407
0.7513	0.7118	0.6750	0.6575	0.6407	0.6086	0.5787	0.5245	0.4768	0.4348	0.3975
0.6830	0.6355	0.5921	0.5718	0.5523	0.5158	0.4823	0.4230	0.3725	0.3294	0.2923
0.6209	0.5674	0.5194	0.4972	0.4761	0.4371	0.4019	0.3411	0.2910	0.2495	0.2149
0.5645	0.5066	0.4556	0.4323	0.4104	0.3704	0.3349	0.2751	0.2274	0.1890	0.1580
0.5132	0.4523	0.3996	0.3759	0.3538	0.3139	0.2791	0.2218	0.1776	0.1432	0.1162
0.4665	0.4039	0.3506	0.3269	0.3050	0.2660	0.2326	0.1789	0.1388	0.1085	0.0854
0.4241	0.3606	0.3075	0.2843	0.2630	0.2255	0.1938	0.1443	0.1084	0.0822	0.0628
0.3855	0.3220	0.2697	0.2472	0.2267	0.1911	0.1615	0.1164	0.0847	0.0623	0.0462
0.3505	0.2875	0.2366	0.2149	0.1954	0.1619	0.1346	0.0938	0.0662	0.0472	0.0340
0.3186	0.2567	0.2076	0.1869	0.1685	0.1372	0.1122	0.0757	0.0517	0.0357	0.0250
0.2897	0.2292	0.1821	0.1625	0.1452	0.1163	0.0935	0.0610	0.0404	0.0271	0.0184
0.2633	0.2046	0.1597	0.1413	0.1252	0.0985	0.0779	0.0492	0.0316	0.0205	0.0135
0.2394	0.1827	0.1401	0.1229	0.1079	0.0835	0.0649	0.0397	0.0247	0.0155	0.0099
0.2176	0.1631	0.1229	0.1069	0.0930	0.0708	0.0541	0.0320	0.0193	0.0118	0.0073
0.1978	0.1456	0.1078	0.0929	0.0802	0.0600	0.0451	0.0258	0.0150	0.0089	0.0054
0.1799	0.1300	0.0946	0.0808	0.0691	0.0508	0.0376	0.0208	0.0118	0.0068	0.0039
0.1635	0.1161	0.0829	0.0703	0.0596	0.0431	0.0313	0.0168	0.0092	0.0051	0.0029
0.1486	0.1037	0.0728	0.0611	0.0514	0.0365	0.0261	0.0135	0.0072	0.0039	0.0021
0.1351	0.0926	0.0638	0.0531	0.0443	0.0309	0.0217	0.0109	0.0056	0.0029	0.0016
0.1228	0.0826	0.0560	0.0462	0.0382	0.0262	0.0181	0.0088	0.0044	0.0022	0.0012
0.1117	0.0738	0.0491	0.0402	0.0329	0.0222	0.0151	0.0071	0.0034	0.0017	0.0008
0.1015	0.0659	0.0431	0.0349	0.0284	0.0188	0.0126	0.0057	0.0027	0.0013	0.0006
0.0923	0.0588	0.0378	0.0304	0.0245	0.0160	0.0105	0.0046	0.0021	0.0010	0.0005
0.0573	0.0334	0.0196	0.0151	0.0116	0.0070	0.0042	0.0016	0.0006	0.0002	0.0001
0.0221	0.0107	0.0053	0.0037	0.0026	0.0013	0.0007	0.0002	0.0001	*	*
0.0085	0.0035	0.0014	0.0009	0.0006	0.0003	0.0001	*	*	*	*

*The factor is zero to four decimal places.

Table A-3 Present Value of an Annuity of $1 per Period for t Periods $= [1 - 1/(1 + r)^t]/r$

Period	Interest Rate								
	1%	**2%**	**3%**	**4%**	**5%**	**6%**	**7%**	**8%**	**9%**
1	0.9901	0.9804	0.9709	0.9615	0.9524	0.9434	0.9346	0.9259	0.9174
2	1.9704	1.9416	1.9135	1.8861	1.8594	1.8334	1.8080	1.7833	1.7591
3	2.9410	2.8839	2.8286	2.7751	2.7232	2.6730	2.6243	2.5771	2.5313
4	3.9020	3.8077	3.7171	3.6299	3.5460	3.4651	3.3872	3.3121	3.2397
5	4.8534	4.7135	4.5797	4.4518	4.3295	4.2124	4.1002	3.9927	3.8897
6	5.7955	5.6014	5.4172	5.2421	5.0757	4.9173	4.7665	4.6229	4.4859
7	6.7282	6.4720	6.2303	6.0021	5.7864	5.5824	5.3893	5.2064	5.0330
8	7.6517	7.3255	7.0197	6.7327	6.4632	6.2098	5.9713	5.7466	5.5348
9	8.5660	8.1622	7.7861	7.4353	7.1078	6.8017	6.5152	6.2469	5.9952
10	9.4713	8.9826	8.5302	8.1109	7.7217	7.3601	7.0236	6.7101	6.4177
11	10.3676	9.7868	9.2526	8.7605	8.3064	7.8869	7.4987	7.1390	6.8052
12	11.2551	10.5753	9.9540	9.3851	8.8633	8.3838	7.9427	7.5361	7.1607
13	12.1337	11.3484	10.6350	9.9856	9.3936	8.8527	8.3577	7.9038	7.4869
14	13.0037	12.1062	11.2961	10.5631	9.8986	9.2950	8.7455	8.2442	7.7862
15	13.8651	12.8493	11.9379	11.1184	10.3797	9.7122	9.1079	8.5595	8.0607
16	14.7179	13.5777	12.5611	11.6523	10.8378	10.1059	9.4466	8.8514	8.3126
17	15.5623	14.2919	13.1661	12.1657	11.2741	10.4773	9.7632	9.1216	8.5436
18	16.3983	14.9920	13.7535	12.6593	11.6896	10.8276	10.0591	9.3719	8.7556
19	17.2260	15.6785	14.3238	13.1339	12.0853	11.1581	10.3356	9.6036	8.9501
20	18.0456	16.3514	14.8775	13.5903	12.4622	11.4699	10.5940	9.8181	9.1285
21	18.8570	17.0112	15.4150	14.0292	12.8212	11.7641	10.8355	10.0168	9.2922
22	19.6604	17.6580	15.9369	14.4511	13.1630	12.0416	11.0612	10.2007	9.4424
23	20.4558	18.2922	16.4436	14.8568	13.4886	12.3034	11.2722	10.3741	9.5802
24	21.2434	18.9139	16.9355	15.2470	13.7986	12.5504	11.4593	10.5288	9.7066
25	22.0232	19.5235	17.4131	15.6221	14.0939	12.7834	11.6536	10.6748	9.8226
30	25.8077	22.3965	19.6004	17.2920	15.3725	13.7648	12.4090	11.2578	10.2737
40	32.8347	27.3555	23.1148	19.7928	17.1591	15.0463	13.3317	11.9246	10.7574
50	39.1961	31.4236	25.7298	21.4822	18.2559	15.7619	13.8007	12.2335	10.9617

(continued)

Table A–3 *(concluded)*

				Interest Rate					
10%	**12%**	**14%**	**15%**	**16%**	**18%**	**20%**	**24%**	**28%**	**32%**
0.9091	0.8929	0.8772	0.8696	0.8621	0.8475	0.8333	0.8065	0.7813	0.7576
1.7355	1.6901	1.6467	1.6257	1.6052	1.5656	1.5278	1.4568	1.3916	1.3315
2.4869	2.4018	2.3216	2.2832	2.2459	2.1743	2.1065	1.9813	1.8684	1.7663
3.1699	3.0373	2.9137	2.8550	2.7982	2.6901	2.5887	2.4043	2.2410	2.0957
3.7908	3.6048	3.4331	3.3522	3.2743	3.1272	2.9906	2.7454	2.5320	2.3452
4.3553	4.1114	3.8887	3.7845	3.6847	3.4976	3.3255	3.0205	2.7594	2.5342
4.8684	4.5638	4.2883	4.1604	4.0386	3.8115	3.6046	3.2423	2.9370	2.6775
5.3349	4.9676	4.6389	4.4873	4.3436	4.0776	3.8372	3.4212	3.0758	2.7860
5.7590	5.3282	4.9464	4.7716	4.6065	4.3030	4.0310	3.5655	3.1842	2.8681
6.1446	5.6502	5.2161	5.0188	4.8332	4.4941	4.1925	3.6819	3.2689	2.9304
6.4951	5.9377	5.4527	5.2337	5.0286	4.6560	4.3271	3.7757	3.3351	2.9776
6.8137	6.1944	5.6603	5.4206	5.1971	4.7932	4.4392	3.8514	3.3868	3.0133
7.1034	6.4235	5.8424	5.5831	5.3423	4.9095	4.5327	3.9124	3.4272	3.0404
7.3667	6.6282	6.0021	5.7245	5.4675	5.0081	4.6106	3.9616	3.4587	3.0609
7.6061	6.8109	6.1422	5.8474	5.5755	5.0916	4.6755	4.0013	3.4834	3.0764
7.8237	6.9740	6.2651	5.9542	5.6685	5.1624	4.7296	4.0333	3.5026	3.0882
8.0216	7.1196	6.3729	6.0472	5.7487	5.2223	4.7746	4.0591	3.5177	3.0971
8.2014	7.2497	6.4674	6.1280	5.8178	5.2732	4.8122	4.0799	3.5294	3.1039
8.3649	7.3658	6.5504	6.1982	5.8775	5.3162	4.8435	4.0967	3.5386	3.1090
8.5136	7.4694	6.6231	6.2593	5.9288	5.3527	4.8696	4.1103	3.5458	3.1129
8.6487	7.5620	6.6870	6.3125	5.9731	5.3837	4.8913	4.1212	3.5514	3.1158
8.7715	7.6446	6.7429	6.3587	6.0113	5.4099	4.9094	4.1300	3.5558	3.1180
8.8832	7.7184	6.7921	6.3988	6.0442	5.4321	4.9245	4.1371	3.5592	3.1197
8.9847	7.7843	6.8351	6.4338	6.0726	5.4509	4.9371	4.1428	3.5619	3.1210
9.0770	7.8431	6.8729	6.4641	6.0971	5.4669	4.9476	4.1474	3.5640	3.1220
9.4269	8.0552	7.0027	6.5660	6.1772	5.5168	4.9789	4.1601	3.5693	3.1242
9.7791	8.2438	7.1050	6.6418	6.2335	5.5482	4.9966	4.1659	3.5712	3.1250
9.9148	8.3045	7.1327	6.6605	6.2463	5.5541	4.9995	4.1666	3.5714	3.1250

Table A–4   Future Value of an Annuity of $1 per Period for t Periods $= [(1 + r)^t - 1]/r$

Period	\multicolumn{9}{c}{Interest Rate}								
	1%	2%	3%	4%	5%	6%	7%	8%	9%
1	1.0000	1.0000	1.0000	1.0000	1.0000	1.0000	1.0000	1.0000	1.0000
2	2.0100	2.0200	2.0300	2.0400	2.0500	2.0600	2.0700	2.0800	2.0900
3	3.0301	3.0604	3.0909	3.1216	3.1525	3.1836	3.2149	3.2464	3.2781
4	4.0604	4.1216	4.1836	4.2465	4.3101	4.3746	4.4399	4.5061	4.5731
5	5.1010	5.2040	5.3091	5.4163	5.5256	5.6371	5.7507	5.8666	5.9847
6	6.1520	6.3081	6.4684	6.6330	6.8019	6.9753	7.1533	7.3359	7.5233
7	7.2135	7.4343	7.6625	7.8983	8.1420	8.3938	8.6540	8.9228	9.2004
8	8.2857	8.5830	8.8932	9.2142	9.5491	9.8975	10.260	10.637	11.028
9	9.3685	9.7546	10.159	10.583	11.027	11.491	11.978	12.488	13.021
10	10.462	10.950	11.464	12.006	12.578	13.181	13.816	14.487	15.193
11	11.567	12.169	12.808	13.486	14.207	14.972	15.784	16.645	17.560
12	12.683	13.412	14.192	15.026	15.917	16.870	17.888	18.977	20.141
13	13.809	14.680	15.618	16.627	17.713	18.882	20.141	21.495	22.953
14	14.947	15.974	17.086	18.292	19.599	21.015	22.550	24.215	26.019
15	16.097	17.293	18.599	20.024	21.579	23.276	25.129	27.152	29.361
16	17.258	18.639	20.157	21.825	23.657	25.673	27.888	30.324	33.003
17	18.430	20.012	21.762	23.698	25.840	28.213	30.840	33.750	36.974
18	19.615	21.412	23.414	25.645	28.132	30.906	33.999	37.450	41.301
19	20.811	22.841	25.117	27.671	30.539	33.760	37.379	41.446	46.018
20	22.019	24.297	26.870	29.778	33.066	36.786	40.995	45.762	51.160
21	23.239	25.783	28.676	31.969	35.719	39.993	44.865	50.423	56.765
22	24.472	27.299	30.537	34.248	38.505	43.392	49.006	55.457	62.873
23	25.716	28.845	32.453	36.618	41.430	46.996	53.436	60.893	69.532
24	26.973	30.422	34.426	39.083	44.502	50.816	58.177	66.765	76.790
25	28.243	32.030	36.459	41.646	47.727	54.865	63.249	73.106	84.701
30	34.785	40.568	47.575	56.085	66.439	79.058	94.461	113.28	136.31
40	48.886	60.402	75.401	95.026	120.80	154.76	199.64	259.06	337.88
50	64.463	84.579	112.80	152.67	209.35	290.34	406.53	573.77	815.08
60	81.670	114.05	163.05	237.99	353.58	533.13	813.52	1253.2	1944.8

(continued)

Table A–4   (concluded)

					Interest Rate					
10%	**12%**	**14%**	**15%**	**16%**	**18%**	**20%**	**24%**	**28%**	**32%**	**36%**
1.0000	1.0000	1.0000	1.0000	1.0000	1.0000	1.0000	1.0000	1.0000	1.0000	1.0000
2.1000	2.1200	2.1400	2.1500	2.1600	2.1800	2.2000	2.2400	2.2800	2.3200	2.3600
3.3100	3.3744	3.4396	3.4725	3.5056	3.5724	3.6400	3.7776	3.9184	4.0624	4.2096
4.6410	4.7793	4.9211	4.9934	5.0665	5.2154	5.3680	5.6842	6.0156	6.3624	6.7251
6.1051	6.3528	6.6101	6.7424	6.8771	7.1542	7.4416	8.0484	8.6999	9.3983	10.146
7.7156	8.1152	8.5355	8.7537	8.9775	9.4420	9.9299	10.980	12.136	13.406	14.799
9.4872	10.089	10.730	11.067	11.414	12.142	12.916	14.615	16.534	18.696	21.126
11.436	12.300	13.233	13.727	14.240	15.327	16.499	19.123	22.163	25.678	29.732
13.579	14.776	16.085	16.786	17.519	19.086	20.799	24.712	29.369	34.895	41.435
15.937	17.549	19.337	20.304	21.321	23.521	25.959	31.643	38.593	47.062	57.352
18.531	20.655	23.045	24.349	25.733	28.755	32.150	40.238	50.398	63.122	78.998
21.384	24.133	27.271	29.002	30.850	34.931	39.581	50.895	65.510	84.320	108.44
24.523	28.029	32.089	34.352	36.786	42.219	48.497	64.110	84.853	112.30	148.47
27.975	32.393	37.581	40.505	43.672	50.818	59.196	80.496	109.61	149.24	202.93
31.772	37.280	43.842	47.580	51.660	60.965	72.035	100.82	141.30	198.00	276.98
35.950	42.753	50.980	55.717	60.925	72.939	87.442	126.01	181.87	262.36	377.69
40.545	48.884	59.118	65.075	71.673	87.068	105.93	157.25	233.79	347.31	514.66
45.599	55.750	68.394	75.836	84.141	103.74	128.12	195.99	300.25	459.45	700.94
51.159	63.440	78.969	88.212	98.603	123.41	154.74	244.03	385.32	607.47	954.28
57.275	72.052	91.025	102.44	115.38	146.63	186.69	303.60	494.21	802.86	1298.8
64.002	81.699	104.77	118.81	134.84	174.02	225.03	377.46	633.59	1060.8	1767.4
71.403	92.503	120.44	137.63	157.41	206.34	271.03	469.06	812.00	1401.2	2404.7
79.543	104.60	138.30	159.28	183.60	244.49	326.24	582.63	1040.4	1850.6	3271.3
88.497	118.16	158.66	184.17	213.98	289.49	392.48	723.46	1332.7	2443.8	4450.0
98.347	133.33	181.87	212.79	249.21	342.60	471.98	898.09	1706.8	3226.8	6053.0
164.49	241.33	356.79	434.75	530.31	790.95	1181.9	2640.9	5873.2	12941.	28172.3
442.59	767.09	1342.0	1779.1	2360.8	4163.2	7343.9	22729.	69377.	*	*
1163.9	2400.0	4994.5	7217.7	10436.	21813.	45497.	*	*	*	*
3034.8	7471.6	18535.	29220.	46058.	*	*	*	*	*	*

*The factor is greater than 99,999.

References

Allen, L., and A. Saunders. "Bank Window Dressing: Theory and Evidence." *Journal of Banking and Finance,* 1992, pp. 585–624.

Altman, E. I. "Managing the Commercial Lending Process." In *Handbook of Banking Strategy,* ed. R. C. Aspinwall and R. A. Eisenbeis. New York: John Wiley & Sons, 1985, pp. 473–510.

The American Banker, December 3, 1998; January 4, 1999, p. 12; June 25, 1999, p. 2; August 5, 1999; December 13, 1999, p. 1.

Bank for International Settlements. "International Banking and Financial Market Developments," *Quarterly Review,* November 1999; Annual Report, June 1999.

_____. *Statistics on Payment Systems in the Group of 10 Countries.* Basle, Switzerland: Bank for International Settlements, Table 5, p. 117; Table 10b, p. 126.

_____. "A New Capital Adequacy Framework." June 1999.

The Banker. February 1998, pp. 41–42.

Banz, R. "The Relationship between Return and Market Value of Common Stocks." *Journal of Financial Economics,* March 1981, pp. 3–18.

Barber, B. M., and T. Odean. "Trading Is Hazardous to Your Wealth: The Common Stock Investment Performance of Individual Investors." *Journal of Finance,* April 2000.

Basu, S. "Investment Performance of Common Stocks in Relation to Their Price-Earnings Ratios: A Test of the Efficient Market Hypothesis." *Journal of Finance,* June 1977, pp. 663–82.

Black, F., and M. Scholes. "The Pricing of Options and Corporate Liabilities." *Journal of Political Economy* 81 (May–June 1973), pp. 637–54 and 737–59.

Bloch, E. *Inside Investment Banking.* 2nd ed. Burr Ridge, IL: McGraw-Hill/Irwin, 1989.

The Bond Buyer. April 19, 1999, p. 7.

Boyd, J. H., and M. Gertler. "Are Banks Dead? Or, Are the Reports Greatly Exaggerated?" Federal Reserve Bank of Minneapolis Research Department, Working Paper, May 1994.

Brealey, R. A., S. C. Myers, and A. J. Marcus. *Fundamentals of Corporate Finance.* New York: McGraw-Hill, 1999, pp. 225–29.

Brook, Y., R. Hendershott, and D. Lee. "The Gains from Takeover Deregulation: Evidence from the End of Interstate Banking Restrictions." *Journal of Finance* 53, no. 6 (1998), pp. 2185–2204.

Business Credit. June 1, 1999, p. 26.

Clark, M., and A. Saunders. "Judicial Interpretation of Glass-Steagall: The Need for Legislative Action." *The Banking Law Journal* 97, 1980, pp. 721–40.

_____. "Glass-Steagall Revisited: The Impact on Banks, Capital Markets, and the Small Investor." *The Banking Law Journal* 97, 1980, pp. 811–40.

Cox, J., and M. Rubenstein, *Options Markets.* Englewood Cliffs, NJ: Prentice-Hall, 1985.

Credit Unions. U.S. Department of Treasury, December 1997, p. 86.

Department of Treasury. Bureau of Public Debt, June 1999; January 20, 2000.

Ellis, K., R. Michaely, and M. O'Hara. "When the Underwriter Is the Market Maker: An Examination of Trading in the IPO Aftermarket." Cornell University, Working Paper, 1999.

Elton, E. J., and M. J. Gruber. *Modern Portfolio Theory and Investment Analysis,* 6th ed. New York: John Wiley & Sons, 1998, Chapter 2.

Euromoney. "A Question of Collateral," November 1995, pp. 46–49.

FASB Statement No. 80. "Accounting for Futures Contracts." FASB, 1984.

Federal Deposit Insurance Corporation. *Quarterly Banking Profile,* Fourth Quarter 1994; First Quarter 1999; Second Quarter 1999; Fourth Quarter 1999.

_____. *Statistics on Banking,* various issues.

Federal Reserve Board. "Flow of Funds Accounts," *Statistical Releases.* Washington, DC: Federal Reserve Board, December 1999.

Federal Reserve Board. "Risk-Based Capital and Interest Rate Risk." Press release, July 30, 1992.

Federal Reserve Board. "The Structure of the Federal Reserve System," May 29, 1999; "Purposes & Functions," July 1999; "Research and Data," December 1999, January 2000; "Selected Interest Rates," January 2000.

Federal Reserve Bulletin. Publication Services, Washington, DC. May 1991; May 1992, Table 1.45; June 1999, Table A12; September 1999, p. 74; November 1999, Table 1.54, p. A.35, Table 1.60; December 1999; January 2000, Table A12; January 2000, Table 1.45; Table 1.46, Table 3.16 various issues.

The Financial Times. September 24, 1998, p. 1; September 25, 1998, p. 44; January 14, 1999, p. 42; June 21, 1999, p. 39; July 1, 1999, p. 39; November 16, 1999, p. 40.

Forbes. "Specialists: Special at Exactly What?" February 1988, pp. 22–23.

Gande, A., M. Puri, and A. Saunders. "Bank Entry, Competition and the Market for Corporate Securities Underwriting." *Journal of Financial Economics* 54, no. 2 (October 1999), pp. 165–96.

General Accounting Office. "Long-Term Capital Management: Regulators Need to Focus Greater Attention on Systematic Risk." GAO/GDD-00-3, October 1999.

Gorton, G., and R. Rosen. "Banks and Derivatives." University of Pennsylvania Wharton School, Working Paper, February 1995.

Groth, J., W. Lewellen, G. Schlarbaum, and R. Lease. "An Analysis of Brokerage House Securities Recommendations." *Financial Analysts Journal*, January–February 1979, pp. 32–40.

Haraf, W. S. "The Collapse of Drexel Burnham Lambert: Lessons for Bank Regulators." *Regulation,* Winter 1991, pp. 22–25.

Higgins, B. "Is a Recession Inevitable This Year?" *Economic Review,* Federal Reserve Bank of Kansas City, January 1988, pp. 3–16.

International Finance Corporation. *Emerging Stock Markets Fact Book 1998,* May 1998.

Jaffe, J. "Special Information and Insider Trading." *Journal of Business*, July 1974, pp. 410–28.

Japan-U.S. Business Report, July 30, 1998.

Kalay, A., and U. Lowenstein. "Predictable Events and Excess Returns: The Case of Dividend Announcements." *Journal of Financial Economics*, September 1985, pp. 423–50.

Kaufman, G. G. "Measuring and Managing Interest Rate Risk: A Primer." *Economic Perspective.* Chicago: Federal Reserve Bank of Chicago, 1984, pp. 16–29.

Krozner, R. "The Evolution of Universal Banking and Its Regulation in Twentieth Century America." In *Universal Banking Financial System Design Reconsidered,* A. Saunders and L. Walter, eds. Burr Ridge, IL: McGraw-Hill/Irwin, 1996.

KMV Corporation. *Credit Monitoring.* San Francisco: KMV Corporation, 1994.

Lakonishok, J., and S. Smidt. "Are Seasonal Anomalies Real? A Ninety-Year Perspective." *Review of Financial Studies*, Winter 1988, pp. 403–25.

Lee, I., S. Lockhead, J. Ritter, and Q. Zhao. "The Cost of Raising Capital." *Journal of Financial Research*, Spring 1996, pp. 59–74.

Lombard, T., J. Roulet, and B. Solnik. "Pricing of Domestic versus Multinational Companies." *Financial Analysts Journal*, March–April 1999, pp. 35–49.

Meier, K. J. *The Political Economy of Regulation: The Case of Insurance.* Albany, NY: State University of New York Press, 1988.

Merton, R. C. "On Option Pricing of Corporate Debt: The Risk Structure of Interest Rates." *Journal of Finance* 29, 1974, pp. 447–70.

Munter, P. H., D. K. Clancy, and C. T. Moores. "Accounting for Financial Futures: A Question of Risk Reduction." *Advances in Accounting Magazine,* 1986, pp. 51–70.

National Credit Union Association. *Midyear Statistics*, 1999; *Quick Facts*, June 1999.

The New York Times, March 24, 1988, p. D1; February 26, 1997, p. D1.

Nunn, K., G. Madden, and M. Gombola. "Are Some Insiders More 'Inside' than Others?" *Journal of Portfolio Management*, Spring 1982, pp. 18–22.

Office of the Comptroller of the Currency. Bank Derivatives Report, First Quarter 1999; Second Quarter 1999.

Peterson, D. "Security Price Reactions to Initial Review of Common Stock by the Value Line Investment Survey." *Journal of Financial and Quantitative Analysis*, December 1987, pp. 483–94.

Risk Magazine. "Called to Account," August 1996, pp. 15–17.

Saunders, A. *Credit Risk Measurement: New Approaches to Value at Risk and Other Paradigms.* New York, NY: John Wiley & Sons, 1999.

Saunders, A., and I. Walter. *Universal Banking in the U.S.?* New York: Oxford University Press, 1994.

Saunders, A., and I. Walter, eds. *Financial System Design: Universal Banking Considered.* Burr Ridge, IL: Irwin/McGraw-Hill Professional Publishing, 1996.

Silber, W. L. "Marketmaker Behavior in an Auction Market: An Analysis of Scalpers in Futures Markets." *Journal of Finance*, September 1984, pp. 937–53.

Stockownership. "Baby Boomer Shareholders." New York Stock Exchange, 1998.

Stoebe, R. "Macrohedging Bank Investment Portfolios." *Bankers Magazine,* November–December 1994, pp. 45–48.

Treasury Bulletin. December 1999, pp. 99–107.

U.S. Department of Commerce, Bureau of Economic Analysis. December 1999.

U.S. Department of Justice. "Horizontal Merger Guideline." April 2, 1992.

U.S. General Accounting Office. "Mutual Funds: Impact on Bank Deposits and Credit Availability." GAO/GGD-95-230, Washington, DC: Government Printing Offices, 1995.

————. GAO/GGD-94-23, 1994, p. 57.

U.S. Treasury, Bureau of Public Debt. May 19, 1999; May 21, 1999; December 22, 1999.

The Wall Street Journal. October 7, 1998, p. A3; October 16, 1998, p. B4; June 3, 1999, p. B1; June 22, 1999, p. A16; August 10, 1999, p. A26; January 7, 2000, p. C17; January 19, 2000, p. C2, C3, C17, C19, C20, C22, C23, C26; January 30, 2000, p. D1; February 11, 2000, p. C19.

Wheelock, D. C. "A Changing Relationship between Bank Size and Profitability." In *Monetary Trends*, Federal Reserve Bank of St. Louis, September 1996, p. 1.

White, L. J. *The S and L Debacle.* New York: Oxford University Press, 1991.

Index

Depository Institutions (Chapters 11–14)

What are depository institutions? (pages 318–320, 343–344)

What are the main assets and liabilities held by depository institutions? (pages 320–328, 348–350, 359–361)

How have depository institutions performed in recent years? (pages 339, 352–354, 362)

Who are the main regulators of depository institutions? (pages 340–341, 351–352, 362)

How is depository institution performance measured? (pages 364–395)

What types of regulations are depository institutions subject to? (pages 398–427)

Pertinent Websites

American Banker	www.americanbanker.com/
Bank for International Settlements	www.bis.org/
Bank of America	www.aba.com/aba/
Bank One	www.bankone.com/
Bank Web Sites	www.mybank.com/
Board of Governors of the Federal Reserve	www.bog.frb.fed.us/
Federal Deposit Insurance Corporation	www.fdic.gov/
Federal Financial Institutions Examination Council	www.ffiec.gov/
National Credit Union Administration	www.ncua.gov/
Office of the Comptroller of the Currency	www.occ.treas.gov/
Office of Thrift Supervision	www.ots.ustreas.gov/treasury/bureaus/ots/ots.html/
The Wall Street Journal	www.wjs.com/

Nondepository Institutions (Chapters 15–19)

What are the various types of nondepository institutions? (pages 446–447, 470–471, 490, 502–503, 525–526)

What are the major assets and liabilities held by each? (pages 452–454, 460–466, 483–487, 494–499, 521–522, 538–540)

What are the major regulations governing nondepository institutions? (pages 454, 467–468, 487–488, 499–500, 523, 540–543)

What are the major lines of business performed by each? (pages 447–452, 455–460, 472–483, 492–493, 504–520, 521–538)

Pertinent Websites

A M. Best	www.ambest.com/
American Banker	www.americanbanker.com/
Associated Press	www.associatedpress.com/
Board of Governors of the Federal Reserve	www.bog.frb.fed.us/
Department of Labor	www.dol.gov/
Investment Company Institute	www.ici.org/
National Association of Insurance Commissioners	www.naic.org/
National Association of Securities Dealers	www.nasd.com/
New York Stock Exchange	www.nyse.com/
Pension Benefit Guaranty Corporation	www.pbgc.gov/
Securities and Exchange Commission	www.sec.gov/
Securities Industry Association	www.sia.com/
Securities Investor Protection Corporation	www.sipc.org/
The New York Times	www.nyt.com/
The Wall Street Journal	www.wjs.com/
Thompson Financial Securities Data	www.tfsd.com/

Types of Risks Incurred by Financial Institutions (Chapter 20)

What are the major risks faced by financial institutions? (pages 547–560)

How are the various risks related? (pages 560–561)

Pertinent Websites

American Banker	www.americanbanker.com/
Board of Governors of the Federal Reserve	www.bog.frb.fed.us/
Federal Deposit Insurance Corporation	www.fdic.gov/
The New York Times	www.nyt.com/